"I wanted to read more because she added frequently asked questions by students and not psychologists, so I understood what she was saying. Also because she wrote like she was talking to students and not doctors or psychologists!"

"I think if I had had this book last semester I would have gotten a better understanding of the course."

"The chapters are way different from the textbook I have. These chapters make it more personal and interesting. It has like a happy tone —like 'I want you to read me' kind of tone."

"The text is easy to understand and takes the reader on a step-by-step basis, until the main point or idea is explained."

"This textbook is marvelous!"

"I think I would even buy this textbook just for the fun of it. I loved the way you have a voice and explain everything in such a way other textbooks don't."

psychology, not just read about it.

PSYCHOLOGY

PSYCHOLOGY

SAUNDRA K. CICCARELLI
Gulf Coast Community College

GLENN E. MEYER
Trinity University

PEARSON

Prentice
Hall

Upper Saddle River, New Jersey 07458

Library of Congress Cataloging-in-Publication Data

Ciccarelli, Saundra K.
    Psychology/Saundra K. Ciccarelli.–1st ed.
       p.   cm.
    Includes bibliographical references and index.
    ISBN 0-13-183959-4
    1. Psychology–Textbooks. I. Title.

BF121.C52 2006
150–dc22   2005051467

Editorial Director: Leah Jewell
Executive Editor: Jessica Mosher
Editorial Assistant: William Grieco
Media Project Manager: David Clevinger
Assessment Editor: Kerri Scott
Director of Marketing: Brandy Dawson
Marketing Manager: Jeanette Moyer
Marketing Assistant: Alexandra Trum
Marketing Development: Burrston House, Ltd.
Editor in Chief, Development: Rochelle Diogenes
Sr. Development Editor: Susanna Lesan
VP/Director of Production and Manufacturing: Barbara Kittle
Sr. Managing Editor: Joanne Riker
Asst. Managing Editor (Production): Maureen Richardson
Production Liaison: Kathleen Sleys

Manufacturing Manager: Nick Sklitsis
Manufacturing Buyer: Sherry Lewis
Director, Image Resource Center: Melinda Reo
Manager, Rights and Permissions: Zina Arabia
Manager, Visual Research: Beth Brenzel
Manager, Cover Visual Research & Permissions: Karen Sanatar
Image Permission Coordinator: Debbie Latronica
Photo Researcher: Barbara Salz
Creative Design Director: Leslie Osher
Interior/Cover Design: Anne Demarinis
Line Art: Mirella Signoretto, Dorling Kindersley, Precision Graphics
Cover Illustration/Photo: Stone/Getty Images
Composition/Full-Service Project Management: Preparé Inc.
Printer/Binder: Courier Companies, Inc.
Cover Printer: Phoenix Color Corp.

Pearson Education Ltd.
Pearson Education Singapore, Pte. Ltd.
Pearson Education, Canada, Ltd.
Pearson Education–Japan
Pearson Education Australia PTY, Limited

Pearson Education North Asia Ltd.
Pearson Educación de Mexico, S.A. de C.V.
Pearson Education Malaysia, Pte. Ltd.
Pearson Education, Upper Saddle River, NJ

10 9 8 7 6 5 4 3 2
0-13-183959-4

Brief Contents

Ciccarelli, *Psychology* is available in both hardcover
(0-13-183959-4) and paperback (0-13-219862-2) versions.

Contents

1

The Science of Psychology 2

2

The Biological Perspective 42

3

Sensation and Perception 82

4

Consciousness: Sleep, Dreams, Hypnosis, and Drugs 124

5

Learning 164

6

Memory 208

7

Development Across the Life Span 248

8

Cognition: Thinking, Intelligence, and Language 292

9

Motivation and Emotion 334

10

Sexuality and Gender 370

11

Stress and Health 404

12

Theories of Personality 442

13

Social Psychology 478

14

Psychological Disorders 520

15

Psychological Therapies 560

Preface

Dear Reader,

Instructors and students alike experience frustration during lectures when students are unprepared for class. My goal in writing this text is to focus on students and motivate them to learn. I set out to write in a style that draws readers into an ongoing dialogue about psychology. My aim is to help introduce readers to psychology—its history, its breadth, its mysteries, and its applications.

I also want to see students inspired to use the study materials that accompany their text. Students want to do well, and they are motivated when goals are clearly laid out and they know content will "be on the test." By creating an integrated learning and assessment package, my co-author and I hope to encourage students to focus on the learning objectives and assist instructors in continually assessing students' progress in mastering these objectives.

I am deeply indebted to the hundreds of reviewers who have taken the time to give me insightful feedback and suggestions on this project as well as the numerous students who have class-tested the material for us. I thank you all for your time and effort.

Sincerely,
Sandy Ciccarelli

LEARNER-CENTERED APPROACH
Curiosity and Dialogue

In recent years there has been an increased focus on a more learner-centered approach in higher education that encourages dialogue and recognizes the importance of actively engaging students. This textbook came about because we recognized the importance of motivating students to read. When we say "read," we mean really read the text, not just skim it looking for answers to some study guide questions or trying to cram it all in the night before the exam. We set out to write in a style that draws the reader into an ongoing dialogue about psychology. We also want to see students inspired to use the study materials integrated with the text. Our goal is to awaken students' curiosity so that they will want to learn more.

Chapter Opening Prologues are designed to capture student interest immediately. Taken from a case study or recent event in the news, these openers are designed to engage students in the material from the very start of the chapter.

Clearly, memories obtained through hypnosis should not be considered as accurate without solid evidence from other sources.

But I've heard about people who remember being abused as children when they are hypnotized. Aren't those memories sometimes real? The fact that some people recover false memories under certain conditions does not mean that child molestation* does not really happen; nor does it mean that a person who was molested might not push that unwanted memory away from conscious thought. Molestation is a sad fact, with one conservative estimate stating that nearly 20 percent of all females and 7 percent of all males have experienced molestation during childhood (Abel & Osborn, 1992). There are also many therapists and psychological professionals who are quite skilled at helping clients remember events of the past without suggesting possible false memories, and they find that clients do remember information and events that were true and able to be verified but were previously unavailable to the client (Dalenberg, 1996). False memory syndrome is not only harmful to the persons directly involved but also makes it much more difficult for genuine victims of molestation to be believed when they do recover their memories of the painful traumas of childhood.

So can we trust any of our memories at all? There is evidence to suggest that false memories cannot be created for just any kind of memory. The *memories* must at least be plausible, according to the research of cognitive psychologist and memory expert

> But I've heard about people who remember being abused as children when they are hypnotized. Aren't those memories sometimes real?

> So can we trust any of our memories at all?

Student Voice Questions encourage students to think critically and communicate. Written by students for students, these questions create a dialogue between the text and the reader.

---

the thing (response of subjects or result of some action) that is measured to see just how the independent variable may have affected it.

The Groups   If researchers do all of this and find that the children's behavior is aggressive, can they say that the aggressive behavior was caused by the violence in the cartoon? No, what has been described so far is not enough. The researchers may find that the children who watch the violent cartoon are aggressive, but how would they know if their aggressive behavior was caused by the cartoon or was just the natural aggressive level of those particular children or the result of the particular time of day they were observed? Those sorts of *confounding variables* (variables that interfere with each other and their possible effects on some other variable of interest) are the kind researchers have to control for in some way. For example, if participants in an experiment were supposed to take only a potassium supplement but also took an iron supplement, any effects the potassium might have had on what the experimenter was measuring would be confused (confounded) with the effects that the iron supplement might have also had. The best way to control for confounding variables is to have two groups of participants: those who watch the violent cartoon, and those

> If researchers do all of this and find that the children's behavior is aggressive, can they say that the aggressive behavior was caused by the violence in the cartoon?

The Hearing Sense: Can You Hear Me Now?

If light works like waves, then do sound waves have similar properties? The properties of sound are indeed similar to those of light, as both senses rely on waves. But the similarity ends there, as the physical properties of sound are different from those of light.

PSYCHOLOGICAL PROPERTIES OF SOUND

3.6 *What is sound?*

Sound waves do not come in little packets the way light comes in photons. Sound waves are simply the vibrations of the molecules of air that surround us. Sound waves

> If light works like waves, then do sound waves have similar properties?

---

some time has passed, the behavior will most likely return as the memory of the punishment gets weaker, allowing spontaneous recovery.

If punishment doesn't work very well, what can a parent do to keep a child from behaving badly?

HOW TO MAKE PUNISHMENT MORE EFFECTIVE   The way to make punishment more effective involves remembering a few simple rules:

1. **Punishment should immediately follow the behavior it is meant to punish.** If the punishment comes long after the behavior, it will not be associated with that behavior.
2. **Punishment should be consistent.** This actually means two things. First, if the parent says that a certain punishment will follow a certain behavior, then the parent

> If punishment doesn't work very well, what can a parent do to keep a child from behaving badly?

Practice Quizzes are included in each chapter at the end of every major section. This embedded assessment encourages students to stop, review, and reinforce their learning before moving on.

PRACTICE QUIZ: HOW MUCH DO YOU REMEMBER?

Pick the best answer.

1. Cognition refers to
   a. behavior that is observable and external.
   b. behavior that is directly measurable.
   c. the mental events that take place while a person is behaving.
   d. memories.

2. In Tolman's maze study, the fact that the group of rats receiving reinforcement only after the tenth day of the study solved the maze far more quickly than did the rats who had been reinforced from the first day can be interpreted to mean that these particular rats
   a. were much smarter than the other rats.
   b. had already learned the maze in the first nine days.
   c. had the opportunity to cheat by watching the other rats.
   d. were very hungry and, therefore, learned much more quickly.

3. Seligman found many similarities between his "helpless" dogs and people suffering from
   a. aggressive behavior syndrome.

CHAPTER 3   SENSATION AND PERCEPTION 121

5. In Bandura's study with the Bobo doll, the children in the group that saw the model punished did not imitate the model at first. They would only imitate the model if given a reward for doing so. The fact that these children had obviously learned the behavior without actually performing it is an example of
   a. latent learning.
   b. operant conditioning.
   c. classical conditioning.
   d. insight learning.

6. Miranda wanted to make a casserole she saw on a food show on TV. She bought the ingredients, put them together, baked it, and served it at dinner that night. To her horror, it tasted awful. She realized that she had left out a key ingredient and vowed next time to write everything down as she watched the show. Miranda's dinner disaster was an example of failing at which of Bandura's four elements of observational learning?
   a. attention
   b. memory
   c. imitation
   d. motivation

Answers: 1-c, 2-b, 3-d, 4-b, 5-a, 6-b.

TEST YOURSELF

Pick the best answer.

1. You find that you have to add 1 teaspoon of sugar to a cup of coffee that already has 5 teaspoons of sugar in it to notice the difference in sweetness. If you have a cup of coffee with 10 teaspoons of sugar in it, how many teaspoons would you have to add to notice the difference in sweetness at least half the time?
   a. 1   c. 4
   b. 2   d. 5

2. Which of your senses habituates rather than adapts to constant stimuli?
   a. vision   c. hearing
   b. touch   d. smell

3. Which of the following terms refers to the psychological effect of the length of light waves?
   a. color   c. saturation
   b. brightness   d. amplitude

4. Which of the following is responsible for controlling how much light enters the eye?
   a. cornea   c. retina
   b. lens   d. iris

5. Which type of retinal cell forms the optic nerve?
   a. rods   c. ganglion cells
   b. cones   d. bipolar cells

6. Which type of retinal cell is responsible for peripheral vision?
   a. rods   c. ganglion cells
   b. cones   d. bipolar cells

7. Which set of colors are the primary colors of light?
   a. red, yellow, and blue   c. blue, green, and yellow
   b. red, blue, and green   d. red, green, and yellow

8. Which of the following properties of sound would be the most similar to the brightness of light?
   a. pitch   c. purity
   b. loudness   d. timbre

9. The thin membrane stretched over the opening to the inner ear is the
   a. pinna.   c. tympanic membrane.
   b. oval window.   d. cochlea.

10. The _____ theory explains how we hear sounds between 100 and 1,000 Hz.
    a. place   c. volley
    b. frequency   d. adaptive

11. If a severe ear infection damages the bones of the middle ear, you may develop _____ hearing impairment.
    a. nerve   c. brain pathway
    b. stimulation   d. conduction

12. The sense of taste is closely related to the sense of
    a. sight.   c. smell.
    b. hearing.   d. touch.

13. The "bumps" on the tongue that are visible to the eye are the
    a. taste buds.   c. taste receptors.
    b. papillae.   d. olfactory receptors.

14. The olfactory receptor cells are located in the
    a. tops of the nasal passages.   c. roof of the mouth.
    b. auditory passages.   d. lining of the outer nose.

15. Which of the following statements about olfactory receptors is TRUE?
    a. Olfactory receptors are replaced every 5 to 8 weeks.
    b. There are fewer than 50 types of olfactory receptors.
    c. Signals from the receptors go through the brain stem and then to the cortex.
    d. Olfactory receptors respond to pressure.

16. In the spinal cord, _____ inhibit(s) the release of substance P.
    a. hormones   c. norepinephrine
    b. serotonin   d. endorphins

17. We know when we are moving up and down in an elevator because of the movement of tiny crystals in the
    a. outer ear.   c. otolith organs.
    b. inner ear.   d. middle ear.

18. Ellis turns around and around in a circle. When he stops, he feels like his head is still spinning. What is responsible for this sensation?
    a. semicircular canals   c. otolith organs
    b. proprioceptors   d. otolith crystals

19. An old comedy routine on television had a character who would line up the heads of people who were very far away from him between his fingers. Then he would pinch his fingers together and say gleefully, "I'm crushing your head, I'm crushing your head." The comedian was playing around with which perceptual constancy?
    a. size constancy   c. brightness constancy
    b. shape constancy   d. color constancy

20. Which Gestalt principle is at work when a ventriloquist moves the dummy's mouth while doing the talking, making it seem like the dummy is talking?
    a. closure   c. contiguity
    b. similarity   d. continuity

21. Researchers have been able to demonstrate depth perception in babies as young as
    a. 1 month.   c. 3 months.
    b. 2 months.   d. 4 months.

22. Which of the following occurs when one object seems to block another object?
    a. convergence   c. overlap
    b. linear perspective   d. texture gradient

23. The Müller-Lyer illusion exists in cultures in which there are
    a. more men than women.   c. lots of trees.
    b. more women than men.   d. buildings with lots of corners.

24. Allison opened her new jigsaw puzzle but soon realized that the puzzle pieces inside had nothing to do with the picture on the box. With no picture to go by, she realized she would have to use
    a. bottom-up processing.   c. perceptual expectancy.
    b. top-down processing.   d. perceptual set.

25. Which supposed ESP ability involves being able to "see" something that is not physically present by touching another object?
    a. precognition
    b. telepathy
    c. clairvoyance
    d. telekinesis

Answers: 1-b, 2-c, 3-a, 4-d, 5-c, 6-a, 7-b, 8-b, 9-c, 10-c, 11-d, 12-c, 13-b, 14-a, 15-a, 16-d, 17-c, 18-a, 19-a, 20-c, 21-b, 22-c, 23-d, 24-a, 25-c.

Test Yourself sample exams are found at the end of every chapter. Both the quizzes and the end-of-chapter tests are in multiple-choice format to replicate the experience most students have with graded assessments.

PSYCHOLOGY IN THE NEWS
Neurofeedback and the Treatment of ADD

5.15 *What is neurofeedback and how is it used?*

A relatively new technique called neurofeedback is used to treat a child's attention problems in the classroom. Although this technique uses the latest in technology, the basic principles behind it are much older. For nearly 60 years, scientists have known how to use feedback of a person's biological information (such as heart rate) to create a state of relaxation (Margolin & Kubic, 1944). **Biofeedback** is the traditional term used to describe this kind of biological feedback of information, and through its use many problems can be relieved or controlled.

biofeedback
the use of feedback about biological conditions to bring involuntary responses such as blood pressure and relaxation under voluntary control.

CURRENT ISSUES IN PSYCHOLOGY
A Look at Abnormality in Various Cultures

14.5 *How is abnormality viewed in other kinds of cultures?*

As mentioned earlier, what's normal in one culture may be abnormal in another culture. **Cultural relativity** is a term that refers to the need to consider the unique characteristics of the culture in which a person with a disorder was nurtured to be able to correctly diagnose and treat the disorder (Castillo, 1997). For example, in most Asian cultures,

CLASSIC STUDIES IN PSYCHOLOGY
REM Madness

Dr. William Dement is generally recognized as one of the world's leading authorities on sleep, sleep deprivation, and sleep disorders. He founded the first sleep disorder clinic at Stanford University in 1970 and has remained active in both research and treatment of sleep problems.

In one of Dement's earliest studies (1960), subjects who were being monitored for sleep stages with an EEG machine were awakened each time they entered REM sleep. Two findings became clear. First, subjects deprived of REM sleep, when allowed to sleep normally, did an unusual amount of extra REM sleep. But also of interest was the fact that the REM-deprived subjects seemed to become paranoid, believing that the experimenter had all kinds of hidden, sinister motives and even experienced hallucinations. These early findings were the source of the *REM myth*, the theory that without dreams, people will become mentally ill.

In later studies (Dement et al., 1969) it was found that REM deprivation did not reliably produce these symptoms of severe mental disturbance. In fact, Dement concluded that the earlier findings may have been an example of the *experimenter effect* (discussed in Chapter One). Dement was very concerned about his subjects' well-being and may have communicated that concern to each subject during the interviews. To make matters worse, in the original experiment he had told the subjects what he thought the probable results of the study might be and provided them with a psychiatrist to whom they could report any unusual symptoms. Clearly, by the third day of REM deprivation the symptoms were most likely due to a combination of sleep deprivation and the power of suggestion.

Dement performed numerous experiments after this one, showing each time that no psychiatric symptoms resulted from REM sleep deprivation alone (unlike the psychotic behavior of a person who is seriously deprived of sleep in general). Popular science magazines still report the REM myth as fact, citing firm scientific support that does not exist. That first experiment, flawed as it was, is the one that many people seem to remember best. Perhaps some people would like to believe that there's a neat little reason for their occasional paranoid thoughts—REM sleep deprivation to the rescue.

Questions for Further Discussion

1. How might REM sleep deprivation studies be conducted?

2. What might be some of the problems encountered by researchers when trying to study sleep in a laboratory setting?

3. Are there any ethical concerns with deliberately disturbing people when they are sleeping?

4. How might the fact that the participants in these studies volunteered to sleep and be awakened under such artificial conditions have affected their behavior?

Dr. William Dement is the leading authority on sleep and sleep deprivation.

Other features of each chapter are special sections covering interesting topics related to the chapter material, especially topics of diversity and cultural interest. These are not set off from the text in boxes; they are part of the narrative, making it more likely that students will read the enriching material. Practice quizzes and end-of-chapter tests include questions on this material, further encouraging students to read.

Each special section ends with **Questions for Further Discussion,** encouraging students to think critically about the content they have just read.

Applying Psychology To Everyday Life:
Using Critical Thinking–Does Astrology Work?

1.16 *How might critical thinking be applied to a real-world example?*

Astrology is a pseudo-psychology that attempts to predict the future and explain personality by using the positions of the stars and planets at the moment of birth. Many people see astrology as a form of entertainment, but others take it quite seriously, planning their daily activities and making important life choices based on their horoscopes. But is there any validity to believing that the positions of the objects in the rest of the universe have any effect at all on one's personality or daily successes or failures? Here's an example of critical thinking applied to astrology:

One thing that is often difficult for students to do is make connections from topics in one chapter to topics in other chapters. Throughout each chapter, when one topic has a relationship to another topic, a L I N K symbol is included with specific chapter and page numbers cited.

15.3   *What were the basic elements of Freud's psychoanalysis?*

Dream interpretation, or the analysis of the elements within a patient's reported dream, formed a large part of Freud's psychoanalytic method. ⓛⓘⓝⓚ *to Chapter Four: Consciousness, pp. 139–140.* Freud believed that repressed material often surfaced in dreams, although in symbolic form. The **manifest content** of the dream was the actual dream and its events, but the **latent content** was the hidden, symbolic meaning of those events that would, if correctly interpreted, reveal the unconscious conflicts that were creating the nervous disorder (Freud, 1900).

6.13   *What kinds of problems do people experience when trying to remember something stored in long-term memory?*

Some people may say that they have "total recall." What they usually mean is that they feel that their memories are more accurate than those of other people. As should be obvious by now, true total recall is not a very likely ability for anyone to have. Here are some reasons why people have trouble recalling information accurately.

THE MISINFORMATION EFFECT   Elizabeth Loftus, in addition to her studies concerning eyewitness testimony, has also done several similar studies that demonstrate the **misinformation effect**. In this effect, misleading information that is presented *after* an event has taken place can affect the accuracy of the memory for that event (Loftus et al., 1978). In one study, subjects viewed a slide presentation of a traffic accident. The actual slide presentation contained a stop sign, but in a written summary of the presentation, the sign was referred to as a yield sign. Subjects who were given this misleading information after viewing the slides were far less accurate in their memories for the kind of sign present than were subjects given no such information. One of the interesting points to be made

Coherent: understandable.

constructive processing
referring to the retrieval of memories in which those memories are altered, revised, or influenced by newer information.

hindsight bias
the tendency to falsely believe, through revision of older memories to include newer information, that one could have correctly predicted the outcome of an event.

misinformation effect
the tendency of misleading information presented after an event to alter the memories of the event itself.

With the **Running Glossary** psychological terms are set in bold in the text and defined in the margins.

For many ESL students a lack of vocabulary is a big stumbling block. If the word is defined on the same page, the student stands a far better chance of understanding what he or she is reading. In this text, these more **Difficult Vocabulary Terms** are defined at the bottom of the page on which they first appear.

A detailed **Chapter Summary** highlights all the important parts of the chapter.

2 ✦ CHAPTER SUMMARY

An Overview of the Nervous System

2.1   *How do all the parts of the nervous system relate to one another?*

• The nervous system is a complex network of cells that carries information to and from all parts of the body.

Neurons and Nerves: Building the Network

2.2   *What are neurons and nerves, and how do they work?*

• The brain is made up of two types of cells, neurons and glial cells.
• Neurons have dendrites, which receive input, a soma or cell body, and axons that carry the neural message to other cells.
• Glial cells separate, support, and insulate the neurons from each other and make up the

• The spinal cord serves two functions. The outer part of the cord transmits messages to and from the brain, whereas the inner part controls lifesaving reflexes such as the pain response.
• Spinal cord reflexes involve sensory neurons, interneurons, and motor neurons, forming a simple reflex arc.
• Great strides are being made in spinal cord repair and the growth of new neurons in the central nervous system.

Psychology in the News: Adult Bone Marrow: New Hope For The Damaged Brain

• Research suggests that stem cells can be obtained from adult bone marrow, making the repair and replacement of damaged neurons more feasible.

A **Concept Map** follows the chapter summary, further emphasizing the key objectives of the chapter in a highly visual manner.

LEARNING OUTCOMES AND ASSESSMENT
Goals and Standards

In recent years many psychology departments have been focusing on core competencies and how methods of assessment can better enhance students' learning. In 2002 the American Psychological Association (APA) established ten recommended goals for the undergraduate psychology major. Specific learning outcomes were established for each of the ten goals, and suggestions were made on how best to tie assessment practices to these goals. For details on the APA learning goals and assessment guidelines, please see **hwww.apa.org/ed/guidehomepage.html.** In writing this text, we have used the APA goals and assessment recommendations as guidelines for structuring content and integrating the teaching and homework materials. Based on APA recommendations, each chapter is structured around detailed learning objectives. All study and testing materials are also organized around these learning objectives, making this text a fully integrated system of study.

2
LEARNING OBJECTIVES

2.1 How do all the parts of the nervous system relate to one another?

2.2 What are neurons and nerves, and how do they work?

2.3 How do neurons communicate with each other and with the body?

2.4 What are the different neurotransmitters?

2.5 How do the brain and spinal cord interact?

2.6 How does the somatic nervous system allow people and animals to interact with their surroundings?

2.7 How does the autonomic nervous system control the body's automatic functions and its reaction to stress?

2.8 How do psychologists study the brain and how it works?

2.9 What are the different structures of the bottom part of the brain and what do they do?

2.10 What are the structures of the brain that control emotion, learning, memory, and motivation?

2.11 What parts of the cortex control the different senses and the movement of the body?

2.12 What parts of the cortex are responsible for higher forms of thought, such as language?

2.13 How does the left side of the brain differ from the right side?

2.14 How do the hormones released by glands interact with the nervous system and affect behavior?

NEUROTRANSMITTERS, MESSENGERS OF THE NETWORK

2.4 *What are the different neurotransmitters?*

The first neurotransmitter to be identified was named *acetylcholine*. It is found at the synapses between neurons and muscle cells. Acetylcholine serves to stimulate the muscle to contract. If acetylcholine receptor sites on the muscle cells are blocked in some way, then the acetylcholine can't get to the site and the muscle will be incapable of contracting—paralyzed, in other words. This is exactly what happens when *curare*, a drug used by South American Indians on their blow darts, gets into the nervous system. Curare's molecules are just similar enough to fit into the receptor site without actually stimulating the cell, making curare an antagonist for acetylcholine.

What would happen if the neurons released too much acetylcholine? The bite of a black widow spider does just that. Its venom stimulates the release of excessive amounts of acetylcholine and causes convulsions and possible death. Black widow spider venom is an agonist for acetylcholine. Acetylcholine is also found in the hippocampus, an area of the brain that is responsible for forming new memories. LINK to Chapter Six: *Memory, p. 237.*

The venom of the black widow spider causes a flood of acetylcholine to be released into the body's muscle system, causing convulsions.

Based on APA outcomes and assessment recommendations, each chapter is structured around detailed **Learning Objectives.** These learning objectives appear in question format at the beginning of the chapter and again at the beginning of relevant text sections. All ancillary materials are also organized around these learning objectives, making this text a fully integrated system of study.

APA UNDERGRADUATE LEARNING GOALS AND OUTCOMES	CICCARELLI LEARNING OBJECTIVES AND TEXT CONTENT
1. Knowledge Base of Psychology **Demonstrate familiarity with the major concepts, theoretical perspectives, empirical findings, and historical trends in psychology.** **1.1** Characterize the nature of psychology as a discipline. **1.2** Demonstrate knowledge and understanding representing appropriate breadth and depth in selected content areas of psychology: theory and research representing general domains, the history of psychology, relevant levels of analysis, overarching themes, and relevant ethical issues. **1.3** Use the concepts, language, and major theories of the discipline to account for psychological phenomena. **1.4** Explain major perspectives of psychology (e.g., behavioral, biological, cognitive, evolutionary, humanistic, psychodynamic, and sociocultural).	**Ch 1:** 1.1–1.6 **Ch 2:** 2.1–2.7m, 2.9–2.14 **Ch 3:** 3.1–3.17 **Ch 4:** 4.1–4.5, 4.7–4.16 **Ch 5:** 5.1–5.5, 5.7–5.10, 5.12–5.22 **Ch 6:** 6.1–6.17 **Ch 7:** 7.2–7.4, 7.6–7.7, 7.9–7.16, 7.18–7.20 **Ch 8:** 8.1–8.11, 8.13–8.18 **Ch 9:** 9.1–9.10, 9.12–9.19 **Ch 10:** 10.1–10.6, 10.9–10.16 **Ch 11:** 11.1–11.3, 11.7–11.10. 11.13 **Ch 12:** 12.1–12.13 **Ch 13:** 13.1–13.23 **Ch 14:** 14.1–14.4, 14.7–14.13, 14.15–14.23 **Ch 15:** 15.1–15.6, 15.8–15.10, 15.21–15.23 Major concepts all reinforced with student study guide materials, on-line homework tools, and instructors' teaching and assessment package

2. Research Methods in Psychology
 	
Understand and apply basic research methods in psychology, including research design, data analysis, and interpretation.
 	
2.1 Describe the basic characteristics of the science of psychology.
 	
2.2 Explain different research methods used by psychologists.
  a. Describe how various research designs address different types of questions and hypotheses
  b. Articulate strengths and limitations of various research designs
  c. Distinguish the nature of designs that permit causal inferences from those that do not
 	
2.3 Evaluate the appropriateness of conclusions derived from psychological research.
  a. Interpret basic statistical results
  b. Distinguish between statistical significance and practical significance
  c. Describe effect size and confidence intervals
  d. Evaluate the validity of conclusions presented in research reports
 	
2.4 Design and conduct basic studies to address psychological questions using appropriate research methods.
  a. Locate and use relevant databases, research, and theory to plan, conduct, and interpret results of research studies
  b. Formulate testable research hypotheses, based on operational definitions of variables
  c. Select and apply appropriate methods to maximize internal and external validity and reduce the plausibility of alternative explanations
  d. Collect, analyze, interpret, and report data using appropriate statistical strategies to address different types of research questions and hypotheses
  e. Recognize that theoretical and sociocultural contexts as well as personal biases may shape research questions, design, data collection, analysis, and interpretation
 	
2.5 Follow the APA Code of Ethics in the treatment of human and nonhuman participants in the design, data collection, interpretation, and reporting of psychological research.
 	
2.6 Generalize research conclusions appropriately based on the parameters of particular research methods.
  a. Exercise caution in predicting behavior based on limitations of single studies
  b. Recognize the limitations of applying normative conclusions to individuals
  c. Acknowledge that research results may have unanticipated societal consequences
  d. Recognize that individual differences and sociocultural contexts may influence the applicability of research findings
	Ch 1: 1.7-1.14, and *Classic Studies in Psychology: Mary Cover Jones and Little Peter* and *Teresa Amabile and the Effect of Extrinsic Reward on Creativity*
	Ch 2: 2.8, and *Classic Studies in Psychology: Through the Looking Glass: Spatial Neglect*
	Ch 3: *Classic Studies: The Visual Cliff*
	Ch 4: *Classic Studies: REM Madness*
	Ch 5: *Psychology in the News: Neurofeedback and Treatment of ADD* and *Classic Studies: Biological Constraints of Operant Conditioning*
	Ch 6: *Classic Studies: Elizabeth Loftus and Eyewitnesses* and *Current Research on Alzheimer's Disease*
	Ch 7: 7.1 and *Classic Studies: Harlow and Contact Comfort*
	Ch 8: *Classic Studies: Terman's Termites*
	Ch 9: *Classic Studies: The Angry/Happy Man*
	Ch 10: 10.7 and *Classic Studies: Masters and Johnson's Observational Study of the Human Sexual Response*
	Ch 12: 12.14-12.17 and *Classic Studies: Geert Hofstede's Four Dimensions of Cultural Personality*
	Ch 13: *Classic Studies: Brown Eyes, Blue Eyes* and *Latané and Darley*
	Ch 15: *Current Issues: What Is EMDR?*
	Appendix 1: Statistics
	Methodology reinforced with student study guide materials, on-line homework tools, and instructors' teaching and assessment package

APA UNDERGRADUATE LEARNING GOALS AND OUTCOMES	CICCARELLI LEARNING OBJECTIVES AND TEXT CONTENT

3. Critical Thinking Skill in Psychology

Respect and use critical and creative thinking, skeptical inquiry, and, when possible, the scientific approach to solve problems related to behavior and mental processes.

3.1 Use critical thinking effectively.

3.2 Engage in creative thinking.

3.3 Use reasoning to recognize, develop, defend, and criticize arguments and other persuasive appeals.

3.4 Approach problems effectively.

Ch 1: 1.15–1.16, *Using Critical Thinking: Does Astrology Work?*
Ch 2: *Applying Psychology to Everyday Life: Differences Between Male and Female Brains*
Ch 3: *Thinking Critically About ESP*
Ch 4: 4.6
Ch 5: 5.6, 5.11
Ch 7: 7.8 and *Current Issues: The Facts and Myths about Immunizations*
Ch 8: 8.12 and *Psychology in the News: Artificial Intelligence (AI)*
Ch 10: *Current Issues: The Intersex Controversy*
Ch 11: 11.15 and *Current Issues: Suicide in America*
Ch 12: 12.8
Ch 13: *Applying Psychology: Anatomy of a Cult*
Ch 14: 14.14 and *Current Issues: Was "Sybil" a True Multiple Personality?*
Ch 15: 15.15, 15.18–15.20, 15.24 and *Applying Psychology: Should Antidepressants Be Prescribed for Children and Adolescents?*
Critical thinking skills reinforced with student study guide materials, online homework tools, and instructors, teaching and assessment package

4. Application of Psychology

Understand and apply psychological principles to personal, social, and organizational issues.

4.1 Describe major applied areas of psychology (e.g., clinical, counseling, industrial/organizational, school, health).

4.2 Identify appropriate applications of psychology in solving problems

4.3 Articulate how psychological principles can be used to explain social issues and inform public policy.

4.4 Apply psychological concepts, theories, and research findings as these relate to everyday life.

4.5 Recognize that ethically complex situations can develop in the application of psychological principles.

Ch 1: 1.16, study skills section
Ch 2: *Psychology in the News: Adult Bone Marrow: New Hope for Damaged Brain*
Ch 3: *Psychology in the News: New Surgery to Help Restore Hearing*
Ch 4: 4.17 and *Psychology in the News: Murderous Dreams* and *Applying Psychology: Are You Sleep Deprived?*
Ch 5: *Applying Psychology: Can You Really Toilet Train Your Cat?*
Ch 6: 6.17–6.18
Ch 7: *Applying Psychology: ADHD-Not Just for Children*
Ch 8: 8.19 and *Applying Psychology: Mental Exercises for Better Cognitive Health*
Ch 9: 9.10–9.11, 9.20 and *Psychology in the News: The Biology of Obesity* and *Applying Psychology: A How-to of Happiness?*
Ch 10: 10.8, 10.17 and *Applying Psychology: How to Protect Yourself from Sexually Transmitted Diseases*
Ch 11: 11.4–11.6, 11.12, 11.14, 11,17 and *Applying Psychology: Focus on Wellness*
Ch 12: *Applying Psychology: Personality Testing on the Internet*
Ch 13: 13.24–13.25
Ch 14: 14.5–14.6 and *Applying Psychology: Seasonal Affective Disorder*
Ch 15: 15.11–15.14, 15.16–15.17
Appendix 2: Applied Psychology
Applications reinforced with student study guide materials, online homework tools, and instructors' teaching and assessment package

5. Values in Psychology

Value empirical evidence, tolerate ambiguity, act ethically, and reflect other values that are the underpinnings of psychology as a science.

5.1 Recognize the necessity for ethical behavior in all aspects of the science and practice of psychology.

5.2 Demonstrate reasonable skepticism and intellectual curiosity by asking questions about causes of behavior.

5.3 Seek and evaluate scientific evidence for psychological claims.

5.4 Tolerate ambiguity and realize that psychological explanations are often complex and tentative.

5.5 Recognize and respect human diversity and understand that psychological explanations may vary across populations and contexts.

5.6 Assess and justify their engagement with respect to civic, social, and global responsibilities.

5.7 Understand the limitations of their psychological knowledge and skills.

Ch 1: 1.2, 1.4 , 1.14–1.16
Ch 2: *Applying Psychology to Everyday Life: Differences Between Male and Female Brains*
Ch 8: 8.10–8.12, 8.17
Ch 9: 9.10–9.12
Ch 10: 10.2–10.8 and *Current Issues: The Intersex Controversy*
Ch 11: 11.5–11.6, 11.15–11.16
Ch 13: 13.12-13.18 and *Classic Studies: Brown Eyes, Blue Eyes* and *Latané and Darley*
Ch 14: 14.5
Values reinforced with content in student study guide, and instructors' teaching and assessment package

APA UNDERGRADUATE LEARNING GOALS AND OUTCOMES	CICCARELLI LEARNING OBJECTIVES AND TEXT CONTENT

6. Information and Technological Literacy

Demonstrate information competence and the ability to use computers and other technology for many purposes.

6.1 Demonstrate information competence at each stage in the following process: formulating a researchable topic, choosing and evaluating relevant resources, and reading and accurately summarizing scientific literature that can be supported by database search strategies.

6.2 Use information and technology ethically and responsibly.

6.3 Demonstrate basic computer skills, proper etiquette, and security safeguards.

Ch 1: 1.7–1.14, and *Classic Studies in Psychology: Mary Cover Jones and Little Peter* and *Teresa Amabile and the Effect of Extrinsic Reward on Creativity*

Ch 2: 2.8, and *Classic Studies in Psychology: Through the Looking Glass: Spatial Neglect*

Ch 3: *Classic Studies: The Visual Cliff*

Ch 4: *Classic Studies: REM Madness*

Ch 5: *Psychology in the News: Neurofeedback and Treatment of ADD* and *Classic Studies: Biological Constraints of Operant Conditioning*

Ch 6: *Classic Studies: Elizabeth Loftus and Eyewitnesses* and *Current Research on Alzheimer's Disease*

Ch 7: 7.1 and *Classic Studies: Harlow and Contact Comfort*

Ch 8: *Classic Studies: Terman's Termites*

Ch 9: *Classic Studies: The Angry/Happy Man*

Ch 10: 10.7 and *Classic Studies: Masters and Johnson's Observational Study of the Human Sexual Response*

Ch 12: 12.14–12.17 and *Classic Studies: Geert Hofstede's Four Dimensions of Cultural Personality*

Ch 13: *Classic Studies: Brown Eyes, Blue Eyes* and *Latané and Darley*

Ch 15: *Current Issues: What Is EMDR?*

Appendix 1: Statistics

Study Guide Chapter 1: summary section on the scientific method and study hints examples 2 , 3, and 4.

Information and technological literacy reinforced with student study guide materials, online homework tools, and instructor's teaching and assessment package

7. Communication Skills

Communicate effectively in a variety of formats.

7.1 Demonstrate effective writing skills in various formats (e.g., essays, correspondence, technical papers, note taking) and for various purposes (e.g., informing, defending, explaining, persuading, arguing, teaching).

7.2 Demonstrate effective oral communication skills in various formats (e.g., group discussion, debate, lecture) and for various purposes (e.g., informing,. defending, explaining, persuading, arguing, teaching).

7.3 Exhibit quantitative literacy. Demonstrate effective interpersonal communication skills.

7.4 Exhibit the ability to collaborate effectively.

Ciccarelli Student Voice questions

Narrative of the text—like a dialogue between author and reader

Test bank essay questions

Instructor's Resources Manual—see student assignments, lecture launchers and classroom activities sections

Ciccarelli online homework and assessment tools

8. Socio-cultural and International Awareness

Recognize, understand, and respect the complexity of sociocultural and international diversity.

8.1 Interact effectively and sensitively with people from diverse backgrounds and cultural perspectives.

8.2 Examine the sociocultural and international contexts that influence individual differences.

8.3 Explain how individual differences influence beliefs, values, and interactions with others and vice versa.

8.4 Understand how privilege, power, and oppression may affect prejudice, discrimination, and inequity Recognize prejudicial attitudes and discriminatory behaviors that might exist in themselves and others.

Ch 1: 1.2, 1.4

Ch 2: *Applying Psychology to Everyday Life: Differences Between Male and Female Brains*

Ch 8: 8.10–8.12, 8.17

Ch 9: 9.10–9.12

Ch 10: 10.2–10.8 and *Current Issues: The Intersex Controversy*

Ch 11: 11.5–11.6, 11.15–11.16

Ch 13: 13.13–13.15 and *Classic Studies: Brown Eyes, Blue Eyes* and *Latané and Darley*

Ch 14: 14.5

Diversity issues also covered in student study guide materials, online homework tools, and instructors' teaching and assessment package

APA UNDERGRADUATE LEARNING GOALS AND OUTCOMES	CICCARELLI LEARNING OBJECTIVES AND TEXT CONTENT

9. Personal Development

Develop insight into their own and other's behavior and mental processes and apply effective strategies for self-management and self-improvement.

9.1 Reflect on their experiences and find meaning in them.

9.2 Apply psychological principles to promote personal development.

9.3 Enact self-management strategies that maximize healthy outcomes.

9.4 Display high standards of personal integrity with others.

Ch 1: 1.16, study skills section

Ch 8: *Applying Psychology: Mental Exercises for Better Cognitive Health*

Ch 9: 9.11 and *Applying Psychology: A How-to of Happiness?*

Ch 10: 10.17 and *Applying Psychology: How to Protect Yourself from Sexually Transmitted Diseases*

Ch 11: 11.4, 11.12, 11.14, 11,17 and *Applying Psychology: Focus on Wellness*

Ch 12: *Applying Psychology: Personality Testing on the Internet*

Ch 13: 13.24–13.25

Ch 14: *Applying Psychology: Seasonal Affective Disorder*

Appendix 2: Applied Psychology

Study Guide: Study Challenge sections

10. Career Planning and Development

Pursue realistic ideas about how to implement their psychological knowledge, skills, and values in occupational pursuits in a variety of settings.

10.1 Apply knowledge of psychology (e.g., decision strategies, life span processes, psychological assessment, types of psychological careers) to formulating career choices.

10.2 Identify the types of academic experience and performance in psychology and the liberal arts that will facilitate entry into the work force, post-baccalaureate education, or both.

10.3 Describe preferred career paths based on accurate self-assessment of abilities, achievement, motivation, and work habits.

10.4 Identify and develop skills and experiences relevant to achieving selected career goals.

10.5 Demonstrate an understanding of the importance of lifelong learning and personal flexibility to sustain personal and professional development as the nature of work evolves.

Ch 1: 1.6

Appendix 2: Applied Psychology

Career planning content also found in student study guide materials, online homework tools, and instructors' teaching and assessment package

TEACHING AND LEARNING PACKAGE
Integration and Feedback

A student **Study Guide** by Brenda Fonseca (Mesa Community College) includes a chapter summary structured around the chapter learning objectives. An innovative study hints section helps students with the most difficult concepts in the chapter. Practice tests are included and a study challenge section helps students use the concepts they are learning to improve their study skills.

As valuable as a good textbook is, it is still only one element of a comprehensive learning package. The teaching and homework package that accompanies *Psychology* is the most comprehensive and integrated package on the market. We have made every effort to provide high-quality instructor supplements that will save you preparation time and enhance the time you spend in the classroom. My coauthor, Glenn Meyer from Trinity University, has overseen the development of each of the components of the teaching and assessment package by working directly with the authors and reviewers to ensure consistency in quality and content. We are grateful to the participants of numerous focus groups who provided feedback on many elements of the integrated package, as well as those instructors and students who reviewed and class tested the materials for us.

SAMPLE EXAM

For the following multiple choice questions, select the answer you feel best answers the question and explain the rationale or reason for your selection in the space provided.

Objective 1.1

1. How is psychology different from philosophy?

a.	Psychology uses the scientific method to answer questions.
b.	Psychology is interested in questions related to human behavior.
c.	There is no difference between philosophy and psychology.
d.	The field of psychology is much older than the field of philosophy.

   Sample Rationale:
   Psychology bases its answers on observations while philosophy answers its questions using logic and reasoning. Both fields are interested in human behavior. The field of psychology is only 125 years old, while philosophy is much older.

2. A researcher is attempting to design a program to help people stop smoking. The goal she is attempting to achieve is to

a.	describe
b.	predict
c.	explain
d.	control

   Sample Rationale:
   She is trying to change people's behaviors. This corresponds to the question of "how" (in other words, "how" do I help people to stop smoking).

3. A researcher is interested in finding out the percentage of adolescents in the U.S. who have depression. The goal he is attempting to achieve is to

a.	describe
b.	predict
c.	explain
d.	control

   | Rationale: | |

AXON

ACTION POTENTIAL

STUDY HINTS

1. As you can see in the "New Terms and Concepts" section, this chapter introduces a large number of new vocabulary terms. You should plan on spending additional time working on these new terms and committing them to memory. Some students find flash cards and study partners helpful for learning this material. For additional assistance, work through the "Study Challenge" at the end of this section. Many students have found it extremely helpful.

2. Some students have a hard time keeping the various research methods straight. It might be helpful to divide the methods into two categories: (1) methods that provide a picture of the structures of the brain and (2) methods that measure the activity of the brain. CT scans were developed before MRIs and do not provide as many details as the MRI does. If you've ever had a CT scan or an MRI performed, you will know that getting an MRI is a much more expensive procedure than a CT scan, although neither procedure is cheap. EEGs only provide information about activity in the outermost part of your brain. PET scans can provide information about activity anywhere in your brain but typically don't provide details about the exact location of the activiy. fMRIs show the activity and the detailed location where the activity is taking place.

Structure of the brain	Activity of the brain
CT scan	EEG
MRI	PET scan
	fMRI

SAMPLE EXAM ANSWERS

1.	a	Psychology bases its answers on observations while philosophy ans[...] questions using logic and reasoning. Both fields are interested in hu[...] behavior. The field of psychology is only 125 years old, while philos[...] much older.
2.	d	She is trying to change people's behaviors. This corresponds to the question of "how" (in other words, "how do I help people to stop smoking).
3.	a	He would like to describe this particular group with regards to depression rates. He is trying to answer the question of "what". What is the current depression rate among U.S. teenagers?
4	d	All of the questions fall [...] the category of describing, predicting, explaining [...]

The **Test Item File** by Dan Bellack (Trident Technical College), Jane Cirillo (Houston Community College), and Glenn Meyer (Trinity University) includes a two-page Total Assessment Guide that lists all of the test items in an easy to reference grid. The Total Assessment Guide organizes all test items by learning objective and questions type.

TOTAL ASSESSMENT GUIDE

Chapter 6
Memory

Topic	Question Type	Factural	Conceptual	Applied
6.1 What is memory? What are the three processes of memory?	Multiple Choice	1, 6, 7, 8, 11	2, 3, 4, 5, 9, 12, 13	10, 172, 140, 141
	True/False	128, 129, 130, 131, 132, 133, 134, 135, 136, 137,		168, 169,
	Short Answer	250, 166, 167	249, 251, 173	
	Essay		261	
6.2 What are some of the different models of how memory works?	Multiple Choice	15, 16, 18, 19, 20, 174, 175, 159, 160		170, 171
	True/False	142, 143, 144, 145, 146, 147		
	Short Answer	252, 253	263	
	Essay		276	
6.3 What is sensory memory?	Multiple Choice	21, 22, 23, 25, 163, 164, 165, 138		139, 162
	True/False	48, 149, 150, 151, 152, 153, 154, 155, 156, 157, 158,		
	Short Answer		161	
	Essay			

52) Professor Beverly approaches questions about human behavior from a perspective which emphasizes bodily events and chemicals, such as hormones, associated with behavior. It is most likely that she accepts which of the following psychological approaches?

A) Learning   B) Biopsychological   C) Cognitive   D) Sociocultural

Explanation: A)
          B) Correct. The biopsychological perspective looks at the relationship between body chemistry and behavior.
          C)
          D) Incorrect. The sociocultural perspective focuses on culture and sociology, not biology.

Diff: 2   Type: MC   Page Ref: 25
Objective: 1.05 What were the contributions of Skinner, Maslow, and Rogers?
User1: Applied

An additional feature for the test bank, currently not found in any other texts, is the inclusion of **rationales for the correct answer and the key distracters** in the multiple choice questions. The rationales help instructors reviewing the content further evaluate the questions they are choosing for their tests and give instructors the option to use the rationales as an answer key for their students.

- The test item file has been thoroughly **class tested** and revised in response to feedback. It has also been reviewed by a developmental editor and a copy editor in order to ensure delivery of the highest quality assessment tool.

- In addition to the high-quality test bank described here, a second bank of over 2000 questions by Fred Whitford (Montana State University) also has been class tested, with item analysis available for each question.

- A powerful new computerized test program helps instructors who are teaching online offer a rich assessment experience. The latest version of Test Gen allows instructors to easily create tests for in-class delivery.

The Instructor's Resource Manual authored by Diane Ashe and Debra Hollister (Valencia Community College) offers an exhaustive collection of resources. For each chapter, you'll find activities, exercises, assignments, handouts, and demos for in-class use, as well as guidelines on integrating the many Ciccarelli media resources into your classroom and syllabus. The material for each chapter is organized by learning objectives in an easy-to-use Chapter Lecture Outline and Resource Integration Guide. This resource saves prep work and helps you maximize your classroom time.

LECTURE LAUNCHERS AND DISCUSSION TOPICS

Lecture/Discussion 1: How Do We Know What We Know?

How do you know that
George Washington was the first president of the United States?
you really have a stomach?

Dependence on observation is one of the hallmarks of science, but it is not the only way humans acquire knowledge. There are, in fact, many questions that cannot be answered by scientific methods and for which other means of acquiring knowledge are more appropriate. Begin by asking the following questions.

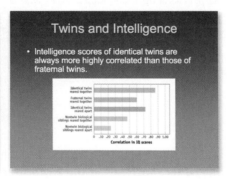

PowerPoint slides by Tammy Barry (University of Southern Mississippi) include illustrations from the text as well as content from a variety of other sources that highlight all of the key points in the text and include easy-to-follow notes on how to customize and enhance your presentations. The PowerPoint presentation is available in print format in the instructor's manual so instructors can review the content of the slides.

Also included are **Classroom Response System questions** by Melissa Acevedo (Valencia Community College) that help generate discussion and provide instant feedback on how your students are responding to the lecture content.

All of the following are sysptoms of ADHD EXCEPT:

1. Feelings of restlessness
2. Not paying attention when spoken to by others
3. Impatient and impulsive
4. Inability to pay attention to details
5. Prolonged atention but to inappropriate aspects of the social situation.

■ Over 130 full-color transparencies are designed to be used in large lecture settings and include illustrations from the text as well as images from a variety of other sources.

This valuable timesaving supplement brings all of the text instructor resources together in one convenient place. The **Instructor's Resource CD-ROM** offers presentation resources, including video clips and PowerPoint presentations customized for the Ciccarelli text. It also includes the electronic files for the Instructor's Resource Manual materials and the Test Item File to help you build your lecture notes.

NEW Introductory Psychology Teaching Films Boxed Set

Offering qualified college adopters an easy-to-use multi-DVD set of videos, organized by topic for easy lecture integration. Includes 100 short video clips of 5–15 minutes in length from many of the most popular video sources for psychology content, such as **ABCNEWS**; the Films for the Humanities series; PBS; Pennsylvania State Media Sales Video Classics, and more!

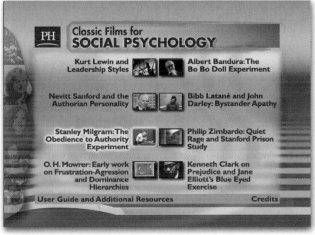

NEW Classic Experiments in Psychology from Pennsylvania State Media, Edited by Dennis Thompson, Georgia State University

This five DVD set includes the best-known classic film footage for key concepts and researchers in the field of psychology. Most clips are from 5–15 minutes in length. The set is available to qualified college adopters. Contact your local Prentice Hall representative for more information.

ONLINE OPTIONS
for *Psychology*

Exciting new program for a compelling online homework/classroom connection

The APA Applying Assessment Strategies in Psychology strongly recommend self-assessment tools and the use of embedded questions and assignments (see **www.apa.org/ed/eval_strategies.html** for more information). Continual feedback is also an important component to successful student progress. The new online learning system offered with *Psychology* is built around the text learning objectives. Students are provided access to chapter-by-chapter diagnostic tests. The tests have a large base of questions distinct from the test bank and other supplementary materials. If students opt to retake a test, different questions are offered on the same objectives. Various question types are used for the diagnostic, including multiple choice, matrix multiple choice, text match, ranking, fill in the blank, and drag and drop. Results from the diagnostic build a customized study plan, and students are provided rich supplementary content to help them learn any objectives they have not yet mastered. The supplementary content includes exercises tied to an e-book, animations, simulations and experiments, as well as audio and video links.

Instructors are provided with the results of the diagnostic tests-by student as well as an aggregate report of their class. Based on the diagnostic results of the class, instructors receive a suggested customized lesson plan based on their own students' results. The customized lesson plan provides opportunity for a compelling classroom experience based on actual student performance. This time-saving feature gives instructors materials specific to the needs of their class and helps to catalogue student progress. Students get an access code that is available at no additional cost with the purchase of a new text for college adoptions.

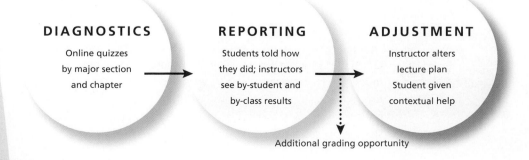

DIAGNOSTICS
Online quizzes by major section and chapter

REPORTING
Students told how they did; instructors see by-student and by-class results

ADJUSTMENT
Instructor alters lecture plan Student given contextual help

Additional grading opportunity

Live!Psych, a library of highly interactive media simulations, animations, and experiments has been developed to teach the key concepts crucial to understanding psychology. Live!Psych simulations and experiments are embedded within students' customized study plans, helping to focus on the concepts they need to master.

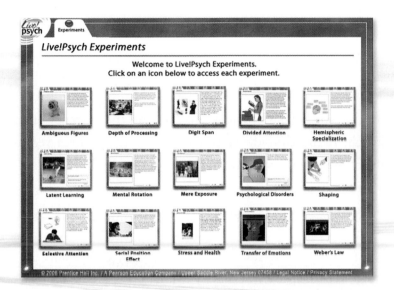

Live!Psych media experiments offer students an interactive way to master the major concepts presented in the text and to reinforce the scientific nature of the discipline. For each experiment, students are given an introduction to the experiment topic, a history and background for the specific experiment, and instructions on how to complete the experiment and several test trials. The student's own individual data from the experiment are gathered, analyzed, and compared to published studies to illustrate the significance of the results.

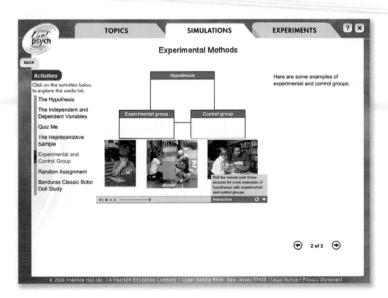

Live!Psych interactive media simulations are designed to get students to interact with the material and to appeal to different learning styles. These media activities were created in consultation with psychology instructors and carefully reviewed by a board of experts to ensure accuracy and pedagogical effectiveness.

OneKey™ offers rich content for instructors teaching full online courses. OneKey™ is the online destination instructors need to present, assess, and communicate with students more effectively than ever.

Also available, online companion website at **www.prenhall.com/ciccarelli**

DEVELOPMENT STORY
Insight and Collaboration

The creation of this text and package is the result of the most extensive development investment in any text that this discipline has ever experienced. We are grateful for the contributions of over 600 instructors and students. More than 150 manuscript reviewers provided invaluable feedback. Expert reviewers in critical topic areas provided feedback on the currency and accuracy of the research. A full-time development editor spent three years going over three drafts of the manuscript editing the prose line-by-line for clarity. More than 50 focus group participants contributed to decisions about text organization, content coverage, and pedagogical innovation. Over 300 students have class-tested the manuscript prior to publication. Student reviewers have also been involved in evaluating the clarity of the writing style and the value of the in-text learning tools and assessment features. We are grateful to all who provided feedback on the manuscript as well as the design—which we hope you find as inviting as we do!

California
Vera Dunwoody, Chaffey College
Steve Isonio, Golden West Community College
Fernando Ortiz, Santa Ana Community College
Michelle Pilati, Rio Hondo College
Angela Sadowski, Chaffey College

Colorado
Karla Gingerich, Colorado State University
Misty Hull, Pikes Peak Community College
Diane Martichuski, University of Colorado at Boulder
Lisa Routh, Pikes Peak Community College

Connecticut
Marlene Adelman, Norwalk Community College
Moises Salinas, Central Connecticut State University
Lawrence Venuk, Naugatuck Valley Community College

Florida
Melissa Acevedo, Valencia Community College–West
Kathleen Bey, Palm Beach Community College–Central
Kelvin Faison, Pasco Hernando Community College
Peter Gram, Pensacola Junior College
Joe Grisham, Indian River Community College
Amy Hackney, Georgia Southern University
Sheryl Hartman, Miami Dade Community College

Debra Hollister, Valencia Community College
Jennifer Peluso, Florida Atlantic University
Jeanine Plowman, Florida State University
Wayne Stein, Brevard Community College–Melbourne
Patricia Stephenson, Miami Dade Community College
Richard Townsend, Miami Dade Community College
Rochelle Warm, Palm Beach Community College–South

Georgia
Deb Briihl, Valdosta State University
Kristen Diliberto-Macaluso, Berry College
Dan Fawaz, Georgia Perimeter College
Adam Goodie, University of Georgia
Amy Hackney, Georgia Southern University

Illinois
Joseph Ferrari, DePaul University
Pablo Gomez, DePaul University
Christine Grela, McHenry County College
Susan Harris-Mitchell, College of DuPage
Karen Owens, College of Lake County
Ada Wainwright, College of DuPage

Indiana
Cathy Alsman, Ivy Tech State College– Terre Haute

Darrell Rudmann, Indiana East University
Don Shull, Ivy Tech–Evansville

Iowa
Lee Skeens. Southeastern Community College

Kansas
Diane Kappen, Johnson County Community College
John Sanders, Garden City Community College
Joe Slobko, Garden City Community College

Kentucky
Kim Case, Northern Kentucky University
Lynn Haller, Morehead State College
Sabra Jacobs, Prestonburg Community College

Louisiana
Brett Heintz, Delgado Community College
Jack Palmer, University of Louisiana –Monroe

Maryland
Misty Kolchakian, Anne Arundel Community College

Massachusetts
Marcelle Bartolo-Abela, Holyoke Community and Baypath Colleges
Shirley Cassarra, Bunker Hill Community College

Michigan
Michael Drissman, Macomb Community College–South
Patricia Lanzon, Henry Ford Community College
Terri Heck, Macomb Community College–South

Mississippi
Shaila Khan, Tougaloo Community College
Randy Vinzant, Jones County Junior College

Missouri
John Gambon, Ozarks Technical College

Nebraska
Patrick Dolan, Drew University
Jean Mandernach, University of Nebraska, Kearney
Keith Matthews, Northeast Community College
James Thomas, University of Nebraska–Omaha

New Jersey
John Ramirez, Middlesex County College
Anthony Zoccolillo, DeVry University

New Mexico
Katherine Demitrakis, Albuquerque Tech–Vocational Institute
Andrea Ericksen, San Juan College
Sarah Erickson, University of New Mexico
Marisa McLeod, Santa Fe Community College
Ron Salazar, San Juan College

New York
Miles Groth, Wagner College
Joe Lao, Teachers College, Columbia University

North Carolina
Beth Barton, Coastal Carolina Community College and University of North Carolina–Wilmington
Micha Pitzen, Coastal Carolina Community College
Stephanie Williford, Coastal Carolina Community College

Ohio
Leslie Angel, Sinclair Community College

Ronald Craig, Cincinnati State College
Lorry Cology, Owens Community College
Diane Feibel, Raymond Walters Community College
Keith Syrja, Owens Community College

Oklahoma
Mike Knight, University of Central Oklahoma

Oregon
Barbara DeFilippo, Lane Community College

Pennsylvania
Daniel Klaus, Community College of Beaver County
Sonya Lott-Harrison, Community College of Philadelphia
Peter Zubritzky, Community College of Beaver County

South Carolina
Dan Bellack, Trident Technical College
Devin Byrd, University of South Carolina–Aiken
William House, University of South Carolina–Aiken
Nancy Simpson, Trident Technical College

Tennessee
Michelle Merwin, University of Tennessee–Martin

Texas
Jane Cirillo, Houston Community College–Southeast
Wanda Clark, South Plains College
Perry Collins, Wayland Baptist University
Wendy Domjan, University of Texas–Austin
James Francis, San Jacinto College–South
Perry Fuchs, University of Texas–Arlington
Judith Keith, Tarrant County Community College–Northeast
Shirin Khosropour, Austin Community College
Richard Kirk, Texas State Technical College
Cynthia Reed, Tarrant County College–Northeast
Eric Reittinger, Texas A&M University
David Shepard, South Texas Community College
Sangeeta Singg, Angelo State University
Peggy Skinner, South Plains College
Tom Wood, Sam Houston State University

Utah
David Yells, Utah Valley State College

Virginia
Molly Lynch, NOVA–Manassas
Bethany Marcus, ECPI College of Technology
James O'Brien, Tidewater Community College
Theresa Tuttle, ECPI College of Technology

West Virginia
Chris LeGrow, Marshall University

Wisconsin
Kathleen Kavanaugh, Milwaukee Area Technical College
Bart Van Voorhis, University of Wisconsin–La Crosse

Text Focus Group
John Creech, Collin County Community College
Vera Dunwoody, Chaffey College
Dan Fawaz, Georgia Perimeter College
Dan Grangaard, Austin Community College
Wayne Hall, San Jacinto college–Central
Susan Hornstein, Southern Methodist University
Shirin Khosropor, Austin Community College

Irv Lichtman, Houston Community College
Michael McCoy, Cape Fear Community College
Wendy Mills, San Jacinto College–North
Annette Nolte, Tarrant County College
Laura Overstreet, Tarrant County College
Gloria Scheff, Broward Community College
Nancy Simpson, Trident Technical College
Joe Tinnin, Richland College
Andrea Zabel, Midland College

Reviewer Conference Participants
Dan Bellack, Trident Technical College
Jane Cirillo, Houston Community College Southeast
Vera Dunwoody, Chaffey College
Perry Fuchs, University of Texas, Arlington
Amy Hackney, Georgia Southern University
Jennifer Peluso, Florida Atlantic University
Cynthia Reed, Tarrant County College–Northeast
Stephanie Williford, Coastal Carolina Community College

Supplements Focus Groups
Kristin Anderson, Houston Community College–Southwest
Susan Anderson, University of South Alabama.
Melissa Avecedo, Valencia Community College
Mike Barber, Lake City Community College
Kathy Bey, Palm Beach Community College
Jack Chuang, San Jacinto College–Central
Jane Cirillo, Houston Community College–Southeast
Wanda Clark, South Plains College
Perry Collins, Wayland Baptist
Jacqueline Cuevas, Midwestern State
Barbara DeFilippo, Lane Community College
Ann Ewing, Mesa Community College
Brenda Fonesca, Mesa Community College
Dan Grangaard, Austin Community College
Sheryl Hartman, Miami Dade College

Karen Hoblit, Victoria College
Debra Hollister, Valencia Community College
Shirin Khospour, Austin Community College
Irv Lichtman, Houston Community College–Northeast
Jerry Marshall, Green River Community College
Marisa McLeod, Santa Fe Community College
Fred Miller, Portland Community College
Jennifer Peluso, Florida Atlantic University
Skip Pollock, Mesa Community College
Genevieve Stevens, Houston Community College–Central
Larry Symon, Western Washington University
Richard Townsend, Miami Dade College
Madeline Wright, Houston Community College–Central
Charles Verschoor, Miami Dade Community College
Andrea Zabel, Midland College
Clare Zaborowski, San Jacinto College–South

Student Reviewers
Maribel Acevedo
Tiffany Anglin
Tracy Marie Augustine
Chris Beard
Kelly Butler
Alina Cole
Ericka Ferrias
James Frier
Maria Guzman
Danielle Marie Ikonomides
Noemi Maldonado
Gricelda Moreno
Shalay Nash
Natalia M. Ramos
Jack Wilkinson
Sharee Wright
Nancy Alvarez
Vanessa Armendariz
Thomas Baker
Lisa Bosecker
Yvronis Charles
Melissa Linn Davis
Kalofa Fregini
Maria G. Gonzalez
Meredith Hawkins
Danna Lowe
Nelida Martinez
Melissa Muldowney
Shana Prado
Pierre A. Saintable
Amanda Wright

Acknowledgments

The saga of this text really began at a lovely little restaurant on the water in beautiful old St. Andrews, Panama City, Florida. It was there that my long-time friends and Prentice Hall employees Cindy Sullivan and Becky Hairelson wheedled, flattered, and gently prodded me into believing that I could write this text and survive to tell the tale. So I must give Cindy and Becky my heartfelt thanks for all their support and for believing in me. I have to thank my husband, Joe Ciccarelli, and my children, Al and Liz, who put up with my being absent for long hours every night and every weekend as the book came together. Among the many other people who have helped and advised me along the way, I must thank Yolanda de Rooy and Leah Jewell for talking me into signing the contract. At least I think that should be a "thank you…" Yolanda and Leah also deserve special thanks for all of the support they have put behind this text. They were the powers at Prentice Hall who committed to spending the time, effort, and money to make this book a reality. Thank you also to Rochelle Diogenes for moral support and great guidance behind the scenes, so to speak. Thanks to Jessica Mosher who managed to bring it all together and keep it (and me) from flying apart at various times, and this despite the fact that she apparently conceived and delivered a baby during her five minutes of spare time. Thanks to Kathleen Sleys for all her great work in checking and re-checking and re-re-checking the manuscript and Jeanette Moyer for arranging a fantastic marketing campaign. Thanks to my co-author, Glenn Meyer, for doing an amazing job of getting all the supplements coordinated. Thanks to Glenn, Dan Bellack, and Jane Cirillo for all of their suggestions and for taking on the heroic task of writing the test bank as the text was being written (and then rewriting the test bank as each "final" version appeared). Leslie Osher and Anne DeMarinis did a marvelous job on the design of the book, thank you! But my most heartfelt thanks must go to Susanna Lesan, who was involved in the editing and review and writing and who knows what else of every word in this textbook, who kept me sane and continually told me that I could do this, and that I was doing it well—I couldn't have done it without you, Susanna, thanks a million!

—*Sandy Ciccarelli*
Gulf Coast Community College
Panama City, Florida
sciccarelli@gulfcoast.edu

I wish to thank Prentice Hall for the opportunity to be involved in this project. I especially want to thank my colleagues, Drs. Dan Bellack and Jane Cirillo for their wisdom and support in this endeavor.

—*Glenn E. Meyer*
Trinity University
San Antonio, Texas

About the Authors

Saundra K. Ciccarelli is a professor at Gulf Coast Community College in Panama City, Florida. She received her doctorate in development psychology from the George Peabody College of Vanderbilt University, Nashville Tennessee. She is a member of Division 2 of the APA. Ciccarelli was originally interested in a career as a researcher in language and intelligence development in developmentally delayed children and adolescents, and had publications in the *American Journal of Mental Deficiency* while still at Peabody. However, she discovered a love of teaching early on in her career. This led Ciccarelli to the position at Gulf Coast Community College, where she has been teaching introductory psychology for over 20 years. Her students love her enthusiasm for the field of psychology and the many anecdotes and examples she uses to bring psychology to life for them. While this is her first textbook, she has authored numerous ancillary materials for several different introductory psychology texts.

Glenn E. Meyer is a professor at Trinity University. He received his doctorate in cognitive psychology from the State University of New York at Buffalo. He has been teaching introductory psychology for over 20 years. His research interests include physiological and cognitive approaches to perception, color vision, human computer interaction, social cognition of aggression and cognitive neuroscience. He has numerous academic publications in journals such as *Science, Nature, Perception, Perception and Psychophyics, Vision Research, The Journal of Experimental Psychology*, and *Child Development*, and has authored several ancillary materials for undergraduate psychology textbooks. He is the supplements coordinator for the Ciccarelli text, authoring much of the ancillary content and overseeing the development of the materials to ensure consistency in content and quality.

Introduction

Secrets for Surviving College:
How to Improve Your Grades

Warning: Reading the following material may lead
to higher grades and lower anxiety!

I want to make better grades, but sometimes it seems that
no matter how hard I study, the test questions turn out
to be hard and confusing and I end up not doing very well.
Is there some trick to getting good grades?

Many students would probably say that their grades are not what they want them to be. They may make the effort, but they still don't seem to be able to achieve the higher grades that they wish they could have. A big part of the problem is that despite many varied educational experiences students are rarely taught how to study. Many students entering college have developed a system of taking notes, reading the textbook, and reviewing for exams that has worked pretty well in the past, but what worked in grade school and high school may not work in college, when the expectations from teachers are higher and the workload is far greater. There are five things students need to know in order to do their absolute best in any college course:

- One's particular learning style.
- How to read a textbook and take notes so that it's understandable the first time.
- How to take notes during lectures.
- How to study for exams.
- How to write term papers.

This Introduction presents various techniques and information for maximizing knowledge and skills in each of these five areas.

Auditory learners need to listen in addition to other forms of learning. This woman is listening to a tape of the textbook she is reading while she looks at the figures and pictures.

Learning Styles: Different Strokes for Different Folks

If everyone learned new information in exactly the same way, life would be so much easier. Teachers would know exactly how to present material so that all students would have an equal opportunity to learn. Unfortunately, that just is not the way it works—people are different in many ways, and one of the ways they differ is in the style of learning that works best for each person.

Exactly what is a **learning style**? In general, a learning style is the particular way in which a person takes in information (Dunn et al., 1989, 2001; Felder, 1993, 1996). People take in information in several ways: through the eyes, by reading text or looking at charts, diagrams, and maps; through the ears, by listening, talking things out, and discussing things with others; and through the sense of touch and the movement of the body, by touching things, writing things down, drawing pictures and diagrams, and learning by doing (Barsch, 1996).

TYPES OF LEARNING STYLES

Learning styles are often classified based on personality theories or theories of intelligence. The number of different learning styles varies with the theory, but most theories of learning styles include **visual learners**, who learn best by seeing, reading, and looking at images; **auditory learners**, who learn best by hearing and saying things out loud; **tactile learners**, who need to touch things; **kinesthetic learners**, who prefer to learn by doing and being active; and **social learners**, who prefer to learn with other people or in groups (Dunn et al., 1989). Most people will find that they have one dominant, or most powerful, learning style along with one or two secondary styles. Notice that several of the learning styles described would work well together: Auditory learners and social learners, for example, work well together, as do tactile and kinesthetic learners, because they are both hands-on kinds of learners. Many theories simply divide people into four basic styles of learning (Barsch, 1996; Dunn et al., 1989; Jester, 2000):

- **Visual/Verbal.** These people learn best when looking at material, particularly things that are written down. Reading the textbook, using classroom notes, and having an instructor who uses overhead projections, writes on the board, or uses visual multimedia presentations are very helpful. Visual/verbal learners, because they focus on reading and taking notes, tend to learn best when studying alone rather than in a group.

- **Visual/Nonverbal.** These are people who are visual learners but learn best through the use of diagrams, pictures, charts, videos, and other image-oriented material rather than printed text. This type of learner, like the visual/verbal learner, also prefers to study alone.

- **Auditory/Verbal.** Auditory/verbal learners take in information best by listening. Group discussions and a lecture format in which the instructor talks about the subject are of the most benefit to this style of learning.

- **Tactile/Kinesthetic.** This style of learner needs a "hands-on" opportunity to learn. Lab classes are very good ways for this type of learner to absorb material. Instructors who do lots of demonstrations and may use field experiences outside of the classroom are good for this style of learner. Some kinesthetic learners benefit from writing notes during a lecture or from writing a summary of their lecture notes afterward.

Notice that the social aspect of learning (studying alone or with others) is included as a part of the description of these four styles. Students who know their learning style can adapt their study habits and note-taking to methods that work best for that style. Finding out one's style is accomplished by taking a simple test. There are a number of

learning style
the particular way in which a person takes in information.

visual learners
people who learn best by seeing, reading, and looking at images.

auditory learners
people who learn best by hearing and saying things out loud.

tactile learners
people who need to touch objects in order to learn about them.

kinesthetic learners
people who prefer to learn by doing and being active.

social learners
people who prefer to learn with other people or in groups.

online assessments for learning styles, or your college's career center may have tests available. Here are a few online assessment sites:

The DVC Learning Style Survey for College (Jester, 2000):
www.metamath.com/lsweb/dvclearn.htm

The Barsch Learning Styles Inventory (Barsch, 1996):
www.xu.edu/lac/Barsch.htm (from Xavier University)

The VARK Questionnaire (Fleming & Mills, 1992):
www.vark-learn.com/English/page.asp?p=questionnaire

DeVry University Online Learning Styles Assessment (DeVry University, 2004):
www.devry.edu/online/online_styles.html

LEARNING STYLES AND LEARNING

Does knowing one's learning style really help improve learning? The research findings have produced mixed results thus far with some finding support for the idea that matching learning styles to teaching styles produces improvement (Braio et al., 1997; Drysdale et al., 2001; Dunn et al., 1986, 1995; Ford & Chen, 2001), but a large survey of the research in this field found little consistent support (Coffield et al., 2004).

From the teacher's point of view, learning styles present a very practical problem. Instructors must teach to the most common level of understanding and may not be able to easily teach for multiple learning styles. The typical instructor may not have a lot of classroom time to do demonstrations, write things on the board, or spend time in discussions, for example. For a student, however, knowing one's learning style can have an impact on note-taking, studying, and reading the textbook. Table 1 presents some study

Some people need to learn in the presence of others, making study groups such as this one an ideal format for the social learner. What are some other study methods that a social learner might use?

TABLE 1 STUDY TIPS FOR DIFFERENT LEARNING STYLES

Visual/Verbal	Visual/Nonverbal	Auditory	Tactile/Kinesthetic
Use different colors of highlighter for different sections of information in text or notes.	Make flash cards with pictures or diagrams to aid recall of key concepts.	Join or form a study group or find a study partner so that you can discuss concepts and ideas.	Sit near the front of the classroom and take notes by jotting down key terms and making pictures or charts to help you remember what you are hearing.
Use flash cards of main points or key terms.	Make charts and diagrams and sum up information in tables.	Talk out loud while studying or into a tape recorder that you can play back later.	When you study, read information out loud while walking back and forth.
Write out key information in whole sentences or phrases in your own words.	Use different highlighter colors for different information but do symbols and diagrams as well as key terms and ideas.	Make speeches.	Study with a friend.
When looking at diagrams, write out a description.	Visualize charts, diagrams, and figures.	Tape the lectures (with permission). Take notes on the lecture sparingly, using the tape to fill in parts that you might have missed.	While exercising, listen to tapes that you have made containing important information.
Use "sticky" notes to remind yourself of key terms and information, and put them in the notebook or text or on a mirror that you use frequently.	Redraw things from memory.	Read notes or text material into a tape recorder or get study materials on tape and play back while driving or doing other chores.	Write out key concepts on a large board or poster.
Visualize spellings of words or facts to be remembered.	Study alone in a quiet place.	When learning something new, state the information in your own words out loud or to a study partner.	Make flash cards, using different colors and diagrams, and lay them out on a large surface. Practice putting them in order.
Rewrite things from memory.			Make a three-dimensional model.
Study alone in a quiet place.			Spend extra time in the lab.
			Go to outside areas such as a museum or historical site to gain information.
			Trace letters and words to remember key facts.
			Use musical rhythms as memory aids, putting information to rhyme or a tune.

tips for visual, auditory, and tactile/kinesthetic learners. All of the techniques listed in this table are good for students who wish to improve both their understanding of a subject and their grades on tests.

Notice that all four of the learning styles make use of some similar methods but in different ways. For example, drawing graphs, charts, and diagrams is a good technique for the visual/nonverbal and the tactile/kinesthetic learners, and both types of visual learners tend to do better when studying alone to improve concentration, whereas both the auditory and the tactile/kinesthetic learners benefit from studying with others and "talking it out."

No matter what the learning style, students must read the textbook to be successful in the course. The next section deals with how to read textbooks for understanding rather than just to "get through" the material.

Reading Textbooks: Textbooks Are Not Meatloaf

There are two common mistakes that people make with regard to reading a textbook. The first mistake is simple: Many people don't bother to read the textbook before going to the lecture that will cover that material. Trying to get anything out of a lecture without reading the material first is like trying to find a new, unfamiliar place without using a map or any kind of directions. It's easy to get "lost." This is especially true because of the assumption that most instructors make when planning their lectures: They assume that the students have already read the assignment. The instructors then use the lecture to expound on the information the students supposedly got from the reading. If the students haven't done the reading, the instructor's lecture isn't going to make a whole lot of sense.

The second mistake that most people make when reading textbook material is to try to read it the same way they would read a novel: They start at the first page and read continuously. With a novel, it's easy to do this because the plot is usually interesting and people want to know what happens next, so they keep reading. It isn't necessary to remember every little detail—all they need to remember are the main plot points. One could say that a novel is like a meatloaf—some meaty parts with lots of filler. Meatloaf can be eaten quickly, without even chewing for very long.

Before reading any chapter in a text, you should survey the chapter by reading the outline and the section headings.

With a textbook, the material may be interesting but not in the same way that a novel is interesting. A textbook is a big, thick steak—all meat, no filler. Just as a steak has to be chewed to be enjoyed and to be useful to the body, textbook material has to be "chewed" with the mind. You have to read slowly, paying attention to every morsel of meaning.

So how do you do that? Probably one of the best-known reading methods is called SQ3R, first used by F. P. Robinson in a book called *Effective Study* (1970). The letters S-Q-R-R-R stand for:

SURVEY   Look at the chapter you've been assigned to read.

- Take a look at the outline at the beginning of the chapter or whatever opening questions, learning objectives, or other material the author has chosen to let you, the reader, know what the chapter is about.

- Flip through the chapter and read the headings of each section, and look at the tables, figures, graphs, and cartoons to get an idea about the kinds of things that you will be learning.
- Finally, quickly read through the chapter summary if there is one.

It might sound like it takes too much time to do this, but you should just be skimming at this point—a couple of minutes is all it should take. Why do this at all? Surveying the chapter, or "previewing" it, as some experts call it, helps you form a framework in your head around which you can organize the information in the chapter when you read it in detail. In Chapter Six, organization is listed as one of the main ways to improve your memory for information. Think of it this way: As mentioned earlier, if you are going to drive to a new place, it's helpful to have a road map to give you an idea of what's up ahead. Surveying the chapter is giving yourself a "road map" for the material in the chapter.

QUESTION   After previewing the chapter, read the heading for the first section. *Just* the first section! Try to think of a question based on this heading that the section should answer as you read. For example, in Chapter One there's a section titled "John B. Watson and Behaviorism." You could ask yourself, "What did Watson do for psychology?" or "What is behaviorism?" Some textbooks even include questions at the start of many sections. In this text, there is a list of learning objectives for the key concepts in the chapter in the form of questions that can be used with the SQ3R method. There are also student questions that can serve the same purpose. These questions, which are based on the author's years of hearing and answering similar questions from students in the classroom, will be in a "balloon" with the picture of a typical student who is asking the question. Now when you read the section, you aren't *just* reading—you're reading to *find an answer*. That makes the material much easier to remember later on.

READ   Now read the section, looking for the answer to your questions. As you read, take notes by making an outline of the main points and terms in the section. This is another area where people make a big mistake. They assume that using a highlighter to mark words and phrases is as good as writing notes. One of the author's former students is conducting research on the difference between highlighting and note-taking, and her preliminary findings are clear: Students who write their own notes during the reading of a text or while listening to a lecture scored significantly higher on their exam grades than students who merely used a highlighter on the text (Boyd & Peeler, 2004). Highlighting requires no real mental effort (no "chewing," in other words), but writing the words down yourself requires you to read the words in depth and understand them. In Chapter Eight, Cognition, you'll learn more about the value of processing information in depth.

RECITE   It may sound silly, but reciting *out loud* what you can remember from the section you've just read is another good way to process the information more deeply and completely. How many times have you thought you understood something, only to find that when you tried to tell it to someone, you didn't understand it at all? Recitation forces you to put the information in your own words, just as writing it down in the form of notes does. Writing it down accesses your visual memory; saying it out loud gives you an auditory memory for the same information. If you have ever learned something well by teaching it to someone else, you already know the

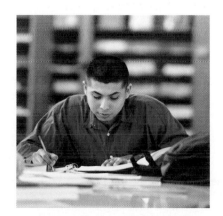

As you read, take notes. Write down key terms and try to summarize the key points of each paragraph and section in the chapter. These notes will be useful when you later review the chapter material.

value of recitation. If you feel self-conscious about talking to yourself, talk into a tape recorder—it makes a great way to review while traveling in the car.

Now repeat the Question, Read, and Recite instructions for each section, taking a few minutes' break after every two or three sections. Why take a break? There's a process that has to take place in your brain when you are trying to form a permanent memory for information, and that process takes a little bit of time. When you take a break every 10 to 20 minutes, you are giving your brain time to do this process. Doing this avoids a common problem in reading texts in which when you find yourself reading the same sentence over and over again because your brain is too overloaded with trying to remember what you just read to continue reading.

RECALL/REVIEW Finally, you've finished reading the entire chapter. If you've used the guidelines listed previously, you'll only have to read the chapter in this depth once instead of having to read it over and over throughout the semester and just before exams. Once you've read the chapter, take a few minutes to try to remember as much of what you learned while reading it as you can. A good way to do this is to take any practice quizzes that might be available, either in your text or a student workbook that goes with the text. Many publishers have Web sites for their textbooks that have practice quizzes available online. If there are no quizzes, read the chapter summary in detail, making sure that you understand everything in it. If there's anything that's confusing, go back to that section in the chapter and read again until you understand it.

Reading textbooks in this way means that you only have to read them once. When it comes time for the final exam, all you will have to do is carefully review your notes to be ready for the exam—you won't have to read the entire textbook all over again. What a time-saver!

How To Take Notes: Printing Out PowerPoint Slides Is NOT Taking Notes

Remember the study showing that highlighting is not as effective as note-taking (Boyd & Peeler, 2004)? One of this researcher's earliest studies was a comparison of students who took notes by hand while listening to a lecture with PowerPoint slides and students who printed out the PowerPoint slides and merely used a highlighter to stress certain ideas on the printout. Students taking notes by hand scored an average of one letter grade higher on exams than did the students who used a highlighter on the printouts. PowerPoint slides are not meant to be notes at all; they are merely talking points that help the instructor follow a particular sequence in lecturing. Typically, the instructor will have more to say about each point on the slide, and that is the information students should be listening to and writing down. In Table 1, the suggestions to use highlighters of different colors are not meant to replace taking notes but instead to supplement the notes you do take.

TAKING NOTES WHILE READING THE TEXT

How should you take notes? As stated earlier, you should try to take notes while reading the chapter by writing down the main points and the vocabulary terms *in your own words* as much as possible. It's important to put the information in your own words because that forces you to think about what you are reading. The more you think about it, the more likely it is that the concepts will become a part of your permanent memory. Remembering to use the techniques for your particular learning style is important, too. For example, auditory learners should try to state ideas out loud in their own words as well as writing them down.

TAKING NOTES DURING THE LECTURE

Taking notes while listening to the lecture is a slightly different procedure. First, you should have your notes from the reading in front of you, and it helps to leave plenty of space between lines to add notes from the lecture. As mentioned in the section on how to read a textbook, a major mistake made by many students is to come to the lecture without having read the material first. This is an EXTREMELY BAD IDEA. In case that didn't sink in the first time, let me repeat it: **Extremely Bad Idea**. If you come to the lecture totally unprepared, you will have no idea what is important enough to write down and what is just the instructor's asides and commentary. Reading the material first gives you a good idea of exactly what is important in the lecture and reduces the amount of notes you take.

If you are an auditory learner, ask the instructor if you can bring a tape recorder to class and tape the lecture. That allows you to listen in class and then play the tape to write down notes later on. Visual learners (especially those who are nonverbal) and tactile learners should try to jot down diagrams, charts, and other visual aids along with written notes.

When you have good notes taken while reading the text and from the lectures, you will also have ready-made study aids for preparing to take exams. The next section deals with the best ways to study for exams.

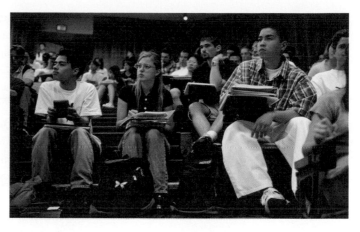

Here are two things that instructors love to see: attentive looks and note-taking during the lecture. How should these students have prepared before coming to this class?

Studying For Exams: Cramming Is Not an Option

There is a right way to study for a test, believe it or not. Here are some good things to remember when preparing for an exam, whether it's a quiz, a unit test, a midterm, or a final (Carter et al., 2002; Reynolds, 2002):

- *Timing is everything:* One of the worst things that students do is waiting until the last minute to study for the exam. Remember the analogy about "chewing" the steak? (Just as a steak has to be chewed to be enjoyed and to be useful to the body, textbook material has to be "chewed" with the mind.) The same concept applies to preparing for an exam: You have to give yourself enough time. If you've read your text material and taken good notes as discussed in the previous sections, you'll be able to save a lot of time in studying for the exam, but you still need to give yourself ample time to go over all of those notes. One helpful thing to do is to make a study schedule in which you plan out (at least a week before the exam) the hours of the day during which you intend to study and the topics you will cover in those hours. Always give yourself more time than you think you will need, just in case something comes up at the last minute to throw off your schedule: unexpected company, car trouble, or other unforeseen events that might require you to forgo studying for one night.

Could this be you? The scattered materials, the frantic phone call to a friend or professor, the tense and worried facial expression are all hallmarks of that hallowed yet useless student tradition, cramming. Don't let this happen to you.

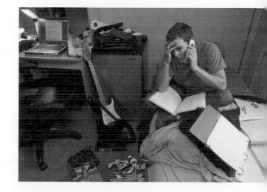

- *Find out as much as you can about the type of test and the material it will cover.* The type of test can affect the way in which you want to study the material. An objective test, for example, such as multiple choice or true/false, is usually fairly close to the text material, so you'll want to be very familiar with the wording of concepts and definitions in the text, although this is not a suggestion to memorize a lot of material. These kinds of tests can include one of three types of questions:

  - **Factual:** Questions that ask you to remember a specific fact from the text material. For example, "Who built the first psychological laboratory?" requires that you recognize a person's name. (The answer is Wilhelm Wundt.)

  - **Applied:** Questions that ask you to use, or apply, information presented in the text. For example, consider the following question from Chapter Five, Learning:

    One-year-old Ben learned to say the word *duck* when his mother showed him a duck in their backyard. That evening he sees a cartoon with a rooster in it and says, "Duck!," pointing to the rooster. Ben is exhibiting _____.
    a. generalization.   **c.** discrimination.
    b. spontaneous recovery.   **d.** shaping.

    This question requires you to take a concept (in this case, generalization) and apply it to a real-world example.

  - **Conceptual:** Questions that demand that you think about the ideas or concepts presented in the text and demonstrate that you understand them by answering questions like the following: "Freud is to _____ as Watson is to _____." (The answers could vary, but a good set would be "the unconscious" and "observable behavior.")

Notice that although memorizing facts might help on the first type of question it isn't going to help at all on the last two. Memorization doesn't always help on factual questions either, because the questions are sometimes worded quite differently from the text. It is far better to understand the information rather than be able to "spit it back" without understanding it. "Spitting it back" is memorization; understanding it is true learning.

Subjective tests, such as essay tests and short answer exams, require that you not only be able to recall and understand the information from the course but also that you are able to organize it in your own words. To study for a subjective test means that you not only need to be familiar with the material, but also you need to be able to write it down. Make outlines of your notes. Rewrite both reading and lecture notes and make flash cards, charts, and drawings. Tactile learners can practice putting the flash cards in order. If you are an auditory or kinesthetic learner, you should talk out loud or study with someone else and discuss the possible questions that could be on an essay test.

Other helpful advice is to look at old tests (if the instructor has made them available) to see what kinds of questions are usually asked. If this is not possible, make sure that you pay close attention to the kinds of questions asked on the first exam so that you will know how to prepare for future tests. Write out your own test questions, as if you were the instructor. Not only does this force you to think about the material the way it will appear on the test, but it also provides a great review tool.

- *Use SQ3R.* You can use the same method that you used to read the text material to go over your notes. Skim through your notes to get an overview of the material that will be on the test. Try to think of possible test questions that the instructor might include on an exam. Reread your notes, referring back to the text if necessary. Recite the main ideas and definitions of terms, either out loud, onto a tape, or to a friend or study group. Review by summarizing sections of material or by making an outline or flash cards that you can use in studying important concepts.

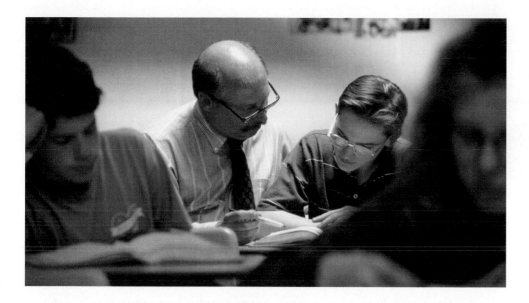

Many students studying for exams ignore one of the most valuable resources to which they have access: the instructor. Most instructors are happy to answer questions or schedule time for students who are having difficulty understanding the material.

- *Take advantage of all the publisher's test materials.* Practice does help, and most textbooks come with a study guide or a Web site. Those materials should have practice quizzes available—take them. Some texts come with a booklet of practice quizzes, as this one does. Take them. The more types of quiz questions you try to answer, the more successful you will be at interpreting the questions on the actual exam. You'll also get a very good idea of the areas that you need to go back and review again.

- *Make use of the resources.* If you find that you are having difficulty with certain concepts, go to the instructor well in advance of the exam for help. (This is another good reason to manage your study time so that you aren't trying to do everything in a few hours the night before the exam.) There are help centers on most college and university campuses with people who can help you learn to study, organize your notes, or tutor you in the subject area.

- *Don't forget your physical needs.* Studies have shown that not getting enough sleep is very bad for memory and learning processes (Stickgold et al., 2001). Try to stop studying an hour or so before going to bed at a reasonable time to give your body time to relax and unwind. Get a full night's sleep if possible. Do not take sleep-inducing medications or drink alcohol, as these substances prevent normal stages of sleep, including the stage that seems to be the most useful for memory and learning (Davis et al., 2003). Do eat breakfast; hunger is harmful to memory and mental performance. A breakfast heavy on protein and light on carbohydrates is the best for concentration and recall (Benton & Parker, 1998; Pollitt & Matthews, 1998; Stubbs et al., 1996).

- *Use your test time wisely.* When taking the test, don't allow yourself to get stuck on one question that you can't seem to answer. If an answer isn't clear, skip that question and go on to others. After finishing all of the questions that you can answer easily, go back to the ones you have skipped and try to answer them again. This accomplishes several things: You get to experience success in answering the questions that you can answer, which makes you feel more confident and relaxed; other questions on the test might act as memory cues for just the information you need for one of those questions you skipped; and once you are more relaxed, you may find that the answers to those seemingly impossible questions are now clear because anxiety is no longer blocking them.

The next section gives some helpful information about another form of assessment: the term paper.

Holding your eyes open is not going to help you study when you are this tired. Sleep has been shown to improve memory and performance on tests, so get a good night's sleep before every exam.

Instructors are a good source of suggestions for paper topics—they know the kind of information they want to be reading and grading in the wee hours of the night.

Writing Papers: Planning Makes Perfect

There are several steps involved in writing a paper, whether it be a short paper or a long one. You should begin all of these steps well in advance of the due date for the paper (not the night before):

1. *Choose a topic.* The first step is to choose a topic for your paper. In some cases, the instructor may have a list of acceptable topics, which makes your job easier. If that is not the case, don't be afraid to go to your instructor during office hours and talk about some possible topics. Try to choose a topic that interests you, one that you would like to learn more about. The most common mistake students make is to pick a topic that is far too broad. For example, the topic "mental retardation" could fill a book. A narrower topic might be one type of mental retardation discussed in detail. Again, your instructor can help you narrow down your topic choices.

2. *Do the research.* Find as many sources as you can that have information about your topic. Don't limit yourself to encyclopedias or textbooks. Go to your school library and ask the librarian to point you in the direction of some good scientific journals that would have information about the topic.

3. *Take notes.* While reading about your topic, make note cards. On the back of the note card (a 3 × 5 card), write the reference that will go along with the reading. (You might also start a document on the computer and type your references into the document as you read, but that only works if you have your computer with you while reading.) References for psychology papers are usually going to be in APA (American Psychological Association) style, which can be found at: **www.apastyle.org.** Write your notes about the reading on the front of the note card. Some people prefer two note cards, one for the notes and one for the reference, so that they can sort them separately.

4. *Decide on the thesis.* The thesis is the central message of your paper—the message you want to communicate to your audience—which may be your instructor, your classmates, or both, depending on the nature of the assignment. Some papers are persuasive, which means they are trying to convince the reader of a particular point of view, such as "Mental retardation is not caused by immunizations." Some papers are informative, providing information about a topic to an audience that may have no prior knowledge, such as "There are several ways to prevent mental retardation."

5. *Write an outline.* Using your notes from all your readings, create an outline of your paper—a kind of "road map" of how the paper will go. Start with an introduction (e.g., a brief definition and discussion of what autism is). Then decide what the body of the paper should be. If your paper is about a type of mental retardation, for example, your outline would include sections about the different causes of that type of retardation. The last section of your outline should be some kind of conclusion. For example, you might have recommendations about how parents of a mentally retarded child can best help that child to develop as fully as possible.

6. *Write a first draft.* Write your paper using the outline and your notes as guides. If using APA style, place citations with all of your statements and assertions. Failure to use citations (which point to the particular reference work from which your information came) is also a common mistake that many students make. Remember not to plagiarize. Plagiarizing is copying information from a source without stating that it is a quotation but instead letting it seem as if it is something you wrote yourself. When

you use a source, you are supposed to explain the information that you are using in your own words and cite the source, as in the following example:

> In one study comparing both identical and fraternal twins, researchers found that stressful life events of the kind listed in the SRRS were excellent predictors of the onset of episodes of major depression (Kendler & Prescott, 1999).

The reference section would have the citation: Kendler, K. S., & Prescott, C. A. (1999). A population-based twin study of lifetime major depression in men and women. *Archives of General Psychiatry* 56(1):39–44.

7. *Let it sit.* Take a few days (if you have been good about starting the paper on time) to let the paper sit without reading it. Then go back over the paper and mark places that don't sound right and need more explanation, a citation, or any other changes. This is much easier to do after a few days away from the paper; your errors will be more obvious.

8. *Write the revised draft.* Some people do more than one draft whereas others do only a first draft and a final. In either case, revise the draft carefully, making sure to check your citations.

In ancient times, people actually had to write or type their first, second, and sometimes third drafts on real paper. The advent of computers with word-processing programs that allow simple editing and revision have no doubt saved a lot of trees from the paper mill. This also means there is no good excuse for failing to write a first draft and for proofreading one's work.

Strategies for Improving Your Memory

Everyone needs a little memory help now and then. Even memory experts use strategies to help them perform their unusual feats of remembering. These strategies may be unique to that individual, but there are many memory "tricks" that are quite simple and available for anyone to learn and use. A memory trick or strategy to help people remember is called a **mnemonic** from the Greek word for memory. Here are a few of the more popular mnemonics, some of which may sound familiar:

• *Linking.* Make a list in which items to be remembered are linked in some way. If trying to remember a list of the planets in the solar system, for example, a person could string the names of the planets together like this: *Mercury* was the messenger god, who carried lots of love notes to *Venus*, the beautiful goddess who sprang from the *Earth's* sea. She was married to *Mars*, her brother, which didn't please her father *Jupiter* or his father *Saturn*, and his uncle *Uranus* complained to the sea god, *Neptune*, who told the god of the underworld, *Pluto*. That sounds like a lot, but once linked in this way, the names of the planets are easy to recall in proper order.

• *The peg word method.* In this method, it is necessary to first memorize a series of "peg" words, numbered words that can be used as keys for remembering items associated with them. A typical series of peg words is:

  • One is a bun

  • Two is a shoe

  • Three is a tree

  • Four is a door

  • Five is a hive

  • Six is bricks

  • Seven is heaven

  • Eight is a gate

  • Nine is a line

  • Ten is a hen

mnemonic
a strategy or trick for aiding memory.

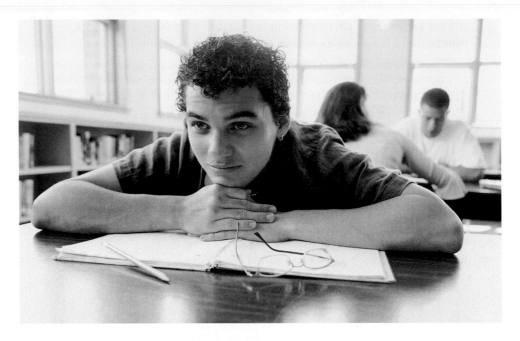

As this student studies, he may be turning the concepts he is learning into images. Using imagery is an excellent mnemonic.

To use this method, each item to be remembered (e.g., on a grocery list) is associated with a peg word and made into an image. If the items to be remembered are cheese, milk, eggs, bread, and sugar, the series of images might be a bun with a big wedge of cheese in it, a shoe with milk pouring out of it, a tree with eggs hanging from it, a door made of a slice of bread, and a hive with little bags of sugar flying around it instead of bees. The images are bizarre, and that actually helps cement the memory. When retrieving the list, all the person has to do is recite, "One is a bun, cheese. Two is a shoe, milk. . ." and so on, and the images will pop up readily.

- *The method of loci (LOW-kee).* This method, often credited to the ancient Romans and sometimes called the Roman Room Method, was actually invented by the Greeks. In both cultures, orators and speech makers used this method to keep track of the points they wanted to make in their speeches, which were often quite long and involved. There were no cue cards or teleprompters, so they had to rely on memory alone. In this method, the person pictures a very familiar room or series of rooms in a house or other building. Each point of the speech is then made into an image and "placed" mentally in the room at certain locations. For example, if the first point was about military spending, the image might be a soldier standing in the doorway of the house throwing money out into the street. Each point would have its place, and all the person would need to do to retrieve the memories would be to take a "mental walk" around the house.

- *Verbal/rhythmic organization.* How do you spell *relief*? If when spelling a word with an *ie* or an *ei* in it, you resort to the old rhyme "I before E except after C, or when sounded as A as in neighbor or weigh," you have made use of a verbal/rhythmic organization mnemonic. "Thirty days hath September, April, June, and November. . ." is another example of this technique. Setting information into a rhyme aids memory because it uses verbal cues, rhyming words, and the rhythm of the poem itself to aid retrieval. Sometimes this method is accomplished through making a sentence by using the first letters of each word to be remembered and making them into new words that form a sentence. The colors of the rainbow are ROY G. BIV (red, orange, yellow, green, blue, indigo, and violet). The notes on the musical staff are: "Every Good Boy Does Fine." There are countless examples of this technique.

- **Put it to music (a version of the rhythmic method).** Some people have had success with making up little songs, using familiar tunes, to remember specific information. The best example of this? The alphabet song.

This Introduction has covered several different ways to help you get more out of not only your psychology class but also all of your college course work. If you follow the advice given in this section for reading, taking notes, studying, writing papers, and improving your memory, you will find that making good grades will be easier than ever before and that you will actually remember a great deal of what you've studied long after the last final exam is over.

Other Resources

There are some excellent books and Web resources available for help in maximizing your studying. Two excellent books are:

Carter, C., Bishop, J., Kravits, S. L., & D'Agostino, J. V. (ed. consultant). (2002). *Keys to college studying: Becoming a lifelong learner.* Upper Saddle River, NJ: Prentice-Hall.

Reynolds, J. (2002). *Succeeding in college: Study skills and strategies.* Upper Saddle River, NJ: Prentice-Hall.

The Virginia Polytechnic Institute and State University has a good online site at **www.ucc.vt.edu/stdysk/stdyhlp.html.**

Another good source created by Joe Landsberger is the Web site Study Guides and Strategies, available at **www.studygs.net.**

PSYCHOLOGY

1

The Science of Psychology

What Can Psychology Do for Me?

Have you ever wondered . . .

. . . why using common sense doesn't always work?
. . . how you could develop a better memory?
. . . if psychics really communicate with the dead?
. . . why it's so easy for little children to learn another language when it's so hard for adults?
. . . what happens when you faint?
. . . if ESP really exists?
. . . why you find some people attractive but not others?
. . . why some people become serial killers?
. . . why you get nervous?
. . . what scores on an IQ test really mean?
. . . how the salesperson managed to talk you into buying more than you wanted to buy?

. . . how different men and women really are?
. . . why you sleep and why you dream?
. . . if hypnosis is real?
. . . why buying lottery tickets can be so addictive?
. . . why people tend to get sick right before final exam week?
. . . why identical twins aren't so identical when it comes to their personalities?

If you've ever been curious about any of these questions, this book is for you. Psychologists study all of these things and more. If you've puzzled about it, thought about doing it, or actually done it, chances are psychology has an explanation for it.

Why study psychology?

Psychology not only helps us understand why other people do the things they do, but it also helps us better understand ourselves and our reactions to other people. Psychology can help you understand how your brain and body are connected, how to improve your learning abilities and memory, and how to deal with the stresses of life, both ordinary and extraordinary. In studying psychology, an understanding of the methods psychologists use is important because research can be flawed, and knowing how research should be done can bring those flaws to light. Finally, the critical thinking that psychology and its methods of research promote can be used to evaluate not just research but also claims of all kinds, including those of advertisers and politicians.

STUDY HELP NOTE: For each section of every chapter in this text there are numbered learning objectives. These learning objectives represent the key questions that students should be able to understand and answer after reading the chapter. They appear at the beginning of each chapter, at the beginning of each relevant section in the chapter, and in the chapter summary.

1.1 What is the definition and what are four primary goals of psychology?

1.2 What were the basic ideas of structuralism and functionalism, and who were the important people in those early fields?

1.3 What were the basic ideas and who were the important people behind the early approaches known as Gestalt, psychoanalysis, and behaviorism?

1.4 What are the basic concepts of the modern perspectives known as psychodynamics, behaviorism, humanism, biopsychology, cognitive psychology, the evolutionary perspective, and the sociocultural perspective?

1.5 What were the contributions of Skinner, Maslow, and Rogers?

1.6 What's the difference between a psychiatrist and a psychologist, and what other types of professionals work in the various areas of psychology?

1.7 Why is psychology a science and what are the steps in using the scientific method?

1.8 How do psychologists use naturalistic and laboratory settings to describe behavior, and what are the advantages and disadvantages associated with these settings?

1.9 How do psychologists use case studies and surveys to describe behavior, and what are some drawbacks to each of these methods?

1.10 What is the correlational technique and what does it tell researchers about relationships?

1.11 How do researchers use operational definitions, independent and dependent variables, experimental and control groups, and random assignment in designing an experiment?

1.12 What are the placebo and the experimenter effects, and how do single-blind and double-blind studies control for those effects?

1.13 How might a real experiment be conducted?

1.14 What are the ethical concerns when conducting research with people and animals?

1.15 What are the basic principles of critical thinking, and how can using critical thinking help people in their everyday lives?

1.16 How might critical thinking be applied to a real-world example?

What Is Psychology?

THE FIELD OF PSYCHOLOGY

Some people believe that psychology is just the study of people and what makes them tick. Psychologists do study people, but they study animals, too. What makes people and animals "tick" is what goes on inside their bodies and brains as well as what they do.

1.1 *What is the definition and what are four primary goals of psychology?*

Psychology is the scientific study of behavior and mental processes. *Behavior* includes all of our outward or overt actions and reactions, such as talking, facial expressions, and movement. *Mental processes* refer to all the internal, covert activity of our minds, such as thinking, feeling, and remembering. Why "scientific?" To study behavior and mental processes in both animals and humans, researchers have to observe them. Whenever a human being is observing anyone or anything, there's always a possibility that the observer will see only what he or she expects to see. Psychologists don't want to let these possible biases* cause them to make faulty observations. They want to be as precise and measure as carefully as they can, so they use the scientific method to study psychology.

PSYCHOLOGY'S GOALS

Every science has goals. In physics, the goals concern learning how the physical world works. In astronomy, the goals are to chart the universe and understand both how it came to be and what it is becoming. In psychology, there are four goals that aim at uncovering the mysteries of human and animal behavior: description, explanation, prediction, and control.

psychology
the scientific study of behavior and mental processes.

---

*Biases: personal judgments based on beliefs rather than facts.

DESCRIPTION: WHAT IS HAPPENING?   The first step in understanding anything is to give it a name. *Description* involves observing a behavior and noting everything about it: what is happening, where it happens, to whom it happens, and under what circumstances it seems to happen.

For example, a teacher might notice that a young girl in his second-grade classroom is behaving oddly. She's not turning in her homework, her grades are slipping badly, and she seems to have a very negative attitude toward school.

That's *what* she is doing. The description of what she is doing gives a starting place for the next goal: *why* is she doing it?

The researcher in the foreground is watching the children through a one-way mirror to get a description of their behavior. Observations such as these are just one of many ways that psychologists have of investigating behavior. Why is it important for the researcher to be behind a one-way mirror?

EXPLANATION: WHY IS IT HAPPENING?   To find out why the girl is doing all these things, the teacher would most likely ask the school counselor to administer some tests. Her parents might be asked to take her to a pediatrician to make sure that there is no physical illness, such as an allergy. They might also take her to a psychologist to be assessed. In other words, they are looking for an *explanation* for her behavior. Finding explanations for behavior is a very important step in the process of forming theories of behavior. A *theory* is a general explanation of a set of observations or facts. The goal of description provides the observations, and the goal of explanation helps to build the theory.

If all the tests seem to indicate that the young girl has a learning problem, such as dyslexia (an inability to read at expected levels for a particular age and degree of intelligence), the next step would be trying to predict what is likely to happen if the situation stays the same.

PREDICTION: WHEN WILL IT HAPPEN AGAIN?   Determining what will happen in the future is a *prediction*. In the example, the psychologist or counselor would predict (based on previous research into similar situations) that this little girl will probably continue to do poorly in her schoolwork and may never be able to reach her full learning potential. Clearly, something needs to be done to change this prediction, and that is the point of the last of the four goals of psychology: changing or modifying behavior.

CONTROL: HOW CAN IT BE CHANGED?   *Control*, or the modification of some behavior, has been somewhat controversial in the past. Some people hear the word *control* and think *brainwashing*, but that is not the focus of this goal. The goal is to change a behavior from an undesirable one (such as failing in school) to a desirable one (such as academic success).

In the example of the young girl, there are certain learning strategies that can be used to help a child (or an adult) who has dyslexia improve reading skills (Aylward et al., 2003; Shaywitz, 1996). The psychologist and educators would work together to find a training strategy that works best for this particular girl.

Not all psychological investigations will try to meet all four of these goals. In some cases, the main focus might be on description and prediction, as it would be for a personality theorist who wants to know what people are like (description) and what they might do in certain situations (prediction). Some psychologists are interested in both description and explanation, as is the case with experimental psychologists who design research to find explanations for observed (described) behavior. Therapists, of course, would be more interested in control, although the other three goals would be important in getting to that goal.

These goals have not really changed in the years since psychology's beginnings, but the methods of achieving them certainly have changed. In the next section, we'll take a look at the early pioneers in psychology.

PRACTICE QUIZ: HOW MUCH DO YOU REMEMBER?

STUDY HELP NOTE: These practice quizzes are spaced throughout each chapter to give students an opportunity to check their understanding of the material in each section and provide practice for exams. The answers to each quiz can be found upside down at the end of each quiz.

Pick the best answer.

1. In the definition of psychology, *behavior* means
  a. internal, covert processes.
  b. mental processes.
  c. outward or overt actions and reactions.
  d. only human behavior.

2. A psychologist is interested in what a particular person might do in a stressful situation. This psychologist is most interested in the goal of
  a. description.   **c.** prediction.
  b. explanation.   **d.** control.

3. Dr. Watson designs a special behavior program for helping children who are bullies learn how to be less aggressive and more successful in social relationships. Dr. Watson is most interested in the goal of
  a. description.   **c.** prediction.
  b. explanation.   **d.** control.

4. The first step in studying animal behavior is to observe animals and record everything they do, when they do it, and what is going on around them when they do it. This meets the goal of
  a. description.
  b. explanation.
  c. prediction.
  d. control.

5. Experimental psychologists, who design experiments to determine the causes of behavior, would be most interested in the goal of
  a. description.
  b. explanation.
  c. prediction.
  d. control.

Answers: 1-c, 2-c, 3-d, 4-a, 5-b.

Psychology Then: The History of Psychology

IN THE BEGINNING: WUNDT, INTROSPECTION, AND THE LABORATORY

How long has ▶ psychology been around—and where did it begin?

How long has psychology been around—and where did it begin? Psychology is a relatively new field in the realm of the sciences, only about 125 years old. It's not that no one thought about what makes people tick before then; on the contrary, there were philosophers,* medical doctors, and physiologists** who thought about little else. Aristotle, who lived from 384–322 B.C., wrote about the relationship of the soul to the body (with the two being aspects of the same underlying structure) in his *De Anima* as well as other works (Durrant, 1993; Everson, 1995). Plato, his teacher (427–347 B.C.), felt that the soul could exist separately from the body, a view that has become known as *dualism* (Jackson, 2001). René Descartes, a seventeenth-century French philosopher and mathematician, agreed with Plato and believed that the pineal gland (a small organ at the base of the brain) was the seat of the soul (Kenny, 1968, 1994). Philosophers tried to understand or explain the human mind and its connection to the physical body, while medical doctors and physiologists wondered about the physical connection between the body and the brain. For example, physician and physicist Gustav Fechner is often credited with performing some of the first scientific experiments that would form a basis for experimentation in psychology with his studies of perception (Fechner, 1860), and physician Hermann von Helmholtz (von Helmholtz, 1852, 1863) performed groundbreaking experiments in visual and auditory perception. (L)(I)(N)(K) *to Chapter Three: Sensation and Perception, p. 98.*

---

*Philosophers: people who seek wisdom and knowledge through thinking and discussion.
**Physiologists: scientists who study the physical workings of the body and its systems.

1.2   *What were the basic ideas of structuralism and functionalism, and who were the important people in those early fields?*

It really all started to come together in a laboratory in Leipzig, Germany, in 1879. It was here that Wilhelm Wundt (VILL-helm Voont, 1832–1920), a physiologist, attempted to apply scientific principles to the study of the human mind. In his laboratory, students from around the world were taught to study the structure of the human mind. Wundt believed that the mind was made up of thoughts, experiences, emotions, and other basic elements. In order to inspect these nonphysical elements, students had to learn to think objectively about their own thoughts—after all, they could hardly read someone else's mind. Wundt called this process **objective introspection**, the process of objectively examining and measuring one's own thoughts and mental activities (Rieber & Robinson, 2001). For example, Wundt might place an object, such as a rock, into a student's hand and have that student tell him everything that he was feeling as a result of having the rock in his hand—all the sensations stimulated by the rock.

German physiologist Wilhelm Wundt participates in an experiment in his laboratory as students look on.

This was really the first attempt by anyone to bring objectivity* and measurement to the concept of psychology. This attention to objectivity, together with the establishment of the first true experimental laboratory in psychology, is why Wundt is known as the "father of psychology."

TITCHENER AND STRUCTURALISM IN AMERICA

One of Wundt's students was Edward Titchener (1867–1927), an Englishman who eventually took Wundt's ideas to Cornell University in Ithaca, New York. Titchener expanded on Wundt's original ideas, calling his new viewpoint **structuralism**, because the focus of study was the structure of the mind. He believed that every experience could be broken down into its individual emotions and sensations (Brennan, 2002). Although Titchener agreed with Wundt that consciousness, the state of being aware of external events, could be broken down into its basic elements, Titchener also believed that the introspection method could be used on thoughts just as it was on physical sensations. For example, Titchener might have asked his students to introspect about things that are blue rather than actually giving them a blue object and asking for reactions to it. Such an exercise might have led to something like the following: "What is blue? There are blue things, like the sky or a bird's feathers. Blue is cool and restful, blue is calm . . ." and so on.

Structuralists would be interested in all of the memories and sensations this woman is experiencing as she smells the rose.

In 1894, one of Titchener's students at Cornell University became famous for becoming the first woman to receive a Ph.D. in psychology (Goodman, 1980; Guthrie, 2004). Her name was Margaret F. Washburn, and she was Titchener's only graduate student for that year. In 1908 she published a book on animal behavior that was considered an important work in that era of psychology, *The Animal Mind* (Washburn, 1908).

Structuralism was a dominant force in the early days of psychology, but it eventually died out in the early 1900s, as the structuralists were busily fighting among themselves over just which key elements of experience were the most important. A competing view arose not long after Wundt's laboratory was established, shortly before structuralism came to America.

Margaret Washburn is shown here in 1926 with other former presidents of the Psychological Society.

---

*Objectivity: expressing or dealing with facts or conditions as they really are without allowing the influence of personal feelings, prejudices, or interpretations.

objective introspection
the process of examining and measuring one's own thoughts and mental activities.

structuralism
early perspective in psychology associated with Wilhelm Wundt and Edward Titchener, in which the focus of study is the structure or basic elements of the mind.

functionalism
early perspective in psychology associated with William James, in which the focus of study is how the mind allows people to adapt, live, work, and play.

Mary Whiton Calkins, despite being denied a Ph.D. degree by Harvard because she was a woman, became the first female president of the American Psychological Society and had a successful career as a professor and researcher.
Source: Archives of the History of American Psychology–The University of Akron

So what happened next? ▶
Where did psychology
go from here?

WILLIAM JAMES AND FUNCTIONALISM

Harvard University was the first school in America to offer classes in psychology in the late 1870s. These classes were taught by one of Harvard's most illustrious instructors, William James (1842–1910). James began teaching anatomy and physiology, but as his interest in psychology developed, he began teaching psychology almost exclusively (Brennan, 2002). His comprehensive textbook on the subject, *Principles of Psychology*, is so brilliantly written that copies are still in print (James, 1890, 2002).

Unlike Wundt and Titchener, James believed that trying to study consciousness was like trying to study the wind. Conscious ideas are constantly flowing in an ever-changing stream, and once you start thinking about what you were just thinking about, what you were thinking about is no longer what you *were* thinking about, it's what you *are* thinking about, and . . . excuse me, I'm a little dizzy. I think you get the picture, anyway.

Instead, James focused on how the mind allows people to *function* in the real world—how people work, play, and adapt to their surroundings, a viewpoint he called **functionalism**. (He was heavily influenced by Charles Darwin's ideas about *natural selection*, in which physical traits that help an animal adapt to its environment and survive are passed on to its offspring, becoming part of the animal's traits.) If physical traits could aid in survival, why couldn't behavioral traits do the same? Animals and people whose behavior helped them to survive would pass those traits on to their offspring, perhaps by teaching or even by some mechanism of heredity.* (Remember that this was early in the days of trying to understand how heredity worked.)

It is interesting to note that one of James's early students was Mary Whiton Calkins, who completed every course and requirement for earning a Ph.D. but was denied that degree by Harvard University because she was a woman. She was allowed to take those classes as a guest only. Calkins eventually established a psychological laboratory at Wellesley College. Her work was some of the earliest research in the area of human memory and the psychology of the self. In 1905, she became the first female president of the American Psychological Society (Furumoto, 1979). Unlike Washburn, Calkins never earned the elusive Ph.D. despite a successful career as a professor and researcher (Guthrie, 2004).

This might be a good place to point out that women were not the only minorities to make contributions in the early days of psychology. In 1920, for example, Francis Cecil Sumner became the first African American to earn a Ph.D. in psychology at Clark University. He eventually became the chair of the psychology department at Howard University and is assumed by many to be the father of African American psychology (Guthrie, 2004). Kenneth and Mamie Clark worked to show the negative effects of school segregation on African American children (Lal, 2002). Hispanic psychologist Jorge Sanchez conducted research in the area of intelligence testing, focusing on the cultural biases in such tests. Since those early days, psychology has seen an increase in all minorities, although the percentages are still far too small when compared to the population at large.

So what happened next? Where did psychology go from here? In the new field of psychology, functionalism offered an alternative viewpoint to the structuralists. But like so many of psychology's early ideas, it is no longer a major perspective. Instead, one can find elements of functionalism in the modern fields of *educational psychology* (studying the application of psychological concepts to education) and *industrial/organizational psychology* (studying the application of psychological concepts to businesses, organizations, and industry), as well as other areas in psychology. ⏺⏺⏺⏺ *to Appendix B, Applied Psychology.* Functionalism also played a part in the development of one of the more modern perspectives, evolutionary psychology, discussed later in this chapter.

---

*Heredity: the transmission of traits and characteristics from parent to offspring through the actions of genes.

GESTALT PSYCHOLOGY: THE WHOLE IS GREATER THAN THE SUM OF ITS PARTS

Meanwhile, back in Germany, other psychologists were attacking the concepts of psychology in yet another way. Max Wertheimer (VERT-hi-mer), like James, objected to the structuralist point of view but for different reasons. Wertheimer felt that psychological events such as perceiving* and sensing** could not be broken down into any smaller elements and still be properly understood. You can take a compact disc player apart, for example, but then you no longer have a CD player—you have a pile of unconnected bits and pieces. As a melody is made up of individual notes and can only be understood if the notes are in their correct relationship to one another, so perception can only be understood as a whole, entire event. Hence, the familiar slogan, "The whole is greater than the sum of its parts." The Gestalt psychologists believed that people naturally seek out patterns ("wholes") in the sensory information available to them. See Figure 1.1 for an example of Gestalt perceptual patterns.

FIGURE 1.1   **A Gestalt Perception**
The eye tends to "fill in" the blanks here and see both of these figures as circles rather than as a series of dots or a broken line.

more than what you started w/

1.3   *What were the basic ideas and who were the important people behind the early approaches known as Gestalt, psychoanalysis, and behaviorism?*

Wertheimer and others devoted their efforts to studying sensation and perception in this new perspective, **Gestalt psychology**. *Gestalt* (Gesh-TALT) is a German word meaning "good form" or "good figure," which fit well with the focus on studying whole patterns rather than small pieces of them. Today, Gestalt ideas are part of the study of *cognitive psychology*, a field focusing not only on perception but also on learning, memory, thought processes, and problem solving; the basic Gestalt principles of perception are still taught within this newer field (Ash, 1998; Kohler, 1992; Wertheimer, 1982). The Gestalt approach has also been influential in psychological therapy, becoming the basis for a major therapeutic technique called *Gestalt therapy*. (L I N K) *to Chapter Fifteen: Psychological Therapies, p. 567.*

SIGMUND FREUD'S PSYCHOANALYSIS

It should be clear by now that psychology didn't start in one place and at one particular time. People of several different viewpoints were trying to promote their own perspective on the study of the human mind and behavior in different places all over the world. Up to now, this chapter has focused on the physiologists who became interested in psychology, and their focus was on understanding consciousness but little else. The medical profession took a whole different approach to psychology.

What about Freud? Everybody talks about him when they talk about psychology. How does he figure into the beginnings of psychology? Sigmund Freud had become a noted physician in Austria while the structuralists argued, the functionalists specialized, and the Gestaltists were looking at the big picture. He was a medical doctor—a neurologist, someone who specializes in disorders of the nervous system—and he and his colleagues had long sought a way to understand the patients who were coming to them for help.

To understand Freud, you have to understand a little about his culture. The late 1800s and early 1900s were the tail end of the "Victorian Age," a time of intense sexual repression. This was a social world in which the word *sex* was never spoken, tables were surrounded by cloth so the bare table "limbs" would not show, and women covered themselves from head to toe in an effort to show as little skin as possible. It is

repression of urges → nervous disorders

◄ What about **Freud?** Everybody talks about him when they talk about psychology. How does he figure into the beginnings of psychology?

Gestalt psychology
early perspective in psychology focusing on perception and sensation, particularly the perception of patterns and whole figures.

---

*Perceiving: becoming aware of something through the senses.   *→perception*
**Sensing: seeing, hearing, feeling, tasting, or smelling something.

Why were so many of ►
his patients women?

Psychoanalyst Sigmund Freud walks with his daughter Anna, also a psychoanalyst.

understandable that many of the people growing up in this era had problems with sexual thoughts that would be perfectly natural in most modern cultures but were considered unnatural and wicked by Freud's culture. Many of those people, most of them women, ended up in Dr. Freud's office.

Why were so many of his patients women? Although "sex" was considered a forbidden area to both men and women on the surface of Victorian society, men were actually allowed to break the rules—in fact, a good Victorian husband was one who sought out a mistress to meet his "worldly" needs and left his saintly pure wife alone after she had borne him several children (Battan, 1999).

Freud's patients suffered from nervous disorders for which he and other doctors could find no physical cause. Therefore, it was thought, the cause must be in the mind, and that is where Freud began to explore. He proposed that there is an *unconscious* (unaware) mind into which we push, or *repress*, all of our threatening urges and desires. He believed that these repressed urges, in trying to surface, created the nervous disorders in his patients (Freud et al., 1990). (L I N K) *to Chapter Twelve: Theories of Personality, p. 446.*

Freud stressed the importance of early childhood experiences, believing that personality was formed in the first six years of life, and that if there were significant problems, those problems must have begun in those early years.

Some of his more well-known followers were Alfred Adler, Carl Jung, and his own daughter, Anna Freud. Anna Freud began what became known as the ego movement in psychology, a movement that produced one of the most famous psychologists in the study of personality development, Erik Erikson. (L I N K) *to Chapter Seven, Development Across the Life Span, pp. 272–282.*

Freud's ideas are still influential today, although in a somewhat modified form. He had a number of followers in addition to those already named, many of whom became famous by altering his theory to fit their own viewpoint, but his basic ideas are still discussed and debated. (L I N K) *to Chapter Twelve: Theories of Personality, p. 454.*

Freudian **psychoanalysis**, the theory and therapy based on his ideas, has been the basis of much modern *psychotherapy* (a process in which a trained psychological professional helps a person gain insights into and change his or her behavior), but another major and competing viewpoint has actually been more influential in the field of psychology as a whole.

JOHN B. WATSON AND BEHAVIORISM

In the early 1900s, John B. Watson had tired of the arguing among the structuralists; he challenged the functionalist viewpoint, as well as psychoanalysis, with his own "science of behavior," or **behaviorism** (Watson, 1924). Watson wanted to bring psychology back to a focus on scientific inquiry, and he felt that the only way to do that was to ignore the whole "consciousness" issue and focus only on *observable behavior*—something that could be directly seen and measured. He based a lot of his ideas on the work of Russian physiologist Ivan Pavlov.

PAVLOV'S CONDITIONED RESPONSE   Pavlov, in his work with dogs, had shown that a reflex (an involuntary reaction) such as salivation, which is normally produced by actually having food in one's mouth, could be caused to occur in response to a totally new and formerly unrelated stimulus,* such as the sound of a bell. He would ring the bell, give the dogs food, and they would salivate. After several rep-

psychoanalysis
the theory and therapy based on the work of Sigmund Freud.

behaviorism
the science of behavior that focuses on observable behavior only.

---

*Stimulus: anything that causes an organism to have a reaction or response.

etitions, the dogs would salivate to the sound of the bell *before* the food was presented—a learned (or "conditioned") reflexive response (Klein & Mowrer, 1989). This process was called *conditioning*. (L)(I)(N)(K) *to Chapter Five: Learning, p. 167.*

OF BABIES AND RATS   Watson was certainly aware of Freud's work and his views on unconscious repression. Freud believed that all behavior stems from some unconscious motivation, whereas Watson believed that all behavior is learned. Freud had stated that a *phobia*, an irrational fear, is really a symptom of an underlying, repressed conflict, and cannot be "cured" without years of psychoanalysis to uncover and understand the repressed material.

Physiologist Ivan Pavlov uses a dog to demonstrate the conditioned reflex to students at the Russian Military Medical Academy.

Watson believed that phobias are learned through the process of conditioning and set out to prove it. He took a baby, known as "Little Albert," and taught him to fear a white rat by making a loud, scary noise every time the infant saw the rat, until finally seeing the rat caused the infant to cry and become fearful (Watson & Rayner, 1920). Even though "Little Albert" was not afraid of the rat at the start, the experiment worked very well—in fact, "Little Albert" became afraid of anything white and fuzzy, including white beards and furry rabbit skins. (This was before there were such things as ethics committees. Today, this study would not be permitted because of the potential psychological harm to the child.)

This sounds really bizarre—what does scaring a baby have to do with the science of psychology? Watson wanted to prove that all behavior was a result of a stimulus–response relationship such as that described by Pavlov. At this particular time in history, Freud and his ideas about unconscious motivation were becoming a dominant force, and Watson felt the need to show the world that a much simpler explanation could be found. Although scaring a baby sounds a little cruel, he felt that the advancement of the science of behavior was worth the relatively brief discomfort of the baby. One of Watson's graduate students later decided to repeat Watson and Rayner's study but added training that would "cancel out" the phobic reaction of the baby to the white rat. For more on this research, see the section on Classic Studies in Psychology that follows.

◀ **This sounds really bizarre—what does scaring a baby have to do with the science of psychology?**

Behaviorism, like psychoanalysis, is still a major perspective in psychology today. It has also influenced the development of other perspectives, such as *cognitive psychology*.

CLASSIC STUDIES IN PSYCHOLOGY
Psychologist Mary Cover Jones and "Little Peter"

Mary Cover was born on September 1, 1897. She graduated from Vassar in 1919 with her bachelor's degree. Rosalie Rayner, John B. Watson's graduate assistant and future wife, was a fellow Vassar graduate and a friend. Mary Cover attended one of Watson's weekend lectures and came away determined to pursue a graduate degree in psychology. Her master's degree was completed in 1920 under the supervision of Watson. In that same year she married another graduate student, Harold Jones (Rutherford, 2000).

Mary Cover Jones was fascinated with the "Little Albert" study and wanted to explore the concept of learned phobias. Beginning with a child known as "Little Peter," Jones began by duplicating Watson and Rayner's 1920 study. She was able to create the same kind of phobic reaction in Peter that had developed in Albert, but she used a white rabbit instead of a rat (Jones, 1924).

Mary Cover Jones, one of the early pioneers of behavior therapy, earned her master's degree under the supervision of John Watson. She had a long and distinguished career, including in 1952 the publication of the first educational television course in child development.

Once the child was conditioned to fear the rabbit, Jones began a process called *counterconditioning*, in which the old conditioning (fear of the rabbit) would be replaced, or countered, by new conditioning. Peter was brought into one corner of a room, while the rabbit was placed in the opposite corner. Peter was then given some food (something he liked quite a bit). Although Peter may have been nervous to have the rabbit in the far corner, the food was right in front of him. He began to eat and experienced the pleasurable sensations associated with eating. This pattern was repeated over several sessions, with the rabbit being brought a little closer each time. Eventually, Peter was no longer showing any fear of the rabbit at all.

How did this work? In Watson and Rayner's original experiment, the white rat was paired with a scary noise. The scary noise caused a fear response, and eventually the rat caused the same fear response because of association with the noise. In Jones's study, this is exactly how Peter came to fear the rabbit. But then the rabbit was paired with yet another stimulus, food, which causes pleasure, not fear. After enough pairings of the food with the rabbit, the newer association of rabbit/food/pleasure replaced the old association of rabbit/noise/fear. The old fear response had been "countered."

Mary Cover Jones went on to become one of the early pioneers of behavior therapy. She was also a key figure in the Oakland Growth Study, a study of 200 fifth- and sixth-grade children that followed their development from the beginnings of puberty to the end of adolescence. It is her work that is often cited when textbooks talk about the benefits and problems associated with early and late maturation in puberty. She and her husband, Harold Jones, published the first educational television course in child development in 1952. After a long and distinguished career, Mary Cover Jones died on July 22, 1987, at the age of 90 (Rutherford, 2000).

Questions for Further Thought

1. What difficulties might early women psychologists like Mary Cover Jones have faced in a field and a culture dominated by men?

2. What kinds of behavior or issues might have been thought inappropriate for women to study in those early days of psychology?

PRACTICE **QUIZ:** HOW MUCH DO YOU REMEMBER?

Pick the best answer.

1. Name which of the following early psychologists would have been most likely to agree with the statement, "The study of the mind should focus on how it allows us to adapt to our surroundings."
   a. Wilhelm Wundt
   b. William James
   c. John Watson
   d. Sigmund Freud

2. Which early perspective would have been LEAST likely to agree with the structuralists?
   a. introspectionism
   b. functionalism
   c. psychoanalysis
   d. Gestalt

3. What did Freud believe controlled most, if not all, of our behavior?
   a. conscious experiences
   b. gestalt perceptions
   c. the unconscious mind
   d. observable experiences

4. Who among the following would be LEAST likely to talk about conscious experiences?
   a. Wundt
   b. James
   c. Watson
   d. Wertheimer

5. Who was the first woman president of the American Psychological Association?
   a. Mary Whiton Calkins
   b. Mary Cover Jones
   c. Margaret Washburn
   d. Eleanor Gibson

6. In the experiment with "Little Peter," what did Mary Cover Jones use as a stimulus to counter Little Peter's fear of the rabbit?
   a. a white rat
   b. food
   c. a loud noise
   d. relaxation

Psychology Now: Modern Perspectives

1.4 *What are the basic concepts of the modern perspectives known as psychodynamics, behaviorism, humanism, biopsychology, cognitive psychology, the evolutionary perspective, and the sociocultural perspective?*

Even today, there isn't one single perspective that is used to explain all human behavior and mental processes. There are actually seven modern perspectives, with two of those being holdovers from the early days of the field.

PSYCHODYNAMIC PERSPECTIVE

Freud's theory is still with us today in use by many professionals in therapy situations. It is far less common today than it was a few decades ago, however, and even those who use his techniques modify them for modern use. In the more modern **psychodynamic perspective**, the focus is still on the unconscious mind and its influence over conscious behavior and on early childhood experiences, but with less of an emphasis on sex and sexual motivations and more emphasis on the development of a sense of self and the discovery of other motivations behind a person's behavior.

Freud had a number of followers who took his original ideas and modified them to their own perspectives. Their students modified those theories, until today there is a kind of neo-Freudianism (Freud et al., 1990; Meadow & Clevans, 1978). Therapists often speak of Freudian complexes and use much of his terminology in their work with clients. Part of the reason that Freudian concepts are so enduring is the lack of any way to scientifically test them and, therefore, show them to be either useful or useless. (L I N K) *to Chapter Twelve, Theories of Personality, p. 454.*

BEHAVIORAL PERSPECTIVE

Like psychoanalysis, behaviorism is still very influential. When its primary supporter, Watson, moved on to greener pastures in the world of advertising, B. F. Skinner became the new leader of the field.

1.5 *What were the contributions of Skinner, Maslow, and Rogers?*

Skinner not only continued research in classical conditioning, but he also developed a theory of how voluntary behavior is learned, called *operant conditioning* (Skinner, 1938). In this theory, behavioral responses that are followed by pleasurable consequences are strengthened, or *reinforced*. For example, a child who cries and is rewarded by getting his mother's attention will cry again in the future. Skinner's work is discussed in much greater depth in Chapter Five, Learning (pp. 177–180). In addition to the psychodynamic and behavioral perspectives, there are five newer perspectives that have developed within the last 50 years.

HUMANISTIC PERSPECTIVE

One of the newer perspectives, often called the "third force" in psychology, was really a reaction to both psychodynamic theory and behaviorism. In the early to mid-1900s, if you were a psychologist you were either a psychoanalyst or a behaviorist—there weren't any other major viewpoints to rival those two. Behaviorism was seen as a very "mechanical" theory—stimulus goes in, response comes out, and what happens in the middle is of no interest. The environment determines behavior and the individual has little input into his or her development. Psychoanalysis wasn't mechanistic, but in that theory the workings of the physical body (in the form of sexual and aggressive instincts) determine behavior, and the individual, once again, has little to do with his or her own destiny.

[handwritten annotations: "maslow" above HUMANISTIC; "free-will (self-actualize)" beside PERSPECTIVE]

psychodynamic perspective
modern version of psychoanalysis that is more focused on the development of a sense of self and the discovery of other motivations behind a person's behavior than sexual motivations.

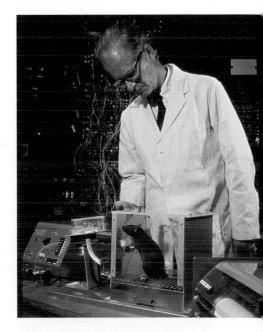

Behaviorist B. F. Skinner puts a rat through its paces. What problems might arise from applying information gained from studies with animals to human behavior?

Humanist Carl Rogers (far right) leads a group therapy session.

—not saying nothing directive.

biopsychological perspective
perspective that attributes human and animal behavior to biological events occurring in the body, such as genetic influences, hormones, and the activity of the nervous system.

Some professionals began to develop a perspective that would allow them to focus on people's ability to direct their own lives. These theorists wanted to shift the focus to the aspects of human nature that make us uniquely human—our appreciation for beauty, for example. In a very real sense, then, this approach owes far more to the early roots of psychology in the field of philosophy, rather than the more scientific fields of medicine and physiology. Humanists held the view that people have *free will*, the freedom to choose their own destiny. Two of the earliest and most famous founders of this view were Abraham Maslow (1908–1970) and Carl Rogers (1902–1987).

Both Maslow and Rogers emphasized the human potential, the ability of each person to become the best person he or she could be (Maslow, 1968; Rogers, 1961). They believed that studying animals in laboratories (as the behaviorists did) or people with nervous disorders (as the psychoanalysts did) could not lead to a better understanding of this human potential for *self-actualization*, as Maslow termed it—achieving one's full potential or actual self. Today, humanism is still very influential in psychotherapy. (L I N K) *to Chapter Fifteen: Psychological Therapies, p. 566.*

BIOPSYCHOLOGICAL PERSPECTIVE

Biopsychology, or the study of the biological bases of behavior and mental processes, isn't really as new a perspective as one might think.

In the **biopsychological perspective**, human and animal behavior is seen as a direct result of events in the body. Hormones, brain chemicals, tumors, and diseases are some of the biological causes of behavior and mental events. (L I N K) *to Chapter Two: The Biological Perspective, pp. 44–75.*

For example, evidence is mounting for a biological cause (perhaps even genetic) for *schizophrenia*, a mental disorder involving delusions (false beliefs), hallucinations (false sensory impressions), and extremely distorted thinking (Brzustowicz et al., 2004; Maziade et al., 1997). (L I N K) *to Chapter Fourteen: Psychological Disorders, pp. 548–549.*

These brain scans show the increasing malfunction of the brains of schizophrenics over a five-year period, highlighting the focus of the biological perspective.

COGNITIVE PERSPECTIVE

Cognitive psychology, which focuses on how people think, remember, store, and use information, became a major force in the field in the 1960s. It wasn't a new idea, as the Gestalt psychologists had themselves supported the study of mental processes of learning. The development of computers, (which just happened to make great models of human thinking), the work of Piaget with children, Chomsky's analysis of Skinner's views of language, and discoveries in biological psychology stimulated an interest in studying the processes of thought. The **cognitive perspective** with its focus on memory, intelligence, perception, thought processes, problem solving, language, and learning has become a major force in psychology. (L I N K) *to Chapter Eight: Cognition, p. 294.*

SOCIOCULTURAL PERSPECTIVE

Another modern perspective in psychology is the **sociocultural perspective**, which actually combines two areas of study: *social psychology*, which is the study of groups, social roles, and rules of social actions, and relationships; and *cultural psychology*, which is the study of cultural norms,* values, and expectations. These two areas are related in that they are both about the effect that people have on one another, either individually or in a larger group, such as a culture (Peplau & Taylor, 1997). (L I N K) *to Chapter Thirteen: Social Psychology, p. 480.*

The sociocultural perspective is important because it reminds people that how they and others behave (or even think) is influenced not only by whether they are alone, with friends, in a crowd, or part of a group but also by the particular culture in which they live. For example, in a classic study covered in Chapter Thirteen (p. 510), researchers Darley and Latané (1968) found that the presence of other people actually *lessened* the chances that a person in trouble would receive help. The phenomenon is called the bystander effect and it is believed to be the result of *diffusion of responsibility*, which is the tendency to feel that someone else is responsible for taking action when others are present. But would this effect appear in other cultures? Shorey (2001), in his discussion of the brutal beating death of a Somali prisoner in a Canadian military facility while bystanders looked on without acting, suggests that it just might. But is Canadian culture too similar to our own to lead us to this conclusion? Would another culture very different from Western culture show the same effect? This is exactly the kind of question that the sociocultural perspective asks and attempts to answer.

EVOLUTIONARY PERSPECTIVE

[handwritten: brain structure]

The **evolutionary perspective** focuses on the biological bases for universal mental characteristics that all humans share. It seeks to explain general mental strategies and traits, such as why we lie, how attractiveness influences mate selection, why fear of snakes is so universal, and why people like music and dancing, among many others.

[handwritten: (fight, flight response)]

In this perspective, the mind is seen as a set of information-processing machines, designed by the same process of natural selection that Darwin (1859) first theorized, allowing human beings to solve the problems we faced in the early days of human evolution—the problems of the early hunters and gatherers. For example, *evolutionary psychologists* (psychologists who study the evolutionary origins of human behavior) would view the human behavior of not eating substances that have a bitter taste (such as poisonous plants) as an adaptive** behavior that evolved as early humans came into contact with such bitter plants. Those who ate the bitter plants would die, while those who spit them out survived to pass their "I don't like this taste" genes on to their offspring, who would pass the genes on to their offspring, and so on, until after a long period of time there is an entire population of humans that naturally avoid bitter tasting substances.

---

*Norms: standards or expected behavior.

**Adaptive: having the quality of adjusting to the circumstances or need; in the sense used here, a behavior that aids in survival.

[handwritten: ① cultural norms influence behavior.]

Psychologists with an evolutionary perspective would be interested in how this couple selected each other as partners.

That explains why ▶
people don't like bitter
stuff, like the white
part of an orange peel,
but that's really a
physical thing. How
would this work for
something
psychological, like
relationships?

That explains why people don't like bitter stuff, like the white part of an orange peel, but that's really a physical thing. How would this work for something psychological, like relationships? Relationships between men and women are one of the many areas in which evolutionary psychologists conduct research. For example, in one study researchers surveyed young adults about their relationships with the opposite sex, asking the participants how likely they would be to forgive either a sexual infidelity or an emotional one (Shackelford et al., 2002). Evolutionary theory would predict that men would find it more difficult to forgive a woman who had sex with someone else than a woman who was only emotionally involved with someone, because the man cannot be sure that the children the woman bears are his (Geary, 2000). Why put all that effort into providing for what could be another man's offspring? Women, on the other hand, should find it harder to forgive an emotional infidelity, as they are always sure that their children are their own, but (in evolutionary terms, mind you) they need the emotional loyalty of the men to provide for those children (Buss et al., 1992; Daly et al., 1982). The results of the study bore out the prediction: men found it harder to forgive a partner's sexual straying and were more likely to break up with the woman than if the infidelity were purely emotional; for women, the opposite results were found.

PRACTICE **QUIZ:** HOW MUCH DO YOU REMEMBER?

Pick the best answer.

1. Which of the following pairs represents the two psychology perspectives that were also part of the historical beginnings of psychology?
   a. humanism and behaviorism
   b. behaviorism and psychodynamics
   c. psychodynamics and humanism
   d. cognitive psychology and psychodynamics

2. Which perspective is known as the "third force" in psychology?
   a. psychoanalysis
   b. behaviorism
   c. cognitive psychology
   d. humanism

3. Elsie suffered a stroke and had to be hospitalized. While in the hospital, she talked in funny, garbled words and seemed to think

that she was being held against her will. Which of the following perspectives BEST explains Elsie's odd behavior?
   a. psychodynamics
   b. cognitive psychology
   c. behaviorism
   d. biopsychology

4. Which perspective would a researcher be taking if she were studying the way children store and retrieve information?
   a. psychoanalysis
   b. behaviorism
   c. cognitive psychology
   d. evolutionary perspective

5. Which of the following historical perspectives gave rise, at least in part, to the evolutionary perspective?
   a. behaviorism
   b. psychoanalysis
   c. structuralism
   d. functionalism

Answers: 1-b, 2-d, 3-d, 4-c, 5-d.

psychiatrist
a medical doctor who has specialized in the diagnosis and treatment of psychological disorders.

psychoanalyst
either a psychiatrist or a psychologist who has special training in the theories of Sigmund Freud and his method of psychoanalysis.

psychiatric social worker
a social worker with some training in therapy methods who focuses on the environmental conditions that can have an impact on mental disorders, such as poverty, overcrowding, stress, and drug abuse.

Types of Psychological Professionals

There are a number of professionals who work in the field of psychology. These professionals have different training, different focuses, and may have different goals from the typical psychologist.

1.6 *What's the difference between a psychiatrist and a psychologist, and what other types of professionals work in the various areas of psychology?*

A **psychiatrist** has a Medical Doctorate (M.D.) degree and is a medical doctor who has specialized in the diagnosis and treatment of psychological disorders. Psychiatrists can prescribe medicine in addition to providing therapy and counseling, and they typically work in private practice or hospital settings.

A **psychoanalyst** is either a psychiatrist (M.D.) or a psychologist (Ph.D., Psy.D., or Ed.D.) who has special training in the theories of Sigmund Freud and his method of psychoanalysis. Psychoanalysts, like psychiatrists, usually work in private practice or hospital settings. (L I N K) *to Appendix B: Applied Psychology.*

A **psychiatric social worker** is trained in the area of social work and usually possesses a Master of Social Work (M.S.W.) degree or a Licensed Clinical Social Work (L.C.S.W.) degree. These professionals focus more on the environmental conditions that can have an impact on mental disorders, such as poverty, overcrowding, stress, and drug abuse. They work out of clinics, hospitals, and social service organizations.

A **psychologist** has no medical training but has a doctorate degree. (A person with a master's degree might be a counselor, therapist, or researcher but is typically not referred to as a psychologist.) Psychologists undergo intense academic training, learning about many different areas of psychology before choosing an area in which to specialize. Because the focus of their careers can vary so widely, psychologists work in many different vocational* settings. Figure 1.2a shows the types of settings in which psychologists work. Although typically psychologists cannot prescribe medications, in some states psychologists can go through special training in the prescription of drugs for certain psychological disorders. Psychologists in the counseling profession must be licensed to practice in their states.

Psychiatric social workers use many tools to help children deal with problems like divorce or abuse. How might using hand puppets help this young girl to talk about the problems in her life?

psychologist
a professional with an academic degree and specialized training in one or more areas of psychology.

*Vocational: having to do with a job or career.

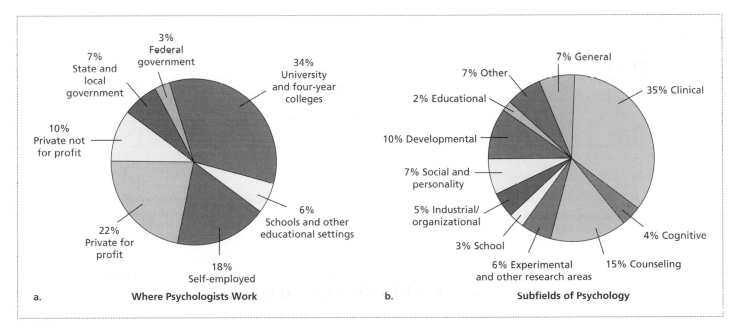

a.   **Where Psychologists Work**

b.   **Subfields of Psychology**

FIGURE 1.2   (a) There are many different work settings for psychologists. Although not obvious from the chart, many psychologists work in more than one setting. For example, a clinical psychologist may work in a hospital setting as well as teaching at a university or college. (b) This pie chart shows the specialty areas of psychologists who recently received their doctorates.
Note: Due to rounding, percentages may not total to 100 percent.
(a) National Science Fundation/Science Resources Statistics. 2001 Survey of Doctorate Recipients. http://www.nsf.gov/sbe/srs/nsf03310pdf/tabl4.pdf
(b) National Science Foundation, Division of Science Resource Statistics, Science & Engineering Doctorate Awards: 2003, NSF 05-300, Project Officer, Joan S. Burrelli (Arlington VA 2004). http://www.nsf.gov/sbe/srs/nsf05300/pdf/front.pdf

AREAS OF SPECIALIZATION

You said not all ▶ psychologists do counseling. But I thought that was all that psychologists do— what else is there?

You said not all psychologists do counseling. But I thought that was all that psychologists do—what else is there? Although many psychologists do participate in delivering therapy to people who need help, there is a nearly equal number of psychologists who do other tasks: researching, teaching, designing equipment and workplaces, and developing educational methods, for example. Also, not every psychologist is interested in the same area of human—or animal—behavior, and most psychologists work in several different areas of interest, as shown in Figure 1.2b, Subfields of Psychology.

There are many other areas as well, as psychology can be used in fields such as health, sports performance, legal issues, business concerns, and even in the design of equipment, tools, and furniture. For a more detailed look at some of these areas in which psychological principles can be applied and a listing of careers that can benefit from a degree in psychology, see (L)(I)(N)(K) *Appendix B: Applied Psychology.*

PRACTICE **QUIZ:** HOW MUCH DO YOU REMEMBER?

Pick the best answer.

1. Which of the following professionals in psychology focuses more on the environmental conditions that affect mental disorders?
   a. psychiatrist   **c.** psychiatric social worker
   b. psychoanalyst   **d.** psychologist

2. Which of the following specialties in psychology deals with diagnosis and treatment of disorders?
   a. clinical   **c.** personality
   b. development   **d.** experimental

3. Max is interested in becoming a psychologist. He is most interested in how people in groups behave differently from people

who act alone. He would most likely specialize in _____ psychology.
   a. comparative   **c.** school
   b. educational   **d.** social

4. Dr. Roaden works in a school system, dealing directly with children who have emotional, academic, and behavioral problems. Dr. Roaden is most likely which type of psychologist?
   a. personality   **c.** school
   b. developmental   **d.** comparative

Answers: 1-c, 2-a, 3-d, 4-c.

Psychology: The Science
WHY PSYCHOLOGISTS USE THE SCIENTIFIC METHOD

Have you ever played the "airport game?" You sit at the airport (bus terminal, doctor's office, or any other place where people come and go and you have a long wait) and try to guess what people do for a living based only on their appearance. Although it's a fun game, the guesses are rarely correct. People's guesses also sometimes reveal the biases that they may have about certain physical appearances: men with long hair are musicians, people wearing suits are executives, and so on. On the other hand, psychology is about trying to determine facts and reduce uncertainty.

1.7   *Why is psychology a science and what are the steps in using the scientific method?*

In psychology, researchers want to see only what is really there, not what their biases might want them to see. The way to do that is by using the **scientific method**, a system for reducing bias and error in the measurement of data.

scientific method
system of gathering data so that bias and error in measurement are reduced.

The first step in any investigation is to have a question to investigate, right? So the first step in the scientific method is this:

1. **Perceiving the Question:** You notice something interesting happening in your surroundings for which you would like to have an explanation. An example might be that you've noticed that your children seem to get a little more aggressive with each other after watching a particularly violent children's cartoon program on Saturday morning. You wonder if the violence in the cartoon could be creating the aggressive behavior in your children. This step is derived from the goal of description: What is happening here?

   Once you have a question, you want an answer. The next logical step is to form a tentative* answer or explanation for the behavior you have seen. This tentative explanation is known as a **hypothesis**.

2. **Forming a Hypothesis:** Based on your initial observations about what's going on in your surroundings, you form an educated guess about the explanation for your observations, putting it into the form of a statement that can be tested in some way. Going back to the previous example, you might say, "Children who watch violent cartoons will become more aggressive."

   The next step is testing the hypothesis. People have a tendency to notice only things that agree with their view of the world, a kind of selective perception called *confirmation bias*. **LINK** *to Chapter Eight, Cognition, p. 303.* For example, if a person is convinced that all men with long hair smoke cigarettes, that person will tend to notice only those long-haired men who are smoking and ignore all the long-haired men who don't smoke. The scientific method is designed to overcome this tendency to look at only the information that confirms people's biases by forcing them to actively seek out information that might *contradict* their biases (or hypotheses). So when you test your hypothesis, you are trying to determine if the factor you suspect has an effect and that the results weren't due to luck or chance. That's why psychologists keep doing research over and over—to get more evidence that hypotheses are "supported."

3. **Testing the Hypothesis:** The method you use to test your hypothesis will depend on exactly what kind of answer you think you might get. You might make more detailed observations or do a survey in which you ask questions of a large number of people, or you might design an experiment in which you would deliberately change one thing to see if it causes changes in the behavior you are observing. In the example, the best method would probably be an experiment in which you select a group of children, show half of them a cartoon with violence and half of them a cartoon with no violence, and then find some way of measuring aggressive behavior in the two groups.

   What do you do with the results of your testing? Of course, testing the hypothesis is all about the goal of getting an explanation for behavior, which leads to the next step.

4. **Drawing Conclusions:** Once you know the results of your hypothesis testing, you will find that either your hypothesis was supported—which means that your little experiment worked, or your measurements supported your initial observations—or it wasn't supported, which means that you need to go back to square one and think of another possible explanation for what you have observed. (Could it be that Saturday mornings make children a little more aggressive? Or Saturday breakfasts?)

The scientific method can be used to determine if children who watch violence on television are more likely to be aggressive than those who do not.

---

*Tentative: something that is not fully worked out or completed as yet.

hypothesis
tentative explanation of a phenomenon based on observations.

The results of any method of hypothesis testing won't be just the raw numbers or measurements. Any data that come from your testing procedure will be analyzed with some kind of statistical method that helps to organize and refine the data. L I N K *to Appendix A: Statistics.* You have come to some conclusion about your investigation's success or failure, you want to let other researchers know what you have found.

You mean you ▶ tell them what happened, even if it failed?

You mean you tell them what happened, even if it failed? Just because one experiment or other study did not find support for the hypothesis does not necessarily mean that the hypothesis is incorrect. Your study might have been poorly designed, or there might have been factors not under your control that interfered with the study. But other researchers are asking the same kinds of questions that you might have asked. They need to know what has already been found out about the answers to those questions so that they can continue investigating, adding more knowledge about the answers to those questions. Even if your own investigation didn't go as planned, that tells other researchers what *not* to do in the future. So the final step in any scientific investigation is reporting the results.

5. **Report Your Results:** At this point, you would want to write up exactly what you did, why you did it, how you did it, and what you found, so that others can learn from what you have already accomplished—or failed to accomplish. Another reason for reporting your results is that even if your research gave you the answer you expected, your investigation might have been done incorrectly, or the results might have been a fluke or due to chance alone. So if others can **replicate** your research (do exactly the same study over again and get the same results), it gives much more support to your findings. This allows others to predict behavior based on your findings as well as using the results of those findings to modify or control behavior, the last two goals in psychology.

This might be a good place to make a distinction between questions that can be scientifically or empirically studied and those that cannot. For example, "What is the meaning of life?" is not a question that can be studied using the scientific or empirical method. Empirical questions are those that can be tested through direct observation or experience. For example, "Has life ever existed on Mars?" is a question that scientists are trying to answer through measurements, experimentation, soil samples, and other methods. Eventually they will be able to say with some degree of confidence that life could have existed or could not have existed. That is an empirical question, because it can be supported or disproved by gathering real evidence. The meaning of life, however, is a question of belief for each person. One does not need proof to *believe*, but scientists need proof (in the form of objectively gathered evidence) to *know*.

In psychology, researchers try to find the answers to empirical questions. Questions that involve beliefs and values are best left to philosophy and religion.

DESCRIPTIVE METHODS

1.8   *How do psychologists use naturalistic and laboratory settings to describe behavior, and what are the advantages and disadvantages associated with these settings?*

There are a number of different ways to investigate the answers to research questions, and which one researchers use depends on the kind of question they want to answer. If they want to simply gather information about what has happened or what is happening, they would want a method that gives them a detailed description.

replicate
in research, repeating a study or experiment to see if the same results will be obtained in an effort to demonstrate reliability of results.

NATURALISTIC OBSERVATION   Sometimes all researchers need to know is what is happening to a group of animals or people. The best way to look at the behavior of animals or people is to watch them behave in their normal environment. That's why animal researchers like Jane Goodall went to the areas where chimpanzees lived and watched them eat, play, mate, and sleep in their own natural surroundings. With people, researchers might want to observe them in their workplaces, homes, or on playgrounds. For example, if someone wanted to know how adolescents behave with members of the opposite sex in a social setting, that researcher might go to the mall on a weekend night.

What is the advantage of naturalistic observation? It allows researchers to get a realistic picture of how behavior occurs because they are actually watching that behavior. In a more artificial setting, like a laboratory, they might get behavior that is contrived or artificial rather than genuine. Of course, there are precautions that must be taken. In many cases, animals or people who know they are being watched will not behave normally anyway, in a process called the **observer effect**, so often the observer needs to remain hidden from view. When researching humans, this is often a difficult thing to do. In the mall setting with the teenagers, a researcher might find that pretending to read a book is a good disguise, especially if one wears glasses to hide the movement of the eyes. Then the researchers would be able to look up at what goes on between the teens without them knowing that they were being watched. In other cases, researchers might use one-way mirrors, or they might actually become participants in a group, a technique called **participant observation**.

Are there disadvantages? Unfortunately, yes. One of the disadvantages of naturalistic observation is the possibility of **observer bias**. That happens when the person doing the observing has a particular opinion about what he or she is going to see or expects to see. If that is the case, sometimes that person sees only those actions that support that expectation and ignores actions that don't fit. A way around that is to have *blind observers*: people who do not know what the research question is and, therefore, have no preconceived notions about what they "should" see. It's also a good idea to have more than one observer, so that the various observations can be compared.

Another disadvantage is that each naturalistic setting is unique and unlike any other. Observations that are made at one time in one setting may not hold true for another time, even if the setting is similar, because the conditions are not going to be exactly the same time after time—researchers don't have that kind of control over the natural world. For example, famed gorilla researcher Diane Fossey had to battle poachers who set traps for the animals in the area of her observations (Mowat, 1988). The presence and activities of the poachers affected the normal behavior of the gorillas she was trying to observe.

LABORATORY OBSERVATION   Sometimes observing behavior in animals or people is just not practical in a natural setting. For example, a researcher might want to observe the reactions of animals to a mirror image of themselves and record the reactions with a camera mounted behind the one-way mirror. That kind of equipment might be difficult to set up in a natural setting. In a laboratory observation, the researcher would bring the animal to the equipment, controlling the type of animal, the number of animals, and everything else that goes on in the laboratory.

Researcher Jane Goodall watches chimpanzees behave in their natural environment. How might her presence have affected the behavior of the chimpanzees?

observer effect
tendency of people or animals to behave differently from normal when they know they are being observed.

participant observation
a naturalistic observation in which the observer becomes a participant in the group being observed.

observer bias
tendency of observers to see what they expect to see.

Psychologists use many kinds of tools to observe behavior. In this scene, a researcher is attaching electrodes to a woman to gather information about her sleep habits.

Simulation
Live!
psych

Observational
Studies

At the top is a computer-generated reconstruction of the damaged skull of Phineas Gage. The red area shows the path taken by the steel rod driven through his skull by an explosion in 1848. At the bottom is a model of his head and next to it the actual skull.

case study
study of one individual in great detail.

representative sample
randomly selected sample of subjects from a larger population of subjects.

As mentioned previously, laboratory settings have the disadvantage of being an artificial situation that might result in artificial behavior—animals and people often react differently in the laboratory than they would in the real world. The main advantage of this method is the degree of control that it gives to the observer.

Both naturalistic and laboratory observations can lead to the formation of hypotheses that can later be tested.

1.9   *How do psychologists use case studies and surveys to describe behavior, and what are some drawbacks to each of these methods?*

CASE STUDIES   Another descriptive technique is called the **case study**, in which one individual is studied in great detail. In a case study, researchers try to learn everything they can about that individual. For example, Sigmund Freud based his entire theory of psychoanalysis on his numerous case studies of his patients in which he gathered information about their childhoods and relationships with others from the very beginning of their lives to the present. ⓛⓘⓝⓚ *to Chapter Twelve: Theories of Personality, p. 445.*

The advantage of the case study is the tremendous amount of detail it provides. It may also be the only way to get certain kinds of information. For example, one famous case study was the story of Phineas Gage, who had a railroad spike driven through his head and suffered a major personality change as a result (Damasio et al., 1994). Researchers couldn't study that with naturalistic observation and an experiment is out of the question. Imagine anyone responding to an ad in the newspaper that read:

Wanted: 50 people willing to suffer nonfatal brain damage for scientific study of the brain. Will pay all medical expenses.

It's pretty certain that anyone who actually answered that ad might already be suffering from some pretty extensive brain damage.

The disadvantage of the case study is that researchers can't really apply the results to other similar people. In other words, they can't assume that if another person had the same kind of experiences growing up that he or she would turn out just like the person in their case study. People are unique and have too many complicating factors in their lives to be that predictable. So what researchers find in one case won't necessarily apply or generalize to others.

SURVEYS   Sometimes what psychologists want to know about is pretty personal—like what people do in their sexual relationships, for example. The only way to find out about very private (covert) behavior is to ask questions.

In the survey method, researchers will ask a series of questions about the topic they are studying. Surveys can be conducted in person in the form of interviews or on the telephone, the Internet, or with a questionnaire. The questions in interviews or on the telephone can vary, but usually the questions in a survey are all the same for everyone answering the survey. In this way, researchers can ask lots of questions and survey literally hundreds of people.

That is the big advantage of surveys, aside from their ability to get at private information. Researchers can get a tremendous amount of data on a very large group of people. Of course, there are disadvantages. One disadvantage is researchers have to be very careful about the group of people they survey. If they want to find out what college freshmen think about politics, for example, they can't really ask every single college freshman in the entire United States. But they can select a **representative sample** from that group. They could randomly* select a certain number of college

*Randomly: in this sense, chosen so that each member of the group has an equal chance of being chosen.

freshmen from several different colleges across the United States, for example. Why randomly? Because the sample has to be *representative* of the **population**, which is the entire group in which the researcher is interested. If researchers selected only freshmen from Ivy League schools, for example, they would certainly get different opinions on politics than they might get from small community colleges. But if they take a lot of colleges and select their *participants* (people who are part of the study) randomly, they will be more certain of getting answers that a broad selection of college students would typically give.

That brings up the other major disadvantage of the survey technique: people aren't always going to give researchers accurate answers. The fact is, people tend to misremember things, distort the truth, and may lie outright—even if the survey is an anonymous* questionnaire. Remembering is not a very accurate process sometimes, especially when people think that they might not come off sounding very desirable or socially appropriate. Some people deliberately give the answer they think is more socially correct rather than their true opinion, so that no one gets offended, in a process called *courtesy bias*. Researchers must take their survey results with a big grain of salt**—they may not be as accurate as they would like them to be.

Both the wording of survey questions and the order in which they appear on the survey can affect the outcome. It is difficult to find a wording that will be understood in exactly the same way by all those who read the question, for example. Questions can be worded in such a way that the desired answer becomes obvious (often resulting in courtesy bias–type answers), or a question that appears at the end of a survey might be answered quite differently than if it had appeared at the beginning.

---

*Anonymous: not named or identified.
**Big grain of salt: a phrase meaning to be skeptical; to doubt the truth or accuracy of something.

population
the entire group of people or animals in which the researcher is interested.

"Next question: I believe that life is a constant striving for balance, requiring frequent tradeoffs between morality and necessity, within a cyclic pattern of joy and sadness, forging a trail of bittersweet memories until one slips, inevitably, into the jaws of death. Agree or disagree?"
© The New Yorker Collection 1989 George Price from cartoonbank.com. All Rights Reserved.

PRACTICE QUIZ: HOW MUCH DO YOU REMEMBER?

Pick the best answer.

1. In the scientific method, the first step is
   a. reporting your results.
   b. perceiving a question.
   c. drawing conclusions.
   d. testing the hypothesis.

2. In a naturalistic observation, the phenomenon in which the behavior of the subjects being observed changes because they are being watched is called
   a. observer bias.
   b. participant observation.
   c. observer effect.
   d. representative sampling.

3. The use of _____ helps to control for the effect of observer bias.
   a. blind observers
   b. a single trained observer
   c. randomly selected observers
   d. none of the above

4. The main disadvantage of a case study is that it is not
   a. easily done due to the large number of subjects.
   b. detailed enough for most research questions.
   c. generalizable to other similar conditions.
   d. biased.

5. Which of the following is the BEST example of a representative sample?
   a. You ask your fellow students to be participants in a study of adult memory.
   b. You ask people from your church to participate in a study of family values.
   c. You choose people shopping in an expensive store in the mall to respond to your survey.
   d. You choose people randomly from the telephone book to respond to your survey.

Answers: 1-b, 2-c, 3-a, 4-c, 5-d.

correlation
a measure of the relationship between two variables.

Simulation
Live! psych
Correlational
Studies

How can a relationship ▶
like that have a
direction?

FINDING RELATIONSHIPS

The methods discussed so far only provide descriptions of behavior. There are really only two methods that allow researchers to know more than just a description of what has happened: correlations and experiments. Correlation is actually a statistical technique, a particular way of organizing numerical information so that it is easier to look for patterns in the information. This method will be discussed here rather than in the statistics appendix found at the back of this text because correlation, like the experiment, is about finding relationships. In fact, the data from the descriptive methods just discussed are often analyzed using the correlational technique.

1.10   *What is the correlational technique and what does it tell researchers about relationships?*

CORRELATIONS   A **correlation** is a measure of the relationship between two or more variables. A *variable* is anything that can change or vary—scores on a test, temperature in a room, gender, and so on. For example, researchers might be curious to know whether or not cigarette smoking is connected to life expectancy—the number of years a person can be expected to live. Obviously, the scientists can't hang around people who smoke and wait to see when those people die. The only way (short of performing a really unethical and lengthy experiment) to find out if smoking behavior and life expectancy are related to each other is to use the medical records of people who have already died. (For privacy's sake, the personal information such as names and social security numbers would be removed, with only the facts such as age, gender, weight, and so on available to researchers.) Researchers would look for two facts from each record: the number of cigarettes the person smoked per day and the age of the person at death.

Now the researcher has two sets of numbers for each person in the study. Those numbers go into a mathematical formula and produce a number called the *correlation coefficient*. The correlation coefficient represents two things: the direction of the relationship and its strength.

How can a relationship like that have a direction? Whenever researchers talk about two variables being related to each other, what they really mean is that knowing the value of one variable allows them to predict the value of the other variable. For example, if researchers found that smoking and life expectancy are indeed related, they should be able to predict how long someone might live if they know how many cigarettes a person smokes in a day. But which way does that prediction work? If a person smokes a lot of cigarettes, does that mean that he or she will live a longer life or a shorter one? Does life expectancy go up or down as smoking increases? That's what is meant by the *direction* of the relationship.

In terms of the correlation coefficient (represented by the small letter *r*), the number researchers get from the formula will either be a positive number or a negative number. If positive, the two variables increase in the same direction—as one goes up, the other goes up; as one decreases, the other also decreases. If negative, the two variables have an inverse* relationship. As one increases, the other decreases. If researchers find that the more cigarettes a person smoked, the younger that person was when he or she died, that would mean that the correlation between the two variables is negative. (As smoking goes up, life expectancy goes down—an inverse relationship.)

---

*Inverse: opposite in order.

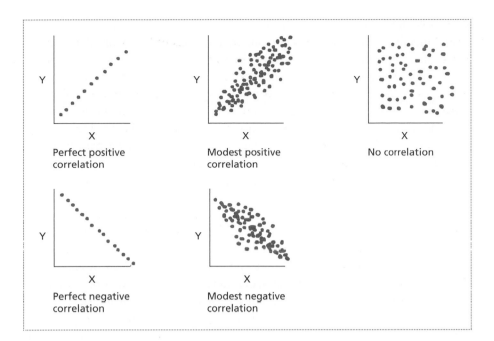

FIGURE 1.3 Five scatterplots showing direction and strength of correlation. It should be noted that perfect correlations, whether positive or negative, rarely occur in the real world.

The strength of the relationship between the variables will be determined by the actual number itself. That number will always range between +1.00 and −1.00. The reason that it cannot be greater than +1.00 or less than −1.00 has to do with the formula and an imaginary line on a graph around which the data points gather, a graph called a scatterplot (see Figure 1.3). If the relationship is a strong one, the number will be closer to +1.00 or to −1.00. A correlation of +.89, for example, would be a very strong positive correlation. That might represent the relationship between scores on the SAT and an IQ test, for example. A correlation of −.89 would be equally strong but negative. That would be more like the correlation researchers would probably find between smoking cigarettes and the age at which a person dies.

Notice that the closer the number is to zero, the weaker the relationship becomes. Researchers would probably find that the correlation coefficient for the relationship between people's weight and the number of freckles they have is pretty close to zero, for example.

Go back to the cigarette thing—if we found that the correlation between cigarette smoking and life expectancy was high, does that mean that smoking causes your life expectancy to be shortened? Not exactly. The biggest error that people make concerning correlation is to assume that it means one variable is the cause of the other. Remember that *correlation does not prove causation.* That means that just because two variables are related to each other, researchers cannot assume that one of them causes the other one to occur. They could both be related to some other variable that is the cause of both. For example, population is the cause of increasing numbers of many kinds of services in a particular area, including churches and bars. The number of churches in any given area can be used to predict the number of bars because the two are correlated through their common link to population, not because churches cause bars to be built or vice versa.

To sum up, a correlation will tell researchers if there is a relationship between the variables, how strong the relationship is, and in what direction the relationship goes. If researchers know the value of one variable, they can predict the value of the other. If they know someone's IQ score, for example, they can predict about what score that person should get on the SAT—not the exact score, just a reasonable estimate. Also, even though correlation does not prove causation, it can provide a starting point for examining causal relationships with another type of study, the experiment.

[handwritten margin notes:]
most likely a 2 pt. decimal.
correlation cannot tell you cause.
correlation ≠ causation

◀ Go back to the cigarette thing—if we found that the correlation between cigarette smoking and life expectancy was high, does that mean that smoking causes your life expectancy to be shortened?

experiment
a deliberate manipulation of a variable to see if corresponding changes in behavior result, allowing the determination of cause-and-effect relationships.

operational definition
definition of a variable of interest that allows it to be directly measured.

independent variable
variable in an experiment that is manipulated by the experimenter.

Simulation
Live!
psych
Experimental
Method

THE EXPERIMENT   The only research method that will allow researchers to determine the cause of a behavior is the **experiment**. In an experiment, researchers deliberately manipulate (change in some purposeful way) the variable they think is causing some behavior while holding all the other variables that might interfere with the experiment's results constant and unchanging. That way, if they get changes in behavior (an effect, in other words), they know that those changes must be due to the manipulated variable. For example, remember the discussion of the steps in the scientific method. It talked about how to study the effects of watching violent cartoons on children's aggressive behavior. The most logical way to study that particular relationship is by an experiment.

First, researchers might start by selecting the children they want to use in the experiment. The best method to do that is the same method they would use for selecting a sample of people to participate in the experiment—random selection. Ideally, researchers would decide on the age they wanted to study. Let's say that they want to know the effects of the experiment on children who are 3 to 4 years old. Then researchers could go to day care centers to randomly select a certain number of children of that age. Of course, that wouldn't include the children who don't go to a day care center. Another way to get a sample in the age range might be to ask several pediatricians to send out letters to parents of children of that age and then randomly select the sample from those children whose parents responded positively.

1.11   *How do researchers use operational definitions, independent and dependent variables, experimental and control groups, and random assignment in designing an experiment?*

The Variables   Another important step is to decide on the variable the researchers want to manipulate (which would be the one they think causes changes in behavior) and the variable they want to measure to see if there are any changes (this would be the effect on behavior of the manipulation). Often deciding on the variables in the experiment comes before selection of the participants or subjects.

In the example of aggression and children's cartoons, the variable that researchers think causes changes in aggressive behavior is the violence in the cartoons. Researchers would want to manipulate that in some way, and in order to do that they have to define the term *violent cartoon*. They would have to find a cartoon that contains violence or make one. Then they would show that cartoon to the participants and try to measure their aggressive behavior afterwards. In measuring the aggressive behavior, they would have to specify exactly what they mean by "aggressive behavior" so that it can be measured. This is called an **operational definition** because it specifically names the operations (steps or procedures) that the experimenter must use to control or measure the variables in the experiment. An operational definition of aggressive behavior might be a checklist of very specific actions

The act of hitting each other with toy swords could be part of an operational definition of aggressive behavior.

such as hitting, pushing, and so on that an observer can mark off as the children do the items on the list. If the observers were just told to look for "aggressive behavior," the researchers would probably get half a dozen or more different interpretations of what aggressive behavior is.

The name for the variable that is manipulated in any experiment is the **independent variable** because it is *independent* of anything the participants do. The participants in the study do not get to choose or vary the independent variable, and their behavior does not affect this variable at all. In the preceding example, the independent variable would be the presence or absence of violence in the cartoons.

The response of the participants to the manipulation of the independent variable *is* a dependent relationship, so the response of the participants that is measured is known as the **dependent variable**. Their behavior, if the hypothesis is correct, should *depend* on whether or not they were exposed to the independent variable, and in the example, the dependent variable would be the measure of aggressive behavior in the children. The dependent variable is always the thing (response of subjects or result of some action) that is measured to see just how the independent variable may have affected it.

The Groups If researchers do all of this and find that the children's behavior is aggressive, can they say that the aggressive behavior was caused by the violence in the cartoon? No, what has been described so far is not enough. The researchers may find that the children who watch the violent cartoon are aggressive, but how would they know if their aggressive behavior was caused by the cartoon or was just the natural aggressive level of those particular children or the result of the particular time of day they were observed? Those sorts of *confounding variables* (variables that interfere with each other and their possible effects on some other variable of interest) are the kind researchers have to control for in some way. For example, if participants in an experiment were supposed to take only a potassium supplement but also took an iron supplement, any effects the potassium might have had on what the experimenter was measuring would be confused (confounded) with the effects that the iron supplement might have also had. The best way to control for confounding variables is to have two groups of participants: those who watch the violent cartoon, and those who watch a nonviolent cartoon for the same length of time. Then the researchers would measure the aggressive behavior in both groups. If the aggressive behavior is significantly greater in the group that watched the violent cartoon (and they would use statistics to determine this), then researchers can say that in this experiment, violent cartoon watching caused greater aggressive behavior.

The name given to the group that gets the independent variable (the violent cartoon in the example) is the **experimental group**, because it is the group that receives the experimental manipulation. The other group, the one that would get either no treatment or some kind of treatment that should have no effect (like the group that watches the nonviolent cartoon in the example), is called the **control group** because it is used to *control* for the possibility that other factors might be causing the effect that is being examined. If researchers were to find that both the group that watched the violent cartoon and the group that watched the nonviolent cartoon were equally aggressive, they would have to assume that the violent content did not influence that behavior at all.

The Importance of Randomization It's been mentioned that the best way to select the participants for any study is randomly, but once researchers have their participants they must be assigned to either the experimental group or the control group. **Random assignment** of each participant to one or the other condition is also the best way to assure control over those other interfering, or *extraneous*, variables. Random assignment means that each participant has an equal chance of being assigned to each condition. If researchers simply looked at the children and put all of the children from one day care center or one pediatrician's recommendations into the experimental group and the same for the control group, they would run the risk of biasing their research. Some day care centers may have more naturally aggressive children, for example, or some pediatricians may have a particular client base in which the children are very passive. So researchers want to take the entire participant group and assign each person randomly to one or the other of the groups in the study. Sometimes this is as simple as picking names out of a hat.

◀ If researchers do all of this and find that the children's behavior is aggressive, can they say that the aggressive behavior was caused by the violence in the cartoon?

CONTROL GROUP   OUT OF CONTROL GROUP.

dependent variable
variable in an experiment that represents the measurable response or behavior of the subjects in the experiment.

experimental group
subjects in an experiment who are subjected to the independent variable.

control group
subjects in an experiment who are not subjected to the independent variable and who may receive a placebo treatment.

random assignment
process of assigning subjects to the experimental or control groups randomly, so that each subject has an equal chance of being in either group.

placebo effect
the phenomenon in which the expectations of the participants in a study can influence their behavior.

1.12   *What are the placebo and the experimenter effects, and how do single-blind and double-blind studies control for those effects?*

Experimental Hazards: The Placebo Effect and the Experimenter Effect   There are a few other problems that might arise in any experiment, even with the use of control groups and random assignment. These problems are especially likely when studying people instead of animals, because people are often influenced by their own thoughts about what's going on in an experiment. For example, say there is a new drug that is supposed to improve memory in people who are in the very early stages of *Alzheimer's disease* (a form of mental deterioration that occurs in some people as they grow old). Ⓛ Ⓘ Ⓝ Ⓚ *to Chapter Six: Memory, p. 240.* Researchers would want to test the drug to see if it really is effective in helping to improve memory, so they would get a sample of people who are in the early stages of the disease, divide them into two groups, give one group the drug, and then test for improvement. They would probably have to do a test of memory both before and after the administration of the drug to be able to measure improvement.

Let me see if I've got ▶
this straight.
The group that
gets the drug
would be the
experimental
group, and the
one that doesn't
is the control
group, right?

Let me see if I've got this straight. The group that gets the drug would be the experimental group, and the one that doesn't is the control group, right? Right, and getting or not getting the drug is the independent variable, whereas the measure of memory improvement is the dependent variable. But there's still a problem with doing it this way. What if the researchers do find that the drug group had greater memory improvement than the group that received nothing? Can they really say that the drug itself caused the improvement? Or is it possible that the participants who received the drug *knew* that they were supposed to improve in memory and, therefore, made a major effort to do so? The improvement may have had more to do with participants' *belief* in the drug than the drug itself, a phenomenon* known as the **placebo effect**: the expectations of the participants in a study can influence their behavior. In medical research, the control group is often given a harmless substitute for the real drug, such as a sugar pill or an injection of salt water, and this substitute

───────────────

*Phenomenon: an observable fact or event.

This elderly woman has Alzheimer's disease, which causes a severe loss of recent memory. If she was given a drug to improve her memory, the researcher could not be certain that any improvement shown was caused by the drug or by the elderly woman's belief that the drug would work. The expectations of any person in an experimental study can affect the outcome of the study, a phenomenon known as the placebo effect.

(which has no medical effect) is called the *placebo*. If there is a placebo effect, the control group will show changes in the dependent variable even though the participants in that group received only a placebo.

There's another way that someone's expectations about the outcome of the experiment can influence the results, even when the participants are animals rather than people. It's called the **experimenter effect**, and it has to do with the experimenter's expectations, not the participants. As discussed earlier in the section about naturalistic observations, sometimes observers are biased—they see what they expect to see. This can also happen in an experiment. If the researcher is doing the measuring of the dependent variable, it's possible that he or she could give the participants clues about how they are supposed to respond—with body language, tone of voice, or even eye contact. It wouldn't be deliberate, but it does happen. It could go something like this in the example: you, the Alzheimer's patient, are in the experimenter's office to take your second memory test after trying the drug. The experimenter seems to pay a lot of attention to you and to every answer that you give in the test, so you get the feeling that you are supposed to have improved a lot. So you try harder, and any improvement you do have may be caused only by your own increased effort, not by the drug. That's the experimenter effect: the behavior of the experimenter caused the participant to change his or her response pattern.

Single-Blind and Double-Blind Studies   Fortunately, there are ways to control for these effects. The classic way to control for the placebo effect is to give the control group an actual placebo—some kind of treatment that doesn't affect behavior at all. In the drug experiment, the placebo would have to be some kind of sugar pill or saline (salt) solution that looks like and is administered just like the actual drug. The participants in both the experimental and the control groups would not know which group they are actually in and whether or not they got the real drug or the placebo. That way, if their expectations have any effect at all on the outcome of the experiment, the experimenter will be able to tell by looking at the results for the control group and comparing them to the experimental group. Even if the control group improves a little, the drug group should improve significantly more if the drug is working. This is called a **single-blind study**, because the participants are "blind" to the treatment they receive.

For a long time, that was the only type of experiment researchers did in psychology. But researchers Robert Rosenthal and Lenore Jacobson reported in their 1968 book, *Pygmalion in the Classroom*, that when teachers were told that some students had a high potential for success and others a low potential, the students showed significant gains or decreases in their performance on standardized tests depending on which "potential" they were supposed to have (Rosenthal & Jacobson, 1968). Actually, the students had been selected randomly and randomly assigned to one of the two groups, "high" or "low." Their performances on the tests were affected by the attitudes of the teachers concerning their potential. This study and similar studies after it highlighted the need to have the experimenter be "blind" as well as the participants in research. So in a **double-blind study**, neither the participants nor the person or persons measuring the dependent variable know who got what. That's why everything in a double-blind experiment gets coded in some way, so that only after all the measurements have been taken can anyone determine who was in the experimental group and who was in the control group.

Other Experimental Designs   In the field of developmental psychology, researchers are always looking for the ways in which a person's age influences his or her behavior. The problem is that age is a variable that cannot be randomly controlled. In a regular experiment, for example, participants can be randomly assigned to the various conditions: drug or placebo, special instructions or no special instructions, and so on.

experimenter effect
tendency of the experimenter's expectations for a study to unintentionally influence the results of the study.

single-blind study
study in which the subjects do not know if they are in the experimental or the control group.

double-blind study
study in which neither the experimenter nor the subjects knows if the subjects are in the experimental or control group.

But participants cannot be randomly assigned to different age groups. It would be like saying, "Okay, these people are now going to be 20, and these others will be 30."

To get around this problem, researchers use alternative designs (called *quasi-experimental designs*) that are not considered true experiments because of the inability to randomly assign participants to the experimental and control groups (Gribbons & Herman, 1997). These designs are discussed more fully in Chapter Seven, Development Across the Life Span, pp. 250–251.

For a good example of a typical experiment, read the following section about Dr. Teresa Amabile's experiment in creativity and rewards.

CLASSIC STUDIES IN PSYCHOLOGY
Teresa Amabile and the Effect of Extrinsic Reward on Creativity

1.13   *How might a real experiment be conducted?*

A very good example of an experiment is a classic study by famed Harvard Business College professor, Dr. Teresa Amabile. Amabile (1982) has made great strides in the study of creativity in both children and adults. In her 1982 study, she randomly selected a group of girls from a local public school. The girls ranged in age from 7 to 11. Dr. Amabile randomly divided them into two groups, an experimental group and a control group. She arranged to have an "art party" at the school after regular class hours and set up an empty classroom as her "laboratory." In this classroom she placed all the materials the children would need to make collages—poster board, paste, and numerous shapes and colors of construction paper. (A collage is just bits of paper or pictures glued onto a poster or paper—no drawing skills are necessary.)

Her hypothesis was that the girls who created art for an *extrinsic* (external) reward, such as toys, would be significantly less creative than the girls who created art for its own sake, or who have *intrinsic* (internal) motivation. On the day of the art party for the experimental group, she showed the children all the materials they would be using and *told them that the best three collages would win prizes.* This instruction was actually one part of her independent variable because she wanted to manipulate the children into believing that they were creating art for an extrinsic reward.

On a different day, she brought the girls in her control group into the same classroom with the same materials, but she told these children that the prizes she showed them at the beginning would be raffled off by drawing names out of a hat at the end of the party. So these children had the same materials, the same amount of time, and the same prizes—but they were making their collages purely for the fun of it, or because of intrinsic motivation.

At the end of the party for *both* groups, she actually raffled off the prizes. It wasn't important that the children in the experimental group actually *win* the prizes with their art, only that they *believed that they would.*

Now all the basic elements of an experiment were in place: the hypothesis (the prediction), the independent variable (the two different sets of instructions), the experimental group (the ones who were told they could win prizes), and the control group (the ones just having fun). From her hypothesis, Amabile's dependent variable has to be how creative the artwork of the children in both groups actually was, but how could she measure something as subjective as creativity?

This is where cleverness comes in. Amabile got several local artists, art critics, and art teachers to come in after the children were gone. She had taped all of the collages (with all the identifying information on the back and, therefore, invisible) to the walls of the school corridors. Each "judge" rated each piece of artwork for its creativity, and then Amabile collected

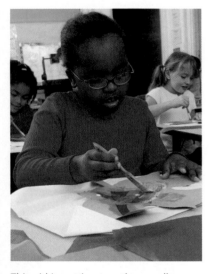

This girl is putting together a collage, using materials very similar to those used in Amabile's classic experiment.

the ratings for each collage, averaged them, and came up with a "creativity score" that she could analyze with statistics. Ⓛ Ⓘ Ⓝ Ⓚ *to Appendix A: Statistics.*

Amabile's hypothesis was indeed supported by the results of her study. The judges' scores for the experimental group (who all believed they were competing for prizes) were consistently and significantly lower than the scores for the control group (Amabile, 1982). So the conclusion is that creativity is decreased when reward is in the picture in the form of prizes or money (as her studies with adults have shown).

Questions for Further Discussion

1. What are some of the factors that might have affected the results of Dr. Amabile's experiment, and how might she have controlled for them?

2. How might the particular school from which Dr. Amabile selected her participants have been an interfering factor in the experiment?

3. How can parents and educators encourage creativity without the use of external rewards?

PRACTICE **QUIZ:** HOW MUCH DO YOU REMEMBER?

Pick the best answer.

1. It's pretty common knowledge that the more you study, the higher your grade will be. What kind of correlation is this relationship?
   a. positive
   b. negative
   c. zero
   d. causal

2. Which of the following would indicate the strongest relationship between two variables:
   a. +1.04
   b. −0.89
   c. +0.75
   d. +0.54

3. In an experiment to test the effects of alcohol on memory, the experimenter gives vodka mixed in orange juice to one group of subjects and orange juice with no vodka to the other group. She then measures the memory skills of both groups by means of a memory test. In this study, the independent variable would be
   a. scores on the memory test.
   b. the presence or absence of vodka in the orange juice.
   c. intelligence.
   d. a placebo.

4. In that same experiment, the control group is the one that gets
   a. only one drink of orange juice with vodka.
   b. a fake test of memory.
   c. only something to eat.
   d. the orange juice without vodka.

5. In a _____ study, neither the experimenter nor the participants know who is in the control group and who is in the experimental group.
   a. placebo
   b. single-blind
   c. double-blind
   d. triple-blind

6. In Dr. Amabile's classic experiment of the effects of reward on creativity, what was the dependent variable?
   a. the special instructions to each group
   b. the collage party
   c. the ratings of creativity from the experts for each child's collage
   d. the size of the collages

Answers: 1-a, 2-b, 3-b, 4-d, 5-c, 6-c.

Ethics of Psychological Research

The study that Dr. Watson did with "Little Albert" and the white rat seems pretty cruel, when you think about it. Do researchers today do that kind of study? Actually, as psychology began to grow and more research with people was being done, psychologists began to realize that some protections had to be put in place. No one wanted to be thought of as a "mad scientist," and if studies were permitted that could actually harm people, the field of psychology might die out pretty quickly. Scientists in other areas of research were also realizing that ethical treatment of the participants in studies had to be ensured in some way. Ethical treatment, of course, means that people who volunteer for a study will be able to expect that no physical or psychological harm should come to them.

◀ The study that Dr. Watson did with "Little Albert" and the white rat seems pretty cruel, when you think about it. Do researchers today do that kind of study?

"He says he wants a lawyer."
© The New Yorker Collection 1999 Tom Chalkley from cartoonbank.com. All Rights Reserved.

1.14 *What are the ethical concerns when conducting research with people and animals?*

Universities and colleges (where most psychological research is carried out) usually have *ethics committees*, groups of psychologists or other professionals who look over each proposed research study and judge it according to its safety and consideration for the participants in the study. These committees look at all aspects of the proposed research, from the written materials that explain the research to the potential subjects to the equipment that may be used in the study itself.

THE GUIDELINES FOR DOING RESEARCH WITH PEOPLE

There are quite a few ethical concerns when dealing with human subjects in an experiment or other type of study. Here is a list of the most common ethical guidelines:

1. *Rights and well-being of participants must be weighed against the study's value to science.* In other words, people come first, research second.

2. *Participants must be allowed to make an informed decision about participation.* This means that researchers have to explain the study to the people they want to include before they do anything to them or with them—even children—and it has to be in terms that the participants can understand. If researchers are using infants, their parents have to be informed and give their consent. This is known as *informed consent.*

3. *Deception must be justified.* In some cases, it is necessary to deceive the participants. If that happens, it has to be because the study wouldn't work any other way, and the participants have to be told after the study exactly why the deception was important. This is called *debriefing.* Debriefing participants helps them understand why they were deceived and the importance of their responses to that deception.

4. *Participants may withdraw from the study at any time.* The participants must be allowed to drop out for any reason. Sometimes people get bored with the study, decide they don't have the time, or don't like what they have to do, for example. Children are particularly likely to decide not to play. Researchers have to let them go, even if it means getting more participants.

5. *Participants must be protected from risks or told explicitly of risks.* For example, if researchers are using any kind of electrical equipment, care must be taken to ensure that no participant will experience a physical shock from faulty electrical equipment.

6. *Investigator must debrief participants, telling the true nature of the study and expectations of results.* This is important in all types of studies but particularly in those involving a deception.

7. *Data must remain confidential.* Freud recognized the importance of confidentiality, referring to his patients in his books and articles with false names. This is also why psychologists and other researchers today tend to report only group results rather than results for a single individual, so that no one could possibly be recognized (American Psychological Association, 1992).

Psychologists also study animals to find out about behavior, often drawing comparisons between what the animals do and what people might do under similar conditions.

But why not
just study the ▶
people in the
first place?

But why not just study the people in the first place? There are some research questions that are extremely important but difficult or impossible to answer by using human participants. Animals live shorter lives, so looking at long-term effects becomes much easier. Animals are also easier to control—the scientist can control diet, living arrangements, and even genetic relatedness. The white laboratory rat has become a recognized species different from ordinary rats, bred with its own kind for many decades until each white rat is essentially a little genetic "twin" of all the others. Animals also engage in much simpler behavior than humans do, making it easier to see the effects of manipulations. But the biggest reason that researchers use animals in some research is that animals can be used in ways that researchers could never use people. For example, it took a long time for scientists to prove that nicotine causes cancer because they had to do correlational studies with people and experiments only with animals. There's the catch—researchers can do many things to animals that they can't do to people. That might seem cruel at first, but when you think that without animal research there would be no vaccines for deadly diseases, no insulin treatments for diabetics, no transplants, then the value of the research and its benefits to humankind far outweigh the hazards to which the research animals are exposed.

There are also ethical considerations when dealing with animals in research, just as there are with humans. With animals, though, the focus is on avoiding exposing them to any *unnecessary* pain or suffering. So if surgery is part of the study, it is done under anesthesia. If the research animal must die in order for the effects of some drug or other treatment to be examined in an autopsy, the death must be accomplished humanely. Animals are used in only about 7 percent of all psychological studies (Committee on Animal Research and Ethics, 2004).

These rabbits are part of a drug-testing study. Their bodies are enclosed in the metal cases to prevent movement during the test. What steps might the researchers using these animals take to treat the animals ethically?

Critical Thinking

What good is all this focus on science and research going to do for me? I live in the real world, not a laboratory. The real world is full of opportunities for scientific thinking. Think about all of those commercials on television for miracle weight loss, hair restoration, or herbal remedies for arthritis, depression, and a whole host of physical and mental problems. Wouldn't it be nice to know how many of these claims people should believe? Wouldn't you like to know how to evaluate claims like these and possibly save yourself some time, effort, and money? That's exactly the kind of "real-world" problem that critical thinking can help sort out.

1.15   *What are the basic principles of critical thinking, and how can using critical thinking help people in their everyday lives?*

THE CRITERIA FOR CRITICAL THINKING

According to Beyer (1995), **critical thinking** means making reasoned judgments. The word *reasoned* means that people's judgments should be logical and well thought out. There are four basic criteria* for critical thinking that people should try to remember when faced with statements about the world around them (Gill, 1991; Shore, 1990):

1. *There are very few "truths" that do not need to be subjected to testing.* Although people may accept religious beliefs and personal values on "faith," everything else in life needs to have supporting evidence. Questions that can be investigated empirically should be examined using established scientific methods. One shouldn't accept anything at face value but should always ask, "How do you know that? What is the evidence?"

2. *All evidence is not equal in quality.* This is one of the most important steps in critical thinking and one that is often overlooked. People need to look at how evidence is gathered before deciding that it provides good support for some idea. For example, there are poorly done experiments, incorrect assumptions based on correlations rather than experiments, and studies in which there was either no control group or no attempt made to control for placebo effects or experimenter effects.

◄ What good is all this focus on science and research going to do for me? I live in the real world, not a laboratory.

critical thinking
making reasoned judgments about claims.

---

*Criteria: standards on which a judgment or decision may be based.

3. *Just because someone is considered to be an authority or to have a lot of expertise does not make everything that person claims automatically true.* One should always ask to see the evidence rather than just take some expert's word for anything. How good is the evidence? Are there other alternative explanations? For example, Linus Pauling, a famous and respected scientist, made claims about the benefits of vitamin C for curing the common cold. Although research is beginning to support the idea that vitamin C may help fight cancer, the research has also found that large doses of this vitamin don't do anything for curing the common cold (Padayatty & Levine, 2001).

4. *Critical thinking requires an open mind.* Although it is good to be skeptical, people don't need to be so skeptical that they actually close their minds to things that are possible. At the same time, it's good to have an open mind, but not so open as to be gullible* or apt to "swallow anything." Critical thinking requires a delicate balance between skepticism and willingness to consider possibilities. For example, scientists have yet to see any convincing evidence that there was once life on Mars. That doesn't mean that scientists totally dismiss the idea of life on Mars, just that there is no convincing evidence *yet*.

PSEUDOPSYCHOLOGIES: WHY DO PEOPLE FALL FOR FAKERY?

I guess I understand ▶
about the
importance of
critical thinking—
there seems to be
a lot of people
out there who
will fall for
anything.

I guess I understand about the importance of critical thinking—there seems to be a lot of people out there who will fall for anything. Actually, the kind of people who fall for the dumbest-sounding scams is rather surprising. Many very intelligent people fall prey to the same kinds of faulty reasoning that less "sophisticated" persons do. Con artists and scammers know the flaws in human nature pretty well, and that's how they survive.

Some of the easiest things to fall for are the **pseudopsychologies**, systems of explaining human behavior that are not based on scientific evidence and that have no real value other than being entertaining (Bunge, 1984). Because people like to try to understand themselves, they often participate in these activities.

People, including some reputable scientists of the Victorian era, used to believe that bumps on the skull were indicators of various personality traits, resulting in the "science" of *phrenology*. Franz Gall, a German anatomy teacher, popularized phrenology in the 1800s. His research was flawed and often quite biased. He also thought that skull size was related to intelligence, and he set out to demonstrate that people of different races had smaller skulls than Caucasians and were, therefore, less intelligent. He deliberately chose skulls of a size to "prove" his assumption.

Another false system is *palmistry*, or the reading of palms. There is overwhelming evidence that the lines of the palm have absolutely no relationship to personality and cannot predict the future (Ben-Shakhar et al., 1986; Dean et al., 1992), yet many people still believe that palm readers are for real. What about handwriting? Surely one's personality would be revealed in handwriting? The pseudo-psychology called *graphology*, or the analysis of personality through handwriting, even has respectable companies using handwriting analysis to select prospective employees, yet graphologists score close to zero on tests of accuracy in personality measurement (Ben-Shakhar et al., 1986).

pseudopsychologies
systems of explaining human behavior that are not based on or consistent with scientific evidence.

---

*Gullible: easily fooled or cheated.

PRACTICE **QUIZ:** HOW MUCH DO YOU REMEMBER?

Pick the best answer.

1. Which of the following is NOT one of the common ethical rules?
   a. Participants have to give informed consent.
   b. Deception cannot be used in any studies with human beings.
   c. The rights and well-being of the participants must come first.
   d. Data must remain confidential.

2. We use animals in research because
   a. animals have simple behavior that makes it easy to see changes.
   b. animals don't live as long as humans and are easier to control.
   c. we can do things to animals that we can't do to people.
   d. all of the above are true.

3. A famous newscaster advertises a new magnetic mattress for controlling pain. If Nathaniel decides to order the mattress because he believes that such a well-known personality should know if it works or not, he has made an error in which of the following?

a. Few "truths" do not need to be tested.
b. All evidence is not equal in quality.
c. Authority or expertise does not make the claims of the authority or expert true.
d. Critical thinking requires an open mind.

4. Critical thinking means making judgments based on
   a. emotional issues.
   b. keeping a closed mind.
   c. reason and logical evaluation.
   d. authority and expertise.

5. Which pseudopsychology claims to understand personality through a study of the bumps on one's skull?
   a. phrenology   **c.** graphology
   b. palmistry   **d.** astrology

Answers: 1-b, 2-d, 3-c, 4-c, 5-a.

Applying Psychology To Everyday Life: Using Critical Thinking–Does Astrology Work?

1.16 *How might critical thinking be applied to a real-world example?*

Astrology is a pseudo-psychology that attempts to predict the future and explain personality by using the positions of the stars and planets at the moment of birth. Many people see astrology as a form of entertainment, but others take it quite seriously, planning their daily activities and making important life choices based on their horoscopes. But is there any validity to believing that the positions of the objects in the rest of the universe have any effect at all on one's personality or daily successes or failures? Here's an example of critical thinking applied to astrology:

1. *Are astrologer's charts up-to-date?* The basic astrological charts were designed over 3,000 years ago. The stars, planets, and constellations are no longer in the same positions in the sky due to changes in the rotation of the Earth's axis over long periods of time—over 24 degrees in just the last 2,000 years (Dean & Kelly, 2000; Kelly, 1980). So a Gemini is really a Cancer and will be a Leo in another 2,000 years.

2. *What exactly is so important about the moment of birth?* Why not the moment of conception? What happens if a baby is born by cesarean section and not at the time it would have been born naturally? Is that person's whole life screwed up?

3. *Why would the stars and planets have any effect on a person? Is it gravity?* The body mass of the doctor who delivers the baby has a far greater gravitational pull on the infant's body than the moon. (Maybe people should use skinny obstetricians?)

Research also shows no connection between astrological signs and personality, careers, skills, marriage rates, divorce rates, or even physical characteristics (Dean & Kelly, 2000; Kelly, 1980). Studies of thousands of predictions by astrologers showed that only a very small percentage of those predictions actually came true (Dean & Kelly, 2000), and the ones that did come true were very vague or easily guessed from current events ("I predict that a famous star will have plastic surgery this year.")

Questions for Further Discussion
   1. Why might reasonably educated people believe in astrology?
   2. Is there any harm in using astrology to make decisions in one's life?

1   CHAPTER SUMMARY

What Is Psychology?

1.1 *What is the definition and what are four primary goals of psychology?*

- Psychology is the scientific study of behavior and mental processes.
- The four goals of psychology are description, explanation, prediction, and control.

Psychology Then: The History of Psychology

1.2 *What were the basic ideas of structuralism and functionalism, and who were the important people in those early fields?*

- In 1879 psychology began as a science of its own in Germany, with the establishment of Wundt's psychology laboratory. He developed the technique of objective introspection.
- Titchener, a student of Wundt, brought psychology in the form of structuralism to America. Structuralism died out in the early twentieth century. Margaret F. Washburn, Titchener's student, was the first woman to receive a Ph.D. in psychology in 1894 and published *The Animal Mind*.
- William James proposed a countering point of view called functionalism, in which the way the mind allows us to adapt is stressed.
- Functionalism influenced the modern fields of educational psychology, evolutionary psychology, and industrial/organizational psychology.

1.3 *What were the basic ideas and who were the important people behind the early approaches known as Gestalt, psychoanalysis, and behaviorism?*

- Wertheimer and others studied sensation and perception, calling the new perspective Gestalt (good figure) psychology.
- Freud proposed that the unconscious mind controls much of our conscious behavior in his theory of psychoanalysis.
- Watson proposed a science of behavior called behaviorism, which focused only on the study of observable stimuli and responses.
- Watson and Rayner demonstrated that a phobia could be learned by conditioning a baby to be afraid of a white rat.

Classic Studies in Psychology: Psychologist Mary Cover Jones and "Little Peter"

- Mary Cover Jones later demonstrated that a learned phobia could be counterconditioned.

Psychology Now: Modern Perspectives

1.4 *What are the basic concepts of the modern perspectives known as psychodynamics, behaviorism, humanism, biopsychology, cognitive psychology, the evolutionary perspective, and the sociocultural perspective?*

- Modern Freudians such as Anna Freud, Jung, and Adler change the emphasis in Freud's original theory into a kind of neo-Freudianism.

1.5 *What were the contributions of Skinnner, Maslow, and Rogers?*

- Skinner's operant conditioning of voluntary behavior became a major force in the twentieth century. He introduced the concept of reinforcement to behaviorism.

- Humanism, which focuses on free will and the human potential for growth, was developed by Maslow and Rogers, among others, as a reaction to the deterministic nature of behaviorism and psychoanalysis.
- Biopsychology emerged as the study of the biological bases of behavior.
- Cognitive psychology is the study of learning, memory, language, and problem solving.
- The principles of evolution and the knowledge we currently have about evolution are used in this perspective to look at the way the mind works and why it works as it does. Behavior is seen as having an adaptive or survival value.

Types of Psychological Professionals

1.6 *What's the difference between a psychiatrist and a psychologist, and what other types of professionals work in the various areas of psychology?*

- Psychiatrists are medical doctors who provide diagnosis and therapy for persons with mental disorders, whereas psychoanalysts are psychiatrists or psychologists with special training in the theory of psychoanalysis.
- Psychiatric social workers are social workers with special training in the influences of the environment on mental illness.
- Psychologists have academic degrees and can do counseling, teaching, and research and may specialize in any one of a large number of areas within psychology.
- There are many different areas of specialization in psychology, including clinical, counseling, developmental, social, and personality as areas of work or study.

Psychology: The Science

1.7 *Why is psychology a science and what are the steps in using the scientific method?*

- The scientific method is a way to determine facts and control the possibilities of error and bias when observing behavior. The five steps are perceiving the question, forming a hypothesis, testing the hypothesis, drawing conclusions, and reporting the results.

1.8 *How do psychologists use naturalistic and laboratory settings to describe behavior, and what are the advantages and disadvantages associated with these settings?*

- Naturalistic observations involve watching animals or people in their natural environments but have the disadvantage of lack of control.
- Laboratory observations involve watching animals or people in an artificial but controlled situation, such as a laboratory.

1.9 *How do psychologists use case studies and surveys to describe behavior, and what are some drawbacks to each of these methods?*

- Case studies are detailed investigations of one subject, whereas surveys involve asking standardized questions of large groups of people who represent a sample of the population of interest.
- Information gained from case studies cannot be applied to other cases. People responding to surveys may not always tell the truth or remember information correctly.

1.10   *What is the correlational technique and what does it tell researchers about relationships?*

• Correlation is a statistical technique that allows researchers to discover and predict relationships between variables of interest.

• Positive correlations exist when increases in one variable are matched by increases in the other variable, whereas negative correlations exist when increases in one variable are matched by decreases in the other variable.

• Correlations cannot be used to prove cause-and-effect relationships.

1.11   *How do researchers use operational definitions, independent and dependent variables, experimental and control groups, and random assignment in designing an experiment?*

• Experiments are tightly controlled manipulations of variables that allow researchers to determine cause-and-effect relationships.

• The independent variable in an experiment is the variable that is deliberately manipulated by the experimenter to see if related changes occur in the behavior or responses of the participants and is given to the experimental group.

• The dependent variable in an experiment is the measured behavior or responses of the participants.

• The control group receives nothing or a placebo treatment.

• Random assignment of participants to groups within an experiment helps to control for individual differences both within and between the groups that might otherwise interfere with the experiment's outcome.

1.12   *What are the placebo and the experimenter effects, and how do single-blind and double-blind studies control for those effects?*

• Experiments in which the subjects do not know if they are in the experimental or control groups are single-blind studies, whereas experiments in which neither the experimenters nor the subjects know this information are called double-blind studies.

Classic Studies in Psychology: Teresa Amabile and the Effect of Extrinsic Reward on Creativity

1.13   *How might a real experiment be conducted?*

• Dr. Teresa Amabile's experiment explored the relationship of rewards and creativity by promising a reward to one group of children for being creative (the experimental group) and not to a second group of children, who were being creative for fun (the control group).

• Her conclusion was that external rewards have a negative effect on creativity.

Ethics of Psychological Research

1.14   *What are the ethical concerns when conducting research with people and animals?*

• Ethical guidelines for doing research with human beings include the protection of rights and well-being of participants, informed consent, justification when deception is used, the right of participants to withdraw at any time, protection of participants from physical or psychological harm, confidentiality, and debriefing of participants at the end of the study.

• Animals in psychological research make useful models because they are easier to control than humans, they have simpler behavior, and they can be used in ways that are not permissible with humans.

Critical Thinking

1.15   *What are the basic principles of critical thinking, and how can using critical thinking help people in their everyday lives?*

• Critical thinking is the ability to make reasoned judgments. The four basic criteria of critical thinking are that there are few concepts that do not need to be tested, evidence can vary in quality, experts and authorities do not automatically make something true, and keeping an open mind is important.

• Faulty reasoning and a failure to use critical thinking can lead to belief in false systems such as palmistry and graphology.

Applying Psychology To Everyday Life: Using Critical Thinking–Does Astrology Work?

1.16   *How might critical thinking be applied to a real-world example?*

• When critical thinking principles are applied to the pseudopsychology of astrology, the conclusion is that astrology does not work. Empirical research findings support this conclusion.

1 KEY TERMS

behaviorism 10
biopsychological perspective 14
case study 22
cognitive perspective 15
control group 27
correlation 24
critical thinking 33
dependent variable 27
double-blind study 29
evolutionary perspective 15
experiment 26
experimental group 27
experimenter effect 29

functionalism 8
Gestalt psychology 9
hypothesis 19
independent variable 26
objective introspection 7
observer bias 21
observer effect 21
operational definition 26
participant observation 21
placebo effect 28
population 23
pseudopsychologies 34
psychiatric social worker 17

psychiatrist 16
psychoanalysis 10
psychoanalyst 16
psychodynamic perspective 13
psychologist 17
psychology 4
random assignment 27
replicate 20
representative sample 22
scientific method 18
single-blind study 29
sociocultural perspective 15
structuralism 7

TEST YOURSELF

STUDY HELP NOTE: These longer quizzes appear at the end of every chapter and cover all the major learning objectives that students should know after reading the chapter. These quizzes also provide practice for exams. The answers to each Test Yourself section can be found printed upside down at the end of the quiz.

Pick the best answer.

1. In the definition of psychology, *mental processes* means
   a. internal, covert processes.
   b. outward behavior.
   c. overt actions and reactions.
   d. only animal behavior.

2. A psychologist is interested in finding out why identical twins have different personalities. This psychologist is most interested in the goal of
   a. description.
   b. explanation.
   c. prediction.
   d. control.

3. Psychologists who give potential employees tests that determine what kind of job those employees might best fit are interested in the goal of
   a. description.
   b. explanation.
   c. prediction.
   d. control.

4. Which early theorist developed his perspective on psychology by basing it on Darwin's "survival of the fittest" doctrine?
   a. Wilhelm Wundt
   b. William James
   c. John Watson
   d. Sigmund Freud

5. "The whole is greater than the sum of the parts" is a statement associated with the perspective of
   a. introspectionism.
   b. functionalism.
   c. psychoanalysis.
   d. Gestalt psychologists.

6. _____ was (were) the focus of Watson's behaviorism.
   a. Conscious experiences
   b. Gestalt perceptions
   c. The unconscious mind
   d. Observable experiences

7. Who is most associated with the technique of introspection?
   a. Wundt
   b. James
   c. Watson
   d. Wertheimer

8. Who was denied a Ph.D. despite completing all the requirements for earning the degree?
   a. Mary Whiton Calkins
   b. Mary Cover Jones
   c. Margaret Washburn
   d. Eleanor Gibson

9. Which perspective focuses on free will and self-actualization?
   a. psychoanalysis
   b. behaviorism
   c. cognitive psychology
   d. humanism

10. Jenna suffers from a nervous tic of washing her hands repeatedly and being unable to resist washing them again and again. Which perspective would explain Jenna's hand-washing behavior as a result of repressed conflicts?
    a. psychodynamics
    b. cognitive psychology
    c. behaviorism
    d. biopsychology

11. Which perspective looks at perception, learning, and memory?
    a. psychoanalysis
    b. behaviorism
    c. cognitive psychology
    d. evolutionary perspective

12. Which perspective assumes that human behavior may have developed in certain directions because it served a useful function in preserving the species?
    a. psychoanalysis
    b. behaviorism
    c. cognitive psychology
    d. evolutionary perspective

13. Which of the following professionals in psychology has the broadest area of interests and functions?
    a. psychiatrist
    b. psychoanalyst
    c. psychiatric social worker
    d. psychologist

14. A person who has suffered a major stroke and is now experiencing severe personality problems because of the damage would best be advised to see a
    a. psychiatrist.
    b. psychoanalyst.
    c. psychiatric social worker.
    d. psychologist.

15. Which of the following specialties in psychology provides diagnosis and treatment for less serious mental problems such as adjustment disorders?
    a. developmental
    b. counseling
    c. personality
    d. experimental

16. In the scientific method, forming an educated guess is called
    a. reporting your results.
    b. perceiving a question.
    c. drawing conclusions.
    d. forming a hypothesis.

17. In a laboratory observation, the main advantage of this method is
    a. the degree of control it allows the observer.
    b. the degree of participation it allows the observer.
    c. the observer effect.
    d. the opportunity for representative sampling.

18. Harlan wanted to write realistically about street gangs, so he pretended to be a teenager and joined a real gang. This is most similar to the method of
    a. laboratory observation.
    b. the observer effect.
    c. the case study.
    d. participant observation.

19. The main advantage of a case study is
    a. the ease of generalizing the results to others.
    b. being able to determine cause and effect.
    c. the amount of detail it provides about an individual.
    d. the large number of people that can be studied at one time.

20. The entire group that a researcher is interested in is called a
    a. sample.
    b. population.
    c. subject pool.
    d. survey.

21. Professor Jones surveyed her six classes and found that students who slept less than five hours the night before the exam received lower exam scores than those students who slept seven hours or more. What kind of correlation is this relationship between hours of sleep and scores?
    a. positive
    b. negative
    c. zero
    d. causal

22. Drinking orange juice is negatively correlated with lowered risk of cancer. Based on this information, which of the following statements is true?
    a. The more orange juice you drink, the higher your risk of cancer.
    b. The more orange juice you drink, the lower your risk of cancer.
    c. The less orange juice you drink, the lower your risk of cancer.
    d. Drinking orange juice causes people to be cancer free.

23. A researcher designs an experiment to test the effects of playing video games on memory. What would be the dependent variable?
    a. scores on a memory test
    b. playing video games
    c. number of hours spent playing video games
    d. the type of video game played

24. In that same experiment, the experimental group would
    a. not play the video games.
    b. take the memory test while the control group would not.
    c. not take the memory test while the control group would.
    d. play the video games.

25. In Dr. Amabile's experiment on creativity and reward, what was the independent variable?
    a. the creativity scores for the collages
    b. the judgments of the art experts
    c. the raffles held at the end of the parties
    d. the special instructions to each group

26. In a _____ study, only the experimenter knows who is in the control group and who is in the experimental group.
    a. placebo   c. double-blind
    b. single-blind   d. triple-blind

27. Double-blind studies control for
    a. the placebo effect.
    b. the experimenter effect.
    c. the placebo effect and the experimenter effect.
    d. extrinsic motivation.

28. Dr. Silverberg conducted a study in which she tests infants for memory ability. Before she can begin her study, she must obtain
    a. permission from the infants.
    b. permission from the parents.
    c. informed consent from the parents.
    d. confidential information from the parents.

29. Several years ago two scientists announced that they had achieved "cold fusion" in the laboratory, but further studies failed to replicate their findings and later they found that the original scientists had used sloppy methods. This highlights which of the following critical thinking principles?
    a. Few "truths" do not need to be tested.
    b. All evidence is not equal in quality.
    c. Authority or expertise does not make the claims of the authority or expert true.
    d. Critical thinking requires an open mind.

30. Which pseudopsychology claims to understand personality through a study of the positions of heavenly bodies?
    a. phrenology   c. astrology
    b. palmistry   d. graphology

Answers: 1-a, 2-b, 3-c, 4-b, 5-d, 6-d, 7-a, 8-a, 9-d, 10-a, 11-c, 12-d, 13-d, 14-a, 15-b, 16-d, 17-a, 18-d, 19-c, 20-b, 21-a, 22-b, 23-a, 24-d, 25-d, 26-b, 27-c, 28-c, 29-b, 30-c.

The Definition of Psychology

Psychology is the scientific study of behavior and mental processes.

1.1

Psychology's Four Goals

▸ Description   ▸ Explanation   ▸ Prediction   ▸ Control

The Beginnings of Psychology

Structuralism and Functionalism

Structuralism: focused on structure or basic elements of the mind

Wundt's psychology laboratory. Germany in 1879: developed the technique of objective introspection

Titchener: Wundt's student, brought structuralism to America

William James and Functionalism: Stressing the way mind allows adaptation

1.2

Gestalt Psychology, Psychoanalysis, and Behaviorism

Gestalt Psychology: Wertheimer and others studied sensation and perception. Known for the statement: *The whole is greater than the sum of its parts.*

Sigmund Freud and Psychoanalysis: unconscious mind controls much of conscious behavior

Watson and Behaviorism: study of observable stimuli and responses

1.3

Psychology: Modern Perspectives

Psychodynamics: modern version of psychoanalyis

Behaviorism: operant conditioning of voluntary behavior (Skinner)

Humanism: emphasizes free will and human potential (Maslow and Rogers)

Biopsychology: behavior as a direct result of events in the body

Cognitive: memory, intelligence, perception, problem solving, and learning

Evolutionary: biological bases for behavior based on evolution

Sociocultural: relationship of social behavior and culture

1.4–1.5

Types of Psychological Professionals

SPECIALTY AREA	MAIN FOCUS
Clinical	Mild to severe psychological disorders
Counseling	Adjustment disorders and milder disorders
Developmental	Age-related changes across the life span
Educational	Educational learning and development
School	Working with children in the schools
Experimental/Cognitive	Thinking, memory, motivation, learning, perception
Social	Study of group behavior and influence on individuals
Personality	Individual differences and development of personality
Physiological	Study of the biological bases of behavior
Comparative	Comparison of animal and human behavior

1.6

CONCEPT MAP

Psychology: The Science

Finding Relationships

Designing an experiment: establishes cause and effect.

Important Elements:

▸ Independent variables—factors that are manipulated

▸ Dependent variables—measured behaviors or responses

▸ Experimental group—the group that receives the treatment of interest

▸ Control group—serves as a comparison and receives no treatment or placebo

▸ Random assignment to groups—controls for individual differences or biases

▸ Operational definitions- definition of a variable of interest

Correlational techniques: predict relationships between variables of interest. Can be positive or negative in direction. Does not prove cause and effect.

1.10–1.11

Placebo Effect and the Experimenter Effect, Single-Blind and Double-Blind Studies

Placebo: when expectations of participants in a study influence their behavior

Experimenter bias: experimenter's expectations may unintentionally influence the results of the study

Single-blind studies: experiments in which the subjects do not know if they are in the experimental or control groups

Double-blind studies: experiments in which neither the experimenters nor the subjects know if they are in the experiment or control group

1.12

Descriptive Methods

Naturalistic observations: watching subjects in natural environments but lacking control

Laboratory observations: in an artificial but controlled situation

Case Studies and Surveys

Case studies involve one subject; surveys involve asking standard-ized questions of a sample of the population

1.8–1.9

The Scientific Method

Determines facts and controls the possibilities of error and bias when observing behavior

Five steps are:

1. perceiving the question
2. forming the hypothesis
3. testing the hypothesis
4. drawing conclusions
5. reporting the results

1.7

Y / X
Perfect positive correlation

Y / X
Modest positive correlation

Y / X
No correlation

Y / X
Perfect negative correlation

Y / X
Modest negative correlation

Research Ethics

Ethical guidelines for doing research with human beings protect the rights and well-being of participants.

Animals in psychological research must not be exposed to unnecessary pain or suffering.

1.14

Critical Thinking

Critical thinking is the ability to make reasoned judgments. Four basic criteria of critical thinking:

1. There are few concepts that do not need to be tested
2. Evidence can vary in quality
3. Experts and authorities do not automatically make something true
4. Keep an open mind

1.15

2

The Biological Perspective

Christopher Reeve—The Man of Steel

On May 27, 1995, the man who brought Superman to life in the movie theaters for a new generation of comic superhero fans fell from his horse during a riding contest. He fell onto his helmeted head, almost perpendicular to the ground. Actor and director Christopher Reeve sustained severe injury to two vertebrae at the top of his spinal cord, paralyzing him from the neck down. He could neither breathe on his own nor feel anything or move anything below his shoulders.

In the years following his accident, Christopher Reeve refused to give up even though doctors told him that he would never regain any of the functions that he had lost. In November 2000, Reeve astonished his doctor, John W. McDonald of Washington University Medical School, by deliberately raising the tip of his left index finger. How could this happen? Until a decade ago, the adult central nervous system was believed to be incapable of repair and regeneration (McDonald et al., 2002).

Dr. McDonald and other researchers at Washington, knowing that more recent studies suggest that central nervous system tissue can regenerate to some degree, developed the Activity-Based Recovery program to exercise the muscles that had lost their function in the hope of stimulating function to return in those muscles (Washington University, 2002). Eventually, Reeve regained sensation over 70 percent of his body, was able to go for long periods without his respirator to help him breathe, and was also able to move his legs and arms while under water (Blakeslee, 2002; Nash, 2004).

Sadly, this courageous actor, director, and tireless crusader for funding for spinal cord injury research lost his fight. Following an infection, he went into cardiac arrest and died on October 10, 2004. Although the "Man of Steel" is gone, his courage and determination will continue to serve as a shining example to other victims of spinal cord injury (Associated Press, 2004).

Why study the nervous system and the glands?

How could we possibly understand any of our behavior, thoughts, or actions without knowing something about the incredible organs that allow us to act, think, and react? If we can understand how the brain, the nerves, and the glands interact to control feelings, thoughts, and behavior, we can begin to truly understand the complex organism called a human being.

2 LEARNING OBJECTIVES

2.1 How do all the parts of the nervous system relate to one another?

2.2 What are neurons and nerves, and how do they work?

2.3 How do neurons communicate with each other and with the body?

2.4 What are the different neurotransmitters?

2.5 How do the brain and spinal cord interact?

2.6 How does the somatic nervous system allow people and animals to interact with their surroundings?

2.7 How does the autonomic nervous system control the body's automatic functions and its reaction to stress?

2.8 How do psychologists study the brain and how it works?

2.9 What are the different structures of the bottom part of the brain and what do they do?

2.10 What are the structures of the brain that control emotion, learning, memory, and motivation?

2.11 What parts of the cortex control the different senses and the movement of the body?

2.12 What parts of the cortex are responsible for higher forms of thought, such as language?

2.13 How does the left side of the brain differ from the right side?

2.14 How do the hormones released by glands interact with the nervous system and affect behavior?

An Overview of the Nervous System

2.1 *How do all the parts of the nervous system relate to one another?*

This chapter will discuss a very complex system of cells, organs, and chemicals that work together to produce behavior, thoughts, and actions. The first part of this complex arrangement is the **nervous system**, a network of cells that carries information to and from all parts of the body. Before beginning the discussion on the cells that make up the nervous system, take a look at Figure 2.1. This figure shows the organization of the various parts of the nervous system and will help in understanding how all the different parts work together in controlling the way people and animals think, act, and feel.

nervous system
an extensive network of specialized cells that carries information to and from all parts of the body.

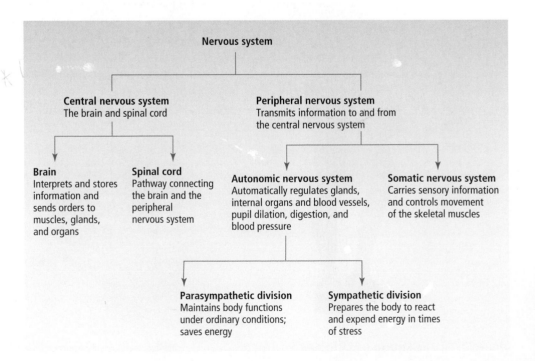

FIGURE 2.1 **An Overview of the Nervous System**

Neurons and Nerves: Building the Network

The field of **neuroscience** is a branch of the life sciences that deals with the structure and functioning of the brain and the neurons, nerves, and nervous tissue that form the nervous system, especially focusing on their relationship to behavior and learning. It was Santiago Ramón y Cajal, a doctor studying slides of brain tissue, who first theorized that the nervous system was made up of individual cells (Ramón y Cajal, translation, 1995).

2.2   *What are neurons and nerves, and how do they work?*

STRUCTURE OF THE NEURON—THE NERVOUS SYSTEM'S BUILDING BLOCK

Although the entire body is composed of cells, each type of cell has a special purpose and function and, therefore, a special structure. Skin cells are flat, but muscle cells are long and stretchy. Most cells do have three things in common: a nucleus, a cell body, and a cell membrane holding it all together. The **neuron** is the specialized cell in the nervous system that receives and sends messages within that system. Neurons are one of the messengers of the body, and that means that they have a very special structure.

The parts of the neuron that receive messages from other cells are called the **dendrites**. The name *dendrite* means "branch," and this structure does indeed look like the branches of a tree. The dendrites are attached to the cell body, or **soma**, which is the part of the cell that contains the nucleus and keeps the entire cell alive and functioning. The **axon** is a fiber attached to the soma, and its job is to carry messages out to other cells. (See Figure 2.2.)

Most people think that the brain is made up entirely of neurons. They may also have heard the old saying that people use only 10 percent of their brains. Neither statement is true, however. People use every cell in the brain for *something*. The fact

neuroscience
a branch of the life sciences that deals with the structure and function of neurons, nerves, and nervous tissue, especially focusing on their relationship to behavior and learning.

neuron
the basic cell that makes up the nervous system and that receives and sends messages within that system.

dendrites
branchlike structures that receive messages from other neurons.

soma
the cell body of the neuron responsible for maintaining the life of the cell.

axon
tube-like structure that carries the neural message to other cells.

[handwritten notes:]
- pain & temp. use same receptors

inside - electrical
between - chemical

FIGURE 2.2   **The Structure of the Neuron**   The electron micrograph on the right shows neurons with axons and dendrites extending from them.

glial cells
grey fatty cells that provide support for the neurons to grow on and around, deliver nutrients to neurons, produce myelin to coat axons, and clean up waste products and dead neurons.

myelin
fatty substances produced by certain glial cells that coat the axons of neurons to insulate, protect, and speed up the neural impulse.

nerves
bundles of axons coated in myelin that travel together through the body.

(millions of neurons)

*6-8 yrs. old: neurons are at peak before losing them.

Simulation
Live! psych

Neurons and Neural Impulses

is that neurons make up only 10 percent of the cells in the brain. The other 90 percent of the brain is composed of **glial cells** that serve as a sort of structure on which the neurons develop and work and which hold the neurons in place. There are several different types of glial cells that perform various functions, such as getting nutrients to the neurons, cleaning up the remains of neurons that have died, and providing insulation for neurons.

Why are the glial cells needed? Well, the neuron's message is going to travel through the cell, and within the cell the message is electrical. That means that if one neuron touches another one in the wrong area, they'll short each other out. So the glial cells act as insulation as well as support.

Neurons aren't found only in the brain. If they are spread all throughout the human body, how are they kept separated? The answer is simple. One special type of glial cell, called a *Schwann cell*, generates a layer of fatty substances called **myelin**. Myelin wraps around the shaft of the axons, forming a protective sheath. It's really the axons that do the bulk of the traveling through the body, with the somas clumped together near the spinal cord. So the axons of those various neurons can travel together throughout the body and never really touch each other directly. It's very similar to the concept of a telephone cable. Within the cable are lots of copper wires coated in plastic. The plastic serves the same insulating purpose for the wires as the myelin sheath does for the axons. Bundled all together, they form a cable that is much stronger and less vulnerable to breakage than any wire alone would be. It works the same way in the nervous system. Bundles of myelin-coated axons travel together in "cables" called **nerves**.

A few other facts about myelin: It not only insulates the neuron, but it also offers a little protection from damage and speeds up the neural message traveling down the axon. As shown in Figure 2.2, sections of myelin bump up next to each other on the axon, similar to the way sausages are linked together. The places where the myelin seems to bump are actually small spaces on the axon called nodes, which are not covered in myelin. When the electrical impulse that is the neural message travels down an axon coated with myelin, it "jumps" between the myelin sheath sections to the places where the axon is accessible at the nodes. That makes the message go much faster down the coated axon than it would down an uncoated axon of a neuron in the brain. This myelin sheath is a very important part of the neuron. The disease called *multiple sclerosis* damages the myelin sheath, which leads to a loss of function in those damaged cells (Allen, 1991).

Axons of neurons found in the body are also coated with a thin membrane called the *neurilemma*, or Schwann's membrane. This membrane, which surrounds the axon and the myelin sheath, serves as a tunnel through which damaged nerve fibers can repair themselves. That's why a severed toe might actually regain some function and feeling if sewn back on in time. Unfortunately, axons of the neurons in the brain and spinal cord do not usually have this coating and are, therefore, more likely to be permanently damaged. (This is one reason why the partial recovery of Christopher Reeve, mentioned in the opening story, was so astonishing.)

▶ Exactly how does this "electrical message" work inside the cell?

Exactly how does this "electrical message" work inside the cell?

GENERATING THE MESSAGE WITHIN THE NEURON— THE NEURAL IMPULSE

A neuron that's at rest—not currently firing a neural impulse or message—is actually electrically charged. The inside of the cell is really a semiliquid solution in which there are charged particles, or *ions*. There is a semiliquid solution surrounding the outside of the cell as well, that also contains ions. The catch is that the ions inside the cell are negatively charged, and the ions outside the cell are positively charged. The cell membrane itself is *permeable*, meaning that some substances that are outside the cell can enter through tiny openings in the membrane, while other substances in the cell can also get outside. The ions inside the cell, which carry a negative charge, are so big that they can't get out. So the inside of the cell is primarily negative when at rest. Outside the cell are positively charged sodium ions that are too big to enter the cell membrane when the cell is at rest. But because the outside sodium ions are positive and the inside ions are negative, and because opposite electrical charges attract each other, the sodium ions will cluster around the membrane. This difference in charges is an electrical potential.

Think of the ions inside the cell as a baseball game inside a stadium (the cell walls). The sodium ions outside the cell are all the fans in the area, and they want to get inside to see the game. When the cell is resting (a state called the **resting potential**, because the cell is at rest), the fans are stuck outside. The sodium ions cannot enter when the cell is at rest, because even though the cell membrane is permeable, the openings are too small at this time for the big sodium ions to enter. But when the cell receives a strong enough stimulation from another cell (meaning that the dendrites are activated), the cell membrane opens up special gates, one after the other, all down its surface that allow the sodium ions (the "fans") to rush into the cell. That causes the inside of the cell to become positive and the outside of the cell to become negative, because all the positive sodium ions are now inside the cell—at the point where the first gate opened. This electrical charge reversal will start at the part of the axon closest to the soma (the first gate) and then proceed down the axon in a kind of chain reaction. (Picture a long hallway with many doors in which the first door opens, then the second, and so on all the way down the hall.) This electrical charge reversal is known as the **action potential** because the electrical potential is now in action rather than at rest. Each action potential sequence takes about one-thousandth of a second, so the neural message travels very fast—from 2 miles per hour in the slowest, shortest neurons to 270 miles per hour in other neurons. (See Figure 2.3.)

Now the action potential is traveling down the axon. When it gets to the end of the axon, something else happens that will be discussed momentarily. Meanwhile, what is happening to the parts of the cell that the action potential has already left behind? How does the cell get the "fans" back outside? Remember, the action potential means that the cell is now positive inside and negative outside at the point where the gate opened. After the action potential passes, the cell membrane literally "pumps" the positive sodium ions back outside the cell, kicking the "fans" out and shutting the gates one by one until the next action potential opens the gates again. The cell becomes negative inside and positive outside, restoring the cell to its resting potential. The neuron is now ready to "fire off" another message.

To sum all that up, when the cell is stimulated, the first gate opens and the electrical charge *at that gate* is reversed. Then the next gate opens and *that* charge is reversed, but in the meantime the *first* gate has been closed and the charge is returning to what it was when it was at rest. The action potential is the *sequence* of gates opening all down the length of the cell.

So if the stimulus that originally causes the neuron to fire is very strong, will the neuron fire more strongly than it would if the stimulus were weak? Neurons actually have a threshold for firing, and all it takes is a stimulus that is just strong enough to get passed that threshold to make the neuron fire. Here's a simple version of how this works: Each neuron is receiving many signals from other neurons. Some of these signals are meant to cause the neuron to fire, whereas others are meant to prevent the neuron from firing. The neuron constantly adds together the effects of the "fire" messages and subtracts the "don't fire" messages, and if the "fire" messages are great enough, the threshold

resting potential
the state of the neuron when not firing a neural impulse.
action potential
the release of the neural impulse consisting of a reversal of the electrical charge within the axon.

So if the stimulus that originally causes the neuron to fire is very strong, will ◀ the neuron fire more strongly than it would if the stimulus were weak?

FIGURE 2.3 **The Neural Impulse Action Potential** In the graph below, voltage readings are shown at a given place on the neuron over a period of 20 or 30 milliseconds (thousandths of a second). At first the cell is resting; it then reaches threshold and an action potential is triggered. After a brief refractory period, the cell returns to its resting potential.

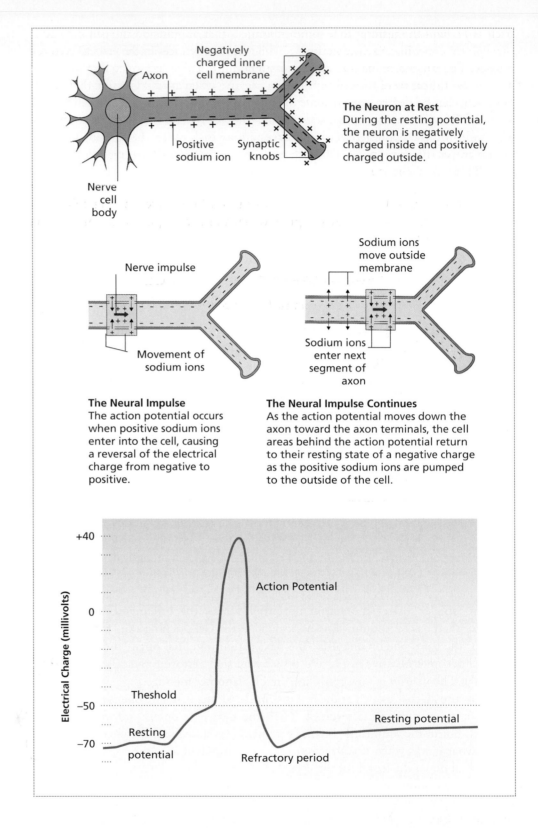

The Neuron at Rest
During the resting potential, the neuron is negatively charged inside and positively charged outside.

The Neural Impulse
The action potential occurs when positive sodium ions enter into the cell, causing a reversal of the electrical charge from negative to positive.

The Neural Impulse Continues
As the action potential moves down the axon toward the axon terminals, the cell areas behind the action potential return to their resting state of a negative charge as the positive sodium ions are pumped to the outside of the cell.

is crossed and the neuron fires. When a neuron does fire, it fires in an **all-or-none** fashion. Neurons are either firing at full strength or not firing at all—there's no such thing as "partial" firing of a neuron. It would be like turning on a light switch—it's either on or it's off. Once the switch is turned to the on position, the light will come on. When it's turned to the off position, the light is off.

all-or-none
referring to the fact that a neuron either fires completely or does not fire at all.

So what's the difference between strong stimulation and weak stimulation? A strong message will cause the neuron to fire more quickly (as if someone flicked the light switch on and off as quickly as possible), and it will also cause more neurons to fire (as if there were a lot of lights going on and off instead of just one). The latter point can be demonstrated quite easily. Just touch lightly on the palm of your hand. You feel a very light pressure sensation. Now push hard in the same spot. You will feel a much stronger pressure sensation, and you can see with your own eyes that more of the skin on the palm of your hand is pushed in by your touch—more skin involved means more neurons firing.

Now that we know how the message travels within the axon of the cell, what is that "something else" that happens when the action potential reaches the end of the axon?

SENDING THE MESSAGE TO OTHER CELLS: THE SYNAPSE

2.3   *How do neurons communicate with each other and with the body?*

chemically process

Look once again at Figure 2.2 on page 45. The end of the axon actually branches out into several "limbs," which are called **axon terminals**. The tip of each axon terminal has a little knob on it. Figure 2.4 shows this knob blown up to giant size. Notice that the knob (called the **synaptic knob** or sometimes the *terminal button*) is not empty. It has a number of little saclike structures in it called **synaptic vesicles**. The word *vesicle* is Latin and means a "little blister" or "fluid-filled sac."

axon terminals
branches at the end of the axon.
synaptic knob
rounded areas on the end of the axon terminals.
synaptic vesicles
saclike structures found inside the synaptic knob containing chemicals.

◀ Now that we know how the message travels within the axon of the cell, what is that "something else" that happens when the action potential reaches the end of the axon?

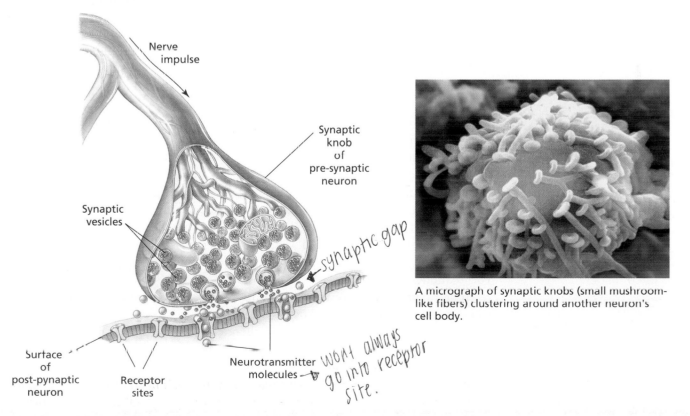

synaptic gap

won't always go into receptor site.

A micrograph of synaptic knobs (small mushroom-like fibers) clustering around another neuron's cell body.

FIGURE 2.4   **The Synapse**   The nerve impulse reaches the synaptic knobs, triggering the release of neuro-transmitters from the synaptic vesicles. The molecules of neurotransmitter cross the synaptic gap to fit into the receptor sites that fit the shape of the molecule.

Simulation

Live! psych

Chemical Messengers

So the ▶
neurotransmitters from one cell cause the next cell to fire, right?

neurotransmitter
chemical found in the synaptic vesicles that, when released, has an effect on the next cell.

synapse (synaptic gap)
microscopic fluid-filled space between the synaptic knob of one cell and the dendrites or surface of the next cell.

receptor sites
holes in the surface of the dendrites or certain cells of the muscles and glands, which are shaped to fit only certain neurotransmitters.

excitatory neurotransmitter
neurotransmitter that causes the receiving cell to fire.

inhibitory neurotransmitter
neurotransmitter that causes the receiving cell to stop firing.

agonists *increase (power↑)*
chemical substances that mimic or enhance the effects of a neurotransmitter on the receptor sites of the next cell, increasing or decreasing the activity of that cell.

antagonists *block cell's responce*
chemical substances that block or reduce a cell's response to the action of other chemicals or neurotransmitters.

Inside the synaptic vesicles are chemicals suspended in fluid. Those chemicals are molecules of substances called **neurotransmitters**. The name is simple enough—they are inside a neuron and they are going to transmit a message. What lies next to the synaptic knob? Right next to it is the dendrite of another neuron. (See Figure 2.4.) Between them is a fluid-filled space called the **synapse** or the **synaptic gap**. Instead of an electrical charge, the vesicles at the end of the axon contain the molecules of neurotransmitters, whereas the surface of the dendrite right next to the axon contains special little locks called **receptor sites**. These locks have a special shape that allows only a particular molecule of neurotransmitter to fit into it, just as only a particular key will fit into a key hole. (The end of the axon containing the neurotransmitters is also called the presynaptic membrane and the surface of the receiving neuron is called the postsynaptic membrane.)

How do the neurotransmitters get across the gap? Recall the action potential making its way down the axon. When that electrical charge reaches the synaptic vesicles, they release their neurotransmitters into the synaptic gap. The molecules then float across the synapse and many of them fit themselves into the receptor sites, activating the next cell. It is this very activation that is the stimulation referred to in the earlier discussion of the action potential.

So the neurotransmitters from one cell cause the next cell to fire, right? That is right—as far as it goes. But the neuron has to have a way to be turned *off* as well as on. Otherwise, when a person burns a finger, the pain signals from those neurons would not stop until the burn was completely healed. Neurons also make connections to muscles and glands. Muscle and gland cells have receptor sites on them, just like on a dendrite, and when the neurotransmitter molecules fit into those receptors, the muscle or gland will be activated or deactivated. Muscles are told to contract or relax, and glands are told to secrete or stop secreting their chemicals. The neurotransmitters found at various synapses around the nervous system (and there are at least 50 to 100 that researchers know about and theoretically several times that number of neurotransmitters) can either "turn cells on" or "turn cells off." The neurotransmitters that turn cells on are referred to as **excitatory neurotransmitters** and the ones that turn cells off are **inhibitory neurotransmitters**.

The molecules of various drugs, if similar enough in shape to the neurotransmitters, can fit into the receptor sites on the receiving neuron just like the neurotransmitters do. By doing so, drugs can affect what happens in the synapse in one of two ways. **Agonists** are chemical substances that can mimic or enhance the effects of a neurotransmitter on the receptor sites of the next cell. This can result in an increase or decrease in the activity of that receiving cell, depending on what the effect of the original neurotransmitter (excitatory or inhibitory) was going to be. So if the original neurotransmitter was excitatory, the effect of the agonist will be to increase that excitation. If it was inhibitory, the effect of the agonist will be to increase that *inhibition*. For example, there are drugs that bind to receptors in the heart muscle (called *beta* receptors) that act as agonists by increasing the action of the neurotransmitter that stimulates the contractions of certain heart valves.

Other drugs act as **antagonists**, chemical substances that block or reduce a cell's response to the action of other chemicals or neurotransmitters. Although an antagonist might sound like it has only an inhibitory effect, it is important to remember that if the neurotransmitter that the antagonist affects is inhibitory itself, the result will actually be an *increase* in the activity of the cell that would normally have been inhibited. *Beta blockers* are drugs that are used to control high blood pressure and (as the name suggests) serve as antagonists by blocking the effects of the neurotransmitters that stimulate the heart's contractions.

This results in slower heart contractions and lowered blood pressure. More examples of agonists and antagonists are discussed later in the context of specific neurotransmitters.

NEUROTRANSMITTERS, MESSENGERS OF THE NETWORK   *& hormones carry info. thru body*

2.4   *What are the different neurotransmitters?*

The first neurotransmitter to be identified was named *acetylcholine*. It is found at the synapses between neurons and muscle cells. Acetylcholine serves to stimulate the muscle to contract. If acetylcholine receptor sites on the muscle cells are blocked in some way, then the acetylcholine can't get to the site and the muscle will be incapable of contracting—paralyzed, in other words. This is exactly what happens when *curare*, a drug used by South American Indians on their blow darts, gets into the nervous system. Curare's molecules are just similar enough to fit into the receptor site without actually stimulating the cell, making curare an antagonist for acetylcholine.

What would happen if the neurons released too much acetylcholine? The bite of a black widow spider does just that. Its venom stimulates the release of excessive amounts of acetylcholine and causes convulsions and possible death. Black widow spider venom is an agonist for acetylcholine. Acetylcholine is also found in the hippocampus, an area of the brain that is responsible for forming new memories. (L I N K) *to Chapter Six: Memory, p. 237.*

Another neurotransmitter is *GABA*, or *γ-aminobutyric acid (or said gamma-aminobutyric acid)*. Whereas acetylcholine is one of the excitatory neurotransmitters, GABA is the most common inhibitory neurotransmitter in the brain. GABA can help to calm anxiety, for example, by binding to the same receptor sites that are affected by tranquilizing drugs and alcohol. In fact, the effect of alcohol is to stimulate the release of excess GABA, which causes the general inhibition of the nervous system associated with getting drunk. This makes alcohol an agonist for GABA. (L I N K) *to Chapter Four: Consciousness, p. 151.*

Serotonin is a neurotransmitter found in the lower part of the brain, and it can act as an excitatory or inhibitory chemical, depending on its location in that brain area. It is associated with sleep, mood, and appetite. Low levels of serotonin activity have been linked to depression, for example. (L I N K) *to Chapter Fourteen: Psychological Disorders, p. 544.*

Dopamine is found in the brain and can have different effects depending on the exact location of its activity. If too little dopamine is released in a certain area of the brain, the result is a disease called Parkinson's—the disease currently being battled by former boxing champ Muhammad Ali and actor Michael J. Fox (Ahlskog, 2003). If too much dopamine is released in another area, the result is a serious mental disorder called schizophrenia (Akil et al., 2003). (L I N K) *to Chapter Fourteen: Psychological Disorders, p. 547.* (See Table 2.1 for a list of some neurotransmitters and their functions.)

Some neurotransmitters actually control the release of other neurotransmitters. These special neurotransmitters are called *neural regulators* or *neural peptides* (Agnati et al., 1992), and one that researchers know a little about is endorphin. *Endorphins* are pain-controlling chemicals in the body. When a person is hurt, a neurotransmitter that signals pain is released. When the brain gets this message, it triggers the release of endorphins. The endorphins bind to receptors that open the gates on the axon.

The venom of the black widow spider causes a flood of acetylcholine to be released into the body's muscle system, causing convulsions.

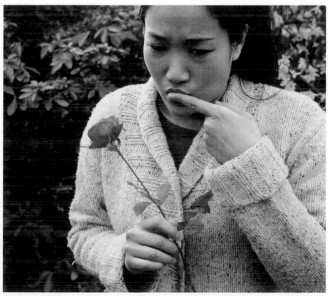

The look on this young woman's face clearly indicates that she has experienced pain in her finger. Pain is a warning signal that something is wrong, in this case that touching the thorns on the stem of the rose was a bad idea. What might be some of the problems encountered by a person who could feel no pain at all?

TABLE 2.1 **NEUROTRANSMITTERS AND THEIR FUNCTIONS**

Neurotransmitters	Functions
Acetylcholine	Involved in memory and stimulates movement.
Serotonin	Involved in mood, sleep, and appetite.
GABA (Gamma-aminobutyric acid)	Involved in sleep and inhibits movement.
Glutamate	Involved in memory formation.
Norepinephrine	Involved in arousal and mood.
Dopamine	Involved in control of movement and sensations of pleasure.
Endorphins	Involved in pain relief.

This causes the cell to be unable to fire its pain signal, and the pain sensations eventually subside.

The name *endorphin* comes from the term *endogenous morphine*. (*Endogenous* means "native to the area"—in this case, native to the body.) Scientists studying the nervous system found receptor sites that fit morphine molecules perfectly and decided that there must be a natural substance in the body that has the same effect as morphine. Endorphins are the reason that heroin and the other drugs derived from opium are so addictive—when people take morphine or heroin, their bodies neglect to produce endorphins. When the drug wears off, they are left with no protection against pain at all, and *everything* hurts. Known as withdrawal, this pain is why most people want more heroin, creating an addictive cycle of abuse. Ⓛ Ⓘ Ⓝ Ⓚ *to Chapter Four: Consciousness, pp. 145–146.*

> **If the neurotransmitters are out there in the synaptic gap and in the receptor sites, what happens to them when they aren't needed anymore?**

If the neurotransmitters are out there in the synaptic gap and in the receptor sites, what happens to them when they aren't needed anymore?

CLEANING UP THE SYNAPSE: REUPTAKE AND ENZYMES

The neurotransmitters have to get out of the receptor sites before the next stimulation can occur. Most neurotransmitters will end up back in the synaptic vesicles in a process called **reuptake**. (Think of a little suction tube, sucking the chemicals back into the vesicles.) That way, the synapse is cleared for the next release of neurotransmitters.

There is one neurotransmitter that is not taken back into the vesicles, however. Because acetylcholine is responsible for muscle activity, and muscle activity needs to happen rapidly and continue happening, it's not possible to wait around for the "sucking up" process to occur. Instead, an enzyme* specifically designed to break apart acetylcholine clears the synaptic gap very quickly. There are enzymes that break down the other neurotransmitters as well.

The neurotransmitter serotonin helps regulate and adjust people's moods, but in some people the reuptake process occurs too quickly. This takes the serotonin out of the synapse before it can fully activate the receptors on the next neuron, leaving the person in a state of depression. Most of the drugs used to treat this condition are called SSRIs (selective serotonin reuptake inhibitors). SSRIs block the reuptake of serotonin, leaving more serotonin available in the synapse to bond with the receptor sites. Eventually, this elevates mood and lifts the depression. Although doctors used

reuptake
process by which neurotransmitters are taken back into the synaptic vesicles.

---
*Enzyme: a complex protein that is manufactured by cells.

to "taper off" the use of antidepressants after the person's depression had lifted, new research has found that keeping a person on a maintenance dose of the drug helps prevent future episodes of depression (Geddes et al., 2003; Taylor et al., 2004).

This section covered the neuron and how neurons communicate. The next section looks at the bigger picture—the nervous system itself. Before reading on, try answering the following questions to test your memory.

PRACTICE QUIZ: HOW MUCH DO YOU REMEMBER?

Pick the best answer.

1. Which part of the neuron receives messages from other cells?
   a. axon
   b. dendrite
   c. soma
   d. myelin

2. Which one of the following is NOT a function of the myelin sheath?
   a. insulation from other axons
   b. speeds up the neural message
   c. protects the nerve fiber from damage
   d. aids in reuptake

3. When the neuron's action potential is released, _____ ions are rushing into the axon through openings on the membrane.
   a. sodium
   b. potassium
   c. chloride
   d. oxygen

4. When the action potential reaches the end of the axon terminals, it causes the release of
   a. an electrical spark that sets off the next neuron.
   b. positively charged ions that excite the next cell.
   c. negatively charged ions that inhibit the next cell.
   d. neurotransmitters that excite or inhibit the next cell.

5. Receiving neurons have special _____ that fit the shape of certain molecules.
   a. synaptic vesicles
   b. gaps
   c. receptor sites
   d. branches

6. Which of the following is associated with sleep, mood, and appetite?
   a. acetylcholine
   b. GABA
   c. serotonin
   d. endorphin

Answers: 1-b, 2-d, 3-a, 4-d, 5-c, 6-c.

The Central Nervous System—The "Central Processing Unit"

The **central nervous system** is composed of the brain and the spinal cord. Both the brain and the spinal cord are composed of neurons and glial cells that control the life-sustaining functions of the body as well as all thought, emotion, and behavior.

2.5   How do the brain and spinal cord interact?

THE BRAIN

The brain is the true core of the nervous system, the part that takes the information received from the senses, makes sense out of it, makes decisions, and sends commands out to the muscles and the rest of the body. Later parts of this chapter will cover the brain in more detail. Without the spinal cord, however, the brain would be useless.

THE SPINAL CORD

The **spinal cord** is a long bundle of neurons that serves two vital functions for the nervous system. Look at the cross-sectional view of the spinal cord in Figure 2.5. Notice that it seems to be divided into two areas, one around the outside and one inside the cord. If it were a real spinal cord, the outer section would appear to be white and the inner section would seem gray. That's because the outer section is composed mainly of axons and nerves, which appear white, whereas the inner section is mainly composed of cell bodies of neurons, which appear gray. The purpose of the outer section is to carry messages from the body up to the brain and from the brain down to the body. It is simply a message "pipeline."

central nervous system (CNS)
part of the nervous system consisting of the brain and spinal cord.

spinal cord
a long bundle of neurons that carries messages to and from the body to the brain that is responsible for very fast, lifesaving reflexes.

FIGURE 2.5 **The Spinal Cord Reflex**
The hammer tap just below the kneecap stimulates the sensory (afferent) nerve fibers, which carry the message up to the interneurons in the middle of the spinal cord. The interneurons then send a message out by means of the motor (efferent) nerve fibers, causing the lower leg to jerk.

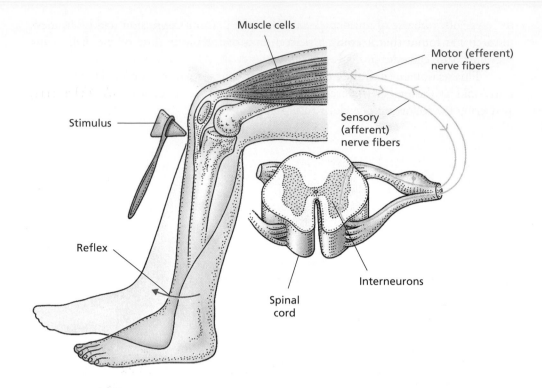

sensory neuron
a neuron that carries information from the senses to the central nervous system. Also called afferent neuron.

motor neuron
a neuron that carries messages from the central nervous system to the muscles of the body. Also called efferent neuron.

interneuron
a neuron found in the center of the spinal cord that receives information from the sensory neurons and sends commands to the muscles through the motor neurons. Interneurons also make up the bulk of the neurons in the brain.

▶ If the spinal cord is such an important link between the body and the brain, what happens if it is damaged?

reflex arc
spinal cord controls reflex
the connection of the sensory neurons to the interneurons to the motor neurons, resulting in a reflex action.

THE REFLEX ARC: THREE TYPES OF NEURONS   The inside section, which is made up of cell bodies separated by glial cells, is actually a primitive sort of "brain." This part of the spinal cord is responsible for certain reflexes—very fast, lifesaving reflexes. To understand how the spinal cord reflexes work, it is important to know there are three basic types of neurons: **sensory** (afferent) **neurons** that carry messages from the senses to the spinal cord, **motor** (efferent) **neurons** that carry messages from the spinal cord to the muscles and glands, and **interneurons** that connect the sensory neurons to the motor neurons (and make up the inside of the spinal cord and the brain itself). Step on a sharp object, for example, and a sensory neuron will send the pain message up to the spinal column where it would enter into the central area of the cord. The interneuron in that central area will then receive the message and send out a response along a motor neuron, causing the foot to be drawn back. This all happens very quickly. If the pain message had to go all the way up to the brain, the response time would be greatly increased and more damage would be done to the toe. So having this kind of **reflex arc** controlled by the spinal cord alone allows for very fast response times.

If the spinal cord is such an important link between the body and the brain, what happens if it is damaged? Damage to the central nervous system was once thought to be permanent. Neurons in the brain and spinal cord were not seen as capable of repairing themselves. When people recovered from a stroke, for example, it was assumed that healthy brain cells took over the function of the damaged ones. Scientists have known for a while now that some forms of central nervous system damage can be repaired by the body's systems, and in recent years great strides have been made in repairing spinal cord damage. The brain actually exhibits a great deal of *plasticity*, the ability to constantly change both the structure and function of many cells in the brain in response to experience and even trauma (Neville & Bavelier, 2000). Scientists have been able to *implant* nerve fibers from outside the spinal cord onto a damaged area and then "coax" the damaged spinal nerves to grow through these "tunnels" of implanted fibers (Cheng et al., 1996). The first human trials have already begun (Bunge & Pearse, 2003). It is also now known that the brain can change itself quite a bit—by adapting neurons to serve new functions when old neurons die or are damaged. Dendrites grow and new synapses are formed in at least some areas of the brain, as people learn new things throughout life (Abraham & Williams, 2003).

Researchers are constantly looking for new ways to repair the brain. For a look at a new and promising treatment for people with diseases such as Parkinson's, Alzheimer's, and damage from strokes, read the following Psychology in the News section.

PSYCHOLOGY IN THE NEWS
Adult Bone Marrow:
New Hope for the Damaged Brain

Scientists have been researching the possibility of transplanting **stem cells** to repair damaged or diseased brain tissue. (See Figure 2.6.) Stem cells can create other cells, such as blood cells, nerve cells, and brain cells (National Institutes of Health, 2000). An ongoing controversy concerns the source of such stem cells, which can be obtained from human embryos, either from terminated pregnancies or fertilization clinics. Many people are opposed to the idea of putting embryos to this use, even if stem cell research promises cures for diseases such as Parkinson's and Alzheimer's, or the repair of damaged spinal cords or brain tissue.

A recent study, reported by author and neurologist Alexander Storch of the University of Ulm in Germany, may hold hope for the future of stem cell treatments without the controversial need to use human embryonic tissue (Storch, 2004). In a paper presented at the American Academy of Neurology in San Francisco, Dr. Storch talked about the possibility of obtaining stem cells from adult bone marrow for use in repairing damaged neural tissue. These cells would not only remove the controversy surrounding embryonic stem cells but would also eliminate any immune system problems in transplanting tissues, because the cells would be taken from the adult's own bone marrow. Storch said that a small amount of bone marrow stem cells can be made to grow and produce a large amount of cells that can be converted into the type of cell needed. Although studies at present are only being conducted on animals, the future may hold promise for people as well.

Questions for Further Discussion

1. If stem cells could be used to create tissues other than nerves and neurons, what other kinds of disorders might become treatable?

2. What problems might arise from doing the first studies with human subjects in this area?

3. How might understanding stem cell reproduction affect cancer research?

Microphotograph of a bone marrow stem cell.

stem cells
special cells found in all the tissues of the body that are capable of manufacturing other cell types when those cells need to be replaced due to damage or wear and tear.

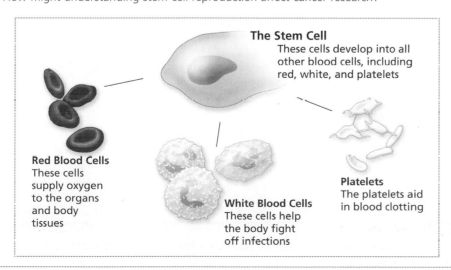

The Stem Cell
These cells develop into all other blood cells, including red, white, and platelets

Red Blood Cells
These cells supply oxygen to the organs and body tissues

White Blood Cells
These cells help the body fight off infections

Platelets
The platelets aid in blood clotting

FIGURE 2.6   **The Stem Cell**   Stem cells are basic cells that differentiate into specific types of cells, such as these blood cells. Stem cells can also become other types of cells, such as brain cells and nerve cells.

Okay, that takes care of the central nervous ▶ system, except for the detail on the brain. How does the central nervous system communicate with the rest of the body?

The Peripheral Nervous System—Nerves on the Edge

Okay, that takes care of the central nervous system, except for the detail on the brain. How does the central nervous system communicate with the rest of the body? The term *peripheral* refers to things that are not in the center or that are on the edges of the center. The **peripheral nervous system** or **PNS** (see Figure 2.7) is made up of all the nerves and neurons that are not contained in the brain and spinal cord. It is this system that allows the brain and spinal cord to communicate with the sensory systems of the eyes, ears, skin, and mouth and allows the brain and spinal cord to control the muscles and glands of the body. The PNS can be divided into two major systems, the **somatic nervous system** and the **autonomic nervous system**.

2.6   *How does the somatic nervous system allow people and animals to interact with their surroundings?*

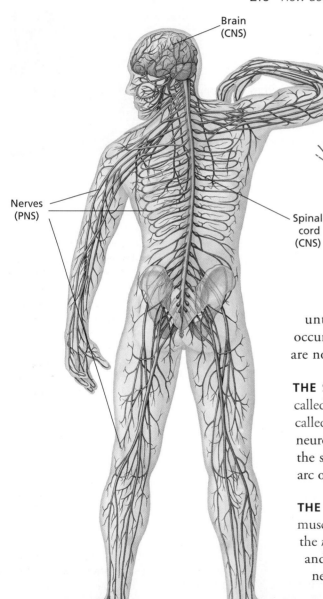

Brain (CNS)

Nerves (PNS)

Spinal cord (CNS)

Voluntary

THE SOMATIC NERVOUS SYSTEM

One of the parts of a neuron is the soma, or cell body (the word *soma* means "body"). In psychology, a lot of terms have the word *soma* in them, which means that the term has something to do with the body. The somatic nervous system is made up of all the nerves carrying messages from the senses to the central nervous system and all of the nerves carrying messages from the central nervous system to the muscles of the body—specifically, the skeletal* muscles that allow people to move their bodies. Notice that it is only the *voluntary muscles* (those that control the movement of the skeleton) that are controlled by the somatic nervous system. When people are walking, raising their hands in class, smelling a flower, or seeing a pretty picture, they are using the somatic nervous system. (As seen in the discussion of spinal cord reflexes, although these muscles are called the voluntary muscles, they can move involuntarily when a reflex response occurs. They are called "voluntary" because they *can* be moved at will but are not limited to only that kind of movement.)

THE SENSORY PATHWAY   Nerves coming from the senses are sometimes called the **sensory pathway**, and the neurons that make up these nerves are called *sensory neurons*. As mentioned in the discussion of the three types of neurons, sensory neurons carry messages from the various sensory organs to the spinal cord, where those messages may form part of a spinal cord reflex arc or may be sent all the way up to the brain.

THE MOTOR PATHWAY   Nerves that carry the messages to the voluntary muscles are called the **motor pathway**, and the neurons in these nerves are the *motor neurons*. Again, motor neurons carry messages from the spinal cord and/or the brain to the muscles and glands. In the case of the somatic nerves, the muscles are only the voluntary, skeletal muscles.

FIGURE 2.7   **The Peripheral Nervous System**

*Skeletal: having to do with the bones of the body, or skeleton.

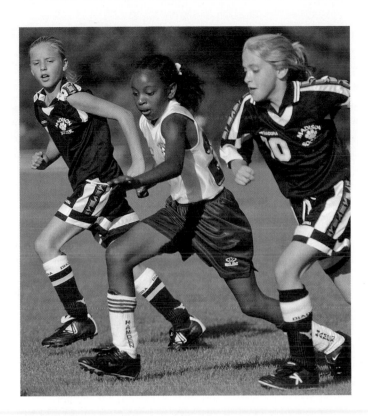

These young soccer players are using their senses and voluntary muscles controlled by the somatic division of the peripheral nervous system. What part of the autonomic nervous system are these girls also using at this time.

Involuntary* muscles, such as the heart, stomach, and intestines, together with glands such as the adrenal glands and the pancreas are all controlled by clumps of neurons located on or near the spinal column. (The words *on* or *near* are used quite deliberately here. The neurons *inside* the spinal column are part of the central nervous system, not the peripheral nervous system.) These large groups of neurons near the spinal column make up the *autonomic nervous system*.

2.7   *How does the autonomic nervous system control the body's automatic functions and its reaction to stress?*

THE AUTONOMIC NERVOUS SYSTEM *don't think about*

The word *autonomic* suggests that the functions of this system are more or less automatic, which is basically correct. Whereas the somatic division of the peripheral nervous system controls the senses and voluntary muscles, the autonomic division controls everything else in the body—organs, glands, and involuntary muscles. The autonomic nervous system itself is divided into two systems, the **sympathetic division** and the **parasympathetic division**. (For a visual representation of how all the various sections of the nervous system are organized, look back at Figure 2.1 on page 44.)

THE SYMPATHETIC DIVISION   The sympathetic division of the autonomic nervous system is primarily located on the middle of the spinal column—running from near the top of the ribcage to the waist area. It may help to think of the name in these terms: The *sympathetic* division is in *sympathy* with one's emotions. In fact, the sympathetic division is usually called the *fight-or-flight system,* because it is allows people

activated automatically

---

*Involuntary: not under deliberate control.

everything not in brain or spinal cord.

peripheral nervous system (PNS)
all nerves and neurons that are not contained in the brain and spinal cord but that run through the body itself.

somatic nervous system
division of the PNS consisting of nerves that carry information from the senses to the CNS and from the CNS to the voluntary muscles of the body.

autonomic nervous system (ANS)
division of the PNS consisting of nerves that control all of the involuntary muscles, organs, and glands.

sensory pathway
nerves coming from the sensory organs to the CNS consisting of sensory neurons.

motor pathway
nerves coming from the CNS to the voluntary muscles, consisting of motor neurons.

sympathetic division (fight-or-flight system)
part of the ANS that is responsible for reacting to stressful events and bodily arousal.

parasympathetic division
part of the ANS that restores the body to normal functioning after arousal and is responsible for the day-to-day functioning of the organs and glands.

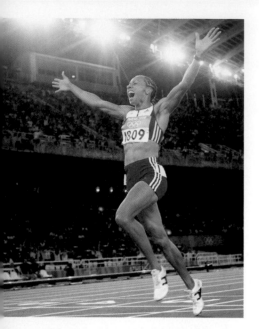

British runner Kelly Holmes at the 2004 Summer Olympics in Athens, Greece. Her sympathetic nervous system is still in high gear, responding to her emotional state.

This marathon runner collapsed where he stood after finishing the race. His parasympathetic nervous system is already slowing his breathing and heart rate as his bodily functions begin to return to normal.

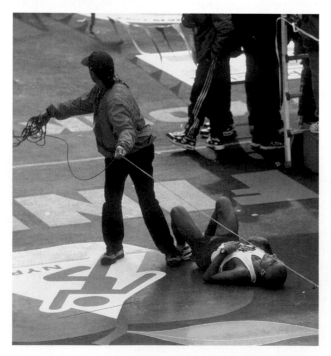

and animals to deal with all kinds of stressful events. **LINK** *to Chapter Eleven: Stress and Health, pp. 419–420.* Emotions during these events might be anger (hence, the term *fight*) or fear (that's the *flight* part, obviously) or even extreme joy or excitement. Yes, even joy can be stressful. The sympathetic division's job is to get the body ready to deal with the stress.

What are the specific ways in which this division readies the body to react? The pupils seem to get bigger, perhaps to let in more light and, therefore, more information. The heart starts pumping faster and harder, drawing blood away from nonessential organs such as the skin (so at first the person may turn pale) and sometimes even the brain itself (so the person might actually faint). Blood needs lots of oxygen before it goes to the muscles, so the lungs work overtime, too (the person may begin to breathe faster). One set of glands in particular receives special instructions. The adrenal glands will be stimulated to release certain stress-related chemicals (members of a class of chemicals released by glands called *hormones*) into the bloodstream. These stress hormones will travel to all parts of the body, but they will only affect certain target organs. Just as a neurotransmitter fits into a receptor site on a cell, the molecules of the stress hormones fit into receptor sites at the various target organs—notably, the heart, muscles, and lungs. This further stimulates these organs to work harder. (There are other hormones for other functions that have nothing to do with stress. For more about hormones and glands, see the last section in this chapter, The Chemical Connection: Endocrine Glands.)

But not every organ or system will be stimulated by the activation of the sympathetic division. Digestion of food and excretion* of waste are not necessary functions when dealing with stressful situations, so these systems tend to be "shut down" or inhibited. Saliva, which is part of digestion, dries right up (ever try whistling when you're scared?). Food that was in the stomach sits there like a lump. Usually, the urge to go to the bathroom will be suppressed, but if the person is really scared the bladder or bowels may actually empty (this is why people who die under extreme stress, such as hanging or electrocution, will release their urine and waste). The sympathetic division is also going to demand that the body burn a tremendous amount of fuel, or blood sugar.

Now, all this is going on during a stressful situation. If the stress ends, the activity of the sympathetic division will be replaced by the activation of the parasympathetic division. If the stress goes on so long that all available energy is used up, the person might actually collapse (as a deer might do when being chased by another animal). This collapse is also a function of the parasympathetic division.

THE PARASYMPATHETIC DIVISION   If the sympathetic division can be called the fight-or-flight system, the parasympathetic division might be called the eat-drink-and-rest system. The neurons of this division are located at the top and bottom of the spinal column, on either side of the sympathetic division neurons (*para* means "beyond" or "next to" and in this sense refers to the neurons located on either side of the sympathetic division neurons).

It might seem as if the parasympathetic division does pretty much the opposite of the sympathetic division, but it's a little more complex than that. The parasympathetic division's job is to restore the body to

---

*Excretion: in this sense, the act of eliminating waste products from the body.

normal functioning after a stressful situation ends. It slows the heart and breathing, constricts the pupils, and reactivates digestion and excretion. Signals to the adrenal glands stop, because the parasympathetic division isn't connected to the adrenal glands. In a sense, the parasympathetic division allows the body to put back all the energy it burned.

Jeannie was in a bad car crash with her family several years ago. They were on their way to lunch when a big pickup truck struck their small car from behind with great force. Although they miraculously escaped with only a few minor bruises and scrapes (due to seat belts and car seats), they found that their appetite was completely gone while they were being checked out in the emergency room (sympathetic system still going strong). When they finally got released and made it to a restaurant, they found themselves eating everything in sight. The parasympathetic division had kicked in with a vengeance.

The parasympathetic division does more than just react to the activity of the sympathetic division. It is the parasympathetic division that is responsible for most of the ordinary, day-to-day bodily functioning. It keeps the heart beating regularly, breathing normal, and digestion going. People spend the greater part of their 24-hour day eating, sleeping, digesting, and excreting. So it is the parasympathetic division that is normally active. At any given moment, then, one or the other of these divisions, sympathetic or parasympathetic, will determine whether people are aroused or relaxed. (See Figure 2.8.)

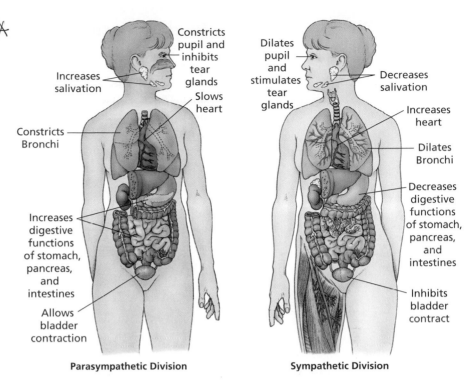

Parasympathetic Division   **Sympathetic Division**

FIGURE 2.8   **Functions of the Parasympathetic and Sympathetic Divisions of the Nervous System**

PRACTICE **QUIZ:** HOW MUCH DO YOU REMEMBER?

Pick the best answer.

1. If you burn your finger, your immediate reaction will probably involve all BUT which of the following?
   a. the brain
   b. the spinal cord
   c. sensory neurons
   d. motor neurons

2. If you are typing on the computer keyboard, the motions of your fingers on the keys are probably being controlled by
   a. the autonomic nervous system.
   b. sensory pathway neurons.
   c. motor pathway neurons.
   d. autonomic neurons.

3. The neurons of the motor pathway control _____.
   a. stress reactions
   b. organs and glands
   c. involuntary muscles
   d. voluntary muscles

4. What type of cell is responsible for the reproduction of other cells of the body?
   a. blood cells
   b. stem cells
   c. neurons
   d. basal cells

5. Which of the following is NOT a function of the sympathetic division?
   a. increasing digestive activity to supply fuel for the body
   b. dilating the pupils of the eyes
   c. increasing the heart rate
   d. increasing the activity of the lungs

6. Which of the following would be active if you are sleeping?
   a. sympathetic division
   b. parasympathetic division
   c. somatic division
   d. motor division

Peeking Inside the Brain

2.8 *How do psychologists study the brain and how it works?*

In ancient times, many early "scientists" would dissect the brains of those who had died—both animals and people—to try to see how the brain worked. The problem, of course, is that it is impossible tell what a structure in the brain is supposed to do if it's dead. A scientist can't even be sure what the brain tissue really looks like when it's inside the skull of a living person instead of sitting on a dissecting table. How can scientists find out what the various parts of the brain do?

CLINICAL STUDIES

One way to get some idea of what the various areas of the brain control is to study animals or people with damage to those areas. In animals, that may mean damaging a part of the brain deliberately. Then researchers test the animal to see what has happened to its abilities. Or they may electrically stimulate some particular area of the animal's brain and watch the result. Both the destruction and stimulation of brain tissue are accomplished by the same basic process. A thin wire insulated everywhere but the very tip is surgically inserted into the brain of the test animal. If brain tissue is to be destroyed, an electrical current strong enough to kill off the neurons at the tip of the wire is sent through it. This is called **deep lesioning**.

If researchers only want to stimulate that area of the brain, the electrical current will be much milder, causing the neurons to react as if they had received a message. This is called *electrical stimulation of the brain*, or *ESB*. Of course, animals aren't people even though some people treat them that way, and researchers can't be sure that a human brain is going to function exactly like the brain of a lower animal.

It should be obvious that researchers can't ask human beings to let them destroy areas of their brains. As stated in Chapter One, anyone who volunteered for that kind of research is probably already suffering from some kind of brain damage. So how do researchers study human brain function? By finding people who already have brain damage and testing those people to see what they can or cannot do. It isn't an ideal way to study the brain, however, as no two case studies of human brain damage are likely to be in exactly the same area of the brain and involve exactly the same amount of damage.

THE EEG

A fairly harmless way to study the activity of the living brain is to record the electrical activity of the neurons just below the skull. This has been done for years, using a device called an **electroencephalograph (EEG)** machine. Small metal disks called microelectrodes are placed directly on the skin covering the skull, using a jelly-like substance to help conduct the electrical messages from the neurons just below. These microelectrodes are attached to wires and the wires are attached to pens that rest on a moving graph paper. The microelectrodes can detect electrical activity, which causes the pens to move up and down on the paper, creating squiggly lines or waves that indicate many things, such as stages of sleep, seizures, and even the presence of tumors. The EEG can also be used to determine which areas of the brain are active during tasks such as reading, writing, and speaking. (See Figure 2.9.)

As can be seen in Figure 2.9a, Very fast, irregular waves called *beta waves* indicate waking activity (third and sixth lines in Figure 2.9a). Slightly more regular and slower waves called *alpha waves* are a sign of relaxation, whereas much slower, larger

deep lesioning
insertion of a thin, insulated wire into the brain through which an electrical current is sent that destroys the brain cells at the tip of the wire.

electroencephalograph (EEG)
machine designed to record the brain wave patterns produced by electrical activity of the surface of the brain.

FIGURE 2.9   **Studying the Brain**   These are four methods researchers use to study the brain: EEGs, CT scans, MRIs, and PET scans. (a) An example of an EEG readout. (b) A CT scan (colored by a computer) showing the detail of a center crosssection of the brain. (c) An MRI (colored by a computer) showing enhanced detail of the same view of the brain as in the CT scan. (d) A PET scan showing activity of the brain, using colors to indicate different levels of activity; areas that are very active are white, whereas areas that are inactive are dark blue.

waves called *delta waves* indicate a deep stage of sleep (first and fifth lines in Figure 2.9a). LINK *to Chapter Four: Consciousness, p. 132.*

Scientists have recently developed a new technique involving the way EEG recordings are interpreted (Makeig et al., 2004). The process allows identification of individual signals coming from the different areas of the brain and is called *Independent Component Analysis (ICA).* ICA allows a more detailed and precise interpretation of the

computed tomography (CT)
brain-imaging method using computer-controlled X-rays of the brain.

magnetic resonance imaging (MRI)
brain-imaging method using radio waves and magnetic fields of the body to produce detailed images of the brain.

positron emission tomography (PET)
brain-imaging method in which a radioactive sugar is injected into the subject and a computer compiles a color-coded image of the activity of the brain with lighter colors indicating more activity.

signals coming from different areas of the brain's surface. Another technique using the EEG is called *event-related potential*, or *ERP.* In ERP, the results of multiple presentations of a stimulus are measured on an EEG and then averaged to remove the variations in random brain activity that occur in the background of any single EEG recording. The result is a measurement of the electrical potential of the brain related to the stimulus event itself or an event-related potential. ERP is being investigated for several different uses. For example, one study has looked at the possibility of using ERP to follow the progression of Alzheimer's disease (Katada et al., 2003), whereas another area of research involves using ERP as a method of lie detection (Allen & Iacona, 1997).

CT SCANS *1970's*

structure?

The EEG only allows researchers to look at the activity of the surface of the brain. Scientists now have several ways to look inside the human brain without harm to the person. One way is to take a series of X-rays of the brain, aided by a computer. This is called a **CT scan** (CT stands for computed tomography, or "mapping" the brain by computer). CT scans can show stroke damage, tumors, injuries, and abnormal brain structure.

MRI SCANS

As good as a CT scan can be, it still doesn't show very small details within the brain. A newer technique called **magnetic resonance imaging**, or **MRI**, provides much more detail, even allowing doctors to see the effects of very small strokes. The person getting an MRI scan will be placed inside a magnetic field. In some cases, the field is inside a big machine and the person is placed inside. This is not a very desirable state if people are even slightly afraid of being in small, enclosed spaces. Newer machines are open to the air and much less unpleasant (but just as noisy). There are even machines that take much less time, called—simply enough—fast MRIs. The magnetic field allows the computer to create a three-dimensional image of the brain and display "slices" of that image on a screen. Although traditional MRI scans only show structure, there is a technique called *functional MRI (fMRI)* in which the computer makes a sort of "movie" of changes in the activity of the brain using images from different time periods.

PET SCANS *(best today)*

Picture of area active

If researchers really want to see the brain in action, though, they might be better off using a **PET scan** (positronic emission tomography). In this method, the person is injected with a radioactive glucose (a kind of sugar). The computer detects the activity of the brain cells by looking at which cells are using up the radioactive glucose and projecting the image of that activity onto a monitor. The computer uses colors to indicate different levels of activity. Areas that are very active usually show up as white or very light, whereas areas that are inactive are dark blue. With this method, researchers can actually have the person perform different tasks while the computer shows what his or her brain is doing during the task.

Okay, now I understand a little more ▶ *about how we look inside the brain. What exactly IS inside the brain?*

Okay, now I understand a little more about how we look inside the brain. What exactly IS inside the brain?

From the Bottom Up: The Structures of the Brain

Now it's time to look at the various structures of the brain, starting from the bottom and working up to the top. (A word of caution: This text won't be discussing every single part of the brain, only the parts interesting to psychologists as explorers of human behavior. Many parts of the brain also overlap in their functions, but a full understanding of the brain is not truly possible within one chapter of an introductory psychology text.)

2.9   *What are the different structures of the bottom part of the brain and what do they do?*

THE BRAIN STEM

MEDULLA   The **medulla** (which, oddly enough, means "marrow" or "inner substance") is located at the top of the spinal column. In Figure 2.10, it is the first "swelling" at the top of the spinal cord, just at the very bottom of the brain. This is the part of the brain that a person would least want to have damaged, as it controls life-sustaining functions such as heartbeat, breathing, and swallowing. (Remember the opening story about Christopher Reeve? His spinal cord damage was so serious because it was high enough to involve part of the medulla. The upper part of the spinal cord and the lower part of the brain are highly interconnected.) It is in the medulla that the nerves coming from and going to the left and right sides of the body cross over, so that the left side of the brain controls the right side of the body and vice versa. It will be useful to remember this crossover when reading about the functions of the left and right sides of the brain in a later part of this chapter.

PONS   The **pons** is the larger "swelling" just above the medulla. This term means "bridge," and the pons is indeed the bridge between the lower parts of the brain and the upper sections. The pons influences sleep and dreaming, coordination of movements on the right and left sides of the body, and arousal. The role that the pons plays in sleep and dreams will be discussed in more detail in Chapter Four. L(I)N(K) *to Chapter Four: Consciousness, p. 140.*

medulla
the first large swelling at the top of the spinal cord, forming the lowest part of the brain, which is responsible for life-sustaining functions such as breathing, swallowing, and heart rate.

pons
the larger swelling above the medulla that connects the top of the brain to the bottom and that plays a part in sleep, dreaming, left–right body coordination, and arousal.

Simulation
Live! psych
Brain Structures and Functions

Cerebral cortex
Controls complex thought processes

Corpus callosum
Connects left and right hemispheres of the brain

Hypothalamus
Part of the forebrain that regulates the amount of fear, thirst, sexual drive, and aggression we feel

Thalamus
Part of the forebrain that relays information from sensory organs to the cerebral cortex

Hippocampus
Plays a role in our emotions, ability to remember, and ability to compare sensory information to expectations

Cerebellum
Part of the hindbrain that controls balance and maintains muscle coordination

Reticular formation
A system of nerves, running from the hindbrain and through the midbrain to the cerebral cortex, controlling arousal and attention

Pituitary gland
Regulates other endocrine glands

Pons
Part of the hindbrain that relays messages between the cerebellum and the cortex

Medulla
Part of the hindbrain where nerves cross from one side of the body to the opposite side of the brain

FIGURE 2.10   **The Major Structures of the Human Brain**

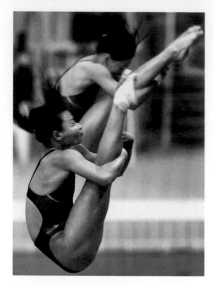

These divers must count on their cerebellum to help them coordinate the many fine muscle commands that allow them to dive in precision. What other kinds of professions depend heavily on the activity of the cerebellum?

So if your cerebellum is ▶ damaged, you might be very uncoordinated?

reticular formation (RF)
an area of neurons running through the middle of the medulla and the pons and slightly beyond that is responsible for selective attention.
cerebellum
part of the lower brain located behind the pons that controls and coordinates involuntary, rapid, fine motor movement.

THE RETICULAR FORMATION   The **reticular formation (RF)** is an area of neurons running through the middle of the medulla and the pons and slightly beyond. These neurons are responsible for people's ability to selectively attend to certain kinds of information in their surroundings. Basically, the RF allows people to ignore constant, unchanging information (such as the noise of an air conditioner) and become alert to changes in information (for example, if the air conditioner stopped, most people would notice immediately).

The reticular formation is also the part of the brain that helps keep people alert and aroused. One part of the RF is called the *reticular activating system (RAS)*, and it stimulates the upper part of the brain, keeping people awake and alert. When a person is driving along and someone suddenly pulls out in front of the vehicle, it is the RAS that brings that driver to full attention. It is also the system that lets a mother hear her baby cry in the night, even though she might sleep through other noises. The RAS has also been suggested by brain-scanning studies as a possible area involved in attention-deficit hyperactivity disorder, in which children or adults have difficulty maintaining attention to a single task (Durston, 2003).

Studies have shown that when the RF of rats is electrically stimulated while they are sleeping, they immediately awaken. If the RF is destroyed (by deep lesioning, for example), they fall into a sleeplike coma from which they never awaken (Moruzzi & Magoun, 1949; Steriade & McCarley, 1990). The RF is also implicated in comas in humans (Plum & Posner, 1985).

CEREBELLUM   At the base of the skull, behind the pons and below the main part of the brain, is a structure that looks like a small brain. (See Figure 2.10 on page 63.) This is the **cerebellum** (meaning "little brain"). The cerebellum is the part of the lower brain that controls all involuntary, rapid, fine motor movement. People can sit upright because the cerebellum controls all the little muscles needed to keep them from falling out of their chair. It also coordinates voluntary movements that have to happen in rapid succession, such as walking, diving, skating, gymnastics, dancing, typing (once it has been learned well), playing a musical instrument, and even the movements of speech. Learned reflexes, skills, and habits are also stored here—which allows them to become more or less automatic. Because of the cerebellum, people don't have to consciously think about their posture, muscle tone, and balance.

So if your cerebellum is damaged, you might be very uncoordinated? Yes. In fact, in a disease called *spinocerebellar degeneration* the first symptoms are tremors, an unsteady walk, slurred speech, dizziness, and muscle weakness. The person suffering from this disease will eventually be unable to walk, stand, or even get a spoon to his or her own mouth (Schöls et al., 1998). These symptoms are similar to what one might see in a person who is suffering from alcohol intoxication.

2.10   *What are the structures of the brain that control emotion, learning, memory, and motivation?*

STRUCTURES UNDER THE CORTEX

The cortex, which is discussed in detail later in this chapter, is the outer wrinkled covering of the brain. But there are a number of important structures located just under the cortex and above the brainstem. Each of these structures plays a part in our behavior. (See Figure 2.11.)

LIMBIC SYSTEM   The **limbic system** (the word *limbic* means "marginal" and these structures are found in the inner margin of the upper brain) includes the thalamus, hypothalamus, hippocampus, and amygdala. In general, the limbic system is involved in emotions, motivation, and learning.

Thalamus   Have you ever had to go to the emergency room of a hospital? You may find yourself getting past the receptionist, but most of the time you will have to wait to see a triage nurse before you ever get to see the doctor—if you ever get to see the doctor. (The word *triage* refers to a process for sorting injured people into groups based on their need for or likely benefit from immediate medical treatment.) Triage nurses will ask people questions about their complaints. They may be able to partially treat minor complaints before the person sees a doctor. Then they will send the person to a treatment room with the equipment that might be needed for the ailment, and eventually the person will see a doctor.

   The **thalamus** ("inner chamber") is in some ways similar to a triage nurse. This somewhat round structure in the center of the brain acts as a kind of relay station for incoming sensory information. Like a nurse, the thalamus might perform some processing of that sensory information before sending it on to the part of the cortex that deals with that kind of sensation—hearing, sight, touch, or taste. Damage to the thalamus might result in the loss or partial loss of any or all of those sensations.

   The sense of smell is unique in that signals from the neurons in the sinus cavity go directly into special parts of the brain called **olfactory bulbs**, just under the front part of the brain. Smell is the only sense that cannot be affected by damage to the thalamus.

Hypothalamus   A very small but extremely powerful part of the brain is located just below and in front of the thalamus (see Figure 2.11). The **hypothalamus** ("below the inner chamber") regulates body temperature, thirst, hunger, sleeping and waking, sexual activity, and emotions. It sits right above the *pituitary gland*, which is called the "master gland" because it controls the functions of all the other endocrine glands that will be discussed later in this chapter. The hypothalamus controls the pituitary, so the ultimate regulation of hormones lies with the hypothalamus.

Hippocampus   The **hippocampus** is the Greek word for "seahorse" and it was given to this structure of the brain because the first scientists who dissected the brain thought it looked like a seahorse. Research has shown that the hippocampus is instrumental in forming long-term (permanent) memories that are then stored elsewhere in the brain (Bigler et al., 1996). Acetylcholine, the neurotransmitter involved in muscle control, is also involved in the memory function of the hippocampus. People who

Thalamus
Part of the forebrain that relays information from sensory organs to the cerebral cortex

Hypothalamus
Part of the forebrain that regulates the amount of fear, thrist, sexual drive, and aggression we feel

Amygdala
Influences our motivation, emotional control, fear response, and interpretations of nonverbal emotional expressions

Hippocampus
Plays a role in our emotions, ability to remember, and ability to compare sensory information to expectations

FIGURE 2.11   **The Limbic System**

limbic system
a group of several brain structures located under the cortex and involved in learning, emotion, memory, and motivation.

thalamus
part of the limbic system located in the center of the brain, this structure relays sensory information from the lower part of the brain to the proper areas of the cortex and processes some sensory information before sending it to its proper area.

olfactory bulbs
two projections just under the front of the brain that receive information from the receptors in the nose located just below.

hypothalamus
small structure in the brain located below the thalamus and directly above the pituitary gland, responsible for motivational behavior such as sleep, hunger, thirst, and sex.

hippocampus
curved structure located within each temporal lobe, responsible for the formation of long-term memories and the storage of memory for location of objects.

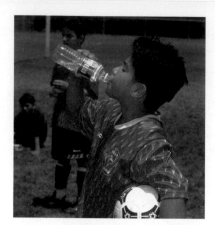

This young boy's thirst is regulated by his hypothalamus.

have Alzheimer's, for example, have much lower levels of acetylcholine in that structure than is normal. The hippocampus is located within the temporal lobes on each side of the brain, and electrical stimulation of the temporal lobe may produce memory-like or dream-like experiences.

The hippocampus may be very close to the area of the brain where the memories for locations of objects are stored as well. Researchers have found that the right parahippocampal gyrus, located alongside the right hippocampus, is more active when a person is planning a travel route (Maguire et al., 1998), which might explain why elderly people who develop memory problems associated with deterioration of the hippocampus also tend to forget where they live, where they parked the car, and similar location problems. Deterioration in the hippocampal area may spread to or affect other nearby areas.

Amygdala   The **amygdala** ("almond") is an area of the brain located near the hippocampus. These two structures seem to be responsible for fear responses and memory of fear. Information from the senses goes to the amygdala before the upper part of the brain is even involved, so that people can respond to danger very quickly, sometimes before they are consciously aware of what is happening. In 1939 researchers found that monkeys with large amounts of their temporal lobes removed—including the amygdala—were completely unafraid of snakes and humans, both normally fear-provoking stimuli (Klüver & Bucy, 1939). This effect came to be known as the *Klüver-Bucy syndrome.* Rats that have damaged amygdala structures will also show no fear when placed next to a cat (Maren & Fanselow, 1996).

PRACTICE **QUIZ:** HOW MUCH DO YOU REMEMBER?

Pick the best answer.

1. Which of the following techniques uses a radioactive sugar to look at the functioning of the brain?
   a. EEG
   b. CT
   c. MRI
   d. PET

2. Which brain structure is most responsible for our balance, posture, and muscle tone?
   a. medulla
   b. cerebellum
   c. reticular formation
   d. pons

3. Which brain structure would most likely result in death if damaged?
   a. medulla
   b. cerebellum
   c. reticular formation
   d. pons

4. If you were to develop a rare condition in which signals from your eyes were sent to the area of the brain that processes sound and signals from the ears were sent to the area of the brain that processes vision, which part of the brain would most likely be damaged?
   a. hippocampus
   b. hypothalamus
   c. thalamus
   d. amygdala

5. If you have problems storing away new memories, the damage is most likely in the _____ area of the brain.
   a. hippocampus
   b. hypothalamus
   c. cerebellum
   d. amygdala

Answers: 1-d, 2-b, 3-a, 4-c, 5-a.

amygdala
brain structure located near the hippocampus, responsible for fear responses and memory of fear.

cortex
outermost covering of the brain consisting of densely packed neurons, responsible for higher thought processes and interpretation of sensory input.

THE CORTEX (perception)

As stated earlier, the **cortex** ("rind" or outer covering) is the outermost part of the brain, which is the part of the brain most people picture when they think of what the brain looks like. It is made up of tightly packed neurons and actually is only about one-tenth of an inch thick on average (Fischl et al., 2001; MacDonald et al., 2000; Zilles, 1990). The tissue appears grayish pink because the tightly packed neural bodies are gray and the small blood vessels appear pink. The cortex is very recognizable because it is full of wrinkles.

Why is the cortex so wrinkled? The wrinkling of the cortex allows a much larger area of cortical cells to exist in the small space inside the skull. If the cortex were to be taken out, ironed flat, and measured, it would be about 2 to 3 square feet. (The owner of the cortex would also be dead, but that's fairly obvious, right?) As the brain develops before birth, it forms a smooth outer covering on all the other brain structures. This will be the cortex, which will get more and more wrinkled as the brain increases in size and complexity. This increase in wrinkling is called *corticalization* and is the real measure of human intelligence.

2.11   *What parts of the cortex control the different senses and the movement of the body?*

THE LOBES AND THEIR SPECIALTIES   The cortex is divided into two sections called the **cerebral hemispheres**, which are connected by a thick, tough band of neural bodies called the **corpus callosum** (literally meaning "hard bodies," as calluses on the feet are hard). (See Figure 2.10.) Each hemisphere can be roughly divided into four sections by looking at the deeper wrinkles, or fissures, in its surface (see Figure 2.12).

– 4 Lobes –

Occipital Lobes   At the base of the cortex, toward the back of the brain is an area called the **occipital lobe** (the term occipital refers to the rear of the head). This area processes visual information from the eyes in the *primary visual cortex*. The *visual association cortex*, also in this lobe, is the part of the brain that helps identify and make sense of the visual information from the eyes. The famed neurologist Oliver Sacks once had a patient who had a tumor in his right occipital lobe area. He could still see objects perfectly well and even describe them in physical terms, but he could not identify them by sight alone. For example, Sacks once gave him a rose to look at. The man turned it around and around and began to describe it as a "red inflorescence" of some type with a green tubular projection. Only when he held it under his nose (stimulating the sense of smell) did he recognize it as a rose (Sacks, 1990). Each area of the cortex has these association areas that help people make sense of sensory information.

Have you ever wondered why people "see stars" sometimes after being hit in the rear of the head? Because the area of the brain at the back of the head processes vision, any stimulation to that area will be interpreted as vision—hence, the "stars."

Parietal Lobes   The **parietal lobes** (*parietal* means "wall") are at the top and back of the brain, just under the parietal bone in the skull. This area contains the **somatosensory cortex**, an area of neurons (see Figure 2.13) running down the front of the parietal lobes on either side of the brain. This area processes information from the skin and internal body receptors for touch, temperature, and body position. The sense of taste may also be processed near this area. The somatosensory cortex is laid out in a rather interesting way—the cells at the top of the brain receive information from the bottom of the body, and as one moves down the area, the signals come from higher and higher in the body. It's almost as if a little upside-down person were laid out along this area of cells.

Temporal Lobes   The **temporal lobes** (*temporal* means "of or near the temples") are found just behind the temples of the head. These lobes contain the *primary auditory cortex* and the *auditory association area*. If a person receives a blow to the

cerebral hemispheres
the two sections of the cortex on the left and right sides of the brain.

corpus callosum
thick band of neurons that connects the right and left cerebral hemispheres.

occipital lobe
section of the brain located at the rear and bottom of each cerebral hemisphere containing the visual centers of the brain.

parietal lobes
sections of the brain located at the top and back of each cerebral hemisphere containing the centers for touch, taste, and temperature sensations.

somatosensory cortex
area of neurons running down the front of the parietal lobes responsible for processing information from the skin and internal body receptors for touch, temperature, body position, and possibly taste.

temporal lobes
areas of the cortex located just behind the temples containing the neurons responsible for the sense of hearing and meaningful speech.

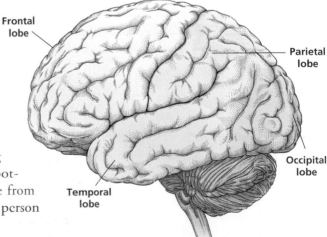

FIGURE 2.12   **The Lobes of the Brain: Occipital, Parietal, Temporal, and Frontal**

These young women are processing the music in their temporal lobes.

The texture, temperature, and softness of the clay are processed in the child's parietal lobes.

side of the head, that person will probably "hear" a ringing sound. Also found in the left temporal lobe is an area that in most people is particularly involved with language.

Frontal Lobes   These lobes are at the front of the brain, hence, the name **frontal lobes**. (It doesn't often get this easy in psychology; feel free to take a moment to appreciate it.) Here are found all the higher mental functions of the brain—planning, personality, memory storage, complex decision making, and (again in the left hemisphere in most people) areas devoted to language. The frontal lobe also helps in controlling emotions by means of its connection to the limbic system. Phineas Gage, mentioned in Chapter One (p. 22) because he suffered damage to his frontal lobe, lacked this emotional control because of the damage to this connection with the limbic system structures, particularly the amygdala. People with damage to this area of the brain may also experience problems with performing mental tasks, getting stuck on one step or one wrong answer and repeating it over and over again (Goel & Grafman, 1995).

The frontal lobes also contain the **motor cortex**, a band of neurons located at the back of each lobe. (See Figure 2.13.) These cells control the movements of the body's voluntary muscles by sending commands out to the somatic division of the peripheral nervous system. The motor cortex is laid out just like the somatosensory cortex right next door in the parietal lobes. This mirror-image layout allows for fast response times between the processing of sensory information and the production of motor responses. For example, if a person's hand touches something squishy, the information about that touch sensation is

FIGURE 2.13 **The Somatosensory and Motor Areas** The motor cortex in the frontal lobe controls the voluntary muscles of the body. Cells at the top of the motor cortex control muscles at the bottom of the body, while cells at the bottom of the motor cortex control muscles at the top of the body. Body parts are drawn larger or smaller according to the number of cortical cells devoted to that body part. For example, the hand has many small muscles and requires a larger area of cortical cells to control it. The somatosensory cortex, located in the parietal lobe just behind the motor cortex, is organized in much the same manner, and receives information about the sense of touch and body position.

MOTOR CORTEX   SOMATOSENSORY CORTEX

received in the somatosensory cortex area right next to the motor cortex area that will let the person pull his or her hand back quickly.

You've mentioned association cortex a few times. Do the other lobes of the brain contain association cortex as well?

THE ASSOCIATION AREAS OF THE CORTEX

2.12   *What parts of the cortex are responsible for higher forms of thought, such as language?*

Association areas are made up of neurons in the cortex that are devoted to making connections between the sensory information coming into the brain and stored memories, images, and knowledge. In other words, association areas help people make sense of the incoming sensory input. Although the association areas in the occipital and temporal lobes have already been mentioned, the bulk of the brain's association cortex is in the frontal lobes. Some special association areas are worth talking about in more detail.

BROCA'S AREA   In the left frontal lobe of most people is an area of the brain devoted to the production of speech. (In a small portion of the population, this area is in the right frontal lobe.) More specifically, this area allows a person to speak smoothly and fluently. It is called *Broca's area* after nineteenth-century neurologist Paul Broca, who first studied people with damage to this area (Leonard, 1997). Damage to Broca's area causes a person to be unable to get words out in a smooth, connected fashion. People with this condition may know exactly what they want to say and understand what they hear others say, but they cannot control the actual production of their own words. Speech is halting and words are often mispronounced, such as saying "cot" instead of "clock" or "non" instead of "nine." This is called **Broca's aphasia**. *Aphasia* refers to an inability to use or understand either written or spoken language (Goodglass et al., 2001).

WERNICKE'S AREA   In the left temporal lobe (again, in most people) is an area called *Wernicke's area*, named after the physiologist and Broca's contemporary, Carl Wernicke, who first studied problems arising from damage in this location. This area of the brain appears to be involved in understanding the meaning of words (Goodglass et al., 2001). A person with **Wernicke's aphasia** would be able to speak fluently and pronounce words correctly, but the words would be the wrong ones entirely. For example, Elsie suffered a stroke to the temporal lobe, damaging this area of the brain. In the emergency room the nurse tried to take her blood pressure, and when the cuff inflated, Elsie said, "Oh, that's so Saturday hard." Now, what does "Saturday hard" mean? Neither the nurse nor Elsie's daughter could figure that one out, but Elsie *thought* she was making sense. She also had trouble understanding what the people around her were saying to her. In another instance, Ernest suffered a stroke at the age of 80 and developed complete aphasia. As he recovered, he showed some telltale signs of Wernicke's aphasia. In one instance, he asked his wife to get him some milk out of the air conditioner. When she told him that he surely meant to say "refrigerator" he got angry and told her he knew what he was saying, "Now get me some milk out of the air conditioner, woman!"

SPATIAL NEGLECT   Remember that not all association areas are in the frontal or temporal lobes. Damage to association areas of the right hemisphere can produce an odd condition called **spatial neglect**. In spatial neglect, a person fails to recognize the left side of the visual field. If that person also has a paralyzed left arm or leg, that person may deny that the arm or leg actually belongs to him or her. Although spatial neglect can affect the left hemisphere, this condition occurs less frequently and in a much milder form than right-hemisphere neglect (Heilman et al., 1993; Springer & Deutsch, 1998).

damage right → influence left

You've mentioned association cortex a few times. Do the other lobes of the brain contain association cortex as well?

frontal lobes
areas of the cortex located in the front and top of the brain, responsible for higher mental processes and decision making as well as the production of fluent speech.

motor cortex
section of the frontal lobe located at the back, responsible for sending motor commands to the muscles of the somatic nervous system.

association areas
areas within each lobe of the cortex responsible for the coordination and interpretation of information, as well as higher mental processing.

Broca's aphasia
condition resulting from damage to Broca's area, causing the affected person to be unable to speak fluently, to mispronounce words, and to speak haltingly.

Wernicke's aphasia
condition resulting from damage to Wernicke's area, causing the affected person to be unable to understand or produce meaningful language.

spatial neglect
condition produced by damage to the association areas of the right hemisphere resulting in an inability to recognize objects or body parts in the left visual field.

CLASSIC STUDIES IN PSYCHOLOGY
Through the Looking Glass: Spatial Neglect

Dr. V. S. Ramachandran reported in his fascinating book, *Phantoms in the Brain* (Ramachandran & Blakeslee, 1998), the case of a woman with spatial neglect. When Ellen's son came to visit her, he was shocked and puzzled by his formerly neat and fastidious* mother's appearance. The woman who had always taken pride in her looks, who always had her hair perfectly done and her nails perfectly manicured, looked messy and totally odd. Her hair was uncombed on the left side. Her green shawl was hanging neatly over her right shoulder but hanging onto the floor on the left. Her lipstick was neatly applied to the right side of her lips, and *only to the right side—the left side of her face was completely bare of makeup!* Yet her eyeliner, mascara, and rouge were all neatly applied to the right side of her face.

What was wrong? The son called the doctor and was told that his mother's stroke had left her with a condition called spatial neglect, in which a person with damage to the right hemisphere of the cortex will ignore everything in the left visual field. It is not that his mother was blind on the left side, just that she would not notice anything there unless her attention was specifically called to it. Her son found that when he pointed out the condition of her makeup to her, she was able to recognize it. He found that she also ignored all of the food on the left side of her plate unless her attention was specifically called to it.

When the doctor examined this woman, he tried to get her to notice her left side by holding up a mirror. She responded correctly when asked what the mirror was and she was able to describe her appearance correctly, but when an assistant held a pen just within the woman's reach, reflected in the mirror on her left side, she tried to reach *through the mirror* to get the pen with her good right hand. When the doctor told her that he wanted her to grab the real object and not the image of it in the mirror, she told him that the pen was *behind* the mirror and even tried to reach around to get it.

Clearly, persons suffering from spatial neglect are not blind at all. They simply can no longer perceive the world in the same way as other people do. For these people, the left sides of objects, bodies, and spaces are somewhere "through the looking glass."

Questions for Further Discussion

1. If a person with spatial neglect only eats the food on the right side of the plate, what could caregivers do to help that person get enough to eat?

2. What other odd things might a person with spatial neglect do that a person with normal functioning would not? What other things might a person with spatial neglect fail to do?

---

*Fastidious: having demanding standards, difficult to please.

> I've heard that some people are right-brained and some are left-brained. Are the two sides of the brain really that different?

THE CEREBRAL HEMISPHERES: ARE YOU IN YOUR RIGHT MIND?

I've heard that some people are right-brained and some are left-brained. Are the two sides of the brain really that different? Most people tend to think of the two cerebral hemispheres as identical twins. Both sides have the same four lobes and are arranged in pretty much the same way. But language seems to be confined to only the left hemisphere in about 90 percent of the population (Toga & Thompson, 2003). What other special tasks do the two halves of the **cerebrum** (the upper part of the brain consisting of the two hemispheres and the structures connecting them) engage in, and how do researchers know about such functions?

2.13   *How does the left side of the brain differ from the right side?*

SPLIT-BRAIN RESEARCH   Roger Sperry was a pioneer in the field of hemisphere specialization. He won a Nobel Prize for his work in demonstrating that the left and right hemispheres of the brain specialize in different activities and functions (Sperry, 1968). In looking for a way to cure epilepsy (severe muscle spasms or seizures resulting from brain damage), Sperry cut through the corpus callosum, the thick band of neurons that joins the two hemispheres. In early research with animals, this technique worked and seemed to have no side effects. The first people to have this procedure done also experienced relief from their severe epileptic symptoms, but testing found that (in a sense) they now had two brains in one body.

The special testing involves sending messages to only one side of the brain, which is now possible because the connecting tissue, the corpus callosum, has been cut. Figure 2.14 shows a picture of a typical split-brain patient seated in front of a screen.

If a picture of a ball is flashed to the right side of the screen, the image of the ball will be sent to the left occipital lobe. The person will be able to say that he or she sees a ball. If a picture of a hammer is flashed to the left side of the screen, the person will not be able to verbally identify the object or be able to state with any certainty that something was seen. But if the left hand (controlled by the right hemisphere) is used, the person can point to the hammer he or she "didn't see." The right occipital lobe clearly saw the hammer, but the person could not verbalize that fact (Sperry, 1968). By doing studies such as these, researchers have found that the left hemisphere specializes in language, speech, handwriting, calculation (math), sense of time and rhythm (which is mathematical in nature), and basically any kind of thought requiring analysis. The right hemisphere appears to specialize in more global (widespread) processing involving perception, visualization, spatial perception, recognition of patterns, faces, emotions, melodies, and expression of emotions. It also comprehends simple language but does not produce speech.

Springer and Deutsch (1998) found that, in general, the left hemisphere processes information in a sequence and is good at breaking things down into smaller parts, or performing analysis. The right hemisphere, by contrast, processes information all at once and simultaneously, a more global or holistic* style of processing. Remember the discussion in Chapter One of the early days of psychology, the structuralists, and the Gestalt psychologists? One could almost say that the left hemisphere of the brain is a structuralist who wants to break everything down into its smallest parts, and the right side of the brain is a Gestaltist, who wants to study only the whole.

cerebrum
the upper part of the brain consisting of the two hemispheres and the structures that connect them.

Experiment
Live!
psych

Hemispheric
Specialization

FIGURE 2.14   **The Split-Brain Experiment**   Roger Sperry created this experiment to demonstrate the specialization of the left and right hemispheres of the brain.

What do you see?

I see a ball.

What do you see?

I see nothing.

---

*Holistic: relating to or concerned with complete systems or wholes.

So there really are ▶
left-brained and
right-brained people?

So there really are left-brained and right-brained people? Actually, unless one is a split-brain patient, the two sides of the brain are always working together as an integrated whole. For example, the right side might recognize someone's face, while the left side struggles to recall the person's name. People aren't really left- or right-brained, they are whole-brained. (Well, most of them, anyway.)

PRACTICE QUIZ: HOW MUCH DO YOU REMEMBER?

Pick the best answer.

1. In which of the following lobes of the cortex would you find the primary auditory area?
   a. frontal
   b. temporal
   c. occipital
   d. parietal

2. Which of the following is the name for the thick band of neurons that connects the left and right sides of the cortex?
   a. fornix
   b. corpus callosum
   c. Wernicke's area
   d. thalamus

3. The higher mental functions, such as thinking and problem solving, are found in the _____ lobe.
   a. frontal
   b. parietal
   c. temporal
   d. occipital

4. In an old *Twilight Zone* episode, a man wakes up one morning to find that people around him are using words that make no sense to him, and they also don't seem to understand him. His wife tells him that their son forgot his dinosaur today, and when he looks puzzled, she holds up the son's lunchbox and repeats, "You know, his dinosaur." This man's predicament is most like which of the following disorders?
   a. Wernicke's aphasia
   b. Broca's aphasia
   c. apraxia
   d. spatial neglect

5. When Dr. Ramachandran's spatial neglect patient was asked to reach for the pen, she
   a. reached to the wrong side of the mirror.
   b. said she couldn't see the pen.
   c. tried to reach through the mirror.
   d. successfully grabbed the pen.

6. If you are a split-brain patient, which of the following would be true?
   a. Objects in your left visual field would be easily named.
   b. Objects in your left visual field are invisible.
   c. Objects in your right visual field would be easily named.
   d. Objects in your right visual field are invisible.

Answers: 1-b, 2-b, 3-a, 4-a, 5-c, 6-c.

The Chemical Connection: The Endocrine Glands

How do the glands fit ▶
into all of this? Aren't
there more glands than
just the adrenal
glands? How do they
affect our behavior?

How do the glands fit into all of this? Aren't there more glands than just the adrenal glands? How do they affect our behavior? Glands are organs in the body that secrete chemicals. Some glands, such as salivary glands and sweat glands, secrete their chemicals directly onto the body's tissues through tiny tubes, or ducts. This kind of gland affects the functioning of the body, but doesn't really affect behavior. (It might affect the behavior of people around a person who is drooling or stinky, though.) Other glands, called **endocrine glands**, have no ducts and secrete their chemicals directly into the bloodstream. (See Figure 2.15.) The chemicals secreted by this type of gland are called **hormones**. As mentioned earlier in the chapter when talking about the sympathetic division of the autonomic nervous system, these hormones flow into the bloodstream, which carries them to their target organs. The molecules of these hormones then fit into receptor sites on those organs to fulfill their function, affecting behavior as they do so.

2.14 *How do the hormones released by glands interact with the nervous system and affect behavior?*

endocrine glands
glands that secrete chemicals called hormones directly into the bloodstream.

hormones
chemicals released into the bloodstream by endocrine glands.

The hormones affect behavior and emotions by controlling muscles and organs such as the heart, pancreas, and sex organs. Some theories of emotion state that the surge in certain hormones actually triggers the emotional reaction (Izard, 1988; Zajonc, 1980, 1984). ⓁⒾⓃⓀ *to Chapter Nine: Motivation and Emotion, p. 357.* Some of the hormones produced by endocrine glands also influence the activity of the brain, producing excitatory or inhibitory effects (Mai et al., 1987).

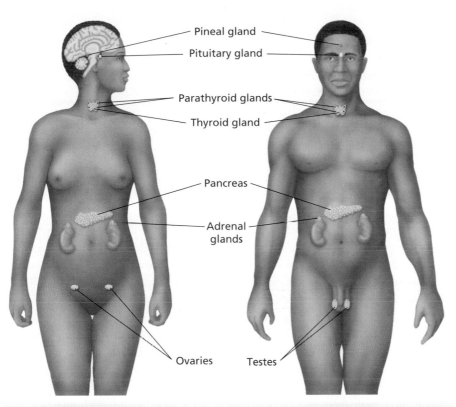

FIGURE 2.15   **The Endocrine Glands**   The endocrine glands secrete hormones directly into the bloodstream, which carries them to organs in the body, such as the heart, pancreas, and sex organs.

THE PITUITARY, MASTER OF THE HORMONAL UNIVERSE

The **pituitary gland** is located in the brain itself, just below the hypothalamus. The hypothalamus controls the glandular system by influencing the pituitary. That is because the pituitary gland is the *master gland*, the one that controls or influences all of the other endocrine glands. One part of the pituitary controls things associated with pregnancy, such as production of milk for nursing infants and the onset of labor, as well as the levels of salt and water in the body. Another part of the pituitary secretes several hormones that influence the activity of the other glands. Most notable of these hormones is a *growth hormone* that controls and regulates the increase in size as children grow from infancy to adulthood.

THE PINEAL GLAND

The **pineal gland** is also located in the brain, nearer to the back. It secretes a hormone called *melatonin*, which regulates the sleep–wake cycle. L I N K *to Chapter Four: Consciousness, p. 127.* Skin color, changes in time.

THE THYROID GLAND

The **thyroid gland** is located inside the neck and secretes a hormone called *thyroxin* that regulates metabolism (how fast the body burns its available energy).

PANCREAS

The **pancreas** controls the level of blood sugar in the body by secreting *insulin* and *glucagons*. If the pancreas secretes too little insulin, it results in *diabetes*. If it secretes too much insulin, it results in *hypoglycemia*, or low blood sugar, which causes a person to feel hungry all the time and often become overweight as a result.

pituitary gland
gland located in the brain that secretes human growth hormone and influences all other hormone-secreting glands (also known as the master gland).

pineal gland
endocrine gland located near the base of the cerebrum that secretes melatonin.

thyroid gland
endocrine gland found in the neck that regulates metabolism.

pancreas
endocrine gland that controls the levels of sugar in the blood.

THE GONADS

The **gonads** are the sex glands, including the **ovaries** in the female and the **testes** in the male. They secrete hormones that regulate sexual behavior and reproduction. They do not control all sexual behavior, though. In a very real sense, the brain itself is the master of the sexual system—human sexual behavior is not controlled totally by instincts and the actions of the glands as in the animal world but also by psychological factors such as attractiveness. L I N K *to Chapter Ten: Sexuality and Gender, pp. 387–389.*

THE ADRENAL GLANDS

Everyone has two **adrenal glands**, one on top of each kidney. The origin of the name is simple enough; *renal* comes from a Latin word meaning "kidney" and *ad* is Latin for "to," so *adrenal* means "to or on the kidney." Each adrenal gland is actually divided into two sections, the *adrenal medulla* and the *adrenal cortex*. It is the adrenal medulla that releases ephinephrine and norepinephrine when people are under stress and that aids in sympathetic arousal.

The adrenal cortex produces over 30 different hormones called *corticoids* (also called steroids) that regulate salt intake, help initiate* and control stress reactions, and also provides a source of sex hormones in addition to those provided by the gonads. One of the most important of these adrenal hormones is *cortisol*, released when the body experiences stress, both physical stress (such as illness, surgery, or extreme heat or cold) and psychological stress (such as an emotional upset). L I N K *to Chapter Eleven: Stress and Health, pp. 420–421.* Cortisol is important in the release of glucose into the bloodstream during stress, providing energy for the brain itself, and the release of fatty acids from the fat cells that provide the muscles with energy.

PRACTICE **QUIZ:** HOW MUCH DO YOU REMEMBER?

Pick the best answer.

1. The endocrine glands secrete chemicals called
   a. pheromones into the bloodstream.
   b. hormones into the bloodstream.
   c. pheromones onto bodily tissues.
   d. hormones onto bodily tissues.

2. Andrew never really grew to be very tall. The doctor told his parents that Andrew's _____ gland did not secrete enough growth hormone, causing his small stature.
   a. pituitary   c. thyroid
   b. adrenal   d. pancreas

3. If the pancreas secretes too little insulin, it causes
   a. diabetes.
   b. hypoglycemia.
   c. hypothyroidism.
   d. virilism.

Answers: 1-b, 2-a, 3-a.

gonads
the sex glands that secrete hormones that regulate sexual development and behavior as well as reproduction.

ovaries
the female gonads.

testes
the male gonads.

adrenal glands
endocrine glands located on top of each kidney that secrete over 30 different hormones to deal with stress, regulate salt intake, and provide a secondary source of sex hormones affecting the sexual changes that occur during adolescence.

Applying Psychology to Everyday Life: Differences Between Male and Female Brains

People have believed for a long time that men and women think differently. Now, brain-scanning techniques such as the MRI have allowed scientists to demonstrate that there are indeed some differences in the way men and women think about certain tasks. Recent studies have found that when both sexes are doing language tasks, Broca's area in the left hemisphere is more active—as it should be. But more than half of the women in the study also used an area on the right side of the brain in the same task (Jaeger et al., 1998; Skrandies et al., 1999). This may explain why women recover from strokes to Broca's area faster and more completely than do men. Women can compensate for the loss of the left-side functions with the right side.

_____

*Initiate: begin or start.

As this woman and man talk, they are each using different hemispheres of the brain to do so.

What are some other differences between male and female use of the hemispheres? Here are just a few:

Mental Process	Males	Females
Emotional Expression	Right	Both sides
Visual/Spatial Perception	Left	Both sides
Vocabulary/Definitions	Left	Both sides
Grammar/Language Mechanics	Left	Left front
Hand Movements	Left	Left front

(Skrandies, Reik, & Kunze, 1999)

In short, women seem to use both sides of their brains for most tasks, processing information not only analytically but globally as well. This might account for stories of "women's intuition" if researchers conclude that intuition is the result of a global sort of insight. Men seem to use the left side of the brain for problem solving, perhaps giving rise to the feeling that men are somehow more logical than women. Are these differences innate? That's a simple answer, but probably an incorrect one. A great deal of environmental training and experience may go into developing these different processing styles. As children, girls in Western cultures are encouraged to use their emotions, to form relationships with others, and to be emotionally sensitive. This may contribute to their tendency to use the right hemisphere in problem solving. Boys in those same cultures, however, are typically taught to hide their emotions, to think calmly and "coolly," contributing to their tendency to rely only on the left hemisphere rather than the emotional right hemisphere (Argyle, 1986; Fischer, 1993; Pittam et al., 1995).

On the other hand, there are physical differences in male and female brains from birth. Researchers have found that a part of the hypothalamus is larger in male brains than in female brains in both rats and humans (Kimura, 2002). Other research once claimed that the corpus callosum that connects the left and right hemispheres is larger in female brains than in male brains, but those findings have now been cast into doubt by more modern brain-imaging techniques, such as the MRI (Bishop & Wahlsten, 1997).

As the newest techniques for looking at the brain are employed in research of this type, scientists will eventually have more specific and detailed answers to questions of gender differences in the brain.

Questions for Further Discussion
1. Why might a focus on the differences in male and female brains become a disadvantage in the world of work?
2. How might parents and educators minimize the differences between boys and girls in cognitive skills?

2 CHAPTER SUMMARY

An Overview of the Nervous System

2.1 How do all the parts of the nervous system relate to one another?

- The nervous system is a complex network of cells that carries information to and from all parts of the body.

Neurons and Nerves: Building the Network

2.2 What are neurons and nerves, and how do they work?

- The brain is made up of two types of cells, neurons and glial cells.
- Neurons have dendrites, which receive input, a soma or cell body, and axons that carry the neural message to other cells.
- Glial cells separate, support, and insulate the neurons from each other and make up 90 percent of the brain.
- Myelin insulates and protects the axons of neurons that travel in the body. These axons bundle together in "cables" called nerves. Myelin also speeds up the neural message.
- Neurons in the peripheral nervous system are also coated with neurilemma, which allows the nerves to repair themselves.

2.3 How do neurons communicate with each other and with the body?

- A neuron contains charged particles called ions. When at rest, the neuron is negatively charged on the inside and positively charged on the outside. When stimulated, this reverses the charge by allowing positive sodium ions to enter the cell. This is the action potential.
- Neurons fire in an all-or-nothing manner. It is the speed and number of neurons firing that tell researchers the strength of the stimulus.
- Synaptic vesicles in the end of the axon terminal release neurotransmitter chemicals into the synapse, or gap, between one cell and the next. The neurotransmitter molecules fit into receptor sites on the next cell, stimulating or inhibiting that cell's firing. There are excitatory and inhibitory synapses.

2.4 What are the different neurotransmitters?

- The first known neurotransmitter was acetylcholine. It stimulates muscles and helps in memory formation. Curare is a poison that blocks its effect.
- GABA is the major inhibitory neurotransmitter; high amounts of GABA are released when drinking alcohol.
- Serotonin is associated with sleep, mood, and appetite.
- Dopamine is associated with Parkinson's and schizophrenia.
- Endorphins are neural regulators that control our pain response.
- Most neurotransmitters are taken back into the synaptic vesicles in a process called reuptake.
- Acetylcholine is cleared out of the synapse by enzymes that break up the molecules.

The Central Nervous System—The "Central Processing Unit"

2.5 How do the brain and spinal cord interact?

- The central nervous system consists of the brain and the spinal cord.

- The spinal cord serves two functions. The outer part of the cord transmits messages to and from the brain, whereas the inner part controls lifesaving reflexes such as the pain response.
- Spinal cord reflexes involve sensory neurons, interneurons, and motor neurons, forming a simple reflex arc.
- Great strides are being made in spinal cord repair and the growth of new neurons in the central nervous system.

Psychology in the News: Adult Bone Marrow: New Hope For The Damaged Brain

- Research suggests that stem cells can be obtained from adult bone marrow, making the repair and replacement of damaged neurons more feasible.

The Peripheral Nervous System—Nerves on the Edge

- The peripheral nervous system is all the neurons and nerves that are not part of the brain and spinal cord and that extend throughout the body.
- There are two systems within the peripheral nervous system, the somatic nervous system and the autonomic nervous system.

2.6 How does the somatic nervous system allow people and animals to interact with their surroundings?

- The somatic nervous system contains the sensory pathway, or neurons carrying messages to the central nervous system, and the motor pathway, or neurons carrying messages from the central nervous system to the voluntary muscles.

2.7 How does the autonomic nervous system control the body's automatic functions and its reaction to stress?

- The autonomic nervous system consists of the parasympathetic division and the sympathetic division. The sympathetic division is our fight-or-flight system, reacting to stress, whereas the parasympathetic division restores and maintains normal day-to-day functioning of the organs.

Peeking Inside the Brain

2.8 How do psychologists study the brain and how it works?

- We can study the brain by using deep lesioning to destroy certain areas of the brain in laboratory animals or by electrically stimulating those areas (ESB).
- We can use case studies of human brain damage to learn about the brain's functions but cannot easily generalize from one case to another.
- The EEG machine allows researchers to look at the activity of the surface of the brain through the use of microelectrodes placed on the scalp and connected to graph paper.
- CT scans are computer-aided X-rays of the brain and show a great deal of brain structure.
- MRI scans use a magnetic field and a computer to give researchers an even more detailed look at the structure of the brain. A related technique, fMRI, allows researchers to look at the activity of the brain over a time period.
- PET scans use a radioactive sugar injected into the bloodstream to track the activity of brain cells, which is enhanced and color-coded by a computer.

From the Bottom Up: The Structures of the Brain

2.9 What are the different structures of the bottom part of the brain and what do they do?

- The medulla is at the very bottom of the brain and top of the spinal column. It controls life-sustaining functions such as breathing and swallowing. The nerves from each side of the body also cross over in this structure to opposite sides.

- The pons is above the medulla and acts as a bridge between the lower part of the brain and the upper part. It influences sleep, dreaming, arousal, and coordination of movement on the left and right sides of the body.

- The reticular formation runs through the medulla and the pons and controls our selective attention and arousal.

- The cerebellum is found at the base and back of the brain and coordinates fine, rapid motor movement, learned reflexes, posture, and muscle tone.

2.10 What are the structures of the brain that control emotion, learning, memory, and motivation?

- The thalamus is the switching station that sends sensory information to the proper areas of the cortex.

- The hypothalamus controls hunger, thirst, sleep, sexual behavior, sleeping and waking, and emotions. It also controls the pituitary gland.

- The limbic system consists of the thalamus, hypothalamus, hippocampus, amygdala, and the fornix.

- The hippocampus is the part of the brain responsible for storing memories and remembering locations of objects.

- The amygdala controls our fear responses and memory of fearful stimuli.

2.11 What parts of the cortex control the different senses and the movement of the body?

- The cortex is the outer covering of the cerebrum and consists of a tightly packed layer of neurons about one-tenth of an inch in thickness. Its wrinkles, or corticalization, allow for greater cortical area and are associated with greater intelligence.

- The cortex is divided into two cerebral hemispheres connected by a thick band of neurons called the corpus callosum.

- The occipital lobes at the back and base of each hemisphere process vision and contain the primary visual cortex.

- The parietal lobes at the top and back of the cortex contain the somatosensory area, which processes our sense of touch, temperature, and body position. Taste is also processed in this lobe.

- The temporal lobes contain the primary auditory area and are also involved in understanding language.

- The frontal lobes contain the motor cortex, which controls the voluntary muscles, and are also where all the higher mental functions occur, such as planning, language, and complex decision making.

2.12 What parts of the cortex are responsible for higher forms of thought, such as language?

- Association areas of the cortex are found in all the lobes but particularly in the frontal lobes. These areas help people make sense of the information they receive from the lower areas of the brain.

- An area called Broca's area in the left frontal lobe is responsible for producing fluent, understandable speech. If damaged, the person has Broca's aphasia in which words will be halting and pronounced incorrectly.

- An area called Wernicke's area in the left temporal lobe is responsible for the understanding of language. If damaged, the person has Wernicke's aphasia in which speech is fluent but nonsensical. The wrong words are used.

Classic Studies in Psychology: **Through the Looking Glass: Spatial Neglect**

- Spatial neglect comes from damage to the association areas on one side of the cortex, usually the right side. A person with this condition will ignore information from the opposite side of the body or the opposite visual field.

2.13 How does the left side of the brain differ from the right side?

- Studies with split-brain patients, in which the corpus callosum has been severed to correct epilepsy, reveal that the left side of the brain seems to control language, writing, logical thought, analysis, and mathematical abilities. The left side also processes information sequentially.

- The right side of the brain processes information globally and controls emotional expression, spatial perception, recognition of faces, patterns, melodies, and emotions. The left hemisphere can speak but the right cannot.

The Chemical Connection: The Endocrine Glands

2.14 How do the hormones released by glands interact with the nervous system and affect behavior?

- Endocrine glands secrete chemicals called hormones directly into the bloodstream, influencing the activity of the muscles and organs.

- The pituitary gland is found in the brain just below the hypothalamus. It has two parts, the anterior and the posterior. It controls the levels of salt and water in the system and, in women, the onset of labor and lactation, as well as secreting growth hormone and influencing the activity of the other glands.

- The pineal gland is also located in the brain. It secretes melatonin, a hormone that regulates the sleep–wake cycle in response to changes in light.

- The thyroid gland is located inside the neck. It controls metabolism (the burning of energy) by secreting thyroxin.

- The pancreas controls the level of sugar in the blood by secreting insulin and glucagons. Too much insulin produces hypoglycemia, whereas too little causes diabetes.

- The gonads are the ovaries in women and testes in men. They secrete hormones to regulate sexual growth, activity, and reproduction.

- The adrenal glands, one on top of each kidney, control the stress reaction through the adrenal medulla's secretion of epinephrine and norepinephrine. The adrenal cortex secretes over 30 different corticoids (hormones) controlling salt intake, stress, and sexual development.

Applying Psychology to Everyday Life: Differences Between Male and Female Brains

- Women seem to use both sides of their brains for most tasks, processing information not only analytically but globally as well, whereas men seem to use the left side of the brain for problem solving.

2 KEY TERMS

action potential 47
adrenal glands 74
agonists 50
all-or-none 48
amygdala 66
antagonists 50
association areas 69
autonomic nervous system (ANS) 56
axon 45
axon terminals 49
Broca's aphasia 69
central nervous system 53
cerebellum 64
cerebral hemispheres 67
cerebrum 70
computed tomography (CT) 62
corpus callosum 67
cortex 66
deep lesioning 60
dendrites 45
electroencephalograph (EEG) 60
endocrine glands 72
excitatory neurotransmitter 50
frontal lobes 68
glial cells 46
gonads 74

hippocampus 65
hormones 72
hypothalamus 65
inhibitory neurotransmitter 50
interneuron 54
limbic system 65
magnetic resonance imaging (MRI) 62
medulla 63
motor cortex 68
motor neuron 54
motor pathway 56
myelin 46
nerves 46
nervous system 44
neuron 45
neuroscience 45
neurotransmitter 50
occipital lobe 67
olfactory bulbs 65
ovaries 74
pancreas 73
parasympathetic division 57
parietal lobes 67
peripheral nervous system (PNS) 56
pineal gland 73
pituitary gland 73

pons 63
positron emission tomography (PET) 62
receptor sites 50
reflex arc 54
resting potential 47
reticular formation (RF) 64
reuptake 52
sensory neuron 54
sensory pathway 56
soma 45
somatic nervous system 56
somatosensory cortex 67
spatial neglect 69
spinal cord 53
stem cells 55
sympathetic division
   (fight-or-flight system) 57
synapse (synaptic gap) 50
synaptic knob 49
synaptic vesicles 49
temporal lobes 67
testes 74
thalamus 65
thyroid gland 73
Wernicke's aphasia 69

TEST YOURSELF

Pick the best answer.

1. In the structure of the neuron, the _____ sends information to other cells.
   a. axon
   b. dendrite
   c. soma
   d. myelin

2. Which type of cell makes up 10 percent of the brain?
   a. glial cells
   b. neurons
   c. stem cells
   d. afferent cells

3. Damaged nerve fibers in the body can repair themselves because they are coated with _____, which forms a protective tunnel around the nerve fibers.
   a. glial
   b. soma
   c. myelin
   d. neurilemma

4. When a neuron is in the resting potential state, where are the sodium ions?
   a. inside the cell
   b. outside the cell
   c. inside the soma
   d. in the synapse

5. How does one neuron communicate with another neuron?
   a. An electrical spark jumps over the gap between cells.
   b. Charged particles leap from one cell to the next.
   c. Chemicals in the end of one neuron float across the gap to fit into holes on the next neuron.
   d. The end of one neuron extends to touch the other neuron.

6. Which neurotransmitter is associated with the control of the pain response?
   a. acetylcholine
   b. GABA
   c. serotonin
   d. endorphin

7. Which of the following is the correct path of a reflex arc?
   a. motor neuron to interneuron to sensory neuron
   b. motor neuron to sensory neuron to interneuron
   c. sensory neuron to interneuron to motor neuron
   d. sensory neuron to motor neuron to the brain

8. Voluntary muscles are controlled by the _____ nervous system.
   a. somatic
   b. autonomic
   c. sympathetic
   d. parasympathetic

9. Your heart races. You begin to breathe faster. Your pupils enlarge and your appetite is gone. Your _____ division has just been activated.
   a. sympathetic
   b. parasympathetic
   c. autonomic
   d. somatic

10. The _____ division controls ordinary, day-to-day bodily functions.
   a. sympathetic
   b. parasympathetic
   c. central
   d. somatic

11. Which of the following techniques for imaging the brain would *not* be advisable for a person with a metal plate in his or her head?
   a. EEG
   b. CT
   c. MRI
   d. PET

12. Which technique of studying the brain actually damages neurons?
   a. EEG
   b. deep lesioning
   c. ESB
   d. MRI

13. Maria suffered a stroke that damaged a part of her brain. She fell into a sleeplike coma and cannot be awakened. If we know that the area of damage is somewhere in the brainstem, which structure is most likely damaged?
   a. medulla
   b. pons
   c. reticular formation
   d. cerebellum

14. Alex, who is two months old, is having his picture taken. The photographer tries to sit him up, but Alex keeps sinking down. Alex cannot sit upright yet because the _____ in his brainstem is not yet fully developed.
   a. medulla
   b. pons
   c. reticular formation
   d. cerebellum

15. Which sense is NOT sent to the cortex by the thalamus?
   a. hearing
   b. smell
   c. taste
   d. vision

16. Which part of the brain is the link between the brain and the glandular system?
   a. hippocampus
   b. thalamus
   c. hypothalamus
   d. amygdala

17. Jeff is undergoing brain surgery to remove a tumor. The surgeon applies electrical simulation to various areas around the tumor, causing Jeff to report tingling sensations in various areas of his skin. The tumor is most likely in which lobe of Jeff's brain?
   a. frontal
   b. temporal
   c. occipital
   d. parietal

18. George has a small stroke that results in a partial paralysis of his left side. The damaged area is most likely in his _____ lobe.
   a. right frontal
   b. left frontal
   c. right parietal
   d. left temporal

19. Linda is recovering from damage to her brain. Her main symptom is a speech problem; instead of saying, "I am going to P. T. (physical therapy) at nine o'clock" she says, "I go . . . P. T. . . . non o'cot." Linda's problem is
   a. spatial neglect
   b. visual agnosia
   c. Broca's aphasia
   d. Wernicke's aphasia

20. Recognizing the face of someone you run into at the mall is a function of the _____ hemisphere; being able to retrieve that person's name from memory is a function of the _____ hemisphere.
   a. left; right
   b. right; left
   c. right; right
   d. left; left

21. Heather is beautifully proportioned, but at 18 years of age she is still no taller than the average 10-year-old. Heather most likely had a problem in her _____ gland(s) while she was growing up.
   a. pituitary
   b. adrenal
   c. thyroid
   d. pineal

22. The action of hormones in the bloodstream is most similar to which of the following?
   a. the action of sodium ions in the action potential
   b. the action of myelin surrounding the axons
   c. the action of glial cells in the brain
   d. the action of neurotransmitters in the synapse

23. Melatonin is secreted by the _____ gland(s).
   a. pituitary
   b. adrenal
   c. thyroid
   d. pineal

24. Which of the following differences between male and female brains has not been supported by research?
   a. Women use both sides of the brain in processing language.
   b. Women recover from strokes more quickly and completely than do men.
   c. The corpus callosum is bigger in men than in women.
   d. The hypothalamus is larger in men than in women.

Answers: 1-a, 2-b, 3-d, 4-b, 5-c, 6-d, 7-c, 8-a, 9-a, 10-b, 11-c, 12-b, 13-c, 14-d, 15-b, 16-c, 17-d, 18-a, 19-c, 20-b, 21-a, 22-d, 23-d, 24-c.

For more sample quizzes and other review activities that will help you get a better grade, be sure to check out your accompanying study guide. To access tests and your own personalized study plan that will help you focus on the areas you need to master before your next class test, be sure to go to the on-line Psychology web site available with the access code packaged with your book.

CONCEPT MAP

The Nervous System
Complex neural network carrying information in your body

2.1

Neurons and Nerves: Building the Network

Structure of the Neuron

Composition of Neurons:
▶ Dendrites, which receive input
▶ Soma or cell body
▶ Axons, which carry neural messages to other cells

Glial cells: separate, support, and insulate the neurons

Myelin: insulates and protects axons and speeds transmission

Nerves: axons bundle together in "cables"

2.2

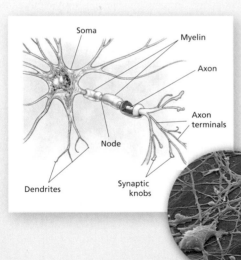

Soma
Myelin
Axon
Axon terminals
Node
Dendrites
Synaptic knobs

The Neural Impulse and Synapse

Action Potentials
At rest:
▶ Neuron is negatively charged on the inside
▶ Outside of the cell is positively charged

Action potential:
▶ Neurons fire in an all-or-nothing manner
  Excitatory transmitters allow positive sodium ions to enter the cell leading to the action potential

Sending the Message to Other Cells: The Synapse
▶ Synaptic vesicles are found at the end of the axon terminal
▶ Action potentials cause transmitter release from the axon terminal
▶ Neurotransmitter molecules fit into dendrites' receptor, stimulating or inhibiting that cell

2.3

Neurotransmitters: Messengers of the Network

Acetylcholine: Stimulates muscle, memory formation

GABA (γ-aminobutyric acid) inhibitory transmitter

Serotonin: associated with sleep, mood, and appetite

Endorphin: neural regulator for pain responses

Dopamine: movement, pleasure sensations

Cleaning Up the Synapse: Reuptake and Enzymes
▶ Most neurotransmitters are taken back into the synaptic vesicles during reuptake
▶ Acetylcholine is cleared out of the synapse by enzymes that break up the molecules

2.4

The Peripheral Nervous System

Somatic Nervous System
▶ Sensory pathway neurons —messages to central nervous system
▶ Motor pathway neurons —central nervous system to voluntary muscles

2.6

Autonomic Nervous System: Its Two Divisions
▶ Sympathetic division is our fight-or-flight system, reacting to stress
▶ Parasympathetic division restores and maintains normal functioning

2.7

The Central Nervous System

The Brain and Spinal Cord

Spinal cord serves two functions:
▸ Transmits messages to and from the brain ▸ Controls life-saving reflexes

2.5

The Brain Stem

Medulla: life-sustaining functions (i.e., breathing, heart rate)

Pons: involved in sleep, dreaming, arousal, coordination of movement

Reticular formation: involved in selective attention and arousal

Cerebellum: motor movement, learned reflexes, posture

2.9

Structures Under the Cortex

Limbic system: thalamus, hypothalamus, hippocampus, amygdala, fornix

Thalamus: switching station that sends sensory information to areas of cortex

Hypothalamus: hunger, thirst, sleep, sexual behavior, sleeping–waking, emotions, pituitary gland

Hippocampus: storing memories and remembering locations of objects

Amygdala: fear responses and memory of fearful stimuli

Fornix: pleasure center, connects hippocampus to cortex

2.10

Studying the Brain

Deep lesioning: destroys certain areas of the brain

ESB: electrical stimulation of the brain

Case studies. EEGs: measure activity of the brain through microelectrodes

CT scans: computer-aided X-rays

MRI: use magnetic energy to measure brain activity

PET scans: use a radioactive sugar to track the activity of brain cells

2.8

MRI

CT scan

PET scan

EEG

The Cortex

▸ Outer covering of the brain
▸ Tightly packed layer of neurons: .01 inch in thickness.
▸ Corticalization or wrinkles allows for greater cortical area
▸ Two cerebral hemispheres connected by corpus callosum

The Cerebral Hemispheres: Are You in Your Right Mind?

Split-brain patients: corpus callosum severed to control epilepsy

Left hemisphere: language, writing, logical thought, information processed sequentially

Right hemisphere: processes information globally, emotional expression, spatial perception, recognition of faces, patterns, melodies, and emotions

2.13

Senses and Movement

Occipital lobe: contains the primary visual cortex

Parietal lobe: somatasensory area, body and chemical senses

Temporal lobe: primary auditory area

Frontal lobe: motor cortex

2.11

Higher Forms of Thought and Language

Association areas: integration of cortical processing

Broca's area: left frontal lobe produces fluent speech.

Wernicke's area: left temporal lobe— understands language

2.12

The Chemical Connection: The Endocrine Glands

Endocrine glands secrete hormones to influence activity of muscles and organs.

Pituitary gland: growth hormone and influences other glands

Pineal gland: melatonin, regulates sleep–wake cycle

Thyroid gland: metabolism by secreting thyroxin

Pancreas: blood sugar by secreting insulin and glucagons

Gonads: hormones regulate sexual growth, activity, reproduction

Adrenal glands: stress reaction with epinephrine and norepinephrine

Adrenal cortex: salt intake, stress, and sexual development

2.14

3

Sensation and Perception

Seeing Sounds and Hearing Colors: Synesthesia

"*There was a piece of music by a group called Uman. The first note was grey and it was like a band of grey with a slight curve to it, and it was a gradient—light grey going to dark grey—it had gold specks on it. The background was black but it was being broken up by other colours, moving shapes of fuchsia and there was a small sound like a click, almost like a drumbeat, something being struck, and as it was struck, a black shape appeared, and the shapes appeared from left to right, going horizontally across the bottom of this—like a movie screen that I was watching. And the shapes were so exquisite, so simple, so pure and so beautiful, I wanted somehow to be able to capture them, but they were moving too quickly and I couldn't remember them all.*"

—Carol Steen (1996), New York artist and synesthete, quoted from ABC Radio National Transcripts, Health Report with Robin Hughes

Ms. Steen is a most unusual artist because she is able to perceive a world where sounds have colors and shapes, an ability she often turns into unusual and beautiful sculptures. A *synesthete* is a person with **synesthesia**, which literally means "joined sensation." People with this condition are rare—about 1 in 25,000. In the synesthete, the signals that come from the sensory organs, such as the eyes or the ears, go to places in the brain in which they weren't originally meant to be, causing those signals to be interpreted as more than one sensation. A fusion of sound and sight is most common, but touch, taste, and even smell can enter into the mix (Cytowic, 1989).

synesthesia
disorder in which the signals from the various sensory organs are processed in the wrong cortical areas, resulting in the sense information being interpreted as more than one sensation.

Why study sensation and perception?

Without sensations to tell us what is outside our own mental world, we would live entirely in our own minds, separate from one another and unable to find food or any other basics that sustain life. Sensations are the mind's window to the world that exists around us. Without perception, we would be unable to understand what all those sensations mean—perception is the process of interpreting the sensations we experience so that we can act upon them.

The ABCs of Sensation

How do we get information from the outside world into our brains? ▶

How do we get information from the outside world into our brains? There is so much information in the world outside the body and brain. That information has to have a way to get into the brain, where it can be used to determine actions and responses. The way into the brain is through the sensory organs and the process of sensation.

WHAT IS SENSATION?

3.1 *What is sensation and how does it enter the central nervous system?*

Sensation is the activation of receptors in the various sense organs. Let's take a closer look at these receptors.

sensation
the activation of receptors in the various sense organs.

just noticeable difference (jnd or the difference threshold)
the smallest difference between two stimuli that is detectable 50 percent of the time.

Light energy enters through the hole in the iris to stimulate the sensory receptors at the back of the eye. *transduction*

SENSORY RECEPTORS The *sensory receptors* are specialized forms of neurons, the cells that make up the nervous system. Instead of receiving neurotransmitters from other cells, these receptor cells are stimulated by different kinds of energy—for example, the receptors in the eyes are triggered by light, whereas vibrations trigger the receptors in the ears.

SENSORY THRESHOLDS

The various sense organs—eyes, ears, nose, skin, and taste buds—are actually quite sensitive to stimulation. People have been investigating sensory abilities for a long time. Ernst Weber (1795–1878) did studies trying to determine the smallest difference between two weights that could be detected. His research led to the formulation known as Weber's law of **just noticeable differences** (**jnd**, or the **difference threshold**). A jnd is the smallest difference between two *plural* stimuli that is detectable 50 percent of the time, and Weber's law simply means that whatever the difference between stimuli might be, it is always a constant—in other words, if the amount of sugar a person would need to add to a cup of coffee that is already sweetened with 5 teaspoons is 1 teaspoon, then the percentage of change needed to detect a just noticeable difference is $\frac{1}{5}$, or 20 percent. So

TABLE 3.1 EXAMPLES OF ABSOLUTE THRESHOLDS	
Sense	**Threshold**
Sight	A candle flame at 30 miles on a clear, dark night
Hearing	The tick of a watch 20 feet away in a quiet room
Smell	One drop of perfume diffused throughout a three-room apartment
Taste	1 teaspoon of sugar in 2 gallons of water
Touch	A bee's wing falling on the cheek from 1 centimeter above

if the coffee has 10 teaspoons of sugar in it, the person would have to add another 20 percent, or 2 teaspoons, to be able to taste the difference half of the time.

Gustav Fechner (1801–1887) expanded on Weber's work by studying something he called the **absolute threshold** (Fechner, 1860). An absolute threshold is the smallest amount of energy needed for a person to consciously detect a stimulus 50 percent of the time it is present. (Remember, the jnd is detecting a difference *between two* stimuli.) For example, how much salt must be added to a glass of water before the change in taste can be detected in at least half of the taste tests? For some examples of absolute thresholds for various senses, see Table 3.1.

I've heard about people being influenced by stuff in movies and on television, things that are just below the level of conscious awareness. Is that true?

SUBLIMINAL PERCEPTION Stimuli that are below the level of conscious awareness are called *subliminal stimuli*. (The word *limin* means "threshold," so *sublimin* means "below the threshold.") These stimuli are just strong enough to activate the sensory receptors but not strong enough for people to be consciously aware of them. Many people believe that these stimuli act upon the unconscious mind, influencing behavior in a process called *subliminal perception*.

Although the following story is now widely recognized as false, it has taken on the status of an urban legend—a story that is so often repeated that people have come to believe that it is true. The story highlights the fears that many people had concerning subliminal perception when psychologists first introduced the concept. The story goes like this: In 1957 a market researcher named James Vicary claimed that over a six-week period, 45,699 patrons at a movie theater in Fort Lee, New Jersey, were shown two advertising messages, *Eat Popcorn* and *Drink Coca-Cola*, while they watched the film *Picnic*. According to Vicary, these messages were flashed for 0.003 second once every 5 seconds. Vicary claimed that over the six-week period the sales of popcorn rose 57.7 percent and the sales of Coca-Cola rose 18.1 percent.

For years, Vicary's claims were often accepted as established facts. The real truth? Vicary never described his study in print. Real researchers were unable to duplicate his findings. Finally, in an interview with *Advertising Age* in 1962, Vicary admitted what many researchers had long suspected: The original study was a complete deception—he never did it (Merikle, 2000; Pratkanis, 1992). Researchers have gathered scientific evidence that subliminal perception does not work in advertising (Bargh et al., 1996; Moore, 1988; Pratkanis & Greenwald, 1988; Trappey, 1996; Vokey & Read, 1985).

So advertisers aren't really trying to control or influence our minds through subliminal perception? Although some advertisers may have tried this, the real world is full of complex motives that are not as easily influenced as one might think (Pratkanis, 1992). Even the so-called "hidden pictures" that some artists airbrush into the art

Experiment
Live! psych
Weber's Law

absolute threshold
the smallest amount of energy needed for a person to consciously detect a stimulus 50 percent of the time it is present.

◄ I've heard about people being influenced by stuff in movies and on television, things that are just below the level of conscious awareness. Is that true?

So advertisers aren't really trying to control or influence our minds
◄ through subliminal perception?

An office area as crowded and busy as this one is full of noise, from conversations to machinery. These office workers are able to concentrate on their own work because they have been habituated to all of the constant noise around them.

This young woman does not feel the piercings on her ear and nose because sensory adaptation allows her to ignore a constant, unchanging stimulation from the metal rings. What else is she wearing that would cause sensory adaptation?

Is that why sometimes I ▶ can smell the odor of the garbage can in the kitchen when I first come home, but after a while the smell seems to go away?

You mean if I stare at ▶ something long enough, it will disappear?

in advertisements aren't truly subliminal—if someone points it out, it can be seen easily enough. Hey, if subliminal study perception really really worked, don't you think that hard authors of textbooks send in psychology me would be some money of the first people to use it?

HABITUATION AND SENSORY ADAPTATION

3.2 *How can some sensations be ignored?*

In Chapter Two, it was stated that the lower centers of the brain sort through sensory stimulation and "ignore" or prevent conscious attention to stimuli that do not change. The brain is only interested in changes in information. That's why people don't really "hear" the noise of the air conditioner unless it suddenly cuts off or the noise made in some classrooms unless it gets very quiet. Although they actually are *hearing* it, they aren't paying attention to it. This is called **habituation** and it is the way the brain deals with unchanging information. L I N K *to Chapter Two: The Biological Perspective, p. 64.*

Is that why sometimes I can smell the odor of the garbage can in the kitchen when I first come home, but after a while the smell seems to go away? The process by which constant and unchanging information from the senses of taste, touch, smell, and vision is "ignored" is a different process from habituation. The difference is that for taste, touch, smell, and vision, any sensory stimulus that does not change is ignored by the actual sensory receptors, not by the lower part of the brain (as in habituation). In **sensory adaptation**, the sensory receptor cells become less responsive to an unchanging stimulus. Without sensory adaptation, clothes would probably drive people crazy because they would be constantly aware of every piece of clothing or jewelry they have on. They would feel the seat of the chair they are sitting on constantly instead of just when they move. Bad odors like the garbage can smell would never go away.

For example, when you eat, the food that you put in your mouth tastes strong at first, but as you keep eating the same thing, the taste does fade somewhat, doesn't it?

You mean if I stare at something long enough, it will disappear? No; the eyes are a little different. Even though the sensory receptors in the back of the eyes would adapt to and become less responsive to a constant visual stimulus, under ordinary circumstances the eyes are never that still. There's a constant movement of the eyes, tiny little vibrations called *saccades* that people don't notice consciously. These movements keep the eyes from adapting to what they see. That's a good thing, because otherwise many students would no doubt go blind from staring off into space.

PRACTICE QUIZ: HOW MUCH DO YOU REMEMBER?

Pick the best answer.

1. The smallest difference between two stimuli that can be detected 50 percent of the time it is present is called
   a. absolute threshold.
   c. sensation.
   b. just noticeable difference.
   d. sensory adaptation.

2. When receptor cells for the senses are activated, the process called _____ has begun.
   a. perception
   c. adaptation
   b. sublimination
   d. sensation

3. You have a piece of candy that you are holding in your mouth. After a while, the candy doesn't taste as strong as it did when you first tasted it. What has happened?
   a. sensory adaptation
   c. threshold adaptation
   b. subliminal perception
   d. perceptual defense

4. Vicary's study of subliminal advertising was remarkable in that
   a. it demonstrated the usefulness of subliminal perception.
   b. people actually bought more colas and popcorn after seeing the movie.
   c. the subliminal stimuli had no effect on buying behavior.
   d. it never happened.

5. Which of your senses does not adapt to a constant stimulus at the level of the receptor cells?
   a. vision
   b. touch
   c. hearing
   d. smell

Answers: 1-b, 2-d, 3-a, 4-d, 5-c.

The Science of Seeing

I've heard that light is waves, but I've also heard that light is made of particles—which is it? Light is a complicated phenomenon. Although scientists have long argued over the nature of light, they finally have agreed that light has the properties of both waves and particles. The following section gives a brief history of how scientists have tried to "shed light" on the mystery of light.

PSYCHOLOGICAL PROPERTIES OF LIGHT: CATCHING THE WAVES

3.3   *What is light?*

Although Isaac Newton believed light to be a function of particles, in 1802 Thomas Young demonstrated that light behaves like waves. Research at the turn of the twentieth century provided evidence for both views—sometimes light behaves like particles and sometimes like waves. It was Albert Einstein who first demonstrated that light is actually both: He proposed tiny "packets" of waves called photons. These photons actually have wavelengths associated with them, hence, the wavelike properties (van der Merwe & Garuccio, 1994).

When people experience light, they are not really aware of its dual nature. There are three psychological aspects to the experience of light: *brightness, color,* and *saturation.*

Brightness is determined by the amplitude of the wave—how high or how low the wave actually is. The higher the wave, the brighter the light will be. Low waves are dimmer. *Color,* or hue, is determined by the length of the wave. Long wavelengths are found at the red end of the *visible spectrum* (the portion of the whole spectrum of light that is visible to the human eye; see Figure 3.1), whereas shorter wavelengths are found at the blue end. *Saturation* refers to the purity of the color people see: A highly saturated red, for example, would contain only red wavelengths, whereas a less saturated red might contain a mixture of wavelengths. For example, when a child is using the red paint from a set of poster paints, the paint on the paper will look like a pure red, but if the child mixes in some white paint, the paint will look pink. The hue is still red but it will be less of a saturated red because of the presence of white wavelengths. Mixing in black or gray would also lessen the saturation.

◀ I've heard that light is waves, but I've also heard that light is made of particles— which is it?

(handwritten notes:)
(brightness)
amplitude-↑=brighter
(hue)
frequency-wavelength

—most of what we see is a mixture

habituation
tendency of the brain to stop attending to constant, unchanging information.
sensory adaptation
tendency of sensory receptor cells to become less responsive to a stimulus that is unchanging.

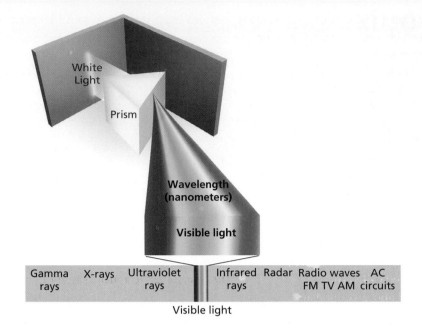

White
Light

Prism

**Wavelength
(nanometers)**

Visible light

| Gamma
rays | X-rays | Ultraviolet
rays | | Infrared
rays | Radar | Radio waves
FM TV AM | AC
circuits |

Visible light

FIGURE 3.1 **The Visible Spectrum**
The wavelengths that people can see
are only a small part of the whole
electromagnetic spectrum.

THE STRUCTURE OF THE EYE

> How does the eye ▶
> know how to interpret
> all of that information?

How does the eye know how to interpret all of that information? The best way to talk about how the eye processes light is to talk about what happens to an image being viewed as the photons of light from that image travel through the eye. Refer to Figure 3.2 to follow the path of the image.

3.4 *How do the parts of the eye work together?*

FROM FRONT TO BACK: THE PARTS OF THE EYE The surface of the eye is covered in a clear membrane called the *cornea*. The cornea not only protects the eye but also is the structure that focuses most of the light coming into the eye (the vision-improv-

Simulation
**Live!
psych**
Human Eye

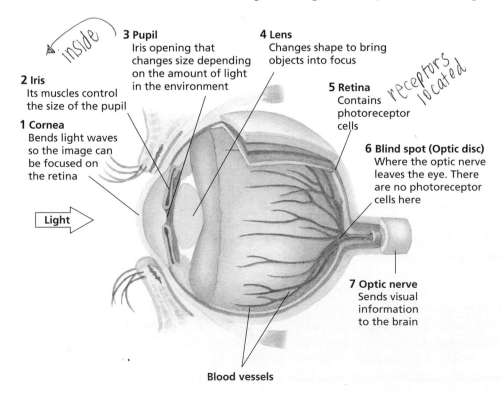

inside

3 Pupil
Iris opening that
changes size depending
on the amount of light
in the environment

4 Lens
Changes shape to bring
objects into focus

2 Iris
Its muscles control
the size of the pupil

5 Retina
Contains
photoreceptor
cells

receptors located

1 Cornea
Bends light waves
so the image can
be focused on
the retina

6 Blind spot (Optic disc)
Where the optic nerve
leaves the eye. There
are no photoreceptor
cells here

Light

7 Optic nerve
Sends visual
information
to the brain

Blood vessels

FIGURE 3.2 **Structure of the Eye**
Light enters the eye through the
cornea and pupil. The iris controls the
size of the pupil. From the pupil, light
passes through the lens to the retina,
where it is transformed into nerve
impulses. The nerve impulses travel to
the brain along the optic nerve.

ing technique called *radial kerototomy* actually uses this fact by making small incisions in the cornea to change the focus in the eye).

The next visual layer is a clear, watery fluid called the *aqueous humor*. This fluid is continually replenished and supplies nourishment to the eye. The light from the visual image then enters the interior of the eye through a hole, called the *pupil*, in a round muscle called the *iris* (the colored part of the eye). The iris can change the size of the pupil, letting more or less light into the eye. That also helps focus the image; people try to do the same thing by squinting.

Behind the iris, suspended by muscles, is another clear structure called the *lens*. The flexible lens finishes the focusing process begun by the cornea and can change its shape from thick to thin in a process called **visual accommodation**, which allows people to focus on objects that are close or far away as shown in Figure 3.3. People lose this ability as the lens hardens through aging (a process called *presbyopia*), causing the need for bifocals, because holding objects at arm's length can no longer be used to compensate.*

Once through the lens, light passes through a large, open space filled with a clear, jelly-like fluid called the *vitreous humor*. This fluid, like the aqueous humor, also nourishes the eye and gives it shape.

RETINA, RODS, AND CONES   The final stop for light within the eye is the *retina*, a light-sensitive area at the back of the eye containing three layers: ganglion** cells, bipolar cells, and the special cells (*photoreceptors*) that respond to the various light waves called **rods** and **cones**. (See Figure 3.4a.) The rods and the cones are the

light is stopped at photoreceptors

*Compensate: to correct for an error or defect.
**Ganglion: a mass of nerve tissue and cells in the peripheral nervous system.

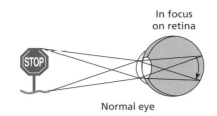

In focus
on retina

Normal eye

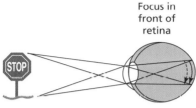

Focus in
front of
retina

Nearsighted eye

Focus
behind
retina

Farsighted eye

FIGURE 3.3   **Common Visual Problems: Nearsightedness and Farsightedness**   This shows the problem of focusing on distant objects when the eyeball is too long (nearsightedness), and the problem of focusing on near objects when the eyeball is too short (farsightedness).

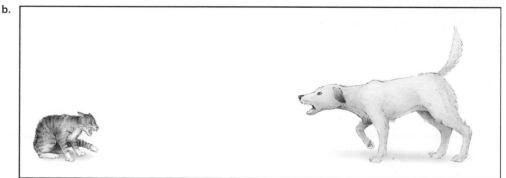

FIGURE 3.4   **The Parts of the Retina** (a) Light passes through ganglion and bipolar cells until it reaches and stimulates the rods and cones. Nerve impulses from the rods and cones travel along a nerve pathway to the brain. On the right of the figure is a photomicrograph of the long, thin rods and the shorter, thicker cones; the rods outnumber the cones by a ration of about twenty to one. (b) The blind spot demonstration. Hold the book in front of you. Close your right eye and stare at the picture of the dog with your left eye. Slowly bring the book closer to your face. The picture of the cat will disappear at some point, because the light from the picture of the cat is falling on your blind spot.

Sometimes when I "space out" and stare at a page, there's a blank spot that forms in what I'm staring at—what is that, adaptation? ▶

visual accommodation
the change in the thickness of the lens as the eye focuses on objects that are far away or close.

rods
visual sensory receptors found at the back of the retina, responsible for noncolor sensitivity to low levels of light.

cones *wavelength*
visual sensory receptors found at the back of the retina, responsible for color vision and sharpness of vision.

blind spot
area in the retina where the axons of the three layers of retinal cells exit the eye to form the optic nerve, insensitive to light.

business end of the retina—the part that actually receives the photons of light and turns them into neural signals to the brain, sending them first to the bipolar cells (called bipolar or "two-ended" because they connect the rods and cones to the cells in the optic nerve) and then to the ganglion cells that form the optic nerve with their axons. (See Figure 3.5.)

Sometimes when I "space out" and stare at a page, there's a blank spot that forms in what I'm staring at—what is that, adaptation?

THE BLIND SPOT The eyes don't adapt to constant stimuli under normal circumstances because of saccadic movements. But if people stare with one eye at one spot long enough, they may see a blank space form, because there is a "hole" in the retina—the place where all the axons of those ganglion cells leave the retina to become the optic nerve. There are no rods or cones here, so this is referred to as the **blind spot**. You can demonstrate the blind spot for yourself by following the directions in Figure 3.4b.

axons all meet @ blind spot

HOW THE EYE WORKS

3.5 *How do the eyes see, and how do the eyes see different colors?*

Rods and cones are each responsible for different aspects of vision. The rods (about 120 million of them in each eye) are found all over the retina except in the very center, which contains only cones. Rods are sensitive to changes in brightness but not to changes in wavelength, so they see only in black and white and shades of gray. They can be very sensitive because they are all on a "party line."

FIGURE 3.5 **Crossing of the Optic Nerve** Light rays enter the eyes to fall upon the retina. Light falling upon the left side of each eye's retina (from the right visual field, shown in yellow) will stimulate a neural message that will travel along the optic nerve to the left visual cortex in the occipital lobe of the left hemisphere. Notice that the message from the left eye goes directly to the left occipital lobe, while the message from the right eye crosses over to the left hemisphere (the optic chiasm is the point of crossover). The optic nerve tissue from both eyes joins together to form the left optic tract before going on to the left occipital lobe. For the left visual field (shown in blue), the messages from both right sides of the retinas will travel along the right optic track to the right visual cortex in the same manner.

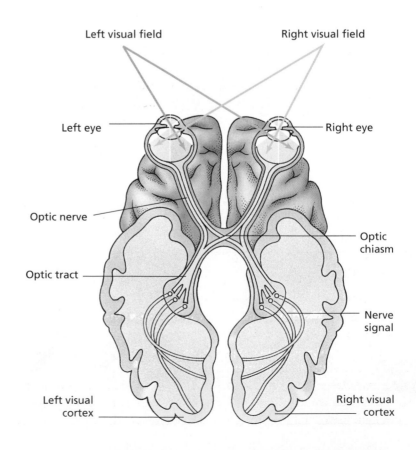

That means that many rods are hooked up to only one bipolar cell, so that if even only one rod is stimulated by a photon of light, the brain perceives the whole area of those rods as stimulated. But because the brain doesn't know exactly what part of the area is actually "calling in" the message, the visual acuity (sharpness) is pretty low. That's why things seen in low levels of light, such as twilight or a dimly lit room, are fuzzy and grayish. Because rods are located on the periphery of the retina, they are responsible for peripheral vision.

Because rods work well in low levels of light, they are also the cells that allow the eyes to adapt to low light. **Dark adaptation** occurs as the eye recovers its ability to see when going from a brightly lit state to a dark state. The brighter the light was, the longer it takes the rods to adapt to the new lower levels of light (Bartlett, 1965). This is why the bright headlights of an oncoming car can leave a person less able to see for a while after the oncoming car has passed. Fortunately, this is usually a temporary condition and the rods readapt to the dark night relatively quickly. Dark adaptation takes about 30 minutes and takes longer as people get older, causing many older persons to be less able to see at night and in darkened rooms (Klaver et al., 1998). This age-related change can cause *night blindness*, in which a person has difficulty seeing well enough to drive at night or get around in a darkened room or house. Some research indicates that taking supplements such as vitamin A can reverse or relieve this symptom in some cases (Jacobsen, et al. 1995).

When going from a darkened room to one that is brightly lit, the opposite process occurs. The cones have to adapt to the increased level of light, and they accomplish this **light adaptation** much more quickly than the rods adapt to darkness—it takes a few seconds at most (Hood, 1998). There are 6 million cones in each eye; of these, 50,000 have a private line to the optic nerve (one bipolar cell for each cone). This means that the cones, found in the very center of the retina in an area called the *fovea*, are the receptors for visual acuity. It also means that the cones need a lot more light to function than the rods do, so cones work best in bright light, which is also when people see things most clearly. Cones are also sensitive to different wavelengths of light, so they are responsible for color vision.

While this deer may see quite well when using its rods at night, the bright headlights of a car will activate the cones. The cones will take a few minutes to fully adapt to the brightness, leaving the deer blinded by the light until then.

dark adaptation
the recovery of the eye's sensitivity to visual stimuli in darkness after exposure to bright lights.

light adaptation
the recovery of the eye's sensitivity to visual stimuli in light after exposure to darkness.

trichromatic theory
theory of color vision that proposes three types of cones: red, blue, and green.

COLOR VISION

You said the cones are used in color vision. There are so many colors in the world—are there cones that detect each color? Or do all cones detect all colors? Although experts in the visual system have been studying color and its nature for many years, at this point in time there is an ongoing theoretical discussion about the role the cones play in the sensation of color.

THEORIES OF COLOR VISION   Two theories about how people see colors were originally proposed in the 1800s. The first is called the **trichromatic** ("three colors") **theory**. First proposed by Thomas Young in 1802 and later modified by Hermann von Helmholtz in 1852, this theory proposed three types of cones: red cones, blue cones, and green cones, one for each of the three primary colors of light.

Wait a minute—I thought the primary colors were red, yellow, and blue. Red, yellow, and blue are the primary colors when talking about *painting*—not when talking about light itself. Paints *reflect* light, and the way reflected light mixes is different

You said the cones are used in color vision. There are so many colors in the world—are ◄ there cones that detect each color? Or do all cones detect all colors?

Wait a minute—I thought the primary ◄ colors were red, yellow, and blue.

afterimages
images that occur when a visual sensation persists for a brief time even after the original stimulus is removed.

opponent-process theory
theory of color vision that proposes four primary colors with cones arranged in pairs: red and green, blue and yellow.

In trichromatic theory, the three types of cones combine to form different colors much as these three colored lights combine.

Hey, now the ▶
afterimage of the flag
has normal colors! Why
does this happen?

from the way direct light mixes. For example, if an artist were to blend red, yellow, and blue paints together, the result would be a mess—a black mess. But if the artist were to blend a red, green, and blue light together by focusing lights of those three colors on one common spot, the result would be white, not black.

In the trichromatic theory, different shades of colors correspond to different amounts of light received by each of these three types of cones. These cones then fire their message to the brain's vision centers. It is the combination of cones and the rate at which they are firing that determine the color that will be seen. For example, if the red and green cones are firing in response to a stimulus at fast enough rates, the color the person sees is yellow. If the red and blue cones are firing fast enough, the result is magenta. If the blue and green cones are firing fast enough, a kind of cyan color (blue-green) appears. Look again at Figure 3.1, the visible spectrum. Adding the long red wavelengths to the much shorter green ones will produce something in the middle—yellow.

In 1964, Brown and Wald identified three types of cones in the retina, each sensitive to one of the primary color wavelengths. The actual colors turn out to be just a little different from Young and Helmholtz's original three: Blue-violet, green-yellow, and yellow-red are the most sensitive wavelengths for these three cones.

THE AFTERIMAGE　The trichromatic theory would, at first glance, seem to be more than adequate to explain how people perceive color. But there's an interesting phenomenon that this theory cannot explain. If a person stares at a picture of the American flag for a little while—say, a minute—and then looks away to a blank white wall or sheet of paper, that person will see an **afterimage** of the flag. Afterimages occur when a visual sensation persists for a brief time even after the original stimulus is removed. The person would also notice rather quickly that the colors of the "flag" in the afterimage are all wrong—green for red, black for white, and yellow for blue. If you follow the directions for Figure 3.6, in which the "flag" is yellow, green, and black, you should see a flag with the usual red, white, and blue.

Hey, now the afterimage of the flag has normal colors! Why does this happen? The phenomenon of the color afterimage is explained by the second theory of color perception, called the **opponent-process theory** (De Valois & Jacobs, 1968; Hurvich, 1969). In this theory, there are actually four primary colors: red, green, blue, and yellow. The cones are arranged in pairs, red with green and blue with yellow. If

FIGURE 3.6　**Color Afterimage**
Stare at the white dot in the center of this oddly colored flag for about thirty seconds. Now look at a white piece of paper or a white wall. Notice that the colors are now the normal, expected colors of the American flag. They are also the primary colors that are opposites of the colors in the picture, and evidence for the opponent process theory of color vision.

one member of a pair is stimulated, the other member cannot be working—so there are no reddish-greens or bluish-yellows.

So how does this cause the color afterimage? If a person tires out one of the members of the pairs (by looking at a red image for about a minute, for example), it weakens that member's ability to inhibit the other cell. When the person then looks away from the red image, there will be a green afterimage as the other member of the pair fires away.

So which theory is the right one? Both theories play a part in color vision. Recently scientists have found that opponent process cells are contained inside the thalamus in an area called the lateral geniculate nucleus (LGN). The LGN is part of the pathway that visual information takes to the occipital lobe. It is when the cones in the retina send signals through the bipolar and retinal ganglion cells that we see the red vs. green pairings and blue vs. yellow pairings. This wave of color processing is then sent up the optic nerve to the thalamus. Together with the retinal cells, the cells in the LGN appear to be the ones responsible for opponent-processing of color vision and the afterimage effect.

So which theory accounts for color blindness? I've heard that there are two kinds of color blindness, people who can't tell red from green and people who can't tell blue from yellow.

COLOR BLINDNESS   From the mention of red-green and yellow-blue color blindness, one might think that the opponent-process theory explains this problem. But in reality color blindness is caused by defective cones in the retina of the eye.

There are really three kinds of color blindness. In a very rare type called *monochrome color blindness*, people either have no cones or have cones that are not working at all. Essentially, if they have cones, they only have one type and, therefore, everything looks the same to the brain—shades of gray. The other two types are caused by the same kind of problem—having one cone that does not

cones = color   rods = black, white, gray

◄ So which **theory is the right one?**

So which **theory accounts for color blindness? I've heard**
◄ **that there are two kinds of color blindness, people who can't tell red from green and people who can't tell blue from yellow.**

The painting on the left was done by a person with normal (trichromatic) color vision. The painting on the right was done by a person with dichromatic red-green color blindness.
Source: From Oliver Sacks's story "The Case of the Colorblind Person" in his book *An Anthropologist on Mars* (1995).

This is the same scene painted by a *monochromat*, a person who sees no color at all. Although some monochromats have no functioning cones and see very poorly, others are like this person and have some functioning cones allowing them to have visual acuity.

FIGURE 3.7 **The Ishihara Color Test**
In the circle on the left, the number 8 is visible only to those with normal color vision. In the circle on the right, people with normal vision will see the number 96, while those with red-green color blindness will see nothing but a circle of dots.

work. If people have *red-green color blindness*, either their red or their green cones are not working. They would see the world in blues, yellows, and shades of gray. If the blue cones are not working, which is less common, they see reds, greens, and shades of gray. To get an idea of what a test for color blindness is like, look at Figure 3.7.

▶ Why are most of the people who are color-blind men?

Why are most of the people who are color-blind men? Because color blindness of one set of cones is inherited in a pattern known as *sex-linked inheritance*, men are much more likely to inherit this disorder than are women. Men can inherit it from their mother's X chromosome* only, whereas women must inherit two defective genes to be color blind.

_____

*X chromosome: chromosome found in the twenty-third pair of chromosomes, associated with female sexual characteristics.

PRACTICE **QUIZ:** HOW MUCH DO YOU REMEMBER?

Pick the best answer.

1. Which of the following terms refers to the psychological effect of the amplitude of light waves?
   a. color
   b. brightness
   c. saturation
   d. hue

2. Which of the following represents the correct path of light through the eye?
   a. iris, cornea, lens, retina
   b. cornea, vitreous humor, iris, lens, aqueous humor, retina
   c. cornea, pupil, lens, vitreous humor, retina
   d. cornea, lens, pupil, iris, retina

3. If you wanted to see a star better at night, what should you do?
   a. Look directly at it, because the cones will focus better at night.
   b. Look off to the side, using the cones in the periphery of the retina.
   c. Look directly at it, because the rods can see sharply at night.
   d. Look off to the side, using the rods in the periphery of the retina.

4. Which theory of color vision accounts better for the afterimage?
   a. trichromatic theory
   b. opponent-process theory
   c. both of the above
   d. neither of the above

5. Which statement about color blindness is true?
   a. There are more men who are color-blind than women.
   b. All color-blind people see only in black and white.
   c. Some color-blind people see only in blue.
   d. Some color-blind people see only in blue and red.

The Hearing Sense: Can You Hear Me Now?

If light works like waves, then do sound waves have similar properties? The properties of sound are indeed similar to those of light, as both senses rely on waves. But the similarity ends there, as the physical properties of sound are different from those of light.

PSYCHOLOGICAL PROPERTIES OF SOUND

3.6   *What is sound?*

Sound waves do not come in little packets the way light comes in photons. Sound waves are simply the vibrations of the molecules of air that surround us. Sound waves do have the same properties of light waves, though—wavelength, amplitude, and *purity*. Wavelengths are interpreted by the brain as the frequency or pitch (high, medium, or low). Amplitude is interpreted as *volume*, how soft or loud a sound is. (See Figure 3.8.) Finally, what would correspond to saturation or purity in light is

◀ If light works like waves, then do sound waves have similar properties?

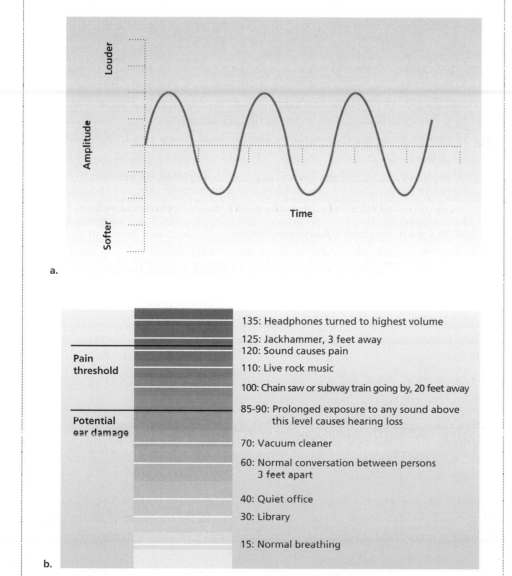

a.

b.

FIGURE 3.8   **Sound Waves and Decibels**   (a) A typical sound wave. The higher the wave, the louder the sound; the lower the wave, the softer the sound. If the waves are close together in time (high frequency), the pitch will be perceived as a high pitch. Waves that are farther apart (low frequency) will be perceived as having a lower pitch. (b) Decibels of various stimuli. A *decibel* is a unit of measure for loudness. Psychologists study the effects that noise has on stress, learning, performance, aggression, and psychological and physical well-being. Research on the hazards of loud noises led the National Basketball Association to put an 85-decibel limit on the sound system played at basketball arenas (Heisler, 1995).

135: Headphones turned to highest volume

125: Jackhammer, 3 feet away
120: Sound causes pain

110: Live rock music

100: Chain saw or subway train going by, 20 feet away

85-90: Prolonged exposure to any sound above this level causes hearing loss

70: Vacuum cleaner

60: Normal conversation between persons 3 feet apart

40: Quiet office

30: Library

15: Normal breathing

Pain threshold

Potential ear damage

"And only you can hear this whistle?"

© The New Yorker Collection 1998 Charles Barsotti from cartoonbank.com. All Rights Reserved.

Is there a pathway ▶ **through the ear, like the layers of the eye?**

Human Ear

called *timbre* in sound, a richness in the tone of the sound. And just as people rarely see pure colors in the world around us, they also seldom hear pure sounds. The everyday noises that surround people do not allow them to hear many pure tones.

Just as a person's vision is limited by the visible spectrum of light, a person is also limited in the range of frequencies he or she can hear. Frequency is measured in cycles (waves) per second, or **hertz (Hz)**. Human limits are between 20 and 20,000 Hz, with the most accurate hearing occurring at around 1,000 Hz. (In comparison, dogs can hear between 50 and 60,000 Hz, whereas dolphins can hear up to 200,000 Hz.) To hear the higher and lower frequencies of a piece of music on a CD, for example, a person would need to increase the amplitude—which explains why some people like to "crank it up."

Is there a pathway through the ear, like the layers of the eye?

THE STRUCTURE OF THE EAR: FOLLOW THE VIBES

The ear is a series of structures, each of which plays a part in the sense of hearing, as shown in Figure 3.9.

3.7 *How do the parts of the ear work together to hear sounds?*

THE OUTER EAR　The *pinna* is the visible, external part of the ear that serves as a kind of concentrator, funneling* the sound waves from the outside into the structure of the ear. People try to mimic this function when they curl their hand around their ear to hear better—they're trying to make the pinna larger.

The pinna is the entrance to the **auditory canal** (or ear canal), the short tunnel that runs down to the *tympanic membrane*, or eardrum. The eardrum is a thin section of skin that tightly covers the opening into the middle part of the ear, just like a drum skin covers the opening in a drum. And just like that drum skin, when sound waves hit the eardrum, it vibrates and causes three tiny bones in the middle ear to vibrate.

THE MIDDLE EAR　Hammer, Anvil, and Stirrup　The three tiny bones in the middle ear are known collectively as the *auditory ossicles* and individually as the hammer, anvil, and stirrup. The names come from the shape of each of the bones. When the eardrum vibrates, the hammer resting against the eardrum also vibrates, causing a chain reaction in the anvil and the stirrup. As the vibrations travel down the bones, they are amplified somewhat. The stirrup, the last bone in the chain, rests against another membrane of tissue called the *oval window*, which in turn covers the entrance to the inner ear.

THE INNER EAR　The oval window vibrates when the stirrup vibrates, setting up another chain reaction within the inner ear.

Cochlea　The inner ear is a snail-shaped structure called the **cochlea**, which is filled with fluid. When the oval window vibrates, it causes the fluid in the cochlea to vibrate. This fluid surrounds a membrane running through the middle of the cochlea called the *basilar membrane*.

Basilar Membrane and the Organ of Corti　The basilar membrane is the resting place of the *organ of Corti*, which contains the receptor cells for the sense of hearing. When the basilar membrane vibrates, it vibrates the organ of Corti, causing it to brush

hertz (Hz)
cycles or waves per second, a measurement of frequency.

auditory canal
short tunnel that runs from the pinna to the eardrum.

cochlea
snail-shaped structure of the inner ear that is filled with fluid.

_____

*Funneling: moving to a focal point.

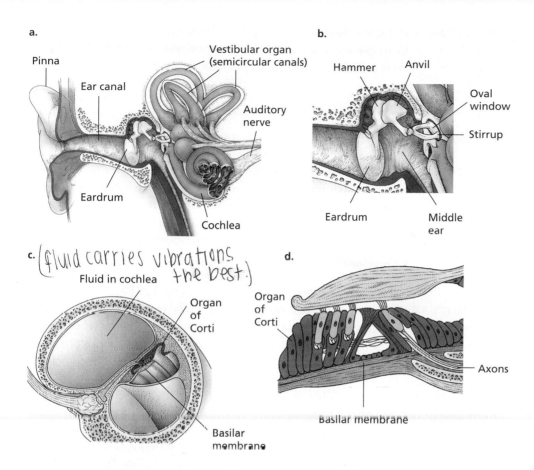

a.
Pinna
Ear canal
Vestibular organ (semicircular canals)
Auditory nerve
Eardrum
Cochlea

b.
Hammer
Anvil
Oval window
Stirrup
Eardrum
Middle ear

c. *(fluid carries vibrations the best.)*
Fluid in cochlea
Organ of Corti
Basilar membrane

d.
Organ of Corti
Axons
Basilar membrane

FIGURE 3.9   **The Structure of the Ear**   (a) This figure shows the entire ear, beginning with the outer ear (pinna, ear canal, and eardrum). The vestibular organ includes the semicircular canals and the otolith organs (inside the round structures just above the cochlea). (b) The middle ear. Sound waves entering through the ear canal cause the eardrum to vibrate, which causes each of the three bones of the middle ear to vibrate, amplifying the sound. The stirrup rests upon the oval window, which transmits its vibration to the fluid in the inner ear. (c) The inner ear. Large spaces are filled with fluid (shown in purple) that vibrates as the oval window vibrates. A thin membrane suspended in this fluid is called the basilar membrane, which contains the organ of Corti, the structure composed of the hair-like cells that send signals to the auditory cortex of the brain by way of the auditory nerve. (d) A close-up view of the basilar membrane (in brown) with the hair cells of the organ of Corti (in dark purple). Notice the axons (small black lines) leaving the hair cells to form the auditory nerve.

against a membrane above it. On the organ of Corti are special cells called *hair cells,* which are the receptors for sound. When these auditory receptors or hair cells are bent up against the other membrane, it causes them to send a neural message through the **auditory nerve** (which contains the axons of all the receptor neurons) and into the brain, where the auditory cortex will interpret the sounds.

(hair cells vibrated trigger sense receptors for sound.)

Thus, the sound waves go in through the pinna and vibrate the eardrum, which then vibrates the hammer, anvil, and stirrup, which in turn vibrate the oval window. This causes the fluid in the cochlea to vibrate, which vibrates the basilar membrane, which then causes the organ of Corti to move up and bend its hair cells, which send signals about hearing to the brain. Of course, the louder the sound in the outside world, the stronger the vibrations that stimulate more of those hair cells, which the brain interprets as loudness.

summary of sound waves going through the ear to brain.

auditory nerve
bundle of axons from the hair cells in the inner ear.

I think I have it ▶ straight— but all of that just explains how soft and loud sounds get to the brain from the outside. How do we hear different kinds of sounds, like high pitches and low pitches?

So the place theory works for pitches above 1,000 Hz, and the frequency theory works for pitches up to 100 Hz. What happens in between? ▶

pitch
psychological experience of sound that corresponds to the frequency of the sound waves; higher frequencies are perceived as higher pitches.

place theory
theory of pitch that states that different pitches are experienced by the stimulation of hair cells in different locations on the organ of Corti.

frequency theory
theory of pitch that states that pitch is related to the speed of vibrations in the basilar membrane.

volley principle
theory of pitch that states that frequencies above 100 Hz cause the hair cells (auditory neurons) to fire in a volley pattern, or take turns in firing.

I think I have it straight—but all of that just explains how soft and loud sounds get to the brain from the outside. How do we hear different kinds of sounds, like high pitches and low pitches?

THEORIES OF PITCH

Pitch, refers to how high or low a sound is. There are two theories about how the brain receives information about pitch.

PLACE THEORY: HEARING IN HIGH PLACES   The older **place theory** was proposed in 1863 by Hermann von Helmholtz of the Young-Helmholtz theory of color vision fame. In this theory, the pitch a person hears depends on where the hair cells that are stimulated are located on the organ of Corti. For example, if the person is hearing a high-pitched sound, all of the hair cells near the oval window will be stimulated, but if the sound is low pitched, all of the hair cells that are stimulated will be located farther away on the organ of Corti.

[handwritten: Problem: organ of corti cannot vibrate @ 20000 Hertz]

FREQUENCY THEORY: THE LOW-DOWN ON PITCH   The **frequency theory**, developed by Ernest Rutherford in 1886, states that pitch is related to how fast the basilar membrane vibrates. The faster this membrane vibrates, the higher the pitch; the slower it vibrates, the lower the pitch. (In this theory, all of the auditory neurons would be firing at the same time.)

So which theory is right? It turns out that both theories are right up to a certain point. In the case of place theory, research has found that for this theory to be right, the basilar membrane has to vibrate unevenly—which it does when the frequency of the sound is *above* 1,000 Hz. For the frequency theory to be correct, the neurons associated with the hair cells would have to fire as fast as the basilar membrane vibrates. This only works up to 100 Hz, because neurons simply can't fire any faster than 100 times per second.

So the place theory works for pitches above 1,000 Hz, and the frequency theory works for pitches up to 100 Hz. What happens in between? The likeliest possibility to explain what happens between 100 and 1,000 Hz is called the **volley principle**. In this explanation, when frequencies are above 100 Hz, the auditory neurons do not all fire at once. Instead, they take turns firing in a process called volleying. If a person heard a tone of 300 Hz, three groups of neurons would take turns sending the message to the brain—the first group for the first 100 Hz, the second group for the next 100 Hz, and so on.

[handwritten margin note: take turns firing]

TYPES OF HEARING IMPAIRMENTS

Hearing impairment is the term used to refer to difficulties in hearing. A person can be partially hearing impaired or totally hearing impaired, and the treatment for hearing loss will vary according to the reason for the impairment.

3.8   *What is a hearing impairment?*

CONDUCTION HEARING IMPAIRMENT   *Conduction hearing impairment* can result from either a damaged eardrum (which would prevent sound waves from being carried into the middle ear properly) or damage to the bones of the middle ear. In the latter case, sounds cannot be conducted from the eardrum to the cochlea. Middle ear damage is often from ear infections that are not treated quickly enough or from chronic ear infections. In this case, hearing aids may be of some use in restoring hearing.

NERVE HEARING IMPAIRMENT   In *nerve hearing impairment*, the problem lies either in the inner ear or in the auditory pathways and cortical areas of the brain. By the time most people are entering late adulthood, they have lost nearly half of their hair cells to the normal aging process. Exposure to loud noises during one's lifetime can cause the hair cells to break and speed up this loss, resulting in earlier hearing problems for many people in middle age.

Because the damage is to the nerves or the brain, nerve hearing impairment cannot be helped with ordinary hearing aids, which are basically sound amplifiers. A new technique for restoring hearing to those with nerve hearing impairment makes use of an electronic device called a *cochlear implant*. This device bypasses the outer and middle ears by sending signals from a microphone worn behind the ear to a sound processor worn on the belt or in a pocket, which then translates those signals into electrical stimuli that are sent to a series of electrodes implanted directly into the brain. (See Figure 3.10.) The brain then processes the electrode information as sound.

With an implant, people can hear some speech and their own speech to a degree that allows more communication with others. See the Psychology in the News section that follows for a report on this surgery as performed on former Miss America, Heather Whitestone.

a.

b.

FIGURE 3.10   **Cochlear Implant**
In a cochlear implant, a microphone implanted just behind the ear picks up sound from the surrounding environment. A speech processor, attached to the implant and worn outside the body, selects and arranges the sound picked up by the microphone. The implant itself is a transmitter and receiver, converting the signals from the speech processor into electrical impulses which are collected by the electrode array in the cochlea and then sent to the brain. This child is able to hear with the help of a cochlear implant. Hearing spoken language during the early years of a child's life helps in the development of the child's own speech.

New Surgery to Help Restore Hearing

3.9   *What can be done to help people with a hearing impairment?*

Several years ago, Heather Whitestone McCallum started running some water into the tub and then got distracted by another chore elsewhere. The tub began to overflow, but Heather could not hear the water running. She was not aware of what was happening until she turned around to see the water flooding the floor.

Heather could not hear the water because the hearing aid that she had worn since she lost most of her hearing in infancy was not powerful enough to let her hear the sound of the water—it only allowed her to hear very loud sounds, such as a siren or a shout from nearby.

In August 2002, Heather received a cochlear implant, an electronic device placed in her inner ear that allows her to hear quite a bit more than sirens (Boswell, 2002). About a month after her implant, she was able to hear the sound of her two infant sons turning on the water in the bathtub—the bathtub they had climbed into themselves. She was able to catch them in the act, possibly saving their lives in the process. Such a feat would not have been possible before the implant, and Heather is quite pleased to be able to hear her children's first words and their cries, and to be able to answer when one of her sons asks her what a certain sound is.

Heather's restored hearing has come at a price, as she has been caught up in a tremendous controversy in the hearing-impaired community. When Heather was first crowned, she was asked if she would get an implant. Her reply was no, her hearing aids were good enough. That was before her sons were born and she realized just how much she was missing by being unable to hear. Some people in the hearing-impaired community have been very critical of her decision to get the implant.

There are people with hearing impairments who believe that it is better to rely totally on lipreading and sign language rather than to have partially restored hearing. These people see being hearing impaired as a trait, like dark skin or curly hair, and think that it is part of their lives and not an illness or a disorder to be cured (Boswell, 2002). Still others see it as the removal of the child from the culture of the hearing impaired, something they compare to the removal of Native American children from their families to send them to white schools, where those children were often forbidden to speak in the language of their tribes.

Other hearing-impaired people have embraced the new technology, especially those people who were not born with a hearing impairment and who remember what it is like to hear. The future promises better hearing and clarity from these implants, but they are not without their drawbacks. If a person has an implant, swimming is not possible, for example. As more and more people choose the implants, the world will no doubt see radical changes in the world of the hearing impaired.

Questions for Further Discussion

1. What are the pros and cons regarding the use of hearing aid devices?

2. Does viewing one's hearing impairment as a trait rather than a disability have any advantages or disadvantages?

3. Should all hearing-impaired people learn to use sign language and lipreading? Why or why not?

Former Miss America Heather Whitestone McCallum signing as she gives a speech. Heather McCallum remains active in the deaf community even though she now has some hearing by means of a cochlear implant.

Pick the best answer.

1. Which of the following properties of sound would be the most similar to the color or hue of light?
   a. pitch   **c.** purity
   b. loudness   **d.** timbre

2. The eardrum is also called the
   a. pinna   **c.** tympanic membrane
   b. oval window   **d.** cochlea

3. The _____ theory explains how we hear sounds above 1,000 Hz.
   a. place   **c.** volley
   b. frequency   **d.** adaptive

4. If the bones of the middle ear begin to deteriorate, you will develop _____ hearing impairment.
   a. nerve   **c.** brain pathway
   b. stimulation   **d.** conduction

5. Hearing-impaired people are less likely to take advantage of new technology to help them hear if they
   a. have been hearing impaired since birth.
   b. were born able to hear for a time.
   c. still remember what it was like to hear.
   d. see their impairment as a disability rather than a difference.

Answers: 1-a, 2-c, 3-a, 4-d, 5-a.

Chemical Senses: It Tastes Good, But It Smells Terrible

gustation
the sensation of a taste.

3.10 *How do the senses of taste and smell work?*

The sense of taste (taste in food, not taste in clothing or friends) and the sense of smell are very closely related. Have you ever noticed that when your nose is all stopped up, your sense of taste is affected, too? That's because the sense of taste is really a combination of taste and smell. Without the input from the nose, there are actually only four, and possibly five, kinds of taste sensors in the mouth.

GUSTATION: HOW WE TASTE THE WORLD

TASTE BUDS   *Taste buds* are the common name for the taste receptor cells, special kinds of neurons found in the mouth that are responsible for the sense of taste, or **gustation**. Most taste buds are located on the tongue, but there are a few on the roof of the mouth, the cheeks, and under the tongue as well. How sensitive people are to various tastes depends on how many taste buds they have; some people have only around 500, whereas others have 20 times that number. The latter are called "supertasters" and need far less seasoning in their food than those with fewer taste buds (Bartoshuk, 1993).

So taste buds are those little bumps I can see when I look closely at my tongue? No, those "bumps" are called *papillae*, and the taste buds line the walls of these papillae. (See Figure 3.11.)

Each taste bud has about 20 receptors that are very similar to the receptor sites on receiving neurons at the synapse. **L I N K** *to Chapter Two, The Biological Perspective, p. 50.* In fact, the receptors on taste buds work exactly like receptor sites on neurons—they receive molecules of various substances that fit into the receptor like a key into a lock. Taste is often called a chemical sense because it works with the molecules of foods people eat in the same way the neural receptors work with neurotransmitters. When the molecules (dissolved in saliva) fit into the receptors, a signal is fired to the brain, which then interprets the taste sensation.

◄ So taste buds are those little bumps I can see when I look closely at my tongue?

a.

Uvula

b.

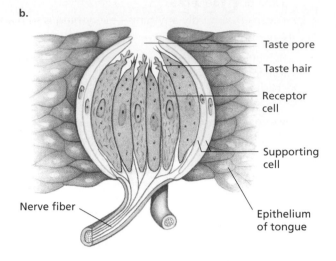

Taste pore

Taste hair

Receptor cell

Supporting cell

Nerve fiber

Epithelium of tongue

c.

FIGURE 3.11 **The Tongue and Taste Buds—A Crosscut View of the Tongue**   (a) The right side of this drawing shows the nerves in the tongue's deep tissue. (b) The taste bud is located inside the papillae, and is composed of several small cells (in pink and blue) that send signals to the brain when stimulated by molecules of food. (c) Microphotograph of the surface of the tongue, showing two different sizes of papillae. The taste buds are located under the surface of the larger red papillae, whereas the smaller and more numerous papillae form a touch-sensitive rough surface that helps in chewing and moving food around the mouth.

What happens to the taste buds when I burn my tongue? Do they repair themselves? I know when I have burned my tongue, I can't taste much for a while, but the taste comes back.

What happens to the taste buds when I burn my tongue? Do they repair themselves? I know when I have burned my tongue, I can't taste much for a while, but the taste comes back. Actually, in general, the taste receptors get such a workout that they have to be replaced every 10 to 14 days (McLaughlin & Margolskee, 1994). And when the tongue is burned, the damaged cells no longer work. As time goes on, those cells get replaced and the taste sense comes back. Ever wonder why some people make a point of cleaning their tongue? The coating that people get on their tongue is no doubt partly composed of dead taste cells.

THE FIVE BASIC TASTES   In 1916 a German psychologist named Hans Henning proposed that there are four primary tastes: sweet, sour, salty, and bitter. In 1996, Lindemann proposed that there is a fifth kind of taste receptor that detects a pleasant "brothy" taste associated with foods like chicken soup, tuna, kelp, cheese, and soy products, among others. Lindemann also proposed that this fifth taste be called _umami,_ a Japanese word that describes the taste. The five taste sensations work together, along with the sense of smell and the texture, temperature, and "heat" of foods, to produce thousands of taste sensations.

How does the sense of smell affect the sense of taste? As you said, when I have a cold I can taste hardly anything—everything is so bland. Everything becomes bland because you can taste only sweet, salty, bitter, sour, and umami—and because your nose is stuffed up with a cold, you don't get all the enhanced variations of those tastes that come from the sense of smell.

THE SENSE OF SCENTS: OLFACTION

Like the sense of taste, the sense of smell is a chemical sense. The ability to smell odors is called **olfaction**, or the **olfactory sense**. (It's pretty easy to remember that, because "old factories" really smell, don't they?)

People don't actually smell with their noses. The outer part of the nose serves the same purpose for odors that the pinna and ear canal serve for sounds: Both are merely ways to get the sensory information to the part of the body that will translate it into neural signals. So the external nose, like the outer ear, is just a collection device.

The part of the olfactory system that turns odors into signals the brain can understand is located at the top of the nasal passages. This area of olfactory receptor cells is only about an inch square in each cavity yet contains about 10 million olfactory receptors. (See Figure 3.12.)

OLFACTORY RECEPTOR CELLS   The *olfactory receptor cells* each have about a half dozen to a dozen little "hairs" that project into the cavity. These "hairs" are called *cilia*. Like taste buds, there are receptor sites on these hair cells that send signals to the brain when stimulated by the molecules of substances that are in the air moving past them.

Wait a minute—you mean that when I'm smelling something like a skunk, there are little particles of skunk odor IN my nose? Yes. When a person is sniffing something, the sniffing serves to move molecules of whatever the person is trying to smell into the nose and into the nasal cavities. That's okay when it's the smell of baking bread, apple pie, flowers, and the like, but when it's skunk, rotten eggs, dead animals—well, try not to think about it too much.

◀ **How does** the sense of smell affect the sense of taste? As you said, when I have a cold I can taste hardly anything—everything is so bland.

Wait a minute—you mean that when I'm smelling something like a skunk, there are little particles of skunk odor ◀ IN my nose?

olfaction (olfactory sense)
the sensation of smell.

FIGURE 3.12   **The Olfactory Receptors**   (a) A cross section of the nose and mouth. This drawing shows the nerve fibers inside the nasal cavity that carry information about smell directly to the olfactory bulb just under the frontal lobe of the brain (shown in green). (b) A diagram of the cells in the nose that process smell. The olfactory bulb is on top, shown in green. Notice the tiny hair-like cells that project into the nasal cavity. These are the receptors for the sense of smell.

Olfactory receptors are like taste buds in another way, too. Olfactory receptors also have to be replaced as they naturally die off, about every 5 to 8 weeks. Unlike the taste buds, there are more than five types of olfactory receptors. In fact, there are at least 1,000 of them.

Don't I remember from Chapter Two that the sense of smell is different in some way from the other senses? Yes, the signals from the olfactory receptors in the nasal cavity do not follow the same path as the signals from all the other senses. Vision, hearing, taste, and touch all go through the medulla (where the signals from one side of the body cross over to the opposite side) and up through the brain stem, the thalamus, and finally to the area of the cortex that processes that particular sensory information. But the sense of smell has its own special place in the brain—the olfactory bulbs.

THE OLFACTORY BULBS   The **olfactory bulbs** are located right on top of the sinus cavity on each side of the brain directly beneath the frontal lobes. (Refer back to Figure 3.12.) The olfactory receptors send their neural signals directly up to these bulbs, bypassing the entire lower brain and its selective attention filter, the reticular formation.

If the olfactory signals bypass the part of the brain that lets us ignore constant and unchanging information, does that mean that we can't "ignore" smells? Fortunately, people can ignore a smell that is constant and unchanging, but it doesn't involve the reticular formation.

Remember when sensory adaptation was covered earlier in the chapter? The text stated that certain sensory receptors become less sensitive to a constant stimulus as time goes by, so that eventually a person no longer perceives the stimulus. This adaptation is why people don't continue to smell the odor of the kitchen garbage can after being home for a while.

Somesthetic Senses: What The Body Knows

So far, this chapter has covered vision, hearing, taste, and smell. That leaves touch. What is thought of as the sense of touch is really several sensations, originating in several different places in—and on—the body. It's really more accurate to refer to these as the body senses, or **somesthetic senses**. The first part of that word, *soma*, means "body," as mentioned in Chapter Two. The second part, *esthetic*, means "feeling," hence, the name. There are three somesthetic sense systems, the **skin senses** (having to do with touch, pressure, temperature, and pain), the **kinesthetic sense** (having to do with the location of body parts in relation to the ground and to each other), and the **vestibular senses** (having to do with movement and body position).

TOUCH, PRESSURE, AND TEMPERATURE

3.11   *How does the sense of touch work, and what happens when people experience pain?*

Here's a good trivia question: What organ of the body is about 20 square feet in size? The answer is the skin. Skin is an organ. Its purposes include more than simply keeping bodily fluids in and germs out; skin also receives and transmits information from the outside world to the central nervous system (specifically, to the somatosensory cortex (L I N K) *to Chapter Two: The Biological Perspective, p. 67.*). Information about light touch, deeper pressure, hot, cold, and even pain is collected by special receptors in the skin's layers.

TYPES OF SENSORY RECEPTORS IN THE SKIN   There are about half a dozen different receptors in the layers of the skin. (See Figure 3.13.) Some of them will respond to only one kind of sensation. For example, the *Pacinian corpuscles* are just beneath the skin and respond to pressure only. There are nerve endings that wrap around the ends of the hair follicles, a fact people may be well aware of when they tweeze their eyebrows. These nerve endings are sensitive to both pain and touch. There are *free*

Don't I remember from ▶ Chapter Two that the sense of smell is different in some way from the other senses?

If the olfactory signals ▶ bypass the part of the brain that lets us ignore constant and unchanging information, does that mean that we can't "ignore" smells?

Her sense of touch is allowing this blind girl to "read" a Braille book with her fingers. The fingertips are extremely sensitive to fine differences in texture, allowing her to distinguish between small dots representing the different letters of the alphabet.

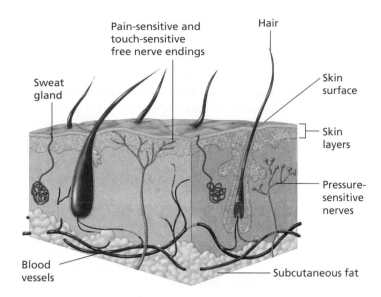

Sweat gland

Pain-sensitive and touch-sensitive free nerve endings

Hair

Skin surface

Skin layers

Pressure-sensitive nerves

Blood vessels

Subcutaneous fat

FIGURE 3.13 **Cross Section of the Skin and Its Receptors** The skin is composed of several types of cells that process pain, pressure, and temperature. Some of these cells are wrapped around the ends of the hairs on the skin and are sensitive to touch on the hair itself, while others are located near the surface and still others just under the top layer of tissue.

nerve endings just beneath the uppermost layer of the skin that respond to changes in temperature and to pressure—and to pain.

How exactly does pain work? Why is it that sometimes I feel pain deep inside? Are there pain receptors there, too? Yes, there are pain nerve fibers in the internal organs as well as receptors for pressure. How else would people have a stomachache or intestinal* pain? Or get that full feeling of pressure when they've eaten too much or their bladder is full?

There are actually different types of pain. There are receptors (called *proprioceptive*** receptors*) that detect pain (and pressure) in the organs, a type of pain called *visceral pain*. But pain sensations in the skin, muscles, tendons, and joints are carried on large nerve fibers and are called *somatic pain*. Somatic pain is the body's warning system that something is being, or is about to be, damaged and tends to be sharp and fast. Another type of somatic pain is carried on small nerve fibers and is slower and more of a general ache. This somatic pain acts as a kind of reminder system, keeping people from further injury by reminding them that the body has already been damaged. For example, if you hit your thumb with a hammer, the immediate pain sensation is of the first kind—sharp, fast, and bright. But later the bruised tissue simply aches, letting you know to take it easy on that thumb.

[handwritten annotation: detect balance]

PAIN—GATE-CONTROL THEORY

The best current explanation for how the sensation of pain works is called *gate-control theory*, first proposed by Melzack and Wall (1965) and later refined and expanded (Melzack & Wall, 1996). In this theory, the pain signals must pass through a "gate" located in the spinal cord. The activity of the gate can be closed by nonpain signals coming into the spinal cord from the body and by signals coming from the brain. The gate is not a physical structure but instead represents the relative balance in neural activity of cells in the spinal cord that receive information from the body and then send information to the brain. *[handwritten: pain can be blocked by other things]*

---

*Intestinal: having to do with the tubes in the body that digest food and process waste material.
**Proprioceptive: coming from inside the body.

How exactly **does pain work? Why is it that sometimes I feel pain deep inside? Are there pain receptors there, too?**

Anhidrosis is a rare genetic disorder that makes 5-year-old Ashlyn unable to feel pain. She must be examined carefully for scrapes and cuts after recess at school because she cannot feel when she hurts herself, putting her at risk for infection. What are some of the problems that Ashlyn and her parents may face as she grows older?

olfactory bulbs
areas of the brain located just above the sinus cavity and just below the frontal lobes that receive information from the olfactory receptor cells.

somesthetic senses
the body senses consisting of the skin senses, the kinesthetic sense, and the vestibular senses.

skin senses
the sensations of touch, pressure, temperature, and pain.

kinesthetic sense
sense of the location of body parts in relation to the ground and each other.

vestibular senses
the sensations of movement, balance, and body position.

I've always heard ▶ that women are able to stand more pain than men. Is that true?

What about motion sickness? I get queasy every time I have to ride in the back seat of a car or travel ▶ on a boat—what kinds of receptors are responsible for that?

Stimulation of the pain receptor cells releases a chemical called *substance P* (for pain, naturally). Substance P released into the spinal cord activates other neurons that send their messages through spinal gates (opened by the pain signal). From the spinal cord, the message goes to the brain, activating cells in the thalamus, somatosensory cortex, areas of the frontal lobes, and the limbic system. The brain then interprets the pain information and sends signals that either open the spinal gates farther, causing a greater experience of pain, or close them, dampening the pain. Of course, this decision by the brain is influenced by the psychological aspects of the pain-causing stimulus. Anxiety, fear, and helplessness intensify pain, while laughter, distraction, and a sense of control can diminish it. (This is why people might bruise themselves and not know it if they were concentrating on something else.) Pain can also be affected by competing signals from other skin senses, which is why rubbing a sore spot can reduce the feeling of pain.

Those same psychological aspects can also influence the release of the *endorphins*, the body's natural version of morphine. ⓛⓘⓝⓚ *to Chapter Two: The Biological Perspective, p. 52.* Endorphins can inhibit the transmission of pain signals in the brain, and in the spinal cord they can inhibit the release of substance P. As discussed in the section on neurotransmitters in Chapter Two, the release of endorphins is perhaps one explanation for "runner's high" (the pleasurable feeling a runner may experience after running a long distance) and the effectiveness of acupuncture.

I've always heard that women are able to stand more pain than men. Is that true? The statement that women are better able to tolerate higher levels of pain than are men is a generalization that has no basis in fact. Some people also have heard that men are very childish about pain and do not cope well with pain, but that is also a myth. The fact is that research has shown that women apparently feel pain more intensely than do men, and they also report pain more often than men do (Chesterton et al., 2003; Faucett et al., 1994; Norrbrink et al., 2003). Men have been shown to cope better with many kinds of pain, possibly because men are often found to have a stronger belief than women that they can control their pain by their own efforts (Jackson et al., 2002).

THE KINESTHETIC SENSE

3.12 *What sense allows the body to know how it is moving and when it is balanced?*

The *proprioceptive receptors (proprioceptors)* located in the skin, joints, muscles, and tendons, mentioned in the discussion of pain, are part of the body's sense of position in space—the location of the arms, legs, and so forth in relation to one another and in relation to the ground. This sense is called *kinesthesia*, from the Greek words *kinein* (to move) and *aesthesis* (sensation). When you close your eyes and raise your hand above your head, you know where your hand is because the proprioceptors tell you about the changes in pressure within the muscles.

What about motion sickness? I get queasy every time I have to ride in the back seat of a car or travel on a boat—what kinds of receptors are responsible for that? Actually, it's not the proprioceptors in the body that make people get sick. The culprits are special structures in the ear that make up the *vestibular sense*—the sense of balance.

THE VESTIBULAR SENSE

The name of this particular sense comes from a Latin word that means "entrance or chamber." The latter definition is probably the one that fits better here, as the structures for this sense are located in the innermost chamber of the ear. There are two kinds of vestibular organs, the otolith organs and the semicircular canals.

The *otolith organs* are tiny sacs found just above the cochlea. These sacs contain a gelatin-like fluid within which tiny crystals are suspended (much like pieces of fruit in a bowl of Jello®). The head moves and the crystals cause the fluid to vibrate, setting off some tiny hair-like receptors on the inner surface of the sac, telling the person that he or she is moving forward, back, sideways, or up and down. (It's pretty much the way the cochlea works but with movement as the stimulus instead of sound vibrations.)

The *semicircular canals* are three somewhat circular tubes that are also filled with fluid and will stimulate hair-like receptors when rotated. There are three tubes so that there is one in each of the three planes of motion. Remember learning in geometry class about the *x*-, *y*-, and *z*-axes? Those are the three planes through which the body can rotate, and when it does, it sets off the receptors in these canals. Ever spin around and around like a top when you were a kid? When you stopped, the fluid in the horizontal canal was still rotating and making you feel dizzy because your body was telling you that you were still moving, but your eyes were telling you that you had stopped.

MOTION SICKNESS   This disagreement between what the eyes say and what the body says is pretty much what causes *motion sickness*, the tendency to get nauseated when in a moving vehicle, especially one with an irregular movement. Normally, the vestibular sense coordinates with the other senses. But for some people, the information from the eyes may conflict a little too much with the vestibular organs, and dizziness, nausea, and disorientation are the result. This explanation of motion sickness is known as **sensory conflict theory** (Oman, 1990). Actually, people can probably blame the dizziness for the nausea—in human evolutionary history, many poisons make a person dizzy, and the most adaptive thing to do is to expel the poison. So although there isn't any poison in a case of motion sickness, the person may "expel" something anyway.

One way some people overcome motion sickness is to focus on a distant point or object. That point won't seem to move like the objects closer to the car window, for example, and so this causes less conflict. This is also how ballerinas and ice skaters manage not to get sick when turning rapidly and repeatedly—they focus their eyes at least once on some fixed object every so many turns.

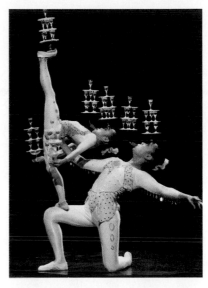

These young Chinese acrobats are balancing real glasses and each other in an amazing feat of coordination and muscular control. They must not only use their vestibular organs to help maintain their balance, but also their kinesthetic sense to be aware of exactly where each body part is in relation to the others.

sensory conflict theory
an explanation of motion sickness in which the information from the eyes conflicts with the information from the vestibular senses, resulting in dizziness, nausea, and other physical discomforts.

PRACTICE **QUIZ:** HOW MUCH DO YOU REMEMBER?

Pick the best answer.

1. The receptors on our taste buds work most like
  a. receptors in the ears.
  b. receptors in the eyes.
  c. receptor sites on neurons.
  d. receptors in the skin.

2. Which of the following statements about olfactory receptors is FALSE?
  a. Olfactory receptors are replaced every few years.
  b. There are at least 1,000 types of olfactory receptors.
  c. Signals from the receptors go directly to the olfactory bulbs in the brain.
  d. Olfactory receptors have hair-like projections called cilia.

3. After some time has passed, you can no longer smell the odor of the paper mill that you noticed when you first walked in your classroom. Which is the most likely reason for this?
  a. The smell has gone away.
  b. You've adapted to the smell, even though it's still there.
  c. Your nose fell asleep.
  d. You fell asleep.

4. Pain sensations in the skin, muscles, tendons, and joints that are carried on large nerve fibers are called
  a. visceral pain.
  b. somatic pain.
  c. referred pain.
  d. indigenous pain.

5. In gate-control theory, substance P
  a. opens the spinal gates for pain.
  b. closes the spinal gates for pain.
  c. is unrelated to pain.
  d. is similar in function to endorphins.

6. A bowl of gelatin with fruit in it will wiggle more than if it contained no fruit. This is most similar to the way the _____ work.
  a. semicircular canals
  b. proprioceptors
  c. otolith organs
  d. none of the above

The ABCs Of Perception

3.13 *What are perception and perceptual constancies?*

whole picture

Perception is the method by which people take all the sensations they experience at any given moment and interpret them in some meaningful fashion. Perception has some individuality to it—no two people will perceive the world in exactly the same way. Two people might be looking at a cloud, for example, and while one thinks it's shaped like a horse, the other thinks it's more like a cow. They both *see* the same cloud, but they *perceive* a different interpretation. As individual as perception might be, there are some rules for how people perceive the world around them. The following section discusses some of these basic principles.

THE CONSTANCIES: SIZE, SHAPE, AND BRIGHTNESS

Rules that the brain has developed

There's an old cartoon that shows a very large man speaking to a very small man. He's saying, "Excuse me for shouting—I thought you were much farther away." This cartoon makes use of the concept of a perceptual constancy* for size. **Size constancy** is the tendency to interpret an object as always being the same size, regardless of its distance from the viewer (or the size of the image it casts on the retina). So if an object that is normally perceived to be about 6 feet tall appears very small on the retina, it will be interpreted as being very far away. Evidence for size constancy has been found in 6-month-old infants (McKenzie et al., 1980), 4-month-olds (Day & McKenzie, 1981), and newborns (Slater et al., 1990). Yet size constancy cannot be fully present at birth, or it must require some kind of environmental stimulation to be maintained, because in cases of people who have been blind since birth and who then have sight restored, size constancy is absent or severely limited (Gregory, 1990; Sacks, 1995).

Another perceptual constancy is the tendency to interpret the shape of an object as constant, even when it changes on the retina. This is called **shape constancy** and is why a person still perceives a coin as a circle even if it is held at an angle that makes it appear to be an oval on the retina. Dinner plates on a table are also seen as round, even though from the angle of viewing they are oval. (See Figure 3.14.)

The third form of perceptual constancy is called **brightness constancy**, the tendency to perceive the apparent brightness of an object as the same even when the light conditions change. If a person is wearing black pants and a white shirt, for example, in broad daylight the shirt will appear to be much brighter than the pants. But if the sun is covered by thick clouds, even though the pants and shirt have less light to reflect than previously, the shirt will still appear to be just as much brighter than the pants as before—because the different amount of light reflected from each piece of clothing is still the same difference as before (Zeki, 2001).

THE GESTALT PRINCIPLES *organize sensory info.*

Remember the discussion of the Gestalt theorists in Chapter One? Those scientists were studying the very same concepts, the rules of human perception. Although Gestalt psychology has become a kind of therapy orientation today, the original focus on perception still remains in the basic principles of perception first laid out by those early pioneers in the field. These principles are based on the idea that people have a natural tendency to force patterns onto whatever they see. Following are some of the basic principles of this tendency to group objects and perceive whole shapes.

FIGURE 3.14 **Shape Constancy**
Three examples of shape constancy are shown here. The opening door is actually many different shapes, yet we still see it as basically a rectangular door. We do the same thing wth a triangle and a circle—although when we look at them from different angles they cast quite differently shaped images on our retina, we experience them as a triangle and a circle because of shape constancy.

perception
the method by which the sensations experienced at any given moment are interpreted and organized in some meaningful fashion.

size constancy
the tendency to interpret an object as always being the same actual size, regardless of its distance.

shape constancy
the tendency to interpret the shape of an object as being constant, even when its shape changes on the retina.

brightness constancy
the tendency to perceive the apparent brightness of an object as the same even when the light conditions change.

*Constancy: something that remains the same, the property of remaining stable and unchanging.

3.14   *What are the Gestalt principles of perception?*

FIGURE–GROUND RELATIONSHIPS   Take a look at the drawing of the cube in Figure 3.15. Which face of the cube is in the front? Look again—do the planes and corners of the cube seem to shift as you look at it?

This is called the Necker cube. It has been around officially since 1832, when a Swiss scientist who was studying the structure of crystals first drew it in his published papers. The problem with this cube is that there are no cues for depth, so the viewer is never really sure which plane or edge is in the back and which is in the front.

A similar illusion can be seen in Figure 3.16. In this picture, the viewer can switch perception back and forth from two faces looking at each other to the outline of a goblet in the middle. Which is the figure in front and which is the background?

Figure–ground relationships refer to the tendency to perceive objects, or figures as existing, on some background. People seem to have a preference for picking out figures from backgrounds even as early as birth, and this is the first visual ability to reappear after a cataract patient regains sight. The illusions in Figures 3.15 and 3.16 are **reversible figures**, in which the figure and the ground can be switched back and forth.

PROXIMITY   Another very simple rule of perception is the tendency to perceive objects that are close to one another as part of the same grouping, a principle called **proximity**, or nearness. (See Figure 3.17.)

SIMILARITY   **Similarity** refers to the tendency to perceive things that look similar as being part of the same group. This is one reason why sports teams wear uniforms that are all the same color—it allows people viewing the game to perceive them as one group even when they are scattered around the field or court.

CLOSURE   **Closure** is the tendency to complete figures that are incomplete. In class, one instructor usually draws a series of curved lines, spaced an inch or so apart, in a circular pattern on the board. When students are asked what they see, they invariably say "a circle." But it isn't a circle at all—just curved lines laid out in a circular formation. The brain fills in the spaces between the arcs to perceive a circle. In the same way, a talented artist can give the impression of an entire face with just a few cleverly placed strokes of the pen or brush—the viewers fill in the details.

CONTINUITY   The principle of **continuity** is easier to see than it is to explain in words. It refers to the tendency to perceive things as simply as possible with a continuous pattern rather than with a complex, broken-up pattern. Look at Figure 3.17 for an example of continuity. Isn't it much easier to see the figure on the left as two wavy lines crossing each other than as the little sections in the diagram to the right?

CONTIGUITY   **Contiguity** isn't shown in Figure 3.17, because it involves not just nearness in space but nearness in time also. Basically, contiguity is the tendency to perceive two things that happen close together in time as being related. Usually the first occurring event is seen as causing the second event. Ventriloquists* make great use of this principle. They make the vocalizations without appearing to move their own mouths but move the dummy's mouth instead. The tendency to believe that the dummy is doing the talking is due largely to contiguity.

There is one other principle of perceptual grouping that was not one of the original principles. It was added to the list (and can be seen at the bottom of Figure 3.17) by Stephen Palmer (Palmer,

---

*Ventriloquist: an entertainer who, through the use of misdirection and skill, makes other objects such as a dummy appear to talk.

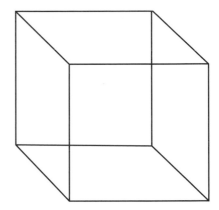

FIGURE 3.15   **The Necker Cube**
This is an example of a reversible figure. It can also be described as an ambiguous figure, since it is not clear which pattern should predominate.

FIGURE 3.16   **Figure-Ground Illusion**
What do you see when you look at this picture? Is it a wine goblet? Or two faces looking at each other? This is an example in which the figure and the ground seem to "switch" each time you look at the picture.

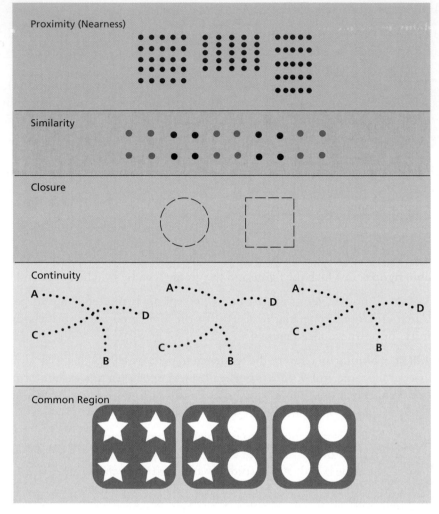

FIGURE 3.17 **Gestalt Principles of Grouping** The Gestalt principles of grouping are shown here. These are the human tendency to organize isolated stimuli into groups on the basis of five characteristics: proximity, similarity, closure, continuity, and common region.

Proximity: The dots on the left can be seen as horizontal or vertical rows—neither organization dominates. But just by changing the proximity of certain dots, as in the other two examples, we experience the dots as vertical columns (middle) or horizontal rows (right).

Similarity: The similarity of color here makes you perceive these dots as forming black squares and color squares rather than two rows of black and colored dots.

Closure: Even though the lines are broken, we still see these figures as a circle and a square—an example of how we tend to "close" or "fill in" missing parts from what we know of the whole.

Continuity: Because of continuity, we are much more likely to see the figure on the left as being made up of two lines, A to B and C to D, than we are to see it as a figure made up of lines A to D and C to B or A to C and B to D.

Common Region: Similarity would suggest that people see two groups, stars and circles. But the colored backgrounds define a visible common region, and the tendency is to perceive three different groups.

figure–ground
the tendency to perceive objects, or figures, as existing on a background.

reversible figures
visual illusions in which the figure and ground can be reversed.

similarity
the tendency to perceive things that look similar to each other as being part of the same group.

proximity
the tendency to perceive objects that are close to each other as part of the same grouping.

closure
the tendency to complete figures that are incomplete.

continuity
the tendency to perceive things as simply as possible with a continuous pattern rather than with a complex, broken-up pattern.

contiguity
the tendency to perceive two things that happen close together in time as being related.

1992). In *common region*, the tendency is to perceive objects that are in a common area or region as being in a group. In Figure 3.17, people could perceive the stars as one group and the circles as another on the basis of similarity. But the colored backgrounds so visibly define common regions that people instead perceive three groups—one of which has both stars and circles in it.

DEPTH PERCEPTION

The ability to see the world in three dimensions is called **depth perception**. It's a handy ability, because without it people would have a hard time judging how far away objects are. How early is depth perception developed? People who have had sight restored have almost no ability to perceive depth if they were blind from birth. Yet, like the constancies, depth perception seems to be present in infants at a very young age. The following Classic Studies in Psychology section presents one of the most famous studies in the field of depth perception.

depth perception
the ability to perceive the world in three dimensions.

CLASSIC STUDIES IN PSYCHOLOGY

The Visual Cliff

3.15   *How do people perceive the world in three dimensions?*

In the late 1950s, psychologist Eleanor Gibson was on a picnic at a local park. She was watching toddlers playing near the edge of a drop-off and began to wonder how the children knew not to step off the drop. (Most people would probably be yelling at the toddlers to get away from the cliff, but most people aren't psychologists.) This simple observation led to one of the most famous experiments in the field of developmental psychology.

Eleanor Gibson and her fellow researcher, Michael Walk, wondered if infants could perceive the world in three dimensions and devised a way to test babies for depth perception (Gibson & Walk, 1960). They built a special table (see Figure 3.18) that had a big drop on one side. The surface of the table on both the top and the drop to the floor were covered in a patterned tablecloth, so that the different size of the patterns would be a cue for depth (remember, in size constancy, if it looks smaller, people assume it is farther away from them). The whole table was then covered by a clear glass top, so that a baby could safely be placed on or crawl across the "deep" side.

The infants tested in this study ranged from 6 months to 14 months old. They were placed on the middle of the table and then encouraged (usually by their mothers) to crawl over either the shallow side or the deep side. Most babies—81 percent—refused to crawl over the deep side, even though they could touch it with their hands and feel that it was solid. They were upset and seemed fearful when encouraged to crawl across. Gibson and Walk interpreted this as a very early sign of the concept of depth perception.

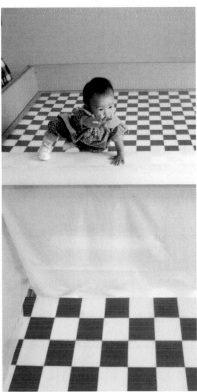

FIGURE 3.18   **The Visual Cliff Experiment**   In the visual cliff experiment, the table has both a shallow and a "deep" side, with glass covering the entire table. When an infant looks down at the deep-appearing side, the squares in the design on the floor look smaller than the ones on the shallow side, forming a visual cue for depth. Notice that this little girl seems to be very reluctant to cross over the deep-appearing side of the table, gesturing to be picked up instead.

Glass only

Glass over patterned surface

Deep side

Shallow side

Floor pattern seen through glass

Questions for Further Discussion

1. Does the fact that 19 percent of the infants did crawl over the deep side of the visual cliff necessarily mean that those infants could not perceive the depth?

2. What other factors might explain the willingness of the 19 percent to crawl over the deep side?

3. Are there any ethical concerns in this experiment?

4. Ducks aren't bothered by the visual cliff at all—why would that be?

Simulation

Live!
psych

Depth
Perception

Of course, the youngest babies in Gibson and Walk's classic study were 6 months old, and that might be old enough to have learned depth cues. In later studies, researchers (Campos et al., 1970) were able to demonstrate depth perception in infants as young as 2 months. These researchers placed very young infants on either the deep side or the shallow side and measured their heart rate. A decreasing heart rate is associated with interest in infants, whereas an increasing rate is associated with fear. The heart rate of the infants did not alter when they were placed on the shallow side but decreased when placed on the deep side. They were interested but not afraid. The older infants in the Gibson and Walk study were old enough to have experience with falling and tumbling down, and it is probably this experience that caused them to fear the depth. Based on the reactions of the infants in the Campos study, it is very likely that the ability to perceive the world in three dimensions is more or less inborn. It is fear of depth that requires learning and experience.

There are various cues for perceiving depth in the world. Some require the use of only one eye (**monocular cues**) and some are a result of the slightly different visual patterns that exist when the visual fields* of both eyes are used (**binocular cues**).

MONOCULAR CUES Monocular cues are often referred to as **pictorial depth cues**, because artists can use these cues to give the illusion of depth to paintings and drawings. Examples of these cues can be seen in Figure 3.19.

1. **Linear perspective:** When looking down a long interstate highway, the two sides of the highway appear to merge together in the distance. This tendency for parallel lines to appear to converge** on each other is called **linear perspective**. It works in pictures because people assume that in the picture, as in real life, the converging lines mean a great distance away from where they are.

2. **Relative size:** The principle of size constancy is at work in **relative size**, when objects that people expect to be of a certain size appear to be small and are, therefore, assumed to be much farther away. Movie makers use this principle to make their small models seem gigantic and in the distance.

3. **Overlap:** If one object seems to be blocking another object, people assume that the blocked object is behind the first one and, therefore, farther away. This cue is also known as **interposition**.

4. **Aerial perspective:** The farther away an object is, the hazier the object will appear to be, a process called **aerial perspective**. This is why distant mountains often look fuzzy, and buildings far in the distance are blurrier than those that are close. At greater distances more tiny particles of dust, dirt, and other pollutants in the air can come between the object and a person's eyes, causing blurred vision.

monocular cues (pictorial depth cues)
cues for perceiving depth based on one eye only.

binocular cues
cues for perceiving depth based on both eyes.

linear perspective
the tendency for parallel lines to appear to converge on each other.

relative size
perception that occurs when objects that a person expects to be of a certain size appear to be small and are, therefore, assumed to be much farther away.

interposition (overlap)
the assumption that an object that appears to be blocking part of another object is in front of the second object and closer to the viewer.

aerial perspective
the haziness that surrounds objects that are farther away from the viewer, causing the distance to be perceived as greater.

*Visual field: the entire area of space visible at a given instant without moving the eyes.
**Converge: come together.

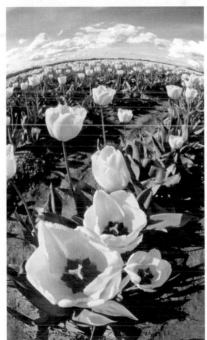

FIGURE 3.19 **Examples of Pictorial Depth Cues** (a) Both the lines of the trees and the sides of the road appear to come together in the distance. This is an example of linear perspective. (b) Notice how the larger pebbles in the foreground seem to give way to smaller and smaller pebbles near the middle of the picture. Texture gradient causes the viewer to assume that as the texture of the pebbles gets finer, the pebbles are getting farther away. (c) In aerial perspective, the farther away something is the hazier it appears because of fine particles in the air between the viewer and the object. Notice that the road and farmhouse in the foreground are in sharp focus while the mountain ranges are hazy and indistinct. (d) The depth clue of relative size appears in this photograph. Notice that the flowers in the distance appear much smaller than those in the foreground. Relative size causes smaller objects to be perceived as farther away from the viewer.

5. **Texture gradient:** If there are any large expanses of pebbles, rocks, or patterned roads (such as a cobblestone street) nearby, go take a look at them one day. The pebbles or bricks that are close to you are very distinctly textured, but as you look farther off into the distance, their texture becomes smaller and finer. **Texture gradient** is another trick used by artists to give the illusion of depth in a painting.

6. **Motion parallax:** The next time you're in a car, notice how the objects outside the car window seem to zip by very fast when they are close to the car, and objects in the distance seem to move more slowly. This discrepancy in motion of near and far objects is called **motion parallax**.

texture gradient
the tendency for textured surfaces to appear to become smaller and finer as distance from the viewer increases.

motion parallax
the perception of motion of objects in which close objects appear to move more quickly than objects that are farther away.

accommodation
as a monocular clue, the brain's use of information about the changing thickness of the lens of the eye in response to looking at objects that are close or far away.

convergence
the rotation of the two eyes in their sockets to focus on a single object, resulting in greater convergence for closer objects and lesser convergence if objects are distant.

binocular disparity
the difference in images between the two eyes, which is greater for objects that are close and smaller for distant objects.

Müller-Lyer illusion
illusion of line length that is distorted by inward-turning or outward-turning corners on the ends of the lines, causing lines of equal length to appear to be different.

7. **Accommodation:** A monocular cue that is not one of the pictorial cues, accommodation makes use of something that happens inside the eye. The lens of the human eye is flexible and held in place by a series of muscles. The discussion of the eye earlier in this chapter mentioned the process of visual accommodation as the tendency of the lens to change its shape, or thickness, in response to objects near or far away. The brain can use this information about **accommodation** as a cue for distance. Accommodation is also called a muscular cue.

BINOCULAR CUES   As the name suggests, these cues require the use of two eyes.

1. **Convergence:** Another muscular cue, **convergence**, refers to the rotation of the two eyes in their sockets to focus on a single object. If the object is close, the convergence is pretty great (almost as great as crossing the eyes). If the object is far, the convergence is much less. Hold your finger up in front of your nose, and then move it away and back again. That feeling you get in the muscles of your eyes is convergence.

2. **Binocular disparity:** Binocular disparity is a scientific way of saying that because the eyes are a few inches apart, they don't see exactly the same image. The brain interprets the images on the retina to determine distance from the eyes. If the two images are very different, the object must be pretty close. If they are almost identical, the object is far enough away to make the retinal disparity very small. You can demonstrate this cue for yourself by holding an object in front of your nose. Close one eye, note where the object is, and then open that eye and close the other. There should be quite a difference in views. But if you do the same thing with an object that is across the room, the image doesn't seem to "jump" or move nearly as much, if at all.

In spite of all the cues for perception that exist, even the most sophisticated perceiver can still fail to perceive the world as it actually is, as the next section demonstrates.

PERCEPTUAL ILLUSIONS

You've mentioned ▶ the word *illusion* several times. Exactly what are illusions, and why is it so easy to be fooled by them?

You've mentioned the word *illusion* several times. Exactly what are illusions, and why is it so easy to be fooled by them? An *illusion* is a perception that does not correspond to reality. People *think* they see something when the reality is quite different. Another way of thinking of illusions is as visual stimuli that "fool" the eye. (Illusions are different from hallucinations in that a hallucination's origin is in the brain itself—a person is seeing or hearing something that is actually not there at all. An illusion is a distorted perception of something that *is* there.)

3.16   *How do visual illusions work?*

MÜLLER-LYER ILLUSION   One of the most famous visual illusions, the **Müller-Lyer illusion**, is shown in Figure 3.20. The distortion happens when the viewer tries to determine if the two lines are exactly the same length. They are identical, but one line looks longer than the other. (It's always the line with the angles on the end facing outward.) Why is this illusion so powerful? The explanation is that most people live in a world with lots of buildings. Buildings have corners. When a person is outside a building, the corner of the building is close to that person, while the walls seem to be moving away. When the person is inside a building, the corner of the room seems to move away from the viewer while the walls are coming closer. In the illusion, the line with the angles facing inward is like the outside of the building, and the one with the angles facing outward is like the inside of the room. In their minds, people "pull" the inward-facing angles toward them like the outside corners of a building, and they make the outward-facing angles "stretch" away from them like the inside corners of the room (Enns & Coren, 1995; Gregory, 1990).

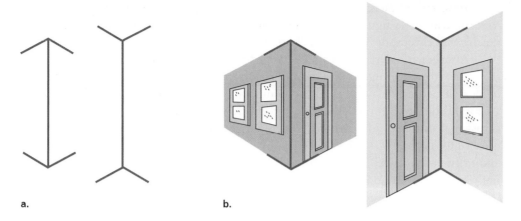

a.   b.

FIGURE 3.20   **The Müller-Lyer Illusion**   (a) Which line is longer? In industrialized Western countries, people generally see the lines in part (a) in situations such as in part (b). According to one theory, they have become so accustomed to seeing right angles in their environment and assume that the short, slanted lines are forming a right angle to the vertical line. They make that assumption because they are accustomed to seeing corners, such as the ones shown in the figure on the right. Consequently, in the figure on the left, they tend to perceive the line on the right as slightly longer than the line on the left.

Segall and colleagues (Segall et al., 1966) found that people in Western cultures, (having carpentered buildings with lots of straight lines and corners (Segall and colleagues refer to this as a "carpentered world") are far more susceptible to this illusion than people from non-Western cultures (having round huts with few corners—an "uncarpentered world"). Gregory (1990) found that Zulus, for example, rarely see this illusion. They live in round huts arranged in circles, use curved tools and toys, and experience few straight lines and corners in their world.

THE MOON ILLUSION   Another common illusion is the *moon illusion*, in which the moon on the horizon* appears to be much larger than the moon in the sky (Plug & Ross, 1994). One explanation for this is that the moon high in the sky is all alone, with no cues for depth surrounding it. But on the horizon, the moon appears behind trees and houses, cues for depth that make the horizon seem very far away. The moon is seen as being behind these objects and, therefore, farther away from the viewer. Because people know that objects that are farther away from them and still seem large are very large indeed, they "magnify" the moon in their minds—a misapplication of the principle of size constancy. This explanation of the moon illusion is called the *apparent distance hypothesis*.

ILLUSIONS OF MOTION   Sometimes people perceive an object as moving when it is really still. One example of this is mentioned in Chapter Thirteen, Social Psychology in the context of a famous experiment in conformity: the *autokinetic effect*. In this effect, a small, stationary light in a darkened room will appear to move or drift because there are no surrounding cues to indicate that the light is *not* moving. Another is the *stroboscopic motion* seen in motion pictures, in which a

slow motion or jerky motion

*Horizon: the place where the earth apparently meets the sky.

Simulation
Live!
psych
Perceptual
Illusions

The moon illusion. When this moon is high in the night sky it will still be the same size to the eye as it is now. Nevertheless, it is perceived to be much larger when on the horizon. In the sky, there are no objects for comparison, but on the horizon, objects such as this tree are seen as being in front of a very large moon.

perceptual set (perceptual expectancy)
the tendency to perceive things a certain way because previous experiences or expectations influence those perceptions.

top-down processing
the use of preexisting knowledge to organize individual features into a unified whole.

bottom-up processing
the analysis of the smaller features to build up to a complete perception.

Experiment
Live!
psych
Ambiguous
Figures

FIGURE 3.21 **Perceptual Set** Look at the drawing in the middle. What do you see? Now look at the drawings on each end. Would you have interpreted the middle drawing differently if you had looked at the drawing of the man or the kneeling woman first?

FIGURE 3.22 **The Devil's Trident** At first glance, this seems to be an ordinary three-pronged figure. But a closer look reveals that the three prongs cannot be real as drawn. Follow the lines of the top prong to see what goes wrong.

rapid series of still pictures will seem to be in motion. Many a student has discovered that drawing little figures on the edges of a notebook and then flipping the pages quickly will also produce this same illusion of movement.

Another movement illusion related to stroboscopic motion is the *phi phenomenon*, in which lights turned on in sequence appear to move. For example, if a light is turned on in a darkened room and then turned off, and then another light a short distance away is flashed on and off, it will appear to be one light moving across that distance. This principle is used to suggest motion in many theater marquee signs, flashing arrows indicating direction that have a series of lights going on and off in a sequence, and even in strings of decorative lighting, such as the "chasing" lights seen on houses at holiday times.

FACTORS THAT INFLUENCE PERCEPTION

Human perception of the world is obviously influenced by things such as culture and misinterpretations of cues. Following are other factors that cause people to alter their perceptions.

3.17 *What factors can influence perception?*

PERCEPTUAL SETS AND EXPECTANCIES People often misunderstand what is said to them because they were expecting to hear something else. People's tendency to perceive things a certain way because their previous experiences or expectations influence them is called **perceptual set** or **perceptual expectancy**. Although expectancies can be useful in interpreting certain stimuli, they can also lead people down the wrong path. For example, look at Figure 3.21. The drawing in the middle is a little hard to identify. People who start looking at these five drawings by looking at the drawing on the far left (which is clearly a man's face) tend to see the middle drawing as a man's face. But people who start looking from the far right (where the drawing is a kneeling woman with one arm over her chest and one touching her knee) see the middle picture as a woman. What you see depends upon what you expect to see.

The way in which people interpret what they perceive can also influence that perception. For example, people can try to understand what they perceive by using information they already have (as is the case in a perceptual expectancy). But if there is no existing information that relates to the new information, they can look at each feature of what they perceive and try to put it all together into one whole.

Anyone who has ever worked on a jigsaw puzzle knows that it's a lot easier to put it together if there is a picture of the finished puzzle to act as a guide. It also helps to have worked the puzzle before—people who have done that already know what it's going to look like when it's finished. In the field of perception, this is known as **top-down processing**—the use of preexisting knowledge to organize individual features into a unified whole. This is also a form of perceptual expectancy.

If the puzzle is one the person has never worked before or if that person has lost the top of the box with the picture on it, he or she would have to start with a small section, put it together, and keep building up the sections until the recognizable picture appears. This analysis of smaller features and building up to a complete perception is called **bottom-up processing** (Cave & Kim, 1999). In this case, there is no expectancy to help organize the perception, making bottom-up processing more difficult in some respects. Fortunately, the two types of processing are used together in perceiving the surrounding world.

Would people of different cultures perceive objects differently because of different expectancies? Some research suggests that this is true. For example, take a look at Figure 3.22.

This figure is often called the "devil's trident." Europeans and North Americans insist on making this figure three dimensional, so they have trouble looking at it—the figure is impossible if it is perceived in three dimensions. But people in more "primitive" native cultures have little difficulty with seeing or even reproducing this figure, because they see it as a two-dimensional drawing, quite literally a collection of lines and circles rather than a solid object (Deregowski, 1969).

PRACTICE **QUIZ:** HOW MUCH DO YOU REMEMBER?

Pick the best answer.

1. The tendency to perceive a quarter as being round even when it is viewed at an angle is called
   a. size constancy.
   c. brightness constancy.
   b. shape constancy.
   d. color constancy.

2. A reversible figure, such as the Necker cube, makes use of which principle of perception?
   a. shape constancy
   c. figure–ground relationships
   b. expectancy
   d. depth perception

3. Which of the following is NOT a monocular cue for depth?
   a. convergence
   c. overlap
   b. linear perspective
   d. texture gradient

4. An illusion
   a. is the same thing as a hallucination.
   b. exists only in the brain cells of the viewer.
   c. is a distorted perception of an actual stimulus.
   d. corresponds directly to reality.

5. Ned found a decaying carcass lying on the beach one day. Looking at the size of the body (which had decomposed quite a bit), Ned decided that it was the body of a sea monster, something like the Loch Ness monster in Scotland. If we know that Ned loves to read about weird, mythical animals, we might expect that he has made an error of perception due to
   a. perceptual set.
   b. perceptual defense.
   c. bottom-up processing.
   d. none of the above

6. The first time Joe had to put together a child's bicycle, it took a long time. But several bicycles later, he's a whiz at constructing them. His improved speed and skill can be attributed to
   a. bottom-up processing.
   b. top-down processing.
   c. perceptual expectancy.
   d. perceptual set.

Answers: 1-b, 2-c, 3-a, 4-c, 5-a, 6-b.

Applying Psychology to Everyday Life: Thinking Critically About ESP

Extrasensory perception (ESP) is usually defined as a claim of perception that occurs without the use of normal sensory channels such as sight, hearing, touch, taste, or smell. People who claim to have one or more of these abilities are commonly called "psychics." It was J. B. Rhine, a professor at Duke University, who first coined the term ESP in 1927 and in fact invented the field of **parapsychology**, the scientific study of ESP, ghosts, and all things that do not normally fall into the realm of ordinary psychology (Rhine, 1935). Dr. Rhine invented the Zener cards (see Figure 3.23) to test for one of the ESP abilities, telepathy.

parapsychology
the study of ESP, ghosts, and other subjects that do not normally fall into the realm of ordinary psychology.

FIGURE 3.23 **Zener Cards** These five shapes, star, circle, cross, wavy lines, and square are used in a test for telepathy, a form of extrasensory perception. One person (the sender) looks at each card after pulling it from a randomly shuffled deck of these five cards and thinks about the image on the card. The person being tested for telepathy, who cannot see the card, is supposed to guess what the shape is. An accuracy rate greater than chance is taken as an indication of telepathic ability.

There are supposedly several different kinds of extrasensory perception. Here's a list of the more common "abilities" that psychics are supposed to have:

1. **Telepathy.** The word literally means "distant feeling" and is commonly used to refer to the claimed ability to read another person's thoughts, or mind reading.

2. **Clairvoyance.** Literally "clear sight," this term refers to the supposed ability to "see" things that are not actually present. This ability is also claimed by many so-called psychic detectives, who believe that they can find lost objects, people, or even the bodies of murder victims by touching objects associated with the people in question.

3. **Precognition.** Precognition is the supposed ability to know something in advance of its occurrence or to predict a future event. Note that precognition is often confused with clairvoyance. The difference is that in clairvoyance, what is "seen" is something that exists at the present time, whereas precognition is supposed to involve "seeing" the future.

Research has been conducted since the time of Rhine's early experiments with mixed results. Many of the earlier methodologies used in researching psychic phenomena were flawed, making their results useless (Randi, 1980, 1982). Critics and skeptics point to the lack of consistent scientific evidence or ability to replicate experiments that seem to support viewing ESP and other psychic abilities as fakery, fraud, and misdirection. Believers claim that ESP is a talent that does not work "on command" and is detrimentally* affected by the presence of skepticism during tests.

Is there a case for ESP, or "psi" as it is sometimes called? Here's a quote from the online *Skeptic's Dictionary*:

Most ESP claims do not get tested, but parapsychologists have attempted to verify the existence of ESP under controlled conditions. Some, like Charles Tart and Raymond Moody, claim success; others, such as Susan J. Blackmore, claim that years of trying to find experimental proof of ESP have failed to turn up any proof of indisputable,** repeatable psychic powers. Defenders of psi claim that the gansfeld (sic) experiments, the CIA's remote viewing experiments and attempts to influence randomizers at Princeton Engineering Anomalies Research have produced evidence of ESP. Psychologists who have thoroughly investigated parapsychological studies, like Ray Hyman and Blackmore, have concluded that where positive results have been found, the work was fraught with fraud, error, incompetence, and statistical legerdemain.† (Carroll, 2002)

One of the most promising research techniques is the ganzfeld experiment, in which a person who is the "receiver" is placed in a room and wears special goggles (Ping-Pong balls cut in half and secured over the eyes) and earphones that produce white noise. This creates a kind of sensory deprivation. A "sender" in another room tries to mentally send images or video clips to the receiver. In one set of studies published in *Psychological Bulletin* (Bem & Honorton, 1994), these experiments seemed to produce a "hit rate" greater than that predicted by chance and were taken as evidence that some kind of mental telepathy had taken place. But later studies that examined all of the ganzfeld studies that had been completed demonstrated that there were no consistent findings across studies, no replication, and found no support for any kind of telepathy (Milton & Wiseman, 2001).

It may be that those who want very badly for there to be such a thing as extrasensory perception, like J. B. Rhine, lose the ability to think critically about the very concepts they are testing.

---

*Detrimentally: harmfully or involving damage.
**Indisputable: unquestionable, unable to be argued against.
†Legerdemain: trickery of any sort; deceit.

3

CHAPTER SUMMARY

The ABCs of Sensation

3.1 What is sensation and how does it enter the central nervous system?

- Sensation is the activation of receptors located in the eyes, ears, skin, nasal cavities, and tongue.
- Sensory receptors are specialized forms of neurons that are activated by different stimuli such as light and sound.
- A just noticeable difference is the point at which a stimulus is detectable half the time it is present.
- Weber's law of just noticeable differences states that the just noticeable difference between two stimuli is always a constant.
- Absolute thresholds are the smallest amount of energy needed for conscious detection of a stimulus at least half the time it is present.
- Subliminal stimuli are just below the level of conscious awareness but have not been shown to affect behavior in day-to-day life.

3.2 How can some sensations be ignored?

- Habituation occurs when the brain ignores a constant stimulus.
- Sensory adaptation occurs when the sensory receptors stop responding to a constant stimulus.

The Science of Seeing

3.3 What is light?

- Brightness corresponds to the amplitude of light waves, whereas color corresponds to the length of the light waves.
- Saturation is the psychological interpretation of wavelengths that are all the same (highly saturated) or varying (less saturated)

3.4 How do the parts of the eye work together?

- Light enters the eye and is focused through the cornea, passes through the aqueous humor, and then through the hole in the iris muscle called the pupil.
- The lens also focuses the light on the retina, where it passes through ganglion and bipolar cells to stimulate the rods and cones.

3.5 How do the eyes see, and how do the eyes see different colors?

- Rods detect changes in brightness but do not see color and function best in low levels of light. They do not respond to different colors and are found everywhere in the retina except the center or fovea.
- Cones are sensitive to colors and work best in bright light. They are responsible for the sharpness of visual information and are found in the fovea.
- Trichromatic theory of color perception assumes three types of cones: red, green, and blue. All colors would be perceived as combinations of these three.
- Opponent-process theory of color perception assumes four primary colors of red, green, blue, and yellow. Cones are arranged in pairs, and when one member of a pair is activated, the other is not.
- Color blindness is either a total lack of color perception or color perception that is limited to yellows and blues or reds and greens only.

The Hearing Sense: Can You Hear Me Now?

3.6 What is sound?

- Sound has three aspects: pitch (frequency), loudness, and timbre (purity).

3.7 How do the parts of the ear work together to hear sounds?

- Sound enters the ear through the visible outer structure, or pinna, and travels to the eardrum and then to the small bones of the middle ear.

- The bone called the stirrup rests on the oval window, causing the cochlea and basilar membrane to vibrate with sound.
- The organ of Corti on the basilar membrane contains the auditory receptors, which send signals to the brain about sound qualities as they vibrate.
- Place theory states that the location of the hair cells on the organ of Corti correspond to different pitches of sound. This explains pitch above 1,000 Hz.
- Frequency theory states that the speed with which the basilar membrane vibrates corresponds to different pitches of sound. This explains pitch below 100 Hz.
- The volley principle states that neurons take turns firing for sounds above 100 Hz and below 1,000 Hz.

3.8 What is a hearing impairment?

- Conduction hearing impairment is caused by damage to the outer or middle ear structures, whereas nerve hearing impairment is caused by damage to the inner ear or auditory pathways in the brain.

Psychology in the News: New Surgery to Help Restore Hearing

3.9 What can be done to help people with a hearing impairment?

- Cochlear implants can restore hearing to those with damage to the hearing nerves in some cases.

Chemical Senses: It Tastes Good, But It Smells Terrible

3.10 How do the senses of taste and smell work?

- Gustation is the sense of taste. Taste buds in the tongue receive molecules of substances, which fit into receptor sites.
- The five basic types of taste are sweet, sour, salty, bitter, and umami (brothy).
- Olfaction is the sense of smell. The olfactory receptors in the upper part of the nasal passages receive molecules of substances and create neural signals that then go to the olfactory bulbs under the frontal lobes.

Somesthetic Senses: What The Body Knows

- The somesthetic senses include the skin senses and the vestibular senses.

3.11 How does the sense of touch work, and what happens when people experience pain?

- Pacinian corpuscles respond to pressure, certain nerve endings around hair follicles respond to pain and pressure, and free nerve endings respond to pain, pressure, and temperature.
- The gate-control theory of pain states that when receptors sensitive to pain are stimulated, a neurotransmitter called substance P is released into the spinal cord, activating other pain receptors by opening "gates" in the spinal column and sending the message to the brain.

3.12 What sense allows the body to know how it is moving and when it is balanced?

- The kinesthetic senses allow the brain to know its position in space through the activity of special receptors called proprioceptors that are responsive to pressure inside the body.
- The vestibular sense also contributes to the body's sense of spatial orientation through the activity of the otolith organs (up and down movement) and the semicircular canals (movement through arcs).
- Motion sickness is explained by sensory conflict theory, in which information from the eyes conflicts with information from the vestibular sense, causing nausea.

The ABCs of Perception

3.13   *What are perception and perceptual constancies?*

- Perception is the interpretation and organization of sensations.
- Size constancy is the tendency to perceive objects as always being the same size, no matter how close or far away they are.
- Shape constancy is the tendency to perceive objects as remaining the same shape even when the shape of the object changes on the retina of the eye.
- Brightness constancy is the tendency to perceive objects as a certain level of brightness, even when the light changes.

3.14   *What are the Gestalt principles of perception?*

- The Gestalt psychologists developed several principles of perception that involve interpreting patterns in visual stimuli. The principles are figure-ground relationships, closure, similarity, continuity, contiguity, and common region.

Classic Studies in Psychology: The Visual Cliff

3.15   *How do people perceive the world in three dimensions?*

- Depth perception is the ability to see in three dimensions. Infants as young as 2 months can detect depth.
- Monocular cues for depth perception include linear perspective, relative size, overlap, aerial perspective, texture gradient, motion parallax, and accommodation.
- Binocular cues for depth perception include convergence and binocular overlap.

3.16   *How do visual illusions work?*

- Illusions are perceptions that do not correspond to reality or are distortions of visual stimuli.
- The Müller-Lyer illusion involves the misperception of two lines of equal length as being different in length because of angles placed on the ends of each line.
- The moon illusion occurs when the moon appears to be larger on the horizon than high in the sky. It is explained by the apparent distance hypothesis, which involves a misinterpretation of size constancy.

3.17   *What factors can influence perception?*

- Perceptual set or expectancy refers to the tendency to perceive objects and situations in a particular way because of prior experiences.
- Top-down processing involves the use of preexisting knowledge to organize individual features into a unified whole.
- Bottom-up processing involves the analysis of smaller features, building up to a complete perception.

Applying Psychology To Everyday Life: Thinking Critically About ESP

- Extrasensory perception (ESP) is a claim of perception that occurs without the use of normal sensory channels such as sight, hearing, touch, taste, or smell.
- ESP claimed abilities include telepathy, clairvoyance, and precognition.
- Research has produced some support for ESP, but critics claim these studies were flawed. Other research has failed to find any support for the claims of ESP.

3 KEY TERMS

absolute threshold 85
accommodation 114
aerial perspective 112
afterimages 92
auditory canal 96
auditory nerve 97
binocular cues 112
binocular disparity 114
blind spot 90
bottom-up processing 116
brightness constancy 108
closure 109
cochlea 96
cones 89
contiguity 109
continuity 109
convergence 114
dark adaptation 91
depth perception 111
figure–ground 109

frequency theory 98
gustation 101
habituation 86
hertz (Hz) 96
interposition (overlap) 112
just noticeable difference (jnd or the differential threshold) 84
kinesthetic sense 104
light adaptation 91
linear perspective 112
monocular cues (pictorial depth cues) 112
motion parallax 113
Müller-Lyer illusion 114
olfaction (olfactory sense) 103
olfactory bulbs 104
opponent-process theory 92
parapsychology 117
perception 108
perceptual set (perceptual expectancy) 116
pitch 98

place theory 98
proximity 109
relative size 112
reversible figures 109
rods 89
sensation 84
sensory adaptation 86
sensory conflict theory 107
shape constancy 108
similarity 109
size constancy 108
skin senses 104
somesthetic senses 104
synesthesia 82
texture gradient 113
top-down processing 116
trichromatic theory 91
vestibular senses 104
visual accommodation 89
volley principle 98

For more sample quizzes and other review activities that will help you get a better grade, be sure to check out your accompanying study guide. To access tests and your own personalized study plan that will help you focus on the areas you need to master before your next class test, be sure to go to the on-line Psychology web site available with the access code packaged with your book.

TEST YOURSELF

Pick the best answer.

1. You find that you have to add 1 teaspoon of sugar to a cup of coffee that already has 5 teaspoons of sugar in it to notice the difference in sweetness. If you have a cup of coffee with 10 teaspoons of sugar in it, how many teaspoons would you have to add to notice the difference in sweetness at least half the time?
a. 1
b. 2
c. 4
d. 5

2. Which of your senses habituates rather than adapts to constant stimuli?
a. vision
b. touch
c. hearing
d. smell

3. Which of the following terms refers to the psychological effect of the length of light waves?
a. color
b. brightness
c. pitch
d. amplitude

4. Which of the following is responsible for controlling how much light enters the eye?
a. cornea
b. lens
c. retina
d. iris

5. Which type of retinal cell forms the optic nerve?
a. rods
b. cones
c. ganglion cells
d. bipolar cells

6. Which type of retinal cell is responsible for peripheral vision?
a. rods
b. cones
c. ganglion cells
d. bipolar cells

7. Which set of colors are the primary colors when mixing light?
a. red, yellow, and blue
b. red, blue, and green
c. blue, green, and yellow
d. red, green, and yellow

8. Which of the following properties of sound would be the most similar to the brightness of light?
a. pitch
b. loudness
c. purity
d. timbre

9. The thin membrane stretched over the opening to the inner ear is the
a. pinna.
b. oval window.
c. tympanic membrane.
d. cochlea.

10. The _____ theory explains how we hear sounds between 100 and 1,000 Hz.
a. place
b. frequency
c. volley
d. adaptive

11. If a severe ear infection damages the bones of the middle ear, you may develop _____ hearing impairment.
a. nerve
b. stimulation
c. brain pathway
d. conduction

12. The sense of taste is closely related to the sense of
a. sight.
b. hearing
c. smell.
d. touch

13. The "bumps" on the tongue that are visible to the eye are the
a. taste buds.
b. papillae.
c. taste receptors.
d. olfactory receptors

14. The olfactory receptor cells are located in the
a. tops of the nasal passages.
b. auditory passages.
c. roof of the mouth.
d. lining of the outer nose.

15. Which of the following statements about olfactory receptors is TRUE?
a. Olfactory receptors are replaced every 5 to 8 weeks.
b. There are fewer than 50 types of olfactory receptors.
c. Signals from the receptors go through the brain stem and then to the cortex.
d. Olfactory receptors respond to pressure.

16. In the spinal cord, _____ inhibit(s) the release of substance P.
a. hormones
b. serotonin
c. norepinephrine
d. endorphins

17. We know when we are moving up and down in an elevator because of the movement of tiny crystals in the
a. outer ear.
b. inner ear.
c. otolith organs.
d. middle ear.

18. Ellis turns around and around in a circle. When he stops, he feels like his head is still spinning. What is responsible for this sensation?
a. semicircular canals
b. proprioceptors
c. otolith organs
d. otolith crystals

19. An old comedy routine on television had a character who would line up the heads of people who were very far away from him between his fingers. Then he would pinch his fingers together and say gleefully, "I'm crushing your head, I'm crushing your head." The comedian was playing around with which perceptual constancy?
a. size constancy
b. shape constancy
c. brightness constancy
d. color constancy

20. Which Gestalt principle is at work when a ventriloquist moves the dummy's mouth while doing the talking, making it seem like the dummy is talking?
a. closure
b. similarity
c. contiguity
d. continuity

21. Researchers have been able to demonstrate depth perception in babies as young as
a. 1 month.
b. 2 months.
c. 3 months.
d. 4 months.

22. Which of the following occurs when one object seems to block another object?
a. convergence
b. linear perspective
c. overlap
d. texture gradient

23. The Müller-Lyer illusion exists in cultures in which there are
a. more men than women.
b. more women than men.
c. lots of trees.
d. buildings with lots of corners.

24. Allison opened her new jigsaw puzzle but soon realized that the puzzle pieces inside had nothing to do with the picture on the box. With no picture to go by, she realized she would have to use
a. bottom-up processing.
b. top-down processing.
c. perceptual expectancy.
d. perceptual set.

25. Which supposed ESP ability involves being able to "see" something that is not physically present by touching another object?
a. precognition
b. telepathy
c. clairvoyance
d. telekinesis

CONCEPT MAP

The ABCs of Sensation

Sensation and the Central Nervous System

Sensation: activation of sense organ receptors

Sensory receptors: specialized neurons activated by stimuli

Thresholds:

▸ **Just noticeable difference:** smallest detectable stimulus change

▸ **Absolute thresholds:** smallest amount of energy for stimulus detection

▸ **Subliminal stimuli:** Not been shown to affect day-to-day behavior

3.1

Ignoring Sensations

Habituation: ignoring a constant stimulus

Sensory adaptation: sensory neurons stop responding to constant stimuli

3.2

Color Vision

Trichromatic and opponent-process theories: two processes that work together

Trichromatic theory of color perception: three types of cones for long, medium, and short wavelengths

Opponent processes: at the ganglion cell level combine long versus medium cones to produce red and green. Medium and long cones combine together versus the short-wavelength cone to produce yellow and blue

Color blindness: total lack of color perception or color perception that is limited to yellows and blues or reds and greens only

The Science of Seeing

Light

Light: form of electromagnetic radiation described by wavelength and amplitude

Color or hue: in part determined by wavelength.

▸ Long wavelengths—red end of the visible spectrum

▸ Shorter wavelengths—blue end of the visible spectrum

Brightness: corresponds to the amplitude of light waves

Saturation: refers to the purity of the color people see

3.3

Parts of the Eye

Pathway of Light:
Cornea →
Pupil →
Lens →
Retina →
(Hits the rods and cones)

3.4

How the Eyes See and How the Eyes See Different Colors

3.5

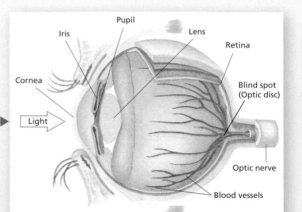

Rods, Cones

Rods: low light levels, no role in color vision, poor acuity, located peripherally

Cones: work at bright light levels, see color, provide central and sharp vision

The Hearing Sense

Sound

Sound consists of pressure waves in the air

Sound has three aspects:

▸ pitch (frequency),
▸ loudness
▸ timbre (purity)

3.6

Parts of the Ear

Sound: → pinna, → eardrum → bones of middle ear (hammer, anvil, stirrup)

Stirrup causes the cochlea and basilar membrane to vibrate with sound

The organ of Corti on the basilar membrane contains the auditory receptors

3.7

Hearing Impairment

Conduction hearing impairment: damage to the outer or middle ear structures

Nerve hearing impairment: damage to the inner ear or auditory pathways

Cochlear implant: an electronic device in the inner ear to restore hearing

3.8

Perception of Pitch

Place theory: organ of Corti hair cells corresponding to pitches above 1,000 Hz

Frequency theory: basilar membrane vibrates corresponding to pitches below 100 Hz

Volley theory: neurons take turns firing for sounds above 100 Hz and below 1,000 Hz

Chemical Senses

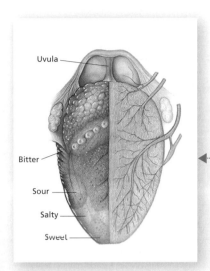

- Uvula
- Bitter
- Sour
- Salty
- Sweet

Gustation— Sense of Taste

Taste buds: contain receptor sites that receive molecules of substances

Five basic types of taste: sweet, sour, salty, bitter, and umami

Olfaction— Sense of Smell

Olfactory receptors receive molecules of substances

Neural signals go to the olfactory bulbs

3.10

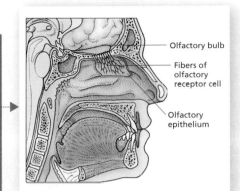

- Olfactory bulb
- Fibers of olfactory receptor cell
- Olfactory epithelium

Somesthetic Senses

Sense of Touch and Pain

Touch:
- Pacinian Corpuscles
- Nerve endings around hair
- Free nerve endings

Gate-control theory of pain:
- Stimulation of pain receptors cause transmitter release into the spinal cord
- Activates other pain receptors by opening "gates" in the spinal column

3.11

Kinesthetic Sense: Movement and Balance

Kinesthetic sense: relays position in space and based on proprioceptors

Vestibular sense: body's sense of spatial orientation

Based on: otolith organs and semicircular canals

3.12

The ABCs of Perception

Perception and Perceptual Constancies

Size constancy: objects seem the same size, no matter their distance

Shape constancy: objects seem same shape despite retinal image changes

Brightness constancy: changes in lighting do not affect brightness perception

3.13

Gestalt Principles of Perception

Figure–ground relationships:
- Closure
- Similarity
- Contiguity
- Continuity
- Common region

3.14

How Do People Perceive the World in Three Dimensions

Depth perception is the ability to see in three dimensions.

Monocular cues (pictorial depth cues): depth cues based on one eye only
- Linear perspective
- Relative size
- Interposition (overlap)
- Aerial perspective
- Texture gradient
- Motion parallax
- Accommodation

Binocular cues: cues for perceiving depth based on both eyes
- Convergence
- Binocular disparity

3.15

Visual Illusions

Müller-Lyer illusion: involves the misperception of two lines of equal length

Moon illusion: moon appears to be larger on the horizon

3.16

Factors That Influence Perception

Perceptual set or expectancy: tendency to perceive according to prior experiences

Top-down processing: knowledge organizes individual features into a unified whole

Bottom-up processing: K analysis of smaller feature builds up to a complete perception

3.17

4

Consciousness: Sleep, Dreams, Hypnosis, and Drugs

A Scream in the Night

Imagine: It's a quiet night. Your 2-year-old son has been asleep for a few hours, and you and your spouse have just gone to bed. As you begin to drift off, you hear a bloodcurdling scream from the baby's room. Both of you leap up and run to the nursery, where you find your infant son, bolt upright in bed, screaming at the top of his not-so-little lungs. You try to calm him down but soon realize that he is not even awake—he is terrified, yet asleep.

That is the experience Jenny and Jim had about once a month for the first few years of their son's life. Their son, Alex, suffered from *night terrors*, a relatively rare sleep disorder that occurs more often in children than adults and more often in boys than girls. It took a few months and some research to find out that they could prevent most of these episodes by making sure that Alex always got a good night's sleep. One of the primary triggers of a night terror is a night or two of lost sleep prior to the night of the episode.

Why study consciousness?

Consciousness, as humans experience it, is the key difference between humans and the lower animals. Waking, sleeping, dreaming, daydreaming, and other forms of conscious awareness make up the better part of the human experience. Drug use is on the rise, not only as recreation but also for many health and psychological conditions, including the treatment of children. It seems obvious that we need to understand how drugs affect our thinking and behavior in everyday life. In a very real sense, to understand consciousness is to understand what it means to be who we are.

4

LEARNING OBJECTIVES

What Is Consciousness?

What exactly is meant by the term *consciousness*? **I've heard it a lot, but I'm not sure that I know everything it means.** *Consciousness* is one of those terms that most people think they understand until someone asks them to define it. Often the first thing people say is something like this: "Oh, consciousness is when you are conscious of what's around you." That isn't really a definition, it's a circular statement. Using the term *conscious* to define *consciousness* is not going to help in understanding what consciousness really is.

> What exactly is meant by the term *consciousness*? I've heard it a lot, but I'm not sure that I know everything it means.

DEFINITION OF CONSCIOUSNESS

4.1 *What does it mean to be conscious, and are there different levels of consciousness?*

A more useful definition of consciousness might be the following: **Consciousness** is people's awareness of everything that is going on around them and inside their own head at any given moment (Farthing, 1992). That includes thoughts, sensations, and feelings. Much of people's time awake is spent in a state called **waking consciousness**, in which their thoughts, feelings, and sensations are clear and organized, and they feel alert. But there are many times in daily activities and in life when people experience states of consciousness that differ from this organized waking state. These variations in consciousness are called altered states of consciousness.

ALTERED STATES OF CONSCIOUSNESS

An **altered state of consciousness** occurs when there is a shift in the quality or pattern of people's mental activity (Tart, 1986). Thoughts may become fuzzy and disorganized and people may feel less alert, or their thoughts may take bizarre turns as they so often do in dreams. There are many pathways to altered states of consciousness: using drugs, daydreaming, being hypnotized, or achieving a meditative state. **LINK** *to Chapter Eleven: Stress and Health, p. 432.* But the most common altered state people experience is the one they spend about a third of their lives in on a nightly basis—sleep.

consciousness
a person's awareness of everything that is going on around him or her at any given moment.

waking consciousness
state in which thoughts, feelings, and sensations are clear, organized, and the person feels alert.

altered state of consciousness
state in which there is a shift in the quality or pattern of mental activity as compared to waking consciousness.

Altered States: Sleep

Have you ever wondered why people have to sleep? They could get so much more work done if they didn't have to sleep, and they would have more time to play and do creative things.

THE NECESSITY OF SLEEP

4.2 *Why do people sleep, and how does sleep work?*

Sleep was once referred to as "the gentle tyrant" (Webb, 1992). People can try to stay awake, and sometimes they may go for a while without sleep, but eventually they *must* sleep. One reason for this is that sleep is one of the human body's *biological rhythms*, natural cycles of activity that the body must go through. Some biological rhythms are monthly, like the cycle of a woman's menstruation, whereas others are far shorter—the beat of the heart is a biological rhythm. But many biological rhythms take place on a daily basis, like the rise and fall of blood pressure and body temperature, or the production of certain body chemicals (Moore-Ede et al., 1982). The most obvious of these is the sleep–wake cycle (Baehr et al., 2000).

THE RHYTHMS OF LIFE: CIRCADIAN RHYTHMS The sleep–wake cycle is a **circadian rhythm**. The term actually comes from two Latin words, *circa* (about) and *diem* (day). So a circadian rhythm is a cycle that takes "about a day" to complete.

For most people, this means that they will experience several hours of sleep at least once during every 24-hour period. The sleep–wake cycle is ultimately controlled by the brain, specifically by an area within the *hypothalamus*, the tiny section of the brain that influences the glandular system. **LINK** *to Chapter Two: The Biological Perspective, p. 65.* *above pituitary*

THE ROLE OF THE HYPOTHALAMUS: THE MIGHTY MITE There was a big fuss over something called melatonin a few years ago—isn't melatonin supposed to make people sleep? Melatonin is only one part of the sleep story. Deep within the hypothalamus is an area called the *suprachiasmatic* (SOO-prah-ki-AS-ma-tik) *nucleus*, the internal clock that tells people when to wake up and when to fall asleep (Quintero et al., 2003; Yamaguchi et al., 2003; Zisapel, 2001). The suprachiasmatic nucleus, or SCN, is sensitive to changes in light. As daylight fades, the SCN tells the *pineal gland* (located in the base of the brain) to secrete the hormone *melatonin* (Bondarenko, 2004; Delagrange & Guardiola-Lemaitre, 1997). As melatonin accumulates, a person will feel sleepy. As the light coming into the eyes increases (as it does in the morning), the SCN tells the pineal gland to stop secreting melatonin, allowing the body to awaken.

There is also ongoing discussion and research into the role of the neurotransmitter serotonin in the regulation of sleep (Veasey, 2003). As the day goes by, serotonin levels in the nervous system increase and seem to produce sleepiness. This would explain why, at the end of the day, it is very hard for people to stay awake past their usual bedtime. The serotonin level is high enough at that time to produce an intense feeling of sleepiness.

Body temperature plays a part in inducing sleep, too. The SCN, as part of the hypothalamus, controls body temperature. The higher the body temperature, the more alert people are; the lower the temperature, the sleepier they are. When people are asleep at night, their body temperature is at its lowest level.

In studies in which volunteers spend several days without access to information about day or night, their sleep–wake cycles lengthened (Czeisler, 1995; Czeisler et al., 1980). The daily activities of their bodies, such as sleeping, waking, waste production, blood pressure rise and fall, and so on, took place over a period of 25 hours rather than 24. Based on this research, it appears that the SCN may be responsible for resetting the body's biological "clock" to a 24-hour cycle every day.

Sleep, according to Webb (1992), is the "gentle tyrant." As this picture shows, when the urge to sleep comes upon a person, it can be very difficult to resist—no matter where that person is at the time. Can you think of a time or place at which you feel asleep without meaning to do so? What do you think were the factors in your "sleep attack?"

◀ There was a big fuss over something called melatonin a few years ago—isn't melatonin supposed to make people sleep?

melatonin— skin pigment

circadian rhythm
a cycle of bodily rhythm that occurs over a 24-hour period.

Microsleeps are a common cause of accidents while driving. If this woman continues to drive while she is this sleepy, she may fall asleep at the wheel for only a few moments. Those few moments can mean disaster—for her and for others on the road with her.

microsleeps
brief sidesteps into sleep lasting only a few seconds.

sleep deprivation
any significant loss of sleep, resulting in problems in concentration and irritability.

Contrary to popular belief, sleep deprivation often affects younger people more than older people, who need less sleep. Does this young man look well rested and able to successfully complete the task of brushing his teeth?

In the same studies, body temperature dropped consistently even in the absence of light (Czeisler et al., 1980). As body temperature dropped, sleep began, giving further support to the importance of body temperature in the regulation of sleep.

THE PRICE OF NOT SLEEPING

4.3   What is the purpose of sleep?

Although people can do without sleep for a while, they cannot do without it altogether. In one experiment, rats were placed on moving treadmills over water. They couldn't sleep normally because they would then fall into the water and be awakened, but they did drift repeatedly into **microsleeps**, or brief sidesteps into sleep lasting only seconds (Goleman, 1982; Konowal et al., 1999). People can have microsleeps, too, and if this happens while they are driving a car or a truck, it's obviously bad news (Dinges, 1995; Lyznicki et al., 1998; Thomas et al., 1998). Microsleep periods are no doubt responsible for a lot of car accidents that occur when drivers have had very little sleep.

What will missing out on one night's sleep do to a person? For most people, a missed night of sleep will result in concentration problems and the inability to do simple tasks that normally would take no thought at all, such as loading a CD into a player. More complex tasks, such as math problems, suffer less than these simple tasks. When sleep loss is complicated by an emotional trauma (such as the death of a loved one), the concentration problems and disorientation may be more severe.

Even so, **sleep deprivation**, or loss of sleep, is a serious problem, which many people have without realizing it. People stay up too late at night during the week, get up before they've really rested to go to work or school, and then try to pay off the "sleep debt" on the weekend. All of that disrupts the normal sleep–wake cycle and isn't good for anyone's health. Students, for example, may stay up all night to study for an important test the next day. In doing so, they will lose more information than they gain, as a good night's sleep is important for memory and the ability to think well. Ⓛ Ⓘ Ⓝ Ⓚ *to Introduction, p. I-9.* Some typical symptoms of sleep deprivation include trembling hands, inattention, staring off into space, droopy eyelids, and general discomfort (Naitoh, Kelly, & Englund, 1989), as well as emotional symptoms such as irritability and even depression. Ⓛ Ⓘ Ⓝ Ⓚ *to Chapter Fourteen: Psychological Disorders, p. 542.* (For more information about sleep deprivation, see the Applying Psychology section at the end of this chapter.)

Just how serious is missing a few nights' sleep? Sleep researchers conducted a study in which healthy adults between the ages of 21 and 38 were randomly placed in one of four restricted sleep conditions (Van Dongen et al., 2003). Participants began the experiment with at least three days of regular sleep and then were either allowed to get only four hours, six hours, or eight hours (this was the control group) of sleep each day for 14 days. A fourth group of participants was totally deprived of sleep (by being kept awake by the researchers) for three days in a row. Measurements of the participants' cognitive abilities and physical alertness were taken every two hours during the scheduled "awake" times. The results showed that even in the six-hour sleep condition, participants' abilities to function mentally and physically were as negatively affected as if they had been entirely deprived of sleep for two nights. All participants in the sleep-deprived and no-sleep conditions were seriously impaired in their functioning and were relatively unaware of the seriousness of the impairment. That the participants did not seem to be aware of their problems in functioning may account for the impression many people have that a few nights of poor sleep is not that serious. The results of this study seem to indicate that even moderate sleep loss is a serious problem.

In one study, researchers found that air traffic controllers such as those pictured here were significantly more impaired in performance after working an eight-hour midnight shift as compared to a day or evening shift of equal length (Heslegrave & Rhodes, 1997).

The Adaptive Theory of Sleep   Okay, so we obviously need to sleep. But what does it do for us? Why do we have to sleep at all? According to the **adaptive theory** of why organisms sleep, sleep is a product of evolution (Webb, 1992). Animals and humans evolved different sleep patterns to avoid predators during the predators' normal hunting times, which are generally at night. If a prey animal (one the predator will eat) is out and about at night, it is likely to be eaten. If instead it is in a safe place sleeping and conserving energy, it remains safe. If this is true, then one would expect prey animals to sleep mostly at night and for shorter periods of time than predator animals, whereas the predator animals can sleep in the daytime and as much as they want. In fact, animals like lions that have very few natural predators sleep nearly 15 hours a day, while animals like gazelles that are prey sleep only a total of 4 hours a day, usually in short naps.

◀ Okay, so we obviously need to sleep. But what does it do for us? Why do we have to sleep at all?

adaptive theory
theory of sleep proposing that animals and humans evolved sleep patterns to avoid predators by sleeping when predators are most active.

This tree-dwelling loris, like most nocturnal animals, has very large eyes. The adaptive theory of sleep assumes that animals in danger from predators tend to sleep at night. With its nightly activities confined safely to the trees, the loris has no need to fear predators at night and instead sleeps during the day.

These lionesses are predators and have no need to sleep at night to protect themselves. They sleep and hunt on and off during the day in perfect safety, while the animals that the lionesses prey upon sleep at night in the safety of dens or other shelter.

FIGURE 4.1 **Sleep Patterns of Infants and Adults** Infants need far more sleep than older children and adults. Both REM sleep and NREM sleep decrease dramatically in the first ten years of life, with the greatest decrease in REM sleep. Nearly 50 percent of an infant's sleep is REM, compared to only about 20 percent for a normal, healthy adult.
(Roffwarg, 1966)

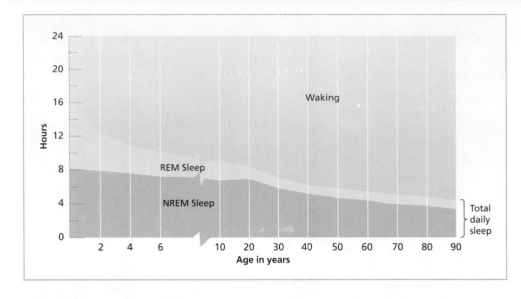

restorative theory
theory of sleep proposing that sleep is necessary to the physical health of the body and serves to replenish chemicals and repair cellular damage.

The Restorative Theory of Sleep The other major theory of why organisms sleep is called **restorative theory**, which states that sleep is necessary to the physical health of the body. During sleep, chemicals that were used up during the day's activities are replenished and cellular damage is repaired (Adam, 1980; Moldofsky, 1995). There is evidence that most bodily growth and repair occur during the deepest stages of sleep, when enzymes responsible for these functions are secreted in higher amounts. This may account for the fact that children in periods of rapid growth need to sleep more and also helps to explain why children who are experiencing disrupted sleep (as is the case in situations of domestic violence) suffer delays in growth (Gilmore & Skuse, 1999; Swanson, 1994).

Which of these theories is correct? The answer is that both are probably needed to understand why sleep occurs the way it does. Adaptive theory explains why people sleep *when* they do, and restorative theory explains why people *need* to sleep.

How Much Sleep Do People Need? How much sleep is enough sleep? The answer varies from person to person because of each person's age and possibly inherited sleep needs (Feroah et al., 2004), but most people need about 7 to 8 hours of sleep each 24-hour period in order to function well. (See Figure 4.1) Some people are short sleepers, needing only 4 or 5 hours, whereas others are long sleepers and need 9 or 10 hours of sleep (McCann & Stewin, 1988).

PRACTICE QUIZ: HOW MUCH DO YOU REMEMBER?

Pick the best answer.

1. When our mental activity undergoes a change in quality or pattern, this is called a(n)
  a. waking consciousness.
  b. altered state of consciousness.
  c. transient state of consciousness.
  d. hallucination.

2. The sleep–wake cycle is a(n) _____ rhythm, normally occurring every 24 hours.
  a. annual
  b. monthly
  c. circadian
  d. nocturnal

3. The suprachiasmatic nucleus instructs the _____ gland to release _____.
  a. pineal; melatonin
  b. pineal; serotonin
  c. pituitary; melatonin
  d. pituitary; serotonin

4. Which of the following does NOT have a role in determining when we sleep?
  a. light and dark information
  b. body temperature
  c. digestion
  d. serotonin

5. Which theory of why we sleep explains why we sleep *when* we do?
  a. restorative theory
  b. adaptive theory
  c. reactive theory
  d. REM theory

THE STAGES OF SLEEP

So are there different kinds of sleep? Do you go from being awake to being asleep and dreaming—is it instant? There are actually two kinds of sleep: **REM (rapid eye movement)** and **non-REM sleep**. REM sleep is a relatively active type of sleep when most of a person's dreaming takes place, whereas non-REM sleep is a much deeper, more restful kind of sleep. There are also several different stages of sleep that people go through each night in which REM sleep and non-REM sleep occur. A machine called an *electroencephalograph (EEG)* allows scientists to see the brain wave activity as a person passes through the various stages of sleep and to determine what type of sleep the person has entered (Aserinsky & Kleitman, 1953). See Figure 4.2 for a look at what happens in each stage of sleep.

A person who is wide awake and mentally active will show a brain wave pattern on the EEG called *beta waves*. Beta waves are very small and very fast. As the person relaxes and gets drowsy, slightly larger and slower **alpha waves** appear. The alpha waves are eventually replaced by even slower and larger **theta waves**.

4.4   *What are the different stages of sleep?*

NON-REM STAGE ONE: LIGHT SLEEP   As theta wave activity increases and alpha wave activity fades away, people are said to be entering Stage One sleep, or light sleep. Several rather interesting things can happen in this non-REM stage of sleep. If people are awakened at this point, they will probably not believe that they were actually asleep. They may also experience vivid visual events called *hypnagogic images* (Mavromatis, 1987; Mavromatis & Richardson, 1984). (The Greek word *hypnos* means "sleep.") These images are bits and pieces of what may eventually become dreams, but are most

◀ So are there different kinds of sleep? Do you go from being awake to being asleep and dreaming—is it instant?

rapid eye movement (REM)
stage of sleep in which the eyes move rapidly under the eyelids and the person is typically experiencing a dream.

NREM (non-REM) sleep
any of the stages of sleep that do not include REM.

alpha waves
brain waves that indicate a state of relaxation or light sleep.

theta waves
brain waves indicating the early stages of sleep.

a.

b.

FIGURE 4.2   **8-hour sleep cycle**   (a) The four stages of sleep and REM sleep comprise the sleep cycle, repeated four or five times during a single night's sleep. A normal sleep cycle takes an average of an hour and a half, with Stage Four being longer in the beginning of the night and REM sleep being longer in the last part of the sleep period, just before awakening. (b) This EEG shows brain activity (bottom line) during REM sleep. The larger graphs in the middle (third and fourth from the top) show muscle activity, which is much slower during REM sleep and accounts for the larger, slower waves on these graphs.

delta waves
long, slow waves that indicate the deepest stage of sleep.

Stages of
Sleep

often seen as flashes of light. Some people have very vivid images that seem realistic. Many researchers now believe that peoples' experiences of ghostly visits, alien abductions, and near-death experiences may be most easily explained by these images (Moody & Perry, 1993). (They can also occur just as people are about to wake up and are then called *hypnopompic images*.)

A much more common occurrence is called the *hypnic jerk* (Mahowald & Schenck, 1996; Oswald, 1959). Have you ever been drifting off to sleep when your knees, legs, or sometimes your whole body gives a big "jerk?" A simple explanation is that the muscles are so tensed up from the day that the brain instructs the body to "shake it out" much the same way people shake their hands to relieve the tension after writing or typing for a long time.

NON-REM STAGE TWO: SLEEP SPINDLES   As people drift further into sleep, the body temperature continues to drop. Heart rate slows, breathing becomes more shallow and irregular, and the EEG will show the first signs of *sleep spindles*, brief bursts of activity lasting only a second or two. Theta waves still predominate in this stage, but if people are awakened during this stage, they will be aware of having been asleep.

NON-REM STAGE THREE AND STAGE FOUR: DELTA WAVES ROLL IN   In the third stage of sleep, the slowest and largest waves make their appearance. These waves are called **delta waves**. In Stage Three, delta waves make up only about 20 to 50 percent of the brain wave pattern.

Once delta waves account for more than 50 percent of total brain activity, the person is said to have entered Stage Four sleep, the deepest stage of sleep. It is during this stage that growth hormones (often abbreviated as GH) are released from the pituitary gland and reach their peak. The body is at its lowest level of functioning. Eventually, the delta waves make up 100 percent of the brain activity for this stage of sleep. See Figure 4.3 to show movement through the sleep stages throughout one night.

People in deep sleep are very hard to awaken. If something does wake them, they may be very confused and disoriented at first. It is not unusual for people to wake up in this kind of disoriented state only to hear the crack of thunder and realize that a storm has come up. Children, who need deep sleep so that their bodies will grow, are even harder to wake up when in this state than are adults.

FIGURE 4.3   **A Typical Night's Sleep**   The graph shows the typical progression through the night of Stages 1–4 and Stage 1 REM sleep. Stage 1–4 are indicated on the x-axis, and REM stages are represented by darker bars on the graph. The REM periods occur about every 90 minutes throughout the night. (Dement, 1974)

The fact that children do sleep so deeply may explain why certain sleep disorders are more common in childhood. In fact, many sleep disorders are more common in boys than in girls because boys sleep more deeply than do girls due to high levels of the male hormone testosterone (Miyatake et al., 1980; Thiedke, 2001).

Stage Four Sleep Disorders   **Sleepwalking,** or **somnambulism**, occurs in about 20 percent of the population and is at least partially due to heredity (Abe et al., 1984; Kales et al., 1980). It is much more common in childhood and also occurs more frequently in boys than in girls. Although the old movies portray sleepwalkers as zombie-like and with arms outstretched, in reality a sleepwalker may do nothing more than sit up in bed. But other sleepwalking episodes may involve walking around the house, looking in the refrigerator or even eating, and getting into the car. One student said that her brother was a sleepwalker, and one morning his family found him sound asleep behind the wheel of the family car in the garage. Fortunately, he couldn't find the keys in his sleep.

Alex, the child whose night terrors were described in the opening story to this chapter, also suffered from sleepwalking. As many somnambulists do, he grew out of this behavior by the time he became an adolescent. His parents also found that preventing sleep loss made sleepwalking a rare occurrence. When Alex did have an episode, he never recalled it the next day. This lack of memory is typical of most sleepwalking episodes. The only real precaution that the families of people who sleepwalk should take is to clear their floors of obstacles and to put not-easy-to-reach locks on the doors. And although it is not dangerous to wake sleepwalkers, they may strike out before awakening.

Night Terrors   As discussed in the prologue, **night terrors** are a rare disorder, although are more likely in children and are likely to disappear as the child grows older (Garland & Smith, 1991). A night terror is essentially a state of panic experienced while sound asleep. People may sit up, scream, run around the room, or flail at some unseen attacker. It is not uncommon for people to feel unable to breathe as well. Considering that people suffering a night terror episode are in a deep stage of sleep and breathing shallowly, one can understand why breathing would seem difficult when they are suddenly active.

Most people do not remember what happened during a night terror episode, although a few people can remember vividly the images and terror they experienced.

But that sounds like the description of a nightmare—what's the difference? There are some very real differences between night terrors and nightmares. Nightmares are usually vividly remembered immediately upon waking. The person having a nightmare will actually be awake, too. A person who has had a nightmare, unlike a person experiencing a night terror, will actually be able to come awake and immediately talk about the bad dream. Perhaps the most telling difference is that nightmares occur during REM sleep rather than deep non-REM sleep, which means that people don't move around in a nightmare as they do in a night terror experience.

REM SLEEP

4.5   *What is dreaming, and what happens if people don't dream?*

Think back to the description of the four stages of sleep. After spending some time in Stage Four, the sleeping person will go back up through Stage Three, Stage Two, and then into a stage in which the eyes move rapidly under the eyelids, the body is almost as aroused as in a waking state, and brain waves resemble beta waves—the kind of brain activity that usually signals wakefulness. (This high level of brain activity has

Sleepwalking is more common among children than adults. Although this young girl may appear to be awake, she is still deeply asleep. When she awakens in the morning, she will have no memory of this sleepwalking episode.

"Wait Don't! It can be dangerous to wake them."
©The New Yorker Collection J. Dator from cartoonbank.com. All Rights Reserved.

◄ But that sounds like the description of a nightmare—what's the difference?

sleepwalking (somnambulism)
occurring during deep sleep, an episode of moving around or walking around in one's sleep.

night terrors
relatively rare disorder in which the person experiences extreme fear and screams or runs around during deep sleep without waking fully.

led some to call this stage *paradoxical sleep*.) The person is still asleep but in the stage known as rapid eye movement sleep (REM).

When a person in REM sleep is awakened, he or she almost always reports being in a dream state (Shafton, 1995). REM sleep is, therefore, associated with dreaming, and 90 percent of dreams actually take place in REM sleep. People do have dreams in the other non-REM (or NREM) stages, but REM dreams tend to be more vivid, more detailed, longer, and more bizarre than the dreams of NREM sleep. NREM dreams tend to be more like thoughts about daily occurrences and far shorter than REM dreams (Foulkes & Schmidt, 1983; Takeuchi et al., 2003).

CLASSIC STUDIES IN PSYCHOLOGY

REM Madness

D r. William Dement is generally recognized as one of the world's leading authorities on sleep, sleep deprivation, and sleep disorders. He founded the first sleep disorder clinic at Stanford University in 1970 and has remained active in both research and treatment of sleep problems.

In one of Dement's earliest studies (1960), subjects who were being monitored for sleep stages with an EEG machine were awakened each time they entered REM sleep. Two findings became clear. First, subjects deprived of REM sleep, when allowed to sleep normally, did an unusual amount of extra REM sleep. But also of interest was the fact that the REM-deprived subjects seemed to become paranoid, believing that the experimenter had all kinds of hidden, sinister motives and even experienced hallucinations. These early findings were the source of the *REM myth*, the theory that without dreams, people will become mentally ill.

In later studies (Dement et al., 1969) it was found that REM deprivation did not reliably produce these symptoms of severe mental disturbance. In fact, Dement concluded that the earlier findings may have been an example of the *experimenter effect* (discussed in Chapter One). Dement was very concerned about his subjects' well-being and may have communicated that concern to each subject during the interviews. To make matters worse, in the original experiment he had told the subjects what he thought the probable results of the study might be and provided them with a psychiatrist to whom they could report any unusual symptoms. Clearly, by the third day of REM deprivation the symptoms were most likely due to a combination of sleep deprivation and the power of suggestion.

Dement performed numerous experiments after this one, showing each time that no psychiatric symptoms resulted from REM sleep deprivation alone (unlike the psychotic behavior of a person who is seriously deprived of sleep in general). Popular science magazines still report the REM myth as fact, citing firm scientific support that does not exist. That first experiment, flawed as it was, is the one that many people seem to remember best. Perhaps some people would like to believe that there's a neat little reason for their occasional paranoid thoughts—REM sleep deprivation to the rescue.

Questions for Further Discussion

1. How might REM sleep deprivation studies be conducted?

2. What might be some of the problems encountered by researchers when trying to study sleep in a laboratory setting?

3. Are there any ethical concerns with deliberately disturbing people when they are sleeping?

4. How might the fact that the participants in these studies volunteered to sleep and be awakened under such artificial conditions have affected their behavior?

Dr. William Dement is the leading authority on sleep and sleep deprivation.

The Need for REM Sleep   Why two kinds of sleep? And why would REM sleep ever be considered restful when the body is almost awake and the brain is so active? REM sleep seems to serve a different purpose than does NREM, or deep sleep. After a very physically demanding day, people tend to spend more time in NREM deep sleep than is usual. But an emotionally stressful day leads to increased time in REM sleep (Horne & Staff, 1983). Perhaps the dreams people have in REM sleep are a way of dealing with the stresses and tensions of the day, whereas physical activity would demand more time for recovery of the body in NREM sleep. Also, if deprived of REM sleep (as would occur with the use of sleeping pills or other depressant drugs), a person will experience greatly increased amounts of REM sleep the next night, a phenomenon called **REM rebound** (Vogel, 1975, 1993).

Nightmares and REM Behavior Disorder   What would happen if we *could* act out our dreams? Would it be like sleepwalking? Being able to act out one's dreams, especially nightmares, is a far more dangerous proposition than sleepwalking. **Nightmares** are bad dreams, and some nightmares can be utterly terrifying. Children tend to have more nightmares than adults do because they spend more of their sleep in the REM state, as discussed earlier. As they age, they have fewer nightmares because they have less opportunity to have them. But some people still suffer from nightmares as adults.

Some people have a rare disorder in which the brain mechanisms that normally inhibit the voluntary muscles fail, allowing the person to thrash around and even get up and act out nightmares. This disorder is called **REM behavior disorder**, which is a fairly serious condition (Shafton, 1995). Usually seen in men over age 60, it can happen in younger men and in women. For more about this disorder, see Psychology in the News: Murderous Dreams that follows.

REM rebound
increased amounts of REM sleep after being deprived of REM sleep on earlier nights.

nightmares
bad dreams occurring during REM sleep.

REM behavior disorder
a rare disorder in which the mechanism that blocks the movement of the voluntary muscles fails, allowing the person to thrash around and even get up and act out nightmares.

◄ What would happen if we *could* act out our dreams? Would it be like sleepwalking?

PSYCHOLOGY IN THE NEWS
Murderous Dreams

4.6   *Can sleepwalking be a defense for committing a crime?*

According to a compilation of information by Dr. Lawrence Martin, Associate Professor at Case Western Reserve University and specialist in pulmonary* and sleep medicine, at least 20 cases of "murder while sleepwalking" have been recorded. The term *sleepwalking* as used in these cases probably refers to the very real condition called REM behavior disorder. Use of this disorder as a defense in a murder trial has sometimes been successful. Here are short descriptions of three well-known cases and their outcomes.

Case One:

Steven Steinberg of Scottsdale, Arizona, was accused of murdering his wife in 1981. The weapon was a kitchen knife and Elena Steinberg was stabbed 26 times. He claimed that he was sleepwalking at the time of the murder and did not remember committing the crime. A jury believed him and acquitted him under the insanity defense—although he admitted that he had indeed killed his wife, he was "temporarily insane" at the time of the murder.

Witnesses at his trial testified that Steinberg may have been sleepwalking or in a dissociative mental state in which the waking, alert part of his consciousness was split apart from the unconscious mind performing the stabbings (Martin, 2004).

*Pulmonary: having to do with the lungs.

Case Two:

Kenneth Parks, a 23-year-old man from Toronto, Canada, had been suffering from severe insomnia stemming from the loss of his job and financial problems. On May 23, 1987, he got up early in the morning, got in his car, and drove 23 kilometers (about 14 miles) to the home of his wife's parents. He stabbed his mother-in-law to death, attacked his father-in-law, and then drove to the police. Once there, he told them that he thought he had killed some people. At that point, he looked down at his hands and seemed to realize for the first time that they were severely cut—several of the tendons in both hands had to be surgically repaired.

Parks had loved his mother-in-law, and there was no history of bad feelings or hostility prior to the attack. He did have a history of sleepwalking and his defense team, which included sleep experts and psychiatrists, concluded that he was indeed unaware of his actions at the time of the crime. He was also acquitted (Denno, 2002; Martin, 2004).

Case Three:

Scott Falater, 43 years old, was accused of murdering his wife in 1997. A neighbor had peeked over the fence separating his property from the Falaters' and witnessed Scott holding his wife's head under water. The neighbor watched Falater pull on gloves and then drag his wife's body over to the pool and dump it in. He called the police, who found a bloody pool and the body of Yamila Falater, with 44 stab wounds.

Falater claimed to be sleepwalking at the time of the murder. Yet the prosecution was able to show that Falater had changed his bloodied clothes, hidden the hunting knife used

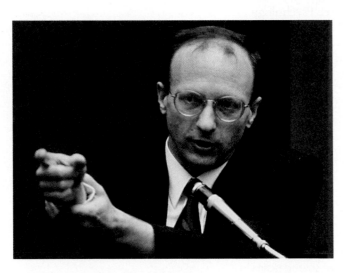

Scott Falater testifies at his trial for the murder of his wife, which he claims he committed while he was sleepwalking.

in the stabbing and his clothes and gloves in a plastic storage container, put the container in a trash bag along with his boots and socks, and then stashed the bag in the spare tire well of his car's trunk—actions that seemed very deliberate and that took much more time to complete than a normal sleep cycle would permit.

Sleep experts hired by the defense stated that Falater's story was possible. The prosecution pointed to marital troubles. Falater's mother and sister backed up his claims of a history of sleepwalking, but his own teenage children denied ever hearing anyone talk about their father's sleepwalking or ever seeing him in that state.

Most damaging to his case was the witness who stated that three weeks before the murder, Falater had been discussing the case of Kenneth Parks and Parks's acquittal for murder based on a sleepwalking defense. The jury found Falater guilty of murder in the first degree. The sentence was life imprisonment with no possibility of parole (Martin, 2004; Tresniowski, 1999).

Questions for Further Discussion

1. Should sleepwalking be a valid defense for a crime as serious as murder? What about other kinds of crimes?

2. What kind of evidence should be required to convince a jury that a crime was committed while sleepwalking?

SLEEP DISORDERS

There are a number of other problems that can occur during sleep in addition to sleepwalking, nightmares, and REM behavior disorder.

4.7 *What kinds of problems can happen during sleep?*

INSOMNIA Most people think that **insomnia** is the inability to sleep. Although that is the literal meaning of the term, in reality insomnia is the inability to get to sleep, stay asleep, or get a good quality of sleep (Kryger, Lavie, & Rosen, 1999). There are many causes of insomnia, both psychological and physiological. Some of the psychological causes are worrying, trying too hard to sleep, or anxiety. Some of the physiological causes are too much caffeine, indigestion, or aches and pain.

In insomnia, a person has trouble getting to sleep, staying asleep, or getting enough sleep. This man is wide awake with insomnia.

There are several steps people can take to help them sleep. Obvious ones are taking no caffeinated drinks or foods that cause indigestion before bedtime, taking medication for pain, and dealing with anxieties in the daytime rather than facing them at night. That last bit of advice is easy to say but not always easy to do. Here are some other helpful hints (Kupfer & Reynolds, 1997):

1. Go to bed only when you are sleepy. If you lie in bed for 20 minutes and are still awake, get up and do something like reading or watching television until you feel sleepy, and then go back to bed.

2. Don't do anything in your bed but sleep. Your bed should be a cue for sleeping, not studying or watching television. Because sleeping is a reflex response, using the bed as a cue for sleeping is a kind of learning called *classical conditioning,* or the pairing of cues and reflex responses. (L)(I)(N)(K) *to Chapter Five: Learning, p. 167.*

3. Don't try too hard to get to sleep, and especially do not look at the clock and calculate how much sleep you aren't getting. That just increases the tension and makes it harder to sleep.

4. Don't take sleeping pills or drink alcohol or other types of drugs that slow down the nervous system (see the category Depressants later in this chapter). These drugs force you into deep sleep and do not allow you to get any REM sleep or the lighter stages. When you try to sleep without these drugs the next night, you will experience REM rebound, which will cause you to feel tired and sleepy the next day. REM rebound is one way to experience the form of insomnia in which a person sleeps but sleeps poorly.

insomnia
the inability to get to sleep, stay asleep, or get a good quality of sleep.

sleep apnea
disorder in which the person stops breathing for nearly half a minute or more.

If none of these things seem to be working, there are sleep clinics and sleep experts who can help people with insomnia. The American Academy of Sleep Medicine has an excellent Web site at **www.aasmnet.org** that has links to find sleep clinics in any area.

SLEEP APNEA Gerald was a snorer. Actually, that's an understatement. Gerald could give a jet engine some serious competition. Snoring is fairly common, occurring when the breathing passages (nose and throat) get blocked. Most people snore only when they have a cold or some other occasional problem, but some people snore every night and quite loudly, like Gerald. It is this type of snoring that is often associated with a condition called **sleep apnea**, in which the person stops breathing for nearly half a minute or more.

This man is wearing a CPAP, or continuous positive air pressure device. The CPAP gently forces air through his nasal passages, keeping his airways open and preventing sleep apnea. Why might wearing a CPAP become a problem for some apnea sufferers?

When breathing stops, there will be a sudden silence, followed shortly by a gasping sound as the person struggles to get air into the lungs. Many people do not wake up while this is happening, but they do not get a good, restful night's sleep because of the apnea.

Apnea is a serious problem. Not only does it disturb nightly sleep, making the person excessively sleepy in the daytime, but also it can cause heart problems (Flemons, 2002). If a person suspects the presence of apnea, a visit to a physician is the first step in identifying the disorder and deciding on a treatment. With mild apnea, treatment may be a device worn on the nose at night to open the nostrils and prevent blockage. Obesity is a primary cause of apnea, especially in men, so another solution might be to lose excess weight. There are also sprays that are supposed to shrink the tissues lining the throat (much as a nasal decongestant spray shrinks the tissues of the nasal passages). Some people sleep with a device that delivers a continuous stream of air under mild pressure, called a *continuous positive airway pressure (CPAP) device*. Others undergo a simple surgery in which the *uvula* (the little flap that hangs down at the back of the throat) and some of the soft tissues surrounding it are removed.

NARCOLEPSY   A genetic disorder affecting one in every two thousand persons, **narcolepsy** is a kind of "sleep seizure." In narcolepsy, the person may slip suddenly into REM sleep during the day (especially when the person experiences strong emotions). Another symptom is excessive daytime sleepiness that results in the person falling asleep throughout the day at inappropriate times and in inappropriate places (Overeem et al., 2001). These sleep attacks may occur many times and without warning, making the operation of a car or other machinery very dangerous for the *narcoleptic* (person who suffers from narcolepsy). The sudden REM attacks are especially dangerous because of the symptom of *cataplexy*, or a sudden loss of muscle tone. This REM paralysis may cause injuries if the person is standing when the attack occurs. The same hypnogogic images that may accompany Stage One sleep may also occur in the narcoleptic person. Table 4.1 has a more detailed list of known sleep disorders.

"On your application it says you have narcolepsy. What is that?"

www.CartoonStock.com

narcolepsy
sleep disorder in which a person falls immediately into REM sleep during the day without warning.

TABLE 4.1 **COMMON SLEEP DISORDERS**

Name of Disorder	Primary Symptoms
Somnambulism	Sitting, walking, or performing complex behavior while asleep
Night terrors	Extreme fear, agitation, screaming while asleep
Restless leg syndrome	Uncomfortable sensations in legs causing movement and loss of sleep
Nocturnal leg cramps	Painful cramps in calf or foot muscles
Hypersomnia	Excessive daytime sleepiness
Circadian rhythm disorders	Disturbances of the sleep–wake cycle such as jet lag and shift work
Enuresis	Urinating while asleep in bed

Pick the best answer.

1. In which stage of sleep is a person who is very hard to awaken?
   a. Stage One   **c.** Stage Three
   b. Stage Two   **d.** Stage Four

2. Which of the following is NOT a characteristic of REM sleep?
   a. paralysis of voluntary muscles
   b. increased heart rate
   c. slower, deeper breathing
   d. increased body temperature

3. Acting out your nightmares is a rare condition called
   a. sleep apnea   **c.** narcolepsy
   b. night terrors   **d.** REM behavior disorder

4. In which disorder does breathing stop for nearly half a minute or more?
   a. sleep apnea   **c.** sleepwalking
   b. night terrors   **d.** narcolepsy

5. Which of the following is bad advice for someone suffering from insomnia?
   a. Do not watch TV or read in bed.
   b. Avoid coffee, tea, and other caffeine-containing products before bed.
   c. Do not study or work in bed.
   d. Lie in bed until you fall asleep, even if it takes several hours.

6. Nightmares occur in _____ sleep, whereas night terrors occur in _____ sleep.
   a. Stage One; Stage Two
   b. REM; NREM
   c. Stage Four; Stage One
   d. NREM; REM

Answers: 1-d, 2-c, 3-d, 4-a, 5-d, 6-b.

Dreams

4.8   Why do people dream, and what do they dream about?

Dreams have long been a source of curiosity. People of ancient times tried to find meaning in dreams. Some saw dreams as prophecy, some as messages from the spirits. But the real inquiry into the process of dreaming began with the publication of Freud's *The Interpretation of Dreams* (1900).

FREUD'S INTERPRETATION: DREAMS AS WISH FULFILLMENT

Sigmund Freud (1856–1939) believed that the problems of his patients stemmed from conflicts and events that had been buried in their unconscious minds since childhood. These early traumas were seen as the cause of *neurotic behavior* in adulthood, in which his patients suffered from symptoms such as a type of paralysis that had no physical basis or repetitive, ritualistic* hand washing. One of the ways Freud devised to get at these early memories was to examine the dreams of his patients, believing that conflicts, events, and desires of the past would be represented in symbolic** form in the dreams.

MANIFEST CONTENT   The *manifest content* of a dream is the actual dream itself. For example, if Chad has a dream in which he is trying to climb out of a bathtub, the manifest content of the dream is exactly that—he's trying to climb out of a bathtub.

LATENT CONTENT   But, of course, Freud would no doubt find more meaning in Chad's dream than is at first evident. He believed that the

---

*Ritualistic: referring to an action done in a particular manner each time it is repeated, according to some specific pattern.
**Symbolic: having the quality of representing something other than itself.

true meaning of a dream lay hidden, or *latent*, and was only expressed in symbols. In the dream, the water in the tub might symbolize the waters of birth, and the tub itself is his mother's womb. Chad may be dreaming about being born in Freudian terms.

Seems like quite a stretch. Wouldn't there be lots of other possible interpretations? Yes, and today many professionals are no longer as fond of Freud's dream analysis as they once were. But there are still some people who insist that dreams have symbolic meaning. For example, dreaming about being naked in a public place is very common, and most dream analyzers interpret that as feeling open and exposed, an expression of childhood innocence, or even a desire for sex. Exactly how the dream is interpreted depends on the other features of the dream and what is happening in the person's waking life.

The development of techniques for looking at the structure and activity of the brain (see Chapter Two, p. 62) has led to an explanation of why people dream that is more concrete than that of Freud.

THE ACTIVATION-SYNTHESIS HYPOTHESIS

Using brain-imaging techniques such as a PET scan (see Chapter Two), researchers have found evidence that dreams are products of activity in the lower brain stem (Hobson, 1988; Hobson & McCarley, 1977; Hobson et al., 2000). This lower area inhibits the neurotransmitters that would allow movement of the voluntary muscles while sending random signals to the areas of the cortex that interpret vision, hearing, and so on.

When signals from the lower brain bombard* the cortex during waking consciousness, the association areas of the cortex interpret those signals as seeing, hearing, and so on. Because those signals come from the real world, this process results in an experience of reality. But when people are asleep, the signals from the brain stem

---

*Bombard: to attack or press.

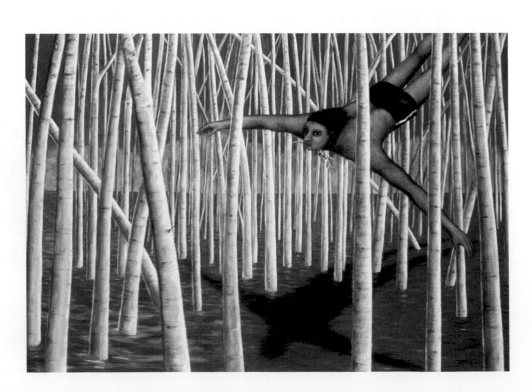

Dreams are often filled with unrealistic and imaginative events and images. A common dream is that of flying, like the man in this painting by American artist Gina Gilmour. What do you think flying might represent in a dream?

are random and not necessarily attached to actual external stimuli, yet the brain must somehow interpret these random signals. It *synthesizes* (puts together) an explanation of the cortex's activation from memories and other stored information.

In this theory, called the **activation-synthesis hypothesis**, a dream is merely another kind of thinking that occurs when people sleep. It is less realistic because it comes not from the outside world of reality but from within people's memories and experiences of the past. The frontal lobes, which people normally use in daytime thinking, are more or less shut down during dreaming, which may also account for the unrealistic and often bizarre nature of dreams (Macquet & Franck, 1996).

My dreams can be really weird, but sometimes they seem pretty ordinary or even seem to mean something. Can dreams be more meaningful? There are dream experts who suggest that dreams may have more meaning than Hobson and McCarley originally theorized. A survey questioning subjects about their dream content, for example, concluded that much of the content of dreams is meaningful, consistent over time, and fits in with past or present emotional concerns rather than being bizarre, meaningless, and random (Domhoff, 1996).

Hobson and colleagues have reworked the activation-synthesis hypothesis to reflect concerns about dream meaning, calling it the **activation-information-mode model**, or **AIM** (Hobson et al., 2000). In this newer version, information that is accessed during waking hours can have an influence on the synthesis of dreams. In other words, when the brain is "making up" a dream to explain its own activation, it uses bits and pieces of the person's experiences from the previous day or the last few days.

This tendency to use information from a person's daily life may also include information that is being suppressed. Suppression is a conscious, deliberate effort to refuse to think about or remember certain events or information. Some theorists see Freud's emphasis on repression (the unconscious forgetting of such information) as suppression. Whether it is called repression or suppression, there is some evidence from cognitive studies that Freud may not have been entirely wrong about the appearance of information a person would rather forget in his or her dreams. For example, in one study of nearly 300 smokers who quit smoking for from one to four weeks, a significant number of participants reported having dreams about smoking and feeling strong negative emotions such as guilt and panic during the dream (Hajek & Belcher, 1991).

WHAT DO PEOPLE DREAM ABOUT?

Do people dream in black and white or color? And do women have different kinds of dreams than men do? Calvin Hall collected over 10,000 dreams and concluded that most dreams reflect the events that occur in everyday life (Hall, 1966). Although most people dream in color, people who grew up in the era of black and white television sometimes have dreams in black and white. There are gender differences, although whether those differences are caused by hormonal/genetic influences, sociocultural influences, or a combination of influences remains to be seen. In his book *Finding Meaning in Dreams*, Dr. William Domhoff (1996) concluded that across many cultures, men more often dream of other males whereas women tend to dream about males and females equally. Men across various cultures also tend to have more physical aggression in their dreams than do women, with women more often being the victims of such aggression in their dreams. Domhoff also concluded that where there are differences in the content of dreams across cultures, the differences make sense in light of the culture's "personality." For example, American culture is considered fairly aggressive when compared to the culture of the Netherlands, and the aggressive content of the dreams in both cultures reflects this difference: There were lower levels of aggression in the dreams of those from the Netherlands when compared to the American dream content.

activation-synthesis hypothesis explanation that states that dreams are created by the higher centers of the cortex to explain the activation by the brain stem of cortical cells during REM sleep periods.

◀ My dreams can be really weird, but sometimes they seem pretty ordinary or even seem to mean something. Can dreams be more meaningful?

◀ Do people dream in black and white or color? And do women have different kinds of dreams than men do?

activation-information-mode model (AIM) revised version of the activation-synthesis explanation of dreams in which information that is accessed during waking hours can have an influence on the synthesis of dreams.

Girls and women tend to dream about people they know, personal appearance concerns, and an emphasis on family and home. Boys and men tend to have more male characters in their dreams, which are also typically in outdoor or unfamiliar settings and may involve weapons, tools, cars, and roads. Men also report more sexual dreams, usually with unknown and attractive partners (Domhoff, 1996; Foulkes, 1982; Van de Castle, 1994).

In dreams people run, jump, talk, and do all of the actions that they do in normal daily life. In fact, nearly 50 percent of the dreams recorded by Hall (1966) had sexual content, although later research has found lower percentages (Van de Castle, 1994). Then there are dreams of flying, falling, trying to do something and failing, all of which are very common dreams, even in other cultures (Domhoff, 1996). So is a dream of being naked in public.

PRACTICE QUIZ: HOW MUCH DO YOU REMEMBER?

Pick the best answer.

1. In Freud's theory, the symbolic content of dreams is called
   a. manifest content.
   b. latent content.
   c. symbolic content.
   d. hidden content.

2. Which dream theory states that dreams are simply the brain's way of explaining random neural activity while sleeping?
   a. Freudian dream theory
   b. dreams for survival theory
   c. activation-synthesis hypothesis
   d. Hall's dreams as reflections of everyday life

3. According to Hobson and McCarley, the _____ area of the brain sends signals to the _____, creating what we interpret as dreams.
   a. cerebellum; forebrain
   b. forebrain; cerebellum
   c. cortex; pons
   d. pons; cortex

4. The _____ lobes "shut down" during dreaming, explaining the often bizarre nature of dreams.
   a. frontal
   b. temporal
   c. occipital
   d. parietal

5. Shelia once had a dream in which she was trying to reach something important but couldn't. The harder she tried, the less she could move—it was like moving in molasses. This is most likely explained by
   a. anxiety.
   b. REM paralysis.
   c. Stage Four paralysis.
   d. a night terror.

Answers: 1-b, 2-c, 3-d, 4-a, 5-b.

Altered States: Hypnosis

Hypnosis is a state of consciousness in which a person is especially susceptible to suggestion. Although a lot of misunderstandings exist about hypnosis, it can be a useful tool when properly managed.

STEPS IN HYPNOTIC INDUCTION

4.9 *What is hypnosis and how does it work?*

There are several key steps in inducing hypnosis. According to Druckman and Bjork (1994), although every hypnotist may have a different style or use different words, these four elements are always present:

1. The hypnotist tells the person to focus on what is being said.

2. The person is told to relax and feel tired.

3. The hypnotist tells the person to "let go" and accept suggestions easily.

4. The person is told to use vivid imagination.

hypnosis
state of consciousness in which the person is especially susceptible to suggestion.

TABLE 4.2 SAMPLE ITEMS FROM THE STANFORD HYPNOTIC SUSCEPTIBILITY SCALE: FORM C (SHSS:C)

Hand lowering	Postural sway
Moving hands apart	Closing eyes
Taste hallucination	Finger lock
Arm rigidity	Hands moving together
Age regression	Cannot say one's name
Hallucinated voice	Visual hallucination
Amnesia	Cannot open eyes

Source: Adapted from Hilgard, E. (1965). *Hypnotic Susceptibility.* New York: Harcourt, Brace & World.

The real key to hypnosis seems to be a heightened state of suggestibility.* People can be hypnotized when active and alert, but only if they are willing to be hypnotized. Only 80 percent of all people can be hypnotized, and only 40 percent are good hypnotic subjects. People who fantasize a lot, who daydream and have vivid imaginations, as well as people who get "really into" whatever task they are doing are more susceptible** to hypnosis than others (Silva & Kirsch, 1992).

A test of *hypnotic susceptibility,* or the degree to which a person is a good hypnotic subject, often makes use of a series of suggestions. The more suggestions the person responds to, the more susceptible that person is. (See Table 4.2 for a list of some common suggestions developed at Stanford University.)

FACT OR MYTH: WHAT CAN HYPNOSIS REALLY DO?

Is it true that people can be hypnotized into doing things that they would never do under normal conditions? Books, movies, and television programs have often misrepresented the effects of hypnosis. Although the popular view is that the hypnotized person is acting involuntarily, the fact is that the hypnotized person is really the one in control. In fact, the hypnotist may only be a guide into a more relaxed state, while the subject actually hypnotizes himself or herself (Kirsch & Lynn, 1995). So relax, you won't be committing any immoral acts or doing anything really objectionable under hypnosis because you are really the one in control. People cannot be hypnotized against their will. The tendency to act as though their behavior is automatic and out of their control is called the *basic suggestion effect* (Kihlstrom, 1985); it gives people an excuse to do things they might not otherwise do because the burden of responsibility for their actions falls on the hypnotist.

Some people say that a hypnotized person can be superstrong or endure pain without feeling it. Is any of that true? No and yes. For a look at what hypnosis can and cannot do, see Table 4.3.

In general, hypnosis is a handy way to help people relax and control pain. These are subjective experiences and very much under people's mental influence. Actual physical behavior is harder to change, and that is why hypnosis is not as effective at changing eating habits or helping people to stop smoking (Druckman & Bjork, 1994). Hypnosis is sometimes used in psychological therapy to help people cope with anxiety or deal with cravings for food or drugs.

◀ Is it true that people can be hypnotized into doing things that they would never do under normal conditions?

◀ Some people say that a hypnotized person can be superstrong or endure pain without feeling it. Is any of that true?

---

*Suggestibility: being readily influenced.
**Susceptible: easily affected emotionally.

TABLE 4.3 **FACTS ABOUT HYPNOSIS**

Hypnosis Can:	**Hypnosis Cannot:**
Create amnesia for whatever happens during the hypnotic session, at least for a brief time (Bowers & Woody, 1996).	Give people superhuman strength. (People may use their full strength under hypnosis, but it is no more than they had before hypnosis.)
Relieve pain by allowing a person to remove conscious attention from the pain (Holroyd, 1996).	Reliably enhance memory. (There's an increased risk of false memory retrieval because of the suggestible state hypnosis creates.)
Alter sensory perceptions. (Smell, hearing, vision, time sense, and the ability to see visual illusions can all be affected by hypnosis.)	Regress people back to childhood. (Although people may *act* like children, they do and say things children would not.)

THEORIES OF HYPNOSIS

There are two views of why hypnosis works. One emphasizes the role of *dissociation*, or a splitting of conscious awareness, whereas the other involves a kind of social role-playing.

HYPNOSIS AS DISSOCIATION: THE HIDDEN OBSERVER   Ernest Hilgard (1991; Hilgard & Hilgard, 1994) believed that hypnosis worked only on the immediate conscious mind of a person, while a part of that person's mind (a "hidden observer") remained aware of all that was going on. It's the same kind of dissociation that takes place when people drive somewhere familiar and then wonder how they got there. One part of the mind, the conscious part, is thinking about dinner or a date or something else, while the other part is doing the actual driving. When people arrive at their destination, they don't really remember the actual trip. In the same way, Hilgard believes that there is a hidden part of the mind that is very much aware of the hypnotic subject's activities and sensations, even though the "hypnotized" part of the mind is blissfully unaware of these same things.

In one study (Miller & Bowers, 1993), subjects were hypnotized and told to put their arms in ice water, although they were instructed to feel no pain. There had to be pain—most people can't even get an ice cube out of the freezer without *some* pain—but subjects reported no pain at all. The subjects who were successful at denying the pain also reported that they imagined being at the beach or in some other place that allowed them to dissociate* from the pain.

HYPNOSIS AS SOCIAL ROLE-PLAYING: THE SOCIAL-COGNITIVE EXPLANATION   The other theory of why hypnosis works began with an experiment in which people who were *not* hypnotized were instructed to behave as if they were (Sarbin & Coe, 1972). These people had no trouble copying many actions previously thought to require a hypnotic state, such as being rigidly suspended between two

Through hypnosis training, this woman can have a much easier and relatively painless experience of childbirth. Pain relief is one of the more practical uses of hypnosis.

*Dissociate: break a connection with something.

chairs. Researchers (Sarbin & Coe, 1972) also found that people who were not familiar with hypnosis, and had no idea what the "role" of a hypnotic subject was supposed to be, could not be hypnotized.

Add to those findings the later findings of Kirsch (2000) that expectancies of the hypnotized person play a big part in how the person responds and what the person does under hypnosis. The **social-cognitive theory of hypnosis** assumes that people who are hypnotized are not in an altered state but are merely playing the role expected of them in the situation. They might believe that they are hypnotized, but in fact it is all a very good performance, so good that even the "subjects" are unaware that they are role-playing. Social roles are very powerful influences on behavior, as anyone who has ever worn a uniform can understand—the uniform stands for a particular role that becomes very easy to play (Zimbardo, 1970; Zimbardo et al., 2000). L I N K to Chapter Thirteen: Social Psychology, p. 507.

PRACTICE **QUIZ:** HOW MUCH DO YOU REMEMBER?

Pick the best answer.

1. Which of the following is NOT one of the steps in inducing hypnosis?
   a. putting the person to sleep
   b. telling the person to relax
   c. telling the person to use vivid imagination
   d. telling the person to "let go"

2. The tendency to act as though your behavior is out of your control and involuntary is called (the)
   a. hypnosis effect.
   b. basic involuntary effect.
   c. basic suggestion effect.
   d. none of the above.

3. Hypnosis has been successfully used to
   a. give a person superhuman strength.
   b. recall memories accurately and completely.
   c. reduce sensations of pain.
   d. regress a person back to infancy.

4. In the _____ theory of hypnosis, the person has a part of the mind that is not hypnotized and that is fully aware of the proceedings.
   a. social-cognitive
   b. dissociative
   c. role-playing
   d. expectancy

Answers: 1-a, 2-c, 3-c, 4-b.

Altered States: Psychoactive Drugs

While some people seek altered states of consciousness in sleep, daydreaming, meditation, or even hypnosis, others try to take a shortcut. They use drugs that alter thinking, perception, memory, or some combination of those abilities called **psychoactive drugs**. Although some of these drugs can be useful under certain circumstances, they all pose risks as well. One of the dangers of such drugs is their potential to create either a physical or psychological dependence, both of which can lead to a lifelong pattern of abuse as well as the risk of taking increasingly larger doses, leading to one of the clearest dangers of dependence: a drug overdose. Drug overdoses do not have to happen only with illegal drugs; even certain additives in so-called natural supplements can have a deadly effect. For example, in January 2003, Steve Bechler, a prospective pitcher for the Baltimore Orioles, died after taking three Ephedra pills on an empty stomach (Shekelle et al., 2003). Ephedra is a substance derived from a shrub found in desert areas and has been used in supplements that claim to promote weight loss.

PHYSICAL DEPENDENCE

4.10   *What is the difference between a physical dependence and a psychological dependence on a drug?*

Drugs that people can become physically dependent on cause the user's body to crave the drug (Abadinsky, 1989; Fleming & Barry, 1992; Pratt, 1991). After using the drug for some period of time, the body becomes unable to function normally without the drug and the person is said to be dependent or addicted.

social-cognitive theory of hypnosis
theory that assumes that people who are hypnotized are not in an altered state but are merely playing the role expected of them in the situation.

psychoactive drugs
drugs that alter thinking, perception, and memory.

DRUG TOLERANCE   One sign of physical dependence is the development of a *drug tolerance* (Pratt, 1991). As the person continues to use the drug, larger and larger doses of the drug are needed to achieve the same initial effects of the drug.

WITHDRAWAL   Another sign of a physical dependence is that the user experiences symptoms of **withdrawal** when deprived of the drug. Depending on the drug, these symptoms can range from headaches, nausea, and irritability to severe pain, cramping, shaking, and dangerously elevated blood pressure. These physical sensations occur because the body is trying to adjust to the absence of the drug. Many users will take more of the drug to alleviate the symptoms of withdrawal, which makes the entire situation worse. In Chapter Five, the text will discuss the concept of *negative reinforcement*, the tendency to continue a behavior that leads to the removal of or escape from unpleasant circumstances or sensations. Negative reinforcement is a very powerful motivating factor, and scores of drug-dependent users exist as living proof of that power.

> But not all drugs produce physical dependence, right? For example, some people say that you can't get physically dependent on marijuana. If that's true, why is it so hard for some people to quit smoking pot?

PSYCHOLOGICAL DEPENDENCE

Not all drugs cause physical dependence; some cause **psychological dependence**, or the feeling that the drug is needed to continue a feeling of emotional or psychological well-being, which is a very powerful factor in continued drug use. The body may not need or crave the drug, and people may not experience the symptoms of physical withdrawal or tolerance, but they will continue to use the drug because they *think* they need it. In this case, it is the rewarding properties of using the drug that cause a dependency to develop. In Chapter Five, this is called *positive reinforcement*, or the tendency of a behavior to strengthen when followed by pleasurable consequences. Negative reinforcement is also at work here, as taking the drug will lower levels of anxiety.

Although not all drugs produce physical dependence, *any* drug can become a focus of psychological dependence. Indeed, because there is no withdrawal to go through and from which to recover, psychological dependencies can last forever. Some people who gave up smoking pot decades ago still say that the craving returns every now and then (Roffman et al., 1988).

The effect of a particular drug depends on the category to which it belongs and the particular neurotransmitter the drug affects. **LINK** *to Chapter Two: The Biological Perspective, pp. 50–51.* This chapter will describe several of the major drug categories: **stimulants** (drugs that increase the functioning of the nervous system), **depressants** (drugs that decrease the functioning of the nervous system), **narcotics** (drugs that are derived from the opium poppy), and the **psychogenic drugs** (those that cause hallucinations as well as marijuana and hashish).

STIMULANTS: UP, UP, AND AWAY

Stimulants are a class of drugs that cause the nervous system and many of the organs connected to it to increase their activity, at least temporarily. In simple terms, stimulants "speed up" the nervous system. Many of these drugs are called "uppers" for this reason.

4.11   *What are some examples of stimulants and the dangers associated with taking them?*

AMPHETAMINES *German made* **Amphetamines** are stimulants that are synthesized (made) in laboratories rather than being found in nature. Among the amphetamines are drugs like Benzedrine, Methedrine, and Dexedrine. Truck drivers use amphetamines to stay

---

But not all drugs produce physical dependence, right? For example, some people say that you can't get physically dependent on marijuana. If that's true, why is it so hard for some people to quit smoking pot? ▶

One of the dangers of psychoactive drugs is that they may lead to physical or psychological dependence. Cocaine is a powerful and addictive stimulant and can be sniffed in through the nose or injected, as the man in this photograph is doing.

awake while driving long hours, and many doctors used to prescribe these drugs as diet pills for overweight people.

Like other stimulants, amphetamines cause the sympathetic nervous system to go into overtime. (L I N K) *to Chapter Two: The Biological Perspective, pp. 57–58.* Stimulants won't give people any extra energy, but they will cause people to burn up whatever energy reserves they do have. They also depress the appetite, which is another function of the sympathetic division. When the energy reserves are exhausted, or the drug wears off, a "crash" is inevitable.

This is why people who take amphetamines often develop a physical dependency on the drug and quickly develop a tolerance. When the "crash" or depression comes, the tendency is to take more pills to get back "up." The person taking these pills finds that it takes more and more pills to get the same stimulant effect. Doses can easily become toxic and deadly. Nausea, vomiting, high blood pressure, and strokes are possible, as is a condition called *amphetamine psychosis*. This condition causes addicts to become delusional (losing contact with what is real) and paranoid. They think people are out to "get" them. Violence is a likely outcome, both against the self and others (Kratofil, Baberg, & Dimsdale, 1996).

Of course, amphetamines are also used to treat narcolepsy, the sleep disorder discussed earlier in this chapter. They are still used as diet pills, but only on a short-term basis and under strict medical supervision. The diet aids people buy over the counter usually contain another relatively mild stimulant, caffeine.

COCAINE Unlike amphetamines, **cocaine** is a natural drug found in coca plant leaves. It produces feelings of euphoria (a feeling of great happiness), energy, power, and pleasure. It also deadens pain and suppresses the appetite. It was used rather liberally by both doctors and dentists (who used it in numbing the mouth prior to extracting a tooth, for example) near the end of the nineteenth century and the beginning of the twentieth century, until the deadly effects of its addictive qualities became known. Many patent medicines contained traces of cocaine, including the famous Coca-Cola™. The good news is that even in 1902, there wasn't enough cocaine in a bottle of cola to affect even a fly, and by 1929, all traces of cocaine were removed (Allen, 1994).

withdrawal
physical symptoms that can include nausea, pain, tremors, crankiness, and high blood pressure, resulting from a lack of an addictive drug in the body systems.

psychological dependence
the feeling that a drug is needed to continue a feeling of emotional or psychological well-being.

stimulants
drugs that increase the functioning of the nervous system.

depressants
drugs that decrease the functioning of the nervous system.

narcotics
a class of opium-related drugs that suppress the sensation of pain by binding to and stimulating the nervous system's natural receptor sites for endorphins.

psychogenic drugs
drugs including hallucinogens and marijuana that produce hallucinations or increased feelings of relaxation and intoxication.

amphetamines
stimulants that are synthesized (made) in laboratories rather than being found in nature.

cocaine
a natural drug derived from the leaves of the coca plant.

Psychoactive Drugs

Far from being illegal, cocaine was once used in many health drinks and medications, such as this toothache medicine used in the late 1800s.

nicotine
the active ingredient in tobacco.

Cocaine is a highly dangerous drug, not just for its addictive properties. Some people have convulsions and may even die when using cocaine for the first time (Lacayo, 1995). It has devastating effects on the children born to mothers who use cocaine, causing learning disabilities, hyperactivity, delayed language development, and tremors, among other symptoms (Blatt et al., 2000; Frank et al., 2001). Laboratory animals have been known to press a lever to give themselves cocaine rather than eating or drinking, even to the point of starvation and death (Iwamoto & Martin, 1988; Ward et al., 1996).

What are the signs of physical dependency? Although cocaine users do not go through the same kind of physical withdrawal symptoms that users of heroin, alcohol, and other physically addictive drugs go through, users will experience a severe mood swing into depression (the "crash"), followed by extreme tiredness, nervousness, an inability to feel pleasure, and paranoia. The brain is the part of the body that develops the craving for cocaine because of chemical changes caused by the drug (Hurley, 1989). There are three basic signs of physical dependency:

- **Compulsive use.** If cocaine is available, the person has to use it. He or she can't say no to it.
- **Loss of control.** Once people start using it, they can't stop until it is all gone or they have exhausted themselves to the point where they can no longer function.
- **Disregard for the consequences of use.** Cocaine addicts will lie, cheat, steal, lose their jobs, damage or break up relationships, and use rent money to buy cocaine—nothing else matters to them but the drug.

As addictive as cocaine is, there is one other stimulant that comes in a very close second. The Surgeon General's Report (Centers for Disease Control and Prevention [CDC], 1992) reports that although crack cocaine (a less pure, cheaper version found on the streets) produces addiction in every person who uses it, nicotine produces addiction in 99 percent of the people who use it.

> Hasn't nicotine just been the victim of a lot of bad press? After all, it's legal, unlike cocaine and heroin. ▶

NICOTINE Hasn't nicotine just been the victim of a lot of bad press? After all, it's legal, unlike cocaine and heroin. Every year, nearly 430,000 people in the United States die from illnesses related to smoking. That's more people than those who die from accidents in motor vehicles, alcohol, cocaine, heroin and other drug abuse, AIDS, suicide, and homicide *combined* (CDC, 2002). Remember, cocaine, heroin, morphine, and many other currently controlled substances or illegal drugs once used to be legal. One has to wonder what would have been the fate of these drugs if as many people had been making money off of them at that time as do those who farm, manufacture, and distribute tobacco products today.

Nicotine is a relatively mild but nevertheless toxic stimulant, producing a slight "rush" or sense of arousal as it raises blood pressure and accelerates the heart, as well as providing a rush of sugar into the bloodstream by stimulating the release of adrenalin (Rezvani & Levin, 2001). As is the case with many stimulants, it also has a relaxing effect on most people (remember the effect of Ritalin on hyperactivity) and seems to reduce stress (Pormerleau & Pormerleau, 1994).

Although fewer Americans are smoking (down to about 25 percent from over 40 percent in the sixties), women and teenagers are actually smoking more than before (CDC, 2002). This is alarming news when one considers the toxic nature of nicotine: In the 1920s and 1930s it was used as an insecticide and is considered to be highly toxic and fast-acting (Gosselin et

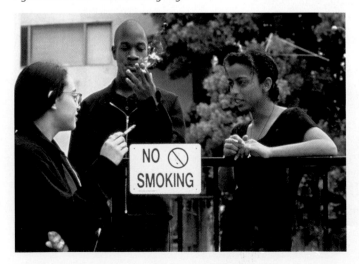

Nicotine is highly addictive, and many smokers will go to great lengths to be able to smoke—including smoking right next to the "No Smoking" sign.

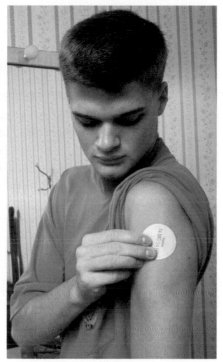

The harmful effects of nicotine are now well known, but many people continue to smoke or chew tobacco in spite of warnings such as this one cautioning pregnant women not to smoke. The nicotine patch this man is placing on his upper arm will deliver a controlled dose of nicotine throughout the time he is wearing it to prevent the physical craving for the drug. As he continues to move to smaller doses, his addiction will lessen and eventually disappear.

al., 1984). Although the amount of nicotine in a cigarette is low, first-time smokers often experience nausea as a result of the toxic effects after just a few puffs.

Quitting is a good idea but hard to accomplish for many people. Although there are a lucky few who can quit "cold turkey" without ever smoking again, the majority of people who quit will start smoking again, even after having quit for years.

Why is it so difficult to quit? Aside from the powerfully addictive nature of nicotine, the physical withdrawal symptoms can be as bad as those resulting from alcohol, cocaine, or heroin abuse (Epping-Jordan et al., 1998). People don't think about nicotine as being as bad as cocaine or heroin because nicotine is legal and easily obtainable, but in terms of its addictive power, it is *more powerful* than heroin or alcohol (Henningfield et al., 1990).

There are many ways to quit, but the most effective methods involve delayed smoking (Cincirpini et al., 1995). In delayed smoking, the smoker begins by delaying that first cigarette of the morning, increasing the delay by a little bit every morning. Next, the total number of cigarettes smoked each day is reduced. There are also medications that can help smokers deal with the cravings for nicotine while they try to quit, as well as nicotine-containing gums and patches (worn on the skin to deliver a measured dose of nicotine in decreasing doses). The gum and patch methods deliver nicotine in a much safer, less addictive way, allowing the smoker to control the cravings until quitting completely (Benowitz, 1996; Henningfield, 1995; Stitzer & De Wit, 1998).

CAFFEINE Although many people will never use amphetamines or take cocaine, and others will never smoke or will quit successfully, there is one stimulant that almost everyone uses, with many using it every day. Of course, this is **caffeine**, the stimulant found in coffee, tea, most sodas, chocolate, and even many over-the-counter drugs.

caffeine
a mild stimulant found in coffee, tea, and several other plant-based substances.

Sleep deprivation causes this man to struggle to wake up. Caffeine can help with alertness but may worsen his sleep deprivation when he tries to get a decent night's sleep tonight.

"Nowadays, Hal is ninety-nine percent caffeine-free."

Caffeine is another natural substance, like cocaine and nicotine, and is found in coffee beans, tea leaves, cocoa nuts, and at least 60 other types of plants (Braun, 1996). It is a mild stimulant, helps maintain alertness, and can increase the effectiveness of some pain relievers such as aspirin. Caffeine is often added to pain relievers for that reason and is the key ingredient in medications meant to keep people awake.

Using coffee to help induce sobriety is a common caffeine myth. All one would get is a wide-awake drunk. Coffee is fairly acidic, too, and acids are not what the stomach of a person with a hangover needs. (And since the subject has come up, drinking more alcohol or "hair of the dog that bit you" just increases the problem later on—the best cure for a hangover is lots of water to put back all the fluids that alcohol takes out of the body and sleep.)

For a comparison of amounts of caffeine in some common foods, see Table 4.4.

DOWN IN THE VALLEY: DEPRESSANTS

Another class of psychoactive drugs is *depressants*, drugs that slow the central nervous system.

4.12 What are some different types of depressants and how can they be harmful?

BARBITURATES OR MAJOR TRANQUILIZERS Commonly known as the *major tranquilizers* (drugs that have a strong depressant effect) or sleeping pills, **barbiturates** are drugs that have a sedative (sleep-inducing) effect. The effects, depending on dosage levels, range from mild sedation or sleepiness to unconsciousness or coma. Overdoses can lead to death as breathing and heart action are stopped. Barbiturates are highly addictive and users can quickly develop a tolerance. Withdrawal can be as serious as convulsions, which are life threatening (Olin, 1993).

Another danger of barbiturate use is the combination of one of these drugs with alcohol, another kind of depressant drug. A person who takes a dose of barbiturates that is not deadly in and of itself may die from the interaction of that dose with alcohol. This is called a *drug interaction* and is a major contributor to many unfortunate deaths.

barbiturates
depressant drugs that have a sedative effect.

TABLE 4.4 AVERAGE CAFFEINE CONTENT OF SOME COMMON FOODS

Product (8 oz. except as noted)	Caffeine (milligrams)
Brewed coffee	60–120
Decaffeinated coffee	2–4
Espresso/cappuccino (1 oz.)	30–50
Tea brewed 1 minute	9–33
Tea brewed 3 minutes	20–46
Tea brewed 5 minutes	20–50
Iced tea (8 oz./12 oz.)	15–24/22–36
Hot cocoa	3–32
Milk chocolate (1 oz.)	1–15
Dark chocolate (1 oz.)	5–35
Jolt soda (8 oz./12 oz.)	47/71
Mountain Dew (8 oz./12 oz.)	36/54
Coca-Cola (8 oz./12 oz.)	31/46
Pepsi (8 oz./12 oz.)	24/36

Source: Barone, J. J., & Roberts, H. R. (1996).

BENZODIAZEPINES OR THE MINOR TRANQUILIZERS   The *minor tranquilizers* (drugs having a relatively mild depressant effect) are called **benzodiazepines**. These drugs are used to lower anxiety and reduce stress. They are considered safer than barbiturates and are now the drugs of choice to treat sleep problems, nervousness, and anxiety. Some of the most common are Valium, Xanax, Halcion, Ativan, and Librium.

Even these minor tranquilizers can be addictive, and large doses can be dangerous, as can an interaction with alcohol or other drugs. Rohypnol is a newer tranquilizer that has become famous as the "date rape" drug. Unsuspecting victims drink something that has been doctored with this drug, which renders them unconscious. Rape or some other form of sexual assault can then be carried out without fear that the victim will remember it or be able to report it (Armstrong, 1997).

ALCOHOL

4.13   *What kind of drug is alcohol and what are the dangers of drinking too much?*

The most commonly used and abused depressant is **alcohol**, the chemical resulting from fermentation or distillation of various kinds of vegetable matter. Anywhere from 10 to 20 million people in the United States suffer from alcoholism. Aside from the obvious health risks to the liver, brain, and heart, alcohol is associated with loss of work time, loss of a job, and loss of economic stability. Alcohol is a major contributing factor in nearly 40 percent of all traffic fatalities in the United States (McGwin, 1999; Williams, 1981).

SIGNS OF ALCOHOL ABUSE   Many people are alcoholics but deny the fact, a common psychological defense. (LINK) *to Chapter Eleven, Stress and Health, p. 433.* They believe that getting drunk, especially in college, is a ritual of adulthood. But drunkenness is a major sign of alcoholism. Some other danger signs are feeling guilty about drinking, drinking in the morning, drinking to recover from drinking, drinking alone, being sensitive about how much one drinks when others mention it, drinking so much that one does and says things one later regrets, drinking enough to have blackouts or memory loss, drinking too fast, lying about drinking, and drinking enough to pass out.

If you are concerned about your own drinking or are worried about a friend or loved one, there is a free and very simple online assessment at this site on the Internet: **www.psychologicaladvice.com/pages/alcohol.html.**

Alcohol is often confused with stimulants. Many people think this because alcohol makes a person feel "up" and euphoric (happy). Actually, alcohol is a depressant that gives the illusion of stimulation, because the very first thing alcohol depresses is a person's natural

benzodiazepines
drugs that lower anxiety and reduce stress.

alcohol
the chemical resulting from fermentation or distillation of various kinds of vegetable matter.

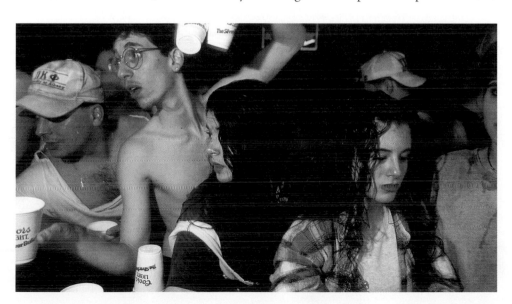

Although many young adults see drinking as a rite of passage into adulthood, few may understand the dangers of "binge" drinking, or drinking four to five drinks within a limited amount of time. Inhibitions are lowered and poor decisions may be made, such as driving while intoxicated. Binge drinking, a popular activity on some college campuses, can also lead to alcoholism.

inhibitions, or the "don'ts" of behavior. Inhibitions are all the social rules people have learned that allow them to get along with others and function in society. Inhibitions also keep people from taking off all their clothes and dancing on the table at a crowded bar—inhibitions are a good thing.

Alcohol, as stated in Chapter Two, indirectly stimulates the release of a neurotransmitter called GABA, the brain's major depressant (Brick, 2003). GABA slows down or stops neural activity. As more GABA is released, the brain's functioning actually becomes more and more inhibited, depressed, or slowed down. The areas of the brain that are first affected by alcohol are unfortunately the areas that control social inhibitions, so alcohol (due to its simulation of GABA) has the effect of depressing the inhibitions. As the effects continue, motor skills, reaction time, and speech are all affected.

Some people might be surprised that only one drink can have a fairly strong effect on some people. People who are not usually drinkers will feel the effects of alcohol much more quickly than those who have built up a tolerance. Women also feel the effects sooner, as their bodies process alcohol differently than men's bodies do. (Women are typically smaller, too, so alcohol has a quicker impact on women.) See Table 4.5 for a look at what constitutes a "drink" and the effects of various numbers of drinks on the system and behavior of the drinker.

PRACTICE **QUIZ:** HOW MUCH DO YOU REMEMBER?

Pick the best answer.

1. What are two signs of physical dependency?
   a. drug tolerance and psychological cravings
   b. psychological cravings and withdrawal
   c. drug tolerance and withdrawal
   d. psychological cravings and nausea

2. Larger and larger doses of amphetamines can lead to a severe mental disturbance and paranoia called
   a. amphetamine neurosis.
   b. amphetamine psychosis.
   c. amphetaminism.
   d. amphetamine toxicity.

3. Which of the following is NOT one of the three signs of cocaine abuse?
   a. withdrawal
   b. compulsive use
   c. loss of control
   d. disregard for consequences

4. Caffeine replaced _____ in patent medicines and over-the-counter preparations in the early 1900s.
   a. cocaine
   b. morphine
   c. opium
   d. nicotine

5. The "date rape" drug, Rohypnol, is one of the _____.
   a. major tranquilizers
   b. barbiturates
   c. minor tranquilizers
   d. opiates

6. Several of her friends suspect that Marnie is using some sort of drug. She is very thin, stays awake for long periods of time, and is often jittery, nervous, and somewhat paranoid. If Marnie is using a drug, it is likely to be
   a. alcohol.
   b. an amphetamine.
   c. sleeping pills.
   d. benzodiazapine.

Answers: 1-c, 2-b, 3-a, 4-a, 5-c, 6-b.

NARCOTICS: I FEEL YOUR PAIN

4.14   *How do narcotics work, and why are they so addictive?*

Narcotics are a class of drugs that suppress the sensation of pain by binding to and stimulating the nervous system's natural receptor sites for endorphins, the neurotransmitters that naturally deaden pain sensations (Olin, 1993). Because they also slow down the action of the nervous system, drug interactions with alcohol and other depressants are possible—and deadly. All narcotics are a derivative of a particular plant-based substance, opium.

OPIUM   **Opium**, made from the opium poppy, has pain-relieving and euphoria-inducing properties that have been known for at least 2,000 years. It was commonly used by ladies of the Victorian era in a form called *laudanum* and was still prescribed as *paregoric* for teething infants in the middle of the twentieth century. (Your own mother or father may have been given paregoric as an infant.) It was not until 1803 that opium was developed for use as a medication by a German physician. The new form—morphine—was hailed as "God's own medicine" (Hodgson, 2001).

opium
substance derived from the opium poppy from which all narcotic drugs are derived.

TABLE 4.5 BLOOD ALCOHOL LEVEL AND BEHAVIOR ASSOCIATED WITH AMOUNTS OF ALCOHOL

A drink is a drink. Each contains half an ounce of alcohol.
So a drink is . . .
- 1 can of beer (12 oz. 4–5% alcohol)
- 1 glass of wine (4 oz. 12% alcohol)
- 1 shot of most liquors (1 oz. 40–50% alcohol)

At times "a drink" is really the equivalent of more than just one drink, like when you order a drink with more than one shot of alcohol in it, or you do a shot followed by a beer.

Average Number of Drinks	Blood Alcohol Level	Behavior
1–2 drinks	.05%	Feeling of well being Release of inhibitions Judgment impaired Coordination and level of alertness lowered Increase risk of collision while driving
3–5 drinks	.10%	Reaction time significantly slowed Muscle control and speech impaired Limited night and side vision Loss of self-control Crash risk greatly increased
6–7 drinks	.15%	Consistent and major increases in reaction time
8–10 drinks	.20%	Loss of equilibrium and technical skills Sensory and motor capabilities depressed Double vision and legal blindness (20/20) Unfit to drive for up to 10 hours
10–14 drinks	.20% and .25%	Staggering and severe motor disturbances
10–14 drinks	.30%	Not aware of surroundings
10–14 drinks	.35%	Surgical anesthesia Lethal dosage for a small percentage of people
14–20 drinks	.40%	Lethal dosage for about 50% of people Severe circulatory/respiratory depression Alcohol poisoning/overdose

Source: Adapted from the *"Moderate Drinking Skills Study Guide."* (2004). Eau-Claire, WI: University of Wisconsin.

MORPHINE **Morphine** was created by dissolving opium in an acid and then neutralizing the acid with ammonia. Morphine was thought to be a wonder drug, although its addictive qualities soon became a major concern to physicians and their patients. Morphine is still used today but in carefully controlled doses and for short periods of time.

HEROIN Ironically, **heroin** was first hailed as the new wonder drug—a derivative of morphine that did not have many of the disagreeable side effects of morphine. The theory was that heroin was a purer form of the drug, and that the impurities in morphine were the substances creating the harmful side effects. It did not take long, however, for doctors and others to realize that heroin was even more powerfully addictive than morphine or opium. Its use as a medicine ceased, but it is still used by many people.

morphine
narcotic drug derived from opium, used to treat severe pain.

heroin
narcotic drug derived from opium that is extremely addictive.

Why are morphine ▶
and heroin so
addictive?

Why are morphine and heroin so addictive? Think back to Chapter Two. That chapter discussed the roles of endorphins in relieving pain. Opium and its derivatives, morphine and heroin, duplicate the action of endorphins so well that the nervous system slows or stops its production of the neurotransmitter. When the drug wears off, there is no protection against any kind of pain, causing the severe symptoms of withdrawal associated with these drugs. The addict who tries to quit using the drug feels such pain that the urge to use again becomes unbearable.

Methadone is also a derivative of opium but does not produce the euphoric "high" of morphine or heroin. It is used to control heroin dependency and can be taken only once a day to control the withdrawal symptoms that would otherwise follow when stopping heroin use (Kahan & Sutton, 1998). Two other drugs, buprenorphine and naltrexone, are also used to treat opiate addictions (Ward et al., 1999).

There are also nondrug treatments that make use of behavioral therapies such as *contingency management therapy*, in which patients earn vouchers for negative drug tests (Tusel et al., 1994). The vouchers can be exchanged for healthier, more desirable items like food. These behavioral therapies can include residential and outpatient approaches. **LINK** *to Chapter Five, Learning, p. 190. Cognitive-behavioral interventions* work to change the way people think about the stresses in their lives and react to those stressors, working toward more effective coping without resorting to heroin.

HALLUCINOGENS: HIGHER AND HIGHER

4.15 *How do hallucinogens work?*

Hallucinogens fall under the category of psychogenic drugs. Hallucinogens actually stimulate the brain into altering its interpretation of sensations (Olin, 1993) and can produce sensory distortions very similar to the disorder *synesthesia* **LINK** *to Chapter Three: Sensation and Perception, p. 82*, in which sensations cross over each other—colors have sound, sounds have smells, and so on. False sensory perceptions, called *hallucinations*, are often experienced, especially with the more powerful hallucinogens. As with other stimulants, there are two basic types—those that are created in a laboratory and those that are from natural sources.

MANUFACTURED HIGHS   There are several drugs that were developed in the laboratory instead of being found in nature. Perhaps because these drugs are manufactured, they are often more potent than drugs found in the natural world.

LSD   LSD, or **lysergic acid diethylamide**, is synthesized from a grain fungus called *ergot*. Ergot fungus commonly grows on rye grain but can be found on other grains as well. First manufactured in 1938, LSD is one of the most potent, or powerful, hallucinogens (Lee & Shlain, 1986). It takes only a very tiny drop of LSD to achieve a "high."

People who take LSD usually do so to get that high feeling. Some people feel that LSD helps them to expand their consciousness or awareness of the world around them. Colors seem more intense, sounds more beautiful, and so on. But the fact is that LSD takes people out of the real world and dumps them into a world of the brain's creation. This is not always a pleasant experience, just as dreams are not always filled with positive emotions. "Bad trips" are quite common, and there is no way to control what kind of "trip" the brain is going to decide to take.

One of the greater dangers in using LSD is the effect it has on a person's ability to perceive reality. Real dangers and hazards in the world may go unnoticed by a person "lost" in an LSD fantasy, and people under the influence of this drug may make poor decisions, such as trying to drive while high.

PCP   Another synthesized drug was found to be so dangerous that it became useful only in veterinary medicine as a tranquilizer. The drug is **PCP** (which stands for *p*henyl *c*yclohexyl *p*iperidine, a name which is often contracted as *phencyclidine*) and can have many

hallucinogens
drugs that cause false sensory messages, altering the perception of reality.

LSD (lysergic acid diethylamide)
powerful synthetic hallucinogen.

PCP
synthesized drug now used as an animal tranquilizer that can cause stimulant, depressant, narcotic, or hallucinogenic effects.

different effects. Depending on the dosage, it can be a hallucinogen, stimulant, depressant, or an analgesic (pain-killing) drug. As with LSD, PCP users can experience hallucinations, distorted sensations, and very unpleasant effects. PCP can also lead to acts of violence against others or suicide (Brecher et al., 1988; Cami et al., 2000). Users may even physically injure themselves unintentionally because PCP causes them to feel no warning signal of pain.

MDMA (Ecstasy)   This last synthetic drug is technically an amphetamine but is capable of producing hallucinations as well. In fact, both **MDMA** (a "designer drug" known on the streets as **Ecstasy** or simply **X**) and PCP are now classified as **stimulatory hallucinogenics**, drugs that produce a mixture of psychomotor stimulant and hallucinogenic effects (Shuglin, 1986). Although many users of MDMA believe that it is relatively harmless, the fact is that it can be deadly. MDMA is a common drug at "raves" or all-night dance parties. One of the properties of this drug is to dehydrate the body and raise body temperature, so it is very important that someone taking this drug drink enough water. But excessive drinking of water can also lead to coma and death, as excess fluid can disrupt the salt content of body tissue, making it impossible for all body parts to function properly. Nightclubs that sponsor raves usually pass out or sell bottled water to offset the dehydration, but in the midst of having fun it is easy for a person to forget to drink enough—or to drink far too much. Adding to the risk is the possibility that Ecstasy users are also consuming alcohol, and that interaction increases the dehydration and rise in body temperature (Leccese et al., 2000).

NONMANUFACTURED HIGHS   A number of substances found in nature can produce hallucinogenic effects. Although some people might refer to these substances as "natural" highs, they are still drugs and still potentially dangerous.

Mescaline   Mescaline comes from the buttons found on the peyote cactus and has long been a part of many Native American religious and spiritual rituals. The duration of its hallucinogenic effects can last longer than those of LSD (Aghajanian & Marek, 1999). Native Americans have used mescaline in combination with sitting in a hut or other enclosed space while water is poured over very hot rocks. This sauna effect, together with the drug, may produce sensations of being out of one's own body or talking with spirits, which is the purpose of these rituals (Lyvers, 2003).

Psilocybin   Psilocybin (sigh-luh-SIGH-bun) is another naturally occurring hallucinogen, contained in a certain kind of mushroom, often referred to as "magic mushrooms." Like mescaline, it has also been used in similar rituals by several native cultures (Aghajanian & Marek, 1999).

Is using mescaline or psilocybin addictive? Neither mescaline nor psilocybin has been shown to create physical dependency, but as with any psychoactive drug, psychological dependency is possible (Lyvers, 2003).

MARIJUANA

4.16   *What is marijuana and what are the risks of using it?*

One of the best known and most commonly abused of the psychogenic drugs, **marijuana** (also call *pot* or *weed*) comes from the leaves and flowers of the hemp plant called *cannabis sativa*. (*Hashish* is the substance scraped from these leaves, and both marijuana and hashish are called *cannabinoids*.) The active ingredient in marijuana is *tetrahydrocannabinol* (THC). Marijuana it is best known for its ability to produce a feeling of well-being, mild intoxication, and mild sensory distortions or hallucinations (Olin, 1993; Tart, 1970).

The effects of marijuana are relatively mild compared to the other hallucinogens. In fact, an inexperienced user who doesn't know what to expect upon smoking that first

Many of these young people enjoying themselves at a rave may be using MDMA, or Ecstasy. The dehydrating effect of the drug, together with the intense dancing and physical activity at raves like this one, can have a deadly effect on the user.

MDMA (Ecstasy or X)
designer drug that can have both stimulant and hallucinatory effects.

stimulatory hallucinogenics
drugs that produce a mixture of psychomotor stimulant and hallucinogenic effects.

mescaline
natural hallucinogen derived from the peyote cactus buttons.

psilocybin
natural hallucinogen found in certain mushrooms.

marijuana (pot or weed)
mild hallucinogen derived from the leaves and flowers of a particular type of hemp plant.

◀ Is using mescaline or psilocybin addictive?

TABLE 4.6 **HOW DRUGS AFFECT CONSCIOUSNESS**

Drug Classification	Common Name	Main Effect
Depressants		
Alcohol	Beer, wine, spirits	Relaxation
Barbiturates (tranquilizers)	Nembutal, Seconal	
Stimulants		
Amphetamines	Methamphetamine, speed, Ritalin, Dexedrine	Stimulation, excitement
Cocaine	Cocaine, crack	
Nicotine	Tobacco	
Caffeine	Coffee, tea	
Narcotics		
Opiates	Morphine, heroin	Euphoria
Psychedelics and Hallucinogens		
	Marijuana, hashish, LSD, Ecstasy	Distorts consciousness, alters perception

This woman is preparing a cannabis (marijuana) cigarette. Cannabis is reported to relieve pain in cases of multiple sclerosis and chronic pain from nerve damage. Such use is controversial as cannabis is classified as an illegal drug in some countries.

marijuana cigarette or *joint* may feel nothing at all. Most people do report a feeling of mild euphoria and relaxation, along with an altered time sense and mild visual distortions. Higher doses can lead to hallucinations, delusions, and the all-too-common paranoia. Most studies of marijuana's effects have concluded that while marijuana can create a powerful psychological dependency, it does not produce physical dependency or physical withdrawal symptoms. Newer studies, however, suggest that long-term marijuana use can produce signs of withdrawal such as irritability, sleep difficulties, and increased aggression (Budney et al., 2001; Kouri et al., 1999).

Even at mild doses, it is not safe to operate heavy machinery or drive a car while under the influence of marijuana. The effect on a person's reaction time and perception of surroundings is too damaging to the ability to make the split-second decisions that are required in driving.

Marijuana is most commonly smoked like tobacco, but some people have been known to eat it baked into brownies or other foods. This is a kind of double duty for the doctored food, as marijuana stimulates the appetite.

Although no one has ever been known to die from an overdose of marijuana, it is not exactly a healthy habit. Marijuana smokers get considerably more *carcinogens* (cancer-causing substances), carbon dioxide, and tar exposure than do the smokers of ordinary cigarettes. This is partly caused by the higher content of these substances in marijuana and partly by the pot smoker's tendency to inhale more deeply and hold the smoke longer than tobacco smokers do (Wu et al., 1988).

Table 4.6 summarizes the various types of drugs, their common names, and their effects on human behavior.

PRACTICE **QUIZ:** HOW MUCH DO YOU REMEMBER?

Pick the best answer.

1. All narcotics are derived from
   a. cannabis.
   b. opium.
   c. mescaline.
   d. morphine.

2. This drug was at first hailed as the new wonder drug, because the impurities that supposedly caused many of the addictive and unpleasant side effects of the previous version had been removed. In fact, _____ was even more addictive and deadly.
   a. laudanum
   b. heroin
   c. morphine
   d. ergot

3. Which of the following hallucinogens is NOT a synthetically created drug?
   a. psylocybin
   b. LSD
   c. PCP
   d. MDMA

4. Of the following, which comes from the peyote cactus?
   a. mescaline   **c.** marijuana
   b. psilocybin   **d.** ergot

5. Which of the following is a long-term effect of marijuana use?
   a. lung cancer   **c.** immune system damage
   b. asthma   **d.** all of the above

6. Which of the following statements about marijuana is TRUE?
   a. Marijuana is not physically addictive.
   b. It is safe to drive under the influence of pot.
   c. Marijuana is healthier than tobacco.
   d. Short-term memory is enhanced by smoking marijuana.

Answers: 1-b, 2-b, 3-a, 4-a, 5-d, 6-a.

Applying Psychology to Everyday Life: Are You Sleep Deprived?

4.17   *How serious is the problem of sleep deprivation?*

Sleep deprivation has long been considered a fact of life for many people, especially college students. Dr. William Dement (1997), one of the most renowned sleep experts in the field, believes that people are ignorant of the detrimental effects of sleep deprivation. Here are some of the facts he points out concerning the widespread nature of sleep deprivation:

- 55 percent of drowsy driving fatalities occur under the age of 25.

- 56 percent of the adult population reports that daytime drowsiness is a problem.

- In a study of 1,000 people who reported no daytime drowsiness, 34 percent were actually found to be dangerously sleepy.

- In samples of undergraduates, nurses, and medical students, 80 percent were dangerously sleep deprived.

Dr. Dement cautions that drowsiness should be considered a red alert. Contrary to many people's belief that drowsiness indicates the first step in falling asleep, he states that drowsiness is the last step—if you are drowsy, you are seconds away from sleep.

In an article published by CNN on its interactive Web site (**www.cnn.com/HEALTH/9703/17/nfm/sleep.deprivation/index.html**), the National Commission on Sleep Disorders (1997) estimates that "sleep deprivation costs $150 billion a year in higher stress and reduced workplace productivity." Sleep deprivation was one of the factors indicated in such disasters as the explosion of the *Challenger*, the Exxon *Valdez* oil spill, and the Chernobyl disaster.

More disturbing facts (data taken from Williamson & Feyer, 2000):

- 30 to 40 percent of all heavy truck accidents can be attributed to driver fatigue.

- Drivers who are awake for 17 to 19 hours were more dangerous than drivers with a blood alcohol level of .05.

- 16 to 60 percent of road accidents involve sleep deprivation (the wide variation is due to the inability to confirm the cause of accidents, as the drivers are often killed).

- Sleep deprivation is linked to higher levels of stress, anxiety, depression, and unnecessary risk taking.

Clearly, sleep deprivation is a serious and all-too-common problem. In today's 24-hour-a-day society, stores are always open, services such as banking and transportation are always available, and many professionals (such as nurses, doctors, and firefighters) must work varying shifts around the clock (Knauth, 1993). As stated earlier, shift work can seriously disrupt the normal sleep–wake cycle, often causing insomnia.

The student in the background is unable to stay awake during his class, indicating that he is seriously sleep deprived. Has this happened to you?

CAUSES OF SLEEP DEPRIVATION

Many of the sleep disorders that were discussed in this chapter are themselves causes of sleep deprivation. Sleep apnea, narcolepsy, sleepwalking, night terrors, and a condition called "restless leg syndrome" in which a person constantly moves his or her legs that are tingly or have crawling sensations are all causes. Yet these problems are not the sole, or most common, cause of sleep deprivation.

The most obvious cause is the refusal of many people to go to sleep at a reasonable time, so that they can get the eight hours of sleep that most adults need in order to function well (Bonnet & Arand, 1995). People want to watch that last bit of news or get a little more work done or party into the wee hours. Another reason for sleep loss is worry. People live in stressful times, and many people worry about a variety of concerns: debts, the stock market, relationships, war, rising crime, and so on. Finally, some medications that people take, both prescription and over-the-counter drugs, interfere with the sleep–wake cycle. For example, decongestants that some people take to relieve sinus congestion may cause a racing heartbeat, preventing them from relaxing enough to sleep.

HOW CAN YOU TELL IF YOU ARE SLEEP DEPRIVED?

According to Fahey (1993), you may be sleep deprived if you:

- actually need your alarm clock to wake up.
- find getting out of bed in the morning is a struggle.
- feel tired, irritable, or stressed out for much of the day.
- have trouble concentrating or remembering.
- fall asleep watching TV, in meetings, lectures, or warm rooms.
- fall asleep after heavy meals or after a low dose of alcohol.
- fall asleep within 5 minutes of getting into bed. (A well-rested person actually takes 15 to 20 minutes to fall asleep.)

If you are interested in learning more about sleep deprivation and sleep disorders that can cause it, try searching the Internet. There are some excellent sites about sleep and sleep disorders, including many with online tests that can help people decide whether or not they have a sleep disorder. Here are a few good sites:

- The Sleep Mall at **www.sleepnet.com/sleeptest.html** has a sleep test that tests for many different kinds of sleep disorders.
- Sleepnet.com at **www.sleepnet.com** also has a sleep test and detailed information about sleep disorders.
- National Sleep Foundation at **www.sleepfoundation.org** has many links to sites with information about sleep, disorders, and sleep tips.

4 CHAPTER SUMMARY

What Is Consciousness?

4.1 *What does it mean to be conscious, and are there different levels of consciousness?*

- Consciousness is a person's awareness of everything that is going on at any given moment. Most waking hours are spent in waking consciousness.
- Altered states of consciousness are shifts in the quality or pattern of mental activity.

Altered States: Sleep

4.2 *Why do people sleep, and how does sleep work?*

- Sleep is a circadian rhythm, lasting 24 hours, and is a product of the activity of the hypothalamus, the hormone melatonin, the neurotransmitter serotonin, and body temperature.

4.3 *What is the purpose of sleep?*

- Adaptive theory states that sleep evolved as a way to conserve energy and keep animals safe from predators that hunt at night.

- Restorative theory states that sleep provides the body with an opportunity to restore chemicals that have been depleted during the day as well as the growth and repair of cell tissue.

- The average amount of sleep needed by most people is about 7 to 8 hours within each 24-hour period.

4.4 *What are the different stages of sleep?*

- Stage One sleep is light sleep.

- Stage Two sleep is indicated by the presence of sleep spindles, bursts of activity on the EEG.

- Stage Three is highlighted by the first appearance of delta waves, the slowest and largest waves, whereas Stage Four is predominantly delta waves, and the body is at its lowest level of functioning.

- Sleepwalking and sleeptalking occur in Stage Four sleep.

- Night terrors are attacks of extreme fear that the victim has while sound asleep.

4.5 *What is dreaming, and what happens if people don't dream?*

- REM sleep occurs four or five times a night, replacing Stage One sleep in the sleep–wake cycle and is accompanied by paralysis of the voluntary muscles.

- Nightmares are bad or unpleasant dreams that occur during REM sleep.

- REM behavior disorder is a rare condition in which REM paralysis fails and the person moves violently while dreaming, often acting out the elements of the dream.

Classic Studies in Psychology: REM Madness

- Early studies of REM sleep seemed to show that a lack of REM sleep would lead to madness, but later research has consistently shown this to be untrue.

Psychology in the News: Murderous Dreams

4.6 *Can sleepwalking be a defense for committing a crime?*

- Sleepwalking has been used as a defense in numerous cases of murder. In many of these cases, the defendant has been acquitted because of the sleepwalking defense.

4.7 *What kinds of problems can happen during sleep?*

- Insomnia is an inability to get to sleep, stay asleep, or get enough sleep.

- Sleep apnea occurs when a person stops breathing for nearly half a minute or more, followed by gasping for breath.

- Narcolepsy is a genetic disorder in which the person suddenly and without warning collapses into REM sleep.

Dreams

4.8 *Why do people dream, and what do they dream about?*

- Manifest content of a dream is the actual dream and its events. Latent content of a dream is the symbolic content, according to Freud.

- Without outside sensory information to explain the activation of the brain cells in the cortex by the pons area, the association areas of the cortex synthesize a story, or dream, to explain that activation in the activation-synthesis hypothesis.

- A revision of activation-synthesis theory, the activation-information-mode model (AIM) states that information experienced during waking hours can influence the synthesis of dreams.

Altered States: Hypnosis

4.9 *What is hypnosis and how does it work?*

- The hypnotist will tell the person to relax and feel tired, to focus on what is being said, to let go of inhibitions and accept suggestions, and to use vivid imagination.

- Hypnosis cannot give increased strength, reliably enhance memory, or regress people to an earlier age or an earlier life, but it can produce amnesia, reduce pain, and alter sensory impressions.

- Hilgard believed that a person under hypnosis is in a state of dissociation, in which one part of consciousness is hypnotized and susceptible to suggestion, while another part is aware of everything that occurs.

- Other theorists believe that the hypnotized subject is merely playing a social role, that of the hypnotized person. This is called the social-cognitive theory of hypnosis.

Altered States: Psychoactive Drugs

4.10 *What is the difference between a physical dependence and a psychological dependence on a drug?*

- Drugs that are physically addictive cause the user's body to crave the drug. When deprived of the drug, the user will go through physical withdrawal.

- Drug tolerance occurs as the user's body becomes conditioned to the level of the drug. After a time, the user must take more and more of the drug to get the same effect.

- In psychological dependence, the user believes that he or she needs the drug to function well and maintain a sense of well-being. Any drug can produce psychological dependence.

4.11 *What are some examples of stimulants and the dangers associated with taking them?*

- Stimulants are drugs that increase the functioning of the nervous system.

- Amphetamines are synthetic drugs such as Benzedrine or Dexedrine. They help people stay awake and reduce appetite but are highly physically addictive.

- Cocaine is highly addictive and can cause convulsions and death in some first-time users.

- Nicotine is a mild stimulant and is very physically addictive.

- Caffeine is the most commonly used stimulant, found in coffee, tea, chocolate, and many sodas.

4.12 *What are some different types of depressants and how can they be harmful?*

- Barbiturates, also known as major tranquilizers, have a sedative effect and are used as sleeping pills.

- The minor tranquilizers are benzodiazepines such as Valium or Xanax.

4.13 *What kind of drug is alcohol and what are the dangers of drinking too much?*

- Alcohol is the most commonly used and abused depressant.

- Alcohol can interact with other depressants.

4.14 *How do narcotics work, and why are they so addictive?*

- Narcotics are pain-relieving drugs of the depressant class that are derived from the opium poppy.

- Opium is the earliest form of this drug.

- Morphine is a more refined version of opium but is highly addictive.

- Heroin was believed to be a purer form of morphine and, therefore, less addictive but in fact is even more powerfully addictive.

- Methadone has the ability to control the symptoms of heroin or morphine withdrawal without the euphoria, or "high," of heroin or morphine.

4.15 *How do hallucinogens work?*

- Hallucinogens are stimulants that alter the brain's interpretation of sensations, creating hallucinations. Three synthetically created hallucinogens are LSD, PCP, and MDMA.
- Three naturally occurring hallucinogens are mescaline, psilocybin, and marijuana.

4.16 *What is marijuana and what are the risks of using it?*

- Marijuana is a mild hallucinogen, producing a mild euphoria and feelings of relaxation in its users. Larger doses can lead to hallucinations and paranoia. It is carcinogenic and impairs learning and memory.

Applying Psychology to Everyday Life: Are You Sleep Deprived?

4.17 *How serious is the problem of sleep deprivation?*

- Sleep deprivation is a serious disorder responsible for a large portion of traffic accidents and fatalities as well as increased stress, depression, anxiety, reduced productivity, and risk-taking behavior.
- Causes of sleep deprivation include sleep disorders such as apnea and narcolepsy, failure of people to go to sleep or stay asleep for an adequate amount of time, worrying, and the influence of some drugs.

4 KEY TERMS

TEST YOURSELF

Pick the best answer.

1. Most of our time awake is spent in a state called _____, in which our thoughts, feelings, and sensations are clear and organized, and we feel alert.
   a. altered state of consciousness
   b. waking consciousness
   c. unconsciousness
   d. working consciousness

2. Which of the following situations is NOT an altered state of consciousness?
   a. You are daydreaming.
   b. You have been drinking beer.
   c. You are concentrating on a math test.
   d. You are asleep.

3. Which of the following is NOT an example of a circadian rhythm?
   a. menstrual cycle
   b. sleep–wake cycle
   c. blood pressure changes
   d. body temperature changes

4. When light begins to fade at the end of the day, the suprachiasmatic nucleus in the _____ signals the pineal gland to release _____.
   a. hippocampus; melatonin
   b. hippocampus; serotonin
   c. hypothalamus; melatonin
   d. hypothalamus; serotonin

5. Which of the following was NOT listed as one of the factors involved in the ability to go to sleep?
   a. body mass
   b. body temperature
   c. serotonin levels
   d. melatonin levels

6. The symptoms of sleep deprivation include all but which of the following?
   a. trembling hands
   b. inability to concentrate
   c. feeling of general discomfort
   d. hypnic jerk

7. You hear about an accident that took place at 3:00 A.M. The car was traveling along and then seemed to drift into the opposing lane of traffic, hitting an oncoming car head on. Given the early morning time, you suspect that the driver of the car that drifted over the center line most likely experienced a
   a. lapse in judgment.
   b. microsleep episode.
   c. hypnogogic episode.
   d. hypnopompic episode.

8. It might be best to say that adaptive theory explains _____, while restorative theory explains _____.
   a. why we *need* to sleep; *when* we sleep
   b. *where* we sleep; why we *need* to sleep
   c. why we *need* to sleep; *where* we sleep
   d. *when* we sleep; why we *need* to sleep

9. What is the first stage of sleep in which, if awakened, you will realize that you were asleep?
   a. Stage One
   b. Stage Two
   c. Stage Three
   d. Stage Four

10. In which stage of sleep do night terrors occur?
    a. Stage One
    b. Stage Two
    c. Stage Three
    d. Stage Four

11. Sleepwalking
    a. is partly hereditary.
    b. occurs more frequently in girls than in boys.
    c. occurs in about 50 percent of the population.
    d. lasts well into late adulthood in most people.

12. Night terrors
    a. are the same thing as nightmares.
    b. are always vividly remembered afterwards.
    c. are more common in children.
    d. take place in one of the lighter stages of sleep.

13. Which of the following statements about REM sleep is false?
    a. The eyes move rapidly back and forth under the eyelids.
    b. Most people report that they were dreaming if awakened.
    c. The body is aroused and brain waves resemble waking beta waves.
    d. Lack of REM sleep produces psychological disorders.

14. If you are in REM sleep but are able to move around and act out your dreams, you may have a rare condition called
    a. REM behavior disorder.
    b. somnambulism.
    c. nightmare disorder.
    d. narcolepsy.

15. If you suddenly and without warning slip into REM sleep during the day, often falling down as you do so, you may have the condition called
    a. sleep apnea.
    b. insomnia.
    c. narcolepsy.
    d. epilepsy.

16. A sleep disorder that may require the use of a machine to force air gently into the nasal passages is called
    a. sleep apnea.
    b. insomnia.
    c. narcolepsy.
    d. cataplexy.

17. Randall tells his therapist that he had a dream about riding on a train that went through a tunnel. The therapist tells Randall that his dream was most likely about sexual intercourse, as the tunnel represents a woman's vagina. Randall's therapist is using the _____ theory of dreams to explain Randall's dream.
    a. activation-synthesis
    b. dreams-for-survival
    c. Hobson/McCarley
    d. Freudian

18. Hypnosis has been shown to do all of the following BUT
    a. induce amnesia for what happens during the hypnotic state.
    b. provide pain relief without medication.
    c. alter sensory perceptions.
    d. regress people back to their early childhood experiences.

19. Jackie used Ecstasy while she was in college, but now that she has a government job she has avoided using any recreational drugs. Although she had no problem quitting, she still finds that every now and then she gets a strong craving to use Ecstasy again. Her craving is most likely the result of
    a. psychological dependence.
    b. physical dependency.
    c. withdrawal.
    d. none of the above.

20. Which of the following is NOT a naturally occurring substance?
    a. nicotine
    b. amphetamine
    c. caffeine
    d. cocaine

21. Which of the following is NOT a depressant?
    a. alcohol
    b. valium
    c. PCP
    d. barbiturate

22. Alcohol actually _____ the release of GABA, a neurotransmitter that inhibits many brain functions.
    a. depresses
    b. decreases
    c. stimulates
    d. prevents

23. _____ was originally thought to be a more pure form of morphine, with fewer side effects.
    a. Heroin
    b. Laudanum
    c. Paregoric
    d. Methadone

24. "Magic mushrooms" are the source of
    a. marijuana.
    b. psilocybin.
    c. mescaline.
    d. Ecstasy.

25. High doses of marijuana can lead to
    a. death.
    b. hallucinations and delusions.
    c. extreme arousal.
    d. none of the above.

26. Which of the following statements concerning sleep deprivation is false?
    a. Driving after 17 to 19 hours without sleep is less dangerous than having a blood alcohol level of 0.05.
    b. Sleep deprivation accounts for 30–40 percent of all accidents involving heavy trucks.
    c. Sleep deprivation accounts for 16–60 percent of all road accidents.
    d. Sleep deprivation can cause stress, anxiety, and depression and increase risky behavior.

Answers: 1-b, 2-c, 3-a, 4-c, 5-a, 6-d, 7-b, 8-d, 9-b, 10-d, 11-a, 12-c, 13-d, 14-a, 15-c, 16-a, 17-d, 18-d, 19-a, 20-b, 21-c, 22-c, 23-a, 24-b, 25-b, 26-a.

For more sample quizzes and other review activities that will help you get a better grade, be sure to check out your accompanying study guide. To access tests and your own personalized study plan that will help you focus on the areas you need to master before your next class test, be sure to go to the on-line Psychology web site available with the access code packaged with your book.

CONCEPT MAP

Consciousness

Consciousness: person's awareness at a given moment   **Altered states:** shifts in quality or pattern of mental activity

4.1

Altered States: Sleep

Sleep

Sleep is part of a circadian rhythm, lasting 24 hours

Product of the activity of:
▶ hypothalamus
▶ hormone melatonin
▶ neurotransmitter serotonin
▶ body temperature

4.2

Purpose of Sleep

Adaptive theory: conserves energy, keeps animals safe from night predators

Restorative theory: opportunity to restore systems, cell tissue growth/repair

4.3

Sleep Disorders

Sleep apnea	breathing stops for about 1/2 minute
Insomnia	inability to fall asleep, stay asleep, get enough sleep
Narcolepsy	genetic disorder causing a collapse into REM sleep
Somnambulism	sitting, walking, performing complex behavior while asleep
Night terrors	extreme fear, agitation, screaming while asleep

4.7

Sleep Deprivation

Causes include sleep disorders such as apnea and narcolepsy, failure of people to go to sleep or stay asleep for an adequate amount of time, worry, drug usage.

4.17

Different Stages of Sleep

Non-REM Stage One sleep: light sleep, hypnagogic images, myoclonic jerks

Stage Two sleep: sleep spindles, bursts of EEG

Stage Three sleep: first appearance of delta waves, growth hormones released

Stage Four sleep: predominantly delta waves, sleepwalking, sleeptalking, and night terrors occur

4.4

REM Sleep and Dreaming

REM sleep occurs four or five times a night

Associated with dreaming (Dement)

Nightmares: unpleasant dreams during REM

REM behavior disorder: REM paralysis fails, acting out dreams

4.5–4.6

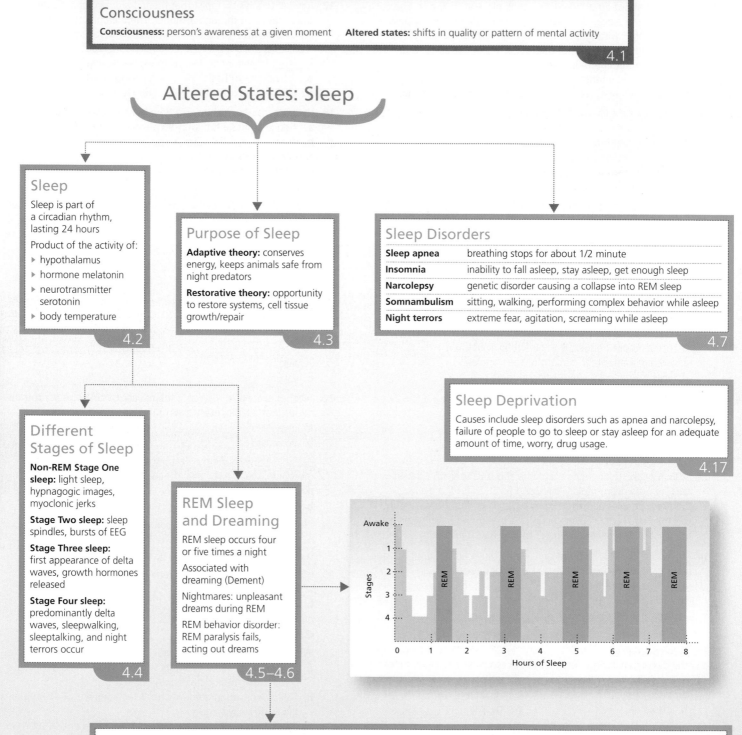

Theories of Dreaming

Freudian theory: conflicts, events, and desires of past represented in symbolic form in dreams.

Manifest content: actual dream and its events.

Latent content: symbolic content, according to Freud.

Activation-synthesis hypothesis: cortical association areas synthesize a dream to explain cortical activation by pons.

Activation-information-mode model: information from waking hours can influence dream synthesis

Dream of Absent Minded Transgressions (DAMiT): tendency of people to dream about information that they have suppressed in waking hours.

4.8

Altered States: Hypnosis

Characteristics of Hypnosis

Hypnosis cannot:
give increased strength, reliably enhance memory, or regress people to an earlier age

Hypnosis can:
produce amnesia, reduce pain, alter sensory impressions

4.9

Theories of Hypnosis

Hilgard—the hidden observer:
Hypnosis is a state of dissociation, in which one part of consciousness is hypnotized, while another part is aware

Social-cognitive theory of hypnosis:
Hypnosis is role-playing due to the social situation

Altered States: Psychoactive Drugs

Physical Dependence and Psychological Drug Dependence

Physically addictive drugs: user's body craves drug. Deprivation causes physical withdrawal

Drug tolerance: body becomes conditioned to level of drug, leads to increased drug dosages

Signs of Physical Dependency:
▶ Compulsive use   ▶ Loss of control
▶ Disregard for the consequences of use.
▶ Psychological dependence: users believe that they need drug to function and for well-being

4.10

Hallucinogens alter brain's interpretation of sensations, creating hallucinations

4.15

Marijuana

Comes from the hemp plant called cannabis sativa.

Hashish is the substance scraped from hemp leaves

4.16

Narcotics and Addiction

▶ **Narcotics** are pain-relieving drugs from opium poppies, bind to endorphin receptors
▶ **Common Narcotics:** opium, morphine, and hero
▶ **Methadone** controls symptoms of heroin or morphine withdrawal

4.14

Stimulants and the Associated Dangers

Stimulants are drugs that increase the functioning of the nervous system: Amphetamines, cocaine, nicotine, and caffeine.

4.11

Depressants are drugs that slow central nervous system

Barbiturates: major tranquilizers, sedative effect, used as sleeping pills

4.12

DRUG CLASSIFICATION	MAIN EFFECT
Depressants Alcohol, barbiturates (tranquilizers)	Relaxation
Stimulants Amphetamines, cocaine, nicotine	Stimulation, excitement
Narcotics Opiates	Euphoria
Psychedelics and Hallucinogens Marijuana, LSD, MDMA	Distort consciousness, alter perception

Alcohol and Its Dangers

Alcohol is the most commonly used and abused depressant.

▶ 10 20 million Americans suffer from alcoholism
▶ 40% of all traffic fatalities in the United States involve alcohol use

4.13

5

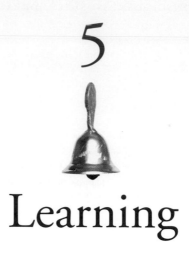

Learning

Why White Coats Made the Baby Scream

When Stephanie was an infant, she was constantly getting sick. This was long before the time when giving immunizations to infants had become routine, which meant that Stephanie spent a lot of her infancy in the doctor's office. Antibiotics were delivered by injection. The shots were obviously painful and caused Stephanie to scream and cry.

Of course, the doctor in his white coat and the nurse in her white uniform were always present, as well as the white paper covering the examining table. It didn't take too many visits before Stephanie would scream when she saw the "white coat" people coming toward her—especially the nurse, who was usually the one who delivered the hated shot.

When she was 1 year old, her mother took her to a photography studio to have her portrait made. In those days, the photographer wore a white jacket to look more professional and took the pictures on a carpeted platform with a white sheet draped across it. Stephanie threw a fit, crying and screaming. The photographer had to take his jacket off and remove the white drape. After about an hour, she was finally calm enough to pose for the picture on a bare platform. Why did Stephanie have this reaction?

Stephanie's reaction to the photo session was a result of a special type of learning called *classical conditioning*. In this type of learning, objects or situations (such as white coats and being up on a table) can become associated or linked with other kinds of situations (such as the pain of injections). Once the association is made, similar objects or situations can cause the same response (e.g., screaming in fear) that the earlier situation causes.

Why study learning?

If we had not been able to learn, we would have died out as a species long ago. Learning is the process that allows us to adapt to the changing conditions of the world around us. We can alter our actions until we find the behavior that leads us to survival and rewards, and we can eliminate actions that have been unsuccessful in the past. Without learning, there would be no buildings, no agriculture, no lifesaving medicines, and no human civilization.

5

Definition of Learning

5.1   *What is learning?*

The term *learning* is one of those concepts whose meaning is crystal clear until one has to put it in actual words. "Learning is when you learn something." "Learning is learning how to do something." A more useful definition is as follows: *Learning* is any relatively permanent change in behavior brought about by experience or practice.

What does "relatively permanent" mean? And how does experience change what we do? The "relatively permanent" part of the definition refers to the fact that when people learn anything, some part of their brain is physically changed to record what they've learned. This is actually a process of memory, for without the ability to remember what happens, people cannot learn anything. Although there is no conclusive proof as yet, research suggests strongly that once people learn something, it is always present somewhere in memory (Barsalou, 1992). They may be unable to "get" to it, but it's there. ⓁⒾⓃⓀ *Chapter Six: Memory, p. 235.*

As for the part about experience or practice, think about the last time you did something that caused you a lot of pain. Are you going to do it again? Of course not. You don't want to experience that pain again, so you change your behavior to avoid the painful consequence.* This is how children learn not to touch hot stoves. Of course, if a person does something that results in a very pleasurable consequence, that person is more likely to do that same thing again. This is another change in behavior. Think back to the prologue. Stephanie's experience with the doctor and the nurse changed her behavior from that of a friendly, outgoing infant to a frightened, screaming child whenever she saw anyone in a white coat coming near her.

So, is any kind of change learning? Not all change is accomplished through learning. Any kind of change in the way an organism *behaves* is learning. Changes like an increase in height or the size of the brain are another kind of change controlled by a genetic blueprint. This kind of change is called *maturation*, and it is not the same as learning. For example, children learn to walk *when* they do because their nervous systems, muscle strength, and sense of balance have reached the point where walking

> What does "relatively ▶ permanent" mean? And how does experience change what we do?

the neighborhood. Jerry Van Amerongen

An instantaneous learning experience.
©Reprinted with special permission of King Features Syndicate.

---

*Consequence: an end result of some action.

is possible for them—all factors controlled by maturation, not by how much practice those children have had in trying to walk. No amount of experience or practice will help that child walk before maturation makes it possible—in spite of what some eager parents might wish.

It Makes Your Mouth Water: Classical Conditioning

In the early 1900s, when Freud was just becoming famous in Europe and the structuralists and functionalists were arguing over consciousness in the ivy-covered halls of American universities, research scientists were unhappy with psychology's focus on mental activity. (L I N K) *to Chapter One: The Science of Psychology, pp. 10–12.* Many were looking for a way to bring some kind of objectivity and scientific research to the field.

It was not a psychologist who accomplished that goal. It was a Russian *physiologist* (a person who studies the workings of the body) named Ivan Pavlov (1849–1936) who accidentally stumbled across the basic principles of a particular kind of learning (Pavlov, 1926).

5.2 *What is classical conditioning and who first studied it?*

Studying the digestive system in his dogs, Pavlov had built a device that would accurately measure the amount of saliva produced by the dogs when they were fed a measured amount of food. Normally, when food is placed in the mouth of any animal, the salivary glands automatically start releasing saliva to help with chewing and digestion. This is a normal *reflex* (involuntary* response) in both animals and humans. The food causes a particular reaction, the salivation. A *stimulus* can be defined as any object, event, or experience that causes a *response*, the reaction of an organism. In the case of Pavlov's dogs, the food is the stimulus and salivation is the response.

Dr. Ivan Pavlov and students working in his laboratory. Pavlov, a Russian physiologist, was the first to study and write about the basic principles of classical conditioning.

PAVLOV AND THE SALIVATING DOGS

What first annoyed and then intrigued Pavlov was that his dogs began salivating when they weren't supposed to be salivating. Some dogs would start salivating when they saw the lab assistant bringing their food, others when they heard clatter of the food bowl from the kitchen, and still others when it was the time of day they were usually fed. Pavlov spent the rest of his career studying what eventually he termed **classical conditioning**, learning to make a reflex response to a stimulus other than the original, natural stimulus that normally produces it.

ELEMENTS OF CLASSICAL CONDITIONING

Pavlov eventually identified several key elements that must be present and experienced in a particular way for conditioning to take place.

5.3 *What are the important concepts in classical conditioning?*

UNCONDITIONED STIMULUS   The original, naturally occurring stimulus mentioned in the preceding paragraph is called the **unconditioned stimulus (UCS)**. The term *unconditioned* means "unlearned" or "naturally occurring." This is the stimulus that ordinarily leads to the reflex, involuntary response. In the case of Pavlov's dogs, the food served is the unconditioned stimulus.

classical conditioning
learning to make a reflex response to a stimulus other than the original, natural stimulus that normally produces the reflex.

unconditioned stimulus (UCS)
a naturally occurring stimulus that leads to an involuntary response.

---

*Involuntary: not under personal control or choice.

UNCONDITIONED RESPONSE   The reflex response to the unconditioned stimulus is called the **unconditioned response (UCR)** for much the same reason. It is unlearned and occurs because of genetic "wiring" in the nervous system. For example, in Pavlov's experiment, the food given to the dogs is the UCS, and the salivation to that food is the UCR.

CONDITIONED STIMULUS   Pavlov determined that almost any kind of stimulus could become associated with the unconditioned stimulus (UCS) if it is paired with the UCS often enough. In his original study, for example, the sight of the food dish itself became a stimulus for salivation *before* the food was given to the dogs. Every time they got food (to which they naturally salivated), they saw the dish. At this point, the dish was called a **neutral stimulus (NS)** because it had no effect on salivation. After being paired with the food so many times, the dish came to produce the same salivation response, although a somewhat weaker one, as did the food itself. When a previously neutral stimulus, through repeated pairing with the unconditioned stimulus, begins to cause the same kind of reflexive response, learning has occurred. The neutral stimulus can now be called a **conditioned stimulus (CS)**. (*Unconditioned* means "unlearned," and *conditioned* means "learned.")

CONDITIONED RESPONSE   The response that is given to the CS is not usually quite as strong as the original unconditioned response (UCR), but it is essentially the same response. However, because it comes as a response to the conditioned stimulus, it is called the **conditioned response (CR)** or sometimes the *conditioned reflex*.

PUTTING IT ALL TOGETHER: PAVLOV'S CANINE CLASSIC, OR DING, DONG, BELL

5.4   *What was Pavlov's classic experiment in conditioning?*

The whole idea of classical conditioning is not as complex as it sounds. What gets tough is keeping all the letters straight: UCS, UCR, CS, and CR. Pavlov did a classic experiment in which he paired the ringing of a bell with the presentation of food to see if the dogs would eventually salivate to the sound of the bell. Since the bell did not normally produce salivation, it was the neutral stimulus (NS) before any conditioning took place. The repeated pairing of the NS and the UCS is usually called *acquisition*, because the organism is in the process of acquiring learning. Figure 5.1 is a chart of how each element of the conditioning relationship worked in Pavlov's experiment.

Notice that the responses, CR and UCR, are the same—salivation. They simply differ in what they are the response *to*. An unconditioned stimulus (UCS) is always followed by an unconditioned response (UCR), and a conditioned stimulus (CS) is always followed by a conditioned response (CR).

Is this rocket science? No, not really. Classical conditioning is actually one of the simplest forms of learning. It's so simple that it happens to people all the time without their even being aware of it. Does your mouth water when you merely *see* an advertisement for your favorite food on television? Does your stomach get upset every time you hear the high-pitched whine of the dentist's drill? These are both examples of classical conditioning.

After all the dog stories, the salivation to the TV ad probably needs no explanation, but what about the dentist's drill? Over the course of many visits, the body comes to associate that sound (CS) with the anxiety or fear (UCR) the person has felt while receiving a painful dental treatment (UCS), and so the sound produces a feeling of anxiety (CR) whether that person is in the chair or just in the outer waiting area.

Classical conditioning in the real world. These children are no doubt salivating to the sound of the ice cream truck's bell, much as Pavlov's dogs were conditioned to respond. What other kinds of stimuli might make a person salivate?

Before Conditioning

Neutral Stimulus (NS)
Bell

No Salivation

During Conditioning

Neutral Stimulus (NS)
Bell

Unconditioned Stimulus (UCS)
Food

Unconditioned Response (UCR)
Salivation

After Conditioning

Conditioned Stimulus (CS)
Bell

Conditioned Response (CR)
Salivation

FIGURE 5.1 **Classical Conditioning**
Before conditioning takes place, the sound of the bell does not cause salivation and is a neutral stimulus, or NS. During conditioning, the sound of the bell occurs just before the presentation of the food (the UCS). The food causes salivation, the UCR. When conditioning has occurred after several pairings of the bell with the food, the bell will begin to elicit a salivation response from the dog without any food. This is learning, and the sound of the bell is now a CS and the salivation to the bell is the CR.

Although classical conditioning happens quite easily, there are a few basic principles that researchers have discovered:

1. The CS must come *before* the UCS. If Pavlov rang the bell just after he gave the dogs the food, they did not become conditioned (Rescorla, 1988).

2. The CS and UCS must come very close together in time—ideally, only several seconds apart. When Pavlov tried to stretch the time between the potential CS and the UCS to several minutes, no association was made. Too much could happen in the longer interval of time to interfere with conditioning (Pavlov, 1926; Wasserman & Miller, 1997).

3. The neutral stimulus must be paired with the UCS several times, often many times, before conditioning can take place (Pavlov, 1926).

4. The CS is usually some stimulus that is distinctive* or stands out from other competing stimuli. The bell was a sound that was not normally present in the laboratory and, therefore, distinct (Pavlov, 1926; Rescorla, 1988).

Could this be you? The anxiety that many people feel while in the dentist's office is a conditioned response, with the dentist's chair and the smells of the office acting as conditioned stimuli.

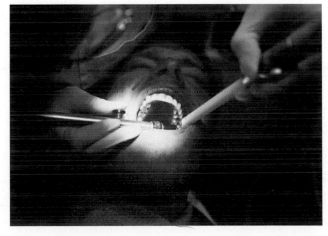

---

*Distinctive: separate, having a different quality from something else.

That seems simple ▶
enough. But I
have to know—did
Pavlov's dogs
salivate to the
doorbell, too?

That seems simple enough. But I have to know—did Pavlov's dogs salivate to the doorbell, too? They certainly could have, if the doorbell were similar in sound to the CS bell, and if the dogs were near enough to hear the doorbell, and assuming Pavlov even *had* a doorbell.

STIMULUS GENERALIZATION AND DISCRIMINATION   Pavlov did find that similar-sounding bells would produce the same conditioned response from his dogs. He and other researchers found that the strength of the response to the similar bells was not as strong as to the original one, but the more similar the other bell tone was to the original bell tone, the more similar the strength of the response was as well (Siegel, 1969). (See Figure 5.2.) The tendency to respond to a stimulus that is only similar to the original conditioned stimulus is called **stimulus generalization**. For example, a person who reacts with anxiety to the sound of a dentist's drill might react with some slight anxiety to a similar-sounding machine, such as an electric coffee grinder.

Of course, Pavlov did not give the dogs any food after the similar bell sounded. They only got food following the correct CS. It didn't take long for the dogs to stop responding (generalizing) to the "fake" bell sounds altogether. Because only the real CS was followed with food, they learned to tell the difference, or *discriminate*, between the "fake" bells and the real one, a process called **stimulus discrimination**. Stimulus discrimination occurs when an organism learns to respond to different stimuli in different ways. For example, although the sound of the coffee grinder might produce a little anxiety in the dental-drill-hating person, after a few uses that sound will no longer produce anxiety because it isn't associated with dental pain.

EXTINCTION AND SPONTANEOUS RECOVERY   What would have happened if Pavlov had stopped giving the dogs food after the real CS? Pavlov did just that, and the dogs gradually stopped salivating to the sound of the bell. When the bell (CS) was repeatedly presented in the absence of the UCS (food, in this case), the salivation (CR) "died out" in a process called **extinction**.

Why does the removal of an unconditioned stimulus lead to extinction of the conditioned response? Look back at Figure 5.1. Once conditioning is acquired, the conditioned stimulus (CS) and conditioned response (CR) will always come *before* the original unconditioned stimulus (UCS). The UCS now serves as a **reinforcer** (strengthener) of the CS–CR association. Remove the reinforcer, and the CR it strengthens will weaken and disappear.

The term *extinction* is a little unfortunate in that it seems to mean that the original conditioned response is totally gone, dead, never coming back, just like the dinosaurs. Remember the definition of learning is any relatively *permanent* change in behavior. The fact is that once people learn something, it's almost impossible to "unlearn" it. People can learn new things that replace it, or lose their way to it in memory, but it's still there. In the case of classical conditioning, this is easily demonstrated.

After extinguishing the conditioned salivation response in his dogs, Pavlov waited a few weeks, putting the bell away. There were no more training sessions and the dogs were not exposed to the bell's ringing in that time at all. But when Pavlov took the bell back out and rang it, the dogs all began to salivate, although it was a fairly weak response and didn't last very long. This brief recovery of the conditioned response proves that the CR is still in there somewhere. It isn't dead and gone, it's just suppressed or inhibited by the lack of an association with the

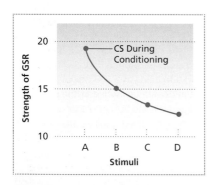

FIGURE 5.2   **Strength of the Generalized Response**   An example of generalization. The subjects had been conditioned originally to a CS (A) of a given frequency. When tested with the original tone, and with tones B, C, and D of differing frequencies, a clear generalization gradient appeared. The closer the frequency of the test tone to the frequency of tone A, the greater was the magnitude of the response to the tone. (Howland, 1937)

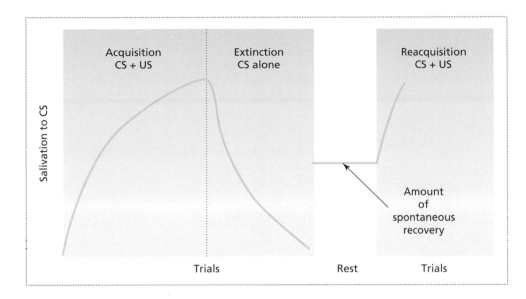

FIGURE 5.3 **Extinction and Spontaneous Recovery** The acquisition, extinction, spontaneous recovery, and reacquisition of a conditioned salivary response. Typically, the measure of conditioning is the number of drops of saliva elicited by the CS on each trial. Note that on the day following extinction, the first presentation of the CS elicits quite a large response.

unconditioned stimulus of food (which is no longer reinforcing the CR). As time passes, this inhibition weakens, especially if the original conditioned stimulus has not been present for a while. In **spontaneous recovery** the conditioned response can briefly reappear when the original CS returns, although the response is usually weak and short-lived. See Figure 5.3 for a graph showing both extinction and spontaneous recovery.

If Pavlov had followed the dogs' spontaneous salivation to the bell with food, their conditioning would have resurfaced in no time at all. This would be an example of retraining. Retraining is made simpler by the fact that the extinguished response isn't really gone, just suppressed.

People experience classical conditioning in many ways. A person who has been hit from behind in a car accident, for example, will spend the next few weeks cringing every time another vehicle gets too close to the rear of the car. That cringing reaction is a conditioned response. The crash itself was the UCS and the closeness of the other cars becomes a CS. People who are allergic to cats sometimes sneeze when they see a *picture* of a cat. Remember the discussion of how to treat insomnia in Chapter Four (p. 137)? One of the recommendations was to avoid reading, working, watching television, or eating in bed. The bed should only be used for sleeping (a reflex) and will eventually become a conditioned stimulus for sleeping.

HIGHER-ORDER CONDITIONING   Another concept in classical conditioning is **higher-order conditioning**. This occurs when a strong conditioned stimulus is paired with a neutral stimulus. The strong CS can actually play the part of a UCS, and the previously neutral stimulus becomes a *second* conditioned stimulus.

For example, let's assume that Pavlov has conditioned his dogs to salivate at the sound of the bell. What would happen if just before Pavlov rang the bell, he snapped his fingers? The sequence would now be "snap-bell-salivation," or "NS-CS-CR." If this happens enough times, the finger snap will eventually also produce a salivation response. The finger snap becomes associated with the bell through the same process that the bell became associated with the food originally and is now another conditioned stimulus.

stimulus generalization
the tendency to respond to a stimulus that is only similar to the original conditioned stimulus with the conditioned response.

stimulus discrimination
the tendency to stop making a generalized response to a stimulus that is similar to the original conditioned stimulus because the similar stimulus is never paired with the unconditioned stimulus.

extinction
the disappearance or weakening of a learned response following the removal or absence of the unconditioned stimulus (in classical conditioning) or the removal of a reinforcer (in operant conditioning).

reinforcer
any event or object that, when following a response, increases the likelihood of that response occurring again.

spontaneous recovery
the reappearance of a learned response after extinction has occurred.

higher-order conditioning
occurs when a strong conditioned stimulus is paired with a neutral stimulus, causing the neutral stimulus to become a second conditioned stimulus.

PRACTICE **QUIZ:** HOW MUCH DO YOU REMEMBER?

Pick the best answer.

1. Which of the following statements about learning is NOT true?
  a. Learning is another word for maturation.
  b. Learning is relatively permanent.
  c. Learning involves changes in behavior.
  d. Learning involves experiences.

2. Ed noticed that whenever he used his electric can opener, his cat would come into the kitchen and act hungry—drooling and mewing pitiably. He reasoned that because he used the can opener to open the cat's food, the sound of the can opener had become a(n)
  a. unconditioned stimulus.
  b. conditioned stimulus.
  c. unconditioned response.
  d. conditioned response.

3. Which of the following statements about conditioning is FALSE, according to Pavlov?
  a. The CS and UCS must come close together in time.
  b. The CS must come immediately after the UCS.
  c. The neutral stimulus and UCS must be paired several times before conditioning takes place.
  d. All of the above are true.

4. The prologue is about Stephanie's fear of white coats as a child. The fact that she was not only afraid of white coats worn by doctors and nurses but also those worn by photographers is an example of
  a. extinction.
  b. spontaneous recovery.
  c. stimulus discrimination.
  d. stimulus generalization.

5. When a conditioned response briefly reappears after it has been extinguished, this is called
  a. spontaneous recovery.
  b. higher-order conditioning.
  c. extinction.
  d. stimulus generalization.

6. The use of a strong CS to create a second CS is called
  a. spontaneous recovery.
  b. higher-order conditioning.
  c. extinction.
  d. stimulus generalization.

Answers: 1-a, 2-b, 3-b, 4-d, 5-a, 6-b.

CONDITIONED EMOTIONAL RESPONSES: RATS!

Later scientists took Pavlov's concepts and expanded them to explain not only animal behavior but also human behavior. One of the earliest of these studies showed that even an emotional response could be conditioned.

5.5   *What is a conditioned emotional response?*

WATSON AND "LITTLE ALBERT"   In the first chapter of this text, John B. Watson was discussed as the founder of *behaviorism.* He firmly believed that all behavior could be explained in terms of learning, including even the *phobias* (irrational fear responses) that the Freudian camp thought were deeply rooted in the unconscious mind. His classic experiment with "Little Albert" and the white rat was a demonstration of learning a phobia (Watson & Rayner, 1920). It was also a very good example of classical conditioning.

Watson paired the presentation of the white rat to the baby with a loud, scary noise. Although the baby was not afraid of the rat, he was naturally afraid of the loud noise and started to cry. Soon, every time the baby saw the rat, he started to cry. In conditioning terms, the loud noise was the UCS, the fear of the noise the UCR, the white rat became the CS, and the fear of the rat (the phobia) was the CR. (See Figure 5.4.) (Of course, no ethics committee today would approve an experiment in which an infant experiences psychological distress like this.)

The learning of phobias is a very good example of a certain type of classical conditioning, the **conditioned emotional response (CER)**. Conditioned emotional responses are some of the easiest forms of classical conditioning to accomplish and our lives are full of them. It's easy to think of fears people might have that are conditioned or learned: a child's fear of the dentist's chair, a puppy's fear of a rolled-up newspaper, or the fear of dogs that is often shown by a person who has been attacked by a dog in the past. But other emotions can be conditioned, too.

conditioned emotional response (CER)
emotional response that has become classically conditioned to occur to learned stimuli, such as a fear of dogs or the emotional reaction that occurs when seeing an attractive person.

FIGURE 5.4   **Conditioning of "Little Albert"**   After Little Albert had been conditioned to fear a white rat, he became afraid of anything white and fuzzy, including John Watson himself with a white fuzzy mask on his face. Can you think of any emotional reactions you experience that might be classically conditioned emotional responses?

The next time you watch television, watch the commercials closely. Advertisers often use certain objects or certain types of people in their ads to generate a certain emotional response in viewers, hoping that the emotional response will become associated with their product. Sexy models, cute little babies, and adorable puppies are some of the examples of stimuli the advertising world uses to tug at our heartstrings, so to speak.

Other television messages are meant to elicit a fear response, such as messages about what drugs will do to your brain. In a classic public service message from the 1980s, a woman holds up an egg and says, "This is your brain." She then drops the egg into a grease-filled, smoking hot skillet and says, "This is your brain on drugs. Any questions?" This spot was supposed to cause disgust by showing the egg being cracked into a filthy-looking skillet and getting immediately fried to a crisp.

It is even possible to become classically conditioned by simply watching someone else respond to a stimulus in a process called **vicarious conditioning** (Bandura & Rosenthal, 1966). Many years ago, children received vaccination shots in school. The nurse lined the children up, and one by one they had to go forward to get a needle in the arm. When some children received their shots, they cried quite a bit. By the time the nurse got near the end of the line of children, they were all crying—many of them before she ever touched needle to skin. They had learned their fear reflex from watching the reactions of the other children.

OTHER CONDITIONED RESPONSES IN HUMANS

Are there any foods that you just can't eat anymore because of a bad experience with them? Believe it or not, your reaction to that food is a kind of classical conditioning.

Many experiments have shown that laboratory rats will develop a **conditioned taste aversion** for any liquid or food they swallow up to six hours before becoming nauseated. Researchers (Garcia et al., 1989; Garcia & Koelling, 1966) found that rats that were given a sweetened liquid and then injected with a drug or exposed to radiation* that caused nausea would not touch the liquid again. (In a similar manner, alcoholics who are given a drug to make them nauseated when they drink alcohol may learn to avoid drinking any alcoholic beverage.)

---

*Radiation: beams of energy.

vicarious conditioning
classical conditioning of a reflex response or emotion by watching the reaction of another person.
conditioned taste aversion
development of a nausea or aversive response to a particular taste because that taste was followed by a nausea reaction, occurring after only one association.

But I thought that it ▶ took several pairings of these stimuli to bring about conditioning. How can classical conditioning happen so fast?

Conditioned taste aversions in nature
This moth is not poisonous to birds, but the Monarch butterfly whose coloring the moth imitates is quite poisonous. Birds find their food by vision and will not eat anything that resembles the Monarch.

But I thought that it took several pairings of these stimuli to bring about conditioning. How can classical conditioning happen so fast?

BIOLOGICAL PREPAREDNESS　Conditioned taste aversions are an example of something called **biological preparedness**. Most mammals, who find their food by smell and taste, will learn to avoid any food that smells or tastes like something they ate just before becoming ill. It's a survival mechanism, because if they kept on eating a "bad" food, they might die. The mammalian* body seems to be prepared to associate smell and taste with getting sick (Garcia & Koelling, 1966; Seligman, 1970). Although most conditioning requires repeated pairings of CS with UCS, when the response is nausea, one pairing seems to be all that is necessary. Taste aversion conditioning is so effective that it has even been used by renowned psychologist Dr. John Garcia and colleagues as a tool to stop coyotes from killing ranchers' sheep and also to stop the ranchers from wiping out the coyote population entirely (Gustavson et al., 1976). Garcia and his fellow researchers laced sheep meat with lithium chloride and left it for the coyotes to find. The coyotes ate the drugged meat, got extremely sick, and avoided eating sheep for quite some time afterwards. The coyotes got to live and the ranchers got to keep their sheep.

It's interesting to note that birds, which find their food by sight, will avoid any object or insect that simply *looks* like the one that made them sick. There is a certain species of moth with coloring that mimics the monarch butterfly. The butterfly is poisonous to birds, but the moth isn't. The moths' mimicry causes birds to avoid eating them, even though they are quite edible. Whereas mammals are biologically prepared to associate taste with illness, birds are biologically prepared to associate visual characteristics with illness (Shapiro et al., 1980).

WHY DOES CLASSICAL CONDITIONING WORK?

There are two ways to explain how one stimulus comes to "stand in" for another. One is the original explanation given by Pavlov, whereas the other is based on a cognitive explanation.

5.6　*Why does classical conditioning work?*

Pavlov believed that the conditioned stimulus, through its association close in time with the unconditioned stimulus, came to activate the same place in the animal's brain that was originally activated by the unconditioned stimulus. He called this process **stimulus substitution**. But if a mere association in time is all that is needed, why would conditioning *fail to happen* when the CS is presented immediately *after* the UCS?

Robert Rescorla (1988) found that the CS has to provide some kind of information about the coming of the UCS in order to achieve conditioning. In other words, the CS must predict that the UCS is coming. In one study, Rescorla exposed one group of rats to a tone, and just after the tone's onset and while the tone was still able to be heard, an electric shock was administered for some of the tone presentations. Soon the rats became agitated** and reacted in fear by shivering and squealing at the onset of the tone, a kind of conditioned emotional response. But with a second group of rats, Rescorla again sounded a tone, but administered the electric shock only

biological preparedness
referring to the tendency of animals to learn certain associations, such as taste and nausea, with only one or few pairings due to the survival value of the learning.

stimulus substitution
original theory in which Pavlov stated that classical conditioning occurred because the conditioned stimulus became a substitute for the unconditioned stimulus by being paired closely together.

---

*Mammalian: having to do with mammals (animals with fur or hair who feed their young with milk from milk glands).
**Agitated: excited, upset.

after the tone *stopped*, not while the tone was being heard. That group of rats responded with fear to the *stopping* of the tone (Rescorla, 1968).

The tone for the second group of rats provided a different kind of information than the tone in the first instance. For the first group, the tone means the shock is coming, whereas for the second group, the tone means there is no shock while the tone is on. It was the particular *expectancy* created by pairing the tone or absence of tone with the shock that determined the particular response of the rats. Because this explanation involves the mental activity of consciously expecting something to occur, it is an example of an explanation for classical conditioning called the **cognitive perspective**.

cognitive perspective
modern theory in which classical conditioning is seen to occur because the conditioned stimulus provides information or an expectancy about the coming of the unconditioned stimulus.

operant conditioning
the learning of voluntary behavior through the effects of pleasant and unpleasant consequences to responses.

PRACTICE **QUIZ:** HOW MUCH DO YOU REMEMBER?

Pick the best answer.

1. In Watson's experiment with "Little Albert," the unconditioned stimulus was
   a. the white rat.
   b. the loud noise.
   c. the fear of the rat.
   d. the fear of the noise.

2. Often people with certain types of cancer must take chemotherapy treatments. The drugs used in these treatments are powerful and usually cause strong nausea reactions. If Cindy had scrambled eggs for breakfast and then took a chemotherapy treatment later that same morning, what might we predict based on conditioned taste aversion research?
   a. Cindy will probably develop a strong liking for scrambled eggs.
   b. Cindy will probably be able to eat scrambled eggs with no nausea at all.
   c. Cindy will probably get nauseated the next time she tries to eat scrambled eggs.
   d. None of the above is likely.

3. Your pet parakeet eats some cooked spaghetti noodles. Later the poor bird gets very ill. What would the research on biological preparedness predict?
   a. The parakeet will probably not eat shell macaroni because it smells similar to spaghetti.
   b. The parakeet will probably not eat shell macaroni because it tastes similar to spaghetti.
   c. The parakeet will probably not eat linguini noodles because they are long and thin and look similar to spaghetti.
   d. The parakeet will eat spaghetti again.

4. The fact that the CS must come immediately *before* the UCS, and not after, is a problem for the _____ theory of why classical conditioning works.
   a. stimulus substitution
   b. cognitive perspective
   c. cognitive substitution
   d. stimulus perspective

5. Rescorla found that the CS must _____ the UCS for conditioning to take place.
   a. replace
   b. come after
   c. come at the same time as
   d. predict

Answers: 1-b, 2-c, 3-c, 4-a, 5-d.

So far, all learning seems to involve reflex behavior. What about how we learn voluntary behavior such as brushing and flossing?

What's in It For Me? Operant Conditioning

5.7 *What is operant conditioning and Thorndike's Law of Effect?*

There are two kinds of behavior that all organisms are capable of doing: involuntary (reflexive) and voluntary. If Inez blinks her eyes because a gnat flies close to them, that's a reflex and totally involuntary. But if she then swats at the gnat to frighten it, that's a voluntary choice. She *had* to blink, but she *chose* to swat.

Classical conditioning is the kind of learning that occurs with reflexive, involuntary behavior. The kind of learning that applies to voluntary behavior is called **operant conditioning**, and it is both different from and similar to classical conditioning.

◄ So far, all learning seems to involve reflex behavior. What about how we learn voluntary behavior such as brushing and flossing?

If Pavlov is the person ▶
to associate with
classical conditioning,
who first studied
operant conditioning?

If Pavlov is the person to associate with classical conditioning, who first studied operant conditioning?

FRUSTRATING CATS: THORNDIKE'S PUZZLE BOX AND THE LAW OF EFFECT

Edward L. Thorndike (1874–1949) was one of the first researchers to explore and attempt to outline the laws of learning voluntary responses, although the field was not yet called operant conditioning. Thorndike placed a hungry cat inside a "puzzle box"

Law of Effect
law stating that if a response is followed by a pleasurable consequence, it will tend to be repeated, and if followed by an unpleasant consequence, it will tend not to be repeated.

FIGURE 5.5   Thorndike puzzle box
A typical Thorndike puzzle box. The cat is placed inside the box and can get out by pushing on the little platform to one side of the door—at first, accidentally. Each time the cat managed to escape, it would be put back into the box until, through trial and error, it knew to push on the platform to open the door.

FIGURE 5.6   Graph of the Time to Learn in Thorndike's Experiment
This is one of the earliest "learning curves" in the history of the experimental study of conditioning. The time required by one of Thorndike's cats to escape from the puzzle box gradually decreased with trials but with obvious reversals.

from which the only escape was to press a lever located on the floor of the box (see Figure 5.5). Cats definitely do *not* like being confined, as anyone who has ever tried to stuff one into a travel box will know (and probably has the scars to prove it), and there's a dish of food *outside* the box, so the cat is highly motivated to get out. Thorndike observed that the cat would move around the box, pushing and rubbing up against the walls in an effort to escape. Eventually, the cat would accidentally push the lever, opening the door. Upon escaping, the cat was fed from a dish placed just outside the box. The lever is the stimulus, the pushing of the lever is the response, and the consequence is both escape (good) and food (even better).

The cat did not learn the connection between the lever and the escape right away. After a number of trials in a box like this one, the cat took less and less time to push the lever to deliberately open the door—it had made an association between pushing the lever and opening the door (see Figure 5.6). Each time the cat rubbed and pushed at the part of the box that had led to freedom and food more quickly.

Based on this research, Thorndike developed the **Law of Effect**: If a response is followed by a pleasurable consequence, it will tend to be repeated. If a response is followed by an unpleasant consequence, it will tend not to be repeated (Thorndike, 1911). This is the basic principle behind learning voluntary behavior. In the case of the cat in the box, pushing the lever was followed by a pleasurable consequence (getting out and getting fed), so pushing the lever became a repeated response.

Who first called it operant conditioning? Thorndike's work began the study of voluntary learning, but the person who has had the greatest influence on the field and who gave it the name *operant conditioning* was B. F. Skinner. He is also known as behaviorism's biggest supporter.

◀ Who first called it operant conditioning?

B. F. SKINNER: THE BEHAVIORIST'S BEHAVIORIST

5.8 *What was Skinner's contribution to operant conditioning?*

B. F. Skinner (1904–1990) was the behaviorist who assumed leadership of the field after John Watson. He was even more determined than Watson that psychologists should study only measurable, observable behavior. In addition to his knowledge of Pavlovian classical conditioning, Skinner found in the work of Thorndike a way to explain all behavior as the product of learning. He even gave the learning of voluntary behavior a special name: *operant conditioning* (Skinner, 1938). Voluntary behavior is that which people and animals do to *operate* in the world. When people perform a voluntary action, it is to get something they want or avoid something they don't want, right? So voluntary behavior, for Skinner, is **operant** behavior, and the learning of such behavior is operant conditioning.

The heart of operant conditioning is the effect of consequences on behavior. Thinking back to the section on classical conditioning, learning a reflex really depends on what comes *before* the response—the unconditioned stimulus and what will become the conditioned stimulus. These two stimuli are the *antecedent* stimuli (antecedent means something that comes before another thing). But in operant conditioning, learning depends on what happens *after* the response—the consequence. In a way, operant conditioning could be summed up as this: "If I do this, what's in it for me?"

THE CONCEPT OF REINFORCEMENT

5.9 *What are the important concepts in operant conditioning?*

"What's in it for me" represents the concept of **reinforcement**, one of Skinner's major contributions to behaviorism. The word itself means to strengthen, and Skinner defined reinforcement as anything that, when following a response, causes that response to be more likely to happen again. Typically, this means that reinforcement is a consequence that is in some way pleasurable to the organism, which relates back to Thorndike's Law of Effect. The "pleasurable consequence" is what's in it for the organism—the reward, so to speak.

Going back to Thorndike's puzzle box research, what was "in it" for the cat? We can see that the escape from the box and the food that the cat received after getting out are both *reinforcement* of the lever-pushing response. Every time the cat got out of the box, it got reinforced for doing so. In Skinner's view, this reinforcement is the reason that the cat learned anything at all. In operant conditioning, reinforcement is the key to learning.

Skinner had his own version of a puzzle box called a "Skinner box" or "operant conditioning chamber" (see Figure 5.7). His early research often involved placing a rat into one of these chambers and training it to push down on a bar to get food.

PRIMARY AND SECONDARY REINFORCERS The events or items that can be used to reinforce behavior are not all alike. Let's say that a friend of yours asks you to help her move some books from the

operant
any behavior that is voluntary.

reinforcement
any event or stimulus, that when following a response, increases the probability that the response will occur again.

"Once it became clear to me that, by responding correctly to certain stimuli, I could get all the bananas I wanted, getting this job was a pushover."

FIGURE 5.7 **A Typical Skinner Box**
This rat is learning to press the bar in the wall of the cage in order to get food (delivered a few pellets at a time in the food trough on lower left). In some cases, the light on the top left might be turned on to indicate that pressing the bar will lead to food, or to warn of an impending shock delivered by the grate on the floor of the cage.

trunk of her car to her apartment on the second floor. She offers you a choice of $25 or a candy bar. Unless you've suffered recent brain damage, you'll most likely choose the money, right? With $25, you could buy more than one candy bar. (At today's prices, you might even be able to afford three.)

Now pretend that your friend offers the same deal to a 3-year-old child who lives downstairs for carrying up some of the paperback books: $25 or a candy bar. Which reward will the child more likely choose? Most children at that age have no real idea of the value of money, so the child will probably choose the candy bar. The money and the candy bar represent two basic kinds of *reinforcers*, items or events that when following a response will strengthen it. The reinforcing properties of money must be learned, but candy gives immediate reward in the form of taste and satisfying hunger.

A reinforcer such as a candy bar that satisfies a basic need like hunger is called a **primary reinforcer**. Examples would be any kind of food (hunger drive), liquid (thirst drive), or touch (pleasure drive). Infants, toddlers, preschool-age children, and animals can be easily reinforced by using primary reinforcers.

A **secondary reinforcer** such as money, however, gets its reinforcing properties from being associated with primary reinforcers in the past. A child who is given money to spend soon realizes that the ugly green paper can be traded for candy and treats—primary reinforcers—and so money becomes reinforcing in and of itself. If a person praises a puppy while petting him (touch, a primary reinforcer), the praise alone will eventually make the puppy squirm with delight.

That sounds very familiar. Isn't this related to classical conditioning? ▶

That sounds very familiar. Isn't this related to classical conditioning? Secondary reinforcers do indeed get their reinforcing power from the process of classical conditioning. After all, the pleasure people feel when they eat, drink, or get a back rub is a reflex response, and any reflex can be classically conditioned to occur to a new stimulus. In the case of money, the candy is a UCS for pleasure (the UCR) and the money is present just before the candy is obtained. The money becomes a CS for pleasure, and people certainly do feel pleasure when they have a lot of that green stuff, don't they?

In the case of the puppy, the petting is the UCS, the pleasure at being touched and petted the UCR. The praise, or more specifically the tone of voice, becomes the CS for pleasure. Although classical and operant conditioning often "work together," as in the creation of secondary reinforcers, they are two different processes. Table 5.1 presents a brief look at how the two types of conditioning differ from each other.

POSITIVE AND NEGATIVE REINFORCEMENT   Reinforcers can also differ in the way they are used. Most people have no trouble at all understanding that following a response with some kind of pleasurable consequence (like a reward) will lead to an increase in the likelihood of that response being repeated. But many people have trou-

primary reinforcer
any reinforcer that is naturally reinforcing by meeting a basic biological need, such as hunger, thirst, or touch.

secondary reinforcer
any reinforcer that becomes reinforcing after being paired with a primary reinforcer, such as praise, tokens, or gold stars.

positive reinforcement
the reinforcement of a response by the addition or experiencing of a pleasurable stimulus.

negative reinforcement
the reinforcement of a response by the removal, escape from, or avoidance of an unpleasant stimulus.

TABLE 5.1 **COMPARING TWO KINDS OF CONDITIONING**

Operant Conditioning	Classical Conditioning
Goal is to increase the rate of an already occurring response.	Goal is to create a new response to a stimulus that doesn't normally produce that response.
Responses are voluntary.	Responses are involuntary and reflexive.
Consequences are important in forming an association.	Antecedent stimuli are important in forming an association.
Reinforcement must be immediate.	CS must occur immediately before the UCS.
An expectancy develops for reinforcement to follow a correct response.	An expectancy develops for UCS to follow CS.

ble understanding that the opposite is also true: Following a response with *the removal or escape* from something *unpleasant* will also increase the likelihood of that response being repeated. Reinforcement does not always mean reward.

There are really only two kinds of things people ever experience as consequences in the world: things they like (food, money, candy, sex, praise, and so on) and things they don't like (spankings, being yelled at, and experiencing any kind of pain, to name a few). There are also only two possibilities for experiencing these two kinds of consequences: Either people experience them directly (such as getting money for working or getting yelled at for misbehaving) or they don't experience them, such as losing an allowance for misbehaving or avoiding a scolding by lying about behavior.

Getting money for working is an example of **positive reinforcement**, the reinforcement of a response by the *addition* or experience of a pleasurable consequence, such as a reward or a pat on the back. That one everyone understands. But avoiding a scolding by lying about one's behavior is an example of negative reinforcement. **Negative reinforcement** is the reinforcement of a response by the removal, escape from, or avoidance of an unpleasant stimulus. Because the behavior (lying) results in *avoiding* an unpleasant stimulus (the scolding), the likelihood that the person will behave that way again (lie in the future) is increased—just as positive reinforcement will increase a behavior's likelihood. People get confused because "negative" sounds like it ought to be something bad, like a kind of punishment. *Punishment* always decreases the likelihood of a behavior happening again. Punishment *weakens* responses, whereas reinforcement (no matter whether it is positive or negative) *strengthens* responses.

I don't understand—I thought that having a toy removed would be an example of negative reinforcement. What's the difference between negative reinforcement and punishment? That is the heart of the confusion: Negative reinforcement occurs when a response is followed by the *removal* of an *unpleasant* stimulus. If something unpleasant has just gone away as a consequence of that response, wouldn't that response tend to happen again and again? If the response increases, the consequence has to be a kind of *reinforcement*. The problem is that the name sounds like it should be some kind of punishment because of the word *negative*, and that's exactly the problem that many people experience when they are trying to understand negative reinforcement. They get negative reinforcement mixed up with the kind of punishment in which a *pleasant* thing is removed (like having your driver's license taken away because you caused a bad accident). Because something is removed (taken away) in both cases, people think that they will both have the effect of punishment, or weakening a response. The difference between them lies in *what* is taken away: In the case of negative reinforcement, it is an unpleasant thing; in the case of this particular form of punishment, it is a pleasant or desirable thing. For a comparison of negative reinforcement and this particular type of punishment by removal, see Table 5.2.

These actors are receiving positive reinforcement in the form of the awards and the applause of the audience.

I don't understand—I thought that having a toy removed would be an example of negative reinforcement. What's the difference between ◀ negative reinforcement and punishment?

If the parents in this restaurant give in to their whining child, they will be positively reinforcing his whining. But they will be receiving negative reinforcement for giving in when the child's obnoxious whining stops.

shaping
the reinforcement of simple steps in behavior that lead to a desired, more complex behavior.

successive approximations
small steps in behavior, one after the other, that lead to a particular goal behavior.

discriminative stimulus
any stimulus, such as a stop sign or a doorknob, that provides the organism with a cue for making a certain response in order to obtain reinforcement.

TABLE 5.2 **NEGATIVE REINFORCEMENT VERSUS PUNISHMENT BY REMOVAL**

Example of Negative Reinforcement	Example of Punishment by Removal
Stopping at a red light to avoid getting in an accident.	Losing the privilege of driving because you got into too many accidents.
Mailing an income tax return by April 15 to avoid paying a penalty.	Having to lose some of your money to pay the penalty for late tax filing.
Obeying a parent before the parent reaches the count of "three" to avoid getting a scolding.	Being "grounded" (losing your freedom) because of disobedience.

Distinguishing between positive reinforcement and negative reinforcement is a little easier. Try to figure out which of the following examples would be positive reinforcement and which would be negative reinforcement:

1. Arnie's father nags him to wash his car. Arnie hates being nagged, so he washes the car so his father will stop nagging.
2. Trey learns that talking in a funny voice gets him lots of attention from his classmates, so now he talks that way often.
3. Allen is a server at a restaurant and always tries to smile and be pleasant because that seems to lead to bigger tips.
4. An Li turns her report in to her teacher on the day it is due because papers get marked down a letter grade for every day they are late.

The answers are as follows:

1. Arnie is being negatively reinforced for washing his car because the nagging (unpleasant stimulus) stops when he does so.
2. Trey is getting positive reinforcement in the form of his classmates' attention.
3. Allen's smiling and pleasantness are positively reinforced by the customers' tips.
4. An Li is avoiding an unpleasant stimulus (the marked-down grade) by turning in her paper on time, which is an example of negative reinforcement.

PRACTICE **QUIZ:** HOW MUCH DO YOU REMEMBER?

Pick the best answer.

1. In Thorndike's puzzle box experiments, the cats were rewarded by
   a. getting out of the box.
   b. getting food.
   c. being petted and praised.
   d. both a and b.

2. _____ is an example of a primary reinforcer, whereas _____ is an example of a secondary reinforcer.
   a. A candy bar; a gold star
   b. A gold star; money
   c. Food; a drink
   d. A gold star; candy

3. _____ occurs when a response is followed by experiencing something pleasurable.
   a. Positive reinforcement
   b. Negative reinforcement
   c. Punishment
   d. Generalization

4. Cindy hates to clean up after dinner. One night she volunteers to bathe the baby before cleaning up. When she finishes with the baby and returns to the kitchen, her husband has cleaned everything up for her. Which of the following statements is most *likely* true?
   a. Cindy will start cleaning up the kitchen before she bathes the baby.
   b. Cindy's husband has positively reinforced her for bathing the baby.
   c. Cindy's husband has negatively reinforced her for bathing the baby.
   d. Cindy will never bathe the baby again.

5. Bennie is afraid of snakes. He won't even look at pictures of them but turns the page or closes the book instead. When he sees a picture of a snake, his anxiety goes up, but when he avoids looking at the picture, his anxiety goes down. It is *most* correct to say that Bennie's avoidance behavior is being
   a. punished because he feels anxious after doing so.
   b. punished because he will never get better.
   c. positively reinforced because he is rewarded by his anxiety going down.
   d. negatively reinforced because he is rewarded by his anxiety going down.

OTHER OPERANT CONCEPTS

Operant conditioning is more than just the reinforcement of simple responses. For example, have you ever tried to teach a pet to do a trick?

Yes, it was really hard. How do the circus trainers get their animals to do all those complicated tricks?

SHAPING   When you see an animal in a circus or in a show at a zoo perform tricks, you are seeing the result of applying the rules of conditioning—both classical and operant—to animals. But the more complex tricks are a form of operant conditioning called **shaping**, in which small steps toward some ultimate goal are reinforced until the goal itself is reached.

For example, if Jody wanted to train his dog to jump through a hoop, he would have to start with some behavior that the dog is already capable of doing on its own. Then he would gradually "mold" that starting behavior into the jump—something the dog is capable of doing but not likely to do on its own. Jody would have to start with the hoop on the ground in front of Rover's face, and then call the dog through the hoop, using the treat as bait. After Rover steps through the hoop (as the shortest way to the treat), Jody should give Rover the treat (positive reinforcement). Then he could raise the hoop just a little, reward him for walking through it again, raise the hoop, reward him . . . until Rover is jumping through the hoop to get the treat. The goal is achieved by reinforcing each **successive approximation** (small steps one after the other that get closer and closer to the goal). This process is shaping (Skinner, 1974).

EXTINCTION, GENERALIZATION, AND SPONTANEOUS RECOVERY IN OPERANT CONDITIONING   *Extinction* in classical conditioning involves the removal of the UCS, the unconditioned stimulus that eventually acts as a reinforcer of the CS–CR bond. It should come as no surprise, then, that extinction in operant conditioning involves the removal of the reinforcement. Have you ever seen a child throw a temper tantrum in the checkout line because the little one wanted some candy or toy? Many exasperated* parents will cave in and give the child the treat, positively reinforcing the tantrum. The parent is also being negatively reinforced for giving in, because the obnoxious** behavior stops. The only way to get the tantrum behavior to stop is to remove the reinforcement, which means no candy, no treat, and if possible, no attention from the parent.

Ignoring one's own child's tantrum in public is a lot harder than ignoring it at home, but it can be done. In fact, most of the other people in the store who witness the tantrum will most likely silently applaud a parent who does not give in and groan inwardly when they see the child's tantrum rewarded.

Just as in classical conditioning, operantly conditioned responses also can be generalized to stimuli that are only similar to the original stimulus. For example, what parent has not experienced that wonderful moment when Baby, who is just learning to label objects and people, refers to every man she sees as "Dada" The name "Dada" is a response to the presence of her own father and is reinforced by his delight and attention to her. But in the beginning, she will generalize her "Dada" response to any man. As other men fail to reinforce her for this response, she'll learn to discriminate between them and her father and only call her father "Dada." In this way, the man who is actually her father becomes a **discriminative stimulus**, which is any stimulus such as a stop sign or a doorknob that provides the organism with a cue for making a certain response in order to obtain reinforcement.

---

*Exasperated: irritated or annoyed.
**Obnoxious: highly offensive or undesirable.

Yes, it was **really hard. How do the circus** ◀ **trainers get their animals to do all those complicated tricks?**

This dog has been trained to help its physically challenged owner. Operant conditioning principles can be used to train animals to do many useful tasks, including opening the refrigerator.

One way to deal with a child's temper tantrum is to ignore it. The lack of reinforcement for the tantrum behavior will eventually result in extinction.

Experiment
Live!
psych

Shaping

Spontaneous recovery (the recurrence of a conditioned response after extinction) will also happen with operant responses. Remember the hoop-jumping dog? Anyone who has ever trained animals to do several different tricks will say that when first learning a new trick, most animals will try to get reinforcers by performing their *old* tricks. Rover might very well have tried to roll over, speak, and shake paws to get that treat before finally walking through the hoop.

PRACTICE **QUIZ:** HOW MUCH DO YOU REMEMBER?

Pick the best answer.

1. Elizabeth's parents want her to put her clothes in the hamper. At first, they praise her for putting the clothes together in one pile. Then they praise her for getting the clothes on the same side of the room as the hamper. When she gets the clothes on top of the hamper, she gets praise. Finally, her parents praise her when she puts her clothes in the hamper. This is an example of
   a. negative reinforcement.　　**c.** extinction.
   b. punishment.　　　　　　　　 **d.** shaping.

2. Marcella starts whining in the grocery store because she wants some candy. Her father refuses to give her candy and ignores her whining. What will happen?
   a. generalization　　　　　　 **c.** spontaneous recovery
   b. extinction　　　　　　　　 **d.** discrimination

3. The first time Giorgio sees a duck, his mother tells him, "That's a duck. Can you say duck?" He repeats the word gleefully. The next day he is watching a cartoon and sees a chicken on the television. He points at the chicken and says "duck!" This is an example of
   a. generalization.　　　　　　 **c.** spontaneous recovery.
   b. extinction.　　　　　　　　 **d.** discrimination.

4. Ella is teaching her parrot a new word. Every time the parrot says a sound that is close to the new word, she gives it a treat. But the parrot keeps repeating other words it has learned in the past, trying to get a treat that way. The parrot is exhibiting
   a. generalization.　　　　　　 **c.** spontaneous recovery.
   b. extinction.　　　　　　　　 **d.** discrimination.

Answers: 1-d, 2-b, 3-a, 4-c.

THE SCHEDULES OF REINFORCEMENT: WHY THE ONE-ARMED BANDIT IS SO SEDUCTIVE

The timing of reinforcement can make a tremendous difference in the speed at which learning occurs and the strength of the learned response. Skinner (1956) found that reinforcing each and every response was not necessarily the best schedule of reinforcement for long-lasting learning.

5.10　*What are the schedules of reinforcement?*

THE PARTIAL REINFORCEMENT EFFECT　Alicia's mother gives her a quarter every night she remembers to put her dirty clothes in the clothes hamper. Bianca's mother gives her a dollar at the end of the week, but only if she has put her clothes in the hamper every night. After a time, the mothers stop giving the girls the money. Which child will stop putting her clothes in the hamper more quickly?

The answer might be surprising. It will more likely be Alicia, who has expected to get a reinforcer (the quarter) after *every single response*. As soon as the reinforcers stop, the behavior extinguishes. Bianca has expected to get a reinforcer only after *seven correct responses*. When the reinforcers stop, Bianca might continue to put the clothes in the hamper for several more days or even another whole week, hoping that the reinforcer will eventually come anyway.

Bianca's behavior illustrates the **partial reinforcement effect** (Skinner, 1956): A response that is reinforced after some, but not all, correct responses will be more resistant to extinction than a response that receives **continuous reinforcement** (a reinforcer for each and every correct response). Imagine being paid for every hamburger you make or every report you turn in. In the real world, people tend to receive partial reinforcement rather than continuous reinforcement for their work.

partial reinforcement effect
the tendency for a response that is reinforced after some, but not all, correct responses to be very resistant to extinction.

continuous reinforcement
the reinforcement of each and every correct response.

Partial reinforcement can be accomplished according to different patterns or schedules. For example, it may be the number of responses that is important, as it would be if one had to sell a certain number of raffle tickets in order to get a prize. On the other hand, it might be a certain interval of time that's important, such as an office safe that can only be opened at a certain time of day. It wouldn't matter how many times one tried to open the safe if the effort didn't come at the right *time*. When it is the number of responses that is important, the schedule is called a *ratio schedule* because a certain number of responses is required for each reinforcer (e.g., 50 raffle tickets for each prize). When the timing of the response is more important, it is called an *interval schedule*.

The other way in which schedules of reinforcement can differ is in whether the number of responses or interval of time is *fixed* (the same in each case) or *variable* (a different number or interval is required in each case). So it is possible to have a fixed ratio schedule, a variable ratio schedule, a fixed interval schedule, and a variable interval schedule (Skinner, 1961).

FIXED RATIO SCHEDULE OF REINFORCEMENT   In a **fixed ratio schedule of reinforcement**, the number of responses required to receive each reinforcer will always be the same number. If Professor Conner were teaching a rat to press a lever to get food pellets, she might require 20 lever pushes for each food pellet, or a fixed ratio of 20 : 1. If she were to graph the rat's progress, she would end up with something like the graph in the upper left corner of Figure 5.8.

fixed ratio schedule of reinforcement schedule of reinforcement in which the number of responses required for reinforcement is always the same.

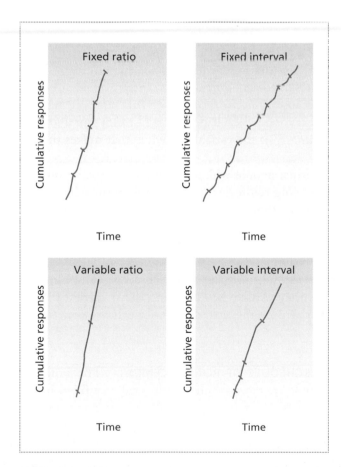

FIGURE 5.8   **Schedules of Reinforcement**   The typical outcomes of four partial reinforcement schedules in the form of cumulative records. Slash mark indicates delivery of reinforcement. The pause after each reinforcement is very characteristic of fixed-ratio schedules, whereas the "scalloped" shape of the record is typical of fixed-interval schedules.

"Remember, every time he gives you a pellet, reinforce that behavior by pulling the lever."

Notice two things about this graph: The rate of responding is very fast and there are little "breaks" in the response pattern immediately after a reinforcer is given. The rapid response rate occurs because the rat wants to get to the next reinforcer just as fast as possible, and the number of lever pushes counts. The pauses or breaks come right after a reinforcer, because the rat knows "about how many" lever pushes will be needed to get to the next reinforcer because it's always the same. Fixed schedules are predictable, and that allows rest breaks.

In human terms, anyone who does piecework, in which a certain number of items have to be completed before payment is given, is reinforced on a fixed ratio schedule. Some sandwich shops give out punch cards that get punched one time for each sandwich purchased. When the card has 10 punches, for example, the person might get a free sandwich.

In Figure 5.8 the graph ▶ on the lower left is also very fast, but it's so much smoother. Why?

VARIABLE RATIO SCHEDULE OF REINFORCEMENT   In Figure 5.8 the graph on the lower left is also very fast, but it's so much smoother. Why? A **variable ratio schedule of reinforcement** is one in which the number of responses changes from one trial to the next. In the rat example, the rat might be expected to push the bar an *average* of 20 times to get reinforcement. That means that sometimes the rat would push the lever only 10 times before a reinforcer comes, but at other times it might take 30 lever pushes or more.

The graph at the lower left of Figure 5.8 shows a curve that is just as rapid a response rate as the fixed ratio schedule because the number of responses still matters. But the graph is much smoother because the rat is taking no rest breaks. It can't afford to do so because it *doesn't know* how many times it may have to push that lever to get the next food pellet. It pushes as fast as it can and eats while pushing. It is the *unpredictability* of the variable schedule that makes the responses more or less continuous.

In human terms, people who shove money into the one-armed bandit, or slot machine, are being reinforced on a variable ratio schedule of reinforcement (they hope). They put their coins in (response), but they don't know how many times they will have to do this before reinforcement (the jackpot) comes. People who do this tend to sit there until they either win or run out of money. They don't dare stop because the "next one" might hit that jackpot. Buying lottery tickets is much the same thing, as is any kind of gambling. People don't know how many tickets they will have to buy, and they're afraid that if they don't buy the next one, that will be the ticket that would have won, so they keep buying and buying.

Slot machines provide reinforcement in the form of money on a variable ratio schedule, making the use of these machines almost addictive. People don't want to stop for fear the next pull of the lever will be that "magic" one that produces a jackpot.

FIXED INTERVAL SCHEDULE OF REINFORCEMENT   The kind of reinforcement schedule most people are more familiar with is called a **fixed interval schedule of reinforcement**, in which a reinforcer is received after a certain, fixed interval of time has passed. If people receive a paycheck once every two weeks (provided that they show up to work in those two weeks), they are being reinforced on this kind of schedule.

As shown in the upper right corner of Figure 5.8, this schedule of reinforcement does not produce as fast a rate of responding as does the fixed ratio schedule. The number of responses doesn't matter in this case, only that at least one response is made during the specific interval of time. In the example with the rat, it might be required to press the lever during a five-minute interval of time. It doesn't have to press the bar fast or even very many times—just once in the five minutes. It is the first correct response after the interval of time has passed that gets reinforced. Eventually, the rat will start pushing the lever only as the interval of time nears its end, causing the scalloping effect you see in the graph. The response rate goes up just before the reinforcer and then drops off immediately after, until it is almost time for the next food pellet.

Paychecks aren't the only kind of fixed schedule that people experience. When do you study the hardest? Isn't it right before a test? If you know when the test is to be given, that's like having a fixed interval of time that is predictable, and you can save your greatest studying efforts until closer to the exam. (Some students save *all* of their studying for the night before the exam, which is not exactly the best strategy.) Another example of a fixed interval schedule would be the way that most people floss and brush their teeth most rigorously* the few days before their next dental exam. In this case, they are probably hoping for negative reinforcement. The cleaner they get their teeth before the appointment, the less time they might have to spend in that chair.

So if a scheduled test is a fixed interval, then would a pop quiz be a variable interval schedule?

VARIABLE INTERVAL SCHEDULE OF REINFORCEMENT Pop quizzes are unpredictable. Students don't know exactly what day they might be given a pop quiz, so the best strategy is to study a little every night just in case there is a quiz the next day. Pop quizzes are good examples of a **variable interval schedule of reinforcement**, in which the interval of time after which the organism must respond in order to receive a reinforcer changes from one time to the next. For example, the rat might receive a food pellet every five minutes *on average*. Sometimes it might be two minutes, sometimes ten, but the rat must push the lever at least once after that interval to get the pellet. Because the rat can't predict how long the interval is going to be, it pushes the bar more or less continuously, producing the smooth graph in the lower right corner of Figure 5.8. Once again, the number of responses is not important, so the rate of responding is not as fast as a variable ratio schedule.

Another example of a variable interval schedule might be the kind of fishing in which people put the pole in the water and wait—and wait, and wait, until a fish takes the bait—if they are lucky. They only have to put the pole in once, but they might refrain from taking it out for fear that just when they do, the biggest fish in the world would swim by. Dialing a busy phone number is also this kind of schedule, as people don't know *when* the call will go through, so they keep dialing and dialing.

---

*Rigorously: strictly, consistently.

variable ratio schedule of reinforcement
schedule of reinforcement in which the number of responses required for reinforcement is different for each trial or event.

fixed interval schedule of reinforcement
schedule of reinforcement in which the interval of time that must pass before reinforcement becomes possible is always the same.

variable interval schedule of reinforcement
schedule of reinforcement in which the interval of time that must pass before reinforcement becomes possible is different for each trial or event.

So if a scheduled test is a fixed interval, then ◄ would a pop quiz be a variable interval schedule?

When people go fishing, they never know how long they may have to dangle the bait in the water before snagging a fish. This is an example of a variable interval schedule of reinforcement and explains why some people, such as this father and son, are reluctant to pack up and go home.

I've heard that ▶
many psychologists
don't recommend
using punishment.
Is that true?

I've heard that many psychologists don't recommend using punishment. Is that true?

PUNISHMENT

5.11 *How does punishment affect behavior?*

Although punishment can be effective in reducing or weakening a behavior, it has several drawbacks. **Punishment** is the opposite of reinforcement. It is any event or stimulus, that when following a response causes that response to be less likely to happen again. The job of punishment is much harder than that of reinforcement. In reinforcement, all one has to do is strengthen a response that is already there. But punishment is used to weaken a response, and getting rid of a response that is already well established is not that easy. Many times punishment only serves to temporarily suppress or inhibit a behavior until enough time has passed that the inhibition itself weakens and disappears. As many parents know, punishing a child's bad behavior doesn't always eliminate the behavior completely. As time goes on, the punishment is forgotten and the bad behavior may occur again in a kind of spontaneous recovery.

In trying to understand why punishment works in some cases and not in others, it will be useful to look at Table 5.3. Contrast the two types of punishment (Gordon, 1989; Skinner, 1953) represented in the table with the two types of reinforcement discussed earlier in the chapter.

PUNISHMENT BY APPLICATION   On the upper right is **punishment by application**, in which something unpleasant (such as a spanking, scolding, or other unpleasant stimulus) is added to the situation or applied. This is the kind of punishment that most people think of when they hear the word *punishment*. This is also the kind of punishment that many child development specialists strongly recommend parents avoid using with their children because it can easily escalate into abuse (Saunders & Goddard, 1998; Straus, 2000; Straus & Stewart, 1999; Straus & Yodanis, 1994; Trocmé et al., 2001). A spanking might be harmless if it is only two or three swats with a hand, but if done in anger or with a belt or other instrument, it becomes abuse.

Punishment by application can be quite severe, and severe punishment does one thing well: It stops the behavior immediately (Bucher & Lovaas, 1967; Carr & Lovass, 1983). It may not stop it permanently, but it does stop it. In a situation in which a child might be doing something dangerous or self-injurious, this kind of punishment is somewhat more acceptable (Duker & Seys, 1995). For example, if a child starts to run into a busy street, the parent might scream at the child to stop and then administer several rather severe swats to the child's rear. If this is not usual behavior on the part of the parent, the child will most likely never run into the street again.

punishment
any event or object that, when following a response, makes that response less likely to happen again.

punishment by application
the punishment of a response by the addition or experiencing of an unpleasant stimulus.

TABLE 5.3 FOUR WAYS TO MODIFY BEHAVIOR

	Reinforcement	Punishment
POSITIVE (Adding)	Something valued or desirable; *Positive Reinforcement* Example: getting a gold star for good behavior in school	Something unpleasant; *Punishment by Application* Example: getting a spanking for disobeying
NEGATIVE (Removing/ Avoiding)	Something unpleasant; *Negative Reinforcement* Example: avoiding a ticket by stopping at a red light	Something valued or desirable; *Punishment by Removal* Example: losing a privilege such as going out with friends

Other than situations of immediately stopping dangerous behavior, severe punishment has too many drawbacks to be really useful. It should also be discouraged because of its potential for leading to abuse (Gershoff, 2000; McMillan et al., 1999; Trocmé et al., 2001):

- Severe punishment may cause the child (or animal) to avoid the punisher instead of the behavior being punished.
- Severe punishment may encourage lying to avoid the punishment (a kind of negative reinforcement).
- Severe punishment creates fear and anxiety, emotional responses that do not promote learning (Baumrind, 1997; Gershoff, 2000; Gershoff, 2002). If the point is to teach something, this kind of consequence isn't going to help.
- Hitting provides a model for aggression (Gershoff, 2000; Milner, 1992).

punishment by removal
the punishment of a response by the removal of a pleasurable stimulus.

PUNISHMENT BY REMOVAL On the lower right of Table 5.3 is a type of punishment called **punishment by removal**, mentioned earlier in the discussion of positive and negative reinforcement. In this type of punishment, behavior is punished by the removal of something pleasurable or desired after the behavior occurs. "Grounding" a teenager is removing the freedom to do what the teenager wants to do and is an example of this kind of punishment. Other examples would be placing a child in time-out (removing the attention of the others in the room), fining someone for disobeying the law (removing money), and punishing aggressive behavior by taking away television privileges. This type of punishment is far more acceptable to child development specialists, as it involves no physical aggression and avoids the problems caused by more aggressive punishments.

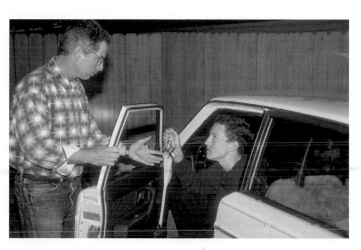

This young man's father is applying punishment by removal as he takes the car keys away from his son.

PROBLEMS WITH PUNISHMENT As mentioned earlier, another problem exists when using severe forms of punishment by application. In using an aggressive type of punishment, such as spanking, the adult is actually modeling (presenting a behavior to be imitated by the child). After all, the adult is using aggression to get what the adult wants from the child. Children sometimes become more likely to use aggression to get what they want when they receive this kind of punishment (Bryan & Freed, 1982; Larzelere, 1986).

Punishment by removal is less objectionable to many parents and educators and is the only kind of punishment that is permitted in many public schools. But this kind of punishment also has its drawbacks. Both punishment by removal and punishment by application are usually only temporary in their effect on behavior. After some time has passed, the behavior will most likely return as the memory of the punishment gets weaker, allowing spontaneous recovery.

If punishment doesn't work very well, what can a parent do to keep a child from behaving badly?

HOW TO MAKE PUNISHMENT MORE EFFECTIVE The way to make punishment more effective involves remembering a few simple rules:

1. **Punishment should immediately follow the behavior it is meant to punish.** If the punishment comes long after the behavior, it will not be associated with that behavior.
2. **Punishment should be consistent.** This actually means two things. First, if the parent says that a certain punishment will follow a certain behavior, then the parent must make sure to follow through and do what he or she promised to do. Second,

◀ If punishment doesn't work very well, what can a parent do to keep a child from behaving badly?

punishment for a particular behavior should stay at the same intensity or increase slightly but never decrease. For example, if a child is scolded for jumping on the bed the first time, the second time this behavior happens the child should also be punished by scolding or by a stronger penalty, such as removal of a favorite toy. But if the first misbehavior is punished by spanking and the second by only a scolding, the child learns to "gamble" with the possible punishment.

3. **Punishment of the wrong behavior should be paired, whenever possible, with reinforcement of the right behavior.** Instead of yelling at a 2-year-old for eating with her fingers, the parent should pull her hand gently out of her plate while saying something such as, "No, we do not eat with our fingers. We eat with our fork," and then placing the fork in the child's hand and praising her for using it. "See, you are doing such a good job with your fork. I'm so proud of you." Pairing punishment (the mild correction of pulling her hand away while saying "No, we do not eat with our fingers") with reinforcement allows parents (and others) to use a much milder punishment and still be effective.

STIMULUS CONTROL: SLOW DOWN, IT'S THE COPS

5.12 *How do operant stimuli control behavior?*

In the beginning of the discussion of operant conditioning, it is stated that there are stimuli associated with learning voluntary behavior, even though it is the consequences of that behavior that create the learning process. These stimuli act as cues in the environment.

DISCRIMINATIVE STIMULI   As stated earlier, a *discriminative stimulus* is any stimulus that provides an organism with a cue for making a certain response in order to obtain reinforcement. For example, a stop sign is a cue for stopping, which is usually followed by negative reinforcement—people don't get a ticket or don't get hit by another vehicle. A doorknob is a cue for where to grab the door in order to successfully open it. In fact, if a door has a knob, people always turn it, but if it has a handle, people usually push it, right? The two kinds of opening devices each bring forth a different response from people, and their reward is opening the door.

   Other examples of discriminative stimuli are all around. What do you do when you are out driving and you see a vehicle with flashing lights in the rear view mirror? You slow down and hope the officer is after someone else. The point is that you *slow down*, and you do that any time you see a vehicle that *might* be a police car or a highway patrol car. People are so well conditioned to respond to the sight of a patrol car by slowing down that the Tennessee Highway Patrol once put empty patrol cars in the rather large medians on the interstates, successfully slowing down holiday traffic while conserving labor.

CLASSIC STUDIES IN PSYCHOLOGY

Biological Constraints on Operant Conditioning

5.13 *What kind of behavior is resistant to conditioning?*

Raccoons are fairly intelligent animals and are sometimes used in learning experiments. In a typical experiment, a behaviorist would use shaping and reinforcement to teach a raccoon a trick. The goal might be to get the raccoon to pick up several coins and drop them into a metal container, for which the raccoon would be rewarded with food. The behaviorist starts by reinforcing the raccoon for picking up a single coin. Then the metal container is introduced and the raccoon is now required to drop the coin into the slot on the container in order to get reinforcement.

It is at this point that operant conditioning seems to fail. Instead of dropping the coin in the slot, the raccoon puts the coin in and out of the slot and rubs it against the inside of the container, then holds it firmly for a few seconds before finally letting it go. When the requirement is upped to two coins, the raccoon spends several minutes rubbing them against each other and dipping them into the container, without actually dropping them in. In spite of the fact that this dipping and rubbing behavior is not reinforced, it gets worse and worse until conditioning becomes impossible.

How can this be? If a behavior is followed by a reinforcer it should be repeated, yet this raccoon is not only failing to repeat the behavior it is being reinforced to do, but also the raccoon is doing behavior that gets no reward at all. Why has operant conditioning failed?

Keller and Marian Breland found themselves pondering that very question because the raccoon study was one of their attempts to condition an animal in this manner (Breland & Breland, 1961). The problem wasn't limited to the raccoon, either. They ran into a similar difficulty with a pig that was being trained to pick up a total of five large wooden coins and put them into a "piggy bank." Although at first successful, the pig became slower and slower at the task over a period of weeks, dropping the coin, rooting (pushing) it around with its nose, picking it up, dropping it again, and rooting some more. This behavior became so persistent that the pig actually did not get enough to eat for the day.

The Brelands concluded that the raccoon and the pig were reverting* to behavior that was instinctual for them. Instinctual behavior is genetically determined and not under the influence of learning. Apparently, even though the animals were at first able to learn the tricks, as the coins became more and more associated with food, the animals began to drift back into the instinctual patterns of behavior that they used with real food. Raccoons rub their food between their paws and dip it in and out of water. Pigs root and throw their food around before eating it. The Brelands called this tendency to revert to genetically controlled patterns **instinctive drift**.

In their 1961 paper describing these and other examples of instinctive drift, the Brelands (both trained by Skinner himself) determined that three assumptions in which most Skinnerian behaviorists believed were not actually true. The three false assumptions:

1. The animal comes to the laboratory a *tabula rasa*, or "blank slate," and can, therefore, be taught anything with the right conditioning.

2. Differences between species of animals are insignificant.

3. All responses are equally able to be conditioned to any stimulus.

As became quickly obvious in their studies with these animals, each animal comes into the world (and the laboratory) with certain genetically determined instinctive patterns of behavior already in place. These instincts differ from species to species, with the result that there are some responses that simply cannot be trained into an animal regardless of conditioning. To quote Breland and Breland (1961),

It is our reluctant conclusion that the behavior of any species cannot be adequately understood, predicted, or controlled without knowledge of its instinctive patterns, evolutionary history, and ecological niche (p. 684).

Questions for Further Discussion

1. What other kinds of limitations do animals have in learning?

2. What kinds of behavior might people do that would be resistant to conditioning?

3. How can these research findings about animal behavior be generalized to human behavior?

---

*Reverting: to go back in action, thought, speech, and so on.

Raccoons commonly dunk their food in and out of water before eating. This "washing" behavior is controlled by instinct and difficult to change even using operant techniques.

instinctive drift
tendency for an animal's behavior to revert to genetically controlled patterns.

APPLYING OPERANT CONDITIONING: BEHAVIOR MODIFICATION

5.14 *What is behavior modification?*

Operant conditioning principles such as reinforcement and shaping have been used for many years to change undesirable behavior and create desirable responses in animals and humans—particularly in school children. The term **behavior modification** refers to the application of operant conditioning to bring about such changes. People might recall their grade school teacher offering gold stars or some other incentive* as a reward for reading a certain number of books or giving a reward like a wooden stick that could be traded in for a treat.

For example, if a teacher wants to use behavior modification to help a child learn to be more attentive during the teacher's lectures, the teacher may do the following:

1. Select a target behavior, such as making eye contact with the teacher.
2. Choose a reinforcer. This may be a gold star applied to the child's chart on the wall, for example.
3. Put the plan in action. Every time the child makes eye contact, the teacher gives the child a gold star. Inappropriate behavior (such as looking out of the window) is not reinforced with gold stars.
4. At the end of the day, the teacher gives the child a special treat or reward for having a certain number of gold stars. This special reward is decided on ahead of time and discussed with the child.

Both gold stars and wooden sticks can be considered *tokens*, secondary reinforcers that can be traded in for other kinds of reinforcers. The use of tokens to modify behavior is called a **token economy**. (L I N K) *to Chapter Fifteen: Psychological Therapies, p. 572.* In the example, the child is collecting gold stars to "buy" the special treat at the end of the day. When one thinks about it, the system of money is very much a token economy. People are rewarded for working for money, which they then trade in for food, shelter, and so on.

Another tool that behaviorists can use to modify behavior is the process of *time-out*. Time-out is a form of mild punishment by removal in which a misbehaving animal, child, or adult is placed in a special area away from the attention of others. Essentially, the organism is being "removed" from any possibility of positive reinforcement in the form of attention. When used with children, time-out should be limited to one minute for each year of age with a maximum time-out of 10 minutes (longer than that and the child can forget why the time-out occurred).

Applied behavior analysis (ABA), is the modern term for a form of behavior modification that uses shaping techniques to mold a desired behavior or response. It can be said to have begun with the work of Lovaas (1964) and his associates, although the basic techniques are those first outlined by Skinner. Lovaas used small pieces of candy as reinforcers to teach social skills and language to children with *autism*. (Autism is a disorder in which the person has great difficulty in communicating with others, often refusing to look at another person. (L I N K) *to Chapter Seven: Development Across the Life Span, p. 263.* People who are autistic may also fail to learn to speak at all, and they normally do not like to be touched. The character played by Dustin Hoffman in the movie *Rainman* was autistic.)

In ABA, skills are broken down to their simplest steps and then taught to the child through a system of reinforcement. Prompts (such as moving a child's face back to look at the teacher or the task) are given as needed when the child is learning a

---

behavior modification
the use of operant conditioning techniques to bring about desired changes in behavior.

token economy
type of behavior modification in which desired behavior is rewarded with tokens.

applied behavior analysis (ABA)
modern term for a form of behavior modification that uses shaping techniques to mold a desired behavior or response.

---

*Incentive: something that encourages a particular action.

skill or refuses to cooperate. As the child begins to master a skill and receives reinforcement in the form of treats or praise, the prompts are gradually withdrawn until the child can do the skill independently. Applied behavior analysis is a growing field with many colleges and universities offering excellent degrees at both the undergraduate and graduate levels. A person graduating from one of these programs may act as a consultant* to schools or other institutions or may set up a private practice. Typical uses for ABA are: dealing with children with disorders, training animals, and developing effective teaching methods for children and adults of all levels of mental abilities (Baer et al., 1968).

*Consultant: someone who offers expert advice or services.

PRACTICE **QUIZ:** HOW MUCH DO YOU REMEMBER?

Pick the best answer.

1. Jessica's mother was upset to find that Jessica had used her crayons to draw flowers on her bedroom wall. Her mother took the crayons away from her and made Jessica wash the drawings off the wall. Which of the following statements is true?
   a. Having her crayons taken away was a form of punishment by removal.
   b. Being made to wash off the drawings was a form of punishment by application.
   c. Having her crayons taken away was a form of negative reinforcement.
   d. Both (a) and (b) are true.

2. Which of the following is NOT a problem with punishment?
   a. The effect of punishment is often temporary.
   b. Severe punishment creates fear and anxiety.
   c. Mild punishment can be paired with reinforcement of the correct behavior.
   d. Aggressive punishment can model aggressive behavior for the child.

3. Professor Elliot told his students that if his door was open, it meant that he was available to them and would gladly answer any questions they might have. But if his door was pushed almost completely shut, it meant that he was busy and would prefer not to answer questions at that time. Professor Elliot's door being open was a _____ for _____.
   a. discriminative stimulus; asking questions
   b. discriminative stimulus; not asking questions
   c. discriminative response; asking questions
   d. discriminative response; not asking questions

4. What is the most likely explanation for why fear caused by severe punishment tends to make the punishment ineffective?
   a. Fear causes the child to remember the behavior that was punished.
   b. Fear creates resentment that makes the child rebellious and disobedient.
   c. Fear interferes with the child's ability to learn from the punishment.
   d. None of the above are true.

5. Applied behavior analysis involves
   a. the process of shaping.
   b. is useful only for teaching autistic children.
   c. is different from behavior modification.
   d. cannot be used with animals.

Answers: 1-d, 2-c, 3-a, 4-c, 5-a.

PSYCHOLOGY IN THE NEWS

Neurofeedback and the Treatment of ADD

5.15 *What is neurofeedback and how is it used?*

A relatively new technique called neurofeedback is used to treat a child's attention problems in the classroom. Although this technique uses the latest in technology, the basic principles behind it are much older. For nearly 60 years, scientists have known how to use feedback of a person's biological information (such as heart rate) to create a state of relaxation (Margolin & Kubic, 1944). **Biofeedback** is the traditional term used to describe this kind of biological feedback of information, and through its use many problems can be relieved or controlled.

biofeedback
the use of feedback about biological conditions to bring involuntary responses such as blood pressure and relaxation under voluntary control.

neurofeedback
form of biofeedback using brain-scanning devices to provide feedback about brain activity in an effort to modify behavior.

In the last decade, a new version of biofeedback that makes use of brain-scanning technology has emerged. Traditionally, biofeedback has used sensors placed on various parts of the body to measure and monitor physical reactions such as muscle tension or body temperature. For example, a person who suffers from high blood pressure can be taught to lower that blood pressure by being given feedback about his or her muscle tension. The person might be hooked up to a monitor that measures muscle tension, and the lower the muscle tension becomes, the lower a sound becomes that is played for the person. Lower muscle tension produces lower blood pressure. The goal would be to get the sound to stay low, and this in and of itself is rewarding, increasing the state of relaxation and lowering blood pressure as a consequence (Benson et al., 1974). The sound is the feedback, and low sounds are the reinforcement for relaxation.

Neurofeedback is the newer version of biofeedback and involves trying to change brain wave activity. In neurofeedback, the person is connected to an *electroencephalograph*, a machine that records the brain's electrical activity. Neurofeedback devices can be integrated into video-game–style programs. In one case a young boy with attention problems was able to make a car on a screen go faster or slower in response to his own changing brain activity, which reflected his mental state of relaxation or excitement (Radford, 2004).

Neurofeedback has been used to treat a number of disorders and conditions in the last few years:

- epilepsy (Sterman, 2000; Sterman & Lantz, 2001)
- anxiety disorders (Egner et al., 2002; Norris et al., 2001)
- depression and anger (Hammond, 2001a; Putnam, 2001)
- drug addiction (Trudeau, 2000)
- chronic fatigue syndrome (Hammond, 2001b; Mueller et al., 2001)
- obsessive-compulsive disorder (Hammond, 2003)
- autism (Jarusiewicz, 2002)
- attention-deficit hyperactivity disorder (Linden et al., 1996; Monastra et al., 2002; Rossiter & La Vaque, 1995)

Playing a video game to help solve problems like anxiety and attention problems? It sounds like a child's dream world.

Questions for Further Discussion

1. What other conditions might neurofeedback be used to treat?
2. How might neurofeedback be used to treat test anxiety?
3. Are there any drawbacks to using video games as a treatment?

"Bathroom? Sure, it's just down that hall to the left, jog right, left, another left, straight past two more lefts, then right, and it's at the end of the third corridor on your right."

Cognitive Learning Theory

5.16 *What is cognitive learning theory?*

In the early days of behaviorism, the original focus of Watson, Skinner, and many of their followers was on observable behavior. Anything that might be occurring inside a person or animal's head during learning was considered to be of no interest to the behaviorist because it could not be seen or directly measured. But in the 1950s and more intensely in the 1960s, many psychologists were becoming aware that *cognition*, the mental events that take place inside a person's mind while behaving, could no longer be ignored (Kendler, 1985). One of these early cognitive learning scientists was Edward Tolman (1886–1959).

TOLMAN'S MAZE-RUNNING RATS: LATENT LEARNING

5.17   *What was Tolman's classic study on latent learning?*

One of psychologist Edward Tolman's best-known experiments in learning involved teaching three groups of rats the same maze, one at a time (Tolman & Honzik, 1930). In the first group, each rat was placed in the maze and rewarded with food for making its way out the other side. The rat was then placed back in the maze, rewarded, and so on until the rat could successfully solve the maze with no errors—the typical maze-learning experience (see Figure 5.9).

The second group of rats was treated exactly like the first, except that they never received any reinforcement upon exiting the maze. They were simply put back in again and again, until the tenth day of the experiment. On that day, the rats in the second group began to receive reinforcement for getting out of the maze. The third group of rats, serving as a control group, was also not reinforced and was not given reinforcement for the entire duration of the experiment.

A strict Skinnerian behaviorist would predict that only the first group of rats would learn the maze successfully because learning depends on reinforcing consequences. At first, this seemed to be the case. The first group of rats did indeed solve the maze after a certain number of trials, whereas the second and third groups seemed to wander aimlessly around the maze until accidentally finding their way out.

On the tenth day, however, something happened that would be difficult to explain using only Skinner's basic principles. The second group of rats, upon receiving the reinforcement for the first time, *should* have then taken as long as the first group to solve the maze. Instead, they began to solve the maze almost immediately (see Figure 5.10).

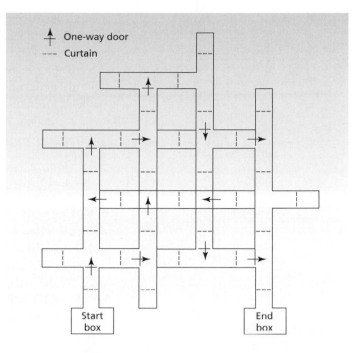

FIGURE 5.9   **A Typical Maze**   This is an example of a maze such as the one used in Tolman's experiments in latent learning. A rat is placed in the start box. The trial is over when the rat gets to the end box.

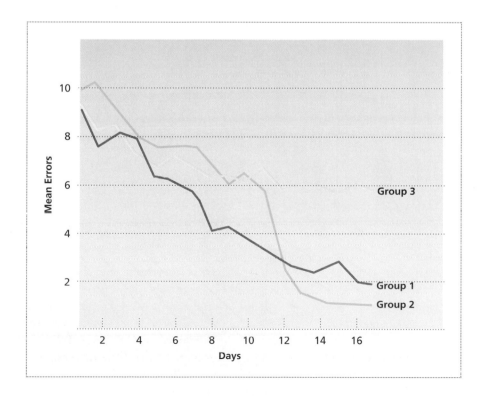

FIGURE 5.10   **Learning Curves for Three Groups of Rats**   In the results of the classic study of latent learning Group 1 was rewarded on each day while Group 2 was rewarded for the first time on Day 11. Group 3 was never rewarded. Note the immediate change in the behavior of Group 2 on Day 12. (Tolman & Honzik, 1930)

latent learning
learning that remains hidden until its application becomes useful.

Experiment
Live! **psych**

Latent
Learning

Tolman concluded that the rats in the second group, while wandering around in the first nine days of the experiment, had indeed learned where all the blind alleys, wrong turns, and correct paths were in the maze. They had simply not *demonstrated* this learning because there was no reason to do so. The learning had remained hidden, or latent, until the rats had a reason to demonstrate their learning by getting to the food. Tolman called this **latent learning**.

SELIGMAN'S DEPRESSED DOGS: LEARNED HELPLESSNESS

5.18 *What is learned helplessness?*

Martin Seligman is now famous for founding the field of *positive psychology*, a new way of looking at the entire concept of mental health and therapy. (L I N K) *to Chapter Nine: Motivation and Emotion, p. 363.* But in the mid- to late 1960s Seligman and his colleagues accidentally discovered an unexpected phenomenon while doing experiments on dogs using classical conditioning (Seligman, 1975). Their original intention was to study escape and avoidance learning. Seligman and colleagues presented a tone followed by a harmless but painful electric shock to one group of dogs (Overmier & Seligman, 1967; Seligman & Maier, 1967). The dogs in this group were harnessed so that they could not escape the shock. The researchers assumed that the dogs would learn to fear the sound of the tone and later try to escape from the tone before being shocked.

These dogs, along with another group of dogs that had not been conditioned to fear the tone, were placed into a special box consisting of a low fence that divided the box into two compartments (see Figure 5.11). The dogs, which were now unharnessed, could easily see over the fence and jump over if they wished—which is precisely what the dogs that had not been conditioned did as soon as the shock occurred. Imagine the researchers' surprise when, instead of jumping over the fence when the tone sounded, the previously conditioned dogs just sat there. In fact, these dogs showed distress but didn't try to jump over the fence *even when the shock itself began.*

FIGURE 5.11 **Seligman's Apparatus** In Seligman's studies of learned helplessness, dogs were placed in a two-sided box. Dogs that had no prior experience with being unable to escape a shock would quickly jump over the hurdle in the center of the box to land on the "safe" side. Dogs that had previously learned that escape was impossible would stay on the side of the box in which the shock occurred, not even trying to go over the hurdle.

Why would the conditioned dogs refuse to move when shocked? The dogs that had been harnessed while being conditioned had apparently learned in the original tone/shock situation that there was nothing they could do to escape the shock. So when placed in a situation in which escape was possible, the dogs still did nothing because they had learned to be "helpless." They believed they could not escape, so they did not try.

I know some people who seem to act just like those dogs—they live in a horrible situation but won't leave. Is this the same thing? Seligman extended this theory of **learned helplessness**, the tendency to fail to act to escape from a situation because of a history of repeated failures in the past, to explain *depression*. Depressed people seem to lack normal emotions and become somewhat apathetic, often staying in unpleasant work environments or bad marriages or relationships rather than trying to escape or better their situation. Seligman proposed that this depressive behavior is a form of learned helplessness. Depressed people may have learned in the past that they seem to have no control over what happens to them (Alloy & Clements, 1998). A sense of powerlessness and hopelessness is common to depressed people, and certainly this would seem to apply to Seligman's dogs as well.

Think about how this might apply to other situations. There are many students who feel that they are bad at math because they have had problems with it in the past. Is it possible that this belief could make them not try as hard or study as much as they should? Isn't this kind of thinking also an example of learned helplessness?

KOHLER'S SMART CHIMP: INSIGHT LEARNING

5.19   *What is insight?*

Another exploration of the cognitive elements of learning came about almost by accident. Wolfgang Köhler (1887–1967) was a Gestalt psychologist who became marooned* on an island in the Canaries (a series of islands off the coast of North Africa) when World War I broke out. Stuck at the primate research lab that had first drawn him to the island, he turned to studies of animal learning.

In one of his more famous studies (Köhler, 1925), he set up a problem for one of the chimpanzees. Sultan the chimp was faced with the problem of how to get to a banana that was placed just out of his reach outside his cage. Sultan solved this problem relatively easily, first trying to reach through the bars with his arm, then using a stick that was lying in the cage to rake the banana into the cage. As chimpanzees are natural tool users, this behavior is not surprising and is still nothing more than simple trial-and-error learning.

But then the problem was made more difficult. The banana was placed just out of reach of Sultan's extended arm with the stick in his hand. At this point there were two sticks lying around in the cage, which could be fitted together to make a single pole that would be long enough to reach the banana. Sultan first tried one stick, then the other (simple trial and error). After about an hour of trying, Sultan seemed to have a sudden flash of inspiration. He pushed one stick out of the cage as far as it would go toward the banana and then pushed the other stick behind the first one. Of course, when he tried to draw the sticks back, only the one in his hand came. He jumped up and down and was very excited, and when Köhler gave him the second stick, he sat on the floor of the cage and looked at them carefully. He then fitted one stick into the other and retrieved his banana. Köhler called Sultan's rapid "perception of relationships" **insight** and determined that insight could not be gained

---

*Marooned: in this sense, being placed on a island from which escape is impossible.

◀ Why would the conditioned dogs refuse to move when shocked?

◀ I know some people who seem to act just like those dogs—they live in a horrible situation but won't leave. Is this the same thing?

learned helplessness
the tendency to fail to act to escape from a situation because of a history of repeated failures in the past.
insight
the sudden perception of relationships among various parts of a problem, allowing the solution to the problem to come quickly.

observational learning
learning new behavior by watching a model perform that behavior.

learning/performance distinction
referring to the observation that learning can take place without actual performance of the learned behavior.

through trial-and-error learning alone (Köhler, 1925). Although Thorndike and other early learning theorists believed that animals could not demonstrate insight, Köhler's work seems to demonstrate that insight requires a sudden "coming together" of all the elements of a problem in a kind of "aha" moment that is not predicted by traditional animal learning studies. More recent research has also found support for the concept of animal insight (Heinrich, 2000; Heyes, 1998; Zentall, 2000), but there is still controversy over how to interpret the results of those studies (Wynne, 1999).

Observational Learning

5.20 *What is observational learning?*

Another type of learning theory that departs from the traditional theories of Pavlov and Skinner and depends at least partly on cognition is that of **observational learning**, the learning of new behavior through the observation of a model (watching someone else who is doing that behavior).

BANDURA AND THE BOBO DOLL

5.21 *What was Bandura's classic Bobo doll study?*

Bandura's classic study in observational learning involved having a preschool child in a room in which the experimenter and a model interacted with toys in the room in front of the child (Bandura, et al., 1961). In one condition, the model interacted with the toys in a nonaggressive manner, completely ignoring the presence of a "Bobo" doll (a punch-bag doll in the shape of a clown). In another condition, the model became very aggressive with the doll, kicking it and yelling at it, throwing it in the air and hitting it with a hammer.

When each child was left alone in the room and had the opportunity to play with the toys, a camera filming through a one-way mirror caught the children who were exposed to the aggressive model beating up on the Bobo doll in exact imitation of the model. The children who saw the model ignore the doll did not act aggressively toward the toy. Obviously, the aggressive children had learned their aggressive actions from merely watching the model—with no reinforcement necessary.

Ah, but would that child have imitated the model if the model had been punished in the film? Wouldn't the <u>consequences</u> of the model's behavior make a difference? In later studies, Bandura showed a film of a model beating up the Bobo doll. In one condition, the children saw the model rewarded afterward. In another, the model was punished. When placed in the room with toys, the children in the first group beat up the doll, but the children in the second group did not. But, when Bandura told the children in the second group that he would give them a reward if they could show him what the model in the film did, each child duplicated the model's actions. Both groups had learned from watching the model, but only the children watching the successful (rewarded) model imitated the aggression with no prompting (Bandura, 1965). Apparently, consequences do matter in motivating a child (or an adult) to imitate a particular model. The tendency for some movies and television programs to make "heroes" out of violent, aggressive "bad guys" is particularly disturbing in light of these findings. In fact, Bandura began this research to investigate possible links between children's exposure to violence on television and aggressive behavior toward others.

The fact that learning can take place without actual performance (a kind of latent learning) is called the **learning/performance distinction**.

Ah, but would that child have imitated the model if the model had been punished in the film? Wouldn't the <u>consequences</u> of the model's behavior make a difference?

Albert Bandura's famous Bobo doll experiment. This doll was used to demonstrate the impact of observing an adult model performing aggressive behavior on the later aggressive behavior of children. The children in these photos are imitating the adult model's behavior even though they believe they are alone and are not being watched.

THE FOUR ELEMENTS OF OBSERVATIONAL LEARNING

Are there other elements of observed behavior that make it more or less likely to be learned? Bandura (1986) concluded, from these studies and others, that observational learning required the presence of four elements.

5.22 *What are the four elements of observational learning?*

◄ Are there other elements of observed behavior that make it more or less likely to be learned?

ATTENTION   To learn anything through observation, the learner must first pay attention to the model. For example, a person at a fancy dinner party who wants to know which utensil to use has to watch the person who seems to know what is correct. Certain characteristics of models can make attention more likely. For example, people pay more attention to those people they perceive as similar to them and to people whom they perceive as attractive.

MEMORY   The learner must also be able to retain the memory of what was done, such as remembering the steps in preparing a dish that was first seen on a cooking show.

IMITATION   The learner must be capable of reproducing, or imitating, the actions of the model. A 2-year-old might be able to watch someone tie shoelaces and might even remember most of the steps, but the 2-year-old's chubby little fingers will not have the dexterity* necessary for actually tying the laces. A person with extremely weak ankles might be able to watch and remember how some ballet move was accomplished but will not be able to reproduce it.

MOTIVATION   Finally, the learner must have the desire to perform the action. That person at the fancy dinner, for example, might not care which fork or which knife is the "proper" one to use. Also, if a person expects a reward because one has been given in the past, or has been promised a future reward (like the children in the second group of Bandura's study), or has witnessed a model getting a reward (like the children in the first group), that person will be much more likely to imitate the observed behavior. Successful models are powerful figures for imitation, but rarely would we be motivated to imitate someone who fails or is punished.

(An easy way to remember the four elements of modeling is to remember the letters AMIM, which stands for the first letters of each of the four elements. This is a good example of using a strategy to improve memory. (L I N K) *to Introduction, p. I-11*).

---

*Dexterity: skill and ease in using the hands.

Pick the best answer.

1. Cognition refers to
   a. behavior that is observable and external.
   b. behavior that is directly measurable.
   c. the mental events that take place while a person is behaving.
   d. memories.

2. In Tolman's maze study, the fact that the group of rats receiving reinforcement only after the tenth day of the study solved the maze far more quickly than did the rats who had been reinforced from the first day can be interpreted to mean that these particular rats
   a. were much smarter than the other rats.
   b. had already learned the maze in the first nine days.
   c. had the opportunity to cheat by watching the other rats.
   d. were very hungry and, therefore, learned much more quickly.

3. Seligman found many similarities between his "helpless" dogs and people suffering from
   a. aggressive behavior syndrome.
   b. mental illness.
   c. schizophrenia.
   d. depression.

4. Köhler determined that Sultan's two-stick solution to the banana problem was an example of insight because it was
   a. the result of trial-and-error learning.
   b. sudden and rapid.
   c. arrived at after a long time period.
   d. intelligent.

5. In Bandura's study with the Bobo doll, the children in the group that saw the model punished did not imitate the model at first. They would only imitate the model if given a reward for doing so. The fact that these children had obviously learned the behavior without actually performing it is an example of
   a. latent learning.
   b. operant conditioning.
   c. classical conditioning.
   d. insight learning.

6. Miranda wanted to make a casserole she saw on a food show on TV. She bought the ingredients, put them together, baked it, and served it at dinner that night. To her horror, it tasted awful. She realized that she had left out a key ingredient and vowed next time to write everything down as she watched the show. Miranda's dinner disaster was an example of failing at which of Bandura's four elements of observational learning?
   a. attention
   b. memory
   c. imitation
   d. motivation

Answers: 1-c, 2-b, 3-d, 4-b, 5-a, 6-b.

Applying Psychology to Everyday Life: Can You Really Toilet Train Your Cat?

5.23   *What is a real-world example of the use of conditioning?*

(This article has been excerpted with permission of the author and cat-trainer extraordinaire, Karawynn Long. Karawynn Long is a published writer and Web designer who lives in Seattle with her family. Sadly, since this article was written, her cat, Misha has passed away. She can be reached at her Web site **www.karawynn.net/mishacat/toilet.html.** The italicized words in brackets are the author's "editorial" comments.)

There have been more books and articles about toilet-training cats than you'd think. In the summer of 1989, when Misha was a small kitten with big ears and enough meow for five cats, I searched out and read a half-dozen of them. And then tried it myself, and discovered there were a couple of things they all failed to mention . . . here's what worked for me and Misha.

The central idea is that the transition from litter box to toilet should be accomplished in a series of stages. [*This is shaping.*] You make a small change and then give your cat time to adjust before you make another small change. If at any time Felix gives the whole thing up and goes on the rug instead, you're pushing him too far too fast; back up a stage or two and try again, more slowly.

READY? FIRST START BY TRAINING YOURSELF . . .

The very most important thing to remember is: Lid Up, Seat Down. Post a note on the back of the door or the lid of the toilet if you think you (or your housemates or guests) might forget. And if you are accustomed to closing the bathroom door when it's empty, you'll have to break that habit too. [*In operant conditioning, this is part of "preparing the training arena."*]

Begin by moving the cat's current litter box from wherever it is to one side of the toilet. Make sure he knows where it is and uses it. Rest (this means doing nothing for a period of between a day and a week, depending on how flappable your cat is). Next put something—a stack of newspapers, a phone book, a cardboard box—under the litter box to raise it, say, about an inch. (Magazines are too slick; you don't want the litter box sliding around and making your cat feel insecure. Tape the litter box down if you need to.) Rest. Get another box or phone book and raise it a little higher. Rest. Continue this process until the bottom of the litter box is level with the top of the toilet seat. (For Misha I raised it about two inches per day.) [*Notice that this is the step-by-step process typically used in shaping.*]

At the beginning of this process, your cat could just step into the litter box; later he began jumping up into it, until at some point he probably started jumping up onto the toilet seat first and stepping into the box from there. Lift the seat on your toilet and measure the inside diameter of the top of the bowl at its widest point. Venture forth and buy a metal mixing bowl of that diameter. Do not (I discovered this the hard way) substitute a plastic bowl. A plastic bowl will not support the cat's weight and will bend, dropping into the toilet bowl and spilling litter everywhere, not to mention startling the cat.

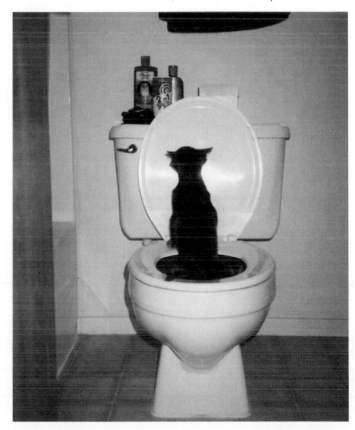

Misha's first attempt without the box. He scored two out of a possible four.

Now you move the litter box over so that it's sitting directly over the toilet seat. (If your cat has shown reluctance over previous changes, you might want to split this into two stages, moving it halfway onto the seat and then fully over.) Take away the stack of phone books or whatever you used. Rest. [*Again, notice that everything has to be done in small steps. This is the heart of the shaping process— requiring too large a step will stop the process.*]

Here's the cool part. Take away the litter box entirely. (Ta da!) Nestle the metal mixing bowl inside the toilet bowl and lower the seat. Fill the bowl with about two inches of litter (all of this is much easier if you have the tiny granules of litter that can be scooped out and flushed).

Naturally, any humans using the toilet at this point will want to remove the metal bowl prior to their own use and replace it afterward. The next week or two the whole process is likely to be something of an annoyance; if you begin to think it's not worth it, just remember that you will never have to clean a litter box again.

Watch your cat using the bathroom in the metal bowl. Count the number of feet he gets up on the toilet seat (as opposed to down in the bowl of litter). The higher the number, the luckier you are and the easier your job is going to be . . .

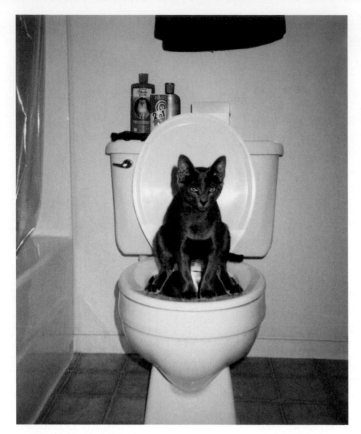

Misha demonstrates proper squatting posture. Note the look of firm concentration.

. . . because next you have to teach him proper squatting posture. Catch him beginning to use the toilet as much of the time as possible and show him where his feet are supposed to go. Just lift them right out of the bowl and place them on the seat (front legs in the middle, hind legs on the outside). If he starts out with three or, heaven forbid, all four feet in the bowl, just get the front two feet out first. Praise him all over the place every time he completes the activity in this position. [*The praise is the positive reinforcement, and should be done with each successful step.*]

(Misha is very doglike in that he craves approval and praise. If your cat is indifferent to this sort of thing, you can also reward him with small food treats and wean him from them later when the toilet behavior has "set." Just keep the treats as small and infrequent as possible—half a Pounce™ or similar treat per occasion should be plenty.) [*If treats are too frequent, it will make it difficult to phase out the reinforcer after the behavior is well learned.*]

When he is regularly using the toilet with his front feet out (and some cats naturally start from this position), begin lifting a hind foot out and placing it on the seat outside the front paws. Your cat will probably find this awkward at first and try to replace the foot in the litter. Be persistent. Move that foot four times in a row if you have to, until it stays there. Praise and/or treat.

Repeat with the other hind foot, until your cat learns to balance in that squat. Once he's getting all four feet regularly on the seat, it's all easy from here.

Which is fortunate, because the last bit is also the most unpleasant. I suggest that you postpone this stage until you have at least a weekend, and preferably several days, when you (or another responsible party) will be at home most of the time. I skipped through this part in about two days; I only hope that your cat allows you to move along that fast.

Begin reducing the litter in the bowl. Go as fast as he'll feel comfortable with, because as the litter decreases, the odor increases. You'll want to be home at this point so that you can praise him and dump out the contents of the bowl immediately after he's finished, to minimize both the smell and the possibility that your cat, in a confused attempt to minimize the smell on his own, tries to cover it up with litter that no longer exists and ends up tracking unpleasantness into the rest of the house.

By the time you're down to a token teaspoonful of litter in the bottom of the bowl, your next-door neighbors will probably be aware of the precise instant your cat has used the toilet. This is as bad as it gets. The next time you rinse out the metal bowl, put a little bit of water in the bottom. Increase the water level each time, just as you decreased the litter level. Remember—if at any point Felix looks nervous enough about the change to give the whole thing up and take his business to the corner behind the door, back up a step or two and try the thing again more slowly. [*Shaping takes a lot of patience, depending on the behavior being shaped and the learning ability of the animal—or person.*]

Once the water in the mixing bowl is a couple of inches deep and your cat is comfortable with the whole thing, you get to perform the last bit of magic. Take the mixing bowl away, leaving the bare toilet. (Lid Up, Seat Down.)

Voila! Your cat is now toilet trained.

Some useful books on using operant conditioning to toilet train cats:

Brotman, E. (2001). *How to Toilet Train Your Cat: The Education of Mango.* Sherman Oaks: CA, Bird Brain Press.

Kunkel, P. & Mead K. P. (1991). *How to Toilet Train Your Cat: 21 Days to a Litter-Free Home.* New York: Workman Publishing Company.

Questions for Further Discussion
1. Why would this technique probably not work with a dog?
2. Are there any safety concerns with teaching a cat in this way?
3. Are there any other difficulties that might arise when doing this training?

CHAPTER SUMMARY

Definition of Learning

5.1 *What is learning?*

- Learning is any relatively permanent change in behavior brought about by experience or practice and is different from maturation that is genetically controlled.

It Makes Your Mouth Water: Classical Conditioning

5.2 *What is classical conditioning and who first studied it?*

- Pavlov accidentally discovered the phenomenon in which one stimulus can, through pairing with another stimulus, come to produce a similar response. He called this classical conditioning.

5.3 *What are the important concepts in classical conditioning?*

- The unconditioned stimulus (UCS) is the stimulus that is naturally occurring and produces the reflex, or involuntary unconditioned response (UCR). Both are called "unconditioned" because they are not learned.
- The conditioned stimulus (CS) begins as a neutral stimulus, but when paired with the unconditioned stimulus eventually begins to elicit the reflex on its own. The reflex response to the conditioned stimulus is called the conditioned response (CR), and both stimulus and response are learned.

5.4 *What was Pavlov's classic experiment in conditioning?*

- Pavlov paired a sound with the presentation of food to dogs and discovered several principles for classical conditioning: The neutral stimulus (NS) and UCS must be paired several times and the CS must precede the UCS by only a few seconds.

- Other important aspects of classical conditioning include stimulus generalization, stimulus discrimination, extinction, spontaneous recovery, and higher-order conditioning.

5.5 *What is a conditioned emotional response?*

- Watson was able to demonstrate that an emotional disorder called a phobia could be learned through classical conditioning by exposing a baby to a white rat and a loud noise, producing conditioned fear of the rat in the baby.
- Conditioned taste aversions occur when an organism become nauseated some time after eating a certain food, which then becomes aversive to the organism.
- Some kinds of conditioned responses are more easily learned than others because of biological preparedness.

5.6 *Why does classical conditioning work?*

- Pavlov believed that the NS became a substitute for the UCS through association in time.
- The cognitive perspective asserts that the CS has to provide some kind of information or expectancy about the coming of the UCS in order for conditioning to occur.

What's in It for Me? Operant Conditioning

5.7 *What is operant conditioning and Thorndike's Law of Effect?*

- Thorndike developed the Law of Effect: A response followed by a pleasurable consequence will be repeated, but a response followed by an unpleasant consequence will not be repeated.

5.8 *What was Skinner's contribution to operant conditioning?*

• B. F. Skinner named the learning of voluntary responses operant conditioning because voluntary responses are what we use to operate in the world around us.

5.9 *What are the important concepts in operant conditioning?*

• Skinner developed the concept of reinforcement, the process of strengthening a response by following it with a pleasurable, rewarding consequence.

• A primary reinforcer is something such as food or water that satisfies a basic, natural drive, whereas a secondary reinforcer is something that becomes reinforcing only after being paired with a primary reinforcer.

• In positive reinforcement, a response is followed by the presentation of a pleasurable stimulus, whereas in negative reinforcement, a response is followed by the removal or avoidance of an unpleasant stimulus.

• Shaping is the reinforcement of successive approximations to some final goal, allowing behavior to be molded from simple behavior already present in the organism.

• Extinction, generalization and discrimination, and spontaneous recovery also occur in operant conditioning.

5.10 *What are the schedules of reinforcement?*

• Continuous reinforcement occurs when each and every correct response is followed by a reinforcer.

• Partial reinforcement, in which only some correct responses are followed by reinforcement, is much more resistant to extinction. This is called the partial reinforcement effect.

• In a fixed ratio schedule of reinforcement, a certain number of responses is required before reinforcement is given.

• In a variable ratio schedule of reinforcement, a varying number of responses is required to obtain reinforcement.

• In a fixed interval schedule of reinforcement, at least one correct response must be made within a set interval of time to obtain reinforcement.

• In a variable interval schedule of reinforcement, reinforcement follows the first correct response made after an interval of time that changes for each reinforcement opportunity.

5.11 *How does punishment affect behavior?*

• Punishment is any event or stimulus that, when following a response, makes that response less likely to happen again.

• In punishment by application, a response is followed by the application or experiencing of an unpleasant stimulus, such as a spanking.

• In punishment by removal, a response is followed by the removal of some pleasurable stimulus, such as taking away a child's toy for misbehavior.

• A person who uses aggressive punishment, such as spanking, can act as a model for aggressive behavior. This will increase aggressive behavior in the one being punished, which is an undesirable response.

• Punishment of both kinds normally has only a temporary effect on behavior.

• Punishment can be made more effective by making it immediate and consistent and by pairing punishment of the undesirable behavior with reinforcement of the desirable one.

5.12 *How do operant stimuli control behavior?*

• Discriminative stimuli are cues, such as a flashing light on a police car or a sign on a door that says "Open," that provide information about what response to make in order to obtain reinforcement.

Classic Studies in Psychology: Biological Constraints on Operant Conditioning

5.13 *What kind of behavior is resistant to conditioning?*

• Instinctive behavior in animals is resistant to conditioning or modification. Although an animal may change its behavior at first through conditioning, the behavior will revert to the instinctual pattern in a process called instinctive drift.

5.14 *What is behavior modification?*

• Operant conditioning can be used in many settings on both animals and people to change, or modify, behavior. This use is termed *behavior modification* and includes the use of reinforcement and shaping to alter behavior.

• Token economies are a type of behavior modification in which secondary reinforcers, or tokens, are used.

• Applied behavior analysis (ABA) is the modern version of behavior modification and makes use of shaping by breaking desired behavior down into discrete steps.

Psychology in the News: Neurofeedback and the Treatment of ADD

5.15 *What is neurofeedback and how is it used?*

• Neurofeedback is a modified version of biofeedback in which the person is connected to an electroencephalograph, a machine that records the brain's electrical activity.

Cognitive Learning Theory

5.16 *What is cognitive learning theory?*

• Cognitive learning theory states that learning requires cognition, or the influence of an organism's thought processes.

5.17 *What was Tolman's classic study on latent learning?*

• Tolman found that rats that were allowed to wander in a maze but were not reinforced still showed evidence of having learned the maze once reinforcement becomes possible. He termed this hidden learning *latent learning*, a form of cognitive learning.

5.18 *What is learned helplessness?*

• Seligman found that dogs that had been placed in an inescapable situation failed to try to escape when it became possible to do so, remaining in the painful situation as if helpless to leave. Seligman called this phenomenon learned helplessness and found parallels between learned helplessness and depression.

5.19 *What is insight?*

• Köhler found evidence of insight, the sudden perception of the relationships among elements of a problem, in chimpanzees.

Observational Learning

5.20 *What is observational learning?*

• Observational learning is learning through watching others perform, or model, certain actions.

5.21 *What was Bandura's classic Bobo doll study?*

• Bandura's famous Bobo doll experiment demonstrated that young children will imitate the aggressive actions of a model even when there is no reinforcement for doing so.

5.22 *What are the four elements of observational learning?*

• Bandura determined that four elements needed to be present for observational learning to occur: attention, memory, imitation, and motivation.

Applying Psychology to Everyday Life: Can You Really Toilet Train Your Cat

5.23 *What is a real-world example of the use of conditioning?*

• Writer Karawynn Long used shaping, reinforcement, and classical conditioning to train her cat to use the toilet in her bathroom instead of a litter box.

5 KEY TERMS

applied behavior analysis (ABA) 190
behavior modification 190
biofeedback 191
biological preparedness 174
classical conditioning 167
cognitive perspective 175
conditioned emotional response (CER) 172
conditioned response (CR) 168
conditioned stimulus (CS) 168
conditioned taste aversion 173
continuous reinforcement 182
discriminative stimulus 181
extinction 170
fixed interval schedule of reinforcement 184
fixed ratio schedule of reinforcement 183
higher-order conditioning 171
insight 195

instinctive drift 189
latent learning 194
Law of Effect 176
learned helplessness 195
learning/performance distinction 196
negative reinforcement 179
neurofeedback 192
neutral stimulus (NS) 168
observational learning 196
operant 177
operant conditioning 175
partial reinforcement effect 182
positive reinforcement 179
primary reinforcer 178
punishment 186
punishment by application 186
punishment by removal 187
reinforcement 177

reinforcer 170
secondary reinforcer 178
shaping 181
spontaneous recovery 171
stimulus discrimination 170
stimulus generalization 170
stimulus substitution 174
successive approximations 181
token economy 190
unconditioned response (UCR) 168
unconditioned stimulus (UCS) 167
variable interval schedule of reinforcement 185
variable ratio schedule of reinforcement 184
vicarious conditioning 173

TEST YOURSELF

Pick the best answer.

1. Learning is
   a. any temporary change in behavior.
   b. a change in behavior due to maturation.
   c. any permanent change in behavior brought about by experience.
   d. any permanent change in behavior due to maturation.

2. In your college dorm, any time you take a shower, someone always flushes the toilet and causes the water in your shower to turn icy cold, making you cringe. After several episodes like this, you find that you tend to cringe whenever you hear a toilet flush, no matter where you are. In this example, what is the conditioned stimulus?
   a. the cold water
   b. the sound of the flushing
   c. the cringing reaction
   d. the sight of a toilet

3. A child has been classically conditioned to fear a white rat. If the child also shows fear when shown a white rabbit, this is called
   a. stimulus generalization.   c. spontaneous recovery.
   b. stimulus discrimination.   d. extinction.

4. You move out of your dorm into an apartment shared with three other people. Unlike the shower in the dorm, this shower does not turn cold when the toilet is flushed, and you eventually stop cringing every time you hear the flushing sound. What has occurred?
   a. stimulus generalization   c. spontaneous recovery
   b. stimulus discrimination   d. extinction

5. When one conditioned stimulus is used to create another, this is called
   a. spontaneous recovery.
   b. extinction.
   c. higher-order conditioning.
   d. shaping.

6. Tenia ate out with some friends and had fried oysters. The next morning she was nauseated and sick for much of the day. The next time she saw someone eating fried oysters, she felt queasy and quickly looked away. Her queasiness at the sight of the fried oysters was probably due to
   a. higher-order conditioning.
   b. a conditioned taste aversion.
   c. stimulus substitution.
   d. stimulus generalization.

7. The fact that some kinds of stimuli (like a taste) are more easily and quickly connected to a response (like nausea) is explained by the concept of
   a. biological preparedness.
   b. psychological preparedness.
   c. instinctive drift.
   d. stimulus substitution.

8. The key to the cognitive perspective of classical conditioning is that the presentation of the conditioned stimulus must
   a. provide information about the coming of the unconditioned response.
   b. provide information about the coming of the unconditioned stimulus.
   c. provide information about the coming of the conditioned response.
   d. act as a substitute for the unconditioned stimulus.

9. In classical conditioning, the _____ are important in learning, but in operant conditioning, it is the _____ that determine whether learning will occur.
   a. antecedents; consequences
   b. consequences; antecedents
   c. rewards; punishments
   d. punishments; rewards

10. Who added the concept of reinforcement to learning theory?
    a. Watson
    b. Thorndike
    c. Skinner
    d. Pavlov

11. Which of the following is an example of a secondary reinforcer?
    a. a candy bar
    b. a glass of water
    c. petting a dog
    d. praising a child

12. Joaquin's parents have given his 2-year-old daughter, Marie, a very noisy jack-in-the-box toy for her birthday. Marie loves to turn the crank and make the puppet pop up, over and over and over. Desperate to have some peace and quiet, Joaquin gives Marie a popsicle, which distracts her and produces the quiet he was craving. But when the popsicle is finished, Marie goes back to the toy, cranking and cranking. Joaquin tries another popsicle. What kind of reinforcement process is taking place in this situation?
    a. Marie is being positively reinforced for playing with the toy by receiving the treat.
    b. Joaquin is being positively reinforced for giving her the treat by the quiet that follows.
    c. Joaquin is being negatively reinforced for giving her the treat by the absence of the noise.
    d. Both (a) and (c) are correct.

13. Sherry wants her dog to "heel" on command. At first she gives the dog a treat for coming to her when she speaks the command, "Heel!" Then she only rewards the dog when it stands at her side when she gives the command and, finally, rewards the dog only when it is at her side and facing front. Sherry is using
    a. higher-order conditioning.
    b. biological readiness.
    c. shaping.
    d. generalization.

14. One-year-old Ben learned to say the word *duck* when his mother showed him a duck in their back yard. That evening he sees a cartoon with a rooster in it and says "duck," pointing to the rooster. Ben is exhibiting
    a. generalization.
    b. discrimination.
    c. spontaneous recovery.
    d. shaping.

15. For every ten boxes of cookies that Lisa sells, her scout troop gets a dollar. Lisa is being reinforced on what schedule?
    a. fixed ratio
    b. fixed interval
    c. variable ratio
    d. variable interval

16. Dennis buys a lottery ticket every Saturday, using the same set of numbers. Although he has only won $25 on one occasion, he keeps buying the tickets. In fact, he's a little afraid that if he doesn't buy a ticket, that would be the one that would win really big. The fact that Dennis seems addicted to buying lottery tickets is a common characteristic of which schedule of reinforcement?
    a. fixed ratio
    b. fixed interval
    c. variable ratio
    d. variable interval

17. Liz failed her math test, so her parents told her that she could not play video games until her grade improved. Her parents are using
    a. positive reinforcement.
    b. negative reinforcement.
    c. punishment by removal.
    d. punishment by application.

18. To make punishment more effective, it should be
    a. very intense.
    b. applied every other time the bad behavior occurs.
    c. an aggressive type, such as spanking.
    d. paired with reinforcement of the correct behavior.

19. Sandy had learned that if her mother was smiling at her when she came into the kitchen, it meant that Sandy would probably be given a treat to eat if she asked nicely. But if her mother was frowning, she would not give Sandy anything and instead would shoo her away. Sandy's mother's facial expression was serving as a
    a. conditioned stimulus.
    b. discriminative stimulus.
    c. positive reinforcer.
    d. negative reinforcer.

20. In applied behavior analysis,
  a. skills are broken down into their smallest steps and then reinforced.
  b. punishment by application is often used to control behavior.
  c. researchers develop new theories of learning rather than actually solving problems.
  d. the basic form of learning used is classical conditioning.

21. Jody has had repeated failures at asking guys out on dates. Finally, she gives up. One day at the office a really nice guy seems interested in her, but she refuses to even approach him. What concept might explain her reluctance?
  a. latent learning
  b. learned helplessness
  c. insight learning
  d. observational learning

22. Jared's father is ill and cannot prepare his famous chili recipe, which Jared has watched his father make many times. When his father tells Jared that he must cook the chili, he panics at first. But then Jared finds that he knows how to put the recipe together anyway. His ability to prepare the recipe is an example of
  a. latent learning.
  b. learned helplessness.
  c. insight learning.
  d. discovery learning.

23. Archimedes was told by the king to find a way to prove that a gold crown was really gold. While in his bath, he noticed the water that his body displaced out of the tub and shouted, "Eureka!" which means "I have found it!" If the crown was really gold, it should displace the same amount of water as an equal amount of real gold. This is a famous example of
  a. latent learning.
  b. learned helplessness.
  c. insight.
  d. observational learning.

24. Jared realized that he had learned how to prepare his father's famous chili recipe by watching his father in the kitchen for many years. This kind of learning is called
  a. discovery learning.
  b. helplessness learning.
  c. insight learning.
  d. observational learning.

25. Barry would really like to learn to do ballroom dancing, but he has a severe limp in his left leg. Although he watches ballroom dancing on television and can remember all the moves and dips, he will be very unlikely to be able to learn to dance this way because he is missing a key element of observational learning. What is it?
  a. attention   **c.** imitation
  b. memory   **d.** motivation

Answers: 1-c, 2-b, 3-d, 4-d, 5-c, 6-b, 7-d, 8-b, 9-a, 10-c, 11-d, 12-d, 13-c, 14-a, 15-a, 16-c, 17-c, 18-d, 19-b, 20-a, 21-b, 22-a, 23-c, 24-d, 25-c.

For more sample quizzes and other review activities that will help you get a better grade, be sure to check out your accompanying study guide. To access tests and your own personalized study plan that will help you focus on the areas you need to master before your next class test, be sure to go to the on-line Psychology web site available with the access code packaged with your book.

CONCEPT MAP

Definition of Learning

Relatively permanent change in behavior caused by experience or practice

5.1

Classical Conditioning

Pavlovian or Classical Conditioning

Phenomenon in which one stimulus can, through pairing with another stimulus, come to produce a similar response

5.2

Concepts in Classical Conditioning

Unconditioned stimulus (UCS): stimulus that automatically evokes involuntary unconditioned response (UCR)

Unconditioned reponses (UCR): response naturally evoked by UCS

Conditioned stimulus (CS): neutral stimulus, paired with the unconditioned stimulus, evokes conditioned response (CR) on its own

Conditioned response (CR): response evoked by CS after CS–UCS pairing

5.3

Conditioned Emotional Responses

Phobias: Watson demonstrated that a phobia could be learned through classical conditioning (e.g. "Little Albert")

Conditioned taste aversions: food producing nausea becomes aversive

Biological preparedness: animals learn certain associations, such as taste and nausea, with only one or few pairings due to the survival value

5.5

Pavlov's Classic Experiment in Conditioning

Presented a sound (CS) followed by food (UCS)

▸ After several pairings, sound alone elicited salivation (CR)

▸ CS must precede UCS

5.4

Operant Conditioning

MAJOR THEORISTS

Thorndike's Law of Effect

A response followed by a pleasurable consequence will be repeated, but a response followed by an unpleasant consequence will not be repeated

5.7

Skinner's Contribution to Operant Conditioning

B. F. Skinner: voluntary response learning—operant conditioning

5.8

Schedules of Reinforcement

Continuous reinforcement: every correct response is followed by a reinforcer

Partial reinforcement: reinforcement is not given after every trial but according to a schedule

Partial reinforcement effect A response rewarded under a partial reinforcement schedule is much more resistant to extinction

5.10

Partial Reinforcement Schedules

Fixed ratio: a certain number of responses are required

Variable ratio schedule: a varying number of responses is required

Fixed interval schedule: correct response made within a set interval

Variable interval schedule: reinforcement follows a varying interval of time

Important Concepts in Operant Conditioning

Primary reinforcer: stimulus that satisfies a basic, natural drive

Secondary reinforcer: stimulus becomes reinforcing after paired with primary reinforcer

Positive reinforcement: stimulus whose presentation increases probability of response

Negative reinforcement: stimulus whose termination increases probability of response

Shaping: reinforcement of successive approximations to some final complex goal

Extinction, generalization and discrimination, and spontaneous recovery: also occur in operant conditioning

5.9

Comparing Two Kinds of Conditioning

OPERANT CONDITIONING	CLASSICAL CONDITIONING
Goal is to increase the rate of an already occurring response.	Goal is to create a new response to a stimulus that doesn't normally produce it.
Responses are voluntary.	Responses are involuntary and reflexive.
Consequences are important in forming an association.	Antecedent stimuli are important in forming an association.
Reinforcement must be immediate.	CS must occur immediately before the UCS.
An expectancy develops for reinforcement to follow a correct response.	An expectancy develops for UCS to follow CS.

Processes of Classical Conditioning

Pavlovian perspective: CS became substitute for UCS through association

Cognitive perspective: CS provides information about arrival of UCS

Other Important Aspects of Classical Conditioning

Stimulus generalization: stimuli similar to UCS will evoke CR but to a lesser degree

Stimulus discrimination: presentation of a stimulus similar to CS without UCS leads to this stimulus not producing generalization

Extinction: disappearance or weakening the CR following the removal of UCS

Spontaneous recovery: reappearance of CR after a pause in extinction trials

Higher-order conditioning: pairing a neutral stimulus with a strong CS, causes the neutral stimulus also to act as a CS

5.6

Cognitive Learning Theory

Learning requires cognition and thought processes

5.16

Tolman's Classic Study on Latent Learning

Latent learning: learning that remains hidden until it becomes useful

Tolman: rats allowed to wander in a maze unreinforced showed evidence of learning the maze when reinforced

5.17

Learned Helplessness

Learned helplessness: tendency to fail to escape because of a history of repeated failures in the past.

Seligman: found that dogs that had been placed in an inescapable situation failed to try to escape later when they could

5.18

Insight— Köhler's Chimps

Insight: sudden perception of relation-ships among various parts of a problem, allowing rapid problem solution

5.19

Punishment and Behavior

Punishment: stimulus, when following a response, makes response less likely

Punishment by application: response is followed by an unpleasant stimulus

Punishment by removal: a response is followed by the removal of some pleasurable stimulus

Aggressive punishment: can act as a model for aggressive behavior

Punishment: normally has only a temporary effect on behavior

5.11

Observational Learning

Operant Stimuli Control of Behavior

Discriminative stimuli: cues that provide information about what response to make in order to obtain reinforcement

Behavioral Resistance to Conditioning

Instinctive behavior in animals is resistant to conditioning or modification

5.12–13

Behavior Modification

Operant conditioning can be to change or modify behavior

Token economies: Secondary reinforcers, or tokens, are used

Applied behavior analysis (ABA): makes use of shaping

Neurofeedback and How it is Used

Neurofeedback: biofeedback method using EEG

5.14–15

Observational Learning

Observational learning: learning through watching others

Vicarious conditioning: classical conditioning by watching the reaction of another

5.20

Bandura's Classic Bobo Doll Study

Bandura's famous Bobo doll experiment: children imitated aggressive actions of a model even when there was no reinforcement for doing so.

5.21

6

Memory

They Tell Me You're My Daughter

Larry was 86 years old and very unhappy. He had always been a person who loved to work in the garden and drive his car around to visit friends back home. Three years ago Larry had fallen and broken a hip. While in the hospital, he got disoriented late one night and fell again, resulting in yet another broken hip. And now, to add insult to injury, his memory was playing tricks on him.

A middle-aged woman kept coming to see him, and it bothered him that he couldn't remember who she was. He had this nagging idea that she was someone he was supposed to know, but he just couldn't remember her name. When he asked the nurse at the assisted living home where he now lived, she told him that the middle-aged woman was his daughter. That just didn't seem right. Larry could not see how she could be his daugh-

ter. After all, his daughter was only a young woman, barely 20 years old.

Every time his daughter who was now in her forties came to visit, she would remind Larry of who she was and how she came to be born. He would eventually be able to see that this older woman was his daughter after all. But each visit would begin the same way, with Larry looking up at her with a puzzled expression and saying, "They tell me you're my daughter, but I just don't see how that can be so."

Why did Larry keep forgetting who his daughter was? His problem with memory was caused by a type of dementia, a serious emotional and mental deterioration. In Larry's case it was caused by a disorder in which narrowing blood vessels in the brain cause tiny strokes, depriving the brain tissue of oxygen and leaving dead areas. Memory problems are one of the first signs of this disorder.

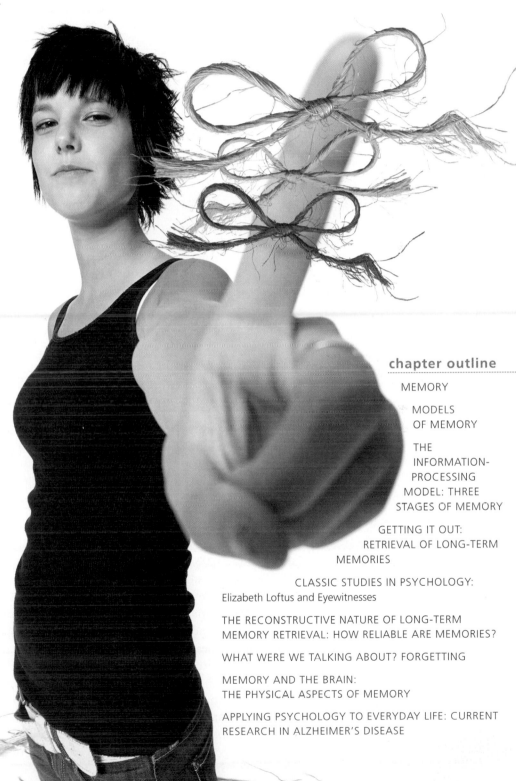

Why study memory?

Without memory, how would we be able to learn anything? The ability to learn is the key to our very survival, and we cannot learn unless we can remember what happened the last time a particular situation arose. Why study forgetting? If we can learn about the ways in which we forget information, we can apply that learning so that forgetting occurs less frequently.

6

LEARNING OBJECTIVES

6.1 What is memory, and what are the three processes of memory?

6.2 What are some of the different models of how memory works?

6.3 What is sensory memory?

6.4 What is short-term or working memory?

6.5 What is long-term memory?

6.6 What are the different types of long-term memory?

6.7 How is information organized that is stored in long-term memory?

6.8 What kinds of cues help people remember?

6.9 How do recall and recognition differ?

6.10 How reliable is eyewitness testimony?

6.11 What is a flashbulb memory?

6.12 How are long-term memories formed?

6.13 What kinds of problems do people experience when trying to remember something stored in long-term memory?

6.14 What is false memory syndrome?

6.15 What are the different causes of forgetting?

6.16 How and where are memories formed in the brain?

6.17 What is amnesia?

6.18 What can be done to help people with Alzheimer's disease?

memory
an active system that receives information from the senses, organizes and alters it as it stores it away, and then retrieves the information from storage.

encoding
the set of mental operations that people perform on sensory information to convert that information into a form that is usable in the brain's storage systems.

Memory (always active)

6.1 *What is memory, and what are the three processes of memory?*

Is memory a place or a process? The answer to that question is not simple. In reading through this chapter, it becomes clear that memory is a process, but that it also has a "place" in the brain as well. Perhaps the best definition of **memory** is an active system that receives information from the senses, organizes and alters it as it stores it away, and then retrieves the information from storage (Baddeley, 1996, 2003).

Although there are several different models of how memory works, all of them involve the same three processes: getting the information into the memory system, storing it there, and getting it back out.

PUTTING IT IN: ENCODING

The first step in the memory system is to get sensory information (sight, sound, etc.) into a form that the brain can use, a process called **encoding**. Encoding is the set of mental operations that people perform on sensory information to convert that information into a form that is usable in the brain's storage systems. For example, when people hear a sound, their ears turn the vibrations in the air into neural messages from the auditory nerve, which makes it possible for the brain to interpret that sound. L I N K *to Chapter Three: Sensation and Perception, p. 97.*

So it sounds like encoding works just ▶ like the senses, which we read about in Chapter Three.

So it sounds like encoding works just like the senses, which we read about in Chapter Three. Encoding is not limited to turning sensory information into signals for the brain, but instead it can take a different form in each of three different storage systems, or stages of memory. In one stage of memory storage, encoding can take the form of rehearsing information over and over to keep it in memory, whereas in another stage encoding involves elaborating on the meaning of the information—but let's elaborate on that later.

The game these people are playing requires retrieval of the words and how to spell them from previously stored memories.

KEEPING IT IN: STORAGE

The next step in memory is to hold on to the information for some period of time, a process called **storage**. This period of time will actually be of different lengths, depending on the stage of memory being used. For example, in one stage of memory people hold on to information just long enough to work with it, about 20 seconds or so. In another stage of memory, people hold on to information more or less permanently.

GETTING IT OUT: RETRIEVAL

The biggest problem many people have is **retrieval**, getting the information they know they have out of storage. Have you ever handed in an essay test and *then* remembered several other things you could have said? Retrieval problems are discussed in a major section of this chapter.

Simulation

Live! psych

Info-Processing Model

Models of Memory

6.2   *What are some of the different models of how memory works?*

Exactly how does memory work? When the storage process occurs, where does that information go and why? Memory experts have proposed several different ways of looking at memory. The model that many researchers feel is the most comprehensive* and perhaps the most influential over the last several decades is the **information-processing model**, an approach that focuses on the way information is processed, or handled, through three different stages of memory. The processes of encoding, storage, and retrieval are seen as part of this model. This theory is covered in greater detail throughout the rest of this chapter, but the other newer models deserve attention as well.

storage
holding onto information for some period of time.

retrieval
getting information that is in storage into a form that can be used.

LEVELS-OF-PROCESSING MODEL processed by "meaning"

The information-processing model assumes that how long a memory will be remembered depends on the stage of memory in which it is stored. Other

information-processing model
model of memory that assumes the processing of information for memory storage is similar to the way a computer processes memory in a series of three stages.

 encoding

---

*Comprehensive: all inclusive, covering everything.

researchers have proposed that how long a memory will be remembered depends on the depth (i.e., the effort made to understand the meaning) to which the information is processed (Cermak & Craik, 1979; Craik & Lockhart, 1972). If the word *BALL* is flashed on a screen, for example, and people are asked to report whether the word was in capital letters or lowercase, the word itself does not have to be processed very much at all—only its visual characteristics need enter into conscious attention. But if those people were to be asked to use that word in a sentence, they would have to think about what a ball is and how it can be used. They would have to process its meaning, not just its "looks," which requires more mental effort. Thinking about the meaning of something is a deeper level of processing and results in longer retention of the word, researchers have found in numerous experiments (Cermak & Craik, 1979; Craik & Tulving, 1975; Watson et al., 1999). This model of memory is called the **levels-of-processing model**.

PARALLEL DISTRIBUTED PROCESSING (PDP) MODEL

In the **parallel distributed processing (PDP) model**, memory is seen as a simultaneous* process, with the creation and storage of memories taking place across a series of mental networks "stretched" across the brain (McClelland & Rumelhart, 1988; Rumelhart et al., 1986).

Supporters of this model base their viewpoint on the way neural processing actually takes place in the brain: Neural connections appear to be organized in a parallel manner as well as in sequential** pathways in the brain (Hinton et al., 1986; Sartori & Umilta, 2000). Instead of information for a memory being processed only in a series of steps, the brain performs several different processes all running at the same time, or parallel,[†] to each other, while at the same time spreading that information across the entire network of neural connections. This allows people to retrieve many different aspects of a memory all at once, allowing much faster reactions and decisions.

So which model is right? "Which model is right?" is not the correct question. The correct question is: Which model explains the findings of researchers about how memory works? The answer to that question is that all of these models, including the information-processing model discussed next and throughout the rest of this chapter, can be used to explain some, if not all, research findings. So although the information-processing model of memory may take "center stage," it is important to remember the concepts of the levels at which information is processed and the way in which those processes may take place while reading the rest of this chapter.

The Information-Processing Model: Three Stages of Memory

The link between cognitive psychology and information-processing theory was discussed briefly in Chapter One. Information-processing theory, which looks at how thought processes such as memory work, uses as its model for human thought the way that a computer functions (Massaro & Cowan, 1993). Data are encoded in a way that the computer can understand and use. The computer stores that

---

Experiment
Live! psych
Depth of Processing

So which model is ▶ right?

levels-of-processing model
model of memory that assumes information that is more "deeply processed," or processed according to its meaning rather than just the sound or physical characteristics of the word or words, will be remembered more efficiently and for a longer period of time.

parallel distributed processing (PDP) model
a model of memory in which memory processes are proposed to take place at the same time over a large network of neural connections.

---

*Simultaneous: all at the same time.
**Sequential: following in time or order.
[†]Parallel: occurring side by side without being connected directly.

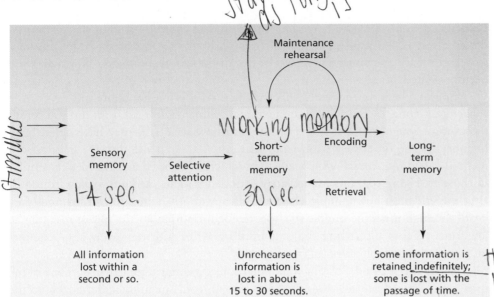

(handwritten annotations on figure:) stays active as long as it is used. / working memory / stimulus / 1-4 sec. / 30 sec. / things will fade over time when not used, sometimes semi erased.

FIGURE 6.1 **Three-Stage Process of Memory** Information enters through the sensory system, briefly registering in sensory memory. Selective attention moves the information into short-term memory, where it is held while attention (rehearsal) continues. If the information receives enough rehearsal, it will enter and be stored in long-term memory.

information on a disk, hard drive, or—these days—a memory stick, and then the data are retrieved out of storage as needed. It was also information-processing theorists who first proposed that there are three stages or types of memory systems (see Figure 6.1): sensory memory, short-term memory, and long-term memory (Atkinson & Shiffrin, 1968).

SENSORY MEMORY: WHY DO PEOPLE DO DOUBLE TAKES?

6.3 *What is sensory memory?* *(handwritten:)* 1st stage

Sensory memory is the first stage of memory, the point at which information enters the nervous system through the sensory systems—eyes, ears, and so on. Think of it as a door that is open for a brief time. Looking through the door, one can see many people and objects, but only some of them will actually make it through the door itself. Sensory memory is a kind of door onto the world.

Information is encoded into sensory memory as neural messages in the nervous system. As long as those neural messages are traveling through the system, it can be said that people have a "memory" for that information that can be accessed if needed. For example, say Elaina is driving down the street, looking at the people and cars on either side of her vehicle. All of a sudden she thinks, "What? Was that man wearing any pants?" and she looks back to check. How did she know to look back? Her eyes had already moved past the possible pants-less person, but some part of her brain must have just processed what she saw (most likely the reticular formation, which notices new and important information). This is called a double take and can only be explained by the presence, however brief, of a memory for what she saw.

There are two kinds of sensory memory that have been studied extensively. They are the iconic (visual) and echoic (hearing) sensory memories. In the sections that follow, these and other types of memories as well as several of the experiments that have added a great deal of information to the understanding of memory will be discussed.

ICONIC SENSORY MEMORY The example of seeing the possibly pants-less person is an example of how visual sensory memory, or **iconic memory**, works. *Icon* is the Greek word for "image." Iconic memory was studied in several classic experiments by George Sperling (1960).

(handwritten margin note:) picture

sensory memory
the very first stage of memory, the point at which information enters the nervous system through the sensory systems.

iconic memory
visual sensory memory, lasting only a fraction of a second.

Rows of Letters	Tone Signaling Which Row to Report
LHTY	High tone
EPNR	Medium tone
SBAX	Low tone

FIGURE 6.2 **Iconic Memory Test**
Sample grid of letters for Sperling's test of iconic memory. To determine if the entire grid existed in iconic memory, Sperling sounded a tone associated with each row after the grid's presentation. Participants were able to recall the letters in the row for which they heard the tone. The graph shows the decrease in the number of letters recalled as the delay in presenting the tone increased.

If iconic memory lasts such a brief time, what use is it to us?

eidetic imagery
the ability to access a visual memory for 30 seconds or more.

Capacity of Iconic Memory   Sperling had found in his early studies that if he presented a row of letters using a machine that allowed very fast presentation, his subjects could only remember about four or five of the letters, no matter how many had been presented.

Sperling became convinced that this method was an inaccurate measure of the capacity of iconic memory because the human tendency to read from top to bottom took long enough that the letters on the bottom of the grid may have faded from memory by the time the person had "read" the letters at the top. He developed a method called the *partial report method*, in which he showed a grid of letters similar to those in Figure 6.2, but immediately sounded a high, medium, or low tone just after the grid was shown. Subjects were told to read off the top row of letters if they heard the high tone, the middle row for the medium tone, or the lowest row for the low tone. As they didn't hear the tone until after the grid went away, they couldn't look at just one row in advance (see Figure 6.2).

Using this method, Sperling found that subjects could accurately report any of the three rows. This meant that the entire grid was in iconic memory and available to the subjects. The capacity of iconic memory is everything that can be seen at one time.

Duration of Iconic Memory   Sperling also found that if he delayed the tone for a brief period of time, after about half a second subjects could no longer recall any of the letters from the grid. The icon had completely faded out of sensory memory in that brief time.

In real life, information that has just entered iconic memory will be pushed out very quickly by new information, a process called *masking* (Cowan, 1988). Research suggests that after only a quarter of a second, old information is replaced by new information.

Although it is rare, some people do have what is properly called **eidetic imagery**, or the ability to access a visual memory over a long period of time. Although the popular term *photographic memory* is often used to mean this rare ability, some people claiming to have "photographic memories" actually mean that they have very good memories. Having a very good memory and having eidetic imagery ability are two very different things. People with eidetic imagery ability might be able to look quickly at a page in a book, then by focusing on a blank wall or piece of paper, "read" the words from the image that still lingers in their sensory memory. Although it might sound like a great ability to have while in college, it actually provides little advantage when taking tests, because it's just like having an open-book test. If a student can't *understand* what's written on the pages, having the book open is useless. It is unknown why some people have this ability, but it is more common in children and tends to diminish by adolescence or young adulthood (Haber, 1979; Leask et al., 1969; Stromeyer & Psotka, 1971).

If iconic memory lasts such a brief time, what use is it to us?

Function of Iconic Memory   Iconic memory actually serves a very important function in the visual system. Chapter Three discussed the way the eyes make tiny little movements called *saccades* that keep vision from adapting to a constant visual stimulus, so that what is stared at steadily doesn't slowly disappear. Iconic memory helps the visual system to view surroundings as continuous and stable in spite of these saccadic movements. It also allows enough time for the brain stem to decide if the information is important enough to be brought into consciousness—like the possibly pants-less person.

ECHOIC SENSORY MEMORY   The other type of sensory memory is **echoic memory**, or the brief memory of something a person has heard. A good example of echoic memory is the "What?" phenomenon. You might be reading or concentrating on the television, and your parent, roommate, or friend walks up and says something to you. You sit there for a second or two, and then say "What? Oh—yes, I'm ready to eat now," or whatever comment is appropriate. You didn't really process the statement from the other person as he or she said it. You heard it, but your brain didn't interpret it immediately. Instead, it took several seconds for you to realize that (1) something was said, (2) it may have been important, and (3) you'd better try to remember what it was. If you realize all this within about 4 seconds (the duration of echoic memory), you will more than likely be able to "hear" an echo of the statement in your head, a kind of "instant replay."

This piano tuner must use echoic sensory memory to tune each of these pianos. What other occupations might find echoic memory to be very useful?

Echoic memory's capacity is limited to what can be heard at any one moment and is smaller than the capacity of iconic memory, although it lasts longer—about 2 to 4 seconds (Schweickert, 1993).

Echoic memory is very useful when a person wants to have meaningful conversations with others. It allows the person to remember what someone said just long enough to recognize the meaning of a phrase. As with iconic memory, it also allows people to hold on to incoming auditory information long enough for the lower brain centers to decide if the information is important enough to become conscious. It is echoic memory that allows a musician to tune a musical instrument, for example. The memory of the tuning fork's tone lingers in echoic memory long enough for the person doing the tuning to match that tone on the instrument.

If the lower centers of the brain do decide that the information is important enough, what happens to the information at that point?

Selective Attention

SHORT-TERM (WORKING) MEMORY
a.k.a.

6.4   *What is short-term or working memory?*

Information moves from sensory memory to the next stage of memory, called **short-term memory (STM)**, through the process of **selective attention** or the ability to focus on only one stimulus from among all sensory input (Broadbent, 1958). When a person is thinking actively about some information, that information is said to be conscious (see Chapter Four). It can also be said to be in short-term memory, the memory system in which information is held for brief periods of time while being used.

Selective attention is responsible for the "cocktail party effect" that has been long established in studies of perception and attention (Cherry, 1953; Handel, 1989). If you've ever been at a party where there's a lot of noise and conversations going on in the background but you are able to notice when someone says your name, you have experienced this effect. The areas of the brain that are involved in selective attention were working even though you were not consciously aware of it, and when that important bit of information (your name) appeared, those areas brought the information to your conscious awareness (Hopfinger et al., 2000; Stuss et al., 2002). The only time this attention filter is not working at its peak is during deep Stage Four sleep, and it is still functioning even then (LaBerge, 1980).

◄ If the lower centers of the brain do decide that the information is important enough, what happens to the information at that point?

echoic memory *sound*
the brief memory of something a person has just heard. *2–4 secs.*

short-term memory (STM) (working memory)
the memory system in which information is held for brief periods of time while being used.

selective attention
the ability to focus on only one stimulus from among all sensory input.

Each person at this gathering is involved in a conversation with others, with dozens of such conversations going on at the same time all around. Yet if a person in another conversation says the name of one of the people in the crowd, that person in the crowd will be able to selectively attend to his or her name. This is known as the "cocktail party" effect.

Short-term memory tends to be encoded in auditory (sound) form. That simply means that people tend to "talk" inside their own heads. Although some images are certainly stored in STM in a kind of "visual sketchpad" (Baddeley, 1986), auditory storage accounts for much of short-term encoding. Even a dancer planning out moves in her head will not only visualize the moves but also be very likely to verbally describe the moves in her head as she plans. An artist planning a painting certainly has visual information in STM but may also keep up an internal dialogue that is primarily auditory. Research in which participants were asked to recall numbers and letters showed that errors were nearly always made with numbers or letters that *sounded like* the target but not with those that *looked like* the target word or number (Conrad & Hull, 1964).

Another way to think about short-term memory is as a *working memory*. This term emphasizes the fact that short-term memory is not merely a "box" into which information is placed but is a working, active system that processes the information it contains at any given moment. One researcher proposed that STM consists of three interrelated systems: a central executive (a kind of "CEO" or "Big Boss") that controls and coordinates the other two systems, a visual "sketchpad" of sorts, and a kind of auditory "recorder" (Baddeley, 1986; Baddeley & Hitch, 1974; Engle & Kane, 2004). The central executive would act as interpreter for both the visual and auditory information in STM. For example, when a person is reading a book, the sketchpad will contain images of the people and events of the particular passage being read while the recorder "plays" the dialogue in the person's head. The central executive helps interpret the information from both systems and pulls it all together.

Let's say you run into someone familiar at the mall. You pull that person's name (perhaps with a little difficulty) from your more permanent memory and visualize that name along with the memory of the last time you saw the person, almost as if you were viewing it on a screen. At the same time, you will hear the name in your head. The central executive pulls these different types of information together and you are able to successfully greet good old Bob.

maintenance rehearsal
practice of saying some information to be remembered over and over in one's head in order to maintain it in short-term memory.

Another way to think about short-term memory is as if it were a kind of desk where you do your work. You might pull some files out of storage (permanent memory) or someone might hand you some files (sensory input). While the files are on your desk, you can see them, read them, and work with them. The "files" are now conscious material and will stay that way as long as they are on the desk. If they are not that important or only necessary for a little while, they get "thrown out" (forgotten as you fail to pay attention to them). If they are important, they might get stored away in the filing system (permanent memory) where they are not conscious until they are once again retrieved—brought out onto the desk.

CAPACITY: THE MAGICAL NUMBER SEVEN   George Miller (1956) wanted to know how much information humans can hold in short-term memory at any one time (or how many "files" will fit on the "desk"). He used a memory test called the *digit-span test,* in which a series of numbers is read to subjects in the experiment who are then asked to recall the numbers in order. Each series gets longer and longer, until the subjects cannot recall any of the numbers in order (see Figure 6.3).

What you will discover is that everyone you test will get past the first two sequences of numbers, but some people will make errors on the six-digit span, about half of the people you test will slip up on the seven-digit span, and very few will be able to get past the nine-digit span without errors. This led Miller to conclude that the capacity of STM is about seven items or pieces of information, plus or minus two items, or from five to nine bits of information. Miller called this the "magical number seven, plus or minus two." So the "desk" isn't really very big and can hold only so many "files."

Chunking   There is a way to "fool" STM into holding more information than is usual. (Think of it as "stacking" related files on the desk.) If the bits of information are combined into meaningful units, or chunks, more information can be held in STM. If someone were to recode the last sequence of numbers as "654-789-3217," for example, instead of 10 bits of information, there would only be three "chunks" that read like a phone number. This process of recoding, or reorganizing, the information is called *chunking.* Chances are that anyone who can easily remember more than eight or nine digits in the digit-span test is probably recoding the numbers into chunks.

[handwritten in left margin: exps. phone #'s & S.S. start]

WHY DO YOU THINK THEY CALL IT SHORT TERM?   How long is the "short" of short-term memory? Research has shown that short-term memory lasts from about 12 to 30 seconds without rehearsal (Atkinson & Shiffrin, 1968; Brown, 1958; Peterson & Peterson, 1959). After that, the memory seems to rapidly "decay" or disappear.

What do you mean by rehearsal? How long can short-term memories last if rehearsal is a factor? Most people learn that saying something they want to remember over and over again in their heads, such as repeating a phone number they need just long enough to dial it, can help them remember longer, a process called **maintenance rehearsal**. With maintenance rehearsal, a person is simply continuing to pay attention to the information to be held in memory, and since attention is how that information got into STM in the first place, it works quite well (Atkinson & Shiffrin, 1968; Rundus, 1971). With this type of rehearsal, information will stay in short-term memory until rehearsal stops. When rehearsal stops, the memory rapidly decays and is forgotten. If anything interferes with maintenance rehearsal, memories are also likely to be lost. For example, if someone is trying to count a stack of dollar bills by reciting each number out loud while counting, and

| 6 8 2 5 |
| 5 7 2 1 4 |
| 3 5 9 7 2 1 |
| 9 2 5 4 6 3 8 |
| 2 8 3 7 1 5 6 9 |
| 7 3 2 4 9 6 8 5 1 |
| 6 5 4 7 8 9 3 2 1 7 |

FIGURE 6.3   **Digit-Span Test** *5-9*
Instructions for the digit-span test: Listen carefully as the instructor reads each string of numbers out loud. As soon as each string is ended (the instructor may say "go"), write down the numbers in the exact order in which they were given.

This woman must hold the phone number she is reading in short-term memory long enough to dial it on the phone next to her.

◄ What do you mean by rehearsal? How long can short-term memories last if rehearsal is a factor?

[handwritten: encoded in auditory form → long term = higher encoding]

Live psych
Digit Span
Experiment

It is very important for this pharmacist to count out the number of pills in the prescription accurately. Short-term memory allows her to remember the last number she counted, but if she is interrupted, she will have to start all over again. Short-term memory is very susceptible to interference.

someone else asks that person the time and interferes with the counting process, the person who is counting will probably forget what the last number was and have to start all over again. Short-term memory helps people keep track of things like counting.

Interference in STM can also happen if the amount of information to be held in STM exceeds its capacity (about five to nine "bits" of information, remember). Information already in STM may be "pushed out" to make room for newer information. This is why it might be possible to remember the first few names of people you meet at a party, but as more names are added, they displace the older names. A better way to remember a person's name is to associate the name with something about the person's appearance, a process that helps move the name from STM into more permanent storage. This more permanent storage is long-term memory, which is the topic of the next section.

PRACTICE **QUIZ:** HOW MUCH DO YOU REMEMBER?

Pick the best answer.

1. Eldon has just finished his essay test and handed it in. As he walks out of the classroom, he realizes that there were a few more things he should have included in the essay. Eldon's problem is in the memory process of
   a. encoding.
   b. storage.
   c. retrieval.
   d. retention.

2. When Edie studies her psychology terms, she tries to tie each concept in to something she already knows. She thinks about the meaning of the concept rather than just saying the words over and over. Which model of memory would best explain Edie's approach to encoding memories?
   a. levels-of-processing
   b. parallel distributed processing
   c. information processing
   d. three stage

3. Long ago (in the dark ages of television), when a television set was turned off it took a while for the last image that was on the screen to fade away. This is most like
   a. iconic memory.
   b. echoic memory.
   c. short-term memory.
   d. long-term memory.

4. Which type of memory allows us to have meaningful conversations?
   a. iconic memory
   b. echoic memory
   c. short-term memory
   d. long-term memory

5. Fethia learned her multiplication facts by repeating them over and over until she had them memorized. Fethia was using what kind of rehearsal?
   a. repetitive
   b. imagery
   c. elaborative
   d. maintenance

Answers: 1-c, 2-a, 3-a, 4-b, 5-d.

LONG-TERM MEMORY

6.5   *What is long-term memory?*

The third stage of memory is **long-term memory (LTM)**, the system into which all the information is placed to be kept more or less permanently. In terms of capacity, LTM is unlimited (Bahrick, 1984; Barnyard & Grayson, 1996). Think about it: Would there ever really come a time when you could not fit one more piece of information into your head? When you could learn nothing more? Perhaps if humans lived much longer lives, there might be a way to "fill up" the brain's memory stores. But in practical terms, there is always room for more information (in spite of what some students may believe).

As for duration,* the name *long-term* says it all. There is a physical change in the brain itself when a long-term memory is formed. This physical change is relatively

long-term memory (LTM)
the system of memory into which all the information is placed to be kept more or less permanently.

*Duration: how long something lasts.

permanent. That means that many of the memories people have stored away for a long, long time—even since childhood—are probably always there. That does not mean that people can always retrieve those memories. The memories may be *available* but not *accessible*, meaning that they are still there, but for various reasons (discussed later under the topic of forgetting) people cannot get to them. It's like knowing that there is a certain item on the back of the top shelf of the kitchen cabinet but having no ladder or step-stool to reach it. The item is there (available), but you can't get to it (not accessible).

I once memorized a poem by repeating it over and over and over—which is maintenance rehearsal, right? I still remember most of the poem, so it must be in long-term memory. So can maintenance rehearsal get information into long-term memory? Information that is rehearsed long enough may actually find its way into long-term memory. After all, it's how most people learned their Social Security number and the letters of the alphabet (although people cheated a little on the latter by putting the alphabet to music, which makes them easier to retrieve). Most people tend to learn poems and the multiplication tables by maintenance rehearsal, otherwise known as rote learning. *Rote* is like "rotating" the information in one's head, saying it over and over again. But maintenance rehearsal is not the most efficient way of putting information into long-term storage, because to get the information back out, one has to remember it almost exactly as it went in. Try this: What is the fifteenth letter of the alphabet? Did you have to recite or sing through the song to get to that letter?

Although many long-term memories are encoded as images (think of the *Mona Lisa*), sounds, smells, and tastes (Cowan, 1988), in general LTM is encoded in meaningful form, a kind of mental storehouse of the meanings of words, concepts, and all the events that people want to keep in mind. Even the images, sounds, smells, and tastes involved in these events have some sort of meaning attached to them that gives them enough importance to be stored long term. If STM can be thought of as a working "surface" or desk, then LTM can be thought of as a huge series of filing cabinets behind the desk, in which files are stored in an organized fashion, according to meaning. Files have to be placed into the cabinets in a certain organized fashion to be useful. How else could anyone ever remember any kind of information quickly, if the files were not in some order? The best way to encode information into LTM in an organized fashion is to make it meaningful through *elaborative rehearsal.*

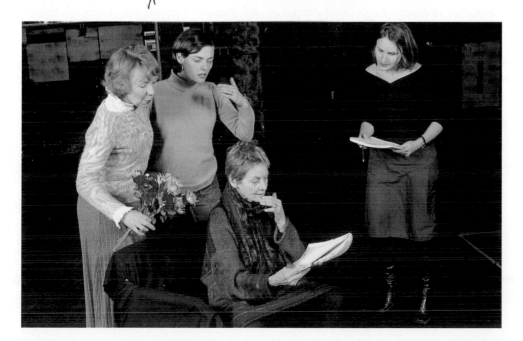

These actresses are memorizing their lines in a play. They will use rehearsal (repeating and practicing their lines over and over) until they can recite their parts perfectly. Their lines will be stored in long-term memory. Is there any way that the actresses could use elaborative rehearsal to help them remember their lines?

◀ I once memorized a poem by repeating it over and over and over—which is maintenance rehearsal, right? I still remember most of the poem, so it must be in long-term memory. So can maintenance rehearsal get information into long-term memory?

elaborative rehearsal
a method of transferring information from STM into LTM by making that information meaningful in some way.

procedural (nondeclarative) memory
type of long-term memory including memory for skills, procedures, habits, and conditioned responses. These memories are not conscious but are implied to exist because they affect conscious behavior.

anterograde amnesia
loss of memory from the point of injury or trauma forward, or the inability to form new long-term memories.

▶ I can remember a lot of stuff from my childhood. Some of it is stuff I learned in school and still remember, and some of it is more personal, like the first day of school. Are there different kinds of long-term memories?

ELABORATIVE REHEARSAL   **Elaborative rehearsal** is a way of transferring information from STM into LTM by making that information meaningful in some way (Postman, 1975). The easiest way to do this is to connect new information with something that is already well known (Craik & Lockhart, 1972; Postman, 1975). For example, the French word *maison* means "house." A person could try to memorize that (using maintenance rehearsal) by saying over and over, "*Maison* means house, *maison* means house." But it would be much easier and more efficient if that person simply thought, "*Maison* sounds like masons, and masons build houses." That makes the meaning of the word tie in with something the person already knows (masons, who lay stone or bricks to build houses) and helps in remembering the French term.

As discussed in the beginning of this chapter, Craik and Lockhart (1972) theorized that information that is more "deeply processed," or processed according to its meaning rather than just the sound or physical characteristics of the word or words, will be remembered more efficiently and for a longer period of time. As the levels-of-processing approach predicts, elaborative rehearsal is a deeper kind of processing than maintenance rehearsal and so leads to better long-term storage (Craik & Tulving, 1975).

I can remember a lot of stuff from my childhood. Some of it is stuff I learned in school and still remember, and some of it is more personal, like the first day of school. Are there different kinds of long-term memories?

TYPES OF LONG-TERM INFORMATION

6.6   *What are the different types of long-term memory?*

Long-term memories include general facts and knowledge, personal facts, and even skills that can be performed. Memory for skills is called *procedural (nondeclarative) memory* because it usually involves a series of steps or procedures; memory for facts is called *declarative memory* because facts are things that are known and can be declared (stated outright). These two types of long-term memory are quite different, as the following sections will explain.

Procedural (Nondeclarative) LTM   *(nonconcious)*   Memories for skills that people know how to do, like tying shoes and riding a bicycle, are a kind of LTM called **procedural (nondeclarative) memory**. Procedural memories also include emotional associations, habits, and simple conditioned reflexes that may or may not be in conscious awareness. **LINK** *to Chapter Five: Learning, p. 168.* Referring back to Chapter Two, the amygdala is the most probable location for emotional associations, such as fear, and the cerebellum in the hindbrain is responsible for storage of memories of conditioned responses, skills, and habits (Squire et al., 1993).

Evidence that separate areas of the brain control procedural memory comes from studies of people with damage to the hippocampus area of the brain. This damage causes them to have **anterograde amnesia**, in which new long-term memories cannot be formed. In one study (Cohen et al., 1985), patients with this disorder were taught how to solve a particular puzzle called the Tower of Hanoi (see Figure 6.4). One of the more famous anterograde amnesia patients, H. M., is discussed in detail later in this chapter on page 238.

Although the patients were able to learn the sequence of moves necessary to solve the puzzle, when brought back into the testing room at a later time they could not remember ever having seen the puzzle before—or, for that matter, the examiner. Each trial was like the first one ever for these patients, as they were unable to store the long-term memory of having been in the room or having met the examiner previously. Yet they were able to solve the puzzle even while claiming that they had never seen it before. Their procedural

Anterograde amnesia does not effect

FIGURE 6.4   **Tower of Hanoi**
The Tower of Hanoi is a puzzle that is solved in a series of steps by moving one disk at a time. A larger disk can never be moved on top of a smaller one. Amnesia patients were able to learn the procedure for solving the puzzle but could not remember that they knew how to solve it.

memories for how to solve the puzzle were evidently formed and stored in a part of the brain separate from the part controlling the memories they could no longer form.

The patients in this study had the kind of memory problems that people with Alzheimer's disease have. Yet even people with Alzheimer's disease do not forget how to walk, talk, fasten clothing, or even tie shoes (although they do lose motor ability because the brain eventually fails to send the proper signals). These are all procedural, nondeclarative memories. They may not be able to tell someone who asks that they know how to do these things, but they can still do them. Alzheimer's disease affects the hippocampus and the frontal cortex (involved in decision making and planning) and eventually affects other areas of the brain after it has progressed nearly to the end (Kanne et al., 1998). In fact, it would be rare to find someone who has lost procedural memory. Literally, these are the kind of memories people "never forget."

AKA.

Procedural memory is often called **implicit memory** because memories for these skills, habits, and learned reflexes are not easily retrieved into conscious awareness. The fact that people have the knowledge of how to tie their shoes, for example, is *implied* by the fact that they can actually tie them. But have you ever tried to tell someone how to tie shoes without using your hands to show them? The subjects in the Tower of Hanoi study provide a good example of implicit memory, as they could solve the puzzle but had no conscious knowledge of how to do so. Such knowledge is in people's memories because they use this information, but they are often not consciously aware of this knowledge (Roediger, 1990). Although procedural memories are implicit, not all implicit memories are necessarily procedural. A memory from one's early childhood of being frightened by a dog, for example, may not be a conscious memory in later childhood but may still be the cause of that older child's fear of dogs. Conscious memories for events in childhood, on the other hand, are usually considered to be a different kind of long-term memory called declarative memory.

facts

Declarative LTM Procedural memory is about the things that people can *do*, but **declarative memory** is about all the things that people can *know*—the facts and information that make up knowledge. People know things such as the names of the planets in the solar system, that adding two and two makes four, and that a noun is the name of a person, place, or thing. These are general facts, but people also know about the things that have happened to them personally. For example, I know what I ate for breakfast this morning and what I saw on the way to work, but I don't know what you had for breakfast or what you might have seen. There are two types of declarative long-term memories, *semantic* and *episodic* (Nyberg & Tulving, 1996).

One type of declarative memory is general knowledge that anyone has the ability to know. Most of this information is what is learned in school or by reading. This kind of LTM is called **semantic memory**. The word *semantic* refers to meaning, so this kind of knowledge is the awareness of the meanings of words, concepts, and terms as well as names of objects, math skills, and so on. This is also the type of knowledge that is used on game shows such as *Jeopardy* and *Who Wants to Be a Millionaire?* Semantic memories, like procedural memories, are relatively permanent. But it is possible to "lose the way to" this kind of memory, as discussed in the section on forgetting.

The other kind of factual memory is the personal knowledge that each person has of his or her daily life and personal history, a kind of autobiographical* memory. Memories of

Procedural knowledge, such as tying one's shoes, often must be learned by doing as it is difficult to put into words. Once this child learns how to tie shoes, the knowledge will always be there to retrieve.

implicit memory
memory that is not easily brought into conscious awareness, such as procedural memory.

declarative memory
type of long-term memory containing information that is conscious and known.

semantic memory
type of declarative memory containing general knowledge, such as knowledge of language and information learned in formal education.

explicit

general Knowledge of language.

---

*Autobiographical: the story of a person's life as told by that person.

I remember well my sensation as we first entered the house. I knew instantly that something was very wrong. I realized that my father's chair had been sat in, as well as my mother's and my own. The porridge we had left on the table to cool had been partially eaten. None of this, however, prepared me for what we were about to discover upstairs....

But sometimes I can't ▶ remember all the names of the planets or what I had for breakfast yesterday. Doesn't that make these memories implicit instead of explicit?

what has happened to people each day, certain birthdays, anniversaries that were particularly special, childhood events, and so on are called **episodic memory**, because they represent episodes from their lives. Unlike procedural and semantic long-term memories, episodic memories tend to be updated and revised more or less constantly. You can probably remember what you had for breakfast today, but what you had for breakfast two years ago on this date is most likely a mystery. Episodic memories that are especially *meaningful*, such as the memory of the first day of school or your first date, are more likely to be kept in LTM (although they may not be as exact as people sometimes assume they are). The updating process is a kind of survival mechanism, because although semantic and procedural memories are useful and necessary on an ongoing basis, no one really needs to remember every little detail of every day. As becomes obvious later, the ability to forget some kinds of information is very necessary.

Episodic and semantic memories are forms of **explicit memory**, memories that are easily made conscious and brought from long-term storage into short-term memory. The knowledge of semantic memories such as word meanings, science concepts, and so on can be brought out of the "filing cabinet" and placed on the "desk" where that knowledge becomes *explicit*, or obvious. The same is often true of personal, episodic memories.

But sometimes I can't remember all the names of the planets or what I had for breakfast yesterday. Doesn't that make these memories implicit instead of explicit? The difference between implicit memories, such as how to balance on a bicycle, and explicit memories, such as naming all the planets, is that it is impossible or extremely difficult to bring implicit memories into consciousness. Explicit memories can be forgotten but always have the potential to be made conscious. When someone reminds you of what you had for breakfast the day before, for example, you will remember that you had that knowledge all along—it was just temporarily "mislaid." For a look at the connections among all these types of LTM, see Figure 6.5.

LONG-TERM MEMORY ORGANIZATION

6.7 *How is information organized that is stored in long-term memory?*

As stated before, LTM has to be fairly well organized for retrieval to be so quick. Can you remember the name of your first grade teacher? If you can, how long did it take you to pull that name out of LTM and "put it on the desk" of STM? It probably took hardly any time at all. Think of it this way: If a person who puts documents in a fil-

FIGURE 6.5 **Types of Long-Term Memories** Long-term memory can be divided into declarative memories, which are factual and typically conscious (explicit) memories, and nondeclarative memories, which are skills, habits, and conditioned responses that are typically unconscious (implicit). Declarative memories are further divided into episodic memories (personal experiences) and semantic memories (general knowledge).

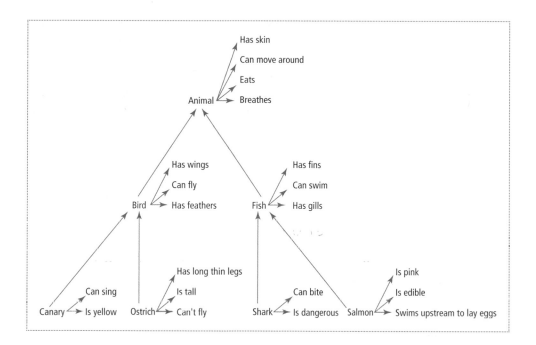

Has skin
Can move around
Eats
Animal — Breathes

Has wings
Can fly
Bird — Has feathers

Has fins
Can swim
Fish — Has gills

Has long thin legs
Is tall
Can sing
Canary — Is yellow
Ostrich — Can't fly

Can bite
Shark — Is dangerous

Is pink
Is edible
Salmon — Swims upstream to lay eggs

FIGURE 6.6   **An Example of a Semantic Network**   In the semantic network model of memory, concepts that are related in meaning are thought to be stored physically near each other in the brain. In this example, canary and ostrich are stored near the concept node for "bird" whereas shark and salmon are stored near "fish." But the fact that a canary is yellow is stored directly with that concept.

ing cabinet just stuffs them in any drawer with no system of organization, when a particular document is needed it requires searching through every drawer. But if documents are filed away alphabetically, and perhaps even according to type of document (deeds in one drawer, power of attorney forms in another, etc.), it becomes very easy to retrieve a particular document.

Research suggests that long-term memory is organized in terms of related meanings and concepts (Collins & Loftus, 1975; Collins & Quillian, 1969). In their original study, Collins and Quillian (1969) had subjects respond "true" or "false" as quickly as possible to sentences such as "a canary is a bird" and "a canary is an animal." Looking at Figure 6.6, it is apparent that information exists in a kind of network, with nodes (focal points) of related information linked to each other in a kind of hierarchy.* To verify the statement "a canary is a bird" requires moving to only one node, but "a canary is an animal" would require moving through two nodes and should take longer. This was exactly the result of the 1969 study, leading the researchers to develop the **semantic network model**, which assumes that information is stored in the brain in a connected fashion, with concepts that are related to each other stored physically closer to each other than concepts that are not highly related (Collins & Quillian, 1969).

The parallel distributed processing model (Rumelhart et al., 1986) discussed earlier in this chapter can be used to explain how rapidly the different points on the networks can be accessed. Although the access of nodes within a particular category (for example, *birds*) may take place in a serial fashion, explaining the different response times in the Collins and Quillian (1969) study, access across the entire network may take place in a parallel fashion, allowing several different concepts to be targeted at the same time (for example, one might be able to think about *birds*, *cats*, and *trees* simultaneously).

Perhaps the best way to think of how information is organized in LTM is to think about the Internet. A person might go to one Web site and from that site link to many other related sites. Each related site has its own specific information but is also linked to many other related sites, and a person can have more than one site open at the same time. This is very similar to the way in which the mind organizes the information stored in LTM.

Hierarchy: an ordered list or series.

episodic memory
type of declarative memory containing personal information not readily available to others, such as daily activities and events.

explicit memory
memory that is consciously known, such as declarative memory.

semantic network model
model of memory organization that assumes information is stored in the brain in a connected fashion, with concepts that are related stored physically closer to each other than concepts that are not highly related.

PRACTICE **QUIZ:** HOW MUCH DO YOU REMEMBER?

Pick the best answer.

1. Of the following, which is the most similar to the concept of long-term memory?
   a. a revolving door
   b. a filing cabinet
   c. a desk top
   d. a computer keyboard

2. Long-term memories are encoded in terms of
   a. sounds.
   b. visual images.
   c. meanings of words and concepts.
   d. all of the above.

3. Which type of LTM is seldom, if ever, lost by people with Alzheimer's disease?
   a. procedural
   b. semantic
   c. episodic
   d. both (b) and (c)

4. In the game show *Who Wants to Be a Millionaire?* contestants are asked a series of questions of general information, although of increasing difficulty. The type of memory needed to access the answers to these kinds of questions is
   a. procedural.
   b. semantic.
   c. episodic.
   d. working.

5. The Internet, with its series of links from one site to many others, is a good analogy for the organization of
   a. short-term memory.
   b. episodic memory.
   c. long-term memory.
   d. procedural memory.

Answers: 1-b, 2-d, 3-a, 4-b, 5-c.

> My problem isn't so much getting information <u>into</u> my head, as finding it later.

When this bride and groom dance together later on in their marriage, they will be able to recall this moment at their wedding and the happiness they felt at that time. State dependent learning makes it easier for people to recall information stored while in a particular emotional state (such as the happiness of this couple) if the recall occurs in a similar emotional state.

Getting It Out: Retrieval of Long-Term Memories

My problem isn't so much getting information <u>into</u> my head, as finding it later. Oddly enough, most people's problems with getting information stored in LTM back out again has to do with *how* they put that information *into* LTM.

RETRIEVAL CUES

6.8   *What kinds of cues help people remember?*

Remember the previous discussion about maintenance rehearsal versus elaborative rehearsal? One of the main reasons that maintenance rehearsal is not a very good way to get information into LTM is that saying something over and over only gives one kind of **retrieval cue** (a stimulus for remembering), the sound of the word or phrase. When people try to remember a piece of information by thinking of what it means and how it fits in with what they already know, they are giving themselves cues for meaning in addition to sound. The more cues stored with a piece of information, the easier the recall of that information will be (Roediger, 2000; Roediger & Guynn, 1996).

Although most people would assume that cues for retrieval would have to be directly related to the concepts being studied, the fact is that almost anything in one's surroundings is capable of becoming a cue. If you usually watch a particular television show while eating peanuts, for example, the next time you eat peanuts you might find yourself thinking of the show you were watching. This connection between surroundings and remembered information is called *encoding specificity.*

ENCODING SPECIFICITY AND STATE-DEPENDENT LEARNING: CONTEXT AND MOOD EFFECTS ON MEMORY RETRIEVAL   Have you ever had to take a test in a different classroom than the one in which you learned the material being tested? Do you think that your performance on that test was hurt by being in a different physical context? Researchers have found strong evidence for the concept of **encoding specificity**, the tendency for memory of any kind of information to be improved if the physical surroundings available when the memory is first formed are also available when the memory is being retrieved (Reder et al., 1974; Tulving & Thomson, 1973). For example, encoding specificity would predict that the best place to take one's chemistry test is in the same room in which you learned the material. Also, it's very common to walk into a room and know that there was something you wanted, but in order to remember it, you have to go back to the room you started in to use your surroundings as a cue for remembering.

In one study, researchers had students who were learning to scuba dive in a pool also learn lists of words while they were either out of the pool or in the pool under the water (Godden & Baddeley, 1975). Subjects were then asked to recall the two lists in each of the two conditions. Words that were learned while out of the pool were recalled significantly better when the subjects were out of the pool, and words that were learned underwater were more easily recalled if the subjects were underwater at the time of recall (see Figure 6.7).

Physical surroundings at the time of encoding a memory are not the only kinds of cues that can help in retrieval. In *state-dependent learning*, memories formed during a particular physiological or psychological state will be easier to recall while in a similar state. State-dependent learning has also been a subject of research (Eich & Metcalfe, 1989). Researchers conducted a study in which they had subjects try to recall words that they had either read or thought up while listening to music that was either happy or sad. The music influenced the mood of the subjects to be either happy or sad while reading or creating the words. When later tested for memory of the words, the words that were read or created while subjects were in a happy mood were recalled better if the mood at recall was also happy but far less well if the mood at recall was sad. The reverse was also true.

Reprinted with special permission of King Features Syndicate.

retrieval cue
a stimulus for remembering.

encoding specificity
the tendency for memory of information to be improved if related information (such as surroundings or physiological state) available when the memory is first formed is also available when the memory is being retrieved.

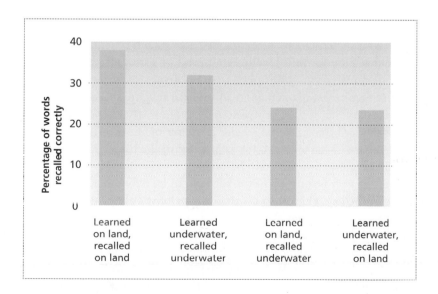

FIGURE 6.7 **Recall of Target Words In Two Contexts** Memory the retrieval of words learned while under water was higher when the retrieval also took place under water. Similarly, words learned while out of the water (on land) were retrieved at a higher rate out of the water.

Reproduced with permission from the British Journal of Psychology, ©The British Psychology Society.

Why do multiple-► choice tests seem so much easier than essay tests?

Recall vs. Recognition

Serial Position

recall
type of memory retrieval in which the information to be retrieved must be "pulled" from memory with very few external cues.

recognition
the ability to match a piece of information or a stimulus to a stored image or fact.

serial position effect
tendency of information at the beginning and end of a body of information to be remembered more accurately than information in the middle of the body of information.

primacy effect
tendency to remember information at the beginning of a body of information better than the information that follows.

6.9 *How do recall and recognition differ?*

Why do multiple-choice tests seem so much easier than essay tests? There are two kinds of retrieval of memories, recall and recognition. It is the difference between these two retrieval methods that makes some kinds of exams seem harder than others. In **recall**, memories are retrieved with few or no external cues, such as filling in the blanks in an application form. **Recognition**, on the other hand, involves looking at or hearing information and matching it to what is already in memory. A word-search puzzle, in which the words are already written down in the grid and simply need to be circled, is an example of recognition. The following section takes a closer look at these two important processes.

RECALL: HMM . . . LET ME THINK

When someone is asked a question such as "Where were you born?" the question acts as the cue for retrieval of the answer. This is an example of recall, as are essay question, short-answer, and fill-in-the-blank tests that are used to measure a person's memory for information (Borges et al., 1977; Gillund & Shiffrin, 1984; Raaijmakers & Shiffrin, 1992).

RETRIEVAL FAILURE: IT'S RIGHT ON THE TIP OF MY TONGUE   Whenever people find themselves struggling for an answer, recall has failed (at least temporarily). Sometimes the answer seems so very close to the surface of conscious thought that it feels like it's "on the tip of the tongue." If people could just get their tongues out there far enough, they could read it. This is sometimes called the *tip of the tongue (TOT)* phenomenon (Brown & McNeill, 1966; Burke et al., 1991). Although people may be able to say how long the word is or name letters that start or even end the word, they cannot retrieve the sound or actual spelling of the word to allow it to be pulled into the auditory "recorder" of STM so that it can be fully retrieved.

How can a person overcome TOT? The best solution is the one "everyone" seems to know: Forget about it. When you "forget about it," the brain apparently continues to work on retrieval. Some time later (perhaps when you run across a similar sounding word in your surroundings), the word or name will just "pop out." This can make for interesting conversations, because when that particular word does "pop out," it usually has little to do with the current conversation.

THE SERIAL POSITION EFFECT   Another interesting feature of recall is that it is often subject to a kind of "prejudice" of memory retrieval, in which information at the beginning and the end of a list, such as a poem or song, tends to be remembered more easily and accurately. This is called the **serial position effect** (Murdock, 1962).

A good demonstration of this phenomenon involves instructing people to listen to and try to remember words that are read to them that are spaced about four or five seconds apart. People typically use maintenance rehearsal by repeating each word in their heads. They are then asked to write as many of the words down as they can remember. If the frequency of recall for each word in the list is graphed, it will nearly always look like the graph in Figure 6.8.

Words at the very beginning of the list tend to be remembered better than those in the middle of the list. This effect is called the **primacy effect** and is due to the fact that the first few words, when the listener has nothing already in STM to interfere with their rehearsal, will receive far more rehearsal time than the words in the middle, which are constantly being replaced by the next word on the list (Craik, 1970; Murdock, 1962). In fact, the first words may actually move into LTM if they are rehearsed long enough, because rote memorization, although not the best way to remember something, can lead to long-term storage.

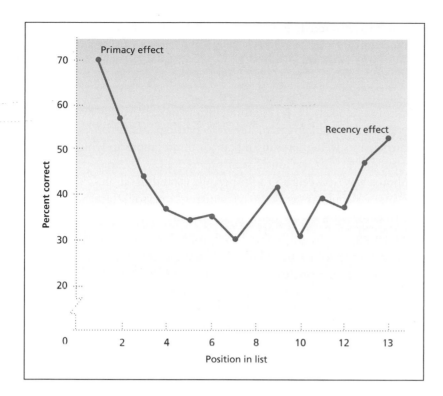

FIGURE 6.8   **Serial Position Effect**
In the serial position effect, information at the beginning of a list will be recalled at a higher rate than information in the middle of the list (primacy effect) because the beginning information receives more rehearsal and may enter LTM. Information at the end of a list is also retrieved at a higher rate (recency effect) because the end of the list is still in STM, with no information coming after it to interfere with retrieval.

At the end of the graph there is another increase in recall. This is the **recency effect** and is usually attributed to the fact that the last word or two was *just heard* and is still in short-term memory for easy retrieval, with no new words entering to "push" the most recent word or words out of memory (Bjork & Whitten, 1974; Murdock, 1962). The serial position effect works with many different kinds of information. In fact, business schools often teach their students that they should try not to be "in the middle" for job interviews. Going first or last in the interview process is much more likely to make a person's interview more memorable.

The serial position effect is often used to demonstrate that there are indeed two memory systems, STM and LTM. Memory researchers point to the primacy effect as a result of LTM storage and the recency effect as a result of STM. But the serial position effect can also apply to LTM exclusively (Baddeley & Hitch, 1974; Roediger & Crowder, 1976). Think about the presidents of the United States. How many of them can you remember? Everyone remembers Washington because he was *first*. After Washington, though, it becomes a struggle to remember who came next for many people. Even if a person can get the first several, the middle presidents are almost impossible to remember. But everyone remembers who is president right now and who was president before him, and so on, up until about the time of childhood (Roediger & Crowder, 1976). In this case, the primacy effect is most likely caused by Washington's importance in history, whereas the recency effect is more likely an effect of the importance of recent events. (Lincoln is the exception to the rule, as most people always remember him as the sixteenth president because of his importance during the Civil War.)

recency effect
tendency to remember information at the end of a body of information better than the information ahead of it.

These people are waiting to be interviewed for a job. The person who is interviewed first and the one who is interviewed last have the greatest chance of being remembered when the time comes for the employer to choose. The serial position effect will cause the impression made by the interviewees who come in the "middle" to be less memorable.

RECOGNITION: HEY, DON'T I KNOW YOU FROM SOMEWHERE?

The other form of memory retrieval is *recognition*, the ability to match a piece of information or a stimulus to a stored image or fact (Borges et al., 1977; Gillund & Shiffrin, 1984; Raaijmakers & Shiffrin, 1992).

'Hey good buddy! Can't kick, big fella.
How you doin'?   What's shakin'?'

©The New Yorker Collection 1988 Lee Lorenz from
cartoonbank.com. All Rights Reserved.

Father Bernard Pagano enters a
courthouse during his time as a suspect
in a series of robberies. He was falsely
identified for the crimes committed by
another man, who eventually confessed
to the robberies. False positives occur
when people mistakenly believe they
have recognized someone or something
that they have actually never seen.

false positive
error of recognition in which people
think that they recognize some
stimulus that is not actually in memory.

automatic encoding
tendency of certain kinds of
information to enter long-term memory
with little or no effortful encoding.

flashbulb memories
type of automatic encoding that occurs
because an unexpected event has
strong emotional associations for the
person remembering it.

Recognition is usually much easier than recall because the cue is the actual object, word, sound, and so on, that one is simply trying to detect as familiar and known. Examples of tests that use recognition are multiple-choice, matching, and true–false tests. The answer is right there and simply has to be matched to the information already in memory.

Recognition tends to be very accurate for images, especially human faces. In one study, over 2,500 photographs were shown to participants at the rate of one every 10 seconds. Participants were then shown pairs of photographs in which one member of each pair was one of the previously seen photographs. Accuracy for identifying the previous photos was between 85 to 95 percent (Standing et al., 1970). This is most likely why many people are good at recognizing a person's face but not as good at being able to come up with the name to go with it.

FALSE POSITIVES   Recognition isn't foolproof, however. Sometimes there is just enough similarity between a stimulus that is not already in memory and one that is in memory so that a **false positive** occurs (Muter, 1978). A false positive occurs when a person thinks that he or she has recognized something or someone but in fact does not have that something or someone in memory.

False positives can become disastrous in certain situations. In one case, in a series of armed robberies in Delaware, word had leaked out that the suspect sought by police might be a priest. When police put Father Bernard Pagano in a lineup for witnesses to identify, he was the only one in the lineup wearing a priest's collar. Seven eyewitnesses identified him as the man who had robbed them. Fortunately for Father Pagano, the real robber confessed to the crimes halfway through Pagano's trial (Loftus, 1987). Eyewitness recognition can be especially prone to false positives, although most people seem to think that "seeing is believing." For more about the problems with eyewitnesses, see the box Classic Studies in Psychology.

CLASSIC STUDIES IN PSYCHOLOGY
Elizabeth Loftus and Eyewitnesses

6.10   *How reliable is eyewitness testimony?*

Elizabeth Loftus is Professor of Psychology and Adjunct Professor of Law at the University of California in Irvine. For over 30 years, Dr. Loftus has been one of the world's leading researchers in the area of memory. Her focus has been on the accuracy of recall of memories—or rather, the inaccuracies of memory retrieval. She has been an expert witness at more than 200 trials, including that of Ted Bundy, the serial killer who was finally executed in Florida (Neimark, 1996).

Loftus and many others have demonstrated time and again that memory is not an unchanging, stable process but rather is a constantly changing one. People continually update and revise their memories of events without being aware that they are doing so, and they incorporate information gained after the actual event, whether correct or incorrect.

Here is a summary of one of Loftus's classic studies concerning the ways in which eyewitness testimony can be influenced by information given after the event in question (Loftus, 1975).

In this experiment, Loftus showed subjects a three-minute video clip taken from the movie *Diary of a Student Revolution*. In this clip, eight demonstrators run into a classroom and eventually leave after interrupting the professor's lecture in a noisy confrontation. At the end of the video, two questionnaires were distributed containing one key question and 90 "filler" questions. The key question for half of the subjects was, "Was the leader of the four demonstrators who entered the classroom a male?" The other half was asked, "Was the leader of the twelve demonstrators who entered the classroom a male?" One week later, a new set of questions was given to all subjects in which the key question was, "How many demonstrators did you see entering the classroom?" Subjects who were previously asked the question incorrectly giving the number as "four" stated an average recall of 6.4 people, while those who read the question incorrectly giving the number as "twelve" recalled an average of 8.9 people. Loftus concluded that subjects were trying to compromise the memory of what they had actually seen—eight demonstrators—with later information. This study, along with the Father Pagano story and many others, clearly demonstrates the heart of Loftus's research. What people see and hear about an event after the fact can easily affect the accuracy of their memories of that event.

Dr. Elizabeth Loftus is an internationally known expert on the accuracy of eyewitness testimony. She is often called on to testify in court cases.

Questions for Further Discussion

1. How might police officers taking statements about a crime avoid getting inaccurate information from eyewitnesses?

2. How might Loftus's research apply to situations in which a therapist is trying to help a client recover memories that may have been repressed? What should that therapist avoid doing?

AUTOMATIC ENCODING: FLASHBULB MEMORIES

6.11   *What is a flashbulb memory?*

Although some long-term memories need extensive maintenance rehearsal or effortful encoding in the form of elaborative rehearsal to enter from STM into LTM, many other kinds of long-term memories seem to enter permanent storage with little or no effort at all, in a kind of **automatic encoding** (Mandler, 1967; Schneider et al., 1984). In these cases, people unconsciously notice a lot of things, such as the passage of time, knowledge of physical space, and frequency of events. For example, a person might make no effort to remember how many times cars have passed down the street but when asked can give an answer of "often," "more than usual," or "hardly any."

A special kind of automatic encoding takes place when an unexpected event or episode in a person's life has strong emotional associations, such as fear, horror, or joy. Memories of highly emotional events can often seem vivid and detailed, as if the person's mind took a "flash picture" of the moment in time. These kinds of memories are called **flashbulb memories** (Neisser, 1982; Neisser & Harsch, 1992; Winningham et al., 2000).

Many people share certain flashbulb memories. People of the "baby boomer" generation remember exactly where they were when the news came that President John F. Kennedy had been shot. Younger generations may remember the explosion of the space shuttles *Challenger* and *Columbia* and certainly remember the horrific events of September 11, 2001. But personal flashbulb memories also exist. These memories tend to be major emotional events, such as the first date, an embarrassing event, or a particularly memorable birthday party.

Why do flashbulb memories seem so vivid and exact? The answer lies in the emotions felt at the time of the event. Emotional reactions stimulate the

little encoding

Events such as the horror of 9/11 are so emotional that the memories for the event are stored automatically. Such "flashbulb" memories seem to be very accurate, as if the person's mind took a flash picture of that moment in time but are actually no more accurate than any other memory.

release of hormones that have been shown to enhance the formation of long-term memories (McEwen, 2000). But is this kind of memory really all that accurate? Although some researchers have found evidence for a high degree of accuracy in flashbulb memories of *major events*, such as the assassination attempt on Ronald Reagan in March 1981, others have found that while flashbulb memories are often convincingly real, they are just as subject to decay and alterations over time as other kinds of memories (Neisser & Harsch, 1992). Apparently, no memories are completely accurate after the passage of time. The next section will discuss some of the reasons for faulty memories.

PRACTICE **QUIZ:** HOW MUCH DO YOU REMEMBER?

Pick the best answer.

1. The best place to take your math exam to ensure good retrieval of math concepts is in
   a. the math classroom.
   b. an auditorium, to prevent cheating.
   c. the English classroom.
   d. the special testing room used for all exams.

2. Sarah can remember names of the first two people she was introduced to at Ted's party, and she can remember the name of the last person she met, but the names of the dozen or so people in between are gone. This is an example of the
   a. encoding specificity effect.
   b. serial position effect.
   c. tip-of-the-tongue effect.
   d. redintegrative effect.

3. This quiz question, as well as of the other quiz questions, makes use of which form of retrieval of memories?
   a. rehearsal   c. recall
   b. relearning   d. recognition

4. Which of the following statements about Loftus's classic study is true?
   a. All of the subjects were able to correctly recall the number of demonstrators.
   b. Subjects given a question stating that there were four demonstrators remembered only three demonstrators.
   c. Subjects given a question stating that there were twelve demonstrators remembered eight demonstrators.
   d. Subjects either increased or decreased the number of demonstrators in an attempt to compromise their memory with the later false information.

5. Which of the following statements about flashbulb memories is false?
   a. They may be formed by the hormones released at emotional moments.
   b. They are vivid and detailed.
   c. They are unusually accurate.
   d. They can be personal or concern world events.

Answers: 1-a, 2-b, 3-d, 4-d, 5-c.

The Reconstructive Nature of Long-Term Memory Retrieval: How Reliable Are Memories?

> I think my memory is ▶ pretty good, but my brother and I often have arguments about things that happened when we were kids. Why don't we have the same exact memories? We were both there!

I think my memory is pretty good, but my brother and I often have arguments about things that happened when we were kids. Why don't we have the same exact memories? We were both there! People tend to assume that their memories are accurate when, in fact, memories are revised, edited, and altered on an almost continuous basis. The reason for the changes that occur in memory has to do with the way in which memories are formed as well as how they are retrieved.

CONSTRUCTIVE PROCESSING OF MEMORIES

6.12   *How are long-term memories formed?*

Many people have the idea that when they recall a memory, they are recalling it as if it were an "instant replay." As new memories are created in LTM, old memories can get "lost," but they are more likely to be changed or altered in some way (Baddeley, 1988). In reality, memories (including those very vivid flashbulb memories) are never quite accurate, and the more time that passes, the more inaccuracies creep in. Psychologist

John Kihlstrom, when talking about Bartlett's (1932) book on the constructive nature of memory, essentially says that ". . . remembering is more like making up a story than it is like reading one printed in a book. For Bartlett, every memory is a blend of knowledge and inference. Remembering is problem-solving activity, where the problem is to give a coherent* account of some past event, and the memory is the solution to that problem" (Kihlstrom, 2002, p. 3).

Think about the example of the filing system used to talk about long-term memory. What if different parts of each file (the sound, the image, the meaning, and so on) are stored in different areas of the filing system? When a person wants to retrieve that piece of information, files have to be pulled out of several places and put back together into the original item. Isn't it very likely that some pieces of the original item will not be retrieved, in fact some may never have been properly stored in the first place, and that some information gets added in that was not originally part of the file?

These men may engage in "Monday morning quarterbacking" as they apply hindsight to their memories of this game. Their memories of the game may be altered by information they get afterwards from the television, newspapers, or their friends.

Loftus, along with other researchers (Hyman, 1993; Hyman & Loftus, 1998, 2002), has provided ample evidence for the **constructive processing** view of memory retrieval. In this view, memories are literally "built" from the pieces stored away at encoding. Each time a memory is retrieved, it may be altered or revised in some way to include new information, or details that were there at encoding and may be left out of the new retrieval.

"remembering is like making up a story"

An example of how memories are reconstructed occurs when people, upon learning the details of a particular event, revise their memories to reflect their feeling that they "knew it all along." They will discard any incorrect information they actually had and replace it with more accurate information gained after the fact. This tendency of people to falsely believe that they would have accurately predicted an outcome without having been told about it in advance is called **hindsight bias** (Bahrick et al., 1996; Hoffrage et al., 2000). Anyone who has ever done some "Monday morning quarterbacking" by saying that they knew all along who would win the game has fallen victim to hindsight bias.

MEMORY RETRIEVAL PROBLEMS

6.13   *What kinds of problems do people experience when trying to remember something stored in long-term memory?*

Some people may say that they have "total recall." What they usually mean is that they feel that their memories are more accurate than those of other people. As should be obvious by now, true total recall is not a very likely ability for anyone to have. Here are some reasons why people have trouble recalling information accurately.

THE MISINFORMATION EFFECT   Elizabeth Loftus, in addition to her studies concerning eyewitness testimony, has also done several similar studies that demonstrate the **misinformation effect**. In this effect, misleading information that is presented *after* an event has taken place can affect the accuracy of the memory for that event (Loftus et al., 1978). In one study, subjects viewed a slide presentation of a traffic accident. The actual slide presentation contained a stop sign, but in a written summary of the presentation, the sign was referred to as a yield sign. Subjects who were given this misleading information after viewing the slides were far less accurate in their memories for the kind of sign present than were subjects given no such information. One of the interesting points to be made

---

*Coherent: understandable.

constructive processing
referring to the retrieval of memories in which those memories are altered, revised, or influenced by newer information.

hindsight bias
the tendency to falsely believe, through revision of older memories to include newer information, that one could have correctly predicted the outcome of an event.

misinformation effect
the tendency of misleading information presented after an event to alter the memories of the event itself.

by this study is that information that comes not only after the original event but also in an entirely different format (i.e., written instead of visual) can cause memories of the event to be incorrectly reconstructed.

RELIABILITY OF MEMORY RETRIEVAL

6.14   *What is false memory syndrome?*

If memory is edited and changed when people are in a state of waking consciousness, alert and making an effort to retrieve information, how much more might memory be changed when people are in an altered state of conscious, such as hypnosis? *False memory syndrome* refers to the creation of inaccurate or false memories through the suggestion of others, often while the person is under hypnosis (Hochman, 1994).

In her 1996 paper, Dr. Elizabeth Bowman has summarized some of the findings about pseudomemories, or false memories, associated with hypnosis. For example, research has shown that, although hypnosis may make it easier to recall some real memories, it also makes it easier to recall false memories. Hypnosis also has been found to increase the confidence people have in their memories regardless of whether those memories are real or false. False memories have been accidentally created by therapist suggestions during hypnotic therapy sessions (especially those that involve age regression). ⓛⓘⓝⓚ *to Chapter Four: Consciousness, pp. 142–144.* For more information on false memory syndrome, visit the Web site at **www.fmsfonline.org**.

There is some recent evidence that false memories are created in the brain in much the same way as real memories are formed, especially when visual images are involved (Gonsalves et al., 2004). Researchers, using MRI scans, looked at brain activity of people who were looking at real visual images and then were asked to imagine looking at visual images. They found that these same people were often unable to later distinguish between the images they had really seen and the imagined images when asked to remember which images were real or imagined. This might explain why asking people if they saw a particular person at a crime scene (causing them to imagine the image of that person) might affect the memories those people have of the crime when questioned some time later—the person they were asked to think about may be falsely remembered as having been present.

Clearly, memories obtained through hypnosis should not be considered as accurate without solid evidence from other sources.

But I've heard about people who remember being abused as children when they are hypnotized. Aren't those memories sometimes real? The fact that some people recover false memories under certain conditions does not mean that child molestation* does not really happen; nor does it mean that a person who was molested might not push that unwanted memory away from conscious thought. Molestation is a sad fact, with one conservative estimate stating that nearly 20 percent of all females and 7 percent of all males have experienced molestation during childhood (Abel & Osborn, 1992). There are also many therapists and psychological professionals who are quite skilled at helping clients remember events of the past without suggesting possible false memories, and they find that clients do remember information and events that were true and able to be verified but were previously unavailable to the client (Dalenberg, 1996). False memory syndrome is not only harmful to the persons directly involved but also makes it much more difficult for genuine victims of molestation to be believed when they do recover their memories of the painful traumas of childhood.

So can we trust any of our memories at all? There is evidence to suggest that false memories cannot be created for just any kind of memory. The *memories* must at least be plausible, according to the research of cognitive psychologist and memory expert

But I've **heard about** ▶ people who remember being abused as children when they are hypnotized. Aren't those memories sometimes real?

So can **we trust any of** ▶ our memories at all?

---
*Molestation: to make improper advances of a sexual nature.

Kathy Pezdek, who with her colleagues has done several studies demonstrating the resistance of children to the creation of implausible false memories (Hyman et al., 1998; Pezdek et al., 1997; Pezdek & Hodge, 1999).

In the 1999 study, Pezdek and Hodge asked children to read five different summaries of childhood events. Two of these events were false, but only one of the two false events was plausible (e.g., getting lost). Although the children were all told that all of the events happened to them as small children, the results indicated that the plausible false events were significantly more likely to be remembered as false memories than were the implausible false events (e.g., getting a rectal enema). A second experiment (Pezdek & Hodge, 1999) found similar results: Children were significantly less likely to form a false memory for an implausible false event than for a plausible false event.

The idea that only plausible events can become false memories runs contrary to the earlier work of Loftus and colleagues and to research concerning some very implausible false memories that have been successfully implanted, such as a memory for satanic rituals and alien abductions (Mack, 1994). Loftus and colleagues (Mazzoni et al., 2001) conducted several experiments in which they found that implausible events could be made more plausible by having the experimenters provide false feedback to the participants, who read articles telling of the implausible events as if they had actually happened to other people. The false feedback involved telling the participants that their responses to a questionnaire about fears were typical of people who had been through one of the false events (much as a well-meaning therapist might suggest to a client that certain anxieties and feelings are typical of someone who has been abused). These manipulations were so successful that participants not only developed false memories for the events but also even contradicted their own earlier statements in which they denied having these experiences in childhood. The researchers concluded that there are two steps that must occur before people will be likely to interpret their thoughts and fantasies about false events as true memories:

1. The event must be made to seem as plausible as possible.
2. Individuals are given information that helps them believe that the event could have happened to them personally.

(false) or memories have to be plausible

PRACTICE QUIZ: HOW MUCH DO YOU REMEMBER?

Pick the best answer.

1. The phenomenon of hindsight bias is an example of the _____ of long-term memory retrieval.
   a. instant replay view
   b. constructive processing view
   c. levels-of-processing view
   d. misinformation effect

2. In Loftus's 1978 study, subjects viewed a slide presentation of an accident. Later, some of the subjects were asked a question about a yield sign when the actual slides contained pictures of a stop sign. When these same subjects were later asked about what kind of sign was at the accident, they were very likely to be confused in this situation. This is an example of the
   a. instant replay effect.
   b. constructive processing effect.
   c. levels-of-processing effect.
   d. misinformation effect.

3. Which of the following statements about memory retrieval while under hypnosis is true?
   a. These memories are more accurate than other kinds of memories.
   b. People recalling memories under hypnosis are more confident in their memories, regardless of accuracy.
   c. Hypnosis makes it harder to recall memories in general.
   d. Age regression through hypnosis can increase the accuracy of recall of early childhood memories.

4. Pezdek and colleagues found that for a person to interpret thoughts and fantasies about false events as true memories
   a. the event must seem as plausible as possible.
   b. the person must believe in repression.
   c. there is very little information provided about the event.
   d. they only need to hear about the event once.

Why do we forget ▶ things? And why do we forget some things but not others?

What Were We Talking About? Forgetting

Why do we forget things? And why do we forget some things but not others?

6.15 *What are the different causes of forgetting?*

Think for a minute: What would it be like if people didn't forget anything? At first, the answer seems to be that such a phenomenal memory would be great, right? Anything people learned would always be there. But what if people *couldn't* forget? That is exactly the problem experienced in the case of A. R. Luria's (1968) famous *mnemonist*, Mr. S. (A mnemonist is a memory expert or someone with exceptional memory ability.) Mr. S. was a performing mnemonist, astonishing his audiences with lists of numbers that he memorized in minutes. But Mr. S. found that he *was unable to forget* the lists. He also could not easily separate important memories from trivial ones, and each time he looked at an object or read a word, images stimulated by that object or word would flood his mind. He eventually invented a way to "forget" things—by writing them on a piece of paper and then burning the paper (Luria, 1968).

The ability to forget seems necessary to one's sanity if the experience of Mr. S. is any indicator. But how fast do people forget things? Are there some things that are harder or easier to forget?

curve of forgetting
a graph showing a distinct pattern in which forgetting is very fast within the first hour after learning a list and then tapers off gradually.

EBBINGHAUS AND THE FORGETTING CURVE

Hermann Ebbinghaus (1913) was one of the first researchers to study forgetting. Because he did not want any verbal associations to aid him in remembering, he created several lists of "nonsense syllables," pronounceable but meaningless (such as GEX and WOL). He memorized a list, waited a specific amount of time, and then tried to retrieve the list, graphing his results each time. The result has become a familiar graph: the **curve of forgetting**. This graph clearly shows that forgetting happens quickly within the first hour after learning the lists and then tapers off gradually. (See Figure 6.9.) In other words, forgetting is greatest just after learning. This curve can be applied to other types of information as well. Although meaningful material is forgotten much more slowly and much less completely, the pattern obtained when testing for forgetting is similar (Conway et al., 1992).

FIGURE 6.9 **Curve of Forgetting**
Ebbinghaus found that his recall of words from his memorized word lists was greatest immediately after learning the list but rapidly decreased within the first hour. After the first hour, forgetting leveled off.

ENCODING FAILURE *not paying close enough attention*

There are several reasons why people forget things. One of the simplest is that some things never get encoded in the first place. Your friend, for example, may have said something to you as he walked out the door, and you may have heard him, but if you weren't paying attention to what he said, it would not get past sensory memory. This isn't forgetting so much as it is **encoding failure**, the failure to process information into memory. Researchers (Nickerson & Adams, 1979) developed a test of encoding failure using images of pennies. Look at Figure 6.10. Which view of a penny is the correct one? People see pennies nearly every day, but how many people actually look at what's on the penny and try to remember it?

FIGURE 6.10   **Which Penny Is Real?**   Most people do not really look at the face of a penny. Which of these pennies represents an actual penny? The answer can be found on the next page.

MEMORY TRACE DECAY THEORY

One of the older theories of forgetting involves the concept of a **memory trace**. A memory trace is some physical change in the brain, perhaps in a neuron or in the activity between neurons, which occurs when a memory is formed (Brown, 1958; Peterson & Peterson, 1959). Over time, if these traces are not used, they may **decay**, fading into nothing. It would be similar to what happens when a number of people walk across a particular patch of grass, causing a path to appear in which the grass is trampled down and perhaps turning brown. But if people stop using the path, the grass grows back and the path disappears.

Forgetting in sensory memory and short-term memory seems easy to explain as decay: Information that is not brought to attention in sensory memory or continuously rehearsed in STM will fade away. But is decay a good explanation for forgetting from long-term memory? When referring to LTM, decay theory is usually called **disuse**, and the phrase "use it or lose it" takes on great meaning (Bjork & Bjork, 1992). Although the fading of information from LTM through disuse sounds logical, there are many times when people can recall memories they had assumed were long forgotten. There must be other factors involved in the forgetting of long-term memories.

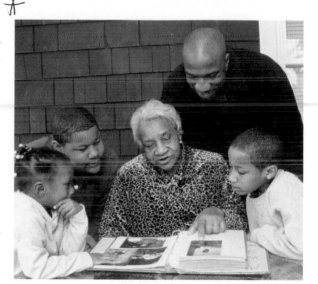

The fact that this woman can remember the things shown in the pictures even after many years makes it unlikely that the memory trace decay theory can explain all forgetting in long-term memory.

INTERFERENCE THEORY

A possible explanation of LTM forgetting is that although most long-term memories may be stored more or less permanently in the brain, those memories may not always be accessible to attempted retrieval because other information interferes (Anderson & Neely, 1995). (And even memories that are accessible are subject to constructive processing, which can lead to inaccurate recall.) An analogy might be this: The can of paint that Phillip wants may very well be on some shelf in his storeroom, but there's so much other junk in its way that he can't see it and can't get to it. In the case of LTM, interference can come from two different "directions."

PROACTIVE INTERFERENCE   Have you ever switched from driving a car with the gearshift on the wheel to one with the gearshift on the floor of the car? If the answer is yes, you probably found that you had some trouble when you first got into the new car. You may have grabbed at the wheel instead of reaching to the gearshift on the floor. The reason you reached for the gearshift in the "old" place

encoding failure
failure to process information into memory.

memory trace
physical change in the brain that occurs when a memory is formed.

decay
loss of memory due to the passage of time, during which the memory trace is not used.

disuse
another name for decay, assuming that memories that are not used will eventually decay and disappear.

People who are used to driving on the right side of the road experience quite a bit of proactive interference when trying to learn to drive in England, where cars are driven on the left. When this man returns home from vacation, he may experience retroactive interference in trying to remember to drive on the right side of the road again.

The answer to Figure 6.10 on page 235 is *A*.

Interference

Proactive Interference

French, learned **beforehand,** interferes proactively

Retroactive Interference

Spanish, learned **afterwards,** interferes retroactively

FIGURE 6.11 **Proactive and Retroactive Interference** If a student were to study for a French exam and then a Spanish exam, interference can occur in two directions. When taking the Spanish exam, the French information studied first may proactively interfere with retrieval of the Spanish information. But when taking the French exam, the more recently studied Spanish information may retroactively interfere with the retrieval of the French information.

proactive interference
memory retrieval problem that occurs when older information prevents or interferes with the retrieval of newer information.

retroactive interference
memory retrieval problem that occurs when newer information prevents or interferes with the retrieval of older information.

is called **proactive interference**: the tendency for older or previously learned material to interfere with the retrieval of newer, more recently learned material. (See Figure 6.11.)

Another example of proactive interference often occurs when someone gets a new cell phone. People in this situation often find themselves remembering their old cell phone number or some of its digits instead of the new cell phone number when they are trying to give the new number to friends.

RETROACTIVE INTERFERENCE When newer information interferes with the retrieval of older information, this is called **retroactive interference**. (See Figure 6.11.) What happens when you change back from the car with the gearshift on the floor to the older car with the gearshift on the wheel? You'll probably reach down to the floor at least once or twice because the newer skill retroactively interferes with remembering the old way of doing it.

How might interference work in each of the following cases?

1. Moving from the United States to England, where people drive on the left instead of the right side of the road.

2. Trying to program your old VCR after having the new one for a year.

3. Moving from one word-processing program to a different one, such as from WordPerfect to Microsoft Word.

The different ways that forgetting occurs are summarized in Table 6.1

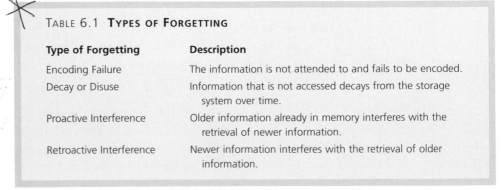

TABLE 6.1 **TYPES OF FORGETTING**

Type of Forgetting	Description
Encoding Failure	The information is not attended to and fails to be encoded.
Decay or Disuse	Information that is not accessed decays from the storage system over time.
Proactive Interference	Older information already in memory interferes with the retrieval of newer information.
Retroactive Interference	Newer information interferes with the retrieval of older information.

PRACTICE **QUIZ:** HOW MUCH DO YOU REMEMBER?

Pick the best answer.

1. Salvatore was introduced to a number of new people on his first day at his new job. According to Ebbinghaus, when should Salvatore expect to have forgotten the greatest number of the names he has just learned?
a. within the first hour after learning the names
b. within the first day after learning the names
c. near the end of the first week on the job
d. near the middle of the first week on the job

2. When a person "forgets" what someone has just said because he wasn't paying attention to the speaker at all, it is an example of the _____ explanation of forgetting.
a. interference
b. memory trace
c. encoding failure
d. repression

3. Decay theory works well to explain forgetting in
a. sensory memory only.
b. short-term memory only.
c. long-term memory only.
d. sensory memory and short-term memory.

4. Edna took sociology in the fall semester and is now taking psychology. Some of the concepts are similar, and Edna finds that she sometimes has trouble recalling some of the major sociology theorists. She keeps getting them confused with psychology theorists. Edna's problem is most likely due to
a. encoding failure.
b. retroactive interference.
c. proactive interference.
d. none of the above.

5. Brian went from the United States, where he grew up, to England. The first week he was there, he had a terrible time remembering to drive on the left side of the road. His problem is most likely due to
a. encoding failure.
b. retroactive interference.
c. proactive interference.
d. none of the above.

Answers: 1-a, 2-c, 3-d, 4-b, 5-c.

Memory and the Brain: The Physical Aspects of Memory

6.16 *How and where are memories formed in the brain?*

The physical change that takes place in the brain when a memory is formed is called the *engram.* Researchers have evidence that specific areas of the brain may be the places in which engrams are formed and that these areas are different for different types of memory. For example, procedural memories seem to be stored in the cerebellum (Boyd & Winstein, 2004; Daum & Schugens, 1996). Research involving PET scanning techniques strongly suggest that short-term memories are stored in the prefrontal cortex (the very front of the frontal lobe) and the temporal lobe (Goldman-Rakic, 1998; Rao et al., 1997).

As for semantic and episodic long-term memories, evidence suggests that these memories are also stored in the frontal and temporal lobes but not in exactly the same places nor in the same location as short-term memories (Weis et al., 2004). In Chapter Two the role of the amygdala was discussed as the place in the brain where our memories of fear are stored.

> **consolidation**
> the changes that take place in the structure and functioning of neurons when an engram is formed.

All that explains is the "where" of memory. Did scientists ever find out the "what" or the exact physical change that happens in the brain when memories are stored?

NEURAL ACTIVITY AND STRUCTURE IN MEMORY FORMATION

Several studies have offered evidence that the engram is not simply one physical change but many: Changes in the number of receptor sites, changes in the sensitivity of the synapse through repeated stimulation (called *long-term potentiation*), and changes in the dendrites and in the proteins within the neurons (Alkon, 1989; Kandel & Schwartz, 1982; Squire & Kandel, 1999). All of these changes serve to increase the neural connections and make connections that already exist more sensitive to stimulation. These changes that take place as an engram is forming are called **consolidation**. Although people may learn quickly, the memory of what has been learned takes some time to form completely.

THE HIPPOCAMPUS AND MEMORY

In the discussion of the *hippocampus* (a part of the limbic system) in Chapter Two (pp. 65–66), it was identified as the part of the brain that is responsible for the formation

◄ All that explains is the "where" of memory. Did scientists ever find out the "what" or the exact physical change that happens in the brain when memories are stored?

changes create new axons (new connections)

of new long-term memories. One of the clearest pieces of evidence of this function comes from the study of a man known as H. M. (Milner et al., 1968).

H. M. was about 17 when he began to suffer from severe epileptic seizures. A few years later, H. M.'s hippocampi were completely removed in an attempt to remove what the surgeon incorrectly believed was the source of the seizures. The last thing H. M. could remember was being rolled on the gurney to the operating room, and that was the last memory he was ever able to form. The hippocampus was not the source of his problem, but it was apparently the source of his ability to store any new information he encountered, because without either hippocampus, he was completely unable to remember anything new. Consolidation had become impossible. He had a magazine that he carried around, reading and rereading the stories, because each time he did so the stories were completely new to him. As with most amnesiacs of this type (although H. M.'s case was quite severe), his procedural memory was still intact. It was only new declarative memory—both semantic and episodic—that was lost.

WHEN MEMORY FAILS: ORGANIC AMNESIA

6.17 *What is amnesia?*

On Christmas Day, 1985, James McDonnell came home to his wife in Larchmont, NY after 14 years of amnesia. He had lost his memory after suffering head injuries in two auto accidents. He had gone to Philadelphia, and had found a job in a restaurant. McDonnell said that his memory returned to him on Christmas Eve when he bumped his head.

There are two forms of severe loss of memory disorders caused by problems in the functioning of the memory areas of the brain.

RETROGRADE AMNESIA   If the hippocampus is that important to the formation of memories, what would happen if it got temporarily "disconnected?" People who are in accidents in which they received a head injury often are unable to recall the accident itself. Sometimes they cannot remember the last several hours or even days before the accident. This type of amnesia (literally, "without memory") is called <u>retrograde amnesia, which is loss of memory from the point of injury backwards</u> (Hodges, 1994). What apparently happens in this kind of memory loss is that the consolidation process, which was busy making the physical changes to allow new memories to be stored, gets disrupted and loses everything that was not already nearly "finished."

Think about this: You are working on your computer, trying to finish a history paper that is due tomorrow. Your computer saves the document every 10 minutes, but you are working so furiously that you've written a lot in the last 10 minutes. Then the power goes out—horrors! When the power comes back on, you find that while all the files you had already saved to your disk are still intact,* your history paper is missing that last 10 minutes' worth of work. This is similar to what happens when someone's consolidation process is disrupted. All memories that were in the process of being stored but not yet permanent are lost.

One of the therapies for severe depression is *ECT*, or *electroconvulsive treatment*. Ⓛ Ⓘ Ⓝ Ⓚ *to Chapter Fifteen: Psychological Therapies, p. 587*. In one study with depressed patients who were being treated with ECT (Squire et al., 1975), patients were tested for their memory of certain television programs both before and after the treatment. Before treatment, recent programs were recalled in more detail and more often than older ones. But after treatment, these patients seemed to forget the *last three years of programs*, remembering only the older ones. Not only does this indicate that memories are lost when consolidation is interrupted (as it is by the seizure caused by the treatment) but also that consolidation may take not just days or months but sometimes years to be completed.

ANTEROGRADE AMNESIA   The kind of amnesia that H. M. experienced is called <u>*anterograde amnesia* or the loss of memories from the point of injury or illness forward</u> (Squire & Slater, 1978). People with this kind of amnesia, like H. M., have difficulty

past memory

present memory

retrograde amnesia
loss of memory from the point of some injury or trauma backwards, or loss of memory for the past.

_____
*Intact: whole or complete.

remembering anything new. This is also the kind of amnesia most often seen in people with *senile dementia*, a mental disorder in which severe forgetfulness, mental confusion, and mood swings are the primary symptoms. (Dementia patients also may suffer from retrograde amnesia in addition to anterograde amnesia.) If retrograde amnesia is like losing a document in the computer because of a power loss, anterograde amnesia is like discovering that your hard drive has become defective—you can read data that are already on the hard drive, but you can't store any new information. As long as you are looking at the data in your open computer window (i. e., attending to it), you can access it, but as soon as you close that window (stop thinking about it), the information is lost because it was never transferred to the hard drive (long-term memory).

This is the reason that elderly people with a dementia such as Alzheimer's will sometimes take several doses of medicine because they cannot remember having already taken a dose. It also makes for some very repetitive conversations, such as being told the same story or asked the same question numerous times in the space of a 20-minute conversation. For more about Alzheimer's disease, see Applying Psychology to Everyday Life on page 240.

INFANTILE AMNESIA   What is the earliest memory you have? Chances are you cannot remember much that happened to you before the age 3. When a person does claim to "remember" some event from infancy, a little investigation usually reveals that the "memory" is really based on what family members have told the person about that event and is not a genuine memory at all. This type of "manufactured" memory often has the quality of watching yourself in the memory as if it were a movie and you were an actor. In a genuine memory, you would remember the event through your own eyes—as if you were the camera.

Why can't people remember events from the first two or three years of life? One explanation of **infantile amnesia** involves the type of memory that exists in the first few years of life, when a child is still considered an infant. Early memories tend to be implicit and, as stated earlier in this chapter, implicit memories are difficult to bring to consciousness. Explicit memory, which is the more verbal and conscious form of memory, does not really develop until after about age 2, when the hippocampus is more fully developed and language skills blossom (Carver & Bauer, 2001).

Katherine Nelson (1993) also gives credit to the social relationships that small children have with others. As children are able to talk about shared memories with adults, they begin to develop their **autobiographical memory**, or the memory for events and facts related to one's personal life story.

infantile amnesia
the inability to retrieve memories from much before age 3.

autobiographical memory
the memory for events and facts related to one's personal life story.

PRACTICE QUIZ: HOW MUCH DO YOU REMEMBER?

Pick the best answer.

1. The physical trace of memory in the brain is called the
   a. memogram.
   c. sonogram.
   b. engram.
   d. pachygram.

2. Katherine is trying to hold the names of the students she just met in her psychology class in short-term memory. According to studies, these short-term memories will be stored in what part of the brain?
   a. cerebellum
   c. amygdala
   b. hippocampus
   d. prefrontal lobes

3. Research suggests that memory formation is a function of
   a. changes in the number of receptor sites.
   b. changes in the sensitivity of the synapse.
   c. changes in the dendrites and proteins within neurons.
   d. all of the above.

4. The role of the _____ in the formation of new long-term memories was first made apparent in the case of H. M., a famous amnesiac.
   a. hippocampus
   c. frontal lobes
   b. amygdala
   d. cerebellum

5. T. J. was in a car accident and suffered a concussion. After he recovered, he found that he could not remember the accident itself or the events of the morning leading up to the accident. T. J. had which kind of amnesia?
   a. retrograde
   b. anterograde
   c. Alzheimer's disease
   d. infantile amnesia

Answers: 1-b, 2-d, 3-d, 4-a, 5-a.

Applying Psychology To Everyday Life: Current Research in Alzheimer's Disease

6.18   *What can be done to help people with Alzheimer's disease?*

Nearly 4 million Americans have Alzheimer's disease, including the late former President Ronald Reagan. It is the most common type of dementia found in adults and the elderly. It has also become the third leading cause of death in late adulthood, with only heart disease and cancer responsible for more deaths (Antuono et al., 2001).

Symptoms usually begin with changes in memory, which may be rather mild at first but which become more severe over time, causing the person to become more and more forgetful about everyday tasks, such as remembering to turn off the stove. Eventually more dangerous forgetting occurs, such as taking extra doses of medication or leaving something cooking on the stove unattended. The person with this disorder repeats things in conversation, thoughts become disorganized, and messages get garbled. As Alzheimer's progresses, the ability to do simple calculations such as balancing a checkbook is lost, along with remembering how to do simple tasks such as bathing or getting dressed. It is a costly disease to care for, and caretakers often face severe emotional and financial burdens in caring for a loved one who is slowly becoming a stranger.

What can be done? There is at present no cure, but in recent years several new medications have been developed that seem to slow the progress of the disease, and new research into the cause gives hope that a cure may one day be a reality. One common treatment is to place the person on a drug such as Aricept®, which blocks the breakdown of acetylcholine, the neurotransmitter involved in the formation of memories. Other drugs to reduce the agitation,* restlessness,

---

*Agitation: excitement or upset.

People with Alzheimer's disease need constant reminders of where they are, what day it is, and what time it is. As the disease progresses, they may forget how to read, rendering these signs useless.

and hallucinations that can come with the disease may be administered. There is some evidence that taking an herbal supplement, gingko biloba, may help the memory problems of some Alzheimer's victims, although this supplement has been shown not to affect the functioning of normal memory (Le Bars et al., 2002). A new drug, memantine, stimulates the proteins responsible for nerve growth and repair and is being tested for effectiveness with Alzheimer's disease (Reiseberg et al., 2003).

Finally, clinical trials are underway to test the effects of statins, drugs that lower cholesterol, on Alzheimer's. A gene that is involved in cholesterol production is also a known risk factor for late-onset Alzheimer's (Zamrini et al., 2004). People taking statins may have a lower than usual risk of Alzheimer's disease.

Questions for Further Discussion

1. What might be some dangers associated with taking an over-the-counter herbal remedy, such as gingko biloba, to treat Alzheimer's or any other medical condition?
2. People are now living much longer than their ancestors, and it is no longer unusual to hear of people who are well over 100 years of age. How might this extension of life expectancy be related to an increased rate of Alzheimer's disease?
3. What kinds of social programs or interventions could help people who are taking care of a relative with Alzheimer's?

CHAPTER SUMMARY

Memory

6.1 *What is memory, and what are the three processes of memory?*

- Memory can be defined as an active system that receives information from the senses, organizes and alters it as it stores it away, and then retrieves the information from storage.
- The three processes are encoding, storage, and retrieval.

Models of Memory

6.2 *What are some of the different models of how memory works?*

- In the levels-of-processing model of memory, information that gets more deeply processed is more likely to be remembered.
- In the parallel distributed processing model of memory, information is simultaneously stored across an interconnected neural network that stretches across the brain.

The Information-Processing Model: Three Stages of Memory

6.3 *What is sensory memory?*

- Iconic memory is the visual sensory memory, in which an afterimage or icon will be held in neural form for about one-fourth to one-half second.
- Echoic memory is the auditory form of sensory memory and takes the form of an echo that lasts for up to 4 seconds.

6.4 *What is short-term or working memory?*

- Short-term memory is where information is held while it is conscious and being used. It holds about seven plus or minus two chunks of information and lasts about 30 seconds without rehearsal.
- STM can be lost through failure to rehearse, decay, interference by similar information, and the intrusion of new information into the STM system, which pushes older information out.

6.5   *What is long-term memory?*

- Long-term memory is the system in which memories that are to be kept more or less permanently are stored and is unlimited in capacity and relatively permanent in duration.

- Information that is more deeply processed, or processed according to meaning, will be retained and retrieved more efficiently.

6.6   *What are the different types of long-term memory?*

- Procedural memories are memories for skills, habits, and conditioned responses. Declarative memories are memories for general facts and personal experiences and include both semantic memories and episodic memories.

- Implicit memories are difficult to bring into conscious awareness, whereas explicit memories are those that a person is aware of possessing.

6.7   *How is information organized that is stored in long-term memory?*

- LTM is organized in the form of semantic networks, or nodes of related information spreading out from a central piece of knowledge.

Getting It Out: Retrieval of Long-Term Memories

6.8   *What kinds of cues help people remember?*

- Retrieval cues are words, meanings, sounds, and other stimuli that are encoded at the same time as a new memory.

- Encoding specificity occurs when physical surroundings become encoded as retrieval cues for specific memories.

- State-dependent learning occurs when physiological or psychological states become encoded as retrieval cues for memories formed while in those states.

6.9   *How do recall and recognition differ?*

- Recall is a type of memory retrieval in which the information to be retrieved must be "pulled" out of memory with few or no cues, whereas recognition involves matching information with stored images or facts.

- The serial position effect, or primacy or recency effect, occurs when the first items and the last items in a list of information are recalled more efficiently than items in the middle of the list.

Classic Studies in Psychology: **Elizabeth Loftus and Eyewitnesses**

6.10   *How reliable is eyewitness testimony?*

- Loftus and others have found that people constantly update and revise their memories of events, adding information to a memory that occurred later even when that information is in error.

6.11   *What is a flashbulb memory?*

- Automatic encoding of some kinds of information requires very little effort to place information into long-term memory.

- Memory for particularly emotional or traumatic events can lead to the formation of flashbulb memories, memories that seem as vivid and detailed as if the person were looking at a snapshot of the event but that are no more accurate than any other memories.

The Reconstructive Nature of Long-Term Memory Retrieval: How Reliable Are Memories?

6.12   *How are long-term memories formed?*

- Memories are reconstructed from the various bits and pieces of information that have been stored away in different places at the time of encoding in a process called constructive processing.

- Hindsight bias occurs when people falsely believe that they knew the outcome of some event because they have included knowledge of the event's true outcome into their memories of the event itself.

6.13   *What kinds of problems do people experience when trying to remember something stored in long-term memory?*

- The misinformation effect refers to the tendency of people who are asked misleading questions or given misleading information to incorporate that information into their memories for a particular event.

6.14   *What is false memory syndrome?*

- Rather than improving memory retrieval, hypnosis makes the creation of false memories more likely.

- False memory syndrome is the creation of false or inaccurate memories through suggestion, especially while hypnotized.

- Pezdek and colleagues assert that false memories are more likely to be formed for plausible false events than for implausible ones.

What Were We Talking About? Forgetting

6.15   *What are the different causes of forgetting?*

- Ebbinghaus found that information is mostly lost within one hour after learning and then gradually fades away. This is known as the curve of forgetting.

- A failure to encode information will not produce a memory.

- Memory trace decay theory assumes the presence of a physical memory trace that decays with disuse over time.

- Forgetting in LTM is most likely due to proactive or retroactive interference.

Memory and the Brain: The Physical Aspects of Memory

- Evidence suggests that procedural memories are stored in the cerebellum, whereas short-term memories are stored in the prefrontal and temporal lobes of the cortex.

- Semantic and episodic memories may be stored in the frontal and temporal lobes as well but in different locations than short-term memory, whereas memory for fear of objects is most likely stored in the amygdala.

6.16   *How and where are memories formed in the brain?*

- Consolidation consists of the physical changes in neurons that take place during the formation of a memory.

- The hippocampus appears to be responsible for the storage of new long-term memories. If it is removed, the ability to store anything new is completely lost.

6.17 *What is amnesia?*

- In retrograde amnesia, memory for the past (prior to the injury) is lost, which can be a loss of only minutes or a loss of several years.

- ECT, or electroconvulsive therapy, can disrupt consolidation and cause retrograde amnesia.

- In anterograde amnesia, memory for anything new becomes impossible, although old memories may still be retrievable.

- Most people cannot remember events that occurred before age 2 or 3. This is called infantile amnesia and is most likely due to the implicit nature of infant memory.

Applying Psychology To Everyday Life: Current Research in Alzheimer's Disease

6.18 *What can be done to help people with Alzheimer's disease?*

- The primary memory difficulty in Alzheimer's is anterograde amnesia, although retrograde amnesia can also occur as the disease progresses.

- There are various drugs in use or in development for use in slowing or stopping the progression of Alzheimer's disease.

6 KEY TERMS

anterograde amnesia 220
autobiographical memory 239
automatic encoding 229
consolidation 237
constructive processing 231
curve of forgetting 234
decay 235
declarative memory 221
disuse 235
echoic memory 215
eidetic imagery 214
elaborative rehearsal 220
encoding 210
encoding failure 235
encoding specificity 225
episodic memory 222
explicit memory 222

false positive 228
flashbulb memories 229
hindsight bias 231
iconic memory 213
implicit memory 221
infantile amnesia 239
information-processing model 211
levels-of-processing model 212
long-term memory (LTM) 218
maintenance rehearsal 217
memory 210
memory trace 235
misinformation effect 231
parallel distributed processing (PDP) model 212
primacy effect 226
proactive interference 236

procedural (nondeclarative) memory 220
recall 226
recency effect 227
recognition 226
retrieval 211
retrieval cue 224
retroactive interference 236
retrograde amnesia 238
selective attention 215
semantic memory 221
semantic network model 223
sensory memory 213
serial position effect 226
short-term memory (STM) (working memory) 215
storage 211

TEST YOURSELF

Pick the best answer.

1. Memory can best be described as
   a. a series of storage bins or boxes.
   b. a process of storage.
   c. an active system that encodes, stores, and retrieves information.
   d. a series of passive data files.

2. In the _____ model of memory, memories are simultaneously created and stored across a mental network.
   a. levels-of-processing
   b. parallel distributed processing
   c. transfer-appropriate processing
   d. information-processing

3. Roberta looked up from her book, realizing that Joaquin had just said something to her. What was it? Oh, yes, he had just asked her if she wanted to go out to dinner. Roberta's ability to retrieve what Joaquin said is due to her
   a. iconic sensory memory.
   b. echoic sensory memory.
   c. short-term memory.
   d. tactile sensory memory.

4. Although Sperling found evidence that iconic memory lasts about half a second, in reality information gets pushed out rather quickly by newer information. Evidence suggests that iconic memory really lasts about _____ of a second.
   a. three-quarters
   b. half
   c. one-quarter
   d. one-tenth

5. The duration of echoic memory is _____ than iconic memory, but its capacity is probably _____.
   a. shorter; larger
   b. longer; smaller
   c. longer; about the same
   d. shorter; about the same

6. When Greg tried to remember the name of his employer's husband, he had trouble getting the right name. At first he thought it might be Sandy or Candy, but finally realized that it was Mandy. Greg's confusion is evidence that short-term memories are primarily encoded in _____ form.
   a. acoustic
   b. visual
   c. tactile
   d. optical

7. Although the capacity of short-term memory is limited, more items can be held in this kind of storage through the process of
   a. chunking.
   b. decoding.
   c. rote rehearsal.
   d. data compression.

8. The best method for encoding long-term memories is probably to use
   a. maintenance rehearsal.
   b. rote rehearsal.
   c. elaborative rehearsal.
   d. sleep learning.

9. The levels-of-processing concept of Craik and Lockhart would suggest that which of the following questions would lead to better memory of the word *frog*?
   a. Does it rhyme with *blog*?
   b. Is it in capital letters?
   c. Is it written in cursive?
   d. Would it be found in a pond?

10. Which type of long-term memory is revised and updated more or less constantly?
    a. procedural
    b. declarative
    c. semantic
    d. episodic

11. Knowledge that we gain from school is called _____ memory.
    a. procedural
    b. declarative
    c. semantic
    d. episodic

12. The semantic network model of memory would suggest that which of the following questions would take longest to answer?
    a. Is a collie a dog?
    b. Is a collie a mammal?
    c. Is a collie an animal?
    d. There would be no difference in answering times.

13. The research of Eich and Metcalf would suggest that if you were really angry when you were learning Spanish, you should be _____ when taking the final exam for best retrieval.
    a. really calm
    b. unemotional
    c. angry
    d. depressed

14. Which of the following is NOT an example of a test using recall?
    a. short answer
    b. essay
    c. fill in the blanks
    d. true–false

15. The serial position effect predicts that the information that will be remembered best from a list will come at the _____ of the list.
    a. beginning
    b. end
    c. middle
    d. beginning and the end

16. Melanie was having a difficult time describing the man who took her purse in the mall parking lot. The officer showed her some pictures of people who had been involved in similar crimes, and she was quickly able to point out the right man. Melanie's situation is a reminder that in comparing recognition to recall, recognition tends to be
    a. easier.
    b. slower.
    c. more difficult.
    d. less accurate.

17. Is eyewitness testimony usually accurate?
    a. Yes, because seeing is believing.
    b. No, because eyewitnesses are not usually honest.
    c. Yes, because eyewitnesses are very confident about their testimony.
    d. No, because there is a great possibility of a "false positive" identification.

18. The passage of time and frequency of events are examples of knowledge that is often subject to
    a. encoding specificity.
    b. automatic encoding.
    c. flashbulb memories.
    d. eidetic imagery.

19. When retrieving a long-term memory, bits and pieces of information are gathered from various areas and put back together in a process called
    a. consolidation.
    b. redintegration.
    c. constructive processing.
    d. automatic processing.

20. Ebbinghaus found that information is forgotten
   a. more rapidly as time goes by.
   b. gradually at first, then increasing in speed of forgetting.
   c. quickly at first, then tapering off gradually.
   d. most quickly one day after learning.

21. A problem with using memory trace decay theory to explain forgetting from long-term memory is that
   a. older people can still remember things from their early years.
   b. there is no physical change in the brain when forming long-term memories.
   c. older memories always get lost, while newer memories always remain.
   d. older people cannot remember events in their childhood.

22. You started out by using WordPerfect and then moved to Microsoft Word because your company demanded that all documents be in Word. If you have trouble with Word, it is most likely due to
   a. proactive interference.
   b. retroactive interference.
   c. anterograde interference.
   d. consolidation problems.

23. The main type of memory problem that people with dementia, including Alzheimer's, typically have is called
   a. psychogenic amnesia.
   b. retrograde amnesia.
   c. retroactive amnesia.
   d. anterograde amnesia.

24. One theory that explains infantile amnesia states that these memories are
   a. never fully stored and, therefore, not available.
   b. explicit and not retrievable consciously.
   c. implicit and not retrievable consciously.
   d. repressed.

25. Gingko biloba extract is supposed to help memory because it
   a. increases the flow of blood to the brain.
   b. clears out the plaques and tangles associated with Alzheimer's.
   c. lowers cholesterol.
   d. speeds up the neural firing mechanisms of the brain.

Answers: 1-c, 2-b, 3-b, 4-c, 5-b, 6-a, 7-a, 8-c, 9-d, 10-d, 11-c, 12-c, 13-c, 14-d, 15-d, 16-a, 17-d, 18-b, 19-c, 20-c, 21-a, 22-a, 23-a, 24-d, 25-a.

For more sample quizzes and other review activities that will help you get a better grade, be sure to check out your accompanying study guide. To access tests and your own personalized study plan that will help you focus on the areas you need to master before your next class test, be sure to go to the on-line Psychology web site available with the access code packaged with your book.

CONCEPT MAP

Memory: Three Processes

Memory: system that actively stores and retrieves information

Three processes are:
- Encoding
- Storage
- Retrieval

6.1

Models of Memory
- Information-processing model
- Levels-of-processing model
- Parallel distributed processing (PDP) model

6.2

Information-Processing Theory: Three Stages of Memory

Long-Term Memory
- Memories are more or less permanent
- Unlimited in capacity
- Deeply processed information is retained and retrieved more efficiently

6.5

Short-Term or Working Memory
- Holds information before storage into LTM or information that is currently in use
- Capacity of 7 ± 2 chunks of information
- Duration of 12 to 30 seconds without rehearsal

Loss of STM contents:
- Failure to rehearse
- Decay
- Interference by similar information
- Intrusion of new information into STM

6.4

Sensory Memory

Iconic memory:
- Visual representation in neural form
- Lasts 1/4 second

Echoic memory:
- Auditory form
- Lasts for up to four seconds

6.3

Types of Long-Term Memory

Procedural memories: skills, habits, and conditioned responses

Declarative memories: general facts and personal experiences. Includes:

Semantic memories: general knowledge, such as knowledge of language and information learned in formal education

Episodic memories: personal information such as daily activities and events.

Implicit memories: difficult to bring into conscious awareness

Explicit memories: person is aware of possessing

6.6

THREE STAGE MODEL OF MEMORY

Maintenance rehearsal

Sensory memory → Selective attention → Short-term memory → Encoding → Long-term memory → Retrieval

All information lost within a second or so.

Unrehearsed information is lost in about 15 to 30 seconds.

Some information is retained indefinitely; some is lost with the passage of time.

Long-Term Memory Organization

Semantic networks: Nodes of related information spreading out from a central piece of knowledge

6.7

Classic Studies in Psychology: Elizabeth Loftus and Eyewitnesses

Eye Witness Testimony Reliability—Elizabeth Loftus

Loftus and others have found:
- People update and revise their memories of events
- Add information to a memory that occurred later
- Revisions occur even if information is in error

6.10

Flashbulb Memory
- Vivid and detailed memories caused by emotional or traumatic events
- No more accurate than any other memories

6.11

RETRIEVAL OF LONG-TERM MEMORIES

Use of Cues for Remembering

Retrieval cue: a stimulus for remembering. Retrieval cues are encoded at same time as new memory

Encoding specificity: physical surroundings become encoded as retrieval cues

State-dependent learning: physiological/psychological states used as retrieval cues

6.8

Differences Between Recall and Recognition

Recall: information must be "pulled" out of memory

Recognition: involves matching information with stored images or facts.

Serial position effect: first items and last items in a list are recalled better than middle items

6.9

SERIAL POSITION EFFECT

Primary effect

Recency effect

Percent correct / Position in list

RECONSTRUCTIVE NATURE OF LONG-TERM MEMORY RETRIEVAL

Long-Term Memory Formation

Constructive processing: memories are reconstructed from information that is stored during encoding

Hindsight bias: tendency to believe, through revision of older memories to include newer information, that one could correctly predict outcome of an event

6.12

Memory Retrieval Problems

Misinformation effect: misleading questions or information may be incorporated into memory

False memory syndrome: creation of false or inaccurate memories through suggestion, hypnosis

6.13–14

Types of Forgetting

TYPES OF FORGETTING	DESCRIPTION
Encoding Failure	The information is not attended to and fails to be encoded.
Decay or Disuse	Information that is not accessed decays from the storage system over time.
Proactive Interference	Older information already in memory interferes with the retrieval of newer information.
Retroactive Interference	Newer information interferes with the retrieval of older information.

6.15

Memory and Brain

Procedural memories: cerebellum

Short-term memories: cortical prefrontal and temporal lobes

Semantic and episodic memories: frontal and temporal lobes

Memory for fear: amygdala

Memory Formation in the Brain

Consolidation: neuronal changes during formation of a memory

Hippocampus: responsible for, new long-term memory storage, removal destroys ability to store anything new

6.16

Amnesia

Retrograde amnesia: past memories lost; can be for minutes or several years

Electroconvulsive therapy: can cause retrograde amnesia

Anterograde amnesia: new memory formation blocked; old memories retrievable

Infantile amnesia: lack of memories before the ages 2–3; due to implicit nature of infant memory

6.17

7

Development Across the Life Span

Home Alone at Two: A Lesson in Survival Instincts

Don separated from his wife, Lisa. She had custody of their 2-year-old daughter, and he had been trying to reach her to check on the little girl. Finally, he contacted the police and found out that his wife had been in jail for nearly three weeks, arrested on an aggravated battery charge. Lisa told him that their daughter was with neighbors, but after knocking on door after door without success, Don finally got the apartment manager to let him into his wife's apartment. There was his precious little child, covered in dirt and dried ketchup. She grabbed him and didn't let go.

The 2-year-old child had survived alone in the apartment for 19 days by eating mustard, ketchup, dried spaghetti, and a few other items she was able to find in the bottom sections of the refrigerator and cupboards of the kitchen and by drinking water from the bathroom sink. When her father found her, she was naked and covered in dried food. Although malnourished, she had managed to find enough to eat to survive until rescued by her father, who was amazed at her relatively good condition.

The day after arriving at the hospital to be treated for malnutrition and dehydration, the plucky little girl was sitting up in her hospital bed, laughing and playing with the nurses.

This true story, which occurred in September 2003, not only shows the power of the survival instinct in human beings but also the adaptive nature of children, even young children, to explore their environment and find ways to cope with adversity.

Why study human development?

Understanding how we come to
be the people we are is a critical
step in understanding ourselves as we
are today as well as who we may
become as we grow older. From the
moment of conception, we are each
headed down a pathway of change,
influenced by our biology, environment,
and social interactions, to a destination
that is the same for all of us. The
twists and turns of the pathway are
what make each of us unique individuals. In this chapter, we'll look at
the influences that help determine our
developmental pathway through life.

7.1 What are some of the special research methods used to study development?

7.2 What is the relationship between heredity and environmental factors in determining development?

7.3 How do chromosomes, genes, and DNA determine a person's characteristics or disorders?

7.4 How do twins develop during pregnancy?

7.5 How do conjoined twins adjust to being connected to each other?

7.6 What happens during the germinal, embryonic, and fetal periods of pregnancy and what are some hazards in prenatal development?

7.7 What kind of physical changes take place in infancy and childhood?

7.8 What are the facts and the myths concerning infant immunizations?

7.9 What are three ways of looking at cognitive development?

7.10 How does language develop?

7.11 How do infants and children develop personalities and form relationships with others?

7.12 What happens in Erikson's first four stages of psychosocial development?

7.13 What are the changes that occur in puberty?

7.14 How do adolescents develop formal operations and moral thinking?

7.15 What happens during the adolescent's search for identity?

7.16 What are the physical and cognitive changes that occur during adulthood and aging?

7.17 How do adults deal with the issues of work, relationships, parenting, aging, and death?

7.18 What are the theories of why aging occurs?

7.19 What are the stages of death and dying?

7.20 How does attention deficit hyperactivity disorder affect adults?

Issues in Studying Human Development

What is development? In the context of life, **human development** is the scientific study of the changes that occur in people as they age, from conception until death. This chapter will touch on almost all of the topics covered in the other chapters of this text, such as personality, cognition, biological processes, and social interactions. But in this chapter, all of those topics will be studied in the context of changes that occur as a result of the process of human development.

7.1 *What are some of the special research methods used to study development?*

As briefly discussed in Chapter One, research in development is affected by the problem of age. In any experiment, the participants who are exposed to the independent variable (the variable in an experiment that is deliberately manipulated by the experimenter) should be randomly assigned to the different experimental conditions. The problem in developmental research is that the age of the people in the study should always be an independent variable, but people cannot be randomly assigned to different age groups.

There are some special designs that are used in researching age-related changes: the **longitudinal design**, in which one group of people is followed and assessed at different times as the group ages; the **cross-sectional design**, in which several different age groups are studied at one time; and the **cross-sequential design**, which is a combination of the longitudinal and cross-sectional designs (Baltes et al., 1988).

The longitudinal design has the advantage of looking at real age-related changes as those changes occur in the same individuals. Disadvantages of this method are the lengthy amount of time, money, and effort involved in following participants over the years as well as the loss of participants when they move away, lose interest, or die. The cross-sectional design has the advantages of being quick, relatively inexpensive, and easier to accomplish than the longitudinal design. The main disadvantage is that one is no longer comparing an individual to that same individual as he or she ages; instead, individuals of different ages are being compared to one another. Differences between age groups are often a problem in developmental research. For example, if

human development
the scientific study of the changes that occur in people as they age from conception until death.

longitudinal design [*Stanford Growth study*]
research design in which one participant or group of participants is studied over a long period of time.

cross-sectional design
research design in which several different age groups of participants are studied at one particular point in time.

cross-sequential design
research design in which participants are first studied by means of a cross-sectional design but also followed and assessed for a period of no more than six years.

TABLE 7.1 A COMPARISON OF TWO DEVELOPMENTAL RESEARCH DESIGNS

Cross-Sectional Design

Different participants of various ages are compared at one point in time to determine age-related *differences*	**Group One** 20-year-old participants	Research done in 2005
	Group Two 40-year-old participants	
	Group Three 60-year-old participants	

Longitudinal Design

The **same** participants are studied at various ages to determine age-related *changes*	**Study One** 20 year old participants	Research done in 1965
	Study Two Same participants are now 40 years old	Research done in 1985
	Study Three Same participants are now 60 years old	Research done in 2005

comparing the IQ scores of 30-year-olds to 80-year-olds to see how aging affects intelligence, questions arise concerning the differing experiences those two age groups have had in educational opportunities that might affect IQ scores in addition to any effects of aging. Table 7.1 shows a comparison between examples of a *longitudinal design* and a *cross-sectional design*.

In studying human development, developmental psychologists have outlined many theories of how these age-related changes occur. There are some areas of controversy, however, and one of these is the issue of nature versus nurture.

NATURE VERSUS NURTURE

7.2   What is the relationship between heredity and environmental factors in determining development?

Nature refers to heredity, the influence of inherited characteristics on personality, physical growth, intellectual growth, and social interactions. **Nurture** refers to the influence of the environment on all of those same things and includes parenting styles, physical surroundings, economic factors, and anything that can have an influence on development that does not come from within the person.

So, is a person like Hitler born that way, or did something happen to make him the person he was? How much of a person's personality and behavior are determined by nature and how much are determined by nurture? This is a key question, and the answer is quite complicated. It is also quite important: Are people like Hitler, the infamous serial killer Ted Bundy, and Timothy McVeigh (the man responsible for the Oklahoma bombing of the Federal Building) the result of bad genes? Or was it bad parenting or life-altering experiences in childhood? Or are they the unique combination of both hereditary and environmental influences? After many years of scientific research, most developmental psychologists now agree that the last possibility is the most likely explanation for most of human development: All that people are and all that people become is the product of an interaction between nature and nurture (Ridley, 1999).

nature
the influence of our inherited characteristics on our personality, physical growth, intellectual growth, and social interactions.

nurture
the influence of the environment on personality, physical growth, intellectual growth, and social interactions.

◀ So, is a person like Hitler born that way, or did something happen to make him the person he was?

The Human Genome Project was completed in 2003 and identified approximately 20,000 to 25,000 genes in the human genetic material.

This does not mean that the controversy no longer exists; for example, intelligence is still a "hot topic" with regard to how much is inherited and how much is learned. There are researchers and theorists who assume a large genetic influence (Bouchard & Segal, 1985; Herrnstein & Murray, 1994; Jensen, 1969) and those who believe that culture, economics, nutrition in early childhood, and educational opportunities have a greater impact (Gardner et al., 1996; Gould, 1996; Rose et al., 1984; Wahlsten, 1997).

Behavioral genetics is a relatively new field in the investigation of the origins of behavior in which researchers try to determine how much of behavior is the result of genetic inheritance and how much is due to a person's experiences. For more on behavioral genetics and links to other sites, go to **www.ornl.gov/ sci/techresources/Human_Genome/elsi/behavior.shtml.**

Prenatal Development

Any study of the human life span must begin with looking at the complex material contained in the cells of the body that carries the instructions for life itself. After discussing the basic building blocks of life, this text will discuss how the processes of conception and the development of the infant within the womb take place.

CHROMOSOMES, GENES, AND DNA

7.3 *How do chromosomes, genes, and DNA determine a person's characteristics or disorders?*

Genetics is the science of heredity. Understanding how genes transmit human characteristics and traits involves defining a few basic terms.

Imagine a long, long ladder. Now imagine that the ladder is made of very soft rubber, and it is twisted around itself along its whole length. **DNA (deoxyribonucleic acid)** is a very special kind of molecule (the smallest particle of a substance that still has all the properties of that substance). DNA consists of two strands, each composed of certain sugars and phosphates. The two strands wind around each other in a spiral, much like the two sides of the ladder wind around each other. Linking the two strands together are certain chemical elements called *amines* or *bases* arranged in a particular pattern. The rungs of the rubber ladder would be like these chemical links. See Figure 7.1 for a more realistic representation of DNA.

Because of DNA's unique shape, each molecule of DNA is linked end to end with the others, forming a very long strand. Sections of this DNA strand are linked by the amines, which are usually referred to by letters A, T, G, and C. Amines are organic structures that contain the genetic codes for building the proteins that make up organic life (hair coloring, muscle, and skin, for example) and that control the life of each cell. Each section of DNA containing a certain sequence (ordering) of these amines is called a **gene**. So a gene is nothing more than a section of the DNA strand that has the same sequence of amines. Genes are located on rod-shaped structures called **chromosomes**, which are found in the nucleus of a cell.

Humans have a total of 46 chromosomes in each cell of their bodies (with the exception of the egg and the sperm). Twenty-three of these chromosomes come from the mother's egg and the other 23 from the father's sperm. Most characteristics are determined by 22 such pairs, called the *autosomes*. The last pair determines the sex of the person. These two chromosomes are called the *sex chromosomes*.

FIGURE 7.1 **DNA Molecule**
In this model of a DNA molecule, the two strands making up the sides of the "twisted ladder" are composed of sugars and phosphates. The "rungs" of the ladder that link the two strands are amines. Amines contain the genetic codes for building the proteins that make up organic life.

Frank and Ernest

I HATE BEING A DNA MOLECULE. THERE'S SO MUCH TO REMEMBER!

© Thaves. Reprinted by permission.

DOMINANT AND RECESSIVE GENES

The 46 chromosomes can actually be arranged in pairs, with one member of each pair coming from the mother and the other member from the father. Think about just one of these pairs for the moment.

In this particular pair of chromosomes, assume that there is a gene for hair color on each chromosome. The actual color of the person's hair will be determined by those two genes, one gene from each parent. If both genes are for brown hair, the person will obviously have brown hair, right? And if both are for blond hair, the person's hair will be blond.

But what if one gene is for brown hair and the other is for blond hair? The answer lies in the nature of each gene. Some genes that are more active in influencing the trait are called **dominant**. A dominant gene will always be expressed in the actual trait, in this case the hair color. A person with a dominant brown hair color gene will have brown hair, no matter what the other gene is, because brown is the most dominant of all the hair colors.

Some genes are less active in influencing the trait and will only be expressed in the actual trait if they are paired with another less active gene. These genes tend to recede, or fade, into the background when paired with a more dominant gene, so they are called

genetics
the science of inherited traits.

DNA (deoxyribonucleic acid)
special molecule that contains the genetic material of the organism.

gene
section of DNA having the same arrangement of chemical elements.

chromosome
tightly wound strand of genetic material or DNA.

dominant
referring to a gene that actively controls the expression of a trait.

◀ But what if one gene is for brown hair and the other is for blond hair?

Brown-eyed parents

B b   B b

B B
Brown-eyed child

B b
Brown-eyed child

b B
Brown-eyed child

b b
Blue-eyed child

FIGURE 7.2 **Dominant and Recessive Genes and Eye Color**
Each of these brown-eyed parents carries one dominant gene for brown eyes (B) and one recessive gene for blue eyes (b). The children represent the possible combinations of the parents' genes. Each parent could pass on the dominant brown eye genes, resulting in a brown-eyed child with no recessive genes (one chance out of four possible combinations). One parent could pass on the dominant gene while the other passes on the recessive gene, resulting in a child with brown eyes who carries the recessive blue eye gene (two chances out of four). Finally, each parent could pass on the recessive blue eye gene, leading to a child with blue eyes who carries two recessive genes for blue eyes (one chance out of four). In other words, each child this couple bears has a 25 percent chance of having blue eyes.

What about red hair? ▶
And how come some people have mixed hair color, like a strawberry blond?

Down syndrome is a form of developmental delay caused by an extra chromosome 21.

recessive
referring to a gene that only influences the expression of a trait when paired with an identical gene.

recessive. Blond hair color is the most recessive color and will only show up in a person's actual hair color if that person has a blond hair color gene from each parent.

What about red hair? And how come some people have mixed hair color, like a strawberry blond? In reality, the pattern of genetic transmission of traits can be a little complicated. Almost all traits are controlled by more than one pair of genes in a process called *polygenic inheritance*. (*Polygenic* means "many genes.") Sometimes certain kinds of genes tend to group themselves with certain other genes, like the genes for blond hair and blue eyes. Other genes are so equally dominant or equally recessive that they combine their traits in the organism. For example, genes for blond hair and red hair are recessive. When a child inherits one of each from his or her parents, instead of one or the other controlling the child's hair color, they may blend together to form a strawberry-blond mix.

GENETIC AND CHROMOSOME PROBLEMS

Several genetic disorders are carried by recessive genes. Diseases carried by recessive genes are inherited when a child inherits two recessive genes, one from each parent. Examples of disorders inherited in this manner are cystic fibrosis (a disease of the respiratory and digestive tracts), sickle cell anemia (a blood disorder), Tay-Sachs disorder (a fatal neurological disorder), and PKU (a problem with digesting a particular protein).

Sometimes the chromosome itself is the problem. Although each egg and each sperm are only supposed to have 23 chromosomes, in the creation of these cells a chromosome can end up in the wrong cell, leaving one cell with only 22 and the other with 24. If either of these cells survives to "mate," the missing or extra chromosome can cause mild to severe problems in development (American Academy of Pediatrics, 1995; Barnes & Carey, 2002; Gardner & Sutherland, 1996).

Examples of chromosome disorders include *Down syndrome*, a disorder in which there is an extra chromosome in what would normally be the twenty-first pair. Symptoms include almond-shaped, wide-set eyes and mental retardation (Barnes & Carey, 2002; Hernandez & Fisher, 1996). Other chromosome disorders occur when there is an extra sex chromosome in the twenty-third pair, such as *Klinefelter's syndrome*, in which the twenty-third set of sex chromosomes is XXY, with the extra X producing a male with reduced masculine characteristics, enlarged breasts, obesity, and excessive height (Bock, 1993), and *Turner's syndrome*, in which the twenty-third pair is actually missing an X, so that the result is a lone X chromosome (Ranke & Saenger, 2001). These females tend to be very short, infertile, and sexually underdeveloped (American Academy of Pediatrics, 1995; Rovet, 1993).

PRACTICE QUIZ: HOW MUCH DO YOU REMEMBER?

Pick the best answer.

1. In a _____ design, several different age groups of participants are studied at one time.
   a. longitudinal
   b. cross-sectional
   c. cross-sequential
   d. cross-longitudinal

2. The design that combines the two other development designs is called
   a. cross-sequential.
   b. cross-sectional.
   c. longitudinal.
   d. cross-longitudinal.

3. In the analogy of the rubber ladder, the sequence of amines would be represented by the _____ of the ladder.
   a. sides
   b. length
   c. rungs
   d. wood

4. Brandon has blue eyes, even though both his mother and father have brown eyes. What do we know about Brandon's parents?
   a. At least one of his parents has a recessive blue eye color gene.
   b. Each of his parents must have one recessive blue eye color gene.
   c. Each of his parents must have one dominant blue eye color gene.
   d. Neither of his parents has a blue eye color gene.

5. Which of the following is a disorder caused by having an extra chromosome?
   a. Tay-Sachs
   b. PKU
   c. cystic fibrosis
   d. Down syndrome

Answers: 1-b, 2-a, 3-c, 4-b, 5-d.

FROM CONCEPTION TO BIRTH

Life begins at the moment of **conception**, the moment at which a female becomes pregnant. From conception to the actual birth of the baby is a period of approximately nine months, during which a single cell becomes a complete infant. It is also during this time that many things can have a positive or negative influence on the developing infant.

THE ZYGOTE AND TWINNING

7.4 How do twins develop during pregnancy?

When an egg (also called an **ovum**) and a sperm unite in the process of **fertilization**, the resulting single cell will have a total of 46 chromosomes and is called a **zygote**. Normally, the zygote will begin to divide, first into two cells, then four, then eight, and so on, with each new cell also having 46 chromosomes, because the DNA molecules produce duplicates of themselves before each division. Eventually, the mass of cells becomes a baby.

There are actually two kinds of twins, resulting from two different unusual occurrences. Twins who are commonly referred to as "identical" are **monozygotic twins**, meaning that the two babies come from one (mono) fertilized egg (zygote). Early in the division process, the mass of cells splits completely—no one knows exactly why—into two separate masses, each of which will develop into a separate infant. The infants will be the same sex and have identical features because they each possess the same set of 46 chromosomes.

The other type of twin is more an accident of timing and is more common in women who are older and who are from certain ethnic groups (Allen & Parisi, 1990; Bonnelykke, 1990; Imaizumi, 1998). A woman's body is only supposed to ovulate (release an egg from the ovary*) once each monthly cycle. Sometimes something goes wrong, and her ovary releases more than one egg at the same time. If two of these eggs are fertilized, the woman may give birth to fraternal or **dizygotic twins** (two eggs), or possibly triplets or some other multiple number of babies. This is also more likely to happen to women who are taking fertility drugs to help them get pregnant. (See Figure 7.3.)

Another form of dizygotic twins is the result of the woman's body releasing an egg in the next monthly cycle, even though the woman is already pregnant. Usually, once the woman is pregnant her body sends a signal to the brain, telling it that no more eggs need to be released. If that signal is too weak or is not sent, she will ovulate again and can become pregnant again. In this type of fraternal twin, one baby may be quite a bit larger than the other because the larger baby is actually older (Bryan & Hallett, 2001).

Twins provide developmental psychologists with another way to look at the contribution of nature and nurture to human development. Researchers may seek out identical twins who have been separated at birth, looking at all the ways those twins are alike in spite of being raised in different environments. L I N K *to Chapter Twelve: Theories of Personality, p. 463.*

What happens when Siamese twins are born? The term *Siamese twins* is really not the most accurate way to describe identical twins who are physically joined together at some point on their bodies. The proper term is *conjoined twins*, and this condition occurs when the mass of cells begins to separate into two masses but remains linked at some particular point. Wherever that point is, the two infants will be physically "stuck" together, sometimes involving only soft tissues, like the original and truly Siamese twins, Chang and Eng, who were joined at the hip, and sometimes

*Ovary: the female sex gland containing the eggs.

---

conception
the moment at which a female becomes pregnant.

ovum
the female sex cell, or egg.

fertilization
the union of the ovum and sperm.

zygote
cell resulting from the uniting of the ovum and sperm.

monozygotic twins
identical twins formed when one zygote splits into two separate masses of cells, each of which develops into a separate embryo.

dizygotic twins
often called fraternal twins, occurring when two eggs each get fertilized by two different sperm, resulting in two zygotes in the uterus at the same time.

Identical twins

1 Accounting for about 1 to 250 births, these are created when a single egg is fertilized by one sperm.

2 The egg splits into halves. Each develops into a fetus with the same genetic composition.

Fraternal twins

1 Twice as common as identicals, fraternals arise when two eggs are released at once.

2 If both are fertilized by separate sperm, two fetuses form. Genetically they are just ordinary siblings.

FIGURE 7.3 **Monozygotic and Dizygotic Twins** Because identical twins come from one fertilized egg (zygote), they are called monozygotic. Fraternal twins, who come from two different fertilized eggs, are called dizygotic.
Source: Kantrowitz and Springen (1987), pp. 60–61.

◄ What happens when Siamese twins are born?

Abby and Britty Hensel are conjoined twins who share one body from the waist down but are two distinctly different individuals.

involving the sharing of certain body parts, like the case of Britty and Abby, which is discussed in the Psychology in the News section that follows.

PSYCHOLOGY IN THE NEWS

Abby and Britty Hensel, Together for Life

7.5 *How do conjoined twins adjust to being connected to each other?*

Brittany, or Britty as her family calls her, loves milk. Her twin sister, Abigail (Abby), despises milk and would rather drink orange juice. Abby likes blue, Britty likes pink. Abby likes oyster crackers in her soup but Britty hates them. Abby loves to eat; Britty thinks food is boring. Abby is the leader but Britty is better at academics. Britty wants to be a pilot, while Abby wants to be a dentist (Miller & Doman, 1996).

Abby and Britty sound like many other siblings, each with separate likes and dislikes as well as different interests. But Abby and Britty are not separate and can never truly be separate, for they have two separate heads yet share one lower body. No more than four sets of surviving conjoined twins in recorded history have this condition. In the case of Abby and Britty Hensel, they each have their own heart and their own stomach but share three lungs. Their spines are joined at the pelvis, and below the waist they have only one set of organs. Each controls one arm and one leg on one side of the body, yet they somehow manage to move as one (Miller & Doman, 1996).

The girls ride a bicycle, swim, and play soccer just like any other girls their age. Yet every action they undertake has to be a miracle of coordination, and they do it without even seeming to think about it. If Britty coughs, *Abby's* hand may reflexively go up to cover Britty's mouth. When Britty is sick, she can't take the medicine for it (her stomach is sensitive) but Abby can take it for her (her stomach isn't sensitive).

In 2002, the girls received surgery to correct a severe curve in each of their spines, the result of their unusual joining of spinal columns (Kaveny, 2001). They each gained about two inches in height and find that to be an advantage on the soccer field. They are healthy and seem to be both happy and well adjusted, surrounded by a loving mother, father, younger brother, and sister.

Questions for Further Discussion

1. What kinds of difficulties might Abby and Britty have in adolescence?
2. How would being conjoined affect career decisions?
3. How can conjoined twins have different personalities?
4. If they decide to have a child (which is physically possible), who will claim the child, or will they both be the baby's mother?

THE GERMINAL PERIOD

7.6 *What happens during the germinal, embryonic, and fetal periods of pregnancy and what are some hazards in prenatal development?*

Once fertilization has taken place, the zygote begins dividing and moving down to the *uterus*, the muscular organ that will contain and protect the developing infant. This process takes about a week, followed by about week during which the mass of cells, now forming a hollow ball, firmly attaches itself to the wall of the uterus. This two-week period is called the **germinal period** of pregnancy. The *placenta* also begins to form during this period. The placenta is a specialized organ that provides nourishment and filters away waste products from the developing baby. The *umbilical cord* also begins to develop at this time, connecting the organism to the placenta.

germinal period
first two weeks after fertilization, during which the zygote moves down to the uterus and begins to implant in the lining.

The three periods of pregnancy are the germinal period, lasting about two weeks, the embryonic period, from about two to eight weeks, and the fetal period, which lasts from eight weeks until the end of pregnancy.

How does it get from the mass of cells to a baby, with eyes, nose, hands, feet, and so on? How do all those different things come from the same original single cell? During the germinal period, the cells begin to differentiate, or develop into specialized cells, in preparation for becoming all the various kinds of cells that make up the human body—skin cells, heart cells, and so on. Perhaps the most important of these cells are the *stem cells*, which stay in a somewhat immature state until needed to produce more cells. Researchers are currently looking into ways to use stem cells found in the umbilical cord to grow new organs and tissues for transplant or to repair neurological damage (Chen & Ende, 2000; Holden & Vogel, 2002; Lu & Ende, 1997). L I N K *to Chapter Two: The Biological Perspective, p. 55.*

THE EMBRYONIC PERIOD   Once firmly attached to the uterus, the developing organism is called an **embryo**. The **embryonic period** will last from two weeks after conception to eight weeks, and during this time the cells will continue to specialize and become the various organs and structures of a human infant. By the end of eight weeks after conception, the embryo is about 1 inch long and has primitive eyes, nose, lips, teeth, little arms and legs, and a beating heart. Although no organ is fully developed or completely functional at this time, nearly all are "there."

2-8 weeks

Critical Periods   As soon as the embryo begins to receive nourishment from the mother through the placenta, it becomes vulnerable to hazards such as diseases of the mother, drugs, and other toxins that can pass from the mother through the placenta to the developing infant. It is during this time of pregnancy that we most clearly see **critical periods**, times during which some environmental influence can have an impact—often devastating—on the development of the infant. The arms, for example,

◀ How does it get from the mass of cells to a baby, with eyes, nose, hands, feet, and so on? How do all those different things come from the same original single cell?

embryo
name for the developing organism from two weeks to eight weeks after fertilization.

embryonic period more acceptable to
the period from two to eight weeks change
after fertilization, during which the (birth
major organs and structures of the defect)
organism develop.

critical periods
times during which certain environmental influences can have an impact on the development of the infant.

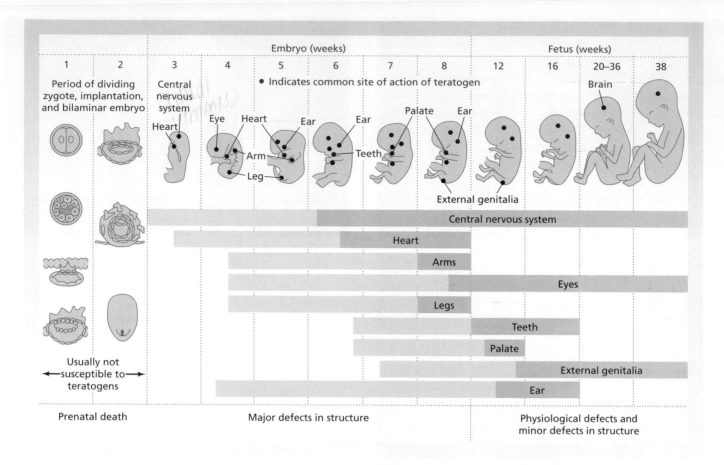

FIGURE 7.4 **Sensitivity to Outside Influences** This chart shows the various time periods during which different organs and bodily structures are most vulnerable to the effects of teratogens. The green areas indicate the possibility of severe structural defects, such as a baby born with no arms, no legs, or a deformed heart. The blue areas indicate more minor structural defects and problems in the way organs and systems may function. Why would the developing organism not be susceptible to teratogens in the first two weeks?

can only be affected during the time that they are developing, whereas the heart can be affected very early in this period. See Figure 7.4 for a look at the particular structures of the developing infant that are most vulnerable at various times during pregnancy.

Prenatal Hazards: Teratogens   Any substance such as a drug, chemical, virus, or other factor that can cause a birth defect is called a **teratogen**. Table 7.2 shows some common teratogens and their possible negative effects on the developing infant.

teratogen
any factor that can cause a birth defect.

fetal period
the time from about eight weeks after conception until the birth of the child.

fetus
name for the developing organism from eight weeks after fertilization to the birth of the baby.

TABLE 7.2 **COMMON TERATOGENS**

Teratogenic Agent	Effect on Development
Rubella	Blindness, deafness, heart defects, brain damage
Marijuana	Irritability, nervousness, tremors; infant is easily disturbed, startles
Cocaine	Decreased height, low birth weight, respiratory problems, seizures, learning difficulties; infant is difficult to soothe
Alcohol	Fetal alcohol syndrome (mental retardation, delayed growth, facial malformation), learning difficulties, smaller than normal heads
Nicotine	Miscarriage, low birth weight, stillbirth, short stature, mental retardation, learning disabilities
Mercury	Mental retardation, blindness
Syphilis	Mental retardation, deafness, meningitis
Caffeine	Miscarriage, low birth weight
Radiation	Higher incidence of cancers, physical deformities
High Water Temperatures	Increased chance of neural tube defects

Source: Shepard, T. H. (2001).

8-birth

THE FETAL PERIOD: GROW, BABY, GROW The **fetal period** is the time from about eight weeks after conception until the birth of the child (now called a **fetus**) and is a period of tremendous growth. The fetus's length increases by about 20 times and its weight increases from about 1 ounce at 2 months to a little over 7 pounds. The organs, while accomplishing most of their differentiation in the embryonic period, continue to develop and become functional. Muscles begin to contract in the third month. In the fourth month, the mother will begin to feel this movement as a tiny "flutter" or "quickening" at first, and by the fifth month, the flutter will become a "kick."

The last few months continue the development of fat and the growth of the body, until about the end of the thirty-eighth week. At that time, the fetus is pushed out of the mother's body in the process of labor and childbirth and becomes a baby. Babies born before 38 weeks are called *preterm* and may need life support to survive. This is especially true if the baby weighs less than about five and a half pounds at birth.

The most likely time for a *miscarriage*, or *spontaneous abortion*, is in the first three months, as the organs are forming and first becoming functional (Speroff et al., 1999). Some 15 to 20 percent of all pregnancies end in miscarriage, many so early that the mother may not have even known she was pregnant (Hill, 1998; Medical Economics Staff, 1994). When a miscarriage occurs, it is most likely caused by a genetic defect in the way the embryo or fetus is developing that will not allow the infant to survive. In other words, there isn't anything that the mother did wrong or that could have been done to prevent the miscarriage.

This pregnant woman is getting a sonogram. Sonograms allow doctors to see any physical deformities and make accurate measurements of gestational age without risk to the mother or the fetus.

PRACTICE **QUIZ:** HOW MUCH DO YOU REMEMBER?

Pick the best answer.

1. The fertilized egg cell is called a
   a. zygote.
   b. ovum.
   c. sperm.
   d. blastocyst.

2. Which of the following statements about Abby and Britty Hensel is FALSE?
   a. They are able to coordinate their actions.
   b. They are remarkably healthy.
   c. They could have been successfully separated.
   d. They are one of only four sets of living dicephalic twins.

3. The first two weeks of pregnancy are called the _____ period.
   a. fetal
   b. embryonic
   c. placental
   d. germinal

4. The period of pregnancy that contains the clearest examples of critical periods is the _____ period.
   a. germinal
   b. embryonic
   c. fetal
   d. gestational

5. Mental retardation and blindness are possible outcomes of the effects of _____ on the developing baby.
   a. alcohol
   b. caffeine
   c. cocaine
   d. mercury

Answers: 1-a, 2-c, 3-d, 4-b, 5-d.

Infancy and Childhood Development

What can babies do? Aren't they pretty much unaware of what's going on around them at first? Surprisingly, babies can do a lot more than researchers used to believe they could. A lot of the early research on infants just after birth was done on babies who were still very drowsy from the general anesthesia that used to be given to their mothers during the labor process. Drowsy babies don't tend to respond well, as one might imagine. In the next few sections, it becomes obvious that infants accomplish a great deal throughout infancy, even in the first few days of life on the outside.

◀ What can babies do? Aren't they pretty much unaware of what's going on around them at first?

PHYSICAL DEVELOPMENT

7.7 *What kind of physical changes take place in infancy and childhood?*

critical ajustments

Immediately after birth, several things start to happen. The respiratory system begins to function, filling the lungs with air and putting oxygen into the blood. The blood now circulates only within the infant's system because the umbilical cord has been cut. Body temperature is now regulated by the infant's own activity and body fat (which acts as insulation) rather than by the amniotic fluid. The digestive system probably takes the longest to adjust to life outside the womb. This is another reason for the excess body fat. It provides fuel until the infant is able to take in enough nourishment on its own. That is why most babies lose a little weight in the first week after birth.

REFLEXES Babies come into this world able to interact with it. Infants have a set of *innate* (existing from birth) involuntary* behavior patterns called *reflexes*. Until an infant is capable of learning more complex means of interaction, reflexes help the infant to survive. Figure 7.5 shows five infant reflexes.

Pediatricians use these and other reflexes to determine whether or not an infant's nervous system is working properly.

---

*Involuntary: in this sense, not under conscious, deliberate control.

FIGURE 7.5 **Five Infant Reflexes**
Shown here are (a) Grasping (b) Moro–startle (c) Rooting (d) Stepping (e) Sucking.
These infant reflexes can be used to check on the health of an infant's nervous system. If a reflex is absent or abnormal, it may indicate brain damage or some other neurological problem.

BABY, CAN YOU SEE ME? BABY, CAN YOU HEAR ME? SENSORY DEVELOPMENT
I've heard that babies can't see or hear very much at birth. Is that true? Although most infant sensory abilities are fairly well developed at birth, some require a bit more time to reach "full power." The sense of touch is the most well developed, which makes perfect sense when one realizes how much skin-to-womb contact the baby has had in the last months of pregnancy. The sense of smell is also highly developed. Breast-fed babies can actually tell the difference between their own mother's milk scent and another woman's milk scent within a few days after birth.

Taste is also nearly fully developed. At birth, infants show a preference for sweets (and human breast milk is very sweet), and by four months have developed a preference for salty tastes (which may come from exposure to the salty taste of their mother's skin). Sour and bitter, two other taste sensations, produce spitting up and the making of horrible faces (Ganchrow et al., 1983).

Hearing is functional before birth but may take a little while to reach its full potential after birth. The fluids of the womb must clear out completely. From birth, newborns seem most responsive to high pitches, as in a woman's voice, and low pitches, as in a male's voice.

The least functional sense at birth is vision. The eye, as stated in Chapter Three, is quite a complex organ. The rods, which see in black and white and have little visual acuity, are fairly well developed at birth, but the cones, which see color and provide sharpness of vision, will take about another six months to fully develop. So the newborn has relatively poor color perception when compared to sharply contrasting lights and darks until about two months of age (Adams, 1987) and has fairly "fuzzy" vision, much as a nearsighted person would have. The lens of the newborn stays fixed until the muscles that hold it in place mature. Until then the newborn is unable to shift what little focus it has from close to far. Thus, newborns actually have a fixed distance for clear vision of about 7 to 10 inches, which is the distance from the baby's face to the mother's face while nursing (Slater, 2000). This focal distance may also be the reason adults almost instinctively hold a baby at about this distance from their own faces.

Newborns also have visual preferences at birth, as discovered by researchers using measures of the time that infants spent looking at certain visual stimuli (Fantz, 1961). They found that infants prefer to look at complex patterns rather than simple ones, three dimensions rather than two, and that the most preferred visual stimulus was a human face. The fact that infants prefer human voices and human faces (DeCasper & Fifer, 1980; DeCasper & Spence, 1986; Fantz, 1964; Maurer & Young, 1983) makes it easier for them to form relationships with their caretakers and to develop language later on.

FROM CRAWLING TO A BLUR OF MOTION: MOTOR DEVELOPMENT   Infants manage a tremendous amount of development in motor skills from birth to about two years of age. Figure 7.6 shows some of the major physical milestones of infancy. When looking at the ages listed, remember that these ages are averages based on large samples of infants. An infant may reach these milestones earlier or later than the average and still be considered to be developing normally.

An infant's normal development is related to many factors such as nutrition, care, and health. One important way to protect an infant's health is to make sure that immunizations against various illnesses are given at the appropriate times. The following section discusses a serious issue concerning immunizations and their importance to the developing child.

◀ I've heard that babies can't see or hear very much at birth. Is that true?

FIGURE 7.6 **Six Motor Milestones** Shown here are (a) Raising head (b) Rolling over (c) Propped up (d) Sitting up (e) Crawling (f) Walking. The motor milestones develop as the infant gains greater voluntary control over the muscles in its body, typically from the top of the body downward. This pattern is seen in the early control of the neck muscles and the much later development of control of the legs and feet.

CURRENT ISSUES IN PSYCHOLOGY

The Facts and Myths About Immunizations

7.8 *What are the facts and the myths concerning infant immunizations?*

In the last few decades, parents of young children have begun to resist getting their infants and young children immunized against childhood diseases such as MMR—measles, mumps, and rubella (German measles). This alarming trend is probably due to a number of factors. First, the parents of these children have grown up in an era in which immunizations during infancy were common, making them unaware of the seriousness of the childhood diseases those immunizations prevent. They have not seen the serious consequences that can result from outbreaks of such diseases: blindness, deafness, mental retardation, and even death (Centers for Disease Control and Prevention, 1999).

Second, many of these parents have become influenced by misinformation that has been placed on the Internet and handed out by concerned but uninformed people that highlights the dangers of immunization (Stratton et al., 2001a, 2001b).

What are some of the myths parents now believe, and what are the facts?

Myth: Children who are given an immunization can get the disease itself.

Fact: Most vaccines are made from dead viruses, and it is impossible to get the disease in this way. Vaccines that use very weak live viruses (like the chicken pox vaccine) might cause a child to develop a mild version of the disease, but the risk is very small and the full-blown disease is far more serious and deadly (Centers for Disease Control and Prevention, 2004; National Institutes of Health, 1998; Offit & Bell, 1998).

Myth: If all the other children in a school are immunized, there's no harm in not immunizing one's own child.

Fact: If one parent is thinking like this, then others are also, and this can lead to an epidemic. One such epidemic of measles happened between 1989 and 1991 in the United States, causing rates of death due to measles to increase by a large number during that period, as well as increases in rates of brain damage due to high fevers (Centers for Disease Control and Prevention, 2004; National Institutes of Health, 1998; Offit & Bell, 1998). Whereas one in 3 million children who receives the measles, mumps, and rubella (MMR) vaccine might experience a reaction serious enough to cause death, one in 500 children who contract the measles will die. Measles causes the death of 1 million children under age 5 each year (Centers for Disease Control and Prevention, 1999, 2000, 2004).

Myth: The vaccine isn't 100 percent effective, so why subject a child to a painful injection?

Fact: Vaccines are one of the most effective weapons we have against disease. They work in 85 percent to 99 percent of cases and greatly reduce your child's risk of serious illness, particularly when more and more people use them (Centers for Disease Control and Prevention, 2000).

Myth: Immunizations cause bad reactions.

Fact: The most common reactions to vaccines are minor, including redness and swelling where the shot was given, fever, and rash. In rare cases immunizations can trigger seizures or severe allergic reactions, but the risk of these is much lower than that of catching the disease if a child is not immunized (Offit & Bell, 1998).

Myth: Immunization is not needed because these diseases have been eliminated.

Fact: Even though these diseases are rare or nonexistent in the United States, they still flourish in other parts of the world. Children must continue to be vaccinated against them because it is easy to come into contact with illnesses through travel (Centers for Disease Control and Prevention, 1994).

Myth: The MMR vaccine causes autism in children.

Fact: Autism is a complex neurological disorder in which the more visible symptoms used for diagnosis, such as language delays and difficulties in speaking, do not appear until two to three years of age. The MMR vaccine is typically given at about one year or shortly after and so seems to be followed by the "onset" of autism. But early signs of autism can now be observed long before the MMR vaccine (Mars et al., 1998), and studies have consistently failed to show any link between the vaccine and autism (Gilberg & Coleman, 2000; Madsen et al., 2002; Taylor et al., 1999). The timing of the vaccine and the first easily visible signs of autism are simply a coincidence.

One of the most important things parents can do for the continued health and safety of their infant is to have the baby immunized, following an approved schedule for each type of vaccine. Immunizations today are safe and effective and prevent dangerous and often deadly childhood diseases, such as rubella.

Questions for Further Discussion

1. What advice would you give a friend who is having a baby concerning vaccinations?

2. Should children who are not vaccinated be allowed to attend public schools?

3. What can be done to encourage parents to have their children immunized?

COGNITIVE DEVELOPMENT

By the time the average infant has reached the age of 1 year, it has tripled its birth weight and added about another foot to its height. The brain triples its weight in the first two years, reaching about 75 percent of its adult weight. By age 5, the brain is at 90 percent of its adult weight. This increase makes possible a tremendous amount of major advances in **cognitive development**, including the development of thinking, problem solving, and memory.

7.9   *What are three ways of looking at cognitive development?*

PIAGET'S THEORY: FOUR STAGES OF COGNITIVE DEVELOPMENT   Early researcher Jean Piaget developed his theory from detailed observations of infants and children, most especially his own three children. Piaget made significant contributions to the understanding of how children think about the world around them, and shifted the view of children's thinking from that of "little adults" to something quite different from adult thinking. Piaget believed that children form mental concepts or **schemes** as they experience new situations and events. For example, if Sandy points to a picture of an apple and tells her child, "that's an apple," the child forms a scheme for "apple" that looks something like that picture. Piaget also believed that children first try to understand new things in terms of schemes they already possess, a process called *assimilation*. The child might see an orange and say "apple" because both objects are round. When corrected, the child might alter the scheme for apple to include "round" and "red." The process of altering or adjusting old schemes to fit new information and experiences is *accommodation* (Piaget, 1952, 1962, 1983).

Piaget also proposed that there are four distinct stages of cognitive development that occur from infancy to adolescence, as shown in Table 7.3 (Piaget, 1952, 1962, 1983).

The Sensorimotor Stage   The **sensorimotor stage** is the first of Piaget's stages. It concerns infants from birth to age 2. In this stage, infants use their senses and motor abilities to learn about the world around them. At first, infants only have the involuntary reflexes present at birth to interact with objects and people. As their sensory and motor development progresses, they begin to interact deliberately with objects, by grasping, pushing, tasting, and so on. Infants move from simple repetitive actions, such as grabbing their toes to complex patterns such as trying to put a shape into a sorting box.

Simulation
Live!
psych
Piaget's
Conservation
Tasks

infant

cognitive development
the development of thinking, problem solving, and memory.

scheme (plural schemas)
a mental concept formed through experiences with objects and events.

sensorimotor stage
Piaget's first stage of cognitive development in which the infant uses its senses and motor abilities to interact with objects in the environment.

TABLE 7.3   **PIAGET'S STAGES OF COGNITIVE DEVELOPMENT**

Stage	Cognitive Development
Sensorimotor Birth to 2 years old	Children explore the world using their senses and ability to move. They develop object permanence and the understanding that concepts and mental images represent objects, people, and events.
Preoperational 2 to 7 years old	Young children can mentally represent and refer to objects and events with words or pictures and they can pretend. However, they can't conserve, logically reason, or simultaneously consider many characteristics of an object.
Concrete Operational 7 to 12 years old	Children at this stage are able to conserve, reverse their thinking, and classify objects in terms of their many characteristics. They can also think logically and understand analogies but only about concrete events.
Formal Operational 12 years old to adulthood	People at this stage can use abstract reasoning about hypothetical events or situations, think about logical possibilities, use abstract analogies, and systematically examine and test hypotheses. Not everyone can eventually reason in all these ways.

Near the end of this period, infants develop a sense of **object permanence**, the knowledge that an object exists even when it is not in sight. For example, the game of "peek-a-boo" is important in teaching infants that Mommy's smiling face is always going to be behind her hands. This is a critical step in developing language, as words themselves are symbols of things that may not be present. Symbolic thought, which is the ability to represent objects in one's thoughts with symbols such as words, becomes possible by the end of this stage, with children of 2 years capable of thinking in simple symbols and planning out actions.

Is that why it's so easy for little children to believe in Santa Claus and the Tooth Fairy when they're little?

The Preoperational Stage *preschool* The **preoperational stage** (ages 2–7) is a time of developing language and concepts. Children, who can now move freely about in their world, no longer have to rely only on senses and motor skills but now can ask questions and explore their surroundings more fully. Pretending and make-believe play become possible because children at this stage can understand, through symbolic thinking, that a line of wooden blocks can "stand in" for a train. They are limited, however, in several ways. They are not yet capable of logical thought—they can use simple mental concepts but are not able to use those concepts in a more rational, logical sense. They tend to be overwhelmed by what they see, so when children of this age see Santa Claus in a book, on television, or at the mall, Santa Claus becomes real to them. It doesn't occur to them to think about how Santa might get to every child's house in one night or why those toys are the same ones they saw in the store just last week. They may be able to count up to 10 or 20, but they won't understand that in the bottom example in Figure 7.7 both rows have the same number of coins. Instead of counting the coins, they are overwhelmed by the longer *appearance* of the top row of coins.

Another limitation is **egocentrism**, the inability to see the world through anyone else's eyes except one's own. For the preoperational child, everyone else must see what the child sees, and what is important to the child must be important to everyone

◄ Is that why it's so easy for little children to believe in Santa Claus and the Tooth Fairy when they're little?

object permanence
the knowledge that an object exists even when it is not in sight.

preoperational stage
Piaget's second stage of cognitive development in which the preschool child learns to use language as a means of exploring the world.

egocentrism
the inability to see the world through anyone else's eyes.

Type of conservation	Initial presentation	Transformation	Question	Preoperational child's answer
Liquids	Two equal glasses of liquid	Pour one into a taller, narrower glass.	Which glass contains more?	The taller one.
Number	Two equal lines of pennies	Increase spacing of pennies in one line.	Which line has more pennies?	The longer one.

FIGURE 7.7 **Conservation Experiment** A typical conservation task consists of pouring equal amounts of water into two glasses of the same size and shape. When the water from one of these glasses is poured into a taller, narrower glass, children who cannot yet conserve tend to focus (centrate) on the height of the water in the second glass, assuming that the second glass now has more water than the first one. In the second example, pennies are laid out in two equal lines. When one line is moved so that the pennies are further apart, the child who cannot yet conserve will centrate on the length of the top line of pennies and assume that there are actually more pennies in that top line.

centration
in Piaget's theory, the tendency of a young child to focus only on one feature of an object while ignoring other relevant features.

conservation
in Piaget's theory, the ability to understand that simply changing the appearance of an object does not change the object's nature.

irreversibility
in Piaget's theory, the inability of the young child to mentally reverse an action.

concrete operations stage
third stage of cognitive development in which the school-age child becomes capable of logical thought processes but is not yet capable of abstract thinking.

formal operations
Piaget's last stage of cognitive development in which the adolescent becomes capable of abstract thinking.

These concrete operational children, seen in a science class, have begun to think logically and are able to solve many kinds of problems that were not possible for them to solve while in the preoperational stage.

else. For example, 2-year-old Vicki, after climbing out of her crib for the third time, was told by her mother, "I don't want to see you in that living room again tonight!" So Vicki's next appearance was made with her hands over her eyes—if she couldn't see her mother, her mother couldn't see *her*. It would also be egocentric, but completely unselfish, if 4-year-old Kenny wants to give his grandmother an action figure for her birthday because that's what *he* would want.

Remember that children in this stage are also overwhelmed by appearances, as in the coin example. A child who complains that his piece of pie is smaller than his brother's may be quite happy once his original piece is cut into two pieces—now he thinks he has "more" than his brother. He has focused only on the number of pieces, not the actual amount of the pie. Focusing only on one feature of some object rather than taking all features into consideration is called **centration**. In the coin example in Figure 7.7, children of this stage will focus on the length of the top line of coins only and ignore the number of coins. Centration is one of the reasons that children in this stage often fail to understand that changing the way something looks does not change its substance. The ability to understand that altering the appearance of something does not change its amount (as in the coin example), its volume, or its mass is called **conservation**.

Preoperational children fail at conservation not only because they centrate (such as the number of pieces of pie) but also because they are unable to "mentally reverse" actions. This feature of preoperational thinking is called **irreversibility**. For example, if a preoperational child sees liquid poured from a short, wide glass into a tall, thin glass, the child will assume that the second glass holds more liquid. This failure to "conserve" (save) the volume of liquid as it takes on a different shape in the tall, thin glass is not only caused by the child's centration on the height of the liquid in the second glass but also by the inability of the child to imagine pouring the liquid back into the first glass and having it be the same amount again. Similar "reasoning" causes children of this age to assume that a ball of clay, when rolled out into a "rope" of clay, is now greater in mass.

Concrete Operations   In the **concrete operations stage** (ages 7–12), children finally become capable of conservation and reversible thinking. Centration no longer occurs as children become capable of considering all the relevant features of any given object. They begin to think more logically about beliefs such as Santa Claus and ask questions, eventually coming to their own more rational conclusions about the fantasies of early childhood. They are in school, learning all sorts of science and math, and are convinced that they know more than their parents at this point. In fact, they become so logical and focused on "the rules" that they find it difficult to alter rules—their thinking is set in "concrete."

This "concrete" thinking is the major limitation of this stage. Children in this stage are unable to deal effectively with *abstract concepts*. Abstract concepts are those that do not have some physical, touchable reality. For example, "freedom" is an abstract concept. People can define it, they can get a good sense of what it means, but there is no "thing" that they can point to and say, "This is freedom." *Concrete concepts*, which are the kind of concepts understood by children of this age, are about objects, written rules, and real things. Children need to be able to see it, touch it, or at least see it in their heads to be able to understand it.

Formal Operations   In the last of Piaget's stages, **formal operations** (age 12 to adulthood), abstract thinking becomes possible. Teenagers not only understand concepts that have no physical reality, but also they get deeply involved in *hypothetical thinking*, or thinking about possibilities and even impossibilities. "What if everyone just got along?" "If women were in charge of countries, would there be fewer wars?"

Piaget did not believe that everyone would necessarily reach formal operations. Studies show that only about half of all adults in the United States reach formal operations (Sutherland, 1992). That does not mean that the adults who do not develop this type of thinking are somehow less intelligent; it simply means that they use a more practical kind of intelligence that suits their particular lifestyle. Successful college students, however, need formal operational thinking to succeed in their college careers, as most college classes require critical thinking, problem-solving abilities, and abstract thinking based on formal operational skills (Powers, 1984).

Educators have put Piaget's ideas into practice by allowing children to learn at their own pace, by "hands-on" experience with objects, and by teaching concepts to children that are at an appropriate cognitive level (Brooks & Brooks, 1993). But Piaget's theory has also been criticized on several points. Some researchers believe that the idea of distinct stages of cognitive development is not completely correct and that changes in thought are more continuous (Courage & Howe, 2002; Feldman, 2003; Schwitzgebel, 1999; Siegler, 1996). Others point out that preschoolers are not as egocentric as Piaget seemed to believe (Flavell, 1999) and that object permanence exists much earlier than Piaget thought (Aguiar & Baillargeon, 2003; Baillargeon, 1986).

Piaget also focused on the child's cognitive development as if the other people in the child's world were not all that important to the acquisition of knowledge and the development of skills. This is not necessarily wrong; children are able to grasp many ideas and concepts through their own thought processes and interactions with objects, discovering basic principles and characteristics of objects in individual play. In contrast, Vygotsky theorized that other people, acting as teachers and mentors, were a crucial part of the cognitive development of the child (Duncan, 1995).

VYGOTSKY'S THEORY: THE IMPORTANCE OF BEING THERE   Russian psychologist Lev Vygotsky developed a theory of how children think that did not match the prevailing political ideas in Russia. After his death from tuberculosis in 1934, his ideas were suppressed by the government but kept alive by his students and later republished. Vygotsky's pioneering work in developmental psychology has had a profound influence on school education in Russia, and interest in his theories continues to grow throughout the world (Bodrova & Leong, 1996). Vygotsky wrote about children's cognitive development but differed from Piaget in his emphasis on the role of others in cognitive development (Vygotsky, 1934/1962, 1978, 1987). Whereas Piaget stressed the importance of the child's interaction with objects as a primary factor in cognitive development, Vygotsky stressed the importance of social interactions with other people, typically more highly skilled children and adults. Vygotsky believed that children develop cognitively when someone else helps them by asking leading questions and providing examples of concepts in a process called **scaffolding**. In scaffolding, the more highly skilled person gives the learner more help at the beginning of the learning process and then begins to withdraw help as the learner's skills improve (Rogoff, 1994).

Vygotsky also proposed that each developing child has a **zone of proximal development (ZPD)**, which is the difference between what a child can do alone versus what a child can do with the help of a teacher. For example, if little Jenny can do math problems up to the fourth-grade level on her own but with the help of a teacher can successfully work problems at a sixth-grade level, her ZPD is two years. Suzi might be the same age as Jenny (and might even score the same on a traditional IQ test), but if Suzi can only work math problems at a fifth-grade level with the help of the teacher, Suzi's ZPD is not as great as Jenny's. This might be a better way of thinking about intelligence: It isn't what you know (as measured by traditional tests), it's what you *can do*.

Other researchers have applied Vygotsky's social focus on learning to the development of a child's memory for personal (autobiographical) events, finding evidence that children learn the culturally determined structures and purposes of personal stories from

scaffolding
process in which a more skilled learner gives help to a less skilled learner, reducing the amount of help as the less skilled learner becomes more capable.

zone of proximal development (ZPD)
Vygotsky's concept of the difference between what a child can do alone and what that child can do with the help of a teacher.

This boy is helping his younger sister learn to read a book. Vygotsky's view of cognitive development states that the help of skilled others aids in making cognitive advances such as this one.

the early conversations they have with their parents. This process begins with the parent telling the story to the very young child, followed by the child repeating elements of the story as the child's verbal abilities grow. The child reaches the final stage at around age 5 or 6 when the child creates the personal story entirely—an excellent example of scaffolding (Fivush et al., 1996; Fivush & Nelson, 2004; Nelson, 1993). Vygotsky's ideas have been put into practice in education through the use of cooperative learning, in which children work together in groups to achieve a common goal, and in reciprocal teaching, in which teachers lead students through the basic strategies of reading until the students themselves become capable of teaching the strategies to others.

INFORMATION-PROCESSING THEORY   One of the models of memory discussed in Chapter Six came from *the information-processing theory*, a theory that looks at the way people deal with information. Memory is one of the main focal points of the information-processing theory and is an important part of infant development.

Infants do have memory abilities because they can be operantly conditioned right after birth (Lipsitt et al., 1966; Siqueland & Lipsitt, 1966). In one classic study, for example (Lipsitt et al., 1966), researchers found that newborns would suck on a pacifier harder to hear their mother's voice rather than some other woman's voice. Their mother's voice acted as reinforcement for sucking harder, implying that they had formed a memory for what had happened the last time they sucked hard.

Infants also *habituate*, or stop responding to a stimulus that is repeated and unchanging, just as adults do. (L I N K) *to Chapter Three: Sensation and Perception, p. 86.* This means that infants must be able to recognize that a certain stimulus is familiar from one time to the next (Bornstein & Benasich, 1986; Slater et al., 1984). Habituation studies have allowed researchers to determine when infants can perceive color, changes in sounds, and so on (Benasich & Tallal, 1996; Bornstein, 1985).

Whereas infant memory is typically nonverbal, the preschool child is capable of using language to form memories. Short-term memory in the preschool years has a smaller capacity than it will in adulthood and is limited to about three items. To make matters worse, the typical 3-year-old can only remember things for about 3 seconds (Gathercole & Hitch, 1993). Preschool children do not yet know how to use strategies such as rehearsal to extend their short-term memories, nor do they know how to elaborate on information that should be stored in long-term memory. The long-term memories of children in the preschool years consist mostly of *episodic* (personal events) and *procedural* (skill) memories, with *semantic* memories (general knowledge) being limited to basic language concepts and word meanings (Nelson, 1978). (L I N K) *to Chapter Six: Memory, pp. 220–222.*

As children grow up and go to school, they are directly taught by teachers and peers how to use memory strategies. They begin to learn how their own memories work, an understanding called *metamemory.* They learn *control strategies* such as rehearsal and organization, and their capacity for short-term memory approaches that of adults. They can, with effort, be taught the same kind of strategies that aid adults in storing and retrieving memories as their command of language grows (Howe & O'Sullivan, 1990; Pierce & Lange, 2000).

It sounds like language is pretty important in all this, is that right?

STAGES OF LANGUAGE DEVELOPMENT

7.10   *How does language develop?*

The development of language is indeed a very important milestone in the cognitive development of a child because language allows children to think in words rather than just images, to ask questions, to communicate their needs and wants to others, and to form concepts (Bloom, 1974; Bloom, 2000). Early views of language development were based on Skinnerian principles of reinforcement. However, Noam Chomsky argued strongly against this. He proposed a LAD (language acquistion device), an innate "program" that contained a schema for human language. The children matched the language they heard against this schema and, thus, language developed in a well-researched sequence (Chomsky, 1957, 1964, 1981, 1986).

There are several stages of language development that all children experience, no matter what culture they live in or what language they will learn to speak (Brown, 1973):

This infant has already learned some of the basics of language, including the use of gestures to indicate meaning and enhance communication.

language development stages

1. **Cooing:** At around 2 months of age, babies begin to make vowel-like sounds.

2. **Babbling:** At about 6 months, infants add consonant sounds to the vowels to make a babbling sound, which at times can almost sound like real speech.

3. **One-word speech:** Somewhere just before or around age 1, most children begin to say actual words. These words are typically nouns and may seem to represent an entire phrase of meaning. They are called *holophrases* (whole phrases in one word) for that reason. For example, a child might say "Milk!" and mean "I want some milk!" or "I drank my milk!"

4. **Telegraphic speech:** At around a year and a half, toddlers begin to string words together to form short, simple sentences using nouns, verbs, and adjectives. "Baby eat," "Mommy go," "Doggie go bye-bye" are examples of telegraphic speech. Only the words that carry the meaning of the sentence are used.

5. **Whole sentences:** As children move through the preschool years, they learn to use grammatical terms and increase the number of words in their sentences, until by age 6 or so they are nearly as fluent as an adult, although the number of words they know is still limited when compared to adult vocabulary.

PRACTICE **QUIZ:** HOW MUCH DO YOU REMEMBER?

Pick the best answer.

1. Which sense is least functional at birth?
   - **a.** touch
   - **b.** taste
   - **c.** smell
   - **d.** vision

2. What is the first voluntary movement that allows an infant to get from one place to another?
   - **a.** sitting without support
   - **b.** rolling over
   - **c.** raising the head when placed face down
   - **d.** standing

3. Which of the following statements concerning vaccinations is FALSE?
   - **a.** The side effects of vaccines are far less harmful than the effects of the diseases they prevent
   - **b.** Most children today do not need immunizations, as the diseases have been eliminated.
   - **c.** Vaccines are one of the most effective ways to prevent the transmission of the diseases they treat.
   - **d.** Vaccinations are particularly important when traveling to other countries where the diseases still exist.

4. In which of Piaget's stages would a child be who has just developed object permanence?
   - **a.** sensorimotor
   - **b.** preoperational
   - **c.** concrete operational
   - **d.** formal operational

5. Vygotsky defines _____ as the difference between what a child can do alone and what that child can do with help.
   - **a.** scaffolding
   - **b.** habituation
   - **c.** zone of proximal development
   - **d.** metamemory

6. "Daddy go bye-bye" is an example of
   - **a.** telegraphic speech.
   - **b.** babbling.
   - **c.** a holophrase.
   - **d.** cooing.

PSYCHOSOCIAL DEVELOPMENT

7.11 *How do infants and children develop personalities and form relationships with others?*

The psychological and social development of infants and children involves the development of personality, relationships, and a sense of being male or female. Although these processes begin in infancy, they will continue in many respects well into adulthood.

Why are some children negative and whiny while others are sweet and good-natured?

TEMPERAMENT   One of the first ways in which infants demonstrate that they have different personalities (long-lasting characteristics that make each person different from other persons) is in their **temperament**, the behavioral and emotional characteristics that are fairly well established at birth. Researchers (Chess & Thomas, 1986; Thomas & Chess, 1977) have been able to identify three basic temperament styles of infants:

1. **Easy:** "Easy" babies are regular in their schedules of waking, sleeping, and eating and are adaptable to change. Easy babies are happy babies and when distressed are easily soothed.
2. **Difficult:** "Difficult" babies are almost the opposite of easy ones. Difficult babies tend to be irregular in their schedules and are very negative about change of any kind. They are loud, active, and tend to be crabby rather than happy.
3. **Slow to warm up:** This kind of temperament is associated with infants who are less negative, quieter, and more regular than difficult children but who are slow to adapt to change. If change is introduced gradually, these babies will "warm up" to new people and new situations.

Of course, not all babies will fall neatly into one of these three patterns—some children may be a mix of two or even all three patterns of behavior, as Chess and Thomas (1986) discovered. Even so, longitudinal research strongly suggests that these temperament styles last well into adulthood (Korn, 1984), although they are somewhat influenced by the environment in which the infant is raised. For example, a "difficult" infant who is raised by parents who are themselves very loud and active may not be perceived as difficult by the parents, whereas a child who is slow to warm up might be perceived as difficult if the parents themselves like lots of change and noise. The first infant is in a situation in which the "goodness of fit" of the infant's temperament to the parents' temperament is very close, but the parents of the second infant are a poor fit in temperament for that less active child (Chess & Thomas, 1986).

I'd sure hate to have a difficult child! How does a baby's temperament affect the way the parents deal with the baby? A baby's temperament is going to be connected to how parents deal with many issues. Babies with easy temperaments allow parents to plan around their schedules, for example. Planning around the varying sleeping and eating behaviors of a difficult infant is much trickier (Bates, 1989; Sheeber & Johnson, 1992). As children grow, their temperament and how well it matches a parent's own temperament becomes an issue in discipline and in the formation of emotional bonds to the parents or other caregivers (Cameron et al., 1989; Goldsmith & Campos, 1982; Skolnick, 1986).

ATTACHMENT   The emotional bond that forms between an infant and a primary caregiver is called **attachment**. Attachment is a very important development in the social and emotional life of the infant, usually forming within the first six months of the infant's life and showing up in a number of ways during the second six months, such as wariness of strangers and fear of being separated from the caregiver. Although attachment to the mother is usually the primary attachment, infants can attach to fathers and to other caretakers as well.

Mary Ainsworth (Ainsworth, 1985; Ainsworth et al., 1978) came up with a special experimental design to measure the attachment of an infant to the caretaker called the *Strange Situation* (exposing an infant to a series of leave-takings and returns of the

Why are some ▶ children negative and whiny while others are sweet and good-natured?

I'd sure hate to have ▶ a difficult child! How does a baby's temperament affect the way the parents deal with the baby?

temperament
the behavioral characteristics that are fairly well established at birth, such as easy, difficult, and slow to warm up.

attachment
the emotional bond between an infant and the primary caregiver.

mother and a stranger). Through this measurement technique Ainsworth and another colleague identified four attachment styles:

1. **Secure:** Infants labeled as secure were willing to get down from their mother's lap when they first entered the room with their mothers. They explored happily, looking back at their mothers and returning to them every now and then (sort of like "touching base"). When the stranger came in, these infants were wary but calm as long as their mother was nearby. When the mother left, the infants got upset. When the mother returned, the infants approached her, were easily soothed, and were glad to have her back.

   [handwritten: -willing to explore / -upset @ separation / -soothed easily]

2. **Avoidant:** In contrast, avoidant babies, although somewhat willing to explore, did not "touch base." They did not look at the stranger or the mother and reacted very little to her absence or her return, seeming to have no interest or concern.

   [handwritten: -unattached / -explore w/o touching in]

3. **Ambivalent:** The word *ambivalent* means to have mixed feelings about something. Ambivalent babies in Ainsworth's study were clinging and unwilling to explore, very upset by the stranger regardless of the mother's presence, protested mightily when the mother left, and were hard to soothe. When the mother returned, these babies would demand to be picked up, but at the same time push the mother away or kick her in a mixed reaction to her return.

   [handwritten: -upset, angry / -insecure attachment]

4. **Disorganized-disoriented:** In subsequent studies, other researchers (Main & Hesse, 1990; Main & Solomon, 1990) found that some babies seemed unable to decide just how they should react to the mother's return. These disorganized-disoriented infants would approach her but with their eyes turned away from her, as if afraid to make eye contact. In general, these infants seemed fearful and showed a dazed and depressed look on their faces.

It should come as no surprise that the mothers of each of the four types of infants also behaved differently from one another. Mothers of secure infants were loving, warm, sensitive to their infant's needs, and responsive to the infant's attempts at communication. Mothers of avoidant babies were unresponsive, insensitive, and coldly rejecting. Mothers of ambivalent babies tried to be responsive but were inconsistent and insensitive to the baby's actions, often talking to the infant about something totally unrelated to what the infant was doing at the time. Mothers of disorganized-disoriented babies were found to be abusive or neglectful in interactions with the infants.

Attachment is not necessarily the result of the behavior of the mother alone, however. The temperament of the infant may play an important part in determining the reactions of the mothers (Goldsmith & Campos, 1982; Skolnick, 1986). For example, an infant with a difficult temperament is hard to soothe. A mother with this kind of infant might come to avoid unnecessary contact with the infant, as did the mothers of the avoidant babies in Ainsworth's studies.

Critics of Ainsworth's Strange Situation research focus on the artificial nature of the design and wonder if infants and mothers would behave differently in the more familiar surroundings of home, even though Ainsworth's experimental observers also observed the infants and mothers in the home prior to the Strange Situation (Ainsworth, 1985). Other research has found results supporting Ainsworth's findings in home-based assessments of attachment (Blanchard & Main, 1979). Other studies have also found support for the concept of attachment styles and stability of attachment over the first six years of life (Lutkenhaus et al., 1985; Main & Cassidy, 1988; Owen et al., 1984; Wartner et al., 1994). Even adult relationships can be seen as influenced by the attachment style of the adult (Bartholomew, 1990; Hazan & Shaver, 1987).

Evidence that similar attachment styles are found in other cultures demonstrates the need to consider attachment as an important first step in forming relationships with others, one which may set the stage for all relationships that follow (Hu & Meng, 1996; Juffer & Rosenboom, 1997; Keromoian & Leiderman, 1986).

In Ainsworth's secure style of attachment, infants will investigate their surroundings while using their mother as a secure base from which to explore. These toddlers are happily playing in this day care environment while their mothers watch. What do you think would happen if one of the mothers started to leave?

CLASSIC STUDIES IN PSYCHOLOGY
Harlow and Contact Comfort

As psychologists began to study the development of attachment, they at first assumed that attachment to the mother occurred because the mother was associated with satisfaction of primary drives such as hunger and thirst. The mother is always present when the food (a primary reinforcer) is presented, so the mother becomes a secondary reinforcer capable of producing pleasurable feelings. **LINK** *to Chapter Five: Learning, p. 178.*

Psychologist Harry Harlow felt that attachment had to be influenced by more than just the provision of food. He conducted a number of studies of attachment using infant Rhesus monkeys (Harlow, 1958). Noticing that the monkeys in his lab liked to cling to the soft cloth pad used to line their cages, Harlow designed a study to examine the importance of what he termed *contact comfort*, the seeming attachment of the monkeys to something soft to the touch.

He isolated eight baby Rhesus monkeys shortly after their birth, placing each in a cage with two surrogate (substitute) "mothers." The surrogates were actually a block of wood covered in soft padding and terry cloth and a wire form, both heated from within. For half of the monkeys, the wire "mother" held the bottle from which they fed, while for the other half the soft "mother" held the bottle. Harlow then recorded the time each monkey spent with each "mother." If time spent with the surrogate is taken as an indicator of attachment, then learning theory would predict that the monkeys would spend more time with whichever surrogate was being used to feed them.

The results? Regardless of which surrogate was feeding them, the monkeys all spent significantly more time with the soft, cloth-covered surrogate. In fact, all monkeys spent very little time with the wire surrogate, even if this was the one with the bottle. Harlow and his colleagues concluded that "contact comfort was an important basic affectional or love variable" (Harlow, 1958, p. 574).

Harlow's work represents one of the earliest investigations into the importance of touch in the attachment process and remains an important part of human development.

The wire surrogate "mother" provides the food for this infant rhesus monkey. But the infant spends all its time with the soft, cloth-covered surrogate. According to Harlow, this demonstrates the importance of contact comfort in attachment.

Questions for Further Discussion

1. Even though the cloth surrogate was warm and soft and seemed to provide contact comfort, do you think that the monkeys raised in this way would behave normally when placed into contact with other monkeys? How might they react?

2. What might be the implications of Harlow's work for human mothers who feed their infants with bottles rather than breast-feeding?

I've heard that you shouldn't pick a baby up every time it cries— that if you do, it might spoil the baby.

ERIKSON'S THEORY: THE FIRST FOUR STAGES I've heard that you shouldn't pick a baby up every time it cries—that if you do, it might spoil the baby. Unfortunately, a lot of people have not only heard this advice but also acted on it by frequently ignoring an infant's crying, which turns out to be a very bad thing for babies. When a baby under 6 months of age cries, it is an instinctive reaction meant to get the caretaker to tend to the baby's needs—hunger, thirst, pain, and even loneliness. Research has shown that babies whose cries are tended to consistently (that is the infant is fed when hungry, changed when wet, and so on) in the early months are more securely attached as late as age 1 than those infants whose caretakers frequently allow the infants to cry when there is a need for attention—hunger, pain, or wetness, for example (Brazelton, 1992; Heinicke et al., 2000). Erikson, a psychodynamic theorist who emphasized the importance of social relationships in the development of personality, would certainly disagree with letting a baby "cry it out," although allowing an infant who has been fed, changed, burped, and checked to cry on occasion will not damage attachment.

Erikson, who trained as a Freudian psychoanalyst but became convinced that social interactions were more important in development than Freud's emphasis on sexual development, believed that development occurred in a series of eight stages, with the first four of these stages occurring in infancy and childhood (Erikson, 1950; Erikson & Erikson, 1997). LINK to *Chapter Twelve: Theories of Personality, p. 453.* Each stage is an emotional *crisis*, or a kind of turning point, in personality, and the crisis in each stage must be successfully met for normal, healthy psychological development.

7.12 *What happens in Erikson's first four stages of psychosocial development?*

Erikson focused on the relationship of the infant and the child to significant others in the immediate surroundings—parents and then later teachers and even peers. Table 7.4 summarizes the conflict in each of the four stages and some of the implications for future development (Erikson, 1950; Erikson & Erikson, 1997).

4 stages of psychosocial development

trust versus mistrust
first stage of personality development in which the infant's basic sense of trust or mistrust develops as a result of consistent or inconsistent care.

autonomy versus shame and doubt
second stage of personality development in which the toddler strives for physical independence.

initiative versus guilt
third stage of personality development in which the preschool-aged child strives for emotional and psychological independence and attemps to satisfy curiosity about the world.

industry versus inferiority
fourth stage of personality development in which the adolescent strives for a sense of competence and self-esteem.

TABLE 7.4 **ERIKSON'S PSYCHOSOCIAL STAGES OF CHILDHOOD**

Stage	Developmental Crisis	Successful Dealing with Crisis	Unsuccessful Dealing with Crisis
1. Infant Birth to 1 year old	**Trust versus Mistrust** Babies learn to trust or mistrust others based on whether or not their needs—such as food and comfort—are met.	If babies' needs are met, they learn to trust people and expect life to be pleasant.	If babies' needs are not met, they learn not to trust.
2. Toddler 1 to 3 years old	**Autonomy versus Shame and Doubt** Toddlers realize that they can direct their own behavior.	If toddlers are successful in directing their own behavior, they learn to be independent.	If toddlers' attempts at being independent are blocked, they learn self-doubt and shame for being unsuccessful.
3. Preschool Age 3 to 5 years old	**Initiative versus Guilt** Preschoolers are challenged to control their own behavior, such as controlling their exuberance when they are in a restaurant.	If preschoolers succeed in taking responsibility, they feel capable and develop initiative.	If preschoolers fail in taking responsibility, they feel irresponsible, anxious, and guilty.
4. Elementary School Age 5 to 12 years old	**Industry versus Inferiority** When children succeed in learning new skills and obtaining new knowledge, they develop a sense of industry, a feeling of competence arising from their work and effort.	When children succeed at learning new skills, they develop a sense of industry, a feeling of competence and self-esteem arising from their work and effort.	If children fail to develop new abilities, they feel incompetent, inadequate, and inferior.

When do little kids learn ▶ the difference between girls and boys?

GENDER ROLE DEVELOPMENT When do little kids learn the difference between girls and boys? Most children begin to realize the difference between girls and boys at about age 2, and most can say which one they are at that age. But knowing one's *sex* (the physical characteristic of being male or female) is not the same thing as knowing the different behavior expected of a male or a female (**gender**). The behavior that goes along with being male or female is heavily influenced by cultural expectations as well as biology, and is referred to as **gender identity**. (LINK) *to Chapter Ten: Sexuality and Gender, p. 374.*

PRACTICE **QUIZ:** HOW MUCH DO YOU REMEMBER?

Pick the best answer.

1. According to Thomas and Chess, a child that is very irregular in sleeping and eating, resists change, and is negative and loud is labeled a(n) _____ child.
   a. easy
   b. difficult
   c. slow-to-warm-up
   d. negative

2. What kind of attachment, according to Ainsworth, is shown by a baby who explores the room, gets upset when the mother leaves but is easily soothed, and is happy to see the mother when she returns?
   a. secure
   b. avoidant
   c. ambivalent
   d. disorganized-disoriented

3. Mothers who were abusive and/or neglectful were associated with the _____ type of attachment.
   a. secure
   b. avoidant
   c. ambivalent
   d. disorganized-disoriented

4. In Erikson's _____ stage of psychosocial development, the child learns self control and begins to feel more capable.
   a. trust versus mistrust
   b. autonomy versus shame and doubt
   c. initiative versus guilt
   d. industry versus inferiority

Answers: 1-b, 2-a, 3-d, 4-c.

Adolescence

Adolescence is the period of life from about age 13 to the early twenties, during which a young person is no longer physically a child but is not yet an independent, self-supporting adult. In the past, adolescence was always defined as the "teens," from ages 13 to 19. But adolescence isn't necessarily determined by chronological age. It also concerns how a person deals with life issues such as work, family, and relationships. So although there is a clear age of onset, the end of adolescence may come early or late for different individuals.

PHYSICAL DEVELOPMENT

I thought that ▶ adolescence was just the physical changes that happen to your body?

I thought that adolescence was just the physical changes that happen to your body?

PUBERTY

7.13 *What are the changes that occur in puberty?*

The clearest sign of the beginning of adolescence is the onset of **puberty**, the physical changes in both *primary sex characteristics* (growth of the actual sex organs such as the penis or the uterus) and *secondary sex characteristics* (changes in the body such as the development of breasts and body hair) that occur in the body as sexual development reaches its peak. (LINK) *to Chapter Ten: Sexuality*

Reprinted with special permission of King Features Syndicate.

and Gender, pp. 372–373. Puberty occurs as the result of a complex series of glandular activities, stimulated by the "master gland" or the pituitary gland when the proper genetically determined age is reached. Certain psychosocial and environmental factors such as stress, exercise, and nutrition may also have an impact on the timing of puberty (Ellis et al., 1999; Graber et al., 1995). The thyroid gland increases the rate of growth, the adrenal glands and sex glands stimulate the growth of characteristics such as body hair, muscle tissue in males, and the menstrual cycle in girls, for example (Grumbach & Kaplan, 1990; Grumbach & Styne, 1998). Puberty often begins about two years after the beginning of the *growth spurt*, the rapid period of growth that takes place at around age 10 for girls and around age 12 for boys.

In addition to an increase in height, physical characteristics related to being male or female undergo rapid and dramatic change. In fact, the rate of growth and development in puberty approaches that of development in the womb. (L)(I)(N)K *to Chapter Ten: Sexuality and Gender, pp. 372–373.* For females, breast tissue begins to enlarge, hips begin to widen, the uterus grows, and eventually the menstrual cycle begins. For boys, the penis and testicles increase in size, muscles become more defined, and the voice begins to deepen. For both sexes, oily secretions increase (causing pimples and even acne in many teens), hair grows on the pubic area and under the arms, and body odor becomes more noticeable. After about four years, the changes of puberty are relatively complete.

gender
the behavior associated with being male or female.

gender identity
perception of one's gender and the behavior that is associated with that gender.

adolescence
the period of life from about age 13 to the early twenties, during which a young person is no longer physically a child but is not yet an independent, self-supporting adult.

puberty
the physical changes that occur in the body as sexual development reaches its peak.

COGNITIVE DEVELOPMENT

If I'm remembering correctly, teenagers should be in Piaget's formal operations stage. So why don't many teenagers think just like adults? The cognitive development of adolescents is less visible than the physical development but still represents a major change in the way adolescents think about themselves, their peers and relationships, and the world around them.

7.14 *How do adolescents develop formal operations and moral thinking?*

PIAGET'S FORMAL OPERATIONS REVISITED Adolescents, especially those who receive a formal high school education, move into Piaget's final stage of formal operations, in which abstract thinking becomes possible. This cognitive advance is primarily due to the final development of the frontal lobes of the brain, the part of the brain that is responsible for organizing, understanding, and decision making (Giedd et al., 1999; Sowell et al., 1999). Teenagers begin to think about hypothetical situations, leading to a picture of what an "ideal" world would be like. Many become convinced that such a world is possible to achieve if only everyone else would just listen to the teenager.

◀ If I'm remembering correctly, teenagers should be in Piaget's formal operations stage. So why don't many teenagers think just like adults?

personal fable
type of thought common to adolescents in which young people believe themselves to be unique and protected from harm.

imaginary audience
type of thought common to adolescents in which young people believe that other people are just as concerned about the adolescent's thoughts and characteristics as they themselves are.

As discussed earlier, Piaget's concept of stages has been criticized as too simplistic. The evidence now points to gradual, continuous cognitive development (Feldman, 2003; Siegler, 1996). Even so, Piaget's theory has had a tremendous impact in the education of children and in stimulating research about children's cognitive development (Satterly, 1987). Children in varying cultures usually come to understand the world in the way that Piaget described, although the age at which this understanding comes varies from one child to another.

Although headed into an adult style of thinking, adolescents are not yet completely free of egocentric thought. At this time in life, however, their egocentrism shows up in their preoccupation* with their own thoughts. They do a lot of introspection (turning inward) and may become convinced that their thoughts are as important to others as they are to themselves. Two ways in which this adolescent egocentrism emerges are the personal fable and the imaginary audience (Elkind, 1985; Lapsley et al., 1986; Vartanian, 2000).

In the **personal fable**, adolescents have spent so much time thinking about their own thoughts and feelings that they become convinced that they are special, one of a kind, and that no one else has ever had these thoughts and feelings before them. "You just don't understand me, I'm different from you" is a common feeling of teens. The personal fable is not without a dangerous side. Because they feel unique, teenagers may feel that they are somehow protected from the dangers of the world and so do not take the precautions that they should. This may result in an unwanted pregnancy, severe injury or death while racing in a car, drinking and driving, and drug use, to name a few possibilities. "It can't happen to me, I'm special" is a risky but common thought.

The **imaginary audience** shows up as extreme self-consciousness in adolescents. They become convinced that *everyone is looking at them* and that they are always the center of everyone else's world, just as they are the center of their own. This explains the intense self-consciousness that many adolescents experience concerning what others think about how the adolescent looks or behaves.

MORAL DEVELOPMENT   Another important aspect in the cognitive advances that occur in adolescence concerns the teenager's understanding of "right" and "wrong." Harvard University professor Lawrence Kohlberg was a developmental psychologist who, influenced by Piaget and others, developed a theory of the development of

---

*Preoccupation: extreme or excessive concern with something.

"Ben is in his first year of high school, and he's questioning all the right things.'

> **Example of a Moral Dilemma**
>
> A woman in Europe was dying from a rare disease. Her only hope was a drug that a local druggist had discovered. The druggist was charging ten times more than it cost him to make it. Heinz, the husband of the dying woman, had desperately tried to borrow money to buy the drug, but he could borrow only half of the amount he needed. He went to the druggist, told him that his wife was dying, and asked to let him pay the druggist later or to sell the drug at a lower cost. The druggist refused, saying that he had discovered the drug and he was going to make money from it. Later, Heinz broke into the druggist's store to steal the drug for his wife. Should Heinz have done that? Why?

FIGURE 7.8   **Example of a Moral Dilemma**
Source: Kohlberg, 1969, p. 379.

moral thinking. Through looking at how people of various ages responded to stories about people caught up in moral dilemmas (see Figure 7.8 for a typical story). Kohlberg (1973) outlined three levels of moral development, or the knowledge of right and wrong behavior. These levels are summarized in Table 7.5, along with an example of each type of thinking.

Although these stages are associated with certain age groups, adolescents and adults can be found at all three levels. For example, a juvenile delinquent tends to be preconventional in moral thinking.

Kohlberg's theory has been criticized as being male oriented, especially since he used only males in his studies (Gilligan, 1982). Carol Gilligan (1982) proposed that men and women have different perspectives on morality: Men tend to judge as moral the actions that lead to a fair or just end, whereas women tend to judge as moral the actions that are nonviolent and hurt the fewest people. Researchers, however, have not found consistent support for gender differences in moral thinking (Walker, 1991).

TABLE 7.5   KOHLBERG'S THREE LEVELS OF MORALITY

Level of Morality	How Rules Are Understood	Example
Preconventional* morality (typically very young children)	The consequences determine morality; behavior that is rewarded is right, that which is punished is wrong.	A child who steals a toy from another child and does not get caught does not see that action as wrong.
Conventional morality (older children, adolescents, and most adults.)	Conformity to social norms is right; nonconformity is wrong.	A child criticizes his or her parent for speeding because speeding is against the stated laws.
Postconventional morality (about 20 percent of the adult population)	Moral principles determined by the person are used to determine right and wrong and may disagree with societal norms.	A reporter who wrote a controversial story goes to jail rather than reveal the source's identity.

(marginal handwritten annotations: "1", "2", "3" next to the three levels)

*The term *conventional* refers to general standards or norms of behavior for a particular society, which will differ from one social group or culture to another.

preconventional morality
first level of Kohlberg's stages of moral development in which the child's behavior is governed by the consequences of the behavior.

conventional morality
second level of Kohlberg's stages of moral development in which the child's behavior is governed by conforming to the society's norms of behavior.

postconventional morality
third level of Kohlberg's stages of moral development in which the person's behavior is governed by moral principles that have been decided on by the individual and which may be in disagreement with accepted social norms. *not achieved by everyone*

PSYCHOSOCIAL DEVELOPMENT

The development of personality and social relationships in adolescence primarily concerns the search for a consistent sense of self or personal identity.

7.15   *What happens during the adolescent's search for identity?*

Actresses Lindsay Lohan, Amanda Seyfried, Lacey Chabert, and Rachel McAdams on the set of Mark S. Waters's comedy movie *Mean Girls*. This movie portrays the ins and outs of peer pressure and the desire to fit in that many adolescents face.

ERIKSON'S IDENTITY VERSUS ROLE CONFUSION   *5th stage*   The psychosocial crisis that must be faced by the adolescent, according to Erikson, is that of **identity versus role confusion** (see Table 7.6 on page 281). In this stage, the teenager must choose from among many options for values in life and beliefs concerning things such as political issues, career options, and marriage (Feldman, 2003). From those options, a consistent sense of self must be found. Erikson believed that teens who have successfully resolved the conflicts of the earlier four stages are much better "equipped" to resist peer pressure and find their own identity during the adolescent years. Those teens who are not as successful come into the adolescent years with a lack of trust in others, feelings of guilt and shame, low self-esteem, and dependency on others. Peer pressure is quite effective on teenagers who desperately want to "fit in" and have an identity of some sort and who feel that others will not want to be with them unless they conform to the expectations and demands of the peer group. They play the part of the model child for the parents, the good student for the teachers, and the "cool" juvenile delinquent to their friends and will be confused about which of the many roles they play are really their own identity.

PARENT/TEEN CONFLICT   Even for the majority of adolescents who end up successfully finding a consistent sense of self, there will be conflicts with parents. Many researchers believe that a certain amount of "rebellion" and conflict is a necessary step in breaking away from childhood dependence on the parents and becoming a self-sufficient* adult. Although many people think that these conflicts are intense and concern very serious behavior, the reality is that most parent/teen conflict is over trivial issues—hair, clothing, taste in music, and so on. On the really big moral issues, most parents and teens would be quite surprised to realize that they are in agreement.

identity versus role confusion
fifth stage of personality development in which the adolescent must find a consistent sense of self.

*Self-sufficient: able to function without outside aid; capable of providing for one's own needs.

PRACTICE **QUIZ:** HOW MUCH DO YOU REMEMBER?

Pick the best answer.

1. Which of the following statements about adolescence is FALSE?
   a. It begins with the onset of puberty.
   b. It is a time during which the young person is no longer a child but is not yet an adult.
   c. It ends when puberty is complete.
   d. It is a time of preoccupation with one's own thoughts.

2. Which term refers to the feeling of being unique and protected?
   a. formal operations
   b. imaginary audience
   c. personal fable
   d. puberty

3. According to Kohlberg, most adolescents are at the _____ level of morality.
   a. preconventional
   b. conventional
   c. postconventional
   d. preliminary

4. According to Erikson, the task of the adolescent is to
   a. find a consistent sense of self.
   b. develop a sense of initiative.
   c. find intimacy with another.
   d. develop a sense of industry.

5. Which of the following issues typically creates a lot of conflict between most teens and their parents?
   a. serious issues of drug and alcohol use
   b. trivial issues of hair, clothing, and music choices
   c. issues of "postconventional" morality
   d. issues of achieving an identity

Adulthood

PHYSICAL DEVELOPMENT: USE IT OR LOSE IT

When exactly does adulthood begin? Adulthood can be thought of as the period of life from the early twenties until old age and death. Exactly when adulthood begins is not always easy to determine. In some cultures, adulthood is reached soon after puberty (Bledsoe & Cohen, 1993; Ocholla-Ayayo et al., 1993). Some people feel that it begins after graduation from high school, whereas others would say adulthood doesn't begin until after graduation from college. Others define it as the point when a person becomes totally self-sufficient with a job and a home separate from his or her parents. In that case, some people are not adults until their late thirties.

◄ **When exactly does adulthood begin?**

7.16 *What are the physical and cognitive changes that occur during adulthood and aging?*

Adulthood can also be divided into at least three periods: young adulthood, middle age, and late adulthood. Physical changes in young adulthood are relatively minimal. The good news is that the twenties are a time of peak physical health, sharp senses, and mature cognitive abilities. The bad news is that even in the early twenties, the signs of aging are already beginning. Oil glands in the neck and around the eyes begin to malfunction, contributing to wrinkles in those areas near the end of the twenties and beginning of the thirties. The thirties may not bring noticeable changes, but vision and hearing are beginning to decline and by around age 40, bifocal lenses may become necessary as the lens of the eye hardens, becoming unable to change its shape to shift focus. Hearing loss may begin in the forties and fifties but often does not become noticeable until the sixties or seventies, when hearing aids may become necessary.

In the forties, skin begins to show more wrinkles, hair turns gray (or falls out), vision and hearing decline further, and physical strength may begin to decline (Frontera et al., 1991). In the fifties, these changes continue. Throughout middle age, weight may increase as the rate at which the body functions slows down but eating increases and less time is spent exercising. Height begins to decrease, with about half an inch of height lost for every 10 years past age 40, although people with the bone-loss disease osteoporosis may lose up to eight inches or more (Cummings & Melton, 2002). Although sexual functioning usually does not decline in middle age, opportunities for sexual activity may be fewer than in the days of young adulthood (Hodsen & Skeen, 1994; Williams, 1995). Children, mortgages, and career worries can put a damper on middle-age romance.

menopause
the cessation of ovulation and menstrual cycles and the end of a woman's reproductive capability.

MENOPAUSE For women, the forties are a time of great physical changes. At this time in life a woman's reproductive organs become unreliable, as levels of the female hormone estrogen decline in preparation for the end of reproduction. The uterus slowly begins to get smaller in size, menstrual cycles become irregular, and some women begin to experience "hot flashes," a sudden sensation of heat and sweating that may keep them up at night. Interestingly, in some cultures, particularly those in which the diet contains high amounts of soy products, hot flashes are almost nonexistent (Cassidy et al., 1994; Lock, 1994). These changes are called the *climacteric*, and the period of five to ten years over which these changes occur is called *perimenopause*. At an average age of 51, most women will cease ovulation altogether, ending their reproductive years. The cessation of ovulation and the menstrual cycle is called **menopause** (Mishell, 2001).

"Elsie is still waiting for postmenopausal zest to kick in.

Do men go through anything like menopause? ▶

andropause
gradual changes in the sexual hormones and reproductive system of males.

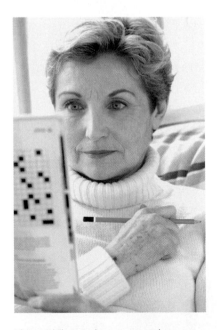

This middle-aged woman works on a crossword puzzle. Mental exercises such as this are one way to keep the brain healthy and fit. What might be some other ways to exercise one's brain?

Do men go through anything like menopause? Men also go through a time of sexual changes, but it is much more gradual and less dramatic than menopause. In males, **andropause** (Carruthers, 2001) may begin in the midtwenties with a decline in several hormones, primarily testosterone (the major male hormone). Physical symptoms are also less dramatic but no less troubling: fatigue, irritability, possible problems in sexual functioning, and reduced sperm count. Males, however, rarely lose all reproductive ability.

EFFECTS OF AGING ON HEALTH   It is in middle age that many health problems first occur, although their true cause may have begun in the young adulthood years. Young adults may smoke, drink heavily, stay up late, and get dark tans, and the wear and tear that this lifestyle causes on their bodies will not become obvious until their forties and fifties.

Some of the common health problems that may show up in middle age are high blood pressure, skin cancer, heart problems, arthritis, and obesity. High blood pressure can be caused by lifestyle factors such as obesity and stress but may also be related to hereditary factors (Rudd & Osterberg, 2002). Sleep problems, such as loud snoring and sleep apnea (in which breathing stops for 10 seconds or more), may also take their toll on physical health. There is some evidence that high blood pressure and apnea are linked, although the link may be as simple as the common cause of obesity (Nieto et al., 2000). The most common causes of death in middle age are heart disease, cancer, and stroke—in that order (McGinnis & Foege, 1993).

COGNITIVE DEVELOPMENT

Intellectual abilities do not decline overall, although speed of processing (or reaction time) does slow down. Compared to a younger adult, a middle-aged person may take a little longer to solve a problem. However, a middle-aged person also has more life experience and knowledge to bring to bear on a problem, which counters the lack of speed. In one study (Salthouse, 1984), for example, older typists were found to outperform younger typists, even though they typed more slowly than the younger subjects. The older typists, because of years of practice, had developed a skill of looking farther ahead in the document they were typing, so that they could type more continuously without looking back at the document. This allowed them to complete their typing more quickly than the younger typists.

CHANGES IN MEMORY   Changes in memory ability are probably the most noticeable changes in middle-age cognition. People find themselves having a hard time remembering a particular word or someone's name. This difficulty in retrieval is probably not evidence of a physical decline (or the beginning of Alzheimer's disease) but is more likely caused by the stresses a middle-aged person experiences and the sheer amount of information that a person of middle years must try to keep straight (Craik, 1994; Launer et al., 1995; Sands & Meredith, 1992).

HOW TO KEEP YOUR BRAIN YOUNG   People who exercise their mental abilities have been found to be far less likely to develop memory problems and even senile dementias such as Alzheimer's in old age (Ball et al., 2002; Colcombe et al., 2003; Fiatarone, 1996). "Use it or lose it" is the phrase to remember. Working challenging crossword puzzles, for example, can be a major factor in maintaining a healthy level of cognitive functioning. Reading, having an active social life, going to plays, taking classes, and staying physically active can all have a positive impact on the continued well-being of the brain (Bosworth & Schaie, 1997; Cabeza et al., 2002; Singh-Manoux et al., 2003).

PSYCHOSOCIAL DEVELOPMENT

7.17 *How do adults deal with the issues of work, relationships, parenting, aging, and death?*

In adulthood, concerns involve career, relationships, family, and approaching old age. The late teens and early twenties may be college years for many, although other young people go to work directly from high school. The task of choosing and entering a career is very serious and a task that many young adults have difficulty accomplishing. A college student may change majors more than once during the first few years of college, and even after obtaining a bachelor's degree many may either get a job in an unrelated field or go on to a different type of career choice in graduate school. Those who are working may also change careers several times (perhaps as many as five to seven times) and may experience periods of unemployment while between jobs.

ERIKSON'S INTIMACY VERSUS ISOLATION: FORMING RELATIONSHIPS In young adulthood, Erikson saw the primary task to be finding a mate. True **intimacy** is an emotional and psychological closeness that is based on the ability to trust, share, and care, while still maintaining one's sense of self. ⓛⓘⓝⓚ *to Chapter Thirteen: Social Psychology, p. 504.* Young adults who have difficulty trusting others and who are unsure of their own identities may find *isolation* instead of intimacy—loneliness, shallow relationships with others, and even a fear of real intimacy. For example, many marriages end in divorce within a few years, with one partner leaving the relationship—and even the responsibilities of parenting—to explore personal concerns and those unfinished issues of identity. Table 7.6 summarizes the last four stages in Erikson's theory.

[handwritten: 6th stage]

intimacy
an emotional and psychological closeness that is based on the ability to trust, share, and care, while still maintaining a sense of self.

TABLE 7.6 ERIKSON'S PSYCHOSOCIAL ADOLESCENT AND ADULT STAGES

Age	State	Developmental Crisis	Successful Dealing with Crisis	Unsuccessful Dealing with Crisis
Adolescence	5	**Identity versus Role Confusion** Adolescents are faced with deciding who or what they want to be in terms of occupation, beliefs, attitudes, and behavior patterns.	Adolescents who succeed in defining who they are and find a role for themselves develop a strong sense of identity.	Adolescents who fail to define their identity become confused and withdraw, or want to inconspicuously blend in with the crowd.
Early adulthood	6	**Intimacy versus Isolation** The task facing those in early adulthood is to be able to share who they are with another person in a close, committed relationship.	People who succeed in this task will have intimate relationships.	Adults who fail at this task will be isolated from other people and may suffer from loneliness.
Middle adulthood	7	**Generativity versus Stagnation** The challenge is to be creative, productive, and nurturant of the next generation.	Adults who succeed in this challenge will be creative, productive, and nurturant, thereby benefiting themselves, their family, community, country, and future generations.	Adults who fail will be passive, and self-centered, feel that they have done nothing for the next generation, and feel that the world is no better off for their being alive.
Late adulthood	8	**Ego Integrity versus Despair** The issue is whether a person will reach wisdom, spiritual tranquility, a sense of wholeness, and acceptance of his or her life.	Elderly people who succeed in addressing this issue will enjoy life and not fear death.	Elderly people who fail will feel that their life is empty and will fear death.

Source: Erikson, 1950/1963, 1968.

generativity
providing guidance to one's children or the next generation, or contributing to the well-being of the next generation through career or volunteer work.

integrity
sense of wholeness that comes from having lived a full life and the ability to let go of regrets; the final completion of the ego.

ERIKSON'S GENERATIVITY VERSUS STAGNATION: PARENTING   In middle adulthood, persons who have found intimacy can now focus outward on others. (See Table 7.6.) Erikson saw this as parenting the next generation and helping them through their crises, a process he called **generativity**. Educators, supervisors, health care professionals, doctors, and community volunteers might be examples of positions that allow a person to be generative. Those who are unable to focus outward but are still dealing with issues of intimacy or even identity are said to be *stagnated*. People who frequently hand the care of their children over to grandparents or other relatives so that they can go out and "have fun" may be unable to focus on anyone else's needs but their own.

PRACTICE **QUIZ:** HOW MUCH DO YOU REMEMBER?

Pick the best answer.

1. The period of five to ten years during which a woman's reproductive system begins to decline is called
   a. climacteric.
   b. perimenopause.
   c. menopause.
   d. all of the above.

2. Which of the following has NOT been shown to help maintain a healthy level of cognitive functioning?
   a. working crossword puzzles
   b. reading
   c. going to plays
   d. sedentary lifestyle

3. Today's worker may change careers as many as _____ times.
   a. one to two
   b. three to five
   c. five to seven
   d. eight to nine

4. According to Erikson, achieving true intimacy is difficult if one's _____ is not already established.
   a. identity
   b. independence
   c. career
   d. marriage

Answers: 1-b, 2-d, 3-c, 4-a.

ERIKSON'S EGO INTEGRITY VERSUS DESPAIR: DEALING WITH MORTALITY   As a person's life enters the stage known as late adulthood, the reality of one's eventual death becomes harder and harder to ignore. (See Table 7.6.) Erikson (1980) believed that at this time, people look back on the life they have lived in a process called a *life review*. In the life review people must deal with mistakes, regrets, and unfinished business. If people can look back and feel that their lives were relatively full and come to terms with regrets and losses, then a feeling of **integrity** or wholeness results. Integrity is the final completion of the identity, or ego. If people have many regrets and lots of unfinished business, they feel *despair*, a sense of deep regret over things that will never be accomplished because time has run out.

Why do people ▶ have to age? What makes us grow older, get wrinkles, and so on?

THEORIES OF AGING

Why do people have to age? What makes us grow older, get wrinkles, and so on? There are a number of theories of why people physically age. One theory states that the hormonal system gets out of balance, causing the immune system that keeps people healthy to start failing. But this theory fails to state why the hormonal system fails in the first place. Another has to do with the effect of outside influences, whereas two others have to do with biological influences.

7.18   *What are the theories of why aging occurs?*

CELLULAR CLOCK THEORY   One of the biologically based theories is the *cellular clock theory* (Hayflick, 1977). In this theory, cells are limited in the number of times they can reproduce to repair damage. Evidence for this theory is the existence of *telomeres*, structures on the ends of chromosomes that shorten each time a cell reproduces (Martin & Buckwalter, 2001). When telomeres are too short, cells cannot reproduce and damage accumulates, resulting in the effects of aging. (Sounds almost like what happens when the warranty is up on a car, doesn't it?)

WEAR-AND-TEAR THEORY The theory that points to outside influences such as stress, physical exertion, and bodily damage is known as the *wear-and-tear theory of aging*. In this theory, the body's organs and cell tissues simply wear out with repeated use and abuse. Damaged tissues accumulate and produce the effects of aging. *Collagen*, for example, is a natural elastic tissue that allows the skin to be flexible. As people age, the collagen "wears out," becoming less and less "stretchy" and allowing skin to sag and wrinkle (Cua et al., 1990; Kligman & Balin, 1989). (This process is not unlike what happens to the elastic in the waistband of one's underwear over time.)

FREE RADICAL THEORY The *free radical theory* is actually the latest version of the wear-and-tear theory in that it gives a biological explanation for the damage done to cells over time. *Free radicals* are oxygen molecules that have an unstable electron (negative particle). They bounce around the cell, stealing electrons from other molecules and increasing the damage to structures inside the cell. As people get older, more and more free radicals do more and more damage, producing the effects of aging (Hauck & Bartke, 2001; Knight, 1998).

I've heard that most older people just want to be left alone and have some peace and quiet. Is that true?

ACTIVITY THEORY **Activity theory** (Havighurst et al., 1968) proposes that an elderly person adjusts more positively to aging when remaining active in some way. Even if a career must end, there are other ways to stay active and involved in life. Elderly people who volunteer at hospitals or schools, those who take up new hobbies or throw themselves full time into old ones, and those who maintain their friendships with others and continue to have social activities have been shown to be happier and live longer than those who withdraw themselves from activity. Contrary to the view of the elderly as voluntarily withdrawing from activities, the withdrawal of many elderly people is not voluntary at all. Others simply stop inviting elderly people to social activities and including them in their lives.

STAGES OF DEATH AND DYING

There are several ways of looking at the process of dying. One of the more well-known theories is that of Elisabeth Kübler-Ross (Kübler-Ross, 1997), who conducted extensive interviews with dying persons and their caretakers.

7.19 What are the stages of death and dying?

Elisabeth Kübler-Ross theorized that people go through five stages of reaction when faced with death (Backer et al., 1994; Kübler-Ross, 1997). These stages are *denial*, in which people refuse to believe that the diagnosis of death is real; *anger*, which is really anger at death itself and the feelings of helplessness to

One way to age successfully and maintain psychological health is to remain active and involved in life. This woman is volunteering in a grade school classroom as a teacher's aide. This not only allows her to feel useful but also helps her to stay mentally alert and socially involved.

I've heard that most older people just want to be left alone and have some peace and quiet. Is that true?

The philosophy behind the hospice concept is to help a person who is dying to face the end of life with dignity and as little pain as possible.

activity theory
theory of adjustment to aging that assumes older people are happier if they remain active in some way, such as volunteering or developing a hobby.

change things; *bargaining*, in which the dying person tries to make a deal, with doctors or even with God; *depression*, which is sadness from losses already experienced (e.g., loss of a job or one's dignity) and those yet to come (e.g., not being able to see a child grow up); and finally *acceptance*, when the person has accepted the inevitable* and quietly awaits death.

Obviously, some people do not have time to go through all of these stages or even go through them in the listed order (Schneidman, 1983, 1994). Some theorists do not agree with the stage idea, seeing the process of dying as a series of ups and downs, with hope on the rise at times and falling to be replaced by a rise in despair or disbelief (Schneidman, 1983, 1994; Weisman, 1972). Still others question the idea of common reactions among dying people, stating that the particular disease or condition and its treatment, the person's personality before the terminal diagnosis, and other life history factors make the process of dying unique and unpredictable (Kastenbaum & Costa, 1977). The danger in holding too strictly to a stage theory is that people may feel there is a "right" way to face death and a "wrong" way, when in fact each person's dying process is unique.

_____

*Inevitable: something that cannot be avoided or escaped.

PRACTICE **QUIZ:** HOW MUCH DO YOU REMEMBER?

Pick the best answer.

1. In Erikson's last crisis, the life review is
   a. a process of assigning blame.
   b. looking back on the life one has lived.
   c. an analysis of one's parents' lives.
   d. the writing of a biography.

2. A sense of completeness of one's ego, or identity, is called
   a. life review.
   b. intelligence.
   c. integrity.
   d. generativity.

3. According to research, if an older person wants to adjust more positively to aging, he or she should
   a. quietly withdraw from social life.
   b. limit his or her range of activities.
   c. disengage from life.
   d. remain active in some way.

4. In which theory of aging do telomeres become the major means of aging cells?
   a. wear-and-tear theory
   b. cellular clock theory
   c. free radical theory
   d. hormonal imbalance theory

5. In the _____ stage of reaction to death and dying, a person may promise to do everything the doctor says if the doctor will say that the person can live a little longer.
   a. denial
   b. anger
   c. bargaining
   d. depression
   e. acceptance

Answers: 1-b, 2-c, 3-d, 4-b, 5-c.

Applying Psychology to Everyday Life: ADHD—Not Just for Children

7.20   *How does attention deficit hyperactivity disorder affect adults?*

Attention deficit hyperactivity disorder, or *ADHD*, has long been recognized and treated in children, but it is only in the last few decades that professionals have come to understand that ADHD can and often does persist into adulthood (Barkley et al., 2001; Goldstein, 1997; Murphy & LeVert, 1995; Nadeau, 1995). The causes of ADHD are not clear, but there is research pointing to a biological basis, and hereditary factors are a large part of that biological influence (Barkley, 1998; Faraone et al., 1993, 2000).

Other contributing factors may include prenatal influences (see the section on teratogens earlier in this chapter), prematurity, high levels of lead in the body, and even prefrontal brain damage. Far from outgrowing this condition, from 30 to 50 percent of all children diagnosed with ADHD will continue to have attentional and behavioral problems as adults that may negatively affect both their professional and personal lives (Barkley et al., 2001; Searight et al., 2000), which could be relieved with treatment.

What are the symptoms of adult ADHD? They are essentially the same as many of the symptoms of children with ADHD but concern issues of work, financial responsibility, and adult activities rather than school and discipline issues that are often seen in children. These symptoms in adults may also be more difficult to separate from other disorders with similar symptoms, such as depression and substance abuse disorders (Searight et al., 2000). Here are a few of the symptoms (Barkley et al., 2001; Wender et al., 2001):

Attention deficit hyperactivity disorder is often thought of as a disorder of childhood, but many adults may also have difficulties staying organized and on task.

- Failing to pay attention to details or making careless mistakes at work.

- Feeling restless, fidgeting with hands or feet, feeling "driven by a motor."

- Failing to listen when spoken to directly, talking excessively, being chronically late.

- Being impulsive and impatient, blurting out answers before questions are completed.

- Losing things needed for tasks, being disorganized, failing to follow through in work, being easily distracted, interrupting others.

The implications for adult life are serious. Adults with ADHD may also suffer from substance abuse disorders such as alcoholism, low self-esteem, anxiety, depression, mood swings, and problems in personal relationships (Hechtman et al., 1984; Wender et al., 2001). Employment may be endangered by what is seen as irresponsible and even disrespectful behavior in the workplace.

What are the treatments for adults with ADHD? Obviously, diagnosis must be the first goal. People who suspect that they might have adult ADHD should consult a medical expert such as a psychiatrist or psychologist who has experience with ADHD. Adults should educate themselves about this disorder and its symptoms so that they can better recognize those symptoms in their own behavior and try to correct or control the behavior.

Medication, just as in some cases of ADHD in children, can also help adults with ADHD, but in addition to treatment with stimulants, treatment of adults with ADHD may include antidepressants as well (Searight et al., 2000). Although children are seldom encouraged to join a support group for their problem, this is an excellent idea for adults with ADHD. Cognitive-behavioral skills training (therapy that focuses on teaching individuals to think about themselves and their lives in a more rational manner, in addition to interpersonal skills), marital counseling, vocational counseling, other forms of psychotherapy, and perhaps changing occupations to ones that more appropriately fit the personality and energy level of the ADHD adult can also be of great value (Goldstein, 1997; Murphy & LeVert, 1995; Nadeau, 1995; Silver, 2000).

Questions for Further Discussion

1. What kinds of symptoms and behavior might show up in a college student with ADHD?

2. What might be appropriate careers for someone with ADHD? What might be careers for which the ADHD adult would not be well suited?

7

CHAPTER SUMMARY

Issues in Studying Human Development

7.1 *What are some of the special research methods used to study development?*

• Three special research methods used in developmental research are the longitudinal design, the cross-sectional design, and the cross-sequential design.

7.2 *What is the relationship between heredity and environmental factors in determining development?*

• The issue of nature (heredity) versus nurture (environmental influences) is the focus of behavioral genetics.

Prenatal Development

7.3 *How do chromosomes, genes, and DNA determine a person's characteristics or disorders?*

• Dominant genes control the expression of a trait, whereas recessive gene traits are only expressed when paired with another recessive gene for the same trait. Almost all traits are the result of combinations of genes working together in a process called polygenic inheritance.

• Chromosome disorders include Down syndrome, Klinefelter's syndrome, and Turner's syndrome, whereas genetic disorders include PKU, cystic fibrosis, sickle cell anemia, and Tay-Sachs disease.

• The fertilized egg cell is called a zygote and divides into many cells, eventually forming the baby.

7.4 *How do twins develop during pregnancy?*

• Monozygotic twins are formed when the zygote splits into two separate masses of cells, each of which will develop into a baby identical to the other. When the two masses do not fully separate, conjoined twins occur.

• Dizygotic twins are formed when the mother's body releases multiple eggs and at least two are fertilized, or when another ovulation occurs even though the mother has already become pregnant.

Psychology in the News: Abby and Britty Hensel, Together for Life

7.5 *How do conjoined twins adjust to being connected to each other?*

• Conjoined twins Abby and Britty Hensel are relatively healthy, well adjusted, and participate fully in many normal activities for young people of their age.

7.6 *What happens during the germinal, embryonic, and fetal periods of pregnancy and what are some hazards in prenatal development?*

• The germinal period is the first two weeks of pregnancy in which the dividing mass of cells (blastocyst) moves down the fallopian tube into the uterus.

• The embryonic period begins at two weeks after conception and ends at eight weeks. The vital organs and structures of the baby form during this period, making it a critical one for teratogens to affect the development of those organs and structures.

• The fetal period is from the beginning of the ninth week until the birth of the baby. During the fetal period, tremendous growth occurs, length and weight increase, and organs continue to become fully functional.

Infancy and Childhood Development

7.7 *What kind of physical changes take place in infancy and childhood?*

• Four critical areas of adjustment for the newborn are respiration, digestion, circulation, and temperature regulation.

• Infants are born with reflexes that help the infant survive until more complex learning is possible. These reflexes include sucking, rooting, Moro (startle), grasping, and Babinski.

• The senses, except for vision, are fairly well developed at birth. Vision is blurry and lacking in full color perception until about 6 months of age. Gross and fine motor skills develop at a fast pace during infancy and early childhood.

Current Issues in Psychology: The Facts and Myths About Immunizations

7.8 *What are the facts and the myths concerning infant immunizations?*

• Immunizations are far less dangerous than the diseases they are designed to prevent and are one of the most effective weapons in the fight against infectious diseases.

7.9 *What are three ways of looking at cognitive development?*

• Piaget's stages include the sensorimotor stage of sensory and physical interaction with the world, preoperational thought in which language becomes a tool of exploration, concrete operations in which logical thought becomes possible, and formal operations in which abstract concepts are understood and hypothetical thinking develops.

• Vygotsky believed that children learn best when being helped by a more highly skilled peer or adult in a process called scaffolding. The zone of proximal development is the difference between the mental age of tasks the child performs without help and those the child can perform with help.

• Information-processing theory states that children improve in their memory capacity as they age, learn to use control strategies to improve memory performance, and gain a better understanding of how their own memories work in a process called metamemory.

7.10 *How does language develop?*

• The stages of language development are cooing, babbling, one-word speech (holophrases), and telegraphic speech. Although some language is learned through imitation and reinforcement, infants may possess a language acquisition device that governs the learning of language during infancy and early childhood.

7.11 *How do infants and children develop personalities and form relationships with others?*

• The three basic infant temperaments are easy (regular, adaptable, and happy), difficult (irregular, nonadaptable, and irritable), and slow to warm up (need to adjust gradually to change).

• The four types of attachment are secure, avoidant (unattached), ambivalent (insecurely attached), and disorganized-disoriented (insecurely attached and sometimes abused or neglected).

Classic Studies in Psychology: Harlow and Contact comfort

• Harlow's classic research with infant Rhesus monkeys demonstrated the importance of contact comfort in the attachment process, contradicting the earlier view that attachment was merely a function of associating the mother with the delivery of food.

7.12 *What happens in Erikson's first four stages of psychosocial development?*

- In trust versus mistrust, the infant must gain a sense of predictability and trust in caretakers or risk developing a mistrustful nature; in autonomy versus shame and doubt the toddler needs to become physically independent.

- In initiative versus guilt the preschool child is developing emotional and psychological independence; in industry versus inferiority school-age children are gaining competence and developing self-esteem.

Adolescence

- Adolescence is the period of life from about age 13 to the early twenties during which physical development reaches completion.

7.13 *What are the changes that occur in puberty?*

- Puberty is a period of about four years during which the sexual organs and systems fully mature and during which secondary sex characteristics such as body hair, breasts, menstruation, deepening voices, and the growth spurt occur.

7.14 *How do adolescents develop formal operations and moral thinking?*

- Adolescents engage in two kinds of egocentric thinking called the imaginary audience and the personal fable.

- Kohlberg proposed three levels of moral development: preconventional morality, conventional morality, and postconventional morality.

7.15 *What happens during the adolescent's search for identity?*

- In Erikson's identity versus role confusion crisis the job of the adolescent is to achieve a consistent sense of self from among all the roles, values, and futures open to him or her.

Adulthood

7.16 *What are the physical and cognitive changes that occur during adulthood and aging?*

- Adulthood begins in the early twenties and ends with death in old age. It can be divided into young adulthood, middle adulthood, and late adulthood.

- The twenties are the peak of physical health; in the thirties the signs of aging become more visible, and in the forties visual problems may occur, weight may increase, strength may decrease, and height begins to decrease.

- Women experience a physical decline in the reproductive system called the climacteric, ending at about age 50 with menopause, when a woman's estrogen levels are at zero and her reproductive capabilities are at an end. Men go through andropause, a less dramatic change in testosterone and other male hormones, beginning in the midtwenties.

- Many health problems such as high blood pressure, skin cancers, and arthritis begin in middle age, with the most common causes of death in middle age being heart disease, cancer, and stroke.

- Reaction times slow down, but intelligence and memory remain relatively stable.

7.17 *How do adults deal with the issues of work, relationships, parenting, aging, and death?*

- Erikson's crisis of young adulthood is intimacy versus isolation, in which the young person must establish an intimate relationship, usually with a mate.

- The crisis of middle adulthood is generativity versus stagnation, in which the task of the middle-aged adult is to help the next generation through its crises, either by parenting, mentoring, or a career that leaves some legacy to the next generation.

- Erikson's final crisis is integrity versus despair, in which an older adult must come to terms with mortality.

7.18 *What are the theories of why aging occurs?*

- Research strongly indicates that remaining active and involved results in the most positive adjustment to aging.

- The cellular clock theory is based on the idea that cells only have so many times that they can reproduce; once that limit is reached, damaged cells begin to accumulate.

- The wear-and-tear theory of physical aging states that as time goes by, repeated use and abuse of the body's tissues cause it to be unable to repair all the damage.

- The free radical theory states that oxygen molecules with an unstable electron move around the cell, damaging cell structures as they go.

7.19 *What are the stages of death and dying?*

- The five stages of reaction to death and dying are denial, anger, bargaining, depression, and acceptance.

Applying Psychology to Everyday Life: ADHD—Not Just for Children

7.20 *How does attention deficit hyperactivity disorder affect adults?*

- Many children with ADHD grow up to be adults with ADHD, affecting their work, relationships, and emotional well-being. ADHD in adults can be treated with medication and/or therapy.

7 KEY TERMS

TEST YOURSELF

Pick the best answer.

1. Differences between age groups would cause the most serious problems for which developmental research method?
  a. longitudinal
  b. cross-cultural
  c. cross-sectional
  d. cross-sequential

2. Cystic fibrosis is a _____ disorder if a person has one gene for the disease but does not have cystic fibrosis.
  a. dominant
  b. recessive
  c. sex-linked
  d. polygenic

3. In _____ syndrome, the twenty-third pair of chromosomes is missing an X, resulting in short, infertile females.
  a. PKU
  b. Down
  c. Klinefelter's
  d. Turner's

4. Which of the following represents dizygotic twins?
  a. One egg is fertilized by two different sperm.
  b. One egg splits and is then fertilized by two different sperm.
  c. Two eggs get fertilized by two different sperm.
  d. Two eggs are fertilized by the same sperm.

5. The spongelike organ that provides nourishment for the growing baby and filters away waste products is called the
  a. fallopian tube.
  b. uterus.
  c. umbilical cord.
  d. placenta.

6. The critical period for pregnancy is the
  a. germinal period.
  b. embryonic period.
  c. fetal period.
  d. last trimester.

7. Mary's baby was born with a smaller than normal head, some facial malformations, and is mentally retarded. Mary most likely _____ during her early pregnancy.
  a. ate fish with mercury in it
  b. drank too much caffeine
  c. drank alcohol
  d. smoked marijuana

8. Which of the following is NOT a risk associated with failing to have a child immunized?
  a. The child may get a deadly disease such as measles or diphtheria.
  b. The child may become immune to the diseases.
  c. Others may be exposed to the diseases that the child can develop.
  d. The child will be more likely to develop a disease with a high fever that can cause brain damage.

9. In the _____ reflex, the baby moves its head toward any light touch to its face.
  a. sucking
  b. startle
  c. rooting
  d. grasping

10. Which of the newborn's senses is the most fully developed at birth?
  a. hearing
  b. vision
  c. smell
  d. touch

11. At what age can the typical infant sit without support?
  a. 3 months
  b. 6 months
  c. 8 months
  d. 12 months

12. By the age of five, the brain is at _____ percent of its adult weight.
  a. 25
  b. 50
  c. 90
  d. 100

13. In which of Piaget's stages does the child become capable of understanding conservation?
  a. sensorimotor
  b. preoperational
  c. formal operational
  d. concrete operational

14. According to Vygotsky, giving a child help in the form of asking leading questions and providing examples is called
  a. scaffolding.
  b. the zone of proximal development.
  c. private speech.
  d. habituation.

15. As children grow from the preschool years into middle childhood, the big changes in the capacity of short-term memory are most likely due to an increase in the use of
  a. metamemory.
  b. control strategies.
  c. habituation.
  d. visual-recognition memory.

16. Little Kashif held his empty cup up to his mother and said, "Milk!" His use of this word is labeled
  a. a holophrase.
  b. telegraphic speech.
  c. babbling.
  d. cooing.

17. As an infant, Liz never liked change, but if you introduce new things gradually, she will eventually accept them without too much fuss. Liz is most likely
  a. easy.
  b. difficult.
  c. slow to warm up.
  d. securely attached.

18. In the Strange Situation, _____ babies were clinging, unwilling to explore, very upset when Mommy left the room, and demanded to be held but pushed her away at the same time when she returned.
a. secure
b. avoidant
c. ambivalent
d. disorganized-disoriented

19. In Erikson's crisis of _____, children are developing a sense of competence and self-esteem.
a. trust versus mistrust
b. autonomy versus shame and doubt
c. initiative versus guilt
d. industry versus inferiority

20. Brandon, at age 3, noticed that only girls seemed to play with things that were pink. Other boys in his preschool would not touch toys that were pink. Now he refuses to let his mother take him down the toy store section that has all the dolls, and when she asks him why, he says, "Because they're all pink, and pink toys are for girls!" Brandon's behavior is best explained by
a. social learning theory.
b. gender schema theory.
c. gender learning theory.
d. social schema theory.

21. Samantha refuses to go to school because her chin has a "huge" pimple on it and she is afraid that everyone will laugh at her and point. Samantha is a victim of
a. the imaginary audience.
b. the personal fable.
c. abstract egocentrism.
d. formal operations.

22. Erikson's fifth stage of psychosocial development is
a. identity versus role confusion.
b. intimacy versus isolation.
c. generativity versus stagnation.
d. integrity versus despair.

23. Vision and hearing begin to decline in the
a. twenties.
b. thirties.
c. forties.
d. fifties.

24. A decline in testosterone in the midtwenties is called
a. perimenopause.
b. menopause.
c. climacteric.
d. andropause.

25. The crisis of middle adulthood, according to Erikson, is
a. identity versus role confusion.
b. intimacy versus isolation.
c. generativity versus stagnation.
d. integrity versus despair.

26. Collagen, an elastic tissue that becomes less elastic as we get older, is a good example of the _____ theory of aging.
a. wear-and-tear
b. cellular clock
c. free radical
d. active

27. According to Kübler-Ross, when bargaining fails, _____ usually results.
a. denial
b. anger
c. depression
d. acceptance

28. Which of the following statements about adult ADHD is true?
a. Children with ADHD almost always grow out of it by adulthood.
b. The symptoms of ADHD in adulthood are similar to those in children.
c. ADHD adults rarely need any treatment at all.
d. Medication is not recommended as a treatment for adult ADHD.

Answers: 1-c, 2-b, 3-d, 4-c, 5-d, 6-b, 7-c, 8-b, 9-c, 10-d, 11-b, 12-c, 13-d, 14-a, 15-b, 16-a, 17-c, 18-c, 19-d, 20-b, 21-a, 22-a, 23-b, 24-d, 25-c, 26-a, 27-c, 28-b.

For more sample quizzes and other review activities that will help you get a better grade, be sure to check out your accompanying study guide. To access tests and your own personalized study plan that will help you focus on the areas you need to master before your next class test, be sure to go to the on-line Psychology web site available with the access code packaged with your book.

CONCEPT MAP

Developmental Research Methods

Longitudinal design: same participants over a long period

Cross-sectional design: participants of different ages

Cross-sequential design: participants first studied cross-sectionally and then followed for 6 years

7.1

Heredity and Environmental Factors

▸ Behavioral genetics—nature (hereditary factors) vs. nurture (environmental influences)
▸ Development occurring as gradually vs. discrete stages

7.2

Prenatal Development

Infancy and Childhood Development

Chromosomes, Genes, DNA and a Person's Characteristics or Disorders

Dominant genes: control the expression of a trait

Recessive genes: expressed when paired with another recessive gene

Traits: results of combinations

Chromosome disorders: Down syndrome, Klinefelter's syndrome, Turner's syndrome

Genetic disorders: PKU, cystic fibrosis, sickle-cell anemia, Tay-Sachs disease

Zygote: fertilized and dividing egg cell

7.3

Physical Changes in Infancy and Childhood

Four critical areas of adjustment for the newborn: respiration, digestion, circulation, and temperature regulation

Infant reflexes aid infant survival: Sucking, Rooting, Moro (startle), Grasping, and Stepping

Senses: except for vision, are fairly well developed at birth.

Vision: blurry and lacking in full color perception until infant is 6 months old

Gross and fine motor skills: develop at a fast pace during infancy and early childhood

7.7

Facts/Myths Concerning Infant Immunizations

▸ Immunizations far less dangerous than the diseases they prevent
▸ Most effective weapons in the fight against infectious diseases

7.8

Monozygotic and Dizygotic Twins

Identical twins

1 Accounting for about 1 to 250 births, these are created when a single egg is fertilized by one sperm.

2 The egg splits into halves. Each develops into a fetus with the same genetic composition.

Fraternal twins

1 Twice as common as identicals, fraternals arise when two eggs are released at once.

2 If both are fertilized by separate sperm, two fetuses form. Genetically they are just ordinary siblings.

7.4

Three Views of Cognitive Development

Piaget's Stages:

▸ **Sensorimotor stage:** sensory and physical interaction
▸ **Preoperational thought:** language—tool of exploration
▸ **Concrete operations:** logical thought possible
▸ **Formal operations:** abstract concepts and hypothetical thinking

Vygotsky's theory:

▸ **Scaffolding:** children learn when helped by peer/adult
▸ **Zone of proximal development:** difference between mental age of tasks child performs without help and with help

Information processing theory:

▸ Children improve in memory capacity as they age
▸ Control strategies improve memory performance
▸ Metamemory: children gain a better understanding of how their own memories work

7.9

Germinal Period, Embryonic, and Fetal Periods—Hazards in Prenatal Development

Germinal period:

▸ First two weeks of pregnancy
▸ Dividing mass of cells (blastocyst) moves down fallopian to uterus

Embryonic period:

▸ Two weeks after conception to eight weeks.
▸ Vital organs and structures form during this period,
▸ Teratogens likely to affect the development of organs & structures

Fetal period:

▸ Beginning of ninth week until birth
▸ Tremendous growth occurs, length and weight increase
▸ Organs continue to become fully functional

7.6

Stages of Language Development

cooing, babbling, one-word speech (holophrases), and telegraphic speech

Language Learning

▸ Some learning through reinforcement and imitation
▸ Infants may possess a language acquisition device (LAD) that governs learning of language during infancy and early childhood

7.10

Development of Personalities and Forming Relationships

Three basic infant temperaments:
- **Easy** (regular, adaptable, and happy)
- **Difficult** (irregular, nonadaptable, irritable)
- **Slow to warm up** (need to adjust gradually)

Four types of attachment: Secure, avoidant, ambivalent, disorganized.

7.11

Erikson's First Four Stages of Psychosocial Development

1. **Trust vs. mistrust:** predictability/trust vs. mistrust
2. **Autonomy vs. shame and doubt:** physical independence
3. **Initiative vs. guilt:** emotional/psychological independence
4. **Industry vs. inferiority:** competence and developing self-esteem

Contact comfort and attachment:
- Harlow's classic research demonstrated the importance of contact comfort
- Contradicted earlier view that attachment was based on mother's food delivery

HARLOW'S EXPERIMENT

7.12

Learning Gender Roles

- Social learning theorists: imitation and reinforcement lead to correct gender behavior
- Gender schema theorists: gender as a concept that is developed over time

7.13

Adolescence

From age 13 to the early twenties— physical development reaches completion

Puberty

- Period of about four years during which the sexual organs and systems fully mature
- Secondary sex characteristics such as body hair, breasts, menarche, deepening voice, and growth spurt occur

7.14

Formal Operations and Moral Thinking

Adolescents engage in two kinds of egocentric thinking: Imaginary audience and personal fable.

Kohlberg: Three levels of moral development: preconventional, conventional, and postconventional morality

7.15

Erikson's Adolescent Identity Versus Role Confusion Crisis

Adolescents try to achieve consistent sense of self from among all the roles, values, and futures open to them

7.16

Adulthood

Adulthood and Aging

Characteristics of aging:
- Twenties: peak of physical health
- Thirties: aging becomes more visible
- Forties: visual problems occur, weight increases, strength and height decrease

Gender issues:
- Women: decline in reproductive capacity ending at about age 50 with menopause
- Men: andropause changes in testosterone and other male hormones

Health problems in aging:
- High blood pressure, arthritis, cancer, skin cancers, heart disease, strokes
- Reaction times slow, intelligence/memory remain stable

7.17

ADHD and Adults

- Children with ADHD grow up to be adults with ADHD
- Affects work, relationships, and emotional well-being
- Can be treated with medication and/or therapy

7.20

Erikson's Stages in Adulthood

Intimacy vs. isolation: young adulthood— establishing intimate relationships

Generativity vs. stagnation: middle adulthood—help the next generation through its crises

Integrity vs. despair: final crisis—coming to terms with mortality

7.18

Theories of Aging

Cellular clock theory: cells have limited reproduction times

Wear-and-tear theory: repeated use and abuse of the body's tissues cause it to be unable to repair all the damage

Free radical theory: oxygen molecules with unstable electrons move around the cell, damaging cell structures as they go

7.19

8

Cognition: Thinking, Intelligence, and Language

How Life Goes On: The Story of Chris Burke

Chris Burke is an actor and a rather successful one at that. He starred in the ABC-TV series *Life Goes On* as Corky Thatcher, winning a Golden Globe award for his performance. A New York City school is named in his honor, he has received numerous film awards, and he continues to guest star in television shows. In 1992, he wrote his autobiography, *A Special Kind of Hero*.

Not too bad for a young man whose parents were told to place him in an institution at birth. Frank and Marian Burke refused to listen to the doctors and treated Chris just like their other children. Chris Burke was born with a condition called **Down syndrome**, a disorder that usually produces a moderate to severe developmental delay as well as some physical abnormalities. In the past, many Down syndrome children were placed in institutions, where they usually made very little progress.

Children diagnosed with Down syndrome today have more educational opportunities and can accomplish much more than was previously believed (Hassold & Patterson, 1998; American Association on Mental Retardation, 2002).

Chris was challenged by his family to always do his best and to be more than the doctors had said he could. He met that challenge head on (Milligan, 1998). An interviewer once asked Chris what it was like for him to live with Down syndrome. He answered, "Having Down syndrome is like being born normal. . . . We are all born in different ways, that is the way I can describe it. I have a normal life." His advice to parents with children born with Down syndrome? "Don't give up on the child. Give the child an education . . . [and] daily love" (Milligan, 1998).

Why study the nature of thought?

To fully understand how we do any of the things we do (such as learning, remembering, and behaving), we need to understand how we think. How do we organize our thoughts? How do we communicate those thoughts to others? What do we mean by intelligence? Why are some people able to learn so much faster than others?

How People Think

thinking (cognition)
mental activity that goes on in the brain when a person is organizing and attempting to understand information and communicating information to others.

mental images
mental representations that stand for objects or events and have a picture-like quality.

Before discussing intelligence and its variations (including Down syndrome), let's talk about what it means to think. People are thinking all the time and talking about thinking as well: "What do you think?" "Let me think about that." "I don't think so." What does it mean to think? **Thinking**, or **cognition** (from a Latin word meaning "to know"), can be defined as mental activity that goes on in the brain when a person is processing information—organizing it, understanding it, and communicating it to others. Thinking includes memory, but it is much more. When people think, they are not only aware of the information in the brain but also are making decisions about it, comparing it to other information, and using it to solve problems.

Thinking also includes more than just a kind of verbal "stream of consciousness." When people think, they often have images as well as words in their minds.

Experiment
Live! psych

Mental Rotation

1st step

MENTAL IMAGERY

8.1 *How do people use mental images to think?*

> So more windows means more time to count them in your head? I guess mentally "walking" through a bigger house in your head would take longer than "walking" ▶ through a smaller one.

As stated in Chapter Six, short-term memories are encoded in the form of sounds and also as visual images, forming a mental picture of the world. Thus, **mental images** (representations that stand in for objects or events and have a picture-like quality) are one of several tools used in the thought process.

Here's an interesting demonstration of the use of mental images. Get several people together and ask them to tell you *as fast as they can* how many windows are in the place where they live. Usually you'll find that the first people to shout out an answer have fewer windows in their houses than the ones who take longer to respond. You'll also notice that most of them look up, as if looking at some image that only they can see. If asked, they'll say that to determine the number of windows, they pictured where they live and simply counted windows as they "walked through" the image.

So more windows means more time to count them in your head? I guess mentally "walking" through a bigger house in your head would take longer than "walking" through a smaller one. That's what researchers think, too. They have found that it does take longer to view a mental image that is larger or covers more distance than a smaller, more compact one (Kosslyn, Ganis, et al., 2001; Ochsner & Kosslyn, 1994). In one study (Kosslyn et al., 1978), participants were asked to look at a map of an imaginary island (see Figure 8.1). On this map were several landmarks, such as a hut, a lake, and a grassy area. After viewing the map and memorizing it, participants were asked to imagine a specific place on the island, such as the hut, and then to "look" for another place, like the lake. When they mentally "reached" the second place, they pushed a button that recorded reaction time. The greater the physical distance on the map between the two locations, the longer it took participants to scan the image for the second location. The participants were looking at their mental image and scanning it just as if it were a real, physical map.

Mental imagery is something people use every day. It helps them remember where they parked the car, find furniture that fits the space they have for it, and relax by creating daydreams. As discussed in the introduction to this text mental imagery is also a very useful tool for remembering things (Paivio, 1971, 1986; Thomas, 2001). L I N K to *Introduction.*

People are even able to mentally rotate, or turn, images (Shepherd & Metzler, 1971). Kosslyn (1983) asked subjects questions such as the following: "Do frogs have lips and a stubby tail?" He found that most people reported visualizing a frog, starting with the face ("no lips") and mentally rotating the image to look for the stubby tail ("yes, there it is").

In the brain, creating a mental image is almost the opposite of seeing an actual image. With an actual image, the information goes from the eyes to the visual cortex of the occipital lobe and is processed, or interpreted, by other areas of the cortex that compare the new information to information already in memory. L I N K to *Chapter Two: The Biological Perspective, p. 67.* In creating a mental image, other areas of the cortex associated with stored knowledge send information to the visual cortex, where the image is perceived in the "mind's eye" (Kosslyn et al., 1993; Sparing et al., 2002). PET scans show areas of the visual cortex being activated during the process of forming an image, providing evidence for the role of the visual cortex in mental imagery (Kosslyn et al., 1993, 1999, 2001).

CONCEPTS Step 2

Images are not the only way in which we think, are they? Mental images are only one form of mental representation. Another aspect of thought processes is the use of concepts. **Concepts** are ideas that represent a class or category of objects, events, or activities. People use concepts to think about objects or events without having to think about all the specific examples of the category. For example, a person can think about "fruit" without thinking about every kind of fruit there is in the world, which would take far more effort and time.

8.2   *What is the nature of a concept?*

Concepts not only contain the important features of the objects or events people want to think about, but also they allow the identification of new objects and events that may fit the concept. For example, dogs come in all shapes, sizes, colors, and lengths of fur. Yet most people have no trouble recognizing dogs as dogs, even though they may never before have seen that particular breed of dog. Friends of the author have a dog called a Briard, which is a kind of sheepdog. In spite of the fact that this dog is easily the size of a small pony, the author had no trouble recognizing it as a dog, although a huge and extremely shaggy one.

FIGURE 8.1   **Kosslyn's Fictional Island**   In Kosslyn's 1978 study, participants were asked to push a button when they had imagined themselves moving from one place on the island to another. As the graph below the picture shows, longer physical distances on the image took longer times for the participants to complete the task.
Source: Kosslyn et al., 1978.

◄ Images are not the only way in which we think, are they?

concepts
ideas that represent a class or category of objects, events, or activities.

Although these apples are different colors, they are all round, similar in size and shape, and symbolize for many people the prototypical fruit. The red apples in particular are a prototype for their category.

Concepts can represent many different levels of objects or events. Concepts can be of a very general form, such as "fruit," called a **superordinate*** concept. The concept "apple" is more specific but can still be a **basic level type**. "Pear," "orange," and "watermelon" would also be basic level. A "Granny Smith apple" would be a **subordinate**** concept, or one that is the most specific example (Mandler, 2000, 2003; Rosch et al., 1976).

Concepts can have very strict definitions, such as the concept of a square as a shape with four equal sides. Concepts defined by specific rules or features are called **formal concepts** and are pretty rigid. To be a square, for example, an object must be a two-dimensional figure with four equal sides and four angles adding up to 360 degrees. If an object has those features, it is not only a square, but also it cannot be anything BUT a square. Science and mathematics are full of formal concepts: acid, limestone, asteroid, and wavelength are a few scientific formal concepts; in geometry, there are triangles, squares, rectangles, polygons, and lines. In psychology, there are double-blind experiments, sleep stages, and conditioned stimuli, to name a few. Each of these concepts must fit very specific features to be considered true examples.

> **But what about things that don't easily fit the rules or features? What if a thing has some, but not all, features of a concept?**

But what about things that don't easily fit the rules or features? What if a thing has some, but not all, features of a concept? In everyday life, people are surrounded by objects, events, and activities that are not as clearly defined as the concepts of science and mathematics. What is a vehicle? Cars and trucks leap immediately to mind, but what about a bobsled? How about a raft? Those last two objects aren't quite as easy to classify as vehicles immediately, but they fit some of the rules for "vehicle." These are examples of **natural concepts**, concepts people form not as a result of the application of a strict set of rules, but rather as the result of their experiences with these concepts in the real world (Ahn, 1998; Barton & Komatsu, 1989; Gelman, 1988; Rosch, 1973). Whereas formal concepts are well defined, natural concepts are "fuzzy" (Hampton, 1998). Is a whale a fish or a mammal? Is a platypus a mammal or a bird? People may know that whales are technically mammals, but whales also share a lot of fish-defining characteristics. Mammals have fur; birds lay eggs and have beaks. The duck-billed platypus has and does all three (has fur, lays eggs, and has a beak), yet it is classified as a mammal, not a bird.

Natural concepts are important in helping people understand their surroundings in a less structured manner than the formal concepts that are taught in school, and they form the basis for interpreting those surroundings and the events that may occur in everyday life.

superordinate concept
the most general form of a type of concept, such as "animal" or "fruit."

basic level type
an example of a type of concept around which other similar concepts are organized, such as "dog," "cat," or "pear."

> **Everyone's experiences aren't going to be the same, right? So how do people develop those basic concepts if they are all having different experiences?**

Everyone's experiences aren't going to be the same, right? So how do people develop those basic concepts if they are all having different experiences?

PROTOTYPES   When someone says "fruit," what's the first image that comes to mind? More than likely, it's a specific kind of fruit like an apple, pear, or orange. It's less likely that someone's first impulse will be to say "guava" or "papaya," or

---

*Superordinate: ranked highest in status or standing.

**Subordinate: ranked lowest in status or standing.

even "banana," unless that person comes from a tropical area. In the United States, apples are a good example of a **prototype**, a concept that closely matches the defining characteristics of the concept (Mervis & Rosch, 1981; Rosch, 1977). Fruit is sweet, grows on trees, has seeds, and is usually round—all very apple-like qualities. Coconuts are sweet and they also grow on trees, but many people in the Northern Hemisphere have never actually seen a coconut tree. They have more likely seen countless apple trees. So people who do have very different experiences with fruit, for instance, will have different prototypes, which are the most basic examples of concepts.

A duck-billed platypus is classified as a mammal yet shares features with birds, such as webbed feet and a bill and also lays eggs. The platypus is an example of a "fuzzy" natural concept. Courtesy of Dave Watts, Nature Picture Library.

What about someone who lives in a tropical area? Would his or her prototype for fruit be different? And would people's prototypes be different in different cultures? More than likely, prototypes develop according to the exposure a person has to objects in that category. So someone who grew up in an area where there are many coconut trees might think of coconuts as more prototypical than apples, whereas someone growing up in the northwestern United States would more likely see apples as a prototypical fruit (Aitchison, 1992). Research suggests that what a person knows about a particular type of object does affect the person's prototype for the category (Lynch et al., 2000; Shafto & Coley, 2003). For example, people who are not that knowledgeable about trees tend to pick a tree that is found where they live as the prototypical tree (such as an oak tree), whereas experts in tree identification tend to select trees that have more ideal characteristics (tall, for example) rather than one specific type of tree. For nonexperts, familiarity was important in selecting a prototype, but for the experts central characteristics more representative of trees in general were the standard (Lynch et al., 2000).

Culture also matters in the formation of prototypes. Research on concept prototypes across various cultures found greater differences and variations in prototypes between cultures that were dissimilar, such as Taiwan and American, than between cultures that are more similar, such as Hispanic Americans and non–Hispanic Americans living in Florida (Lin & Schwanenflugel, 1995; Lin, Schwanenflugel, & Wisenbaker, 1990; Schwanenflugel & Rey, 1986).

How do prototypes affect thinking? People tend to look at potential examples of a concept and compare them to the prototype to see how well they match—which is why it takes most people much longer to think about olives and tomatoes as fruit because they aren't sweet, one of the major characteristics of the prototype of fruit (Rosch & Mervis, 1975). Table 8.1 presents some prototypical examples of the concepts "vehicle" and "fruit" as well as less typical examples.

No matter what type, concepts are one of the ways people deal with all the information that bombards* their senses every day and allows them to organize their perceptions of the world around them. Concepts not only help people think, but also they are an important tool in *problem solving*, a type of thinking that people engage in every day and in many different situations.

*Bombards: attacks again and again.

�◀ **What about someone who lives in a tropical area? Would his or her prototype for fruit be different? And would people's prototypes be different in different cultures?**

subordinate concept
the most specific category of a concept, such as one's pet dog or a pear in one's hand.

formal concepts
concepts that are defined by specific rules or features.

natural concepts
concepts people form as a result of their experiences in the real world.

prototype
an example of a concept that closely matches the defining characteristics of a concept.

problem solving
process of cognition that occurs when a goal must be reached by thinking and behaving in certain ways.

trial and error (mechanical solution)
problem-solving method in which one possible solution after another is tried until a successful one is found.

algorithms
very specific, step-by-step procedures for solving certain types of problems.

Simulation
Live! psych

Problem Solving

TABLE 8.1 **FROM PROTOTYPES TO ATYPICAL EXAMPLES (MOST TYPICAL TO LEAST TYPICAL)**	
Vehicles	**Fruit**
Car	Orange
Bus	Apple
Train	Peach
Bicycle	Grape
Airplane	Strawberry
Boat	Grapefruit
Wheelchair	Watermelon
Sled	Date
Skates	Tomato
Elevator	Olive

Source: Adapted from Rosch & Mervis, 1975, p. 576.

▶ Problem solving is certainly a big part of any college student's life. Is there any one "best" way to go about solving a problem?

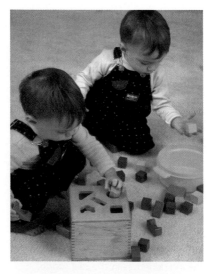

These children try one piece after another until finding the piece that fits. This is an example of trial-and-error learning.

PROBLEM SOLVING AND DECISION MAKING

Problem solving is certainly a big part of any college student's life. Is there any one "best" way to go about solving a problem? Put a coin in a bottle and then cork the opening. How can you get the coin out of the bottle without pulling out the cork or breaking the bottle? (For the solution, see p. 300.)

As stated earlier, images and concepts are mental tools that can be used to solve problems. For the preceding problem, you are probably trying to create an image of the bottle with a coin in it. Problem solving occurs when a goal must be reached by thinking and behaving in certain ways. Problems range from figuring out how to cut a recipe in half to understanding complex mathematical proofs to deciding what to major in at college. There are several different ways in which people can think in order to solve problems.

8.3 *What methods do people use to solve problems and make decisions?*

TRIAL AND ERROR (MECHANICAL SOLUTIONS) One method is to use **trial and error**, also known as a **mechanical solution**. Trial and error refers to trying one solution after another until finding one that works. For example, if Shelana has forgotten the PIN number for her online banking Web site, she can try one combination after another until she finds the one that works, if she has only a few such PINs that she normally uses. Mechanical solutions can also involve solving by *rote*, or a learned set of rules. This is how word problems were solved in grade school, for example. One type of rote solution is to use an algorithm.

ALGORITHMS **Algorithms** are specific, step-by-step procedures for solving certain types of problems. Algorithms will always result in a correct solution, if there is a correct solution to be found, and you have enough time to find it. Mathematical formulas are algorithms. When librarians organize books on bookshelves, they also use an algorithm: Place books in alphabetical order within each category, for example. Many puzzles, like a Rubik's Cube®, have a set of steps that, if followed exactly, will always result in solving the puzzle. But algorithms aren't always practical to use.

For example, if Shelana didn't have a clue what those four numbers might be, she *might* be able to figure out her forgotten PIN number by trying *all possible combinations* of four digits, 0 through 9. She would eventually find the right four-digit combination—provided she hasn't starved to death or died of old age. Computers, however, can run searches like this one very quickly, so the systematic search algorithm is a useful part of some computer programs.

HEURISTICS Unfortunately, humans aren't as fast as computers and need some other way to narrow down the possible solutions to only a few. One way to do this is to use a heuristic. A **heuristic**, or "rule of thumb," is a simple rule that is intended to apply to many situations. Whereas an algorithm is very specific and will always lead to a solution, a heuristic is an educated guess based on prior experiences that helps narrow down the possible solutions for a problem. For example, if a student is typing a paper in a word-processing program and wants to know how to format the page, he or she could try to read an entire manual on the wordprocessing program. That would take a while. Instead, the student could type "format" into the help feature's search program or click on the word "Format" on the tool bar. Doing either action greatly reduces the amount of information the student will have to look at to get an answer. Using the help feature or clicking on the appropriate tool bar word will also work for similar problems.

Will using a rule of thumb always work, like algorithms? Using a heuristic is faster than using an algorithm in many cases, but unlike algorithms, heuristics will *not* always lead to the correct solution. What you gain in speed is sometimes lost in accuracy. For example, one kind of heuristic (called a *representative heuristic*) for categorizing objects simply assumes that any object (or person) that shares characteristics with the members of a particular category is also a member of that category. This is a handy tool when it comes to classifying plants but doesn't work as well when applied to people. Are all people with dark skin from Africa? Does everyone with red hair also have a bad temper? Are all blue-eyed blondes from Sweden? See the point? The representative heuristic can be used—or misused—to create and sustain stereotypes (Tversky & Kahneman, 1974).

A useful heuristic that works much of the time is to work backward from the goal. For example, if you want to know the shortest way to get to the new bookstore in town, you already know the goal, which is finding the bookstore. There are probably several ways to get there from your house, and some shorter than others. Assuming you have the address of the store, the best way to determine the shortest route is to look up the location of the store on a map of the city and then trace a route back to where you live.

What if my problem is writing a term paper? Starting at the end isn't going to help me much! Sometimes it's better to break a goal down into subgoals, so that as each subgoal is achieved, the final solution is that much closer. Writing a term paper, for example, can seem overwhelming until it is broken down into steps: choose a topic, research the topic, organize what has been gathered, write one section at a time, and so on. Other examples of heuristics include making diagrams to help organize the information concerning the problem or testing possible solutions to the problem one by one and eliminating those that do not work.

Another kind of heuristic is **means–end analysis**, in which a person determines the difference between the current situation and the goal and then tries to reduce that difference by various means (methods). For example, Katrina wanted a certain kind of invitation for her wedding, but buying it already made was very expensive and well

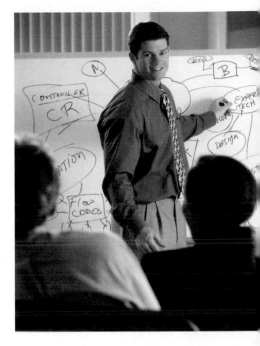

One rule of thumb, or heuristic, involves breaking down a goal into subgoals. The man standing in front of the white board has diagrammed the steps needed to reach the company's goal.

What if my problem is writing a term paper? Starting at the end isn't going to help me much!

heuristic
an educated guess based on prior experiences that helps narrow down the possible solutions for a problem. Also known as a "rule of thumb."

means–end analysis
heuristic in which the difference between the starting situation and the goal is determined and then steps are taken to reduce that difference.

not as specific as algorithms

Simulation
Live! psych

Algorithms and
Heuristics

Sometimes I have to ▶
find answers to
problems one step
at a time, but in
other cases the
answer seems to
just "pop" into my
head all of a
sudden. Why do some
answers come so
easily to mind?

over her budget. She ordered one sample of the invitation and examined it carefully. It had a pocket inside that held the response cards for people to send back to Katrina, a decorative seashell tied onto the outside of the card with fancy ribbon, and a small box instead of an envelope. Her goal was to make 200 of these invitations by hand. Her subgoals were to find the paper, take the invitation carefully apart to see how to put one together, buy the little shells, find and buy the right size boxes for mailing, and assemble the invitations. What might have seemed an impossible task became doable once it was broken down into smaller subgoals.

INSIGHT   Sometimes I have to find answers to problems one step at a time, but in other cases the answer seems to just "pop" into my head all of a sudden. Why do some answers come so easily to mind? When the solution to a problem seems to come suddenly to mind, it is called *insight.* Chapter Five (p. 195) discussed Köhler's (1925) work with Sultan the chimpanzee, which demonstrated that even some animals can solve problems by means of a sudden insight. In humans, insight often takes the form of an "aha!" moment—the solution seems to come in a flash. A person may realize that this problem is similar to another one that he or she already knew how to solve or might see that an object can be used for a different purpose than its original one, like using a dime as a screwdriver.

Remember the problem of the bottleneck discussed earlier in this chapter? The task was to get the coin out of the bottle without removing the cork or breaking the bottle. The answer is simple: Push the cork into the bottle and shake out the coin. Aha!

Insight is not really a magical process, although it can seem like magic. What usually happens is that the mind simply reorganizes a problem, sometimes while the person is thinking about something else (Durso et al., 1994).

Here's a problem that can be solved with insight: Marsha and Marjorie were born on the same day of the same month of the same year to the same mother and the same father yet they are not twins. How is that possible? Think about it and then look for the answer at the end of this section.

In summary, thinking is a complex process involving the use of mental imagery and various types of concepts to organize the events of daily life. Problem solving is a special type of thinking that involves the use of many tools, such as trial-and-error thinking, algorithms, and heuristics, to solve different types of problems.
Answer: Marsha and Marjorie are two of a set of triplets. Gotcha!

For a look at how some scientists are trying to develop machines that can think in a similar fashion to a human, see the following special section.

PSYCHOLOGY IN THE NEWS
Artificial Intelligence (AI)

8.4   *What is artificial intelligence?*

Many people might think that interest in **artificial intelligence (AI)**, or the creation of a machine that can think like a human, is a relatively recent phenomenon. But the idea of a mechanical "man" or robot is ancient. In Greek mythology, the god Hephaestus created a bronze man called Talos 1, the guardian of Crete. In a sense, Mary Shelley's *Frankenstein* (1818/1969) was an artificially created being as well. The first use of the term *robot* was in Karel Capek's famous play *"R. U. R."* (*Rossum's Universal Robots*) in 1923 (Capek & Capek, 1923).

By the 1950s, robots were big in the field of science fiction. Isaac Asimov (1968) became famous for his Three Laws of Robotics, laws that ensured that no human would ever be harmed

artificial intelligence (AI)
the creation of a machine that can think like a human.

by a robot (perhaps a reaction to the Frankenstein story). The laws, which have become popularized again in the 2004 film *I, Robot*, are:

1. A robot may not injure a human being or, through inaction, allow a human being to come to harm.

2. A robot must obey orders given it by human beings except where such orders would conflict with the First Law.

3. A robot must protect its own existence as long as such protection does not conflict with the First or Second Law (Asimov, 1950).

Will Smith faces an army of robots on the set of the movie *I, Robot*, which was loosely based on Isaac Asimov's famous book.

It was John McCarthy (1959) who first coined the term *artificial intelligence* at a conference devoted to the subject. Today artificial intelligence is represented in computer programs such as Deep Blue, a chess program that allowed a computer to beat the world chess champion, Garry Kasparov, in 1997 (Kasparov had beaten Deep Blue in 1996, four games to two). In 2003, Kasparov played Deep Blue's "descendent," Deep Junior and managed only a draw. Deep Junior, unlike Deep Blue, was programmed to consider only the strongest possible positions in detail (Knight, 2003). Interestingly, Deep Blue was programmed to use heuristics, the same kind of decision-making processes that humans use when playing chess. Deep Junior used algorithms (the more typical way in which computers are programmed). Deep Junior was able to play Kasparov to a draw using strategies that were less like human thinking than Deep Blue's strategies.

Should scientists be trying to create artificial intelligence that mimics human thought processes? That is one of the arguments among researchers in the field of AI (Hoffmann, 1998; Weizenbaum, 1976). Scientists will no doubt continue to try to refine robotic machines that can be used to go where humans cannot safely go, such as the depths of the oceans and the farthest reaches of our solar system. Will those machines think like machines, think like humans, or use a blend of machine and human cognitive processes? Only the future knows.

Questions for Further Thought

1. How might having hands and feet make a robot more useful for certain tasks?

2. What are some of the concerns that might arise if human-shaped robots become a reality?

3. In what other areas of life might robots become useful?

4. Should a robot be able to function without human supervision or control?

Chess genius Gary Kasparov plays against the artificial intelligence program Deep Junior. The outcome was a draw.

PRACTICE **QUIZ:** HOW MUCH DO YOU REMEMBER?

Pick the best answer.

1. Mental images
   a. represent abstract ideas.
   b. have a picture-like quality.
   c. consist entirely of unconscious information.
   d. are always prototypes.

2. Knowing that the definition of psychology is the scientific study of behavior and mental processes is an example of a
   a. prototypical concept.   c. formal concept.
   b. natural concept.   d. mental image.

3. A "rule of thumb" is another name for a
   a. heuristic.   c. trial-and-error solution.
   b. algorithm.   d. means–end analysis.

4. What type of problem-solving strategy would be best to use when solving a problem in algebra class?
   a. heuristic   c. trial-and-error solution
   b. algorithm   d. means–end analysisk

5. Miguel was struggling with the answer to one of the questions on his psychology midterm. Seeing that the answer was not going to come easily, he went on to answer some of the other easier questions. Then, suddenly, the answer to the problematic question just seemed to "pop" into his head. Miguel's experience is an example of
   a. means–end anlaysis.
   b. a heuristic.
   c. an algorithm.
   d. insight.

6. The main difference between the AI programs Deep Blue and Deep Junior is that Deep Blue used _____ whereas Deep Junior was programmed to use _____.
   a. algorithms; heuristics
   b. heuristics; rules of thumb
   c. heuristics; algorithms
   d. algorithm; rules of thumb

Answers: 1-b, 2-c, 3-a, 4-b, 5-d, 6-c.

PROBLEMS WITH PROBLEM SOLVING

Methods of problem solving such as using insight are not foolproof. Sometimes a solution to a problem remains just "out of reach" because the elements of the problem are not arranged properly or because people get stuck in certain ways of thinking that act as barriers to solving problems. Such ways of thinking occur more or less automatically, influencing attempts to solve problems without any conscious awareness of that influence. Here's a classic example:

Two strings are hanging from a ceiling but are too far apart to allow a person to hold one and walk to the other. Nearby is a table with a pair of pliers on it. The goal is to tie the two pieces of string together. How? For the solution to this problem, see page 305.

People can become aware of automatic tendencies to try to solve problems in ways that are not going to lead to solutions and in becoming aware can abandon the "old" ways for more appropriate problem-solving methods. Three of the most common barriers* to successful problem solving are functional fixedness, mental sets, and confirmation bias.

——————————

*Barriers: something that blocks one's path; an obstacle preventing a solution.

The string problem: How do you tie the two strings together if you cannot reach them both at the same time?

FIGURE 8.2   **The String Problem**

8.5 *What are the barriers to solving problems?*

FUNCTIONAL FIXEDNESS   One problem-solving difficulty involves thinking about objects only in terms of their typical uses, which is a phenomenon called **functional fixedness** (literally, "fixed on the function"). Have you ever searched high and low for a screwdriver to fix something around the house? All the while there are several objects close at hand that could be used to tighten a screw: a butter knife, a key, or even a dime in your pocket. Because the tendency is to think of those objects in terms of cooking, unlocking, and spending, we sometimes ignore the less obvious possible uses. The string problem is an example of functional fixedness. The pair of pliers is often seen as useless until the person realizes it can be used as a weight. (See page 305.)

Alton Brown, renowned chef and star of the Food Network's *Good Eats* cooking show, is a big fan of what he calls "multitaskers," kitchen items that can be used for more than one purpose. For example, a cigar-cutter can become a tool for cutting carrots, green onions, and garlic. Obviously, Chef Brown is not a frequent victim of functional fixedness.

MENTAL SETS   Functional fixedness is actually a kind of **mental set**, which is defined as the tendency for people to persist in using problem-solving patterns that have worked for them in the past. Solutions that have worked in the past tend to be the ones people try first, and people are often hesitant or even unable to think of other possibilities. Look at the accompanying figure.

Can you draw four straight lines so that they pass through all nine dots *without lifting your pencil from the page*?

People are taught from the earliest grades to stay within the lines, right? That tried-and-true method will not help in solving the dot problem. The solution involves drawing the lines beyond the actual dots, as seen in Figure 8.3 on page 307.

CONFIRMATION BIAS   Another barrier to logical thinking called **confirmation bias** is the tendency to search for evidence that fits one's beliefs while ignoring any evidence to the contrary. This is similar to a mental set, except that what is "set" is a belief rather than a method of solving problems. For example, believers in ESP tend to remember the few studies that seem to support their beliefs and psychic predictions that worked out while at the same time "forgetting" the cases in which studies found no proof or psychics made predictions that failed to come true. They remember only that which confirms their bias toward a belief in the existence of ESP.

CREATIVITY

So far, we've only talked about logic and pretty straightforward thinking. How do we come up with totally new ideas, things no one has thought of before? Not every problem can be answered by using information already at hand and the rules of logic in applying that information. Sometimes a problem requires coming up with entirely new ways of looking at the problem or unusual, inventive solutions. This

functional fixedness
a block to problem solving that comes from thinking about objects in terms of only their typical functions.

mental set
the tendency for people to persist in using problem-solving patterns that have worked for them in the past.

confirmation bias
the tendency to search for evidence that fits one's beliefs while ignoring any evidence that does not fit those beliefs.

So far, we've only talked about logic and pretty straightforward thinking. How do we ◀ come up with totally new ideas, things no one has thought of before?

Pablo Picasso was one of the most creative artists of his time. Here he is seen drawing an abstract of a woman in the air with a flashlight, using multiple exposures of the camera. What does his ability to "hold" the light image in his head long enough to complete the abstract tell us about his iconic memory?

Cynthia Breazeal is a researcher at the Artificial Intelligence Lab at MIT. Here she is pictured with the robot she designed called Kismet. Designed to help with the study of infant emotional expressions, Kismet can display several "moods" on its face as emotional expressions. This is divergent thinking at its best—a "baby" that won't cry, wet, or demand to be fed.

kind of thinking is called **creativity**: solving problems by combining ideas or behavior in new ways (Csikszentmihalyi, 1996).

8.6   *What is creative thinking?*

DIVERGENT AND CONVERGENT THINKING   The logical method for problem solving that has been discussed so far is based on a type of thinking called **convergent thinking**. In convergent thinking, a problem is seen as having only one answer and all lines of thinking will eventually lead to (converge on) that single answer by using previous knowledge and logic (Ciardiello, 1998). For example, the question "In what ways are a pencil and a pen alike?" can be answered by listing the features that the two items have in common: Both can be used to write, have similar shapes, and so on, in a simple comparison process. Convergent thinking works well for routine problem solving but may be of little use when a more creative solution is needed.

Divergent thinking is the reverse of convergent thinking. Here a person starts at one point and comes up with many different, or divergent, ideas or possibilities based on that point (Finke, 1995). For example, if someone were to ask the question, "What is a pencil used for?" the convergent answer would be "to write." But if the question is put this way: "How many different uses can you think of for a pencil?" the answers multiply: "writing, poking holes, a weight for the tail of a kite, a weapon."

What are the characteristics of a creative, divergent thinker? Theorists in the field of creative thinking have found through examining the habits of highly creative people that the most productive periods of divergent thinking for those people tend to occur when they are doing some task or activity that is more or less automatic, such as walking or swimming (Csikszentmihalyi, 1996; Gardner, 1993a; Goleman, 1995). These automatic tasks take up some attentional processes, leaving the remainder to devote to creative thinking. The fact that all of one's attention is not focused on the problem is actually a benefit because divergent thinkers often make links and connections at a level of consciousness just below alert awareness so that ideas can flow freely without being censored* by the higher mental processes (Goleman, 1995). In other words, having part of one's attention devoted to walking, for example, allows the rest of the mind to "sneak up on" more creative solutions and ideas.

Divergent thinkers will obviously be less prone to some of the barriers to problem solving, such as functional fixedness. For example, what would most people do if it suddenly started to rain while they are stuck in their office with no umbrella? How many people would think of using a see-through vinyl tote bag as a makeshift umbrella?

Creative, divergent thinking is often a neglected topic in the education of young people. Although some people are naturally more creative, it is possible to develop one's creative ability. The ability to be creative is important—coming up with topics for a research paper, for example, is something that many students have trouble doing. Cross-cultural research (Basadur et al., 2002; Colligan, 1983) has found that divergent thinking and problem-solving skills can be easily taught in cultures such as that of Japan and the Omaha Native Americans. In these cultures creativity in many areas is not normally prized and the preference is to hold to well-established traditions,

---

*Censored: blocked from conscious awareness as unacceptable thoughts.

TABLE 8.2 STIMULATING DIVERGENT THINKING

Brainstorming	Generate as many ideas as possible in a short period of time, without judging each idea's merits until all ideas are recorded.
Keeping a Journal	Carry a journal to write down ideas as they occur or a recorder to capture those same ideas and thoughts.
Freewriting	Write down or record everything that comes to mind about a topic without revising or proofreading until all of the information is written or recorded in some way. Organize it later.
Mind or Subject Mapping	Start with a central idea and draw a "map" with lines from the center to other related ideas, forming a mental image of the concepts and their connections.

creativity
the process of solving problems by combining ideas or behavior in new ways.

convergent thinking
type of thinking in which a problem is seen as having only one answer, and all lines of thinking will eventually lead to that single answer, using previous knowledge and logic.

divergent thinking
type of thinking in which a person starts from one point and comes up with many different ideas or possibilities based on that point.

such as that of traditional dances that have not varied for centuries. See Table 8.2 for some ways to become a more divergent thinker.

Many people have the idea that creative people are also a little different from other people. There are artists and musicians, for example, who actually encourage others to see them as eccentric. But the fact is that creative people are actually pretty normal. According to Csikszentmihalyi (1997),

1. Creative people usually have a broad range of knowledge about a lot of subjects and are good at using mental imagery.

2. Creative people aren't afraid to be different—they are more open to new experiences than many people, and they tend to have more vivid dreams and daydreams than others do.

3. Creative people value their independence.

4. Creative people are often unconventional in their work but not otherwise.

Solution to the String Problem

The solution to the string problem is to use the pliers as a pendulum to get the second string closer to you.

PRACTICE **QUIZ:** HOW MUCH DO YOU REMEMBER?

Pick the best answer.

1. Al goes out one frosty morning to find that his car is covered with a layer of thick frost. He needs to get to work and looks for his ice scraper. Unable to find it, he thinks a moment, goes into the house, and returns with a hard plastic spatula from the kitchen. In using the spatula as a makeshift ice scraper, Al has overcome
   a. functional fixedness.
   b. confirmation bias.
   c. creativity bias.
   d. confirmation fixedness.

2. Randall believes that aliens crashed in the western United States in the 1950s. When looking for information about this on the Internet, he ignores any sites that are skeptical of his belief and only visits and talks with his friends about the sites that support his belief. This is an example of
   a. functional fixedness.
   b. confirmation bias.
   c. creativity bias.
   d. confirmation fixedness.

3. When a problem is seen as having only one answer, with all lines of thinking leading to that answer, this is known as _____ thinking.
   a. divergent
   b. creative
   c. convergent
   d. mental set

4. Which of the following statements about creative people is *TRUE?*
   a. They are not very good at mental imagery.
   b. They are not afraid to be different.
   c. They value their dependence on others.
   d. They are often very conventional in their work.

I know I've **heard and** ▶
even used the term a
lot, but exactly what is
intelligence?

I know I've heard and even used the term a lot, but exactly what is intelligence?

Intelligence

Think back to the story of Chris Burke in the prologue. His parents were told to place him in an institution, but instead they chose to raise him as any other child would be raised, with astonishing and very positive results. Why would the doctors have given his parents such negative and limiting advice? The doctors were basing their predictions on assumptions about intelligence, but not everyone is in agreement on just what intelligence truly is.

DEFINITION

8.7   *What is the definition of intelligence?*

What is intelligence? Is it a score on some test, or is it practical knowledge of how to get along in the world? Is it making good grades or being a financial success or a social success? Ask a dozen people and you will probably get a dozen different answers. Psychologists have come up with a workable definition that combines many of the ideas just listed: They define **intelligence** as the ability to learn from one's experiences, acquire knowledge, and use resources effectively in adapting to new situations or solving problems (Sternberg & Kaufman, 1998; Wechsler, 1975). These are the characteristics that people need to be able to survive in their culture.

It doesn't sound like ▶
that would be easy to
measure on a
test—how
do IQ tests
work,
anyway?

It doesn't sound like that would be easy to measure on a test—how do IQ tests work, anyway?

MEASURING INTELLIGENCE

The measurement of intelligence by some kind of test is a concept that is less than a century old. It began when educators in France realized that some students needed more help with learning than others did. If a way could be found to identify these students, they could be given a different kind of education than the more capable students.

8.8   *How do intelligence tests measure intelligence?*

BINET'S MENTAL ABILITY TEST   In those early days, a French psychologist named Alfred Binet was asked by the French Ministry of Education to design a formal test of intelligence that would help identify children who were unable to learn as quickly or as well as others, so that they could be given remedial education. Eventually, he and colleague Théodore Simon came up with a test that not only distinguished between fast and slow learners but also between children of different age groups as well (Binet & Simon, 1916). They noticed that the fast learners seemed to give answers to questions that older children might give, whereas the slow learners gave answers that were more typical of a younger child. Binet decided that the key element to be tested was a child's *mental age*, or the average age at which children could successfully answer a particular level of questions.

STANFORD-BINET AND IQ   Terman (1916), a researcher at Stanford University, adopted German psychologist William Stern's method for comparing mental age and *chronological age* (number of years since birth) for use with the translated and revised Binet test. Stern's (1912) formula was to divide the mental age (MA) by the chronological age (CA) and multiply the result by 100 to get rid of any decimal points. The resulting score is called an **intelligence quotient**, or **IQ**. (A quotient is a number that results from dividing one number by another.)

$$IQ = MA/CA \times 100$$

intelligence
the ability to learn from one's experiences, acquire knowledge, and use resources effectively in adapting to new situations or solving problems.

intelligence quotient (IQ)
a number representing a measure of intelligence, resulting from the division of one's mental age by one's chronological age and then multiplying that quotient by 100.

For example, if a child who is 10 years old takes the test and scores a mental age of 15 (is able to answer the level of questions typical of a 15-year-old), the IQ would look like this:

$$IQ = 15/10 \times 100 = 150$$

The quotient has the advantage of allowing testers to compare the intelligence levels of people of different age groups.

Today, the Stanford-Binet Intelligence Scales, Fifth Edition (SB5)(Roid, 2003) is often used by educators to make decisions about the placement of students into special educational programs. Most children are given this test at around the second grade, or age 7 or 8. See Table 8.3 for descriptions of some items from the SB5.

THE WECHSLER TESTS   Although the original Stanford-Binet Test is now in its fifth edition and includes different questions for people of different age groups, it is not the only IQ test that is popular today. David Wechsler (1981, 1990, 1991) was the first to devise a series of tests designed for specific age groups (also given to an individual, not just groups, as is the Stanford-Binet test). Originally dissatisfied with the fact that the Stanford-Binet was designed for children but being administered to adults, he developed an IQ test specifically for adults. He later designed tests specifically for older school-age children and preschool children as well as those in the early grades. The Wechsler Adult Intelligence Scale (WAIS-IV), Wechsler Intelligence Scale for Children (WISC-IV), and the Wechsler Preschool and Primary Scale of Intelligence (WPPSI-III) are the three versions of this test, and in the United States these tests are now used more frequently than the Stanford-Binet. These tests differ from the Stanford-Binet in that they each have a verbal and a performance (nonverbal) scale, as well as providing an overall score of intelligence. The verbal component scale tests vocabulary, comprehension, and general knowledge, whereas the performance component scale tests such skills as arranging blocks to match a pattern, identifying missing parts in pictures, and putting pictures representing a story in order. Table 8.4 has some sample verbal and performance items from the WAIS-IV.

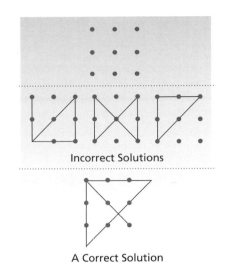

Incorrect Solutions

A Correct Solution

FIGURE 8.3   **The Solution to the Dot Problem**   When people try to solve this problem, a mental set causes them to think of the dots as representing a box, and they try to draw the line while staying in the box. The only way to connect all nine dots without lifting the pencil from the paper is to draw the lines so they extend out of the box of dots—literally "thinking outside the box."

TABLE 8.3   CRITERION-REFERENCED INTERPRETATION OF THE CSS FULL SCALE IQ SCORES ON THE SB5 FOR AGE EQUIVALENTS AGE 5 AND ABOVE

CSS Scale	Age Equivalent	Selected Tasks (SB5 Activity, Item and Level, Subtest Abbreviation)
530	> 21 years	Vocabulary, defines a difficult word (Item 44, VKN)
525	> 21 years	Verbal Analogies, completes a difficult analogy (Item 2, level 6, VFR)
520	> 21 years	Vocabulary, defines a difficult word (Item 34, VKN)
515	> 21 years	Position & Direction, correctly answers story of someone walking a direction, then turning left, etc. (Item 2, Level 6, VVS)
510	16 years, 2 months	Verbal Quantitative, answers word problem about bringing correct amount of water in pint cans (Item 2, Level 5, VQR)
505	12 years, 9 months	Verbal Absurdities, finds absurdity about icebergs (Item 3, Level 4, VFR)
500	10 years, 0 months	Picture Absurdities, identifies error in position of continents (Item 4, Level 4, NVKN)
495	8 years, 8 months	Verbal Quantitative, counts blocks in three-dimensional model (Item 2, Level 4, VQR)
490	7 years, 8 months	Verbal Absurdities, finds absurdity in story of injury (Item 2, Level 4, NVFR)
485	6 years, 10 months	Last Word, recalls last word in sentences about cars and dogs (Item 2c, Level 4, VWM)
480	6 years, 1 month	Picture Absurdities, identifies absurdity in picture of envelope (Item 2, Level 4, NVKN)
475	5 years, 6 months	Form Patterns, forms the "walking person" pattern (Item 1, Level 3, NVVS)
470	5 years, 0 months	Vocabulary, defines the word for a common fruit (Item 16, VKN

Note: Actual age-equivalent scores offered through the SB5 extend to less than 2 years, 0 months.

Abbreviations are as follows: CSS — Change-Sensitive Score, FR — Fluid Reasoning, KN — Knowledge, NV — Nonverbal, CR = Quantitative Reasoning, V = Verbal, VS = Visual-Spatial Processing, WM = Working Memory.

Source: Roid, 2003. Riverside Publishing Company.

> ### TABLE 8.4 PARAPHRASED SAMPLE ITEMS FROM THE WECHSLER ADULT INTELLIGENCE SCALE (WAIS)
>
> **Verbal Scale**
>
> | | |
> |---|---|
> | Information | What is steam made of? What is pepper? Who wrote *Tom Sawyer*? |
> | Comprehension | Why is copper often used in electrical wire?
What is the advantage of keeping money in a bank? |
> | Arithmetic | Three women divided eighteen golf balls equally among themselves. How many golf balls did each person receive?
If two buttons cost $.15, what will be the cost of a dozen buttons? |
> | Similarities | In what way are a circle and a triangle alike? In what way are a saw and a hammer alike? |
> | Vocabulary | What is a hippopotamus? What does "resemble" mean? |
>
> **Performance Scale**
>
> | | |
> |---|---|
> | Picture Arrangement | A story is told in three or more cartoon panels placed in the incorrect order; put them together to tell the story. |
> | Picture Completion | Point out what's missing from each picture. |
> | Block Design | After looking at a pattern or design, try to arrange small cubes in the same pattern. |
> | Object Assembly | Given pieces with part of a picture on each, put them together to form such objects as a hand or a profile. |
> | Digit Symbol | Learn a different symbol for each number and then fill in the blank under the number with the correct symbol. (This test is timed.) |

Simulated items similar to those in the *Wechsler Adult Intelligence Scale*, Third Edition (2005).

TEST CONSTRUCTION: GOOD TEST, BAD TEST?

8.9 *How are intelligence tests constructed?*

All tests are not equally good tests. Some tests might be easy to use, but if they don't actually measure what they are supposed to measure, they are useless. They are thought of as "invalid" (untrue) tests. **Validity** is the degree to which a test actually measures what it's supposed to measure. Other tests may fail to give the same results on different occasions for the same person when that person has not changed—also useless. These would be considered unreliable tests. **Reliability** of a test refers to the test producing consistent results each time it is given to the same individual or group of people. For example, if Nicholas takes a personality test today and then again in a month or so, the results should be very similar if the personality test is reliable. And what does a test score mean? To what, or whom, is it compared?

Take the hypothetical example of Professor Stumpwater, who for reasons best known only to him believes that intelligence is related to a person's golf scores. Let's say that he develops an adult intelligence test based on golf scores. What do we need to look at to determine if his test is a good one?

validity
the degree to which a test actually measures what it's supposed to measure.

reliability
the tendency of a test to produce the same scores again and again each time it is given to the same people.

Standardization of Tests   First of all, we would want to look at how he tried to standardize his test. *Standardization* refers to the process of giving the test to a large group of people that represents the kind of people for whom the test is designed. Standardization groups are chosen randomly from the population for whom the test is intended and, like all samples, must be representative of that population. (L)(I)(N)(K) *to Appendix A: Statistics.* If a test is designed for children, for example, then a large sample of randomly selected children would be given the test. All test subjects would take the test under the same conditions. In the professor's case, this would mean that he would have to allow his sample members to play the same number of rounds of golf on the same course under the same weather conditions, and so on.

Norms   The scores from the standardization group would be called the *norms*, the standards against which all others who take the test would be compared. Most tests of intelligence follow a *normal curve*, or a distribution in which the scores are the greatest around the *mean*, or average, and become less and less the farther from the mean they occur (See Figure 8.4). (L)(I)(N)(K) *to Appendix A: Statistics.*

In Figure 8.4 percentages represent the percentage of scores falling under a section of the curve for each *standard deviation (SD)* from the mean on the Wechsler IQ test. The standard deviation is the average variation of scores from the mean.

When instructors "grade on the curve," they are using the normal curve to determine who gets what grade. The scores that fall in the middle of the curve would receive a C, whereas the scores that fall below C would receive an F or a D, and those falling above C would receive a B or an A, depending on where the scores fall compared to the middle.

In the case of the professor's golf test, he might find that a certain golf score is the average, which he would interpret as average intelligence. People who scored extremely well on the golf test would be compared to the average, as well as people with unusually poor scores.

The normal curve allows IQ scores to be more accurately estimated. The old IQ scoring method using the simple formula devised by Stern produces raw IQ scores that start to become meaningless as the person's chronological age passes 16 years. (Once a person becomes an adult, the idea of questions that are geared for a particular age group loses its power. For example, what kind of differences would there be between questions designed for a 30-year-old versus a 40-year-old?) Test designers replaced the old ratio IQ of the earlier versions of IQ tests with **deviation IQ scores**, which are based on the normal curve distribution (Eysenck, 1994): IQ is assumed to be normally distributed with a mean IQ of 100 and a typical standard deviation of about 15 (the standard deviation can vary according to the particular test).

deviation IQ scores
a type of intelligence measure that assumes that IQ is normally distributed around a mean of 100 with a standard deviation of about 15.

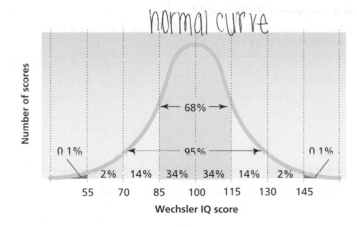

FIGURE 8.4   **The Normal Curve**

These high school students are taking a standardized intelligence test. How fair is it to expect all of these young people, many from different cultural backgrounds, to interpret every question on the test in the exact manner that the test designer intended?

▶ **Just because an IQ test gives the same score every time a person takes it doesn't mean that the score is actually measuring real intelligence, right?**

With respect to validity and reliability, the professor's test fares poorly. If the results of the professor's test were compared with other established intelligence tests, there would probably be no relationship at all. Golf scores have nothing to do with intelligence, so the test is not a valid, or true, measure of intelligence.

On the other hand, his test might work well for some people and poorly for others on the question of reliability. Some people who are good and regular golfers tend to score about the same for each game that they play, so for them, the golf score IQ would be fairly reliable. But others, especially those who do not play golf or play infrequently, would have widely varying scores from game to game. For those people, the test would be very unreliable, and if a test is unreliable for some, it's not a good test.

A test can fail in validity but still be reliable. If for some reason Professor Stumpwater chose to use height as a measure of intelligence, an adult's score on Stumpwater's "test" would always be the same, as height does not change by very much after the late teens. But the opposite is not true. If a test is unreliable, how can it accurately measure what it is supposed to measure? For example, adult intelligence remains fairly constant. If a test meant to measure that intelligence gives different scores at different times, it's obviously not a valid measure of intelligence.

Just because an IQ test gives the same score every time a person takes it doesn't mean that the score is actually measuring real intelligence, right? That's right—think about the definition of intelligence for a moment: the ability to learn from one's experiences, acquire knowledge, and use resources effectively in adapting to new situations or solving problems. How can anyone define what effective use of resources might be? Does everyone have access to the same resources? Is everyone's "world" necessarily perceived as being the same? Intelligence tests are useful measuring devices but should not necessarily be assumed to be measures of all types of intelligent behavior, or even good measures for all groups of people, as the next section discusses.

IQ TESTS AND CULTURAL BIAS   The problem with trying to measure intelligence with a test that is based on an understanding of the world and its resources is that not everyone comes from the same "world." People raised in a different culture, or even a different economic situation, from the one in which the designer of an IQ test is raised are not likely to perform well on such a test.

Because of differences among cultures, it is very difficult to design an intelligence test that is completely free of *cultural bias*, a term referring to the unfair advantage that a person from the same culture (or socioeconomic background) as the one from which the test is designed would have over those who are from different cultural or socioeconomic backgrounds (Helms, 1992). If people raised in an Asian culture are given a test designed within a traditional Western culture, many items on the test might make no sense to them. For example, one kind of question might be: Which one of the five is least like the other four?

DOG - CAR - CAT - BIRD - FISH

The answer is supposed to be "car," which is the only one of the five that is not alive. But a Japanese child, living in a culture that relies on the sea for so much of its food and culture, might choose "fish," because none of the others are found in the ocean. That child's test score would be lower but not because the child is not intelligent.

> **TABLE 8.5 SAMPLE OF THE DOVE COUNTERBALANCE GENERAL INTELLIGENCE TEST**
>
> 1. A "handkerchief head" is:
>   a. a cool cat,
>   b. a porter,
>   c. an Uncle Tom,
>   d. a hoddi,
>   e. a preacher.
>
> 2. Cheap chitlings (not the kind you purchase at a frozen food counter) will taste rubbery unless they are cooked long enough. How soon can you quit cooking them to eat and enjoy them?
>   a. 45 minutes,
>   b. 2 hours,
>   c. 24 hours,
>   d. 1 week (on a low flame),
>   e. 1 hour.
>
> 3. What are the "Dixie Hummingbirds"?
>   a. part of the KKK,
>   b. a swamp disease,
>   c. a modern gospel group,
>   d. a Mississippi Negro paramilitary group,
>   e. deacons.
>
> 4. "Money don't get everything it's true"
>   a. but I don't have none and I'm so blue,
>   b. but what it don't get I can't use,
>   c. so make do with what you've got,
>   d. but I don't know that and neither do you.
>
> The answers are as follows:
>
> 1. c.   2. c.   3. c.   4. b.

Source: Dove, A. (1971).

In 1971, Adrian Dove designed an intelligence test to highlight the problem of cultural bias. Dove, an African American sociologist, created the Dove Counterbalance General Intelligence Test (later known as the Chitling Test) in an attempt to demonstrate that a significant language/dialect barrier exists among children of different backgrounds. Look at Table 8.5 and take a sample of the test.

A person who is not from the African American culture of the northeastern United States will probably score very poorly on this test. African American people from different geographical regions don't always do well on this test either. The point is simply this: Tests such as these are created by people who are from a particular culture and background. Test questions and answers that the creators might think are common knowledge may relate to their own experiences and not to people of other cultures, backgrounds, or socioeconomic levels.

Attempts have been made to create intelligence tests that are as free of cultural influences as is humanly possible. Many test designers have come to the conclusion that it may be impossible to create a test that is completely free of cultural bias (Carpenter et al., 1990). Instead, they are striving to create tests that are at least *culturally fair.* These tests use questions that do not create a disadvantage for people whose culture differs from that of the majority. Many items on a "culture fair" test require the use of nonverbal abilities such as rotating objects rather than items about verbal knowledge that might be culturally specific.

If intelligence tests are so flawed, why do people still use them? The one thing that IQ tests do well is predict academic success for those who score at the higher and lower ends of the normal curve. (For those who score in the average range of IQ, the predictive value is less clear.) The kinds of tests students are given in school are often similar to intelligence tests, and so people who do well on IQ tests typically do well on other kinds of academically oriented tests as well, such as the Scholastic Aptitude Test (SAT), the American College Test (ACT), the Graduate Record Exam (GRE), and actual college examinations. These achievement tests are very similar to IQ tests but are administered to groups of people rather than to individuals.

◀ If intelligence **tests are so flawed, why do people still use them?**

PRACTICE QUIZ: HOW MUCH DO YOU REMEMBER?

Pick the best answer.

1. Using the Stanford-Binet IQ formula, what IQ would a person have whose mental age is 10 and whose chronological age is 15?
   a. 150
   b. 1.50
   c. 0.67
   d. 67

2. Darla is four years old. The intelligence test that would most likely be used to determine her IQ is the
   a. WAIS-IV.
   b. WISC-IV.
   c. WPPSI-III.
   d. Dove Test.

3. Professor Beckett designed an IQ test. To standardize this test, the professor should be careful to do which of the following?
   a. Use only a small sample to prevent possible cheating on the test.
   b. Select the people in the sample from the population of people for whom the test is designed.
   c. Select only university professors to take the test so that they can critique the questions on the test.
   d. Test each member of the sample under different conditions.

4. _____ would be the problem in a test that provides a consistent score for some people each time it is administered but yields different scores for other people.
   a. Reliability   c. Standardization
   b. Validity   d. Normalization

Answers: 1-d, 2-c, 3-b, 4-a.

---

developmentally delayed
condition in which a person's behavioral and cognitive skills exist at an earlier developmental stage than the skills of others who are the same chronological age. A more acceptable term for mental retardation.

INDIVIDUAL DIFFERENCES IN INTELLIGENCE

Another use of IQ tests is to identify people who differ from those of average intelligence by a great degree. Although one such group is composed of those who are sometimes called "geniuses" (who fall at the extreme high end of the normal curve for intelligence), the other group is made up of people who, for various reasons, are considered intellectually delayed and whose IQ scores fall well below the mean on the normal curve.

MENTAL RETARDATION (DEVELOPMENTAL DELAY)

8.10   *What is mental retardation and what causes it?*

IQ ≠ 70

Mental retardation is defined in two ways. First, the person's IQ score must fall below 70, or two standard deviations below the mean on the normal curve. Second, the person's *adaptive behavior* (skills that allow people to live independently, such as being able to work at a job, the ability to communicate well with others, and grooming skills such as being able to get dressed, eat, and bathe with little or no help) is severely below a level appropriate for the person's age. It occurs in about 3 percent of the population (The Arc, 1982) and affects an estimated 6.2 to 7.5 million people (American Association on Mental Retardation, 2002). Although the term *mental retardation* is still commonly used to refer to the condition, people with this condition are now called **developmentally delayed**, meaning that their behavioral and cognitive skills exist at an earlier developmental stage than the skills of others who are the same chronological age (Smith & Mitchell, 2001). *function slower*

So how would a professional go about deciding whether or not a ▶ child is developmentally delayed? Is the IQ test the primary method?

So how would a professional go about deciding whether or not a child is developmentally delayed? Is the IQ test the primary method? Diagnosis of developmental delay, according to the American Association on Mental Retardation guidelines (Janicki et al., 1995), should not depend upon only IQ tests scores alone but also on the strengths and weaknesses of the person in four areas:

1. **Intellectual and adaptive behavior skills.** In addition to scores on IQ tests, the person's ability to use language, reading, and writing, ability to understand and handle money transactions, social skills such as following rules and being responsible, and adaptive behavior such as job skills and hygiene should be assessed.

2. **Psychological and emotional considerations.** Personality traits and levels of emotional maturity vary in persons who are developmentally delayed just as they do in others and should also be considered in making a diagnosis of the degree of retardation and recommendations for care and education. A person who has an easygoing personality, for example, might receive different care recommendations and educational opportunities than a person who is highly anxious or temperamental.*

3. **Physical and health considerations.** When retardation is the result of physical conditions such as severe malnourishment,** it may be possible to improve the person's intellectual and behavioral skills through intervention, resulting in a higher assessment of functioning.

This middle-aged man is named Jack. Jack lives in a small town in Arkansas and serves as a deacon in the local church. He is loved and respected and leads what, for him, is a full and happy life. Jack also has Down syndrome. Like Chris Burke in the opening story, Jack has managed to find his place in the world.

4. **Environmental considerations.** Intervention may also be possible in some forms of retardation that are the result of exposure to unhealthy living conditions that can affect brain development. Examples of such conditions are lead poisoning from eating paint chips (Lanphear et al., 2000), exposure to PCBs (Darvill et al., 2000), prenatal exposure to mercury (Grandjean et al., 1997) as well as other toxicants (Ericksson et al., 2001; Eskenazi et al., 1999; Schroeder, 2000), poor nutrition resulting in inadequate development of the brain, or a lack of mental stimulation in one's surroundings during the formative years of infancy and childhood (Shah, 1991).

Classifications Developmental delay can vary from mild to extremely severe. Even with their flaws, IQ test scores are still used to classify the various levels of delay, as can be seen in Table 8.6.

---

*Temperamental: sensitive and moody.
**Malnourishment: a serious medical condition resulting from a lack of appropriate or adequate food intake.

TABLE 8.6 **CLASSIFICATIONS OF DEVELOPMENTAL DELAY**

Classification	Range of IQ Scores	Adaptive Limitations	Percentage of Developmentally Delayed Population
Mild	55–70	Can reach sixth-grade skill level. Capable with training of living independently and being self-supporting.	90%
Moderate	40–55	Can reach second-grade skill level. Can work and live in sheltered environments with supervision.	6%
Severe	25–40	Can learn to talk and perform basic self-care but needs constant supervision.	3%
Profound	Below 25	Very limited ability to learn, may only be able to learn very simple tasks, poor language skills and limited self-care.	1%

Source: Table based on classifications in American Psychiatric Association. (2000).

So what causes ▶
developmental delay?
It's not just
environmental factors,
like lead or mercury
poisoning, is it?

Causes   So what causes developmental delay? It's not just environmental factors, like lead or mercury poisoning, is it? The causes listed earlier as environmental considerations of the American Association on Mental Retardation guidelines are said to produce *familial retardation* (Schroeder, 2000), a delay related to living in poverty conditions and one that usually produces relatively mild retardation.

The three most common biological causes of developmental delay are Down syndrome, fetal alcohol syndrome, and fragile X syndrome. *Fetal alcohol syndrome* is a condition that results from exposing a developing embryo to alcohol and intelligence levels range from below average to developmentally delayed (Olson & Burgess, 1997). In *fragile X syndrome*, a male has a thin, frail-looking area on his X chromosome of the twenty-third pair. As children, people with this syndrome are typically mildly developmentally delayed but shift to being severely or profoundly developmentally delayed as adults (Dykens et al., 1994).

There are many other causes of developmental delay (Murphy et al., 1998). Lack of oxygen at birth, damage to the fetus in the womb from diseases, infections, or drug use by the mother, and even diseases and accidents during childhood can lead to developmental delay.

One thing should always be remembered: Developmental delay affects the person's intellectual capabilities. Developmentally delayed people are just as responsive to love and affection as anyone else and need to be loved and to have friends just as all people do. Intelligence is only one characteristic; warmth, friendliness, caring, and compassion also count for a great deal and should not be underrated. Just ask Chris Burke or any of the people whose lives have been touched by his.

GIFTEDNESS

8.11   *What is giftedness?*

At the other end of the intelligence scale* are those who fall on the upper end of the normal curve (see Figure 8.4) above an IQ of 130 (about 2 percent of the population). The term applied to these people is **gifted**, and if the IQ falls above 140 (less than half of 1 percent of the population), the term is often *genius.* Some people use the term *genius* only for people with extremely high IQs or with other qualities that are extreme, such as creativity (Kamphaus, 1993).

I've heard ▶
that geniuses
are sometimes a little
"nutty" and odd. Are
geniuses, especially the
really high IQ ones, "not
playing with a full deck,"
as the saying goes?

I've heard that geniuses are sometimes a little "nutty" and odd. Are geniuses, especially the really high IQ ones, "not playing with a full deck," as the saying goes? People have long held many false beliefs about people who are very, very intelligent. One common phrase around the turn of the twentieth century was "early ripe, early rot," which meant that people expected young geniuses to lose their genius early in life (Shurkin, 1992). Other beliefs were that gifted people are weird and socially awkward, physically weak, and more likely to suffer from mental illnesses. From these beliefs comes the "mad scientist" of the cinema (think "Dr. Evil" of *Austin Powers*) and the "evil genius" of literature—Dr. Frankenstein, Dr. Jekyll, and Superman's archenemy,** Lex Luthor, to name a few.

These beliefs were shattered by a groundbreaking study that was initiated in 1921 by Lewis M. Terman, a psychologist at Stanford University. Terman (1925)

gifted
the 2 percent of the population falling on the upper end of the normal curve and typically possessing an IQ of 130 or above.

---

*Scale: a graded series of tests or performances used in rating individual intelligence or achievement.

**Archenemy: a main enemy; the most important enemy.

selected 1,528 children to participate in a longitudinal study (L I N K) *to Chapter Seven: Development Across the Life Span, p. 250.* These children, 857 boys and 671 girls, had IQs (as measured by the Stanford-Binet) ranging from 130 to 200.

The early findings of this major study (Terman & Oden, 1947) demonstrated that the gifted were socially well adjusted and often skilled leaders. They were also above average in height, weight, and physical attractiveness, putting an end to the myth of the weakling genius. Terman was also able to demonstrate that his gifted children were not only *not* more susceptible to mental illness than the general population—they were actually more resistant to mental illnesses. Only those with the highest IQs (180 and above) were found to have some social and behavioral adjustment problems *as children* (Janos, 1987).

Terman's "Termites," as they came to be called, were also typically successful as adults. They earned more academic degrees and had higher occupational and financial success than their average peers (at least, the men in the study had occupational success—women at this time did not typically have careers outside the home). Researchers Zuo and Cramond (2001) examined some of Terman's gifted people to see if their identity formation as adolescents (see Chapter Seven, page 278) was related to later occupational success. They found that most of the more successful "Termites" had in fact successfully achieved a consistent sense of self, whereas those who were less successful had not done so.

A book by Joan Freeman called *Gifted Children Grown Up* (Freeman, 2001) describes the results of a similar longitudinal study of 210 gifted and nongifted children in Great Britain. One of the more interesting finds from this study is that gifted children who are "pushed" to achieve at younger and younger ages, sitting for exams long before their peers would do so, often grow up to be disappointed, somewhat unhappy adults. Freeman (2001) points to differing life conditions for the gifted as a major factor in their success, adjustment, and well being: Some lived in poverty and some in wealth, for example. Yet another longitudinal study (Torrance, 1993) found that in both gifted students and gifted adults there is more to success in life than intelligence and high academic achievement. In that study, liking one's work, having a sense of purpose in life, a high energy level, and persistence were also very important factors. If the picture of the genius as mentally unstable is a myth, so, too, is the belief that being gifted will always lead to success, as even Terman found in his original study. For more on Terman's famous study, see the Psychology in the News section that follows.

United Media/United Feature Syndicate, Inc.

Stanford University psychologist Lewis Terman is pictured at his desk in 1942. Terman spent a good portion of his career researching children with high IQ scores and was the first to use the term "gifted" to describe these children.

 CLASSIC STUDIES IN PSYCHOLOGY
Terman's Termites

8.12   *Does being intellectually gifted guarantee success in life?*

Terman's (1925) longitudinal study is still going on today, although many of his original subjects have passed away and those who remain are in their eighties. Terman himself died in 1956, but several other researchers (including Robert Sears, one of the original "Termites") have kept track of the remaining "Termites" over the years (Holahan & Sears, 1996).

As adults, the "Termites" were relatively successful, with a median income in the 1950s of $10,556, compared to the national median at that time of $5,800 a year. Most of them had graduated from college, many earning advanced degrees. Their occupations included doctors, lawyers, business executives, university professors, scientists, and even one famous science fiction writer and an Oscar-winning director (Edward Dmytryk, director of the 1954 *The Caine Mutiny*, among others).

By 2000, only about 200 "Termites" were still living. Although the study was marred by several flaws, it still remains one of the most important and rich sources of data on an entire generation. Terman's study was actually the first truly longitudinal study (see Chapter Seven) ever to be accomplished, and scientists have gotten data about the effects of phenomena such as World War II and the influence of personality traits on how long one lives from the questionnaires filled out by the participants over the years.

Terman and Oden (1959) compared the 100 most successful men in the group to the 100 least successful by defining "successful" as holding jobs that related to or used their intellectual skills. The more successful men earned more money, had careers with more prestige, and were healthier and less likely to be divorced or alcoholics than the less successful men. The IQ scores were relatively equal between the two groups, so the differences in success in life had to be caused by some other factor or factors. Terman and Oden found that the successful adults were different from the others in three ways: They were more goal oriented, more persistent in pursuing those goals, and were more self-confident than the less successful "Termites."

What were the flaws in this study? Terman acquired his participants by getting recommendations from teachers and principals, not through random selection, so that there was room for bias in the pool of participants from the start. It is quite possible that the teachers and principals were less likely, especially in 1921, to recommend students who were "troublemakers" or different from the majority. Consequently, Terman's original group consisted of almost entirely white, urban, and middle-class children, with the majority (856 out of 1,528) being male. There were two African Americans, six Japanese Americans, and one Native American.

Another flaw is the way Terman interfered in the lives of his "children." In any good research study, the investigator should avoid becoming personally involved in the lives of the participants of the studies to reduce the possibility of biasing the results. Terman seemed to find it nearly impossible to remain objective (Leslie, 2000). He became like a surrogate father to many of them, even going so far as to write a letter urging authorities to give Edward Dmytryk every consideration as they tried to determine whether 14-year-old runaway Edward was indeed being abused by his father or just telling a tall tale. Terman's letter did the trick, and Edward went to a good foster home and grew up to become a famous Hollywood director of 23 films. In another incident, one of Terman's Japanese American participants and family was in danger of being sent to an internment camp (essentially a prison camp) during World War II. They wrote to Terman and he again wrote a letter, this time to the government, vouching for the family's loyalty and arguing that they should not be interned. They were not interned. These are just two of the many ways in which Terman not only observed his participants but also influenced the course of their lives above and beyond their own intelligence levels.

Flawed as it may have been, Terman's groundbreaking study did accomplish his original goal of putting to rest the myths that existed about genius in the early part of the twentieth century. Gifted children and adults are no more prone to mental illnesses or odd behavior than any other group, and they also have their share of failures as well as successes. Genius is obviously not the only factor that influences success in life—personality and experiences are strong factors as well. For example, the homes of the children in the top 2 percent of Terman's group had an average of 450 books in their libraries, a sign that the parents of these children valued books and learning, and these parents were also more likely to be teachers, professionals, doctors, and lawyers. The experiences of these gifted children growing up would have been vastly different from those in homes with less emphasis on reading and lower occupational levels for the parents.

Questions for Further Discussion

1. In Terman and Oden's 1959 study of the successful and unsuccessful "Termites," what might be the problems associated with the definition of "successful" in the study?

2. Thinking back to the discussion of research ethics in Chapter One (pp. 31–33), what ethical violations may Terman have committed while involved in this study?

3. If gifted children thrive when growing up in more economically sound and educationally focused environments, what should the educational system strive to do to nourish the gifted? Should the government get involved in programs for the gifted?

PRACTICE **QUIZ:** HOW MUCH DO YOU REMEMBER?

Pick the best answer.

1. Jarod is 35 years old, but his mind has never gone beyond the level of a second-grade child. Jarod would be classified as _____ developmentally delayed.
   a. mildly
   b. moderately
   c. severely
   d. profoundly

2. A male with a mild developmental delay that becomes more severe as he ages probably suffers from
   a. Down syndrome.
   b. fetal alcohol syndrome.
   c. hydrocephaly.
   d. fragile X syndrome.

3. Elizabeth was tested while in grade school, and was found to have an IQ of 134. Elizabeth's intelligence level can be labeled as
   a. average.
   b. somewhat above normal.
   c. gifted.
   d. genius.

4. Which of the following statements about the successful "Termites" in the Terman and Oden (1959) study is NOT true?
   a. The successful men earned more money.
   b. The successful men were more likely to be divorced.
   c. The unsuccessful men were less healthy.
   d. The unsuccessful men held jobs of lower prestige.

Answers: 1-b, 2-d, 3-c, 4-b.

THEORIES OF INTELLIGENCE

It still seems strange to think that "intelligence" can be measured by one little number—it seems almost too simple. Although Terman's view of intelligence as measured by a single number is still in use, other researchers have proposed different definitions of and ways to measure intelligence, which can be seen as the result of several different abilities. It is the number of abilities and their nature that result in the different views of intelligence that follow.

8.13   *What are the theories of intelligence and how do they differ?*

SPEARMAN'S G FACTOR   Spearman (1904) saw intelligence as two different abilities, both measurable by intelligence tests. The ability to reason and solve problems was labeled **g factor** for *general intelligence*, whereas a person's ability to excel in certain areas such as music, business, or art was labeled **s factor** for *specific intelligence*. A traditional IQ test would most likely measure g factor, but Spearman believed that superiority in one type of intelligence predicts superiority overall. Although his early research found some support for specific intelligences, other researchers (Guilford,

◄ It still seems **strange** to think that "intelligence" can be measured by one little number—it seems almost too simple.

g factor
the ability to reason and solve problems, or general intelligence.

s factor
the ability to excel in certain areas, or specific intelligence.

triarchic theory of intelligence
Sternberg's theory that there are three kinds of intelligences: analytical, creative, and practical.

analytical intelligence
the ability to break problems down into component parts, or analysis, for problem solving.

creative intelligence
the ability to deal with new and different concepts and to come up with new ways of solving problems.

TABLE 8.7 **GARDNER'S NINE INTELLIGENCES**

Type of Intelligence	Description	Sample Occupation
Verbal/linguistic	Ability to use language	Writers, speakers
Musical	Ability to compose and/or perform music	Musicians, even those who do not read musical notes but can perform and compose
Logical/mathematical	Ability to think logically and to solve mathematical problems	Scientists, engineers
Visual/spatial	Ability to understand how objects are oriented in space	Pilots, astronauts, artists, navigators
Movement	Ability to control one's body motions	Dancers, athletes
Interpersonal	Sensitivity to others and understanding motivation of others	Psychologists, managers
Intrapersonal	Understanding of one's emotions and how they guide actions	Various people-oriented careers
Naturalist	Ability to recognize the patterns found in nature	Farmers, landscapers, biologists, botanists
Existentialist	Ability to see the "big picture" of the human world by asking questions about life, death, and the ultimate reality of human existence	Various careers, philosophical thinkers

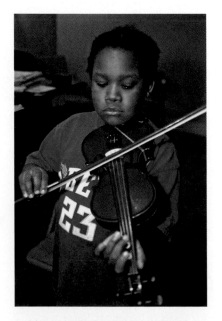

This child is displaying only one of the many forms that intelligence can take, according to Gardner's multiple intelligences theory.

1967; Thurstone, 1938) felt that Spearman had oversimplified the concept of intelligence. Intelligence began to be viewed as composed of numerous factors. In fact, Guilford (1967) proposed that there were 120 types of intelligence.

GARDNER'S MULTIPLE INTELLIGENCES   One of the later theorists to propose the existence of several kinds of intelligence was Gardner (1993b, 1999a). Although many people use the terms *reason*, *logic*, and *knowledge* as if they are the same ability, Gardner believes that they are different aspects of intelligence, along with several other abilities. He originally listed seven different kinds of intelligence but has recently (Gardner, 1998) added an eighth type and then a ninth (Gardner, 1999b). The nine types of intelligence are described in Table 8.7.

The idea of multiple intelligences has great appeal, especially for educators, in spite of the fact that there is little scientific evidence that such intelligences are anything more than different abilities and that those abilities are not necessarily the same thing as what is typically meant by *intelligence* (Hunt, 2001).

STERNBERG'S TRIARCHIC THEORY   Sternberg (1988, 1997) has theorized that there are three kinds of intelligence. Called the **triarchic theory of intelligence** (*triarchic* means "three"), this theory is similar to Aristotle's theory that intelligence is composed of theoretical, productive, and practical aspects.

In Sternberg's theory, the three aspects are *analytical, creative*, and *practical intelligence*. **Analytical intelligence** refers to the ability to break problems down into component parts, or analysis, for problem solving. This is the type of intelligence that is measured by intelligence tests and academic achievement tests, or "book smarts" as some people like to call it. **Creative intelligence** is the ability to deal with new and different concepts and to come up with new ways of solving problems (divergent thinking, in other words). **Practical intelligence** is best described as "street smarts," or the ability to use information to get along in life. People with a high degree of practical intelligence know how to be tactful, how to manipulate situations to their advantage, and how to use inside information to increase their odds of success.

How might these three types of intelligence be illustrated? All three might come into play when planning and completing an experiment. For example:

Analytical: Being able to run a statistical analysis on data from the experiment.

Creative: Being able to design the experiment in the first place.

Practical: Being able to get funding for the experiment from donors.

Practical intelligence has become a topic of much interest and research. Sternberg (1996, 1997) has found that practical intelligence predicts success in life but has a surprisingly low relationship to academic (analytical) intelligence. In fact, the higher one's degree of practical intelligence, the less likely that person is to succeed in a university or other academic setting.

EMOTIONAL INTELLIGENCE   What about people who have a lot of "book smarts" but not much common sense? There are people like that, who never seem to get ahead in life, in spite of having all that so-called intelligence. It is true that not everyone who is intellectually able is going to be a success in life (Mehrabian, 2000). Often the people who are most successful are those who didn't do all that well in the regular academic setting.

One of the early explanations for why people who succeed in life often did poorly in school and those who did well in school did not excel in the "real" world was that success relies on a certain degree of **emotional intelligence**, the awareness of and ability to manage one's own emotions as well as the ability to be self-motivated, to feel what others feel, and to be socially skilled (Persaud, 2001).

The concept of emotional intelligence was first introduced by Salovey and Mayer (1990) and later expanded upon by Goleman (1995). Goleman proposed that emotional intelligence is a more powerful influence on success in life than more traditional views of intelligence. One who is emotionally intelligent possesses self-control of emotions such as anger, impulsiveness, and anxiety. Empathy, the ability to understand what others feel, is also a component, as are an awareness of one's own

Sternberg's practical intelligence is a form of "street smarts" that includes the ability to adapt to one's environment and solve practical problems. These girls are giving their younger brother a drink of water by using a folded leaf as an impromptu cup.

practical intelligence
the ability to use information to get along in life and become successful.

emotional intelligence
the awareness of and ability to manage one's own emotions as well as the ability to be self-motivated, able to feel what others feel, and socially skilled.

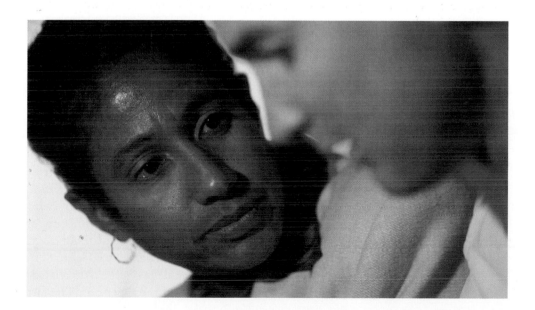

Emotional intelligence includes empathy, which is the ability to feel what others are feeling. This doctor is not only able to listen to her patient's problems but also able to show by her facial expression, body language, and gestures that she understands how the patient feels.

emotions, sensitivity, persistence even in the face of frustrations, and the ability to motivate oneself (Salovey & Mayer, 1990).

That all sounds very nice, ▶
but how can anything
like this be measured? Is
there research to
support this idea?

That all sounds very nice, but how can anything like this be measured? Is there research to support this idea? In one study, researchers asked 321 participants to read passages written by nonparticipants and try to guess what the nonparticipants were feeling while they were writing (Mayer & Geher, 1996). The assumption was that people who were good at connecting thoughts to feelings would also have a high degree of empathy and emotional intelligence. The participants who more correctly judged the writers' emotional experiences (assessed by both how well each participant's emotional judgments agreed with a group consensus and the nonparticipant's actual report of feelings) also scored higher on the empathy measure and lower on the defensiveness measure. These same participants also had higher SAT scores (self-reported), leading Mayer and colleagues to conclude not only that emotional intelligence is a valid and measurable concept but also that general intelligence and emotional intelligence may be related: Those who are high in emotional intelligence are also smarter in the traditional sense (Mayer et al., 2000).

Although his own work and that of his colleagues provide empirical support for the concept of emotional intelligence, Mayer (1999) has criticized the presentation of emotional intelligence in popular magazines and best-selling (but nonscientific) books by stating in an online article for the American Psychology Association,

". . . the popular literature's implication—that highly emotionally intelligent people possess an unqualified advantage in life—appears overly enthusiastic at present and unsubstantiated by reasonable scientific standards."

THE NATURE/NURTURE CONTROVERSY REGARDING INTELLIGENCE

8.14 *What is the influence of heredity and environment on the development of intelligence?*

Are people born with all of the "smarts" they will ever have, or does experience and learning count for something in the development of intellect? The influence of nature (heredity or genes) and nurture (environment) on personality traits has long been debated in the field of human development (see Chapter Seven, p. 251), and intelligence is one of the traits that has been examined closely.

TWIN STUDIES   The problem with trying to separate the role of genes from that of environment is that controlled, perfect experiments are neither practical nor ethical. Instead, researchers find out what they can from *natural experiments*, circumstances existing in nature that can be examined to understand some phenomenon. *Twin studies* are an example of such circumstances.

Identical twins are those who originally came from one fertilized egg and, therefore, share the same genetic inheritance. Any differences between them on a certain trait, then, should be caused by environmental factors. Fraternal twins come from two different eggs, each fertilized by a different sperm, and share only the amount of genetic material that any two siblings would share. Ⓛ Ⓘ Ⓝ Ⓚ *to Chapter Seven: Development Across the Life Span, p. 255.* By comparing the IQs of these two types of twins reared together (similar environments) and reared apart (different environments), as well as persons of other degrees of relatedness, researchers can get a general, if not exact, idea of how much influence heredity has over the trait of intelligence (see Figure 8.5).

As can be easily seen from the chart, the greater the degree of genetic relatedness, the stronger the correlation is between the IQ scores of those persons. The fact

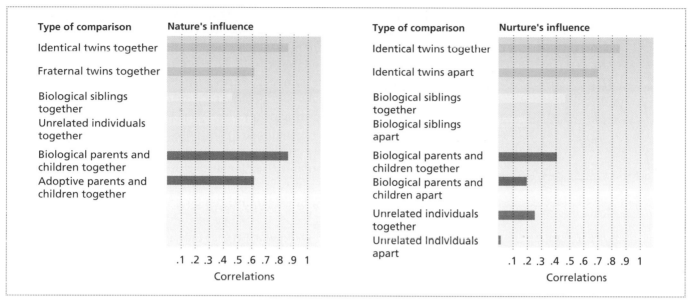

FIGURE 8.5 **Correlations between IQ Scores of Persons with Various Relationships** In the graph on the left, the degree of genetic relatedness seems to determine the agreement (correlation) between IQ scores of the various comparisons. For example, identical twins, who share 100 percent of their genes are more similar in IQ than fraternal twins, who share only about 50 percent of their genes, even when raised in the same environment. In the graph on the right, identical twins are still more similar to each other in IQ than are other types of comparisons, but being raised in the same environment increases the similarity considerably.

that genetically identical twins show a correlation of 0.86 means that the environment must play a part in determining some aspects of intelligence as measured by IQ tests. If heredity alone were responsible, the correlation between genetically identical twins should be 1.00. At this time, researchers have determined that the estimated *heritability* (proportion of change in IQ within a population that is caused by hereditary factors) for intelligence is about 0.50 or 50 percent (Plomin & DeFries, 1998).

Wait a minute—if identical twins have a correlation of 0.86, wouldn't that mean that intelligence is 86 percent inherited? Although the correlation between identical twins is higher than the estimated heritability of 0.50, that similarity is not entirely due to the twin's genetic similarity. Twins who are raised in the same household obviously share very similar environments as well. Even twins who are reared apart are usually placed in homes that are similar in socioeconomic and ethnic background—more similar than one might think. So when twins who are genetically similar are raised in similar environments, their IQ scores are also going to be similar.

Heritability is worth a little more explanation because findings show that genes have significant influence on human behavior. A trait like height is one that is highly heritable; in a group of people who are all nearly equal in nourishment, for example, differences between them in height will be caused almost entirely by differences in their genes. But something like table manners is very low in heritability; table manners are a result of experience and upbringing, not genetics (Dickens & Flynn, 2001).

One of the things that people need to understand about heritability is that estimates of heritability apply only to changes in IQ within a *group* of people, *not to the individual people themselves*. Each individual is far too different in experiences, education, and other nongenetic factors to predict exactly how a particular set of genes will interact with those factors in that one person. It is only differences among people *in general* that can be investigated for the influence of genes (Dickens & Flynn, 2001). Genes always interact with environmental factors, and in some cases extreme environments can modify even very heritable traits, as would happen in the case of a severely malnourished child's growth pattern.

◀ Wait a minute—if identical twins have a correlation of 0.86, wouldn't that mean that intelligence is 86 percent inherited?

"I don't know anything about the bell curve, but I say heredity is everything".

©The New Yorker Collection 1994 Charles Barsotti from cartoonbank.com. All Rights Reserved.

THE BELL CURVE AND MISINTERPRETATION OF STATISTICS In 1994, Herrnstein and Murray published the controversial book *The Bell Curve*, in which they cite large amounts of statistical studies (never published in scientific journals prior to the book) that led them to make the claim that IQ is largely inherited. These authors go further by also implying that people from lower economic levels are poor because they are unintelligent.

In their book, Herrnstein and Murray made several statistical errors and ignored the effects of environment and culture. First, they assumed that IQ tests actually do measure intelligence. As discussed earlier, IQ tests are not free of cultural or socioeconomic bias. So all they really found was a correlation between race and *IQ*, not race and *intelligence*. Second, they assumed that intelligence itself is very heavily influenced by genetics, with a heritability factor of about 0.80. The current estimate of the heritability of intelligence is about 0.50 (Plomin & DeFries, 1998).

Herrnstein and Murray also failed to understand that heritability only applies to differences that can be found *within* a group of people as opposed to those *between* groups of people or individuals (Gould, 1981). Heritability estimates can only be made truly from a group that was exposed to a similar environment.

One of their findings was that Japanese Americans are at the top of the IQ ladder, a finding that they attribute to racial and genetic characteristics. They seem to ignore the cultural influence of intense focus on education and achievement by Japanese American parents (Neisser et al., 1996). Scientists (Beardsley, 1995; Kamin, 1995) have concluded that, despite the claims of *The Bell Curve*, there is no real scientific evidence for genetic differences in intelligence *between* different racial groups. A series of studies, using blood-group testing for racial grouping (different racial groups have different rates of certain blood groups, allowing a statistical estimation of ancestry), found no significant relationship between ethnicity and IQ (Neisser et al., 1996).

Although *The Bell Curve* stated that Japanese Americans are genetically superior in intelligence, the book's authors overlook the influence of cultural values. Japanese American parents put much time and effort into helping their children with schoolwork.

PRACTICE QUIZ: HOW MUCH DO YOU REMEMBER?

Pick the best answer.

1. According to Spearman, a traditional IQ test would most likely measure
  a. practical intelligence.
  b. specific intelligence.
  c. general intelligence.
  d. emotional intelligence.

2. In Gardner's view, astronauts, navigators, and artists would be high in _____ intelligence.
  a. verbal/linguistic
  b. visual/spatial
  c. interpersonal
  d. intrapersonal

3. Sternberg has found that _____ intelligence is a good predictor of success in life but has a low relationship to _____ intelligence.
  a. practical; academic
  b. practical; creative
  c. academic; practical
  d. academic; creative

4. Which of the following was NOT one of the errors of the authors of *The Bell Curve*?
  a. They assumed that IQ tests are good measures of intelligence.
  b. They found a correlation between race and IQ, not race and intelligence.
  c. They assumed that intelligence was heavily influenced by genetics.
  d. They assumed that heritability applied only to differences within groups of people.

Language

8.15 *What is the definition of language?*

Language is a system for combining symbols (such as words) so that an infinite* number of meaningful statements can be made for the purpose of communicating with others. Language allows people not only to communicate with one another but also to represent their own internal mental activity. In other words, language is a very important part of how people think. Whereas Chapter Seven discussed the theories of language development, this chapter's focus concerns the characteristics of language.

THE LEVELS OF LANGUAGE ANALYSIS

8.16 *What are the different elements of a language and its structure?*

The structures of languages all over the world share common characteristics. Languages involve word order, word meanings, the rules for making words into other words, the sounds that exist within a language, the rules for practical communication with others, and the meanings of sentences and phrases.

GRAMMAR   **Grammar** is the system of rules governing the structure and use of a language. It includes rules for the order of words known as syntax and morphology, the study of the formation of words.

SYNTAX   **Syntax** is a system of rules for combining words and phrases to form grammatically correct sentences. Consider the following sentence: "Where does the American president live?" The adjective *American* comes before the noun *president*, and the verb is a complex one involving both *does* and *live*. In English, this makes perfect sense. In Spanish, the word order of the sentence with the exact same meaning would be: "*¿Dónde vive el presidente norteamericano?*" Literally translated, it says "Where lives the president American?" which is incorrect syntax in English but perfectly correct in Spanish. As one can imagine, syntax is quite important. Just a simple mix-up can cause sentences to be completely misunderstood. For example, "John kidnapped the boy" has a different meaning from "John, the kidnapped boy" although all four words are the same (Lasnik, 1990).

One last example of the importance of syntax can be found in the lobby of a Moscow hotel across from a monastery: "You are welcome to visit the cemetery where famous composers, artists, and writers are buried daily except Thursday." So if people want to watch famous composers, artists, and writers being buried, they should not go to this monastery on Thursday.

MORPHEMES   **Morphemes** are the smallest units of meaning within a language. For example, the word *playing* consists of two morphemes, *play* and *ing*. *Play* is a good example of a *free morpheme*, one that has meaning as it stands alone, whereas *ing* is an example of a *bound morpheme*, which has no meaning by itself but is attached to another morpheme, changing its grammatical function.

Morphemes themselves are governed by **semantics**, rules for determining the meaning of words and sentences. Sentences, for example, can have the same semantic meaning while having different syntax: "Johnny hit the ball" and "the ball was hit by Johnny."

PHONEMES   **Phonemes** are the basic units of sound in a language. The *a* in the word *car* is a very different phoneme from the *a* in the word *day*, even though it is the same letter of the alphabet. The difference is in how we say the sound of the *a* in each word.

---

*Infinite: unlimited, without end.

---

language
a system for combining symbols (such as words) so that an unlimited number of meaningful statements can be made for the purpose of communicating with others.

grammar
the system of rules governing the structure and use a of language.

syntax
the system of rules for combining words and phrases to form grammatically correct sentences.

morphemes
the smallest units of meaning within a language.

semantics
the rules for determining the meaning of words and sentences.

phonemes
the basic units of sound in language.

Phonemes are more than just the different ways in which we pronounce single letters, too. *Th*, *sh*, and *au* are also phonemes. Phonemes for different languages are also different, and one of the biggest problems for people who are trying to learn another language is the inability to both hear and pronounce the phonemes of that other language. Although infants are born with the ability to recognize all phonemes (Werker & Lalonde, 1988), after about nine months, that ability has deteriorated and the infant recognizes only the phonemes of the language to which the infant is exposed (Boyson-Bardies et al., 1989).

How many phonemes are there? The number of phonemes in English is estimated at 35 to 40 (Calvert, 1992). The different estimates are the result of disagreements among linguists as to exactly how certain phonemes differ from other phonemes. Other languages can have as few as 10 (in the Pirahã language spoken by Pirahã people of Brazil) or as many as 141 (in the !Kung language spoken in certain areas of Africa).

PRAGMATICS The **pragmatics** of language have do with the practical aspects of communicating with others, or the social "niceties" of language. Simply put, pragmatics involve knowing things like how to take turns in a conversation, the use of gestures to emphasize a point or indicate a need for more information, and the different ways in which one speaks to different people (Yule, 1996). For example, adults speak to small children differently than they do to other adults by using simpler words. Both adults and children use higher pitched voices and many repeated phrases when talking to infants. Part of the pragmatics of language includes knowing just what rhythm and emphasis to use when communicating with others, called *intonation*. When speaking to infants, adults and children are changing the inflection when they use the higher pitch and stress certain words differently than others. Some languages, such as Japanese, are highly sensitive to intonation, meaning that changing the pronunciation of a particular word can change its meaning entirely (Beckman & Pierrehumbert, 1986). For example, the Japanese name "Yoshiko" should be pronounced with the accent or stress on the first syllable: YO-she-koh. This pronunciation of the name means "woman-child." But if the stress is placed on the second syllable (yo-SHE-ko), the name means "woman who urinates."

THE RELATIONSHIP BETWEEN LANGUAGE AND THOUGHT

8.17 *Does language influence the way people think?*

As with the controversy of nature versus nurture, researchers have long debated the relationship between language and thought. Does language actually influence thought, or does thinking influence language?

LINGUISTIC RELATIVITY HYPOTHESIS For quite some time, the hypothesis that language shapes and influences thoughts was accepted by many theorists, although there were some who believed that thoughts influence the development of langue, such as Jean Piaget (1926). Known as the Sapir-Whorf hypothesis after the two theorists, Edward Sapir and his student, Benjamin Lee Whorf, this hypothesis assumed that the thought processes and concepts within any culture are determined by the words of the culture (Sapir, 1921; Whorf, 1956). It has come to be known as the **linguistic relativity hypothesis**, meaning that thought processes and concepts are controlled by (relative to) language. That is, the words people use determine much of the way in which they think about the world around them.

One of the most famous examples used by Whorf to support this idea was that of the Inuits, Native Americans living in the Arctic. Supposedly, the Inuits have many more words for *snow* than do people in other cultures. One estimate was 23 different words, while other estimates have ranged in the hundreds. Unfortunately, this anec-

How many phonemes are there?

Pragmatics involves the practical aspects of communicating. This young mother is talking and then pausing for the infant's response. In this way, the infant is learning about taking turns, an important aspect of language development. What kinds of games do adults play with infants that also aid the development of language?

pragmatics
aspects of language involving the practical ways of communicating with others, or the social "niceties" of language.

linguistic relativity hypothesis
the theory that thought processes and concepts are controlled by language.

dotal evidence has turned out to be false being more myth than reality (Pullum, 1991). In fact, English speakers also have many different words for snow (sleet, slush, powder, dusting, and yellow, to name a few).

Is there evidence for the linguistic relativity hypothesis? Neither Sapir nor Whorf provided any scientific studies that would support their proposition. There have been numerous studies by other researchers, however. For example, in one study researchers assumed that a language's color names would influence the ability of the people who grew up with that language to distinguish among and perceive colors. The study found that basic color terms did directly influence color recognition memory (Lucy & Shweder, 1979). But an earlier series of studies of the perception of colors (Rosch-Heider, 1972; Rosch-Heider & Olivier, 1972) had already found just the opposite effect: Members of the Dani tribe, who have only two names for colors, were no different in their ability to perceive all of the colors than were the English speakers in the study. More recent studies (Davics, 1998a, 1998b; Laws et al., 1995; Pinker & Bloom, 1990) support Rosch-Heider's findings and the idea of a **cognitive universalism** (concepts are universal and influence the development of language) rather than linguistic relativity.

Other research suggests that although the linguistic relativity hypothesis may not work for fine perceptual discriminations such as those in the Rosch-Heider studies, it may be an appropriate explanation for concepts of a higher level. In one study, researchers showed pictures of two animals to preschool children (Gelman & Markham, 1986). The pictures were of a flamingo and a bat. The children were told that the flamingo feeds its baby mashed-up food but the bat feeds its baby milk. Then they were shown a picture of a blackbird (which looked more like the bat than the flamingo). Half of the children were told that the blackbird was a bird, while the other children were not. When asked how the blackbird fed its baby, the children who had been given the bird label were more likely to say that it fed its baby mashed-up food than were the children who were not given the label, indicating that the preschoolers were making inferences about feeding habits based on category membership rather than perceptual similarity—the word *bird* helped the children who were given that label to place the blackbird in its proper higher-level category.

Psychologists cannot deny the influence of language on problem solving, cognition, and memory. Sometimes a problem can simply be worded differently to have the solution become obvious, and memory (LINK) *to Chapter Six: Memory, p. 219.* is certainly stored in terms of the semantics of language. Language can definitely influence the perception of others as well—"computer geek" and "software engineer" might be used to describe the same person, but one phrase is obviously less flattering and the image brought to mind is different for the two terms. In the end, trying to determine whether language influences thoughts or thoughts influence language may be like trying to determine which came first, the chicken or the egg.

ANIMAL STUDIES IN LANGUAGE   I've heard that chimpanzees can be taught to use sign language. Is this for real, or are the chimps just performing tricks like the animals you can see in the circus or the zoo? There are really two questions about animals and language. The first is "can animals communicate?" and the second is "can animals use language?" The answer to the first question is a definite "yes." Animals communicate in many ways. They use sounds such as the rattle of a rattlesnake or the warning growl of an angry dog. There are also physical behaviors, such as the "dance" of honeybees that tells the other bees where a source of pollen is (Gould & Gould, 1994). But the answer to the second question is more complicated because language is defined as the use of symbols, and symbols are things that stand for something else. Words are symbols, and gestures can be symbols. But the gestures used by animals are instinctual, meaning they are controlled by the animal's genetic makeup. The honeybee doing the "dance"

cognitive universalism
theory that concepts are universal and influence the development of language.

I've heard that chimpanzees can be taught to use sign language. Is this for real, or are the chimps just performing tricks like the animals you can see in the circus or the zoo?

is controlled completely by instinct, as is the growling dog. In human language, symbols are used quite deliberately and voluntarily, not by instinct, and abstract symbols have no meaning until people assign meaning to them.

8.18 *Are animals capable of learning language?*

Can animals be taught to use symbols that are abstract? There have been attempts to teach animals how to use sign language (as animals lack the vocal structure to form spoken words), but many of these attempts were simply not "good science." The most successful of these experiments (which is not without its critics as well) has been with Kanzi, a bonobo chimpanzee trained to press abstract symbols on a computer keyboard (Savage-Rumbaugh & Lewin, 1994). Kanzi actually was not the original subject of the study—his mother, Matata, was the chimp being trained. She did not learn many of the symbols, but Kanzi watched his mother use the keyboard and appeared to learn how to use the symbols through that observation. At last count, Kanzi could understand about 150 spoken English words. Trainers who speak to him are not in his view, so he is not responding to physical cues or symbols. He has managed to follow correctly complex instructions up to the level of a $2\frac{1}{2}$-year-old (Savage-Rumbaugh et al., 1998). The most recent studies with Kanzi have him making sounds that seem to have consistent meaning across different situations (Tagliatatela et al., 2003). Nearly 100 videotaped hours of Kanzi engaged in day-to-day activites were analyzed for these sounds. The researchers were able to identify four sounds that seemed to represent banana, grapes, juice, and the word *yes*. (However, remember that four sounds do not come close to making an entire language.)

Other studies with dolphins (Herman et al., 1993) and a parrot (Pepperberg, 1998) have also met with some success. Is it real language? The answer seems to be a qualified "yes." The qualification is that none of the animals that have achieved success so far can compare to the level of language development of a 3-year-old human child (Pinker, 1995). However, linguists still debate whether these animals are truly learning language if they are not also learning how to use syntax—combining words into grammatically correct sentences as well as being able to understand the differences between sentences such as "The girl kissed the boy" and "The boy kissed the girl." As yet, there is no evidence that any of the animals trained in language have been able to master syntax (Demers, 1988; Johnson, 1995; Pinker, 1995).

Kanzi looks at the keyboard used in teaching language to chimpanzees. Kanzi's language abilities were learned through watching the researchers train his mother rather than directly—much as a human infant learns through listening to the speech of adults.

PRACTICE **QUIZ:** HOW MUCH DO YOU REMEMBER?

Pick the best answer.

1. The system of rules for combining words and phrases to make meaningful sentences is called
    a. grammar.
    b. phonics.
    c. syntax.
    d. morphology.

2. Grammar includes all but which of the following aspects of language?
    a. tone
    b. sounds
    c. order
    d. meaning

3. The sounds of the letters b, z, c, and d are examples of
    a. morphemes.
    b. phonemes.
    c. semantics.
    d. syntax.

4. The Dani have only two words for color yet can distinguish between many different colors. This finding supports the language theory of
    a. Sapir and Whorf.
    b. Lucy and Shweder.
    c. Pullum.
    d. Rosch.

5. The quality of language produced by animals cannot yet compare to the level achieved by a _____ human.
    a. 1-year-old
    b. 2-year-old
    c. 3-year-old
    d. 5-year-old

Answers: 1-c, 2-a, 3-b, 4-b, 5-c.

Applying Psychology to Everyday Life: Mental Exercises for Better Cognitive Health

8.19 *What are some ways to improve thinking?*

The brain is not a muscle, but it needs exercise to stay "fit" just as muscles do. Research has shown that people who regularly work crossword puzzles, take classes, read, and stay mentally active are less likely to develop senile dementia than those who fail to use their minds (Ball et al., 2002; Cabeza et al., 2002; Wilson et al., 2002).

The following exercises are taken from *Brain Fitness* (LePoncin, 1990). Monique LePoncin is the founder of the French National Institute for Research on the Prevention of Cerebral Aging. The exercises that follow are based on the various mental abilities that have been researched in human thought processes, such as memory and perception. Many of these can be done while traveling to or from work, shopping, or doing other errands, during breaks, or even when in the bathroom.

PERCEPTIVE ABILITY EXERCISES

1. For sight, try to look at an object such as a photograph or a person you pass on the street. Draw it (or him or her) immediately to exercise short-term memory. At the end of the week, redraw the seven things you have observed during the seven days—an exercise of long-term memory.

2. For smell and taste (which do decline with age), try to identify the ingredients in whatever food you are eating at a friend's house or in a restaurant. Concentrate on the herbs and spices, and ask the host or wait staff to confirm your guesses.

3. For memory, try to memorize the dishes on your favorite restaurant's menu. If you want a greater challenge, memorize the prices, too. At the end of the day, try to write as many of the dishes and prices down as you can.

4. For hearing as well as memory, try to recognize callers on the phone before they identify themselves. Memorize the phone numbers and then write down both the people and the numbers of those with whom you spoke at the end of the day. Repeat at the end of the week for the entire week.

5. Another exercise for smell as well as touch is to try to identify objects with your eyes closed.

6. Visuospatial abilities are used to estimate distances, areas, and volumes (handy when packing a suitcase or storing items away in a box). When you walk into a room, try to determine how many people are on your right and on your left, as well as where the objects in the room are, as quickly as you can. Draw maps of the places you have visited when you return home, and draw them again the next day.

7. Working jigsaw puzzles as quickly as possible will exercise your ability to build a logical whole from different elements.

8. Exercising logical thinking can be accomplished by using memory systems to remember the items you need to buy in the store rather than using a list. Any of the systems mentioned in the Introduction will work. Play card games, board games that use strategy like chess or checkers, and do word games like crosswords, anagrams, and word searches. Don't play the same games all the time; mix them up for variety.

9. Exercise your verbal abilities by listening to the news and writing down the main points at some later time in the day. When reading a chapter of a book, try to imagine having to summarize it as briefly as possible to someone who has not read it. Do the same thing for the whole book when finished.

One of the best ways to exercise not only logical thinking abilities but also divergent thinking abilities is to work a type of crossword puzzle called a "cryptic crossword." In these puzzles, the clues themselves are various kinds of word puzzles, riddles, and hidden meanings. In each clue, there is a literal definition or clue for the word as well as a second definition that might be a pun or an anagram, or the word itself might be hidden within the clue.

For example, the clue "Digital mice run out" would lead to the word *numeric*, an anagram of "mice run." The word *out* is the clue that "mice run" needs to be rearranged to provide the answer for the normal clue "digital." Or a clue such as "Gasp here—shortstop's trapping balls" leads to the answer "spheres," which is actually hidden in the words *gasp here shortstop*. That phrase is "trapping" the word and the real definition is "balls." People may have to cheat outrageously as they learn how to "think outside the box" for this type of puzzle, but they will eventually improve and find that they are much more creative in their thinking than they were before they tried cryptics. (Warning: cryptic crosswords can be addictive.)

Many cryptic crosswords can be found on the Internet or in puzzle magazines. Here are a few of the better sites:

Teresa's Cryptic Crosswords: **www.execulink.com/~tagies**

Webber's Cryptic Crosswords: **http://thinks.com/crosswords/cryptic/cryptic.htm**

The Globe and Mail (a daily cryptic crossword that you work online): **www.globeandmail.com/crosswords**

Questions for Further Discussion
1. What other kinds of mental activities might help to keep the brain fit?
2. Should doctors suggest mental fitness exercises to their patients?
3. What media sources (e.g., television, magazines) exist that help to promote mental fitness?

8   *Intelligence= problem solving*

CHAPTER SUMMARY

How People Think

- Thinking (cognition) is mental activity that occurs in the brain when information is being organized, stored, communicated, or processed.

8.1   *How do people use mental images to think?*

- Mental images represent objects or events and have a picture-like quality.

8.2   *What is the nature of a concept?*

- Concepts are ideas that represent a class or category of events, objects, or activities.
- Prototypes are examples of a concept that more closely match the defining characteristics of that concept.

8.3   *What methods do people use to solve problems and make decisions?*

- Problem solving consists of thinking and behaving in certain ways to reach a goal.
- Mechanical solutions include trial-and-error learning and rote solutions.
- Algorithms are a type of rote solution in which one follows step-by-step procedures for solving certain types of problems.
- A heuristic or "rule of thumb" is a strategy that narrows down the possible solutions for a problem.
- Insight is the sudden perception of a solution to a problem.

Psychology in the News: Artificial Intelligence (AI)

8.4   *What is artificial intelligence?*

- Artificial intelligence refers to the attempt to create a machine that thinks like a human being.
- Although some computers have been designed that can play chess and perform in similar ways to a human, the true flexibility of human thought processes has yet to be developed in a machine.

8.5   *What are the barriers to solving problems?*

- Functional fixedness is the tendency to perceive objects as having only the use for which they were originally intended and, therefore, failing to see them as possible tools for solving other problems.
- Confirmation bias is the tendency to search for evidence that confirms one's beliefs, ignoring any evidence to the contrary.

8.6   *What is creative thinking?*

- Divergent thinking involves coming up with as many different answers as possible. This is a kind of creativity (combining ideas or behavior in new ways).
- Creative people are usually good at mental imagery and have knowledge on a wide range of topics, are unafraid to be different, value their independence, and are often unconventional in their work but not in other areas.

Intelligence

8.7   *What is the definition of intelligence?*

- Intelligence is the ability to understand the world, think rationally or logically, and use resources effectively when faced with challenges or problems.

8.8   *How do intelligence tests measure intelligence?*

- The Stanford-Binet Intelligence Test yields an IQ score that is determined by dividing the mental age of the person by the chronological age and multiplying that quotient by 100.
- The Wechsler Intelligence Tests yield a verbal score and a performance score as well as an overall score of intelligence.

8.9   *How are intelligence tests constructed?*

- Standardization, validity, and reliability are all important factors in the construction of an intelligence test.
- Deviation IQs are based on the normal curve, defining different levels of intelligence based on the deviation of scores from a common mean.
- IQ tests are often criticized for being culturally biased.

8.10   *What is mental retardation and what causes it?*

- Mental retardation or developmental delay is a condition in which IQ falls below 70 and adaptive behavior is severely deficient for a person of a particular chronological age.
- The four levels of delay are: Mild: 55–70 IQ; Moderate: 40–55 IQ; Severe: 25–40 IQ; and Profound: Below 25 IQ.
- Causes of developmental delay include deprived environments as well as chromosome and genetic disorders and dietary deficiencies.

8.11   *What is giftedness?*

- Gifted persons are defined as those having IQ scores at the upper end of the normal curve (130 or above).

Classic Studies in Psychology: Terman's Termites

8.12   *Does being intellectually gifted guarantee success in life?*

- Terman conducted a longitudinal study that demonstrated that gifted children grow up to be successful adults for the most part.
- Terman's study has been criticized for a lack of objectivity because Terman became too involved in the lives of his participants, even to the point of interfering on their behalf.

8.13   *What are the theories of intelligence and how do they differ?*

- Spearman proposed general intelligence, or g factor, as the ability to reason and solve problems, whereas specific intelligence, or s factor, is the ability to excel in certain areas such as music or business.
- Gardner proposed nine different types of intelligence, ranging from verbal, linguistic, and mathematical to interpersonal and intrapersonal intelligence.
- Sternberg proposed three types of intelligence: analytical, creative, and practical.
- Emotional intelligence is viewed as a powerful influence on success in life.

8.14   *What is the influence of heredity and environment on the development of intelligence?*

- Stronger correlations are found between IQ scores as genetic relatedness increases. Heritability of IQ is estimated at 0.50.
- In 1994, Herrnstein and Murray published *The Bell Curve* in which they made widely criticized claims about the heritability of intelligence.

Language

8.15 *What is the definition of language?*

• Language is a system for combining symbols so that an infinite number of meaningful statements can be created and communicated to others.

8.16 *What are the different elements of a language and its structure?*

• Grammar is the system of rules by which language is governed and includes the rules for using phonemes, morphemes, and syntax. Pragmatics refers to practical aspects of language.

8.17 *Does language influence the way people think?*

• Sapir and Whorf originally proposed that language controls and helps the development of thought processes and concepts, an idea that is known as the linguistic relativity hypothesis.

• Other researchers have found evidence that concepts are universal and directly influence the development of language, called the cognitive universalism viewpoint.

8.18 *Are animals capable of learning language?*

• Studies with chimpanzees, parrots, and dolphins have been somewhat successful in demonstrating that animals can develop a basic kind of language, including some abstract ideas.

• Controversy exists over the lack of evidence that animals can learn syntax, which some feel means that animals are not truly learning and using language.

Applying Psychology to Everyday Life: Mental Exercises for Better Cognitive Health

8.19 *What are some ways to improve thinking?*

• Mental activity that requires creativity and the use of memory abilities, such as working crossword puzzles and reading books, can help to keep the brain fit.

8 KEY TERMS

algorithms 298
analytical intelligence 318
artificial intelligence (AI) 300
basic level type 296
cognitive universalism 325
concepts 295
confirmation bias 303
convergent thinking 304
creative intelligence 318
creativity 304
developmentally delayed 312
deviation IQ scores 309
divergent thinking 304
emotional intelligence 319
formal concepts 296

functional fixedness 303
g factor 317
gifted 314
grammar 323
heuristic 299
intelligence 306
intelligence quotient (IQ) 306
language 323
linguistic relativity hypothesis 324
means–end analysis 299
mental images 294
mental set 303
morphemes 323
natural concepts 296
phonemes 323

practical intelligence 319
pragmatics 324
problem solving 298
prototype 297
reliability 308
s factor 317
semantics 323
subordinate concept 296
superordinate concept 296
syntax 323
thinking (cognition) 294
trial and error (mechanical solution) 298
triarchic theory of intelligence 318
validity 308

TEST YOURSELF

Pick the best answer.

1. Mental activity that goes on in the brain when a person is processing information is called
  a. mentation.
  b. a concept.
  c. thinking.
  d. mental imagery.

2. Concepts that are formed as a result of everyday experience, which are not always well defined, are known as _____ concepts.
  a. formal
  b. natural
  c. prototypical
  d. mental

3. On a popular quiz show, contestants are asked to match the audience in naming certain items. One contestant, when asked to "name a type of vehicle" replied "wheelchair!" The audience groaned, because they knew that the contestant was pretty far off the mark. The contestant should have picked a vehicle that was closer to a _____ for vehicles to match the audience's response.
  a. formal concept
  b. natural concept
  c. fuzzy concept
  d. prototype

4. Algorithms are a type of _____
   a. mechanical solution.
   b. heuristic.
   c. rule of thumb.
   d. means–end analysis.

5. The _____ heuristic can be used to create and maintain stereotypes.
   a. availability
   b. representative
   c. insight
   d. means–end analysis

6. Which of the following artificial intelligence programs was able to beat world chess champion Garry Kasparov?
   a. Deep Blue
   b. Deep Purple
   c. Deep Junior
   d. Deep Senior

7. When people persist in trying to solve a problem the same way they have always gone about solving problems, they have developed
   a. a mental set.
   b. functional fixedness.
   c. confirmation bias.
   d. transformation bias.

8. Which of the following questions would be more likely to produce divergent thinking?
   a. "What is a stapler?"
   b. "How do you spell *stapler*?"
   c. "How many uses can you think of for a stapler?"
   d. "What does a stapler look like?"

9. Which of the following is NOT part of the definition of intelligence?
   a. ability to adapt
   b. ability to solve problems
   c. ability to be creative
   d. ability to use resources effectively

10. Keneisha is only 11 years old, but she can answer questions that most 15-year-olds can answer. Fifteen is Keneisha's
   a. chronological age.
   b. mental age.
   c. IQ.
   d. standard age.

11. Which of the following makes the Wechsler tests different from the Stanford-Binet?
   a. The Wechsler tests are administered to individuals.
   b. The Wechsler is designed only for children.
   c. The Stanford-Binet is designed only for adults.
   d. The Wechsler provides both a verbal and a performance score.

12. A test that gives similar scores for a person each time the person takes it is considered to be a _____ test.
   a. reliable
   b. valid
   c. standardized
   d. creative

13. When a test allows a person from one particular background to have an unfair advantage over persons from other backgrounds, it is called
   a. culturally free.
   b. culturally fair.
   c. culturally biased.
   d. unreliable.

14. In familial retardation, the degree of retardation is typically
   a. severe.
   b. profound.
   c. moderate.
   d. mild.

15. Denny has a flat upper lip, wide-set eyes, and problems with his heart in addition to being mildly retarded. Denny most likely suffers from
   a. Down syndrome.
   b. fetal alcohol syndrome.
   c. fragile X syndrome.
   d. cretinism.

16. In Terman's study of gifted children, social and behavioral problems were found only in those
   a. with IQs of 150 or higher.
   b. with IQs of 180 or higher.
   c. with IQs of 180 or higher in adulthood.
   d. with IQs of 180 or higher in childhood.

17. According to Sternberg, "street smarts" is another way of talking about which kind of intelligence?
   a. analytical
   b. creative
   c. practical
   d. emotional

18. Which type of intelligence, according to Sternberg, would most likely be measured by traditional intelligence tests?
   a. analytical
   b. creative
   c. practical
   d. emotional

19. Goleman has proposed that _____ intelligence is a more powerful influence on success in life than other forms of intelligence.
   a. analytical
   b. creative
   c. practical
   d. emotional

20. The current estimate of heritability of intelligence is
   a. 0.90.
   b. 0.86.
   c. 0.50.
   d. 0.34.

21. The basic units of sound are called
   a. morphemes.
   b. phonemes.
   c. semantics.
   d. syntax.

22. The linguistic relativity hypothesis states that
   a. language shapes thoughts.
   b. thoughts shape language.
   c. language and thought develop independently.
   d. language and thought influence each other.

23. Which of the following is NOT one of the animals that has been taught to use language with some success?
   a. chimpanzee
   b. parrot
   c. dog
   d. dolphin

24. State which of the following words is the most likely answer to the cryptic clue: "Part of a vehicle's engine mistakenly ate ink."
   a. intake
   b. carburetor
   c. spark plug
   d. distributor

Answers: 1-c, 2-b, 3-d, 4-a, 5-b, 6-a, 7-a, 8-c, 9-c, 10-b, 11-d, 12-a, 13-c, 14-d, 15-b, 16-d, 17-c, 18-a, 19-d, 20-c, 21-b, 22-a, 23-c, 24-a.

For more sample quizzes and other review activities that will help you get a better grade, be sure to check out your accompanying study guide. To access tests and your own personalized study plan that will help you focus on the areas you need to master before your next class test, be sure to go to the on-line Psychology web site available with the access code packaged with your book.

Cognition

Occurs when information is being organized, stored, communicated, or processed

Nature of a Concept

Concepts: ideas that represent a class or category of events, objects, or activities

Prototypes: concepts that closely match defining characteristics of a concept

8.2

Mental Images

represent objects or events and have a picture-like quality

8.1

CONCEPT MAP

Intelligence Tests and Measuring Intelligence

Stanford-Binet Intelligence Test: yields an IQ score

IQ = MA/CA x 100

Wechsler Intelligence Tests: yield a verbal and a performance score as well as an overall score of intelligence

8.7

Problem Solving

THE NORMAL CURVE

Problem Solving and Decision Making

Problem solving consists of thinking and behaving in certain ways to reach a goal

Mechanical solutions: trial-and-error learning and rote solutions

Algorithms: methods of problem solving that always guarantee a solution

Heuristics: strategies that narrow down possible solutions for a problem but do not guarantee a solution

Insight: sudden perception of a solution to a problem

8.3

Creative Thinking

Divergent thinking: coming up with as many different answers as possible

8.5

Intelligence Test Construction

Important factors in test construction: Standardization, validity, and reliability

Deviation IQs: based on deviations of the mean of a normal curve

IQ tests: often criticized for being culturally biased

8.8

Barriers to Problem Solving

Functional fixedness: perceiving objects as having only one use, failing to see other uses

Confirmation bias: searching for evidence that confirms one's beliefs, ignoring contrary evidence

8.4

Intelligence

Ability to understand the world, think rationally or logically, and use resources effectively when faced with challenges or problems

8.6

Artificial Intelligence

▸ Artificial intelligence: attempt to create a machine that thinks like a human being
▸ Computers have been designed that play chess and perform in similar ways to humans
▸ True flexibility of human thought has yet to be developed in a machine

8.9

Theories of Intelligence

Spearman proposed
▸ **General intelligence or g factor:** ability to reason and solve problems
▸ **Specific intelligence or s factor:** ability to excel in certain areas

Gardner: proposed eight different types of intelligence (from verbal, linguistic, and mathematical to interpersonal and intrapersonal intelligence)

Sternberg proposed three types of intelligence: analytical, creative, and practical

Emotional intelligence: viewed as a powerful influence on success in life

8.13

Influence of Heredity and Environment on Intelligence

▸ Stronger correlations are found between IQ scores as genetic relatedness increases
▸ Heritability of IQ is estimated at 0.50

8.14

Mental Retardation and Its Causes

Mental retardation or developmental disability:
▸ Condition in which IQ falls below 70
▸ Adaptive behavior severely deficient at a particular chronological age

Causes include: deprived environments, chromosome and genetic disorders, and dietary deficiencies

8.10

Giftedness

Gifted persons: having IQ scores at the upper end of the normal curve (130 or above)

8.11

Being Intellectually Gifted— Terman's Termites

Terman demonstrated that gifted children usually grow up to be successful adults

8.12

Language

System for combining symbols so that an infinite number of meaningful statements can be created and communicated to others

8.15

Elements and Structure of Language

Grammar: system of rules by which language is governed

Parts of language:
▸ **phonemes**—basic units of sound in language
▸ **morphemes**—smallest units of meaning within a language
▸ **syntax**—system of rules for combining words and phrases

Pragmatics: practical aspects of language

8.16

Language and Thinking

Sapir and Whorf linguistic relativity hypothesis: language controls and helps development of thought processes and concepts

Cognitive universalism viewpoint: concepts are universal and directly influence the development of language

8.17

Animal Language

▸ Chimpanzees, parrots, and dolphins have demonstrated a basic kind of language, including some abstract ideas
▸ Controversy exists over lack of evidence that animals can learn syntax

8.18

Improving Thinking

Mental activity requiring creativity and memory can help keep brain fit.

8.19

9

Motivation and Emotion

Walking Tall

Debi R. was a relatively healthy woman in her early fifties when her back began to bother her. Her doctor recommended surgery to relieve two bad disks in her back. Her disks had begun to slip out of place, causing the pain in her back.

After the surgery, the pain was still there. The surgeon operated again the next day, saying that another disk had ruptured. When Debi began to recover, she found that she could not move her legs or feel her feet—she was partially paralyzed. Several months later the truth was revealed that the doctor had operated on the wrong side of her disks the first time and then made matters worse by operating again while her tissues were still swollen. Debi was told that she might never walk again.

That was over a year ago. Today, Debi still has pain but can walk with only a cane to aid in her balance. She still has numbness in her feet, but she is no longer confined to a wheelchair. How did she do it? She refused to accept the predictions of the doctors and she worked extremely hard to achieve the goal of walking again. She did everything the therapists told her to do, and when the therapy was stopped, she continued on her own. She is finally at the point where she can walk for short distances with no help at all.

Debi was able to overcome her disability because she was highly *motivated* to do so. She also overcame her fears about not being able to walk and manages her feelings about the pain and the unfairness of what happened to her so that her outlook on life remains sunny and joyful. Each day brings a new hope that more progress will be made. Debi isn't even close to giving up.

Why study motivation and emotion?

The study of motivation not only helps us understand why we eat and drink the way we do, but also why some people are more driven to achieve than others. Emotions are a part of everything we do, affecting our relationships with others and our own health, as well as influencing important decisions. In this chapter, we will explore the motives behind our actions and the origins and influences of emotions.

chapter outline

Approaches to Understanding Motivation

9.1   *What is motivation?*

"How much would you pay for all the secrets of the universe? Wait, don't answer yet. You also get this six-quart covered combination spaghetti pot and clam steamer. Now, how much would you pay?"

©The New Yorker Collection 1981 Michael Maslin from cartoonbank.com. All Rights Reserved.

motivation

the process by which activities are started, directed, and continued so that physical or psychological needs or wants are met.

extrinsic motivation

type of motivation in which a person performs an action because it leads to an outcome that is separate from or external to the person.

instincts

the biologically determined and innate patterns of behavior that exist in both people and animals.

Motivation is the process by which activities are started, directed, and continued so that physical or psychological needs or wants are met (Petri, 1996). The word itself comes from the Latin word, *movere*, which means "to move." Motivation is what "moves" people to do the things they do. For example, when a person is relaxing in front of the television and begins to feel hungry, the physical need for food might cause the person to get up, go into the kitchen, and search for something to eat. If the hunger is great enough, the person might even cook something. The physical need of hunger caused the action (getting up), directed it (going to the kitchen), and sustained the search (finding or preparing something to eat). Hunger is only one example, of course. Loneliness may lead to calling a friend or going to a place where there are people. The desire to get ahead in life motivates many people to go to college. Just getting out of bed in the morning is motivated by the need to keep a roof over one's head and food on the table by going to work.

There are different types of motivation. Sometimes people are driven to do something because of an external reward of some sort (or the avoidance of an unpleasant consequence), as when someone goes to work at a job to make money and avoid losing possessions such as a house or a car **LINK** *to Chapter Five: Learning, p. 186.* When the motivation is external (coming from outside the self), it is called **extrinsic motivation.** In extrinsic motivation, a person performs an action because it leads to an outcome that is separate from the person (Ryan & Deci, 2000). Other examples would be giving a child money for every "A" on a report card, offering a bonus to an employee for increased performance, or tipping a server in a restaurant for good service. The child, employee, and server are motivated to work for the external or extrinsic rewards.

INSTINCT APPROACHES

9.2   *What are instinct approaches to motivation?*

One of the earliest approaches to motivation focused on the biologically determined and innate patterns of behavior that exist in both people and animals called **instincts.** Just as animals are governed by their instincts to do things such as migrating, nest building, mating, and protecting their territory, early researchers proposed that human beings may also be governed by similar instincts (James, 1890; McDougall, 1908). According to these **instinct approach** theorists, in humans the instinct to reproduce is responsible for sexual behavior, and the instinct for territorial protection may be related to aggressive behavior.

William McDougall (1908) proposed a total of 18 instincts for humans, including curiosity, flight (running away), pugnacity (aggressiveness), and acquisition (gathering possessions). As the years progressed, psychologists added more and more instincts to the list until there were thousands of proposed instincts. However, none of these early theorists did much more than give names to these instincts. Although there were plenty of descriptions, such as "submissive people possess the instinct of submission," there was no attempt to explain why these instincts exist in humans, if they exist at all (Petri, 1996).

Freud's psychoanalytic theory still includes the concept of instincts that reside in the id (the part of the personality containing all the basic human needs and drives). ⓛⓘⓝⓚ *to Chapter Twelve: Theories of Personality, p. 446.* Even so, instinct approaches have faded away because, although they could describe human behavior, they could not explain it. But these approaches did accomplish one important thing by forcing psychologists to realize that some human behavior is controlled by hereditary factors. This idea remains central in the study of human behavior today.

DRIVE-REDUCTION APPROACHES

9.3   *What are drive-reduction approaches to motivation?*

The next approach to gain support involved the concepts of needs and drives. A **need** is a requirement of some material (such as food or water) that is essential for survival of the organism. When an organism has a need, it leads to a psychological tension as well as a physical arousal that motivates the organism to act in order to fulfill the need and reduce the tension. This tension is called a **drive** (Hull, 1943).

Drive-reduction theory proposes just this connection between internal physiological states and outward behavior. In this theory, there are two kinds of drives. **Primary drives** are those that involve survival needs of the body such as hunger and thirst, whereas **acquired (secondary) drives** are those that are learned through

psychological tension

instinct approach
approach to motivation that assumes people are governed by instincts similar to those of animals.

need
a requirement of some material (such as food or water) that is essential for survival of the organism.

drive
a psychological tension and physical arousal arising when there is a need that motivates the organism to act in order to fulfill the need and reduce the tension.

drive-reduction theory
approach to motivation that assumes behavior arises from physiological needs that cause internal drives to push the organism to satisfy the need and reduce tension and arousal.

primary drives
those drives that involve needs of the body such as hunger and thirst.

acquired (secondary) drives
those drives that are learned through experience or conditioning, such as the need for money or social approval.

(left) The human body needs water, especially when a person is working hard or under stress, as this man appears to be. Thirst is a survival need of the body, making it a primary drive, according to drive reduction theory. What other kinds of needs might be primary drives?

(right) Some people are driven to do strenuous, challenging activities even when there is no physical need to do so. When a drive is acquired through learning, it is called an acquired or secondary drive. Fulfilling an acquired drive provides secondary reinforcement. What might this rock climber find reinforcing about scaling this steep cliff?

exp. contact comfort

homeostasis
the tendency of the body to maintain a
steady state.

maintain a balance (controlled by the brain)

experience or conditioning, such as the need for money, social approval, or the need of recent former smokers to have something to put in their mouths. If this sounds familiar, it should. The concepts of primary and secondary reinforcers from Chapter Five are related to these drives. Primary reinforcers satisfy primary drives, and secondary reinforcers statisfy acquired, or secondary drives. Ⓛ Ⓘ Ⓝ Ⓚ *to Chapter Five: Learning, p. 177.*

This theory also includes the concept of **homeostasis**, or the tendency of the body to maintain a steady state. One could think of homeostasis as the body's version of a thermostat—thermostats keep the temperature of a house at a constant level, and homeostasis does the same thing for the body's functions. When there is a primary drive need, the body is in a state of imbalance. This stimulates behavior that brings the body back into balance, or homeostasis. For example, if Jarrod's body needs food, he feels hunger and the state of tension/arousal associated with that need. He will then seek to restore his homeostasis by eating something, which is the behavior stimulated to reduce the hunger drive (see Figure 9.1).

Although drive-reduction theory works well to explain the actions people take to reduce tension created by needs, it does not explain all human motivation. Why do people eat when they are not really hungry? People don't always seek to reduce their inner arousal, either—sometimes they seek to increase it. Bungee-jumping, parachuting as a recreation, rock climbing, and watching horror movies are all activities that increase the inner state of tension and arousal, and many people love doing these activities. Why would people do things like these if it doesn't reduce some need or restore homeostasis? The answer is complex: There are different types of needs, different effects of arousal, different incentives, and different levels of importance attached to many forms of behavior. The following theories explore some of these factors in motivation.

DIFFERENT STROKES FOR DIFFERENT FOLKS: NEEDS   Obviously, motivation is about needs. Drive-reduction theory talks about needs, Maslow talks about needs, and many other theories of motivation include the concept of needs or something similar. In many of these theories, most needs are the result of some inner physical drive (such as hunger or thirst) that demands to be satisfied. Even Maslow begins with such physical needs, although later he includes more psychological needs such as self-esteem and companionship. Harvard University psychologist David C. McClelland (1961, 1987) proposed a theory of motivation that highlights the importance of three psychological needs not typically considered by the other theories: achievement, affiliation, and power.

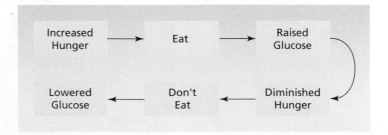

FIGURE 9.1   **Homeostasis**   In homeostasis, the body maintains balance in the body's physical states. For example, this diagram shows how increased hunger (a state of imbalance) prompts a person to eat. Eating increases the level of glucose (blood sugar), causing the feelings of hunger to reduce. After a period without eating, the glucose levels become low enough to stimulate the hunger drive once again, and the entire cycle is repeated.

9.4 *What are three types of needs?*

Need for Achievement: How to Succeed by Excelling at Everything   The **need for achievement** (abbreviated as **nAch** in McClelland's writings) involves a strong desire to succeed in attaining goals, not only realistic ones but also challenging ones. People who are high in nAch look for careers and hobbies that allow others to evaluate them because these high achievers also need to have feedback about their performance in addition to the achievement of reaching the goal. Although many of these people do become wealthy, famous, and publicly successful, others fulfill their need to achieve in ways that lead only to their own personal success, not material riches—they just want the challenge.

Achievement motivation appears to be strongly related to success in school, occupational success, and the quality and amount of what a person produces (Collins et al., 2004; Gillespie et al., 2002; Spangler, 1992). The chapter-opening story of Debi R. is a good example of the need for achievement. Debi's desire to overcome her physical difficulties and walk once again had nothing to do with becoming successful or wealthy, but she certainly showed a strong desire to achieve a challenging goal.

Carol Dweck's Self-Theory of Motivation   How do people get to be high achievers? According to motivation and personality psychologist Carol Dweck (1999), the need for achievement is closely linked to personality factors, including a person's view of how *self*, the beliefs one holds about one's abilities and relationships to others, can affect the understanding of how much a person's actions can influence his or her success. This concept is related to the much older notion of *locus of control*, in which people who assume that they have control over what happens in their lives are considered to be *internal* in locus of control, and those who feel that their lives are controlled by powerful others, luck, or fate are considered to be *external* in locus of control (Mac-Donald, 1970; Rotter, 1966).

Dweck has amassed a large body of empirical research, particularly in the field of education, to support the idea that people's "theories" about their own selves can affect their level of achievement motivation and their willingness to keep trying to achieve success in the face of failure (Dweck, 1986; Dweck & Elliott, 1983; Dweck & Leggett, 1988; Elliott & Dweck, 1988). According to this research, people can form one of two belief systems about intelligence, which in turn affects their motivation to achieve. One type of person believes that intelligence is fixed, unchanging, and independent of anything the person might want to do to change that intelligence. The other type of person believes that intelligence is changeable and can be shaped by experiences and effort in small increases, or increments. Those who believe intelligence is fixed often demonstrate an external locus of control, assuming that their actions cannot change their circumstances. They are prone to developing learned helplessness, the tendency to stop trying to achieve a goal because past failure has led them to believe that they cannot succeed. **LINK** *to Chapter Five: Learning, p. 194.* Their goals involve trying to "look smart" and outperform others ("See, at least I did better than she did"). They tend to give up easily or try to avoid situations in which they might fail, often ensuring their own failure when doing so. For example, how many students, when faced with a challenging task like a term paper or a major test, end up avoiding coming to class, delaying any start on studying or writing until the last minute, or even developing some long-lasting illness that prevents them from having to face the challenge (at least for a while)?

This does not mean that students with this view of intelligence are always unsuccessful. In fact, Dweck's research (1999) suggests that students who have had a

---

need for achievement (nAch)
a need that involves a strong desire to succeed in attaining goals, not only realistic ones but also challenging ones.

desire for sucess

◄ How do people get to be high achievers?

Many people are driven by a need to attain both realistic and challenging goals. This young girl seems eager to provide an answer to the teacher's question, and the teacher's positive feedback will help foster the girl's need for achievement.

need for affiliation (nAff)
the need for friendly social interactions and relationships with others.

need for power (nPow)
the need to have control or influence over others.

stimulus motive
a motive that appears to be unlearned but causes an increase in stimulation, such as curiosity.

Donald Trump stands triumphant at the opening of his Trump International Hotel and Tower in New York. Many people who are as wealthy as "The Donald" continue to buy new houses, new businesses, clothing, and cars (among other things) even though they do not need them. This is an example of the need for power at work. How might this need for power be expressed in a person's relationships with others, such as a spouse, employee, or friend?

long history of successes may be most at risk for developing a learned helplessness after a big failure precisely because their previous successes have led them to believe in their own fixed intelligence. For example, a child who had never earned anything less than an "A" in school who then receives his first "C" might become depressed and refuse to do any more homework, ensuring future failure.

On the other hand, those who believe that intelligence is changeable show an internal locus of control and believe that their own actions and efforts will improve their intelligence; they work at developing new strategies and get involved in new tasks, with the goal of increasing their "smarts." They are motivated to master tasks and don't allow failure to destroy their confidence in themselves or prevent them from trying again and again, using new strategies each time.

Based on this and other research, Dweck recommends that parents and teachers encourage children to value the learning process more than "looking smart" by always having the right answer (and only responding when sure of that answer, for example). Errors should not be viewed as failures but as a way to improve future performance on the road to mastering whatever the goal in question is. Essentially, this means praising efforts and the methods that children use to make those efforts, not just successes or ability. Instead of saying, "You're right, how smart you are," the parent or teacher should say something such as, "You are really thinking hard," or "That was a very clever way to think about this problem." In the past, teachers and parents have been told that praise is good and criticism is bad—it might damage a child's self-esteem. Dweck believes that constructive criticism, when linked with praise of effort and the use of strategies, will be a better influence on the child's self-esteem than endless praise that can become meaningless when given indiscriminately.

Need for Affiliation: Popularity Rules   Another psychological need is for friendly social interactions and relationships with others. Called the **need for affiliation (nAff)**, people high in this need seek to be liked by others and to be held in high regard by those around them. This makes high affiliation people good team players, whereas a person high in achievement just might run over a few team members on the way to the top.

Need for Power: The One Who Dies with the Most Toys Wins   The final psychological need proposed by McClelland is the **need for power (nPow)**. Power is not about reaching a goal but about having control over other people. People high in this need would want to have influence over others and make an impact on them. They want their ideas to be the ones that are used, regardless of whether or not their ideas will lead to success. Status and prestige are important, so these people wear expensive clothes, live in expensive houses, drive fancy cars, and dine in the best restaurants. Whereas someone who is a high achiever may not need a lot of money to validate the achievement, someone who is high in the need for power typically sees the money (and cars, houses, jewelry, and other "toys") as the achievement. The subtitle for this section is a saying from a popular bumper sticker but is really a comment on the more negative aspect of the need for power. For the person high in the need for power, it's all about who has the most expensive "toys" in the end.

AROUSAL APPROACHES

9.5   *What are arousal approaches to motivation?*

Another explanation for human motivation involves the recognition of yet another type of need, the need for stimulation. A **stimulus motive** is one that appears to be unlearned but causes an increase in stimulation. Examples would be curiosity, playing, and exploration.

"adrenaline junkies"

In **arousal theory**, people are said to have an optimal (best or ideal) level of tension. Task performances, for example, may suffer if the level of arousal is too high (such as severe test anxiety) or even if the level of arousal is too low (such as boredom). For many kinds of tasks, a moderate level of arousal seems to be best. This relationship between task performance and arousal is called the **Yerkes-Dodson law** (Teigen, 1994; Yerkes & Dodson, 1908). However, this effect is modified by the difficulty level of the task: Easy tasks demand a somewhat "high-moderate" level for optimal performance, whereas difficult tasks require a "low-moderate" level. Figure 9.2 shows this relationship in graphic form.

Maintaining an optimal level of arousal, then, may involve reducing tension or creating it (Hebb, 1955). For example, a child who is bored may "go looking for trouble," as many parents have experienced. Husbands or wives who are underaroused may pick a fight with their spouse. Students who experience test anxiety (a high level of arousal) may seek out ways to reduce that anxiety in order to improve test performance. Students who are not anxious at all may not be motivated to study well, lowering their test performance. Many arousal theorists believe that the optimal level of arousal for most people under normal circumstances is somewhere in the middle, neither too high nor too low.

If people are supposed to be seeking a level of arousal somewhere around the middle, why do some people love to do things like bungee-jumping? Even though the average person might require an average level of arousal to feel content, there are some people who need less arousal and some who need more. The person who needs more arousal is called a **sensation seeker** (Zuckerman, 1979, 1994). Sensation seekers seem to need more complex and varied sensory experiences than do other people. The need does not always have to involve danger. For example, students who travel to other countries to study tend to score higher on scales of sensation seeking than do students who stay at home (Schroth & McCormack, 2000). Table 9.1 has some sample items from a typical sensation-seeking scale.

In one study (Putnam & Stifter, 2002), researchers found evidence of "sensation-seeking" behavior in children as young as age 2. In this study, 90 children were studied at the ages of 6, 12, 24, and 25 months. In a test of the youngest participants, the babies were shown two sets of toys: a block, a plate, and a cup; or a flashing light, a toy beeper, and a wind-up dragon. The first set was considered a low-intensity stimulus whereas the second set was labeled a high-intensity stimulus. The infants who

like bell curve

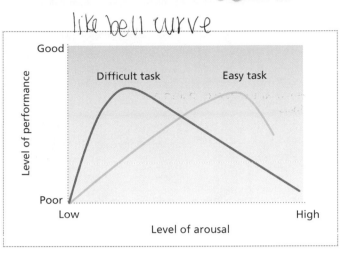

FIGURE 9.2 **Arousal and Performance** The optimal level of arousal for task performance depends on the difficulty of the task. We generally perform easy tasks well if we are highly aroused (green) and accomplish difficult tasks well if we are not very aroused (red).

◀ If people are supposed to be seeking a level of arousal somewhere around the middle, why do some people love to do things like bungee-jumping?

arousal theory
theory of motivation in which people are said to have an optimal (best or ideal) level of tension that they seek to maintain by increasing or decreasing stimulation.

Yerkes-Dodson law
law stating performance is related to arousal; moderate levels of arousal lead to better performance than do levels of arousal that are too low or too high. This effect varies with the difficulty of the task: easy tasks require a high-moderate level while more difficult tasks require a low-moderate level.

sensation seeker
someone who needs more arousal than the average person.

TABLE 9.1 **SAMPLE ITEMS FROM THE ZUCKERMAN-KUHLMAN PERSONALITY QUESTIONNAIRE**

Scale Item	Sensation Seeking
I sometimes do "crazy" things just for fun.	High
I prefer friends who are excitingly unpredictable.	High
I am an impulsive person.	High
Before I begin a complicated job, I make careful plans.	Low
I usually think about what I am going to do before doing it.	Low

Source: Adapted from Zuckerman, M. (2002).

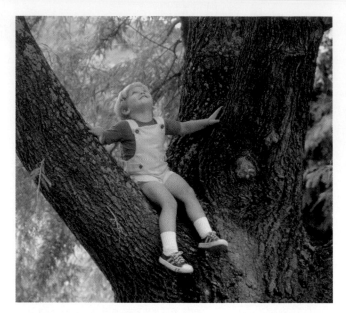

This daring preschool boy has climbed high into this massive tree, and looks as though he might try to climb higher still.

> Last Thanksgiving, I had ▶ eaten about all I could. Then my aunt brought out a piece of her wonderful pumpkin pie and I couldn't resist—I ate it, even though I was not at all hungry. What makes us do things even when we don't have the drive or need to do them?

incentives ~~reinforcements, rewards~~
things that attract or lure people into action.

incentive approaches
theories of motivation in which behavior is explained as a response to the external stimulus and its rewarding properties.

reached out for the toys more quickly, and reached for the high-intensity toys in particular, were labeled "approach motivated."

The same children at age 2 were given an opportunity to explore a black box with a hole in one side. The children who were labeled "low approach motivated" at 6 and 12 months were unwilling to put a hand into the hole to see what might be in the box, whereas the "high-approach-motivated" children not only put their hands in but also in some cases tried to climb into the box.

Is sensation seeking something people have when they are born? Although it is tempting to think of 6-month-old children as having little in the way of experiences that could shape their personalities, the fact is that the first six months of life is full of experiences that might affect children's choices in the future. For example, a very young infant might, while being carried, stick a hand into some place that ends up causing pain. This experience might affect that infant's willingness in the future to put his or her hand in something else through the simple learning process of operant conditioning. **L I N K** *to Chapter Five: Learning, pp. 175–179.* Determining the origins of sensation seeking will have to wait for further research.

INCENTIVE APPROACHES

Last Thanksgiving, I had eaten about all I could. Then my aunt brought out a piece of her wonderful pumpkin pie and I couldn't resist—I ate it, even though I was not at all hungry. What makes us do things even when we don't have the drive or need to do them? It's true that sometimes there is no physical need present, yet people still eat, drink, or react as if they did have a need. Even though that piece of pie was not necessary to reduce a hunger drive, it was very rewarding, wasn't it? And on past occasions, that pie was also delicious and rewarding, so there is anticipation of that reward now. The pie, in all its glorious promise of flavor and sweetness, becomes an incentive to eat. **Incentives** are things that attract or lure people into action. In fact, the dictionary (Merriam-Webster, 2003) lists *incentive* as meaning the same thing as *motive*.

9.6 *What are incentive approaches to motivation?*

In **incentive approaches**, behavior is explained in terms of the external stimulus and its rewarding properties. These rewarding properties exist independently of any need or level of arousal and can cause people to act only upon the incentive. Thus, incentive theory is actually based, at least in part, on the principles of learning that were discussed in Chapter Five (pp. 175–177).

One of the earliest incentive approaches clearly demonstrates the relationship to learning, particularly the early cognitive learning theories found in the work of Edward Tolman (1932). **Expectancy-value theories** are a class of incentive theories based on the work of Tolman and others (Lewin, 1936; Rotter, 1954). In general, these theories assume that the actions of humans cannot be predicted or fully understood without understanding the beliefs, values, and the importance that people attach to those beliefs and values at any given moment in time. Tolman's work with animals (the latent learning studies with rats discussed in Chapter Five, p. 193) demonstrated that organisms are capable of remembering what had happened in the past, anticipating future events, and adjusting their own actions according to those cognitive expectancies (a set of beliefs about what will happen in the future based on past experiences). Kurt Lewin (1936) applied these concepts to people in his field theory of decision making, while Julian Rotter's (1954) social learning theory included expectancy as one of the three factors that predict people's behavior.

By itself, the incentive approach does not explain the motivation behind all behavior. Many theorists today see motivation as a result of both the "push" of internal needs or drives and the "pull" of a rewarding external stimulus. For example, sometimes a person may actually be hungry (the push) but choose to satisfy that drive by selecting a candy bar instead of a rice cake. The candy bar has more appeal to most people and it, therefore, has more "pull" than the rice cake. (Frankly, to most people, just about anything has more pull than a rice cake.)

HUMANISTIC APPROACHES: MASLOW'S HIERARCHY OF NEEDS

9.7   *What is Maslow's hierarchy of needs?*

A final approach to the study of motivation is based on the work of Abraham Maslow (1987). Maslow was one of the early humanistic psychologists who rejected the dominant theories of psychoanalysis and behaviorism in favor of a more positive view of human behavior Ⓛ🛈🅝🅚 *to Chapter One: The Science of Psychology, p. 13.* Maslow proposed that there are several levels of needs that a person must strive to meet before achieving the highest level of personality fulfillment. According to Maslow, **self-actualization** is the point that is seldom reached at which people have satisfied the lower needs and achieved their full human potential.

These needs include both deficiency needs and growth needs. Deficiency needs are needs of the body, such as the need for food or water, whereas growth needs are for desires like having friends or feeling good about oneself. For a person to achieve self-actualization, which is the highest level of growth needs, the primary, basic needs must first be fulfilled. Figure 9.3 shows the typical way to represent Maslow's series of needs as a pyramid with the most basic needs for survival at the bottom and the highest needs at the top. This type of ranking is called a hierarchy.*

The lowest level of the pyramid consists of physiological needs such as food, water, and rest. Once those needs are met, safety becomes important and involves feeling secure. Belongingness and love are the needs for friends and companions as well as to be accepted by others, and self-esteem is the need to feel that one has accomplished something good or earned the esteem of others. Although Maslow's original hierarchy included only one more level of self-actualization needs, Maslow later inserted two other needs just below this level (Maslow, 1971; Maslow & Lowery, 1998). Just above the esteem needs on the hierarchy come the cognitive needs, or the need to know and understand the world. This need is typical of an academic person who learns for the sake of gathering knowledge. Above the cognitive needs are the aesthetic needs, which include the need for order and beauty and are typical of artistic people. Once all these needs are met, it is possible to be concerned about self-actualization needs, or needs that help a person reach his or her full potential and capabilities as a human being. Although it does not appear in Figure 9.3, Maslow also added a higher need called transcendence above the self-actualization needs (Maslow, 1971). Transcendence involves helping others to achieve their full potential. This aspect of Maslow's

---

*Hierarchy: a graded or ranked series.

expectancy-value theories
incentive theories that assume the actions of humans cannot be predicted or fully understood without understanding the beliefs, values, and the importance that a person attaches to those beliefs and values at any given moment in time.

self-actualization
according to Maslow, the point that is seldom reached at which people have sufficiently satisfied the lower needs and achieved their full human potential.

FIGURE 9.3   **Maslow's Hierarchy of Needs**   Maslow proposed that human beings must fulfill the more basic needs, such as physical and security needs, before being able to fulfill the higher need of self-actualization.

Self-actualization needs: to find self-fulfillment and realize one's potential

Aesthetic needs: symmetry, order, and beauty

Cognitive needs: to know, understand, and explore

Esteem needs: to achieve, be competent, gain approval and recognition

Belongingness and love needs: to be with others, be accepted, and belong.

Safety needs: to feel secure and safe, out of danger

Physiological needs: hunger, thirst, fatigue, etc.

hierarchy is very similar to a stage in another theorist's work. Erik Erikson theorized a stage in personality development called generativity, in which people focus on helping the next generation through earlier crises of personality development. (L)(I)(N)(K) *to Chapter Seven: Development Across the Life Span, pp. 281–282.*

People move up the pyramid as they go through life, gaining wisdom and the knowledge of how to handle many different situations. But a shift in life's circumstances can result in a shift down to a lower need. For example, someone might be near the top, fulfilling the need for growth in ways that lead to self-actualization (appreciation of beauty, need for truth and justice, and helping others to grow, for example). But if that person loses her job and cannot find another one for quite some time, her money will start running out. She might take a job that is not good for her self-esteem out of love for her family and the need to provide a safe place for them to live (by being able to make the house payments) and food for them to eat. She would be starting at the level of love and working her way back up. Moving up and down and then back up can occur frequently—even from one hour to the next. Times in a person's life in which self-actualization is achieved, at least temporarily, are called **peak experiences.** For Maslow, the process of growth and self-actualization is the striving to make peak experiences happen again and again.

Here's an example that might help in understanding this hierarchy. In the movie *Castaway,* Tom Hanks's character is stranded on a deserted island. His first concern is to find something to eat and fresh water to drink—without those two things, he cannot survive. Even while he is building a crude shelter, he is still thinking about how to obtain food. Once he has those needs met, however, he gets lonely. He finds a soccer ball, paints a handprint and then a crude face on it, and names it "Wilson." He talks to the soccer ball as if it were a person, at first as a kind of way to talk out the things he needs to do and later as a way of staying relatively sane. The need for companionship is *that* strong.

Maslow's theory has had a powerful influence on the field of management (Heil et al., 1998). Douglas McGregor, in his explanations of two different styles of management (McGregor, 1960), relates the older and less productive "Theory X" to Maslow's lower needs and the newer, more productive style of management called "Theory Y" to the higher needs. (L)(I)(N)(K) *to Appendix B: Applied Psychology.* In spite of this influence, Maslow's theory is not without its critics. There are several problems that others have highlighted, and the most serious is that there is little scientific support (Drenth et al., 1984). Like Sigmund Freud, Maslow developed his theory based on his own personal observations of people rather than any empirically gathered observations or research. Although many people report that while they were starving, they could think of nothing but food, there is anecdotal evidence in the lives of many people, some of them quite well known, that the lower needs do not have to be satisfied before moving on to a higher need (Drenth et al., 1984). For example, artists and scientists throughout history have been known to deny their own physical needs while producing great works (a self-actualization need). Abraham Lincoln and Edgar Allen Poe both suffered from a severe mood disorder called bipolar affective disorder, (L)(I)(N)(K) *to Chapter Fourteen: Psychological Disorders, pp. 542–543,* which causes the sufferer to have severe periods of depression and insecurity. This should have placed them on the lowest levels of the hierarchy, yet Lincoln and Poe are responsible for some of the most memorable deeds and works in history (Fieve, 1997).

Maslow's work was based on his studies of Americans. Cross-cultural research suggests that the order of needs on the hierarchy does not always hold true for other cultures, particularly those cultures with a stronger tendency than the culture of the United States to avoid uncertainty, such as Greece and Japan. In those countries security needs are much stronger than self-actualization needs in determining motivation (Hofstede, 1980; Hofstede et al., 2002). This means that people in those cultures value job security more than

In the movie *Castaway,* the character played by actor Tom Hanks feels the need for a companion so badly that he names this soccer ball "Wilson." He comes to think of "Wilson" as such a good friend that he almost fails in his attempt to escape the island on which he is stranded to "rescue" the ball when it falls off his make-shift raft.

peak experiences
according to Maslow, times in a person's life during which self-actualization is temporarily achieved.

they do job satisfaction (holding an interesting or challenging job). In countries such as Sweden and Norway that stress the quality of life as being of greater importance than what a person produces, social needs may be more important than self-actualization needs (Hofstede et al., 2002). **LINK** *to Chapter Twelve: Theories of Personality, pp. 465–466.*

Other theorists have developed and refined Maslow's hierarchy. Clayton Alderfer developed one of the more popular versions of this refinement. In his theory, the hierarchy has only three levels: *existence needs*, which include the physiological needs and basic safety needs that provide for the person's continued existence; *relatedness needs*, which include some safety issues as well as belongingness and self-esteem needs and are related to social relationships; and *growth needs*, which include some self-esteem issues and the self-actualization needs that help people develop their full potential as human beings (Alderfer, 1972).

Alderfer believed that more than one need could be active at a time and that progression up and down the hierarchy is common as one type of need assumes greater importance at a particular time in a person's life than other needs. This makes Alderfer's hierarchy of needs less rigid and more in line with observations about life's "ups and downs."

SELF-DETERMINATION THEORY (SDT)

9.8 What is the self-determination theory of motivation?

Another theory of motivation that is similar to Maslow's hierarchy of needs is the **self-determination theory (SDT)** of Ryan and Deci (2000). In this theory, there are three inborn and universal needs that help people gain a complete sense of self and whole, healthy relationships with others. The three needs are *autonomy*, or the need to be in control of one's own behavior and goals (i.e., self-determination); *competence*, or the need to be able to master the challenging tasks of one's life; and *relatedness*, or the need to feel a sense of belonging, intimacy, and security in relationships with others. These needs are common in several theories of personality; the relatedness need is, of course, similar to Maslow's belongingness and love needs, and both autonomy and competence are important aspects of Erikson's theory of psychosocial personality development (Erikson, 1950, 1980). **LINK** *to Chapter Seven: Development Across the Life Span, pp. 272–273, 278, 281.*

Ryan, Deci, and their colleagues (Deci et al., 1994; Ryan & Deci, 2000) believe that satisfying these needs can best be accomplished if the person has a supportive environment in which to develop goals and relationships with others. Such satisfaction will not only foster healthy psychological growth but also increase the individual's **intrinsic motivation**, which is the type of motivation in which a person performs an action because the act itself is rewarding or satisfying in some internal manner. In the Classic Studies in Psychology section in Chapter One (p. 30), psychologist Teresa Amabile (Amabile et al., 1976) found that children's creativity was affected by the kind of motivation for which they worked, and extrinsic motivation (in which motivation to act occurs because the action leads to an outcome that is separate from the person) decreased the degree of creativity shown in their artwork.

Evidence suggests that intrinsic motivation is increased or enhanced when a person not only feels competence (through experiencing positive feedback from others and succeeding at what are perceived to be challenging tasks) but also a sense of autonomy or the knowledge that his or her actions are self-determined rather than controlled by others (deCharms, 1968; Deci & Ryan, 1985).

Previous research has found a negative impact on intrinsic motivation when an external reward is given for the performance (Deci et al., 1999), but a more recent paper discusses the results of other studies that find negative effects only for tasks that are not interesting in and of themselves (Cameron et al., 2001). When the task itself is interesting to the person (as might be an assignment that an instructor or manager has explained

[handwritten margin note: a.k.a. social context influences action]

"That is the correct answer, Bill, but I'm afraid you don't win anything for it."
©The New Yorker Collection 1986 Lee Lorenz from cartoonbank.com. All Rights Reserved.

in terms of its importance and future value), external rewards may increase intrinsic motivation, at least in the short term. Although this recent finding is intriguing, further research is needed to determine if the long-term effects of extrinsic rewards on intrinsic motivation are consistently negative, as the bulk of the research has shown up to now.

But don't we sometimes do things for both kinds of motives? There are usually elements of both intrinsic and extrinsic motives in many of the things people do. Most teachers, for example, work for money to pay bills (the extrinsic motive) but may also feel that they are helping young children to become better adults in the future, which makes the teachers feel good about themselves (the intrinsic motive).

> **But don't we sometimes do things for both kinds of motives?** ▶

PRACTICE **QUIZ:** HOW MUCH DO YOU REMEMBER?

Pick the best answer.

1. The process by which activities are started, directed, and sustained to meet a person's wants is called a(n)
   a. drive.
   b. incentive.
   c. motivation.
   d. instinct.

2. People high in the need for _____ want to be liked by others and are good team players.
   a. achievement
   b. affiliation
   c. power
   d. emotion

3. In the _____ approach, people are said to have an optimal level of tension.
   a. drive-reduction
   b. arousal
   c. incentive
   d. humanistic

4. The most basic needs in Maslow's hierarchy are _____ needs.
   a. esteem
   b. love
   c. safety
   d. physiological

5. Jamal gets a new toy for every good grade on his report card in first grade. Jamal is receiving
   a. intrinsic motivation.
   b. extrinsic motivation.
   c. need motivation.
   d. intrinsic rewards.

Answers: 1-c, 2-b, 3-b, 4-d, 5-b.

What, Hungry Again? Why People Eat

The eating habits of people today have become a major concern and a frequent topic of news programs, talk shows, and scientific research. There are countless pills, supplements, and treatments to help people eat less and others to help people eat more. Eating is not only a basic survival behavior; it is also a form of entertainment for many.

PHYSIOLOGICAL COMPONENTS OF HUNGER

Why do we eat? I mean, what causes us to feel hungry in the first place? There are actually several factors involved in the hunger drive. Cannon (Cannon & Washburn, 1912) believed that stomach contractions, or "hunger pangs," caused hunger and that the presence of food in the stomach would stop the contractions and appease the hunger drive. Oddly enough, having an empty stomach is not the deciding factor in many cases. Although the stomach does have sensory receptors that respond to the pressure of the stretching stomach muscles as food is piled in and that send signals to the brain indicating that the stomach is full (Geliebter, 1988), people who have had their stomachs removed still get hungry (Janowitz, 1967).

> Why do we eat? I mean, what causes us to feel hungry in the first place? ▶

9.9 *What happens in the body to cause hunger?*

One factor in hunger seems to be the insulin response that occurs after we begin to eat. **Insulin** and **glucagons** are hormones that are secreted by the pancreas to control the levels of fats, proteins, and carbohydrates in the whole body, including glucose (blood sugar). Insulin reduces the level of glucose in the bloodstream, for example, whereas glucagons increase the level. Insulin, normally released in greater amounts after eating has begun, causes a feeling of more hunger because of the drop

insulin *decreasing*
a hormone secreted by the pancreas to control the levels of fats, proteins, and carbohydrates in the body by reducing the level of glucose in the bloodstream.

glucagons *↳ 80-120*
hormones that are secreted by the pancreas to control the levels of fats, proteins, and carbohydrates in the body by increasing the level of glucose in the bloodstream.

increasing

in blood sugar levels. Carbohydrates, especially those that are highly refined (such as table sugar, white flour, and white potatoes), cause the insulin level to spike even more than other foods do because there is such a large amount of glucose released by these foods at one time. High blood sugar leads to more insulin released, which leads to a low blood sugar level, increased appetite, and the tendency to overeat. That is the basic principle behind many of the newest diets that promote low-carbohydrate intake. The proponents of these new diets argue that if people control the carbohydrates, they can control the insulin reaction and prevent hunger cravings later on.

THE ROLE OF THE HYPOTHALAMUS   The stomach and the pancreas are only two of the factors in hunger. In Chapter Two the role of the hypothalamus in controlling many kinds of motivational stimuli, including hunger, was seen as a result of its influence on the pituitary. But the hypothalamus itself has two separate areas, controlled by the levels of glucose and insulin in the body, which appear to control eating behavior.

The *ventromedial hypothalamus (VMH)* may be involved in stopping the eating response when glucose levels go up (Neary et al., 2004). In one study, rats whose VMH areas (located to the front and center of the hypothalamus) were damaged would no longer stop eating—they ate and ate until they were quite overweight (Hetherington & Ranson, 1940). (See Figure 9.4 for a picture of a rat with this kind of damage.) However, they did not eat everything in sight. They actually got rather picky, only overeating on food that appealed to them (Ferguson & Keesey, 1975; Parkinson & Weingarten, 1990). In fact, if all the food available to them was unappealing, they did not become obese and in some cases even lost weight.

The other part of the hypothalamus, located on the side, is called the *lateral hypothalamus (LH)* and seems to influence the onset of eating when insulin levels go up (Neary et al., 2004). Damage to this area caused rats to stop eating to the point of starvation. They would eat only if force-fed and still lost weight under those conditions (Anand & Brobeck, 1951; Hoebel & Teitelbaum, 1966).

WEIGHT SET POINT AND BASAL METABOLIC RATE   Obviously, the role of the hypothalamus in eating behavior is complex. Some researchers (Leibel et al., 1995; Nisbett, 1972) believe that the hypothalamus affects the particular level of weight that the body tries to maintain, called the **weight set point.** Injury to the hypothalamus does raise or lower the weight set point rather dramatically, causing either drastic weight loss or weight gain.

Metabolism, the speed at which the body burns available energy, and exercise also play a part in the weight set point. Some people are no doubt genetically wired to have faster metabolisms, and those people can eat large amounts of food without gaining weight. Others have slower metabolisms and may eat a normal or even less than normal amount of food and still gain weight or have difficulty losing it (Bouchard et al., 1990). (Some people swear they can gain weight by just *looking* at a piece of cake!) Regular, moderate exercise also helps offset the slowing of metabolism and the accompanying increase in the weight set point (Tremblay et al., 1999).

The rate at which the body burns energy when a person is resting is called the **basal metabolic rate (BMR)** and is directly tied to the set point. If a person's BMR decreases (as it does in adulthood), that person's weight set point increases. Table 9.2

FIGURE 9.4   **Obese Laboratory Rat**
This rat has reached a high level of obesity because its ventromedial hypothalamus has been deliberately damaged in the laboratory. The result is a rat that no longer receives signals of being satiated, and so the rat continues to eat and eat and eat.

weight set point
the particular level of weight that the body tries to maintain.

basal metabolic rate (BMR)
the rate at which the body burns energy when the organism is resting.

TABLE 9.2 **AVERAGE BASAL METABOLIC RATES FOR A FEMALE AND MALE**				
Age Range	**Ages 10–18**	**Ages 19–30**	**Ages 31–60**	**Ages 61–80**
Female (5½ ft.)	1770	1720	1623	1506
Male (6 ft.)	2140	2071	1934	1770

shows the changes in BMR of a typical woman and man as age increases from 10 years to 80 years. Notice that the BMR decreases more dramatically as the age of the person increases. Adolescents have a very high BMR and, therefore, a lower weight set point, meaning they can eat far more than an adult of the same size and not gain weight. But when that adolescent becomes an adult, the BMR begins to decline. If the eating habits of the teenage years are maintained, excessive weight gain is not far behind. (In some people, the excessive weight gain may be mostly "behind.")

If you would like to calculate your own BMR, there are numerous Internet sites that allow a person to enter data such as height, age, weight, and activity level. The BMR is then automatically calculated according to a standard formula. Simply type "basal metabolic rate calculator" into your Web search engine to find these sites.

SOCIAL COMPONENTS OF HUNGER

9.10　*How do social factors influence hunger?*

People often eat when they are not really hungry. There are all sorts of social cues that tell people to eat, such as the convention of eating breakfast, lunch, and dinner at certain times. A large part of that "convention" is actually the result of classical conditioning. (L I N K) *to Chapter Five: Learning, pp. 167–169.* The body becomes conditioned to respond with the hunger reflex at certain times of the day; through association with the act of eating, those times of the day have become conditioned stimuli for hunger. Sometimes a person who has just eaten a late breakfast will still "feel" hungry at noon, simply because the clock says it's time to eat. People also respond to the appeal of food. How many times has someone finished a huge meal only to be tempted by that luscious-looking dessert on the dessert cart?

Food can also be used in times of stress as a comforting routine, an immediate escape from whatever is unpleasant (Dallman et al., 2003). Rodin (1981, 1985) found that the insulin levels that create hunger may actually increase *before* food is eaten (similar to the way Pavlov's dogs began salivating before they received their food). Like getting hungry at a certain time of day, this physiological phenomenon may also be due to classical conditioning: In the past, eating foods with certain visual and sensory characteristics led to an insulin spike, and this pairing occurred so frequently that now just looking at or smelling the food produces the spike before the food is consumed (Stockhorst, 1999). This may explain why some people (who are called "externals" because of their tendency to focus on the external features of food rather than internal hunger) are far more responsive to these external signals—they produce far more insulin in response to the *anticipation* of eating than do nonexternals, or people who are less affected by external cues (Rodin, 1985).

Cultural factors and gender also play a part in determining hunger and eating habits. In one study, a questionnaire about eating habits was given to both men and women from the United States and Japan. Although no significant differences in what initiates eating existed for men in either culture, women in the United States were found to be much more likely to start eating for emotional reasons, such as depression. Japanese women were more likely to eat because of hunger signals or social demands (Hawks et al., 2003). In this same study, both men and women from the United States were more likely to eat while watching television or movies than were Japanese men and women. Both culture and gender must be taken into account when studying why and under what circumstances people eat.

MALADAPTIVE EATING PROBLEMS

9.11　*What are some problems in eating behavior?*

It would be nice if people all over the world ate just the amount of food that they needed and were able to maintain a healthy, normal weight. Unfortunately, that is not the case for many people. Some people weigh far more than they should, whereas others weigh far less.

(Top) Cultural factors play an important part in why people eat. Women in Japan have been found to be motivated to eat by hunger and social demands, as this woman and her family are doing.
(Bottom) Women in the United States may eat because they are depressed or for other emotional reasons, rather than just to appease hunger or in a social situation. Obviously, this woman does not need the social trappings of a bowl, dining table, and the company of others to motivate her eating habits—unless you count the cat.

Why do some people get so fat? Is it just overeating?

OBESITY   There are several factors that create *obesity*, a condition in which the body weight of a person is 20 percent or more over the ideal body weight for that person's height. Actual definitions of obesity vary. Some definitions consider 20 to 30 percent to be overweight and limit obesity to 30 percent. Others state that men are obese at 20 percent over the ideal weight and women at 30 percent. However it is defined, a significant factor in obesity is heredity. There appear to be several sets of genes, some on different chromosomes, that influence a person's likelihood of becoming obese (Barsh et al., 2000). If there is a history of obesity in a particular family, each family member has a risk of becoming obese that is double or triple the risk of people who do not have a family history of obesity (Bouchard, 1997).

Another factor is certainly overeating. Around the world, as developing countries get stronger economics and their food supplies become stable, the rates of obesity increase dramatically and quickly (Barsh et al., 2000). Foods become more varied and enticing* as well, and an increase in variety is associated with an increase in eating beyond the physiological need to eat (Raynor & Epstein, 2001). In industrialized societies when workers spend more hours in the workplace, there is less time available for preparing meals at home and more incentive to dine out (Chou et al., 2004). When the "dining out" choices include fast food and soft drinks, as is so often the case, obesity rates increase. In sum, as cultures become more industrialized and follow Western cultural lifestyles, negative aspects such as obesity of those lifestyles also increase.

As mentioned earlier, metabolism slows down as people age. Aside from not changing the eating habits of their youth, as they earn more income people also often increase the amount of food they consume, thereby assuring a weight gain that may lead to obesity. At about 31 percent, the United States has the highest rate of obesity in the world (Friedman, 2000, 2003; Marik, 2000; Mokdad et al., 2001).

In recent years, a hormone called *leptin* has been identified as one of the factors that controls appetite, which may also play an important role in obesity. The role of leptin is discussed in Psychology in the News, which follows.

---

*Enticing: attractive; desirable.

◀ Why do some people get so fat? Is it just overeating?

leptin
a hormone that, when released into the bloodstream, signals the hypothalamus that the body has had enough food and reduces the appetite while increasing the feeling of being full.

PSYCHOLOGY IN THE NEWS
The Biology of Obesity

9.12   *What biological factors play a part in obesity?*

Why are some people so naturally slender, whereas others seem likely to get fat? Scientists now believe that a hormone called **leptin** plays a key role in appetite control. Leptin is a protein that is secreted as a *hormone* (a chemical that travels by way of the blood to all parts of the body) by the fatty tissues of the body. When released into the bloodstream, leptin signals the hypothalamus that the body has had enough food, reducing appetite and increasing the feeling of being full, or satiated (Friedman & Halaas, 1998).

Leptin enters the bloodstream from the fat cells, traveling to the hypothalamus in the brain where it binds to receptors and causes the hypothalamus to signal the

YOUR LOST WEIGHT

"Ready to head back?"

This family is becoming more typical in the United States as obesity rates continue to rise. How much of the excess weight on each of these family members is caused by poor choices in diet and lack of exercise, and how much might be caused by inherited biological factors, such as a resistance to the hormone leptin?

body to either stop eating or to eat more. High levels of leptin, which are produced when enough food is consumed, cause the appetite to decrease, whereas low levels of leptin signal a condition of starvation and lead to increased appetite and the urge to eat (Brunner et al., 1997). This is the normal feedback loop for appetite control in the brain.

Having found this link, scientists experimented on obese mice by giving them a high dosage of the hormone, which should lead to a decrease in appetite and weight loss. Although at first the results seemed promising, more recent studies have found that certain strains of obese mice do not lose weight when leptin levels are increased, suggesting a resistance to leptin—their bodies can respond only to certain levels of leptin, and when the levels go too high, the body stops responding, allowing appetite to remain out of control (Friedman, 2003).

To make matters worse, the genes that once helped people survive famine and times of want may be the very genes that are now responsible for the rise in obesity (Friedman, 2003). Essentially, humans once lived in two major groupings: the hunter-gatherers, who had to take food as they could get it and often faced very lean times; and the herder-farmers, who lived in areas where cultivating food and raising domesticated animals was possible. The hunter-gatherer population would benefit most from genes that allowed their bodies to store energy very efficiently against the lean times.

What aided the hunter-gatherer population in ancient times, then, may be what is causing people descended from that population to store excess amounts of energy—the obese are storing up for a famine that does not come: "Obesity is not a personal failing. In trying to lose weight, the obese are fighting a difficult battle—a battle against biology, a battle that only the intrepid take on and one in which only a few prevail" (Friedman, 2003, p. 856.)

Questions for Further Discussion

1. What might the research with leptin-resistant mice imply for some obese people?

2. Many obese people face discrimination in many forms. If obesity is, at least in part, controlled by hormonal and genetic factors, how might the attitudes of others toward the obese change?

ANOREXIA NERVOSA   Jennifer is an attractive 20-year-old overachiever who rigidly maintains her weight with diet, exercise, and self-discipline. Although she is thin, she still is dissatisfied with her appearance and weight and strives to lose more. Jennifer is 5 feet, 6 inches tall and weighs only 85 pounds (Rideout, 2005). Why does Jennifer think she needs to lose more weight?

Anorexia nervosa is a condition in which a person (typically young and female) reduces eating to the point that a weight loss of 15 percent below expected body weight or more is the result. At a weight loss of 40 percent below expected body weight, hospitalization is necessary. Hormone secretion becomes abnormal, especially in the thyroid and adrenal glands. The heart muscles become weak and heart rhythms may alter. Other physical effects of anorexia include diarrhea, loss of muscle tissue, loss of sleep, and low blood pressure.

Some anorexics will eat in front of others but then force themselves to throw up or take large doses of laxatives. They are often obsessed with exercising and with

anorexia nervosa
a condition in which a person reduces eating to the point that a weight loss of 15 percent below the ideal body weight or more occurs.

food—cooking elaborate meals for others while eating nothing themselves. They have extremely distorted body images, seeing fat where others see only skin and bones.

What causes anorexia is not yet fully understood. Some theories involve biological explanations. Others point to psychological factors such as a rejection of sexual maturity (anorexia usually begins in the early teens and often causes menstruation to cease), sexual abuse, perfectionism with a desire to control as many aspects of one's life as possible, and family dysfunction (Abraham & Llewellyn-Jones, 2001; Mitchell, 1985).

What can be done to treat anorexia? If the anorexic weight loss is severe (40 percent or more below expected normal weight), dehydration, severe chemical imbalances, and possibly organ damage may result. Hospitalization should occur before this dangerous point is reached. In the hospital the anorexic's physical needs will be treated, even to the point of force-feeding in extreme cases. Anorexia nervosa is classified as a clinical (mental) disorder in The *Diagnostic and Statistical Manual of Mental Disorders, Version IV-Text Revision or DSM-IV-TR* (American Psychiatric Association, 2000), which is a listing of disorders and their symptoms used by psychological professionals to make a diagnosis. LINK *to Chapter Fourteen: Psychological Disorders, p. 527.* As a result, psychological counseling will also be part of the hospital treatment, which may last from two to four months. Those anorexics who are not so severely malnourished as to be in immediate danger can be treated outside of the hospital setting, typically receiving supportive psychotherapy, behavioral therapy, and perhaps group therapy. Family therapy is nearly always indicated in cases in which the family of the anorexic is contributing in some way to the behavior. LINK *to Chapter Fifteen: Psychological Therapies, p. 577.* (The author was recently told of a mother and daughter who were both developing anorexia, with the mother encouraging the behavior in her daughter.) The prognosis for full recovery is not as hopeful as it should be because only 40 to 60 percent of all anorexics who receive treatment will make such a recovery. For some anorexics who do gain weight, the damage to the heart and other body systems may still be so great that an early death is a possibility (Neumarker, 1997).

The following Web sites provide access to information, help, and professional referrals for people with anorexia and other eating disorders:

- **www.mentalhealth.com/dis/p20-et01.html** (information and links to other Web pages)
- **www.anad.org/site/anadweb** (National Association of Anorexia and Associated Disorders)
- **www.findinfo.com/anorexia.htm** (links provided to self-help and professional sites)

BULIMIA In her late twenties, Carrie is the expected weight for her height but obsesses about food. She alternates between starving herself and then gorging on large amounts of food. After gorging, she makes herself throw up to rid her body of the food she has just eaten. Typically, she gorges on fattening, sugary foods such as cookies, ice cream, and breads (Rideout, 2005). Why does Carrie eat like this?

Bulimia is a condition in which a person develops a cycle of "binging" or overeating enormous amounts of food at one sitting, and "purging" or deliberately vomiting after eating (Hay & Bacaltchuk, 2002). There are some similarities to anorexia: The victims are usually female, are obsessed with their appearance, diet excessively, and believe themselves to be fat even when they are quite obviously not fat. But bulimics are typically a little older than anorexics at the onset of the disorder—early twenties rather than early puberty. Like Carrie, bulimics often maintain a normal weight, making it difficult to detect. The most obvious difference is that the bulimic will eat, and eat to excess, binging on huge amounts of food (as much as 50,000 calories in one sitting). A typical binge may include a gallon of ice cream, a package of cookies, and a gallon of milk—all consumed as quickly as possible.

Mary Kate Olson is a young actress who has, with her sister Ashley, made it very big in Hollywood. The tabloids have accused her of being anorexic and of undergoing treatment for anorexia. Whether this is true or false is yet to be confirmed, but in this photograph she does appear to be very thin. Hollywood is a major contributor to the concept of very thin women as beautiful and desirable. This is a far cry from the days of sex symbol Marilyn Monroe, who was rumored to be a size 12.

bulimia
a condition in which a person develops a cycle of "binging" or overeating enormous amounts of food at one sitting, and "purging" or deliberately vomiting after eating.

But wait ▶ a minute—if they're so concerned about gaining weight, why do they binge at all?

But wait a minute—if they're so concerned about gaining weight, why do they binge at all? Bulimics have very distorted views of how much food is too much food, and eating one cookie while trying to control weight can lead to a binge—after all, since the diet is completely blown, why not go all out?

One might think that bulimia is not as damaging to the health as anorexia. After all, the bulimic is in no danger of starving to death. But bulimia comes with many serious health consequences: severe tooth decay and erosion of the lining of the esophagus from the acidity of the vomiting, enlarged salivary glands, potassium, calcium, and sodium imbalances that can be very dangerous, damage to the intestinal tract from overuse of laxatives, heart problems, fatigue, and seizures (Berg, 1999).

As with anorexia, there have been many proposed causes. Several research studies indicate a genetic component for both bulimia and anorexia (Fumeron et al., 2001; Strober et al., 2000; Vink et al., 2001). Psychological issues of control have also been cited, but biological evidence suggests that brain chemistry, and in particular the neurotransmitter *serotonin*, is involved in both bulimia and anorexia (Fumeron et al., 2001; Jimerson et al., 1997). Other studies point to the role of leptin, a hormone that has also been implicated in obesity and discussed in the previous Psychology in the News section (Ferron et al., 1997).

Treatment of bulimia, which like anorexia is listed as a clinical (mental) disorder in the *DSM-IV-TR* (American Psychiatric Association, 2000), can involve many of the same measures taken to treat anorexia: hospitalization, drugs that affect serotonin levels, and psychotherapy. The prognosis for the bulimic's recovery is somewhat more hopeful than that of anorexia. Cognitive therapy, which involves helping clients to understand how illogical and irrational their thought patterns have become, has been successful in treating bulimia (DeAngelis, 2002). A cognitive therapist is very direct, forcing clients to see how their beliefs do not stand up when considered in "the light of day" and helping them form new and more constructive ways of thinking about themselves and their behavior. L I N K *to Chapter Fifteen: Psychological Therapies, p. 573.* Table 9.3 lists just a few of the more visible signs and symptoms of eating disorders.

CULTURE AND EATING DISORDERS Although many researchers have believed eating disorders, especially anorexia, to be culture-bound syndromes that only show up in cultures obsessed with being thin (as many Western cultures are), eating disorders are also found in other cultures (Miller & Pumariega, 1999). What differs between Western and non-Western cultures is the rates at which such disorders appear. For example, Chinese and Chinese American women are far less likely to suffer from eating disorders than are non-Hispanic white women (Pan, 2000). Why wouldn't Chinese American women be more likely to have eating disorders after being exposed to the Western cultural obsession with thinness? Pan (2000) assumes that whatever Chi-

TABLE 9.3 **POSSIBLE SIGNS OF EATING DISORDERS**

Dramatic weight loss in a relatively short period of time

Obsession with calories and fat content of food

Hiding food in strange places

Hair loss, pale appearance to the skin

Bruised or callused knuckles, bloodshot eyes with light bruising under the eyes

Frequent trips to the bathroom following meals

Obsession with continuous exercise

Wearing baggy clothes to hide body shape or weight loss

Reading books about weight loss and eating disorders

Complaints of often feeling cold

nese cultural factors "protect" Chinese women from developing eating disorders may also still have a powerful influence on Chinese American women.

One problem with looking at anorexia and bulimia in other cultures is that the behavior of starving oneself may be seen in other cultures as having an entirely different purpose than in Western cultures. One key component of anorexia, for example, is a fear of being fat, a fear that is missing in many other cultures. Yet women in those cultures have starved themselves for other socially recognized reasons: religious fasting or unusual ideas about nutrition (Castillo, 1997).

Anorexia and bulimia have also been thought to occur only rarely in African American women, but that characterization seems to be changing. Researchers are seeing an increase in anorexia and bulimia among young African American women of all socioeconomic levels (Crago et al., 1996; Mintz & Betz, 1998; Pumariega & Gustavson, 1994). If clinicians and doctors are not aware that these disorders can affect more than the typical white, young, middle- to upper-middle-class woman, important signs and symptoms of eating disorders in nonwhite or non-Western people may allow these disorders to go untreated until it is too late.

PRACTICE **QUIZ:** HOW MUCH DO YOU REMEMBER?

Pick the best answer.

1. Which of the following is not one of the physiological factors in hunger?
   a. stomach
   b. pancreas
   c. hypothalamus
   d. corpus callosum

2. As the basal metabolic rate decreases, the weight set point
   a. decreases.
   b. increases.
   c. stays the same.
   d. varies up and down.

3. People who are _____ respond to the anticipation of eating with higher insulin levels.
   a. internals
   b. externals
   c. intrinsic
   d. extrinsic

4. Scientists believe that some people become obese because their ancestors were _____ and more likely to store up fat for future times of famine.
   a. herder-farmers   c. hunter-gatherers
   b. agriculturalists   d. big overeaters

5. One of the main differences between anorexia and bulimia is that the anorexic
   a. is obsessed about body weight.
   b. tends to be female.
   c. never binges on food.
   d. can suffer from heart problems.

6. Bulimia, unlike anorexia,
   a. produces an obsession with food.
   b. is hard to detect because the person's weight is often normal.
   c. is not physically harmful.
   d. involves starvation.

Answers: 1-d, 2-b, 3-b, 4-c, 5-c, 6-b.

The first half of this chapter has looked at the motives that drive human behavior. But people do more than just behave; there are feelings that accompany every human action. The second half of the chapter explores the world of human emotions and how those emotions are connected to both thinking and actions.

Emotion

What part does the way we feel about things play in all of our daily activities—what exactly causes feelings? Although strict behaviorists in the tradition of Watson and Skinner would prefer not to think about it, human beings are full of feelings, or emotions. Although emotions may be internal processes, there are outward physical signs of what people are feeling as well.

What part does the way we feel about things play in all of our daily ◄ activities—what exactly causes feelings?

*State of arousal doesn't change for ∂ emotion.(always the same regardless of the emotion)

THE THREE ELEMENTS OF EMOTION

9.13   *What are the three elements of emotion?*

The Latin word meaning "to move" is the source of both words used in this chapter over and over again—*motive* and *emotion*. **Emotion** can be defined as the "feeling" aspect of consciousness, characterized by a certain physical arousal, a certain behavior that reveals the feeling to the outside world, and an inner awareness of feelings.

THE PHYSIOLOGY OF EMOTION   Physically, when a person experiences an emotion, there is an arousal created by the sympathetic nervous system. ⓛⓘⓝⓚ *to Chapter Two: The Biological Perspective, pp. 57–58.* The heart rate increases, breathing becomes more rapid, the pupils dilate, and the mouth may become dry. Think about the last time you were angry and then about the last time you were frightened. Weren't the physical symptoms pretty similar? Although facial expressions do differ between various emotional responses (Ekman, 1980; Ekman et al., 1969; Ekman & Friesen, 1978), emotions are difficult to distinguish from one another on the basis of outward bodily reactions alone. In fact, it is quite easy to mistake a person who is actually afraid or angry as being aroused if the person's face is not clearly visible, which can lead to much miscommunication and misunderstanding. However, in the laboratory using devices to measure the heart rate, blood pressure, and skin temperature, researchers have found that different emotions are associated with different physiological reactions: Fear is associated with a decrease in skin temperature, whereas anger is associated with an increase in skin temperature and a greater increase in blood pressure, for example (Levenson, 1992; Levenson et al., 1992).

Just what parts of the brain are involved in various aspects of emotion? As discussed in Chapter Two, the *amygdala*, a small area located within the limbic system on each side of the brain, is associated with fear in both humans and animals (Davis & Whalen, 2001; Fanselow & Gale, 2003) and is also involved in the facial expressions of human emotions (Morris et al., 1998). When the amygdala is damaged in rats, they cannot be classically conditioned to fear new objects—they apparently cannot remember to be afraid (Davidson et al., 2000; Fanselow & Gale, 2003). In humans, damage to the amygdala has been associated with similar effects (LaBar et al., 1995) and with impairing the ability to determine emotions from looking at the facial expressions of others (Adolphs & Tranel, 2003).

Emotions even work differently depending on which side of the brain is involved. Researchers have found that negative feelings such as sadness, anxiety, and depression seem to be a function of primarily the left hemisphere of the brain (Ahern & Schwartz, 1985; Davidson et al., 1990; Papousek & Schulter, 2002). In the most recent study (Papousek & Schulter, 2002), the electrical activity of the brain was tracked using an electroencephalograph (EEG). ⓛⓘⓝⓚ *to Chapter Two: The Biological Perspective, pp. 60–62.* When anxiety and depression were high, so was the activity on the left side of the brain. But when anxiety and depression were reduced, activity levels dropped in the left hemisphere and increased in the right hemisphere.

The ability to interpret the facial expressions of others as a particular emotion also seems to be a function of one side of the brain more than the other. Researchers have found that when people are asked to identify the emotion on another person's face, the right hemisphere is more active than the left, particularly in women (Voyer & Rodgers, 2002). This difference begins weakly in childhood but increases in adulthood, with children being less able to identify negative emotions as well as positive emotions when compared to adults (Barth & Boles, 1999; Lane et al., 1995). This finding is consistent with early research that assigns the recognition of faces to the right hemisphere (Berent, 1977; Ellis, 1983).

THE BEHAVIOR OF EMOTION: EMOTIONAL EXPRESSION   How do people behave when in the grip of an emotion? There are facial expressions, body movements, and actions that indicate to others how a person feels. Frowns, smiles, and sad expressions

emotion
the "feeling" aspect of consciousness, characterized by a certain physical arousal, a certain behavior that reveals the emotion to the outside world, and an inner awareness of feelings.

FIGURE 9.5   **Facial Expressions of Emotion**   Facial expressions appear to be universal. For example, these faces are interpreted as showing (a) anger, (b) fear, (c) disgust, (d) happiness, (e) surprise, and (f) sadness by people of cultures all over the world. Although the situations that cause these emotions may differ from culture to culture, the expression of particular emotions remains strikingly the same.

combine with hand gestures, the turning of one's body, and spoken words to produce an understanding of emotion. People fight, run, kiss, and yell, along with countless other actions stemming from the emotions they feel.

Facial expressions can vary across different cultures, although some aspects of facial expression seem to be universal. (See Figure 9.5 for some examples of universal facial expressions.) Charles Darwin (1898) was one of the first to theorize that emotions were a product of evolution and, therefore, universal—all human beings, no matter what their culture, would show the same facial expression because the facial muscles evolved to communicate specific information to onlookers. For example, an angry face would signal to onlookers that they should act submissively or expect a fight. Although Darwin's ideas were not in line with the behaviorist movement of the early and middle twentieth century, which promoted environment rather than heredity as the cause of behavior, other researchers have since found evidence that there is a universal nature to at least seven basic emotions (Ekman, 1973; Ekman & Friesen, 1969, 1971). Even children who are blind from birth can produce the appropriate facial expressions for any given situation without ever having witnessed those expression on others, which strongly supports the idea that emotional expressions have their basis in biology rather than in learning (Charlesworth & Kreutzer, 1973; Fulcher, 1942).

In their research, Ekman and Friesen found that people of many different cultures (Japanese, Europeans, Americans, and even the Fore tribe of New Guinea) can consistently recognize at least seven facial expressions: anger, fear, disgust, happiness, surprise, sadness, and contempt (Ekman & Friesen, 1969, 1971). Although the emotions and the related facial expressions appear to be universal, exactly when, where, and how an emotion is expressed may be determined by the culture. There are **display rules** that can vary from culture to culture (Ekman, 1973; Ekman & Friesen, 1969). Display rules are

Simulation

Live psych

Facial Expressions and Emotion

display rules
learned ways of controlling displays of emotion in social settings.

learned ways of controlling displays of emotion in social settings. For example, Japanese people have strict social rules about showing emotion in public situations—they simply do not show emotion, remaining cool, calm, and collected, at least on the *outside*. But if in a more private situation, as a parent scolding a child within the home, the adult's facial expression easily would be recognized as "angry" by people of any culture. The emotion is universal and the way it is expressed on the face is universal, but whether it is expressed or displayed depends on the learned cultural rules for displaying emotion.

Display rules seem to vary by the type of culture in which they occur. For example, display rules are different between cultures that are individualistic (placing the importance of the individual above the social group) and those that are collectivistic (placing the importance of the social group above that of the individual). While the culture of the United States is individualistic, for example, the culture of Japan is collectivistic. At least part of the difference between the two types of display rules may be due to these cultural differences (Edelmann & Iwawaki, 1987; Hofstede, 1980; Hofstede et al., 2002). ⓛⓘⓝⓚ *to Chapter Twelve: Theories of Personality, pp. 465–466.*

SUBJECTIVE EXPERIENCE: LABELING EMOTION The third component of emotion is interpreting the subjective feeling by giving it a label: anger, fear, disgust, happiness, sadness, shame, interest, and so on. Another way of labeling this component is to call it the "cognitive component," because the labeling process is a matter of retrieving memories of previous similar experiences, perceiving the context of the emotion, and coming up with a solution—a label.

The label a person applies to a subjective feeling is at least in part a learned response influenced by that person's language and culture. Such labels may differ in people of different cultural backgrounds. For example, a recent study (Tsai et al., 2004) found that Chinese Americans who were still firmly rooted in their original Chinese culture were far more likely to use labels to describe their emotions that referred to bodily sensations (such as "dizzy") or social relationships (such as "friendship") than were more "Americanized" Chinese Americans and European Americans.

In another study, even the subjective feeling of happiness showed cultural differences (Kitayama & Markus, 1994). In this study, Japanese students and students from the United States were found to associate a general positive emotional state with entirely different circumstances. In the case of the Japanese students, the positive state was more associated with friendly or socially engaged feelings. The students from the United States associated their positive emotional state more with feelings that were socially disengaged, such as pride. This finding is a further reflection of the differences between cultures that are either collectivistic or individualistic.

So which of the three elements is the most important? And in what order do they come? Does a feeling have any meaning before it is named? In the early days of psychology, it was assumed that feeling a particular emotion led first to a physical reaction and then to a behavioral one. Seeing a snarling dog in one's path causes the feeling of fear, which stimulates the body to arousal, followed by the behavioral act of running. People are aroused because they are afraid. (See Figure 9.6.)

Experiment
Live!
psych
Transfer of Emotions

So which of the three elements is the most important? And in what order do they come? Does a feeling have any meaning before it is named? ▶

FIGURE 9.6 **Common Sense Theory of Emotion** In the common-sense theory of emotion, a stimulus (snarling dog) leads to an emotion of fear, which then leads to bodily arousal (in this case, indicated by shaking).

Common sense theory

"I'm shaking because I'm afraid"

Stimulus

First response

Second response

FEAR

Snarling dog

Conscious fear

ANS arousal

JAMES-LANGE *reaction first, then feel (label)*

9.14   *What is the James-Lange theory of emotion?*

William James (1884, 1890, 1894), who was also the founder of the functionalist perspective in the early history of psychology (L I N K) *to Chapter One: The Science of Psychology, p. 8*, disagreed with this early viewpoint. He believed that the order of the components of emotions was quite different. At nearly the same time, a physiologist and psychologist in Denmark, Carl Lange (1885), came up with an explanation of emotion so similar to that of James that the two names are used together to refer to the theory—the **James-Lange theory of emotion**. (See Figure 9.7.)

James-Lange theory

"I'm afraid because I'm shaking"

Stimulus	First response	Second response
Snarling dog	ANS arousal, changes in body	Conscious fear

FIGURE 9.7   **James-Lange Theory of Emotion**   In the James-Lange theory of emotion, a stimulus leads to bodily arousal first, which is then interpreted as an emotion.

In this theory, a stimulus of some sort (for example, the large snarling dog) produces a physiological reaction. This reaction, which is the arousal of the "fight-or-flight" sympathetic nervous system (wanting to run), produces bodily sensations such as increased heart rate, dry mouth, and rapid breathing. James and Lange believed that the physical arousal led to the labeling of the emotion (*fear*). Simply put, "I am afraid because I am aroused," "I am embarrassed because my face is red," "I am nervous because my stomach is fluttering," and "I am in love because my heart rate increases when I look at her or him."

What about people who have spinal cord injuries that prevent the sympathetic nervous system from functioning? Although James-Lange would predict that these people should show decreased emotion because the arousal that causes emotion is no longer there, this does not in fact happen. Several studies of people with spinal cord injuries report that these people are capable of experiencing the same emotions after their injury as before, sometimes even more intensely (Bermond et al., 1991; Chwalisz et al., 1988).

"I can't explain it. I see that guy coming up the walkway and I go postal."

©The New Yorker Collection 1998 Leo Cullum from cartoonbank.com. All Rights Reserved.

CANNON-BARD *same time*

9.15   *What is the Cannon-Bard theory of emotion?*

Physiologists Walter Cannon (1927) and Philip Bard (1934) theorized that the emotion and the physiological arousal occur more or less at the same time. Cannon, an expert in sympathetic arousal mechanisms, did not feel that the physical changes caused by different emotions were distinct enough to allow them to be perceived as different emotions. Bard expanded on this idea by stating that the sensory information that comes into the brain is sent simultaneously (by the thalamus) to both the cortex and the organs of the sympathetic nervous system. The fear and the bodily reactions are, therefore, experienced at the same time—not one after the other. "I'm afraid and running and aroused!" (See Figure 9.8.)

This theory, known as the **Cannon-Bard theory of emotion**, also had its critics. Lashley (1938) stated that the thalamus would have to be pretty sophisticated to make sense of all the possible human emotions and relay them to the proper areas of the cortex and body. It would seem that other areas of the brain must be involved in processing emotional

James-Lange theory of emotion theory in which a physiological reaction leads to the labeling of an emotion.

Cannon-Bard theory of emotion theory in which the physiological reaction and the emotion are assumed to occur at the same time.

FIGURE 9.8 **Cannon-Bard Theory of Emotion** In the Cannon-Bard theory of emotion, a stimulus leads to activity in the brain, which then sends signals to arouse the body and interpret the emotion at the same time.

Stimulus   First response   Second response

Cannon-Bard theory

"I'm shaking and feeling afraid at the same time"

Snarling dog

Subcortical brain activity

ANS arousal, changes in body

FEAR

Conscious fear

reactions. The studies of people with spinal cord injuries, which seem to suggest that emotions can be experienced without feedback from the sympathetic organs to the cortex and cited as a criticism of the James-Lange theory, seem at first to support the Cannon-Bard version of emotions: People do not need feedback from those organs to experience emotion. However, there is an alternate pathway that carries information from these organs to the cortex; this is the *vagus nerve*, one of the cranial nerves (LeDoux, 1994). This makes the case for Cannon-Bard a little less convincing.

SCHACHTER-SINGER AND COGNITIVE AROUSAL THEORY

9.16 *What is the cognitive arousal theory of emotion?*   cues,emotion

The early theories talked about the emotion and the physical reaction, but what about the mental interpretation of those components? In their **cognitive arousal theory,** Schachter and Singer (1962) proposed that two things have to happen before emotion occurs: the physical arousal and a labeling of the arousal based on cues from the surrounding environment. These two things happen at the same time, resulting in the labeling of the emotion. (See Figure 9.9.)

For example, if a person comes across a snarling dog while taking a walk, the physical arousal (heart racing, eyes opening wide) is accompanied by the thought (cognition) that this must be fear. Then and only then will the person experience the fear emotion. In other words, "I am aroused in the presence of a scary dog; therefore, I must be afraid." Evidence for this theory was found in what is now a classic experiment, described in the Classic Studies in Psychology on the following page.

cognitive arousal theory
theory of emotion in which both the physical arousal and the labeling of that arousal based on cues from the environment must occur before the emotion is experienced.

FIGURE 9.9 **Schachter's Cognitive Arousal Theory of Emotion** Schachter's cognitive arousal theory is similar to the James-Lange theory, but adds the element of cognitive labeling of the arousal. In this theory, a stimulus leads to both bodily arousal and the labeling of that arousal (based on the surrounding context), which leads to the experience and labeling of the emotional reaction.

Stimulus   First response   Second response

Schachter's cognitive arousal theory

"This snarling dog is dangerous and that makes me feel afraid."

Snarling dog

Cognitive appraisal

ANS arousal, changes in body

FEAR

Conscious fear

CLASSIC STUDIES IN PSYCHOLOGY
The Angry/Happy Man

9.17   *What happened in Schachter and Singer's classic study of emotion?*

In 1962, Stanley Schachter and Jerome Singer designed an experiment to test their theory that emotions are determined by an interaction between the physiological state of arousal and the label, or cognitive interpretation, that a person places on the arousal. Male student volunteers were told that they were going to answer a questionnaire about their reactions to a new vitamin called Suproxin. In reality, they were all injected with a drug called epinephrine, which causes physical arousal in the form of increased heart rate, rapid breathing, and a reddened face—all responses that happen during a strong emotional reaction.

Each student then participated in one of two conditions. In one condition, a confederate* posing as one of the participants started complaining about the experimenter, tearing up his questionnaire and storming out. In the other condition, there was one man who acted more like he was very happy, almost giddy and playing with some of the objects in the room. The "angry" man and the "happy" man in both conditions deliberately behaved in the two different ways as part of the experiment.

After both conditions had played out, participants in each of the two conditions were asked to describe their own emotions. The participants who had been exposed to the "angry" man interpreted their arousal symptoms as anger, whereas those exposed to the "happy" man interpreted their arousal as happiness. In all cases, the actual cause of arousal was the epinephrine and the physical symptoms of arousal were identical. The only difference between the two groups of participants was their exposure to the two different contexts. Schachter and Singer's theory would have predicted exactly these results: Physiological arousal has to be interpreted cognitively before it is experienced as a specific emotion.

Although this classic experiment stimulated a lot of research, much of that research has failed to find much support for the cognitive arousal theory of emotion (Reisenzein, 1983, 1994). What this theory did do, however, is highlight the importance of cognition in determining emotions, a concept that has been revisited in some more modern theories of emotion.

Questions for Further Discussion

1. How might observing the emotions of others under more normal circumstances (i.e., not in a drugged state) affect a person's own emotional state?

2. According to Schachter and Singer's theory, for your first date with a person, should you choose a happy movie or a sad one?

3. In this experiment, what was the independent variable manipulated by the experimenters? What was the dependent variable?

4. This experiment used deception, as the participants were not told the true nature of the injection they received. What kind of ethical problems might have arisen from this deception? What problems would the experimenters have had in getting this study approved by an ethics committee today?

---

*Confederate: someone who is cooperating with another person on some task.

THE FACIAL FEEDBACK HYPOTHESIS: SMILE, YOU'LL FEEL BETTER

9.18   *What is the facial feedback hypothesis?*

In his (1898) book *The Expression of the Emotions in Man and Animals*, Charles Darwin stated that facial expressions evolved as a way of communicating intentions, such

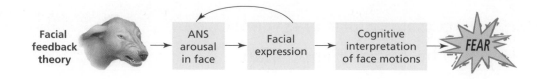

FIGURE 9.10 **Facial Feedback Hypothesis of Emotion** In the facial feedback theory of emotion, a stimulus such as this snarling dog causes arousal and a facial expression. The facial expression then provides feedback to the brain about the emotion. The brain then interprets the emotion and may also intensify it.

Does that mean that I ▶ don't smile because I'm happy—I'm happy because I smile?

The facial feedback hypothesis assumes that changing your own facial expression can change the way you feel. Smiling makes people feel happy, and frowning makes people feel sad. This effect seems to have an impact on the people around us as well. If this is true, this smiling man may make the airline steward handing him his food feel good, too. Is it hard for you to stay in a bad mood when the people around you are smiling and laughing?

as threat or fear, and that these expressions are universal within a species rather than specific to a culture. He also believed (as in the James-Lange theory) that when such emotions are expressed freely on the face, the emotion itself intensifies—meaning that the more one smiles, the happier one feels.

Modern psychologists have proposed a theory of emotion that is consistent with much of Darwin's original thinking. Called the **facial feedback hypothesis**, this explanation assumes that facial expressions provide feedback to the brain concerning the emotion being expressed, which in turn not only intensifies the emotion but also actually *causes* the emotion (Buck, 1980; Ekman, 1980; Ekman & Friesen, 1978; Keillor et al., 2002). (See Figure 9.10.)

Does that mean that I don't smile because I'm happy—I'm happy because I smile? Not only does this explanation assume that the facial expression causes the emotion, but also there is evidence that seeing other people's facial expressions can cause people to change their own facial expressions to match. People who are shown pictures of faces that are happy, for example, show activation of their own muscles around the mouth that would be used to smile, whereas people looking at angry faces show activation in the eyebrows, as if frowning (Dimberg et al., 2000).

One fairly recent study does cast some doubt on the validity of this hypothesis. If the facial feedback hypothesis is correct, then people who have facial paralysis on both sides of the face should be unable to experience emotions in a normal way. But a case study conducted on just such a person revealed that although she was unable to express emotions on her paralyzed face, she could respond emotionally to slides meant to stimulate emotional reactions, just as anyone else would (Keillor et al., 2002). Clearly, the question of how much the actual facial expression determines the emotional experience has yet to be fully answered.

For more about the psychology of happiness, see the section Applying Psychology to Everyday Life at the end of this chapter.

LAZARUS AND THE COGNITIVE-MEDIATIONAL THEORY

9.19 *What is cognitive-mediational theory?*

As mentioned in the Classic Studies in Psychology section, Schachter and Singer's (1962) study stressed the importance of cognition, or thinking, in the determination of emotions. One of the more modern versions of cognitive emotion theories is Lazarus's **cognitive-mediational theory** of emotion (1991). In this theory, the most important aspect of any emotional experience is how the person interprets, or appraises, the stimulus that causes the emotional reaction. To *mediate* means to "come between" and in this theory, the cognitive appraisal mediates by coming between the stimulus and the emotional response to that stimulus.

Lazarus's
Cognitive-mediational
theory → Appraisal of threat → FEAR → Bodily response

FIGURE 9.11   **Lazarus's Theory of Emotion**   In Lazarus's cognitive-mediational theory of emotion, a stimulus causes an immediate appraisal (e.g., "The dog is snarling and not behind a fence, so this is dangerous"). The cognitive appraisal results in an emotional response, which is then followed by the appropriate bodily response.

For example, remember the person who encountered a snarling dog while walking through the neighborhood? According to Lazarus, the appraisal of the situation would come *before* both the physical arousal and the experience of emotion. If the dog is behind a sturdy fence, the appraisal would be something like "no threat." The most likely emotion would be annoyance, and the physical arousal would be minimal. But if the dog is not confined, the appraisal would more likely be "danger—threatening animal!" which would be followed by an increase in arousal and the emotional experience of fear. In other words, it's the *interpretation* of the arousal that results in the emotion of fear, not the labeling as in the Schachter-Singer model, and the interpretation comes first. (See Figure 9.11).

Not everyone agrees with this theory, of course. Some researchers believe that emotional reactions to situations are so fast that they are almost instantaneous, which would leave little time for a cognitive appraisal to occur first (Zajonc, 1998). Others (Kihlstrom et al., 2000) have found that the human brain can respond to a physical threat before conscious thought enters the picture. The simple spinal cord reflex of pain withdrawal discussed in Chapter Two (p. 54) is an example of this—the reflex occurs so quickly that the brain itself is not involved, and the experience of pain is consciously felt *after* the injured body part is jerked away from the painful stimulus. Ⓛⓘⓝⓚ *to Chapter Two: The Biological Perspective, p. 54.*

Which theory is right? Human emotions are so incredibly complex that it might not be out of place to say that all of the theories are correct to at least some degree. In certain situations, the cognitive appraisal might have time to mediate the emotion that is experienced (such as falling in love), whereas in other situations, the need to act first, think and feel later is more important. (See Figure 9.12.)

facial feedback hypothesis
theory of emotion that assumes that facial expressions provide feedback to the brain concerning the emotion being expressed, which in turn causes and intensifies the emotion.

cognitive-mediational theory
theory of emotion in which a stimulus must be interpreted (appraised) by a person in order to result in a physical response and an emotional reaction.

PRACTICE QUIZ: HOW MUCH DO YOU REMEMBER?

Pick the best answer.

1. Which of the following is NOT one of the three elements of emotion?
   a. subjective experience
   b. behavior
   c. attention
   d. physical reaction

2. The theory of emotion that states that the thalamus sends sensory information to the cortex and the sympathetic organs at the same time is the _____ theory.
   a. James-Lange
   b. Cannon-Bard
   c. Schachter-Singer
   d. facial feedback

3. In Schachter and Singer's classic study, participants who were exposed to the "angry" man interpreted their physiological arousal as _____, whereas those who were exposed to the "happy" man interpreted their arousal as _____.
   a. angry; happy
   b. happy; angry
   c. happy; happy
   d. angry; angry

4. Gerald smiles a lot at the office, which makes his coworkers feel happier, too. This effect is best explained by which of the following theories of emotion?
   a. James-Lange
   b. cognitive-mediational
   c. Schachter-Singer
   d. facial feedback

5. In the _____ theory of emotion, the most important aspect of an emotional experience is the interpretation, or appraisal, of the stimulus.
   a. cognitive-mediational
   b. Cannon-Bard
   c. James-Lange
   d. facial feedback

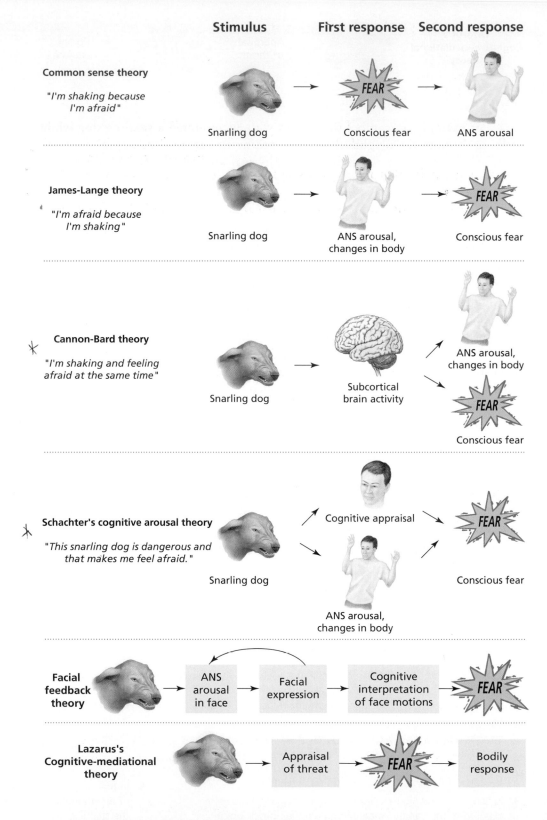

FIGURE 9.12   **Comparison of Theories of Emotion**   These figures represent the six different theories of emotion as discussed in the text.

Applying Psychology to Everyday Life: A How-To of Happiness?

9.20   *What is the positive psychology movement?*

One emotion that is probably nearest and dearest to most people is happiness, a state of well-being and contentment that is much to be desired. Social psychologist David G. Myers is widely recognized as a leader in the field of research into happiness. He is also one of the supporters of the **positive psychology movement**, a viewpoint that recommends shifting the focus of psychology away from the negative (abuse, anxiety, depression, all the things that can go wrong) to a more positive focus on strengths, well-being, and the pursuit of happiness (Myers, 1993).

According to Myers and others (Lyubomirsky et al., 2001; Myers, 1993; Schwartz et al., 2002), happiness is the key to many things: the perception of the world as a safer place, healthier and more satisfying lives, and even the ability to make decisions more easily. Happy people are also more likely to help others (Pizarro & Salovey, 2002; Salovey et al., 2000).

So how can people become happier? In his popular book, *The Pursuit of Happiness*, Myers (1993) lists 10 suggestions for becoming happier that are based on his many years of research:

1. **Realize that enduring happiness doesn't come from success.** Money, power, and fame do not guarantee happiness. If people don't have wealth, they may be in miserable, unhappy circumstances, but the reverse is not necessarily true: Money really doesn't buy happiness. Psychiatrists and clinical psychologists often have very wealthy, successful people as clients.

2. **Take control of your time.** People who feel in control of their lives by good time management skills are also happier people. Setting goals and breaking those goals down into steps can help a person see progress on a daily basis. Make lists and cross off items as they are finished.

3. **Act happy.** Put on a happy face. When people smile, it releases chemicals that make them feel better, and when they frown, the opposite occurs. Think happy, talk happy, act happy, and you will be happier.

4. **Seek work and leisure activities that engage your skills.** Doing things that are challenging without being overwhelming can result in more happiness in both work and leisure activities. There can be more happiness in tending one's garden than in taking a world tour.

5. **Join the "movement" movement.** Exercise, particularly aerobic exercise, will not only help you to feel better and look better physically, but also it relieves depression and anxiety. Get moving and get happier.

6. **Give your body the sleep it wants.** Sleep deprivation is bad for the mind, the body, and the mood. Sleep-deprived people are crabby, whereas people who have time to sleep and rest adequately are typically happier.

positive psychology movement a viewpoint that recommends shifting the focus of psychology away from the negative aspects to a more positive focus on strengths, well-being, and the pursuit of happiness.

In the pursuit of happiness, many people find that helping others increases their own happiness. These volunteers are experiencing that kind of happiness as they fill sandbags to help control the flooding of a nearby river.

7. **Give priority to close relationships.** A good social support system just can't be beat. Friends offer support and help to get you through the bad times. Take time to nurture friendships and relationships.

8. **Focus beyond the self.** Not only do happy people help other people more readily, but also they are happier for doing so. Helping others makes people feel good.

9. **Keep a gratitude journal.** Writing down the positive things that you have, such as a good thing that happened today, the friends you saw, and things that you did and enjoyed, also boost a sense of well-being. Stop and smell the roses.

10. **Nurture your spiritual self.** People with a strong sense of faith also tend to be happier. Communities based on shared belief systems about faith provide a good support system. These communities can also give a person a sense of purpose and provide hope during times of stress. People involved in these communities also tend to help others, too (see number 8).

9

CHAPTER SUMMARY

Approaches to Understanding Motivation

9.1 *What is motivation?*

• Motivation is the process by which activities are started, directed, and sustained so that physical or psychological needs are fulfilled.

9.2 *What are instinct approaches to motivation?*

• Instinct approaches proposed that some human actions may be motivated by instincts, which are innate patterns of behavior found in both people and animals.

9.3 *What are drive reduction approaches to motivation?*

• Drive-reduction approaches state that when an organism has a need (such as hunger), the need leads to psychological tension that motivates the organism to act, fulfilling the need and reducing the tension.

• Primary drives involve needs of the body whereas acquired (secondary) drives are those learned through experience. Homeostasis is the tendency of the body to maintain a steady state.

9.4 *What are three types of needs?*

• The need for achievement is a strong desire to succeed in getting to one's goals, both realistic and challenging.

• The self-theory of emotion links the need for achievement to the concept of locus of control. A belief in control over one's life leads to more attempts to achieve, even in the face of failure. Those who believe that they have little control over what happens to them are more likely to develop learned helplessness.

• The need for affiliation is the desire to have friendly social interactions and relationships with others and a desire to be held in high regard by others.

• The need for power concerns having control over others, influencing them and having an impact on them. Status and prestige are important to people high in this need.

9.5 *What are arousal approaches to motivation?*

• In arousal theory, a person has an optimal level of arousal to maintain. People who need more arousal than others are called sensation seekers.

9.6 *What are incentive approaches to motivation?*

• In the incentive approach, an external stimulus may be so rewarding that it motivates a person to act toward that stimulus rather than another stimulus or to satisfy a drive.

9.7 *What is Maslow's hierarchy of needs?*

• Maslow proposed a hierarchy of needs, beginning with basic physiological needs and ending with self-actualization needs. The more basic needs must be met before the higher needs can be fulfilled.

9.8 *What is the self-determination theory of motivation?*

• Self-determination theory (SDT) is a model of motivation in which three basic needs are seen as necessary to an individual's successful development: autonomy, competence, and relatedness.

• Intrinsic motivation occurs when people act because the act itself is satisfying or rewarding, whereas extrinsic motivation occurs when people receive an external reward (such as money) for the act.

What, Hungry Again? Why People Eat

9.9 *What happens in the body to cause hunger?*

• The physiological components of hunger include signals from the stomach and the hypothalamus and the increased secretion of insulin.

• When the basal metabolic rate slows down, the weight set point increases and makes weight gain more likely.

9.10 *How do social factors influence hunger?*

• The social components of hunger include social cues for when meals are to be eaten, cultural customs and food preferences, and the use of food as a comfort device or escape from unpleasantness.

• Some people may be externals who respond to the anticipation of eating by producing an insulin response, increasing the risk of obesity.

9.11 *What are some problems in eating behavior?*

• Maladaptive eating problems include obesity, anorexia, and bulimia.

Psychology in the News: The Biology of Obesity

9.12 *What biological factors play a part in obesity?*

• Scientists have researched the role of leptin, a hormone that controls the feeling of being full, in obesity.

• Genetics may play a part in anorexia and bulimia, as well as insensitivity to leptin, a hormone that controls appetite.

Emotion

9.13 *What are the three elements of emotion?*

• Emotion is the "feeling" aspect of consciousness and includes physical, behavioral, and subjective components.

9.14 *What is the James-Lange theory of emotion?*

• The James-Lange theory states that a stimulus creates a physiological response that then leads to the labeling of the emotion.

9.15 *What is the Cannon-Bard theory of emotion?*

• The Cannon-Bard theory asserts that the physiological reaction and the emotion are simultaneous, as the thalamus sends sensory infor-mation to both the cortex of the brain and the organs of the sympathetic nervous system.

9.16 *What is the cognitive arousal theory of emotion?*

• In Schachter and Singer's cognitive arousal theory, both the physiological arousal and the actual interpretation of that arousal must occur before the emotion itself is experienced. This interpretation is based on cues from the environment.

Classic Studies in Psychology: The Angry/Happy Man

9.17 *What happened in Schachter and Singer's classic study of emotion?*

• Those participants who were exposed to the "angry" man interpreted their physical arousal as anger, whereas those who were exposed to the "happy" man interpreted their physical arousal as happiness.

9.18 *What is the facial feedback hypothesis?*

• In the facial feedback hypothesis, facial expressions provide feedback to the brain about the emotion being expressed on the face, intensifying the emotion.

9.19 *What is cognitive-mediational theory?*

• In the cognitive-mediational theory of emotion, the cognitive component of emotion (the interpretation) precedes both the physiological reaction and the emotion itself.

Applying Psychology to Everyday Life: A How-To of Happiness?

9.20 *What is the positive psychology movement?*

• The positive psychology movement is a viewpoint that recommends shifting the focus of psychology away from negative aspects such as abuse, anxiety, depression, and all the things that can go wrong to a more positive focus on strengths, well-being, and the pursuit of happiness.

• David Myers has determined 10 things people can do to improve and increase happiness.

9 KEY TERMS

TEST YOURSELF

Pick the best answer.

1. The approach to motivation that forced psychologists to consider the hereditary factors in motivation was the _____ approach.
   a. arousal
   b. drive-reduction
   c. instinct
   d. incentive

2. The need for money is an example of a(n) _____ drive.
   a. primary
   b. acquired
   c. innate
   d. instinctive

3. Jocelyn needs to be the one whose ideas are always used and craves prestige among others. She drives an expensive car and wears nothing but the most expensive clothes. Jocelyn is high in the need for
   a. achievement.
   b. affiliation.
   c. power.
   d. attention.

4. People who are always looking for a challenge may be high in the need for
   a. achievement.
   b. affiliation.
   c. power.
   d. attention.

5. Evidence from a study with 2-year-olds who were given an opportunity to explore a black box with a hole in it suggests that sensation seeking may be
   a. learned.
   b. abnormal.
   c. acquired over time.
   d. innate.

6. Gene is trying to choose a snack. There is a bowl of fruit on the table, but there's also a candy bar that he bought yesterday. The fact that Gene feels drawn to choose the candy bar instead of the fruit is an example of the power of
   a. needs.
   b. drives.
   c. incentives.
   d. arousal.

7. According to Maslow, a person who wants to become self-actualized must first satisfy
   a. higher needs before other more basic needs.
   b. more basic needs such as food and safety.
   c. needs for creativity, justice, and the appreciation of beauty.
   d. needs for achievement, affiliation, and power.

8. Shontia works at a day care center. The pay is low and the hours are long, but she loves being around children and has no desire to look for a higher-paying job. Shontia's motivation appears to be
   a. intrinsic.
   b. extrinsic.
   c. selfish.
   d. external.

9. When we eat, the pancreas releases _____, which lowers blood sugar and can increase the feeling of hunger.
   a. glucose
   b. insulin
   c. thyroxin
   d. adrenaline

10. The structure in the brain that, when damaged, causes rats to stop eating is called the
    a. ventromedial pituitary.
    b. lateral hippocampus.
    c. ventromedial hypothalamus.
    d. lateral hypothalamus.

11. The rate at which your body burns energy when at rest is called the
    a. basal metabolic rate.
    b. weight set point.
    c. basal set point.
    d. weight metabolic rate.

12. According to Rodin, externals are people who may produce insulin in response to anticipating food as a result of
    a. genetic tendencies.
    b. biological sensitivity.
    c. classical conditioning.
    d. operant conditioning.

13. If there is a history of obesity in a family, each family member has _____ of becoming obese compared to people without such a family history.
    a. the same risk
    b. double or triple the risk
    c. five times the risk
    d. less risk

14. Leptin is a _____ involved in appetite control.
    a. hormone
    b. fatty tissue
    c. organ
    d. neurotransmitter

15. Unlike anorexics, bulimics
    a. often purge themselves to stay thin.
    b. are obsessed with being too fat.
    c. can do damage to their health.
    d. may appear to be normal in weight.

16. The role of _____, a neurotransmitter that is also implicated in obesity, may provide clues to both bulimia and anorexia.
    a. serotonin
    b. insulin
    c. dopamine
    d. norepinephrine

17. Your heart is racing, your breathing is rapid, and your mouth is dry. What emotion are you experiencing?
    a. anger
    b. fear
    c. happiness
    d. It is not always possible to distinguish one emotion from another by physiological reactions only.

18. The _____ theory of emotion would predict that people with spinal cord injuries that prevent them from experiencing sympathetic arousal would show decreased emotion.
    a. James-Lange
    b. Cannon-Bard
    c. Schachter-Singer
    d. facial feedback

19. In Schachter and Singer's classic study, participants were physically aroused by
    a. exposure to a "happy" man.
    b. exposure to an "angry man.
    c. receiving epinephrine.
    d. watching an exciting film.

20. The theory of emotion that owes a lot to Darwin's work is the _____ theory.
    a. James-Lange
    b. Cannon-Bard
    c. Schachter-Singer
    d. facial feedback

21. Researchers have found that the human brain
    a. must be consciously aware of a threat before responding.
    b. can respond to a threat before it becomes conscious of the threat.
    c. is not involved in emotions at all.
    d. is important in the spinal cord pain withdrawal reflex.

22. According to Myers, which of the following would NOT lead to increased happiness?
    a. getting enough sleep
    b. acting happy
    c. focusing on oneself
    d. managing one's time

Answers: 1-c, 2-b, 3-c, 4-a, 5-c, 6-c, 7-b, 8-a, 9-b, 10-d, 11-a, 12-c, 13-b, 14-a, 15-d, 16-a, 17-d, 18-d, 19-c, 20-d, 21-b, 22-c.

For more sample quizzes and other review activities that will help you get a better grade, be sure to check out your accompanying study guide. To access tests and your own personalized study plan that will help you focus on the areas you need to master before your next class test, be sure to go to the on-line Psychology web site available with the access code packaged with your book.

Approaches to Motivation

Motivation: process by which activities are started, directed, and sustained to fulfill physical or psychological needs

9.1

Instinct Approaches to Motivation

Human and animal actions may be motivated by innate behavior patterns

9.2

Drive-Reduction Approaches to Motivation

Drive-reduction approaches: needs (such as hunger) motivate the organism to act, fulfilling the need and reducing psychological tension

Homeostasis: tendency of the body to maintain a steady state

Primary drives: involve survival needs of the body

Secondary drives: those learned through experience

9.3

HOMEOSTASIS

Increased Hunger → Eat → Raised Glucose

Lowered Glucose ← Don't Eat ← Diminished Hunger

Three Types of Needs

Need for achievement: desire to succeed in getting to one's goals, both realistic and challenging

Need for affiliation: desire to have friendly social interactions and be held in high regard by others

Need for power: desire to have control over others, influence them, and have an impact on them

9.4

Eating Behaviors

Causes of Hunger

Physiological components: signals from the stomach, increased secretion of insulin, and actions of hypothalamus

Weight gain: when the basal metabolic rate slows down, the weight set point increases and makes weight gain more likely

9.9

Social Factors and Hunger

▶ Social cues for when meals are to be eaten
▶ Cultural customs and food preferences
▶ Use of food as a comfort device or escape
▶ Externals respond to anticipation of eating by producing insulin, increasing risk of obesity

9.10

Problems in Eating Behavior

Obesity

Anorexia: weight loss of 15 percent below the ideal body weight

Bulimia: cycle of "binging" and "purging"

9.11

Possible Signs of Eating Disorders

Dramatic weight loss in a relatively short period of time

Obsession with calories and fat content of food

Hiding food in strange places

Hair loss, pale appearance to the skin

Bruised or callused knuckles, bloodshot eyes with light bruising under the eyes

Frequent trips to the bathroom following meals

Obsession with continuous exercise

Wearing baggy clothes to hide body shape or weight loss

Reading books about weight loss and eating disorders

Complaints of often feeling cold

Biological Factors in Obesity

Leptin: hormone that controls the feeling of being full

Genetics: may play a part in anorexia and bulimia, insensitivity to leptin

9.12

CONCEPT MAP

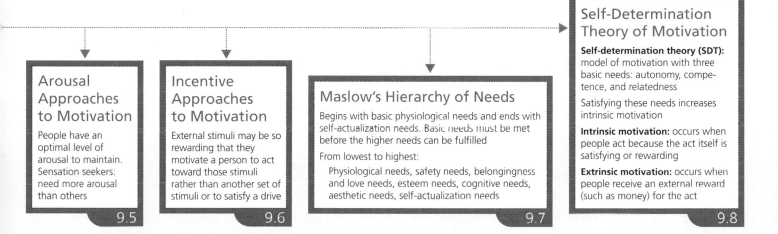

Self-Determination Theory of Motivation

Self-determination theory (SDT): model of motivation with three basic needs: autonomy, competence, and relatedness

Satisfying these needs increases intrinsic motivation

Intrinsic motivation: occurs when people act because the act itself is satisfying or rewarding

Extrinsic motivation: occurs when people receive an external reward (such as money) for the act

9.8

Arousal Approaches to Motivation

People have an optimal level of arousal to maintain. Sensation seekers: need more arousal than others

9.5

Incentive Approaches to Motivation

External stimuli may be so rewarding that they motivate a person to act toward those stimuli rather than another set of stimuli or to satisfy a drive

9.6

Maslow's Hierarchy of Needs

Begins with basic physiological needs and ends with self-actualization needs. Basic needs must be met before the higher needs can be fulfilled

From lowest to highest:

Physiological needs, safety needs, belongingness and love needs, esteem needs, cognitive needs, aesthetic needs, self-actualization needs

9.7

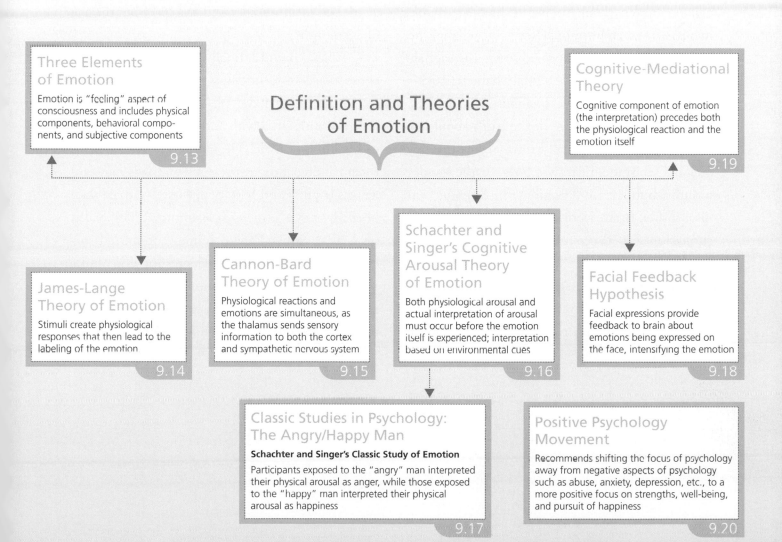

Definition and Theories of Emotion

Three Elements of Emotion

Emotion is "feeling" aspect of consciousness and includes physical components, behavioral components, and subjective components

9.13

Cognitive-Mediational Theory

Cognitive component of emotion (the interpretation) precedes both the physiological reaction and the emotion itself

9.19

James-Lange Theory of Emotion

Stimuli create physiological responses that then lead to the labeling of the emotion

9.14

Cannon-Bard Theory of Emotion

Physiological reactions and emotions are simultaneous, as the thalamus sends sensory information to both the cortex and sympathetic nervous system

9.15

Schachter and Singer's Cognitive Arousal Theory of Emotion

Both physiological arousal and actual interpretation of arousal must occur before the emotion itself is experienced; interpretation based on environmental cues

9.16

Facial Feedback Hypothesis

Facial expressions provide feedback to brain about emotions being expressed on the face, intensifying the emotion

9.18

Classic Studies in Psychology: The Angry/Happy Man

Schachter and Singer's Classic Study of Emotion

Participants exposed to the "angry" man interpreted their physical arousal as anger, while those exposed to the "happy" man interpreted their physical arousal as happiness

9.17

Positive Psychology Movement

Recommends shifting the focus of psychology away from negative aspects of psychology such as abuse, anxiety, depression, etc., to a more positive focus on strengths, well-being, and pursuit of happiness

9.20

10

Sexuality and Gender

Sexual Reassignment: The Story of David Reimer

Brenda Reimer spent her childhood feeling awkward and out of place. She was a tomboy and never wanted to play with the typical "girl" toys of childhood. When puberty began, Brenda's troubles increased as her hormones began to change her body, but not in the expected ways. Instead, she seemed to develop *male* sexual characteristics—deepening voice and increasing muscles.

Brenda was unaware of the truth about herself—she had been born a normal healthy boy, one of a set of identical twin boys. At the age of 8 months, both Bruce ("Brenda's" birth name) and his brother Brian were circumcised. Brian's circumcision was successful, but Bruce was horribly mutilated with more than half of his penis removed in the botched operation. Bruce's parents sought advice from various medical professionals, one of whom recommended reassigning

Bruce's gender as female. Further surgery was done to complete the physical transformation into a female. He was renamed Brenda, dressed as a girl, and in all ways treated as a girl from the age of 18 months.

When "Brenda" finally learned the truth, he chose at age 14 to undergo reconstructive surgery to return his male physical characteristics, renamed himself David, and lived more than half of his life as a male. He married a woman with three children from a previous marriage and said he was happier and better adjusted as a male than he ever was as a "female" (Colapinto, 2000). Sadly, on May 4, 2004, David Reimer committed suicide following a number of depressing downturns in his life: the loss of his job, the breakup of his marriage, and the death of his twin brother. He was 38 years old (Walker, 2004).

Why study sexuality and gender?

Human sexual behavior is responsible for the reproduction of the human race, but it is also one of the most important motivators of human behavior. Gender, the identification of a person as male or female, affects not only how people think of themselves but also their relationships with others as friends, lovers, and coworkers and how those others think of them as well.

10 ⚥

10.1   What are the physical differences between females and males?

10.2   What is gender?

10.3   How much influence do biology and learning have on gender role development?

10.4   What are the theories about how children learn their gender roles?

10.5   What is gender stereotyping?

10.6   What is androgyny?

10.7   What are the differences in thinking, social behavior, and personality between women and men?

10.8   What is the controversy concerning the treatment of intersexed infants?

10.9   What happens in the bodies of women and men during sexual intercourse?

10.10   How did Masters and Johnson investigate the human sexual response?

10.11   How did Kinsey study human sexual behavior?

10.12   What were the findings of the Janus Report?

10.13   What are the different sexual orientations and how do they develop?

10.14   What are the sexual dysfunctions caused by physical problems or stress?

10.15   What are the sexual dysfunctions known as paraphilias?

10.16   What are sexually transmitted diseases?

10.17   How can people protect themselves and prevent the spread of STDs?

The Physical Side of Human Sexuality

David Reimer's life was turned upside down because of a confusion between his original physical sex and the gender that his doctor and parents tried to determine for him after those physical sexual characteristics were altered. Before discussing the issue of gender and gender identity, it may help to understand the physical structures of the human sexual system and the function of those structures. These structures differ for females and males and develop at different times in an individual's life.

10.1   *What are the physical differences between females and males?*

THE PRIMARY SEX CHARACTERISTICS

The sexual organs include structures that are present at birth and those that develop during *puberty*, the period of physiological changes that takes place in the sexual organs and reproductive system during late middle childhood and adolescence. **LINK** *to Chapter Seven: Development Across the Life Span, pp. 274–275.*

FEMALE PRIMARY SEX CHARACTERISTICS   Primary sex characteristics are those physical characteristics that are present in the infant at birth. In the female, these characteristics include the **vagina** (the tube leading from the outside of the body to the opening of the womb), **uterus** (the womb), and **ovaries** (the female sex glands). (See Figure 10.1.) Primary sex characteristics are directly involved in human reproduction.

MALE PRIMARY SEX CHARACTERISTICS   In males, the primary sex characteristics include the penis, the **testes** or **testicles** (the male sex glands), the **scrotum** (an external pouch that holds the testes), and the **prostate gland** (a gland that secretes most of the fluid that carries the male sex cells, or sperm). (See Figure 10.1.)

THE SECONDARY SEX CHARACTERISTICS

Secondary sex characteristics develop during puberty and are only indirectly involved in human reproduction. These characteristics serve to distinguish the male

---

primary sex characteristics
sexual organs present at birth and directly involved in human reproduction.

vagina
the tube that leads from the outside of a female's body to the opening of the womb.

uterus
the womb in which the baby grows during pregnancy.

ovaries
the female sexual glands.

testes (testicles)
the male sex glands.

scrotum
external sack that holds the testes.

prostate gland
gland that secretes most of the fluid holding the male sex cells or sperm.

secondary sex characteristics
sexual organs and traits that develop at puberty and are indirectly involved in human reproduction.

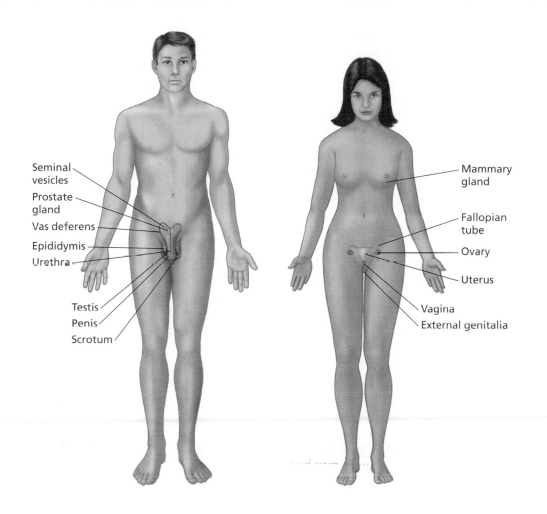

FIGURE 10.1   **Male and Female Sexual Organs**   These figures show the sexual organs of men and women. With the exception of breast tissue development in the female, which occurs during puberty, all of these structures develop during the prenatal period.

Seminal vesicles
Prostate gland
Vas deferens
Epididymis
Urethra
Testis
Penis
Scrotum

Mammary gland
Fallopian tube
Ovary
Uterus
Vagina
External genitalia

menstrual cycle
monthly shedding of the blood and tissue that line the uterus in preparation for pregnancy when conception does not occur.

mammary glands
glands within the breast tissue that produce milk when a woman gives birth to an infant.

from the female and may act as attractants to members of the opposite sex, ensuring that sexual activity and reproduction will occur. They are also, in many cases, a physical necessity for reproduction.

FEMALE SECONDARY SEX CHARACTERISTICS   In females, secondary sex characteristics include a growth spurt that begins at about ages 10 to 12 and is over about one year after their first **menstrual cycle** (in which the blood and tissue lining of the uterus exit the body through the vagina if there is no pregnancy to support), enlarged breasts about two years after the growth spurt, wider hips to allow the passage of the fetus through the pelvic bones, pubic hair, and fat deposits on the buttocks and thighs. Some secondary sex characteristics also involve the growth and development of the primary sexual organs. In females, this occurs when the **mammary glands** in the breasts become capable of producing milk for an infant and when the menstrual cycle begins usually at about ages 12 to 13 (Kreipe, 1992; Lee, 1995).

MALE SECONDARY SEX CHARACTERISTICS   The secondary sex characteristics of males include a deepening voice, facial and chest hair, pubic hair, and the development of coarser skin texture, as well as a large increase in height that continues beyond the growth spurt of the female. The male growth spurt occurs about two years later than the female growth spurt, but males

Puberty changes come about two years earlier for girls than for boys, including the growth spurt. This dancing couple are both thirteen years old, but the physical difference in height is quite obvious.

How does the **person's body know which sexual characteristics to develop? Aren't some babies born** ▶ **with sex organs belonging to both sexes?**

continue to gain height until the late teens. Although the larynx (voice box) increases in size in both sexes, it increases so much in males that part of the tissue forming it becomes visible under the skin of the neck in a structure known as the Adam's apple. Primary sex characteristics also undergo changes during puberty, including the production of sperm and the growth of the penis and testes, which will eventually allow the male to function sexually and reproduce (Kreipe, 1992; Lee, 1995).

How does the person's body know which sexual characteristics to develop? Aren't some babies born with sex organs belonging to both sexes? The primary sex characteristics develop as the fetus is growing in the womb. During the early part of pregnancy, two organs called the *gonads* form in the embryo. At this point, the gonads are undifferentiated: neither male nor fully female. These gonads will eventually develop into either the female sex glands or the male sex glands. If the chromosomes of the twenty-third pair contain two female or X chromosomes, the gonads will develop into the ovaries. If the twenty-third pair contains a Y chromosome, the undifferentiated gonads will become the testes. If the gonads become ovaries, these glands will then release female hormones (**estrogens**) and the infant develops female sex organs. If the gonads become testes, male hormones or **androgens** will be released, causing the development of the male sexual organs.

estrogens
female sex hormones.

androgens
male sex hormones.

gender
the psychological aspects of being male or female.

gender roles
the culture's expectations for masculine or feminine behavior, including attitudes, actions, and personality traits associated with being male or female in that culture.

gender typing
the process of acquiring gender role characteristics.

gender identity
the individual's sense of being male or female.

The Psychological Side of Human Sexuality: Gender

10.2 *What is gender?*

Whereas sex can be defined as the physical characteristics of being male or female, **gender** is defined as the psychological aspects of being masculine or feminine. The expectations of one's culture, the development of one's personality, and one's sense of identity are all affected by the concept of gender.

GENDER ROLES AND GENDER TYPING

Gender roles are the culture's expectations for behavior of a person who is perceived as male or female, including attitudes, actions, and personality traits associated with a particular gender within that culture (Tobach, 2001; Unger, 1979). **Gender typing** is the process by which people learn their culture's preferences and expectations for proper "masculine" and "feminine" behavior. The process of developing a person's **gender identity** (a sense of being male or female) is influenced by both biological and environmental factors (in the form of parenting and other child-rearing behaviors), although which type of factor has greater influence is still controversial.

Wait a minute—the ▶ **story about David Reimer's case makes it sound like biology wins out over upbringing, doesn't it?**

Wait a minute—the story about David Reimer's case makes it sound like biology wins out over upbringing, doesn't it? Most researchers today would agree that biology has an important role in gender identity, at least in certain aspects of gender identity and behavior (Diamond & Sigmundson, 1997; Reiner, 1999, 2000). In one study, 25 genetically male children who were born with ambiguous genitalia were surgically altered and raised as girls. Now older children and teenagers, they prefer male play activities. Fourteen of these children have openly declared themselves to be boys (Reiner, 2000). Even David Reimer's doctor, who was one of the original supporters of the view that upbringing is the key determining factor in gender identity, no longer holds such an extreme position (Money, 1994).

Gender identity, like physical sex, is also not always as straightforward as males who are masculine and females who are feminine. People's sense of gender identity does not always match their external appearance or even the sex chromosomes that determine whether they are male or female (Califia, 1997; Crawford & Unger, 2004; White, 2000). Biology and environment both have an influence on the concept of a person's gender identity. In a disorder called *gender identity disorder* a person feels that he or she is occupying the body of the wrong sex; a man may feel that he was meant to be a woman or a woman may feel that she was meant to be a man (American Psychiatric Association, 2000). Some people with this disorder feel so strongly that they are in the wrong sex that they have surgery to become the sex they feel they were always meant to be. These people are generally termed *transsexuals*. Other people are born with ambiguous gender and may also have issues with gender identity (see the Current Issues in Psychology section on p. 382).

Many Native American tribes have long recognized the role of the male *winkte* (the Lakota word for "wants to be like a woman") in their societies and traditionally were not only tolerant of such different individuals but also had important places for them in the social structure as caretakers of children, cooks, and menders and creators of clothing, and even had certain rituals for bestowing luck upon a hunt (Medicine, 2002). Although some winkte (now often referred to as people with "two spirits") were homosexuals, many were not and would now be recognized as having an alternate gender identity. Unfortunately, as tribes have modernized and become more integrated into the larger European-dominated culture of the United States, the tolerant attitudes of other Native Americans toward the winkte have begun to be replaced with homophobic attitudes and aggressive behavior toward those who are different in this way (Medicine, 2002). Although the causes of gender identity disorder are not fully understood, there is some evidence for both prenatal influences and early childhood experiences as causes (Stein, 1984; Ward, 1992; Zhou et al., 1995).

10.3   *How much influence do biology and learning have on gender role development?*

BIOLOGICAL INFLUENCES   What are the biological influences on gender? Aside from the obvious external sexual characteristics of the genitals, there are also hormonal differences between men and women. Some researchers believe that exposure to these hormones during fetal development not only causes the formation of the sexual organs but also predisposes the infant to behavior that is typically associated with one gender or the other. There have been several studies of infant girls who were exposed to androgens before birth (for example, some drugs to prevent miscarriages are male hormones). In these studies, the girls were found to be tomboys during early childhood—preferring to play with typically "boy" toys, wrestling and playing rough, and playing with boys rather than with other girls (Berenbaum & Snyder, 1995; Money & Mathews, 1982; Money & Norman, 1987). However, when these girls grew up, they became more typically "female" in their desire for marriage and motherhood, which many of these same researchers took as evidence that upbringing won out over the hormonal influences.

Was their early tomboy nature due to the influence of the male hormones? This is difficult to prove, as the parents of these girls were told about their infants' exposure to male hormones during the pregnancy and may have formed assumptions about the effects of such masculinizing hormones on their children. It is entirely possible that these girls were simply allowed, or even encouraged, to be more "masculine" as small children because the parents were expecting them to be masculine. As these same girls grew older, they were exposed to the gender role expectations of teachers, friends, and the media, which may have influenced them to become more like the feminine gender stereotype in contrast to their earlier "masculine" style of behavior.

A recent study examined the way in which men and women respond to visual sexual stimuli and found that although men and women may report being equally

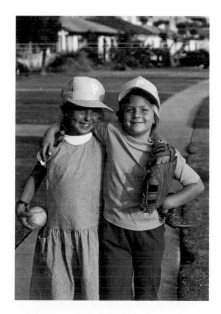

In studies where infant girls were exposed to androgens (male hormones) while in their mothers' wombs, the girls became "tomboys" as children, preferring to play with typically masculine toys and participate in male-dominated play activities. Yet when these same girls grew into puberty and adulthood, they became more feminine in their behavior. What do these findings mean for the nature/nurture controversy?

aroused by erotic pictures, what happens in their brains is quite different (Hamann et al., 2004). Using a brain-scanning technique called *functional magnetic resonance imaging (fMRI)*, the researchers found that the amygdala and hypothalamus areas of the limbic system (areas involved in emotional and sexual responses) were more strongly active in men than in women who viewed the pictures. ⓛⓘⓝⓚ *to Chapter Two: The Biological Perspective, pp. 65–66, 75.* The researchers concluded that the male brain's enhanced reaction might be a product of natural selection, as early human males who could quickly recognize a sexually receptive female would have had a greater opportunity to mate and pass on their genes to their offspring.

ENVIRONMENTAL INFLUENCES   Even if the girls who were exposed to androgens prenatally were initially influenced by these hormones, it seems fairly clear that their later "reversion" to more feminine ways was at least somewhat influenced by the pressures of society. In most cultures, there are certain roles that males and females are expected to play (gender roles, in other words), and the pressure that can be brought to bear on a person who does not conform to these expectations can be tremendous. In most Western cultures, the pressure to be masculine is even greater for males than the pressure to be feminine is for girls. The term tomboy is not generally viewed as an insult, but there are no terms for a boy who acts in a feminine manner that are not insulting—sissy, for example, is not a nice term at all. And although studies of parents' influence on their children's gender typing show that both parents have an impact, they also show that the fathers are almost always more concerned about their sons showing male gender behavior than their daughters showing female gender behavior (Lytton & Romney, 1991).

CULTURE AND GENDER   A person's culture is also an environmental influence. Previous cross-cultural research has found relatively little influence of cultural differences on gender roles and ideas of masculine and feminine behavior (Best & Williams, 2001). Studies have found that the most obvious influences of culture on male and female gender roles and behavior have been in the area of traditional versus nontraditional views. In the traditional view, women are seen as more responsible for domestic duties: child-rearing, home care, cooking, and so on. Men are seen as more responsible for the external activities of working to feed the family and chores that require heavy physical labor, such as farming or construction work. For a long time, the traditional view of the roles of the sexes prevailed in cross-cultural research, which some have seen as caused by the biological differences between men and women: Men are not only physically stronger in upper body strength that might be needed for heavy physical labor but also are freer than women in some senses, as women are the bearers of children and the ones who must breast-feed their infants (Best & Williams, 2001).

In the past few decades, however, a change has occurred in cultures that are of different "personalities." Cultures that are more individualistic and have fairly high standards of living are becoming more nontraditional, especially for women in those cultures, whereas the more traditional views seem to be held by collectivistic cultures that have less wealth, although even in the latter, women were more likely to be less traditional than men (Gibbons et al., 1991). Other studies have found that the most nontraditional ideas about gender roles and gender behavior are found in countries such as the Netherlands, Germany, Italy, and England, whereas the most traditional ideas predominate in African and Asian countries such as Nigeria, Pakistan, and Japan (Best & Williams, 2001). The United States, often seen as very nontraditional by researchers, actually was somewhere in the middle in these studies, perhaps due to the large variation in subcultures that exists within this multicultural country. Environment, even in the form of culture, seems to play at least a partial and perhaps dominant role in gender behavior.

In Chapter Two, the Applying Psychology section (p. 74) reviewed some of the differences in male and female brain activity. Even in these biological differences, the influence of the environment in the form of parenting and cultural expectations cannot be ruled out as potential causes. Psychologist Eleanor Maccoby (1998) believes that the biological differences between males and females help to create different contexts in which boys and girls are raised; the aggressive nature of boys, for example, causes them to engage in more rough-and-tumble play and competitive games than girls. One thing is clear: The issue of differences between men and women is one that will be discussed, debated, and the researched for some time to come.

Although Asian cultures are often more traditional in the roles that men and women play within society, even in these cultures gender roles are becoming more flexible, as this male preschool teacher in a Chinese classroom demonstrates. Why might gender roles in these traditional countries be changing?

PRACTICE QUIZ: HOW MUCH DO YOU REMEMBER?

Pick the best answer.

1. Which of the following is not a primary sex characteristic?
   a. uterus
   b. penis
   c. enlarging breasts
   d. ovaries

2. Which of the following is FALSE concerning secondary sex characteristics?
   a. They are directly concerned with reproduction.
   b. They serve to attract members of the opposite sex.
   c. They typically develop during puberty.
   d. They include the appearance of pubic hair.

3. Developing a person's sense of being male or female is called
   a. gender role.
   b. gender identity.
   c. gender typing.
   d. gender stereotyping.

4. Which of the following is not a biological influence on gender?
   a. hormones secreted during fetal development
   b. the influence of hormones taken by the pregnant mother
   c. exposure to playmates of a particular gender
   d. sex chromosomes

5. In _____ cultures, gender roles are seen as more traditional, whereas in _____ cultures they may be more nontraditional, especially for women.
   a. individualistic; collectivistic
   b. collectivistic; individualistic
   c. European; Asian
   d. affluent; poor

Answers: 1-c, 2-a, 3-b, 4-c, 5-b.

THEORIES OF GENDER ROLE DEVELOPMENT

10.4   *What are the theories about how children learn their gender roles?*

How do children acquire the knowledge of their society or culture's gender role expectations? How does that knowledge lead to the development of a gender identity? Although early psychodynamic theorists such as Freud, **LINK** *to Chapter Twelve: Theories of Personality, p. 450*, believed that children would learn their gender identities as a natural consequence of resolving the sexual conflicts of early childhood, many modern theorists focus on learning and cognitive processes for the development of gender identity and behavior.

SOCIAL LEARNING THEORY Social learning theory, which emphasizes learning through observation and imitation of models, attributes* gender role development to those processes. Children observe their same-sex parents behaving in certain ways and imitate that behavior. When the children imitate the appropriate gender behavior, they are reinforced with positive attention. Inappropriate gender behavior is either ignored or actively discouraged (Fagot & Hagan, 1991; Mischel, 1966).

Of course, parents are not the only gender role models available to children. In addition to older brothers and sisters, family friends, teachers, and peers, children are exposed to male and female behavior on the television and other media. In fact, television, movies, and children's books are often filled with very traditional male and female roles. In these books, doctors are males and nurses are female far more often than the other way around, for example. Although some children's books and television programs make a genuine effort to present males and females in nontypical occupations, there are far more that maintain traditional roles for men and women.

As children develop the concept of gender, they begin to imitate the behavior of those they see as similar to themselves. This young boy is "shaving" just like his father. As he grows, he will also incorporate his father's masculine behavior and ideas about what it is to be male into his own personality.

GENDER SCHEMA THEORY A theory of gender role development that combines social learning theory with cognitive development is called **gender schema theory** (Bem, 1987, 1993). In this theory based on the Piagetian concept of schemas (see Chapter Seven), children develop a schema, or mental pattern, for being male or female in much the same way that they develop schemas for other concepts such as "dog," "bird," and "big." As their brains mature, they become capable of distinguishing among various concepts. For example, a "dog" might at first be anything with four legs and a tail, but as a child encounters dogs and other kinds of animals and is given instruction, "dog" becomes more specific and the schema for "dog" becomes well defined.

In a similar manner, children develop a concept for "boy" and "girl." Once that schema is in place, children can identify themselves as "boy" or "girl" and will notice other members of that schema. They notice the behavior of other "boys" or "girls" and imitate that behavior. Rather than being simple imitation and reinforcement, as in social learning theory, children acquire their gender role behavior by organizing that behavior around the schema of "boy" or "girl." Evidence for this theory includes the finding that children can discriminate between male and female faces and voices before age 1 (Martin, 2000), a sign that the world is already being organized into those two concepts.

GENDER STEREOTYPING

10.5 *What is gender stereotyping?*

A **stereotype** is a concept that can be held about a person or group of people that is based on very superficial characteristics. A **gender stereotype** is a concept about males or females that assigns various characteristics to them on the basis of nothing more than being male or female.

gender schema theory
theory of gender identity acquisition in which a child develops a mental pattern, or schema, for being male or female and then organizes observed and learned behavior around that schema.

stereotype
a concept held about a person or group of people that is based on superficial, irrelevant characteristics.

gender stereotype
a concept held about a person or group of people that is based on being male or female.

*Attributes: explains as a cause.

MALE AND FEMALE GENDER STEREOTYPES   Consider the following joke: "Why is it so hard for women to find men who are sensitive and caring? Because those men already have boyfriends." This joke makes light of the stereotype that "real men" are insensitive and unemotional and suggests that any man who has these traits must be a homosexual. The male gender stereotype generally includes the following characteristics: aggressive, logical, decisive, unemotional, insensitive, nonnurturing, impatient, and mechanically talented. The female stereotype typically includes these characteristics: illogical, changeable, emotional, sensitive, naturally nurturing, patient, and all-thumbs when it comes to understanding machines. Notice that each of these stereotypes has both positive and negative characteristics.

There are some researchers who believe that accepting stereotyping of any kind, even positive stereotyping, can lead to **sexism**, or prejudice about males and females. In fact, some researchers (Glick & Fiske, 2001) claim that acceptance of positive stereotypes can lead to **benevolent sexism**, prejudice that is more socially acceptable but still leads to men and women being treated unequally. Not all men are mechanically talented, nor are all women naturally nurturing, for example. A positive stereotype for men is that they are strong and protective of women, implying that women are weak and need protection, just as the positive female stereotype of natural nurturance of children implies that males cannot be nurturing. Such stereotypes, although somewhat "flattering" for the sex about whom they are held, can be harmful to the other sex.

10.6   What is androgyny?

ANDROGYNY   Psychologist Sandra Bem (1975, 1981) has developed the concept of **androgyny** to describe people whose personalities reflect the "best of both worlds," allowing them to be more flexible in everyday behavior and career choices. People who fall into the gender role stereotypes, according to Bem, often find themselves limited in their choices for problem solving because of the stereotype's constraints on "proper" male or female behavior.

For example, let's say that a man, through an unhappy circumstance, is left in charge of his three small children. If he is a male who has "bought into" the male stereotype, he has no confidence in his ability to raise these children by himself. He may rush into another relationship with a woman just to provide his children with a "mother." Similarly, a "traditional" female who is left without a husband might have difficulty in dealing with raising sons and with a task as simple as mowing the lawn. Researchers have found that when traditional males, traditional females, and androgynous people are compared in terms of the degree of depression they experience when their lives are filled with many negative events, the androgynous people experience less than half the depression experienced by traditional men and only a third of the depression experienced by traditional women (Roos & Cohen, 1987). Figure 10.2 shows the results of this study.

There's a very good example of the limitations of gender stereotypes and how they can even be dangerous in a popular movie of the last decade, *Jurassic Park*. In one scene, the elderly, somewhat disabled designer of the park, a man, is reluctant to give a gun to the female scientist, stating that he doesn't "feel right" about it—as he is a man, he feels he should face the danger rather than the woman, who should stay where it is safe. He was allowing himself to be limited by his male concept of self.

sexism
prejudice about males and/or females leading to unequal treatment.

benevolent sexism
acceptance of positive stereotypes of males and females that leads to unequal treatment.

androgyny
characteristic of possessing the most positive personality characteristics of males and females regardless of actual sex.

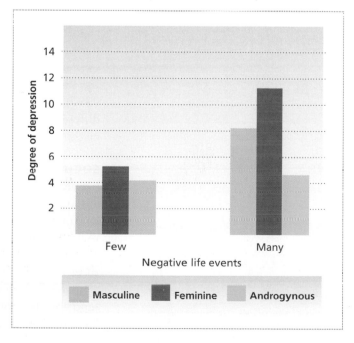

FIGURE 10.2   **Depression as Influenced by Negative Life Events**   These bar graphs show that men who are masculine and women who are feminine in their gender roles experience a significant increase in depression when they are exposed to an increased number of life events. The same is not true for people with an androgynous gender role. How might being androgynous allow a person to be more adaptable?

"It's a guy thing."
©The New Yorker Collection 1995 Donald Reilly from cartoonbank.com. All Rights Reserved.

Instead, the woman scientist jerks the gun out of his hands and says, "We'll talk about sexism in survival situations when I get back." She is *not* a stereotypical female who feels that men should do all the dangerous work. She is androgynous. She is brave, independent, assertive—all typical "male" characteristics, but she is also nurturing and sensitive. She is not limited in her actions by stereotyped beliefs about what she should and should not do but rather makes her decisions based on the *situation* and the behavior it calls for, regardless of gender.

GENDER DIFFERENCES

10.7 *What are the differences in thinking, social behavior, and personality between women and men?*

Although there are clear biological differences in males and females, even to the point of affecting the size of certain structures in the brain (Allen et al., 1989; Allen & Gorski, 1991; Zhou et al., 1995), what sort of differences exist in the behavior of males and females? Are those differences due to biology, socialization, or a combination of the two influences?

COGNITIVE DIFFERENCES Researchers have long held that females score higher on tests of verbal abilities than do males but that males score higher on tests of mathematical skills and spatial skills (Diamond, 1991; Voyer et al., 1995). (See Figure 10.3.) Another study, using MRI technology, found that men listen with the left hemisphere only, whereas women listen with both hemispheres, suggesting that women pay attention to the tone and emotion of statements as well as the content (Lurito et al., 2000). Early explanations of these differences in cognitive functioning involved physical differences in the way each sex used the two hemispheres of the brain and hormonal differences (Witelson, 1991). Other research, however, strongly suggests that psychological and social issues may be more responsible for these differences, as these differences have become less and less obvious (Hyde & Plant; 1995; Kimura, 1999; Voyer et al., 1995; Watt, 2000). That the differences seem to be disappearing as society has begun to view the two genders as more equal in ability is taken as a sign that more equal treatment in society has reduced the gender difference.

More evidence that the gender differences between males and females in certain cognitive areas are disappearing comes from a study showing that girls actually begin their school experience with math and science skills that are equal to those of the boys of their age group, but that by the time they finish high school, the girls have become less skilled in those two areas than boys (American Association of University Women, 1992; Sadker & Sadker, 1994). Six years later, a follow-up study showed that these differences had all but disappeared as the girls improved their skills (American Association of University Women, 1998).

SOCIAL AND PERSONALITY DIFFERENCES The differences normally cited between men and women in the ways they interact with others and in their personality traits are often the result of stereotyped thinking about the sexes. It is difficult to demonstrate differences that are not caused by the way boys and girls are socialized as they grow up. Boys are taught to hold in their emotions, not to cry, to be "strong" and "manly." Girls are encouraged to form emotional attachments, be emotional, and to be open about their feelings with others.

In communication, research suggests that when men talk to each other, they tend to talk about current events, sports, and other events. This has been called a "report" style of communication and seems to involve switching topics frequently and

Tasks Favoring Men

Men tend to perform better than women on certain spatial tasks. They do well on tests that involve mentally rotating an object or manipulating it in some fashion, such as imagining turning this three-dimensional object:

or determining where the holes punched in a folded piece of paper will fall when the paper is unfolded:

Men also are more accurate than women in target-directed motor skills, such as guiding or intercepting projectiles:

They do better on disembedding tests, in which they have to find a simple shape, such as the one on the left, once it is hidden within a more complex figure:

And men tend to do better than women on tests of mathematical reasoning:

| 1,100 | If only 60 percent of seedlings will survive, how many must be planted to obtain 660 trees? |

Tasks Favoring Women

Women tend to perform better than men on tests of perceptual speed, in which subjects must rapidly identify matching items—for example, pairing the house on the far left with its twin:

In addition, women remember whether an object, or a series of objects, has been displaced.

On some tests of ideational fluency, for example, those in which subjects must list objects that are the same color, and on tests of verbal fluency, in which participants must list words that begin with the same letter, women also outperform men:

| L - - - | Limp, Livery, Love, Laser Liquid, Low, Like, Lag, Live, Lug, Light, Lift, Liver, Lime Leg, Load, Lap, Lucid... |

Women do better on precision manual tasks—that is, those involving fine-motor coordination—such as placing the pegs in holes on a board.

And women do better than men on mathematical calculation tests:

| 77 | $14 \times 3 - 17 + 52$ |
| 43 | $2(15 + 3) + 12 - \dfrac{15}{3}$ |

Source: D. Kimura, "Sex Differences in the Brain", *Scientific American*, Vol. 267 (3). September 1992.

FIGURE 10.3   **Male/Female Cognitive Differences**

attempts to dominate the conversation by certain members of the group. In contrast, women tend to use a "relate" style of communication with each other, revealing a lot about their private lives and showing concern and sympathy. They tend to interrupt each other less and let everyone participate in the conversation (Argamon et al., 2003; Coates, 1986; Pilkington, 1998; Swann, 1998).

PRACTICE **QUIZ**: HOW MUCH DO YOU REMEMBER?

Pick the best answer.

1. Studies have shown that _____ are more concerned about appropriate gender behavior in their children, particularly their _____ children.
   a. fathers; male
   b. fathers; female
   c. mothers; male
   d. mothers; female

2. Alex sees his father hammering some nails into a loose board on their house. Later, Alex takes his toy hammer and pretends to hammer in some imaginary nails. Of which theory of gender development would this be a good example?
   a. gender schema theory
   b. gender role theory
   c. psychoanalytic theory
   d. social learning theory

3. In an older movie, a male character is suddenly left with a small baby for whom he must now care. Desperate for help, he calls his fiancée, thinking that she will know what to do because she's a woman, and women are natural mothers. The character's thinking in this instance is an example of
   a. androgyny.
   b. schema error.
   c. benevolent sexism.
   d. negative stereotyping.

4. Susanna is a mother to her two children, but she also has a career as a professor at a university. She is nurturant and sensitive to her children's needs, able to express her emotions outwardly, independent and assertive, and thinks problems through calmly and logically. Susanna is a good example of a person who is
   a. masculine.
   b. feminine.
   c. transsexual.
   d. androgynous.

5. Research has shown that men tend to talk to each other about
   a. private concerns.
   b. their feelings.
   c. relationships.
   d. current events.

CURRENT ISSUES IN PSYCHOLOGY

The Intersex Controversy

10.8 *What is the controversy concerning the treatment of intersexed infants?*

The Intersexed Person

On rare occasions, an infant is born with sexual organs that are ambiguous*—not clearly male or female. This is the more common form of **hermaphroditism**, the condition of possessing both male and female sex organs. (The term comes from the name of a Greek god, Hermaphroditus, who was said to have both male and female characteristics.) It is very rare to find a person who truly has both ovary and testicle material in one body. More commonly, the development of the external genitals is affected by either chromosome defects or the presence of the wrong hormones at a critical time in the development of the fetus in the womb (Hutcheson & Snyder, 2004). In this case, a female clitoris might look more like a penis, or a penis might be so small as to resemble a clitoris.

People with hermaphroditism now prefer the term **intersexed** or **intersexual**, meaning "between the sexes." Approximately 1 out of 1,500 children are born with this condition (Dreger, 1998, 1999). In the middle to late 1900s, the medical profession's answer to the intersexed person was to recommend surgery to make the child more clearly one sex or the other—often in direct contradiction with the child's actual chromosomal sex. A male with an abnormally small penis might have his testicles removed, his penis reduced, and a vagina constructed to make him female. His parents would be told to dress and think of their child as a girl, when in fact he would be a castrated boy. It was easier in those days to construct "females," as a functioning penis was not yet possible with surgery, but a "functioning"

hermaphroditism
the condition of possessing both male and female sexual organs.

intersexed, intersexual
a person who possesses ambiguous sexual organs, making it difficult to determine actual sex from a visual inspection at birth.

---

*Ambiguous: not clearly one thing or another; capable of being interpreted in more than one way.

vagina was. Being intersexed was regarded, and still is by many medical professionals, as an abnormality that must be "fixed."

The **intersex** controversy consists of a large number of intersexed individuals who, having developed ways of communicating with one another through the Internet and within organizations, are no longer happy with being designated as "abnormal" and forced into surgical alterations while still infants. Parents who resist such surgical treatments are sometimes subjected to intense pressure by the doctors involved. Sexual reassignment is still very common in early infancy and often leads to adolescents or young adults like David Reimer who reject the reassignment and face depression and anxiety (Diamond & Sigmundson, 1997; Dreger, 1999). This rejection of the attempt to "retrain" gender identity indicates that nature, not nurture, may be far more important in determining a person's identity as male or female.

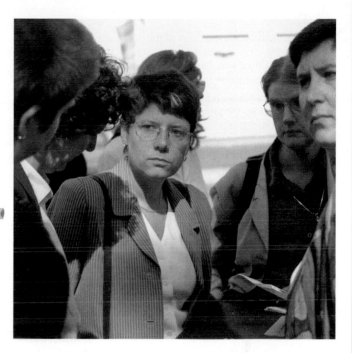

Some adults who were born intersexed and experienced the surgery and sexual reassignment as infants are now angry about having their rights violated and being subjected to such a radical procedure without consent (Kessler, 1998). The Intersex Society of North America (ISNA) was formed in 1994 to give support to intersexed people and strongly recommends that doctors not seek to perform surgical procedures on intersexed children. The goal is to remove the veil of secrecy, so that a child who is intersexed can be informed at a relatively early age (far earlier than adolescence) of this condition and that a decision might need to be made in the future about surgery. This allows intersexed persons to make the decision for themselves.

Cheryl Chase is an intersexual, a person who has mixed or ambiguous male and female sex organs. She, along with many other intersexuals, is working to stop the practice of surgically altering intersexual infants who are unable to give their own consent for what Chase and colleagues consider to be unnecessary surgery.

Questions for Further Discussion

1. What are the possible advantages and disadvantages to waiting until later in childhood to surgically alter an intersexed child?

2. Should an intersexed person have the right to make the decision to have or not have surgery?

3. Should parents of an intersexed infant have the right to make that decision?

4. How might the removal of a male's foreskin in the circumcision process be a similar ethical issue?

I've heard that men and women experience sex differently—is that true? How is it different?

Human Sexual Behavior

In 1957, gynecologist Dr. William Masters and psychologist Virginia Johnson began what would become a controversial* study of the human sexual response in 700 men and women volunteers (Masters & Johnson, 1966). At that time in history, human sexuality was still a relatively forbidden topic to all but young adults, who were exploring the concepts of "free love" and engaging in premarital sex far more openly than in the past. A later section of this chapter discusses the work of Alfred Kinsey (Kinsey et al., 1948; Kinsey et al., 1953), who conducted a major survey of different types of sexual activity; Masters and Johnson devised equipment that would measure the physical responses that occur during sexual activity. They used this equipment to measure physiological activity in both men and women volunteers who either were engaging in actual intercourse or masturbation. Although many conservative and religious people were outraged by this research, it remains as one of the most important studies of the human sexual response.

◄ I've heard that men and women experience sex differently—is that true? How is it different?

---

*Controversial: leading to arguments or opposing viewpoints.

intersex
alternate term for hermaphroditism.

orgasm
a series of rhythmic contractions of the muscles of the vaginal walls or the penis, also the third and shortest phase of sexual response.

seminal fluid
fluid released from the penis at orgasm that contains the sperm.

resolution
the final phase of the sexual response in which the body is returned to a normal state.

refractory period
time period in males just after orgasm in which the male cannot become aroused or achieve erection.

SEXUAL RESPONSE

10.9 *What happens in the bodies of women and men during sexual intercourse?*

Masters and Johnson (1966) found four stages of a sexual response cycle in their groundbreaking research. (See the Classic Studies in Psychology section that follows for a more detailed look at how this landmark research was accomplished.) Although these stages are similar in both men and women, there are some differences. Also, the transition between the stages is not necessarily as well defined as the descriptions of the stages might seem to describe, and the length of time spent in any one phase can vary from experience to experience and person to person.

PHASE ONE: EXCITEMENT This first phase is the beginning of sexual arousal and can last anywhere from one minute to several hours. Pulse rate increases, blood pressure rises, breathing quickens, and the skin may show a rosy flush, especially on the chest or breast areas. In women, the clitoris swells, the lips of the vagina open, and the inside of the vagina moistens in preparation for intercourse. In men, the penis becomes erect, the testes pull up, and the skin of the scrotum tightens. Nipples will harden and become more erect in both sexes, but especially in the female.

PHASE TWO: PLATEAU In the second phase of the sexual response, the physical changes that began in the first phase are continued. In women, the outer part of the vagina swells with increased amounts of blood to that area, while the clitoris retracts under the clitoral hood but remains highly sensitive. The outer lips of the vagina become redder in color. In men, the penis becomes more erect and may release a few drops of fluid. At this point, it is unlikely that the male will lose his erection. This phase may last only a few seconds to several minutes.

PHASE THREE: ORGASM The third phase is the shortest of the three stages and involves a series of rhythmic muscular contractions known as the **orgasm**. In women, this involves the muscles of the vaginal walls and can happen multiple times, lasting slightly longer than the orgasm experience of the male. In men, the orgasmic contractions of the muscles in and around the penis trigger the release of **seminal fluid**, the fluid that contains the male sex cells, or sperm. Men typically have only one intense orgasm.

Didn't someone once say that women can have two different kinds of orgasms, and one of them is better than the other? Sigmund Freud (1931) once theorized that an orgasm stimulated by manipulation of the clitoris rather than stimulation of the vagina was a less mature sexual response for women. This may be attributed to the time period, one in which men were held to be superior to women and masturbation (which would involve stimulating the clitoris in a woman) was seen as morally wrong and mentally damaging. Masters and Johnson (1966) were able to demonstrate that there is no physiological difference between a vaginal orgasm and a clitoral one.

PHASE FOUR: RESOLUTION The final phase of the sexual response is **resolution**, the return of the body to its normal state before arousal began. The blood that congested the blood vessels in the various areas of the genitals recedes; the heart rate, blood pressure, and breathing all reduce to normal levels during this phase. In women, the clitoris descends, the color of the vaginal lips returns to normal, and the lips close once more. In men, the erection is lost, the testes descend, and the scrotal sack thins again. Also, men have a **refractory period** during which they cannot achieve another erection, lasting anywhere from several minutes to several hours for different individuals. The older the man gets, the longer the refractory period tends to extend. Women do not have a refractory period and in fact can achieve another series of orgasms if stimulation continues.

Didn't someone ▶ once say that women can have two different kinds of orgasms, and one of them is better than the other?

For more on the historic Masters & Johnson study, see the Classic Studies in Psychology section that follows. (See also Figures 10.4 and 10.5.)

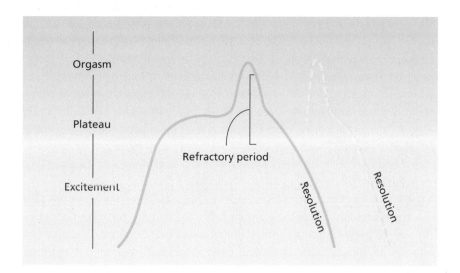

FIGURE 10.4   **The Male Sexual Response Cycle**   A male experiences sexual arousal (excitement), a plateau lasting a few seconds to a few minutes, orgasm, and then experiences a refractory period during which another erection is not yet possible. This refractory period can last for several minutes to several hours and tends to increase in length with age. Resolution, in which the body returns to its prearousal state, is last.

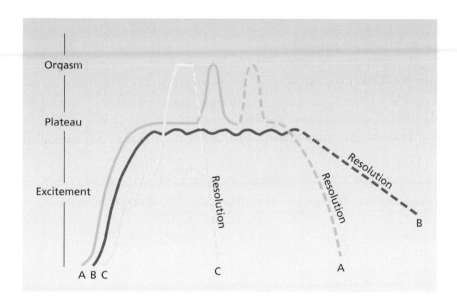

FIGURE 10.5   **The Female Sexual Response Cycle**   Women can experience several different patterns of sexual response. In pattern A, a woman experiences excitement, a plateau, and orgasm in a similar manner to a man. Unlike a man, the woman does not have a refractory period and can experience several orgasms before entering resolution. In pattern B, there is a longer plateau period but no orgasm, and in pattern C, the woman goes from excitement to orgasm to a quick resolution without experiencing a plateau period.

CLASSIC STUDIES IN PSYCHOLOGY

Masters and Johnson's Observational Study of the Human Sexual Response

10.10   *How did Masters and Johnson investigate the human sexual response?*

William Masters and Virginia Johnson pioneered the first direct observational study of human sexual behavior. Their study stirred up tremendous controversy in an era that feared that the study of human sexuality would undermine the structure of the family and society. Masters obtained permission from his department chair at the Washington University School of Medicine in St. Louis, Missouri, in 1954. He then assembled an advisory board composed of the police commissioner, a newspaper publisher, and several

Dr. William Masters and Dr. Virginia Johnson examined human sexuality by measuring physiological responses in a laboratory. Their subjects were volunteers, many of whom were prostitutes, a fact which caused an uproar when their research became public.

prominent religious leaders, in addition to the university's chancellor. Together, they accomplished a feat that seems incredible in today's media-driven world: They convinced the press to keep completely quiet about this research into human sexuality for the next 12 years (Kolodny, 2001).

Such research had to be done discretely, as even Masters's choice of subjects was controversial. His initial studies in 1955 and 1956 were done entirely with prostitutes. He conducted interviews with them and observed them at work. Although this research was never published, he used the opportunity to think about what kind of instrumentation he would need to properly measure the sexual responses in a more controlled setting. Together with psychologist Dr. Virginia Johnson, Masters devised equipment that would allow them to measure sexual responses in humans in a laboratory setting. These machines were similar to a polygraph machine (a lie detector) but much more complex in their design and the particular physiological responses (for example, heart rate, body temperature) they measured. Masters and Johnson also used photography and direct observation in the laboratory settings, using prostitutes and other volunteers as subjects.

The publication of *Human Sexual Response* in 1966 was the end result of the 12 years of research. Masters and Johnson became instant celebrities and the book itself became a bestseller. This was the beginning of a partnership that lasted over 30 years. That partnership not only changed many people's attitudes about what was sexually normal but also challenged many sexual myths and created the field of sex therapy. Although direct observational studies can have the disadvantage of affecting the participant's behavior, the work of Masters and Johnson has remained some of the most important work in the field of human sexuality and is still used in sex therapy and sex education and by infertility and conception experts (Kolodny, 2001; Masters, Johnson, & Kolodny, 1995.)

Questions for Further Discussion

1. Would researchers today be able to convince the press (newspapers, magazines, and television) to keep research into human sexuality secret, as Masters did?

2. What problems with their research might have come from the fact that many of their participants were prostitutes?

3. In what ways might this kind of research be easier to conduct today?

4. In what ways might this kind of research be more difficult to conduct today?

PRACTICE **QUIZ:** HOW MUCH DO YOU REMEMBER?

Pick the best answer.

1. People who are intersexual
   a. are also homosexuals.
   b. are psychologically disordered.
   c. want to be allowed to make any surgical decisions for themselves.
   d. are people who suffer from gender identity disorder but are physically normal.

2. Which of the following was NOT one of the reasons that Masters and Johnson's research was considered controversial?
   a. They used prostitutes as participants.
   b. They were doing a study about sexual behavior.
   c. No one had ever studied sexual behavior before this.
   d. They were observing and taking pictures of people engaging in sexual activity.

3. In which of the phases of sexual response does the genital area undergo a series of muscular contractions?
   a. excitement
   b. plateau
   c. orgasm
   d. resolution

4. Which phase of the sexual response is typically the longest?
   a. excitement
   b. plateau
   c. orgasm
   d. resolution

5. In which phase does the refractory period occur for men?
   a. excitement
   b. plateau
   c. orgasm
   d. resolution

DIFFERENT TYPES OF SEXUAL BEHAVIOR

While Masters and Johnson focused their research on the physiological responses that occur during the sexual act, other researchers had already been studying the different forms of sexual behavior. The study of sexual behavior is not the study of the sex act, but rather when, with whom, and under what circumstances sexual acts take place. Although there were other attempts to study human sexual behavior before the mid-twentieth-century studies of Alfred Kinsey (Kinsey, et al. 1948; Kinsey et al., 1953), his original work remains an important source of information concerning the different ways in which people engage in the sex act. A movie based on Kinsey's life and work was released in the United States in 2004. Even more than half a century later, Kinsey's work is still so controversial that many movie theaters in the United States refused to show the film.

These are actual headlines from various newspapers, all featuring the media's response to Kinsey's controversial survey of human sexual behavior, the Kinsey Report, first published in 1948. How might Kinsey's research be treated today?

10.11 *How did Kinsey study human sexual behavior?*

THE KINSEY STUDY In 1948, zoologist Alfred Kinsey published a controversial report on the results of a massive survey of sexual behavior collected from 1938 and on (Kinsey et al., 1948). His findings concerning the frequency of behavior such as masturbation, anal sex, and premarital sex rocked many people, who were apparently not ready to believe that so many people had tried alternative sexual behaviors. Kinsey believed that sexual orientation was not an either/or situation in which one is either completely heterosexual or completely homosexual but instead that sexual orientation is on a continuum,* with some people falling at either extreme and some falling closer to the middle. The idea that there were many people who fit into that middle range of sexual orientation was shocking and, for many, unbelievable. (See Table 10.1.)

Kinsey used highly trained interviewers who conducted face-to-face interviews with the participants, who were all male in the original study. A later survey was published in 1953 that dealt exclusively with females (Kinsey et al., 1953). The participants were volunteers supposedly from both rural and urban areas and from different socioeconomic, religious, and educational backgrounds. In reality, a large portion of

*Continuum: a sequence of values, elements, or behavior that varies by small degrees.

TABLE 10.1 **KINSEY AND COLLEAGUES' (1948) RATING SCALE FOR SEXUAL ORIENTATION**

0	1	2	3	4	5	6
Exclusively heterosexual	Predominantly heterosexual; only incidentally homosexual	Predominantly heterosexual; more than incidentally homosexual	Equally heterosexual and homosexual	Predominantly homosexual; more than incidentally heterosexual	Predominantly homosexual; only incidentally heterosexual	Exclusively homosexual

Source: Reprinted with permission of the Kinsey Institute for Research in Sex, Gender, and Reproduction, Inc.

TABLE 10.2 KEY FINDINGS FROM KINSEY'S SEXUAL BEHAVIOR SURVEYS

Males reporting anal sex with spouse: 11 percent.

Nearly 46 percent of males had bisexual experiences.

Between 6 and 14 percent of females had bisexual experiences.

Whereas nearly 21 percent of the males had experienced intercourse at age 16, only 6 percent of females had done so.

Males reporting premarital sex: 67 to 98 percent (varied by economic level).

Females reporting premarital sex: 50 percent.

Nearly 50 percent of all married males had some extramarital experiences, whereas 26 percent of married females had extramarital experiences.

About 10 percent of males were predominantly homosexual.

Between 2 and 6 percent of females were predominantly homosexual.

Males who reported masturbating: 92 percent.

Females who reported masturbating: 62 percent.

Gebhard, P. H., & Johnson, A. B. (1979/1998).

Alfred Kinsey conducted many of his interviews face-to-face, as seen here. How might having to answer questions about one's sexual behavior be affected by Kinsey's presence?

the participants were well-educated, urban, young Protestants. Table 10.2 lists some of the more interesting findings of the Kinsey study.

Although Kinsey's data are still quoted in many discussions of sexual behavior, his original surveys were far from perfect. As stated earlier, the participants were almost exclusively white, middle class, and college educated. Older people, those who lived in rural regions, and less educated people were not well represented. Some critics claimed that Kinsey gave far more attention to sexual behavior that was considered unusual or abnormal than he did to "normal" sexual behavior (Geddes, 1954). Also, Kinsey's surveys were no less susceptible to the exaggerations, falsifications, and errors of any method using self-report techniques. Finally, a face-to-face interview might cause some people being interviewed to be inhibited about admitting to certain kinds of sexual behavior, or others might exaggerate wildly, increasing the likelihood of inaccurate data.

10.12 *What were the findings of the Janus Report?*

THE JANUS REPORT In 1993, Dr. Samuel S. Janus and Dr. Cynthia L. Janus published the results of the first large-scale study of human sexual behavior since those of Kinsey (1948) and Masters and Johnson (1966). This national survey, begun in 1983, sampled 3,000 people from all 48 mainland states. Professors in the fields of sociology, psychology, psychiatry, history, biology, and political science received special training in the survey method and supervised experienced graduate student researchers who also collected survey data.

Data were collected through interviews and mass questionnaires. Survey respondents ranged in age from 18 to over 65 years, from all levels of marital status, educational backgrounds, and geographical regions in the United States.

One finding of this massive survey was that nearly eightly percent of men and seventy percent of women had masturbated (although about a fourth to a third stated that this occurred rarely). Other responses indicated that nineteen percent of men and nearly eight percent of women were involved in full sexual intercourse by age fourteen. Premarital sex was more commonly reported in men than in women (sixty-seven percent for males, forty-six percent for females), and men were nearly twice as likely as women to report having at least one extramarital affair. While more than a fifth of the male respondents and only slightly fewer female respondents reported having at least one homosexual experience, only nine percent of males and five percent of females identified themselves as predominantly homosexual.

In addition to these findings, *The Janus Report on Sexual Behavior* also looked at **sexual deviance** (sexual behavior that is unacceptable according to social norms), single people's sexual behavior, marriage, divorce, the decision to have children, and how religion, political orientation, education, wealth, and geographical region affect sexual behavior.

SEXUAL ORIENTATION

The term **sexual orientation** refers to a person's sexual attraction for members of a particular sex. One of the more important questions that researchers are trying to answer is whether sexual orientation is the product of learning and experience or is biological in origin.

10.13   *What are the different sexual orientations and how do they develop?*

HETEROSEXUAL   The most common sexual orientation is **heterosexual**, in which people are sexually attracted to members of the opposite physical sex, as in a man being attracted to a woman or vice versa. (The Greek word *hetero* means "other," so *heterosexual* means "other sexual" or attraction for the other sex.) Heterosexuality is a socially acceptable form of sexual behavior in all cultures.

HOMOSEXUAL   It is difficult to get an accurate percentage for **homosexual** orientation or sexual attraction to members of one's own sex. (The Greek word *homo* means "same.") The problem concerns the discrimination, prejudice, and mistreatment that homosexual people face in most cultures, making it more likely that a homosexual person will lie about his or her sexual orientation to avoid such negative treatment. The most recent surveys estimate that about 9 percent of men and 5 percent of women are homosexuals, meaning that their sexual orientation is exclusively or predominantly homosexual (Janus & Janus, 1993). However, the same surveys indicate that 22 percent of men and 17 percent of women have had at least one homosexual experience. Apparently, it is not unusual for people to experiment with alternative sexual behavior while deciding their true sexual identity.

DEVELOPMENT OF SEXUAL ORIENTATION   Is homosexuality a product of the environment, biology, or both? This is a very controversial issue for both heterosexuals and homosexuals (Diamond, 1995). If homosexuality is a product of upbringing

sexual deviance
behavior that is unacceptable according to societal norms and expectations.

sexual orientation
a person's sexual attraction preference for members of a particular sex.

heterosexual
person attracted to the opposite sex.

homosexual
person attracted to the same sex.

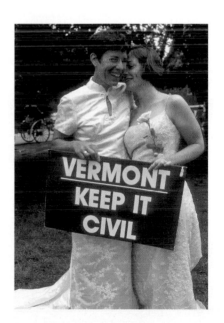

These women are celebrating their wedding day. Vermont is one of very few states that allow a civil union between same-sex couples. Whether or not sexual orientation is determined by biology or by environmental influences is an important question, and the answer to this question will have far-reaching consequences.

TABLE 10.3 **WHEN GAY OR BISEXUAL COLLEGE STUDENTS SAY THEY BECAME AWARE OF THEIR SEXUAL ORIENTATION**

Age	Female	Male
Grade school	11%	17%
Junior high	6%	20%
High school	46%	50%
College	37%	13%

Source: Elliott, L., & Brantley, C. (1997).

and environmental experiences, it can be assumed to be a behavior that can be changed, placing a burden of choice to be "normal" or "abnormal" squarely on the shoulders of homosexual people. If it is biological, either through genetic influences or hormonal influences during pregnancy, then it can be seen as a behavior that is no more a choice than whether the infant is born a male or a female. The implications of homosexuality as biological leads to some volatile* issues: If it is not a choice or a learned behavior pattern, then society will no longer be able to expect or demand that homosexuals change their sexual behavior or orientation. Homosexuality becomes an issue of diversity rather than deviance.

In the past several decades, a large body of research in the areas of biological differences in the brains of heterosexual and homosexual males, genetic influences on sexual orientation, and even prenatal influences on sexual orientation has been amassed by various scientists. One of the earliest studies, for example, found that severe stress experienced by pregnant women during the second trimester of pregnancy (the time during which the sexual differences in genitalia are formed) results in a significantly higher chance of any male children becoming homosexual in orientation (Ellis et al., 1988).

A controversial study by Simon LeVay (1991) found an area of the hypothalamus (which, as discussed in Chapter Two, controls the pituitary gland and, through that gland, the sex glands and andrenal glands that influence sexual behavior and development) that is three times larger in men than in women. LeVay examined the brain structures of 19 homosexual males (all of whom had died of AIDS), 16 heterosexual males (six of whom had died of AIDS), and six deceased women whose sexual orientation was unknown. He found that the same area of the hypothalamus that is larger in men than in women was also two to three times larger in heterosexual men than in homosexual men. Although there have been some researchers who objected to his findings (Byne, 1995) on the basis of the small number of people he studied as well as the possible complications that might have been the result of the AIDS virus, LeVay has remained steadfast in his insistence that his findings are valid (LeVay & Hamer, 1994). Of course, LeVay's findings are correlational, and correlation does not mean that one thing causes the other. **LINK** *to Chapter One: The Science of Psychology, p. 25.* It is possible that the differences in the size of the hypothalamus might be due to increased or decreased sexual activity, for example. There may have been other differences in lifestyle that account for the size difference, or the fact that LeVay was examining dead tissue, which may undergo changes after death that vary over

*Volatile: explosive.

time. Just because there is a relationship between sexual orientation and size of the hypothalamus does not mean that the size of the hypothalamus causes sexual orientation. More research may shed light on this question.

In a recent study that may be interpreted as support of LeVay's findings, researchers discovered that male sheep, or rams, with an exclusively homosexual preference for other rams rather than female sheep (ewes) also have a significantly smaller than normal area in the hypothalamus of their brains when compared to rams that are exclusively heterosexual (Roselli et al., 2004). Like the LeVay (1991) study, the brain structure of the homosexual rams in this study was physically more similar to the brain structure of ewes. These findings, unlike those of LeVay, could not have been influenced by the AIDS virus. However, it is important to remember that these findings, just as LeVay's do, represent a correlation only. Neither the findings of the LeVay nor the Roselli studies can be interpreted as showing that the cause of homosexuality is definitely biological, much less that it is a specific area of the hypothalamus that causes sexual orientation to be determined.

The evidence for genetic influences on sexual orientation is increasingly convincing. In studies of male and female homosexuals who have identical twins, fraternal twins, or adopted siblings, researchers found that 52 percent of the identical twin siblings were also gay, compared to 22 percent of the fraternal twins and only 11 percent of the adopted brothers and sisters (Bailey & Pillard, 1991). In a similar study with lesbian women only, 48 percent of identical twins were also gay compared to 16 percent of the fraternal twins and 6 percent of the adopted siblings (Bailey et al., 1993). Other research along similar lines has supported these findings (Bailey et al., 2000; Dawood et al., 2000). However, these findings should be interpreted cautiously as well. Twin studies are difficult to conduct without the influence of environment on behavior. Even twins who are raised apart tend to be reared in similar environments, so that the influence of learning and experience on sexual orientation cannot be entirely ruled out.

There is some evidence that homosexuality may be transmitted by genes carried on the X chromosome, which is passed from mother to son but not from father to son. In 33 out of 40 homosexual brothers, Hamer and colleagues (Hamer et al., 1993) found an area on the X chromosome (in a location called Xq28) that contains several hundred genes that the homosexual brothers had in common in every case, even though other genes on that chromosome were different. This was taken as evidence that the brothers had both inherited a set of genes, donated on the mother's X chromosome, that might be responsible for their sexual orientation. These findings have since been supported in other research (Hu et al., 1995; Turner, 1995).

One of the most common behavioral findings about male homosexuals is that they are consistently feminine as children, according to developmental psychologist J. Michael Bailey (Bailey & Zucker, 1995). Bailey has determined that about three-fourths of feminine boys (defined as boys who are uninterested in sports, rough play, desire to be girls, or have a reputation as a "sissy") are homosexual as adults, a far greater rate than in the general population of males. Bailey and colleague Ken Zucker interpret these findings as further support for the biological foundations of sexual orientation. Of course, those differences in childhood behavior could also have been the result of attention and other forms of reinforcement from the social environment. It is simply a very difficult task to separate the environmental influences on any aspect of behavior from the biological ones.

One thing is certain: The issue of what causes sexual orientation will continue to generate research and controversy for a long time to come.

If people have had a ▶ homosexual experience as well as heterosexual ones, does that make them bisexuals?

If people have had a homosexual experience as well as heterosexual ones, does that make them bisexuals?

BISEXUAL A person who is **bisexual** may be either male or female and is attracted to both sexes. Although, as stated in the survey results, a portion of the population has had experiences with both sexes, this does not make these people bisexual, except in the most literal sense, and only for that period of experimentation. In other words, people can have bisexual experiences but are not bisexuals unless this becomes their preferred, stable, sexual identity.

Bisexual people do not necessarily have relationships with both men and women at the same time and may vary in the degree of attraction to one sex or the other over time. Many bisexuals may not act on their desires but instead have a long-term monogamous relationship with only one partner.

PRACTICE **QUIZ:** HOW MUCH DO YOU REMEMBER?

Pick the best answer.

1. The first scientifically based survey of human sexual behavior was designed and carried out by
a. personality psychologists.
b. a physiological psychologist.
c. a zoologist.
d. a psychiatrist.

2. In Kinsey's original data, more _____ than _____ reported having bisexual experiences.
a. homosexuals; heterosexuals
b. heterosexuals; homosexuals
c. women; men
d. men; women

3. Which group was NOT one of the groups poorly represented in the Kinsey study?
a. older people   c. people with little education
b. white, middle-class   d. people living in rural areas

4. Compared to the Kinsey data, the data from the Janus Report revealed the age of the first sexual experience for about 20 percent of the men and 8 percent of the women to be
a. 14.   c. 17.
b. 16.   d. 12.

5. LeVay found evidence that homosexual males have a difference from heterosexual males in what area of the brain?
a. thalamus   c. hypothalamus
b. cortex   d. corpus callosum

Answers: 1-c, 2-d, 3-b, 4-a, 5-c.

Sexual Dysfunctions

bisexual
person attracted to both men and women.

sexual dysfunction
a problem in sexual functioning.

What about when people have problems with sex, like impotence? A **sexual dysfunction** is a problem with sexual functioning, or the actual physical workings of the sex act. Sexual dysfunctions can be caused by organic factors, sociocultural factors, individual psychological problems, or problems in relationships. More commonly, such problems may stem from a combination of two or more of these factors.

Organic factors include physical problems such as illnesses, side effects from medication, the effects of surgeries, physical disabilities, and even the use of illegal and legal drugs, such as cocaine, alcohol, and nicotine. Chronic illnesses such as diabetes, cancer, or strokes also belong in this category of factors.

Sociocultural influences on sexual attitudes and behavior also exist and may be a source of psychological stress leading to sexual dysfunction. In the United States and some other Western cultures, people may have experienced instruction from their parents (both direct teaching and indirect) that actually helped them to form negative attitudes toward sex and sexual activities, such as masturbation. Some religious upbringing may also foster a sense of guilt about sex and interest in sex. In one study, a relationship between conservative, religious traditionalism and sexual attitudes was found for married members of Jewish, Protestant, and Catholic faiths (Purcell, 1985). The research showed that the more conservative and traditional the

"Believe me. You're just thinking about it too much."
©The New Yorker Collection 1998 Robert Mankoff from cartoonbank.com. All Rights Reserved.

married couples were, the less interest and pleasure they took in sexual activity, and the more they experienced guilt, shame, and sexual inhibitions. In non-Western cultures, such as that of India, sex may be seen as not only a duty of married couples, but also a joy to be celebrated within the context of producing children (Gupta, 1994). In particular, women in India may have an entirely different attitude toward sex because a woman's status in Indian culture depends greatly upon her ability to bear children.

Psychological stressors also include individual psychological problems, such as low self-esteem, anxiety over performance of the sex act, depression, self-consciousness about one's body image, anxiety disorders, or a history of previous sexual abuse or assault. For example, women who were sexually molested in childhood are two to four times more likely to suffer from pain in the pelvic area on a chronic basis (Reiter & Milburn, 1994).

Another source of psychological stress leading to sexual dysfunctions is the relationship between the two sexual partners. The sexual dysfunction may be only an outward symptom of an underlying problem with the relationship. Example of such problems might be unresolved arguments, resentment of the partner who feels he or she has less power and influence over the relationship, lack of trust, infidelities, lack of physical attractiveness to the partner, or even lack of sexual skills on the part of one or both partners (Alperstein, 2001).

ORGANIC OR STRESS-INDUCED DYSFUNCTIONS

10.14 *What are the sexual dysfunctions caused by physical problems or stress?*

The **organic or stress-induced dysfunctions** are the type of sexual problems that are caused by physical disorders, such as nerve damage, or by psychological stress, such as worry and anxiety. Sexual dysfunctions involve problems in three possible areas of sexual activity: sexual interest, arousal, and response.

How common are problems like these—aren't they pretty rare? A nationwide survey found that about 43 percent of women and 31 percent of men report having some sort of sexual dysfunction (Laumann et al., 1999). In the stress-filled world that many people live in today, it isn't all that surprising to find such a high degree of dysfunction. In fact, the figures may actually be higher than those reported in the survey. As stated in Chapter One, one of the hazards of doing survey research is that people don't always tell the truth. If a person is going to lie about sexual problems, the most likely lie (or distorted truth) would probably be to deny or minimize such problems.

Table 10.4 lists some of the more common physical sexual dysfunctions that may be caused by organic factors or psychological stressors such as those discussed at the beginning of this section.

organic or stress-induced dysfunction sexual problem caused by physical disorder or psychological stress.

◄ How common are problems like these— aren't they pretty rare?

TABLE 10.4 ORGANIC OR STRESS-INDUCED DYSFUNCTIONS

Sexual Desire Disorders	Hypoactive Sexual Desire Disorder: Ongoing, abnormally low desire for sexual activity.
	Sexual Aversion Disorder: Fear and disgust of sexual contact.
Sexual Arousal Disorders	Female Sexual Arousal Disorder: Desire for sexual activity is present, but physical discomfort and a lack of pleasure are experienced during sexual activity.
	Male Erectile Disorder: A male cannot maintain an erection long enough to complete the sexual act.
Orgasmic Disorders	Male Orgasmic Disorder: A male cannot achieve orgasm through vaginal stimulation, even though fully aroused.
	Female Orgasmic Disorder: A female cannot achieve an orgasm even though fully aroused.
	Premature Ejaculation: Some men experience orgasm shortly after penetration, which can cause feelings of sexual inadequacy because the partner does not have time to achieve orgasm.
Sexual Pain Disorders	Vaginismus: Persistent contractions of the vaginal muscles, causing sexual intercourse to be painful or impossible.
	Dyspareunia: Pain in the genitals that can occur before, during, or after intercourse, which can be experienced by either sex.

Erectile dysfunction is a major concern to many men, who are unable to engage in sexual intercourse with their partners. Medications such as Viagra help some men function once again. Does this ad seem to promise more than just the revival of sexual functioning?

I've heard about ▶
tranvestites—are they
gay? And are
there women
transvestites also?

paraphilia
a sexual disorder in which the person's preferred method of sexual arousal and fulfillment is through sexual behavior that is unusual or socially unacceptable.

For all of the sexual dysfunctions, treatment can include medication, psychotherapy, hormone therapy, stress reduction, and behavioral training. For example, Masters and Johnson (1970) recommended a technique called *sensate focus* for treatment of premature ejaculation, in which each member of a couple engages in a series of exercises meant to focus attention on his or her own sensual experiences during various stages of sexual arousal and activity. Male erectile disorder is now commonly treated with drug therapy.

THE PARAPHILIAS

10.15 *What are the sexual dysfunctions known as paraphilias?*

Another major category of sexual problems is behavioral rather than physical in nature. **Paraphilia** (also called *atypical sexual behavior*) is a disorder in which the person either prefers, or must, achieve sexual arousal and fulfillment through sexual behavior that is unusual or not socially acceptable. In some cases, the atypical sexual behavior is illegal and destructive as well. The term *paraphilia* comes from two Greek words meaning "beyond love," and these disorders are truly "beyond" normal, socially acceptable behavior. Notice that this a culturally defined term—in some cases, sexual behavior that is considered abnormal or even illegal in one culture may be quite acceptable in another culture. Whereas some of this alternate sexual behavior is considered to be a "kinkier" form of sexual expression, in some cases the behavior indicates a mental illness and may also be a criminal offense. Table 10.5 lists some of the paraphilias along with brief definitions of each.

I've heard about transvestites—are they gay? And are there women transvestites also? Actually, most transvestites are heterosexual males who may be married and enjoy normal sexual relationships with their wives. The transvestite who cross-dresses for sexual excitement should not be confused with a homosexual male who cross-dresses to attract other males. As for women, there seems to be little evidence that women who wear men's clothing do so for sexual arousal purposes. In fact, it is quite socially acceptable in modern Western society for women to wear clothing that once was considered male. Westerners think nothing of a woman wearing pants, a suit jacket, and even a tie but would look oddly at a man wearing a skirt or a dress, right? In a sense, then, if the culture does not prevent a woman from wearing male-type clothing, there is no "shock" value to doing so—and this may be a big factor in the excitement for men who wear women's clothing. The risk of being "found out" adds to the sexual thrill.

TABLE 10.5 **PARAPHILIAS**

Festishism	An object or part of the body becomes the focus of sexual interest and arousal, such as shoes, feet, or underwear.
Exhibitionism	The exposure of normally clothed parts of the body to unsuspecting and typically unwilling viewers, such as a "flasher."
Voyeurism	Obtaining sexual arousal and gratification through watching other people engage in sexual behavior or undress, such as a "Peeping Tom."
Frotteurism	Becoming sexually aroused or gratified through rubbing up against an unwilling person, usually in a crowded public place.
Necrophilia	A kind of fetishism in which the sexual arousal comes from touching or having intercourse with a corpse.
Transvestism	A kind of fetishism in which sexual arousal and pleasure comes from wearing the clothing of the opposite sex.

PEDOPHILIA **Pedophilia** is a sexual deviancy that is illegal and considered immoral in almost every culture if it is carried out. The *DSM-IV-TR* (American Psychiatric Association, 2000) describes a **pedophile** as a person who has recurring sexual thoughts, fantasies, or behavior toward prepubescent children (children who have not yet entered puberty). These urges are considered criminal acts if they are acted upon. A person must be at least 16 years old and have an age difference of at least five years between the person and the object of the sexual fantasies to be considered a pedophile.

Contrary to the image most people have of a "dirty old man," the typical pedophile is a young adult male who may be sexually attracted to either females or males of the right age. Many pedophiles are married and have sexual relationships with their wives, yet still engage in their pedophilic fantasies or behavior. Female pedophiles are rare, but they do exist.

Treatments for the paraphilias can include psychotherapy, conditioning techniques, and even hormone therapy in some cases of pedophilia. ⓛⓘⓝⓚ *to Chapter Fifteen: Psychological Therapies, p. 562.*

There are several possible causes of the different paraphilias. Fetishism is often explained as a kind of classical conditioning, in which the object or body part, because of its presence during sexual activity and arousal (the unconditioned stimulus and response), becomes a kind of conditioned stimulus for sexual arousal (the conditioned response). ⓛⓘⓝⓚ *to Chapter Five: Learning, pp. 167–168.* **Transvestism** can be explained in much the same way. Interestingly, transvestism is more common in cultures in which the male is the major earner of the money, causing some researchers to wonder if cross-dressing may become a way for some men to temporarily assume the female role as a way of relieving the stress of being the breadwinner (Munroe, 1980).

Exhibitionism has been explained as a fear of rejection in sexual situations, so that the "flasher" who exposes himself and then runs gets to feel somehow masculine and powerful without the fear of rejection (Miner & Dwyer, 1997). Feelings of inferiority and sexual inadequacy are often given as explanations for paraphilias.

Sexually Transmitted Diseases

10.16   *What are sexually transmitted diseases?*

One of the consequences of unprotected sexual contact is the transmission of certain diseases. Some of these diseases affect the sex organs themselves, whereas others have broader and more life-threatening effects. The bacterial infections are quite treatable with antibiotics, but those caused by viruses are more difficult to treat and are often incurable. Even the treatable bacterial infections can cause serious problems if left untreated, and some bacterial infections are difficult to detect because the symptoms in at least one sex are not all that noticeable. For example, *chlamydia*, listed in Table 10.6, is easily treatable but may go undetected in women because there are few symptoms or no symptoms noticed. If left untreated, chlamydia can cause *pelvic inflammatory disorder (PID)*, a condition that can damage the lining of the uterus and the fallopian tubes as well as the ovaries and other nearby structures. Ten percent of women in the United States will develop PID during their child-bearing years (Miller & Graves, 2000). Table 10.7 lists some of the more common sexually transmitted diseases and their causes.

pedophilia
deriving sexual arousal and pleasure from touching or having sexual relations with prepubescent (nonsexually mature) children or fantasizing about such contact.

pedophile
a person who has recurring sexual thoughts, fantasies, or engages in sexual actions toward prepubescent (nonsexually mature) children.

transvestism
deriving sexual arousal and pleasure from dressing in the clothing of the opposite sex.

These posters warning against sexually transmitted diseases hang in a youth center in San Francisco, California. Adolescents often fail to take precautions against such diseases and are becoming sexually active at younger ages, making them a high-risk group for STDs.

TABLE 10.6 COMMON SEXUALLY TRANSMITTED DISEASES

STD	Cause	Symptoms
Chlamydia	Bacterial infection that grows within the body's cells like a virus.	Swollen testicles, discharge, burning during urination. Women may experience no symptoms.
Syphilis	Bacterial infection.	Sores that appear on or in the genital area and can spread to other body parts and the brain.
Gonorrhea	Bacterial infection that grows rapidly in warm, moist areas of the body (mouth, anus, throat, genitalia).	In men, a foul-smelling, cloudy discharge from penis, burning upon urination. In women, inflamed cervix, light vaginal discharge.
Genital Herpes	Herpes simplex virus.	Sores on the genital area. Itching, burning, throbbing, "pins-and-needles" sensations where sores are about to appear.
Genital Warts	Human papillomavirus (HPV).	Warty growths on the genitalia.
AIDS	Human immunodeficiency virus (HIV).	Severe malfunction and eventual breakdown of the immune system.

AIDS or acquired immune deficiency syndrome sexually transmitted viral disorder that causes deterioration of the immune system and eventually results in death due to complicating infections that the body can no longer fight.

AIDS

Without a doubt, the one sexually transmitted disease that nearly everyone knows something about is **AIDS**, or **acquired immune deficiency syndrome**. AIDS is caused by a viral infection, specifically the *human immunodeficiency virus*, or *HIV*. A person who has the HIV infection does not necessarily have AIDS, but is at risk for developing AIDS in the future. HIV wears down the body's immune system, making the body vulnerable to infections and viruses that normally would not cause a problem. When a person with the HIV virus develops one of these "opportunistic" infections, or when the person's T-cell count goes below a certain level, the person is said to have AIDS (Folkman & Chesney, 1995).

I've heard a lot of ▶ stories about how people can get AIDS. What's the real story?

I've heard a lot of stories about how people can get AIDS. What's the real story? HIV can be transmitted to a person from anyone who has the infection, even if that person doesn't look sick. He or she might not have tested positive for HIV yet but still be able to transmit the virus in one of three ways:

- Having unprotected sexual contact.
- Sharing a needle (used to take drugs).
- Giving birth to a baby while infected. The virus can be transmitted to the baby in this way, as can breast-feeding the baby while infected (Kourtis et al., 2001).

Blood, vaginal fluid, semen, and breast milk are the main ways in which AIDS is passed from the infected person to an uninfected person. Contrary to a lot of myths about AIDS, there is no scientific proof or documented cases of AIDS being passed through tears or saliva. Kissing an infected person will not result in transmission, although it is possible to transmit the virus through oral sex or, rarely, through deep kissing when there are open sores or bleeding gums in the mouth of either party.

Can't a person get AIDS ▶ from blood transfusion?

Can't a person get AIDS from blood transfusion? Before the medical world knew as much about AIDS as it does today, some people did acquire AIDS through transfusions of infected blood. However, the blood supply used for transfusions is now screened very carefully, resulting in an extremely low risk of getting AIDS through a transfusion.

In the United States, there are about 800,000 to 900,000 people who are HIV-positive. Over 300,000 people are currently living with AIDS, and there are about 40,000 new infections each year (UNAIDS, 2003). The fastest-growing population of people with HIV infections is now women. In heterosexual contact, the virus is 17

These young men, all gay, are attending a counseling session at a community-based AIDS clinic. They do not necessarily have AIDS; the purpose of this particular group is to help educate these men and others like them in ways to prevent HIV infections. With no cure as yet, prevention is the best defense against AIDS.

times more likely to be passed from the man to the woman than from the woman to the man, although the latter does occur (Padian et al., 1991). In the mid-1990s, AIDS was a leading cause of death, especially in young adults. However, newer treatments have cut the AIDS death rate significantly.

The first symptoms of an HIV infection are often mistaken for the flu—fever, sore muscles, swollen lymph glands, and skin rashes. It takes a few weeks for your immune system to make antibodies, which are what the HIV test detects, so it is possible to have the infection and transmit it before ever having enough antibodies to test positive. Once infected, the person can remain relatively healthy for up to 10 years or so, but all the while the immune system is being damaged by the virus.

Four of the more common opportunistic infections that can hallmark the onset of AIDS in an HIV infected person are *pneumocystis pneumonia*, a type of lung infection, *Kaposi's sarcoma*, a skin cancer, *cytomegalovirus*, an infection that usually occurs in the eyes, and *candida*, a fungal infection in the mouth, throat, or vagina (Laguna et al., 1997). These diseases can also bring about serious weight loss and other health problems and, if left untreated, will result in death.

What are the treatments for AIDS, and how long can a person live who has it? How long individuals can live with AIDS depends on several factors, including how healthy they were before the infection, whether they can avoid exposure to the infections that wear down the body, and whether they take the medications that are now used to treat HIV and AIDS. Some people die fairly quickly, whereas others stay relatively healthy for years, even without the medications.

The medications used to treat HIV are *antiretrovirals*, drugs that inhibit a particular enzyme that the virus needs in order to take over the body's systems (Kaufmann et al., 2000). Some of the more common antiretrovirals are AZT, didanosine, and zalcitibine, to name a few. The goal is to slow the virus down. When opportunistic infections occur, they are treated aggressively as well with the drugs best suited to each specific infection. Researchers are getting closer and closer to a vaccine that will prevent the HIV infection, although the results of human trials are not yet available. The first double-blind human trial of an AIDS vaccine was completed and reported in early 2005, and although the vaccine did not prevent HIV infections, scientists see the results of the clinical trial as a foundation on which they can build future trials (Gilbert et al., 2005).

The Applying Psychology in Everyday Life section at the end of this chapter has information on ways to prevent the transmission of AIDS and other sexually transmitted diseases.

◀ What are the treatments for AIDS, and how long can a person live who has it?

PRACTICE **QUIZ:** HOW MUCH DO YOU REMEMBER?

Pick the best answer.

1. Which of the following is not sexual dysfunction stemming from an organic physical disorder?
   a. sexual desire disorder
   b. frotteurism
   c. male erectile disorder
   d. sexual aversion disorder

2. In _____, the person may have the desire for sexual activity but be unable to physically participate.
   a. sexual desire disorder
   b. sexual pain disorder
   c. sexual arousal disorder
   d. orgasmic disorder

3. Which of the following statements about transvestites is FALSE?
   a. Most transvestites are homosexuals.
   b. Transvestites get sexual excitement from wearing the clothing of the opposite sex.
   c. Most transvestites are married.
   d. There is little evidence of women transvestites in Western cultures.

4. If left untreated, _____ can cause pelvic inflammatory disorder in women.
   a. chlamydia
   b. syphilis
   c. genital warts
   d. AIDS

5. There is no scientific, documented proof of AIDS being passed to another through
   a. childbirth.
   b. blood transfusions.
   c. sharing a needle.
   d. tears or saliva.

6. One of the most common opportunistic infections associated with AIDS is _____, an infection usually occurring in the eyes.
   a. pneumocystis pneumonia
   b. Kaposi's sarcoma
   c. cytomegalovirus
   d. candida

Answers: 1-b, 2-c, 3-a, 4-a, 5-d, 6-c.

Applying Psychology to Everyday Life: How to Protect Yourself from Sexually Transmitted Diseases

10.17   *How can people protect themselves and prevent the spread of STDs?*

Although this section may not seem like an application of psychological principles at first, part of psychology involves learning adaptive behavior and, often, how to change maladaptive behavior. The advice in this section will hopefully lead to both kinds of behavioral change. Information is one of the best defenses, after all.

There are several precautions that can help prevent the spread of many sexually transmitted diseases. Although not all methods work equally well for every disease, people who are at risk of infection through their sexual behavior or intravenous drug use should try to use every method of prevention that is available to them. Langford (2002) suggests taking several preventative measures:

- *Use condoms.* The use of condoms can help prevent transmission of diseases through vaginal contact. Condoms do not provide complete protection but do decrease the chances of contracting disease as well as unwanted pregnancy if used properly. Other methods of birth control do not prevent disease transmission, so it is necessary to use a condom in addition to these methods if disease control is the goal.

- *Have a sexual relationship with one uninfected partner.* The risk of infection increases with the number of sexual partners.

- *Don't share needles or other drug equipment.* Even vitamin injections, which are legal, can transmit a disease if a needle is shared. Tattooing or body piercing should also be avoided or great care taken to ensure that the needles are sterile.

- *If you are sexually active, especially if you have more than one partner, have regular exams for sexually transmitted diseases.* Early detection means easier and more effective treatment.

- *Learn the common symptoms for sexually transmitted diseases.* If you think you might be infected, get help right away.

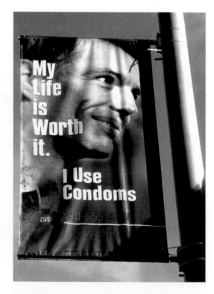

Not too many years ago, no one would have dared to advertise condoms in such a public manner. The only consequences of unsafe sex were unwanted pregnancies and serious, but not necessarily life-threatening sexually transmitted diseases. With the onslaught of the AIDS virus, safe sex has taken on a whole new meaning.

- *Talk openly with your partner about diseases and condom use.* Never leave your protection up to someone else; it's up to you to take precautions.
- *Realize that abstinence is the only 100 percent effective prevention.* Delaying having sex for the first time greatly reduces the chances of getting a sexually transmitted disease. The younger a person is at the first sexual experience, the greater the risk of disease.

Questions for Further Discussion

1. How important is it for parents to talk to their children about sexually transmitted diseases?
2. At what age should parents begin informing their children about the dangers of STDs?
3. Should the dangers of sexually transmitted diseases be a part of a regular public school education, and if so, at what grade level should such education begin?
4. What are some other precautions that people can take to prevent STDs?

10

CHAPTER SUMMARY

The Physical Side of Human Sexuality

10.1 *What are the physical differences between females and males?*

- The female sexual organs present at birth are the primary sex characteristics of vagina, uterus, and ovaries.
- The female sexual organs that develop during puberty are secondary sex characteristics consisting of the growth spurt, onset of the menstrual cycle, breast development, widening hips, pubic hair, fat deposits, and further growth and development of the uterus, vagina, and ovaries.
- The primary male sex characteristics are the penis, scrotum, testicles, and prostate gland.
- The secondary male sex characteristics are an enlarged larynx (Adam's apple), deepening voice, facial and chest hair, pubic hair, coarser skin texture, and a large increase in height.

The Psychological Side of Human Sexuality: Gender

10.2 *What is gender?*

- Gender is the psychological aspects of being male or female.
- Gender roles are the culture's expectations for male and female behavior and personality.
- Gender typing is the process by which people in a culture learn the appropriate gender role behavior.
- Gender identity is a person's sense of being male or female.

10.3 *How much influence do biology and learning have on gender role development?*

- There are both biological influences, in the form of hormones and chromosomes, and environmental influences, in the form of parenting, surroundings, and culture on the formation of gender identity.

10.4 *What are the theories about how children learn their gender roles?*

- Social learning theorists believe that gender identity is formed through reinforcement of appropriate gender behavior as well as imitation of gender models.
- Gender schema theorists believe that gender identity is a mental schema that develops gradually, influenced by the growth of the brain and organization of observed male or female behavior around the schema.

10.5 *What is gender stereotyping?*

- Gender stereotyping occurs when people assign characteristics to a person based on the person's male or female status rather than actual characteristics.

10.6 *What is androgyny?*

- Androgyny describes people who do not limit themselves to the male or female stereotyped characteristics, instead possessing characteristics associated with both traditional masculine and feminine roles.

10.7 *What are the differences in thinking, social behavior, and personality between women and men?*

- Cognitive differences between men and women include a male advantage in mathematical and spatial skills and a female superiority in verbal skills. These differences are now less than they were previously.
- Males and females are socially taught to interact differently and express emotions differently. Men tend to talk with each other in a "report" style, whereas women tend to talk to each other in a "relate" style.

Current Issues in Psychology: The Intersex Controversy

10.8 *What is the controversy concerning the treatment of intersexed infants?*

- Intersexed persons were historically seen as damaged, often being subjected to cruelty and even death.
- Many intersexed persons today would like to be recognized as a normal sexual variation rather than being considered deformed.

Human Sexual Behavior

10.9 *What happens in the bodies of women and men during sexual intercourse?*

- Masters and Johnson found four phases of human sexual response: arousal, plateau, orgasm, and resolution.

Classic Studies In Psychology: Masters and Johnson's Observational Study of the Human Sexual Response

10.10 *How did Masters and Johnson investigate the human sexual response?*

- Masters and Johnson used volunteers, some of whom were prostitutes, and both observed and measured their physiological responses during all phases of sexual intercourse.

10.11 *How did Kinsey study human sexual behavior?*

• Alfred Kinsey conducted a series of sexual behavior surveys in the late 1940s and early 1950s, revealing some highly controversial findings about the kinds of sexual behavior common among people in the United States, including homosexuality, premarital sex, and extramarital sex.

10.12 *What were the findings of the Janus Report?*

• Janus and Janus, in the mid-1990s, published the results of a large-scale survey of sexual behavior in the United States. Their survey results did not differ widely from those of Kinsey but looked at many more types of sexual behavior and factors related to sexual behavior than did Kinsey's surveys.

10.13 *What are the different sexual orientations and how do they develop?*

• Heterosexuals are attracted to people of the opposite sex and represent the largest sexual orientation.

• Homosexuals are primarily attracted to people of the same sex and make up about 9 percent of men and 5 percent of women.

• Bisexuals are people who are attracted to both males and females.

Sexual Dysfunctions

• Sexual dysfunctions are problems with sexual functioning. They may be caused by physical problems, stress, or psychological problems.

10.14 *What are the sexual dysfunctions caused by physical problems or stress?*

• Organic or stress-induced dysfunctions are caused by a physical problem or by stress and can affect sexual interest, arousal, and response.

• These disorders include hypoactive sexual desire, sexual aversion, female sexual arousal disorder, male erectile disorder, male orgasmic disorder, female orgasmic disorder, premature ejaculation, vaginismus, and dyspareunia.

10.15 *What are the sexual dysfunctions known as paraphilias?*

• The paraphilias are thought to be psychological in origin and involve sexual behavior that is unusual or not socially acceptable as a preferred way of achieving sexual pleasure.

• The paraphilias include fetishism, exhibitionism, voyeurism, frotteurism, necrophilia, transvestism, and pedophilia.

Sexually Transmitted Diseases

10.16 *What are sexually transmitted diseases?*

• Sexually transmitted diseases can affect the sexual organs and the ability to reproduce and may result in pain, disfigurement, and even death.

• Some common bacterial sexually transmitted diseases are chlamydia, syphilis, and gonorrhea. These diseases are treatable with antibiotics.

• Viral sexually transmitted diseases include genital herpes (caused by the herpes simplex virus that also causes cold sores) and genital warts (caused by the human papillomavirus). Neither can be cured and both can lead to complications such as increased risk of cancer.

• Acquired immune deficiency syndrome (AIDS) is a lethal virus that is transmitted through an exchange of blood, vaginal fluid, semen, or breast milk. Having unprotected sex with an infected person, sharing a needle with an infected person, or giving birth to or breast-feeding a baby while infected are the methods of transmission.

• AIDS wears down the immune system, opening the body up to infections that, over time, will result in death. There are drug treatments but no cure.

Applying Psychology to Everyday Life: How to Protect Yourself from Sexually Transmitted Diseases

10.17 *How can people protect themselves and prevent the spread of STDs?*

• People can avoid contracting or spreading sexually transmitted diseases by using condoms, having only one partner, abstaining from sex, avoiding IV drug use, knowing the symptoms of the various diseases, and getting regular physicals.

10 KEY TERMS

AIDS or acquired immune deficiency syndrome 396	heterosexual 389	refractory period 384
androgens 374	homosexual 389	resolution 384
androgyny 379	intersex 383	scrotum 372
benevolent sexism 379	intersexed, intersexual 382	secondary sex characteristics 372
bisexual 392	mammary glands 373	seminal fluid 384
estrogens 374	menstrual cycle 373	sexism 379
gender 374	organic or stress-induced dysfunction 393	sexual deviance 389
gender identity 374	orgasm 384	sexual dysfunction 392
gender roles 374	ovaries 372	sexual orientation 389
gender schema theory 378	paraphilia 394	stereotype 378
gender stereotype 378	pedophile 395	testes (testicles) 372
gender typing 374	pedophilia 395	transvestism 395
hermaphroditism 382	primary sex characteristics 372	uterus 372
	prostate gland 372	vagina 372

For more sample quizzes and other review activities that will help you get a better grade, be sure to check out your accompanying study guide. To access tests and your own personalized study plan that will help you focus on the areas you need to master before your next class test, be sure to go to the on-line Psychology web site available with the access code packaged with your book.

TEST YOURSELF

Pick the best answer.

1. Which statement about primary sex characteristics is TRUE?
   a. They are directly involved in human reproduction.
   b. They develop during puberty.
   c. They are the same for males and females.
   d. They include the formation of breasts and growth of the beard.

2. The culture's expectations for male and female behaviors are called
   a. gender roles.
   b. gender typing.
   c. gender identity.
   d. gender constancy.

3. What happened to the girls who were exposed to masculinizing hormones prenatally?
   a. They were unaffected by the hormones.
   b. They became lesbians.
   c. They became tomboys as adolescents and young adults.
   d. They became more traditionally feminine as they grew older.

4. In gender schema theory, gender identity
   a. first forms as a mental concept of "boy" or "girl."
   b. is acquired through simple imitation of models.
   c. occurs through observational learning.
   d. is acquired through positive reinforcement of appropriate gender behavior.

5. Which characteristic is NOT one of the male stereotyped characteristics?
   a. aggressive
   b. unemotional
   c. changeable
   d. impatient

6. A person is said to be _____ if that person possesses both masculine and feminine personality traits that are typically positive.
   a. a hermaphrodite
   b. androgynous
   c. intersexed
   d. bisexual

7. Research suggests that differences between males and females in mathematics and verbal skills may be caused by psychological and social issues rather than biology because
   a. these differences have increased in recent years.
   b. these differences have decreased in recent years.
   c. these differences have remained constant.
   d. females now score higher than males in mathematics.

8. An intersexed person is
   a. a person who has sex with both men and women.
   b. another name for a homosexual.
   c. a person born with ambiguous sexual organs.
   d. another name for a heterosexual.

9. Orgasm occurs in
   a. Phase One.
   b. Phase Two.
   c. Phase Three.
   d. Phase Four.

10. The refractory period is a time during which
    a. a woman cannot have another orgasm.
    b. a man cannot have another erection.
    c. a man can be erect but not have an orgasm.
    d. a woman cannot be aroused.

11. Which of the following studies of sexual behavior was not a survey?
    a. the Kinsey Report
    b. the Janus Report
    c. Masters and Johnson's study
    d. All of the above were surveys.

12. The most recent surveys indicate that about _____ percent of men and _____ percent of women are predominantly homosexual.
    a. 22; 17
    b. 15; 10
    c. 5; 9
    d. 9; 5

13. Bisexual people
    a. have multiple relationships with men and women at the same time.
    b. are equally attracted to both sexes.
    c. can be either male or female.
    d. rarely have long-term, monogamous relationships.

14. Which of the following is not one of the three areas affected by sexual dysfunctions?
    a. sexual reproduction
    b. sexual arousal
    c. sexual interest
    d. sexual response

15. _____ is more a problem of timing than anything else.
    a. Male orgasmic disorder
    b. Female orgasmic disorder
    c. Dyspareunia
    d. Premature ejaculation

16. A woman who experiences intense contractions of the vaginal muscles, making intercourse painful, is suffering from
    a. vaginismus.
    b. dysparenunia.
    c. sexual interest disorder.
    d. sexual aversion.

17. Touching or rubbing up against an unwilling person is called
    a. voyeurism.
    b. frotteurism.
    c. fetishism.
    d. necrophilia.

18. Which of the following involves touching a dead body?
    a. voyeurism
    b. exhibitionism
    c. necrophilia
    d. transvestism

19. Which of the following statements about pedophiles is FALSE?
    a. They are mostly male.
    b. They can be attracted to children of either sex.
    c. They are mostly married with adult sexual relationships with their wives.
    d. They are typically older men.

20. Which of the following sexually transmitted diseases is not caused by a bacterial infection?
    a. genital herpes
    b. chlamydia
    c. syphilis
    d. gonorrhea

21. Charles has noticed a foul-smelling, cloudy discharge from his penis and burning when he urinates. Charles probably has
    a. genital herpes.
    b. chlamydia.
    c. syphilis.
    d. gonorrhea.

22. A person is not said to have AIDS until
    a. infected with HIV.
    b. the T-cell count goes below a certain level.
    c. Kaposi's sarcoma develops.
    d. the HIV bacteria count reaches a certain level.

23. Which of the following is not one of the recommendations for preventing the spread of sexually transmitted diseases?
    a. Assume that your partner will take care of prevention.
    b. Have one sexual partner who has been tested and is negative.
    c. Use condoms.
    d. Abstain from having sexual relations.

Answers: 1-a, 2-a, 3-d, 4-a, 5-c, 6-b, 7-b, 8-c, 9-c, 10-b, 11-c, 12-d, 13-c, 14-a, 15-d, 16-a, 17-b, 18-c, 19-c, 20-a, 21-d, 22-b, 23-a.

Physical Side of Human Sexuality

Female sexual organs (primary sex characteristics) present at birth: vagina, uterus, and ovaries

Female sexual organs/characteristics that develop during puberty (secondary sex characteristics):
- Growth spurt
- Menarche
- Breast development
- Widening hips
- Pubic hair
- Fat deposits
- Further growth and development of uterus, vagina, and ovaries

Male primary sex characteristics: penis, scrotum, testicles, and prostate gland

Secondary male sex characteristics:
- Enlarged larynx (Adam's apple)
- Deepening voice
- Facial and chest hair
- Pubic hair
- Coarser skin texture
- Large increase in height

10.1

Psychological Side of Human Sexuality: Gender

Gender: psychological aspects of being male or female

Gender roles: culture's expectation for male and female behavior and personality

Gender typing: process by which people in a culture learn appropriate gender role behavior

Gender identity: person's sense of being male or female

10.2

Influences of Biology and Learning on Gender Role Development

Biological influences: hormones and chromosomes

Environmental influences: parenting, surroundings, and culture

10.3

Theories of Children Learning Gender Roles

Social learning theory

Gender schema theory

10.4

Gender Stereotyping

Occurs when people assign characteristics to a person based on the person's male or female status rather than actual characteristics

10.5

Androgyny

- People who do not limit themselves to male or female stereotyped characteristics
- Possession of characteristics associated with both traditional masculine and feminine roles

10.6

Gender Differences in Thinking, Social Behavior, and Personality

Cognitive differences:
- Male advantage in mathematical and spatial skills
- Female superiority in verbal skills

Emotional differences:
- Males and females are socially taught to interact differently and express emotions differently

10.7

Current Issues in Psychology: The Intersex Controversy

- Intersexed persons were historically seen as damaged
- Many intersexed persons today would like to be recognized as a normal sexual variation

10.8

Sexual Behavior Studies

Physical Responses During Sexual Intercourse

Masters and Johnson found four phases of human sexual response: arousal, plateau, orgasm, and resolution

10.9

Kinsey's Study of Human Sexual Behavior

▸ Sexual behavior surveys in the late 1940s and early 1950s
▸ Highly controversial findings of sexual behavior, including homosexuality, premarital sex, and extramarital sex

10.11

Masters and Johnson's Investigation of the Human Sexual Response

Masters and Johnson used volunteers and prostitutes to observe and measure physiological responses during sexual intercourse

10.10

Janus Report Findings (mid-1990s)

▸ Results did not differ widely from those of Kinsey
▸ Looked at more types of sexual behavior and factors than Kinsey

10.12

Kinsey and Colleagues' (1948) Rating Scale for Sexual Orientation

0	1	2	3	4	5	6
Exclusively heterosexual	Predominantly heterosexual; only incidentally homosexual	Predominantly heterosexual; more than incidentally homosexual	Equally heterosexual and homosexual	Predominantly homosexual; more than incidentally heterosexual	Predominantly homosexual; only incidentally heterosexual	Exclusively homosexual

Source: Reprinted with permission of the Kinsey Institute for Research in Sex, Gender, and Reproduction, Inc.

Sexually Transmitted Diseases

Different Sexual Orientations and Their Development

▸ Heterosexuals: attracted to people of the opposite sex; the largest sexual orientation
▸ Homosexuals: primarily attracted to people of the same sex; about 9 percent of men and 5 percent of women
▸ Bisexuals: attracted to both males and females

10.13

Sexually Transmitted Diseases

▸ Bacterial diseases: chlamydia, syphilis, and gonorrhea
▸ Viral sexually transmitted diseases: genital herpes, genital warts
▸ Acquired immune deficiency syndrome (AIDS)

10.16

Protecting Against and Preventing the Spread of STDs

▸ Using condoms
▸ Having only one monogamous partner
▸ Abstaining from sex
▸ Avoiding IV drug use
▸ Knowing symptoms of the various diseases
▸ Getting regular physicals

10.17

Sexual Dysfunctions Caused by Physical Problems or Stress

Organic or stress-induced dysfunctions:
▸ caused by physical problems or by stress   ▸ can affect sexual interest, arousal, and response

Disorders include: hypoactive sexual desire, sexual aversion, female sexual arousal disorder, male erectile disorder, male orgasmic disorder, female orgasmic disorder, premature ejaculation, and vaginismus dyspareunia

10.14

Paraphilias

Paraphilias: Sexual behavior that is unusual or not socially acceptable

Paraphilias include: fetishism, exhibitionism, voyeurism, frotteurism, necrophilia, transvestism, and pedophilia

10.15

11

Stress and Health

A Tale of Two Siblings

Although Nan had always been in relatively good health, when she was 81 her husband of more than 60 years died. Then she began to suffer falls, breaking first one hip and then the other, an ankle, a wrist, and her collarbone all at different times—she'd just start recovering from one injury when another would occur. By the time she was approaching her ninetieth birthday, she was dealing with chronic pain and the loss of her favorite activities—gardening and quilting. Despite all this, Nan manages to find joy in each day and remains a vital part of her children and grandchildren's lives.

Although Bill, Nan's older brother, had to use a cane to get around because of arthritis and a bad back, he was able to control his aches and pains with medication. He had also lost his wife of many years but seemed to adjust to the loss and his widowhood fairly well. He had six grown children and many grandchildren who would come to visit him regularly, and he still had one daughter, a middle-aged woman with mild Down syndrome, living at home with him. She was capable of helping with much of the housework. One day, the daughter heard a loud, frightening noise and went to check on her father. A horrible sight greeted her—her father had shot himself in the head with his shotgun. There was no note, and he had given no one any clue that he was considering taking his life.

How could Bill, who was in far less pain and far less lonely than his sister, fail so miserably at coping with the ordinary stresses of everyday living that he chose to end his own life? How can Nan, who lives each day in pain but manages to deal with her life stresses, continue to live and enjoy life? What factors might be responsible for the vastly different coping abilities of this brother and his sister?

Why study health and stress?

How are they related? Stress is not a rare experience but something that all people experience in varying degrees every day. This chapter will explore the sources of stress in daily life, the factors that can make the experience of stress easier or more difficult, and how stress influences our physical and mental health, as well as ways to cope with the stresses of everyday life and extraordinary experiences.

11

Stress

Life is really about change. Every day, each person faces some kind of challenge, big or small. Just deciding what to wear to work or school can be a challenge for some people, while others find the drive to the workplace or school the most challenging part of the day. There are decisions to be made and changes that will require adapting plans already made. Sometimes there are actual threats to well-being—an accident, a fight with the boss, a failed exam, or losing a job, to name a few. All of these challenges, threats, and changes require people to respond in some way.

DEFINITION OF STRESS

11.1 *What is stress?*

Stress is the term used to describe the physical, emotional, cognitive, and behavioral responses to events that are appraised* as threatening or challenging.

Stress can show itself in many ways. Physical problems can include unusual fatigue, sleeping problems, frequent colds, and even chest pains and nausea. People under stress may behave differently, too: pacing, eating too much, crying a lot, smoking and drinking more than usual, or physically striking out at others by hitting or throwing things. Emotionally, people under stress experience anxiety, depression, fear, and irritability, as well as anger and frustration. Mental symptoms of stress include problems in concentration, memory, and decision making, and people under stress often lose their sense of humor.

I feel like that ▶ most of the time!

I feel like that most of the time! Most people experience some degree of stress on a daily basis, and college students are even more likely to face situations and events that require them to make changes and adapt their behavior: Assigned readings, papers, studying for tests, juggling jobs, car problems, relationships, and dealing with deadlines are all examples of things that can cause a person to experience stress. Some people feel the effects of stress more than others because what is appraised as a threat by one person might be appraised as an opportunity by another. (For example, think how you and your friends might respond differently to the opportunity to write a 10-page paper for extra credit in the last three weeks of the semester.) Stress-causing events are called **stressors**; they can come from within a person or from an external source and range from relatively mild to severe.

stress
the term used to describe the physical, emotional, cognitive, and behavioral responses to events that are appraised as threatening or challenging.

stressors
events that cause a stress reaction.

_____

*Appraised: in this sense, evaluated or judged in terms of importance or significance.

WHAT ARE STRESSORS?

Events that can become stressors range from being stuck behind a person in the 10-items-or-less lane of the grocery store who has twice that amount to dealing with the rubble left after a tornado or a hurricane destroys one's home. Stressors can range from the deadly serious (hurricanes, fires, crashes, combat) to the merely irritating and annoying (delays, rude people, losing one's car keys). Stressors can even be imaginary, as when a couple puts off doing their income tax return, imagining that they will have to pay a huge tax bill, or when a parent imagines the worst happening to a teenage child who isn't yet home from an evening out.

Taking a test is just one of many possible stressors in a college student's life. What aspects of college life have you found to be stressful? Do other students experience the same degree of stress in response to the same stressors?

Actually, there are two kinds of stressors: those that cause **distress**, which occurs when people experience unpleasant stressors, and those that cause *eustress*, which results from positive events that still make demands on a person to adapt or change. Marriage, a job promotion, and having a baby may all be positive events for most people, but they all require a great deal of change in people's habits, duties, and even lifestyle, thereby creating stress. Hans Selye (1936) originally coined the term *eustress* to describe the stress experienced when positive events require the body to adapt.

In an update of Selye's original definition, researchers now define **eustress** as the optimal amount of stress that people need to promote health and well-being. The arousal theory of Chapter Nine is based on the idea that a certain level of stress, or arousal, is actually necessary for people to feel content (Zuckerman, 1994). ⓛⓘⓝⓚ *to Chapter Nine: Motivation and Emotion, pp. 340–342.* That arousal can be viewed in terms of eustress. Many students are aware that experiencing a little anxiety or stress is helpful to them because it motivates them to study, for example. Without the eustress created by the impending exam, many students might not study very much or at all.

What about the student who is so stressed out that everything he's studied just flies right out of his head? Obviously, a high level of anxiety concerning an impending exam that actually interferes with the ability to study or to retrieve the information at exam time is not eustress but is, in fact, distress. The difference is not only in the degree of anxiety but also in how the person interprets the exam situation. Interpretation, or appraisal, is the topic of the next section.

COGNITIVE FACTORS IN STRESS: LAZARUS'S COGNITIVE APPRAISAL APPROACH

11.2   *What are the cognitive factors in stress?*

Cognitive psychologist Richard Lazarus developed a cognitive view of stress called the *cognitive–mediational theory* of emotions, in which the way people think about and appraise a stressor is a major factor in how stressful that particular stressor becomes (Lazarus, 1991, 1999; Lazarus & Folkman, 1984). ⓛⓘⓝⓚ *to Chapter Nine: Motivation and Emotion, pp. 360–361.* According to Lazarus, there is a two-step process in assessing the degree of threat or harm of a stressor and how one should react to that stressor. (See Figure 11.1.)

PRIMARY APPRAISAL   The first step in appraising a stressor is called **primary appraisal**, which involves estimating the severity of the stressor and classifying it as a threat (something that could be harmful in the future), a challenge (something to be met and defeated), or a harm or loss that has already occurred. If the stressor is appraised as a threat, negative emotions may arise that inhibit the person's ability to cope with the threat. For example, a student who has not read the text or taken good notes will certainly appraise an upcoming exam as threatening. If the stressor is seen as a challenge, however, it is possible to plan to meet that challenge, which is a more positive and less

◄ What about the student who is so stressed out that everything he's studied just flies right out of his head?

distress
the effect of unpleasant and undesirable stressors.

eustress
the effect of positive events, or the optimal amount of stress that people need to promote health and well-being.

primary appraisal
the first step in assessing a stress, which involves estimating the severity of a stressor and classifying it as either a threat or a challenge.

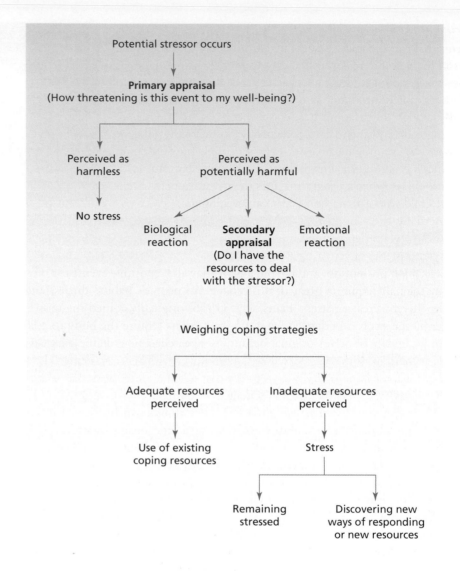

stressful approach. For example, the student who has studied, read, and feels prepared is much more likely to appraise the upcoming exam as an opportunity to do well.

Perceiving a stressor as a challenge instead of a threat makes coping with the stressor or the harm it may already have caused more likely to be successful, whereas perceiving it as an embarrassment or imagining failure or rejection is more likely to lead to increased stress reactions, negative emotions, and an inability to cope well (Folkman, 1997; Lazarus, 1993). Think positive!

SECONDARY APPRAISAL   In **secondary appraisal**, people who have identified a threat or harmful effect must estimate the resources that they have available for coping with the stressor. Resources might include social support, money, time, energy, ability, or any number of potential resources, depending on the threat. If resources are perceived as adequate or abundant, the degree of stress will be considerably less than if resources are missing or lacking. Using the example of the student and the upcoming exam, a student who feels that she has the time to study and the ability to understand the material in that time will feel much less distress than the student who has little time to study and doesn't feel that she understood much of the lectures covered on the exam.

As another example, let's say that a person's position at a firm has just been downsized. That's a fairly big stressor in most situations, but the degree of stress experienced and the coping abilities of that person will depend on both primary appraisal and sec-

secondary appraisal
the second step in assessing a threat, which involves estimating the resources available to the person for coping with the stressor.

ondary appraisal. In most cases, primary appraisal might go something like this: "I've lost my job! I need a job, so this is bad, very bad!" ("This is a threat!") The secondary appraisal might result in the following: "I don't have much money in savings, and the job market for my skills is pretty bad right now. I don't have anyone I can borrow money from or live with while I'm looking for more work. I'm going to lose everything!" ("I don't have the resources to deal with this!") Contrast that person's situation with this person's situation: "I've been let go, but that's not so bad. I wanted to look for a new job anyhow." ("This is a challenge.") The secondary appraisal might be: "I have some money in savings, and I can live with my brother for a while if nothing turns up quickly—I should be fine." ("I have the resources to deal with this.") Which person is going to experience more stress and have more health problems as a consequence?

The next section deals with three types of stressors: catastrophes, major life changes, and hassles.

11.3   *What kinds of experiences can cause stress?*

CATASTROPHES   Losing one's home in a tornado is an example of a stressor called a **catastrophe**, an unpredictable event that happens on a large scale and creates tremendous amounts of stress and feelings of threat. Wars, hurricanes, floods, fires, airplane crashes, and other disasters are catastrophes. The terrorist-driven destruction of the World Trade Center in New York City on September 11, 2001, is a prime example of a catastrophe. In one study, nearly 8 percent of the people living in the area near the attacks developed a severe stress disorder, and nearly 10 percent reported symptoms of depression even as late as two months after the attack (Galea et al., 2002). Even people who lived nowhere near New York City were affected by the horrifying events of that day and the days that followed. Researchers at the University of Michigan surveyed people from all over the United States. They found that nearly two-thirds of those surveyed were still having trouble concentrating and sleeping as long as three weeks after the tragedy (Wahlberg, 2001).

Post-Traumatic Stress Disorder (PTSD)   The severe stress disorder suffered by people after 9/11 is a type of anxiety disorder called **post-traumatic stress disorder**, or **PTSD**. Although many of these people experienced symptoms of anxiety, recurring nightmares, sleep disturbances, problems in concentration, and moments in which they seemed to "relive" the event in dreams and flashbacks, such reactions usually faded considerably within a month after the event. This more temporary condition is called *acute stress disorder*. When the symptoms persist for more than a month, the condition becomes post-traumatic stress disorder. Treatment of this disorder may involve psychotherapy and the use of drugs to control anxiety. LINK *to Chapter Fifteen: Psychological Therapies, pp. 564–586.*

Women seem to be more vulnerable to PTSD than men. Researchers have found that women have almost twice the risk of developing PTSD than do men, and that the likelihood increases if the traumatic experience took place before the woman was 15 years old (Breslau et al., 1997, 1999).

MAJOR LIFE CHANGES   Thankfully, most people do not have to face the extreme stress of a catastrophe. But stress is present even in relatively ordinary life experiences. Sometimes there are big events, such as marriage, job loss, or going to college, that require a person to make adjustments and changes—and adjustments and changes are really the core of stress, according to early researchers in the field (Holmes & Rahe, 1967).

The Social Readjustment Rating Scale (SRRS)   Holmes and Rahe (1967) believed that any life event that required people to change, adapt, or adjust their lifestyles would result in stress. Like Selye, they assume that both negative events (such as getting fired) and positive

This photograph shows people fleeing from the December 2004 tsunami (a giant tidal wave) in Phuket, Thailand. A catastrophe such as this tsunami is a large-scale and unpredictable event that creates intense and often prolonged feelings of stress and threat.

catastrophe
an unpredictable, large-scale event that creates a tremendous need to adapt and adjust as well as overwhelming feelings of threat.

Post-Traumatic Stress Disorder (PTSD)
a disorder resulting from exposure to a major stressor, with symptoms of anxiety, nightmares, poor sleep, reliving the event, and concentration problems, lasting for more than one month.

Social Readjustment Rating Scale (SRRS)
assessment that measures the amount of stress in a person's life over a one-year period resulting from major life events.

events (such as getting a promotion) demand that a person adjust in some way, and so both kinds of events are associated with stress. Holmes and Rahe devised a way to measure the amount of stress in a person's life by having that person add up the total "life change units" associated with each major event in their **Social Readjustment Rating Scale (SRRS)** (see Table 11.1). The "life change units" came from sampling 394 people, who were told that marriage represented 50 life change units on a scale from 0 (no changes required) to 100 (extreme changes required). By adding up the points associated with life events that have happened to a person within the past 12 months, a good estimate of the degree of stress being experienced by that person can be obtained.

The researchers found that scores on the SRRS could be associated with increased risk of illness or accidents. (Table 11.1 is not a complete listing of the events and associated life change units and should not be used to calculate a stress "score.") Scores of 150 or below were not associated with any significant problems, but scores between 150 and 199 were considered a "mild life crisis" and associated with a 33 percent increase in chance of illness or accident. Scores between 200 and 299 were labeled "moderate life crisis" and associated with a 50 percent increase in risk, whereas scores over 300 were considered a "major life crisis" and represented an 80 percent increase in risk (Holmes & Masuda, 1973). Simply put, if a person's score is 300 or above, that person has a very high chance of becoming ill or having an accident in the

TABLE 11.1 **SAMPLE ITEMS FROM THE SOCIAL READJUSTMENT RATING SCALE (SRRS)**

Major Life Event	Life Change Units
Death of spouse	100
Divorce	75
Marital separation	65
Jail term	63
Death of a close family member	63
Personal injury or illness	53
Marriage	50
Dismissal from work	47
Marital reconciliation	45
Pregnancy	40
Death of close friend	37
Change to different line of work	36
Change in number of arguments with spouse	36
Major mortgage	31
Foreclosure of mortgage or loan	30
Begin or end school	26
Change in living conditions	25
Change in work hours or conditions	20
Change in residence/schools/recreation	19
Change in social activities	18
Small mortgage or loan	17
Vacation	13
Christmas	12
Minor violations of the law	11

Source: Adapted from Holmes, T. H., & Rahe, R. H. (1967).

near future. Illness includes not only physical conditions such as high blood pressure, ulcers, or migraine headaches but mental illness as well. In one study, researchers found that stressful life events of the kind listed in the SRRS were excellent predictors of the onset of episodes of major depression (Kendler & Prescott, 1999).

The SRRS was later revised (Miller & Rahe, 1997) to reflect changes in the ratings of the events in the 30 intervening years. Miller and Rahe found that overall stress associated with many of the items on the original list had increased by about 45 percent from the original 1967 ratings.

How can stress cause a person to have an accident? Many studies conducted on the relationship between stress and accidents in the workplace have shown that people under a lot of stress tend to be more distracted and less cautious and, therefore, place themselves at a greater risk for having an accident (Hansen, 1988; Sherry, 1991; Sherry et al., 2003).

The SRRS as it was originally designed seems more appropriate for adults who are already established in their careers. There are versions of the SRRS that use as life events some of those things more likely to be experienced by college students. One of these more recent versions is the **College Undergraduate Stress Scale (CUSS)** that is represented in its entirety in Table 11.2 (Renner & Mackin, 1998). This scale looks quite different from Holmes and Rahe's original scale because the stressful events listed and rated include those that would be more common or more likely to happen to a college student. (Try it—add up the life change units from the events that you personally have experienced within the last year and then determine your level of risk according to Holmes and Rahe's original scoring system described earlier.)

Falling asleep in class? How can falling asleep in class be stressful? It's what happens when the professor catches you that's stressful, isn't it? Ah, but if you fall asleep in class, even if the professor doesn't catch on, you'll miss the lecture notes. You might then have to get the notes from a friend, find enough money to pay for the copy machine, try to read your friend's handwriting, and so on—all stressful situations. Actually, all the events listed on both the SRRS and the CUSS are stressful not just because some of them are emotionally intense but also because there are so many little details, changes, adjustments, adaptations, frustrations, and delays that are caused by the events themselves. The death of a spouse, for example, rates 100 life change units because it requires the greatest amount of adjustment in a person's life. A lot of those adjustments are going to be the little details: planning the funeral, deciding what to do with the spouse's clothes and belongings, getting the notice in the obituaries, answering all of the condolence cards with a thank-you card, dealing with insurance and changing names on policies, and on and on and on. In other words, major life events create a whole host of hassles.

HASSLES   Although it's easy to think about big disasters and major changes in life as sources of stress, the bulk of the stress we experience daily actually comes from little frustrations, delays, irritations, minor disagreements, and similar annoyances. These daily annoyances are called **hassles** (Lazarus, 1993; Lazarus & Folkman, 1984). Experiencing major changes in one's life is like throwing a rock into a pond: There will be a big splash, but the rock itself is gone. What is left behind are all the ripples in the water that came from the impact of the rock. Those "ripples" are the hassles that arise from the big event.

Lazarus and Folkman (1984) developed a "hassles" scale that has items such as "misplacing or losing things" and "troublesome neighbors." A person taking the test for hassles would rate each item in the scale in terms of how much of a hassle that

◀ **How can stress** cause a person to have an accident?

◀ **Falling asleep in** class? How can falling asleep in class be stressful? It's what happens when the professor catches you that's stressful, isn't it?

College Undergraduate Stress Scale (CUSS)
assessment that measures the amount of stress in a college student's life over a one-year period resulting from major life events.

hassles
the daily annoyances of everyday life.

TABLE 11.2 **COLLEGE UNDERGRADUATE STRESS SCALE (CUSS)**

Event	Rating
Being raped	100
Finding out that you are HIV-positive	100
Death of a close friend	97
Contracting a sexually transmitted disease (other than AIDS)	94
Concerns about being pregnant	91
Finals week	90
Oversleeping for an exam	89
Flunking a class	89
Having a boyfriend or girlfriend cheat on you	85
Financial difficulties	84
Writing a major term paper	83
Being caught cheating on a test	83
Two exams in one day	80
Getting married	76
Difficulties with parents	73
Talking in front of a class	72
Difficulties with a roommate	66
Job changes (applying, new job, work hassles)	65
A class you hate	62
Confrontations with professors	60
Maintaining a steady dating relationship	55
Commuting to campus or work, or both	54
Peer pressures	53
Being away from home for the first time	53
Getting straight A's	51
Fraternity or sorority rush	47
Falling asleep in class	40

Source: Adapted from Renner, M. J., & Mackin, R. S. (1998).

particular item was for the person. The ratings range between 0 (no hassle or didn't occur) to 3 (extremely severe hassle). Whereas the major life events of Holmes and Rahe's scale (1967) may have a long-term effect on a person's chronic physical and mental health, the day-to-day minor annoyances, delays, and irritations that affect immediate health and well-being are far better predictors of short-term illnesses such as headaches, colds, backaches, and similar symptoms (Burks & Martin, 1985; DeLongis et al., 1988). In one study, researchers found that among 261 participants who experienced headaches, scores on a scale measuring the number and severity of daily hassles were significantly better predictors of headaches than were scores on a life events scale (Fernandez & Sheffield, 1996). The researchers also found that it was not so much the number of daily hassles that predicted headaches but rather the perceived severity of the hassles.

A recent study has indicated that hassles may also come from quite different sources depending on a person's developmental stage (Ellis et. al., 2001). In this study, researchers surveyed 270 randomly selected people from the ages 3–75. The participants were asked to check off a list of daily hassles and pleasures associated with having "bad days" and "good days," respectively, as well as ranking the hassles in terms of frequency and severity of impact. For children ages 3–5, getting teased was the biggest daily hassle. For children in the 6–10 age group, the biggest hassle was getting bad grades. Children 11–15 years old reported feeling pressured to use drugs, whereas older adolescents (ages 16–22) cited trouble at school or work. Adults found fighting among family members the greatest source of stress, whereas the elderly people in the study cited a lack of money.

In that same study, the researchers were somewhat surprised to find that elderly people were much more strongly affected by such hassles as going shopping, doctor's appointments, and bad weather than the children and younger adults. It may be that while a young person may view going shopping as an opportunity to socialize, older adults find it threatening: Physically, they are less able to get to a place to shop and may have to rely on others to drive them and help them get around and, thus, may take much more time for shopping and doing errands than a younger person would. Mentally, shopping could be seen as threatening because of a lack of financial resources to pay for needed items. Even the need to make decisions might be seen as unpleasant to an older person.

Children in the preschool age range find teasing by their peers to be the biggest daily hassle they experience. This boy is obviously upset by the teasing of the other children, who are making fun of his glasses. What other hassles might a child in this age range experience?

PRACTICE **QUIZ:** HOW MUCH DO YOU REMEMBER?

Pick the best answer.

1. The optimal amount of stress that people need to promote their health and sense of well-being is called
   a. intensity.
   c. eustress.
   b. distress.
   d. acute stress.

2. According to Lazarus, secondary appraisal involves
   a. estimating the severity of the stressor.
   b. classifying the stressor as a threat or challenge.
   c. deciding whether the stressor is a problem.
   d. estimating the resources a person has available for coping.

3. Anxiety, recurring nightmares, sleep disturbances, and concentration problems that occur for more than one month after a major stressor are symptoms of
   a. acute stress disorder.
   b. post-traumatic stress disorder.
   c. pre-traumatic stress disorder.
   d. general stress disorder.

4. Research has shown that _____ have a long-term effect on physical and mental health, but _____ have a greater impact on short-term health.
   a. hassles; major life events
   b. major life events; hassles
   c. major life events; catastrophes
   d. hassles; castastrophes

5. The College Undergraduate Stress Scale rates being raped as equally stressful when compared with which of the following?
   a. death of a close family member
   b. concerns about being pregnant
   c. being accused of rape
   d. finding out that one is HIV-positive

Answers: 1-c, 2-d, 3-b, 4-b, 5-d.

SOURCES OF STRESS

Although several specific sources of stress (e.g., marriage, car problems, etc.) have already been mentioned, the reasons why people find these events stressful fall into several categories.

pressure
the psychological experience produced by urgent demands or expectations for a person's behavior that come from an outside source.

frustration
the psychological experience produced by the blocking of a desired goal or fulfillment of a perceived need.

11.4   *What are some sources of stress in everyday life?*

PRESSURE   When there are urgent demands or expectations for a person's behavior coming from an outside source, that person is experiencing **pressure**. Pressure occurs when people feel that they must work harder, faster, or do more, as in meeting a deadline or studying for final exams.

Time pressure is one of the most common forms of pressure. Although some people claim to "work well under pressure," the truth is that pressure can have a negative impact on a person's ability to be creative. Psychologist Teresa Amabile has gathered research within actual work settings strongly indicating that when time pressure is applied to workers who are trying to come up with creative, innovative ideas, creativity levels decrease dramatically—even though the workers may think they have been quite productive because of the effort they have made (Amabile et al., 2002).

UNCONTROLLABILITY   Another factor that increases a person's experience of stress is the degree of control that the person has over a particular event or situation. The less control a person has, the greater the degree of stress. Researchers, in both clinical interviews and experimental studies, have found that lack of control in a situation actually increases post-traumatic stress syndrome symptoms (Breier et al., 1987).

In two studies carried out in a nursing home with the elderly residents as the participants, researchers Rodin and Langer (Langer & Rodin, 1976; Rodin & Langer, 1977) gave the residents each a houseplant. Decisions about watering and how much sun each plant should have were up to each resident. These residents, who comprised the experimental group, were also given choices such as whether they wanted to see a weekly movie, on which of the two evenings that the movie was shown did they want to attend, and in what area or room they would like to see their visitors. Participants in the control group, although also given plants, were told that the nurses would take care of the plants and were not encouraged to make decisions for themselves. The follow-up study took place a year and a half later. Using participation in activities, measures of happiness, and other assessments, the researchers found that those who had more control over their lives and who had been given more responsibility were more vigourous, active, and sociable than those in the control group.

The stress-increasing effects of lack of control explain the relationship between unpredictability and stress as well. When potentially stressful situations are unpredictable, as in police work, the degree of stress experienced is increased. An unpredictable situation is one that is not controllable, which may at least partially explain the increase in stress. In one study, rats were either given an electric shock after a warning tone or given a shock with no warning. The rats receiving the unpredictable shocks developed severe stomach ulcers (Weiss, 1972).

FRUSTRATION   **Frustration** occurs when people are blocked or prevented from achieving a desired goal or fulfilling a perceived need. As a stressor, frustration can be *external*, such as when a car breaks down, a desired job offer doesn't come through after all, or experiencing a theft of one's belongings. Losses, rejections, failures, and delays are all sources of external frustration.

Obviously, some frustrations are minor and others are more serious. The seriousness of a frustration is affected by how important the goal or need actually is. A person who is delayed in traffic while driving to the mall to do some shopping just for fun will be less frustrated than a person who is trying to get to the mall before it closes to get that last-minute forgotten and important anniversary gift.

Internal frustrations, also known as *personal frustrations*, occur when the goal or need cannot be attained because of internal or personal characteristics. For example,

"I suppose this puts my new bike on the back burner?"

someone who wants to be an astronaut might find that severe motion sickness prevents him or her from such a goal. If a man wants to be a professional basketball player but is only 5 feet tall and weighs only 85 pounds, he may find that he cannot achieve that goal because of his physical characteristics. A person wanting to be an engineer but who has no math skills would find it difficult to attain that goal.

There are several typical responses that people make when frustrated. The first is *persistence*, or the continuation of efforts to get around whatever is causing the frustration. Persistence may involve making more intense efforts or changing the style of response. For example, anyone who has ever put coins into a drink machine only to find that the drink does not come out has probably (1) pushed the button again, more forcefully, and (2) pushed several other buttons in an effort to get some kind of response from the machine. If neither of these strategies works, many people may hit or kick the machine itself in an act of aggression.

Aggression, or actions meant to harm or destroy, is unfortunately another typical reaction to frustration. Early psychologists in the field of behaviorism proposed a connection between frustration and aggression, calling it the *frustration–aggression hypothesis* (Dollard et al., 1939; Miller et al., 1941). (L)(I)(N)(K) *to Chapter Thirteen: Social Psychology, p. 505.* Although they believed that some form of frustration nearly always precedes aggression, that does not mean that frustration *always* leads to aggression. In fact, aggression is a frequent and persistent response to frustration, but it is seldom the first response. In a reformulation of the frustration–aggression hypothesis, Berkowitz (1993) stated that frustration creates an internal "readiness to aggress" but that aggression will not follow unless certain external cues are also present. For example, if the human source of a person's frustration is far larger and stronger in appearance than the frustrated person, aggression is an unlikely outcome!

Okay, so if the person who ticked you off is bigger than you—if aggression isn't possible—what can you do? One could try to reason with the person who is the source of frustration. Reasoning with someone is a form of persistence. Trying to "get around" the problem is another way in which people can deal with frustration. Another possibility is to take out one's frustrations on less threatening, more available targets in a process called **displaced aggression**. Displaced aggression is a form of **displacement**, one of the psychological defense mechanisms discussed a little later on in this chapter. Anyone who has ever been frustrated by things that occurred at work or school and then later yelled at another person (such as a spouse, parent, child, etc.) has experienced displaced aggression. The person one really wants to strike out at is one's boss, the teacher, or whoever or whatever caused the frustration in the first place. That could be dangerous, so the aggression is reserved for another less threatening or weaker target. For example, unemployment and financial difficulties are extremely frustrating, as they block a person's ability to maintain a certain standard of living and acquire possessions. In one study, male unemployment and single parenthood were the two factors most highly correlated to rates of child abuse (Gillham et al., 1998). Unemployment is also one of the factors correlated most highly with the murder of abused women, creating four times the risk of murder for women in abusive relationships (Campbell & Wolf, 2003). Both studies are examples of displaced aggression toward the weaker targets of children and women. Such targets often become *scapegoats*, or habitual targets of displaced aggression.

aggression
actions meant to harm or destroy.

displaced aggression
taking out one's frustrations on some less threatening or more available target, a form of displacement.

displacement
psychological defense mechanism in which emotional reactions and behavioral responses are shifted to targets that are more available or less threatening than the original target.

◄ Okay, so if the person who ticked you off is bigger than you—if aggression isn't possible—what can you do?

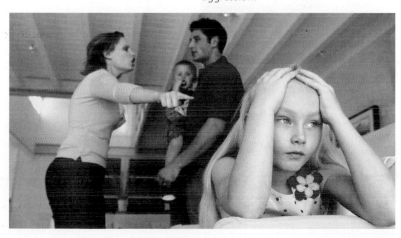

These parents are fighting in front of their obviously distressed daughter. In some instances, a child who experiences this kind of frustration might act out aggressively toward a sibling or a pet in a form of displaced aggression.

escape or withdrawal
leaving the presence of a stressor, either literally or by a psychological withdrawal into fantasy, drug abuse, or apathy.

Scapegoats are often pets, children, spouses, and even minority groups (who are seen as having less power).

Another possible reaction to frustration is **escape or withdrawal**. Escape or withdrawal can take the form of leaving, dropping out of school, quitting a job, or ending a relationship. Some people manage a psychological escape or withdrawal into apathy (ceasing to care about or act upon the situation), fantasy (which is only a temporary escape), or the use of drugs. Obviously the latter can lead to even more problems.

A far more drastic and permanent form of escape is suicide, the taking of one's own life. People who hear about someone's suicide are nearly always mystified by that choice. How can things be so bad that death seems the only option? For current facts about suicide, its causes, and what can be done to prevent it, see the Current Issues in Psychology section that follows.

CURRENT ISSUES IN PSYCHOLOGY

Suicide in America

11.5 *Why do people commit suicide?*

Hare are the facts:

- In 1996, among teenagers and young adults suicide took more lives than cancer, heart disease, AIDS, birth defects, strokes, pneumonia, the flu, and chronic lung diseases *combined*.
- More people die from suicide than from homicide.
- Rates of suicide increase with age and are highest for those over 65.
- The most common method of committing suicide is with a firearm.
- Men are more likely to complete a suicide (and men are more likely to use firearms), but women make more attempts.
- From 1980 to 1996 the rate of suicides among children 10 to 14 years of age increased by 100 percent.

All of these facts are taken from *The Surgeon General's Call to Action to Prevent Suicide*, published in 1999 by the Office of the Surgeon General of the United States (Satcher, 1999). Many of these facts might come as a surprise. Remember Bill in the opening story, the sibling who took his own life? He was over 65, male, and used a firearm to kill himself—all factors predicted by the Surgeon General's report.

What are the signs of impending suicide? Sometimes there are none, but depression ●LINK● to Chapter Fourteen: Psychological Disorders, pp. 541–542, is one of the most common mental disorders associated with suicide, and depression does have signs:

- feelings of hopelessness or emptiness
- lack of energy or fatigue
- *anhedonia*, or the inability to feel pleasure or enjoyment
- irritability
- sleeping problems, either too much sleep or too little
- eating more or less than usual
- physical symptoms that persist, such as headaches, stomachaches, or pain

Suicide prevention hot-line centers are designed to provide help and support to people who are on the verge of committing suicide. Volunteers, such as the one pictured here, act as concerned listeners for the depressed people who call in to the hotline centers.

People who are depressed and intend to commit suicide usually do talk about it, and this communication should always be taken seriously. There is a long-standing belief that "people who talk about it just want attention and won't really follow through," but this is not at all true. Talking about committing suicide is a kind of "dress rehearsal," and people who intend to commit suicide may clear out desks and lockers, settle their finances, write out wills, and even seem in relatively good spirits because they have made the decision to "end it" and are looking forward to the escape (Satcher, 2001).

What can be done to prevent suicides? Here are some guidelines from the American Foundation for Suicide Prevention (**www.afsp.org**):

- Listen with a sincere attitude of concern
- Avoid giving unasked-for advice
- Ask them if they have experienced feeling like this before and how they managed to cope with it then
- Share a time when you felt the same way and assure them that things can and will change
- Ask them if they are feeling suicidal
- Stay with them; do something together
- If you have immediate concern, call the police for emergency intervention
- Give them the number for the suicide prevention hot line and make sure they call:
- Toll-Free and 24 Hours: 1-800-SUICIDE or 1-800-784-2433

Above all, a person who tries to prevent a suicide and fails should not feel responsible. In the end, if a person committed to the act of suicide succeeds, there was nothing that any bystander could really do to prevent it.

Questions for Further Thought

1. How might a parent's suicide affect the children left behind?
2. How might a teenager's suicide affect parents and siblings?
3. What are the financial implications for those left behind?

CONFLICT Conflict occurs when a person feels pulled toward or drawn to two or more desires or goals but can only achieve or experience one. Lewin (1935) defined three types of conflicts, and his definitions are still used by today's researchers in the area of conflict and conflict resolution.

11.6 *What are the different types of conflicts people must face?*

Approach–Approach Conflict In an **approach–approach conflict**, a person experiences attraction to two desires or goals, each of which is attractive. Typically, this type of conflict, often called a "win-win situation" is relatively easy to resolve and does not involve a great deal of stress. Because both goals are desirable, the only stress involved is having to choose between them, acquiring one and losing the other. An example of this might be the need to choose between the chocolate cake or key lime pie for dessert or from among several good choices for a date to the prom. "Six on one hand, half a dozen on the other" is a phrase that sums up this conflict nicely. As can be seen in Figure 11.2, moving toward either goal will result in an increase in the approach value of that goal (the "ball" can easily roll down the "hill" after approaching either goal).

conflict
psychological experience of being pulled toward or drawn to two or more desires or goals, only one of which may be attained

approach–approach conflict
conflict occurring when a person must choose between two desirable goals.

FIGURE 11.2 **Conflict diagrams**   These diagrams represent three possible types of conflicts. In these diagrams, the ball represents the person who must make a decision. In an approach–approach conflict (first diagram), both goals (represented by the bottoms of the two hills) are equally desirable. Once one of these goals is chosen, the choice becomes very easy—it's all downhill. In an avoidance–avoidance conflict (the second diagram), both goals (tops of the two hills) are equally undesirable, but one must be chosen. Since movement toward either goal is an "uphill battle," people caught in these situations often delay making any kind of choice. In an approach–avoidance conflict (third diagram), the goal has both desirable and undesirable aspects. At first, the desirable aspects are most obvious, making it easy to "roll down the hill." But as the person gets closer to the goal (top of the hill), the undesirable aspects get stronger, making the goal harder to reach.

avoidance–avoidance conflict
conflict occurring when a person must choose between two undesirable goals.

approach–avoidance conflict
conflict occurring when a person must choose or not choose a goal that has both positive and negative aspects.

This couple is picking out an engagement ring, a rite of passage for many young adults. The decision to marry is often an approach-avoidance conflict, with the "pulls" of companionship, intimacy, and family and the "pushes" of added responsibilities, a lack of privacy, disagreements, and financial pressures.

Avoidance–Avoidance Conflict   Avoidance–avoidance conflicts are much more stressful. In this conflict, the choice is between two or more goals or events that are unpleasant. This type of conflict is so common that there are numerous phrases to symbolize it: "Caught between a rock and a hard place," "Between the devil and the deep blue sea," "Out of the frying pan into the fire," and "lose-lose situation" are some of these phrases. Because neither alternative is pleasant, many people avoid making a choice by delaying decisions (Tversky & Shafir, 1992). For example, given the choice of risky back surgery or living with the pain, some people would wait, hoping that the pain would go away on its own and relieve them of the need to make a choice. People who are fearful of dental procedures might face the conflict of suffering the pain of a toothache or going to the dentist. In Figure 11.2, movement toward either choice increases the negative aspect of that choice (the "ball" has an increasingly steeper climb as the goal is approached), resulting in the person staying put, unable to move toward one choice or the other.

Approach–Avoidance Conflict   Approach–avoidance conflicts are a little different in that they only involve one goal or event. That goal or event may have both positive and negative aspects that make the goal appealing and unappealing at the same time. For example, marriage is a big decision to make for anyone and usually has both its attractive features, such as togetherness, sharing good times, and companionship, and also its negative aspects, such as disagreements, money issues, and mortgages. This is perhaps the most stressful of all of the types of conflict, causing many people to vacillate* or be unable to decide for or against the goal or event. The author experienced a very stressful approach–avoidance conflict when deciding to write this textbook: On the one hand, there would be money, prestige, and the challenge of doing something new. On the other hand, a tremendous amount of effort and time would be required to write the text, which would take time and energy away from other areas of life. Another example is the offer of a promotion that would require a person to move to a city he or she doesn't like—more money and higher status but all the hassles of

---

*Vacillate: to go back and forth between one decision and another.

moving and living in a less than perfect place. In Figure 11.2, the approach value of the goal is represented by how easy it is to start toward the goal, but as the goal is approached, the negative factors increase in strength (the "hill" gets steeper and harder to climb as the goal is neared), causing indecision.

What if I have to choose between two things, and each of them has good points and bad points?

Multiple Approach–Avoidance Conflicts When the choice is between two goals that have both positive and negative elements to each goal, it is called a **double approach–avoidance conflict.** For example, what if a person had the choice of buying a house out in the country or in the city? The house in the country has its attractions: privacy, fresh air, and quiet. But there would be a long commute to one's job in the city. A house in the city would make getting to work a lot easier, but then there are the negative aspects of pollution, noise, and crowded city streets. Each choice has both good and bad points. This type of conflict also tends to lead to vacillation. Other examples of this type of conflict might be trying to decide which of two people one wants to date or which of two majors one needs to choose.

It is fairly common to face **multiple approach–avoidance conflicts** in daily life. In a multiple approach–avoidance conflict, one would have more than two goals or options to consider, making the decision even more difficult and stressful. For many college students, deciding on a career is actually this type of conflict.

◀ **What if I have to choose between two things, and each of them has good points and bad points?**

double approach–avoidance conflict conflict in which the person must decide between two goals, with each goal possessing both positive and negative aspects.

multiple approach–avoidance conflict conflict in which the person must decide between more than two goals, with each goal possessing both positive and negative aspects.

PRACTICE **QUIZ:** HOW MUCH DO YOU REMEMBER?

Pick the best answer.

1. When people have to work harder, do more work, or work faster, they are experiencing
   a. frustration.
   b. uncontrollability.
   c. pressure.
   d. conflict.

2. The stress-increasing effects of uncontrollability are related to the effects of _____ on stress.
   a. frustration
   b. unpredictability
   c. pressure
   d. conflict

3. Eduardo is on his way to an important job interview when his car breaks down on the highway. Eduardo is likely to experience what kind of frustration?
   a. external
   b. internal
   c. personal
   d. uncontrollable

4. The first response that people typically make to frustration is
   a. persistence.
   b. increasing efforts.
   c. varying efforts.
   d. aggression.

5. People who are depressed and may be suicidal often suffer from _____, a condition in which the person has lost the ability to experience pleasure.
   a. irritability
   b. anhedonia
   c. neural numbness
   d. learned helplessness

6. Jasmine has just been offered an opportunity to teach at a small college in a rural area of Kansas. On the one hand, she really needs a job and the money it would bring would allow her to pay off some debts. But the college is in a very small town far away from any major cities and has very little to offer in the way of amusements. She would also be far away from her family and friends. Jasmine is facing what type of conflict in deciding whether or not to accept the job?
   a. approach–approach
   b. avoidance–avoidance
   c. approach–avoidance
   d. double approach–avoidance

Answers: 1-c, 2-b, 3-a, 4-a, 5-b, 6-c.

Factors in the Stress Reaction

When I get all stressed out, I feel pretty terrible. What's the effect of stress on my body? Chapter Two discussed in detail the function of the *autonomic nervous system* (ANS), the part of the human nervous system that is responsible for all automatic, involuntary, and life-sustaining activities. The ANS consists of two divisions, the *parasympathetic* and the *sympathetic*. It is the sympathetic nervous system (the "fight-or-flight" system) that reacts when the human body is subjected to stress: Heart rate increases, digestion slows or shuts

◀ When I get all stressed out, I feel pretty terrible. What's the effect of stress on my body?

General Adaptation Syndrome (GAS) the three stages of the body's physiological reaction to stress, including alarm, resistance, and exhaustion.

down, and energy is sent to the muscles to help deal with whatever action the stressful situation requires. The parasympathetic system returns the body to normal, day-to-day functioning after the stress is ended. If the stress is great enough and lasts long enough, the parasympathetic system may shut the body down, causing a collapse into what some people might call "nervous exhaustion." Both systems figure prominently in a classic theory of the body's physiological reactions to stress, the general adaptation syndrome.

THE GENERAL ADAPTATION SYNDROME

11.7 *What is happening in the body when a person experiences stress?*

Psychologist Hans Selye was the founder of the field of research concerning stress and its effects on the human body. He studied the sequence of physiological reactions that the body goes through when adapting to a stressor. This sequence (see Figure 11.3) is called the **general adaptation syndrome (GAS)** and consists of three stages (Selye, 1956):

- *Alarm:* When the body first reacts to a stressor, the sympathetic nervous system is activated. The adrenal glands release hormones that increase heart rate, blood pressure, and the supply of blood sugar, resulting in a burst of energy. Reactions such as fever, nausea, and headache are common.

Simulation
Live!
psych

Selye's Syndrome

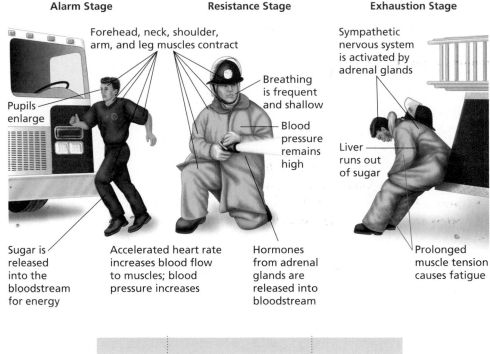

Alarm Stage

Forehead, neck, shoulder, arm, and leg muscles contract

Pupils enlarge

Sugar is released into the bloodstream for energy

Resistance Stage

Breathing is frequent and shallow

Blood pressure remains high

Accelerated heart rate increases blood flow to muscles; blood pressure increases

Hormones from adrenal glands are released into bloodstream

Exhaustion Stage

Sympathetic nervous system is activated by adrenal glands

Liver runs out of sugar

Prolonged muscle tension causes fatigue

FIGURE 11.3 **General Adaptation Syndrome** The diagram at the top shows some of the physical reactions to stress in each of the three stages of the general adaptation syndrome. The diagram at the bottom shows the relationship of each of the three stages to the individual's ability to resist a stressor. In the alarm phase, resistance rapidly increases as the body mobilizes its defense systems. In the resistance stage, the body is working at a much increased level of resistance, using resources until the stress ends or the resources run out. In the exhaustion stage, the body is no longer able to resist as resources have been depleted, and at this point disease and even death are possible.

Resistance to stress →

Shock

Normal level of resistance to stress

Phase 1 Alarm

Phase 2 Resistance

Phase 3 Exhaustion

- *Resistance:* As the stress continues, the body settles into sympathetic division activity, continuing to release the stress hormones that help the body fight off, or resist, the stressor. The early symptoms of alarm lessen and the person or animal may actually feel better. This stage will continue until the stressor ends or the organism has used up all of its resources.

- *Exhaustion:* When the body's resources are gone, resistance ends, the parasympathetic division activates, and exhaustion occurs. Exhaustion can lead to the formation of stress-related diseases (i.e., high blood pressure or a weakened immune system) or the death of the organism if outside help is unavailable (Stein-Behrens et al., 1994).

Alarm and resistance are stages that people experience many times throughout life, allowing people to adapt to life's demands (Selye, 1976). It is the prolonged secretion of the stress hormones during the stage of resistance that can lead to the most harmful effects of stress. It was this aspect of Selye's work that convinced other researchers of the connection between stress and certain "diseases of adaptation" as Selye termed them. The most common of these diseases are ulcers and high blood pressure.

IMMUNE SYSTEM AND STRESS

11.8 *What is the relationship between stress and the immune system?*

As Selye first discovered, the **immune system** (the system of cells, organs, and chemicals in the body that responds to attacks on the body from diseases and injuries) is affected by stress. The field of **psychoneuroimmunology** concerns the study of the effects of psychological factors such as stress, emotions, thinking, and behavior on the immune system (Cohen & Herbert, 1996; Kiecolt-Glaser et al., 1995, 1996, 2002). Researchers in this field have found that stress triggers the same response in the immune system that infection triggers (Maier & Watkins, 1998). Certain molecules are created by immune cells when the immune cells encounter an infection in the body. The immune cells surround the bacteria or other infectious material and release the special molecules into the bloodstream. From there, these molecules activate receptor sites on the *vagus nerve*, the longest nerve that connects the body to the brain. It is the activation of these receptor sites that signals the brain that the body is sick, causing the brain to respond by further activation of the immune system.

Stress activates this same system but starts in the brain rather than in the bloodstream. The same chemical changes that occur in the brain when it has been alerted by the vagus nerve to infection in the body occurred in laboratory animals when they were kept isolated from other animals or given electric shocks (Maier & Watkins, 1998). This has the effect of "priming" the immune system, allowing it to more successfully resist the effects of the stress, as in Selye's resistance stage of the GAS.

So stress actually increases the activity of the immune system? But then how does stress end up causing those diseases, like high blood pressure? The positive effects of stress on the immune system only seem to work when the stress is not a continual, chronic condition. As stress continues, the body's resources begin to fail in the exhaustion phase of the general adaptation to stress (Kiecolt-Glaser et al., 1987, 1995, 1996; Prigerson et al., 1997). In one study, college students who were undergoing a stressful series of exams were compared to a group of similar students relaxing during a time of no classes and no exams (Deinzer et al., 2000). The exam group tested significantly lower for immune system chemicals that help fight off disease than did the relaxing control group, even as long as 14 days after the exams were over. The suppression of immune system functioning by stress apparently can continue even after the stress itself is over.

One reason that the early stress reaction is helpful but prolonged stress is not might be that the stress reaction, in evolutionary terms, is really only meant for a

immune system
the system of cells, organs, and chemicals of the body that responds to attacks from diseases, infections, and injuries.

psychoneuroimmunology
the study of the effects of psychological factors such as stress, emotions, thoughts, and behavior on the immune system.

Simulation
Live! psych
Immune System

So stress actually increases the activity of the immune system? But then how does stress end up causing those diseases, like high blood pressure?

FIGURE 11.4 **Stress Duration and Illness**   In this graph, the risk of getting a cold virus increases greatly as the months of exposure to a stressor increase. While a stress reaction can be useful in its early phase, prolonged stress has a negative impact on the immune system, leaving the body vulnerable to illnesses such as a cold.
Source: Cohen et al., 1998.

short-term response, such as running from a predator (Sapolsky, 2004). That level of intense bodily and hormonal activity isn't really meant to go on and on, as it does for human beings in the modern, stress-filled life we now know. Humans experience the stress reaction over prolonged periods of times and in situations that are not necessarily life threatening, leading to a breakdown in the immune system. (See Figure 11.4.)

HEART DISEASE   Of course, anything that can weaken the immune system can have a negative effect on other bodily systems. The sympathetic system (active during stress) cannot work at the same time as the parasympathetic system, and vice versa. It is the parasympathetic system, remember, that is responsible for normal, day-to-day functioning of the body, including repairs and "system maintenance," so to speak. For example, stress has been shown to put people at a higher risk for heart attacks and strokes at least in part because the liver, which is activated during parasympathetic functioning, does not have a chance to clear the fat and cholesterol from the bloodstream, leading to clogged arteries and eventually the possibility of heart attacks. In one recent study, middle-aged men were questioned about stress, diet, and lifestyle factors and were examined for biological risk factors for heart disease: obesity, high blood sugar, high triglycerides (a type of fatty acid found in the blood), and low levels of HDL or "good" cholesterol. (See Figure 11.5.) Stress and the production of stress hormones were found to be strongly linked to all four factors: The more stress the workers were exposed to in their work environment and home life, the more likely they were to exhibit these risk factors (Brunner et al., 2002).

Stress can also lead to certain unhealthy behaviors, such as drinking alcohol; smoking; eating all the wrong, high-fat, high-calorie "comfort" foods; and the avoidance of exercise—all factors associated with poor health.

CANCER   Cancer is not one disease but rather a collection of diseases that can affect any part of the body. Unlike normal cells, which divide and reproduce according to genetic instructions and stop dividing according to those same instructions, cancer cells divide without stopping. The resulting tumors affect the normal functioning of the organs and systems they invade, causing organs to fail and eventually killing the organism. People, animals, and plants can have cancer.

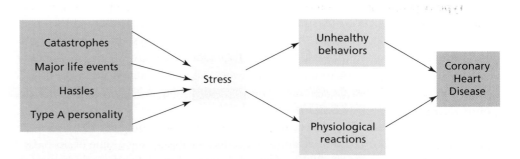

FIGURE 11.5 **Stress and Coronary Heart Disease**   The box on the left represents various sources of stress (Type A personality refers to someone who is ambitious, always working, and usually hostile). In addition to the physical reactions that accompany the stress reaction, an individual under stress may be more likely to engage in unhealthy behavior such as overeating, drinking alcohol or taking other kinds of drugs, avoiding exercise, and acting out in anger or frustration. This kind of behavior also contributes to an increased risk of coronary heart disease.

Although stress cannot give a person cancer, stress can have a suppressing effect on the immune system, making the unchecked growth of cancer more likely. In particular, an immune system cell called a **natural killer cell** has as its main functions the suppression of viruses and the destruction of tumor cells (Herberman & Ortaldo, 1981). Stress has been shown to depress the release of natural killer cells, making it more difficult for the body's systems to fight cancerous growths (Zorilla et al., 2001). In other research, stress has been linked to the accumulation of genetic errors that can lead to the formation of cancer cells and tumors: Stress causes the release of hormones that, over time, can cause mistakes in the instructions given by the genes to the cells of the body. As these mistakes "pile up" over the years, cells can begin to grow out of control, causing the growth of tumors and possibly cancer (Kiecolt-Glaser et al., 2002).

The physical effects of stress on the body and the immune system are only part of the picture of the influence of stress in daily life. The next section looks at the psychological impact of stress on health and well-being.

THE PSYCHOLOGY OF STRESS: HOW PERSONALITY AND STRESS ARE RELATED

11.9   *What is the relationship between stress and personality?*

Even as long ago as the early 1930s, psychologists have had evidence that personality characteristics are a major factor in predicting health. A longitudinal study begun in 1932 (Lehr & Thomae, 1987) found that personality was almost as important to longevity (how long people live) as genetic, physical, and lifestyle factors. Other researchers have found that people who live to be very old—into their nineties and even over 100 years—tend to be relaxed, easygoing, cheerful, and active. People who have opposite personality traits such as aggressiveness, stubbornness, inflexibility, and tenseness typically do not live as long as the average life expectancy (Levy et al., 2002).

Those personality traits are some of the factors associated with two personality types that have been related to how people deal with stress and the influence of certain personality characteristics on coronary heart disease.

TYPE A AND TYPE B   In 1974, medical doctors Meyer Freidman and Ray Rosenman published a book titled *Type A Behavior and Your Heart.* The book was the result of studies spanning three decades of research into the influence of certain personality characteristics and coronary heart disease (Friedman & Kasanin, 1943; Friedman & Rosenman, 1959; Rosenman et al., 1975). Since then, numerous researchers have explored the link between what Friedman called Type A and Type B personalities. Type A people are workaholics—they are very competitive, ambitious, hate to waste time, and are easily annoyed. There is a constant sense of pressure and a strong tendency to try to do several things at once. Often successful but frequently unsatisfied, they always seem to want to go faster and do more, and they get easily upset over small things. A typical Type A finds it difficult to relax and do nothing—Type A people take work with them on vacation, a laptop to the beach, and do business over the phone in the car.

In 1961, the *Western Collaborative Group Study* (Rosenman et al., 1975) assessed 3,500 men and followed them for eight years. For example, participants were asked to agree or disagree with statements such as "I can relax without guilt," in which strong agreement indicate a Type B personality. The results were that Type A men were three times more likely to develop heart disease than Type B men. Type B people are not that competitive or driven, tend to be easygoing and slow to anger, and seem relaxed and at peace. Type B people are more likely to take a book to the beach to cover up their face than to actually read the book. (See Figure 11.6.)

natural killer cell
immune system cell responsible for suppressing viruses and destroying tumor cells.

Type A personality
person who is ambitious, time conscious, extremely hardworking, and tends to have high levels of hostility and anger as well as being easily annoyed.

Type B personality
person who is relaxed and laid-back, less driven and competitive than Type A, and slow to anger.

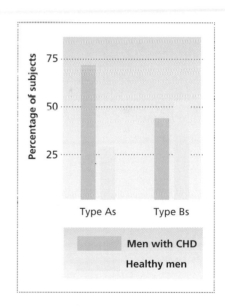

FIGURE 11.6   **Personality and Coronary Heart Disease**   The two bars on the left represent men with Type A personalities. Notice that within the Type A men, there are more than twice as many who suffer from coronary heart disease as those who are healthy. The two bars on the right represent men with Type B personalities. Far more Type B personalities are healthy than Type A personalities, and there are almost twice as many Type A personalities suffering from heart disease as Type B personalities.
Source: Miller et al., 1991.

Although Type A men and women may be successful in the world of business, their anger and hostility put them at high risk of coronary heart disease. How would anger and hostility be able to affect the heart?

Experiment
Live!psych
Stress/Health

What about people ▶ who don't blow their top but try to keep everything in instead? Wouldn't that be bad for a person's health?

Type C personality
pleasant but repressed person, who tends to internalize his or her anger and anxiety and who finds expressing emotions difficult.

The *Framingham Heart Study* found that the risk of coronary heart disease for women who work and are also Type A is four times that of Type B working women (Eaker & Castelli, 1988). Other research has narrowed the key factors in Type A personality and heart disease to one characteristic: hostility* (Frederickson et al., 1999; Matthews et al., 2004; Williams, 1999; Williams et al., 1980). Williams and his colleagues used the *Minnesota Multiphasic Personality Inventory*, a personality test that looks for certain characteristics that include the level of hostility. LINK to Chapter Twelve: Theories of Personality, p. 470. In this study, 424 patients who had undergone exploratory surgery for coronary heart disease were examined, and the presence of heart disease was related both to being Type A and to being hostile, with hostility being the more significant factor in the hardening of the arteries to the heart (Williams et al., 1980).

There are numerous studies supporting the link between hostility and increased risk of coronary heart disease. A study of hostility levels and risk factors for heart disease in over 4,000 young adults found that increases in hostility over a five-year follow-up study were associated with a rise in high blood pressure, one of the major risk factors of heart disease (Markovitz et al., 1997). Another study of anger in young men and their risk for premature heart disease found that over a period of slightly more than three decades, the young men who had exhibited high levels of hostility in their youth were far more likely to develop premature cardiovascular disease, particularly heart attacks, than were those men who had lower levels of anger and hostility (Chang et al., 2002). Similar studies found that hostility in college-aged male and females was significantly related to increased risk of heart disease, particularly if levels of hostility rose in middle age (Brondolo et al., 2003; Siegler et al., 2003).

Even children may not escape the hostility–heart disease link. A recent study has found that children and adolescents who scored high on assessments of hostility were more likely to show physical changes such as obesity, resistance to insulin, high blood pressure, and elevated levels of triglycerides three years after the initial measurements of hostility had been made (Raikkonen et al., 2003).

What about people who don't blow their top but try to keep everything in instead? Wouldn't that be bad for a person's health?

TYPE C   A third personality type was identified by researchers Temoshok and Dreher (1992) as being associated with a higher incidence of cancer. Type C people tend to be very pleasant and try to keep the peace but find it difficult to express emotions, especially negative ones. They tend to internalize their anger and often experience a sense of despair over the loss of a loved one or a loss of hope. They are often lonely. These personality characteristics are strongly associated with cancer, and people who have cancer and this personality type often have thicker cancerous tumors as well (Eysenck, 1994; Temoshok & Dreher, 1992). Just as the stress of hostility puts the cardiovascular systems of Type A people at greater risk, the internalized negative emotions of the Type C personality may increase the levels of harmful stress hormones, weaken the immune system, and slow recovery.

THE HARDY PERSONALITY   Not all Type A people are prone to heart disease. There are some people who actually seem to thrive on stress instead of letting stress wear

---

*Hostility: feelings of conflict, anger, and ill will that are long lasting.

them down. These people have what is called the **hardy personality**, a term first coined by psychologist Suzanne Kobasa (1979). Hardy people (call them "Type H") differ from ordinary, hostile Type A people and others who suffer more ill effects due to stress in three ways:

- Hardy people have a deep sense of *commitment* to their values, beliefs, sense of identity, work, and family life.

- Hardy people also feel that they are in *control* of their lives and what happens to them.

- Hardy people tend to interpret events in primary appraisal differently than people who are not hardy. When things go wrong, they do not see a frightening problem to be avoided but instead a *challenge* to be met and answered.

"He always times '60 minutes.'"
©The New Yorker Collection 1983 Mischa Richter from cartoonbank.com. All Rights Reserved

Why would those three characteristics lessen the negative impact of stress? Commitment makes a person more willing to make sacrifices and deal with hardships than if commitment were lacking. Think about it: Have you ever had a job that you hated? Every little frustration and every snag were very stressful, right? Now think about doing something you love to do. The frustrations and snags that inevitably come with any endeavor just don't seem quite as bad when you are doing something you really want to do, do they?

As for control, uncontrollability is one of the major factors cited as increasing stress, as was discussed earlier in this chapter. Seeing events as challenges rather than problems also changes the level of stress experienced, a difference similar to that felt when riding a roller coaster: If riding the coaster is your own idea, it's fun; if someone makes you ride it, it's not fun.

The four personality types discussed so far could be summed up this way: If life gives you lemons,

- Type A people get enraged and throw the lemons back, having a minor heart attack while doing so.

- Type C people don't say anything but fume inside where no one can see.

- Type B people gather all the lemons and make lemonade.

- Hardy people gather the lemons, make lemonade, sell it, turn it into a franchise business, and make millions.

EXPLANATORY STYLE: OPTIMISTS AND PESSIMISTS   In addition to personality type, there are other personal factors that have an influence on people's reactions to stressors. One of these factors is the attitude that people have toward the things that happen to them in life.

Optimists are people who always tend to look for positive outcomes. For an optimist, a glass is half full, whereas for a pessimist, the glass is half empty. **Pessimists** seem to expect the worst to happen. Researchers have found that optimism is associated with longer life and increased immune system functioning. Mayo Clinic researchers conducted a longitudinal study of optimists and pessimists (as assessed by a scale) over a period of 30 years (Maruta et al., 2002). The results for pessimists were not good: They had a much higher death rate than did the optimists, and those that were still living in 1994 had more problems with physical and emotional health, more pain, less ability to take part in social activities, and less energy than optimists. The optimists had a 50 percent lower risk of premature death and were more calm, peaceful, and happy than the pessimists (Maruta et al., 2002). An earlier study linked being optimistic to higher levels of helper T cells (immune system cells that direct and

Type Z behavior
©The New Yorker Collection 1987 Donald Reilly from cartoonbank.com. All Rights Reserved.

hardy personality
a person who seems to thrive on stress but lacks the anger and hostility of the Type A personality

optimists
people who expect positive outcomes.

pessimists
people who expect negative outcomes.

increase the functioning of the immune system) and higher levels of natural killer cells, the body's antivirus, anticancer cells (Segerstrom et al., 1998).

Martin Seligman is a social learning psychologist who developed the concept of *learned helplessness* (LINK) *to Chapter Five: Learning, p. 194,* and began the positive psychology movement. Seligman (2002) has outlined four ways in which optimism may affect how long a person lives:

1. Optimists are less likely to develop learned helplessness, the tendency to stop trying to achieve a goal that has been blocked in the past.

2. Optimists are more likely than pessimists to take care of their health by preventive measures (such as going to the doctor regularly and eating right) because they believe that their actions make a difference in what happens to them. (Remember, this is a characteristic of hardy people as well.)

3. Optimists are far less likely than pessimists to become depressed and depression is associated with mortality because of the effect of depression on the immune system.

4. Optimists have more effectively functioning immune systems than pessimists, perhaps because they experience less psychological stress.

Seligman (1998) has also found that optimists are more successful in their life endeavors than pessimists. Optimistic politicians win more elections, optimistic students get better grades, and optimistic athletes win more contests.

Whoa—optimistic students get better grades? How do I become an optimist? Sign me up! Optimism is mostly a matter of controlling mood or emotional reactions to situations. Psychiatrist Dr. Susan Vaughan (2000) has some good advice for optimistic people who want to keep a positive outlook:

• *Alternative thinking:* Optimists tend to take bad things that happen less personally, coming up with alternative explanations for why the bad thing happened. For example, optimists tend to attribute poor exam grades to the difficulty of that particular material or to not having enough time to study. They appraise it as a challenge and assume that they will perform more successfully in the future.

• *Downward social comparison:* Many people make themselves feel better by comparing their performance to that of less competent others, making them feel better and protecting self-esteem. Optimists use *downward social comparison* frequently.

• *Relaxation:* Optimists use relaxation as a way to improve mood, such as exercising, meditating, or reading a good book.

HOW TO BECOME AN OPTIMISTIC THINKER The way to become an optimist is to monitor one's own thinking. Recognition of negative thoughts is the first step, followed by disputing those same negative thoughts (Seligman, 2002). The problem is that most people don't really think about their thoughts or characterize them as negative or pessimistic, which means that the damaging effects of such thinking are left uncontrolled. Here's a plan to follow to become an optimistic thinker:

1. When a bad mood strikes, stop and think about what just went through your head.

2. When you've recognized the negative statements, treat them as if they came from someone else—someone who is trying to make your life miserable. Think about the damage the statement is doing to you.

3. Argue with those thoughts. Challenge each negative statement and replace it with a more positive statement.

▶ Whoa—optimistic students get better grades? How do I become an optimist? Sign me up!

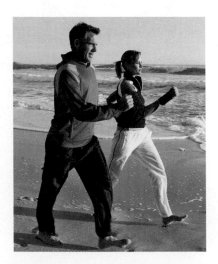

Regular exercise increases the functioning of the immune system and helps give people a sense of control over their health. Having a sense of control decreases feelings of stress, which also helps the immune system to function well.

Example:

1. "I'll never get this term paper finished, it's too hard and there's so much going on that it's impossible!" What words in this statement makes it pessimistic? "Never" is a long time. Why is it too hard? Is it really impossible, or just difficult? Is it just one part of the paper that seems so hard, or is it the whole thing?

2. That statement isn't going to help me at all, it just makes me feel worse and that makes me unmotivated to work on the paper.

3. I can finish the term paper. I'm just going to have to devote more time to working on it. I can make a timetable for finishing the different parts of the paper and stop spending so much time watching television and escaping into other activities that can wait until the paper is finished. I've been in situations like this before and managed, so I can manage now, too.

Notice that the third way of thinking is much more positive and hopeful. It includes ways to get around what seemed too hard or impossible in the negative statement. Essentially, the last step in becoming a more optimistic thinker is to learn to argue with yourself and correct distorted or faulty thinking.

How can I recognize distorted thinking when it's my own thoughts in the first place? Recognizing faulty thinking can be difficult at first. The following questions may help people to hone in on negative thinking:

1. In thinking about the thoughts you have had in the last few hours, how many of them were negative thoughts? How could you change those thoughts to be more positive?

2. When thinking about people you know who make a lot of negative self-statements or who are always minimizing their efforts or putting themselves down, how does their behavior make you feel? How do you think their behavior makes them feel?

◀ How can I recognize distorted thinking when it's my own thoughts in the first place?

PRACTICE **QUIZ:** HOW MUCH DO YOU REMEMBER?

Pick the best answer.

1. In the _____ stage of the GAS, the person may actually start to feel better.
   a. alarm
   b. resistance
   c. exhaustion
   d. termination

2. The activation of the immune system response by stress differs from the activation of that system by illness in that
   a. illness activates areas in the brain first.
   b. stress increases the release of natural killer cells.
   c. stress activates a different immune response than does illness.
   d. stress activates areas in the brain first.

3. Adam is very ambitious and driven to succeed. He is easily angered, always wants to be working, and finds it hard to relax. According to research, Adam
   a. is at a high risk for coronary heart disease.
   b. is a hardy personality.
   c. is a Type B personality.
   d. is a Type C personality.

4. Which of the following is NOT one of the three "C's" of the hardy personality?
   a. commitment
   b. callousness
   c. control
   d. challenge

5. Optimism has been associated with all of the following except
   a. taking care of one's health.
   b. increased rates of learned helplessness.
   c. lower rates of depression.
   d. healthy immune systems.

burnout
negative changes in thoughts, emotions, and behavior as a result of prolonged stress or frustration.

acculturative stress
stress resulting from the need to change and adapt a person's ways to the majority culture.

social support system
the network of family, friends, neighbors, coworkers, and others who can offer support, comfort, or aid to a person in need.

THE SOCIAL FACTORS IN STRESS

11.10 *What is the relationship between stress and social factors?*

As stated earlier, much of the stress in everyday life comes from having to deal with other people and with the rules of social interaction. Overcrowding, for example, is a common source of stress and may be one reason for the increasing rise of *road rage*, or the tendency for drivers to become excessively enraged by ordinary traffic frustrations, sometimes resulting in serious injuries, assaults, and even death (AAA Foundation for Traffic Safety, 1997). Two of the more prominent social factors in creating stressful living conditions are both economically based: poverty and job stress.

POVERTY   Living in poverty is stressful for many reasons. Lack of sufficient money to provide the basic necessities of life can lead to many stressors for both adults and children: overcrowding, lack of medical care, increased rates of disabilities due to poor prenatal care, noisy environments, increased rates of illness (such as asthma in childhood) and violence, and substance abuse (Aligne et al., 2000; Bracey, 1997; Leroy & Symes, 2001; Park et al., 2002; Renchler, 1993; Rouse, 1998; Schmitz et al., 2001).

JOB STRESS   Even if a person has a job and is making an adequate salary, there are stresses associated with the workplace that add to daily stressors. Some of the typical sources of stress in the workplace include the workload, a lack of variety or meaningfulness in work, lack of control over decisions, long hours, poor physical work conditions, and lack of job security (Murphy, 1995).

Stress at work can result in the same symptoms as stress from any other source: headaches, high blood pressure, indigestion, and other physical symptoms; anxiety, irritability, anger, depression, and other psychological symptoms; and behavioral symptoms such as overeating, drug use, poor job performance, or changes in family relationships (Anschuetz, 1999).

There are times when I ▶ **feel like I've just had it with school and all the work the teachers pile on—is that something like workplace stress?**

There are times when I feel like I've just had it with school and all the work the teachers pile on—is that something like workplace stress?

Burnout   One of the more serious effects of workplace stress is a condition called burnout. **Burnout** can be defined as negative changes in thoughts, emotions, and behavior as a result of prolonged stress or frustration (Miller & Smith, 1993). Symptoms of burnout are extreme dissatisfaction, pessimism, lowered job satisfaction, and a desire to

Poverty can lead to many conditions that increase the degree of stress experienced by both adults and children. These children, for example, may face an increased risk of malnutrition, illness, and exposure to violence because of the conditions under which they must live.

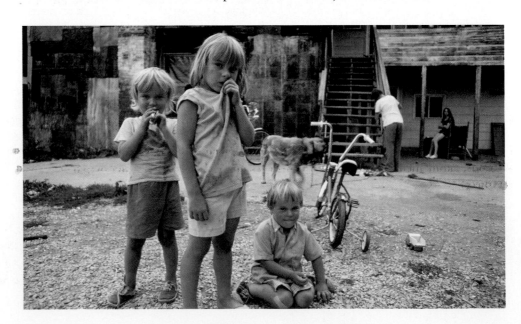

quit. Although burnout is most commonly associated with job stress, college students can also suffer from burnout when the stresses of college life—term papers, exams, assignments and the like—become overwhelming.

HOW CULTURE AFFECTS STRESS   When a person from one culture must live in another culture, that person may experience a great deal of stress. *Acculturation* means the process of adapting to a new or different culture, often the dominant culture (Sodowsky et al., 1991). The stress resulting from the need to change and adapt to the dominant or majority culture is called **acculturative stress** (Berry & Kim, 1998; Berry & Sam, 1997).

The method that a minority person chooses to enter into the majority culture can also have an impact on the degree of stress that minority person will experience (Berry & Kim, 1988). One method is *integration*: The individual tries to maintain a sense of the original cultural identity while also trying to form a positive relationship with members of the dominant culture. For example, an integrated person will maintain a lot of original cultural traditions within the home and with immediate family members, but will dress like the majority culture and adopt some of those characteristics as well. For people who choose integration, acculturative stress is usually low (Ward & Rana-Deuba, 1999).

In *assimilation*, the minority person gives up the old cultural identity and completely adopts the majority culture's ways. In the early days of the United States, many immigrants were assimilated into the mainstream American culture, even changing their names to sound more "American." Assimilation leads to moderate levels of stress, most likely due to the loss of cultural patterns and rejection by other members of the minority culture who have not chosen assimilation (LaFromboise et al., 1993; Lay & Nguyen, 1998).

Separation is a pattern in which the minority person rejects the majority culture's ways and tries to maintain the original cultural identity. Members of the minority culture refuse to learn the language of the dominant culture, and they live where others from their culture live, socializing only with others from their original culture. Separation results in a fairly high degree of stress, and that stress will be even higher if the separation is forced (by discrimination from the majority group) rather than voluntary (self-imposed withdrawal from the majority culture).

The greatest acculturative stress will most likely be experienced by people who have chosen to be *marginalized*, neither maintaining contact with the original culture nor joining the majority culture. They essentially live on the "margins" of both cultures without feeling or becoming part of either culture. Marginalized individuals do not have the security of the familiar culture of origin or the acceptance of the majority culture and may suffer a loss of identity and feel alienated from others (Roysircai-Sodowsky & Maestas, 2000). Obviously, marginalized people have little in the way of a social support system to help them deal with both everyday stresses and major life changes.

I hear the term social support system all the time now. Exactly what is it?

THE POSITIVE BENEFITS OF SOCIAL SUPPORT   A **social support system** is the network of friends, family members, neighbors, coworkers, and others who can offer help to a person in need. That help can take the form of advice, physical or monetary support, information, emotional support, love and affection, or companionship. Research has consistently shown that having a good social support system is of critical importance in a person's ability to cope with stressors: People with good social support systems are less likely to die from illnesses or injuries than those without such support (Kulik & Mahler, 1989, 1993). Marriage, itself a form of social support, is a good predictor of healthy aging and longevity (Gardner & Oswald, 2004; Vaillant, 2002). Social support has been found to have a positive effect on the immune system (Holt-Lunstad et al., 2003) and improves the mental

(Top) This Buddhist group is celebrating Songkran, the New Year, by performing their cultural ritual of pouring water over their elder's palms. Although they are wearing clothing typical of people living in Los Angeles, California, where the ceremony is taking place, they still maintain some of their old cultural traditions.
(Bottom) Miss Cambodian American appears in a parade in California. She is also fully integrated into the American culture of beauty pageants but still maintains her ethnic identity as a Cambodian American.

◀ I hear the term social support system all the time now. Exactly what is it?

College is often stressful for a young adult who is away from home for the first time. This young woman is being consoled by her fellow students. Social support is one of the most important keys to handling the stresses of any situation. What are some other things the young woman could do to ease her homesickness?

health and physical functioning of people who have *lupus*, a chronic inflammatory disease that can affect nearly any part of the body (Sutcliffe et al., 1999; Ward et al., 1999) as well as those with cancer and HIV (Carver & Antoni, 2004; Gonzalez et al., 2004).

Social support can make a stressor seem less threatening because people with such support know that there is help available. Having people to talk to about one's problems reduces the physical symptoms of stress—talking about frightening or frustrating events with others can help people think more realistically about the threat, for example, and talking with people who have had similar experiences can help put the event into perspective. L I N K *to Chapter Fifteen: Psychological Therapies, pp. 576–577.* The negative emotions of loneliness and depression, which are less likely to occur with someone who has social support, can adversely affect one's ability to cope (Beehr et al., 2000; Weisse, 1992). Positive emotions, on the other hand, have a decidedly beneficial effect on health, helping people recover from stressful experiences more quickly and effectively (Tugade & Fredrickson, 2004). Positive emotions are more likely to occur in the presence of friends and family.

How people think about a stressor is also a powerful influence on their ability to cope, as the next section will discuss.

PRACTICE QUIZ: HOW MUCH DO YOU REMEMBER?

Pick the best answer.

1. Which of the following is NOT a typical source of stress in the workplace?
   a. heavy workload
   b. lack of variety
   c. lack of shift work
   d. lack of job security

2. Which of the following is NOT a symptom of burnout:
   a. pessimism
   b. dissatisfaction
   c. optimism
   d. desire to quit

3. Larysa moved from Ukraine to the United States. She learned to speak and write English, changed her last name so that it would sound more "American," and no longer maintains any of her old culture's styles of dress or customs. Larysa has used which method of entering the majority culture?
   a. integration   c. separation
   b. assimilation   d. marginalization

4. Social support
   a. has a positive benefit on health.
   b. can improve the physical functioning of cancer patients.
   c. can improve the physical functioning of people with HIV.
   d. shows all of the above.

Answers: 1-c, 2-c, 3-b, 4-d.

Coping With Stress

I have exams and my ▶ job and my relationship to worry about, so I feel pretty stressed out—how do people deal with all the stress they face every day?

I have exams and my job and my relationship to worry about, so I feel pretty stressed out—how do people deal with all the stress they face every day? So far, this chapter has talked about what stress is and the factors that can magnify the effects of stress, as well as the effects of stress on a person's physical health. Part of dealing with stress is in knowing those kinds of things so that changes can be made in the factors that are controllable. **Coping strategies** are actions that people can take to master, tolerate, reduce, or minimize the effects of stressors, and they can include both behavioral strategies and psychological strategies.

11.11   *What are two ways that people can deal with stress?*

PROBLEM-FOCUSED COPING

One type of coping strategy is to work on eliminating or changing the stressor itself. When people try to eliminate the source of a stress or reduce its impact through their own actions, it is called **problem-focused coping** (Folkman & Lazarus, 1980; Lazarus,

1993). For example, a student might have a problem understanding a particular professor. The professor is knowledgeable but has trouble explaining the concepts of the course in a way that this student can understand. Problem-focused coping might include talking to the professor after class, asking fellow students to clarify the concepts, getting a tutor, or forming a study group with other students who are also having difficulty to pool the group's resources.

EMOTION-FOCUSED COPING

Problem-focused coping can work quite well but is not the only method people can use. Most people use both problem-focused coping and **emotion-focused coping** to successfully deal with controllable stressful events (Folkman & Lazarus, 1980; Lazarus, 1993; Stowell et al., 2001). Emotion-focused coping is a strategy that involves changing the way a person feels or emotionally reacts to a stressor. This reduces the emotional impact of the stressor and makes it possible to deal with the problem more effectively. For example, the student who is faced with a professor who isn't easy to understand might share his concerns with a friend, talking it through until calm enough to tackle the problem in a more direct manner. Emotion-focused coping also works for stressors that are uncontrollable and for which problem-focused coping is not possible. Someone using emotion-focused coping may decide to view the stressor as a challenge rather than a threat, decide that the problem is a minor one, write down concerns in a journal, or even ignore the problem altogether.

Ignore it? But won't that just make matters worse? True, ignoring a problem is not a good strategy when there is something a person can actively do about solving the problem. But when it is not possible to change or eliminate the stressor, or when worrying about the stressor can be a problem itself, ignoring the problem is not a bad idea. Researchers working with people who had suffered heart attacks found that those people who worried about a future attack were more likely to suffer from symptoms of post-traumatic stress, such as nightmares and poor sleep (both factors that increase the risk of a future heart attack), than were the people who tried to ignore their worries (Ginzburg et al., 2003).

Using humor can also be a form of emotion-focused coping, as the old saying "laughter is the best medicine" suggests. A recent study on the effects of laughter found that laughter actually boosted the action of the immune system by increasing the work of natural killer cells (cells that attack viruses in the body). In this study, participants were shown a humor video for one hour. Blood samples were taken 10 minutes before the viewing, 30 minutes into the viewing, 30 minutes after viewing, and 12 hours after viewing the humor video. There were significant increases in natural killer cell activity and nearly half a dozen other immune system cells and systems, with some effects lasting the full 12 hours after the video ended (Berk et al., 2001).

Emotion-focused coping is highly related to several forms of psychological defenses first proposed by Sigmund Freud, as the next section discusses.

PSYCHOLOGICAL DEFENSE MECHANISMS

11.12   *What are the psychological defense mechanisms?*

In Freud's writings on psychoanalysis, he stated that when people experience anxiety (stress) from conflicts between the demands of the body's needs and desires and society's rules for proper behavior, there are certain unconscious* distortions of thought that

This young woman is writing about her feelings and experiences in her diary. Writing about feelings in this way can be a form of emotion-focused coping.

◄ Ignore it? But won't that just make matters worse?

coping strategies
actions that people can take to master, tolerate, reduce, or minimize the effects of stressors.

problem-focused coping
coping strategies that try to eliminate the source of a stress or reduce its impact through direct actions.

emotion-focused coping
coping strategies that change the impact of a stressor by changing the emotional reaction to the stressor.

---

*Unconscious: in Freud's theory, the part of the mind that holds conflicts, urges, and thoughts of which the person is not aware.

"I'm sorry, I'm not speaking to anyone tonight. My defense mechanisms seem to be out of order."

This man is practicing Zen yoga meditation. Meditation increases relaxation and helps to lower blood pressure and muscle tension.

psychological defense mechanisms
unconscious distortions of a person's perception of reality that reduce stress and anxiety.

meditation
mental series of exercises meant to refocus attention and achieve a trancelike state of consciousness.

concentrative meditation
form of meditation in which a person focuses the mind on some repetitive or unchanging stimulus so that the mind can be cleared of disturbing thoughts and the body can experience relaxation.

can protect their sense of self from that anxiety (Freud, 1915). LINK *to Chapter Twelve: Theories of Personality, p. 448.* These unconscious distortions of the perception of reality are called **psychological defense mechanisms** and were further explained by Freud's daughter, Anna Freud (1946). Although Freudian theory has fallen in and out of favor over the last century, the concept of these defense mechanisms has remained quite useful in clinical psychology as a way of describing people's defensive behavior and irrational thinking.

Table 11.3 lists, defines, and gives examples of some of the more common defense mechanisms.

It may have become obvious that nearly all of these techniques are forms of emotion-focused coping strategies, although their misuse can easily lead to more problems, as many of Freud's patients discovered.

Unlike much of the rest of Freud's psychoanalytic theory, research in cognitive psychology has uncovered some scientific support for the concept of unconscious coping mechanisms at work when people experience stress (Cramer, 2000). Although many psychologists in the 1970s and early 1980s rejected the idea of the unconscious mind's influence on conscious behavior, recent studies in cognitive perception have found support for the influence of experiences for which there is no conscious memory on task performance (Dehaene et al., 2001; Greenwald et al., 1996; Kihlstrom, 1987). These studies deal with the phenomenon of implicit memory. LINK *to Chapter Six: Memory, p. 221.* Implicit memory, also called procedural memory, is a form of long-term memory in which habits, skills, conditioned responses, emotional associations, and other well-learned procedures are stored. These memories affect conscious behavior, as in being able to balance on a bicycle, but are not stored in conscious awareness and cannot easily be brought into conscious awareness.

MEDITATION AS A COPING MECHANISM

11.13 *How can meditation help relieve stress?*

Meditation is a mental series of exercises meant to refocus attention and achieve a trancelike state of consciousness. LINK *to Chapter Four: Consciousness, p. 126.* Meditation can produce a state of relaxation that can aid in coping with the physiological reactions to a stressful situation.

CONCENTRATIVE MEDITATION Have you ever found yourself staring out into space, or at some little spot on the wall or table, only to realize that your mind has been a complete blank for the last several minutes?

The state just described is really nothing more than **concentrative meditation**, the form of meditation best known to the general public. In concentrative meditation, the goal is to focus the mind on some repetitive or unchanging stimulus (such as a spot or the sound of one's own heart beating) so that the mind can forget daily hassles and problems and the body can relax. In fact, Benson (Benson, 1975; Benson et al., 1974a, 1974b) found that meditation produces a state of relaxation in which blood pressure is lowered, alpha waves (brain waves associated with relaxation) are increased, and the amounts of melatonin secreted at night (the hormone that helps induce sleep) are increased.

Some people say that if you meditate for only twenty minutes a day, you don't have to sleep at night. That would be nice—think how much more could be

TABLE 11.3 **THE PSYCHOLOGICAL DEFENSE MECHANISMS**

Defense Mechanism and Definition	Example
Denial: refusal to recognize or acknowledge a threatening situation.	Ben is an alcoholic who denies being an alcoholic.
Repression: "pushing" threatening or conflicting events or situations out of conscious memory.	Elise, who was sexually abused as a child, cannot remember the abuse at all.
Rationalization: making up acceptable excuses for unacceptable behavior.	"If I don't have breakfast, I can have that piece of cake later on without hurting my diet."
Projection: placing one's own unacceptable thoughts onto others, as if the thoughts belonged to them and not to oneself.	Keisha is attracted to her sister's husband but denies this and believes the husband is attracted to her.
Reaction formation: forming an emotional reaction or attitude that is the opposite of one's threatening or unacceptable actual thoughts.	Matt is unconsciously attracted to Ben but outwardly voices an extreme hatred of homosexuals.
Displacement: expressing feelings that would be threatening if directed at the real target onto a less threatening substitute target.	Sandra gets reprimanded by her boss and goes home to angrily pick a fight with her husband.
Regression: falling back on childlike patterns as a way of coping with stressful situations.	Four-year-old Jeff starts wetting his bed after his parents bring home a new baby.
Identification: trying to become like someone else to deal with one's anxiety.	Marie really admires Suzy, the most popular girl in school, and tries to copy her behavior and dress.
Compensation (substitution): when a person tries to make up for areas in which a lack is perceived by becoming superior in some other area.	Reggie is not good at athletics, so he puts all of his energies into becoming an academic scholar.
Sublimation: turning socially unacceptable urges into socially acceptable behavior.	Alain, who is very aggressive, becomes a professional hockey player.

accomplished with those extra hours. Unfortunately, although certain meditation groups do make some rather wild claims for meditation, research has shown none of them to be true (Murphy & Donavan, 1997). What research does show is that concentrative meditation is a good way to relax and lower blood pressure in adolescents and adults, men and women, and both whites and African Americans (Barnes et al., 1997; Schneider et al., 1995; Wenneberg et al., 1997). It isn't the only way, as reading a good book or taking a warm bath also produces relaxation. Even simply resting for the same amount of time as one might meditate can be just as relaxing. The advantage of meditation is that people can do it almost anywhere, even in the classroom just before a big test. (It would be a little difficult to take a warm bath then.)

Other research has suggested that concentrative meditation can reduce the levels of chronic pain (Kabat-Zinn et al., 1986), reduce the symptoms of anxiety, depression, and hostility (Kabat Zinn et al., 1985), and reduce stress levels in cancer patients (Speca et al., 2000). Reducing stress levels in cancer patients through meditation will increase the likelihood of recovery and reduce the incidence of recurrence.

denial
psychological defense mechanism in which the person refuses to acknowledge or recognize a threatening situation.

repression
psychological defense mechanism in which the person refuses to consciously remember a threatening or unacceptable event, instead pushing those events into the unconscious mind.

rationalization
psychological defense mechanism in which a person invents acceptable excuses for unacceptable behavior.

projection
psychological defense mechanism in which unacceptable or threatening impulses or feelings are seen as originating with someone else, usually the target of the impulses or feelings.

reaction formation
psychological defense mechanism in which a person forms an opposite emotional or behavioral reaction to the way he or she really feels to keep those true feelings hidden from self and others.

displacement
redirecting feelings from a threatening target to a less threatening one.

regression
psychological defense mechanism in which a person falls back on childlike patterns of responding in reaction to stressful situations.

identification
defense mechanism in which a person tries to become like someone else to deal with anxiety.

compensation (substitution)
defense mechanism in which a person makes up for inferiorities in one area by becoming superior in another area.

sublimation
channeling socially unacceptable impulses and urges into socially acceptable behavior.

receptive meditation
form of meditation in which a person attempts to become aware of everything in immediate conscious experience, or an expansion of consciousness.

RECEPTIVE MEDITATION   The other kind of meditation is less well known and not as easily achieved. It is called **receptive meditation** and involves trying to expand consciousness outward. The best description of what this is like is to think about a time when you were overawed by nature. Perhaps you were standing at the ocean's edge on a starry night and became suddenly aware of how vast the universe really is. Or perhaps you were walking in the woods and listening to all the little sounds of the birds and animals surrounding you. Your attention was focused outward rather than inward, and this is similar to the state that this type of meditation tries to achieve.

THE EFFECTS OF MEDITATION   Regardless of which form of meditation people choose to try, the effects are similar (Murphy & Donavan, 1997). Meditation for only 20 minutes can produce lowered blood pressure in people with hypertension (high blood pressure). It can calm anxiety, help people get to sleep, and help people deal with stress.

HOW CULTURE AFFECTS COPING

11.14   *What are the cultural influences on stress?*

Imagine this scene: You are driving out in the country when you come upon an elderly man working on a large wooden box, polishing it with great care. You stop to talk to the man and find out that the box is his own coffin, and he spends his days getting it ready, tending to it with great care. He isn't frightened of dying and doesn't feel strange about polishing his own coffin. How would you react?

If you were from the same rural area of Vietnam as the elderly man, you would probably think nothing strange is going on. For elderly people in the Vietnamese culture, thoughts of death and the things that go along with dying, such as a coffin, are not as stressful as they are to people from Western cultures. In fact, *stress* isn't all that common a term in Vietnamese society compared to Western societies (Phan & Silove, 1999).

In the case of people living in Vietnam and even Vietnamese immigrants to other countries, mental illness is explained by an imbalance between the male and female elements of a person, or by a loss of soul, evil spirits, or a weakening of the nerves. Coping with stress in Vietnamese culture may include rituals, consulting a fortune-teller, or eating certain foods (Phan & Silove, 1999).

Obviously, culture is an important factor in the kinds of coping strategies an individual may adopt and even in determining the degree of stress that is experienced.

These Peruvian villagers in a cemetery are honoring their loved ones who have passed away. The Day of the Dead is not only a celebration of the lives of those who have passed on but also a celebration for the living, who use this holiday to gain a sense of control over one of life's most uncontrollable events—death itself. What rituals or ceremonies do people of other cultures use to cope with death?

Mental health professionals should make an effort to include an assessment of a person's cultural background as well as immediate circumstances when dealing with adjustment problems due to stress.

HOW RELIGION AFFECTS COPING

11.15 *Can being religious help people cope with stress?*

A belief in a higher power can also be a source of great comfort in times of stress. There are several ways that religious beliefs can affect the degree of stress people experience and the ability to cope with that stress (Hill & Butter, 1995; Pargament, 1997).

First, most people who hold strong religious beliefs belong to a religious organization and attend regular religious functions, such as services at a synagogue, mosque, temple, or church. This membership can be a vital part of a person's social support system. People do not feel alone in their struggle, both literally because of the people who surround them in their religious community and spiritually because of the intangible presence of their deity (Koenig et al., 1999).

Another way that religion helps people cope involves the rituals and rites that help people feel better about personal weaknesses, failures, or feelings of inadequacy (Koenig et al., 2001). These include rituals such as confession of sins or prayer services during times of stress. Finally, religious beliefs can give meaning to things that otherwise seem to have no meaning or purpose, such as viewing death as a pathway to a paradise, or the destruction of one's home in a natural disaster as a reminder to place less attachment on material things.

Many religions also encourage healthy behavior and eating habits through their prohibitions on such activities as overeating, drinking alcohol, smoking, drug use, and sexual activity outside marriage. Some research even suggests that people with religious commitments live longer than those who have no such beliefs, although this is correlational research and should not be interpreted as concluding that religious belief causes longer life expectancies (Hummer et al., 1999; Koenig et al., 1999; Strawbridge et al., 1997; Thoresen & Harris, 2002).

PRACTICE QUIZ: HOW MUCH DO YOU REMEMBER?

Pick the best answer.

1. When a person tries to cope by eliminating or changing the stressor directly, it is known as
   a. a defense mechanism.
   c. self-focused coping.
   b. problem-focused coping.
   d. emotion-focused coping.

2. Darrell is convinced that a woman supervisor in his office is very attracted to him, even though she has given him no outward signs of interest in him. He watches her frequently and makes excuses to be near her or to talk to her. He interprets everything she says as a veiled reference to her desire for him. If Darrell's supervisor actually has no romantic interest in him, we might conclude that Darrell is
   a. rationalizing.
   c. projecting.
   b. repressing.
   d. regressing.

3. Rusty drinks beer all day long, often passing out in a stupor after several hours of steady drinking. Yet he refuses to admit that he has a drinking problem, saying that "it's only beer" and continuing to drink. Rusty is most likely using which defense mechanism?
   a. denial
   c. displacement
   b. repression
   d. reaction formation

4. Kareem is relaxing in a chair with his eyes closed. As he sits quietly, he is focusing on the sound of his own breathing and clearing his mind of other thoughts. Kareem is practicing
   a. sensory deprivation.
   b. concentrative meditation.
   c. receptive meditation.
   d. implosive meditation.

5. Which of the following is NOT one of the ways that religion helps people reduce or cope with stress?
   a. Religion can provide a strong social support system.
   b. Religion includes rituals that can help people feel better about their failings.
   c. Most religions promote healthy lifestyles.
   d. Religion isolates people from those who are different.

Applying Psychology to Everyday Life: Focus on Wellness

11.16 *What are some ways to promote wellness in one's life?*

Wellness can be defined as the practice of behaviors and lifestyle choices that promote both physical and mental health. Here are some helpful hints on how to promote wellness in one's own life:

- *Exercise.* No one likes to admit it, but exercise is the best way to become healthier. Exercise makes the heart healthier, raises the body's metabolic rate to help maintain a healthy weight, raises good cholesterol and lowers bad cholesterol, strengthens bones, improves sleep quality, reduces tiredness, increases natural killer cell activity to help ward off viruses and cancer, and is a great way to reduce the effects of stress (Fiatarone et al., 1993; Manson et al., 2002).

- *Get involved with others.* The benefits of social support have already been highlighted in this chapter. Make some new friends or join a social organization. Make it a point to do things with other people. Have friends over to dinner or go out shopping with others.

- *Get some sleep.* Most people in the busy, hectic modern world simply do not get enough sleep. As discussed in Chapter Four, sleep serves to restore the body physically and provides a way to manage stress during dreaming. Try to get at least seven to eight hours of sleep each night, including weekends. Try to go to bed and get up at the same time every day to maintain your sleep–wake cycle. Sleep deprivation can lead to a lower production of natural killer cells, which are a necessary and vital part of the immune system (Irwin et al., 1994, 1996).

- *Eat healthy foods.* It's also very easy to eat all the wrong things in today's world. Fortunately, even fast-food restaurants are offering more salads and grilled items to promote healthier eating. Eat breakfast every day, making sure to include a good amount of protein in that meal. Protein in the morning helps improve concentration and alertness, and eating breakfast helps you to avoid overeating at lunch or dinner. Eating breakfast has even been shown to decrease the risk of stroke, obesity, and diabetes (Pereira et al., 2003). Be sure to include some healthy snacks at least twice a day.

- *Have some fun.* Playing is important! Schedule some time to just relax, play a game with a friend, read a book, or do something fun. Playing helps prevent burnout.

- *Manage your time.* One of the things that can create a lot of stress is feeling overwhelmed when there are lots of tasks to do. Make a list of the tasks you need to accomplish, putting the most important and urgent ones first. Check each item off the list as you finish it. This gives you a sense of control over your day's activities and rewards you with a sense of accomplishment each time you can check off an item.

- *Take a deep breath.* When feeling stressed, take a moment to cope. Take some deep breaths to help calm yourself and relax tension. If you're so stressed that you feel like crying, find a quiet, private place and cry—crying can relieve stress.

Playing a game, especially one that involves having fun with your friends, is a great way to maintain a sense of wellness and stay physically healthy–especially if the game involves exercise!

11

CHAPTER SUMMARY

Stress

11.1   What is stress?

• Stress occurs when events are identified as threatening or challenging.

• Stress that has a negative impact is called distress. Eustress is the optimal amount of stress that people need to function well.

11.2   What are the cognitive factors in stress?

• The cognitive appraisal approach states that how people think about a stressor determines, at least in part, how stressful that stressor will become.

• The first step in appraising a stressor is called primary appraisal, in which the person determines whether an event is threatening, challenging, or of no consequence. Threatening events are more stressful than those seen as challenging.

• The second step is secondary appraisal, in which the person assesses the resources available to deal with the stressor, such as time, money, and social support.

11.3   What kinds of experiences can cause stress?

• Catastrophes are events such as floods or crashes that can result in high levels of stress, including acute stress disorder and post-traumatic stress disorder.

• Major life changes create stress by requiring adjustments. Major life changes have an impact on chronic health problems and risk of accidents.

• The daily frustrations and irritations experienced by people, called hassles, have an impact on day-to-day health.

11.4   What are some sources of stress in everyday life?

• Four sources of stress are pressure, uncontrollability, frustration, and conflict.

• Frustration, which can be internal or external, may result in persistence, aggression, displaced aggression, or withdrawal.

Current Issues in Psychology: Suicide in America

11.5   Why do people commit suicide?

• Suicidal behavior is highly linked to depression. People who talk about suicide should be taken seriously and need help.

11.6   What are the different types of conflicts people must face?

• There are four types of conflicts: approach–approach, avoidance–avoidance, approach–avoidance, and multiple approach–avoidance.

Factors in the Stress Reaction

• The autonomic nervous system consists of the sympathetic system, which responds to stressful events, and the parasympathetic system, which restores the body to normal functioning after the stress has ceased.

11.7   What is happening in the body when a person experiences stress?

• The general adaptation syndrome is the body's reaction to stress and includes three stages of reaction: alarm, resistance, and exhaustion.

11.8   What is the relationship between stress and the immune system?

• Stress causes the immune system to react as though an illness or invading organism has been detected, increasing the functioning of the immune system.

• As the stress continues or increases, the immune system can begin to fail.

11.9   What is the relationship between stress and personality?

• Type A personalities are ambitious, time conscious, hostile and angry workaholics who are at increased risk of coronary heart disease, primarily due to their anger and hostility.

• Type B personalities are relaxed and easygoing and have one-third the risk of coronary heart disease as do Type A personalities, if male, and one-fourth the risk if female and working outside the home.

• Type C personalities are pleasant but repressed, internalizing their negative emotions.

• Hardy people are hard workers who lack the anger and hostility of the Type A personality, instead seeming to thrive on stress.

• Optimists look for positive outcomes and experience far less stress than pessimists, who take a more negative view.

11.10   What is the relationship between stress and social factors?

• Several social factors can increase the effects of stress: poverty, stresses on the job or in the workplace, and entering a majority culture that is different from one's culture of origin.

• Burnout is a condition that occurs when job stress is so great that the person develops negative thoughts, emotions, and behavior as well as an extreme dissatisfaction with the job and a desire to quit.

• The four methods of acculturation are integration, assimilation, separation, and marginalization.

• Social support systems are important in helping people cope with stress.

Coping with Stress

11.11   What are two ways that people can deal with stress?

• Problem-focused coping is used when the problem can be eliminated or changed so that it is no longer stressful or so that the impact of the stressor is reduced.

• Emotion-focused coping is often used with problem-focused coping and involves changing one's emotional reactions to a stressor.

11.12   What are the psychological defense mechanisms?

• Psychological defense mechanisms are unconscious distortions of perceived reality and can be a form of emotion-focused coping.

11.13   How can meditation help relieve stress?

• Meditation can produce a state of relaxation and reduce the physical reactions common to stressful situations.

• Concentrative meditation involves focusing inward on some repetitive stimulus, such as one's breathing. Receptive meditation involves focusing outward to expand conscious awareness.

11.14   What are the cultural influences on stress?

• Different cultures perceive stressors differently, and coping strategies will also vary from culture to culture.

11.15   Can being religious help people cope with stress?

• People with religious beliefs also have been found to cope better with stressful events.

Applying Psychology to Everyday Life: Focus on Wellness

11.16   What are some ways to promote wellness in one's life?

• Factors that promote wellness include exercise, social activities, getting enough sleep, eating healthy foods, having fun, managing one's time, and practicing good coping skills.

11 KEY TERMS

TEST YOURSELF

Pick the best answer.

1. Which of the following is a cognitive symptom of stress?
   a. frequent colds
   b. anxiety
   c. overeating
   d. memory problems

2. How do today's researchers differ from Selye in their view of eustress?
   a. They feel that eustress is more harmful than distress.
   b. They have not found evidence for eustress.
   c. They believe that a certain level of eustress is necessary to promote health.
   d. They believe that distress can be helpful instead of harmful.

3. Appraising a stressor as a challenge results in
   a. more stress.
   b. less stress.
   c. less successful coping.
   d. increased negative emotions.

4. Unpredictable, large-scale events that create a great deal of stress and feelings of threat are called
   a. major life events.
   b. catastrophes.
   c. hassles.
   d. major hassles.

5. After the car accident, Yoshiko suffered from nightmares and other sleeping problems, and she could not concentrate on her work. After about two weeks, these symptoms disappeared and she was able to work and sleep normally again. Yoshiko was suffering from
   a. acute stress disorder.
   b. post-traumatic stress disorder.
   c. mild stress reaction.
   d. shell shock.

6. Lisa's score on the SRRS was 380. According to Holmes and Rahe, Lisa is probably suffering from a
   a. mild life crisis.
   b. moderate life crisis.
   c. major life crisis.
   d. mild stress disorder.

7. Researchers found that the _____ of daily hassles was a far better predictor of headaches than were scores on a life events scale.
   a. number
   b. type
   c. positive quality
   d. perceived severity

8. Differences in the way men and women respond to daily hassles
   a. are greatest during the college years.
   b. decrease with age.
   c. were not supported by research.
   d. are present for older adults but not for college students.

9. Which of the following is NOT a source of stress as discussed in the text?
   a. pressure
   b. uncontrollability
   c. predictability
   d. frustration

10. Who reformulated the frustration–aggression hypothesis?
    a. Dollard
    b. Berkowitz
    c. Miller
    d. Lazarus

11. Rachel's employer gives her a bad review, making Rachel feel lousy. When she arrives at home, she yells at her husband and children. Rachel is displaying
    a. escape.
    b. withdrawal.
    c. displacement.
    d. projection.

12. Trying to decide between two of your favorite desserts is an example of a(n) _____ conflict.
    a. approach–approach
    b. avoidance–avoidance
    c. approach–avoidance
    d. multiple approach–avoidance

13. Phrases such as "caught between a rock and a hard place" and "out of the frying pan, into the fire" refer to _____ conflicts.
    a. approach–approach
    b. avoidance–avoidance
    c. approach–avoidance
    d. multiple approach–avoidance

14. When a person has to make a choice among several goals and each goal has both its good points and its bad points, the person is experiencing a(n) _____ conflict.
    a. approach–approach
    b. avoidance–avoidance
    c. approach–avoidance
    d. multiple approach–avoidance

15. In which of Selye's stages is death a possible outcome?
- **a.** alarm
- **c.** reaction
- **b.** resistance
- **d.** exhaustion

16. Joe rarely takes any work home, preferring to leave his work worries at the office. He is not ambitious and likes to have a lot of leisure time when it is possible. He is also easygoing and doesn't lose his temper often, preferring to avoid conflict. Which of the following statements about Joe is most likely true?
- **a.** Joe is a Type A personality.
- **b.** Joe is a Type B personality.
- **c.** Joe is a Type C personality.
- **d.** Joe's risk of coronary heart disease is high.

17. Tad seems to thrive on stress and feels very much in control of his life. He would probably be labeled a _____ personality.
- **a.** Type A
- **c.** Type C
- **b.** Type B
- **d.** hardy

18. Which of the following is NOT one of the three methods suggested by Vaughan to promote a positive, optimistic mood?
- **a.** alternative thinking
- **c.** using a scapegoat
- **b.** relaxation
- **d.** downward social comparison

19. Acculturative stress is lowest for people who choose _____ as their method of entering the majority culture.
- **a.** integration
- **c.** separation
- **b.** assimilation
- **d.** marginalization

20. Shawna is having trouble in algebra. She goes to the school's academic help center for tutoring and spends extra time working algebra problems at home. Shawna's method of coping is
- **a.** problem focused.
- **c.** defensive focused.
- **b.** emotion focused.
- **d.** internal.

21. Jerome, an 8-year-old boy, constantly teases one of the girls in his third-grade classroom. He calls her names and chases her on the playground, telling other boys that she has "cooties." If Jerome's real feelings are more like attraction to this girl, we can say that Jerome is exhibiting
- **a.** displacement.
- **c.** reaction formation.
- **b.** projection.
- **d.** sublimation.

22. Meditation has been shown to accomplish all of the following except
- **a.** relaxation.
- **b.** reduction in blood pressure.
- **c.** reduce the need for sleep.
- **d.** reduce symptoms of anxiety.

23. Who among the following probably has the least ability to cope effectively with stress?
- **a.** Marian, a very religious person
- **b.** Mei Ling, who comes from a culture that emphasizes the family
- **c.** Jackie, who has few friends and whose family lives far away from her
- **d.** Lenora, who meditates every day

24. Which of the following is NOT one of the guidelines for preventing suicide?
- **a.** listen with sincerity
- **b.** ask the person if he or she feels suicidal
- **c.** share a time when you felt the same way
- **d.** give the person advice even if he or she doesn't ask for it

25. Which of the following is one of the ways to promote wellness in one's life?
- **a.** Get enough sleep.
- **b.** Eat whatever you want, as long as it tastes good.
- **c.** Don't worry about managing your time.
- **d.** Avoid getting too involved with other people.

Answers: 1-d, 2-c, 3-b, 4-b, 5-a, 6-c, 7-d, 8-d, 9-c, 10-b, 11-a, 12-a, 13-b, 14-d, 15-d, 16-b, 17-d, 18-c, 19-a, 20-a, 21-c, 22-c, 23-c, 24-d, 25-a.

For more sample quizzes and other review activities that will help you get a better grade, be sure to check out your accompanying study guide. To access tests and your own personalized study plan that will help you focus on the areas you need to master before your next class test, be sure to go to the on-line Psychology web site available with the access code packaged with your book.

Stress

> **Stress** occurs when events are identified as threatening or challenging
> **Distress:** stress with a negative impact
> **Eustress:** optimal amount of stress needed to function well

11.1

Cognitive Factors in Stress: Lazarus's Cognitive Appraisal Approach

How people think about a stressor determines, at least in part, how stressful that stressor will become

1. **First step is primary appraisal:** person determines whether an event is threatening, challenging, or of no consequence. Threatening events are more stressful than those seen as challenging
2. **Second step is secondary appraisal:** person assesses resources available to deal with the stressor

11.2

Experiences That Can Cause Stress

Catastrophes: result in high levels of stress, including acute stress disorder and post-traumatic stress disorder

Major life changes: create stress by requiring adjustments; increased risk of chronic health problems and accidents

Hassles: daily frustrations/irritations, have impact on daily health

11.3

Sources of Stress in Everyday Life

Four sources of stress are: pressure, uncontrollability, frustration, and conflict

Frustrations:
> can be internal or external
> may result in persistence, aggression, displaced aggression, or withdrawal

11.4

Body and Stress

General Adaptation Syndrome: body's reaction to stress, includes

Three Stages of Reaction:
1. alarm
2. resistance
3. exhaustion

11.7

Causes of Suicide

Suicidal behavior:
> Linked to depression
> People who talk about suicide should be taken seriously

11.5

Different Types of Conflicts

Conflict Types:
> approach–approach
> approach–avoidance
> avoidance–avoidance
> multiple approach–avoidance

Factors in the Stress Reaction—Autonomic Nervous System:
> **Sympathetic system:** responds to stressful events
> **Parasympathetic system:** restores body to normal functioning after stress

11.6

Two Foci That Can Deal with Stress

> **Problem-focused coping:** used when problem can be eliminated or changed so no longer stressful or impact of stressor reduced
> **Emotion-focused coping:** used with problem-focused coping, involves changing one's emotional reactions

11.11

Psychological Defense Mechanisms

> Unconscious distortions of perceived reality
> Form of emotion-focused coping

11.12

Stress and Personality

Type A personalities:
▸ ambitious, time conscious, hostile, and angry workaholics
▸ increased risk of coronary heart disease, due to anger and hostility

Type B personalities
▸ relaxed, easygoing
▸ one-third the risk of coronary heart disease if male
▸ one-fourth the risk if female and working outside the home

Type C personalities
▸ pleasant but repressed   ▸ internalize their negative emotions

Hardy people:
▸ hard workers who lack the anger and hostility   ▸ seem to thrive on stress

Optimists
▸ look for positive outcomes   ▸ experience far less stress than pessimists

11.9

Stress and the Immune System

▸ Stress increases the functioning of the immune system
▸ As the stress continues or increases, the immune system can begin to fail

11.8

Relationship Between Stress and Social Factors

Social factors that increase the effects of stress:
▸ Poverty   ▸ Stresses on the job
▸ Entering a different majority culture

Burnout: person develops negative thoughts, emotions, and behavior; extreme dissatisfaction with the job; desire to quit

Four Methods of Acculturation: integration, assimilation, separation, marginalization, and marginalization

11.10

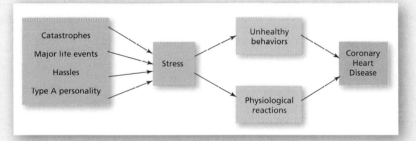

Coping with Stress

Meditation and Relieving Stress

Meditation:
▸ can produce a state of relaxation
▸ reduce the physical reactions to stress

Concentrative meditation:
▸ involves focusing inward on some repetitive stimulus, such as one's breathing

Receptive meditation:
▸ involves focusing outward to expand conscious awareness

11.13

Cultural Influences on Stress

▸ Different cultures perceive stressors differently
▸ Coping strategies vary according to culture

11.14

Religion and Coping with Stress

Religious people cope better with stressful events

11.15

Promoting Wellness in One's Life

Factors that promote wellness:
▸ exercise
▸ social activities
▸ getting enough sleep
▸ eating healthily
▸ having fun
▸ managing one's time
▸ practicing good coping skills

11.16

12

Theories of Personality

Not-So-Identical Twins

Many people have heard the story of the "Jim" twins, James Arthur Springer and James Edward Lewis, identical twins separated at the age of 1 month. At age 39 Springer and Lewis were the first set of twins studied by University of Minnesota psychologist Thomas Bouchard, who examined the differences and similarities between identical and fraternal twins raised apart from each other (Bouchard et al., 1990).

The two "Jims" shared interests in mechanical drawing and carpentry, a love of math and a dread of spelling in high school, and smoked and drank the same amount. It is understandable that many researchers attribute these similarities to the shared genetic material of the "Jim" twins. But Springer and Lewis were both raised in Ohio by parents from relatively similar socioeconomic backgrounds—how much of their similarity to each other might be due to those conditions? And how would genetics explain that they both divorced women named Linda before marrying women named Betty? Are there genes for "divorce Linda, marry Betty?" Obviously not.

Then there's the case of Oskar and Jack. Like the "Jim" twins, they also exhibited a number of similarities in personality and behavior. No one would accuse Oskar and Jack of being raised in similar environments, however. Born in Trinidad at the time Hitler was rising to power, Jack Yufe was raised by their Jewish father in Trinidad as a Jew, while their mother took Oskar Stohr to occupied Czechoslovakia, where he attended a Nazi-run school and was at one time a Hitler youth. In terms of environment, Oskar and Jack were not-so-identical twins.

If the researchers in the twin study had dug a little deeper, they would also have found countless differences between the twins in the study. To automatically assume that similarities between identical twins are all caused by genetic influences and that differences are caused by environmental influences is bad science. The fact is that any two randomly selected people will find that they have countless things in common, none of which is likely to be caused by hereditary factors.

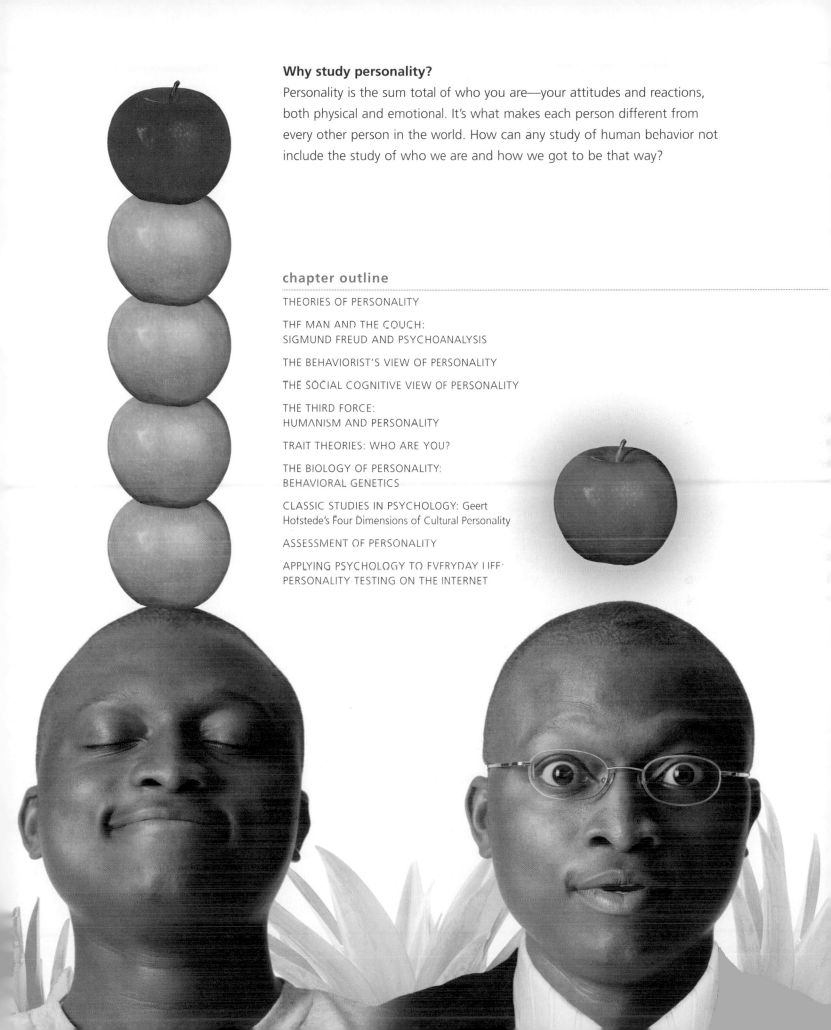

Why study personality?

Personality is the sum total of who you are—your attitudes and reactions, both physical and emotional. It's what makes each person different from every other person in the world. How can any study of human behavior not include the study of who we are and how we got to be that way?

12

Theories of Personality

12.1 *What is personality?*

As stated in the opening story, **personality** is the unique way in which each individual thinks, acts, and feels throughout life. Personality should not be confused with **character**, which refers to value judgments made about a person's morals or ethical behavior, nor should it be confused with **temperament**, the enduring characteristics with which each person is born, such as irritability or adaptability. Both character and temperament are vital parts of personality, however.

Personality is an area of the still relatively young field of psychology in which there are several ways in which the characteristic behavior of human beings can be explained. One reason that there is not yet one single explanation of personality that all can agree on is that personality is still difficult to measure precisely and scientifically. At present, there are four main perspectives, or viewpoints, in personality theory:

- *The psychoanalytic perspective* had its beginnings in the work of Sigmund Freud and still exists today. It focuses on the role of the unconscious mind in the development of personality. This perspective is also heavily focused on biological causes of personality differences.

- *The behaviorist perspective* is based on the theories of learning as discussed in Chapter Five. This approach focuses on the effect of the environment on behavior.

- *The humanistic perspective* first arose as a reaction against the psychoanalytic and behaviorist perspectives and focuses on the role of each person's conscious life experiences and choices in personality development.

- *The trait perspective* differs from the other three in its basic goals: The psychoanalytic, behaviorist, and humanistic perspectives all seek to explain the process that causes personality to form into its unique characteristics, whereas trait theorists are more concerned with the end result—the characteristics themselves. Although some trait theorists assume that traits are biologically determined, others make no such assumption.

personality
the unique and relatively stable ways in which people think, feel, and behave.

character
value judgments of a person's moral and ethical behavior.

temperament
the enduring characteristics with which each person is born.

preconscious mind
level of the mind in which information is available but not currently conscious.

The Man and the Couch: Sigmund Freud and Psychoanalysis

FREUD'S CULTURAL BACKGROUND

It's hard to understand how Freud developed his ideas about personality without knowledge of the world in which he and his patients lived. Born in the Austro-Hungarian Empire in 1856, Freud's family moved to Vienna when he was only 4 years old. He lived there until 1938, when Germany occupied Austria, and Freud, of Jewish background, moved to England to escape the Nazis. During this time period, Europe was in what is commonly known as the Victorian Age, named for Queen Victoria of Great Britain. The Victorian Age, as was discussed in Chapter One, was a time of sexual repression. People growing up in this period were told by their church that sex should take place only in the context of marriage and then only to make babies. To enjoy sexual intercourse was considered a sin.

Men were understood to be unable to control their "animal" desires at times, and a good Victorian husband would father several children with his wife and then turn to a mistress for sexual comfort, leaving his virtuous* wife untouched. Women, especially those of the upper classes, were not supposed to have sexual urges. It is no wonder that many of Freud's patients were wealthy women with problems stemming from unfulfilled sexual desires or sexual repression. Freud's "obsession" with sexual explanations for abnormal behavior seems more understandable in light of his cultural background and that of his patients.

Freud came to believe that there were layers of consciousness in the mind. His belief in the influence of the unconscious mind on conscious behavior, published in *The Psychopathology of Everyday Life* (Freud, 1901), shocked the Victorian world.

THE DIVISIONS OF THE MIND

12.2   *How did Freud view the divisions of the conscious mind?*

Freud believed that the mind was divided into three parts: the preconscious, conscious, and unconscious minds (Freud, 1904). (See Figure 12.1.)

THE PRECONSCIOUS MIND   According to Freud, the **preconscious mind** is a level of the mind where all of the information, events, concerns, and thoughts that a person is not aware of at the moment are kept. These bits and pieces of the mind can be easily brought into conscious awareness, however, when the need arises. If this sounds like long-term memory, there's a good reason for that: Essentially, what Freud was talking about then is very much like what researchers now refer to as *explicit long-term memory,* or the relatively permanent and accessible storage of experiences. **LINK** *to Chapter Six: Memory, p. 222.*

Sigmund Freud (1856–1939), founder of the psychodynamic movement in psychology.

FIGURE 12.1   **Freud's Conception of the Personality**   This iceberg represents the three levels of the mind. The part of the iceberg visible above the surface is the conscious mind. Just below the surface is the preconscious mind, everything that is not yet part of the conscious mind. Hidden deep below the surface is the unconscious mind, feelings, memories, thoughts, and urges that cannot be easily brought into consciousness. While two of the three parts of the personality (ego and superego) exist at all three levels of awareness, the id is completely in the unconscious mind.

*Virtuous: morally excellent.

THE CONSCIOUS MIND Freud believed that the **conscious mind** is all of the things of which a person is aware at any given moment. Whatever is uppermost in one's mind is in the conscious mind.

That sounds almost like short-term memory! Yes, it is very similar to *short-term memory*, or the memory system in which information is held while it is being used. Freud's terms may be different, but the concepts are basically the same as those used by cognitive psychologists to talk about memory.

THE UNCONSCIOUS MIND The **unconscious mind** (also called "the unconscious") was the real departure for the professionals of Freud's day, however. Freud theorized that there is a part of the mind that remains hidden at all times, surfacing only in symbolic form in dreams and in some of the behavior people engage in without knowing why they have done so. Even when a person makes a determined effort to bring a memory out of the unconscious mind, it will not appear directly, according to Freud. Freud believed that the unconscious mind was the most important determining factor in human behavior and personality. Ⓛ Ⓘ Ⓝ Ⓚ *to Chapter Four: Consciousness, p. 139.*

One of the ways that the unconscious can influence conscious behavior, for example, is in everyday speech. Have you ever meant to say one thing, only to have it come out as something entirely different? For example, a psychologist preparing an article condemning Freud's theories began her paper by writing, "Fraud's theory. . . ." In this example, the psychologist obviously meant to say "Freud" but another word altogether came out—a word that Freud would have said revealed the woman's true feelings. This tendency to reveal oneself through errors of speech is called a *Freudian slip*, a slip of the tongue that appears to be accidental but that may provide a clue to the individual's unconscious wishes or urges. Chapter Fifteen discusses other methods used by Freud to uncover the unconscious mind.

THE DIVISIONS OF THE PERSONALITY

12.3 *According to Freud, what are the three parts of the personality and how do they interact?*

Freud also believed, based on his observations of his patients, that personality itself could be divided into three parts. The way these three parts of the personality develop and interact with one another became the heart of his theory (Freud, 1923, 1933, 1940).

ID: IF IT FEELS GOOD, DO IT The first and most primitive part of the personality, present in the infant, is the **id**. *Id* is a Latin word that means "it." The id is a completely unconscious, amoral part of the personality that exists at birth, containing all of the basic biological drives: hunger, thirst, self-preservation, and sex, for example. When these drives are active, the person will feel an increase in not only physical tension but also in psychological tension that Freud called the **libido**, the instinctual energy that may come into conflict with the demands of a society's standards for behavior. When libidinal energy is high, it's unpleasant for the person, so the goal is to reduce the libido by fulfilling the drive: Eat when hungry, drink when thirsty, and satisfy the sex drive when the need for pleasure is present. Freud emphasized the sexual aspect of libido more than many of his later followers did, seeing the struggle to reduce libido yet somehow conform to social rules, such as "sex is wrong outside of marriage."

Wait a minute—Freud thought babies have sex drives? Yes, Freud thought babies have sex drives, which shocked and outraged his colleagues and fellow Victorians. By "sex drive" he really meant "pleasure drive," the need to seek out pleasurable sensations. People do seem to be pleasure-seeking creatures, and even infants seek pleasure from sucking and chewing on anything they can get into their mouths. In fact, thinking about what infants are like when they are just born provides a good pic-

---

That sounds almost like short-term memory! ▶

conscious mind
level of the mind that is aware of immediate surroundings and perceptions.

unconscious mind
level of the mind in which thoughts, feelings, memories, and other information are kept that are not easily or voluntarily brought into consciousness.

id
part of the personality present at birth and completely unconscious.

libido
the instinctual energy that may come into conflict with the demands of a society's standards for behavior.

Wait a minute—Freud thought babies have sex drives? ▶

ture of the id. Infants are demanding, irrational, illogical, and impulsive. They want their needs satisfied immediately, and they don't care about anyone else's needs or desires. (A word of caution: The fact that infant behavior seems to fit Freud's concept of the id is not proof that the id exists. It simply means that Freud came up with the concept of the id to fit what he already knew about infants.)

Freud called this need for satisfaction the **pleasure principle**, which can be defined as the desire for immediate gratification of needs with no regard for the consequences. The pleasure principle can be summed up simply as "if it feels good, do it."

EGO: THE EXECUTIVE DIRECTOR   People normally try to satisfy an infant's needs as quickly as possible. Infants are fed when hungry, changed when wet, and tended to whenever they cry. But as infants begin to grow, adults start denying them their every wish. There will be things they cannot touch or hold, and they must learn to wait for certain things, such as food. Freud would say that reality has reared its ugly head, and the id simply cannot deal with the reality of having to wait or not getting what it wants. Worse still would be the possibility of punishment as a result of the id's unrestrained actions.

According to Freud, to deal with reality, a second part of the personality develops called the **ego**. The ego, from the Latin word for "I," is mostly conscious and is far more rational, logical, and cunning than the id. The ego works on the **reality principle**, which is the need to satisfy the demands of the id and reduce libido only in ways that will not lead to negative consequences. This means that sometimes the ego decides to deny the id its desires because the consequences would be painful or too unpleasant.

Here's a hypothetical example: If a 6-month-old sees an object and wants it, she will reach out and grab it despite her parent's frantic cries of "No, no!" The parent will literally have to pry the object out of the baby's hands, with the baby protesting mightily all the while. But if that same child is about 2 years old, when she reaches for the object and the parent shouts "No!" she will most likely draw back her hand without grabbing the object because her ego has already begun to develop. In the first case, the infant has only the id to guide her behavior, and the id wants to grab the object and doesn't care what the parent says or does. But the 2-year-old has an ego, and that ego knows that the parent's "No!" may very well be followed by punishment, an unpleasant consequence. The 2-year-old will make a more rational, more logical decision to wait until the parent isn't looking and *then* grab the object and run.

A simpler way of stating the reality principle, then, is "if it feels good, do it, but only if you can get away with it."

SUPEREGO: THE MORAL WATCHDOG   If everyone acted on the reality principle, the world would be pretty scary. How does knowing right from wrong come into Freud's theory? Freud called the third and final part of the personality, the moral center of personality, the **superego**. The superego (also Latin, meaning "over the self") develops as a preschool-aged child learns the rules, customs, and expectations of society. There are actually two parts to the superego: the *ego ideal* and the *conscience*. The **ego ideal** is a kind of measuring device. It is the sum of all the ideal, or correct and acceptable, behavior that the child has learned about from parents and others in the society. All behavior is held up to this standard and judged by the second part of the superego, the **conscience**. The conscience is the part of the personality that makes people feel pride when they do the right thing and guilt, or *moral anxiety*, when they do the wrong thing. It is not until the conscience develops that children have a sense of right and wrong. (Note that the term *conscience* is

If everyone acted on the reality principle, the world would be pretty scary. How does knowing right from wrong come into Freud's theory?

fixation
disorder in which the person does not fully resolve the conflict in a particular psychosexual stage, resulting in personality traits and behavior associated with that earlier stage.

psychosexual stages
five stages of personality development proposed by Freud and tied to the sexual development of the child.

oral stage
first stage occurring in the first year of life in which the mouth is the erogenous zone and weaning is the primary conflict.

anal stage
second stage occurring from about 1 to 3 years of age, in which the anus is the erogenous zone and toilet training is the source of conflict.

anal expulsive personality
a person fixated in the anal stage who is messy, destructive, and hostile.

anal retentive personality
a person fixated in the anal stage who is neat, fussy, stingy, and stubborn.

a different word from *conscious*. They may look and sound similar, but they represent totally different concepts.)

THE ANGEL, THE DEVIL, AND ME: HOW THE THREE PARTS OF THE PERSONALITY WORK TOGETHER   Anyone who has ever watched cartoons while growing up has probably seen these three parts of the personality shown in animated form. For example, one cartoon featured a (famous) duck getting out of bed to go to school. He didn't want to go to school, and spied his fishing pole in the corner. Out pops this little devil image of the duck, telling him to skip school and go fishing instead. As he reaches for the fishing pole, out pops a little angel image that shames him into going on to school. Images such as these still appear in animated films, with one of the more recent examples in *The Emperor's New Groove* when a character argues with his angel and devil over disposing of the emperor. The devil is the id, the angel is the superego, and the poor critter caught in the middle is the ego.

So, the id makes demands, the superego puts restrictions on how those demands can be met, and the ego has to come up with a plan that will quiet the id but satisfy the superego. Sometimes the id or the superego does not get its way, resulting in a great deal of anxiety for the ego itself. This constant state of conflict is Freud's view of how personality works; it is only when the anxiety created by this conflict gets out of hand that disordered behavior arises.

The *psychological defense mechanisms* are ways of dealing with stress through unconsciously distorting one's perception of reality. These defense mechanisms were mainly outlined and studied by Freud's daughter, Anna Freud, who was a psychoanalyst (Benjafield, 1996; A. Freud, 1946). In order for the three parts of the personality to function, the constant conflict among them must be managed, and Freud assumed that the defense mechanisms were one of the most important tools for dealing with the anxiety caused by this conflict. A list of the defense mechanisms, their definitions, and examples of each appears in Table 11.3 in Chapter Eleven. (L)(I)(N)(K) *to Chapter Eleven: Stress and Health, p. 433.*

PRACTICE **QUIZ:** HOW MUCH DO YOU REMEMBER?

Pick the best answer.

1. Although Chien's parents have told him that he attended his grandmother's funeral when he was 9 years old, he has no memory of the funeral. According to Freud, Chien's memory of the funeral may be in the _____ mind.
   a. preconscious
   b. conscious
   c. conscience
   d. unconscious

2. Which of Freud's parts of the personality is most like a director?
   a. id
   b. ego
   c. superego
   d. ego ideal

3. According to Freud, which part of the personality makes the person feel pride when doing the right thing?
   a. ego
   b. superego
   c. ego ideal
   d. conscience

4. In Freud's view of the personality, the "devil" would be seen as the
   a. conscience.
   b. id.
   c. ego.
   d. superego.

Answers: 1-d, 2-b, 3-d, 4-b.

So the id exists at birth, but the other two parts of the personality develop later—how much later? When is personality finished? ▶

STAGES OF PERSONALITY DEVELOPMENT

So the id exists at birth, but the other two parts of the personality develop later—how much later? When is personality finished? For Freud, the three parts of the personality develop in a series of stages. Because he focused heavily on the sex drive, he believed that the stages were determined by the developing sexuality of the child. At each stage, a different *erogenous zone*, or area of the body that produces pleasurable feelings, becomes important and can become the source of conflicts. Conflicts that are not fully resolved can result in **fixation**, or getting "stuck" to some degree in an earlier stage of development. The child may grow into an adult but will still carry emotional and psychological "baggage" from that earlier fixated stage.

Because the personality, or *psyche*, develops as a result of sexual development, Freud called these the **psychosexual stages** of personality development.

12.4   *What are the stages of personality development in Freudian theory?*

ORAL STAGE: ORAL FIXATION   The first stage is called the **oral stage** because the erogenous zone is the mouth. This stage occurs from the birth of the infant to about 1 or $1\frac{1}{2}$ years and is dominated by the id. The conflict that can arise here, according to Freud, will be over weaning (taking the mother's breast away from the child, who will now drink from a cup). Weaning that occurs too soon or too late can result in too little or too much satisfaction of the child's oral needs, resulting in the activities and personality traits associated with an orally fixated adult personality: overeating, drinking too much, chain smoking, talking too much, nail biting, gum chewing, and a tendency to be either too dependent and optimistic (when the oral needs are overindulged) or too aggressive and pessimistic (when the oral needs are underindulged).

Freud believed that mothers should breast-feed their infants to satisfy an infant's need for oral gratification in the oral stage of psychosexual development. The age at which an infant was weaned from the breast was a critical factor in psychoanalytic theory.

ANAL STAGE: THE ODD COUPLE AND ANAL FIXATION   As the child becomes a toddler (1 or $1\frac{1}{2}$ years to 3 years), Freud believed that the erogenous zone moves from the mouth area to the anus. This stage is called the **anal stage**.

It moves where?—you can't be serious! It does sound strange, but remember that Freud was really talking about the focus of pleasure. He believed that children in this stage got a great deal of pleasure from both withholding and then releasing their feces at will. This allows children to develop self-control as well as please their parents, both desirable goals for children of this age. Of course, when people have the urge to relieve themselves, it does feel physically good to get rid of that pressure. That's the "sensual" pleasure to which Freud was most likely referring.

Obviously, Freud thought that the main area of conflict here is toilet training, the demand that the child use the toilet at a particular time and in a particular way. This invasion of reality is part of the process that stimulates the development of the ego during this stage. Fixation in the anal stage, from toilet training that is too harsh, can take one of two forms. The child who rebels openly against the demands of the parents and other adults will refuse to go in the toilet, instead defecating where and when he or she feels like doing it. According to Freud, this translates in the adult as a person who sees messiness as a statement of personal control and who is somewhat destructive and hostile. These **anal expulsive personalities** (so called because they expelled their feces as children purposefully) are what most people would call "slobs."

The other anal fixation is the child who is terrified of making a mess and rebels passively—refusing to go at all or retaining the feces. No mess, no punishment. As adults, they are stingy, stubborn, and excessively neat. This type is called the **anal retentive personality**. A classic movie (later a television program) called *The Odd Couple* involved two people, one a classic anal expulsive personality and the other a classic anal retentive personality, trying to live with each other peacefully. The comedy was very popular for a long time, probably because people could relate to the characters so well. Most people either know someone who is like one of those two personalities or *are* one of those two personalities.

It moves where?—you can't be serious!

Early psychoanalytic theory highlighted the importance of toilet training in the anal stage of psychosexual development. A child in this stage was thought to derive pleasure from learning to control his or her bodily functions. The ego also develops during this stage.

According to Freud, children in the phallic stage develop a natural curiosity about sexual differences. This girl and boy are at just the right age to have noticed that they have physical differences.

ROLE MODEL

CHIP OFF THE OLD BLOCK

phallic stage
third stage occurring from about 3 to 6 years of age, in which the child discovers sexual feelings.

Oedipus complex
situation occurring in the phallic stage in which a child develops a sexual attraction to the opposite-sex parent and jealousy of the same-sex parent.

identification
defense mechanism in which a person tries to become like someone else to deal with anxiety.

PHALLIC STAGE   As the child grows older (3 to 6 years), the erogenous zone finally shifts to the genitals. Children have discovered the differences between the sexes by now, and most have also engaged in perfectly normal self-stimulation of the genitals, or masturbation. One can only imagine the horror of the Victorian parent who discovered a child engaged in masturbation. People of that era believed that masturbation led to all manner of evils, including mental illness.

This awakening of sexual curiosity and interest in the genitals is the beginning of what Freud termed the **phallic stage.** The word *phallic* comes from the Greek word *phallos* and means "penis."

Are there separate stages for girls? Actually, Freud believed that the penis was the focus of this stage for both boys *and* girls. Children at this age nearly always engage in that childhood "game" called "I'll show you mine if you'll show me yours." Freud believed that boys, upon seeing that the girl had no penis, would think that the penis can be lost or cut off and develop a fear of losing the penis called *castration anxiety*. Girls, he believed, would feel that they were missing something vital and could not be complete without it, leading to feelings of inferiority and *penis envy*. If this seems an odd focus on male anatomy, remember the era—the Western world at that time was very male oriented and male dominated. Fortunately, nearly all psychoanalysts have long since abandoned the concept of penis envy (Horney, 1939, 1973; Slipp, 1993). The conflict in the phallic stage centers on the awakening sexual feelings of the child. Freud essentially believed that boys develop both sexual attraction to their mothers and jealousy of their fathers during this stage, a phenomenon called the **Oedipus complex.** (Oedipus was a king in a Greek tragedy who unknowingly killed his father and married his mother.) One of Freud's followers, Carl Jung, proposed that the term *Oedipus* be reserved only for males and that the complex in females be termed the *Electra complex*, after a female character in another Greek tragedy (Jung, 1933).

The sexual attraction is not that of an adult male for a female but more of a sexual curiosity that becomes mixed up with the boy's feelings of love and affection for his mother. Of course, his jealousy of his father leads to feelings of anxiety and fears that his father, a powerful authority figure, might get angry and do something terrible—remember that castration anxiety? To deal with this anxiety, two things must occur by the time the phallic stage ends. The boy will *repress* his sexual feelings for his mother and *identify* with his father. **Identification,** as discussed in Chapter Eleven, is a defense mechanism used to combat anxiety. The boy tries to be just like his father in every way, taking on the father's behavior, mannerisms, values, and moral beliefs as his own, so that Daddy won't be able to get angry with the boy. Girls go through a similar process, with their father the target of their affections and their mother as the rival, although the mother is not as feared by girls as the father is by boys because there is no castration anxiety for girls.

Freud believed that the superego develops as a result of identifying with the same-sex parent. Remember, according to Freud all this is *supposed to happen*—sexual attraction to opposite-sex parent, jealousy of same-sex parent, anxiety from these two emotional reactions, and sexual repression and identification to resolve the complex.

What happens when things go wrong? If a child does not have a same-sex parent with whom to identify, or if the opposite-sex parent encourages the sexual attraction, fixation can occur. Fixation in the phallic stage usually involves immature sexual attitudes as an adult. People who are fixated in this stage, according to Freud, will often exhibit promiscuous* sexual behavior and be very vain. The vanity is seen as a cover-up for feelings of low self-worth arising from the failure to resolve the complex, and the lack of moral sexual behavior stems from the failure of identification and the inadequate formation of the superego. Additionally, men with this fixation may be "mama's boys" who never quite grow up, and women may look for much older father figures to marry.

Now the child is about 6 years old and, if passage through the first three stages was successfully accomplished, has all three parts of the personality in place. What next? The personality may be in place, but the place it is in is only 6 years old. Freud named two more periods, one a kind of "holding pattern" and the other the final coming to terms with one's own sexuality.

LATENCY: BOYS HAVE COOTIES AND GIRLS ARE YUCK Remember that by the end of the phallic stage, children have pushed their sexual feelings for the opposite sex into the unconscious in another defensive reaction, repression. From age 6 to the onset of puberty, children will remain in this stage of hidden, or *latent*, sexual feelings, so this stage is called **latency**. In this stage, children grow and develop intellectually, physically, and socially but not sexually. This is the age at which boys play with other boys, girls play only with girls, and each thinks the opposite sex is pretty awful.

GENITAL STAGE When puberty does begin, the sexual feelings that were once repressed can no longer be ignored. Bodies are changing and sexual urges are once more allowed into consciousness, but these urges will no longer have the parents as their targets. When children are 3, their parents are their whole world. When they are 13, their parents have to walk 20 paces behind them in the mall so none of the 13-year-olds' friends will see them. Instead, the focus of sexual curiosity and attraction will become other adolescents or rock stars, movie stars, and other objects of adoration. Since Freud tied personality development into sexual development, the genital stage represented the final process in Freud's personality theory as well as the entry into adult social and sexual behavior. Table 12.1 summarizes the stages of the psychosexual theory of personality development.

THE NEO-FREUDIANS

12.5 *How did Jung, Adler, Horney, and Erikson modify Freud's theory?*

At first Freud's ideas were met with resistance and ridicule by the growing community of doctors and psychologists. Eventually, a number of early psychoanalysts, objecting to Freud's emphasis on biology and particularly on sexuality, broke away from a strict interpretation of psychoanalytic theory, instead altering the focus of **psychoanalysis** (the term Freud applied to both his explanation of the workings of the unconscious mind and the development of personality and the therapy he based on that theory) to the impact of the social environment. At the same time they retained many of Freud's original concepts such as the id, ego, superego, and the defense mechanisms. These early psychoanalysts became the **neo-Freudians**, or "new" Freudian psychoanalysts. This section briefly covers some of the more famous neo-Freudians.

latency
fourth stage occurring during the school years, in which the sexual feelings of the child are repressed while the child develops in other ways.

psychoanalysis
Freud's term for both the theory of personality and the therapy based on it.

neo-Freudians
followers of Freud who developed their own competing theories of psychoanalysis.

---
*Promiscuous: having sexual relations with more than one partner.

TABLE 12.1 FREUD'S PSYCHOSEXUAL STAGES

Stage	Age	Focus of Pleasure	Focus of Conflicts	Difficulties at This Stage Affect Later...
Oral	Birth to $1\frac{1}{2}$ years old	Oral activities (such as sucking, feeding, and making noises with the mouth)	Weaning	• Ability to form interpersonal attachments • Basic feelings about the world • Tendency to use oral forms of aggression, such as sarcasm • Optimism or pessimism • Tendency to take charge or be passive
Anal	$1\frac{1}{2}$ to 3 years old	Bowel and bladder control	Toilet training	• Sense of competence and control • Stubbornness or willingness to go along with others • Neatness or messiness • Punctuality or tardiness
Phallic	3 to 6 years old	Genitals	Identification with parent of the same sex as the child	• Development of conscience and guilt • Pride or humility
Latency	6 years old to puberty	Social skills (such as the ability to make friends) and intellectual skills Dormant period in terms of psychosexual development	School, play, same-sex friendships	• Ability to get along with others
Genital	Puberty to death	Sexual behavior	Sexual relationship with partner	• Immature love or indiscriminate hate • Uncontrollable working or inability to work

Note: Freud thought that the way a person finds pleasure or is prevented from satisfying urges for pleasure at each stage affects personality. Thus, like Erikson's stage model, described in Chapter Seven, Freud's model argues that the way a person deals with particular psychological challenges or potential areas of conflict has long-term effects on personality.

JUNG　Carl Gustav Jung disagreed with Freud about the nature of the unconscious mind. Jung believed that the unconscious held much more than personal fears, urges, and memories. He believed that there was not only a **personal unconscious**, as described by Freud, but a **collective unconscious** as well (Jung, 1933).

According to Jung, the collective unconscious contains a kind of "species" or "racial" memory, memories of ancient fears and themes that seem to occur in many folktales and cultures. These collective, universal human memories were called *archetypes* by Jung. There are many archetypes, but two of the more well known are the *anima/animus* (the feminine side of a man/the masculine side of a woman) and the *shadow* (the dark side of personality, called the Devil in Western cultures). The side of one's personality that is shown to the world is termed the *persona*.

ADLER　Alfred Adler was also in disagreement with Freud over the importance of sexuality in personality development. Adler (1954) developed the theory that as young, helpless children, people all develop feelings of inferiority when comparing themselves to the more powerful, superior adults in their world. The driving force behind all human endeavors, emotions, and thoughts for Adler was not the seeking of pleasure but the seeking of superiority. The defense mechanism of *compensation*, in which people try to overcome feelings of inferiority in one area of life by striving to be superior in another area, figured prominently in Adler's theory. L I N K to *Chapter Eleven: Stress and Health, p. 433*

Carl Jung (1875–1961) was a Swiss psychoanalyst who eventually broke away from Freud's emphasis on the sexual content of the unconscious mind. He formed his own theory of analysis known as analytical psychology.

Dr. Alfred Adler (1870–1937) relaxes at his desk in this 1930s' photograph. Adler was one of the early psychoanalysts trained by Sigmund Freud, but believed that feelings of inferiority rather than growing sexuality were the keys to personality development.

Dr. Karen Horney (1885–1952) took issue with Freud's emphasis on sexuality, especially the concept of penis envy. She emphasized the importance of feelings of basic anxiety in personality development during early childhood.

Dr. Erik Erikson (1902–1994), was originally an educator. This may have influenced his version of psychoanalytic theory, which emphasized the development of the ego and the importance of social relationships with parents, peers, and other people on personality development.

Adler (1954) also developed a theory that the birth order of a child affected personality. Firstborn children with younger siblings feel inferior once those younger siblings get all the attention and often overcompensate by becoming overachievers. Middle children have it slightly easier, getting to feel superior over the dethroned older child while dominating younger siblings. They tend to be very competitive. Younger children are supposedly pampered and protected but feel inferior because they are not allowed the freedom and responsibility of the older children. Although some researchers have found evidence to support Adler's birth order theory (Stein, 2001; Sulloway, 1996), and some have even linked birth order to career choices (Leong et al., 2001; Watkins & Savickas, 1990), other researchers point to sloppy methodology and the bias of researchers toward the birth order idea (Beer & Horn, 2001; Freese et al., 1999; Ioannidis, 1998).

HORNEY   Karen Horney (1967, 1973) did not study directly with Freud but studied his work and taught psychoanalysis at the Psychoanalytic Institutes of Berlin and New York. She left the institute because of disagreements with Freud over the differences between males and females and the concept of penis envy, with which she strongly disagreed. She countered with her own concept of "womb envy," stating that men felt the need to compensate for their lack of child-bearing ability by striving for success in other areas (Burger, 1997).

Rather than focusing on sexuality, Horney focused on the child's sense of **basic anxiety**, the anxiety created in a child born into a world that is so much bigger and more powerful than the child. While people whose parents gave them love, affection, and security would overcome this anxiety, others with less secure upbringings would develop **neurotic personalities** and maladaptive ways of dealing with relationships. Some children, according to Horney, try to deal with their anxiety by moving toward people, becoming dependent and clingy. Others move against people, becoming aggressive, demanding, and cruel. A third way of coping would be to move away from people by withdrawing from personal relationships.

ERIKSON   Erik Erikson (1950, 1959, 1982) was an art teacher who became a psychoanalyst by studying with Anna Freud. He also broke away from Freud's emphasis on sex, preferring instead to emphasize the social relationships that are important at every stage of life. Erikson's eight psychosocial stages were discussed in detail in Chapter Seven. **LINK** to Chapter Seven: *Development Across the Life Span*, pp. 272, 278, 281.

personal unconscious
Jung's name for the unconscious mind as described by Freud.

collective unconscious
Jung's name for the memories shared by all members of the human species.

archetypes
Jung's collective, universal human memories.

basic anxiety
anxiety created when a child is born into the bigger and more powerful world of older children and adults.

neurotic personalities
maladaptive ways of dealing with relationships in Horney's theory.

It sounds as if all of ▶
these theorists
became famous by
ditching some of
Freud's original
ideas. Is Freud
even worth
studying
anymore?

It sounds as if all of these theorists became famous by ditching some of Freud's original ideas. Is Freud even worth studying anymore?

CURRENT THOUGHTS ON FREUD AND PSYCHOANALYSIS

12.6 *How does modern psychoanalytic theory differ from that of Freud?*

Although Freud's psychoanalytic theory seems less relevant in today's sexually saturated world, many of his concepts have remained useful and still form a basis for many modern personality theories. As mentioned in Chapter Eleven, the idea of the defense mechanisms has research support. The concept of an unconscious mind also has some research support. As strange as the idea of an unconscious mind that guides behavior must have seemed to Freud's contemporaries, modern researchers have had to admit that there are influences on human behavior that exist outside of normal conscious awareness. Although much of this research has taken place in the area of hypnosis and subliminal perception (Borgeat & Goulet, 1983; Bryant & McConkey, 1989; Kihlstrom, 1987, 1999, 2001), other researchers have looked at the concept of implicit memory and implicit learning (Frensch & Runger, 2003). ⓁⒾⓃⓀ *to Chapter Six: Memory, p. 221.*

For example, in one study people who were experiencing surgery under general anesthesia* (and presumably unconscious) were exposed to pairs of associated words, such as *bread–butter*. While in the recovery area, they were tested for recall and recognition of the individual items and were unable to remember any of the items. However, when later presented with the first word of each pair, these people were significantly more likely to respond with the original associated word than were people who had not been exposed to the pairs. This was true even though the surgical patients had no conscious memory of having heard the pairs of words prior to testing (Kihlstrom et al., 1998).

This might be a good time to point out a very important fact about Freud's theory: He did no experiments to arrive at his conclusions about personality. His theory is based on his own observations (case studies) of numerous patients. Basing his suppositions on their detailed memories of their childhoods and life experiences, he interpreted their behavior and reminiscences to develop his theory of psychoanalysis. He felt free to interpret what his patients told him of their childhoods as fantasy or fact, depending on how well those memories fit in with his developing theory. For example, many of Freud's patients told him that they were sexually abused by fathers, brothers, and other close family members. Freud was apparently unable to accept these memories as real and decided that they were fantasies, making them the basis of the Oedipal conflict.

Freud based much of his interpretations of a patient's problems on the interpretations of dreams and the results of the patient's free association (talking about anything without fear of negative feedback). These "sources" of information are often criticized as being too ambiguous and without scientific support for the validity of his interpretations. The very ambiguity of these sources of information allowed Freud to fit the patient's words and recollections to Freud's own preferred interpretation, as well as increasing the possibility that Freud's own suggestions and interpretations to the patient might alter the actual memories of the patient, who would no doubt be in a very suggestible state of mind during therapy (Grünbaum, 1984).

Another criticism of Freud's theory concerns the people upon whose dreams, recollections, and comments the theory of psychoanalysis was based. Freud's clients

*Anesthesia: loss of sensation and, in some cases, consciousness.

were almost all wealthy Austrian women living in the Victorian era of sexual repression. Critics state that basing his theory on observations made with such a group of clients promoted his emphasis on sexuality as the root of all problems in personality, as women of that social class and era were often sexually frustrated. Freud rarely had clients who did not fit this description, and so his theory is biased in terms of sexual frustrations (Robinson, 1993).

Although most professionals today view Freud's theory with a great deal of skepticism, his influence on the modern world cannot be ignored. Freudian concepts have had an impact on literature, movies, and even children's cartoons. People who have never taken a course in psychology are familiar with some of Freud's most basic concepts, such as the defense mechanisms. He was also one of the first theorists to emphasize the importance of childhood experiences on personality development—in spite of the fact that he never studied children.

It has only been in the last several decades that people have had the necessary tools to examine the concepts of the unconscious mind. One can only wonder how Freud might have changed his theory in light of what is known about the workings of the human brain and the changes in society that exist today.

habits
in behaviorism, sets of well-learned responses that have become automatic.

PRACTICE **QUIZ:** HOW MUCH DO YOU REMEMBER?

Pick the best answer.

1. An area of the body that produces pleasurable sensations is called the _____ zone.
   - **a.** erogenous
   - **b.** fixation
   - **c.** Oedipal
   - **d.** phallic

2. In which psychosexual stage might fixation result in a person who is excessively neat and fussy?
   - **a.** oral
   - **b.** anal
   - **c.** phallic
   - **d.** genital

3. In which psychosexual stage does the defense mechanism of identification figure prominently?
   - **a.** oral
   - **b.** anal
   - **c.** phallic
   - **d.** latency

4. In which psychosexual stage are the sexual feelings repressed?
   - **a.** oral
   - **b.** anal
   - **c.** phallic
   - **d.** latency

5. According to Jung, the part of the mind containing universal human memories is called the _____ unconscious.
   - **a.** personal
   - **b.** cognitive
   - **c.** collective
   - **d.** animistic

6. Which of the neo-Freudians discussed in the text talked about neurotic personalities as moving toward people, moving against people, or moving away from people?
   - **a.** Jung
   - **b.** Adler
   - **c.** Horney
   - **d.** Erikson

Answers: 1-a, 2-b, 3-c, 4-d, 5-c, 6-c.

The Behaviorist's View of Personality

At the time that Freud's theory was shocking the Western world, another psychological perspective was also making its influence known. In Chapter Five the theories of classical and operant conditioning were discussed in some detail. *Behaviorists*, researchers who use the principles of conditioning to explain the actions and reactions of both animals and humans, have a very different view of personality.

12.7 *How do behaviorists explain personality?*

For the behaviorist, personality is nothing more than a set of learned responses or **habits** (DeGrandpre, 2000; Dollard & Miller, 1950). In the strictest traditional view of Watson and Skinner, everything a person or animal does is a response to some environmental stimulus that has been reinforced or strengthened by reward in some way.

So how does rewarding certain behavior end up becoming some kind of personality pattern? Think about how a traditional behaviorist might explain a shy personality. Beginning in childhood, a person might be exposed to a parent with a rather harsh discipline style (stimulus). Avoiding the attention of that parent would result in

So how does rewarding certain behavior end up becoming some ◀ kind of personality pattern?

social cognitive learning theorists
theorists who emphasize the importance of both the influences of other people's behavior and of a person's own expectancies on learning.

social cognitive view
learning theory that includes cognitive processes such as anticipating, judging, memory, and imitation of models.

reciprocal determinism
Bandura's explanation of how the factors of environment, personal characteristics, and behavior can interact to determine future behavior.

self-efficacy
individual's perception of how effective a behavior will be in any particular circumstance.

fewer punishments and scoldings, so that avoidance response is negatively reinforced—the "bad thing" or punishment is avoided by keeping out of sight and quiet. Later, that child might generalize that avoidance response to other authority figures and adults, such as teachers. In this way, a pattern (habit) of shyness would develop.

Of course, many learning theorists today do not use only classical and operant conditioning to explain the development of the behavior patterns referred to as personality. **Social cognitive learning theorists**, who emphasize the importance of both the influences of other people's behavior and of a person's own expectancies on learning, hold that observational learning, modeling, and other cognitive learning techniques can lead to the formation of patterns of personality. (L I N K) *to Chapter Five: Learning, pp. 192–196.*

The Social Cognitive View of Personality

One of the more well-researched learning theories that includes the concept of cognitive processes as influences on behavior is the social cognitive theory of Albert Bandura. In the **social cognitive view**, behavior is governed not just by the influence of external stimuli and response patterns but also by cognitive processes such as anticipating, judging, and memory as well as learning through the imitation of models.

BANDURA'S RECIPROCAL DETERMINISM AND SELF-EFFICACY

Bandura (1989) believes that three factors influence one another in determining behavior: the environment, the behavior itself, and personal or cognitive factors that the person brings into the situation from earlier experiences (see Figure 12.2). These three factors each affect the other two in a reciprocal, or give-and-take, relationship. Bandura calls this relationship **reciprocal determinism**.

As can be seen in Figure 12.2, the environment includes the actual physical surroundings, the other people who may or may not be present, and the potential for reinforcement in those surroundings. The intensity and frequency of the behavior will not only be influenced by the environment but will also have an impact on that environment. The person brings into the situation previously reinforced responses (personality, in other words) and mental processes such as thinking and anticipating.

Here's how this might work: Richard walks into a classroom filled with other students, but no teacher is present at this time. (This is the *environment*.) Part of Richard's *person* characteristics includes the desire to have attention from other people by talking loudly and telling jokes, which has been very rewarding to him in the past (past reinforcements are part of his cognitive processes, or expectancies of future rewards for his behavior). Also in the past, he has found that he gets more attention when an authority figure is not present. His *behavior* will most likely be to start talking and telling jokes, which will continue if he gets the reaction he expects from his fellow students. If the teacher walks in (the *environment* changes), his behavior will change. If the other students don't laugh, his behavior will change. In the future Richard might be less likely to behave in the same way because his expectations for reward (a cognitive element of his *person* variables) are different.

One of the more important person variables that Bandura talks about is **self-efficacy**, a person's perception of how effective a behavior will be in any particular circumstance (Bandura, 1998). (Self-efficacy is not the same concept as *self-esteem*, which is the positive values a person places on his or her sense of worth.)

FIGURE 12.2 **Reciprocal Determinism** In Bandura's model of reciprocal determinism, three factors influence behavior: the environment, which consists of the physical surroundings and the potential for reinforcement; the person (personal/cognitive characteristics that have been rewarded in the past); and the behavior itself, which may or may not be reinforced at this particular time and place.

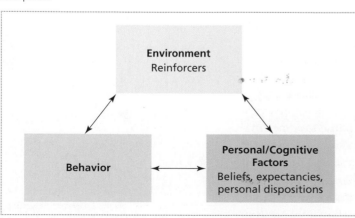

Environment
Reinforcers

Behavior

Personal/Cognitive Factors
Beliefs, expectancies, personal dispositions

People's sense of self-efficacy can be high or low, depending on what has happened in similar circumstances in the past (success or failure), what other people tell them about their competence, and their own assessment of their abilities. For example, if Fiona has an opportunity to write an extra-credit paper to improve her grade in psychology, she will be more likely to do so if her self-efficacy is high: She has gotten good grades on such papers in the past, her teachers have told her that she writes well, and she knows she can write a good paper. According to Bandura, people high in self-efficacy are more persistent and expect to succeed, whereas people low in self-efficacy expect to fail and tend to avoid challenges (Bandura, 1998).

CURRENT THOUGHTS ON THE SOCIAL COGNITIVE VIEW

The social cognitive view of personality, unlike traditional behaviorism, does include mental processes and their influence on behavior. Unlike psychoanalysis, the concepts in this theory can and have been tested under scientific conditions (DeGrandpre, 2000; Domjan et al., 2000; Skinner, 1989). Bandura's classic "Bobo doll" study, described in Chapter Five, for example, made use of experimentation (Bandura, 1965). Although some critics think that human personality and behavior are too complex to explain as the result of cognitions and external stimuli interacting, others point out that this viewpoint has enabled the development of therapies based on learning theory that have become effective in changing undesirable behavior. Ⓛ Ⓘ Ⓝ Ⓚ *to Chapter Fifteen: Psychological Therapies, pp. 569–573.*

The Third Force: Humanism and Personality

12.8 *How do humanists explain personality?*

As first discussed in Chapter One, in the middle of the twentieth century the pessimism of Freudian psychoanalysis with its emphasis on conflict and animalistic needs, together with the emphasis of behaviorism on external control of behavior, gave rise to a third force in psychology: the **humanistic perspective**. Humanists such as Carl Rogers and Abraham Maslow wanted psychology to focus on the things that make people uniquely human, such as subjective emotions and the freedom to choose one's own destiny. As Maslow's theory was discussed more fully in Chapter Nine, in this chapter the discussion of the humanistic view of personality will focus on the theory of Carl Rogers.

CARL ROGERS AND SELF-CONCEPT

12.9 *What was Roger's view of the self?*

Like Maslow, Rogers (1961) believed that human beings are always striving to fulfill their innate capacities and capabilities and to become everything that their genetic potential will allow them to become. This striving for fulfillment is called the **self-actualizing tendency**. An important tool in human self-actualization is the development of an image of oneself, or the **self-concept**. The self-concept is based on what people are told by others and how the sense of **self** is reflected in the words and actions of important people in one's life, such as parents, siblings, coworkers, friends, and teachers.

REAL AND IDEAL SELF   Two important components of the self-concept are the **real self** (one's actual perception of characteristics, traits, and abilities that form the basis of the striving for self-actualization) and the **ideal self** (the perception of what one

---

humanistic perspective
the "third force" in psychology that focuses on those aspects of personality that make people uniquely human, such as subjective feelings and freedom of choice.

self-actualizing tendency
the striving to fulfill one's innate capacities and capabilities.

self-concept
the image of oneself that develops from interactions with important, significant people in one's life.

self
archetype that works with the ego to manage other archetypes and balance the personality.

real self
one's perception of actual characteristics, traits, and abilities.

ideal self
one's perception of whom one should be or would like to be.

"It's always 'Sit,' 'Stay,' 'Heel'—never 'Think,' 'innovate,' 'Be yourself.'"

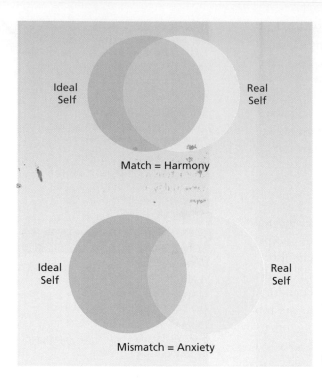

FIGURE 12.3   **Real and Ideal Selves**
According to Rogers, the self-concept includes the real self and the ideal self. The real self is a person's actual perception of traits and abilities, where as the ideal self is the perception of what a person would like to be or thinks he or she should be. When the ideal self and the real self are very similar (matching), the person experiences harmony and contentment. When there is a mismatch between the two selves, the person experiences anxiety and may engage in neurotic behavior.

positive regard
warmth, affection, love, and respect that come from significant others in one's life.

unconditional positive regard
positive regard that is given without conditions or strings attached.

What kind of people ▶
are considered to be
fully functioning? Is it
the same thing as
being self-actualized?

should be or would like to be). The ideal self primarily comes from those important, significant others in one's life, most often the parents. Rogers believed that when the real self and the ideal self are very close or similar to each other, people feel competent and capable, but when there is a mismatch between the real and ideal selves, anxiety and neurotic behavior can be the result. (See Figure 12.3.)

The two halves of the self are more likely to match if they aren't that far apart at the start. When one has a realistic view of the real self, and the ideal self is something that is actually attainable, there usually isn't a problem of a mismatch. It is when a person's view of self is distorted or the ideal self is impossible to attain that problems arise. Once again, it is primarily how the important people (who can be either good or bad influences) in a person's life react to the person that determines the degree of agreement between real and ideal selves.

CONDITIONAL AND UNCONDITIONAL POSITIVE REGARD   Rogers defined **positive regard** as warmth, affection, love, and respect that come from the significant others (parents, admired adults, friends, and teachers) in people's experience. Positive regard is vital to people's ability to cope with stress and to strive to achieve self-actualization. Rogers believed that **unconditional positive regard**, or love, affection, and respect with no strings attached, is necessary for people to be able to explore fully all that they can achieve and become. Unfortunately, some parents, spouses, and friends give **conditional positive regard**, which is love, affection, respect, and warmth that depend, or seem to depend, on doing what those people want.

Here is an example: As a freshman, Sasha was thinking about becoming a math teacher, a computer programmer, or an elementary school teacher. Karen, also a freshman, already knew that she was going to be a doctor. While Sasha's parents had told her that what she wanted to become was up to her and that they would love her no matter what, Karen's parents had made it very clear to her as a small child that they expected her to become a doctor. She was under the very strong impression that if she tried to choose any other career, she would lose her parents' love and respect. Sasha's parents were giving her unconditional positive regard, but Karen's parents (whether they intended to do so or not) were giving her conditional positive regard. Karen was obviously not as free as Sasha to explore her potential and abilities.

For Rogers, a person who is in the process of self-actualizing, actively exploring potentials and abilities and experiencing a match between real and ideal selves, is a **fully functioning person**. Fully functioning people are in touch with their own feelings and abilities and are able to trust their innermost urges and intuitions (Rogers, 1961). To become fully functioning, a person needs unconditional positive regard. In Rogers's view, Karen would not have been a fully functioning person.

What kind of people are considered to be fully functioning? Is it the same thing as being self-actualized? Although the two concepts are highly related, there are some subtle differences. Self-actualization is a goal that people are always striving to reach, according to Maslow (1987). **LINK** to *Chapter Nine: Motivation and Emotion, pp. 343–344.* In Rogers's view, only a person who is fully functioning is capable of reaching the goal of self-actualization. To be fully functioning is a necessary step in the process of self-actualization. Maslow (1987) listed several people that he considered to be self-actualized people: Albert Einstein, Mahatma Gandhi, and

Eleanor Roosevelt, for example. These were people that Maslow found to have the self-actualized qualities of being creative, autonomous, and unprejudiced, for example. In Rogers's view, these same people would be seen as having trusted their true feelings and innermost needs rather than just going along with the crowd, a description that certainly seems to apply in these three cases.

CURRENT THOUGHTS ON THE HUMANISTIC VIEW OF PERSONALITY

Humanistic views of personality paint a very rosy picture. Some critics believe that the picture is a little too rosy, ignoring the more negative aspects of human nature. For example, would humanistic theory easily explain the development of sociopathic personalities who have no conscience or moral nature? Or could a humanist explain the motivation behind terrorism?

Humanistic theory is also very difficult to test scientifically. Little research support exists for this viewpoint, which is almost more of a philosophical view of human behavior rather than a psychological explanation. Its greatest impact has been in the development of therapies to promote self-growth and help people better understand themselves and others. (LINK) to Chapter Fifteen: Psychological Therapies, pp. 566–569.

conditional positive regard
positive regard that is given only when the person is doing what the providers of positive regard wish.

fully functioning person
a person who is in touch with and trusting of the deepest, innermost urges and feelings.

trait theories
theories that endeavor to describe the characteristics that make up human personality in an effort to predict future behavior.

trait
a consistent, enduring way of thinking, feeling, or behaving.

PRACTICE QUIZ: HOW MUCH DO YOU REMEMBER?

Pick the best answer.

1. According to behaviorists, personality is
   a. driven by unconscious forces.
   b. a set of learned responses.
   c. motivated by a striving for success.
   d. a collection of specific traits.

2. Which of the following is not one of Bandura's three factors in reciprocal determinism?
   a. environment   c. traits
   b. the person   d. behavior

3. Sandy is playing a trivia game with her friends. When it is her turn, she gets the category of geography. She knows very little about geography and has never done well in this category in the past, so her sense of self-efficacy is likely to be
   a. low.   c. just right.
   b. high.   d. unaffected by the game.

4. Eddie knows that he is pretty good at art, but his parents have never encouraged him to develop art as a career because they don't feel that artists have "real" jobs. As a result, Eddie feels that he should concentrate on a more practical career to please his parents. If Eddie is working to be who he should be, according to his parents, he is being influenced by his
   a. self-concept.   c. superego.
   b. real self.   d. ideal self.

5. Rogers believed that in order for people to become fully functioning, they must receive _____ from the important people in their lives.
   a. unconditional positive regard
   b. conditional positive regard
   c. positive reinforcement
   d. positive modeling

Answers: 1-b, 2-c, 3-a, 4-d, 5-a.

Trait Theories: Who Are You?

12.10   *What is the trait perspective?*

As discussed in the introduction to this chapter, **trait theories** are less concerned with the explanation for personality development and changing personality than they are with describing personality and predicting behavior based on that description. A **trait** is a consistent, enduring way of thinking, feeling, or behaving, and trait theories attempt to describe personality in terms of a person's traits.

ALLPORT

One of the earliest attempts to list and describe the traits that make up personality can be found in the work of Gordon Allport (Allport & Odbert, 1936). Allport and his colleague H. S. Odbert literally scanned the dictionary for words that could be

"Can't you give him one of those personalities in a bottle I keep reading about?"

surface traits
aspects of personality that can easily be seen by other people in the outward actions of a person.

source traits
the more basic traits that underlie the surface traits, forming the core of personality.

introversion
dimension of personality in which people tend to withdraw from excessive stimulation.

traits, finding about 18,000, then paring that down to 200 traits after eliminating synonyms. Allport believed (with no scientific evidence, however) that these traits were literally wired into the nervous system to guide one's behavior across many different situations and that each person's "constellation" of traits was unique. (In spite of Allport's lack of evidence, behavioral geneticists have found support for the heritability of personality traits, and these findings are discussed in the next section of this chapter.)

CATTELL AND THE 16PF

Two hundred traits is still a very large number of descriptors. How might an employer be able to judge the personality of a potential employee by looking at a list of 200 traits? A more compact way of describing personality was needed. Raymond Cattell (1990) defined two types of traits as surface traits and source traits. Surface traits are like those found by Allport, representing the personality characteristics easily seen by other people. Source traits are those more basic traits that underlie the surface traits. For example, shyness, being quiet, and disliking crowds might all be surface traits related to the more basic source trait of **introversion**, a tendency to withdraw from excessive stimulation.

Using a statistical technique that looks for groupings and commonalities in numerical data called *factor analysis*, Cattell discovered 16 source traits (Cattell, 1950, 1966), and although he later determined that there might be another seven source traits to make a total of 23 (Cattell & Kline, 1977), he developed his assessment questionnaire, *The Sixteen Personality Factor Questionnaire* (16PF) (Cattell, 1995) based on just 16 source traits (see Figure 12.4). These 16 source traits are seen as trait dimensions, or continuums, in which there are two opposite traits at each end with many possible degrees of the traits possible along the dimension. For example, someone scoring near the reserved end of the reserved/outgoing dimension would be more introverted than someone scoring in the middle or at the opposite end.

FIGURE 12.4　**Cattell's Self-Report Inventory**　This is an example of personality profiles based on Cattell's 16PF self-report inventory. The two groups represented are airline pilots and writers. Notice that airline pilots, when compared to writers, tend to be more controlled, relaxed, self-assured, and far less sensitive. Writers, on the other hand, were more imaginative and better able to think abstractly.
Source: Cattell, 1973; Cattel et al., 1993.

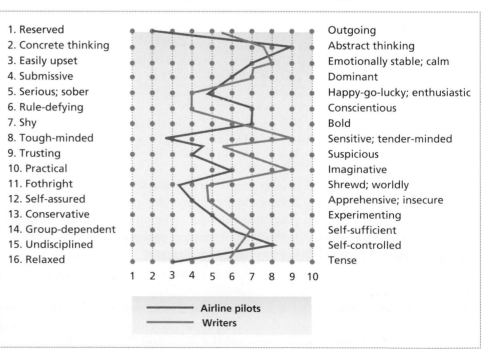

1. Reserved		Outgoing
2. Concrete thinking		Abstract thinking
3. Easily upset		Emotionally stable; calm
4. Submissive		Dominant
5. Serious; sober		Happy-go-lucky; enthusiastic
6. Rule-defying		Conscientious
7. Shy		Bold
8. Tough-minded		Sensitive; tender-minded
9. Trusting		Suspicious
10. Practical		Imaginative
11. Forthright		Shrewd; worldly
12. Self-assured		Apprehensive; insecure
13. Conservative		Experimenting
14. Group-dependent		Self-sufficient
15. Undisciplined		Self-controlled
16. Relaxed		Tense

1　2　3　4　5　6　7　8　9　10

——— Airline pilots
——— Writers

THE BIG FIVE: OCEAN, OR THE FIVE-FACTOR MODEL OF PERSONALITY

Sixteen factors are still quite a lot to discuss when talking about someone's personality. Later researchers attempted to reduce the number of trait dimensions to a more manageable number, with several groups of researchers arriving at more or less the same five trait dimensions (Botwin & Buss, 1989; Jang et al., 1998; McCrae & Costa, 1996). These five dimensions have become known as the **five-factor model**, or the **Big Five** (see Table 12.2), and represent the core description of human personality—that is, the only dimensions necessary to understand what makes us tick.

As shown in the table, these five trait dimensions can be remembered by using the acronym OCEAN, in which each of the letters is the first letter of one of the five dimensions of personality.

- **Openness** can best be described as a person's willingness to try new things and be open to new experiences. People who try to maintain the status quo and who don't like to change things would score low on openness.
- **Conscientiousness** refers to a person's organization and motivation, with people who score high in this dimension being those who are careful about being places on time and careful with belongings as well. Someone scoring low on this dimension, for example, might always be late to important social events or borrow belongings and fail to return them or return them in poor condition.
- **Extraversion** is a term first used by Carl Jung (1933), who believed that all people could be divided into two personality types: **extraverts** and **introverts**. Extraverts are outgoing and sociable, whereas introverts are more solitary and dislike being the center of attention.
- **Agreeableness** refers to the basic emotional style of a person, who may be easygoing, friendly, and pleasant (at the high end of the scale) or grumpy, crabby, and hard to get along with (at the low end).
- **Neuroticism** refers to emotional instability or stability. People who are excessive worriers, overanxious, and moody would score high on this dimension, whereas those who are more even-tempered and calm would score low.

Costa and McCrae believed that these five traits were not interdependent. In other words, knowing someone's score on extraversion would not give any information about scores on the other four dimensions, allowing for a tremendous amount of variety in personality descriptions.

five-factor model (Big Five)
model of personality traits that describes five basic trait dimensions.

openness
one of the five factors; willingness to try new things and be open to new experiences.

conscientiousness
the care a person gives to organization and thoughtfulness of others; dependability.

extraversion
dimension of personality referring to one's need to be with other people.

extraverts
people who are outgoing and sociable.

introverts
people who prefer solitude and dislike being the center of attention.

agreeableness
the emotional style of a person that may range from easygoing, friendly, and likeable to grumpy, crabby, and unpleasant.

neuroticism
degree of emotional instability or stability.

TABLE 12.2 **THE BIG FIVE**

High Scorer Characteristics	Factor (OCEAN)	Low Scorer Characteristics
Creative, artistic, curious, imaginative, nonconforming	**Openness (O)**	Conventional, down-to-earth, uncreative
Organized, reliable, neat, ambitious	**Conscientiousness (C)**	Unreliable, lazy, careless, negligent, spontaneous
Talkative, optimistic, sociable, affectionate	**Extraversion (E)**	Reserved, comfortable being alone, stays in the background
Good-natured, trusting, helpful	**Agreeableness (A)**	Rude, uncooperative, irritable, aggressive, competitive
Worrying, insecure, anxious, temperamental	**Neuroticism (N)**	Calm, secure, relaxed, stable

Source: Adapted from McRae & Costa, P. T. (1990).

trait–situation interaction
the assumption that the particular circumstances of any given situation will influence the way in which a trait is expressed.

behavioral genetics
field of study devoted to discovering the genetic bases for personality characteristics.

CURRENT THOUGHTS ON THE TRAIT PERSPECTIVE

12.11 *How do trait theorists today view personality?*

Some theorists have cautioned that personality traits will not always be expressed in the same way across different situations. Walter Mischel, a social cognitive theorist, has emphasized that there is a **trait–situation interaction**, in which the particular circumstances of any given situation are assumed to influence the way in which a trait is expressed (Mischel & Shoda, 1995). An outgoing extravert, for example, might laugh, talk to strangers, and tell jokes at a party. That same person, if at a funeral, would still talk and be open, but the jokes and laughter would be less likely to occur.

As mentioned earlier, the five-factor model has been studied and tested by numerous researchers. Cross-cultural studies have found evidence of these five trait dimensions in 11 different cultures, including Japan, the Philippines, Germany, China, and Peru (Digman, 1990; John et al., 1988; McCrae et al., 2000; Paunonen et al., 1996). This cultural commonality raises the question of the origins of the Big Five trait dimensions: Are child-rearing practices across all those cultures similar enough to result in these five aspects of personality, or could these five dimensions have a genetic component that transcends cultural differences? The next section will discuss the evidence for a genetic basis of the Big Five.

PRACTICE QUIZ: HOW MUCH DO YOU REMEMBER?

Pick the best answer.

1. Who believed that traits existed as part of the nervous system?
  a. Costa and McCrae   **c.** Cattell
  b. Allport   **d.** Rogers

2. According to Cattell, traits that are numerous and can easily be seen by other people are called _____ traits.
  a. central
  b. cardinal
  c. surface
  d. source

3. In the Big Five theory of personality, "C" stands for
  a. conscientiousness.   **c.** contrariness.
  b. consciousness.   **d.** complexity.

4. Elsie's daughter gave her a microwave oven for her birthday. Elsie has never used a microwave and is scared to use this one. Instead, she lets it sit in her kitchen and refuses to let her daughter teach her how to use it. Elsie would probably score very low on
  a. agreeableness.   **c.** introversion.
  b. neuroticism.   **d.** openness.

Answers: 1-b, 2-c, 3-a, 4-d.

The Biology of Personality: Behavioral Genetics

What about ▶ genetics? How much of our personality is inherited?

What about genetics? How much of our personality is inherited? The field of **behavioral genetics** is devoted to the study of just how much of an individual's personality is due to inherited traits. Animal breeders have known for a long time that selective breeding of certain animals with specific desirable traits can produce changes not only in size, fur color, and other physical characteristics but also in the temperament of the animals (Isabel, 2003; Trut, 1999). As stated earlier in this chapter, temperament consists of the characteristics with which each person is born and is, therefore, determined by biology to a great degree. If the temperaments of animals can be influenced by manipulating patterns of genetic inheritance, then it is only one small step to assume that at least those personality characteristics related to temperament in human beings may also be influenced by heredity.

Animal breeders have an advantage over those who are studying the influence of genes in human behavior. Those who breed animals can control the mating of certain animals and the conditions under which those animals are raised. Human research cannot ethically or practically develop that degree of control and so must fall back on the accidental "experiments" of nature and opportunity, studies of twins and adopted persons.

12.12   *What part do biology and heredity play in personality?*

TWIN STUDIES

The difference between monozygotic (identical) and dizygotic (fraternal) twins was discussed in Chapter Seven. (L I N K) *to Chapter Seven: Development Across the Life Span, p. 255.* As discussed previously, identical twins share 100 percent of their genetic material, having come from one fertilized egg originally, whereas fraternal twins share only about 50 percent of their genetic material as any other pair of siblings would. By comparing identical twins to fraternal twins, especially when twins can be found who were not raised in the same environment (like Oskar and Jack or the "Jim" twins in the opening story), researchers can begin to find evidence of possible genetic influences on various traits, including personality. (See Figure 12.5.)

The results of the Minnesota twin study have revealed that identical twins are more similar than fraternal twins or unrelated people in intelligence, leadership abilities, the tendency to follow rules, and the tendency to uphold traditional cultural expectations (Bouchard, 1997; Finkel & McGue, 1997); nurturance,* empathy,**

Simulation
Live!
psych

Heritability of Personality

---

*Nurturance: affectionate care and attention.
**Empathy: the ability to understand the feelings of others.

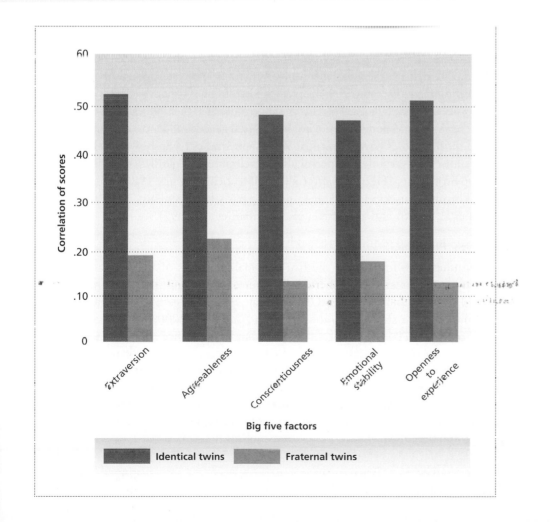

FIGURE 12.5   **Personalities of Identical and Fraternal Twins**
Identical and fraternal twins differ in the way they express the Big Five personality factors. The scores of identical twins have a correlation of about 50 percent, whereas those of fraternal twins have a correlation of only about 15 to 20 percent. These findings give support to the idea that some aspects of personality are genetically based.
Source: Loehlin (1992)

James Arthur Springer and James Edward Lewis, otherwise known as the "Jim" twins. Although separated shortly after birth and reunited at age 39, they exhibited many similarities in personality and personal habits. While genetics may explain some of these similarities, what other factors might also be at work?

and assertiveness (Neale et al., 1986); and aggressiveness (Miles & Carey, 1997). This similarity holds even if the twins are raised in separate environments.

ADOPTION STUDIES

Another tool of behavioral geneticists is to study adopted children and their adoptive and birth families. If studying genetically identical twins raised in different environments can help investigators understand the genetic influences on personality, then studying *unrelated* people who are raised in the *same* environment should help investigators discover the influence of environment. By comparing adopted children to their adoptive parents and siblings and, if possible, to their biological parents who have not raised them, researchers can uncover some of the shared and nonshared environmental and genetic influences on personality.

Adoption studies have confirmed what twin studies have shown: Genetic influences account for a great deal of personality development, regardless of shared or non-shared environments (Hershberger et al., 1995; Loehlin et al., 1985; Loehlin et al., 1998). Through this kind of study, a genetic basis has been suggested for shyness (Plomin et al., 1988) and aggressiveness (Brennan et al., 1997).

CURRENT FINDINGS

Several studies have found that the five personality factors of the five-factor model have nearly a 50 percent rate of heritability* across several cultures (Bouchard, 1994; Jang et al., 1996; Loehlin, 1992; Loehlin et al., 1998). Together with the results of the Minnesota twin study and other research (Lubinski, 2000; Lykken & Tellegen, 1996; Plomin, 1994), the studies of genetics and personality seem to indicate that variations in personality traits are about 25 to 50 percent inherited (Jang et al., 1998). This also means that environmental influences apparently account for about half of the variation in personality traits as well.

Although the five factors have been found across several cultures, this does not mean that different cultures do not have an impact on personality. For more on this topic, see the Classic Studies in Psychology section that follows.

---

*Heritability: the degree to which the changes in some trait within a population can be considered to be due to genetic influences.

CLASSIC STUDIES IN PSYCHOLOGY
Geert Hofstede's Four Dimensions of Cultural Personality

12.13   *What were Hofstede's dimensions of cultural personality?*

In the early 1980s, organizational management specialist Geert Hofstede conducted a massive study into the work-related values of employees of IBM, a multinational corporation (Hofstede, 1980; Hofstede et al., 2002). The study surveyed workers in 64 countries across the world. Hofstede analyzed the data collected from this survey and found four basic dimensions of personality along which cultures differed.

1. **Individualism/collectivism:** *Individualistic cultures* tend to have loose ties between individuals, with people tending to look after themselves and their immediate families only. Members of such cultures have friends based on shared activities and interests and may belong to many different loosely organized social groups. Autonomy,* change, youth, security of the individual, and equality are all highly valued. In a *collectivistic culture*, people are from birth deeply tied into very strong in-groups, typically extended families that include grandparents, aunts and uncles, and cousins. Loyalty to the family is highly stressed, and the care of the family is placed before the care of the individual. Group membership is limited to only a few permanent groups that have tremendous influence over the individual. The values of this kind of culture are duty, order, tradition, respect for the elderly, group security, and respect for the group status and hierarchy.** Whereas the United States and Great Britain are examples of individualistic cultures, Japan, China, Korea, Mexico, and Central America are much more collectivistic.

2. **Power distance:** This dimension refers to the degree to which the less powerful members of a culture accept and even expect that the power within the culture is held in the hands of a select few rather than being more evenly distributed. Countries such as the Philippines, Mexico, many Arab countries, and India were found to be high in such expectations, whereas countries such as Austria, Sweden, Australia, Great Britain, and the United States were low in power distance.

3. **Masculinity/femininity:** Referring to how a culture distributes the roles played by men and women within a culture, this dimension varies more for the men within a culture than for the women. "Masculine" cultures are assertive and competitive, although more so for men than for women, and "feminine" cultures are more modest and caring. Both men and women in "feminine" countries have similar, caring values, but in "masculine" countries, the women are not quite as assertive and competitive as the men, leading to a greater difference between the sexes in masculine countries. Japan, Austria, Venezuela, Italy, Switzerland, Mexico, Ireland, Jamaica, the United States, Great Britain, and Germany were found to be masculine countries, whereas Sweden, Norway, the Netherlands, Denmark, Costa Rica, Yugoslavia, Finland, Chile, Portugal, Thailand, and Guatemala were ranked as more feminine.

4. **Uncertainty avoidance:** Some cultures are more tolerant of uncertainty, ambiguity,† and unstructured situations. Cultures that do not tolerate such uncertainty and lack of structure tend to have strict rules and laws, lots of security and safety measures, and tend

---

*Autonomy: the quality of being self-directed or self-controlled.
**Hierarchy: in this sense, a body of persons in authority over others.
†Ambiguity: the quality of being uncertain and indistinct.

(Top) Senator John Edwards and John Kerry, along with their wives, mingle with potential voters at a Wendy's® restaurant in Newburgh, New York, during the 2004 presidential race. Power distance involves the degree to which people, such as those watching these influential politicians, accept the fact that control of their lives rests in the hands of a select few. How often do you think people such as these senators eat at restaurants like this one when it isn't an election year?
Stephen Crowley/The New York Times

(Bottom) King Mohammed VI of Morocco is pictured on a pilgrimage to Jeddah in Saudi Arabia. Notice that the king and the people of power with him are kept well away from the general public. While this is partly for security reasons, it also indicates a high degree of power distance in this culture.

toward a philosophical/religious belief of One Truth (and "we have it!"). Cultures that are more accepting of uncertainty are more tolerant of different opinions and have fewer rules. They tend to allow many different religious beliefs to exist side by side and are less anxious and emotional than people in uncertainty-avoiding countries. Uncertainty-avoiding countries include Greece, Portugal, Guatemala, Uruguay, Belgium, El Salvador, Japan, Yugoslavia, and Peru, whereas those that are more tolerant of uncertainty include Singapore, Jamaica, Denmark, Sweden, Hong Kong, Ireland, Great Britain, Malaysia, India, Philippines, the United States, Canada, and Indonesia.

Note that the Big Five personality dimensions of Costa and McCrae (1990) are not necessarily in competition with Hofstede's dimensions. Hofstede's dimensions are *cultural personality traits*, whereas those of the Big Five refer to individuals.

Questions for Further Discussion

1. Was your own culture listed for any of these dimensions? If so, do you agree with the personality dimension assigned to your culture?

2. If your culture was not listed for a personality dimension, where do you think your culture would fall on that dimension?

Assessment of Personality

> **With all the different theories of personality, how do people find out what kind of personality they have?**

With all the different theories of personality, how do people find out what kind of personality they have? The methods for measuring or assessing personality vary according to the theory of personality used to develop those methods, as one might expect. However, most psychological professionals doing a personality assessment on a client do not necessarily tie themselves down to one theoretical viewpoint only, preferring to take a more *eclectic* view of personality. The eclectic view is a way of choosing the parts of different theories that seem to best fit a particular situation, rather than using only one theory to explain a phenomenon. In fact, looking at behavior from all four perspectives can often bring insights into a person's behavior that would not easily come from taking only one perspective. Many professionals will not only use several different perspectives but also several of the assessment techniques that follow. Even so, certain methods are more commonly used by certain kinds of theorists, as can be seen in Table 12.3.

Personality assessments may also differ in the purposes for which they are conducted. For example, sometimes a researcher may administer a personality test of some sort to participants in a research study so that the participants may be classified according to certain personality traits. There are personality tests available to people who simply want to learn more about their own personalities. Finally, clinical and counseling psychologists, psychiatrists, and other psychological professionals use personality assessment in the diagnosis of disorders of personality. (L)(I)(N)(K) *to Chapter Fourteen: Psychological Disorders, p. 527.*

INTERVIEWS

12.14 *What are the advantages and disadvantages of using interviews to measure personality?*

Some therapists ask questions and note down the answers in a survey process called an **interview**. (L)(I)(N)(K) *to Chapter One: The Science of Psychology, p. 22.* This type of interview, unlike a job interview, is likely to be *unstructured* and flow naturally from the beginning comments between the client and the psychologist.

"Do you mind if I say something helpful about your personality?"

©The New Yorker Collection 1997 Robert Weber from cartoonbank.com. All Rights Reserved.

interview

method of personality assessment in which the professional asks questions of the client and allows the client to answer, either in a structured or unstructured fashion.

TABLE 12.3 **WHO USES WHAT METHOD?**

Type of Assessment	Most Likely Used By . . .
Interviews	Psychoanalysts, Humanistic Therapists
Projective Tests:	Psychoanalysts
Rorschach	
Thematic Apperception Test	
Behavioral Assessments:	Behavioral and Social-Cognitive Therapists
Direct Observation	
Rating Scales	
Frequency Counts	
Personality Inventories:	Trait Theorists
Sixteen Personality Factor Questionnaire (16PF)	
Neuroticism/Extraversion/Openness	
<None>Personality Inventory (NEO-PI)	
Myers-Briggs Type Indicator (MBTI)	
Eysenck Personality Questionnaire (EPQ)	
Keirsey Temperament Sorter II	
California Psychological Inventory (CPI)	

PROBLEMS WITH INTERVIEWS   So an interview is a kind of self-report process, right? Yes, when psychologists interview clients, clients must report on their innermost feelings, urges, and concerns—all things that only they can directly know. The same problems that exist with self-report data (such as surveys) exist with interviews. Clients can lie, distort the truth, misremember, or give what they think is a socially acceptable answer instead of true information. Interviewers themselves can be biased, interpreting what the client says in light of their own belief systems or prejudices. Freud certainly did this when he refused to believe that his patients had actually been sexually molested as children, preferring to interpret that information as a fantasy instead of reality (Russell, 1986).

Another problem with interviews is something called the **halo effect**, which is a tendency to form a favorable or unfavorable impression of someone at the first meeting, so that all of that person's comments and behavior after that first impression will be interpreted to agree with the impression—positively or negatively. The halo effect can happen in any social situation, including interviews between a psychological professional and a client. First impressions really do count, and people who make a good first impression because of clothing, personal appearance, or some other irrelevant* characteristic will seem to have a "halo" hanging over their heads—they can do no wrong after that (Lance et al., 1994; Thorndike, 1920). (Sometimes the negative impression is called the "horn effect.")

PROJECTIVE TESTS

12.15   *How are projective tests used to explore personality, and what are the problems with projective tests?*

Psychoanalysts have a goal in dealing with their clients that other personality theorists do not share: The psychoanalyst wishes to uncover the unconscious conflicts, desires, and urges that affect the client's conscious behavior. No other theorist assigns such importance to the unconscious mind, so psychoanalysts use assessment methods that are meant to "get at" those unconscious, hidden emotions and events.

◄ So an interview is a kind of self-report process, right?

halo effect
tendency of an interviewer to allow positive characteristics of a client to influence the assessments of the client's behavior and statements.

---

*Irrelevant: not applying to the case or example at hand.

FIGURE 12.6 **Rorschach Inkblot Example** One of the Rorschach inkblots. A person being tested is asked to tell the interviewer what he or she sees in this inkblot. Answers are neither right nor wrong, but may reveal unconscious concerns. What do you see in this inkblot?

FIGURE 12.7 **Thematic Apperception Test Example** A sample from the Thematic Apperception Test (TAT). When you look at this picture, what story does it suggest to you? Who are the people? What is their relationship?

Think about the definition of the defense mechanism of **projection**: placing, or "projecting," one's own unacceptable thoughts onto others, as if the thoughts actually belonged to those others. What if a person could project unacceptable, unconscious thoughts onto some harmless, ambiguous stimulus, like a picture? For example, have you ever tried to see "shapes" in the clouds? You might see a house where another person might see the same cloud as a horse. The cloud isn't really either of those things but can be *interpreted* as one or the other, depending on the person doing the interpretation. That makes a cloud an ambiguous stimulus—one that is capable of being interpreted in more than one way.

In just this way, psychoanalysts (and a few other psychologists) show their clients ambiguous visual stimuli and ask the clients to tell them what they see. The hope is that the client will project those unconscious concerns and fears onto the visual stimulus, revealing them to the analyst. Tests using this method are called **projective tests.** Although such tests can be used to explore one's personality, they are most commonly used as a diagnostic tool to uncover problems in personality.

THE RORSCHACH INKBLOTS One of the more well-known projective tests is the Rorschach inkblot test, developed in 1921 by Swiss psychiatrist Hermann Rorschach (ROR-shok). There are 10 inkblots, five in black ink on a white background and five in colored inks on a white background. (See Figure 12.6 for an example of a Rorschach-type inkblot.)

People being tested are asked to look at each inkblot and simply say whatever it might look like to them. Using predetermined categories and responses commonly given by people to each picture (Exner, 1980), psychologists score responses on key factors, such as reference to color, shape, figures seen in the blot, and response to the whole or to details.

Rorschach tested thousands of inkblots until he narrowed them down to the 10 in use today. They are still frequently used to describe personality, diagnose mental disorders, and predict behavior (Watkins et al., 1995; Weiner, 1997).

THE TAT First developed in 1935 by psychologist Henry Murray and his colleagues (Morgan & Murray, 1935), the **Thematic Apperception Test (TAT)** consists of 20 pictures, all black and white, that are shown to a client. The client is asked to tell a story about the person or people in the picture, who are all deliberately drawn in ambiguous situations (see Figure 12.7).

Again, the story developed by the client is interpreted by the psychoanalyst, who looks for revealing statements and projection of the client's own problems onto the people in the pictures.

These are only two of the more well-known projective tests. Other types of projective tests include the Sentence Completion test, Draw-A-Person, and House-Tree-Person. In the Sentence Completion test, the client is given a series of sentence beginnings, such as "I wish my mother . . ." or "Almost every day I feel . . ." and asked to finish the sentence, whereas in the Draw-A-Person and House-Tree-Person, the client is asked to draw the named items.

But how can anyone know if the interpretation is correct? Isn't there a lot of room for error?

But how can anyone know if the interpretation is correct? Isn't there a lot of room for error?

PROBLEMS WITH PROJECTIVE TESTS Projective tests are by their nature very subjective (valid only within the person's own perception), and interpreting the answers of clients is almost an art. It is certainly not a science and is not known for its accuracy. Problems lie in the areas of reliability and validity. In Chapter Eight, *reliability* was defined as the tendency of a test to give the same score every time it is administered to the same person or group of people, and *validity* was defined as the ability of the test to measure what it is intended to measure. Projective tests, with no standard grading scales, have both low reliability and low validity (Gittelman-Klein, 1978; Lilienfield, 1999; Wood et al., 1996). A person's answers to the Rorschach, for example, might be quite different from one day to the next, depending on the person's mood and what scary movie might have been on television the previous night.

Projective tests may sound somewhat outdated in today's world of MRIs and PET scans, but many practicing clinical psychologists and psychiatrists still use this type of testing (Butcher & Rouse, 1996; Camara et al., 2000). Some psychologists believe that the latest versions of these tests and others like them still have practical use and some validity (Ganellen, 1996; Weiner, 1997), especially when a client's answers on these tests are used as a starting point for digging deeper into the client's recollections, concerns, and anxieties. However, more reliable and objective methods for assessing personality are available, as the next section discusses.

Somehow, I can't see a behaviorist using any of these tests, they're too"mental"— do behaviorists even measure personality?

BEHAVIORAL ASSESSMENTS

12.16   *How can behavioral assessments be used in assessing personality?*

Behaviorists do not typically want to "look into the mind." Because behaviorists assume that personality is merely habitually learned responses to stimuli in the environment, the preferred method for a behaviorist would be to watch that behavior unfold in the real world. In **direct observation**, the psychologist observes the client engaging in ordinary, everyday behavior, preferably in the natural setting of home, school, or workplace, for example. A therapist who goes to the classroom and observes that tantrum behavior only happens when a child is asked to do something involving fine motor abilities (like drawing or writing) might be able to conclude that the child has difficulty with those skills and throws a tantrum to avoid the task.

Other methods often used by behavioral therapists and other assessors are rating scales and frequency counts. In a **rating scale**, a numerical rating is assigned, either by the assessor or the client, for specific behaviors (Nadeau et al., 2001). In a **frequency count**, the assessor literally counts the frequency of certain behaviors within a specified time limit. Educators make use of both rating scales and frequency counts to diagnose behavioral problems such as attention deficit disorder and aspects of personality such as social skill level through the various grade levels.

PROBLEMS WITH BEHAVIORAL ASSESSMENTS   Problems with these assessments can include the observer effect (when a person's behavior is affected by being watched) and observer bias, which can be controlled by having multiple observers and correlating their observations with each other. **Ⓛ Ⓘ Ⓝ Ⓚ** *to Chapter One: The Science of Psychology, p. 24.* As with any kind of observational method, there is no control over the external environment. A person observing a client for a particular behavior may not see that behavior occur within the observation time—much as some car problems never seem to show up when the mechanic is examining the car.

PERSONALITY INVENTORIES

12.17   *What are the different kinds of personality inventories used to measure personality?*

Trait theorists are typically more interested in personality descriptions. They tend to use an assessment known as a **personality inventory**, a questionnaire that has a standard list of questions and only requires certain specific answers, such as "yes," "no," and "can't decide." The standard nature of the questions (everyone gets the same list) and the lack of open-ended answers make these assessments far more objective and reliable than projective tests (Garb et al., 1998), although they are still a form of self-report. One such personality

---

projection
defense mechanism involving placing, or "projecting," one's own unacceptable thoughts onto others, as if the thoughts actually belonged to those others and not to oneself.

projective tests
personality assessments that present ambiguous visual stimuli to the client and ask the client to respond with whatever comes to mind.

Rorschach inkblot test
projective test that uses 10 inkblots as the ambiguous stimuli.

Thematic Apperception Test (TAT)
projective test that uses 20 pictures of people in ambiguous situations as the visual stimuli.

subjective
referring to concepts and impressions that are only valid within a particular person's perception and may be influenced by biases, prejudice, and personal experiences.

direct observation
assessment in which the professional observes the client engaged in ordinary, day-to-day behavior in either a clinical or natural setting.

rating scale
assessment in which a numerical value is assigned to specific behavior that is listed in the scale.

frequency count
assessment in which the frequency of a particular behavior is counted.

personality inventory
paper and pencil or computerized test that consists of statements that require a specific, standardized response from the person taking the test.

inventory is Cattell's 16PF, described earlier in this chapter. Costa and McCrae (2000) have recently revised their original *Neuroticism/Extraversion/Openness Personality Inventory (NEO-PI)*, which is based on the five-factor model of personality traits (discussed on page 461). Another inventory in common use is the *Myers-Briggs Type Indicator (MBTI)*. This inventory is based on the ideas of Carl Jung and looks at four personality dimensions. The sensing/intuition (S/I) dimension includes people who prefer to rely on what they can see, hear, and so on through their own physical senses (*sensing*) and, on its opposite end, those who look for patterns and trust their hunches (*intuition*). Sensing people are very detail oriented, preferring to work only with the known facts, whereas intuitive people are more willing to use metaphors, analogies, and look for possibilities. The thinking/feeling (T/F) dimension runs from those who prefer to use logic, analysis, and experiences that can be verified as facts (*thinkers*) to those who tend to make decisions based on their personal values and emotional reactions (*feeling*). Introversion/extroversion (I/E) is the same classic dimension that began with Jung and is represented in nearly every personality theory, including the Big Five. Perceiving/judging (P/J) describes those who are willing to adapt and modify decisions, be spontaneous, and who are naturally curious and tend to put off making a final decision so that all possibilities are covered (*perceiving*) as well as those who are the opposite: the action-oriented, decisive, get-the-task-done-and-don't-look-back type (*judging*). These four dimensions can differ for each individual, resulting in 16 (4 × 4) possible personality types: ISTJ, ISTP, ISFP, ISFJ, and so on (Briggs & Myers, 1998). The Myers-Briggs is often used to assess personality to help people know the kinds of careers for which they may best be suited.

For example, a person who scored high on the extravert, sensing, thinking, and judging dimensions would be an ESTJ. A typical description of this personality type would be a person who needs to analyze information and bring order to the outer world. Such people are organizers, energetic in completing tasks, and practical. They also take their responsibilities seriously and expect others to do so as well. School administrators, for example, are often ESTJs.

Other common personality tests include the Eysenck Personality Questionnaire (Eysenck & Eysenck, 1993), the Keirsey Temperament Sorter II (Keirsey, 1998), the California Psychological Inventory (Gough, 1995), and the Sixteen Personality Factor Questionnaire (Cattell, 1994).

THE MMPI-2　By far the most common personality inventory is the *Minnesota Multiphasic Personality Inventory, Version II*, or *MMPI-2*, which specifically tests for abnormal behavior patterns in personality (Butcher & Rouse, 1996; Butcher et al., 2000, 2001). This questionnaire consists of 567 statements such as "I am often very tense" or "I believe I am being plotted against." The person taking the test must answer "true," "false," or "cannot say." The MMPI has 10 clinical scales and eight validity scales in addition to numerous subscales. Each scale tests for a particular kind of behavior. The behavior patterns include relatively mild personality problems such as excessive worrying and shyness as well as more serious disorders such as schizophrenia and depression. Ⓛ Ⓘ Ⓝ Ⓚ *to Chapter Fourteen: Psychological Disorders, pp. 542, 544.*

How can you ▶ tell if a person is telling the truth on a personality inventory?

How can you tell if a person is telling the truth on a personality inventory? *Validity scales*, which are built into any well-designed psychological inventory, are intended to indicate whether or not a person taking the inventory is responding honestly. Responses to certain items on the test will indicate if people are trying to make themselves look better or worse than they are, for example, and certain items are repeated throughout the test in a slightly different form, so that anyone trying to "fake" the test will have difficulty responding to those items consistently (Butcher et al., 2001). For example, if one of the statements is "I am always happy" and a person responds "true" to that statement, the suspicion would be that this person is trying to look better than he or she really is. If several of the validity scale questions are answered in this way, the conclusion is that the person is not being honest.

PROBLEMS WITH PERSONALITY INVENTORIES   The advantage of personality inventories over projective tests and interviews is that inventories are standardized (i.e., everyone gets exactly the same questions and the answers are scored in exactly the same way). In fact, responses to inventories are often scored on a computer. Observer bias and bias of interpretation are simply not possible because this kind of assessment is objective rather than subjective. The validity and reliability of personality inventories are generally recognized as being greatly superior to that of projective tests (Anastasi & Urbina, 1997).

There are some problems, however. The validity scales, for example, are a good check against cheating, but they are not perfect. Some people are still able to fake their answers and respond in what they feel are the socially appropriate ways (Anastasi & Urbina, 1997; Hicklin & Widiger, 2000). Other problems have to do with human nature itself: Some people may develop a habit of picking a particular answer rather than carefully considering the statement, whereas others may simply grow tired of responding to all those statements and start picking answers at random.

PRACTICE **QUIZ:** HOW MUCH DO YOU REMEMBER?

Pick the best answer.

1. Which of the following is not one of the traits found to have a genetic component in studies of identical twins?
   a. intelligence
   b. leadership abilities
   c. antagonism
   d. aggressiveness

2. The five-factor model trait dimensions have been shown to have
   a. no relevance in other cultures.
   b. only a 20 percent rate of heritability.
   c. relevance only for Western cultures.
   d. about a 50 percent rate of heritability across cultures.

3. Which of the following countries would be most likely to have an individualistic trait, according to Hofstede?
   a. Japan
   b. Vietnam
   c. England
   d. Brazil

4. Which of the following methods would NEVER be used by a behaviorist?
   a. interview
   b. projective test
   c. direct observation
   d. personality inventory

5. Which method of personality assessment offers the most objective measurement?
   a. interview
   b. projective test
   c. direct observation
   d. personality inventory

6. Observer bias would be a problem for any of the following methods except
   a. interview.
   b. projective test.
   c. direct observation.
   d. personality inventory.

Answers: 1-c, 2-d, 3-c, 4-b, 5-d, 6-d.

Applying Psychology To Everyday Life: Personality Testing on the Internet

12.18   *How good are the personality tests people can take on the Internet?*

Most people enjoy finding out something about themselves. In fact, that's part of the attraction of the pseudopsychological methods of astrology and graphology, as discussed in Chapter One. People want to know, "What am I really like?"

There are a number of online personality tests available, with more appearing on almost a daily basis. Some of these tests are fairly well thought out, based on much larger, validated tests, and can give the casual "surfer" some insight into personality traits. Here are two sample Web sites with fairly serious tests:

- Keirsey Temperament Sorter (based on Jung's theory):
  www.advisorteam.com/temperament_sorter/register.asp?partid=1
- Five-Factor Test (based on the five-factor model):
  http://users.wmin.ac.uk/~buchant/wwwffi

One of the more unusual online personality tests is the Color Test, which has the person select certain colored shapes by clicking on them with the mouse. The Color Test is based on the work of Swiss color psychologist Dr. Max Lüscher, a color consultant for industrial concerns (Lüscher, 1969). Color psychologists study the effects of color on mood, attention, and other human factors and most often work in the field of consumer or marketing psychology, helping businesses and industries select color schemes for products, Web pages, and physical surroundings that will maximize sales and productivity (Bellizzi & Crowley, 1983; Guerin et al., 1995). There are several Internet sites that allow people to take a free Color Test, such as the one at **www.colorquiz.com**.

The Color Test as devised by Lüscher consists of eight cards, each a different color, which are randomly placed color side up in front of the person to be tested. The person is asked to choose the color card that is most attractive, which is then recorded and removed, and the person is asked to choose the most attractive color from those that remain. This is repeated until only one card is left. Various tables in Lüscher's book are used to interpret the color choices.

Although colors have been shown to have an effect on the body's physical reactions, with red creating higher measurements of blood pressure, respiration, heart rate, and eyeblink frequency and blue the lowest (Dominy & Lucas, 2001; Kaiser, 1984), there is little scientifically derived research to support the association of certain colors with certain personality traits (Brauen & Bonta, 1979; Holmes et al., 1984; McAloon & Lester, 1979). The results of color personality tests sound suspiciously like the general readings given by astrologers and graphologists: "Does not wish to be involved in differences of opinion, contention or argument, preferring to be left in peace. Wants to make a favorable impression and be recognized. Needs to feel appreciated and admired. Sensitive and easily hurt if no notice is taken of him or if he is not given adequate acknowledgment." How many of these statements are true of you or someone you know? This is a good example of the *Barnum Effect* in action—keep the statement general with a little something for everyone, and it will please nearly everyone.

Still, it can be fun to participate in tests like these, so long as people remember that a real personality test should be administered under controlled conditions by an expert. One of the dangers in taking online personality tests (and especially those in magazines) too seriously, for example, is that there is no person-to-person contact to help put the results in perspective, which can lead people to believe that they are in big trouble—even though their results are not that different from other people's results. It can be a little like "medical student disease," in which medical students read up on exotic diseases and become convinced that they have them all until the teacher reassures them. People taking an online personality test may believe they have some serious psychological disorder because they don't know how to interpret the results of the test.

One final word of advice: Online testing can be good entertainment, but real problems should be handled by real professionals.

Questions for Further Discussion

1. What might be some other dangers of taking a personality test online?
2. What should a person look for when trying to judge the quality of an online personality test?

12 CHAPTER SUMMARY

Theories of Personality

12.1 *What is personality?*

- Personality is the unique way individuals think, feel, and act. It is different from character and temperament but includes those aspects.

- The four perspectives in the study of personality are the psychoanalytic, behavioristic (including social cognitive theory), humanistic, and trait perspectives.

The Man and the Couch: Sigmund Freud and Psychoanalysis

12.2 *How did Freud view the divisions of the conscious mind?*

- The three divisions of the mind are the conscious, preconscious, and unconscious. The unconscious can be revealed in dreams and Freudian slips of the tongue.

12.3   *According to Freud, what are the three parts of the personality and how do they interact?*

- The three parts of the personality are the id, ego, and superego.
- The id works on the pleasure principle and the ego works on the reality principle.
- The superego is the moral center of personality, containing the ego ideal and the conscience, and is the source of moral anxiety.
- The conflicts between the demands of the id and the rules and restrictions of the superego lead to anxiety for the ego, which uses defense mechanisms to deal with that anxiety.

12.4   *What are the stages of personality development in Freudian theory?*

- The personality develops in a series of psychosexual stages: oral (id dominated), anal (ego develops), phallic (superego develops), latency (period of sexual repression), and genital (sexual feelings reawaken with appropriate targets).
- The Oedipus and Electra complexes (sexual "crushes" on the opposite-sex parent) create anxiety in the phallic stage, which is resolved through identification with the same-sex parent.
- Fixation occurs when conflicts are not fully resolved during a stage, resulting in adult personality characteristics reflecting childhood inadequacies.

12.5   *How did Jung, Adler, Horney, and Erikson modify Freud's theory?*

- The neo-Freudians changed the focus of psychoanalysis to fit their own interpretation of the personality.
- Jung developed a theory of a collective unconscious.
- Adler proposed feelings of inferiority as the driving force behind personality and developed birth order theory.
- Horney developed a theory based on basic anxiety and rejected the concept of penis envy.
- Erikson developed a theory based on social rather than sexual relationships, covering the entire life span.

12.6   *How does modern psychoanalytic theory differ from that of Freud?*

- Current research has found support for the defense mechanisms and the concept of an unconscious mind that can influence conscious behavior, but other concepts cannot be scientifically researched.

The Behaviorist's View of Personality

12.7   *How do behaviorists explain personality?*

- Behaviorists define personality as a set of learned responses or habits.

The Social Cognitive View of Personality

- The social cognitive view of personality includes the concept of reciprocal determinism, in which the environment, characteristics of the person, and the behavior itself all interact.
- Self-efficacy is a characteristic in which a person perceives a behavior as more or less effective based on previous experiences, the opinions of others, and perceived personal competencies.
- Behaviorist personality theory has scientific support but is criticized as being too simplistic.

The Third Force: Humanism and Personality

12.8   *How do humanists explain personality?*

- Humanism developed as a reaction against the negativity of psychoanalysis and the deterministic nature of behaviorism.

12.9   *What was Roger's view of the self?*

- Carl Rogers proposed that self-actualization depends on proper development of the self-concept.
- The self-concept includes the real self and the ideal self. When these two components do not match or agree, anxiety and disordered behavior are the results.

- Unconditional positive regard from important others in a person's life helps the formation of the self-concept and the congruity of the real and ideal selves, leading to a fully functioning person.
- Humanistic theory is not scientifically researched but has been effective in therapy situations.

Trait Theories: Who Are You?

12.10   *What is the trait perspective?*

- Trait theorists describe personality traits in order to predict behavior.
- Allport first developed a list of about 200 traits and believed that these traits were part of the nervous system.
- Cattell reduced the number of traits to between 16 and 23 with a computer method called factor analysis.
- Several researchers have arrived at five trait dimensions that have research support across cultures, called the Big Five or five-factor model. The five factors are openness, conscientiousness, extraversion, agreeableness, and neuroticism.

12.11   *How do trait theorists today view personality?*

- Cross-cultural research has found support for the five-factor model of personality traits in a number of different cultures.
- Future research will explore the degree to which child-rearing practices and heredity may influence the five personality factors.
- Behavior genetics is a field of study of the relationship between heredity and personality.

The Biology of Personality: Behavioral Genetics

12.12   *What part do biology and heredity play in personality?*

- Studies of twins and adopted children have found support for a genetic influence on many personality traits, including intelligence, leadership abilities, traditionalism, nurturance, empathy, assertiveness, neuroticism, and extraversion.

Classic Studies In Psychology: Geert Hofstede's Four Dimensions of Cultural Personality

12.13   *What were Hofstede's dimensions of cultural personality?*

- Hofstede's cross-cultural management study revealed four basic dimensions of personality along which cultures may vary: individualism/collectivism, power distance, masculinity/femininity, and uncertainty avoidance.

Assessment of Personality

12.14   *What are the advantages and disadvantages of using interviews to measure personality?*

- Interviews are used primarily by psychoanalysts and humanists and can include structured or unstructured interviews.
- Disadvantages of interviews can include the halo effect and bias of the interpretation on the part of the interviewer.

12.15   *How are projective tests used to explore personality, and what are the problems with projective tests?*

- Projective tests are based on the defense mechanism of projection and are used by psychoanalysts. Projective tests include the Rorschach inkblot test and the Thematic Apperception Test.
- Projective tests can be useful in finding starting points to open a dialogue between therapist and client but have been criticized for being low in reliability and validity.

12.16   *How can behavioral assessments be used in assessing personality?*

- Behavioral assessments are primarily used by behaviorists and include direct observation of behavior, rating scales of specific behavior, and frequency counts of behavior.
- Behavioral assessments have the disadvantage of the observer effect, which causes an observed person's behavior to change, and observer bias on the part of the person doing the assessment.

12.17 *What are the different kinds of personality inventories used to measure personality?*

- Personality inventories are typically developed by trait theorists and provide a detailed description of certain personality traits. They are objective tests rather than subjective.
- The NEO-PI is based on the five-factor model, whereas the Myers-Briggs Type Indicator is based on Jung's theory of personality types.
- The MMPI-2 is designed to detect abnormal personality.
- Personality inventories include validity scales to prevent cheating, but such measures are not perfect and cheating is sometimes possible.

Applying Psychology to Everyday Life: Personality Testing on the Internet

12.18 *How good are the personality tests people can take on the Internet?*

- There are numerous personality tests available on the Internet, although all of them are not equal in quality, reliability, or validity.
- One danger in taking an online personality test is the lack of professional interpretation of the results of such tests.

12 KEY TERMS

TEST YOURSELF

Pick the best answer.

1. Which of the following is the definition of personality?
   a. the characteristics with which each person is born
   b. the moral and ethical behavior of a person
   c. the unique way an individual thinks, feels, and acts
   d. changes in behavior according to experiences

2. Freud's emphasis on sex and sexual development was mostly due to
   a. his own problems with sexuality.
   b. the culture within which he and his patients existed at the time.
   c. an increase in sexual deviancy across Europe in the nineteenth century.
   d. the influence of his colleagues.

3. Which of Freud's parts of the personality is the most like short-term memory?
   a. conscious   c. unconscious
   b. preconscious   d. subconscious

4. Stephen wants a new MP3 player he saw in the local electronics store, but he doesn't have enough money to pay for it. Which structure of Stephen's personality would urge him to take the player while no one in the store was looking?
   a. id   c. superego
   b. ego   d. libido

5. Which structure of the personality, according to Freud, works on the reality principle?
   a. id
   b. ego
   c. superego
   d. libido

6. The _____ develops in the _____ stage as a result of identification.
   a. ego; oral
   b. id; oral
   c. superego; phallic
   d. superego; latency

7. Three-year-old Brandon has watched his father, a chef, when he prepares meals for the family. This year, Brandon has asked for a play kitchen for his birthday. Freud would say that Brandon is beginning the process of _____ as a way of resolving his Oedipal conflict.
   a. compensation
   b. identification
   c. sublimation
   d. denial

8. According to Adler, middle children tend to be
   a. overachieving.
   b. competitive.
   c. resentful of the freedom of the older child.
   d. filled with feelings of inferiority.

9. Research has begun to show some support for which of Freud's concepts?
   a. the existence of an id, ego, and superego
   b. the order of the psychosexual stages
   c. the concept of an unconscious mind
   d. the existence of the Oedipus complex

10. To explain a person's personality, behaviorists would look to
    a. early childhood emotional traumas.
    b. the kind of love, warmth, and affection given to the person by his or her parents.
    c. the early experiences of rewards and punishments for certain behavior.
    d. the constellation of personality traits possessed by the person.

11. For Bandura, one of the most important person variables in determining personality is
    a. self-efficacy.
    b. self-concept.
    c. self-determination.
    d. self-motivation.

12. Unlike psychoanalysis, the social cognitive view of personality
    a. tries to explain how people become the people they are.
    b. stresses the importance of early childhood in personality development.
    c. is fully able to explain all the complexities of human behavior.
    d. has been scientifically tested.

13. The striving for fulfillment of one's potential is called
    a. self-concept.
    b. self-efficacy.
    c. self-actualization.
    d. the ideal self.

14. According to Rogers, anxiety and neurotic behavior result from
    a. unconscious conflicts and desires.
    b. a mismatch between the real and ideal self.
    c. receiving too much unconditional positive regard from significant others.
    d. learned habits of behavior.

15. Which of the following viewpoints has different goals from the other three?
    a. psychoanalytic
    b. behaviorism
    c. humanism
    d. trait theory

16. How many source traits did Cattell use in developing his personality inventory?
    a. 5
    b. 10
    c. 16
    d. 23

17. The five-factor model of personality traits includes all but which of the following?
    a. openness
    b. self-sufficiency
    c. extraversion
    d. neuroticism

18. Dr. Phillips is constantly late for his classes and often shows up late for his office hours, leaving students waiting in the hallway outside his door for nearly an hour at times. Using the five-factor model, which dimension would show a very low score for Dr. Phillips?
    a. self-sufficiency
    b. openness
    c. agreeableness
    d. conscientiousness

19. The study of the inherited portions of personality is called
    a. twin studies.
    b. adoptive studies.
    c. behavioral genetics.
    d. adoptive genetics.

20. According to Hofstede, cultures that have many strict rules and laws, lots of security and safety measures, and that tend to hold only one philosophical or religious belief are high in
    a. individualism.
    b. power distance.
    c. masculinity.
    d. uncertainty avoidance.

21. If a client is having trouble talking about what is bothering him, a psychoanalyst might turn to a(n) _____ to probe the client's unconscious conflicts.
    a. objective test
    b. projective test
    c. personality inventory
    d. observational study

22. The Rorschach test has people
    a. tell stories about a picture with people in it.
    b. answer hundreds of questions about their feelings and thoughts.
    c. perform tasks while an observer watches through a one-way mirror.
    d. look at ambiguous visual stimuli and tell what they think it is.

23. Which type of assessment would have the least problem with reliability?
    a. subjective test
    b. projective test
    c. personality inventory
    d. observational study

24. Which of the following is not a type of behavioral assessment?
    a. direct observation
    b. Thematic Apperception Test
    c. rating scale
    d. frequency count

25. Which of the following is based on the five-factor model?
    a. NEO-PI
    b. MBTI
    c. MMPI-2
    d. 16PF

Answers: 1-c, 2-b, 3-a, 4-a, 5-b, 6-c, 7-b, 8-b, 9-c, 10-c, 11-a, 12-d, 13-c, 14-b, 15-d, 16-c, 17-b, 18-d, 19-c, 20-d, 21-b, 22-d, 23-c, 24-b, 25-a.

For more sample quizzes and other review activities that will help you get a better grade, be sure to check out your accompanying study guide. To access tests and your own personalized study plan that will help you focus on the areas you need to master before your next class test, be sure to go to the on-line Psychology web site available with the access code packaged with your book.

CONCEPT MAP

Personality: unique way individuals think, feel, and act

Four perspectives are:
1. Psychoanalytic
2. Behaviorist (including social cognitive theory)
3. Humanist
4. Trait

12.1

Theories of Personality

PSYCHOANALYTIC

BEHAVIORIST

Jung, Adler, Horney, and Erickson's Modifications of Freud

Jung: theory of a collective unconscious

Adler: feelings of inferiority as the force behind personality

Horney: theory based on basic anxiety, rejected penis envy concept

Erikson: developed a theory based on social relationships

12.5

Modern Psychoanalytic Theory

Research supports defense mechanisms, unconscious mind. Other concepts are unable to be scientifically researched

12.6

Behaviorist Theories of Personality

Personality: set of learned responses or habits

Social cognitive: concept of reciprocal determinism: the environment, person, and behavior interact

Self-efficacy: person perceives behavior as more or less effective based on previous experiences, opinions of others, perceived personal competencies

12.7

Freud's View of the Conscious Mind

Three Divisions: Conscious, Preconscious, and Unconscious

12.2

Freud's Three Parts of the Personality: Id, Ego and Superego

- **Id:** works on the pleasure principle
- **Ego:** works on the reality principle
- **Superego:** is the moral center of personality

Conflict between id and superego leads to anxiety for ego

12.3

Freudian Stages of Personality Development

Personality develops in a series of psychosexual stages:
- Oral (id dominated)
- Anal (ego develops)
- Phallic (superego develops)
- Latency (period of sexual repression)
- Genital (sexual feelings)

Oedipus and Electra complexes:
- Create anxiety in the phallic stage
- Resolved through identification with the same-sex parent

Fixation: occurs when conflicts are not fully resolved during a stage

12.4

Interviews as Measures of Personality

- Interviews used primarily by psychoanalysts and humanists
- Can include structured or unstructured interviews
- Disadvantages: halo effect and biased interpretations

12.14

RORSCHACH INK BLOT

THEMATIC APPERCEPTION TEST

Projective Tests

- Based on defense mechanism of projection
- Include Rorschach inkblots and Thematic Apperception Test
- Criticized for being low in reliability and validity

12.15

HUMANIST
THE THIRD FORCE: HUMANISM AND PERSONALITY

TRAIT

Roger's View of the Self

Self-actualization: depends on proper development of the self-concept

Self-concept: includes real self, ideal self

Unconditional positive regard: positive regard that is given without conditions

Humanistic theory: not scientifically researched

12.9

Humanist Theories of Personality

Reaction against negativity of psychoanalysis and behaviorism's determinism

12.8

The Trait Perspective

Trait theorists: describe personality traits in order to predict behavior

Allport: list of about 200 traits

Cattell: 16 and 23 traits

Big Five or Five-Factor Model
- Openness
- Conscientiousness
- Extraversion
- Agreeableness
- Neuroticism

12.10

Trait Theorists Today

- Cross-cultural research: supports the five-factor model
- Future research: explores child-rearing practices, heredity, and five-factor model
- Behavior genetics: study of relationship between heredity and personality

12.11

Roles of Biology and Heredity in Personality

Studies of twins and adopted children support a genetic influence on personality

12.12

Hofstede's Four Dimensions of Cultural Personality

1. Individualism/collectivism   2. Power distance
3. Masculinity/feminity   4. Uncertainty avoidance

12.13

Assessment of Personality

Behavioral Assessments Used in Assessing Personality

- Include direct observation, rating scales, and frequency counts
- Disadvantages: observer effect and observer bias

12.16

Personality Inventories

- Developed by trait theorists
- Provide detailed description of personality traits
- Objective tests rather than subjective
  - NEO-PI: based on the five-factor model
  - Myers-Briggs Type Indicator: based on Jung's theory of personality types
  - MMPI-2: designed to detect abnormal personality

12.17

Personality Tests on the Internet

- There are numerous personality tests available on the Internet, although all of them are not equal in quality, reliability, or validity
- One danger in taking an online personality test is the lack of a professional to interpret results

12.18

13

Social Psychology

The Unresponsive Bystander: Why Did No One Help?

It was a cold early morning on March 13, 1964, when Catherine "Kitty" Genovese was attacked and killed by a man who later claimed that he just couldn't get the idea of murdering someone out of his head. Kitty had driven into the parking lot of the apartment building in which she lived at about 3:15 A.M. The killer was waiting in the darkness. Kitty spotted him and ran for the safety of her apartment building, but the man was faster and jumped on her back, stabbing her repeatedly. Kitty was heard to scream, "Oh my God! He stabbed me! Please help me!" But no one came to help. The man left and Kitty crawled into an entryway, but the man returned, raped her, and then stabbed her to death. The entire attack took nearly half an hour.

A police investigation determined that at least 38 people heard or watched some part of the fatal attack from their apartment windows. People turned on their lights and opened their windows to look out at the struggle going on below. Incredibly, not one of these people—Kitty's neighbors—called the police until after the attack was over. Why did no one try to help Kitty? There were lots of excuses: Many people assumed that someone else had already called the police. Others "didn't want to get involved." Some assumed that it was a lover's spat, and one man simply stated, "I was tired." Are people really this cold and heartless? What was the problem here?

Why study social psychology?

If people lived in total isolation from other people, there would be no reason to study the effect that other people have on the behavior of individuals and groups. But human beings are social creatures—we live with others, work with others, and play with others. The people who surround us all of our lives have an impact on our beliefs and values, decisions and assumptions, and the way we think about other people in general. Why are some people prejudiced toward certain other people? Why do we obey some people but not others? What causes us to like, to love, or to hate others? The answers to all these questions and many more can be found in the study of social psychology.

13.1 What makes people want to conform to the actions of others?

13.2 What is groupthink?

13.3 What are four common ways to gain the compliance of another?

13.4 What makes people obey the instructions or orders of others?

13.5 How does the presence of other people affect a person's performance on a task?

13.6 What are the three components of an attitude and how are attitudes formed?

13.7 How can attitudes be changed?

13.8 What happens when a person's attitudes don't match the person's actions?

13.9 What are social categorization and implicit personality theories?

13.10 How do people try to explain the actions of others?

13.11 What is the difference between prejudice and discrimination?

13.12 Why are people prejudiced, and how can prejudice be stopped?

13.13 What factors cause people to be attracted to each other?

13.14 What is love, and what are the different forms that love can take?

13.15 How is aggressive behavior determined by biology and learning?

13.16 What is altruism?

13.17 What is the bystander effect?

13.18 What did Latané and Darley discover about the presence of others and helping behavior?

13.19 What decisions have to be made before a person will help someone else?

13.20 Why do people join cults?

Chapter One defined psychology as the scientific study of behavior and mental processes, including how people think and feel. The field of social psychology also looks at behavior and mental processes but includes as well the social world in which we exist, as we are surrounded by others to whom we are connected and by whom we are influenced in so many ways. It is not the same field as *sociology*, which is the study and classification of human societies. Sociology studies the big picture: how entire groups of people live, work, and play. Although social psychology does look at group behavior, it is more concerned with the individual person within the group and the influence of the group on the person.

Social psychology is the scientific study of how a person's behavior, thoughts, and feelings are influenced by the real, imagined, or implied presence of others. Although there are several sections in this chapter, there are really only three main areas under discussion: *social influence,* the ways in which a person's behavior can be affected by other people; *social cognition,* the ways in which people think about other people; and *social interaction,* the positive and negative aspects of people relating to others.

Social Influence: Conformity, Compliance, and Obedience

People live in a world filled with other people. An infant is born into a world with adults who have an impact on the infant's actions, personality, and growth. Adults must interact with others on a daily basis. Such interactions provide ample opportunity for the presence of other people to directly or indirectly influence the behavior, feelings, and thoughts of each individual in a process called **social influence**. There are many forms of social influence. People can influence others to follow along with their own actions or thoughts, to agree to do things even when the person might prefer to do otherwise, and to be obedient to authorities. The mere presence of others can even influence the way people perform tasks successfully or unsuccessfully.

Simulation
Live! psych
Conformity

social psychology
the scientific study of how a person's thoughts, feelings, and behavior are influenced by the real, imagined, or implied presence of others.

social influence
the process through which the real or implied presence of others can directly or indirectly influence the thoughts, feelings, and behavior of an individual.

CONFORMITY

13.1   *What makes people want to conform to the actions of others?*

Have you ever noticed someone looking up at something? Did the urge to look up to see what that person was looking at become so strong that you actually found yourself looking up? This common practical joke always works, even when people suspect that it's a joke. It clearly demonstrates the power of **conformity**: changing one's own behavior to more closely match the actions of others.

"Sure, I follow the herd — not out of brainless obedience, mind you, but out of a deep and abiding respect for the concept of community."

In 1936, social psychologist Muzafer Sharif conducted a study in which participants were shown into a darkened room and exposed to a single point of light. Under those conditions, a point of light will seem to move because of tiny, involuntary movements of the eye. Ⓛ Ⓘ Ⓝ Ⓚ to *Chapter Three: Sensation and Perception, p. 86.* The participants were not told of this effect and reported the light moved anywhere from a few inches to several feet. When a confederate (a person chosen by the experimenter to deliberately manipulate the situation) also gave estimates, the original participants began to make estimates of motion that were more and more similar to those of the confederate (Sherif, 1936). This early experiment on conformity has been criticized because the judgments being made were ambiguous* (i.e., the light wasn't really moving so any estimate within reason would sound good); would participants be so easily swayed if the judgments were more specifically measurable and certain?

ASCH'S CLASSIC STUDY ON CONFORMITY   Solomon Asch (1951) conducted his classic study of conformity by having participants gather in a room. They were told that they were participating in an experiment on visual judgment. They were then shown a white card with three black lines of varying lengths followed by another white card with only one line on it. The task was to determine which line on the first card was most similar to the line on the second card (see Figure 13.1).

In reality, only the last person in the group was a real participant. The others were all confederates (people following special directions from the experimenter) who were instructed to pick the same *incorrect* line from the comparison lines. Would the last person, having heard the others pick what seemed to be the wrong answer, change to conform to the group's opinion? Surprisingly, the participants conformed to the group answer a little over one-third of the time. Asch also found that the number of confederates mattered: Conformity increased with each new confederate until there were four confederates; more than that did not increase the participants' tendency to conform (Asch, 1951). In a later experiment, Asch (1956) found that conformity decreased if there was just one confederate who gave the correct answer—apparently, if participants knew that there was at least one other person whose answer agreed with their own, the evidence of their own eyes won out over the pressure to conform to the group.

More recent research in the United States has found less conformity among participants, perhaps suggesting that the Asch conformity effect was due to the more conforming nature of people in the era and culture of the American 1950s (Lalancette & Standing, 1990; Nicholson et al., 1985; Perrin & Spencer, 1980). In other cultures, however, studies have found conformity effects similar to those in Asch's study (Neto, 1995). Still others have found even greater effects of conformity in collectivist cultures such as Hong Kong, Japan, and Zimbabwe (Bond & Smith, 1996; Kim & Markus, 1999).

---

*Ambiguous: having no clear interpretation or able to be interpreted in many ways rather than just one way.

Standard Line

1   2   3

Comparison Line

FIGURE 13.1   **Stimuli Used in Asch's Study**   Participants in Asch's famous study on conformity were first shown the three comparison lines. They were then shown the standard line and asked to determine to which of the three comparison lines the standard line was most similar. Which line would you pick? What if you were one of several people, and everyone who answered ahead of you chose Line number three? How would that affect your answer?
Source: Adapted from Asch (1956).

conformity
changing one's own behavior to match that of other people.

What about gender ▶ —are men or women more conforming?

Many historical events have been at least partly caused by the phenomenon of groupthink. The explosion of the U.S. space shuttle *Challenger* on January 28, 1986, which killed all seven astronauts on board, is one of those events. Several people later admitted that they had doubts about the safety of launching on schedule but were afraid to speak up.

I have a friend who watches all those infomercials on the shopping channels and buys stuff that isn't worth the money or ▶ that doesn't work like it's supposed to work. Why do people fall for pitches like that?

What about gender—are men or women more conforming? Research shows that gender differences are practically nonexistent unless the situation involves behavior that is not private. If it is possible to give responses in private, conformity is no greater for women than for men, but if a public response is required, women do tend to show more conformity than men (Eagly, 1987; Eagly et al., 2000). This effect may be due to the socialization that women receive in being agreeable and supportive; however, the difference in conformity is quite small.

13.2   *What is groupthink?*

THE HAZARDS OF GROUPTHINK   Consider that in the 1961 Bay of Pigs disaster one of the completely unsupported assumptions made by the group advising President Kennedy was that the Cuban exiles would be able to get those still living in Cuba to rise up to overthrow Castro. No single member of the group of advisors was willing to disagree with the group's outward agreement on this assumption. (The Cubans never organized a revolt and Castro is still in power. The Cuban exiles who were supposed to find support among the Cubans still living in Cuba were captured and later ransomed back by the United States.) This is a classic example of an error that can occur in situations when the pressure to conform to the group norm outweighs any evidence that the group norm is wrong. This kind of thinking, in which people feel it is more important to maintain the group's cohesiveness than to consider the facts more realistically, is called **groupthink** (Hogg & Hains, 1998; Janis, 1972, 1982; Schafer & Crichlow, 1996). Other examples include the sinking of the *Titanic* in 1912 (the group responsible for designing and building the ship assumed she was unsinkable and did not even bother to include enough lifeboats on board for all the passengers) and the *Challenger* disaster of 1986 in which a part on the shuttle was known by a few to be unacceptable (but no one spoke up to delay the launch).

Why does groupthink happen? Social psychologist Irving Janis (1972, 1982), who originally gave this phenomenon its name, lists several "symptoms" of groupthink. For example, group members may come to feel that the group can do no wrong, is morally correct, and will always succeed, creating the illusion of invulnerability.* Group members also tend to hold stereotyped views of those who disagree with the group's opinions, causing members to think that those who oppose the group have no worthwhile opinions. They exert pressure on individual members to conform to group opinion, prevent those who might disagree from speaking up, and even censor themselves so that the group's mind-set will not be disturbed in a "don't rock the boat" mentality. Self-appointed "mind-guards" work to protect the leader of the group from contrary viewpoints. (See Table 13.1.)

Several things can be done to minimize the possibility of groupthink (Hart, 1998; McCauley, 1998; Moorhead et al., 1998). For example, leaders should remain impartial and the entire group should seek the opinions of people outside the group. Any voting should be done on secret ballots rather than by a show of hands, and it should be made clear that group members will be held responsible for decisions made by the group.

COMPLIANCE

I have a friend who watches all those infomercials on the shopping channels and buys stuff that isn't worth the money or that doesn't work like it's supposed to work. Why do people fall for pitches like that? Marketing products is really very much a psychological process. In fact, the whole area of **consumer psychology** is devoted to figuring out how to get people to buy things that someone is selling.

---

*Invulnerability: quality of being unable to be attacked or harmed.

TABLE 13.1 **CHARACTERISTICS OF GROUPTHINK**

Characteristic	Description
Invulnerability	Members feel they cannot fail.
Rationalization	Members explain away warning signs and help each other rationalize their decision.
Lack of introspection	Members do not examine the ethical implications of their decision because they believe that they cannot make immoral choices.
Stereotyping	Members stereotype their enemies as weak, stupid, or unreasonable.
Pressure	Members pressure each other not to question the prevailing opinion.
Lack of disagreement	Members do not express opinions that differ from the group consensus.
Self-deception	Members share in the illusion that they all agree with the decision.
Insularity	Members prevent the group from hearing disruptive but potentially useful information from people who are outside the group.

Source: Janis (1972, 1982).

L I N K *to Appendix B: Applied Psychology.* But infomercials are not the only means by which people try to get others to do what they want them to do. **Compliance** occurs when people change their behavior as a result of another person or group asking or directing them to change. The person or group asking for the change in behavior typically doesn't have any real authority or power to command a change; when that happens, it is called *obedience*, which is the topic of the next major section of this chapter.

A number of techniques that people use to get the compliance of others clearly show the relationship of compliance to the world of marketing, as they refer to techniques that door-to-door salespersons would commonly use.

13.3 *What are four common ways to gain the compliance of another?*

FOOT-IN-THE-DOOR TECHNIQUE   Let's say that a neighbor asks you to keep an eye on his house while he is on vacation. You agree, thinking that it's a rather small request. Later that day, or perhaps even in the same conversation, the neighbor asks if you would kindly water his plants while he's gone. This is a little bit more involved and requires more of your time and energy—will you do it? If you are like most people, you probably will comply with this second larger request.

When compliance with a smaller request is followed by a larger request, people are quite likely to comply because they have already agreed to the smaller one and they want to behave consistently with their previous response (Cialdini et al., 1995; Dillard, 1990, 1991; Freedman & Fraser, 1966). This is called the **foot-in-the-door technique** because the first small request acts as an opener. (Salespeople once literally stuck a foot in the door to prevent the occupant from shutting it so they could continue their sales pitch, hence, the name.)

DOOR-IN-THE-FACE TECHNIQUE   Closely related to the foot-in-the-door technique is its opposite: the **door-in-the-face technique** (Cialdini et al., 1975). In this method, the larger request comes first, which is usually refused. This is followed by a second smaller and more reasonable request that often gets compliance. An example

groupthink
kind of thinking that occurs when people place more importance on maintaining group cohesiveness than on assessing the facts of the problem with which the group is concerned.

consumer psychology
branch of psychology that studies the habits of consumers in the marketplace.

compliance
changing one's behavior as a result of other people directing or asking for the change.

foot-in-the-door technique
asking for a small commitment and, after gaining compliance, asking for a bigger commitment.

door-in-the-face technique
asking for a large commitment and being refused, and then asking for a smaller commitment.

of this would be if the neighbor first asked you to take care of his dog and cat in your home. After you refused to do so, the neighbor might ask if you would at least water his plants, which you would probably do.

This technique relies on the **norm of reciprocity**, which basically assumes that if someone does something for a person, the person should do something in return. (Gouldner, 1960). This is also the principle used by those organizations that give out free, unasked-for samples, such as the free address stickers that come with many requests for charitable donations.

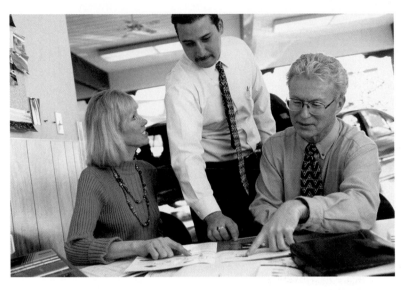

This couple is in the process of buying a new car. Car salespeople often use the low-ball technique by quoting what sounds like a reasonable price to potential buyers. Once this couple has committed to buying a particular car, they may find that there are other costs tacked onto that original price, such as additional options, extended warranties, and other fees. Can you think of other instances when something like this has happened to you?

LOWBALL TECHNIQUE Another compliance technique, also common in the world of sales, is called the **lowball technique** (Burger & Petty, 1981). In this technique, once a commitment is made, the cost of that commitment is increased. (In the sense used here, *cost* does not necessarily mean money; *cost* can also mean time, effort, or other kinds of sacrifices.) For example, let's say that a professor agrees to write a textbook for a publishing company. Once committed to that process, the professor discovers that the task involves not only writing but also traveling to meet with editors, working nights and weekends to meet deadlines, and making the commitment to take time off from her teaching job to finish the text on time for publication. (This example is purely hypothetical, of course.)

A more common example will occur to anyone who has ever bought a car. The commitment to buy the car at one low price is quickly followed by the addition of other costs: extended warranties, additional options, taxes and fees, and so on, causing the buyer to spend more money than originally intended.

THAT'S-NOT-ALL TECHNIQUE Finally, there is the now familiar technique of the infomercial salesperson: the **that's-not-all technique**. In this compliance tactic, the person doing the persuading makes an offer, but before the target of the offer can make a decision, the persuader throws in something extra to make the deal look even better (Burger, 1986). See if this sounds familiar:

"But wait—that's not all! If you act now, we'll send you this 15-piece set of genuine faux carving knives as a bonus!"

By offering something that the consumer did not ask for in the first place, the persuader has once again activated the norm of reciprocity. Now the consumer feels as though the persuader has "given" something and the consumer should respond by giving in to the persuader's request to buy the product.

Cultural differences exist in people's susceptibility to these techniques. For the foot-in-the-door technique in particular, research has shown that people in individualist cultures (such as the United States) are more likely to comply with the second request than are people in collectivist cultures (such as Japan). The research suggests that people in collectivist cultures are not as concerned with being consistent with previous behavior because they are less focused on their inner motivation than are people in individualist cultures, who are more concerned with their inner motives and consistency (Cialdini et al., 1999; Petrova et al., 2003). (LINK) *to Chapter Twelve: Theories of Personality, pp. 465–466.*

norm of reciprocity
assumption that if someone does something for a person, that person should do something for the other in return.

lowball technique
getting a commitment from a person and then raising the cost of that commitment.

that's-not-all technique
a sales technique in which the persuader makes an offer and then adds something extra to make the offer look better before the target person can make a decision.

OBEDIENCE

obedience
changing one's behavior at the
command of an authority figure.

13.4   *What makes people obey the instructions or orders of others?*

There is a difference between the concepts of compliance, which is agreeing to change one's behavior because someone else asks for the change, and **obedience**, which is changing one's behavior at the direct order of an authority figure. A salesperson who wants a person to buy a car has no real power to force that person to buy, but an authority figure is a person with social power—such as a police officer, a teacher, or a work supervisor—who has the right to demand certain behavior from the people under the authority figure's command or supervision.

How far will people go in obeying the commands of an authority figure? What factors make obedience more or less likely? These are some of the questions that researchers have been investigating for many years. The answers to these questions became very important not only to researchers but also to people everywhere after the atrocities committed by the soldiers in Nazi Germany—soldiers who were "just following orders."

MILGRAM'S SHOCKING RESEARCH   Social psychologist Stanley Milgram set out to find answers to these questions. He was aware of Asch's studies of conformity and wondered how much impact social influence could have on a behavior that was more meaningful than judging the length of lines on cards. He designed what has become one of the most famous (even notorious*) experiments in the history of psychology.

Through ads placed in the local newspaper, Milgram recruited people who were told that they would be participating in an experiment to test the effects of punishment on learning behavior (Milgram, 1964a, 1974). Although there were several different forms of this experiment with different participants, the basic premise was the same: The participants believed that they had randomly been assigned to either the "teacher" role or the "learner" role, when in fact the "learner" was an actor already aware of the situation. The "teacher" was given a sample 45-volt shock from the chair in which the "learner" was strapped during the experiment. The task for the learner was a simple memory test for paired words.

The "teacher" was seated in front of a machine through which the shocks would be administered and the level of the shocks changed. (See Figure 13.2.) For each mistake

---

*Notorious: widely and unfavorably known.

FIGURE 13.2   **Control Panel in Milgram's Experiment**   In Stanley Milgram's classic study on obedience, the participants were presented with a control panel like this one. Each participant ("teacher") was instructed to give electric shocks to another person (the "learner," who only pretended to be shocked). Notice the labels under the switches. At what point do you think you would have refused to continue the experiment?

Voltage of "Shock"	Learner's Script
TABLE 13.2 **SAMPLE SCRIPT ITEMS FROM MILGRAM'S CLASSIC EXPERIMENT**	
150	"Ugh!! Experimenter! That's all. Get me out of here. I told you I had heart trouble. My heart's starting to bother me now. Get me out of here, please. My heart's starting to bother me. I refuse to go on. Let me out."
210	"Ugh!! Experimenter! Get me out of here. I've had enough. I *won't* be in this experiment any more."
300	(*Agonized scream*) "I absolutely refuse to answer any more. Get me out of here. You can't hold me here. Get me out. Get me out of here."
330	(*Intense and prolonged agonized scream*) "Let me out of here. Let me out of here. My heart's bothering me. Let me out, I tell you. (*Hysterically*) Let me out of here. Let me out of here. You have no right to hold me here. Let me out! Let me out! Let me out of here! Let me out! Let me out!"

Source: Milgram (1964a, 1974).

made by the "learner," the "teacher" was instructed to increase the level of shock by 15 volts. The "learner" (who was not actually shocked) followed a carefully arranged script, showing discomfort, asking for the experiment to end, screaming, and even falling silent as if unconscious—or dead. (See Table 13.2 for samples of the scripted responses of the "learner.") As the "teachers" became reluctant to continue administering the shocks, the experimenter in his authoritative white lab coat said, for example, "The experiment requires you to continue" or "You must continue," and reminded the "teacher" that the experimenter would take full responsibility for the safety of the "learner."

How many of the participants continued to administer what they believed were real shocks? Milgram surveyed psychiatrists, college students, and other adults prior to the experiments for their opinions on how far the participants would go in administering shocks. Everyone predicted that the participants would all refuse to go on at some point, with most believing that the majority of the participants would start refusing as soon as the "learner" protested—150 volts. None of those he surveyed believed that any participant would go all the way to the highest voltage.

So were they right? Far from it—in the first set of experiments, 65 percent of the "teachers" went all the way through the experiment's final 450-volt shock level, although many were obviously uncomfortable and begged to be allowed to stop. Of those "teachers" who did protest and finally stop, not one of them stopped before reaching 300 volts!

So what happened? Were those people sadists? Why would they keep shocking someone like that? No one was more stunned than Milgram himself. He had not believed that his experiments would show such a huge effect of obedience to authority. These results do not appear to be some random "fluke" resulting from a large population of sadistic people residing in the area. These experiments have been repeated at various times, in the United States and in other countries, and the percentage of participants who went all the way consistently remained between 61 and 66 percent (Blass, 1999).

So what happened? Were those people sadists? ▶ Why would they keep shocking someone like that?

That's incredible—I just don't believe that I could do something like that to someone else.

◀ That's incredible—I just don't believe that I could do something like that to someone else.

EVALUATION OF MILGRAM'S RESEARCH   Researchers have looked for particular personality traits that might be associated with high levels of obedience but have not found any one trait or group of traits that consistently predicts who will obey and who will not in experiments similar to Milgram's original studies (Blass, 1991). The people who "went all the way" were not necessarily more dependent or susceptible to being controlled by others; they were simply people like most other people, caught in a situation of "obey or disobey" the authority. Although some have suggested that Milgram's results may have been due to the same kind of foot-in-the-door technique of persuasion as discussed earlier, with participants more likely to go on with each next demanding step of the experiment because they had already agreed to the smaller increments of shock, as yet no research supports this idea (Gilbert, 1981).

Milgram's research also raised a serious ethical question: How far should researchers be willing to go to answer a question of interest? Some have argued that the participants in Milgram's studies may have suffered damaged self-esteem and serious psychological stress from the realization that they were willing to administer shocks great enough to kill another person, just on the say-so of an experimenter (Baumrind, 1964). Milgram (1964b) responded to the criticism by citing his follow-up study of the participants, in which he found that 84 percent of the participants were glad to have been a part of the experiment and only 1.3 percent said that they were sorry they had been in the experiment. A follow-up psychiatric exam one year later also found no signs of harm or trauma in the participants. Even so, most psychologists do agree that under the current ethical rules that exist for such research, this study would never be allowed to happen today. (L I N K) *to Chapter One: The Science of Psychology, pp. 31–33.*

SOCIAL FACILITATION AND SOCIAL LOAFING

13.5   *How does the presence of other people affect a person's performance on a task?*

In addition to the influence that others can have on a person's actions and attitudes, social influence can affect the success or failure of an individual's task performance. The difficulty of the task seems to determine the particular effect of the presence of others as well: If a task is easy, the presence of other people seems to improve performance. If the task is difficult, the presence of others actually has a negative effect on performance. The positive influence of others on performance is called **social facilitation**, whereas the negative influence is sometimes called *social impairment* (Aiello & Douthitt, 2001; Michaels et al., 1982; Zajonc, 1965).

In both social facilitation and social impairment, the presence of other people acts to increase arousal (Zajonc, 1965, 1968; Zajonc et al., 1970). Social facilitation occurs because the presence of others creates just enough increased arousal to improve performance. But the presence of others when the task is difficult produces too high a level of arousal, resulting in impaired performance. (L I N K) *to Chapter Nine: Motivation and Emotion, p. 341.*

All people are not the same, and it would be foolish to expect the rules of social influence to affect different individuals in exactly the same way. For example, people who are lazy tend not to do as well when other people are also working on the same

social facilitation
the tendency for the presence of other people to have a positive impact on the performance of an easy task.

At first the man in the foreground seems to be paying attention to the woman making the presentation. But if you look carefully at his computer screen, you'll see he's actually engaging in some serious social loafing. How do you think his colleagues around the room might feel about his behavior?

task, but they can do quite well when working on their own. This phenomenon is called **social loafing** (Karau & Williams, 1993, 1997; Latané et al., 1979). The reason for this is that it is easier for a lazy person (a "loafer") to hide laziness when working in a group of people because it is less likely that the individual will be evaluated alone—the group will be the focus of the evaluation, and someone in the group will most likely be concerned enough about the evaluation to make sure that the task is completed successfully. The social loafer doesn't feel the need to make any real effort, preferring to let the other members of the group do the work. But when the social loafer is working alone, the focus of evaluation will be on that person only. In that case, the loafer works harder because there is no one else to whom the work can be shifted.

Social loafing depends heavily on the assumption that personal responsibility for a task is severely lessened when working with a group of other people. One study suggests that although Americans may readily make that assumption, Chinese people, who come from a more interdependent cultural viewpoint, tend to assume that each individual within the group is still nearly as responsible for the group's outcome as the group at large (Menon et al., 1999). Chinese people are, therefore, less likely to exhibit social loafing than are people in the United States.

PRACTICE **QUIZ:** HOW MUCH DO YOU REMEMBER?

Pick the best answer.

1. A person's conformity in a situation like the Asch line study is most likely to be strongest when
   a. the person is in the room with only one other person.
   b. at least one other person agrees with the person.
   c. that person is from Hong Kong.
   d. that person is from the United States.

2. In groupthink, members of the group
   a. have an illusion of invulnerability.
   b. avoid stereotyping those who hold an opposing viewpoint.
   c. like to "rock the boat" every now and then.
   d. sometimes question the moral "rightness" of the group.

3. When members of a cult are trying to enlist a new recruit, they start by asking the recruit to make a small commitment, such as attending a short meeting or helping out at a social function. Then the commitments get more involved, such as staying for a longer period of time and eventually for major donations of money and moving in with the cult members. This is most like which of the following techniques?
   a. foot-in-the-door technique
   b. door-in-the-face technique
   c. lowball technique
   d. that's-not-all technique

4. Which of the following has been shown to be true concerning the "teachers" in Milgram's experiment?
   a. Most of the "teachers" were sorry to have been a part of the experiment.
   b. They were found to be psychologically weak-minded people.
   c. Only a very small percentage showed any signs of psychological problems after one year.
   d. They were not ordinary people.

5. Alex, who is in the honors program, failed to do his share of the work on the group project with his four classmates. Alex was most likely engaging in
   a. social facilitation.
   b. social impairment.
   c. social loafing.
   d. social influencing.

Answers: 1-c, 2-a, 3-a, 4-c, 5-c.

social loafing
the tendency for people to put less effort into a simple task when working with others on that task.

attitude
a tendency to respond positively or negatively toward a certain person, object, idea, or situation.

Attitudes

One area of social cognition concerns the formation and influence of attitudes on the behavior and perceptions of others. An **attitude** can be defined as a tendency to respond positively or negatively toward a certain idea, person, object, or situation (Triandis, 1971). This tendency, developed through peoples' experiences as they live and work with others, can affect the way they behave toward those ideas, people, objects, and situations and can include opinions, beliefs, and biases. In fact, attitudes influence the way people view these things *before* they've actually been exposed to them (Petty et al., 2003).

What do you mean—how can an attitude have an effect on something that hasn't happened yet? Attitudes are not something people have when they are born. They are learned through experiences and contact with others and even through direct instruction from parents, teachers, and other important people in a person's life. Because attitudes involve a positive or negative evaluation of things, it's possible to go into a new situation, meet a new person, or be exposed to a new idea with one's "mind already made up" to like or dislike, agree or disagree, and so on (Eagly & Chaiken, 1993; Petty et al., 2003). For example, children are known for making up their minds about certain foods before ever tasting them, simply because the foods are "green." Those children may have tried a green food in the past and disliked it and now are predisposed* to dislike any green food, whether they've tasted it or not.

THE ABC MODEL OF ATTITUDES

13.6   *What are the three components of an attitude and how are attitudes formed?*

Attitudes are actually made up of three different parts, or components, as shown in Figure 13.3. These components should not come as a surprise to anyone who has been reading the other chapters in this text because, throughout the text, references have been made to personality and traits being composed of the ways people think, feel, and act. By using certain terms to describe these three things, psychologists have come up with a handy way to describe the three components of attitudes (Eagly & Chaiken, 1993, 1998)

AFFECTIVE COMPONENT   The *affective component* of an attitude is the way a person feels toward the object, person, or situation. *Affect* is used in psychology to mean "emotions" or "feelings," so the affective component is the emotional component. For example, some people might feel that country music is fun and uplifting.

---

*Predisposed: referring to a tendency to respond in a particular way based on previous experience.

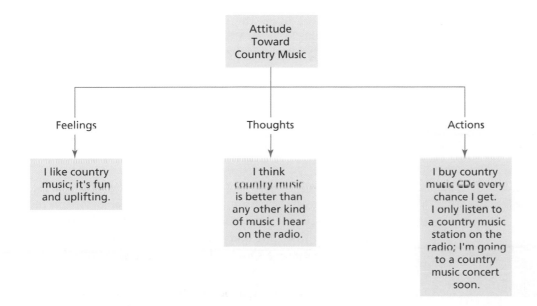

FIGURE 13.3   **Three Components of an Attitude**   Attitudes consist of the way a person feels and thinks about something, as well as the way the person chooses to behave. If you like country music you are also likely to think that country music is good music. You are also more likely to listen to this style of music, buy this type of music, and even go to a performance. Each of the three components influences the other two.

BEHAVIOR COMPONENT The *behavior component* of an attitude is the action that a person takes in regard to the person, object, or situation. For example, a person who feels that country music is fun is likely to turn to a country music station on the car radio, buy country music CDs, or go to a country music concert.

COGNITIVE COMPONENT Finally, the *cognitive component* of an attitude is the way a person thinks about the person, object, or situation. These thoughts, or cognitions, include beliefs and ideas about the focus of the attitude. For example, the country music lover might believe that country music is superior to other forms of music.

> **So if you know what someone thinks or feels about something, you can predict what that person will do, right?**

So if you know what someone thinks or feels about something, you can predict what that person will do, right? Oddly enough, attitudes turn out to be pretty poor predictors of actual behavior in a number of controlled research studies. One survey of such research conducted in the 1960s found that what people say and what people do are often two very different things (Wicker, 1971). Studies conducted in the decades that followed found that attitudes predict behavior only under certain conditions. For example, in one study researchers found that although people indicated on a survey that they believed in protecting the environment and would be willing to pay more for fruits and vegetables raised under such conditions, those same people were seen to buy the ecology-friendly fruit only in grocery stores in areas of higher income levels where consumers actually had the financial means to "put their money where their mouth was" (Clarke et al., 1999). Those who did not live in a higher-income area gave what they probably saw as a socially desirable answer on the survey but then allowed the external influence of a lower income to determine their actual behavior.

Another factor in matching attitudes and behavior concerns how specific the attitude itself is. People may hold a general attitude about something without reflecting that attitude in their actual behavior. For example, doctors generally hold the attitude that people should do everything they can to protect their health and promote wellness, yet many doctors still smoke tobacco, fail to exercise, and often get too little sleep. But a very specific attitude, such as "exercise is important to my immediate health" will more likely be associated with the behavior of exercising (Ajzen, 2001; Ajzen & Fishbein, 2000).

Some attitudes are stronger than others, and strong attitudes are more likely to predict behavior than weak ones. A person who quit smoking because of failing health might have a stronger attitude toward secondhand smoking than someone who quit smoking on a dare, for example. The importance or salience* of a particular attitude in a given situation also has an impact on behavior—the more important the attitude appears, the more likely the behavior will match the attitude. Someone who is antismoking might be more likely to confront a smoker breaking the rules in a hospital, for example, than a smoker outside the building (Eagly & Chaiken, 1998).

Although many people might have the attitude that buying an ecology-friendly vehicle such as this 2001 Toyota Prius (a hybrid vehicle that can run on either gasoline or electricity) is a good idea, only those who can afford to buy such a vehicle will do so. Attitudes may predict people's behavior but only when people also have the means to act on their beliefs will the predicted behavior actually occur.

ATTITUDE FORMATION

Attitude formation is the result of a number of different influences with only one thing in common: They are all forms of learning.

DIRECT CONTACT One way in which attitudes are formed is by direct contact with the person, idea, situation, or object that is the focus of the attitude. For example, a child who tries Brussels sprouts for the first time and dislikes them will form a negative attitude about Brussels sprouts. Later that negative attitude may

---

*Salience: importance or having the quality of being obvious or easily seen.

be generalized to other foods that are green or have a similar taste.

DIRECT INSTRUCTION   Another way attitudes are formed is through direct instruction, either by parents or some other individual. Parents may tell their children that smoking cigarettes is dangerous and unhealthy, for example. Some children will form a negative attitude about smoking as a result.

INTERACTION WITH OTHERS   Sometimes attitudes are formed because the person is around other people with that attitude. If a person's friends, for example, all hold the attitude that smoking is cool, that person is more likely to think that smoking is cool as well (Eddy et al., 2000; Hill, 1990). The attitudes and behavior of teachers, parents, and siblings matter as well. Researchers found that a nonsmoking mother, teacher, or brother had a strong influence on both girls and boys (who are less likely to smoke), although the influence of all three on boys seemed to fade over a seven-year follow-up study (Shean et al., 1994).

VICARIOUS CONDITIONING (OBSERVATIONAL LEARNING)   Many attitudes are learned through the observation of other people's actions and reactions to various objects, people, or situations. Just as a child whose mother shows a fear of dogs may develop a similar fear, a child whose mother or father shows a positive attitude toward classical music may grow into an adult with a similarly positive attitude. The emotional components of an attitude can be learned by observing the emotional reactions of others, and the behavioral components can be observed and imitated.

Attitudes are not only influenced by other people in a person's immediate world but also by the larger world of the educational system (many attitudes may be learned in school or through reading books) and the mass media of magazines, television, and the movies—a fact of which advertisers and marketing experts are well aware (Gresham & Shimp, 1985; MacKenzie et al., 1986).

Don't Get Left in the Rain
Smoking just isn't cool.

AMERICAN CANCER SOCIETY

This public service message is aimed at changing the attitudes of young people who smoke. Most nonsmokers will not confront a person who is smoking in an appropriate area, as the young woman in this photo is doing. But if the young woman were in a hospital waiting room, others would be more likely to confront her. Smoking in an area that is clearly not appropriate would be more important to those with antismoking attitudes.

ATTITUDE CHANGE: THE ART OF PERSUASION

Sometimes people learn attitudes that aren't necessarily good ones, right? So can attitudes change? Because attitudes are learned, they are also subject to change with new learning. The world is full of people, companies, and other organizations that want to change peoples' attitudes. It's all about the art of **persuasion**, the process by which one person tries to change the belief, opinion, position, or course of action of another person through argument, pleading, or explanation.

13.7   *How can attitudes be changed?*

Persuasion is not a simple matter. There are several factors that become important in predicting how successful any persuasive effort at attitude change might be. These factors include:

- **Source:** the *communicator* is the person delivering the message. There is a strong tendency to give more weight to people who are perceived as experts, as well as those who seem trustworthy, attractive, and similar to the person receiving the message (Eagly & Chaiken, 1975; Petty & Cacioppo, 1986, 1996; Priester & Petty, 1995).
- **Message:** The actual message should be clear and well organized (Booth-Butterfield, 1996). It is usually more effective to present both sides of an argument to an

◀ Sometimes people learn attitudes that aren't necessarily good ones, right? So can attitudes change?

persuasion
the process by which one person tries to change the belief, opinion, position, or course of action of another person through argument, pleading, or explanation.

elaboration likelihood model
model of persuasion stating that people will either elaborate on the persuasive message or fail to elaborate on it, and that the future actions of those who do elaborate are more predictable than those who do not.

central-route processing
type of information processing that involves attending to the content of the message itself.

peripheral-route processing
type of information processing that involves attending to factors not involved in the message, such as the appearance of the source of the message, the length of the message, and other noncontent factors.

It said earlier in the chapter that sometimes what people say and what they do are very different. I once pointed this out to a friend of ▶ mine who was behaving this way, and he got really upset over it. Why did he get so upset?

How the jurors in this courtroom interpret and process the information they are given will determine the outcome of the trial. Those who listen carefully to what is said by persons involved in the trial are using central-route processing. There may be some jurors, however, who are more affected by the appearance, dress, attractiveness, or tone of voice of the lawyers, defendant, and witnesses. When people are persuaded by factors other than the message itself, it is called peripheral-route processing.

audience that has not yet committed to one side or the other (Crowley & Hoyer, 1994; Petty & Cacioppo, 1996; Petty et al., 2003). Messages that are directed at producing fear are more effective if they produce only a moderate amount of fear and also provide information about how to avoid the fear-provoking consequences (Kleinot & Rogers, 1982; Meyrick, 2001; Petty, 1995; Rogers & Mewborn, 1976).

- **Target Audience:** The characteristics of the people who are the intended target of the message of persuasion are also important in determining the effectiveness of the message. The age of the audience members can be a factor, for example. Researchers have found that people who are in the young adult stage of the late teens to the mid-twenties are more susceptible to persuasion than are older people (Visser & Krosnick, 1998).

How easily influenced a person is will also be related to the way people tend to process information. In the **elaboration likelihood model** of persuasion (Petty & Cacioppo, 1986), it is assumed that people either elaborate on what they hear (the facts of the message) or they do not elaborate at all, preferring to pay attention to the surface characteristics of the message (length, who delivers it, how attractive the message deliverer is, etc.). Two types of processing are hypothesized in this model: **central-route processing**, in which people attend to the content of the message, and **peripheral-route processing**, a style of information processing that relies on peripheral cues (cues outside of the message content itself) such as the expertise of the message source, the length of the message, and other factors that have nothing to do with the message content. This style of processing causes people not to pay attention to the message itself but instead to base their decisions on those peripheral factors (Petty & Cacioppo, 1986; Stiff & Mongeau, 2002). For example, the author once participated on a jury panel in which one woman voted "guilty" because the defendant had "shifty eyes" and not because of any of the evidence presented.

COGNITIVE DISSONANCE: WHEN ATTITUDES AND BEHAVIOR CLASH

It said earlier in the chapter that sometimes what people say and what they do are very different. I once pointed this out to a friend of mine who was behaving this way, and he got really upset over it. Why did he get so upset? When people find themselves

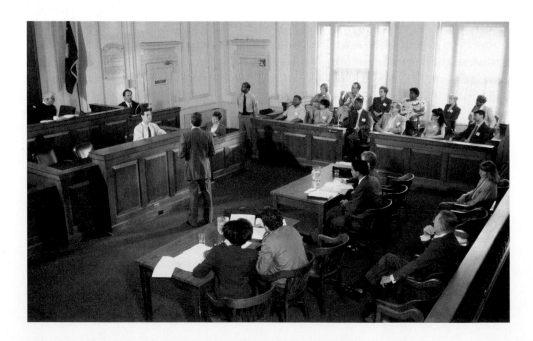

doing things or saying things that don't match their idea of themselves as smart, nice, or moral, for example, they experience an emotional discomfort known as **cognitive dissonance** (Aronson, 1997; Festinger, 1957). Most people need to see themselves as smart, moral, and rational. When people are confronted with the knowledge that something they have done or said was a dumb move, immoral, or illogical, they suffer an inconsistency in cognitions. For example, they may have a cognition that says "I'm pretty smart" but also the cognition "That was a dumb thing to do," which causes a dissonance. (*Dissonance* is a term referring to an inconsistency or lack of agreement.)

13.8   *What happens when a person's attitudes don't match the person's actions?*

When people experience cognitive dissonance, the result is unpleasant and the motivation is to change something so that the unpleasant feelings are reduced or eliminated. There are three basic things that people can do to reduce cognitive dissonance:

1. Change the conflicting behavior to make it match the attitude.
2. Change the current conflicting cognition to justify the behavior.
3. Form new cognitions to justify the behavior.

Take the example of Larry, who is a college graduate and a cigarette smoker. On one hand, Larry is educated enough to know that cigarette smoking is extremely harmful, causing lung problems, cancer, and eventually death. On the other hand, Larry enjoys his smoking, feeling that it calms him and helps him deal with stress—not to mention the fact that he's thoroughly addicted and finds it difficult to quit. His attitude (smoking is bad for you) doesn't match his behavior. Larry is experiencing cognitive dissonance and knows he needs to do something to resolve his dilemma.*

If Larry chooses the first way of dealing with cognitive dissonance, he'll quit smoking, no matter how difficult it is. As long as he is working at changing the conflicting behavior, his dissonance will be reduced. But what if he can't quit? He might decide that smoking isn't as bad as everyone says it is, which changes his original conflicting attitude (Option Two). He might also form a new attitude by deciding that if he smokes "light" cigarettes, he's reducing his risk enough to justify continuing smoking (Option Three).

In a classic experiment conducted at Stanford University, psychologist Leo Festinger and colleague James Carlsmith (1959) recruited male volunteers to participate in a study. Each participant was given an hour-long, incredibly boring task: sorting wooden spools into batches of 12 and turning wooden pegs about 90 degrees to the right. The experimenters then asked the participant to help out because a student assistant had failed to show up. Could the participant convince the female subjects in the waiting room that the task was fun and interesting? While half of the participants were paid only $1 to try to convince the waiting women, the other participants were paid $20. (In the late 1950s, $20 was a considerable sum of money—the average income was $5,000, the average car cost $3,000, and gas was only 25 cents a gallon.)

At the time of this study, many researchers would have predicted that the more the participant was paid to lie, the more the participant would come to like the task because the participant was getting more reinforcement ($20) for doing so. But what actually happened was that those participants who were paid only $1 for lying actually convinced themselves that the task was interesting and fun. The reason is cognitive dissonance: Participants who were paid only $1 experienced distress at thinking that they would lie to someone for only a dollar. Therefore, they must not be lying—the task really was pretty interesting, after all, and fun, too! Those who were paid more experienced no dissonance because they knew exactly why they were lying—for lots of money—and the money was a sufficient amount to explain their behavior to

*Dilemma: a problem involving a difficult choice.

cognitive dissonance
sense of discomfort or distress that occurs when a person's behavior does not correspond to that person's attitudes.

impression formation
the forming of the first knowledge that a person has concerning another person.

social cognition
the mental processes that people use to make sense of the social world around them.

their satisfaction. Although most people don't want to be thought of as liars, getting paid enough money to fill the gas tank of one's car three or four times over was incentive enough to tell what probably seemed to be a harmless fib. Those who were paid only $1 had to change their attitude toward the task so that they would not really be lying and could maintain their self-image of honesty. (See Figure 13.4.)

PRACTICE QUIZ: HOW MUCH DO YOU REMEMBER?

Pick the best answer.

1. Which of the following represents the cognitive component of an attitude?
   a. "I just love Italian food!"
   b. "Tonight, we're going to that new Italian restaurant."
   c. "Italian food is the best of the European cuisines."
   d. "I'm going to make lasagna tonight."

2. Lilly's mother always listens to the classic rock station on her car radio, so Lilly has grown up hearing that music and noticing how much her mother enjoys of it. Now Lilly says that classic rock is her favorite music, too. Lilly's attitude toward classic rock was most likely acquired through
   a. direct contact.
   b. direct instruction.
   c. interaction with others.
   d. vicarious conditioning.

3. Physical attractiveness is most involved in which of the following aspects of persuasion?
   a. the source
   b. the message
   c. the audience
   d. the media

4. Which of the following is not one of the elements of effective persuasion?
   a. the source or communicator
   b. characteristics of the message
   c. presence of supporters
   d. characteristics of the audience

5. "I didn't like the sermon at all today. It was too long, and that preacher wasn't dressed up enough" would be an example of which type of processing?
   a. central-route processing
   b. peripheral-route processing
   c. cognitive-route processing
   d. visual-route processing

6. In the famous Festinger experiment, participants were paid either $1 or $20 to lie to people in the waiting room about how interesting the task really was. The participants who convinced themselves that the task really was fun were the ones who were
   a. paid immediately.
   b. paid after one day.
   c. paid only $1.
   d. paid $20.

Answers: 1-c, 2-d, 3-a, 4-c, 5-b, 6-c.

Inducement	Attitude
$1	+1.35
$20	– 0.5
Control	– .45

*Based on a –5 to +5 scale, where –5 means "extremely boring" and +5 means "extremely interesting"

FIGURE 13.4 **Cognitive Dissonance: Attitude Toward a Task** After completing a boring task, some participants were paid $1 and some $20 to convince others waiting to do the same task that the task was interesting and fun. Surprisingly, the participants who were paid only $1 seemed to change their own attitude toward the task, rating it as interesting, while those paid $20 rated the task no differently than a control group.
Source: Adapted from Festinger and Carlsmith (1959).

Impression Formation and Attribution

When one person meets another for the first time, it is the first opportunity either person will have to make initial evaluations and judgments about the other. That first opportunity is a very important one in **impression formation**, the forming of the first knowledge a person has about another person. Impression formation includes assigning the other person to a number of categories and drawing conclusions about what that person is likely to do—it's really all about prediction. In a sense, when first meeting another person, the observer goes through a process of concept formation similar to that discussed in Chapter Eight. Impression formation is another kind of social cognition.

There is a *primacy effect* in impression formation: The first time people meet someone, they form an impression of that person that persists even though they may later have other contradictory information about that person (DeCoster & Claypool, 2004; Luchins, 1957). So the old saying is pretty much on target: First impressions do count.

Impression formation is one of a number of phenomena that are all part of **social cognition**, the mental processes that people use to make sense out of the social world around them.

SOCIAL CATEGORIZATION

13.9 *What are social categorization and implicit personality theories?*

One of the processes that occur when people meet someone new is the assignment of that person to some kind of category or group. This assignment is usually based on characteristics the new person has in common with other people or groups with whom the perceiver has had prior experience. This **social categorization** is mostly automatic and occurs without conscious awareness of the process (Macrae & Bodenhausen, 2000). Although this is a natural process (human beings are just born categorizers ⓁⒾⓃⓀ *to Chapter Eight: Cognition, pp. 295–296*), sometimes it can cause problems. When the characteristics used to categorize the person are superficial* ones that have become improperly attached to certain ideas, such as "red hair equals a bad temper," social categorization can result in a **stereotype**, a set of characteristics that people believe are shared by all members of a particular social category (Fiske, 1998). Stereotypes are very limiting, causing people to misjudge what others are like and often to treat them differently as a result. Add the process of stereotyping to the primacy effect, and it becomes easy to see how important first impressions really are. That first impression not only has more importance than any other information gathered about a person later on but may include a stereotype that is resistant to change as well (Hilton & von Hipple, 1996; Hugenberg & Bodenhausen, 2003).

It sounds as though we'd be better off if people didn't use social categorization. Social categorization does have an important place in the perception of others. It allows people to access a great deal of information that can be useful about others, as well as helping people to remember and organize information about the characteristics of others (Macrae & Bodenhausen, 2000). The way to avoid falling into the trap of stereotyping someone is to be aware of existing stereotypes and apply a little critical thinking: "Okay, so he's a guy with a tattoo on his arm. That doesn't mean that he's overly aggressive—it just means he has a tattoo."

IMPLICIT PERSONALITY THEORIES

The categories into which people place others are based on something called an **implicit personality theory**. Implicit personality theories are sets of assumptions that people have about how different types of people, personality traits, and actions are all related and form in childhood (Dweck et al., 1995; Erdley & Dweck, 1993). For example, many people have an implicit personality theory that includes the idea that happy people are also friendly people and people who are quiet are shy. Although these assumptions or beliefs are not necessarily true, they do serve the function of helping to organize *schemas*, or mental patterns that represent (in this case) what a person believes about certain "types" of people. (The concept of schema here is similar to the complex patterns proposed by Piaget. ⓁⒾⓃⓀ *to Chapter Seven: Development Across the Life Span, p. 264.*) Of course, the schemas formed in this way can easily become stereotypes when people have limited experience with others who are different from them, especially in superficial ways such as skin color or other physical characteristics (Levy et al., 1998).

There is some evidence to suggest that implicit personality theories may differ from culture to culture as well as from individual to individual. For example, one study found that Americans and Hong Kong Chinese people have different implicit personality theories about how much the personality of an individual is able to change. Whereas Americans assume that personality is relatively fixed and unchanging, Chinese people native to Hong Kong assume that personalities are far more changeable (Chiu et al., 1997).

***

*Superficial: on the surface.

social categorization
the assignment of a person one has just met to a category based on characteristics the new person has in common with other people with whom one has had experience in the past.

stereotype
a set of characteristics that people believe is shared by all members of a particular social category.

implicit personality theory
sets of assumptions about how different types of people, personality traits, and actions are related to each other.

◄ It sounds as though we'd be better off if people didn't use social categorization.

At this job fair in Shanghai, China, thousands of applicants wait hopefully in line for an opportunity to get a job interview. Making a good first impression is important in any job interview situation, but when the competition numbers in the thousands, the people who will most likely get interviews are those who are neatly dressed and well groomed.

attribution
the process of explaining one's own behavior and the behavior of others.

attribution theory
the theory of how people make attributions.

situational cause
cause of behavior attributed to external factors, such as delays, the action of others, or some other aspect of the situation.

dispositional cause
cause of behavior attributed to internal factors such as personality or character.

fundamental attribution error (actor-observer bias)
the tendency to overestimate the influence of internal factors in determining behavior while underestimating situational factors.

The people involved in this accident are likely to be late for classes or work. This is a good example of a genuine situational cause for tardiness.

But what else determines which type ▶ of cause a person will use? For example, what determines how people explain the behavior of someone they don't already know or like?

ATTRIBUTION

13.10   *How do people try to explain the actions of others?*

Another aspect of social cognition is the need people seem to have to explain the behavior of other people. Have you ever watched someone who was doing something you didn't understand? Chances are you were going through a number of possible explanations in your head: "Maybe he's sick, or maybe he sees something I can't see," and so on. It seems to be human nature to want to know why people do the things they do, and if no obvious answer is available, people tend to come up with their own reasons. People also need an explanation for their own behavior. This need is so great that if an explanation isn't obvious, it causes the distress known as cognitive dissonance. The process of explaining both one's own behavior and the behavior of other people is called **attribution**.

CAUSES OF BEHAVIOR   **Attribution theory** was originally developed by social psychologist Fritz Heider (1958) as a way of not only explaining why things happen but also why people choose the particular explanations of behavior that they do. There are basically two kinds of explanations—those that involve an external cause and those that assume that causes are internal.

When the cause of behavior is assumed to be from external sources, such as the weather, traffic, educational opportunities, and so on, it is said to be a **situational cause**. The observed behavior is assumed to be caused by whatever situation exists for the person at that time. For example, if John is late, his lateness might be explained by heavy traffic or car problems.

On the other hand, if the cause of behavior is assumed to come from within the individual, it is called a **dispositional cause**. In this case, it is the person's internal personality characteristics that are seen as the cause of the observed behavior. Someone attributing John's behavior to a dispositional cause, for example, might assume that John was late because his personality includes being careless of his and other people's time.

There's an emotional component to these kinds of attributions as well. When people are happy in a marriage, for example, researchers have found that when a spouse's behavior has a positive effect, the tendency is to attribute it to an internal cause ("he did it because he wanted me to feel good"). When the effect is negative, the behavior is attributed to an external cause ("she must have had a difficult day"). But if the marriage is an unhappy one, the opposite attributions occur: "He is only being nice because he wants something from me" or "She's being mean because it's her nature to be crabby" (Fincham et al., 2000; Karney & Bradbury, 2000).

FUNDAMENTAL ATTRIBUTION ERROR   But what else determines which type of cause a person will use? For example, what determines how people explain the behavior of someone they don't already know or like? The most well-known attributional bias is the **fundamental attribution error**, which is the tendency for people to overestimate the influence of another person's internal characteristics on behavior and underestimate the influence of the situation. In other words, people tend to explain the actions of others based on what "kind" of person they are rather than looking for outside causes such as social influences or situations (Harman, 1999; Jones & Harris, 1967; Weiner, 1985). (For example, people hearing about Milgram's "shock" study tend to assume that something is wrong with the "teachers" in the study rather than explaining their behavior within the circumstances of the situation.)

But why do we do that? Why not assume an external cause for everyone? When people observe themselves, they are very aware of the situational influences on their own behavior. For example, Tardy John was actually the one driving to work, and he knows that heavy traffic and a small accident made him late to work—he was *there*, after all. But someone else looking at John's behavior doesn't have the opportunity to see all of the possible situational influences and has only John himself in focus and, thus, assumes that John's tardiness is caused by some internal personality flaw.

Other research has shown that when students are given an opportunity to make attributions about cheating, they make the fundamental attribution error: If others are cheating, it's because they are not honest people, but if the students themselves were cheating it would be because of the situation (Bogle, 2000).

Can the tendency to make these errors be reduced? There are several strategies for making errors in attribution less likely. One is to notice how many other people are doing the same thing. As a college professor, the author often has students who come in late. When it is only one student and it happens frequently, the assumption is that the student is not very careful about time (dispositional cause). But when a large number of students come straggling in late, the assumption becomes "there must be a wreck on the bridge," which is a situational attribution. In other words, if a lot of people are doing it, it is probably caused by an outside factor.

Another trick is to think about what you would do in the same situation. If you think that you might behave in the same way, the cause of behavior is probably situational. People should also make the effort of looking for causes that might not be obvious. If John were to look particularly "stressed out," for example, the assumption might be that something stressed him out, and that "something" might have been heavy traffic.

Although the fundamental attribution error has been found in American culture (Jones & Harris, 1967), would the same error occur in a culture that is very different from American culture, such as in Japan? This is the question asked by researchers Masuda and Kitayama (2004), who had both American and Japanese participants ask a target person to read a prewritten attitudinal statement. The participants were then asked to give their opinion on the target's real attitude. American participants made the classic error, assuming that the target's attitude matched the reading. The Japanese participants, however, showed no such error. A summary of the research in cross-cultural differences in attribution provides further support for the idea that the fundamental attribution error is not a universal one (Peng et al., 2000). The work of Miller (1984) and many other researchers (Cha & Nam, 1985; Choi & Nisbett, 1998; Choi et al., 1999; Lee et al., 1996; Morris & Peng, 1994; Morris et al., 1995; Norenzayan et al., 1999) strongly suggests that in more interdependent, collectivist cultures found in Hong Kong, Japan, and Korea people tend to assume that external situational factors are more responsible for the behavior of other people than are internal dispositional factors—a finding that is exactly the reverse of the fundamental attribution error so common in individualist Western cultures such as the United States.

◄ But why do we do that? Why not assume an external cause for everyone?

Simulation
Live! psych
Attributions

PRACTICE **QUIZ:** HOW MUCH DO YOU REMEMBER?

Pick the best answer.

1. Which of the following statements about stereotypes is FALSE?
   a. Stereotypes are forms of social categories.
   b. Stereotypes are sets of characteristics that people believe are true for all members of a particular social category.
   c. Stereotypes are governed by the recency effect.
   d. Stereotypes are very limiting and can cause discrimination.

2. Mental patterns that represent what a person believes about certain types of people are called
   a. schemas.
   b. stereotypes.
   c. attributions.
   d. attitudes.

3. Elizabeth's room is almost always a mess. Her parents attribute this to Elizabeth's laziness. This is an example of a _____ cause.
   a. situational
   b. dispositional
   c. dispensational
   d. superficial

4. John was late to class, and his friend Eddie assumes that John simply doesn't care about being on time. But when Eddie is late the next day, he blames it on heavy traffic. Eddie has made the
   a. egocentric error.
   b. fundamental attribution error.
   c. assumption error.
   d. false consensus error.

5. In Asian cultures, people tend to explain the behavior of others as a result of
   a. bad genes.
   b. internal dispositions.
   c. situational factors.
   d. personality traits.

Answers: 1-c, 2-a, 3-b, 4-b, 5-c.

On September 6, 1957, this high school in Little Rock, Arkansas, became integrated, allowing African American students to attend school with white students. The practice of segregating black and white school children was discrimination, and the desegregation laws were aimed at stopping that discrimination. But the attitudes of prejudice persisted even after the legal discrimination was stopped, and to some degree still exist today. The courts can make laws against discrimination, but changing prejudicial attitudes is much more difficult.

prejudice
negative attitude held by a person about the members of a particular social group.

discrimination
treating people differently because of prejudice toward the social group to which they belong.

Prejudice and Discrimination

Social influence and social cognitions are two of three main areas included in the field of social psychology. The third major area has to do with social interactions with others, or the relationships between people, both casual and intimate. Social interactions are all too often affected by the prejudices that people hold about other groups of people.

13.11   *What is the difference between prejudice and discrimination?*

In talking about attitudes, the idea that some attitudes—stereotypes—can be formed by using only superficial information about a person or group of people was discussed. When a person holds an unsupported and often negative attitude about the members of a particular social group, it is called **prejudice**. When prejudicial attitudes cause members of a particular social group to be treated differently than others in situations that call for equal treatment, it is called **discrimination**. Prejudice is the attitude and discrimination is the behavior that can result from that attitude. Although laws can be made to minimize discriminatory behavior, it is not possible to have laws against holding certain attitudes. In other words, discrimination can be controlled and in some cases eliminated, but the prejudicial attitude that is responsible for the discrimination cannot be so easily controlled or eliminated.

TYPES OF PREJUDICE AND DISCRIMINATION

There are many kinds of prejudice. There are also many kinds of discrimination that occur as a result of prejudice. There's ageism, or prejudicial attitudes toward the elderly; sexism; racism, or prejudice toward those from different ethnic groups; prejudice toward those from different religions, those from different economic levels, those who are overweight, those who are too thin, and so on. Prejudice can also vary in terms of what type of people or groups make the most likely targets. In any society, there will always be **in-groups** and **out-groups**, or "us" versus "them." The in-group is all the people with whom a particular person identifies and the out-groups are everyone else (Brewer, 2001; Hewstone et al., 2002; Tajfel & Turner, 1986). The formation of in-groups and out-groups begins in childhood (Ruble et al., 2004) and continues as children become adults.

Once an in-group is established, prejudice toward and discriminatory treatment of the out-group or groups soon follow (Brewer, 2001). Members of the out-groups are usually going to become stereotyped according to some superficial characteristic, such as skin color or hair color, and getting rid of a stereotype once formed is difficult at best (Cameron et al., 2001; Hamilton & Gifford, 1976).

The **realistic conflict theory** of prejudice describes the formation of prejudice and the onset of discriminatory treatment that are closely tied to the degree of conflict between the in-group and the out-group (Horowitz, 1985; Taylor & Moghaddam, 1994). Because the examples of this from history and modern times are so numerous, it is possible to list only a few: the conflict between the early Crusaders and the Muslims, between the Jewish people and the Germans, the hatred between the Irish Catholics and the Irish Protestants, and the conflict between the native population of you-name-the-country and the colonists who want that land. The section that follows is a classic study that illustrates how easily in-groups and out-groups can be formed and how quickly prejudice and discrimination follow.

"First, can we agree that it's a big back yard?"
©The New Yorker Collection 2002 Charles Barsotti from cartoonbank.com. All Rights Reserved.

CLASSIC STUDIES IN PSYCHOLOGY

Brown Eyes, Blue Eyes

In a small town in Iowa in 1968, a few days after the assassination of Dr. Martin Luther King, Jr., a second-grade teacher named Jane Elliot tried to teach her students a lesson in prejudice and discrimination. She divided her students into two groups, those with blue eyes and those with brown eyes.

On the first day of the lesson, the blue-eyed children were given special privileges, such as extra time at recess and getting to leave first for lunch. She also told the blue-eyed children that they were superior to the brown-eyed children, telling the brown-eyed children not to bother taking seconds at lunch because it would be wasted. She kept the blue-eyed children and the brown-eyed children apart (Peters, 1971).

Although Elliot tried to be critical of the brown-eyed out-group, she soon found that the blue-eyed children were also criticizing, belittling, and were quite vicious in their attacks on the brown-eyed children. By the end of the day, the blue-eyed children felt and acted superior, and the brown-eyed children were miserable. Even the lowered test scores of the brown-eyed children reflected their misery. Two days later, the brown-eyed children became the favored group and the effects from the first two days appeared again but in reverse this time: The blue-eyed children began to feel inferior and their test scores dropped.

The fact that test scores reflected the treatment received by the out-group is a stunning one, raising questions about the effects of prejudice and discrimination on the education of children who are members of stereotyped out-groups. That the children were so willing to discriminate against their own classmates, some of whom were their close friends before the experiment, is also telling. In his book about this classroom experiment, *A Class Divided*, Peters (1971) reported that the students who were part of the original experiment, when reunited 15 years later to talk about the experience, said that they believed that this early experience with prejudice and discrimination helped them to become less prejudiced as young adults.

Questions for Further Discussion

1. Is there anything about this experiment that you find disturbing?
2. How do you think adults might react in a similar experiment?
3. Are there any ethical concerns with what Elliot did in her classroom?
4. What kinds of changes might have occurred in the personalities and performances of the children if the experiment had continued for more than two days with each group?

in-groups
social groups with whom a person identifies; "us."

out-groups
social groups with whom a person does not identify; "they."

realistic conflict theory
theory stating that prejudice and discrimination will be increased between groups that are in conflict.

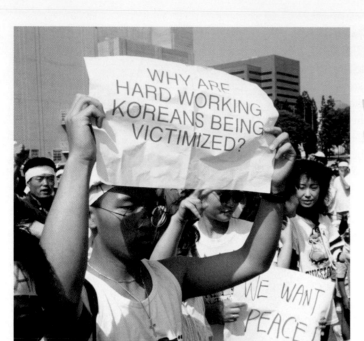

These Korean demonstrators were protesting the riots that followed the 1992 not guilty verdict of the four police officers who were videotaped beating Rodney King. The riots lasted six days, killing 42 people and damaging 700 buildings in mainly Korean and other Asian-American neighborhoods. As the most recent immigrants to the area, the Asian-American population of Los Angeles, California became the scapegoats for aggression.

SCAPEGOATING   Conflicts between groups are usually greater when there are other pressures or stresses going on, such as war, economic difficulties, or other misfortunes. When such pressures exist, the need to find a *scapegoat* becomes stronger. A scapegoat is a person or a group, typically a member or members of an out-group, who serves as the target for the frustrations and negative emotions of members of the in-group. (The term comes from the ancient Jewish tradition of sending a goat out into the wilderness with the symbolic sins of all the people on its head.)

Scapegoats are going to be the group of people with the least power, and the newest immigrants to any area are typically those who have the least power at that time. That is why many social psychologists believe that the rioting that took place in Los Angeles, California, in the spring of 1992 occurred in the areas it did. This was the time of the infamous Rodney King beating. Rodney King was an African American man who was dragged out of his car onto the street and severely beaten by four police officers. The beating was caught on tape by a bystander. At the trial, the officers were found not guilty of assault with a deadly weapon. This decision was followed by a series of violent riots (Knight, 1996).

The puzzling thing about these riots is that the greatest amount of rioting and violence did not take place in the neighborhoods of the mostly white police officers or in the African American neighborhoods. The rioting was greatest in the neighborhoods of the Asian Americans and Asians who were the most recent immigrants to the area. When a group has only recently moved into an area, as the Asians had, that group has the least social power and influence in that new area. So the rioters took out their frustrations *not* on the people seen as directly responsible for those frustrations but on the group of people with the least power to resist.

HOW PEOPLE LEARN PREJUDICE

13.12   *Why are people prejudiced, and how can prejudice be stopped?*

As was clearly demonstrated in the brown eyes–blue eyes experiment discussed in the Classic Studies in Psychology section, even children have their prejudiced attitudes. Is all prejudice simply a matter of learning, or are there other factors at work? Several theories have been proposed to explain the origins and the persistence of prejudice. In **social cognitive** theory, prejudice is seen as an attitude that is formed as other attitudes are formed, through direct instruction, modeling, and other social influences on learning.

social cognitive
referring to the use of cognitive processes in relation to understanding the social world.

social identity theory
theory in which the formation of a person's identity within a particular social group is explained by social categorization, social identity, and social comparison.

social identity
the part of the self-concept including one's view of self as a member of a particular social category.

social comparison
the comparison of oneself to others in ways that raise one's self-esteem.

SOCIAL IDENTITY THEORY   In **social identity theory**, three processes are responsible for the formation of a person's identity within a particular social group and the attitudes, concepts, and behavior that go along with identification with that group (Tajfel & Turner, 1986). The first process is *social categorization*, as discussed earlier in this chapter. Just as people assign categories to others (such as black, white, student, teacher, and so on) to help organize information about those others, people also assign themselves to social categories to help determine how they should behave. A *reference group* is a group of people to whom people compare themselves, and one's social category determines the reference group that will be used. The second element of social identity theory is *identification*, or the formation of one's **social identity**. A social identity is the part of one's self-concept that includes the view of oneself as a member of a particular social group. This identification process includes the idea of the in-group. The third aspect of social identity theory is **social comparison**, Festinger's (1954) concept in which people compare themselves to others to improve their own self-esteem: "Well, at least I'm better off than that person."

With respect to prejudice, social identity theory helps to explain why people categorize or stereotype others, the in-group sense of "us versus them" that people adopt toward out-groups, and people's need to increase their own self-esteem by looking down on others.

STEREOTYPE VULNERABILITY   As discussed previously, stereotypes are the widespread beliefs a person has about members of another group. Not only do stereotypes affect the way people perceive other people, but also stereotypes can affect the way people see themselves and their performance (Snyder et al., 1977). **Stereotype vulnerability** refers to the effect that a person's knowledge of another's stereotyped opinions can have on that person's behavior (Steele, 1992, 1997). Research has shown that when people are aware of stereotypes that are normally applied to their own group by others, they feel anxious about behaving in ways that might support that stereotype. This fear results in anxiety and self-consciousness that have negative effects on their performance in a kind of **self-fulfilling prophecy**, or the effect that expectations can have on outcomes.

Stereotype vulnerability is highly related to *stereotype threat*, in which members of a stereotyped group are made anxious and wary of any situation in which their behavior might confirm a stereotype (Hyde & Kling, 2001; Steele, 1999). In one study, researchers administered a difficult verbal test to both Caucasian and African American participants (Steele & Aronson, 1995). Half of the African American participants were asked to record their race on a demographic* question before the test, making them very aware of their minority status. Those participants showed a significant decrease in scores on the test when compared to the other participants, both African American and Caucasian, who did not answer such a demographic question. They had more incorrect answers, had slower response times, answered fewer questions, and demonstrated more anxiety when compared to the other participants (Steele & Aronson, 1995). Similar effects of stereotype threat on performance also have been found in women (Gonzales et al., 2002; Steele, 1997; Steele et al., 2002).

OVERCOMING PREJUDICE

The best weapon against prejudice is education: learning about people who are different from you in many ways. The best way to learn about others is to have direct contact with them and learning to see them as people rather than "as outsiders or strangers." *Intergroup contact* is very common in college settings, for example, where students and faculty from many different backgrounds live, work, and study together. Because they go through many of the same experiences (midterms, finals, and so on), people from these diverse** backgrounds find common ground to start building friendships and knowledge of each other's cultural, ethnic, or religious differences.

EQUAL STATUS CONTACT   Contact between social groups can backfire under certain circumstances, however, as seen in a famous study (Sherif et al., 1961) called the "Robber's Cave." In this experiment conducted at a summer camp called Robber's Cave, 22 white, well-adjusted 11- and 12-year-old boys were divided into two groups. The groups each lived in separate housing and were kept apart from each other for daily activities. During the

---

*Demographic: having to do with the statistical characteristics of a population.
**Diverse: different, varied.

stereotype vulnerability
the effect that people's awareness of the stereotypes associated with their social group has on their behavior.

self-fulfilling prophecy
the tendency of one's expectations to affect one's behavior in such a way as to make the expectation more likely to occur.

Simulation
Live! psych
Prejudice

Intergroup contact is one of the best ways to combat prejudice. When people have an opportunity to work together, as the students in this diverse classroom do, they get to know each other on common ground. Can you think of the first time you had direct contact with someone who was different from you? How did that contact change your viewpoint?

equal status contact
contact between groups in which the groups have equal status, with neither group having power over the other.

"jigsaw classroom"
educational technique in which each individual is given only part of the information needed to solve a problem, causing the separate individuals to be forced to work together to find the solution.

second week, after in-group relationships had formed, the researchers scheduled highly competitive events pitting one group against the other. Intergroup conflict quickly occurred, with name-calling, fights, and hostility emerging between the two groups.

The third week involved making the two groups come together for pleasant, noncompetitive activities, in the hopes that cooperation would be the result. Instead, the groups used the activities of the third week as opportunities for more hostility. It was only after several weeks of being forced to work together to resolve a series of crises (created deliberately by the experimenters) that the boys lost the hostility and formed friendships between the groups. When dealing with the crises, the boys were forced into a situation of **equal status contact**, in which they were all in the same situation with neither group holding power over the other. Equal status contact has been shown to reduce prejudice and discrimination. It appears that personal involvement with people from another group must be cooperative and occur when all groups are equal in terms of power or status to have a positive effect on reducing prejudice (Pettigrew & Tropp, 2000; Robinson & Preston, 1976).

THE "JIGSAW CLASSROOM" One way to ensure that contact between people from different backgrounds will occur in a cooperative fashion is to make success at a task depend on the cooperation of each person in a group of people of mixed abilities or statuses. If each member of the group has information that is needed to solve the problem at hand, a situation is created in which people must depend on one another to meet their shared goals (Aronson et al., 1978). Ordinarily, school classrooms are not organized along these lines but are instead more competitive and, therefore, more likely to create conflict between people of different abilities and backgrounds.

In a **"jigsaw classroom,"** students have to work together to reach a specific goal. Each student is given a "piece of the puzzle," or information that is necessary for solving the problem and reaching the goal (Aronson et al., 1978; Clarke, 1994). Students then share their information with other members of the group. Interaction between diverse students is increased, making it more likely that those students will come to see each other as partners and form friendly relationships rather than labeling others as members of an out-group and treating them differently. This technique works at the college level as well as in the lower school grades (Johnson et al., 1991; Lord, 2001).

PRACTICE **QUIZ:** HOW MUCH DO YOU REMEMBER?

Pick the best answer.

1. The behavioral component of prejudice is
   a. discrimination.
   b. stereotyping.
   c. implicit personality theorizing.
   d. holding a negative attitude toward a person.

2. The most likely predictor of the development of prejudice and discrimination between two groups is the degree of _____ between the groups.
   a. differences   c. distance
   b. conflict   d. emotionality

3. In teacher Jane Elliot's classic study, the most startling finding was that the
   a. blue-eyed children were kinder to their brown-eyed peers.
   b. brown-eyed children were less prejudiced.
   c. test scores of each group decreased when it was the out-group.
   d. children were unwilling to discriminate with respect to the others.

4. Which of the following is not an element of social identity theory?
   a. reference group
   b. social identity
   c. social comparison
   d. superordinate goals

5. Which situation would be least likely to result in a decrease of prejudice?
   a. asking people to work on separate projects but in the same room
   b. asking people to work on a common task
   c. giving each person a piece of information to share with the others to solve a problem
   d. people of various backgrounds helping rescue others from a flood

Answers: 1-a, 2-b, 3-c, 4-d, 5-a.

Liking and Loving: Interpersonal Attraction

Prejudice pretty much explains why people don't like each other. What does psychology say about why people like someone else? There are some "rules" for those whom people like and find attractive. Liking or having the desire for a relationship with someone else is called **interpersonal attraction**, and there's a great deal of research on the subject. (Who wouldn't want to know the rules?)

THE RULES OF ATTRACTION

13.13   *What factors cause people to be attracted to each other?*

Several factors are involved in the attraction of one person to another, including both superficial physical characteristics, such as physical beauty and proximity, as well as elements of personality.

PHYSICAL ATTRACTIVENESS   When people think about what attracts them to other people, one of the topics that usually arises is the physical attractiveness of the other person. Some research suggests that physical beauty is one of the main factors that influence people's choices for selecting people they want to know better, although other factors may become more important in the later stages of relationships (Eagly et al., 1991; Feingold, 1992; White, 1980).

PROXIMITY—CLOSE TO YOU   The closer together people are physically, such as working in the same office building or living in the same dorm, the more likely they are to form a relationship. **Proximity** refers to being physically near someone else. People choose friends and lovers from the pool of people available to them, and availability depends heavily on proximity.

One theory about why proximity is so important involves the idea of repeated exposure to new stimuli. The more people experience something, whether it is a song, a picture, or a person, the more they tend to like it. The phrase "it grew on me" refers to this reaction. When people are in physical proximity to each other, repeated exposure may increase their attraction to each other.

BIRDS OF A FEATHER—SIMILARITY   Proximity does not guarantee attraction, just as physical attractiveness does not guarantee a long-term relationship. People tend to like being around others who are *similar* to them in some way. The more people find they have in common with others—such as attitudes, beliefs, and interests—the more they tend to be attracted to those others (Hartfield & Rapson, 1992; Moreland & Zajonc, 1982; Neimeyer & Mitchell, 1998). Similarity as a factor in relationships makes sense when seen in terms of validation of a person's beliefs and attitudes. When other people hold the same attitudes and beliefs and do the same kinds of actions, it makes a person's own concepts seem more correct or valid.

WHEN OPPOSITES ATTRACT   Isn't there a saying about "opposites attract"? Aren't people sometimes attracted to people who are different instead of similar? There is often a grain of truth in many old sayings, and "opposites attract" is no exception. Some people find that forming a relationship with another person who has *complementary* qualities, or characteristics in the one person that fill a need in the other, can be very rewarding (Carson, 1969; Schmitt, 2002). Research does not support this view of attraction, however. It is similarity, not complementarity, that draws people together and helps them stay together (Berscheid & Reis, 1998; McPherson et al., 2001).

interpersonal attraction
liking or having the desire for a relationship with another person.

proximity
physical or geographical nearness.

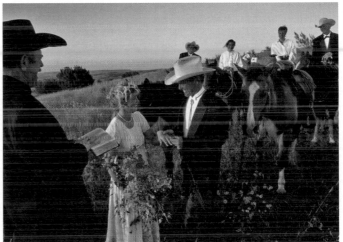

Proximity and similarity are two of the powerful forces governing interpersonal attraction. This woman and man are getting married in a traditional cowboy wedding ceremony. They met because of working in similar careers, and they share similar values as a result.

◀ Isn't there a saying about "opposites attract"? Aren't people sometimes attracted to people who are different instead of similar?

reciprocity of liking
tendency of people to like other people who like them in return.

RECIPROCITY OF LIKING   Finally, people have a very strong tendency to like people who like them, a simple but powerful concept referred to as **reciprocity of liking**. In one experiment, researchers paired college students with other students (Curtis & Miller, 1986). Neither student in any of the pairs knew the other member. One member of each pair was randomly chosen to receive some information from the experimenters about how the *other* student in the pair felt about the first member. In some cases, target students were led to believe that the other students liked them and, in other cases, that the targets disliked them.

When the pairs of students were allowed to meet and talk with each other again, they were friendlier, disclosed more information about themselves, agreed with the other person more, and behaved in a warmer manner *if they had been told* that the other student liked them. The other students came to like these students better as well, so liking produced more liking.

The only time that liking someone does not seem to make that person like the other in return is if a person suffers from feelings of low self-worth. In that case, finding out that someone likes you when you don't even like yourself makes you question his or her motives. This mistrust can cause you to act unfriendly to that person, which makes the person more likely to become unfriendly to you in a kind of self-fulfilling prophecy (Murray et al., 1998).

LOVE IS A TRIANGLE—ROBERT STERNBERG'S TRIANGULAR THEORY OF LOVE

13.14   *What is love, and what are the different forms that love can take?*

Dictionary definitions of love refer to a strong affection for another person due to kinship, personal ties, sexual attraction, admiration, or common interests.

But those aren't all the same kind of relationships. I love my family and I love my friends but in different ways. Psychologists generally agree that there are different kinds of love. One psychologist, Robert Sternberg, outlined a theory of what he determined were the three main components of love and the different types of love that combinations of these three components can produce (Sternberg, 1986, 1988, 1997).

THE THREE COMPONENTS OF LOVE   According to Sternberg, love consists of three basic components: intimacy, passion, and commitment.

Intimacy, in Sternberg's view, refers to the feelings of closeness that one has for another person or the sense of having close emotional ties to another. Intimacy in this sense is not physical but psychological. Friends have an intimate relationship because they disclose things to each other that most people might not know, they feel strong emotional ties to each other, and they enjoy the presence of the other person.

Passion is the physical aspect of love. Passion refers to the emotional and sexual arousal a person feels toward the other person. Passion is not simply sex; holding hands, loving looks, and hugs can all be forms of passion.

Commitment involves the decisions one makes about a relationship. A short-term decision might be, "I think I'm in love." An example of a more long-term decision is, "I want to be with this person for the rest of my life."

THE LOVE TRIANGLES   A love relationship between two people can involve one, two, or all three of these components in various combinations. The combinations can produce seven different forms of love, as can be seen in Figure 13.5.

> But those aren't all the same kind of relationships. I love my family and I love my friends but in different ways. ▶

FIGURE 13.5   **Sternberg's Triangular Theory of Love**   This diagram represents the seven different kinds of love that can result from combining the three components of love: intimacy, passion, and commitment. Notice that some of these types of love sound less desirable or positive than others. What is the one key element missing from the less positive types of love?
Source: Adapted from Sternberg (1986b).

Liking
Intimacy only

Romantic Love
Intimacy + Passion

Consummate Love
Intimacy + Passion + Commitment

Companionate Love
Intimacy + Commitment

Infatuation
Passion only

Fatuous Love
Passion + Commitment

Empty Love
Commitment only

Two of the more familiar and more heavily researched forms of love from Sternberg's theory are romantic love and companionate love. When intimacy and passion are combined, the result is the more familiar **romantic love**, which is sometimes called passionate love by other researchers (Bartels & Zeki, 2000; Diamond, 2003; Hartfield, 1987). Romantic love is often the basis for a more lasting relationship. In many Western cultures, the ideal relationship begins with liking, then becomes romantic love as passion is added to the mix, and finally becomes a more enduring form of love as a commitment is made.

When intimacy and commitment are the main components of a relationship, it is called **companionate love**. In companionate love, people who like each other, feel emotionally close to each other, and understand one another's motives have made a commitment to live together, usually in a marriage relationship. Companionate love is often the binding tie that holds a marriage together through the years of parenting, paying bills, and lessening physical passion (Gottman & Krokoff, 1989; Steinberg & Silverberg, 1987). In many non-Western cultures, companionate love is seen as more sensible. Choices for a mate on the basis of compatibility are often made by parents or matchmakers rather than the couple themselves (Duben & Behar, 1991; Hortaçsu, 1999; Jones, 1997; Thornton & Hui-Sheng, 1994).

Finally, when all three components of love are present, the couple has achieved *consummate love*, the ideal form of love that many people see as the ultimate goal. This is also the kind of love that may evolve into companionate love when the passion lessens during the middle years of a relationship's commitment.

The concept of romantic love, in which two people first feel a passionate attraction for each other and then develop an intimate relationship, is a relatively new one and more typical of Western cultures. In many other cultures marriages are arranged by the parents of the young couple and based on similarity of personality and commitment, as in this Hindu wedding taking place in Jaipur, India. It is assumed that intimacy and passion will develop over the course of their marriage.

PRACTICE **QUIZ:** HOW MUCH DO YOU REMEMBER?

Pick the best answer.

1. Which of the following is not one of the reasons given by the text for interpersonal attraction?
  a. physical attractiveness   **c.** personality
  b. similarity   **d.** proximity

2. The more you see someone, the more likely you are to _____ that person.
  a. dislike   **c.** grow tired of
  b. like   **d.** be annoyed by

3. A person who is very low in self-worth is less likely to be affected by the
  a. halo effect.   **c.** need complementarity effect.
  b. mere exposure effect.   **d.** reciprocity of liking effect.

4. According to Sternberg, the emotional and physical arousal a person feels for another is the _____ component of love.
  a. intimacy   **c.** commitment
  b. passion   **d.** psychological

Answers: 1-c, 2-b, 3-d, 4-b.

Aggression and Prosocial Behavior

Unfortunately, violence toward others is another form of social interaction. When one person hurts or tries to destroy another person deliberately, either with words or with physical behavior, psychologists call it **aggression**. One common cause of aggressive behavior is frustration, which occurs when a person is prevented from reaching some desired goal. The concept of aggression as a reaction to frustration is known as the frustration–aggression hypothesis (Berkowitz, 1993; Miller et al., 1941). There are many sources of frustration that can lead to aggressive behavior. Pain, for example, produces negative sensations that are often intense and uncontrollable, leading to frustration and often aggressive acts against the nearest available target (Berkowitz,

romantic love
type of love consisting of intimacy and passion.

companionate love
type of love consisting of intimacy and commitment.

aggression
behavior intended to hurt or destroy another person.

1993). Loud noises, excessive heat, the irritation of someone else's cigarette smoke, and even awful smells can lead people to act out in an aggressive manner (Anderson, 1987; Rotton et al., 1979; Rotton & Frey, 1985; Zillmann et al., 1981).

Frustration is not the only source of aggressive behavior. Many early researchers, including Sigmund Freud (1930), believed that aggression was a basic human instinct. In Freud's view, aggression was part of the death instinct that drove human beings to destroy both others and themselves, and he believed that if aggression were not released it would cause illness. But if aggression is an instinct present in all humans, it should occur in far more similar patterns across cultures than it does. Instinctual behavior, as often seen in animals, is not modifiable by environmental influences. Modern approaches try to explain aggression as a biological phenomenon or a learned behavior.

AGGRESSION AND BIOLOGY

13.15   *How is aggressive behavior determined by biology and learning?*

There is some evidence that human aggression has at least partially a genetic basis. Studies of twins have shown that if one identical twin has a violent temper, the identical sibling will most likely also have a violent temper. This agreement between twins' personalities happens more often with identical twins than with fraternal twins (Miles & Carey, 1997; Rowe et al., 1999). It may be that some gene or complex of genes makes certain people more susceptible to aggressive responses under the right environmental conditions.

As discussed in Chapter Two, certain areas of the brain seem to control aggressive responses. The amygdala and other structures of the limbic system have been shown to trigger aggressive responses when stimulated in both animals and humans (Adams, 1968; Albert & Richmond, 1977; LaBar et al., 1995; Scott et al., 1997). Charles Whitman, the Tower of Texas sniper, who in 1966 killed his mother, his wife, and then shot and killed 12 more people before finally being killed by law enforcement officers, left a note asking for an examination of his brain. An autopsy did reveal a tumor that was pressing into his amygdala (Lavergne, 1997).

There are also chemical influences on aggression. Testosterone, a male sex hormone, has been linked to higher levels of aggression in humans (Archer, 1991). This may help to explain why violent criminals tend to be young, male, and muscular. They typically have high levels of testosterone and low levels of serotonin, another important chemical found in the brain (Alexander et al., 1986; Brown & Linnoila, 1990; Coccaro & Kavoussi, 1996; Dabbs et al., 2001; Robins, 1996).

Don't some people ▶ get pretty violent after drinking too much? Does alcohol do something to those brain chemicals?

Don't some people get pretty violent after drinking too much? Does alcohol do something to those brain chemicals? Alcohol does have an impact on aggressive behavior. Psychologically, alcohol acts to release inhibitions, making people less likely to control their behavior even if they are not yet intoxicated. Biologically, alcohol affects the functioning of many neurotransmitters and in particular is associated with a decrease in serotonin (Virkkunen & Linnoila, 1996). In one study, volunteers were asked to administer electric shocks to an unseen "opponent" in a study reminiscent of Milgram's shock experiment. The actual responses to the shock were simulated by a computer, although the volunteers believed that the responses were coming from a real person. The volunteers were told it was a test of reaction time and learning (Bushman, 1997). Volunteers participated both before consuming alcohol and after consuming alcohol. Participants were much more aggressive in administering stronger shocks after drinking.

THE POWER OF SOCIAL ROLES

Although frustration, genetics, body chemicals, and even the effects of drugs can be blamed for aggressive behavior to some degree, much of human aggression is also influenced by learning. The social learning theory explanation for aggression states that aggressive behavior is learned by watching aggressive models get reinforced for their aggressive behavior (Bandura, 1980; Bandura et al., 1961). **LINK** *to Chapter Five: Learning, p. 196.* Aggressive models can be parents, siblings, friends, or people on television.

There is some evidence to suggest that even taking on a particular *social role*, such as that of a soldier, can lead to an increase in aggressive behavior. A **social role** is the pattern of behavior that is expected of a person who is in a particular social position. For example, "doctor" is a social role that implies wearing a white coat, asking certain types of questions, and writing prescriptions, among other things. A deeply disturbing experiment was conducted by famed social psychologist Philip Zimbardo at Stanford University in 1971. The experiment was recorded on film from the beginning to a rather abrupt end: about 70 young men, most of whom were college students, volunteered to participate for two weeks. They were told that they would be randomly assigned the social role of either a guard or a prisoner in the experiment. The "guards" were given uniforms and instructions not to use violence but to maintain control of the "prison." The "prisoners" were booked at a real jail, blindfolded, and transported to the campus "prison," actually the basement of one of the campus buildings. On day 2, the prisoners staged a revolt (not planned as part of the experiment), which was quickly crushed by the guards. The guards then became increasingly more aggressive, using humiliation to control and punish the prisoners. For example, prisoners were forced to clean out toilet bowls with their bare hands. The staff observing the experiment had to release five of the prisoners who became so upset that they were physically ill. The entire experiment was canceled on the fifth day, after one of the prisoners reported to Zimbardo that what the experimenters were doing to the young men was terrible (Zimbardo, 1971).

The conclusions of Zimbardo and his colleagues highlighted the influence that a social role, such as that of "guard," can have on perfectly ordinary people. Although history is full of examples of people behaving horribly to others while filling a particular role, one need not travel very far into the past to find an example. During the war in Iraq in 2003, an army reserve general was suspended from duty while an investigation into reported prisoner abuses was conducted. Between October and December 2003, investigators found numerous cases of cruel, humiliating, and other startling abuses of the Iraqi prisoners by the army military police stationed at the prison of Abu Ghraib (Hersh, 2004). Among the cruelties reported were pouring cold water on naked detainees, beating them with a broom handle or chair, threatening them with rape, and one case of actually carrying out the threat. How could any normal person have done such things? The "guards" in the Stanford prison study were normal people, but the effect of putting on the uniform and taking on the social role of guard changed their behavior radically. Is it possible that a similar factor was at work at Abu Ghraib? The behavior of the guards at Abu Ghraib was not part of a formal, controlled study, so further research will be needed to determine to what degree the social roles at work in situations like this influence the kind of behavior seen in this real-life example.

This photograph shows a "guard" searching a "prisoner" in Zimbardo's famous Stanford prison experiment. The students in the experiment became so deeply involved in their assigned roles that Zimbardo had to cancel the experiment after only five days—less than half the time originally scheduled for the study.

social role
the pattern of behavior that is expected of a person who is in a particular social position.

A U.S. soldier threatens an Iraqi prisoner at the Abu Ghraib prison in Iraq. Investigators into alleged abuses at this prison found numerous sadistic and brutal acts committed by U.S. military personnel upon the prisoners. One brigadier general in charge of the prison was suspended. At the time of publication of this text, other legal actions were still being considered.

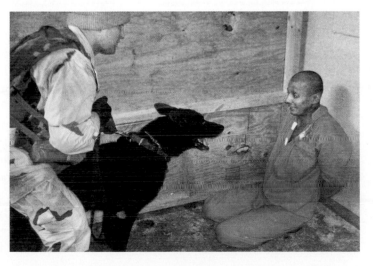

No one can deny that abused children are exposed to powerful models of aggression. Their abusing parents get reinforced for their aggressive behavior when they get what they want from the child. No one can deny that there are people who were abused who go on to become abusers. Contrary to popular belief, most children who suffer abuse do *not* grow up to become abusers themselves—in fact, only one-third of abused children do so (Kaufman & Zigler, 1993; Oliver, 1993). Instead of becoming abusers themselves, some abused children receive help and overcome the damage from their childhood, whereas others withdraw, isolating themselves rather than becoming abusive (Dodge et al., 1990).

I've heard ▶ that violent television programs can cause children to become more aggressive. How true is that?

VIOLENCE IN THE MEDIA AND AGGRESSION   I've heard that violent television programs can cause children to become more aggressive. How true is that? Bandura's early study on the effects of an aggressive model viewed over a movie screen on small children was one of the first attempts to investigate the effect of violence in the media on children's aggressive behavior (Bandura et al., 1961). Since then, researchers have examined the impact of television and other media violence on the aggressive behavior of children of various ages. The conclusions have all been similar: Children who are exposed to high levels of violent media are more aggressive than children who are not (Baron & Reiss, 1985; Bushman & Huesmann, 2000; Centerwall, 1989; Geen & Thomas, 1986; Huesmann & Miller, 1994; Huesmann et al., 1997; Huesmann et al., 2003; Villani, 2001). These studies have found that there are several contributing factors involving the normal aggressive tendencies of the child, with more aggressive children preferring to watch more aggressive media as well as the age at which exposure begins: the younger the child, the greater the impact. Parenting issues also have an impact, as the aggressive impact of television is lessened in homes where aggressive behavior is not tolerated and punishment is not physical.

Violent video games have also come under fire as causing violent acting-out in children, especially young adolescents. The tragic shootings at schools all over the United States have, at least in part, been blamed on violent video games that the students seemed to be imitating. This was especially a concern in the Littleton, Colorado, shootings because the adolescent boys involved in those incidents had not only played a violent video game in which two shooters killed people who could not fight back but also had made a video of themselves in trench coats, shooting school athletes. This occurred less than a year before these same boys killed 13 of their fellow students at Columbine High School and wounded 23 others (Anderson & Dill, 2000). In one study, second-grade boys were allowed to play either an aggressive or a nonaggressive video game. After playing the game, the boys who had played the aggressive video game demonstrated more verbal and physical aggression both to objects around them and to their playmates while playing in a free period than boys who had played the nonagressive video game (Irwin & Gross, 1995).

In a massive meta-analysis of research into the connection between violent media and aggressive behavior in children, social psychologist Craig Anderson and colleagues found clear and consistent evidence that even short-term exposure to violent media significantly increases the likelihood that children will engage in both physical and verbal aggression as well as aggressive thoughts and emotions (Anderson et al., 2003). Clearly, violent video games do correlate with increased aggression levels of the children who play them, both young children and adolescents (Anderson, 2003; Anderson & Bushman, 2001).

PROSOCIAL BEHAVIOR

Another and far more pleasant form of human social interaction is **prosocial behavior**, or socially desirable behavior that benefits others rather than bringing them harm.

13.16   *What is altruism?*

ALTRUISM   One form of prosocial behavior that almost always makes people feel good about other people is **altruism**, or helping someone in trouble with no expectation of reward and often without fear of one's own safety. Although no one is surprised by the behavior of a mother who enters a burning house to save her child, some people are often surprised when total strangers step in to help, risking their own lives for people they do not know.

Sociobiologists, scientists who study the evolutionary and genetic bases of social organizations in both animals and humans, see altruistic behavior as a way of preserving one's genetic material, even at the cost of one's own life. This is why the males of certain species of spiders, for example, seem to willingly become "dinner" for the female mates they have just fertilized, ensuring the continuation of their genes through the offspring she will produce (Koh, 1996). It also explains the mother or father who risks life and limb to save a child. But why do people risk their own lives to help total strangers? More importantly, why do people sometimes refuse to help when their own lives are not at risk, as in the case of Kitty Genovese presented in the opening story?

WHY PEOPLE WON'T HELP   The opening story about Kitty Genovese's murder shocked most people when reported in the news in March 1964. People were outraged by the apparent indifference and lack of sympathy for the poor woman's plight. Why did those people simply stand by and watch or listen? Social psychologists would explain that the lack of response to Kitty Genovese's screams for help was not due to indifference or a lack of sympathy but instead to the presence of other people. When other people are present at the scene or are assumed to be present, individuals are affected by two basic principles of social psychology: the bystander effect and diffusion of responsibility.

13.17   *What is the bystander effect?*

Bystander Effect   The **bystander effect** refers to the finding that the likelihood of a bystander (someone observing an event and close enough to offer help) to help someone in trouble decreases as the number of bystanders increases. If only one person is standing by, that person is far more likely to help than if there is another person, and the addition of each new bystander decreases the possibility of helping behavior even more (Darley & Latané, 1968; Eagly & Crowley, 1986; Latané & Darley, 1969). In the case of Kitty Genovese, there were 38 "bystanders" at the windows of the apartment buildings, and none of them helped.

But why does the number of bystanders matter? **Diffusion of responsibility** is the phenomenon in which a person fails to take responsibility for either action or inaction because of the presence of other people who are seen to share the responsibility (Leary & Forsyth, 1987). Diffusion of responsibility is a form of attribution in which people explain why they acted (or failed to act) as they did because of others. "I was just following orders," "Other people were doing it," and "There were a lot of people there, and I thought one of them would do something" are all examples of statements made in such situations. Kitty Genovese received no help because there were too many potential "helpers," and not one of the people listening to her cries for help took the responsibility to intervene—they thought surely someone else was doing something about it.

For more on the bystander effect, the Classic Studies in Psychology section that follows reviews one of the more famous social psychology experiments.

prosocial behavior
socially desirable behavior that benefits others.

altruism
prosocial behavior that is done with no expectation of reward and may involve the risk of harm to oneself.

bystander effect
referring to the effect that the presence of other people has on the decision to help or not help, with help becoming less likely as the number of bystanders increases.

diffusion of responsibility
occurring when a person fails to take responsibility for actions or for inaction because of the presence of other people who are seen to share the responsibility.

◀ But why does the number of bystanders matter?

CLASSIC STUDIES IN PSYCHOLOGY
Latané and Darley

13.18 *What did Latané and Darley discover about the presence of others and helping behavior?*

After the Kitty Genovese murder, psychologists became curious about why the bystanders did not call the police right away or try to help in some other way. Two social psychologists, Bibb Latané and John Darley, began a series of research projects to determine the different conditions under which help might or might not be given. In their classic 1969 study, they conducted several experiments, one of which is summarized here.

Participants were filling out questionnaires in a room that began to fill with smoke. Some participants were alone in the room, whereas in another condition there were three participants in the room. In a third condition one participant was in the room with two confederates of the experimenter, who were instructed to notice the smoke but ignore it afterwards. In the "participant alone" condition, three-fourths of the participants left the room to report the smoke. In the "three participants" condition, only a little over one-third of the participants reported the smoke, whereas only one-tenth of the participants who were in the room with confederates did so. Interviews with the participants who failed to report the smoke found that participants did not perceive the smoke as threatening.

In all of the researchers' experiments, participants were less likely to respond to a possible emergency situation when there were others present than when participants were alone. One bystander cannot diffuse responsibility to others, but two or more can.

Questions for Further Discussion

1. What other reasons could participants in this experiment have for not responding?
2. What might be some of the factors that distinguish the participants who did try to help from those who did not?
3. Are there any ethical concerns with research such as this?

FIGURE 13.6 **Elements Involved in Bystander Response** As you can see in the accompanying graph, the time taken to report smoke and the percent of people reporting smoke both depended upon how many people were in the room at the time the smoke was observed. If a person was alone, he or she was far more likely to report the smoke and report it more quickly than when there were three people. (Latané & Darley, 1968).

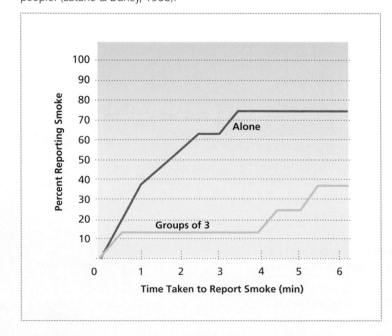

13.19 *What decisions have to be made before a person will help someone else?*

FIVE DECISION POINTS IN HELPING BEHAVIOR In all of the experiments reported in the preceding section, there were people who did try to help in every condition. What kind of decision-making process might they have gone through before deciding to help? What are the requirements for deciding when help is needed? Darley and Latané (1968) identified several decision points that a bystander must face before helping someone in trouble. These decision points are outlined in Table 13.3.

Aside from the factors listed in the table, there are other influences on the decision to help. For example, the more ambiguity* there is in a situation, the less likely it becomes that the situation will be defined as an emergency. If there are

---

*Ambiguity: having the quality of being difficult to identify specific elements of the situation.

TABLE 13.3 HELP OR DON'T HELP: FIVE DECISION POINTS

Decision Point	Description	Factors Influencing Decision
Noticing	Realizing that there is a situation that might be an emergency.	Hearing a loud crash or a cry for help.
Defining an Emergency	Interpreting the cues as signaling an emergency.	Loud crash is associated with a car accident, people are obviously hurt.
Taking Responsibility	Personally assuming the responsibility to act.	A single bystander is much more likely to act than when others are present (Latané & Darley, 1969).
Planning a Course of Action	Deciding how to help and what skills might be needed.	People who feel they have the necessary skills to help are more likely to help.
Taking Action	Actually helping	Costs of helping (e.g., danger to self) must not outweigh the rewards of helping.

other people nearby, especially if the situation is ambiguous, bystanders may rely on the actions of the others to help determine if the situation is an emergency or not. Since all the bystanders are doing this, it is very likely that the situation will be seen as a non-emergency because no one is moving to help.

Another factor is the mood of the bystanders. People in a good mood are generally more likely to help than people in a bad mood, but oddly enough, they are not as likely to help if helping would destroy the good mood. Gender of the victim is also a factor, with women more likely to receive help than men if the bystander is male, but not if the bystander is female. Physically attractive people are more likely to be helped. Victims who look like "they deserve what is happening" are also less likely to be helped. For example, a man lying on the side of the street who is dressed in shabby clothing and appears to be drunk will be passed by, but if he is dressed in a business suit, people are more likely to stop and help. Racial and ethnicity differences between victim and bystander also decrease the probability of helping (Richards & Lowe, 2003; Tukuitonga & Bindman, 2002).

PRACTICE **QUIZ:** HOW MUCH DO YOU REMEMBER?

Pick the best answer.

1. Which of the following has not been studied as a cause of aggressive behavior?
   a. frustration
   b. pain
   c. alcohol
   d. marijuana

2. The area of the brain that is most involved in aggression is the
   a. amygdala.
   b. pineal gland.
   c. cerebellum.
   d. cortex.

3. Which of the following statements is true?
   a. Abused children always grow up to become abusers.
   b. Abused children rarely grow up to become abusers.
   c. Abused children grow up to become abusers about one-third of the time.
   d. Children who were not abused do not grow up to become abusers.

4. According to the bystander effect, Leshan is more likely to get help if there is (are)
   a. no other people standing nearby.
   b. only one other person standing nearby.
   c. several people standing nearby.
   d. a crowd of people standing nearby.

5. In the Latané and Darley experiment, subjects were most likely to help when
   a. they were alone in the room.
   b. they were with a friend.
   c. there were three other people in the room.
   d. there was one stranger in the room.

6. Once a situation has been defined as an emergency, the next step in the decision-making process is
   a. noticing.
   b. taking action.
   c. taking responsibility.
   d. planning a course of action.

cult
any group of people with a particular religious or philosophical set of beliefs and identity.

Applying Psychology to Everyday Life: Anatomy of a Cult

13.20 *Why do people join cults?*

The term **cult** literally refers to any group of people with a particular religious or philosophical set of beliefs and identity. In the strictest sense of the word, the Roman Catholic Church and Protestantism are cults within the larger religion of Christianity. But most people associate the term *cult* with a negative connotation*: a group of people whose religious or philosophical beliefs and behavior are so different from that of mainstream organizations that they are viewed with suspicion and seen as existing on the fringes of "normal" behavior. Although many cults exist without much notice from more mainstream groups, at times members of cults have horrified the public with their actions.

One of the most well-remembered and often cited examples of a cult gone horribly wrong was that of the People's Temple in Jonestown, Guyana, headed by Jim Jones. Originally a Christian offshoot, the People's Temple became a cult under Jones's dictatorial leadership. In 1978, when Jones felt threatened by reporters coming to Guyana, he instructed the entire cult of over 900 people to commit suicide by either drinking cyanide-laced drinks or shooting each other. A total of 914 people died, including 274 children (WorldIQ.com, 2002).

More recently, the followers of the Heaven's Gate cult, who believed that aliens in a spaceship were coming in the tail of the Hale-Bopp comet in 1997, committed suicide under the leadership of Marshall Applewhite. They believed that their souls would be taken up by the comet aliens.

Why would any person get so caught up in cult beliefs that suicide, and in some cases, murder becomes a desired behavior? What kind of person joins a cult in the first place? Although there is no particular personality profile associated with cult membership, cult members do appear to have been in some psychological distress at the time of recruitment by the cult. People who are under a lot of stress, dissatisfied with their lives, unassertive, gullible, dependent, feel a desire to belong to a group, and who are unrealistically idealistic ("we can solve all the world's problems if everyone will just love each other") are the most likely targets of cult recruitment (Langone, 1996). Young people rebelling against parental authority or trying to become independent of families are prime targets.

Cult leaders also have certain techniques of persuasion that are common to most cult organizations. The first step is usually something called "love-bombing" by current cult members, who shower the recruit with affection and attention and claim to understand just how the potential cult member feels. Then efforts are made to isolate the recruit from family and friends who might talk them out of joining. This is accomplished in part by keeping the recruits so busy with rigid rituals, ways of dress, meditations, and other activities that they do not allow the recruit time to think about what is happening. All of these activities also serve to wear down the resistance of the recruits. Cults also teach their members how to stop questioning thoughts or criticisms, which are typically seen as sins or extremely undesirable behavior. Access to people and information outside the cult is either kept to a well-guarded minimum or totally shut off (Singer & Lalich, 1995; Zimbardo & Hartley, 1985).

In 1978, the Reverend Jim Jones, leader of the People's Temple in Jonestown, Guyana, ordered his followers to drink poisoned drinks or shoot each other. Of the cult members, 640 adults were dead and 274 children were either killed by their own hands or those of their parents.

*Connotation: the meaning of a word or concept that is more suggestive than directly stated.

Commitments to the cult are small at first, such as attending a music concert or some other cult function. Eventually, a major step is requested by the cult, such as quitting one's job, turning over money or property to the cult, or similar commitments. Leaving a cult is quite difficult, as members of the cult in good standing will often track down a "deserter." Parents, friends, and other family members have been known to hire special "deprogrammers" to help their loved one recover from cult membership, willingly or unwillingly. Sometimes people actually have to "kidnap" their loved one out of the cult environment. Nevertheless, as difficult as it is to leave, 90 percent or more of cult members do eventually get out (Barker, 1983; Galanter, 1983).

Cults have existed all through recorded history and will probably continue to exist in the future. In 1995, there were between 3,000 and 5,000 cults in the United States alone (Singer & Lalich, 1995). Most cults do not pose a physical threat to their members or others, but the examples of the followers of Jim Jones, David Koresh, and Osama bin Laden clearly demonstrate that cults, like any group of people, can become deadly.

Questions for Further Discussion
1. In what ways are the methods used by cults on new recruits similar to the methods used by the military when training new soldiers?
2. Is it ethical for the family members of an adult to "kidnap" and deprogram a cult member?
3. Which methods of compliance do cults seem to use to recruit new members?

13 CHAPTER SUMMARY

- Social psychology is the scientific study of how a person's thoughts, feelings, and behavior are influenced by the real, imagined, or implied presence of other people.

Social Influence: Conformity, Compliance, and Obedience

13.1 *What makes people want to conform to the actions of others?*

- Asch used a set of comparison lines and a standard line to experiment with conformity, finding that subjects conformed to group opinion about one-third of the time, increased as the number of confederates rose to four, and decreased if just one confederate gave the correct answer.

- Cross-cultural research has found that collectivistic cultures show more conformity than individualistic cultures. Gender differences do not exist in conformity unless the response is not private, in which case women are more conforming than men.

13.2 *What is groupthink?*

- Groupthink occurs when a decision-making group feels that it is more important to maintain group unanimity and cohesiveness than to consider the facts realistically.

- Minimizing groupthink involves impartial leadership, seeking outside opinions, stating problems in an objective manner, breaking large groups into subgroups, encouraging questions and alternate solutions, using secret ballots, and holding group members responsible for the decisions made by the group.

- Compliance occurs when a person changes behavior as a result of another person asking or directing that person to change.

13.3 *What are four common ways to gain the compliance of another?*

- Four common ways of getting compliance from others are the foot-in-the-door technique, the door-in-the-face technique, the lowball technique, and the that's-not-all technique.

13.4 *What makes people obey the instructions or orders of others?*

- Milgram did experiments in which he found that 65 percent of people obeyed the authority figure of a psychology professor even if it meant hurting, injuring, or possibly killing another person with an electric shock.

13.5 *How does the presence of other people affect a person's performance on a task?*

- When the performance of an individual on a relatively easy task is improved by the presence of others, it is called social facilitation. When the performance of an individual on a relatively difficult task is negatively affected by the presence of others, it is called social impairment.

- When a person who is lazy is able to work in a group of people, that person often performs less well than if the person were working alone in a phenomenon called social loafing.

Attitudes

- Attitudes are tendencies to respond positively or negatively toward ideas, persons, objects, or situations.

13.6 *What are the three components of an attitude and how are attitudes formed?*

- The three components of an attitude are the affective (emotional) component, the behavioral component, and the cognitive component.

- Attitudes are often poor predictors of behavior unless the attitude is very specific or very strong.

- Direct contact with the person, situation, object, or idea can help form attitudes.
- Attitudes can be formed through direct instruction from parents or others.
- Interacting with other people who hold a certain attitude can help an individual form that attitude.
- Attitudes can also be formed through watching the actions and reactions of others to ideas, people, objects, and situations.

13.7 How can attitudes be changed?

- Persuasion is the process by which one person tries to change the belief, opinion, position, or course of action of another person through argument, pleading, or explanation.
- The key elements in persuasion are the source of the message, the message itself, and the target audience.
- In the elaboration likelihood model, central-route processing involves attending to the content of the message itself, whereas peripheral-route processing involves attending to factors not involved in the message, such as the appearance of the source of the message, the length of the message, and other noncontent factors.

13.8 What happens when a person's attitudes don't match the person's actions?

- Cognitive dissonance is an emotional disturbance that occurs when a person's actions do not match the person's attitudes.
- Cognitive dissonance is lessened by changing the conflicting behavior, changing the conflicting attitude, or forming a new attitude to justify the behavior.

Impression Formation and Attribution

- Impression formation is the forming of the first knowledge a person has about another person.
- The primacy effect in impression formation means that the very first impression one has about a person tends to persist even in the face of evidence to the contrary.
- Impression formation is part of social cognition, or the mental processes that people use to make sense out of the world around them.

13.9 What are social categorization and implicit personality theories?

- Social categorization is a process of social cognition in which a person, upon meeting someone new, assigns that person to a category or group on the basis of characteristics the person has in common with other people or groups with whom the perceiver has prior experience.
- One form of a social category is the stereotype, in which the characteristics used to assign a person to a category are superficial and believed to be true of all members of the category.
- An implicit personality theory is a form of social cognition in which a person has sets of assumptions about different types of people, personality traits, and actions that are assumed to be related to each other.
- Schemas are mental patterns that represent what a person believes about certain types of people. Schemas can become stereotypes.

13.10 How do people try to explain the actions of others?

- Attribution is the process of explaining the behavior of others as well as one's own behavior.
- A situational cause is an explanation of behavior based on factors in the surrounding environment or situation.
- A dispositional cause is an explanation of behavior based on the internal personality characteristics of the person being observed.

- The fundamental attribution error is the tendency to overestimate the influence of internal factors on behavior while underestimating the influence of the situation.

Prejudice and Discrimination

13.11 What is the difference between prejudice and discrimination?

- Prejudice is a negative attitude that a person holds about the members of a particular social group. Discrimination occurs when members of a social group are treated differently because of prejudice toward that group.
- There are many forms of prejudice, including ageism, sexism, racism, and prejudice toward those who are too fat or too thin.
- In-groups are the people with whom a person identifies, whereas out-groups are everyone else at whom prejudice tends to be directed.
- Conflict between groups increases prejudice and discrimination according to realistic conflict theory.
- Scapegoating refers to the tendency to direct prejudice and discrimination at out-group members who have little social power or influence. New immigrants are often the scapegoats for frustration and anger of the in-group.

Classic Studies In Psychology: Brown Eyes, Blue Eyes

- A schoolteacher divided her class into brown-eyed children and blue-eyed children to teach them a lesson about prejudice. The children quickly began to discriminate toward whichever group was the out-group during a certain time period.

13.12 Why are people prejudiced, and how can prejudice be stopped?

- Social cognitive theory views prejudice as an attitude acquired through direct instruction, modeling, and other social influences.
- Social identity theory sees a person's formation of a social sense of self within a particular group as being due to three things: social categorization (which may involve the use of reference groups), social identity (the person's sense of belonging to a particular social group), and social comparison (in which people compare themselves to others to improve their own self-esteem).
- Stereotype vulnerability refers to the effect that a person's knowledge of the stereotypes that exist against that person's social group can have on that person's behavior.
- People who are aware of stereotypes may unintentionally come to behave in a way that makes the stereotype real in a self-fulfilling prophecy.
- Intergroup contact is more effective in reducing prejudice if the groups have equal status.
- Prejudice and discrimination can also be reduced when a superordinate goal that is large enough to override all other goals needs to be achieved by all groups.
- Prejudice and discrimination are reduced when people must work together to solve a problem because each person has an important key to solving the problem, creating a mutual interdependence. This technique used in education is called the "jigsaw classroom."

Liking and Loving: Interpersonal Attraction

- Interpersonal attraction refers to liking or having the desire for a relationship with another person.

13.13 What factors cause people to be attracted to each other?

- People tend to form relationships with people who are in physical proximity to them.
- People are attracted to others who are similar to them in some way.

- People may also be attracted to people who are different from themselves, with the differences acting as a complementary support for areas in which each may be lacking.
- People tend to like other people who like them in return, a phenomenon called the reciprocity of liking.

13.14 *What is love, and what are the different forms that love can take?*

- Love is a strong affection for another person due to kinship, personal ties, sexual attraction, admiration, or common interests.
- Sternberg states that the three components of love are intimacy, passion, and commitment.
- Romantic love is intimacy with passion, companionate love is intimacy with commitment, and consummate love contains all three components.

Aggression and Prosocial Behavior

- Aggression is behavior intended to hurt or destroy another person, which may be physical or verbal. Frustration is a major source of aggression.

13.15 *How is aggressive behavior determined by biology and learning?*

- Biological influences on aggression may include genetics, the amygdala and limbic system, and testosterone and serotonin levels.
- Social roles are powerful influences on the expression of aggression. Social learning theory states that aggression can be learned through direct reinforcement and through the imitation of successful aggression by a model.
- Studies have concluded that violent television, movies, and video games stimulate aggressive behavior, both by increasing aggressive tendencies and providing models of aggressive behavior.
- Prosocial behavior is behavior that is socially desirable and benefits others.

13.16 *What is altruism?*

- Altruism is prosocial behavior in which a person helps someone else without expectation of reward or recognition, often without fear for his or her own safety.

13.17 *What is the bystander effect?*

- The bystander effect means that people are more likely to get help from others if there are one or only a few people nearby rather than a larger number. The more people nearby, the less likely it is that help will be offered.
- When others are present at a situation in which help could be offered, there is a diffusion of responsibility among all the bystanders, reducing the likelihood that any one person or persons will feel responsibility for helping.

Classic Studies In Psychology: **Latané and Darley**

13.18 *What did Latané and Darley discover about the presence of others and helping behavior?*

- Researchers Latané and Darley found that people who were alone were more likely to help in an emergency than people who were with others.

13.19 *What decisions have to be made before a person will help someone else?*

- The five steps in making a decision to help are noticing, defining an emergency, taking responsibility, planning a course of action, and taking action.

Applying Psychology to Everyday Life: Anatomy of a Cult

13.20 *Why do people join cults?*

- People who join cults tend to be under stress, unhappy, unassertive, gullible, dependent, want to belong, and idealistic. Young people are also likelier to join cults than are older people.
- Cults use love-bombing, isolation, rituals, and activities to keep the new recruits from questions and critical thinking. Cults also use the foot-in-the-door technique.

13 KEY TERMS

aggression 505
altruism 509
attitude 488
attribution 496
attribution theory 496
bystander effect 509
central-route processing 492
cognitive dissonance 493
companionate love 505
compliance 483
conformity 481
consumer psychology 482
cult 512
diffusion of responsibility 509
discrimination 498
dispositional cause 496
door-in-the-face technique 483
elaboration likelihood model 492
equal status contact 502

foot-in-the-door technique 483
fundamental attribution error
    (actor-observer bias) 496
groupthink 482
implicit personality theory 495
impression formation 494
in-groups 498
interpersonal attraction 503
"jigsaw classroom" 502
lowball technique 484
norm of reciprocity 484
obedience 485
out-groups 498
peripheral-route processing 492
persuasion 491
prejudice 498
prosocial behavior 509
proximity 503
realistic conflict theory 499

reciprocity of liking 504
romantic love 505
self-fulfilling prophecy 501
situational cause 496
social categorization 495
social cognition 494
social cognitive 500
social comparison 500
social facilitation 487
social identity 500
social identity theory 500
social influence 480
social loafing 488
social psychology 480
social role 507
stereotype 495
stereotype vulnerability 501
that's-not-all technique 484

TEST YOURSELF

Pick the best answer.

1. Studies have found the degree of conformity to be greater in _____ cultures.
   a. collectivistic
   b. individualistic
   c. Western
   d. European

2. To prevent groupthink, members of a group should do all but which of the following?
   a. Have the leader of the group remain impartial.
   b. Seek outside opinions.
   c. Discourage questions and alternate solutions.
   d. Use secret ballots.

3. Maria's fellow professor asked her to teach an honors class in the spring. Maria agreed only to find out after agreeing that teaching such a course also meant that she would have to attend meetings of the honors professors, go to honors-oriented conventions, and take on special advising duties. Maria had fallen victim to the _____ technique.
   a. foot-in-the-door
   b. door-in-the-face
   c. lowball
   d. that's-not-all

4. Some researchers believe that Milgram's results were a form of the _____ technique of persuasion.
   a. foot-in-the-door
   b. door-in-the-face
   c. lowball
   d. that's-not-all

5. Sandy loves to play pool and has become quite good at the game. Lately, she has noticed that she seems to play better when there are people watching her than when she is playing alone. This difference in Sandy's playing is most likely the result of
   a. social facilitation.
   b. social impairment.
   c. social loafing.
   d. social laziness.

6. Jerry goes to a lot of dog races because he enjoys them and loves to see the dogs run. For Jerry, going to the dog races a lot represents the _____ component of an attitude.
   a. psychological
   b. behavioral
   c. cognitive
   d. affective

7. The public service messages that encourage parents to sit down with their children and talk frankly about drugs are promoting which method of attitude formation?
   a. direct contact
   b. direct instruction
   c. vicarious conditioning
   d. observational learning

8. Researchers have found that a _____ degree of fear in a message makes it more effective, particularly when it is combined with _____.
   a. maximum; information about how to prevent the fearful consequences
   b. minimum; threats
   c. moderate; threats
   d. moderate; information about how to prevent the fearful consequences

9. Sandy was a juror in the trial for a man accused of stealing guns from a sporting goods store. The defendant was not very well-spoken and came from a very poor background, but Sandy listened carefully to the evidence presented and made her decision based on that. Sandy was using _____ processing.
   a. central-route
   b. peripheral-route
   c. cognitive-route
   d. visual-route

10. Which of the following is not one of the three things people do to reduce cognitive dissonance?
    a. change their behavior
    b. change their attitude
    c. form a new attitude
    d. ignore the conflict

11. Gerard goes to his job interview dressed in patched blue jeans, a torn t-shirt, and sandals. His hair is uncombed and he hasn't shaved in a few days. Obviously, Gerard knows nothing about
    a. cognitive dissonance.
    b. attitude formation.
    c. impression formation.
    d. groupthink.

12. Sets of assumptions that people have about how different types of people, personality traits, and actions are all related to each other are called
    a. social categorization.
    b. implicit personality theories.
    c. urban legends.
    d. stereotypes.

13. If behavior is assumed to be caused by internal personality characteristics, this is known as
    a. a situational cause.
    b. a dispositional cause.
    c. a fundamental attribution error.
    d. actor-observer bias.

14. The people with whom a person identifies most strongly are called the
    a. referent group.
    b. in-group.
    c. out-group.
    d. "them" group.

15. Prejudice and discrimination are least likely to develop in which of the following situations?
    a. two different groups of immigrants competing for jobs
    b. two different religious groups, in which each believes that its religion is the right one
    c. two different groups, with one group being blamed for the economic difficulties of the other
    d. two different groups dealing with the aftermath of a hurricane

16. The _____ explanation of prejudice assumes that the same processes that help form other attitudes form prejudiced attitudes.
    a. scapegoat
    b. authoritarian
    c. social cognitive
    d. psychodynamic

17. Patrick is very proud of his Irish heritage and thinks of himself as an Irish American. Patrick has a strong
    a. social identity.
    b. reference group.
    c. social category.
    d. stereotype vulnerability.

18. The self-fulfilling prophecy is a negative outcome of
    a. social identity.
    b. reference grouping.
    c. scapegoating.
    d. stereotype vulnerability.

19. The "Robber's Cave" experiment showed the value of _____ in combating prejudice.
    a. "jigsaw classrooms"
    b. equal status contact
    c. subordinate goals
    d. stereotyping vulnerability

20. Sarah found her soulmate, Jon, when she moved to a small town in Florida. According to research in interpersonal attraction, the most likely explanation for them to "find" each other is
    a. karma.
    b. personal attractiveness.
    c. fate.
    d. proximity.

21. According to Sternberg, married (committed) people who also have intimacy and passion are in the form of love called _____ love.

   a. companionate
   b. romantic
   c. affectionate
   d. consummate

22. The concept of aggression as a basic human instinct driving people to destructive acts was part of early _____ theory.

   a. humanistic
   b. behavioral
   c. psychoanalytical
   d. cognitive

23. The neurotransmitter that seems most involved in aggression is

   a. testosterone.
   b. serotonin.
   c. dopamine.
   d. norepinephrine.

24. Violent video games have been blamed for all but which of the following?

   a. increased levels of aggression in children
   b. increased levels of aggression in adolescents
   c. increased levels of altruism in children
   d. increased incidents of school shootings

25. To which two processes do most social psychologists attribute the failure of Kitty Genovese's neighbors to help her?

   a. bystander effect and altruism
   b. aggression and diffusion of responsibility
   c. altruism and diffusion of responsibility
   d. bystander effect and diffusion of responsibility

26. Cries for help, shouting, and loud noises all help with which step in the decision process for helping?

   a. noticing
   b. defining an emergency
   c. taking responsibility
   d. taking action

27. Cults use all of the following except _____ to gain new members.

   a. love-bombing
   b. isolation
   c. "foot-in-the-door" technique
   d. talking with parents of the recruit

Answers: 1-a, 2-c, 3-c, 4-a, 5-a, 6-d, 7-b, 8-d, 9-a, 10-d, 11-c, 12-b, 13-b, 14-b, 15-d, 16-c, 17-a, 18-d, 19-b, 20-d, 21-d, 22-c, 23-b, 24-c, 25-d, 26-b, 27-d.

For more sample quizzes and other review activities that will help you get a better grade, be sure to check out your accompanying study guide. To access tests and your own personalized study plan that will help you focus on the areas you need to master before your next class test, be sure to go to the on-line Psychology web site available with the access code packaged with your book.

CONCEPT MAP

Social psychology: study of thoughts, feelings, and behavior influenced by real, imagined, or implied presence of other people

Behavior

Conforming to the Actions of Others

Asch: Conformity increases with size of group, decreases with confederates

13.1

Groupthink

Decision makers maintain group unanimity even if incorrect

Minimizing groupthink involves:
▸ Impartial leadership
▸ Seeking outside opinions
▸ Stating problems in an objective manner
▸ Breaking large groups into subgroups
▸ Encouraging questions/ alternate solutions
▸ Using secret ballots
▸ Holding group members responsible

13.2

Compliance

Occurs when a person changes behavior as a result of another's influence

Four Common Ways to Gain Compliance
▸ Foot-in-the-door technique
▸ Door-in-the-face technique
▸ Low-ball technique
▸ That's-not-all technique

13.3

Obeying the Instructions of Others

Milgram: 65% of people obeyed a professorial authority figure even if it meant possibly hurting a person

13.4

Presence of Others Affects Task Performance

Social Facilitation: performance on a task is improved by others' presence

Social Impairment: performance on an easy task is impaired by others' presence

Social Loafing: people work less in a group than when alone

13.5

Thoughts

ATTITUDES

Attitudes: tendencies to respond positively or negatively toward ideas, persons, objects, or situations

IMPRESSION FORMATION AND ATTRIBUTION

Impression Formation: first knowledge a person has about another person; process that people use to make sense of the world

Primacy effect: first impression one has about a person tends to persist

Three Components of Attitudes and Attitude Formation

1. Affective (emotional) component
2. Behavioral component
3. Cognitive component

Factors in Attitude Formation:
▸ Attitudes are poor predictors of behavior
▸ Direct contact
▸ Direct instruction from parents or others
▸ Interacting with others
▸ Watching actions and reactions of others

13.6

Attitude Change

Persuasion: changing beliefs or actions of another

Key elements in persuasion:
▸ Source of the message
▸ Message itself
▸ Target audience

Elaboration Likelihood Model:
▸ Central-route processing: attending to message content
▸ Peripheral-route processing: attending to factors not involved in message

13.7

Cognitive Dissonance— Attitude Mismatch

Mismatch: Emotional disturbance when a person's actions do not match attitudes

Lessened by: changing conflicting behaviors and attitudes, forming new attitudes

13.8

Social Categorization and Implicit Personality Theories

Social categorization: assignment to a category

Stereotype: assignment of characteristics

Implicit personality theory: sets of assumptions about different types of people

Schemas: belief patterns about people

13.9

Explaining Actions

Attribution: process of explaining behavior

Situational cause: explaining behavior surrounding environment or situation

Dispositional cause: explaining behavior based on internal personality characteristics

Fundamental attribution error: overestimating internal factors' influence on behavior

13.10

Aggression

Behavior intended to hurt others

Biological factors: genetics, amygdala and limbic system, testosterone/serotonin

Learned Factors

▸ **Social learning theory:** reinforcement and imitation of successful aggression
▸ **Media:** violent television, movies, and video games can stimulate aggressive behavior
▸ **Frustration:** may be linked to aggression

13.15

Altruism

Prosocial behavior in which a person helps someone else without expectation of reward or recognition, often without fear for one's own safety

13.16

Bystander Effect

Presence of others can cause a diffusion of responsibility among all the bystanders

13.17

Latané and Darley's Studies of Helping Behavior

People who were alone were more likely to help in an emergency than people who were with others

13.18

The Helping Decision—Five Steps

1. Noticing   2. Defining an emergency   3. Taking responsibility
4. Planning a course of action   5. Taking action

13.19

Feelings

PREJUDICE AND DISCRIMINATION

Prejudice and Discrimination

Prejudice: negative attitudes

Discrimination: differential treatment

In-groups: group person identifies with

Out-groups: treated with prejudice

13.11

Causes of Prejudice

▸ **Social cognitive theory:** acquired through instruction, modeling, and social influences
▸ **Social identity theory:** sense of self from social categorization, identity, comparison
▸ **Stereotype vulnerability:** stereotypes may become a self-fulfilling prophecy

Reducing Prejudice

▸ **Equal status-contact:** no group holds power over the others; reduces prejudice
▸ **Jigsaw classroom:** mutual problem solving

13.12

LIKING AND LOVING

Factors in Attraction

▸ Proximity
▸ Similarity
▸ Complementary differences
▸ Reciprocity of liking

13.13

Sternberg's Triangular Theory of Love

Liking
Intimacy only

Romantic Love
Intimacy + Passion

Consummate Love
Intimacy + Passion + Commitment

Companionate Love
Intimacy + Commitment

Infatuation
Passion only

Fatuous Love
Passion + Commitment

Empty Love
Commitment only

13.14

14

Psychological Disorders

The Harsh Reality of Postpartum Psychosis

What could drive a mother to kill her own children? In Toronto, a 37-year-old woman jumped in front of a subway train with her 6-month-old infant in her arms. Another young mother shut herself and her three children in the garage with the car running. Yet another mother in Texas drowned her five children in the bathtub. Experts believe that these women were suffering from a rare form of depression that is caused by sudden hormonal changes just after a woman gives birth. This condition is called postpartum psychosis (Ahokas et al., 2000; Brockington et al., 1982; Hamilton, 1982; Mahe & Dumaine, 2001).

Postpartum psychosis may include actual false beliefs or delusions (such as believing that the baby is possessed by a demon), hallucinations (one woman thought her baby was a rat trying to bite her), frantic energy, and an unwillingness to eat or sleep in addition to the **postpartum depression** symptoms (Rohde & Marneros, 1993).

Research into this condition has suggested that postpartum psychosis is most likely caused by internal, biological factors rather than any cultural or societal expectations because this disorder is found in many cultures, both Western and non-Western, as well as in both technological and traditional societies (Kumar, 1994). Other research highlights the possible role of lack of estrogen, the female hormone that is lower than usual right after childbirth (Ahokas et al., 2000; Mahe & Dumaine, 2001).

Whatever the cause, how can the delusions and hallucinations seem real enough to these women to cause them to harm their own children? Why does this condition become so severe in some women, whereas many others have only a mild form of it? What factors cause a person to cross over the line from normal to abnormal behavior?

postpartum psychosis
a rare and severe form of depression that occurs in women just after giving birth and includes delusional thinking and hallucinations.

postpartum depression
depression occurring within a year after giving birth in about 10 percent of women and that includes intense worry about the baby, thoughts of suicide, and fears of harming the baby.

Why study abnormal behavior?
Because it is all around us, which raises many questions: How should one react? What should be done to help? What kind of person develops a mental illness? Could this happen to someone close? The key to answering these questions is to develop an understanding of just what is meant by abnormal behavior and the different ways in which behavior can depart from the "normal" path.

chapter outline

14 ✈

What Is Abnormality?

I've heard people call ▶ a lot of different things other people do "crazy" or "weird." How do psychologists decide when people are really mentally ill and not just a little odd?

I've heard people call a lot of different things other people do "crazy" or "weird." How do psychologists decide when people are really mentally ill and not just a little odd? Exactly what is meant by the term *abnormal behavior?* Abnormal compared to what? Who gets to decide what is normal and what is not? Has the term always meant what it means now? These are just a few questions that come to mind when thinking about the study of abnormal behavior, or **psychopathology** (Wen-Shing & Strelzer, 1997). As can be seen in the following section, definitions of abnormality have depended on cultural ways of explaining behavior down through the ages.

A BRIEF HISTORY OF PSYCHOLOGICAL DISORDERS

14.1 *How did people in earlier times explain mental illness?*

As early as 3000 B.C., archaeologists have found human skulls bearing the evidence of an ancient surgical technique. The skulls have holes cut into them, and the holes were made while the person was still living. In fact, many of the holes show evidence of healing, meaning that the person survived the process. The process of cutting holes into the skull of a living person is called *trepanning* (also spelled *trephining*). Although trepanning is still done today to relieve pressure of fluids on the brain, in ancient times the reason may have had more to do with releasing the "demons" possessing the poor victim (Gross, 1999). Ancient peoples might well have assumed that people who were behaving oddly were possessed by evil spirits. As trepanning had to be rather unpleasant, the disordered person may very well have tried hard to be "normal" after treatment, too.

Hippocrates, a Greek physician during the time in which the rest of the world and even many Greeks believed in the demon possession explanation of mental illness, challenged that belief with his assertion that illnesses of both the body and the mind were the result of imbalances in the body's vital fluids, or *humors.* Although Hippocrates was not correct in his assumptions about the humors of the body (phlegm, black bile, blood, and

psychopathology
the study of abnormal behavior.

yellow bile), his was the first recorded attempt to explain abnormal behavior as due to some biological process.

Moving forward in time, people of the Middle Ages believed in spirit possession (through the teachings of the Roman Catholic Church) and the treatment of choice was a religious one: *exorcism*, or the formal casting out of the demon through a religious ritual. During the Renaissance, belief in demon possession (in which the possessed person was at least seen as a victim) gave way to a belief in witchcraft, and mentally ill persons were most likely called witches and put to death.

WHAT IS ABNORMAL?

Defining abnormal behavior or abnormality is not as simple as it might seem at first. The easy way out is to say that abnormal behavior is behavior that is not normal, but what does that mean?

14.2   *What are the different ways in which abnormal behavior can be defined?*

STATISTICAL DEFINITION   One way to define *normal* and *abnormal* is to use a statistical definition. Frequently occurring behavior would be considered normal, and behavior that is rare would be abnormal. That kind of definition works fine with a behavior such as talking to others, as the two rarer possibilities would be not talking to anyone at all and talking too much to too many people—both of which would be considered abnormal. What about a behavior such as happiness? Is a medium level of happiness really the "norm" most people strive to reach? A total lack of happiness would be abnormal, but should a person who is very happy really be labeled abnormal? Statistical definitions of abnormality wouldn't work for intelligence either, as only mental retardation (the lower end of a distribution of intelligence in a population) would be considered undesirable and abnormal (Troisi & McGuire, 2002). People possessing a higher degree of intelligence than is "normal" are actually highly respected.

SOCIAL NORM DEVIANCE   Another way of defining abnormality is to see it as something that goes against the norms or standards of the society in which the individual lives. For example, refusing to wear clothing in a society that does not permit nudity would be seen as abnormal. But deviance (variation) from social norms is not always labeled as negative, abnormal behavior, as in a person who decides to become a monk and live in a monastery in the United States. That would be unusual behavior and not what the society considers a standard behavior, but it wouldn't be a sign of abnormality.

Using social nonconformity as a criterion for abnormality also creates a problem when dealing with different cultures. Behavior that would be labeled disordered in one culture may be quite acceptable in another. (See the Current Issues in Psychology section later in this chapter.) Even within one culture, the **situational context** (the social or environmental setting of a person's behavior) can make a difference in how behavior is labeled. For example, if a man comes to a therapist complaining of people listening in on his phone conversations and spying on all his activities, the therapist's first thought might be that the man is suffering from feelings of persecution. But if the man then explains that he is in a witness protection program, the complaints take on an entirely different and quite understandable tone.

El Hechizo ("The Spell"), by Spanish artist Francisco Goya. It portrays witches, demons, and other evil spirits tormenting a poor young man and represents what ancient people believed was the cause of mental illness: demon possession.
Francisco Goya, "El Hechizo", 1787-88, Fundacion Lazaro Gaidiano.

situational context
the social or environmental setting of a person's behavior.

"Correct me if I'm wrong, but hasn't the fine line between sanity and madness gotten finer?"

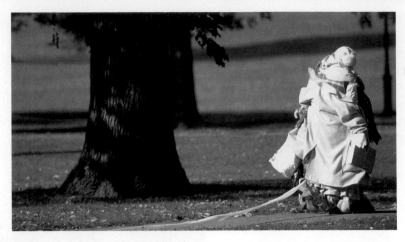

This homeless person has piled on so much clothing that is it impossible to tell if it is a man or a woman. Homeless people are sometimes mentally ill people who have not been able to keep their jobs or find work because of their mental illness, and they often feel that they have nowhere to go for help. Which of the ways to determine if behavior is abnormal seems to apply to this situation?

So how do ▶ psychologists decide what is abnormal?

SUBJECTIVE DISCOMFORT   One good sign of abnormality is when the person experiences a great deal of **subjective discomfort**, or emotional distress while engaging in a particular behavior. A woman who suffers from a fear of going outside her house, for example, would experience a great deal of anxiety when trying to leave home and distress over being unable to leave. However, all behavior that might be considered abnormal does not necessarily create subjective discomfort in the person committing the act—a serial killer, for example, does not experience emotional distress after taking someone's life, and some forms of disordered behavior involve showing no emotions at all.

INABILITY TO FUNCTION NORMALLY   Behavior that does not allow a person to fit into society or function normally can also be labeled abnormal. This kind of behavior is termed **maladaptive**, meaning that the person finds it hard to adapt to the demands of day-to-day living. Maladaptive behavior includes behavior that may initially help a person cope but has harmful or damaging effects. For example, a woman who cuts herself to relieve anxiety does experience initial relief but is harmed by the action. Maladaptive behavior is a key element in the definition of abnormality.

THE FINAL DEFINITION OF ABNORMALITY

So how do psychologists decide what is abnormal? Perhaps the shortest definition of abnormality or **psychological disorders** is any pattern of behavior that causes people significant distress, causes them to harm themselves or others, or harms their ability to function in daily life. To get a clear picture of abnormality, it is often necessary to take all of the factors discussed thus far into account. Clinical psychologists and other psychological professionals must consider several different criteria in determining whether or not a behavior is abnormal (at least two of these criteria must be met to form a diagnosis of abnormality):

1. Is the behavior unusual, such as experiencing severe panic when faced with a stranger or being severely depressed in the absence of any stressful life situations?
2. Does the behavior go against social norms?
3. Does the behavior cause the person significant subjective discomfort?
4. Is the behavior maladaptive?
5. Does the behavior cause the person to be dangerous to self or others, as in the case of someone who tries to commit suicide or attacks other people without reason?

Models of Abnormality

What causes ▶ psychological disorders?

What causes psychological disorders? In Chapter Twelve several different theories of personality were discussed. These theories of personality can be used to describe and explain the formation of not only ordinary behavior and personality but disordered behavior and abnormal personality as well. How one explains disordered behavior, then, depends on which theoretical model is used to explain personality in general.

THE BIOLOGICAL MODEL: MEDICAL CAUSES FOR PSYCHOLOGICAL DISORDERS

14.3   *How are psychological disorders related to the brain and body chemistry?*

One model that was not discussed in Chapter Twelve is the **biological model**, which proposes that psychological disorders have a biological or medical cause (Gamwell &

subjective discomfort
emotional distress or emotional pain.

maladaptive
anything that does not allow a person to function within or adapt to the stresses and everyday demands of life.

Tomes, 1995). This model explains disorders such as anxiety, depression, and schizophrenia as caused by chemical imbalances, genetic problems, brain damage and dysfunction, or some combination of those causes.

The biological or medical model has had a great deal of influence, especially in the language used to describe disorders: *mental illness*, *symptoms of disorder*, and terms such as *diagnosis*, *mental patient*, *mental hospital*, *therapy*, and *remission* all come from medical terminology. The use of such terms, although still widespread, may tend to bias the assumptions of professionals who are not psychiatrists or medical doctors toward a biological cause for disordered behavior.

THE PSYCHOLOGICAL MODELS

Although biological explanations of psychological disorders are influential, they are not the only ways or even the first ways in which disorders are explained. There are several psychological models that attempt to explain disordered behavior as the result of various forms of emotional, behavioral, or thought-related malfunctioning.

14.4   *How can psychological disorders be explained by the different viewpoints in psychology?*

PSYCHOANALYSIS: HIDING PROBLEMS   The psychoanalytic model, based on the work of Freud and his followers, ⓛⓘⓝⓚ *to Chapter Twelve: Theories of Personality, p. 446.* explains disordered behavior as the result of repressing, or hiding, one's threatening thoughts, memories, and concerns in the unconscious mind (Carducci, 1998). These repressed thoughts and urges try to resurface, and disordered behavior develops as a way of keeping the thoughts repressed. For example, a woman who has unacceptable thoughts of sleeping with her brother-in-law might be compelled to wash her hands every time those thoughts threaten to become conscious, ridding herself symbolically of the "dirty" thoughts.

BEHAVIORISM: LEARNING PROBLEMS   Behaviorists, who define personality as a set of learned responses, have no trouble explaining disordered behavior as being learned just like normal behavior (Skinner, 1971; Watson, 1913). For example, when Joanne was a small child, a spider dropped onto her leg, causing Joanne to scream and react with fear. Her mother came running and made a big fuss over her, soothing her and giving her lots of attention. The next time Joanne saw a spider, she screamed again because of the prior fear-provoking incident. She also was rewarded with the attention of everyone in the room. Eventually, Joanne would experience a fear reaction and scream if someone just said the word *spider*. Behaviorists would say that Joanne's fear of the spider was classically conditioned to occur to the mere sight of a spider or even the word, and her screaming reaction was positively reinforced by all the attention and soothing.

COGNITIVE PERSPECTIVE: THINKING PROBLEMS   Cognitive psychologists, who study the way people think, remember, and mentally organize information, see abnormal behavior as resulting from illogical thinking patterns (Mora, 1985). A depressed person, for example, may be taking small problems and blowing them out of proportion: "I flunked my algebra test, my life is ruined!" A cognitive psychologist might explain Joanne's fear of spiders as distorted thinking: "All spiders are vicious and will bite me, and I will die!" Joanne's particular thinking patterns put her at a higher risk of depression and anxiety than those of a person who thinks more logically.

Actor Tony Shaloub stars as TV detective Adrian Monk. Monk suffers from obsessive-compulsive disorder, which often makes his detective work difficult. Here he wears a sterile glove so that he can use a public telephone without fear of contamination by germs.

psychological disorders
any pattern of behavior that causes people significant distress, causes them to harm others, or harms their ability to function in daily life.

biological model
model of explaining behavior as caused by biological changes in the chemical, structural, or genetic systems of the body.

cognitive psychologists
psychologists who study the way people think, remember, and mentally organize information.

A Look at Abnormality in Various Cultures

14.5 *How is abnormality viewed in other kinds of cultures?*

As mentioned earlier, what's normal in one culture may be abnormal in another culture. **Cultural relativity** is a term that refers to the need to consider the unique characteristics of the culture in which a person with a disorder was nurtured to be able to correctly diagnose and treat the disorder (Castillo, 1997). For example, in most Asian cultures, mental illness is often seen as a shameful thing that brings disgrace to one's family. It may be seen as something inherited and, therefore, something that would hurt the marriage chances of other family members, or it may be seen as stemming from something the family's ancestors did wrong in the past (Ritts, 1999; Ying, 1990). This leads many Asian people suffering from disorders that would be labeled as depression or even schizophrenia to report bodily symptoms rather than emotional or mental ones because bodily ailments are more socially acceptable (Fedoroff & McFarlane, 1998; Lee, 1995; Ritts, 1999).

Some disorders called **culture-bound syndromes** are only found in particular cultures. Here are a few examples, together with the culture in which they are found (Ritts, 1999):

- *Koro:* Found primarily in China and a few other South Asian and East Asian countries, koro involves a fear that one's genitals are shrinking (Pfeiffer, 1982).

- *Taijin-kyofu-sho (TKS):* TKS is found primarily in Japan and also involves excessive fear and anxiety, but in this case it is the fear that one will do something in public that is socially inappropriate or embarrassing such as blushing, staring, or having an offensive body odor (Kirmayer, 1991).

- *Susto:* Susto is a kind of magical fright found among the Kechua-speaking Latino Indians of the Andes. It is seen as a "loss of soul" triggered by some frightening experience, after which the person falls to the ground and experiences appetite and weight loss, weakness, problems sleeping, depression, and apathy* (Pfeiffer, 1982).

- *Amok:* The term comes from Southeast Asia but similar concepts are found in Latin America as well as in certain Native American tribes. Amok results from a perceived insult or slight, which is followed by a period of brooding and then a violent or aggressive outburst, during which the person may attack others and may not remember doing so (Pfeiffer, 1982).

- *Anorexia nervosa:* The eating disorder, anorexia, in which individuals starve themselves to become thin, is typically found only in Western cultures such as the United States and Great Britain (Bemporad, 1997; Garner & Garfinkel, 1980). There is some evidence that the incidence rates in other non-Western cultures are changing as exposure to Western culture through the media increases (Ritenbaugh et al., 1992) and that in some cultures starvation is not motivated by a desire to be thin but rather by eccentric nutritional ideas or religious fasting (Castillo, 1997; Rieger et al., 2001).

Questions for Further Discussion

1. Think about your own culture. Is there a disorder or behavior that seems to be unique to that culture?

2. Are there superstitions or magical beliefs in your culture or social group that could become the basis for a disorder?

cultural relativity
the need to consider the unique characteristics of the culture in which behavior takes place.

culture-bound syndromes
disorders found only in particular cultures.

*Apathy: lack of feeling or emotion; indifference to surroundings.

PRACTICE **QUIZ:** HOW MUCH DO YOU REMEMBER?

Pick the best answer.

1. Who would be most likely to assume that psychological disorders are caused by an imbalance in the fluids of the body?
   a. an ancient Egyptian physician
   b. a modern psychiatrist
   c. an ancient Greek physician
   d. a physician of the Middle Ages

2. Lisa has started having feelings of fearfulness about going to school. She has begun to suffer from headaches and stomachaches and has missed several days of school already. Lisa's condition is abnormal from the _____ definition.
   a. statistical
   b. situational context
   c. social deviance
   d. subjective discomfort

3. Which model of abnormality explains abnormal behavior as caused by illogical thinking?
   a. psychoanalytic
   b. cognitive
   c. behavioral
   d. biological

4. Elliot is attracted to his beautiful cousin, Ginny, but knows that she is too closely related to him. He believes he has successfully overcome this forbidden attraction but still finds that every time Ginny is near him he is overwhelmed with feelings of anxiety and feels the need to wash his hands. Which model of abnormality would most likely explain Elliot's behavior?
   a. psychoanalytic
   b. cognitive
   c. behavioral
   d. biological

5. In Japan, the disorder called _____ centers around a fear of doing something embarrassing or socially inappropriate.
   a. koro
   b. taijin-kyofu-sho
   c. susto
   d. amok

Answers: 1-c, 2-d, 3-b, 4-a, 5-b.

Diagnostic and Statistical Manual, Version IV, Text Revision (*DSM-IV-TR*)

14.6 *How do psychologists decide what kind of disorder a person has?*

In 1952, the first edition of the *Diagnostic and Statistical Manual of Mental Disorders (DSM)* was published to help psychological professionals diagnose psychological disorders. The current version of the *DSM* is called the *Diagnostic and Statistical Manual of Mental Disorders, Version IV, Text Revision* or *DSM-IV-TR* (American Psychiatric Association, 2000). (The Text Revision version did not change any categories from the older *DSM-IV* but added new text material to the existing categories.)

CATEGORIES IN THE *DSM-IV-TR*

14.7 *What are the different types of psychological disorders and how common are they?*

The *DSM-IV-TR* describes about 250 different psychological disorders. Each disorder is described in terms of its symptoms, the typical path the disorder takes as it progresses, and a checklist of specific criteria that must be met in order for the diagnosis of that disorder to be made. The manual also divides these disorders and relevant facts about the person being diagnosed along five different categories, or axes (see Table 14.1). A psychologist or psychiatrist assesses the person on each of these five axes.

Axis I, Clinical Disorders, contains the disorders that bring most people to the attention of a psychological professional. With one exception, all of the psychological disorders are listed on this axis. The exception is the personality disorders, which are listed on Axis II along with mental retardation. The reason for this is that unlike most psychological disorders that appear at some later point in a person's life, personality disorders seem to exist almost from birth and are relatively stable and enduring. This almost innate quality makes personality disorders more similar to a condition such as mental retardation, which also exists as a part of the individual's biological makeup.

Axis III includes physical disorders that affect a person's psychological *adjustment*, such as juvenile diabetes, chromosome disorders such as Klinefelter's syndrome, and high blood pressure. (In psychology, the term *adjustment* refers to a person's ability to

TABLE 14.1 **THE AXES OF THE *DSM-IV-TR***

Axis	Type of Information	Description in Brief
Axis I	Clinical Disorders and Other Conditions That May Be a Focus of Clinical Attention.	Psychological disorders that impair functioning and are stressful and factors that are not disorders but that may affect functioning, such as academic or social problems.
Axis II	Personality Disorders Mental Retardation	Rigid, enduring, maladaptive personality patterns.
Axis III	General Medical Conditions	Chronic and acute illnesses and medical conditions that may have an impact on mental health.
Axis IV	Psychosocial and Environmental Problems	Problems in the physical surroundings of the person that may have an impact on diagnosis, treatment, and outcome.
Axis V	Global Assessment of Functioning	Overall judgment of current functioning, including mental, social, and occupational.

Adapted from the American Psychiatric Association, *DSM-IV-TR* (2000).

function normally in everyday life.) Axis IV contains information about problems in the person's life that might affect adjustment, such as the death of a loved one, the loss of a job, or poverty. Finally, Axis V is an overall judgment made by the psychological professional of the person's mental health and adjustment, literally a rating on a scale of 0 to 100. For example, scores of 91–100 would be interpreted as superior functioning, 71–80 as temporary problems due to stress, and 41–50 would indicate serious symptoms.

For a listing and brief description of the disorders found on Axis I, see Table 14.2.

TABLE 14.2 **AXIS I DISORDERS OF THE *DSM-IV-TR***

Disorder	Examples
Disorders usually first diagnosed in infancy, childhood, or adolescence	Learning disabilities, ADHD, bedwetting, speech disorder
Delirium, dementia, amnesia, and other cognitive disorders	Alzheimer's, Parkinson's, amnesia due to physical causes
Psychological disorders due to a general medical condition	Personality change because of a brain tumor
Substance-related disorders	Alcoholism, drug addictions
Schizophrenia and other psychotic disorders	Schizophrenia, delusional disorders, hallucinations, paranoid psychosis
Mood disorders	Depression, mania, bipolar disorders
Anxiety disorders	Panic disorder, phobias, stress disorders
Somatoform disorders	Hypochondria, conversion disorder
Factitious disorders	Pathological lying, Munchausen syndrome
Dissociative disorders	Multiple personality, amnesia not due to physical causes
Sexual and gender identity disorders	Sexual desire disorders, paraphilias
Eating disorders	Anorexia, bulimia
Sleep disorders	Insomnia, sleep terror disorder, sleepwalking, narcolepsy
Impulse-control disorders not elsewhere classified	Kleptomania, pathological gambling, pyromania
Adjustment disorders	Mixed anxiety, conduct disturbances

HOW COMMON ARE PSYCHOLOGICAL DISORDERS?

That table has a pretty long list of disorders, but most people don't get these problems, right? Actually, psychological disorders are more common than most people might think. In any given year, about 22 percent of adults over age 18 suffer from a mental disorder (NIMH, 2001; Regier et al., 1993, 2001). That comes to about 44 million people in the United States. Four of the ten leading causes of disability in the United States and other developed countries are psychological disorders of some kind, with major depression leading the list (Murray & Lopez, 1996; NIMH, 2001). In fact, it is quite common for people to suffer from more than one mental disorder at a time, such as a person with depression who also has a substance abuse disorder, or a person with an anxiety disorder who suffers from sleep disorders as well (NIMH, 2001). Table 14.3 has percentages of selected psychological disorders in the United States. (Note that this table does not include all of the disorders that occur in the 44 million adults in the United States mentioned earlier in this paragraph.)

Before describing the various categories and types of disorders, a word of caution: It's very easy to see oneself in these disorders. As mentioned in Chapter Twelve, medical students often become convinced that they have every one of the symptoms for some rare, exotic disease they have been studying. Psychology students studying abnormal behavior can also become convinced that they have some mental disorder, a problem that can be called *psychology student's syndrome.* The problem is that so many psychological disorders are really ordinary variations in human behavior taken to an extreme. For example, some people are natural-born worriers. They look for things that can go wrong around every corner. That doesn't make them disordered—it makes them pessimistic worriers. It doesn't become a disorder until the worrying gets out of hand or takes place when there's nothing to worry about or go wrong. So if you start "seeing" yourself or even your friends and family in any of the following discussions, don't panic—all of you are *probably* okay.

◀ That table has a pretty long list of disorders, but most people don't get these problems, right?

TABLE 14.3 **OCCURRENCE OF PSYCHOLOGICAL DISORDERS IN THE UNITED STATES**

Category of Disorder	Specific Disorder	Percentage/Number*
Depressive Disorders	Major depressive disorder	5%/9.9 million
	Dysthymic disorder	5.4%/10.9 million
	Bipolar disorder	1.2%/2.3 million
Schizophrenia	All types	1.1%/2.2 million
Anxiety Disorders	Panic disorder	1.7%/2.4 million
	Obsessive-compulsive disorder	2.3%/3.3 million
	Post-traumatic stress disorder	3.6%/5.2 million
	Generalized anxiety disorder	2.8%/4.0 million
	Social phobia	3.7%/5.3 million
	Agoraphobia	2.2%/3.2 million
	Specific phobia	4.4%/6.3 million

*Percentage of adults over age 18 affected annually/actual number within the population where available, in the United States.

Adapted from NIMH (2001).

anxiety disorders
disorders in which the main symptom is excessive or unrealistic anxiety and fearfulness.

free-floating anxiety
anxiety that is unrelated to any realistic, known source.

phobia
an irrational, persistent fear of an object, situation, or social activity.

Statistically speaking, about one out of every five of the people in this crowd probably suffers from some form of psychological disorder.

Anxiety Disorders: What, Me Worry?

14.8 *What are the different types of anxiety disorders and their symptoms?*

The category of **anxiety disorders** includes all disorders in which the most dominant symptom is excessive or unrealistic anxiety. Anxiety can take very specific forms, such as a fear of a specific object, or it can be a very general emotion, such as that experienced by someone who is worried and doesn't know why.

But doesn't everybody have anxiety sometimes? What makes it a disorder? There's a difference between anxiety that is realistic and has a known source and the kind of anxiety found in disorders. If final exams are coming up and a student hasn't studied enough, that student's anxiety is understandable and realistic. But a student who has studied, has done well on all the exams, and is very prepared who still worries excessively about passing is showing an unrealistic amount of anxiety. People who are in danger of losing their job might experience quite a bit of anxiety, but its source is obvious and understandable. But people whose life is going well and for whom nothing bad is looming in the future who still feel extremely anxious may be experiencing an anxiety disorder. **Free-floating anxiety** is the term given to anxiety that seems to be unrelated to any realistic, known factor, and it is often a symptom of an anxiety disorder (Freud & Gay, 1977).

Post-traumatic and acute stress disorders are also anxiety disorders but were discussed more thoroughly in Chapter Eleven and will not be repeated here.

PHOBIC DISORDERS: WHEN FEARS GET OUT OF HAND

One of the more specific anxiety disorders is a **phobia**, an irrational, persistent fear of something. The "something" might be an object or a situation or may involve social situations.

But doesn't ▶ everybody have anxiety sometimes? What makes it a disorder?

When I have to get up in front of the class to do a presentation, I get really nervous. Is this fear a common phobia? ▶

When I have to get up in front of the class to do a presentation, I get really nervous. Is this fear a common phobia?

SOCIAL PHOBIAS (SOCIAL ANXIETY DISORDER)   **Social phobias** (also called *social anxiety disorders*) involve a fear of interacting with others or being in a social situation and are some of the most common phobias people experience (WHO International Consortium in Psychiatric Epidemiology, 2000). People with a social phobia are afraid of being evaluated in some negative way by others, so they tend to avoid situations that could lead to something embarrassing or humiliating. They are very self-conscious as a result. Common types of social phobia are stage fright, fear of public speaking, and fear of urinating in a public restroom. Not surprisingly, people with social phobias often have a history of being shy as children (Sternberger et al., 1995).

SPECIFIC PHOBIAS   A **specific phobia** is an irrational fear of some object or specific situation, such as a fear of dogs, or a fear of being in small, enclosed spaces (**claustrophobia**). Other specific phobias include a fear of injections (*trypanophobia*), fear of dental work (*odontophobia*), fear of blood (*hematophobia*), and fear of heights (**acrophobia**). For a listing of common phobias, see Table 14.4.

AGORAPHOBIA   A third type of phobia is **agoraphobia**, a Greek name that literally means "fear of the marketplace." Although that makes it sound like a social phobia, agoraphobia is a little more complicated. It is actually the fear of being in a place or situation (social or not) from which escape is difficult or impossible if something should go wrong (APA, 2000). So agoraphobics are often afraid of not only crowds but also crossing bridges, traveling in a car or plane, eating in restaurants, and sometimes even of leaving the house. To be in any of these situations or to even think about being in such situations can lead to extreme feelings of anxiety and even panic attacks (see the section on page 532 about panic attacks).

If a person has agoraphobia, it might be difficult to even go to work or to the store, right? Exactly. People with specific phobias can usually avoid the object or situation without too much difficulty and people with social phobias may simply avoid jobs and situations that involve meeting people face-to-face. But people with agoraphobia cannot avoid their phobia's source because it is simply being outside in the real world. A severe case of agoraphobia can make a person's home a prison, leaving the person trapped inside unable to go to work, shop, or engage in any kind of activity that requires going out of the home.

Although leading man Harrison Ford has often played confident, bold characters in films, he describes himself as being terrified of public speaking. At a banquet of the American Film Institute he received a lifetime achievement award. He was unable to express his thanks in the manner he would have liked, speaking in barely audible whispers.

◀ If a person has agoraphobia, it might be difficult to even go to work or to the store, right?

TABLE 14.4 **COMMON PHOBIAS AND THEIR SCIENTIFIC NAMES**

Fear of	Scientific Name
Washing and bathing	Ablutophobia
Spiders	Arachnophobia
Lightning	Ceraunophobia
Dirt, germs	Mysophobia
Snakes	Ophidiophobia
Darkness	Nyctophobia
Fire	Pyrophobia
Foreigners, strangers	Xenophobia
Animals	Zoophobia

Source: Adapted from Culbertson (2003).

social phobia
fear of interacting with others or being in social situations that might lead to a negative evaluation.

specific phobia
fear of objects or specific situations or events.

claustrophobia
fear of being in a small, enclosed space.

acrophobia
fear of heights.

agoraphobia
fear of being in a place or situation from which escape is difficult or impossible.

"Is the Itsy Bitsy Spider obsessive-compulsive?"
©The New Yorker Collection 2003 Michael Shaw from cartoonbank.com.
All Rights Reserved.

I knew someone who ▶
had just had a baby, and
she spent the first few
nights home with the
baby checking it to see if
it was breathing—is that
an obsessive-compulsive
disorder?

OBSESSIVE-COMPULSIVE DISORDER

Sometimes people get a thought running through their head that just won't go away, like when a song gets stuck in one's mind. If that particular thought causes a lot of anxiety, it can become the basis for an **obsessive-compulsive disorder** or OCD, a disorder in which intruding* thoughts that occur again and again (obsessions, such as a fear that germs are on one's hands) are followed by some repetitive, ritualistic behavior (compulsion, such as repeated hand washing) meant to lower the anxiety caused by the thought (Soomro, 2001).

Some other examples of obsessive thoughts and compulsive behaviors include an obsession with having left something undone, resulting in the constant checking and rechecking of one's work or thinking that one might do something to harm a loved one, leading to counting and recounting the knives in the kitchen.

I knew someone who had just had a baby, and she spent the first few nights home with the baby checking it to see if it was breathing—is that an obsessive-compulsive disorder? No, almost all new parents check their infant's breathing frequently at first. Remember *psychology student's syndrome?* Everyone has a little obsessive thinking from time to time or has some little ritual that just makes them feel better. One woman liked to check on both of her children just before she went to bed, saying a little prayer for their safekeeping each night. She didn't feel *compelled* to do the checking and the prayer, however. If she had been a true obsessive-compulsive, she would *always have to perform the check and the prayer*, even if it meant getting out of bed or going to wherever the children were sleeping. If she had for some reason been unable to complete the ritual, she would also have experienced extreme anxiety or distress. The distress caused by a failure or inability to successfully complete the compulsive behavior is a defining feature of OCD. In fact, the woman's children might not have been allowed to sleep anywhere else because of her fear that she could not complete the ritual. It's really a matter of degree.

PANIC DISORDER

Anna, a 14-year-old, was sitting in science class watching a film. All of a sudden, she started feeling really strange. Her ears seemed to be stuffed with cotton and her vision was very dim. She was cold, had broken out in a sweat, and felt extremely afraid for no good reason. Her heart was racing and she immediately became convinced that she was dying. A friend sitting behind her saw how pale she had become and tried to ask her what was wrong, but Anna couldn't speak. She was in a state of panic and couldn't move. The friend got the teacher's attention, who motioned to Anna to come over to him. Although she would have sworn she couldn't move, she stood up to go to him and immediately everything returned to normal.

Sound familiar? Anna's symptoms are the classic symptoms of a **panic attack**, a sudden onset of extreme panic with various physical symptoms: racing heart, rapid breathing, a sensation of being "out of one's body," dulled hearing and vision, sweating, and dry mouth (Kumar & Oakley-Browne, 2002). Many people who have a panic attack think that they are having a heart attack and can experience pain as well as panic, but a panic attack is not a diagnosable medical disorder. Psychologically, the person having a panic attack is in a state of terror, thinking that this is it, death is happening, and many people may feel a need to escape. The attack happens without warning and quite suddenly. Although some panic attacks can last as long as half an hour, some last only a few minutes, with most attacks peaking within 10 to 15 minutes.

obsessive-compulsive disorder
disorder in which intruding, recurring thoughts or obsessions create anxiety that is relieved by performing a repetitive, ritualistic behavior (compulsion).

panic attack
sudden onset of intense panic in which multiple physical symptoms of stress occur, often with feelings that one is dying.

---

*Intruding: forcing one's way in; referring to something undesirable that enters awareness.

Having a panic attack is not that unusual, especially for adolescent girls and young adult women (Eaton et al., 1994). Researchers have also found evidence that cigarette smoking greatly increases the risk of panic attacks in adolescents and young adults (Johnson, 2000; Zvolensky et al., 2003). Regardless of the age of onset, it is only when panic attacks become so frequent that they affect a person's ability to function in day-to-day life that they become a **panic disorder**. When a fear of having panic attacks in a public place prevents the person from going out into unfamiliar or exposed places, it is called **panic disorder with agoraphobia**.

Many people try to figure out what triggers a panic attack and avoid the situation if possible. If driving a car sets off an attack, they don't drive. If being in a crowd sets off an attack, they don't go where crowds are. It is easy to see how having panic disorder can often lead to agoraphobia. Psychologists and psychiatrists will classify a person as having either a panic disorder with agoraphobia or a panic disorder without agoraphobia.

Actress Sigourney Weaver portrayed an FBI criminal profiler who was attacked by a serial killer in the 1995 movie "Copycat." Her character developed severe panic disorder with agoraphobia, preventing her from leaving her home. In this still from the film, she is suffering from a panic attack in an elevator in an attempt to escape the killer.

GENERALIZED ANXIETY DISORDER

What about people who are just worriers? Can that become a disorder? Remember free-floating anxiety? That's the kind of anxiety that has no real source and may be experienced by people with **generalized anxiety disorder**, in which excessive anxiety and worries (apprehensive expectations) occur more days than not for at least six months. People with this disorder may also experience anxiety about a number of events or activities (such as work or school performance). These feelings of anxiety persist six months or more and have no real source that can be pinpointed, nor can the person control the feelings even if an effort is made to do so.

People with this disorder are just plain worriers (Ruscio et al., 2001). They worry about money, their children, their lives, their friends, the dog, and anything else that they think might possibly go wrong. They feel tense and edgy, get tired easily, and may have trouble concentrating. They have muscle aches and tension; they experience sleeping problems and are often irritable—all signs of stress. The problem is that the stress comes from their worrying rather than from any real external source. General anxiety disorder is often found occurring with other anxiety disorders and depression.

Once again, it is a matter of degree and source: People with generalized anxiety disorder worry more excessively than people who are normal worriers, and they are worried over things that would cause other people no real concern.

◀ What about people who are just worriers? Can that become a disorder?

CAUSES OF ANXIETY DISORDERS

14.9   *How do psychologists explain the causes of anxiety disorders?*

Different perspectives on how personality develops offer different explanations for anxiety disorders. For example, the *psychoanalytic model* sees anxiety as a kind of danger signal that repressed urges or conflicts are threatening to surface (Freud & Gay, 1977). A phobia is seen as a kind of displacement, in which the phobic object is actually only a symbol of whatever the person has buried deep in his or her unconscious mind—the true source of the fear. A fear of knives might mean a fear of one's own aggressive tendencies, or a fear of heights may hide a suicidal desire to jump.

Behaviorists disagree with this interpretation. They believe that anxious behavioral reactions are learned. They see phobias, for example, as nothing more than classically conditioned fear responses, as was the case with "Little Albert" (Rachman, 1990; Watson & Rayner, 1920). ⓛⓘⓝⓚ *to Chapter Five: Learning, p. 172.* Remember Joanne,

panic disorder
disorder in which panic attacks occur frequently enough to cause the person difficulty in adjusting to daily life.

panic disorder with agoraphobia
fear of leaving one's familiar surroundings because one might have a panic attack in public.

generalized anxiety disorder
disorder in which a person has feelings of dread and impending doom along with physical symptoms of stress, which lasts six months or more.

magnification
the tendency to interpret situations as far more dangerous, harmful, or important than they actually are.

all-or-nothing thinking
the tendency to believe that one's performance must be perfect or the result will be a total failure.

overgeneralization
the tendency to interpret a single negative event as a never-ending pattern of defeat and failure.

minimization
the tendency to give little or no importance to one's successes or positive events and traits.

Experiment
Live!
psych

Disorders

who was afraid of spiders? She received a lot of attention when she had a phobic reaction. When her friends stopped giving her this attention every time she overreacted to seeing a spider or hearing the word, the reaction was almost completely extinguished.

Cognitive psychologists see anxiety disorders as the result of illogical, irrational thought processes. One way in which people with anxiety disorders show irrational thinking (Beck, 1976, 1984) is through **magnification**, or the tendency to "make mountains out of molehills" by interpreting situations as being far more harmful, dangerous, or embarrassing than they actually are. In panic disorder, for example, a person might interpret a racing heartbeat as a sign of a heart attack instead of just a momentary arousal.

Another distorted thought process is **all-or-nothing thinking**, in which a person believes that his or her performance must be perfect or the result will be a total failure. **Overgeneralization** (a single negative event interpreted as a never-ending pattern of defeat), jumping to conclusions without facts to support that conclusion, and **minimization** (giving little or no emphasis to one's successes or positive events and traits) are other examples of irrational thinking.

Evidence exists that *biological* factors contribute to anxiety disorders. Generalized anxiety disorder, for example, has been linked to an imbalance in several neurotransmitters in the nervous system, including serotonin and GABA (Brawman-Mintzer & Lydiard, 1997; Rynn et al., 2000). Recent research has linked panic disorder to a possible defect in the way serotonin binds to its receptors in the nervous system (Neumeister et al., 2004). Some evidence suggests that these chemical imbalances may have a genetic component, meaning that anxiety disorders such as obsessive-compulsive disorder, phobias, and panic disorder can be passed from parent to child through more than just observational learning (Karayiorgou et al., 1997; Lesch et al., 1996; Logue et al., 2003).

Anxiety disorders are found around the world, although the particular form the disorder takes might be different in various cultures. For example, in some Latin American cultures anxiety can take the form of "ataque de nervios," or "attack of nerves," in which the person may have fits of crying, shout uncontrollably, experience sensations of heat, and become very aggressive, either verbally or physically. These attacks usually come after some stressful event such as the death of a loved one (APA, 2000). The Current Issues in Psychology section earlier in this chapter mentioned several syndromes found in certain cultures, such as koro and TKS, that are essentially types of phobias specific to those cultures. Panic disorder is found almost universally at about the same rate all over the world (Weissman et al., 1997).

PRACTICE **QUIZ:** HOW MUCH DO YOU REMEMBER?

Pick the best answer.

1. Which of the following is NOT a correct match?
   a. Axis V—Global Assessment of Functioning
   b. Axis I—Personality Disorders
   c. Axis III—General Medical Conditions
   d. Axis IV—Psychosocial and Environmental Problems

2. An irrational fear of blood would be a
   a. social phobia.
   b. specific phobia.
   c. type of agoraphobia.
   d. type of acrophobia.

3. Jennifer worries that someone might come into her house at night while she is sleeping and helpless. She checks the locks on the doors and windows several times before she can relax enough to go to bed. Her constant checking of the locks is most similar to
   a. a compulsion.
   b. an obsession.
   c. a panic disorder.
   d. a phobia.

4. Bud's relatives are concerned that he worries too much. He worries about little things going wrong, he worries about big things going wrong, and sometimes it seems as though he's worrying because there's nothing to worry about. He worries so much that he has a hard time getting things done. Bud most likely has
   a. panic disorder.
   b. obsessive-compulsive disorder.
   c. generalized anxiety disorder.
   d. post-traumatic stress disorder.

5. Sandy has the tendency to make everything seem so much worse than it usually is. Beck would say that Sandy has a tendency to
   a. overgeneralize.
   b. minimize.
   c. do all-or-nothing thinking.
   d. magnify.

Answers: 1-b, 2-b, 3-a, 4-c, 5-d.

Somatoform Disorders: Sickness as a State of Mind

14.10   *What are the different kinds of somatoform disorders?*

Another category of abnormal behavior involves the belief that one is physically ill, which is often accompanied by the experience of physical symptoms even though there is no physical illness or problem. Disorders in which people believe they are sick when they are not are called **somatoform disorders**. *Somatoform* means that these disorders take the form of a bodily (somatic) ailment but are not real physical disorders. Although there is no real physical cause, the symptoms are very real to the person experiencing them.

I've heard of something like this—but I thought the name of it was psychosomatic disorder? Somatoform disorders are actually quite different from **psychosomatic disorders**. In a psychosomatic disorder (now called **psychophysiological disorder**), the bodily ailments are real physical ailments caused or worsened by stress. The two disorders are often confused. Unlike psychophysiological disorders, somatoform disorders are *not* real physical ailments, and although the symptoms are real to the person experiencing them, they are quite literally "all in one's head."

HYPOCHONDRIASIS

Hypochondriasis (or the older name *hypochondria*) is one of the better-known somatoform disorders. In this disorder, a person worries excessively and almost constantly about getting ill. Although this may sound like an anxiety disorder, the specific worry about illness is the distinguishing feature of this disorder. People with this disorder become very preoccupied with bodily symptoms, which may be real but unimportant in reality or imagined (Phillips, 2001). They go to doctors and health clinics frequently, looking for some medical professional who will tell them what dreadful disease they have (Magarinos et al., 2002). People with this disorder are often called *hypochondriacs*.

SOMATIZATION DISORDER

A similar somatoform disorder is **somatization disorder**, in which the person complains about a specific physical symptom or symptoms, such as pain, nausea, difficulty swallowing, or trouble catching one's breath (Kellner, 1986). People with this disorder also go to doctors a lot, but they show less worry and more "drama." They tend to get very emotional when describing their symptoms, using phrases like "unbearable" and "beyond description" to describe their pain or other symptom, and they tend to become very dependent on the medical professional, demanding attention and even threatening suicide to get that attention in some cases. The symptoms also seem to multiply and shift frequently, with the main symptom being pain one day and shortness of breath on another, for example (Swartz, 1990). Like the hypochondriac, a person with somatization disorder is not creating symptoms just to fool others. Although it might be obvious to others, people with these disorders do not see the connection between their anxiety and their bodily symptoms.

CONVERSION DISORDER

Conversion disorder is limited to those functions controlled by the somatic nervous system. It is not seen as frequently today as in the past. Symptoms are the loss of motor and/or sensory functions (APA, 2000). A person may experience dramatic and

somatoform disorders
disorders that take the form of bodily illnesses and symptoms but for which there are no real physical disorders.

psychosomatic disorder
disorder in which psychological stress causes a real physical disorder or illness.

psychophysiological disorder
modern term for psychosomatic disorder.

◄ I've heard of something like this—but I thought the name of it was psychosomatic disorder?

"You know, Burkhart, if you're so damn afraid of the flu maybe you should just stay home."

hypochondriasis
somatoform disorder in which the person is terrified of being sick and worries constantly, going to doctors repeatedly, and becoming preoccupied with every sensation of the body.

somatization disorder
somatoform disorder in which the person dramatically complains of a specific symptom such as nausea, difficulty swallowing, or pain for which there is no real physical cause.

conversion disorder
somatoform disorder in which the person experiences a specific symptom in the somatic nervous system's functioning, such as paralysis, numbness, or blindness, for which there is no physical cause.

FIGURE 14.1 **Glove Anesthesia**
Glove anesthesia is a disorder in which the person experiences numbness from the wrist down (see the drawing on the left). However, real nerve damage would produce numbness down one side of the arm and hand, as shown in the drawing on the right. Thus, because glove anesthesia is anatomically impossible, it is actually a sign of a conversion disorder.

specific symptoms such as blindness, paralysis, deafness, or numbness of certain body parts, none of which have real physical causes. Typically, the problems occur along with some other psychological disorder, such as depression, at a time when there is a stressful situation either already happening or threatening to happen (Hurwitz, 1989).

There are some simple ways to recognize conversion disorders. People with such disorders tend to exhibit a kind of indifference or lack of concern about the symptom, which is understandable if the person has unconscious knowledge that the symptom is not real (Silver, 1996). Another is that the symptom is anatomically impossible, as is the case with blindness for which there is no corresponding damage to the eyes, optic nerve, or parts of the brain responsible for vision. (See Figure 14.1.) Finally, conversion disorder symptoms disappear when the person is asleep, hypnotized, under anesthesia, or unconscious (Parobek, 1997; Silver, 1996). Like somatization disorder, conversion disorder usually occurs when a stressful situation has also occurred or is threatening to occur, such as a soldier facing the return to combat.

CAUSES OF SOMATOFORM DISORDERS

14.11 *What causes somatoform disorders?*

Freud believed that this type of disorder was a way of making anxiety caused by the repression of traumatic events or unacceptable impulses into a physical symptom. The physical symptom was seen as providing some relief from anxiety at first. For example, a woman who was anxious about unwanted sexual thoughts might become "paralyzed" from the waist down, ensuring that she had no way to act on those thoughts. Behaviorists believe that the telling factors in somatoform disorders are that such behavior results in two kinds of reinforcement: positive reinforcement in the form of attention from doctors, family members, and others; and negative reinforcement from being able to avoid whatever stressful situation is associated with the disorder. A hypochondriac, for example, who believes that his heart is about to give out might resist going back to work or doing strenuous chores around the house, a soldier with conversion paralysis need not face combat again, and a child with a somatization stomachache gets to stay home and avoid the big math exam that day.

Cognitive psychologists would again point to the tendency to magnify symptoms and allow false beliefs to dominate one's thinking.

Turning one's anxiety into physical symptoms is not found in Western culture alone. Somatoform-type disorders are found in many countries, although the specific symptoms may vary from culture to culture (Mezzick et al., 1996). For example, in *dhat* syndrome, young Asian men are excessively afraid that a loss of seminal fluid is depleting their bodies of energy and vitality and often go to doctor after doctor seeking help—exactly what a hypochondriac does (Chadda & Ahuja, 1990).

Dissociative Disorders: Altered Consciousness

14.12 *What are the dissociative disorders?*

Dissociative disorders involve a break, or dissociation, in consciousness, memory, or a person's sense of identity. This "split" is easier to understand when thinking about how people sometimes drive somewhere and then wonder how they got there—they don't remember the trip itself at all. This sort of "automatic pilot" driving happens when the route is familiar and frequently traveled. One part of the conscious mind was thinking about work, school, or whatever was uppermost in the mind while lower centers of consciousness were driving the car, stopping at signs and lights, and turning

dissociative disorders
disorders in which there is a break in conscious awareness, memory, the sense of identity, or some combination.

when needed. This split in conscious attention is very similar to what happens in dissociative disorders. The difference is that in the disorders the dissociation is much more pronounced and involuntary.

DISSOCIATIVE AMNESIA: WHO AM I?

In **dissociative amnesia**, one cannot remember personal information such as one's own name or specific personal events—the kind of information contained in episodic long-term memory. ⓛⓘⓝⓚ *to Chapter Six: Memory, p. 221.* This memory loss is usually associated with a stressful or emotionally traumatic experience, such as rape or childhood abuse (Chu et al., 1999; Kirby et al., 1993), and cannot be easily explained by simple forgetfulness. It can be a loss of memory for only one small segment of time, or it can involve a total loss of one's past personal memories. For example, a soldier might be able to remember being in combat but cannot remember witnessing a friend get killed, or a person might forget his or her entire life. These memories usually resurface, sometimes quickly, and sometimes after a long delay. In one case, a veteran of the Second World War had amnesia for the time during which he was captured, tortured, and escaped from the Far East. He did not recall these memories, or the fact that he had been an intelligence agent at the time, until 37 years later (Cassiday & Lyons, 1992).

Dissociative amnesia may sound like retrograde amnesia, but it differs in its cause. In retrograde amnesia, the memory loss is typically caused by a physical injury, such as a blow to the head. In dissociative amnesia, the cause is psychological rather than physical. The "blow" is a mental one, not a real one. People with dissociative amnesia do not forget how to drive or any of the skills they previously had, and they can still talk and use the kind of information found in semantic memory. It is only the personal information that is suppressed. ⓛⓘⓝⓚ *to Chapter Twelve: Theories of Personality, pp. 445–446.*

On Christmas Day 1985, James McDonnell came home to his wife in Larchmont, New York, after 14 years of amnesia. After suffering two separate head injuries in auto accidents, he lost his memory. He went to Philadelphia and found a job in a restaurant. On Christmas Eve, Mr. McDonnell bumped his head and recovered all of his memories. This picture shows the happy reunion with his wife. What kinds of emotional and psychological adjustments do you think Mr. McDonnell and his family might have had to make upon his sudden return?

DISSOCIATIVE FUGUE: WHO AM I AND HOW DID I GET HERE?

The Latin word *fugere* means "flight" and is the word from which the term *fugue* is taken. A **dissociative fugue** occurs when a person suddenly travels away from home (the flight) and afterwards cannot remember the trip or even personal information such as identity. The person may become confused about identity, sometimes even taking on a whole new identity in the new place (Nijenhuis, 2000). Such flights usually take place after an emotional trauma and are more common in times of disasters or war.

As an example, look at the story of John Doe, so named by the physician who first saw him in the emergency room. John had no belongings and didn't know his name. He had no memories about his life before waking up on a park bench that morning, eight hours before. He seemed physically healthy, in his forties, and was dressed neatly and casually. He was clear and coherent* and seemed mentally stable, except for his loss of memory. Following a lead provided by the tag in his jacket, John was identified as a lawyer from a town 500 miles away who had been reported missing by his wife two days earlier. He had been criminally charged with embezzling from his clients and had been under such pressure that he had told his wife, "I don't know if I can take much more of this without losing my mind." Instead of losing his mind, John lost himself (Morrison, 1995).

dissociative amnesia
loss of memory for personal information, either partial or complete.

dissociative fugue
traveling away from familiar surroundings with amnesia for the trip and possible amnesia for personal information.

---

*Coherent: logically and consistently ordered or structured.

dissociative identity disorder
disorder occurring when a person seems to have two or more distinct personalities within one body.

DISSOCIATIVE IDENTITY DISORDER: HOW MANY AM I?

Perhaps the most controversial dissociative disorder is **dissociative identity disorder**, formerly known as multiple personality disorder. In this disorder, a person seems to experience at least two or more distinct personalities existing in one body. There may be a "core" personality, who usually knows nothing about the other personalities and is the one who experiences "blackouts" or losses of memory and time. Fugues are common in dissociative identity disorder, with the core personality experiencing unsettling moments of "awakening" in an unfamiliar place or with people who call the person by another name (Kluft, 1984).

First reported in the nineteenth century as a clinical disorder, many believe that cases of so-called "spirit" or "demon possession" were possibly people with this disorder. Freudian psychoanalysts believe that multiple personalities come about as a way of coping with extreme stress, usually in early childhood. Many people who have been diagnosed as "multiples" are women with a history of childhood sexual or physical abuse. It is thought that the dissociation occurs as one aspect of personality emerges to deal with the stress while the rest of the personality remains safely "hidden" in the unconscious mind. Psychoanalysts attempt to "reintegrate" the individual personalities into the core personality, which is a fancy way of saying that the person has to reclaim that part of the personality as part of the whole (Kluft, 1988). (Non-Freudian psychologists, psychiatrists, and therapists use other forms of psychotherapy and/or drugs in the treatment of this disorder.)

With the publication of several famous books such as *The Three Faces of Eve* (Thigpen & Cleckley, 1992) and *Sybil* (Schreiber, 1973) and movies made from those books, dissociative identity disorder became well known to the public. Throughout the 1980s, the publishing world saw numerous books, some fiction, and some a blend of fiction and fact, about this disorder, and psychological professionals began to diagnose this condition at an alarming rate—"multiple personality," as it was then known, had become the "fad" disorder of the late twentieth century, according to some researchers (Aldridge-Morris, 1989; Boor, 1982; Cormier & Thelen, 1998; Showalter, 1997).

In the last decade, the diagnosis of dissociative identity disorder has come under scrutiny* with many professionals now beginning to doubt the validity of previous diagnoses. Even the famous case of "Sybil" has been criticized as a case of the therapist actually "creating" the multiple personalities in her client through suggestion and even direct instruction. (For more on this controversial case, see the following Current Issues in Psychology section.) Some psychological professionals believe that dissociative identity disorder is actually a misdiagnosis of borderline personality disorder or some other form of anxiety disorder (Lauer et al., 1993).

Christine Costner Sizemore is the real face behind *The Three Faces of Eve,* the book that first brought dissociative identity disorder into the public eye. Ms. Sizemore is a successful writer and artist and has been free of symptoms for many years.

Is it a real disorder that ▶ some people fake, or is there really no such thing as multiple personality?

Is it a real disorder that some people fake, or is there really no such thing as multiple personality? There are some skeptics who believe that there is no such disorder at all and that clients who demonstrate different "personalities" are simply acting out to get the attention of the therapist or are responding to what the therapist seems to want (Gleaves, 1996). In one study, ordinary people were given instructions in how to play the role of a multiple personality and were able to exhibit the "symptoms" associated with the disorder quite effectively (Spanos et al., 1985). However,

---

*Scrutiny: a close examination.

just because someone can act out having the flu does not mean that the flu does not really exist, so being able to reproduce the symptoms of dissociative identity disorder by acting does not automatically mean that such a disorder does not exist. The question is not really, "Does dissociative identity disorder exist?" but rather, "What causes a person to exhibit the symptoms of dissociative identity disorder?" If the cause is suggestions from the therapist or deliberate deception, then there is a problem. If the symptoms of dissociative identity disorder are a sign of a person in deep psychological trouble, then the "reality" of those "personalities" becomes somewhat meaningless—the person is in trouble and needs help in either case (Arrigo & Pezdek, 1998; McHugh, 1993).

CAUSES OF DISSOCIATIVE DISORDERS

14.13   *How do dissociative disorders develop?*

Psychoanalytic theory, of course, sees the repression of threatening or unacceptable thoughts and behavior at the heart of all disorders, and the dissociative disorders in particular seem to have a large element of repression—motivated forgetting—in them. In the psychoanalytic view, loss of memory or disconnecting one's awareness from a stressful or traumatic event is adaptive in that it reduces the emotional pain (Dorahy, 2001). Dissociation in Freudian theory is a defense mechanism and is associated with emotional or physical trauma (A. Freud, 1946).

Cognitive and behavioral explanations for dissociative disorders are connected: The person may feel guilt, shame, or anxiety when thinking about disturbing experiences or thoughts and start avoiding thoughts about them. This "thought avoidance" is negatively reinforced by the reduction of the anxiety and unpleasant feelings and eventually will become a habit of "not thinking about" these things. This is similar to what many people do when faced with something unpleasant, such as an injection or a painful procedure such as having a root canal. They "think about something else." In doing that, they are deliberately not thinking about what is happening to them at the moment and the experience of pain is decreased. People with dissociative disorders may simply be better at doing this sort of "not thinking" than other people are.

Also, consider the positive reinforcement possibilities for a person with a dissociative disorder: attention from others and help from professionals. Shaping may also play a big role in the development of some cases of dissociative identity disorder. The therapist may unintentionally pay more attention to a client who talks about "feeling like someone else," which may encourage the client to report more such feelings and even elaborate on them. In the wake of the books and movies about multiples, many therapists no doubt were looking very hard for signs of multiple personality in their clients.

There are some possible biological sources for dissociations, as well. Researchers have found that people with **depersonalization disorder** (a mild dissociative disorder in which people feel detached and disconnected from themselves, their bodies, and their surroundings) have lower brain activity in the areas responsible for their sense of body awareness than do people without the disorder (Simeon et al., 2000). Others have found evidence that people with dissociative identity disorders show significant differences in PET scan activity taken when different "personalities" are present (Reinders et al., 2001).

Dissociative disorders can also be found in other cultures. *Amok*, the trancelike state in which a person suddenly becomes highly agitated and violent (found in Southeast Asia and Pacific Island cultures), is usually associated with no memory for the period during which the "trance" lasts (Suryani & Jensen, 1993).

depersonalization disorder
dissociative disorder in which a person feels detached and disconnected from themselves, their bodies, and their surroundings.

Shirley Ardell Mason is pictured here as she looked in 1970 while serving as an assistant art professor at Rio Grande College in Ohio. Upon her death in 1998, neighbors in her Lexington, Kentucky hometown were stunned to discover that Ms. Mason was the famous multiple personality, "Sybil."

CURRENT ISSUES IN PSYCHOLOGY

Was "Sybil" a True Multiple Personality?

14.14 *What is the controversy surrounding the famous case of "Sybil"?*

Shirley Ardell Mason spent the last 25 years of her life in Lexington, Kentucky, living quietly as the town's resident artist. When she died on February 26, 1998, of breast cancer at age 75, all but a very few people were surprised to learn that the former college art teacher was in fact the most famous psychiatric patient in the world—"Sybil" (Miller & Kantrowitz, 1999). Her diagnosis and treatment for dissociative identity disorder (DID), known then as multiple personality disorder or MPD, became known worldwide with the publication of writer Flora Rita Schreiber's landmark book, *Sybil*, in 1973, followed by a 1976 made-for-television movie starring actress Sally Fields as "Sybil."

But were Shirley's 16 alternate personalities real, or did her psychiatrist, Dr. Wilbur, unintentionally "create" a case of multiple personality? Two sources of evidence suggest strongly that "Sybil," was not a multiple personality until Dr. Wilbur suggested that "Sybil," under hypnosis and the effects of sodium pentothal, a powerful mind-altering drug, talk about her feelings as other people with other names and identities. In an excerpt from audiotapes of the sessions between Wilbur and book author Schreiber, Wilbur says, "And I said, 'Well, there's a personality who calls herself Peggy.' And uh, I said, 'She is pretty assertive. . . . She can do things you can't,' and she (Sybil) was very, uh, obviously perturbed by this . . . And I said . . . 'She wouldn't do anything you wouldn't approve of. She might do something that you wouldn't think of doing.' " This quote seems to have Wilbur actually telling Shirley how she should think of her other "personalities." In another tape, Schreiber is heard dismissing a letter written by Shirley Mason to Dr. Wilbur, in which Shirley denies having multiple personalities (Spiegel & Borch-Jacobsen, 1997).

Evidence was also offered by Dr. Herbert Spiegel, who was Shirley's therapist when Dr. Wilbur was out of town. Spiegel, basing his opinion on both his own sessions with Shirley and the contents of the tapes, concluded that the so-called personalities came out of Wilbur's technique of giving names to various emotional states experienced by her client (Spiegel & Borch-Jacobsen, 1997). More ominous is his recall of telling the book's author, Schreiber, that "Sybil" did not have multiple personalities. He says that Schreiber replied, "If we don't call it multiple personality, the publisher won't want it, it won't sell."

If many cases of dissociative identity disorder are not real, how can the people who are diagnosed with this disorder act so much like different "people" that even professionals are fooled? Spanos (1994, 1996) conducted studies in which he found that ordinary college students, under hypnosis, would show signs of a "second personality." He concludes that many cases of DID may actually be misdiagnosed because of clients' tendencies to "play the role" of a multiple personality, a social role that has become quite well known through books and movies.

Lending further support to the idea that dissociative identity disorder may be a disorder created by therapists in a particular social context, like the hysteria of the Freudian age, is the fact that the disorder is confined to North American culture with very few cases in Britain and none in Asian cultures such as Japan and India (Cohen et al., 1995; Fujii et al., 1998; Merskey, 1992).

One fact is clear: Before the publication of *Sybil*, there were only 76 reported *current* cases of DID (Braun, 1986) and only 200 cases of DID in all recorded medical history up to that time (Ofshe & Watters, 1994). After the book, the number of diagnosed cases of DID began to skyrocket. By 1984, there were 1,000 cases; by 1989, there were 4,000 cases, and in the 1990s psychiatrists and psychologists were estimating that there were 20,000 to 30,000 people suffering from DID (Van Til, 1997).

Questions for Further Discussion

1. If the famous case of "Sybil" turns out to be a mistaken diagnosis, does that mean that all other diagnoses of dissociative identity disorder are also mistaken?

2. What kind of precautions could therapists take to avoid "creating" certain symptoms of disorder in their clients?

PRACTICE **QUIZ:** HOW MUCH DO YOU REMEMBER?

Pick the best answer.

1. Which one is not a real physical disorder?
   a. psychosomatic disorder
   b. psychophysiological disorder
   c. somatoform disorder
   d. disease of adaptation

2. Lisa has started having feelings of fearfulness about going to school. She has begun to suffer from headaches and stomachaches and has missed several days of school already. Lisa's illnesses are probably a form of
   a. phobic disorder.
   b. somatization disorder.
   c. generalized anxiety disorder.
   d. dissociative disorder.

3. Carlo wakes up in a strange motel room. He doesn't know where he is or how he got there, and he's not sure what day it is. This is most likely an episode of dissociative
   a. amnesia.
   b. fugue.
   c. identity disorder
   d. multiple personality.

4. The fact that the dissociative disorders seem to have a large element of repression in them is related to the _____ explanation of disorders.
   a. behavioral
   b. cognitive
   c. biological
   d. psychoanalytic

5. Which of the following is NOT one of the reasons for doubting the diagnosis of "Sybil" as a true multiple personality?
   a. "Sybil" had an abusive early childhood.
   b. Her doctor made suggestions to her about her "personalities."
   c. Her doctor used hypnosis and drugs, which may have created a very suggestible state in "Sybil."
   d. The author of the book told a psychiatrist that the book would only sell if "Sybil" was labeled a multiple personality.

Answers: 1-c, 2-b, 3-b, 4-d, 5-a.

Mood Disorders: The Effect of Affect

14.15 *What are the different types of mood disorders?*

In psychological terms, the word **affect** is used to mean "emotion" or "mood." **Mood disorders** are a disturbance in emotion and are also referred to as affective disorders. Although the range of human emotions runs from deep, intense sadness and despair to extreme happiness and elation, under normal circumstances people stay in between those extremes—neither too sad nor too happy but content. (See Figure 14.2.) It is when stress or some other factor pushes a person to one extreme or the other that mood disorders can result. Mood disorders can be relatively mild (straying only a short distance from the "average") or they can be extreme (existing at either extreme of the range).

There are two relatively mild mood disorders, although their mildness does not mean that people suffering from these disorders do not need help. **Dysthymia** comes

"I've got the bowl, the bone, the big yard. I know I should be happy."
©The New Yorker Collection 1992 Mike Twohy from cartoonbank.com. All Rights Reserved.

Extreme Sadness	Mild Sadness	Normal Emotions	Mild Emotions	Extreme Elation

FIGURE 14.2   **The Range of Emotions**   Most people experience a range of emotions over the course of a day or several days, such as mild sadness, calm contentment, or mild elation and happiness. A person with a mood disorder experiences emotions that are extreme and, therefore, abnormal.

affect
in psychology, an emotional reaction.

mood disorders
disorders in which mood is severely disturbed.

dysthymia
a moderate depression that lasts for two years or more and is typically a reaction to some external stressor.

But doesn't everybody get a little "down" sometimes? When does being sad become a disorder? ▶

from Greek words meaning "bad spirit" and is a form of mild, chronic* depression that lasts for at least two years or more (Klein et al., 2000). **Cyclothymia** means "spirit that moves in circles" and involves a cycle of being sad, then feeling quite happy, and then returning to sad, happy, sad, happy, and so on, with the cycle lasting two years or more. The episodes of elation are called *hypomania*, meaning "low mania." (*Mania* is extremely excessive activity and elation or irritability.) Like dysthymia, it usually begins in childhood or adolescence and includes times of normal feelings that may last less than two months at a time (APA, 2000).

But doesn't everybody get a little "down" sometimes? When does being sad become a disorder? It is normal to get sad every now and then and even to have a mild "mood swing" on occasion (the "mild" positions on Figure 14.2). But people experiencing normal sadness or moodiness usually return to normal relatively quickly. There's also usually a reason for the sadness—something bad has happened, an opportunity was lost, somebody is sick or has died, and so on. Although both dysthymia and cyclothymia can be triggered by an outside, stressful event, they go on too long to be considered normal reactions that need no treatment or attention.

MAJOR DEPRESSION

When a deeply depressed mood comes on fairly suddenly and either seems to be too severe for the circumstances or exists without any external cause for sadness, it is called **major depression**. Major depression would fall at the far extreme of sadness on Figure 14.2. People suffering from major depression are depressed for most of every day, take little or no pleasure in any activities, feel tired, have trouble sleeping or sleep too much, experience changes in appetite and significant weight changes, experience excessive guilt or feelings of worthlessness, have trouble concentrating, and may have thoughts of death or suicide, including suicide attempts. Some people with this disorder also suffer from delusional thinking and may experience hallucinations. Most of these symptoms occur on a daily basis, lasting for the better part of the day (APA, 2000).

FIGURE 14.3 **Prevalence of Major Depression** As the most common mood disorder, major depression has seen an increase in diagnosis with each decade. From 1936 to 1945, the prevalence of major depression in the population was about 3 percent, with the onset of symptoms occurring at around ages 18 to 20. By 1966 to 1975, the prevalence had jumped to about 23 percent of the population, and the age of onset had dropped to the early teens.

Major depression is the most common of the diagnosed mood disorders and is about twice as common in women as it is in men (APA, 2000). (See Figure 14.3.) This is true even across various cultures (Blazer et al., 1994; Weissman et al., 1993). There are many possible explanations for this gender difference, including the different hormonal structure of the female system (menstruation, hormonal changes during and after pregnancy, menopause, etc.) and different social roles played by women in the culture (Blehar & Oren, 1997). Research has found little support for hormonal influences in general, instead finding that the role of hormones and other biological factors in depression is unclear. Instead, studies have found that the degree of differences between male and female rates of depression is decreasing and is nonexistent in college students and single adults, leading some to conclude that social factors such as marital status, career type, and number of children may have more importance in creating the gender difference than biological differences (McGrath et al., 1992; Nolen-Hoeksema, 1990; Weissman & Klerman, 1977).

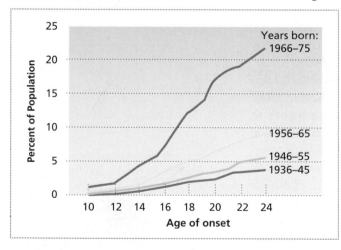

BIPOLAR DISORDERS

Major depression is sometimes referred to as a *unipolar disorder* because the emotional problem exists at only one end, or "pole," of the emotional range. When a person suffers

cyclothymia
disorder that consists of mood swings from moderate depression to hypomania and lasts two years or more.

major depression
severe depression that comes on suddenly and seems to have no external cause.

---

*Chronic: long-lasting or occurring frequently over a long period of time.

Former President Clinton's mental health advisor Tipper Gore, the wife of then Vice President Al Gore, listens to *60 Minutes* correspondent Mike Wallace as he tells of his suffering from clinical depression. They were both attendees at the White House Conference on Mental Health at Howard University on June 7, 1999.

from severe mood swings that go all the way from severe depression to **manic** episodes (excessive excitement, energy, and elation), that person is said to suffer from a **bipolar disorder**, meaning that emotions cycle between the two poles of possible emotions (APA, 2000). Unlike cyclothymia, there is usually no external cause for the extreme ups and downs of the bipolar person. The depressive phases of a bipolar person are indistinguishable from major depression but give way to manic episodes that may last from a few weeks to a few months. In these manic episodes, the person is extremely happy or euphoric* without any real cause to be so happy. Restlessness, irritability, an inability to sit still or remain inactive, and seemingly unlimited energy are also common. The person may seem silly to others and can become aggressive when not allowed to carry out the grand (and sometimes delusional) plans that are often the hallmark of the manic phase. Speech may be rapid and jump from one topic to another. Oddly, people in the manic state are often very creative until their lack of organization renders their attempts at being creative useless (Blumer, 2002; McDermott, 2001; Rothenberg, 2001).

That sounds almost like a description of an overactive child—can't sit still, can't concentrate—are they related? The answer to that question is actually part of an ongoing controversy. There does seem to be a connection between attention deficit hyperactivity disorder (ADHD) and the onset of bipolar disorder in adolescence (Carlson et al., 1998), but only a small percentage of children with ADHD go on to develop bipolar disorder. The symptoms of bipolar disorder include irrational thinking and other manic symptoms that are not present in ADHD (Geller et al., 1998). Confusion between the two disorders arises because hyperactivity (excessive movement and an inability to concentrate) is a symptom of both disorders.

CAUSES OF MOOD DISORDERS

14.16   *What are the causes of mood disorders?*

Explanations of depression and other mood disorders include psychoanalytic, learning, biological, and genetic theories. Psychoanalytic theories see depression as anger turned inward on the person. This anger, originally aimed at parents or other authority figures who are too threatening to receive the expressions of anger directly, gets

manic
having the quality of excessive excitement, energy, and elation or irritability.

bipolar disorder
severe mood swings between major depressive episodes and manic episodes.

That sounds almost like a description of an overactive child—can't sit still, can't concentrate— ◀ are they related?

Award-winning actress Patty Duke was finally diagnosed with bipolar disorder in 1982. She credits her treatment with lithium as saving her life.

---

*Euphoric: having a feeling of vigor, well-being, or high spirits.

repressed by the child and later is displaced to the self in the form of self-blame and self-hate (O'Conner, 1994; O'Conner et al., 1997).

Learning theorists link depression to learned helplessness (Seligman, 1975, 1989), whereas social cognitive theorists point to distortions of thinking such as blowing negative events out of proportion and minimizing positive, good events (Beck, 1976, 1984). In the social cognitive view, depressed people continually have negative, self-defeating thoughts about themselves, which depress them further in a downward spiral of despair. Learned helplessness (discussed in Chapter Five) has been linked to an increase in such self-defeating thinking and depression in studies with people who have experienced uncontrollable, painful events (Abramson et al., 1978, 1980). This link does not necessarily mean that negative thoughts *cause* depression; it may be that depression increases the likelihood of negative thoughts (Gotlib et al., 2001).

Biological explanations of mood disorders focus on the effects of brain chemicals such as serotonin, norepinephrine, and dopamine; drugs used to treat depression and mania typically affect the levels of these three neurotransmitters, either alone or in combination (Cohen, 1997; Cummings & Coffey, 1994).

Genes may also play a part in mood disorders. The fact that the more severe mood disorders are not a reaction to some outside source of stress or anxiety but rather seem to come from within the person's own body, together with the tendency of mood disorders to appear in genetically related individuals at a higher rate, suggests rather strongly that inheritance may play a significant part in these disorders (Barondes, 1998; Farmer, 1996). More than 65 percent of people with bipolar disorder have at least one close relative with either bipolar disorder or major depression (NIMH Genetics Workgroup, 1998). Twin studies have shown that if one identical twin has either major depression or bipolar disorder, the chances that the other twin will also develop a mood disorder are about 40 to 70 percent (Muller-Oerlinghausen et al., 2002).

PRACTICE QUIZ: HOW MUCH DO YOU REMEMBER?

Pick the best answer.

1. Jorge lost his father three years ago. Since then, he has experienced occasional bouts of sadness and depression. Although he usually feels quite happy, sometimes the sadness returns. Jorge's relatively mild mood swings most likely indicate
   a. dysthymia.
   b. cyclothymia.
   c. major depression.
   d. bipolar disorder.

2. Macha woke up one morning in a very sad mood and couldn't think of any reason why she should feel that way. The feeling got worse as the day went on, and although in the days and weeks to follow she occasionally felt normal, she had more sad days than normal. Her feelings were so intense that she couldn't sleep, ate too much, and couldn't take joy in anything. Macha is most likely suffering from
   a. dysthymia.
   b. cyclothymia.
   c. major depression.
   d. bipolar disorder.

3. Vicki was always coming up with grand plans for making money, none of which lasted very long before she abandoned them. The latest scheme is to buy a huge tract of land and build an expensive "dude" ranch where people can come to learn how to train their horses, eat at a four-star restaurant, and stay in luxury accommodations—all this in spite of the fact that Vicki and her husband don't have the money to buy the land, knowledge of how to run a hotel, or have a four-star chef handy. Vicki may have
   a. dysthymia.
   b. cyclothymia.
   c. major depression.
   d. bipolar disorder.

Answers: 1-b, 2-c, 3-d.

schizophrenia
severe disorder in which the person suffers from disordered thinking, bizarre behavior, hallucinations, and is unable to distinguish between fantasy and reality.

Schizophrenia: Altered Reality

Once known as *dementia praecox*, a Latin-based term meaning "out of one's mind before one's time," **schizophrenia** was renamed by Eugen Bleuler, a Swiss psychiatrist, to better illustrate the division (*schizo-*) within the brain (*phren*) among thoughts, feelings, and behavior that seems to take place in people with this disorder (Bleuler,

1911; Möller & Hell, 2002). Because the term literally means "split mind," it has often been confused with dissociative identity disorder, which was at one time called "split personality." A more modern definition of schizophrenia describes it as a long-lasting **psychotic** disorder (involving a severe break with reality), in which there is an inability to distinguish what is real from fantasy as well as disturbances in thinking, emotions, behavior, and perception.

SYMPTOMS

14.17 *What are the main symptoms of schizophrenia?*

Schizophrenia includes several different kinds of symptoms. Disorders in thinking are a common symptom and are called **delusions.** Although delusions are not prominent in all forms of schizophrenia, they are the symptom that most people associate with this disorder. Delusions are false beliefs about the world that the person holds and that tend to remain fixed and unshakable even in the face of evidence that disproves the delusions. Common schizophrenic delusions include *delusions of persecution*, in which people believe that others are trying to hurt them in some way; *delusions of reference*, in which people believe that other people, television characters, and even books are specifically talking to them; *delusions of influence*, in which people believe that they are being controlled by external forces, such as the devil, aliens, or cosmic forces; and *delusions of grandeur*, in which people are convinced that they are powerful people who can save the world or have a special mission (APA, 2000).

Dr. John Nash is a famous mathematician who won the Nobel Prize for mathematics in 1994. His fame, however, is more due to the fact that Nash once suffered from a form of schizophrenia in which he experienced delusions of persecution. He at one time believed that aliens were trying to contact him through the newspaper (delusions of reference). His life story and remarkable recovery from schizophrenia are portrayed in the 2001 movie *A Beautiful Mind*, which starred Russell Crowe as Nash (Kuhn & Nasar, 2001; Nasar, 1998).

Delusional thinking alone is not enough to merit a diagnosis of schizophrenia, as there is a separate category of psychotic disorders called **delusional disorders**, in which the primary symptom is some form of delusion. In schizophrenia, other symptoms must be present (APA, 2000; Black & Andreason, 1999). Speech disturbances are common: Schizophrenic people will make up words, repeat words or sentences persistently, string words together on the basis of sounds (called *clanging*, such as "come into house, louse, mouse, mouse and cheese, please, sneeze"), and experience sudden interruptions in speech or thought. Thoughts are significantly disturbed as well, with schizophrenic people having a hard time linking their thoughts together in a logical fashion.

People with schizophrenia may also have **hallucinations**, in which they hear voices or see things or people that are not really there. Hearing voices is actually more common and one of the key symptoms in making a diagnosis of schizophrenia. Hallucinations involving touch, smell, and taste are less common but also possible. Although the movie portrayed Nash as having visual hallucinations, he says that he actually heard voices that he eventually learned to ignore (Nasar, 1998).

Emotional disturbances are also a key feature of schizophrenia. **Flat affect** is a condition in which the person shows little or no emotion. Emotions can also be excessive and/or inappropriate—a person might laugh when it would be more appropriate to cry or show sorrow, for example.

The person's behavior may also become disorganized and extremely odd. For example, some forms of schizophrenia are accompanied by periods of complete

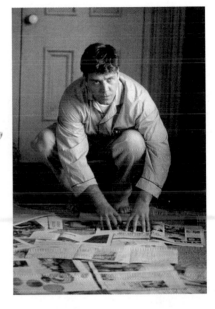

Actor Russell Crowe portrayed schizophrenic genius John Forbes Nash in the 2001 film *A Beautiful Mind.*

psychotic
the break away from an ability to perceive what is real and what is fantasy.

delusions
false beliefs held by a person who refuses to accept evidence of their falseness.

delusional disorder
a psychotic disorder in which the primary symptom is one or more delusions.

hallucinations
false sensory perceptions, such as hearing voices that do not really exist.

flat affect
a lack of emotional responsiveness.

disorganized

type of schizophrenia in which behavior is bizarre and childish and thinking, speech, and motor actions are very disordered.

catatonic

type of schizophrenia in which the person experiences periods of statue-like immobility mixed with occasional bursts of energetic, frantic movement and talking.

paranoid

type of schizophrenia in which the person suffers from delusions of persecution, grandeur, and jealousy, together with hallucinations.

undifferentiated

type of schizophrenia in which the person shows no particular pattern, shifting from one pattern to another, and cannot be neatly classified as disorganized, paranoid, or catatonic.

This photograph shows Keith, Deanna, Joshua, and Luck Laney of New Chapel Hill, Texas, in seemingly happier times. On May 12, 2003, Deanna Laney killed her two young sons by crushing their heads with rocks, believing that God had ordered her to kill her children. On the day of the killings, Deanna suffered a number of visual and auditory hallucinations. Mrs. Laney was found innocent by reason of insanity in 2004 and has been committed to a maximum security state hospital, where she is undergoing treatment for paranoid schizophrenia.

immobility, whereas still others may involve weird facial grimaces and odd gesturing. According to the American Psychiatric Association (2000), at least two or more of the following symptoms must be present frequently for at least one month to diagnose schizophrenia: delusions, hallucinations, disturbed speech, disturbed emotions, and disturbed behavior.

Attention is also a problem for many schizophrenics. They seem to have trouble "screening out" information and stimulation that they don't really need, causing them to be unable to focus on information that is relevant (Asarnow et al., 1991).

CATEGORIES OF SCHIZOPHRENIA

14.18 *What are the different types of schizophrenia?*

Although all schizophrenics share the symptoms already discussed to a certain degree, the way in which these symptoms show up in behavior can be used to distinguish among several different types of schizophrenia. There are five basic categories and two major types of schizophrenia (APA, 2000). The two types differ in the kind of symptoms that predominate.

DISORGANIZED **Disorganized** schizophrenics are very confused in speech, have vivid and frequent hallucinations, and tend to have very inappropriate affect (emotion) or flat affect. They are very socially impaired, unable to engage in the normal social rituals of daily life. Giggling, silliness, nonsensical speech, and neglect of cleanliness are common. They may not bathe or change clothing and may have problems with urinating or defecating in public, either because of incontinence or a deliberate wish to shock those watching.

CATATONIC Although it is becoming rare, **catatonic** schizophrenia involves very disturbed motor behavior. The person doesn't respond to the outside world and either doesn't move at all, maintaining often odd-looking postures for hours on end (a condition known as *catatonia*) or moves about wildly in great agitation. It's as if there are only two "speeds" for the catatonic, totally off or totally on.

PARANOID The **paranoid** schizophrenic suffers from hallucinations and delusions. Auditory* hallucinations are common, and the delusions are typically persecution, grandeur, or extreme jealousy of another or several other persons. Although their thinking is not as scattered as that of the disorganized schizophrenic, their delusions tend to be bizarre** but very systematic.

UNDIFFERENTIATED Sometimes a person with schizophrenic symptoms does not consistently show signs of one of the three previous categories but may instead shift from one pattern to another or show no consistent pattern. This person is usually labeled as having **undifferentiated** schizophrenia.

RESIDUAL Some people have a major episode of schizophrenia that ends, leaving the person in a state between an active episode of schizophrenia and, in some cases, full recovery. If they no longer show the major symptoms of delusions and hallucinations but still have some residual (leftover) symptoms such as negative beliefs, poor language skills, or some unusual ideas and perceptions, they might be given the label

---

*Auditory: having to do with hearing.
**Bizarre: extremely unusual or weird.

of **residual** schizophrenic. They would be considered a little "odd" by others but would be able to function in daily life, unlike a person who is suffering from an active episode of schizophrenia.

Another way of categorizing schizophrenia is to look at the kind of symptoms that predominate. **Positive symptoms** appear to reflect an excess or distortion of normal functions, such as hallucinations and delusions. **Negative symptoms** appear to reflect a decrease of normal functions, such as poor attention or lack of affect (APA, 2000).

Positive symptoms are associated with overactivity in the dopamine areas of the brain. Dopamine-reducing drugs used to treat schizophrenia are usually effective on these symptoms and the outlook for recovery is generally good (Davis et al., 1991; Penn, 1998; Rosenzweig et al., 1996).

Negative symptoms include the inability to filter out stimuli to focus attention, flat affect, problems with producing speech, apathy, and withdrawal from others. Negative symptoms, unlike positive symptoms, are associated with *lower* than normal activity in the dopamine systems of the brain and problems in the functioning of the frontal lobe. Studies have found that schizophrenics with negative symptoms have decreased blood flow to the frontal lobe areas (Davis et al., 1991; Perlstein et al., 2001). Unfortunately, this also means that the outlook for recovery from negative-symptom schizophrenia is not good, as these symptoms do not respond well to medications that are effective with positive-symptom schizophrenia.

CAUSES OF SCHIZOPHRENIA

14.19 *What are the possible causes of schizophrenia?*

In psychoanalytic theory, schizophrenia was thought to be the result of a severe breakdown in the ego, which was overwhelmed by the infantile demands of the id. In this theory, the ego retreats into an earlier, more childish stage of development and can no longer distinguish between the fantasies of the id and the realities of the world. It was thought that this regression results from a disturbed relationship between mother and child. Critics of this view point out that schizophrenic people are more than simply childish and infantile in their behavior, engaging in bizarre behavior, delusions, and hallucinations that are not common to infants or young children. Psychoanalysts have not been successful in attempts to link early childhood experiences with later development of schizophrenia (Cioffi, 1998).

Behaviorists do not try to account for the onset of schizophrenia but focus on how the particular behavioral symptoms of the different types of schizophrenia might be shaped through the processes of reinforcement and extinction. For example, a person with catatonic schizophrenia might have gained attention from remaining in a statue-like pose, making such poses more likely in the future. Modeling may also play a part in the behavioral explanation of schizophrenia, as patients in a hospital may see the bizarre behavior of other patients get rewarded with attention and later imitate similar behavior. This does not explain how people who have never been exposed to other schizophrenics develop their behavior, however.

Cognitive theorists see the irrational beliefs of the schizophrenic as a more severe form of illogical thinking than is found in anxiety and mood disorders. Cognitive-behavioral treatments of schizophrenia symptoms have had some success in reducing, but not completely erasing, those symptoms (Bradshaw, 1997, 1998). It would seem that cognitive and behavioral theories are more useful in developing treatments to reduce the severity of schizophrenic symptoms than as models for explaining the causes of schizophrenia.

Biological explanations of schizophrenia have generated a significant amount of research pointing to genetic origins, chemical influences (dopamine), and brain

residual
type of schizophrenia in which there are no delusions and hallucinations, but the person still experiences negative thoughts, poor language skills, and odd behavior.

positive symptoms
symptoms of schizophrenia that are excesses of behavior or occur in addition to normal behavior; hallucinations, delusions, and distorted thinking.

negative symptoms
symptoms of schizophrenia that are less than normal behavior or an absence of normal behavior; poor attention, flat affect, and poor speech production.

The woman on the right suffers from schizophrenia, as does 1 percent of the population worldwide. Medication, such as that being given by the nurse on the left, can help some schizophrenic people lead relatively normal lives. Others must remain in institutions.

structural defects (frontal lobe defects and deterioration of neurons) as the causes of schizophrenia (Gottesman & Shields, 1982; Harrison, 1999; Kety et al., 1994). Dopamine was first suspected when amphetamine users began to show schizophrenia-like psychotic symptoms. One of the side effects of amphetamine usage is to increase the release of dopamine in the brain. Drugs used to treat schizophrenia decrease the activity of dopamine, and the prefrontal cortex (an area of the brain involved in planning and organization of information) of people with schizophrenia has been shown to produce lower levels of dopamine than normal (Acar et al., 2003; Harrison, 1999).

Further support for a biological explanation of schizophrenia comes from studies of the incidence of the disorder across different cultures. If schizophrenia were caused mainly by environmental factors, the expectation would be that rates of schizophrenia would vary widely from culture to culture. In fact, the rate of schizophrenia is approximately 1 percent of the population, regardless of the culture (Torrey, 1987).

Family, twin, and adoption studies have provided strong evidence that genes are a major means of transmitting schizophrenia. The highest risk for developing schizophrenia if one has a blood relative with the disorder is faced by monozygotic (identical) twins, who share 100 percent of their genetic material, with a risk factor of about 50 percent (Gottesman & Shields, 1976, 1982; Gottesman et al., 1987). Dizygotic twins, who share about 50 percent of their genetic material, have about a 17 percent risk, the same as a child with one schizophrenic parent. As genetic relatedness decreases, so does the risk. (See Figure 14.4.)

Adoption studies also support the genetic basis of schizophrenia. In one study, the biological and adoptive relatives of schizophrenic adoptees were compared to a control group of adoptees without schizophrenia but from similar backgrounds and conditions (Kety et al., 1994). The adoptees with schizophrenia had relatives with schizophrenia but *only among their biological relatives*. When the prevalence of schizophrenia was compared

FIGURE 14.4 **Genetics and Schizophrenia** This graph shows a definite pattern: the greater the degree of genetic relatedness, the higher the risk of schizophrenia in individuals related to each other. The only individual to carry a risk even close to that of identical twins (who share 100 percent of their genes) is a person who is the child of two schizophrenic parents. *Source:* Gottesman (1991).

between the biological relatives of the schizophrenic adoptees and the biological relatives of the control group, the rate of the disorder in the relatives of the schizophrenic group was 10 times higher than in the control group (Kety et al., 1994).

There's something I don't understand. If one identical twin has the gene and the disorder, shouldn't the other one always have it, too? Why is the rate only 50 percent? If schizophrenia were entirely controlled by genes, identical twins would indeed both have the disorder at a risk of 100 percent, not merely 50 percent. Obviously, there is some influence of environment on the development of schizophrenia. One model that has been proposed is the **stress-vulnerability model**, which assumes that persons with the genetic "markers" for schizophrenia have a physical vulnerability to the disorder but will not develop schizophrenia unless they are exposed to environmental or emotional stress at critical times in development, such as puberty (Harrison, 1999; Weinberger, 1987). That would explain why only one twin out of a pair might develop the disorder when both carry the genetic markers for schizophrenia—the life stresses for the affected twin were different from those of the one who remained healthy.

◀ **There's something I don't understand. If one identical twin has the gene and the disorder, shouldn't the other one always have it, too? Why is the rate only 50 percent?**

Personality Disorders: I'm Okay, It's Everyone Else Who's Weird

14.20 *What are the different kinds of personality disorders?*

Personality disorders are a little different from other psychological disorders in that the disorder does not affect merely one aspect of the person's life, such as a higher than normal level of anxiety or a set of distorted beliefs, but instead affects the entire life adjustment of the person. The disorder is the personality itself, not one aspect of it. In personality disorder, a person has an excessively rigid, maladaptive pattern of behavior and ways of relating to others (APA, 2000). This rigidity and inability to adapt to social demands and life changes make it very difficult for the individual with a personality disorder to fit in with others or have relatively normal social relationships. There are three basic categories of personality disorders listed in the *DSM-IV-TR* (APA, 2000): those in which the people are seen as odd or eccentric by others, those in which the behavior of the person is very dramatic or erratic, and those in which the main emotion is anxiety or fearfulness. There are 10 recognized types of personality disorders (see Table 14.5).

"But enough about my problems, you're the one who called 911."

ANTISOCIAL PERSONALITY DISORDER

One of the most well researched of the personality disorders is **antisocial personality disorder**. People with antisocial personality disorder are literally "against society." The antisocial person, sometimes called a *sociopath*, habitually breaks the law, disobeys rules, tells lies, and uses other people without worrying about their rights or feelings. In Freudian terms, the antisocial personality has no superego or a very weak superego and, therefore, has no real conscience to create guilt feelings when the person does something morally wrong. As a consequence, people with this disorder typically feel no remorse or guilt at lying, cheating, stealing, or even more serious crimes such as murder.

The first thing that usually comes to most people's minds when they hear the term *sociopath* is the *serial killer*, a person who kills others for the excitement and thrill of killing without feeling any guilt. However, most antisocial personalities are not

stress-vulnerability model
explanation of disorder that assumes a biological sensitivity, or vulnerability, to a certain disorder will develop under the right conditions of environmental or emotional stress.

personality disorders
disorders in which a person adopts a persistent, rigid, and maladaptive pattern of behavior that interferes with normal social interactions.

antisocial personality disorder
disorder in which a person has no morals or conscience and often behaves in an impulsive manner without regard for the consequences of that behavior.

TABLE 14.5 **THE PERSONALITY DISORDERS**

Personality Disorder	Description
Odd or Eccentric Types	
Paranoid	Extreme suspicion of others; mistrustful, often jealous
Schizoid	Loners who are cool, distant, and unwilling and unable to form close relationships with others
Schizotypal	Difficulty in forming social relationships, odd and eccentric behavior, tendency to hold magical beliefs
Dramatic or Erratic Types	
Antisocial	Lacking in conscience or morals; users and con artists who experience no regret or strong emotions
Borderline	Moody, unstable, lacking in a clear sense of identity, clinging to others
Histrionic	Tendency to overreact and use excessive emotions to draw attention from and manipulate others. Love to be the center of attention
Narcissistic	Extremely vain and self-involved
Anxious or Fearful Types	
Avoidant	Fearful of social relationships, tend to avoid social contacts unless absolutely necessary
Dependent	Needy, want others to make decisions for them
Obsessive-Compulsive	Controlling, focused on neatness and order to an extreme degree

killers. Typically they borrow money or belongings and don't bother to repay the debt or return the items, they are impulsive, they don't keep their commitments either socially or in their jobs, and they tend to be very selfish, self-centered, manipulative, and unable to feel deep emotions.

There is a definite gender difference in antisocial personality disorder with nearly three to six times as many males diagnosed with this disorder as females (APA, 2000; Paris, 2004).

BORDERLINE PERSONALITY DISORDER

People with **borderline personality disorder** have relationships with other people that are intense and relatively unstable. They are often moody, manipulative, and untrusting of others. Periods of depression are not unusual, and some may engage in excessive spending, drug abuse, or suicidal behavior (suicide attempts may be part of the manipulation the borderline personality uses against others in a relationship). Emotions are often inappropriate and excessive, leading to confusion with *histrionic personality disorder*. What makes the borderline different is the confusion over identity issues, in which the person may be unable to focus on consistent life goals, career choices, friendships, and even sexual behavior (APA, 2000).

The frequency of this disorder in women is nearly two to three times greater than in men (APA, 2000; Swartz et al., 1990). Numerous causes such as genetic or hormonal influences, childhood experiences with incest or other abuse, and a poor mother–infant relationship during the years in which the identity is forming have all been suggested as a cause of the disorder (Torgersen, 2000; Widiger & Weissman, 1991; Zanarini, 2000).

borderline personality disorder
maladaptive personality pattern in which the person is moody, unstable, lacks a clear sense of identity, and often clings to others.

CAUSES OF PERSONALITY DISORDERS

14.21   *What causes personality disorders?*

Psychoanalytic theorists have blamed an inadequate resolution to the Oedipus complex for the formation of personality disorders. In particular, the antisocial personality can be described as lacking a fully developed superego. More recently, these theories focus on problems in the development of the ego in the anal stage as being responsible for disorders such as narcissism and borderline disorders.

Cognitive-learning theorists do not talk about innate personality traits, normal, disordered, or otherwise. Instead, these theorists talk about how specific behavior can be learned over time through the processes of reinforcement, shaping, and modeling. More cognitive explanations involve the belief systems formed by the personality disordered persons, such as the paranoia, extreme self-importance, and fear of being unable to cope by oneself of the paranoid, narcissistic, and dependent personalities, for example.

There is some evidence of genetic factors in personality disorders. Close biological relatives of people with disorders such as antisocial, schizotypal, and borderline are more likely to have these disorders than those who are not related, for example (APA, 2000; Battaglia et al., 1995; Faraone et al., 1999; Nigg & Goldsmith, 1994). Adoption studies of children whose biological parents had antisocial personality disorder show an increased risk for that disorder in those children, even though raised in a different environment by different people (APA, 2000).

One interesting finding in genetic studies is that some research shows a greater risk of schizophrenia in relatives of people with schizotypal personality disorder (Kendler & Walsh, 1995; Webb & Levinson, 1993). Only a small proportion of people with schizotypal personality disorder go on to develop full-blown schizophrenia, however (APA, 2000).

Other causes of personality disorders have been suggested. Antisocial personalities are emotionally unresponsive to stressful or threatening situations when compared to others, which may be one reason that they are not afraid of getting caught (Arnett et al., 1997; Blair et al., 1995; Lykken, 1995). This unresponsiveness seems to be linked to lower than normal levels of stress hormones in antisocial persons (Lykken, 1995).

Disturbances in family relationships and communication have also been linked to personality disorders and, in particular, to antisocial personality disorder (Benjamin, 1996; Livesley, 1995). Childhood abuse, neglect, overly strict parenting, overprotective parenting, and parental rejection have all been put forth as possible causes, making the picture of the development of personality disorders a complicated one. It is safe to say that many of the same factors (genetics, social relationships, and parenting) that help to create ordinary personalities also create disordered personalities.

PRACTICE QUIZ: HOW MUCH DO YOU REMEMBER?

Pick the best answer.

1. Charles believed that a famous song by a popular musical group carried a special, secret message meant only for him. This would be an example of a delusion of
   a. persecution.
   b. reference.
   c. influence.
   d. grandeur.

2. In an old movie, a madman made weird faces and sounds, jumped about wildly in his cell, and laughed and giggled constantly. This bizarre behavior is typical of the _____ schizophrenic.
   a. disorganized
   b. catatonic
   c. paranoid
   d. residual

3. Which type of schizophrenic is most likely to have delusions of grandeur?
   a. disorganized
   b. catatonic
   c. paranoid
   d. residual

4. Which of the following statements about antisocial personality disorder is TRUE?
   a. Most people with this disorder are vicious killers.
   b. Most people with this disorder are men.
   c. People with this disorder suffer terrible guilt but commit crimes anyway.
   d. People with this disorder feel emotions very deeply and intensely.

seasonal affective disorder (SAD)
a mood disorder caused by the body's reaction to low levels of sunlight in the winter months.

phototherapy
the use of lights to treat seasonal affective disorder or other disorders.

Applying Psychology To Everyday Life: Seasonal Affective Disorder (SAD)

14.22   *What is seasonal affective disorder and how can it be treated?*

Some people find that they only get depressed at certain times of the year. In particular, depression seems to set in during the winter months and goes away with the coming of spring and summer. If this describes you or someone you know, it could be **seasonal affective disorder (SAD)**. SAD is a mood disorder that is caused by the body's reaction to low levels of light present in the winter months (Partonen & Lonnqvist, 1998).

Think back to Chapter Four and the discussion of the role of the *suprachiasmatic nucleus* (SCN) of the hypothalamus in the brain. Light entering the eye travels through the optic nerve and through the SCN. The SCN controls the secretion of the hormone *melatonin* from the pineal gland in the brain, and that hormone is released in greater amounts as darkness and the need for sleep cause the SCN to stimulate the pineal gland. When daylight comes, the SCN tells the pineal gland to stop producing melatonin and the body is able to wake up.

What happens in SAD is simple. In some people, especially those who live in northern climates where winter is long and the days are very short, the biological clock that is controlled by the SCN gets out of "step." This can cause feelings of tiredness, lack of energy, and daytime sleepiness that the mind interprets as depression. Other symptoms include excessive eating, a craving for sugary and starchy foods, excessive sleeping, and weight gain. The worst months for SAD are January and February, and true SAD disappears in the spring and summer.

Treatment of SAD can include antidepressant drugs, but one of the most effective treatments is **phototherapy**, or daily exposure to bright light (Terman, 2001). Lamps are used to create an "artificial daylight" for a certain number of hours during each day, and the person with SAD sits under that light. Milder symptoms can be controlled with more time spent outdoors when the sun is shining and increasing the amount of sunlight that comes into the workplace or home. (See Figure 14.5.)

This woman is experiencing full-spectrum light therapy, one of the main treatments recommended for people suffering from seasonal affective disorder, or SAD.

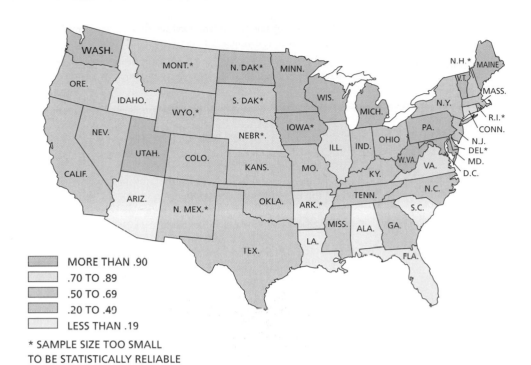

FIGURE 14.5 **Prevalence of SAD in the United States**   These data, gathered by Steven G. Potkin and his associates (from Wurtman & Wurtman, 1989), indicate considerably higher rates of seasonal affective disorder (SAD) in the northern latitudes. For example, Washington, Minnesota, and Maine have more than three times the levels of SAD as Florida, Louisiana, and Arizona. Shorter winter days in the more northern areas are thought to trigger a change in the brain's biochemistry resulting in SAD.

MORE THAN .90
.70 TO .89
.50 TO .69
.20 TO .49
LESS THAN .19

* SAMPLE SIZE TOO SMALL
TO BE STATISTICALLY RELIABLE

14

CHAPTER SUMMARY

What Is Abnormality?

- Psychopathology is the study of abnormal behavior.

14.1 *How did people in earlier times explain mental illness?*

- In ancient times holes were cut in an ill person's head to let out evil spirits in a process called trepanning. Hippocrates believed that mental illness came from an imbalance in the body's four humors, whereas in the Middle Ages the mentally ill were labeled as witches.

14.2 *What are the different ways in which abnormal behavior can be defined?*

- Abnormal behavior can be defined as behavior that is statistically rare, is deviant from social norms, causes subjective discomfort, does not allow normal, day-to-day functioning, or causes a person to be dangerous to self or others.

Models of Abnormality

14.3 *How are psychological disorders related to the brain and body chemistry?*

- In biological models of abnormality, the assumption is that mental illnesses are caused by chemical or structural malfunctions in the nervous system.

14.4 *How can psychological disorders be explained by the different viewpoints in psychology?*

- Psychoanalytic theorists assume that abnormal behavior stems from repressed conflicts and urges that are fighting to become conscious.
- Behaviorists see abnormal behavior as learned.

- Cognitive theorists see abnormal behavior as coming from irrational beliefs and illogical patterns of thought.

Current Issues in Psychology: A Look at Abnormality in Various Cultures

14.5 *How is abnormality viewed in other kinds of cultures?*

- Cultural relativity refers to the need to consider the norms and customs of another culture when diagnosing a person from that culture with a disorder.
- Culture-bound syndromes are disorders found only in certain cultures.

Diagnostic and Statistical Manual, Version IV, Text Revision (*DSM-IV-TR*)

14.6 *How do psychologists decide what kind of disorder a person has?*

- *Diagnostic and Statistical Manual, Version IV, Text Revision* is a manual of psychological disorders and their symptoms.

14.7 *What are the different types of psychological disorders and how common are they?*

- There are five axes in the *DSM-IV-TR*, which include clinical disorders, personality disorders, general medical conditions, psychosocial and environmental problems, and a global assessment of functioning.
- Over one-fifth of all adults over age 18 suffer from a mental disorder in any given year. Major depression is one of the most common psychological disorders worldwide.

Anxiety Disorders: What, Me Worry?

14.8   What are the different types of anxiety disorders and their symptoms?

- Anxiety disorders are all disorders in which the most dominant symptom is excessive and unrealistic anxiety.

- Phobias are irrational, persistent fears. The three types of phobias are social phobias, specific phobias, and agoraphobia.

- Obsessive-compulsive disorder consists of an obsessive, recurring thought that creates anxiety and a compulsive, ritualistic, and repetitive behavior that reduces that anxiety.

- Panic disorder is the sudden and recurrent onset of intense panic for no reason, with all the physical symptoms that can occur in sympathetic nervous system arousal, and is sometimes accompanied by agoraphobia.

- Generalized anxiety disorder is a condition of intense and unrealistic anxiety that lasts six months or more.

14.9   How do psychologists explain the causes of anxiety disorders?

- Psychoanalytic explanations point to repressed urges and desires that are trying to come into conscious, creating anxiety that is controlled by the abnormal behavior.

- Behaviorists state that disordered behavior is learned through both positive and negative reinforcement.

- Cognitive psychologists believe that excessive anxiety comes from illogical, irrational thought processes.

- Biological explanations of anxiety disorders include chemical imbalances in the nervous system, in particular serotonin and GABA systems.

- Genetic transmission may be responsible for anxiety disorders among related persons.

Somatoform Disorders: Sickness as a State of Mind

14.10   What are the different kinds of somatoform disorders?

- Somatoform disorders are the belief that one is physically ill, although there is no corresponding physical ailment, and include hypochondriasis, somatization disorder, and conversion disorder.

14.11   What causes somatoform disorders?

- Psychoanalytic explanations of somatoform disorders assume that anxiety is turned into a physical symptom.

- Behavioral explanations point to the negative reinforcement experienced when the "ill" person escapes unpleasant situations such as combat.

- Cognitive explanations assume that people magnify their physical symptoms and normal bodily changes into ailments out of irrational fear.

Dissociative Disorders: Altered Consciousness

14.12   What are the dissociative disorders?

- Dissociative disorders involve a break in consciousness, memory, or both. These disorders include dissociative amnesia, dissociative fugue, and dissociative identity disorder.

14.13   How do dissociative disorders develop?

- Psychoanalytic explanations point to repression of memories, seeing dissociation as a defense mechanism against anxiety.

- Cognitive and behavioral explanations see dissociative disorders as a kind of avoidance learning.

- Biological explanations point to lower than normal activity levels in the areas responsible for body awareness in people with dissociative disorders.

Current Issues in Psychology: Was "Sybil" a True Multiple Personality?

14.14   What is the controversy surrounding the famous case of "Sybil"?

- There is taped evidence to suggest that the psychiatrist treating "Sybil," the famous multiple personality case, may have suggested to "Sybil" that she view her emotions as separate personalities.

Mood Disorders: The Effect of Affect

14.15   What are the different types of mood disorders?

- Mood disorders, also called affective disorders, are severe disturbances in emotion.

- Dysthymia is a moderate depression that is typically a reaction to some external stressor, whereas cyclothymia consists of moderate mood swings usually tied to an external stressor.

- Major depression has a sudden onset and is extreme sadness and despair, typically with no obvious external cause. It is the most common of the mood disorders and is twice as common in women as in men.

- Bipolar disorders are severe mood swings from major depressive episodes to manic episodes of extreme elation and energy with no obvious external cause.

14.16   What are the causes of mood disorders?

- Psychoanalytic theories see depression as anger at authority figures from childhood turned inward on the self.

- Learning theories link depression to learned helplessness.

- Cognitive theories see depression as the result of distorted, illogical thinking.

- Biological explanations of mood disorders look at the function of serotonin, norepinephrine, and dopamine systems in the brain.

- Mood disorders are more likely to appear in genetically related people with higher rates of risk for closer genetic relatives.

Schizophrenia: Altered Reality

- Schizophrenia is a split between thoughts, emotions, and behavior. It is a long-lasting psychotic disorder in which reality and fantasy become confused.

14.17   What are the main symptoms of schizophrenia?

- Symptoms of schizophrenia include delusions (false beliefs about the world), hallucinations, emotional disturbances, attentional difficulties, disturbed speech, and disordered thinking.

14.18   What are the different types of schizophrenia?

- The five types of schizophrenic behavior are disorganized, catatonic, paranoid, undifferentiated, and residual.

- Positive symptoms are excesses of behavior associated with increased dopamine activity, whereas negative symptoms are deficits in behavior associated with decreased dopamine activity.

14.19 *What are the possible causes of schizophrenia?*

• Psychoanalytic theories see schizophrenia as resulting from a severe breakdown of the ego, which has become overwhelmed by the demands of the id and results in childish, infantile behavior.

• Behaviorists focus on how reinforcement, observational learning, and shaping affect the development of the behavioral symptoms of schizophrenia.

• Cognitive theorists see schizophrenia as severely irrational thinking.

• Biological explanations focus on dopamine, structural defects in the brain, and genetic influences in schizophrenia. Rates of risk of developing schizophrenia increase drastically as genetic relatedness increases with the highest risk faced by an identical twin whose twin sibling has schizophrenia.

Personality Disorders: I'm Okay, It's Everyone Else Who's Weird

14.20 *What are the different kinds of personality disorders?*

• Personality disorders are extremely rigid, maladaptive patterns of behavior that prevent a person from normal social interactions and relationships.

• In antisocial personality disorder a person has no conscience and uses people for personal gain. A rare form is the serial killer.

• In borderline personality disorder a person is clingy, moody, unstable in relationships, and suffers from problems with identity.

14.21 *What causes personality disorders?*

• Psychoanalysts blame an inadequate resolution to the Oedipal complex for personality disorders, stating that this results in a poorly developed superego.

• Cognitive-learning theorists see personality disorders as a set of learned behavior that has become maladaptive—bad habits learned early on in life. Belief systems of the personality disordered person are seen as illogical.

• Biological relatives of people with personality disorders are more likely to develop similar disorders, supporting a genetic basis for such disorders.

• Biological explanations look at the lower than normal stress hormones in antisocial personality disordered persons as responsible for their low responsiveness to threatening stimuli.

• Other possible causes of personality disorders may include disturbances in family communications and relationships, childhood abuse, neglect, overly strict parenting, overprotective parenting, and parental rejection.

Applying Psychology to Everyday Life: Seasonal Affective Disorder (SAD)

14.22 *What is seasonal affective disorder and how can it be treated?*

• Seasonal affective disorder, or SAD, is a form of depression that is related to low levels of exposure to light during the winter months.

• Treatment consists of light exposure, called phototherapy.

14 KEY TERMS

TEST YOURSELF

Pick the best answer.

1. A few days after giving birth to her daughter, Natane felt anxious about being a new mother and found herself crying for no good reason at odd moments throughout the day. If Natane sometimes feared she might hurt her baby or had thoughts of suicide, she most likely was experiencing
   a. postpartum depression.
   b. postpartum psychosis.
   c. postpartum neurosis.
   d. the baby blues.

2. What was the most likely reason that ancient peoples performed trepanning on others?
   a. to relieve fluid pressure on the brain
   b. to look into the brain to see what was wrong
   c. to release evil spirits that were in the person's head
   d. to restore balance to the body's humors

3. Michael decided to give up his job teaching at a small community college in Florida and become a monk. He moved to a nearby town with a monastery, took his vows, and is now living quite happily as a member of that religious order. By what definition might Michael's behavior be considered abnormal?
   a. statistical
   b. subjective discomfort
   c. maladaptive
   d. harmful to self

4. Which model of abnormality talks about rewards, shaping, and imitation as ways of developing abnormal behavior?
   a. psychoanalytic   c. cognitive
   b. behavioral   d. biological

5. Which of the following disorders is a type of sexual fear?
   a. taijin-kyofu-sho   c. susto
   b. amok   d. koro

6. Which axis of the *DSM-IV-TR* would a therapist use to classify the loss of a person's job?
   a. I   c. III
   b. II   d. IV

7. When anxiety is unrelated to any known, realistic factor, it is called
   a. free-floating anxiety. c. a phobia.
   b. panic.   d. acute.

8. Alex hates to go over bridges. This is a mild form of
   a. social phobia.   c. agoraphobia.
   b. specific phobia.   d. claustrophobia.

9. Professor Cantrell always checked the door to his office before leaving for class, lunch, or home. He would pull it closed and then rattle the doorknob three times to make sure that it was locked. He does this because he keeps thinking that he hasn't really locked it well. His thoughts about this are a form of
   a. obsession.   c. anxiety attack.
   b. compulsion.   d. door phobia.

10. When a person experiences sudden attacks of intense fear, racing heart, dizziness, and other physical signs of stress, and refuses to go away from home for fear one of these attacks will happen again, it is most properly called
    a. an anxiety attack.
    b. a panic attack.
    c. panic disorder.
    d. panic disorder with agoraphobia.

11. Daria went to great lengths to plan her mother's seventieth surprise birthday party. "Oh, if she finds out about this, the whole thing will be ruined, it'll be a disaster!" Her sister tried to tell her that even if the party ended up not being a surprise, their mother would be happy and have fun, but Daria was convinced that it would be horrible. According to a cognitive theorist, Daria is engaging in
    a. minimization.
    b. all-or-nothing thinking.
    c. overgeneralization.
    d. magnification.

12. Henri was a soldier during World War I. He and his best friend were scouting ahead when a mine blew up nearby, killing his friend and wounding Henri in the leg. When Henri woke up after the surgeons repaired his leg, he found that he could not see. The doctors told him that there should be nothing wrong with his eyes, but he still could not see, though he tried. This was most likely a
    a. somatization disorder.
    b. hypochondriac disorder.
    c. conversion disorder.
    d. psychosomatic disorder.

13. Dissociative amnesia is different from retrograde amnesia because
    a. only memories of the past are lost in retrograde amnesia.
    b. the ability to form new memories is lost in retrograde amnesia.
    c. dissociative amnesia is caused by a physical blow to the head.
    d. dissociative amnesia is caused by psychological trauma.

14. The fact that people with dissociative identity disorder have different PET scan readouts when in their different "personalities" is evidence for the _____ explanation of dissociative disorders.
    a. biological   c. behavioral
    b. psychoanalytic   d. cognitive

15. Which term does not belong?
    a. bipolar   c. dysthymia
    b. hypochondria   d. major depression

16. Which mood disorder consists of mostly manic episodes with only a few episodes of depression?
    a. bipolar   c. dysthymia
    b. unipolar   d. major depression

17. Which mood disorder is a consistently sad mood?
    a. bipolar
    c. mania
    b. cyclothymia
    d. major depression

18. A character in an old movie was a street person who wore aluminum foil on his head to protect his brain from the thought-controlling rays of the government. This is an example of a _____ delusion
    a. persecution
    c. influence
    b. reference
    d. grandeur

19. Which of the following is not a typical symptom of schizophrenia?
    a. overly rational thinking
    c. delusions
    b. inappropriate emotions
    d. hallucinations

20. In which category of schizophrenia would a person be who shifts patterns of behavior?
    a. catatonic
    c. paranoid
    b. disorganized
    d. undifferentiated

21. David Koresh, leader of the ill-fated Branch Davidians in Waco, Texas, believed that he was "God's Anointed One," who would bring about the end of the world. This is a _____ delusion.
    a. jealous
    b. grandiose
    c. persecutory
    d. somatic

22. Relatives of people who have schizotypal personality disorder have an increased risk of developing _____ when compared to unrelated persons.
    a. major depression
    b. affective psychosis
    c. antisocial personality disorder
    d. schizophrenia

Answers: 1-a, 2-c, 3-a, 4-b, 5-d, 6-d, 7-a, 8-c, 9-a, 10-d, 11-b, 12-c, 13-d, 14-a, 15-b, 16-a, 17-d, 18-c, 19-a, 20-d, 21-b, 22-d.

For more sample quizzes and other review activities that will help you get a better grade, be sure to check out your accompanying study guide. To access tests and your own personalized study plan that will help you focus on the areas you need to master before your next class test, be sure to go to the on-line Psychology web site available with the access code packaged with your book.

Abnormality

Abnormality: Psychopathology—Study of Abnormal Behavior

Definitions of Abnormal Behavior

▸ Behavior that is statistically rare
▸ Deviates from social norms
▸ Causes subjective discomfort
▸ Does not allow normal, day-to-day functioning
▸ Causes person to be dangerous to self or others

14.2

Psychological Disorders

MODELS OF ABNORMALITY

Biological Models of Abnormality

Mental illness is caused by chemical or structural malfunctions in nervous system

14.3

Psychological Viewpoints of the Causes of Abnormal Behavior

Psychoanalytic models: repressed conflicts and urges trying to surface to consciousness

Behaviorists: learned responses

Cognitive theorists: irrational beliefs and illogical thought patterns

14.4

Professional Descriptions of Abnormal Behavior

Diagnostic and Statistical Manual, Version IV, Text Revision: manual of psychological disorders and symptoms

14.6

Different Psychological Disorders and Their Frequency of Occurrence

Five axes in the DSM-IV-TR:
1. Clinical disorders
2. Personality disorders
3. General medical conditions
4. Psychosocial and environmental problems
5. Global assessment of functioning

1 out of 5 people above 18 years old suffers from a mental disorder in a given year

Major depression is the most common psychological disorder

14.7

ANXIETY DISORDERS

Anxiety Disorders and Symptoms

Anxiety disorders: excessive/unrealistic anxiety

Phobias: irrational, persistent fears; three types of phobias: social, specific, and agoraphobia

Obsessive-compulsive disorder: obsessive thoughts and compulsive behavior

Panic disorder: intense panic, physical symptoms from sympathetic nervous system

Generalized anxiety disorder: intense and unrealistic anxiety lasting at least six months

14.8

SOMATOFORM DISORDERS

Somatoform disorders: belief that one is physically ill with no physical ailment

Types: hypochondriasis, somatization disorder, and conversion disorder

14.10

Causes of Anxiety Disorders

Psychoanalytic explanations: repressed urges and desires trying to come into consciousness, creating anxiety that is controlled by abnormal behavior

Behaviorists: disordered behavior is learned through reinforcement

Cognitive psychologists: excessive anxiety from illogical, irrational thought processes

Biological explanations:
▸ Chemical imbalances in nervous system, in particular serotonin and GABA systems
▸ Genetics may be responsible for anxiety disorders among related persons

14.9

Causes of Somatoform Disorders

Psychoanalytic explanations: anxiety is turned into a physical symptom

Behavioral explanations: negative reinforcement experienced when the "ill" person escapes unpleasant situations

Cognitive explanations: people magnify physical symptoms and normal bodily changes out of irrational fear

14.11

CONCEPT MAP

DISSOCIATIVE DISORDERS

Break in consciousness, memory, or both

Types:
▶ Dissociative amnesia
▶ Dissociative fugue
▶ Dissociative identity disorder

14.12

Causes of Dissociative Disorders

Psychoanalytic: repression of memories, dissociation as a defense against anxiety

Cognitive and behavioral explanations: type of avoidance learning.

Biological explanations: lower activity levels in areas responsible for body awareness

14.13

The Controversial Case of "Sybil"

Evidence suggests that the psychiatrist treating Sybil may have suggested that she view her emotions as separate personalities

14.14

MOOD DISORDERS: THE EFFECT OF AFFECT

Different Types of Mood Disorders

Mood disorders also called affective disorders: severe disturbances in emotion

Dysthymia: moderate depression — reaction to some external stressor

Cyclothymia: moderate mood swings usually tied to an external stressor

Major depression: sudden onset, extreme sadness/despair, no obvious external cause

Bipolar disorders: severe mood swings from depressive episodes to manic episodes

14.15

Causes of Mood Disorders

Psychoanalytic: depression as anger at authority figures from childhood turned inward on self

Learning theories: link depression to learned helplessness

Cognitive theories: depression seen as result of distorted, illogical thinking

Biological explanations: function of serotonin, norepinephrine, and dopamine systems

Genetics: more likely to appear in genetically related people

14.16

SCHIZOPHRENIA: ALTERED REALITY

Schizophrenia: split between thoughts, emotions, and behavior

Main Symptoms of Schizophrenia

delusions, attentional difficulties, hallucinations, disturbed speech, emotional disturbances, disordered thinking

14.17

Five Types of Schizophrenia

▶ Disorganized   ▶ Catatonic   ▶ Paranoid   ▶ Undifferentiated   ▶ Residual

14.18

Possible Causes of Schizophrenia

Psychoanalytic: severe breakdown of the ego, due to infantile demands of id

Behaviorists: reinforcement, observational learning lead to behavioral symptoms

Cognitive theorists: severe irrational thinking

Biological: dopamine, structural defects in the brain, and genetic causes

14.19

PERSONALITY DISORDERS

Different Types of Personality Disorders

extremely rigid, maladaptive behavior patterns prevent normal social interactions and relationships

Antisocial: person has no conscience and uses people for personal gain, a rare form is the serial killer

Borderline: person is clingy, moody, unstable in relationships, and suffers from problems with identity

14.20

Causes of Personality Disorders

Psychoanalysis: inadequate resolution to the Oedipal complex resulting in a poorly developed superego.

Cognitive-learning: learned behavior that has become maladaptive; illogical belief systems

Biological explanations: lower-than-normal stress hormones in antisocial personality; genetic bases

Other possible causes: disturbances in family communications and relationships, childhood abuse, neglect, overly strict parenting, overprotective parenting, and parental rejection

14.21

Seasonal Affective Disorder

Seasonal affective disorder (SAD): form of depression related to the winter months' low levels of sunshine

Treatment: light exposure — phototherapy

14.22

15

Psychological Therapies

Treating Panic Disorder

Marie began having panic attacks at the age of 14. When she started having attacks at school, the school began sending her home. Marie's mother took her to see a child psychiatrist, who diagnosed Marie with mild panic disorder.

The psychiatrist recommended two types of treatment: cognitive psychotherapy and a carefully monitored drug treatment. The cognitive psychotherapy included sessions in which the psychiatrist would let Marie talk about her feelings and fears, and then he would show her where her thinking was going a little off track. The goal of cognitive therapy is to help clients see how their thinking patterns can be self-defeating and illogical. The psychiatrist explained to Marie that panic disorder did not mean that she was "crazy." A small area in her brain that would normally react to fear-provoking situations was "misfiring," making her body think that there was reason to be afraid and causing the panic symptoms. He explained that it was like having a smoke detector that went off when there was no smoke and no fire.

The drug treatment consisted of daily doses of an antidepressant medication; the dosage was very small at first and was increased gradually until Marie was on a maximum dose. During the course of the drug treatment, the cognitive therapy sessions continued. Marie's panic attacks disappeared completely, and she was able to gradually discontinue taking the drug. Within one year, Marie was able to end her therapy, having successfully conquered her panic.

Marie's story is a successful one, but the stories of other people with psychological disorders are not always resolved so simply. Different disorders require different kinds of therapies, and not all disorders can be completely eliminated. Therapies can take many forms, depending on the particular psychological explanation of disorder that is the basis of the therapy and the specific disorder that needs to be treated.

Why is it important to study therapies for psychological disorders?
There are almost as many therapy methods as there are disorders. Correctly matching the type of therapy to the disorder can mean the difference between a cure or a crisis. It is important to know the choices available for treatment and how they relate to the different kinds of disorders so that an informed decision can be made and the best possible outcome can be achieved for mental health and wellness.

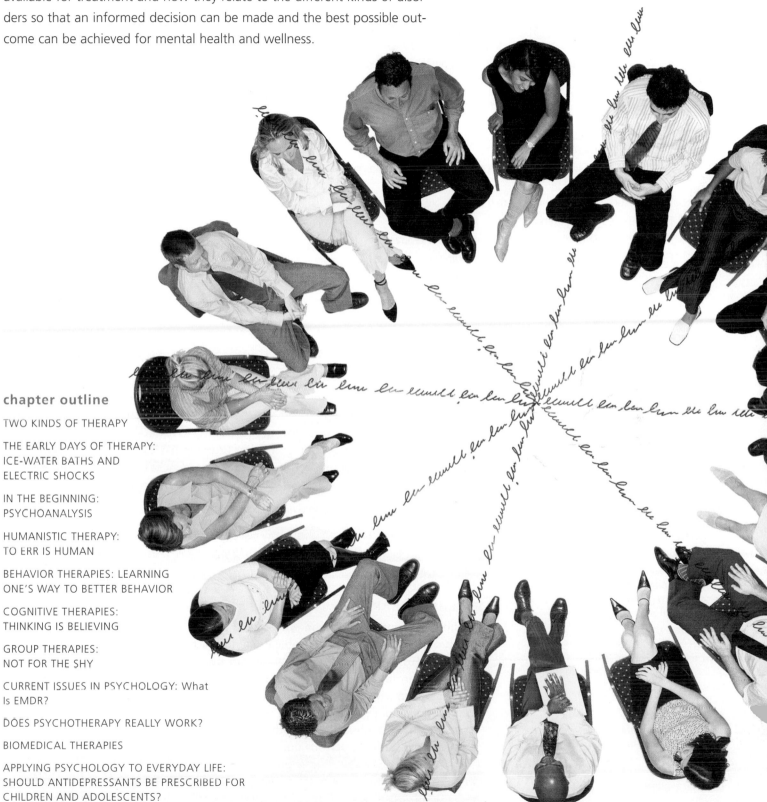

15.1 What are the two ways in which psychological disorders can be treated?

15.2 How were psychological disorders treated in the past?

15.3 What were the basic elements of Freud's psychoanalysis?

15.4 How is psychoanalysis conducted and viewed today?

15.5 What are the basic elements of Rogers's person-centered therapy?

15.6 What is Gestalt therapy?

15.7 How are humanistic therapies viewed today?

15.8 How do behavior therapists use classical conditioning to treat disordered behavior?

15.9 How do behavior therapists use operant conditioning to treat disordered behavior?

15.10 How successful are behavior therapies?

15.11 What is cognitive therapy?

15.12 What are the goals of cognitive-behavioral therapy?

15.13 What is rational-emotive behavior therapy?

15.14 How successful are cognitive and cognitive-behavioral therapies?

15.15 What are the advantages and disadvantages of group therapy?

15.16 What are the different types of group therapy?

15.17 For whom is group therapy most likely to be a useful form of treatment?

15.18 Does eye-movement desensitization reprocessing really work?

15.19 How effective is psychotherapy?

15.20 Is psychotherapy's effectiveness affected by cultural, ethnic, or gender differences?

15.21 What are the various types of drugs used to treat psychological disorders?

15.22 How is electroconvulsive therapy used to treat severe psychological disorders?

15.23 What is the history of psychosurgery, and how is it used today?

15.24 What are the dangers of treating children and adolescents with antidepressant drugs?

Two Kinds of Therapy

When talking about treating psychological disorders, there are two main types of **therapy** (treatment methods aimed at making people feel better and function more effectively). In the type of therapy that is usually more effective, people tell the therapist about their problems, and the therapist listens and tries to help them understand those problems or change the behavior that causes them. The second type of therapy uses biological methods to bring the symptoms under control.

15.1 *What are the two ways in which psychological disorders can be treated?*

The kind of therapy that involves talking things out with a professional is called **psychotherapy**, whereas the kind of therapy that uses biological methods is called **biomedical therapy**.

PSYCHOTHERAPY

Psychotherapy probably began when some tribal shaman (holy man or magician) helped a tribe member whose problems could not be helped by the medicine man of the tribe (Torrey, 1986). Psychotherapy can be performed in many different ways. Sometimes an individual talks with a professional on a one-to-one basis. At other times, a person with certain psychological problems might become part of a group of people with similar problems that is led by a professional.

The goal of almost all psychotherapy is to help both mentally healthy and psychologically disordered persons understand themselves better (Goin, 2005; Wolberg, 1977). Because understanding of one's motives and actions is called *insight*, therapies aimed mainly at this goal are called **insight therapies**. A therapy that is directed more at changing behavior than providing insights into the reasons for that behavior (as used by Marie's psychiatrist in the opening story) is called **action therapy**.

therapy
treatment methods aimed at making people feel better and function more effectively.

psychotherapy
therapy for mental disorders in which a person with a problem talks with a psychological professional.

biomedical therapy
therapy for mental disorders in which a person with a problem is treated with biological or medical methods to relieve symptoms.

insight therapies
therapies in which the main goal is helping people to gain insight with respect to their behavior, thoughts, and feelings.

action therapy
therapy in which the main goal is to change disordered or inappropriate behavior directly.

BIOMEDICAL THERAPY

The other main type of therapy uses some biological treatment in the form of a medical procedure to bring about changes in the person's disordered behavior. Biomedical therapies include the use of drugs, as in the case of Marie in the opening story, surgical methods, and electrical shock treatments. It is important to understand that biomedical therapy alone does nothing but alleviate the symptoms of the disorder, such as anxiety, depression, or attentional problems. Although in some cases controlling the symptom may be all that is needed, most professionals would agree that any biomedical therapy of a psychological disorder should be accompanied by some form of psychotherapy as well, as Marie's psychiatrist chose to do (Keller et al., 2000). This ensures that any underlying psychological problems that may be the source of the symptoms are also treated, preventing a recurrence of the problem or the development of some other kind of symptom.

The Early Days of Therapy: Ice-Water Baths and Electric Shocks

15.2   *How were psychological disorders treated in the past?*

Life for the mentally ill was not pleasant in most parts of the world for many years. As discussed in Chapter Thirteen, people with severe mental illnesses were often thought to be possessed by demons or evil spirits, and the "treatments" to rid the person of these spirits were severe and deadly. Even in the supposedly more enlightened times of the last two hundred years or so, the mentally ill did not always receive humane* treatment.

EARLY TREATMENT OF THE MENTALLY ILL

I've seen movies about mental hospitals and they didn't look like great places to be even now—how bad was it back then? What did people do with relatives who were ill that way? The first truly organized effort to do something with mentally ill persons began in England in the middle of the sixteenth century. Bethlehem Hospital in London (later known as "Bedlam") was converted into an asylum (a word meaning "place of safety") for the mentally ill. In reality, the first asylums were little more than prisons where the mentally ill were chained to their beds. "Treatments" consisted of bloodletting (which more often than not led to death or the need for lifelong care for the patient), beatings, ice baths in which the person was submerged until passing out or suffering a seizure, and induced vomiting in a kind of spiritual cleansing (Hunt, 1993). This cleansing or purging was meant to rid the body of physical impurities so that the person's mind and soul could function more perfectly.

PINEL'S REFORMS

It was not until 1793 that efforts were made to treat the mentally ill with kindness and guidance—known as "moral treatment"—rather than beating them or subjecting them to the harsh physical purging that had been commonplace. It was at this time that Philippe Pinel personally unchained the inmates at the Bicêtre Asylum in Paris, France, beginning the movement of humane treatment of the mentally ill (Brigham, 1844; Curtis, 1993).

---

*Humane: marked by compassion, sympathy, or consideration for humans (and animals).

I've seen movies about mental hospitals and they didn't look like great places to be even now—how bad was it back then? What did people do with relatives who ◀ were ill that way?

In this famous painting by French artist Robert Fleury, French psychiatrist Dr. Phillippe Pinel orders the chains removed from patients at a Paris asylum for insane women. Pinel was one of the first psychiatrists to recommend humane treatment of the mentally ill.

So what exactly happens ▶ in psychoanalysis? I've heard lots of stories about it, but what's it really like?

In this picture of a more traditional psychoanalytic therapy session, the patient is lying on a couch while the doctor sits behind her, unseen. Freud recommended this arrangement so that the patient would be unable to see the doctor taking notes or reacting to the patient's revelations, making it more likely that the patient would talk freely.

psychoanalysis
an insight therapy based on the theory of Freud, emphasizing the revealing of unconscious conflicts.

manifest content
the actual content of one's dream.

latent content
the symbolic or hidden meaning of dreams.

In The Beginning: Psychoanalysis

So what exactly happens in psychoanalysis? I've heard lots of stories about it, but what's it really like? In a sense, Freud took the old method of physical cleansing to a different level. Instead of a physical purge, cleansing for Freud meant removing all the "impurities" of the unconscious mind that he believed were responsible for his patients' psychological and nervous disorders. (Freud was a medical doctor and referred to the people who came to him for help as "patients.") The impurities of the unconscious mind were considered to be disturbing thoughts, socially unacceptable desires, and immoral urges that originated in the id, the part of the personality that is itself unconscious and driven by basic needs for survival and pleasure. **LINK** to *Chapter Twelve: Theories of Personality, p. 446.*

Because these unconscious thoughts were used by the person to prevent anxiety and would not be easily brought into conscious awareness, Freud designed a technique to help his patients feel more relaxed, open, and able to explore their innermost feelings without fear of embarrassment or rejection. This method was called **psychoanalysis**, an insight therapy that emphasizes revealing the unconscious conflicts, urges, and desires that are assumed to cause disordered emotions and behavior (Freud, 1904; Mitchell & Black, 1996). This is the original reason for the couch in Freud's version of psychoanalysis; people lying on the couch were more relaxed and would, Freud thought, feel more dependent and childlike, making it easier for them to get at those early childhood memories. An additional plus was that he could sit behind the patients at the end of the couch and take notes. Without the patients being able to see his reactions to what they said, they remained unaffected by his reactions.

Freud also made use of two techniques to try to get at the repressed information in his patients' unconscious minds. These techniques were the interpretation of dreams and allowing patients to talk freely about anything that came to mind.

DREAM INTERPRETATION

15.3 *What were the basic elements of Freud's psychoanalysis?*

Dream interpretation, or the analysis of the elements within a patient's reported dream, formed a large part of Freud's psychoanalytic method. **LINK** to *Chapter Four: Consciousness, pp. 139–140.* Freud believed that repressed material often surfaced in dreams, although in symbolic form. The **manifest content** of the dream was the actual dream and its events, but the **latent content** was the hidden, symbolic meaning of those events that would, if correctly interpreted, reveal the unconscious conflicts that were creating the nervous disorder (Freud, 1900).

FREE ASSOCIATION

The other technique for revealing the unconscious mind was a method originally devised by Freud's coworker, Josef Breuer (Breuer & Freud, 1895). Breuer encouraged his patients to freely say whatever came into their minds without fear of being negatively evaluated or condemned. As the patients talked, they began to reveal things that were loosely associated with their flow of ideas, often revealing what Breuer felt were hidden, unconscious concerns. Freud adopted this method, believing that repressed impulses and other material were trying to "break free" into consciousness and would eventually surface in his patients' **free associations**.

RESISTANCE

A key element in psychoanalysis was the analysis of **resistance**, the point at which the patient becomes unwilling to talk about certain topics. Freud believed that resistance from the patient meant that the conversation was coming uncomfortably close to repressed material.

TRANSFERENCE

In revealing more and more of their innermost feelings to the doctor, patients would begin to trust the therapist who accepted anything they said and did not criticize or punish them for saying it, as they once trusted their parents. Freud believed that the therapist would then become a symbol of a parental authority figure from the past in a process he called **transference**. In transference, the patient would at first transfer positive feelings for some authority figure from the past such as a mother or father. When the therapist remained neutral and seemingly unresponsive, the patient would transfer negative feelings.

EVALUATION OF PSYCHOANALYSIS

15.4   *How is psychoanalysis conducted and viewed today?*

Freud's original theory, on which he based his interpretations of his patients' revelations, has been criticized for several flaws, as discussed in Chapter Twelve. These included the lack of scientific research to support his claims, his unwillingness to believe some of the things revealed by his patients when those revelations did not fit into his view of the world, and his almost obsessive need to assume that problems with sex and sexuality were at the heart of nearly every nervous disorder.

Although some psychoanalysts today still use Freud's original methods, which could take years to produce results, modern psychoanalysts have greatly modified the way a psychoanalytic session is conducted. The couch is gone, and the *client* (a term used to put the therapist and the person seeking help on a more equal basis, instead of the doctor–patient concept) may sit across a desk from the therapist or in chairs. The client may stand or walk about. Rather than remaining quiet until the client says something revealing, the modern psychoanalyst is far more **directive**, asking questions, suggesting helpful behavior, and giving opinions and interpretations earlier in the relationship, which helps speed up the therapeutic process. Today's psychoanalysts also focus less on the id as the motivator of behavior, instead looking more at the ego or sense of self as the motivating force behind all actions (Prochaska & Norcross, 2003). Some psychoanalysts also focus on the process of transference more than on other typical aspects of traditional psychoanalysis, leading to the more general method called **psychodynamic therapy**.

Even so, the psychodynamic technique requires the client to be fairly intelligent and verbally able to express his or her ideas, feeling, and thoughts effectively. People who are extremely withdrawn or who suffer from the more severe psychotic disorders are not good candidates for this form of psychotherapy. People who have nonpsychotic adjustment disorders, such as anxiety, somatoform, or dissociative disorders, are more likely to benefit from psychodynamic therapy.

"Don't worry. Fantasies about devouring the doctor are perfectly normal."

free association
Freudian technique in which a patient was encouraged to talk about anything that came to mind without fear of negative evaluations.

resistance
occurring when a patient becomes reluctant to talk about a certain topic, either changing the subject or becoming silent.

transference
In psychoanalysis, the tendency for a patient or client to project positive or negative feelings for important people from the past onto the therapist.

directive
therapy in which the therapist actively gives interpretations of a client's statements and may suggest certain behavior or actions.

psychodynamic therapy
a newer and more general term for therapies based on psychoanalysis, with an emphasis on transference, shorter treatment times, and a more direct therapeutic approach.

PRACTICE QUIZ: HOW MUCH DO YOU REMEMBER?

Pick the best answer.

1. Psychotherapies that attempt to change disordered behavior directly are known as _____ therapies.
   a. insight
   b. action
   c. biomedical
   d. psychoanalytic

2. In the sixteenth century, purging or _____ was sometimes used as a means to rid the body of physical impurities so that the person's mind and soul could improve.
   a. ice bathing
   b. bloodletting
   c. beating
   d. spiritual cleansing

3. In _____, a psychoanalyst encouraged the patient to talk about whatever came to mind.
   a. free association
   b. dream interpretation
   c. resistance
   d. transference

4. The psychoanalyst knows that repressed information is just "below the surface" of the conversation when the patient begins to experience
   a. free association.
   b. dream interpretation.
   c. resistance.
   d. transference.

5. Compared to traditional psychoanalysis, modern psychodynamic therapy is
   a. more directive.
   b. less directive.
   c. more action oriented.
   d. more focused on the id.

Answers: 1-b, 2-d, 3-a, 4-c, 5-a.

---

nondirective
therapy style in which the therapist remains relatively neutral and does not interpret or take direct actions with regard to the client, instead remaining a calm, nonjudgmental listener while the client talks.

So the key to getting over unhappiness would be to get ▶ the real and ideal selves closer together? How does a therapist do that?

Humanistic Therapy: To Err Is Human

Unlike psychodynamic therapists, humanistic theorists do not focus on unconscious, hidden conflicts. Instead, humanists focus on conscious, subjective experiences of emotion and people's sense of self, as well as more immediate experiences in their daily lives rather than early childhood experiences of the distant past (Cain & Seeman, 2001; Rowan, 2001; Schneider et al., 2001). The two most common therapy styles based on humanistic theory are Carl Rogers's person-centered therapy and Fritz Perls's Gestalt therapy, both forms of insight therapy.

TELL ME MORE: ROGERS'S PERSON-CENTERED THERAPY

15.5 *What are the basic elements of Rogers's person-centered therapy?*

Chapter Twelve discussed the basic elements of Rogers's theory of personality, which emphasizes the sense of self (Rogers, 1961). To sum it up quickly, Rogers proposed that everyone has a *real self* (how people see their actual traits and abilities) and an *ideal self* (how people think they should be). The closer the real and ideal selves match up, the happier and more well adjusted the person. To have these two self-concepts match, people need to receive *unconditional positive regard*, which is love, warmth, respect, and affection without any conditions attached. If people think that there are conditions put on the love and affection they receive, their ideal selves will be determined by those conditions and become more difficult to achieve, resulting in a mismatch of selves and unhappiness.

So the key to getting over unhappiness would be to get the real and ideal selves closer together? How does a therapist do that? Rogers believed that the goal of the therapist should be to provide the unconditional positive regard that has been absent from the troubled person's life. He also believed that the person would actually have to do most of the work, talking out problems and concerns in an atmosphere of warmth and acceptance from the therapist, so he originally called the people in this therapy relationship "clients" instead of "patients," to put the therapeutic* relationship on a more equal footing. As a result, Rogers's therapy is very **nondirective** because the person actu-

---

*Therapeutic: providing or assisting in a cure.

ally does all the real work, with the therapist merely acting as a sounding board. Later, the term *client* was changed to the even more neutral term *person*. His therapy is now called **person-centered therapy** because the person is truly the center of the process.

FOUR BASIC ELEMENTS   Rogers saw four key elements as being necessary in any successful person–therapist relationship.

Reflection   **Reflection** refers to the technique the therapist must use to allow clients to continue to talk and have insights without the interference of the therapist's interpretations and possible biases. The only way to ensure that a therapist will not control the stream of ideas coming from clients is for the therapist to simply restate what people have already said in slightly different words but with the same exact meaning. Reflection, is literally a kind of mirroring of clients' statements. Here's an example from one of Rogers's own therapy sessions with a client (Meador & Rogers, 1984, p. 143):

Client:

I just ain't no good to nobody, never was, and never will be.

Rogers:

Feeling that now, hm? That you're just no good to yourself, no good to anybody. Never will be any good to anybody. Just that you're completely worthless, huh?—Those really are lousy feelings. Just feel that you're no good at all, hm?

Client:

Yeah.

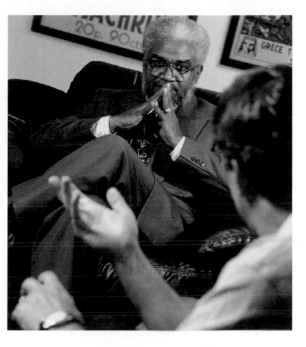

A Rogerian person-centered therapist listens with calm acceptance to anything the client says. A sense of empathy with the client's feelings is also important.

Unconditional Positive Regard   Another key element of person-centered therapy is the warm, accepting, completely uncritical atmosphere that the therapist must create for clients. This involves having respect for clients and their feelings, values, and goals, even if they are different from those of the therapist; it is called **unconditional positive regard**.

Empathy   The therapist also has to be able to acknowledge what clients are feeling and experiencing by using a kind of understanding called **empathy**. This involves listening carefully and closely to what clients are saying and trying to feel what they feel. Therapists must also avoid getting their own feelings mixed up with clients' feelings.

Authenticity   Finally, the therapist must show **authenticity** in a genuine, open, and honest response to the client. It is easier for some professionals to "hide" behind the role of the therapist, as was often the case in psychoanalysis. In person-centered therapy, the therapist has to be able to tolerate a client's differences without being judgmental.

GESTALT THERAPY

15.6   *What is Gestalt therapy?*

Another humanistic therapy based on Gestalt ideas is called **Gestalt therapy**. The founder of this therapeutic method is Fritz Perls, who believed that people's problems often stemmed from hiding important parts of their feelings from themselves. If some part of a person's personality, for example, is in conflict with what society says is acceptable, the person might hide that aspect behind a false "mask" of socially acceptable behavior. As happens in Rogers's theory when the real and ideal selves do not match, in Gestalt theory the person experiences unhappiness and maladjustment when the inner self does not match the mask (Perls, 1951, 1969).

person-centered therapy
a nondirective insight therapy based on the work of Carl Rogers in which the client does all the talking and the therapist listens.

reflection
therapy technique in which the therapist restates what the client says rather than interpreting those statements.

unconditional positive regard
referring to the warmth, respect, and accepting atmosphere created by the therapist for the client in person-centered therapy.

empathy
the ability of the therapist to understand the feelings of the client.

authenticity
the genuine, open, and honest response of the therapist to the client.

Gestalt therapy
form of directive insight therapy in which the therapist helps clients to accept all parts of their feelings and subjective experiences, using leading questions and planned experiences such as role-playing.

In Gestalt therapy, the therapist looks at the whole person—career, family, relationships, and body language. What do the people sitting on the couch seem to be saying with their body language?

That sounds pretty much like the same thing, only with slightly different words. How is Gestalt therapy different from person-centered therapy?

That sounds pretty much like the same thing, only with slightly different words. How is Gestalt therapy different from person-centered therapy? The two therapy types are similar because they are both based in humanism. But whereas person-centered therapy is nondirective, allowing the client to talk out concerns and eventually come to insights with only minimal guidance from the therapist, Gestalt therapists are very directive. This means that a Gestalt therapist does more than simply reflect back clients' statements; instead, a Gestalt therapist actually leads clients through a number of planned experiences, with the goal of helping clients to become more aware of their own feelings and take responsibility for their own choices in life, both now and in the past. These experiences might include a dialogue* that clients have with their own conflicting feelings in which clients actually argue both sides of those feelings. Clients may talk with an empty chair to reveal their true feelings toward the person represented by the chair or take on the role of a parent or other person with whom they have a conflict so that the clients can see things from the other person's point of view.

The Gestalt therapist actually confronts the client's own statements. For example, if a client complains of tenseness in his hands, the therapist would direct him to talk about how *he* feels, not how his hands feel. Once the client realizes, through active prompting from the therapist, that the tenseness is of his own creation, he can begin to control it and choose not to be tense (Perls, 1969).

But now Gestalt therapy is beginning to sound almost like psychoanalysis with its focus on the past. How are they different?

But now Gestalt therapy is beginning to sound almost like psychoanalysis with its focus on the past. How are they different? Unlike psychoanalysis, which focuses on the *hidden past*, Gestalt therapy focuses on the *denied past*. Gestalt therapists do not talk about the unconscious mind. They believe everything is conscious but that it is possible for some people to simply refuse to "own up" to having certain feelings or to deal with past issues. The Gestalt therapist is more concerned about the client's "here and now" than some murky early childhood experiences. Part of that "here and now" includes attention to the body language of the client during therapy

---

*Dialogue: a conversation or exchange of ideas between two or more persons.

sessions. Body language, feelings both stated and unstated, and the events going on in the client's life at the time of therapy are the *gestalt* (the "whole picture") that gives this technique its name.

EVALUATION OF THE HUMANISTIC THERAPIES

15.7 *How are humanistic therapies viewed today?*

Humanistic therapies have been used not only to treat mental disorders but also to help people make career choices, deal with workplace problems, and serve as a form of marriage counseling. Person-centered therapy in particular is a very ethical form of therapy because it is so nondirective: There's nothing that the therapist says that the client has not already said, so the therapist runs no risk of misinterpretation.

Unfortunately, humanistic therapies have several of the same drawbacks as psychoanalysis. There is little experimental research to support the basic ideas on which this type of therapy is founded, but humanists have always preferred to use case studies to build their theories. People must be intelligent, verbal, and able to express their thoughts, feelings, and experiences in a logical manner, which makes humanistic therapies a somewhat less practical choice for treating the more serious mental disorders such as schizophrenia.

> **behavior therapies**
> action therapies based on the principles of classical and operant conditioning and aimed at changing disordered behavior without concern for the original causes of such behavior.

PRACTICE QUIZ: HOW MUCH DO YOU REMEMBER?

Pick the best answer.

1. Humanistic therapies are different from psychoanalysis because the humanistic therapies are
   a. more directive.
   b. action oriented.
   c. focused only on conscious thoughts and behavior.
   d. insight therapies.

2. Which of the following is not one of the four basic elements of Rogers's person-centered therapy?
   a. conditional positive regard
   b. empathy
   c. reflection
   d. authenticity

3. Which of the following types of therapy makes the greatest use of body language?
   a. psychoanalysis   c. Gestalt therapy
   b. person-centered therapy d. Rogerian therapy

4. Franklin's therapist has him talk to an empty chair and pretend that he is talking to his father. Franklin's therapist is most likely a _____ therapist.
   a. psychodynamic
   b. person-centered
   c. Gestalt
   d. Freudian

Answers: 1-c, 2-a, 3-c, 4-c.

Behavior Therapies: Learning One's Way to Better Behavior

The last chapter talked about how behaviorists have a very different way of looking at abnormality—it's all learned. So do behaviorists do any kind of therapy? That's right—the basic concept behind behaviorism is that all behavior, whether "normal" or "abnormal," is learned through the same processes of classical and operant conditioning. Unlike the psychodynamic and humanistic therapies, **behavior therapies** are action based rather than insight based. Their aim is to change behavior through the use of the same kinds of learning techniques that people (and animals) use to learn any new responses. The abnormal or undesirable behavior is not seen as a symptom of anything else but rather is the problem itself. Learning created the problem, and new learning can correct it (Onken et al., 1997; Skinner, 1974; Sloan & Mizes, 1999).

◀ The last chapter talked about how behaviorists have a very different way of looking at abnormality—it's all learned. So do behaviorists do any kind of therapy?

behavior modification or applied behavior analysis
the use of learning techniques to modify or change undesirable behavior and increase desirable behavior.

systematic desensitization
behavior technique used to treat phobias, in which a client is asked to make a list of ordered fears and taught to relax while concentrating on those fears.

counterconditioning
replacing an old conditioned response with a new one by changing the unconditioned stimulus.

aversion therapy
form of behavioral therapy in which an undesirable behavior is paired with an aversive stimulus to reduce the frequency of the behavior.

This device allows the delivery of high levels of nicotine to the smoker in a process known as rapid smoking. Rapid smoking is an aversive technique for helping people to quit smoking and is based on the classical conditioning principle of counter-conditioning.

THERAPIES BASED ON CLASSICAL CONDITIONING

15.8 *How do behavior therapists use classical conditioning to treat disordered behavior?*

Classical conditioning is the learning of involuntary responses by pairing a stimulus that normally causes a particular response with a new, neutral stimulus. After enough pairings, the new stimulus will also cause the response to occur. LINK *to Chapter Five: Learning, pp. 167–168.* Through classical conditioning, old and undesirable reflex responses can be replaced by desirable ones. There are several techniques that have been developed using this type of learning to treat disorders such as phobias, obsessive-compulsive disorder, and similar anxiety disorders.

Using learning techniques to change undesirable behavior and increase desirable behavior has a long history (Hughes, 1993; Lovaas, 1987; Lovaas et al., 1966). Originally called **behavior modification**, the more recent version of these techniques is **applied behavior analysis**. Both terms refer to the use of conditioning techniques to modify behavior.

SYSTEMATIC DESENSITIZATION The technique of **systematic desensitization**, in which a therapist guides the client through a series of steps meant to reduce fear and anxiety, really began with the work of Watson and the classic research study of "Little Albert" (Watson & Rayner, 1920). LINK *to Chapter One: The Science of Psychology, p. 11.* In that study, Watson created a phobic response to a rat by repeatedly pairing exposure to the rat with a loud, scary noise. His intentions, carried out by Mary Cover Jones in a later study (Jones, 1924), were to undo the damage by pairing the rat (now an object creating fear) with a pleasure-producing stimulus, such as food. LINK *to Chapter One: The Science of Psychology, pp. 11–12.* This **counterconditioning** (conditioning to correct the original learning) forms the basis for desensitization procedures (Paul & Shannon, 1966; Rimm & Masters, 1987; Wolpe, 1958, 1991).

Systematic desensitization is normally used to treat phobic disorders and consists of a three-step process. First, the client must learn to relax through deep muscle relaxation training. Next, the client and the therapist construct a list, beginning with the object or situation that causes the least fear to the client and working up to the object or situation that produces the greatest degree of fear. Finally, under the guidance of the therapist the client begins at the first item on the list that causes minimal fear and looks at it, thinks about it, or actually confronts it, all while remaining in a relaxed state. The idea is that the phobic object or situation is a conditioned stimulus that the client has learned to fear because it was originally paired with a real fearful stimulus—just as "Little Albert" learned to fear the rat because of the noise. By pairing the old conditioned stimulus (the fear object) with a new relaxation response that is incompatible* with the emotions and physical arousal associated with fear, the person's fear is reduced and relieved. The person then proceeds to the next item on the list of fears (called a *hierarchy of fears*) until the phobia is gone.

AVERSION THERAPY Another way to use classical conditioning is to reduce the frequency of undesirable behaviors, such as smoking or overeating, by teaching the client to pair an aversive (unpleasant) stimulus with the stimulus that results in the undesirable response in a process called **aversion therapy**. For example, someone who wants to stop smoking might go to a therapist who uses a *rapid-smoking* technique, in which the client is allowed to smoke but must take a puff on the cigarette every five or six seconds. As nicotine is a poison, such rapid smoking produces nausea and dizziness, both unpleasant effects.

---

*Incompatible: referring to two or more things that cannot exist together or at the same time.

Rapid smoking is a version of counterconditioning. In the terms of classical conditioning in Chapter Five, the old conditioned stimulus (CS) is the cigarette including the act of putting it in one's mouth, lighting up, and so on. These things were originally paired with the nicotine, which was the unconditioned stimulus (US) that produced a pleasurable stimulation response (UR). Taking a cigarette becomes pleasurable before the nicotine even has a chance to have its effect (CR), through the association of the two stimuli.

Rapid smoking becomes a new unconditioned stimulus (US) that produces *new* and very unpleasant responses, such as nausea and dizziness (URs), rather than pleasurable ones. When paired with the act of putting a cigarette in the mouth (CS), lighting up (CS), and so on, those old conditioned stimuli now become associated with the new unpleasant responses. Putting a cigarette in one's mouth after this conditioning triggers a new conditioned response of nausea. In fact, for some people even the thought of "lighting up" becomes nauseating (Smith, 1988). Studies have shown that people using this method have managed to remain smoke-free for relatively long periods of time (Chapelon-Clavel et al., 1997; Hajek & Stead, 2000), although some health professionals consider the quality of these studies to be poor (Joanna Briggs Institute, 2001).

Another good example of aversion therapy is the use of a drug called *disulfiram*, commonly known by the brand name Antabuse®, to treat alcoholism (Petrakis et al., 2002). This medicine, when properly prescribed and monitored by a doctor or psychiatrist, results in several aversive reactions when combined with alcohol. The person may experience nausea, vomiting, anxiety, and even more serious symptoms, making this drug an effective deterrent for drinking for people who are unable to quit by other means.

Could you use aversion therapy to help someone with a phobia? Because phobias are already very unpleasant, aversive conditioning is not the most useful method of therapy. But although desensitization remains one of the more common therapies for phobias, it does not always bring quick results.

FLOODING   One method that does help a person deal with a phobia more quickly is **flooding**. Like systematic desensitization, flooding involves exposing the person with a phobia to the phobic object or situation. But this exposure is rapid and intense, rather than slow and gradual (Gelder, 1976; Olsen, 1975) and produces extinction of the conditioned fear response rather than replacing the old fear response with a different response. For example, a person who has a phobia of dogs might be exposed to a (very friendly) small dog that is actually in the room with the person. If the person cannot leave the room or avoid the dog (which would actually reinforce the fear through the removal of an unpleasant stimulus, otherwise known as negative reinforcement), the fear will eventually extinguish because *nothing bad happens*. The exposure might have to be repeated several times but usually brings results within a few sessions of only one or two hours each. Notice that there are really two steps in this therapy: exposure to the feared stimulus or situation and prevention of the once-typical avoidance response. This technique is also called *exposure and response prevention* for that reason. Flooding has also been successfully used to treat post-traumatic stress disorder (Foa et al., 2000; Keane et al., 1989) and obsessive-compulsive disorder through exposure to the anxiety-provoking situations (Foa & Franklin, 2000).

THERAPIES BASED ON OPERANT CONDITIONING

15.9   *How do behavior therapists use operant conditioning to treat disordered behavior?*

Operant conditioning techniques include reinforcement, extinction, shaping, and modeling to change the frequency of voluntary behavior. (L I N K) *to Chapter Five: Learning, pp. 177, 181, 196.* In the treatment of psychological disorders, the goal is to reduce the frequency of undesirable behavior and increase the frequency of desirable responses.

◀ Could you use aversion therapy to help someone with a phobia?

flooding
technique for treating phobias and other stress disorders in which the person is rapidly and intensely exposed to the fear-provoking situation or object and prevented from making the usual avoidance or escape response.

One of the advantages of using operant conditioning to treat a problem behavior is that results are usually quickly obtained rather than having to wait through years of more insight-oriented forms of therapy. When bringing the behavior under control (rather than finding out why it occurs in the first place) is the goal, operant and other behavioral techniques are very practical. There's an old joke about a man whose fear of things hiding under his bed is cured by a behavioral therapist in one night. The therapist simply cut the legs off the bed.

MODELING   **Modeling**, or learning through the observation and imitation of a model, is discussed in Chapter Five. The use of modeling as a therapy is based on the work of Albert Bandura, which states that a person with specific fears or someone who needs to develop social skills can learn to do so by watching someone else (the model) confront those fears or demonstrate the needed social skills (Bandura et al., 1969). In **participant modeling**, a model demonstrates the desired behavior in a step-by-step, gradual process. The client is encouraged by the therapist to imitate the model in the same gradual, step-by-step manner (Bandura, 1986; Bandura et al., 1974). The model can be a person actually present in the same room with the client or someone seen on videotape.

Behavioral therapists can give parents or others advice and demonstrations on how to carry out behavioral techniques. Once a person knows what to do, modeling is a fairly easy technique. Modeling has been effective in helping children with dental fears (Klorman et al., 1980; Ollendick & King, 1998), social withdrawal (O'Connor, 1972), obsessive-compulsive disorder (Roper et al., 1975), and phobias (Hintze, 2002).

USING REINFORCEMENT   **Reinforcement** is the strengthening of a response by following it with some pleasurable consequence (positive reinforcement) or the removal of an unpleasant stimulus (negative reinforcement). Reinforcement of both types can form the basis for treatment of people with behavioral problems.

Token Economies   In a **token economy**, objects that can be traded for food, candy, treats, or special privileges are called *tokens*. Clients earn tokens for behaving correctly or accomplishing behavioral goals and can later exchange those tokens for things that they want. They may also lose tokens for inappropriate behavior. This trading system is a token economy. ⓁⒾⓃⓀ *to Chapter Five: Learning, p. 190.* Token economies have also been used successfully in modifying the behavior of relatively disturbed persons in mental institutions, such as schizophrenic people or depressed persons (Dickerson et al., 1994; Glynn, 1990; McMonagle & Sultana, 2002).

Contingency Contracting   Another method based on the use of reinforcement involves making a **contingency contract** with the client (Salend, 1987). This contract is a formal agreement between therapist and client (or teacher and student, or parent and child) in which both parties' responsibilities and goals are clearly stated. Such contracts are useful in treating specific problems such as drug addiction (Talbott & Crosby, 2001), educational problems (Evans & Meyer, 1985; Evans et al., 1989), and eating disorders (Brubaker & Leddy, 2003).

For example, a typical contingency contract between a child and a parent would have one section that states the purpose of the contract (for example, "harmony in the home") and then a specific list of behaviors that the child agrees to complete, such as "completing homework," "making my bed," and "using a respectful tone when speaking to Mom or Dad." There will also be a list of penalties associated with failing to perform each of these tasks. This written statement of the rules and penalties makes it clear to children that if they fail to perform a task, they are choosing the punishment. The parents will also have a section stating the privileges that the child will earn

modeling
learning through the observation and imitation of others.

participant modeling
technique in which a model demonstrates the desired behavior in a step-by-step, gradual process while the client is encouraged to imitate the model.

reinforcement
the strengthening of a response by following it with a pleasurable consequence or the removal of an unpleasant stimulus.

token economy
the use of objects called tokens to reinforce behavior in which the tokens can be accumulated and exchanged for desired items or privileges.

contingency contract
a formal, written agreement between the therapist and client (or teacher and student) in which goals for behavioral change, reinforcements, and penalties are clearly stated.

when performing the tasks as agreed, such as free time to watch television, use of the car, or purchase of a special toy. The child and the parents sign the agreement.

Why does it work? The contingency contract puts everything down in "black and white." The stated tasks, stated penalties, and stated rewards are consistent, making discipline easier on both the child and the parents. There is no "wiggle room" for either child or parents to reinterpret the rules or back down on a promised privilege. Consistency is one of the most effective tools in using both rewards and punishments to mold behavior. (L I N K) *to Chapter Five: Learning, pp. 187–188.*

USING EXTINCTION   **Extinction** involves the removal of a reinforcer to reduce the frequency of a particular response. In modifying behavior, operant extinction often involves removing one's attention from the person when that person is engaging in an inappropriate or undesirable behavior. With children, this removal of attention may be a form of **time-out,** in which the child is removed from the situation that provides reinforcement (Kazdin, 1980). In adults, a simple refusal by the other persons in the room to acknowledge the behavior is often successful in reducing the frequency of that behavior. For example, recall Joanne, the spider-phobic woman. (L I N K) *to Chapter Fourteen: Psychological Disorders, p. 525.* Her friends subjected Joanne to a kind of extinction process by refusing to fuss over her reactions, resulting in a reduction in both severity and frequency of her phobic reactions.

EVALUATION OF BEHAVIOR THERAPIES

15.10   *How successful are behavior therapies?*

Behavior therapies may be more effective than other forms of therapy in treating specific behavioral problems, such as bedwetting, overeating, drug addictions, and phobic reactions (Burgio, 1998, Wetherell, 2002). More serious psychological disorders, such as severe depression or schizophrenia, do not respond as well overall to behavioral treatments, although improvement of specific symptoms can be achieved (Glynn, 1990; McMonagle & Sultana, 2002). Bringing symptoms under control is an important step in allowing a person to function normally in the social world, and behavior therapies are a relatively quick and efficient way to eliminate or greatly reduce such symptoms.

Cognitive Therapies: Thinking Is Believing

15.11   *What is cognitive therapy?*

Cognitive therapy (Beck, 1979; Freeman et al., 1989) is focused on helping people change their ways of thinking. Rather than focusing on the behavior itself, the cognitive therapist focuses on the distorted* thinking and unrealistic beliefs that lead to maladaptive behavior (Hollon & Beck, 1994), especially those distortions relating to depression (Abela & D'Allesandro, 2002; McGinn, 2000). The goal is to help clients test, in a more objective, scientific way, the truth of their beliefs and assumptions. Then they can recognize thoughts that are distorted and negative and replace them with more positive, helpful thoughts. Because the focus is on changing thoughts rather than gaining deep insights into their causes, this kind of therapy is an action therapy.

---

*Distorted: twisted out of true meaning.

extinction
the removal of a reinforcer to reduce the frequency of a behavior.

time-out
an extinction process in which a person is removed from the situation that provides reinforcement for undesirable behavior, usually by being placed in a quiet corner or room away from possible attention and reinforcement opportunities.

cognitive therapy
therapy in which the focus is on helping clients recognize distortions in their thinking and replace distorted, unrealistic beliefs with more realistic, helpful thoughts.

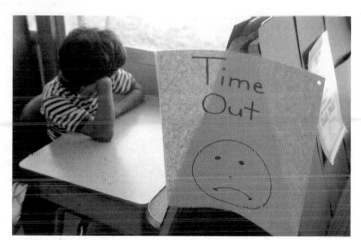

This boy is sitting in the "time-out" corner at his school. By removing the attention that he found rewarding, the teacher is attempting to extinguish the behavior that earned the boy a time-out. Do you see anything in this time-out corner that might make it less effective?

◀ What are these
unrealistic beliefs?

arbitrary inference
distortion of thinking in which a person draws a conclusion that is not based on any evidence.

selective thinking
distortion of thinking in which a person focuses on only one aspect of a situation while ignoring all other relevant aspects.

overgeneralization
distortion of thinking in which a person draws sweeping conclusions based on only one incident or event and applies those conclusions to events that are unrelated to the original.

magnification and minimization
distortions of thinking in which a person blows a negative event out of proportion to its importance (magnification) while ignoring relevant positive events (minimization).

personalization
distortion of thinking in which a person takes responsibility or blame for events that are unconnected to the person.

cognitive-behavioral therapy (CBT)
action therapy in which the goal is to help clients overcome problems by learning to think more rationally and logically.

Those questions sound ▶
like critical thinking,
like what was discussed
in Chapter One.

BECK'S COGNITIVE THERAPY

What are these unrealistic beliefs? Cognitive therapy focuses on the distortions of thinking. **LINK** to *Chapter Twelve: Theories of Personality, pp. 456–457.* Here are some of the more common distortions in thought that can create negative feelings and unrealistic beliefs in people:

- **Arbitrary inference:** This refers to "jumping to conclusions" without any evidence. *Arbitrary* means to decide something based on nothing more than personal whims. Example: "Suzy canceled our lunch date—I'll bet she's seeing someone else!"

- **Selective thinking:** In selective thinking, the person focuses only on one aspect of a situation, leaving out other relevant* facts that might make things seem less negative. Example: Peter's teacher praised his paper but made one comment about needing to check his punctuation. Peter assumes that his paper is lousy and that the teacher really didn't like it, ignoring the other praise and positive comments.

- **Overgeneralization:** Here a person draws a sweeping conclusion from one incident and then assumes that the conclusion applies to areas of life that have nothing to do with the original event. Example: "I insulted my algebra teacher. I'll flunk and I'll never be able to get a decent job—I'll end up on welfare."

- **Magnification and minimization:** Here a person blows bad things out of proportion while not emphasizing the good things. Example: A student who has received good grades on every other exam believes that the "C" she got on the last quiz means she's not going to succeed in college.

- **Personalization:** In personalization, an individual takes responsibility or blame for events that are not really connected to the individual. Example: When Sandy's husband comes home in a bad mood because of something that happened at work, she immediately assumes that he is angry with her.

A cognitive therapist tries to get clients to look at their beliefs and test them to see how accurate they really are. The first step is to identify an illogical or unrealistic belief, which the therapist and client do in their initial talks. Then the client is guided by the therapist through a process of asking questions about that belief, such as "When did this belief of mine begin?" or "What is the evidence for this belief?"

Those questions sound like critical thinking, like what was discussed in Chapter One. Cognitive therapy really is a kind of critical thinking, but it is thinking specifically about one's own thoughts and beliefs rather than outside events and experiences. Just as cognitive psychology grew out of behaviorism **LINK** to *Chapter One: The Science of Psychology, pp. 11, 14–15,* therapies using cognitive methods have behavioral elements within them as well, leading to the term **cognitive-behavioral therapy (CBT).**

15.12 *What are the goals of cognitive-behavioral therapy?*

Cognitive-behavioral therapy, or CBT, focuses on the present rather than the past (like behaviorism) but also assumes that people interact with the world with more than simple, automatic reactions to external stimuli. People observe the world and the people in the world around them, make assumptions and inferences** based on those observations or cognitions, and then decide how to respond (Rachman & Hodgson, 1980). As a form of cognitive therapy, CBT also assumes that disorders come from illogical, irrational cognitions and that changing the thinking patterns to

---

*Relevant: having importance with regard to the situation.
**Inferences: conclusions drawn from observations and facts.

more rational, logical ones will relieve the symptoms of the disorder, making it an action therapy. Cognitive-behavioral therapists may also use any of the tools that behavioral therapists use as well to help clients alter their actions. The three basic goals of any cognitive-behavioral therapy follow.

1. Relieve the symptoms and help clients resolve the problems.
2. Help clients develop strategies that can be used to cope with future problems.
3. Help clients change the way they think from irrational, self-defeating thoughts to more rational, self-helping, positive thoughts.

ELLIS AND RATIONAL-EMOTIVE BEHAVIOR THERAPY (REBT)

15.13   *What is rational-emotive behavior therapy?*

Albert Ellis proposed a version of CBT called **rational-emotive behavioral therapy (REBT)**, in which clients are taught a way to challenge their own irrational beliefs with more rational, helpful statements (Ellis, 1997, 1998). Here are some examples of irrational beliefs:

- Everyone should love and approve of me (if they don't, I am awful and unlovable).
- When things do not go the way I wanted and planned, it is terrible and I am, of course, going to get very disturbed. I can't stand it!

But I've felt that way at times. Why are these statements so irrational? Notice that these statements have one thing in common: It's either all or nothing. Can a person really expect the love and affection of every single person? Is it really realistic to expect things to work as planned every time? REBT is about challenging these types of "my way or nothing" statements, helping people to realize that life can be good without being "perfect." In REBT, therapists take a very directive role, challenging the client when the client makes statements like those listed earlier, assigning homework, using behavioral techniques to modify behavior, and arguing with clients about the rationality of their statements. Take the following example of a hypothetical exchange between a shy client and a REBT therapist:

Client:

I'm just so shy, I can't bring myself to talk to anyone.

Therapist:

Really? You're talking to me, aren't you?

Client:

But that's different, I know you.

Therapist:

You didn't know me when you started coming to see me, yet you were able to talk to me, right? So obviously, you can talk to other people when you want to talk, right?

Client:

Well. . .maybe. But it's hard for me to just start up a conversation with someone I've never met.

Therapist:

But "hard" isn't the same as "impossible," is it? When you go home tonight, I want you to look at some person you don't know on the bus, the train, the sidewalk, and just say, "Hi." That's all, just "hi." Do that at least twice a day until you see me again, and each time you do it, buy yourself a little treat.

rational-emotive behavior therapy (REBT)
cognitive-behavioral therapy in which clients are directly challenged in their irrational beliefs and helped to restructure their thinking into more rational belief statements.

◀ But I've felt that way at times. Why are these statements so irrational?

TABLE 15.1 **CHARACTERISTICS OF PSYCHOTHERAPIES**

Type of Therapy	Goal	Key People
Psychodynamic therapy	Insight	Freud
Person-centered therapy	Insight	Rogers
Gestalt therapy	Insight	Perls
Behavior therapy	Action	Watson, Jones, Skinner, Bandura
Cognitive therapy	Action	Beck
CBT	Action	Various professionals
REBT	Action	Ellis

EVALUATION OF COGNITIVE AND COGNITIVE-BEHAVIORAL THERAPIES

15.14 *How successful are cognitive and cognitive-behavioral therapies?*

Cognitive and cognitive-behavioral therapies are less expensive than the typical insight therapy because they are comparatively short-term therapies. As in behavior therapy, clients do not have to dig too deep for the hidden sources of their problems. Instead, cognitive-based therapies get right to the problems themselves, helping clients deal with their symptoms more directly. In fact, one of the criticisms of these therapies as well as behavior therapies is that they treat the symptom, not the cause. However, it should be noted that in the cognitive viewpoint, the maladaptive thoughts are seen as the cause of the problems, not merely the symptoms. There is also an element of potential bias because of the therapist's opinions as to which thoughts are rational and which are not (Westen, in press).

Nevertheless, cognitive and cognitive-behavioral therapies have considerable success in treating many types of disorders, including depression, stress disorders, anxiety disorders, and even some types of schizophrenia (Clark et al., 1989; DeRubeis et al., 1999; Holcomb, 1986; Jay & Elliot, 1990; Kendall, 1983; McGinn, 2000; Meichenbaum, 1996). As an offshoot of behaviorism, the learning principles that are the basis of cognitive-behavioral therapies are considered empirically sound (Masters et al., 1987).

For a summary of the various types of psychotherapies discussed up to this point, see Table 15.1.

Group Therapies: Not For the Shy

An alternative to individual therapy, in which the client and the therapist have a private, one-on-one session, is to gather a group of clients with similar problems together and have the group discuss problems under the guidance of a single therapist (Yalom, 1995).

15.15 *What are the advantages and disadvantages of group therapy?*

ADVANTAGES OF GROUP THERAPY

There are several advantages to group therapy:

- Lower cost. Because the therapist can see several clients at one time, this type of therapy is usually less expensive than individual therapy.

- Exposure to the ways in which other people view and handle the same kinds of problems.

In group therapy, several people who share similar problems gather with a therapist to discuss their feelings and concerns. The presence of others who are going through the same kind of emotional difficulties can be comforting, as well as providing the opportunity for insights into one's own problems by hearing about the problems of others.

- The opportunity for both the therapist and the person to see how that person interacts with others.

- Social and emotional support from people who have problems that are similar or nearly identical to one's own. This advantage is an important one; studies have shown that breast cancer patients who were part of a group therapy process had much higher survival and recovery rates than those who received only individual therapy or no psychotherapy (Fawzy et al., 1993; Spiegel et al., 1989).

DISADVANTAGES OF GROUP THERAPY

Group therapy is not appropriate for all situations, and there can be disadvantages:

- The therapist is no longer the only person to whom secrets and fears are revealed, which may make some people reluctant to speak freely.

- The client must share the therapist's time during the session.

- An extremely shy person may have great difficulty speaking up in a group setting.

- People with severe psychiatric disorders involving paranoia, such as schizophrenia, may not be able to tolerate group therapy settings.

A survey and comparison of the effectiveness of both individual and group therapy found that group therapy is only effective if it is long term and that it is more effective when used to promote skilled social interactions rather than attempting to decrease the more bizarre symptoms of delusions and hallucinations (Evans et al., 2000).

BiZarRo by Dan Piraro

Would anyone in the group like to respond to the way Frank is dealing with his anger?

®Dan Piraro. Reprinted with special permission of King Features Syndicate.

TYPES OF GROUP THERAPIES

15.16 *What are the different types of group therapy?*

There are also several ways in which group therapy can be accomplished. The therapist may use either an insight or cognitive-behavioral style, although person-centered, Gestalt, and behavior therapies seem to work better in group settings than psychoanalysis and cognitive-behavioral therapies (Andrews, 1989).

In addition to the variations in the style of therapy, the group structure can also vary. There may be small groups formed of related persons or other groups of unrelated persons that meet without the benefit of a therapist. Their goal is to share their problems and provide social and emotional support for each other.

FAMILY COUNSELING One form of group therapy is **family counseling** or **family therapy**, in which all of the members of a family who are experiencing some type of problem—marital problems, problems in child discipline, or sibling rivalry, for example—are seen by the therapist as a group. The therapist may also meet with one or more family members individually at times, but the real work in opening the lines of communication among family members is accomplished in the group setting (Frankel & Piercy, 1990; Pinsoff & Wynne, 1995). The family members may include grandparents, aunts and uncles, and in laws as well as the core family. This is because family therapy focuses on the family as a whole unit or system of interacting "parts." No one person is seen as "the problem" because all members of the family system are part of the problem: They are experiencing it, rewarding it, or by their actions or inactions causing it to occur in the first place.

Take the example of the author's cousin, George. George was what most people would label a "brat." He refused to do chores, was rude to his mother and others, and destroyed his toys to gain attention. Why did George need that attention? His father had not wanted children and ignored

family counseling (family therapy) a form of group therapy in which family members meet together with a counselor or therapist to resolve problems that affect the entire family.

In family therapy, all family members participate in therapy sessions with the therapist guiding them through open communication. Although it appears that the young boy in the corner is the focus of this session, all family members are encouraged to see how their own behavior may contribute to the problem behavior.

self-help groups (support groups) a group composed of people who have similar problems and who meet together without a therapist or counselor for the purpose of discussion, problem solving, and social and emotional support.

George—except when George was misbehaving. George's mother would not allow his father to spank him, and she allowed George to be rude. When George destroyed a toy, his mother would buy him a new one. Clearly, the problems within this family system are not all the fault of George alone.

The goal in family therapy, then, is to discover the unhealthy ways in which family members interact and communicate with one another and change those ways to healthier, more productive means of interaction. Family therapists work not only with families but also with couples who are in a committed relationship with the goal of improving communication, helping the couple to learn better ways of solving their problems and disagreements, and increasing feelings of intimacy and emotional closeness (Christensen et al., 1995; Heavey et al., 1993).

SELF-HELP GROUPS Therapists are often in short supply, and they also charge money for leading group therapy sessions. Many people may also feel that a therapist who has never had a drug problem cannot truly understand their problem, for example, and may feel that someone who has experienced addiction and beaten it is more capable of providing real help. This, rather than just concerns about money, is the main reason some people choose to meet with others who have problems similar to their own on a voluntary basis, with no therapist in charge. Called **self-help groups** or **support groups**, these groups are usually formed around the particular problem. Some examples of self-help groups are Alcoholics Anonymous, Overeaters Anonymous, and Narcotics Anonymous, all of which have groups meeting all over the country at almost any time of the day or night. There are countless smaller support groups for nearly every condition imaginable including anxiety, phobias, having a parent with a dementia, having difficult children, depression, and dealing with stress—just to name just a few. The advantages of self-help groups are that they are free and provide the social and emotional support that any group session can provide (Bussa & Kaufman, 2000). Self-help groups do not have leaders but instead have people who volunteer monthly or weekly to lead individual meetings. So the person who is in charge of organizing the meetings is also a member of the group with the same problem as all the other members.

In this meeting of one of the oldest self-help groups in the country, the person standing at the front of the room is not a specialist or a therapist, but just a member of the group. She has the same problem as all of the other people in the room, which is the strength of this type of program—people are more likely to trust and open up to someone who has struggled as they have.

15.17 *For whom is group therapy most likely to be a useful form of treatment?*

EVALUATION OF GROUP THERAPY Group therapy can provide help to people who might be unable to afford individual psychotherapy. It can also provide social and emotional support to people who may improve significantly from simply knowing that they are not the only people to suffer from whatever their particular problem may be. People who are not comfortable in social situations or who have trouble speaking in front of others may not find group therapy as helpful as those who are more verbal and social by nature. It is also important to note that group therapy can be used in combination with individual and biomedical therapies.

PRACTICE **QUIZ:** HOW MUCH DO YOU REMEMBER?

Pick the best answer.

1. Jeremy is trying to stop biting his fingernails. He wears a rubber band around each of his wrists, and whenever he finds himself biting his nails he snaps the band. Jeremy is using a form of _____ to modify his nail-biting behavior.
   a. systematic desensitization   **c.** flooding
   b. aversion therapy   **d.** extinction

2. The reality television shows that deliberately force people to face their "worst fears" are most similar to which therapy technique?
   a. systematic desensitization   **c.** flooding
   b. aversion therapy   **d.** extinction

3. At Skinner Elementary School, teachers pass out "skinner bucks" to students who turn in papers on time, obey the teacher, and finish their homework. The paper "bucks" can be used at the end of the week to trade for special treats or game-playing time on the classroom computer. This system most resembles a
   a. participant modeling technique.
   b. contingency contract.
   c. group extinction procedure.
   d. token economy.

4. Which of the following would be an unlikely strategy for a rational-emotive behavior therapist to use in treating a client?
a. arguing with the client's statements
b. repeating what the client has just said without interpreting it
c. giving the client homework
d. pointing out irrational beliefs to the client

5. Maya is upset because her supervisor teased her about turning in her report several hours late. Although her supervisor was quite pleased with the report itself and told Maya that her work was excellent, Maya remains unhappy. Beck would say that Maya is guilty of
a. arbitrary inference.   **c.** personalization.
b. selective thinking.   **d.** defective thinking.

6. Which person might benefit the least from a group therapy environment?
a. Suzanne, who has a phobia of cats
b. Richard, who has a drinking problem
c. Jasmine, who is painfully shy
d. Elena, who suffers from depression

7. Six members of Ron's statistics class would meet every Saturday to go over their notes and try to figure out what the teacher had told them during his rambling lectures. If part of every Saturday's session is spent sharing feelings about the teacher and venting their anger and resentment, Ron's study group could be said to serve as
a. a support group.   **c.** awareness training group.
b. family therapy.   **d.** guided discovery group.

CURRENT ISSUES IN PSYCHOLOGY

What Is EMDR?

15.18   *Does eye-movement desensitization reprocessing really work?*

Graduate psychology student Francine Shapiro was walking through a local park thinking about some old memories that bothered her. As she moved her eyes rapidly back and forth, she discovered that her disturbing thoughts seemed to disappear. She quickly found 70 volunteers to try this eye-movement technique and they, too, found their disturbing thoughts, fears, and anxieties decreasing as they moved their eyes rapidly back and forth (Butler, 1993). Shapiro eventually earned her doctorate by developing a controlled study in which 22 survivors of rape, war, or childhood abuse were given one hour of what Shapiro called **eye-movement desensitization reprocessing**, or **EMDR**. All participants reported that their memories had lost a great deal of their fearfulness or anxiety and that they felt considerably better after undergoing the process (Shapiro, 1989).

EMDR has since become a popular therapy with many practicing clinicians for treatment of post-traumatic stress disorder or PTSD **LINK** to *Chapter Eleven: Stress and Health, p. 409*, phobias, and other anxiety-related disorders, although PTSD remains the disorder for which this new therapy is most commonly used.

Essentially, the client is instructed to think of a negative memory and an image that represents that memory (Shapiro, 1989, 1995). At this point, the client focuses on the memory while visually following the therapist's rapidly moving fingers back and forth, until the anxiety or fear has been eliminated. This is the "eye-movement desensitization" part of the process. The client is also asked to focus on some negative self-statement ("I am unlovable") during the EMDR session, and when the fear and anxiety have been removed, the client focuses on a positive thought ("I am lovable") while looking for signs of stress or tension. If such signs exist, they will be treated with more sessions of EMDR. This is the "reprocessing" part of EMDR, in which they negative cognitions are reprocessed into positive, helpful ones.

But just how new and different is this technique? Shapiro has supporters who have done studies that showed EMDR to be an effective therapy for stress and anxiety disorders of various types (Silver, et al. 1995; Wilson et al., 1995). Other researchers have found that EMDR is not always effective (Montgomery & Ayllon, 1994; Muris et al., 1998; Oswalt et al., 1993), nor is it any more effective (as Shapiro and her followers have claimed) than simple muscle relaxation or

eye-movement desensitization reprocessing (EMDR)
controversial form of therapy for post-traumatic stress disorder and similar anxiety problems in which the client is directed to move the eyes rapidly back and forth while thinking of a disturbing memory.

exposure therapy, which are two more traditional methods (Vaughan et al., 1994). Still others point to the lack of objectivity in how clients' "recovery" is measured, pointing out that many of the earlier studies were done without actually verifying the presence of a diagnosed disorder in the client and that the therapists themselves personally collected all data (much of it self-report and, therefore, possibly inaccurate) from the clients, leading to the possibility of experimenter bias or the experimenter effect (Hurst & Milkewicz, 2000).

Robert Carroll, in *The Skeptic's Dictionary* article on EMDR (Carroll, 2000), states that each time a new study shows that some part of EMDR does not work the way Shapiro originally theorized that it would, Shapiro changes the theoretical explanation of how EMDR works to allow the new research to fit. For example, research has shown that the eye movements are not actually necessary; simple finger tapping or alternating tones in each ear also produces the same results (Butler, 1993; Renfry & Spates, 1994). Shapiro then admitted that the eye movements are not essential and shifted the focus of the therapy to the reprocessing of thoughts (Carroll, 2000). This constant revision makes the theory impossible to disprove and sounds suspiciously like what many proponents of pseudo-psychologies do when confronted with evidence against their basic ideas (Lohr et al., 1995, 1998). Until enough studies are done that control for experimenter bias and that use objective measurements of recovery, EMDR will no doubt remain a popular but controversial method of therapy.

Questions for Further Discussion

1. Could EMDR be a radically different form of systematic desensitization or exposure therapy, or could it be the simple exposure that brings about the relief reported by clients?

2. If a therapy such as EMDR does produce results, what could be the harm in allowing people to take advantage of it? How might that be similar to a placebo effect?

Does Psychotherapy Really Work?

> There sure are a lot of psychotherapies, but do any of them really work?

There sure are a lot of psychotherapies, but do any of them really work? One of the earliest studies to look at the effectiveness of psychotherapy was Hans Eysenck's survey of 19 different studies reporting on the improvement or lack of improvement of clients' conditions using psychoanalysis and **eclectic therapies**, in which the therapist used not one but several different techniques of psychotherapy (Eysenck, 1957). Eysenck compared the results of these studies with studies of people who were institutionalized for mental disorders but given no psychotherapy. Instead, these people received food, shelter, and care for their basic needs and formed the control group. (The studies in question were done in the 1930s, a time period when such custodial care was unfortunately common.) Eysenck concluded that the people receiving psychotherapy did not recover at any higher rate than those who had no psychotherapy and that the passage of time alone could account for all recovery.

STUDIES OF EFFECTIVENESS

15.19   *How effective is psychotherapy?*

This classic survey created a major controversy within the world of clinical and counseling psychology. Other researchers began their own studies to find evidence that would contradict Eysenck's findings. One such effort reviewed studies that the researchers considered to be well controlled and concluded that the psychotherapies did not differ from one another in effectiveness (Luborsky et al., 1975). Of course, that can mean either that the psychotherapies were all equally effective or that they were all equally ineffective.

eclectic therapies
therapy style that results from combining elements of several different therapy techniques.

There are numerous problems with studying the effectiveness of psychotherapy. Controlled studies can be done using an experimental group of people who receive a particular psychotherapy and a control group of people who are put on a waiting list, but this is less than ideal. The control group is not getting the attention from the therapist, for one thing, and so there would be no placebo-effect expectations about getting better because of therapy (Shapiro & Shapiro, 1997). Also, not all therapies take the same amount of time to be effective. For example, psychoanalysis, even in its short form, takes longer than a behavioral therapy. In a short-term study, behavioral therapy would obviously look more effective. Action therapies such as behaviorism measure the success of the therapy differently than do insight therapies; in a behavioral therapy the reduction of the undesired behavior is easy to objectively measure, but gaining insights and feelings of control, self-worth, self-esteem, and so on are not as easily evaluated (Shadish et al., 2002).

Studies that do not use empirical* procedures but instead try to determine if the clients have been helped by the therapy in general are plagued by problems such as experimenter bias (the therapist expects the therapy to work and is also the one assessing the progress of the client), the inaccuracies of self-report information, and the same placebo effect cited by Shapiro and Shapiro (Seligman, 1995; Wampold, 1997).

Nevertheless, more recent surveys have shown that people who have received psychotherapy believe that they have been helped more often than not (*Consumer Reports*, 1995; Kotkin et al., 1996). The *Consumer Reports* research was a survey of the magazine's readers in which those who had been or were currently clients in psychotherapy rated the effectiveness of the therapy they received. Here are the findings from a summary of this and several other similar surveys (Lambert & Ogles, 2003; Seligman, 1995; Thase, 1999):

- An estimated 75–90 percent of people feel that psychotherapy has helped them.

- The longer a person stays in therapy, the greater the improvement.

Other studies have found that some psychotherapies are more effective for certain types of disorders (Hollon et al., 2002) but that no one psychotherapy is the most effective or works for every type of problem. Remember, all of the survey information is subject to the same flaws as any other survey information: errors in memory, inaccurate self-reporting, deliberate mistruths, and in this case even the placebo effect because subjects who pay for therapy more than likely expect to feel better (whether the therapy works or not).

CHARACTERISTICS OF EFFECTIVE THERAPY

So how does a person with a problem know what kind of therapist to go to? How do you pick a good one? As discussed in Chapter Twelve, most psychological professionals today take an eclectic view of psychotherapy, using a combination of methods or switching methods to fit the particular client's needs or specific problems. A client with a phobia may benefit from both behavioral therapy and cognitive therapy, for example. Clients who have more long-term goals of understanding themselves better might be more comfortable with psychoanalysis or one of the humanistic therapies. Finding an effective therapy (or therapist) is not so much finding one therapy that works overall but finding a specific therapy that works for a specific problem.

Several factors are important in any successful, effective therapy (Hubble et al., 1999; Seligman, 1998; Stiles et al., 1998). The most important aspect of a successful psychotherapy is the relationship between the client and the therapist, known as the

◀ So how does a person with a problem know what kind of therapist to go to? How do you pick a good one?

---

*Empirical: capable of being verified or disproved by observation or experiment.

therapeutic alliance
the relationship between therapist and client that develops as a warm, caring, accepting relationship characterized by empathy, mutual respect, and understanding.

therapeutic alliance. This relationship should be caring, warm, and accepting, and be characterized by empathy, mutual respect, and understanding. Therapy should also offer clients a protected setting in which to release emotions and reveal private thoughts and concerns and should help clients understand why they feel they way they do and provide them with ways to feel better. (One of the main problems with radio and television psychologists, of course, is the lack of a private, protected setting for clients. Part of the danger lies in assuming that television or radio therapists actually have any real training in psychology or therapy. Many people call themselves therapists without the proper background, as the term *therapist* is not a licensed term, whereas *psychologist* and *psychiatrist* are.)

CULTURAL, ETHNIC, AND GENDER CONCERNS IN PSYCHOTHERAPY

15.20 *Is psychotherapy's effectiveness affected by cultural, ethnic, or gender differences?*

Consider the following situation (adapted from Wedding, 2004).

K. is a 24-year-old Korean American. She lived with her parents, who were both born and reared in Korea before moving to the United States as adults. She came to a therapist because she was depressed and unhappy with her lack of independence. Her father was angry about her plans to marry a non-Korean. Her therapist immediately began assertiveness training and role-playing to prepare K. to deal with her father. The therapist was disappointed when K. failed to keep her second appointment.

This example of an actual case demonstrates a problem that exists in the therapist–client relationship for many clients when the ethnicity or culture of the client is different from that of the therapist. This cultural difference makes it difficult for therapists to understand the exact nature of their clients' problems and for clients to benefit from therapies that do not match their needs (Matsumoto, 1994; Moffic; 2003; Wedding, 2004). The values of different cultures and ethnic groups are not universally the same. How, for example, could a female therapist who is white, from a upper-middle-class family, and well educated hope to understand the problems of a Hispanic adolescent boy from a poor family living in substandard housing? Gender, ethnicity, and economic background are all vastly different.

In the case of K., for example, the therapist mistakenly assumed that the key to improving K.'s situation was to make her more assertive and independent from her family, particularly her father. This Western idea runs counter to Korean cultural values. Korean culture stresses interdependence, not independence. The family comes first, obedience to one's elders is highly valued, and "doing one's own thing" is not acceptable. K.'s real problem may have been her feelings of guilt about her situation and her father's anger. She may have wanted help in dealing with her family situation and her feelings about that situation, not help in becoming more independent.

For therapy to be effective, the client must continue in treatment until a successful outcome is reached. K. never came back after the first session. One of the problems that can occur when the culture or ethnic backgrounds of the client and therapist are mismatched, as in K.'s case, is that the therapist may project his or her values onto the client, failing to achieve true empathy with the client's feelings or even to realize what the client's true feelings are and causing the client to drop out of therapy. Studies of such situations have found that members of minority racial or ethnic groups drop out of therapy at a significantly higher rate than the majority group clients (Brown et al., 2003; Cooper et al., 2003; Flaherty & Adams, 1998; Sue, 1977, 1992; Sue et al., 1994; Vail, 1976; Vernon & Roberts, 1982).

Are differences in gender that important? For example, do women prefer female therapists while men would rather talk to another man? Research on gender and therapist–client relationships varies. When talking about white middle-class clients, it seems that both men and women prefer a female therapist (Jones et al., 1987). But African American clients were more likely to drop out of therapy if the therapist was the *same* sex as the client (Vail, 1976), male Asian clients seemed to prefer a male therapist, and female Asian clients stayed in therapy equally long with either male or female therapists (Flaherty & Adams, 1998; Flaskerud, 1991). (Although several of the references cited are older ones, they represent the most recent studies for these specific findings.)

Four barriers to effective psychotherapy exist when the culture or ethnic backgrounds of client and therapist are different (Sue & Sue, 2003):

1. **Language.** Speaking different languages becomes a problem in understanding what both client and therapist are saying and in psychological testing (Betancourt & Jacobs, 2000; Lewis, 1996).

2. **Cultural values.** Differing cultural values can cause therapists to fail at forming an empathetic relationship (Sattler, 1977; Wedding, 2004).

3. **Social class.** Clients from impoverished backgrounds may have values and experiences that the therapist cannot understand (Wedding, 2004).

4. **Nonverbal communication.** Body language, or nonverbal communication, can also differ between cultures and ethnicities. The physical distance between the client and therapist, the use of gestures, and eye contact, for example, can cause misunderstandings during the session and in interpretation of the client's moods and intentions (Galanti, 1997; Like et al., 1996). People in some cultures are content with long periods of silence while others are not, direct eye contact is desirable in some cultures and offensive in others, and even facial expressions of emotion vary from very expressive (as with Hispanic people) to nonexpressive (as with many Asian people).

The American Psychiatric Association (2000a) has included a guide for therapists concerning cultural issues and culture-bound syndromes such as *koro*. **L**◯**N**◯**K** *to Chapter Fourteen: Psychological Disorders, p. 526.* All therapists need to make an effort to become aware of cultural differences, culture-bound syndromes, and possible gender issues.

◀ Are differences in gender that important? For example, do women prefer female therapists while men would rather talk to another man?

Reprinted with special permission of King Features Syndicate.

CYBERTHERAPY: THERAPY IN THE COMPUTER AGE

Although psychotherapy is usually accomplished by the client or clients speaking face-to-face with the therapist, a new type of therapy is now available to people in need who own a computer. **Cybertherapy** refers to psychotherapy that is offered on the Internet, and the people who practice it are called *cybertherapists*. Although this method of delivery may have the advantages of lower or no cost, availability of therapy opportunities for those unable to get to a therapist easily (such as people living in a remote or rural area), access to support groups online, and relative anonymity, there are dangers. There is no guarantee that the cybertherapist has any credentials or training in psychotherapy, and because there is no face-to-face or even voice-to-voice contact in most forms of cybertherapy, the therapist has no access to body language or vocal tones in trying to assess a client's emotional and psychological state. For further information on this subject, an excellent list of the various forms that cybertherapy can take and the strengths and weaknesses of each has been developed by Dr. Azy Barak, a psychologist at the University of Haifa in Israel and an expert in Internet psychotherapy (Barak, 1999).

cybertherapy
psychotherapy that is offered on the Internet. Also called online, Internet, or Web therapy or counseling.

biomedical therapies
therapies that directly affect the biological functioning of the body and brain.

psychopharmacology
the use of drugs to control or relieve the symptoms of psychological disorders.

antipsychotic drugs
drugs used to treat psychotic symptoms such as delusions, hallucinations, and other bizarre behavior.

Biomedical Therapies

Just as a therapist trained in psychoanalysis is more likely to use that technique, a therapist whose perspective on personality and behavior is biological will most likely turn to medical techniques to manage disordered behavior. Even psychotherapists who are not primarily biological in orientation may combine psychotherapy with medical treatments that are supervised by a medical doctor working with the psychologist. As medical doctors, psychiatrists are almost inevitably biological in perspective and, thus, use **biomedical therapies** (directly affecting the biological functioning of the body and brain) in addition to any psychotherapy technique they may favor. This was the case with Marie, the young girl from the opening story.

The biomedical therapies fall into three categories: drug therapy, shock therapy, and surgical treatments.

PSYCHOPHARMACOLOGY

15.21 *What are the various types of drugs used to treat psychological disorders?*

The use of drugs to control or relieve the symptoms of a psychological disorder is called **psychopharmacology**. Although these drugs are sometimes used alone, they are more often combined with some form of psychotherapy and are more effective as a result (Kearney & Silverman, 1998; Keller et al., 2000). There are four basic categories of drugs used to treat psychotic disorders, anxiety disorders, the manic phase of mood disorders, and depression.

ANTIPSYCHOTIC DRUGS Drugs used to treat psychotic symptoms, such as hallucinations, delusions, and bizarre behavior, are called **antipsychotic drugs**. The three categories of antipsychotic drugs are *typical neuroleptics, atypical neuroleptics,* and *partial dopamine agonists.* The first of the typical neuroleptics to be developed was *chlorpromazine* (Jones & Pilowsky, 2002). The term *neuroleptic* comes from the French word *neuroleptique,* which means "to have an effect on neurons." Table 15.2 lists several of these antipsychotic drugs and their side effects.

These drugs work by blocking certain dopamine receptors in the brain, thereby reducing the effect of dopamine in synaptic transmission (Csernansky et al., 2002). However, because they block more pathways in the dopamine system than are involved in psychosis, they tend to cause problems such as *tardive dyskinesia,* a syndrome causing the person to make repetitive, involuntary jerks and movements of the face, lips, legs, and body (Jones & Pilowsky, 2002).

The atypical neuroleptics also suppress dopamine but to a much greater degree in the one dopamine pathway that seems to cause psychotic problems. These drugs also block or partially block certain serotonin receptors, resulting in fewer negative side effects and sometimes even improvement in the more negative symptoms of schizophrenia such as withdrawal, apathy, and reduced communication (Jones & Pilowsky, 2002).

Clozapine, an atypical neuroleptic, can cause a potentially fatal reduction in the white blood cells of the body's immune system in a very small percentage of people. For this reason, the blood of patients on clozapine is closely monitored (Jones & Pilowsky, 2002).

How long do people generally have to take these antipsychotic medications? In some cases, a person might have a psychotic episode that lasts only a few months or a few years and may need drug treatment only for that time. But in most cases, especially in schizophrenia that starts in adolescence or young adulthood, the medication must be taken for the rest of the person's life.

How long do people generally have to take these antipsychotic medications? ▶

TABLE 15.2 **TYPES OF DRUGS USED IN PSYCHOPHARMACOLOGY**

Classification	Treatment Areas	Side Effects	Examples
Antipsychotic: Typical Neuroleptic	Positive (excessive) symptoms such as delusions or hallucinations	Motor problems, tardive dyskinesia	Chlorpromazine Droperidol Haliperodol
Antipsychotic: Atypical Neuroleptic	Positive and some negative symptoms of psychoses	Fewer than typical neuroleptics; clozapine may cause serious blood disorder	Risperidone Clozapine Aripirazole
Antianxiety: Minor Tranquilizers	Symptoms of anxiety and phobic reactions	Slight sedative effect; potential for physical dependence	Xanax Ativan Valium
Antimanic	Manic behavior	Potential for toxic buildup	Lithium Anticonvulsant drugs
Antidepressants: MAOIs	Depression	Weight gain, constipation dry mouth, dizziness, headache, drowsiness, insomnia, some sexual arousal disorders	Iproniazid Isocarboxazid Phenelzine sulfite Tranylcypromine sulfite
Antidepressants: Tricyclics	Depression	Skin rashes, blurred vision, lowered blood pressure, weight loss	Imipramine Desipramine Amitriptyline Doxepin
Antidepressants: SSRIs	Depression	Nausea, nervousness, insomnia, diarrhea, rash, agitation, some sexual arousal problems	Fluoxetine Hydrochloride sertraline Hydrochloride Paroxetine Hydrochloride

Long-term use of neuroleptics, particularly the older typical drugs, has been associated with a decrease in cognitive functioning (Terry et al., 2002, 2003). A newer class of atypical neuroleptics called partial dopamine agonists, affect the release of dopamine rather than blocking its receptors in the brain (Tamminga, 2002). (An *agonist* is any chemical substance that can stimulate a reaction within the synapse. Ⓛ Ⓘ Ⓝ Ⓚ *to Chapter Two: The Biological Perspective, p. 50.*) By 2005 the only one of these drugs that had been approved by the Food and Drug Administration for use in the treatment of schizophrenia was aripirazole. The hope is that these newer drugs will not only produce fewer negative side effects but also have less impact on the thought processes of those persons taking these drugs. In one recent study, the atypical neuroleptics were also found to lower the risk of violent behavior in schizophrenic patients who are receiving their medication through community-based treatment centers (Swanson et al., 2004).

ANTIANXIETY DRUGS   There are currently two kinds of drugs used to treat anxiety disorders from mild anxiety to the more serious anxiety of social phobias, simple

antianxiety drugs
drugs used to treat and calm anxiety reactions, typically minor tranquilizers.

antidepressant drugs
drugs used to treat depression and anxiety.

phobias, and panic disorder. The traditional **antianxiety drugs** are the minor tranquilizers or *benzodiazepines* such as Xanax, Ativan, and Valium. All of these drugs have a sedative effect and in the right dose can relieve symptoms of anxiety within half an hour of taking the drug (Uretsky, 2002). Although many side effects are possible, the main concern in using these drugs is their potential for abuse (NIDA, 2002).

In the last several years the use of the benzodiazepines to treat anxiety has declined, and physicians and therapists have begun to prescribe **antidepressant drugs** to treat anxiety disorders such as panic disorder, obsessive-compulsive disorder, and post-traumatic stress disorder. Although the antidepressants take from three to five weeks to show any effect, they are not as subject to abuse as the minor tranquilizers and have fewer of the same side effects.

ANTIMANIC DRUGS For many years, the treatment of choice for bipolar disorder and episodes of mania has been *lithium*, a metallic chemical element that in its salt form (lithium carbonate) evens out both the highs and the lows of bipolar disorder. It is generally recommended that treatment with lithium continue at maintenance levels in people with recurring bipolar disorder. Lithium affects the way sodium ions in neuron and muscle cells are transported, although it is not clear exactly how this affects mood. Side effects typically disappear quickly, although the use of lithium has been associated with weight gain. Diet needs to be controlled when taking lithium because lowered levels of sodium in the diet can cause lithium to build up to toxic levels, as can any substance that removes water from the body such as the caffeine in sodas, tea, and coffee.

Anticonvulsant drugs, normally used to treat seizure disorders, have also been used to treat mania. Examples are carbamazepine, valproic acid (Depakote), and lamotrigine. These drugs can be as effective in controlling mood swings as lithium and can also be used in combination with lithium treatments (Bowden et al., 2000; Thase & Sachs, 2000). When bouts of mania include psychotic symptoms (as in affective psychosis), patients are often treated with antipsychotic drugs in addition to a combination of anticonvulsants or antidepressants (Tohen et al., 2003).

ANTIDEPRESSANT DRUGS As is so often the case in scientific discoveries, the first types of drugs used in the treatment of depression were originally developed to treat other disorders. Iproniazid, for example, was used to treat tuberculosis symptoms in the early 1950s and was found to have a positive effect on mood, becoming the first modern *antidepressant* (Trujillo & Chinn, 1996). This drug became the first of the *monamine oxidase inhibitors (MAOIs)*, a class of antidepressants that blocks the activity of an enzyme called monamine oxidase. Monamine oxidase is the brain's "cleanup worker" because its primary function is to break down the neurotransmitters norepinephrine, serotonin, and dopamine—the three neurotransmitters most involved in control of mood. Under normal circumstances, the excess neurotransmitters are broken down *after* they have done their "job" in mood control. In depression, these neurotransmitters need more time to do their job, and the MAOIs allow them that time by inhibiting the enzyme's action.

Some common MAOIs in use today are isocarboxazid (Marplan), phenelzine sufate (Nardil), and tranylcypromine sulfate (Parnate). These drugs can produce some unwanted side effects, although in most cases the side effects decrease or disappear with continued treatment: weight gain, constipation, dry mouth, dizziness, headache, drowsiness or insomnia, and sexual arousal disorders are possible. People taking MAOIs should also be careful about eating certain smoked, fermented, or pickled foods, drinking certain beverages, or taking some other medications due to a risk of severe high blood pressure in combination with these substances (Geddes & Butler, 2002).

The second category of antidepressant drug to be developed is called the *tricyclic antidepressants*. These drugs were discovered in the course of developing treatments for schizophrenia (Trujillo & Chinn, 1996). Tricyclics, so called because of their molecular structure consisting of three rings (cycles), increase the activity of serontonin and norepinephrine in the nervous system by inhibiting their reuptake into the synaptic vesicles of the neurons. L I N K to Chapter Two: The Biological Perspective, *p. 52*. Some common tricyclics are imipramine (Tofranil), desipramine (Norpramin, Pertofrane), amitriptyline (Elavil), and doxepin (Sinequan, Adapin). Side effects of these drugs, which may also decrease over the course of treatment, are very similar to those of the MAOIs but can also include skin rashes, blurred vision, lowered blood pressure, and weight loss (APA, 2000b; Geddes & Butler, 2002).

The effect of the MAOIs and the tricyclics on the action of the three critical neurotransmitters led researchers to try to develop drugs that would more specifically target the critical neural activity involved in depression with fewer negative side effects. This led to the development of the *selective serotonin reuptake inhibitors (SSRIs)*, drugs that inhibit the reuptake process of only serotonin. This causes fewer side effects while still providing effective antidepressant action, making these drugs relatively safe when compared to the older antidepressants. But like the other two classes of antidepressants, the SSRIs may take from two to six weeks to produce effects. Some of the better-known SSRIs are fluoxetine hydrochloride (Prozac), sertraline hydrochloride (Zoloft), and paroxetine hydrochloride (Paxil). Side effects, although fewer in number and less intense than the other drugs, can include nausea, nervousness, insomnia, diarrhea, rash, agitation, and some sexual arousal problems (APA, 2000b; Geddes & Butler, 2002). Table 15.2 summarizes the various types of drugs used to treat psychological disorders.

For a look at a current controversy concerning antidepressants, see the Applying Psychology to Everyday Life section at the end of this chapter.

ELECTROCONVULSIVE THERAPY

15.22 *How is electroconvulsive therapy used to treat severe psychological disorders?*

Many people are—well—*shocked* to discover that **electroconvulsive therapy (ECT)** is still in use to treat cases of severe depression. ECT involves the delivery of an electric shock to either one side or both sides of a person's head, resulting in a seizure or convulsion of the body and the release of a flood of neurotransmitters in the brain (APA, 2001). The result is an almost immediate improvement in mood, and ECT is used not only in severe cases of depression that have not responded to drug treatments or psychotherapy but also in the treatment of several other severe disorders that are not responding to those alternate treatments, such as schizophrenia and severe mania (APA, 2001).

How did somebody come up with the idea to shock people who were mentally ill? Was it a kind of punishment back in the early days of mental institutions? In the 1930s, doctors actually were researching the possible uses of inducing seizures in treating schizophrenia, although the seizures were induced through means of a drug (camphor) in those early experiments. It was Italian researchers Cerletti and Bini who first used electricity to induce a seizure in a schizophrenic man, who fully recovered after only 11 such treatments (Endler, 1988; Fink, 1984; Shorter, 1997). Soon doctors were using ECT on every kind of severe mental disorder. In those early days, no anesthesia was used because the shock was severe enough to result in a loss of consciousness (most of the time). Broken bones, bitten tongues, and fractured teeth were not unusual "side effects."

electroconvulsive therapy (ECT) form of biomedical therapy to treat severe depression in which electrodes are placed on either one or both sides of a person's head and an electric current is passed through the electrodes that is strong enough to cause a seizure or convulsion.

Electroconvulsive therapy consists of applying an electric shock to one or both sides of the head. The result is rapid improvement in mood. It has been shown to be most effective in treating severe depression that has not responded to medication.

How did somebody come up with the idea to shock people who were mentally ill? Was it a kind of punishment back in the early days of mental institutions?

What are some of the side effects? Wasn't there something from an earlier chapter about this therapy ▶ affecting memory?

bilateral ECT
electroconvulsive therapy in which the electrodes are placed on both sides of the head.

unilateral ECT
electroconvulsive therapy in which the electrodes are placed on only one side of the head and the forehead.

psychosurgery
surgery performed on brain tissue to relieve or control severe psychological disorders.

prefrontal lobotomy
psychosurgery in which the connections of the prefrontal lobes of the brain to the rear portions are severed.

bilateral cingulotomy
psychosurgical technique in which an electrode wire is inserted into the cingulated gyrus area of the brain with the guidance of a magnetic resonance imaging machine for the purpose of destroying that area of brain tissue with an electric current.

But I thought ▶ lobotomies left most people worse off than before—didn't it take away their emotions or something?

ECT received more negative attention as it was portrayed in the classic 1975 film *One Flew Over the Cuckoo's Nest,* in which the little understood treatment was applied as a punishment and made to look like one. In reality, today's ECT is far more controlled and humane. It can only be used to treat severe disorders, not to control unruly behavior, and written and informed consent is required in most states. ECT has been found to be most useful for severe depression that has not responded to medications or psychotherapy and in cases where suicide is a real possibility or has already been attempted. ECT works more quickly than antidepressant medications, so it can play an important role in helping to prevent suicide attempts (APA, 2001).

What are some of the side effects? Wasn't there something from an earlier chapter about this therapy affecting memory? ECT does have several negative side effects, some of which last longer than others. Memory is definitely affected, as ECT disrupts the consolidation process and prevents the formation of long-term memories. ⓁⒾ Ⓝ Ⓚ *to Chapter Six: Memory, p. 237.* This causes both retrograde amnesia, the loss of memories for events that happen close to the time of the treatment, and anterograde amnesia, the rapid forgetting of new material (APA, 2001; Lisanby et al., 2000; Weiner, 2000). The retrograde effects can extend to several months before and a few weeks after treatment and the older memories may return with time, whereas the anterograde amnesia is more temporary, clearing up in a few weeks after treatment. Only a very few patients suffer more severe and long-lasting cognitive difficulties, and it is not easy to determine whether these difficulties originate with the treatment or the disorder the person exhibits (Smith, 2001).

ECT as it is done today makes an effort to reduce as many side effects as possible. The modern patient is given muscle relaxants to reduce the effects of the convulsion as well as a very short-term anesthetic. In some cases, the electrodes used to induce the shock are placed on both sides of the head (**bilateral ECT**) and in others only on one side and the forehead (**unilateral ECT**). Unilateral ECT causes less severe muscular convulsions and less severe memory and cognitive problems and has been shown to be just as effective as bilateral ECT (Sackeim et al., 2000).

PSYCHOSURGERY

15.23 *What is the history of psychosurgery, and how is it used today?*

Just as surgery involves cutting into the body, **psychosurgery** involves cutting into the brain to remove or destroy brain tissue for the purpose of relieving symptoms of mental disorders. One of the earliest and best-known psychosurgical techniques is the **prefrontal lobotomy**, in which the connections of the prefrontal lobes of the brain to the rear portions of the brain are severed. The lobotomy was developed in 1935 by Portuguese neurologist Dr. Antonio Egas Moniz, who was awarded the Nobel prize in medicine for his contribution to psychosurgery (Cosgrove & Rauch, 1995; Freeman & Watts, 1937).

But I thought lobotomies left most people worse off than before—didn't it take away their emotions or something? Although it is true that some of the early lobotomy patients did seem less agitated, anxious, and delusional, it is also true that some early patients did not survive the surgery (about 6 percent died, in fact) and others were left with negative changes in personality: apathy, lack of emotional response, intellectual dullness, and childishness, to name a few. Fortunately, the development of antipsychotic drugs, beginning with chlorpromazine, together with the results of long-term studies that highlighted serious side effects of lobotomies, led to the discontinuation of lobotomies as a psychosurgical technique (Cosgrove & Rauch, 1995; Swayze, 1995). Some famous recipients of the last decades of lobotomies (and the disorders for which the procedure was performed) were actress Francis Farmer (alcoholism), Rosemary Kennedy, sister of John F. Kennedy (mild mental retardation), and Rose Williams, sister of playwright Tennessee Williams (schizophrenia).

Are there any psychosurgical techniques in use today since the lobotomy is no longer used? The lobotomy is gone, but there is a modern replacement called the **bilateral cingulotomy**, in which magnetic resonance imaging LINK to *Chapter Two: The Biological Perspective, p. 62,* is used to guide an electrode to a specific area of the brain called the cingulated gyrus. This area connects the frontal lobes to the limbic system, which controls emotional reactions. By running a current through the electrode, a very small and specific area of brain cells can be destroyed. This process is called *deep lesioning.* LINK to *Chapter Two: The Biological Perspective, p. 60.* Cingulotomies have been shown to be effective in about one-third to one-half of cases of major depression, bipolar disorder, and certain forms of obsessive-compulsive disorder that have not responded to any other therapy techniques (Dougherty et al., 2002; Spangler et al., 1996). Because this is deliberate brain damage and quite permanent, all other possible treatments must be exhausted before a bilateral cingulotomy will be performed and, unlike the early days of lobotomies, it can be performed only with the patient's full and informed consent (Rodgers, 1992; Spangler et al., 1996). In fact, because of the ethical, social, and legal implications of psychosurgery in general, today only a very small number of such surgeries are carried out in a few medical centers across the world (Cosgrove & Rauch, 1995).

The woman on the left is Rosemary Kennedy, sister of President John F. Kennedy. The man on the right is her father, U.S. Ambassador to Great Britain Joseph Kennedy. About six years after this photograph was taken, Rosemary, who was mildly mentally retarded and whose behavior had become difficult to control, was subjected to a prefrontal lobotomy. The results were disastrous, and she remained institutionalized until her death on January 7th, 2005.

PRACTICE QUIZ: HOW MUCH DO YOU REMEMBER?

Pick the best answer.

1. Which of the following statements about the effectiveness of psychotherapy is FALSE?
   a. In surveys, 75 to 90 percent of people reported that therapy has helped them.
   b. The longer a person stays in therapy, the less effective it is.
   c. Psychotherapy without drugs seems to work as well as psychotherapy with drugs.
   d. No one psychotherapy is effective for all disorders.

2. For psychotherapy to be effective,
   a. the therapist must provide a protected setting for clients to reveal their feelings.
   b. the therapist should maintain emotional distance from the client.
   c. clients and therapists should avoid warmth in their relationship.
   d. therapists should choose one style of therapy for all of their clients.

3. Of the following, all are potential barriers to effective therapy listed by Sue & Sue (2003) when culture or ethnic backgrounds of therapist and client are different except
   a. language.
   b. cultural values.
   c. social class.
   d. gender.

4. The newest drugs being developed to treat psychotic symptoms are the
   a. typical neuroleptics.
   b. atypical neuroleptics.
   c. anticonvulsants.
   d. partial dopamine agonists.

5. For which disorders have antidepressants NOT been used?
   a. panic disorder
   b. dissociative amnesia
   c. obsessive-compulsive disorder
   d. post-traumatic stress disorder

6. Electroconvulsive shock therapy is useful in preventing suicide attempts because it
   a. is more effective than drug therapies.
   b. has few negative side effects.
   c. works more quickly than antidepressants.
   d. makes people happy.

7. The risk of permanent brain damage is greatest with
   a. cybertherapy.
   b. ECT.
   c. psychosurgery.
   d. bilateral ECT.

Answers: 1-b, 2-a, 3-d, 4-d, 5-b, 6-c, 7-c.

Applying Psychology to Everyday Life: Should Antidepressants Be Prescribed for Children and Adolescents?

15.24 *What are the dangers of treating children and adolescents with antidepressant drugs?*

In recent years there has been a growing controversy over the use of antidepressant drugs for treatment of depression and anxiety-related disorders in adolescents (Breggin, 2003, 2004; Breggin & Breggin, 1994). Although such drugs are approved for use by the Food and Drug Administration in adults, in late 2004 the FDA began requiring drug manufacturers to include a "black box" warning (the most serious type of warning in the labeling of prescription drugs) for all antidepressant drugs (FDA MedWatch Safety Alert, 2004). The warning includes a description of an increased risk of suicide in both children and adolescents and suggests that they be closely monitored. Although the new warning does not forbid the use of these drugs in children and teens, it does strongly urge professionals to weigh the possible benefits of the drug against the possible negative effects.

Wait a minute—how can a drug that's meant to help depression increase the risk of suicide? Children and adolescents are often affected differently by drugs used to treat various disorders in adults. The hormonal and neurological systems—including the serotonin systems—of younger people are not yet fully functional, and drugs that would be harmless in an older person may have harmful side effects in young people. The effects of antidepressants on children and adolescents, however, are not clearly understood.

In one major study published in 2001, researchers conducted what was at that time the largest clinical trial of antidepressant use in cases of adolescent depression (Keller et al., 2001). The researchers concluded that using antidepressants in adolescents was both safe and effective. But in April 2004, researchers published the results of a meta-analysis (a comprehensive scientific review) of both the published and unpublished studies conducted by drug companies that produce antidepressants (Whittington et al., 2004). It was found that although the published research supported the safety of these drugs for use with children and adolescents, the unpublished research indicated that four out of the five drugs tested could lead to increased risk of suicide in children from ages 5 to 18. Prozac was the only antidepressant that did not have an increased risk of suicide for this age group.

Does this mean that children and adolescents should not be given these drugs to treat other conditions? At least one of the drugs in the 2004 study is approved for use in treating obsessive-compulsive disorder in children. When this drug (and possibly others like it) is used to treat anxiety-related disorders rather than depression, there is no apparent increase in risk of suicide.

Obviously, the use of these drugs to treat depression is risky, especially when the research shows that there are safer drugs and alternative treatments. One study found that treating adolescents with a major depression disorder was more successful when the use of the approved antidepressant was combined with psychotherapy (March et al., 2004). Doctors and psychiatrists should exercise caution in prescribing powerful psychoactive drugs meant for adult bodies and nervous systems to younger persons.

Questions for Further Discussion

1. Why would the combination of psychotherapy and drug therapy be more effective in treating depression in adolescents?

2. How much input should a child be permitted to have in his or her treatment process?

▶ Wait a minute—how can a drug that's meant to help depression increase the risk of suicide?

Depression is not only an adult disorder; children and adolescents such as this sad young boy also suffer from depression. Using antidepressant drugs to treat depression in children and adolescents is controversial. What other methods could be used to treat depression in this age group?

15   CHAPTER SUMMARY

Two Kinds of Therapy

15.1   What are the two ways in which psychological disorders can be treated?

- Psychotherapy involves a person talking to a psychological professional about the person's problems.
- Psychotherapy for the purpose of gaining understanding into one's motives and actions is called insight therapy, whereas psychotherapy aimed at changing disordered behavior directly is called action therapy.
- Biomedical therapy uses a medical procedure to bring about changes in behavior.

The Early Days of Therapy: Ice-Water Baths and Electric Shocks

15.2   How were psychological disorders treated in the past?

- Mentally ill people began to be confined to institutions called asylums in the mid-1500s. Treatments were harsh and often damaging.
- Philippe Pinel became famous for demanding that the mentally ill be treated with kindness, personally unlocking the chains of inmates at Bicêtre Asylum in Paris, France.

In the Beginning: Psychoanalysis

- Sigmund Freud developed a treatment called psychoanalysis that focused on releasing a person's hidden, repressed urges and concerns from the unconscious mind.

15.3   What were the basic elements of Freud's psychoanalysis?

- Psychoanalysis uses interpretation of dreams, free association, positive and negative transference, and resistance to help patients reveal their unconscious concerns.

15.4   How is psychoanalysis conducted and viewed today?

- Freud's original therapy technique is criticized for its lack of scientific research and his own personal biases that caused him to misinterpret much of what his patients revealed.
- Modern psychodynamic therapists have modified the technique so that it takes less time and is much more direct, and they do not focus on the id and sexuality as Freud did.

Humanistic Therapy: To Err Is Human

- Humanistic therapies focus on the conscious mind and subjective experiences to help clients gain insights.

15.5   What are the basic elements of Rogers's person-centered therapy?

- Person-centered therapy is very nondirective, allowing the client to talk through problems and concerns while the therapist provides a supportive background.
- The four basic elements of person-centered therapy are reflection of the client's statements by the therapist, unconditional positive regard given to the client by the therapist, the empathy of the therapist for the client, and the authenticity of the therapists in the client's perception.

15.6   What is Gestalt therapy?

- Gestalt therapy is more directive, helping clients to become aware of their feelings and to take responsibility for their choices in life.
- Gestalt therapists try to help clients deal with things in their past that they have denied and will use body language and other nonverbal cues to understand what clients are really saying.

15.7   How are humanistic therapies viewed today?

- Humanistic therapies are also not based in experimental research and work best with intelligent, highly verbal persons.

Behavior Therapies: Learning One's Way to Better Behavior

- Behavior therapies are action therapies that do not look at thought processes but instead focus on changing the abnormal or disordered behavior itself through classical or operant conditioning.

15.8   How do behavior therapists use classical conditioning to treat disordered behavior?

- Classical conditioning techniques for changing behavior include systematic desensitization, aversion therapy, and flooding.

15.9   How do behavior therapists use operant conditioning to treat disordered behavior?

- Therapies based on operant conditioning include modeling, reinforcement and the use of token economies, and extinction.

15.10   How successful are behavior therapies?

- Behavior therapies can be effective in treating specific problems, such as bedwetting, drug addictions, and phobias, and can help improve some of the more troubling behavioral symptoms associated with more severe disorders.

Cognitive Therapies: Thinking Is Believing

15.11   What is cognitive therapy?

- Cognitive therapy is oriented toward teaching clients how their thinking may be distorted and helping clients to see how inaccurate some of their beliefs may be.
- Some of the cognitive distortions in thinking include arbitrary inference, selective thinking, overgeneralization, magnification and minimization, and personalization.

15.12   What are the goals of cognitive-behavioral therapy?

- Cognitive-behavioral therapies are action therapies that work at changing a person's illogical or distorted thinking.
- The three goals of cognitive-behavioral therapies are to relieve the symptoms and solve the problems, to develop strategies for solving future problems, and to help change irrational, distorted thinking.

15.13 *What is rational-emotive behavior therapy?*

- Rational-emotive behavior therapy is a directive therapy in which the therapist challenges clients' irrational beliefs, often arguing with clients and even assigning them homework.

15.14 *How successful are cognitive and cognitive-behavioral therapies?*

- Although CBT has seemed successful in treating depression, stress disorders, and anxiety, it is criticized for focusing on the symptoms and not the causes of disordered behavior.

Group Therapies: Not for the Shy

15.15 *What are the advantages and disadvantages of group therapy?*

- Group therapy has the advantages of low cost, exposure to other people with similar problems, social interaction with others, and social and emotional support from people with similar disorders or problems.

- Disadvantages of group therapy can include the need to share the therapist's time with others in the group, the lack of a private setting in which to reveal concerns, the possibility that shy people will not be able to speak up within a group setting, and the inability of people with severe disorders to tolerate being in a group.

15.16 *What are the different types of group therapy?*

- Group therapy can be accomplished using many styles of psychotherapy and may involve treating people who are all part of the same family, as in family counseling.

- Group therapy can also be accomplished without the aid of a trained therapist in the form of self-help or support groups composed of other people who have the same or similar problems.

15.17 *For whom is group therapy most likely to be a useful form of treatment?*

- Group therapy is most useful to persons who cannot afford individual therapy and who may obtain a great deal of social and emotional support from other group members.

Current Issues in Psychology: What Is EMDR?

15.18 *Does eye-movement desensitization reprocessing really work?*

- Eye-movement desensitization reprocessing, or EMDR, involves moving the eyes back and forth rapidly while concentrating on disturbing thoughts. The disturbing thoughts are supposed to be controlled or eliminated by this process.

- Although studies seem to show that it is effective in treating stress and anxiety disorders, other research has found that it is not always effective and criticize the way in which recovery is measured in the supportive studies. More controlled studies are needed.

Does Psychotherapy Really Work?

- Eysenck's early survey of client improvement seemed to suggest that clients would improve as time passed, with or without therapy.

15.19 *How effective is psychotherapy?*

- Surveys of people who have received therapy suggest that psychotherapy is more effective than no treatment at all.

- Surveys reveal that from 75 to 90 percent of people who receive therapy improve, the longer a person stays in therapy the better the improvement, and psychotherapy works as well alone as with drugs.

- Some types of psychotherapy are more effective for certain types of problems, and no one psychotherapy method is effective for all problems.

- Effective therapy should be matched to the particular client and the particular problem, there should exist a therapeutic alliance between therapist and client, and a protected setting in which clients can release emotions and reveal private thoughts is essential.

15.20 *Is psychotherapy's effectiveness affected by cultural, ethnic, or gender differences?*

- When the culture, ethnic group, or gender of the therapist and the client differs, misunderstandings and misinterpretations can occur due to differences in cultural/ethnic values, socioeconomic differences, gender roles, and beliefs.

- The four barriers to effective psychotherapy that exist when the backgrounds of client and therapist differ are language, cultural values, social class, and nonverbal communication.

- Cybertherapy is therapy that is offered on the Internet. Cybertherapists may or may not be trained in psychotherapy, but cybertherapy offers the advantages of anonymity and therapy for people who cannot otherwise get to a therapist.

Biomedical Therapies

- Biomedical therapies include the use of drugs, induced convulsions, and surgery to relieve or control the symptoms of mental disorders.

15.21 *What are the various types of drugs used to treat psychological disorders?*

- Antipsychotic drugs are used to control delusions, hallucinations, and bizarre behavior and include the typical neuroleptics, atypical neuroleptics, and partial dopamine agonists.

- Antianxiety drugs are used to treat anxiety disorders and include the benzodiazepines and certain antidepressant drugs.

- Antimanic drugs are used to treat bipolar disorder and include lithium and certain anticonvulsant drugs.

- Antidepressant drugs are used in the treatment of depression and include monamine oxidase inhibitors (MOAIs), tricyclic antidepressants, and selective serotonin reuptake inhibitors (SSRIs).

15.22 *How is electroconvulsive therapy used to treat severe psychological disorders?*

- Electroconvulsive therapy, or ECT, is used to treat severe depression, bipolar disorder, and schizophrenia and involves the use of a muscle relaxant, a short-term anesthetic, and relatively mild muscular contractions.

15.23 *What is the history of psychosurgery, and how is it used today?*

• One of the earliest psychosurgeries was the prefrontal lobotomy, in which the front part of the frontal lobe was cut away from the back part of the brain, producing effects ranging from a disappearance of symptoms to a lack of emotional response and mental retardation.

• Modern psychosurgery includes the bilateral cingulotomy, used to treat major depression, bipolar disorders, and certain forms of obsessive-compulsive disorder that have not responded to other forms of treatment.

Applying Psychology to Everyday Life: Should Antidepressants Be Prescribed for Children and Adolescents?

15.24 *What are the dangers of treating children and adolescents with antidepressant drugs?*

• When both published and unpublished studies are taken into account, research has shown that all but one antidepressant drug has been associated with an increased risk of suicide when used to treat depression in children and adolescents.

• Prozac, the one safe antidepressant for children and adolescents, has been found to be more effective when combined with psychotherapy.

15

KEY TERMS

action therapy 562

antianxiety drugs 586

antidepressant drugs 586

antipsychotic drugs 584

arbitrary inference 574

authenticity 567

aversion therapy 570

behavior modification or applied behavior analysis 570

behavior therapies 569

bilateral cingulotomy 589

bilateral ECT 588

biomedical therapies 584

biomedical therapy 562

cognitive therapy 573

cognitive-behavioral therapy (CBT) 574

contingency contract 572

counterconditioning 570

cybertherapy 583

directive 565

eclectic therapies 580

electroconvulsive therapy (ECT) 587

empathy 567

extinction 573

eye-movement desensitization reprocessing (EMDR) 579

family counseling (family therapy) 577

flooding 571

free association 565

Gestalt therapy 567

insight therapies 562

latent content 564

magnification and minimization 574

manifest content 564

modeling 572

nondirective 566

overgeneralization 574

participant modeling 572

personalization 574

person-centered therapy 567

prefrontal lobotomy 588

psychoanalysis 564

psychodynamic therapy 565

psychopharmacology 584

psychosurgery 588

psychotherapy 562

rational-emotive behavior therapy (REBT) 575

reflection 567

reinforcement 572

resistance 565

selective thinking 574

self-help groups (support groups) 578

systematic desensitization 570

therapeutic alliance 582

therapy 562

time-out 573

token economy 572

transference 565

unconditional positive regard 567

unilateral ECT 588

TEST YOURSELF

Pick the best answer.

1. Larisa is going to a therapist to gain a better understanding of what makes her do the things she does. This type of therapy is known as _____ therapy.
   a. insight
   b. action
   c. behavioral
   d. biomedical

2. It was _____ who is most credited with the "moral treatment" movement for using kindness and guidance with the mentally ill.
   a. Sigmund Freud
   b. Josef Breuer
   c. Jean Martin Charcot
   d. Philippe Pinel

3. The actual content of a dream is the _____ content, according to Freud.
   a. repressed
   b. latent
   c. manifest
   d. sexual

4. The psychoanalyst does not start interpreting what the patient has said until _____ has occurred.
   a. positive transference
   b. negative transference
   c. free association
   d. dream analysis

5. In _____, a person-centered therapist must show an honest and open response to the client and not hide behind the professional role of therapist.
   a. reflection
   b. unconditional positive regard
   c. empathy
   d. authenticity

6. Gestalt therapy differs from person-centered therapy because
   a. it is based in humanistic theory.
   b. it focuses on the unconscious mind.
   c. it is directive rather than nondirective.
   d. it is an insight therapy.

7. What kind of person would probably get the least benefit from a humanistic therapy?
   a. one who is bright but confused about self-image
   b. one who is very talkative and open in discussing feelings
   c. oe who enjoys exploring the inner workings of the mind
   d. one who has a hard time putting things into words in a logical manner

8. Lashonna was afraid of dogs. She wanted to get over this fear, so she began by thinking about seeing a dog but staying calm. Then she walked past her neighbor's dog in its fenced yard until she no longer felt afraid. Next, she visited a pet store and petted a dog while the salesclerk held it. Finally, she bought herself a puppy and was no longer afraid. Lashonna's method is most like
   a. systematic desensitization.
   b. aversion therapy.
   c. flooding.
   d. extinction.

9. When the exposure to a feared object is rapid and intense rather than slow and gradual, it is called
   a. systematic desensitization.
   b. aversion therapy.
   c. flooding.
   d. extinction.

10. Carra sat down with her daughter, Morgan, and together they wrote out a list of things that Morgan was expected to do each day and the rewards she would get if she accomplished them, as well as the penalties she would face if she did not do them. This is most like which technique?
    a. token economy   c. extinction
    b. time-out   d. contingency contracting

11. Which therapy style can be compared to a drill sergeant–private style of therapeutic relationship?
    a. person-centered   c. rational-emotive behavioral
    b. Gestalt   d. cognitive

12. Which of the following is not one of the three goals of cognitive-behavioral therapy?
    a. helping the client gain insight
    b. relieving the symptoms and resolving the problems
    c. helping the client develop strategies for future problem solving.
    d. helping the client to think in a more rational, self-helping way.

13. Stephan finds a piece of paper with a phone number he does not recognize on his wife's dresser. He immediately assumes that his wife is seeing someone else and that the phone number belongs to that man. Beck would say that Stephan has engaged in what type of distorted thinking?
    a. arbitrary inference
    b. selective thinking
    c. overgeneralization
    d. personalization

14. Which of the following is a disadvantage of group therapy?
    a. Clients share the therapist's time.
    b. Clients see how other people have handled the problem.
    c. Clients get social support from others.
    d. Clients interact with others socially.

15. When Carson began acting out, her parents took her to a therapist who suggested that her parents may have caused the problem by using the wrong kind of discipline. The kind of therapy that might best help Carson would probably be
    a. a support group of other disturbed children.
    b. an insight therapy.
    c. a cognitive therapy.
    d. family therapy.

16. Which of the following is not one of the problems in studying the effectiveness of psychotherapy?
    a. All therapies take the same amount of time to be effective.
    b. Control groups have no expectations about getting better.
    c. Some therapies measure success differently and are not easily evaluated.
    d. There may be experimenter bias.

17. Cindy is a white, upper-middle-class graduate student in clinical psychology doing her first internship in juvenile court. Her first client is an angry 15-year-old African American boy. Which of the following might be barriers to effective therapy in this situation?
a. social class
b. gender
c. cultural values
d. All of these might be barriers.

18. When a person on an antipsychotic drug develops repetitive, involuntary jerks and movements of the face, lips, legs, and body, this is called
a. the "Thorazine" shuffle.
b. neuroleptic syndrome.
c. tardive dyskinesia.
d. psychotic syndrome.

19. The use of antianxiety drugs to treat anxiety disorders is gradually being phased out in favor of treatment with _____ drugs.
a. antidepressant
b. antimanic
c. antipsychotic
d. sedative

20. Which neurotransmitter is not one of the three that seem to be involved in depression and the drugs that treat depression?
a. norepinephrine
b. serotonin
c. dopamine
d. epinephrine

21. Before the use of electricity, seizures were induced in psychotic patients by means of
a. ice cold water.
b. bloodletting.
c. camphor.
d. opium.

22. In bilateral cingulotomy, the
a. front of the brain is cut away from the back.
b. a thin wire electrode is used to destroy a small area of brain tissue.
c. an electric shock is used to stimulate certain areas of the brain.
d. a drug is injected into the brain to destroy a small area of brain tissue.

23. One antidepressant drug was found to be safe and most effective in treating adolescent depression when combined with
a. other antidepressant drugs.
b. psychotherapy.
c. EMDR.
d. psychosurgery.

Answers: 1-a, 2-d, 3-c, 4-b, 5-d, 6-c, 7-d, 8-a, 9-c, 10-d, 11-c, 12-a, 13-a, 14-a, 15-d, 16-a, 17-c, 18-c, 19-a, 20-d, 21-c, 22-b, 23-b.

For more sample quizzes and other review activities that will help you get a better grade, be sure to check out your accompanying study guide. To access tests and your own personalized study plan that will help you focus on the areas you need to master before your next class test, be sure to go to the on-line Psychology web site available with the access code packaged with your book.

Two Ways of Treating Psychological Disorders

1. **Psychotherapy:**
   ▶ **Insight therapy:** understanding one's motives
   ▶ **Action therapy:** changing disordered behavior
2. **Biomedical therapy:** medical procedures for changes in behavior

15.1

Psychological Disorders in the Past

Mid-1500s: mentally ill people confined in harsh and often damaging asylums

Philippe Pinel: demanded that the mentally ill be treated with kindness

Psychoanalysis: Freud developed psychoanalysis: focused on hidden, repressed urges and concerns from unconscious

15.2

Psychotherapy

PSYCHOANALYSIS

Basic Elements of Freud's Psychoanalysis: Used to Reveal the Unconscious

▶ Dream interpretation
▶ Free association
▶ Resistance
▶ Positive and negative transference

15.3

Today's View of Psychoanalysis

Freud's theory criticized for:
▶ Lack of scientific research
▶ Personal biases causing misinterpretations of patients

Modern modifications:
▶ Takes less time
▶ More direct
▶ Does not focus on id, sexuality

15.4

HUMANISTIC THERAPIES

Humanistic Therapies: focus on conscious mind and subjective experience

Rogers's Person-Centered Therapy

▶ Nondirective
▶ Client talks through problems
▶ Therapist provides supportive background

Four Basic Elements:
▶ Reflection of client's statements by therapist
▶ Unconditional positive regard given to the client by the therapist
▶ Empathy of therapist for the client
▶ Authenticity of therapist in client's perception

15.5

Fritz Perl's Gestalt Therapy

▶ More directive than person-centered therapy
▶ Focuses on the here and now
▶ Empty chair exercise

15.6

Today's Views of Humanistic Therapies

▶ Not based in experimental research
▶ Work best with intelligent, highly verbal persons

15.7

Does Psychotherapy Really Work?

Eysenck's early survey: suggested clients improve with time, with or without therapy

Effectiveness of Psychotherapy

▶ Surveys suggest psychotherapy is more effective than no treatment
▶ 75 to 90 percent of people who receive therapy improve
▶ Longer therapy is better
▶ Some psychotherapies more effective for certain problems
▶ Therapy should be matched to client and problem

15.19

Psychotherapy's Effectiveness and Cultural, Ethnic, or Gender Differences

▶ Misunderstandings and misinterpretations can occur
▶ Barriers to effective psychotherapy: language, cultural values, social class, nonverbal communication

15.20

BEHAVIOR THERAPIES

▶ Do not look at thought processes   ▶ Use conditioning to alter behavior

Behavior Therapists and Classical Conditioning

Uses: systematic desensitization, aversion therapy, flooding

15.8

Behavior Therapists and Operant Conditioning

Uses: modeling, reinforcement and the use of token economies, extinction

15.9

Effectiveness of Behavior Therapy

Effective in treating bedwetting, drug addictions, phobias, and behavioral symptoms associated with severe disorders

15.10

COGNITIVE THERAPIES—THINKING IS BELIEVING

Cognitive Therapy

Teaches client thinking may be distorted

15.11

Goals of Cognitive-Behavioral Therapy

▶ Change illogical or distorted thinking
▶ Relieve symptoms/problems
▶ Develop strategies to solve future problems
▶ Change irrational, distorted thinking

15.12

Rational-Emotive Behavior Therapy

Directive therapy — therapist challenges client's irrational beliefs, often arguing with clients, assigning homework

15.13

Effectiveness of Cognitive Therapies

▶ Successful in treating depression, stress disorders, anxiety
▶ Criticized for focusing on symptoms and not causes

15.14

GROUP THERAPY

Advantages and Disadvantages of Group Therapy

Advantages: Low cost, exposure to others, social interaction, and social/emotional support from others

Disadvantages: lack of privacy to reveal concerns, shy people won't speak up, people may not tolerate groups

Group therapy: can be accomplished using many styles of psychotherapy and may involve family counseling, self-help, or support groups

15.15–17

Biomedical Therapies

Drug Treatments

Antipsychotic drugs: control delusions, hallucinations, and bizarre behavior, include neuroleptics, atypical neuroleptics, and partial dopamine agonists

Antianxiety drugs: treat anxiety disorders, include benzodiazepines and antidepressant drugs

Antimanic drugs: treat bipolar disorder, include lithium and anticonvulsant drugs

Antidepressant drugs: treat depression; include monoamine oxidase inhibitors (MAOIs), tricyclic antidepressants, and selective serotonin reuptake inhibitors (SSRIs)

15.21

Electroconvulsive Therapy

Treats severe depression, bipolar disorder, and schizophrenia — uses muscle relaxant, short-term anesthetic, mild muscular contractions

15.22

Psychosurgery

Earliest form: prefrontal lobotomy can produce symptom disappearance, lack of emotional response, or mental retardation

Modern forms: bilateral cingulotomy, used to treat major depression, bipolar disorders, and certain forms of obsessive-compulsive disorder

15.23

Dangers of Treating Children and Adolescents with Antidepressant Drugs

▶ All but one antidepressant drug are associated with increased suicide risk when used to treat depression in children and adolescents
▶ Prozac more effective when combined with psychotherapy

15.24

Appendix A

STATISTICS IN PSYCHOLOGY

A.1 *Why do psychologists use statistics?*

Why study statistics?

Psychology is a science, and scientists must have ways of describing, summarizing, and analyzing the numerical data gathered through systematic observation and experimentation. Statistics allow researchers to do all of these things in a meaningful, logical fashion.

Many students in psychology wonder why the field uses seemingly such complicated mathematics. The answer is easy. Psychologists base their field on research findings. Data are collected and they have to be analyzed. Statistics is the field that gives us the tools to do that.

Psychologists have to be able to do two things with the data they collect. The first is to summarize the information from a study or experiment. This is the role of **descriptive statistics**. The second is to make judgments and decisions about the data. We are interested if groups differ from each other. We are also interested in how one group of variables is related to another. This second emphasis is known as **inferential statistics**.

Statistical analysis is a way of trying to account for the error that exists in almost any body of data. A **statistic** is typically a number that represents some measure of central tendency or variability. These are described later. Statistics are calculated from a **sample**. The same number calculated from a population is called a **parameter**. If you asked what the average height of teenage males was, and you calculated the average from just your high school, that average, mean would be a statistic. If you tested every teenage male on earth, the average would be a parameter. As you can see parameters are very rarely calculated. Thus, **statistics** is the branch of mathematics that is concerned with the collection and interpretation of data from samples (Agresti & Finlay, 1997; Aron et al., 2005). Psychology is only one of many fields that use the following types of statistics.

Descriptive Statistics

Descriptive statistics are a way of organizing numbers and summarizing them so that they can be understood. There are two main types of descriptive statistics:

- *Measures of Central Tendency.* Measures of central tendency are used to summarize the data and give you one score that seems typical of your sample.
- *Measures of Variability.* Measures of variability are used to indicate how spread out the data are. Are they tightly packed or are they widely dispersed?

descriptive statistics
a way of organizing numbers and summarizing them so that patterns can be determined.

inferential statistics
statistical analysis of two or more sets of numerical data to reduce the possibility of error in measurement and to determine if the differences between the data sets are greater than chance variation would predict.

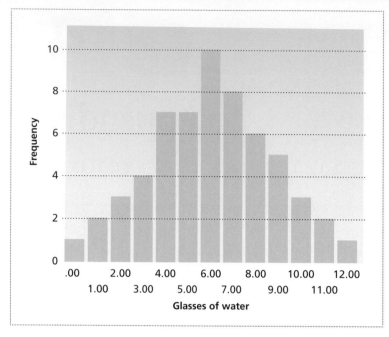

FIGURE A.1   **A Histogram**
Histograms, or bar graphs, provide a visual way to look at data from frequency distributions. In this graph, for example, the height of the bars indicates that most people drink between 4 to 8 glasses of water (represented by the five highest bars in the middle of the graph).

statistic
a measure of central tendency or variability computed from a sample.

sample
group of subjects selected from a larger population of subjects, usually selected randomly.

parameter
a number representing some measure of central tendency or variability within a population.

statistics
branch of mathematics concerned with the collection and interpretation of numerical data.

frequency distribution
a table or graph that shows how often different numbers or scores appear in a particular set of scores.

histogram
a bar graph showing a frequency distribution.

polygon
line graph showing a frequency distribution.

The actual descriptive statistics are best understood after we explain the concept of a frequency distribution.

A.2   *What types of tables and graphs represent patterns in data?*

One way psychologists get started in a research project is to look at their data, but just looking at a list of numbers wouldn't do much good. So we make a graph or chart. Then we can look for patterns.

FREQUENCY DISTRIBUTIONS

A **frequency distribution** is a table or graph that shows how often different numbers, or scores, appear in a particular set of scores. For example, let's say that you have a sample of 59 people, the size of an introductory psychology class. You ask them how many glasses of water they drink each day. You could represent the answers as shown in Table A.1. Just by looking at this table, it is clear that typical people drink between 4 to 8 glasses of water a day.

Tables can be useful, especially when dealing with small sets of data. Sometimes a more visual presentation gives a better "picture" of the patterns in a data set, and that is when researchers use graphs to plot the data from a frequency distribution. One common kind of graph is a **histogram**, or a bar graph. Figure A.1 shows how the same data from Table A.1 would look in a bar graph.

Another type of graph used in frequency distributions is the **polygon**, a line graph. Figure A.2 shows the same data in a polygon graph.

THE NORMAL CURVE

Frequency polygons allow researchers to see the shape of a set of data easily. For example, the number of people drinking glasses of water in Figure A.2 is easily seen to be centered about 6 glasses (central tendency) but drops off below 3 glasses and above 9 glasses a day (variability). Our frequency polygon has a high point and the frequency decreases on both sides.

TABLE A.1   **A FREQUENCY DISTRIBUTION**

Number of Glasses per Day	Number of People out of 59 (Frequency)
0	1
1	2
2	3
3	4
4	7
5	7
6	10
7	8
8	6
9	5
10	3
11	2
12	1

FIGURE A.2   **A Polygon**
A polygon is a line graph that can represent the data in a frequency distribution in much the same way as a bar graph, but allows the shape of the data set to be easily viewed.

normal curve
a special frequency polygon in which the scores are symmetrically distributed around the mean, and the mean, median, and mode are all located on the same point on the curve with scores decreasing as the curve extends from the mean.

bell curve
alternate name for the normal curve, which is said to be shaped like a bell.

A common frequency distribution of this type is called the **normal curve**. It has a very specific shape and is sometimes called the **bell curve**. Look at Figure A.3. This curve is almost a perfect normal curve, and many things in life are not that perfect. The normal curve is used as a model for many things that are measured, such as intelligence, height, or weight, but even those measures only come close to a perfect distribution (provided large numbers of people are measured). One of the reasons that the normal curve is so useful is that it has very specific relationships to measures of central tendency and a measurement of variability, known as the standard deviation.

OTHER DISTRIBUTION TYPES   Distributions aren't always normal in shape. Some distributions are described as *skewed*. This occurs when the distribution is not even on both sides of a central score with the highest frequency (like in our example). Instead, the scores are concentrated toward one side of the distribution. Let's go back to our distribution of water drinking. Look at the frequency polygon shown in Figure A.4.

FIGURE A.3   **The Normal Curve**
The normal curve, also known as the bell curve because of its unique shape, is often the way in which certain characteristics such as intelligence or weight are represented in the population. The highest point on the curve typically represents the average score in any distribution.

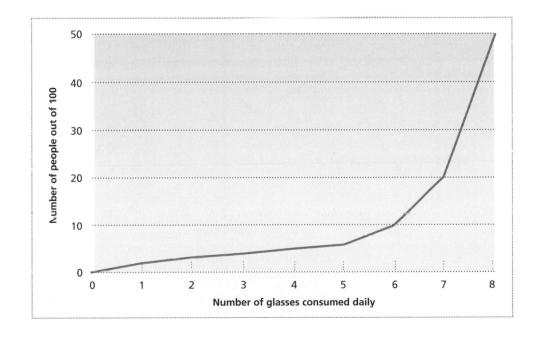

FIGURE A.4   **A Frequency Polygon**
Skewed distributions are those in which the most frequent scores occur at one end or the other of the distribution, as represented by this frequency polygon in which most people are seen to drink at least 7 to 8 glasses of water each day.

FIGURE A.5 Skewed Distribution
These frequency polygons show how distributions can be skewed in two different directions. The graph on the left represents the frequency of heights among hobbits (the little people from the fantasy *Lord of the Rings*) and is positively skewed because the long "tail" goes to the right, or positive direction. The graph on the right shows the frequency of heights among NBA basketball players and is negatively skewed—the tail points to the left.

> A frequency ▶
> distribution looks like a
> good way to look at a
> set of numbers, but
> there's still a lot to look
> at—isn't there some
> way to sum it all up?

In this case, most scores are piled up in the high end with most people drinking 7 or 8 glasses of water a day. The graph in Figure A.5 shows a **skewed distribution**. Skewed distributions are called positively or negatively skewed, depending on where the scores are concentrated. A concentration in the high end, like our figure, would be called **negatively skewed**. A concentration in the low end would be called **positively skewed**. The direction of the extended tail determines whether it is positively (tail to right) or negatively (tail to left) skewed. Here's an example. What do you think about the distribution of heights of hobbits (the little guys from the *Lord of the Rings*) and NBA basketball players (who are usually tall)? Might not these frequency distributions of height be appropriate?

Some frequency polygons show two high points rather than just one (see Figure A.6) and are called **bimodal distributions**. In this example, we have a distribution of test scores and we see that one group of students seemed to do well and one group didn't. Bimodal distributions usually indicate that you have two separate groups being graphed in one polygon. What would the distribution of height for men and women look like?

MEASURES OF CENTRAL TENDENCY

A frequency distribution looks like a good way to look at a set of numbers, but there's still a lot to look at—isn't there some way to sum it all up? There are several ways to sum up numerical data. One way is to find out what a "typical" score might be, or some central number around which all the others seem to fall. This kind of summation is called a **measure of central tendency**, or the number that best represents the central part of a frequency distribution. There are three different measures of central tendency: the mean, the median, and the mode.

A.3 *What types of statistics examine central tendencies in data?*

MEAN The most commonly used measure of central tendency is the **mean**, the arithmetic average of a distribution of numbers. That simply means that you add up

skewed distribution
frequency distribution in which most of the scores fall to one side or the other of the distribution.

negatively skewed
a distribution of scores in which scores are concentrated in the high end of the distribution.

positively skewed
a distribution of scores in which scores are concentrated in the low end of the distribution.

bimodal distribution
frequency distribution in which there are two high points rather than one.

measures of central tendency
numbers that best represent the most typical score of a frequency distribution.

mean
the arithmetic average of a distribution of numbers.

FIGURE A.6 A Bimodal Distribution When a distribution is bimodal, it means that there are two high points instead of just one. For example, in the midterm grades represented on this graph there are two "most frequent" scores—60 and 80. This most likely represents two groups of students, with one group being less successful than the other.

all the numbers in a particular set and then divide them by how many numbers there are. This is usually the way teachers get the grade point average for a particular student, for example. If Rochelle's grades on the tests she has taken so far are 86, 92, 87, and 90, then the teacher would add $86 + 92 + 87 + 90 = 355$, and then divide 355 by four (the number of scores) to get the mean, or grade point average, of 88.75. Here is the formula for the mean:

$$\text{Mean} = \Sigma X/N$$

What does this mean?

- Σ is a symbol called sigma. It is a Greek letter and it is also called the summation sign.
- X represents a score. Rochelle's grades are represented by X.
- ΣX means add up or sum all the X scores or $\Sigma X = 86 + 92 + 87 + 90 = 355$.
- N means the number of scores. In this case, there are four grades.

We then divide the sum of the scores (ΣX) by N to get the mean or

$$\text{Mean} = \Sigma X/N = \frac{355}{4} = 88.75$$

The mean is a good way to find a central tendency if the set of scores clusters around the mean with no extremely different scores that are either far higher or far lower than the mean.

MEDIAN   I remember that sometimes my teacher would "curve" the grades for a test, and it was always bad when just one person did really well and everyone else did lousy—is that what you mean about extremely different scores? Yes, the mean doesn't work as well when there are extreme scores, as you would have if only two students out of an entire class had a perfect score of 100 and everyone else scored in the seventies or lower. If you want a truer measure of central tendency in such a case, you need one that isn't affected by extreme scores. The **median** is just such a measure. A median is the score that falls in the middle of an *ordered* distribution of scores. Half of the scores will fall above the median, and half of the scores will fall below it. If the distribution contains an odd number of scores, it's just the middle number, but if the number of scores is even, it's the average of the two middle scores. The median is also the 50th percentile. Look at Table A.2 for an example of the median.

The mean IQ of this group would be 114.6, but the median would be 101 (the average between Evan with 102 and Fethia with 101, the average of the two middle numbers). This may not look like much of a difference, but it's really a change of about 13.5 IQ points—a big difference. Also, think about measures of income in a particular area. If most people earn around $23,000 per year in a particular area, but there are just a few extremely wealthy people in the same area who earn $1,000,000 a year, a mean of all the annual incomes would no doubt make the area look like it was doing much better than it really is economically. The median would be a more accurate measure of the central tendency of such data.

median
the middle score in an ordered distribution of scores, or the mean of the two middle numbers; the 50th percentile.

◄ I remember that sometimes my teacher would "curve" the grades for a test, and it was always bad when just one person did really well and everyone else did lousy—is that what you mean about extremely different scores?

TABLE A.2 **INTELLIGENCE TEST SCORES FOR 10 PEOPLE**

Name	Allison	Ben	Carol	Denise	Evan	Fethia	George	Hal	Inga	Jay
IQ	240	105	103	103	102	100	100	100	98	95

mode
the most frequent score in a distribution of scores.

bimodal
condition in which a distribution has two modes.

MODE   The **mode** is another measure of central tendency in which the most frequent score is taken as the central measure. In the numbers given in the preceding example, the mode would be 100 because that number appears more times in the distribution than any other. Three people have that score. This is the simplest measure of central tendency and is also more useful than the mean in some cases, especially when there are two sets of frequently appearing scores. For example, suppose a teacher notices that on the last exam the scores fall into two groups, with about 15 students making a 95 and another 14 students making a 67. The mean *and* the median would probably give a number somewhere between those two scores—such as 80. That number tells the teacher a lot less about the distribution of scores than the mode would because, in this case, the distribution is **bimodal**—there are two very different yet very frequent scores.

MEASURES OF CENTRAL TENDENCY AND THE SHAPE OF THE DISTRIBUTION
When the distribution is normal or close to it, the mean, median, and mode are the same or very similar. There is no problem. When the distribution is not normal, then the situation requires a little more explanation.

Skewed Distributions   If the distribution is skewed, then the mean is pulled in the direction of the tail of the distribution. The mode is still the highest point and the median is between the two. Let's look at an example. In Figure A.7 we have a distribution of salaries at a company. A few people make a low wage, most make a midlevel wage, and the bosses make a lot of money. This gives us a positively skewed distribution with the measures of central tendency placed as in the figure. As mentioned earlier, with such a distribution, the median would be the best measure of central tendency to report. If the distribution were negatively skewed (tail to the left), the order of the measures of central tendency would be reversed.

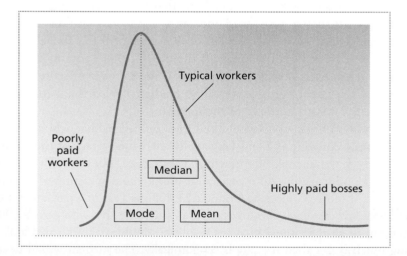

FIGURE A.7   **Positively Skewed Distribution**   In a skewed distribution, the high scores on one end will cause the mean to be pulled toward the tail of the distribution, making it a poor measure of central tendency for this kind of distribution. For example, in this graph many workers make very little money (represented by the mode) while only a few workers make a lot of money (the tail). The mean in this case would be much higher than the mode because of those few high scores distorting the average. In this case, the median is a much better measure of central tendency because it tends to be unaffected by extremely high or extremely low scores such as those in this distribution.

Bimodal Distributions If you have a bimodal distribution, then none of the measures of central tendency will do you much good. You need to discover why you have seemingly two groups in your one distribution.

MEASURES OF VARIABILITY

A.4 *What types of statistics examine variations in data?*

Descriptive statistics can also determine how much the scores in a distribution differ, or vary, from the central tendency of the data. These **measures of variability** are used to discover how "spread out" the scores are from each other. The more the scores cluster around the central scores, the smaller the measure of variability will be, and the more widely the scores differ from the central scores, the larger this measurement will be.

There are two ways that variability is measured. The simpler method is by calculating the **range** of the set of scores, or the difference between the highest score and the lowest score in the set of scores. The range is somewhat limited as a measure of variability when there are extreme scores in the distribution. For example, if you look at Table A.2, the range of those IQ scores would be 240 − 95, or 145. But if you just look at the numbers, you can see that there really isn't that much variation except for that one high score of 240.

The other measure of variability that is commonly used is the one that is related to the normal curve, the **standard deviation**. This measurement is simply the square root of the average squared difference, or deviation, of the scores from the mean of the distribution. The mathematical formula for finding the standard deviation looks complicated, but it is really nothing more than taking each individual score, subtracting the mean from it, squaring that number (because some numbers will be negative and squaring them gets rid of the negative value), and adding up all of those squares. Then this total is divided by the number of scores and the square root of that number is the standard deviation. In the IQ example, it would go like this:

$$\text{Standard Deviation Formula} \quad SD = \sqrt{[\Sigma(X - M)^2/N]}$$

The mean (M) of the 10 IQ scores is 114.6. To calculate the standard deviation we:

1. Subtract each score from the mean to get a deviation score → $(X - M)$
2. We square each deviation score → $(X - M)^2$
3. We add them up. Remember that's what the sigma (Σ) indicates → $\Sigma(X - M)^2$
4. We divide the sum of the squared deviation by N (the number of scores) → $\Sigma(X - M)^2/N$
5. We take the square root ($\sqrt{\ }$) of the sum for our final step. $\sqrt{[\Sigma(X - M)^2/N]}$

The process is laid out in Table A.3.

The standard deviation is equal to 41.9. What that tells you is that this particular group of data deviates, or varies, from the central tendencies quite a bit—there are some very different scores in the data set, or in this particular instance, one extremely different score.

This procedure may look very complicated. Let us assure you that computers and calculators you can buy for $8.00 can figure out the standard deviation simply by entering the numbers and pressing a button. No one does a standard deviation by hand anymore.

measures of variability
measurement of the degree of differences within a distribution or how the scores are spread out.

range
the difference between the highest and lowest score in a distribution.

standard deviation
the square root of the average squared deviations from the mean of scores in a distribution; a measure of variability.

TABLE A.3 FINDING THE STANDARD DEVIATION

Score	Deviation from the Mean $(X - M)$	Squared Deviation $(X - M)^2$
240.00	125.40 (ex. 240 − 114.60 = 125.40)	15,725.16 (125.40^2 = 15,725.16)
105.00	−9.60	92.16
103.00	−11.60	134.56
103.00	−11.60	134.56
102.00	−12.60	158.76
100.00	−14.60	213.16
100.00	−14.60	213.16
100.00	−14.60	213.16
98.00	−16.60	275.56
95.00	−19.60	384.16

Sum of Scores (ΣX) = 1,146.00	$(\Sigma X - M)$ = 0.00	$(\Sigma X - M)^2$ = 17,544.40

Mean = $(\Sigma X)/N$
   = 1,146/10 = 114.60

Standard Deviation
   $= \sqrt{[\Sigma(X - M)^2/N]}$
   $= \sqrt{17,544.40/10}$ = 41.9

How does the standard deviation relate to the normal curve? Let's look at the classic distribution of IQ scores. It has a mean of 115 and a standard deviation of 15 as set up by the test designers. It is a bell curve. With a true normal curve, researchers know exactly what percent of the population lies under the curve between each standard deviation from the mean. For example, notice that in the percentages in Figure A.8, one standard deviation above the mean has 34.13 percent of the population represented by the graph under that section. These are the scores between the IQs of 100 and 115. One standard deviation below the mean (−1) has exactly the same percent, 34.13, under that section—the scores between 85 to 100. This means that 68.26 percent of the population falls within one standard deviation from the mean, or one average "spread" from the center of the distribution. For example, "giftedness" is normally defined as having an IQ score that is two standard deviations *above* the mean. On the Wechsler Intelligence Scales, this means having an IQ of 130 or greater because the Wechsler's standard deviation is 15. But if the test a person takes to determine giftedness is the Stanford-Binet, the IQ score must be 132 or greater because the standard deviation of that test is 16, not 15.

Although the "tails" of this normal curve seem to touch the bottom of the graph, in theory they go on indefinitely, never touching the base of the graph. In reality, though, any statistical measurement that forms a normal curve will have 99.72 percent of the population it measures falling within three standard deviations either above or below the mean. Because this relationship between the standard deviation and the normal curve does not change, it is always possible to compare different test scores or sets of data that come close to a normal curve distribution. This is done by computing a *z* **score** which indicates how many stan-

z score
a statistical measure which indicates how far away from the mean a particular score is in terms of the number of standard deviations which exist between the mean and that score.

Standard Deviations	-4	-3	-2	-1	0	1	2	3	4
Weschler IQ	40	55	70	85	100	115	130	145	160
Stanford-Brown IQ	36	52	68	84	100	116	132	148	164
Cumulative %	0.003	0.135	2.275	15.856	50.00	84.134	97.725	99.865	99.997

FIGURE A.8   **IQ Normal Curve**   Scores on intelligence tests are typically represented by the normal curve. The dotted vertical lines each represent one standard deviation from the mean, which is always set at 100. For example, an IQ of 116 on the Stanford-Binet represents one standard deviation above the mean, and the area under the curve indicates that 34.13 percent of the population falls between 100 and 116 on this test.

dard deviations you are away from the mean. It is calculated by subtracting the mean from your score and dividing by the standard deviation. For example, if you had an IQ of 115, your z score would be 1.0. If you had an IQ of 70, your z score would −2.0. So on any exam if you had a high z score you did well. A low z score means you didn't do that well. The formula for a z score is:

$$Z = (X - M)/SD$$

Inferential Statistics

A.5   *How can statistics be used to determine if differences in sets of data are large enough to be due to something other than chance variation?*

Descriptive methods of statistics are not useful when it comes to comparing sets of numbers or scores to see if there are differences between them that are great enough to be caused by something other than chance variation. **Inferential statistics** consist of statistical techniques that allow researchers to determine the difference between results of a study that are meaningful and those that are merely due to chance variations. Inferential statistics also allow researchers to draw conclusions, or make *inferences*, about the results of research and about whether those results are only true for the specific group of animals or people involved in the study or whether the results can be applied to, or *generalized* to, the larger population from which the study participants were selected.

For example, in Dr. Amabile's classic study described in Chapter One, there were a lot of variables that she simply could not control completely, even with random assignment of her participants to the two conditions (L I N K) *to Chapter One: The Science of Psychology, p. 30.* There was no guarantee that random assignment would take away all of the interfering effects of having children with different artistic abilities at the beginning of the study, or who had breakfast and who didn't, or whether or not some children really didn't want those tacky old prizes anyway. So maybe any difference found between the two groups was due to pure luck or chance and not the independent variable under study.

In any analysis that compares two or more sets of data, there's always the possibility of error in the data that comes from either within the group (all participants in one group, for example, will not be exactly like each other) or differences between groups (the experimental group and the control group are formed with different people, so there are differences between the two groups that have nothing to do with the manipulations of the experimenter). When researchers want to know if the differences they find in the data that come from studies like Dr. Amabile's are large enough to be caused by the experimental manipulation and *not* just by the chance differences that exist within and between groups, they have to use a kind of statistical technique that can take those chance variations into account. These kinds of statistical analysis use inferential statistics.

Inferential statistical analysis also allows researchers to determine how much confidence they should have in the results of a particular experiment. As you might remember, results from other kinds of studies that look for relationships—observations, surveys, and case studies—are often analyzed with descriptive statistics, especially correlations. But experiments look for *causes* of relationships, and researchers want to have some evidence that the results of their experiments really mean what they think they mean.

There are many different kinds of inferential statistical methods. The method that is used depends on the design of the experiment, such as the number of independent and dependent variables or the number of experimental groups. All inferential statistics have one thing in common—they look for differences in group measurements that are **statistically significant**. Statistical significance is a way to test differences to see how likely those differences are to be real and not just caused by the random variations in behavior that exist in everything animals and people do.

For example, in Dr. Amabile's study, her results showed that the collages of the children who were promised the prizes (an extrinsic reward) were judged to be less creative than those of the children who created collages just for fun. But was that difference between the creativity scores of the two groups a real difference, or was it merely due to chance variations in the children's artistic creations? Dr. Amabile used an inferential test on her results that told her that the difference was too big to be just chance variations, which means her results were *significant*—they were most likely to be real differences. How likely? Tests of significance give the researcher the probability that the results of their experiment were caused by chance and not by their experimental manipulation. For example, in one test called a *t*-test, the scores of the children's artwork would have been placed into a formula that would result in a single number (t) that evaluates the probability that the difference between the two groups means is due to pure chance or luck. That number would be compared to a value that exists in a table of possible t values, which tells the researcher the probability of the result is due to chance or luck. If the number obtained by the calculation is bigger than the value in the table, there will be a probability associated with that number in the table. The probability, symbolized by the letter p, will tell the researcher the probability of the difference was due to chance. In Dr. Amabile's case, the probability was $p < .05$, which means the probability that the results were due to chance alone was less than 5 out of 100. Another way of stating the same result is that Dr. Amabile could be 95 percent certain that her results were real and not due to chance. Dr. Amabile would, thus, report that the study found a **significant difference**, which means a difference thought not to be due to chance.

statistically significant
referring to differences in data sets that are larger than chance variation would predict.

***t*-test**
type of inferential statistical analysis typically used when two means are compared to see if they are significantly different.

significant difference
a difference between groups of numerical data that is considered large enough to be due to factors other than chance variation.

There are several statistic techniques to test if groups are different from each other. Here are some common ones you might encounter if you read journal articles.

- *t*-test—determines if two means are different from each other
- *F*-test or analysis of variance—determines if three or more means are different from each other. Can also evaluate more than one independent variable at a time.
- chi-square—compares frequencies of proportions between groups to see if they are different. For example, the proportion of women hired at a company is too low and might indicate discrimination. *Chi* is pronounced like the beginning of the word *Kite*. Don't say *chee*. It will be ugly.

If you do take a statistics course, you will find out that most analyses are done by computers and you don't have to manually go through the long formulas.

A.6 *How are statistics used to predict one score from another?*

We've already talked about the correlation coefficient. Let's see how psychologists can predict one variable from another using it ⓛⓘⓝⓚ to *Chapter One: The Science of Psychology, pp. 24–25.*

correlation coefficient
a number that represents the strength and direction of a relationship existing between two variables.

THE CORRELATION COEFFICIENT

A *correlation* is a measure of the relationship between two or more variables. For example, if you wanted to know if scores on the SAT are related to grade point average, you could get SAT scores and GPAs from a group of people and enter those numbers into a mathematical formula, which will produce a number called the **correlation coefficient**. The correlation coefficient represents the direction of the relationship and its strength. Chapter One (pp. 24–25) discusses correlation in more detail and also emphasizes that correlation does not allow the assumption that one variable causes the other.

Is the formula for the correlation coefficient really complicated? Actually, the definitional formula for finding a correlation coefficient is not very complicated. Here it is:

$$r = \frac{\Sigma Z_x Z_y}{n}$$

The *r* is the *correlation coefficient*, the number representing the strength and direction of the relationship between the two variables. Z_x and Z_y are the Z scores for each score. If you remember, the Z score tells you how many standard deviations a score is away from the mean. You would calculate the Z_x and Z_y for each subject, multiply, and add them up. Then divide by the number of subjects. There is a very complicated looking formula based on the raw scores.

$$r = \frac{\Sigma XY - \dfrac{\Sigma X \Sigma Y}{N}}{\sqrt{\left(\Sigma X^2 - \dfrac{(\Sigma X)^2}{N}\right)\left(\Sigma Y^2 - \dfrac{(\Sigma Y)^2}{N}\right)}}$$

Don't worry. You can do all this work on inexpensive calculators or on computers using common statistical programs or spreadsheets. Let's take the following example of two sets of scores, one on a test of drawing ability with scores from 1 (poor) to 5 (excellent) and the other on a test of writing ability using the same scale:

◄ Is the formula for the correlation coefficient really complicated?

	Drawing (X)	Writing (Y)
Student 1	3	5
Student 2	1	2
Student 3	2	3
Student 4	4	4
Student 5	1	3
Student 6	4	6
Student 7	2	3
Student 8	3	4
Student 9	5	5
Student 10	1	2

If we plugged our data set into our calculator or spreadsheet, we would find that r (the correlation coefficient) equals 0.86. That would indicate a fairly strong correlation. If you go on in statistics, you will find out how to see if the correlation coefficient we calculated is statistically significant or, if you recall, not due to just dumb luck when we picked our subjects. In our case, the r is very significant and would happen by chance only 1 in 100 times!

Remember that the correlation coefficient has values that range between $+1.0$ and -1.0. The closer the r is to these values, the stronger the relationship. A positive r means a positive relationship, whereas a negative r means a negative relationship.

Our example had us trying to see if two scores were related. It is also possible to see if three or more scores are related with various techniques. The most common one is called multiple regression.

A.7 *Why are skills in statistics important to psychology majors?*

We have taken a look at describing data, seeing if groups differ from each other and seeing if two variables are related to each other. Those are the basic ideas of psychological statistics. The more advanced techniques are just bigger and better versions of these ideas. Many psych students sometimes panic at the thought of taking statistics. However, it is crucial to the field and not really that hard if you put your mind to it and don't freeze yourself up. Here's a practical hint. Students with good research and statistical skills are much more employable and make more money than those who don't try to master research skills. It's nice to care about people but you need all the skills you can get in today's world. Statistics and research design is one really profitable set of skills.

A

CHAPTER SUMMARY

A.1 *Why do psychologists use statistics?*

• Statistics is a branch of mathematics that involves the collection, description, and interpretation of numerical data.

Descriptive Statistics

• Descriptive statistics are ways of organizing numbers and summarizing them so that they can be understood.

• Inferential statistics are ways of determining if groups are different and if two or more variables are related.

A.2 *What types of tables and graphs represent patterns in data?*

• Frequency distributions are tables or graphs that show the patterns in a set of scores and can be a table, a bar graph or histogram, or a line graph or polygon.

A.3 *What types of statistics examine central tendencies in data?*

• Measures of central tendency are ways of finding numbers that best represent the center of a distribution of numbers and include the mean, median, and mode.

- The normal curve is a special frequency polygon that is symmetrical and has the mean, median, and mode as the highest point on the curve.

A.4 *What types of statistics examine variations in data?*

- Measures of variability provide information about the differences within a set of numbers and include the range and the standard deviation.

Inferential Statistics

A.5 *How can statistics be used to determine if differences in sets of data are large enough to be due to something other than chance variation?*

- Inferential statistics involves statistical analysis of two or more sets of numerical data to reduce the possibility of error in measurement and determine statistical significance of the results of research.

A.6 *How are statistics used to predict one score from another?*

- The correlation coefficient is a number that represents the strength and direction of a relationship existing between two variables.

A.7 *Why are skills in statistics important to psychology majors?*

- Students who understand the process of research and the statistical methods used in research are more desirable to many university and business institutions than those who lack such skills.

TEST YOURSELF

Pick the best answer.

1. The correlation coefficient provides all of the following types of information EXCEPT:
   a. whether or not there is a relationship between the variables.
   b. the strength of the relationship between the variables.
   c. the cause of the relationship between the variables.
   d. the direction of the relationship between the variables.

2. Another name for a bar graph is a
   a. polygon.
   b. histogram.
   c. normal curve.
   d. line graph.

3. A table that shows how often different scores appear in a set of scores is called a frequency
   a. polygon.
   b. histogram.
   c. normal curve.
   d. distribution.

4. In the set of numbers 2, 2, 2, 3, 5, 5, 6, 8, 15, the median would be
   a. 5.75.
   b. 5.33.
   c. 5.
   d. 2.

5. In the same set of numbers in Question 4, the mode would be
   a. 5.75.
   b. 5.33.
   c. 5.
   d. 2.

6. In a skewed distribution, the scores
   a. have two high points instead of one.
   b. fall to one side of the distribution.
   c. are evenly distributed around the mean.
   d. fall on both sides of the mean.

7. The normal curve is a special kind of
   a. frequency distribution.
   b. scattergram.
   c. measure of central tendency.
   d. pie chart.

8. The normal curve has a special relationship with the
   a. range.
   b. median.
   c. standard deviation.
   d. mode.

9. In the normal curve,
   a. the mean, median, and mode are all on the highest point of the curve.
   b. the mean is on the highest point while the median and mode are on either side of the mean.
   c. the median is on the highest point while the mean and mode are on either side of the median.
   d. the standard deviation is located at the highest point of the curve.

10. What approximate percent of the population is said to fall between one standard deviation above and one standard deviation below the mean on a normal curve?
   a. 50 percent
   b. 34 percent
   c. 100 percent
   d. 68 percent

11. Errors in data
   a. come only from within a group.
   b. come only from between different groups.
   c. come from BOTH between and within groups.
   d. can be completely eliminated by random assignment.

12. When the goal is to compare sets of numbers or scores to see if the differences between them are greater than chance variations, researchers use
   a. descriptive statistics.
   b. inferential statistics.
   c. analytical statistics.
   d. their intuitions.

13. Inferential statistics are used when researchers want to know about
   a. the range of the highest to lowest scores.
   b. causes of differences in data.
   c. central tendencies in data.
   d. variability in data.

14. Dr. Asimov finds that the results of his *t*-test are significant at $p < .01$. That means that he can be
   a. totally certain that the results are not due to chance.
   b. totally certain that the results are due to chance.
   c. 1 percent certain that the results are not due to chance.
   d. 1 percent certain that the results are due to chance.

Answers: 1-c, 2-b, 3-d, 4-c, 5-d, 6-b, 7-a, 8-c, 9-a, 10-d, 11-c, 12-b, 13-b, 14-d.

For more sample quizzes and other review activities that will help you get a better grade, be sure to check out your accompanying study guide. To access tests and your own personalized study plan that will help you focus on the areas you need to master before your next class test, be sure to go to the on-line Psychology web site available with the access code packaged with your book.

Appendix B

APPLIED PSYCHOLOGY AND PSYCHOLOGY CAREERS

A Parent–Teacher Meeting

Why study applied psychology?

Many different kinds of psychologists study or work in many different fields. Whereas early psychologists were still discovering the processes that govern the human mind, today's psychologists are more often applying information and principles gained from research to people in the real world. Why study careers in psychology? With so many different areas of focus, a career in psychology can be varied and exciting. There is much more to psychology than helping people who have mental health problems.

Peggy was a little startled when she received a phone call from her daughter Katrina's grade school counselor. The counselor asked Peggy to come to the school the following afternoon for a conference with Katrina's teachers. At the conference, Peggy was relieved to learn that Katrina, far from being in trouble at school, had been tested and found to be a gifted child. Gifted children are those who score on the upper end of intelligence tests, and Katrina had scored very well indeed.

The counselor and teachers explained that Katrina, as a gifted child, needed to have a special educational plan drawn up to ensure that she received the education best suited to her abilities. This plan is called an **individualized educational program**, or **IEP** (Sellin & Birch, 1981; U.S. Department of Education, 2000). An IEP is required for children with special needs, such as learning problems or intellectual delay, but many school districts also require an IEP for gifted children as well.

Peggy was asked to look at the plan Katrina's teachers and counselor had developed, which included a summary of Katrina's current performance levels and both short-term and long-term goals for her educational future. For example, the counselor and teachers wanted to work on helping Katrina develop better organizational skills and improve her handwriting. Peggy was asked for her input, and then she and the teachers and counselor signed the IEP for Katrina. They told Peggy that a new IEP would be developed for Katrina each year.

Peggy's experience with the IEP is one small example of how psychology can be used in the real world, in this case, by those in the field of *educational psychology* who examine the process of learning and look for ways to improve learning in children and adults. Educational psychology is one of many areas in which psychological principles can be applied to issues and concerns of everyday life. This appendix will look at just some of the areas of applied psychology, as well as the types of careers open to someone who studies psychology today.

What Is Applied Psychology?

B.1   *What is the definition of applied psychology?*

The term **applied psychology** refers to using findings from psychological research to solve real-world problems. The psychological professional, who might be a psychiatrist, psychologist, or even a psychiatric social worker as described here and in Chapter One, may do testing or use some other type of assessment and then describe a plan of action intended to solve whatever problem is of concern. In the opening story, the problem revolved around delivering the best possible education to a gifted child. The counselor tested Katrina in several different ways to determine not only her gifted status but also areas in which she needed help, such as her organizational skills. Then the counselor and teachers used that information to devise Katrina's IEP. This is a practical application of psychological tools to a real problem—the counselor literally "applies" psychology.

It seems to me that psychology could be useful in a lot of different areas, not just education. In fact, wasn't that what all those "Applying Psychology" sections at the end of each chapter were about anyway? Every chapter in this text (and even this appendix) does end with some application of psychology to the real world. The field of applied psychology isn't just one field but rather a lot of different areas that all share the common goal of using psychology in a practical way. A large number of areas can be considered applied psychology, including one of the broadest areas of psychology: clinical and counseling psychology. There are health psychologists who examine the effects of stress on physical as well as mental health, educational and school psychologists, sports psychologists who help athletes prepare themselves mentally for competition, human factors psychologists who deal with the way people and machines interact, forensic psychologists who deal with psychological issues within the legal system, and industrial/organizational (I/O) psychologists who deal with the work environment. There are also environmental psychologists who look at the interaction of people with their surroundings at work, in social settings, and in schools, homes, and other buildings. Those surroundings include not just the physical structures but also the particular population of people who live, work, and play in those surroundings. Other psychologists look at the factors that influence people to buy certain products or the best ways to market a product and examine the buying habits of the typical consumer.

This appendix includes information on the different types of psychological professionals and the type of education required and gives a brief overview of many of the specialized areas in psychology. The rest of this appendix briefly explores how psychology can be used in a practical way in several different areas of life: the environment, law, education, sports, and the world of work.

▶ It seems to me that psychology could be useful in a lot of different areas, not just education. In fact, wasn't that what all those "Applying Psychology" sections at the end of each chapter were about anyway?

individualized educational program (IEP)
a special education plan drawn up by teachers for children with special needs such as giftedness or mental retardation.

applied psychology
the use of psychological concepts in solving real-world problems.

Psychology as a Career

When most people think of psychology as a potential career, they assume certain things about the profession: For example, to help people with their problems one has to be a psychologist, all psychologists are doctors, and all psychologists counsel mentally ill people. None of these things is completely true.

TYPES OF PSYCHOLOGICAL PROFESSIONALS

B.2 *What are the different types of psychological professionals?*

There are several types of professionals who work in psychology. These professionals have different training with different focuses and may have different goals. Chapter One (pp. 16–17) briefly describes the differences among these types of professionals, and that material is expanded in the following descriptions.

PSYCHIATRISTS A **psychiatrist** has a medical doctorate (M.D.) degree and is a medical doctor who has specialized in the diagnosis and treatment of psychological disorders. Like any other medical doctor who may specialize in emergency medicine, treating the diseases of the elderly, treating infants and children, or any other special area of medicine, psychiatrists are able to write prescriptions and perform medical procedures on their patients. They simply have special training in the diagnosis and treatment of disorders that are considered to be mental disorders, such as schizophrenia, depression, or extreme anxiety. Because they are medical doctors, they tend to have a biopsychological perspective on the causes and treatments for such disorders.

PSYCHOANALYSTS A **psychoanalyst** is either a psychiatrist (M.D.) or a psychologist (Doctor of Philosophy or Ph.D.) who has special training in the theories of Sigmund Freud and his method of psychoanalysis. Psychoanalysts of today may be more direct and take less time to get to the heart of a client's problems, but they still follow many of Freud's original principles and methods.

PSYCHIATRIC SOCIAL WORKERS A **psychiatric social worker** is trained in the area of social work and usually possesses a master of social work (M.S.W) degree or a licensed clinical social work (L.C.S.W.) degree. These professionals focus more on the environmental conditions that can have an impact on mental disorders, such as poverty, overcrowding, stress, and drug abuse. They may administer psychotherapy (talking with clients about their problems) and often work in a clinical setting that may have other types of psychological professionals available.

PSYCHOLOGISTS A **psychologist** has no medical training. Instead, psychologists undergo intense academic training, learning about many different areas of psychology prior to choosing an area in which to specialize. Psychologists may have either a doctor of philosophy (Ph.D.) or doctor of psychology (Psy.D.) degree. (People who hold a master of science or M.S. degree are not usually called psychologists except in a few states. They can be called therapists or counselors, or they may be teachers or researchers.)

What's the difference between a Ph.D. and a Psy.D.? The Ph.D. is a type of degree that usually indicates the highest degree of learning available in almost any subject area—psychology, the study of languages, education, philosophy, the sciences, and many others. It is typically very research oriented, and earning the degree usually requires a previous master's degree in addition to course work for the doctorate itself, as well as a dissertation—a scholarly work of research in the area of focus that is as long as a book and may even be published as a book.

psychiatrist
a medical doctor who specializes in the diagnosis and treatment of psychological disorders.

psychoanalyst
either a psychiatrist or a psychologist who has special training in the theories of Sigmund Freud and his method of psychoanalysis.

psychiatric social worker
a social worker with some training in therapy methods who focuses on the environmental conditions that can have an impact on mental disorders, such as poverty, overcrowding, stress, and drug abuse.

psychologist
a professional with an academic degree and specialized training in one or more areas of psychology.

Psychologists specialize in many different areas and work in many different settings. This child psychologist is evaluating the young boy by using puppets and dolls to encourage the boy to talk about his

◀ What's the difference between a Ph.D. and a Psy.D.?

The Psy.D. is a relatively new type of degree developed in the late 1970s that is focused less on research and more on the practical application of psychological principles (Peterson, 1976, 1982). In addition to academic course work such as that required for the Ph.D., this degree may require a major paper instead of a dissertation, with the difference being that the paper is not a report of research designed and conducted by the student but is rather a large-scale term paper. Each year of a Psy.D. program will also require the student to participate in a practicum, an actual experience with observing and eventually conducting therapy and treatments under supervision.

Unlike psychiatrists, psychologists typically cannot prescribe medicines or perform medical procedures. There are some states that allow psychologists to prescribe medication if they have received special education in the use of prescription drugs. In 2002, New Mexico became the first state to allow psychologists to prescribe medications (Josefso, 2002). Prior to this legislation, Guam was the only country to allow psychologists to prescribe drugs to their clients. The reasoning behind this move, for which the American Psychological Association has been lobbying since 1984, involves both cost and the wait for mental health services. If a person sees a psychologist and then has to go to a psychiatrist for medical prescriptions, the cost can be prohibitive. There are also fewer psychiatrists in some states than in others, causing long waits for mental health services from those doctors—delays that can sometimes lead to an increase in suicide rates for patients who are not getting the help they need. This was the main thrust behind the New Mexico legislation, as suicide rates there were 75 percent higher than in the rest of the nation (Josefso, 2002). In 2004, Louisiana became the second state to allow this privilege to psychologists (Spencer, 2004).

Although some psychologists take the special training to become psychoanalysts, many do not. Psychologists who are counselors or therapists may use one or more techniques that have little to do with Freud's original ideas (L I N K) *to Chapter Fifteen, Psychological Therapies, pp. 564–576.* In fact, many psychologists do no counseling at all. There are psychologists who only teach at colleges or universities, those who do only research in those same institutions or for industries, and those who do a combination of teaching and research. Other psychologists are involved in designing equipment and workplaces, developing educational methods, or working as consultants to businesses and the court system.

Although becoming a psychologist requires a doctorate degree of some kind, there are many career fields that can benefit from a four-year degree in psychology as the basis of that career.

CAREERS WITH A BACHELOR'S DEGREE IN PSYCHOLOGY

B.3 *What kinds of careers are available to someone with a bachelor's degree in psychology?*

Although people earning only the baccalaureate (bachelor's) degree in psychology cannot be called psychologists or provide therapy in a private practice, there are many career fields open to such a person. A bachelor's degree in psychology can be highly flexible and adaptable to many different kinds of careers (Schwartz, 2000). In the 1994–1995 *Psychology Baccalaureate Survey* conducted by the American Psychological Association (Grocer & Kohout, 1997), people with bachelor's degrees in psychology found careers in the following areas:

- education and teaching
- consulting and statistical analysis
- administration or clerical services
- professional services
- sales
- health and health-related services
- research and development or research and development management

Constance Newman (left) is a Peace Corps volunteer. Using skills she developed while obtaining a bachelor's degree in psychology, Constance is trying to help this Mbankono woman understand the importance of having her child immunized against diseases such as measles.

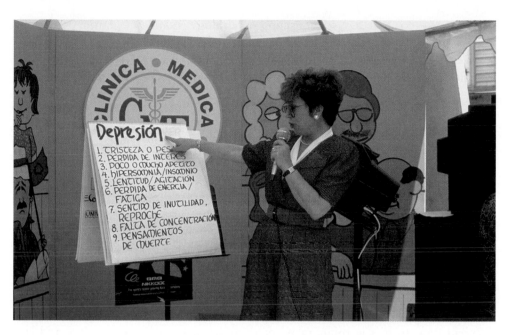

Many people with a bachelor's degree in psychology work in health-related fields, such as this woman who is lecturing about depression at a medical clinic.

Other possible careers include marketing researcher, social worker, and communications specialist (Schwartz, 2000). With its emphasis on critical thinking and empirical observation, psychology trains people for a variety of potential workplace environments and requirements. Psychology is an excellent major even if you intend to do graduate work in some other career: Business, law, child care, teaching, and management are only a few of the areas that relate to psychology.

AREAS OF SPECIALIZATION

You said that some psychologists just teach or do research. What kind of research do they do? There are many different areas in which psychologists may focus their energies. They conduct experiments, surveys, observations, and so on to gather more information for their particular field of interest, to find support for current theories, or to develop new ones. Let's look at some of the areas in which psychologists may specialize.

B.4   *What are the areas of specialization in psychology?*

CLINICAL PSYCHOLOGY   Even though not all psychologists do counseling or therapy, many psychologists do just that. **Clinical psychology** is the most similar of the areas to psychiatry. Clinical psychologists, like psychiatrists, diagnose and treat psychological disorders in people. However, the clinical psychologist can use no drugs or medical therapies (with the exceptions discussed earlier, of course) but instead relies on listening to the client's problems, administering psychological tests, and then helping the client to make positive changes in his or her life by providing explanations for the client's behavior and feelings as well as advising the client on how to make changes. Some clinical psychologists work with many different kinds of people, whereas others specialize in a certain age group, such as children or the elderly, or in a certain type of disorder, such as depression or schizophrenia. They may work in private practice or in hospitals or clinics, and many may also have teaching careers at colleges or universities (L⬤NK) *to Chapter One: The Science of Psychology, pp. 16–18.*

◄ You said that some psychologists just teach or do research. What kind of research do they do?

clinical psychology
area of psychology in which the psychologists diagnose and treat people with psychological disorders that may range from mild to severe.

counseling psychology
area of psychology in which the psychologists help people with problems of adjustment.

developmental psychology
area of psychology in which the psychologists study the changes in the way people think, relate to others, and feel as they age.

experimental psychology
area of psychology in which the psychologists primarily do research and experiments in the areas of learning, memory, thinking, perception, motivation, and language.

social psychology
area of psychology in which the psychologists focus on how human behavior is affected by the presence of other people.

personality psychology
area of psychology in which the psychologists study the differences in personality among people.

physiological psychology
area of psychology in which the psychologists study the biological bases of behavior.

COUNSELING PSYCHOLOGY   Counseling psychology is similar to clinical psychology in that this type of psychologist diagnoses and treats problems. The difference is that a counseling psychologist usually works with people who have less severe problems, such as adjustment to stress, marriage, family life, work problems, and so on. They work in many of the same settings as clinical psychologists but are less likely to work in hospital settings. Counseling psychologists and clinical psychologists make up nearly 60 percent of all psychologists currently in the field (NSF/NIH/USED/NEH/USDA/NASA, 2000) (L I N K) *to Chapter One: The Science of Psychology, p. 17.*

DEVELOPMENTAL PSYCHOLOGY   Developmental psychology is an area that focuses on the study of change, or development. Developmental psychologists are interested in changes in the way people think, in how people relate to others, and in the ways people feel over the entire span of life. These psychologists work in academic settings such as colleges and universities and may do research in various areas of development. They do not provide therapy (L I N K) *to Chapter Seven: Development Across the Life Span, pp. 250–252.*

EXPERIMENTAL PSYCHOLOGY   Experimental psychology encompasses several different areas such as learning, memory, thinking, perception, motivation, and language. The focus of these psychologists, however, is on doing research and conducting studies and experiments with both people and animals in these various areas. They tend to work in academic settings, especially in large universities (L I N K) *to Chapter One: The Science of Psychology, p. 17.*

SOCIAL PSYCHOLOGY   Social psychology is an area that focuses on how human behavior is affected by the presence of other people. For example, social psychologists explore areas such as prejudice, attitude change, aggressive behavior, and interpersonal attraction. Although most social psychologists work in academic settings, teaching and doing research, some work in federal agencies and big business doing practical (applied) research. In fact, many social psychologists are experimental psychologists who perform their experiments in real-world settings rather than the laboratory to preserve the natural reactions of people. When people are in an artificial setting, they often behave in self-conscious ways, which is not the behavior the researcher wishes to study (L I N K) *to Chapter Thirteen: Social Psychology, p. 480.*

PERSONALITY PSYCHOLOGY   Personality psychology focuses on the differences in personality among people. These psychologists may look at the influence of heredity on personality. They study the ways in which people are both alike and different. They look at the development of personality and do personality assessment. They may be involved in forming new theories of how personality works or develops. Personality psychologists work in academic settings, doing research and teaching (L I N K) *to Chapter Twelve: Theories of Personality, p. 444.*

Developmental psychologists study the changes that occur in children and adults as people age. The researcher in the foreground is videotaping this mother and infant as the infant is tested for various developmental skills. Why do you think the researcher is using a videotape rather than just writing down notes?

PHYSIOLOGICAL PSYCHOLOGY   Physiological psychology is an area that focuses on the study of the biological bases of behavior. Many professionals now refer to this area as *neuroscience* or *biopsychology*. Physiological psychologists study the brain, nervous system, and the influence of the body's chemicals, such as hormones and the chemicals in the brain, on human behavior. They study the effects of drug use and the genetic influences that may exist on some kinds of abnormal and normal human behavior, such as schizophrenia or aspects of intelligence. Most physiological psychologists, like experimental psychologists, work in an academic setting **LINK** *to Chapter Two: The Biological Perspective, p. 44.*

COMPARATIVE PSYCHOLOGY **Comparative psychology** is an area that focuses exclusively on animals and animal behavior. By comparing and contrasting animal behavior with what is already known about human behavior, comparative psychologists can contribute to the understanding of human behavior by studying animals. Studying animal behavior also helps people to learn how to treat animals more humanely and to coexist with the animals in a common environment. Comparative psychologists might work in animal laboratories in a university or may do observation and studies of animals in the animals' natural habitats.

Psychologists in these areas may do research that is directed at discovering basic principles of human behavior (basic research) or they may engage in research designed to find solutions to practical problems of the here and now (applied research). There are many other areas in which psychologists may specialize that focus almost exclusively on applied research. These areas are those most often associated with applied psychology.

Psychology and Health, Education, Sports, Law, and the Environment

B.5 *How does psychology interact with the fields of health, education, sports, law, and the environment?*

PSYCHOLOGY AND HEALTH

Health psychology focuses on the relationship of human behavior patterns and stress reactions to physical health with the goal of improving and helping to maintain good health while preventing and treating illness. A health psychologist might design a program to help people lose weight or stop smoking, for example. Stress management techniques are also a major focus of this area. Health psychologists may work in hospitals, clinics, medical schools, health agencies, academic settings, or private practice.

In one recent study, health psychologists examined the effects of social support and social burden (strain in social activities, negative experiences, and the need for taking care of others) on the number of times women went for breast cancer screening in a special study of breast cancer (Messina et al., 2004). The researchers found that women who had more social support and less of a social burden tended to go for screenings more often than women who had less social support and more social demands. Those with higher social demands and less support tended to rely more on self-examination at home rather than clinical tests. Relying only on self-examination without the support of clinical tests such as mammography puts these women at greater health risk. This is a good example of the kind of research that health psychologists conduct. Other areas studied by health psychologists include the influence of optimistic attitudes on the progress of disease, the link between mental distress and health, and the promotion of wellness and hope in an effort to prevent illness **LINK** *to Chapter Eleven: Stress and Health, p. 436.*

PSYCHOLOGY AND EDUCATION

Educational psychology is concerned with the study of human learning. As educational psychologists come to understand some of the basic aspects of learning, they develop methods and materials for aiding the process of learning. For example, educational psychologists helped to design the phonics method of teaching children to read. This type of psychologist may have a doctorate of education (Ed.D.) rather than a Ph.D. and typically works in academic settings.

comparative psychology
area of psychology in which the psychologists study animals and their behavior for the purpose of comparing and contrasting it to human behavior.

health psychology
area of psychology in which the psychologists focus on the relationship of human behavior patterns and stress reaction to physical health.

educational psychology
area of psychology in which the psychologists are concerned with the study of human learning and development of new learning techniques.

This woman is a health psychologist. She is helping this girl to control her fear of receiving an injection by letting her act out giving an injection to a special doll.

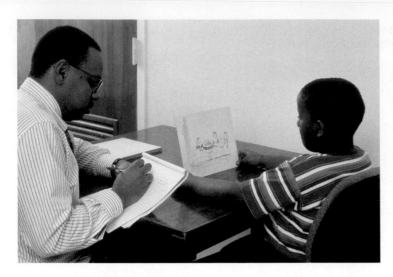

School psychologists often administer tests to assess a child's intelligence or psychological well-being. The young boy's description of the drawing he is holding will help this psychologist determine the boy's emotional state.

What types of research might an educational psychologist conduct? The December 2004 issue of *Journal of Educational Psychology* included articles on the role that students' emotions play in classroom discussions, a method of teaching third-graders to solve mathematical problems, two articles on improving reading comprehension, the effects of parental involvement on children's success in school, and the variables in classroom environments that lead students to cheat or not cheat—just to name a few.

School psychology is related to, but not at all the same as, educational psychology. Whereas educational psychologists may do research and develop new learning techniques, school psychologists may take the results of that research or those methods and apply them in the actual school system. School psychologists work directly with children in the school setting. They do testing and other forms of assessment to place children in special programs or to diagnose educational problems such as dyslexia or attention deficit disorder. They may act as consultants to teachers, parents, and educational administrators. Counseling students is actually a relatively small part of the job of a school psychologist, although counseling takes a much bigger role when tragedies strike a school. When traumatic events such as the unexpected and tragic death of a classmate or even larger-scale tragedies such as the numerous school shootings of the past decade take place, school psychologists are often called on to offer help and counseling to students.

PSYCHOLOGY AND SPORTS

Sports psychology is a relatively new and fast-growing field in which the main focus is on helping athletes and others involved in sports activities prepare mentally, rather than just physically, for participation in sports. The idea behind this field is that a superior physical performance is not enough to guarantee success; rather, the mind must be prepared for the activity by setting clear, short-term goals, holding positive thoughts, using visualization of the goal, stopping negative thoughts, and other techniques based primarily in the cognitive perspective. For example, a sports psychologist might have a basketball player who has been having trouble getting the ball into the net do visualization exercises, mentally seeing himself throw the ball into the net again and again. The famous basketball player, Michael Jordan, attributed much of his success to his ability to remain focused under the most intense pressure. There were other players who were stronger or taller, but Jordan's ability to be calm and direct his energies exactly where he needed them to go is no doubt one of the main factors that set this sports superstar above the crowd. Sports psychologists work in athletic organizations and may have a private practice or do consulting work. (For more on the techniques used in sports psychology, see the Applying Psychology to Everyday Life section at the end of this appendix.)

PSYCHOLOGY AND THE LAW

Psychologists have often been involved in the world of legal matters in various ways. Social psychologists often do research in the areas of criminal behavior and may consult with attorneys or other agents of the court system on such topics as witness credibility, jury selection, and the kind of influences that exist for decision-making processes. Developmental psychologists may become involved in determining the accuracy of and influences on the testimony of children and adolescents, as well as the needs of children caught up in a custody battle between divorced or divorcing parents. Cognitive psychologists may become expert witnesses on the accuracy of memory and eyewitness testi-

school psychology
area of psychology in which the psychologists work directly in the schools, doing assessments, educational placement, and diagnosing educational problems.

sports psychology
area of psychology in which the psychologists help athletes and others to prepare themselves mentally for participation in sports activities.

mony or ways to determine the truth or falsehood of statements made by witnesses or defendants. Clinical psychologists may deliver their services directly to prisoners in prisons and jails or may conduct assessments of intelligence and/or mental status to determine whether or not a person charged with a crime should stand trial.

All of the forms of psychological involvement in legal matters mentioned here can be considered as part of the growing field of **forensic psychology**. Forensic psychology is the practice of psychology related to the legal system and involves examining criminal evidence and aiding law enforcement investigations into criminal activities. As discussed earlier, some forensic psychologists provide information and advice to legal officials such as lawyers or judges, some act as expert witnesses, some actually diagnose and treat criminals within the prison system, and others may administer psychological tests to criminal defendants. Forensic psychologists may aid either the prosecution or the defense in a trial by helping determine which potential jurors would be the best or worst choices. This type of professional may do consulting work in addition to a regular private practice in clinical or counseling psychology or may work entirely within the justice system as a police psychologist, a profiler of serial criminals for federal agencies, or a full-time jury expert, for example.

Forensic psychologists and psychiatrists are often called upon to give testimony in court cases. In this photo, Dr. Park Dietz testifies to the mental state of an accused murderer.

PSYCHOLOGY AND THE ENVIRONMENT

Another broad area in which psychological principles can be applied to solve practical problems is the area of managing the environment. **Environmental psychology** is an area that focuses on the relationship between human behavior and the environment in which the behavior takes place, such as an office, store, school, dormitory, or hospital. Because the concern of researchers in this field deals directly with behavior in a particular setting, research is always conducted in that setting rather than in a laboratory. Environmental psychologists may work with other professionals such as urban or city planners, economists, engineers, and architects, helping those professionals to plan the most efficient buildings, parks, housing developments, or plants, for example.

forensic psychology
area of psychology concerned with people in the legal system, including profiling of criminals, jury selection, and expert witnessing.

environmental psychology
area of psychology in which the focus is on how people interact with and are affected by their physical environments.

PRACTICE QUIZ: HOW MUCH DO YOU REMEMBER?

Pick the best answer.

1. Which of the following professionals in psychology focuses more on the environmental conditions that affect mental disorders?
   a. psychiatrist
   b. psychoanalyst
   c. psychiatric social worker
   d. psychologist

2. Which of the following specialties in psychology is most similar to the medical field of psychiatry?
   a. clinical
   b. counseling
   c. personality
   d. experimental

3. Max is interested in becoming a psychologist. He is most interested in how people become attracted to other people. He would most likely specialize in _____ psychology.
   a. comparative
   b. developmental
   c. sports
   d. social

4. The study of the effects of psychological stress on the growth rate of cancer cells would most likely be the work of a _____ psychologist.
   a. environmental
   b. forensic
   c. health
   d. sports

5. Which type of psychologist would be more likely to administer an IQ test to a child to determine the child's eligibility for a gifted program?
   a. educational
   b. school
   c. developmental
   d. personality

industrial/organizational (I/O) psychology

area of psychology concerned with the relationships between people and their work environment.

human factors psychology

area of industrial/organizational psychology concerned with the study of the way humans and machines interact with each other.

Psychology and Work

B.6 *What are industrial/organizational psychology and human factors psychology?*

Work is a tremendous part of many people's lives. People often spend more time at work than they do with their families or in social activities. One of the largest branches of applied psychology focuses on how psychology can help people in management, productivity, morale, and many other areas of the world of work.

Industrial/organizational (I/O) psychology is concerned with the relationships between people and their work environments. I/O psychologists may help in personnel selection, administer job performance assessments, design work schedules that help workers adjust to new time periods of work hours with less difficulty, or design new work areas to increase morale and productivity. Psychologists in this field may study the behavior of entire organizations. They are often hired by corporations and businesses to deal with the hiring and assessment of employees. They may research and develop ways for workers to be more efficient and productive. They may work in business, government agencies, and academic settings.

A certain kind of I/O specialist, called a *human factors engineer*, focuses on designing machines, furniture, and other devices that people have to use so that those devices are the most practical, comfortable, and logical for human use. **Human factors psychology** consists of these researchers and designers who study the way humans and machines interact with each other. They may work in the design of appliances, airplane controls, and the operation of computers or other mechanical devices. Human factors psychologists tend to work directly in the businesses that design and manufacture the machines they study.

Industrial/organizational psychology got its start near the beginning of the twentieth century with the work of Walter D. Scott, a former student of famed physiologist and founder of the first psychological laboratory, Wilhelm Wundt. Scott applied psychological principles to hiring, management, and advertising techniques (Schultz & Schultz, 2004). He also wrote one of the first books about the application of psychology to industry and advertising, called *The Theory and Practice of Advertising* (Scott, 1908). Another early figure in the newly developing field of industrial/organizational psychology was Hugo Munsterberg, a psychologist also trained by Wundt who conducted research on such varied topics as the power of prayer and eyewitness testimony (Hothersall, 1995). Munsterberg wrote a book about eyewitness testimony called *On the Witness Stand* (1907) and later wrote *Psychology and Industrial Efficiency* (1913).

The field became important during World War I when the army needed a way to test the intelligence of potential recruits. Psychologist Robert Yerkes, who would later become known for his groundbreaking research in comparative psychology while working with the great apes, developed the Army Alpha and Army Beta tests. The Army Alpha test was used with applicants who were able to read, whereas the Army Beta test was administered to applicants who were illiterate (McGuire, 1994; Yerkes, 1921).

In the mid-1920s a series of studies conducted by Elton Mayo for the Western Electric Company (Franke & Kaul, 1978; Parsons, 1992; Roethlisberger & Dickson, 1939) broadened the field. These were the first studies to view the workplace as a social system rather than simply a production line. Rather than treating workers as simply other pieces of equipment, these studies suggested that allowing workers some input into the decision-making

Human factors psychologists design machines that are more practical and comfortable for people to use. For example, this keyboard is designed to reduce the risk of pain in the wrists and increase accuracy in typing.

process not only improved worker morale* but also reduced workers' resistance to changes in the workplace. These studies led the way for others to examine how management of employees and production could be improved. Management theories and strategies may also be applied to other kinds of settings such as schools, colleges, and universities. The following section takes a closer look at the development of these theories.

MANAGEMENT THEORIES

Traditionally managers dealt with workers by assuming that workers did not want to work and, in fact, that workers preferred to be told what to do. This assumption led to developing policies and rules about what workers should and should not do. **Scientific management** was one of the first real attempts to increase the efficiency of workers (Kanigel, 1997; Taylor, 1911). This became a very important goal in the 1920s as industries were struggling to keep up with the demands for mass-produced products following World War I. Proponents of scientific management believed that there was only one best way to perform any particular task. They also assumed that paying money for performing tasks was the only motivator appropriate in the workplace.

In the 1960s, a newer theory of management began to emerge. Douglas McGregor (1960) felt that the older style of management that assumed workers were unmotivated and in need of direction was not the best relationship of managers to the people they managed. He dubbed this old way as "Theory X" and then described his newer style of management as "Theory Y." In Theory Y, work is seen as something that can and should be meaningful for employees, who will actually want to work as long as the work is meaningful to them. Rather than leading people to work under such external controls as the threat of job loss or demotion, managers should help employees feel that they have an investment or commitment in the company's goals. The idea, of course, is that an employee who feels committed to or invested in the goals of the company will be self-motivated, and good performance will be rewarded not simply by paychecks but also by a sense of pride and accomplishment in one's work. McGregor was heavily influenced by the work of Abraham Maslow (1943) and his satisfaction of needs model of motivation ⬤LINK⬤ to Chapter Nine: Motivation and Emotion, pp. 343–345.

These women were participants in one of the early industrial/organizational psychology experiments conducted by Elton Mayo for the Western Electric Company.

MANAGEMENT STRATEGIES

McGregor's Theory Y led to the development of newer strategies for managing workers in the workplace. One of these was *participant management*, in which an effort is made to involve all employees from all levels of the company in the decision-making process. Another related strategy is *management by objectives*, in which specific goals are stated for each employee. Reaching those stated goals or objectives can then serve as a measurement of productivity and performance, and employees know exactly what

*Morale: a sense of common purpose, enthusiasm, confidence, and loyalty.

scientific management
older theory of management, also known as Theory X, in which it is assumed that workers do not want to work and only do so because they are getting paid, and also that there is only one correct way to perform any task.

"Maybe you're right, maybe it won't ward off evil spirits, but maybe it will, and these days who wants to take a chance?

they have to do in order to succeed at their job. If employees feel that they have direct input into all of the decisions made by the company, then they feel personally invested in the product that the company produces. If they know exactly what objectives toward which to direct their efforts, they can monitor their progress and feel a sense of accomplishment as each objective is met (Coye & Belohlav, 1995).

Another innovative management strategy that falls under the concept of participant management is the notion of *quality circles* (Deming, 2000). Quality circles are composed of groups of employees who all work on similar tasks or who share responsibility for a certain area of production. They typically meet on a regular basis to discuss problems and propose solutions for those problems, thus maintaining or improving the quality of the product for which they are responsible.

These management techniques can be applied to situations other than manufacturing of machinery, cars, or other kinds of tangible products. For example, quality circles have been used successfully in the fields of education (Hirshfield, 1983) and health care (Schillemans et al., 1989).

OTHER AREAS IN INDUSTRIAL/ORGANIZATIONAL PSYCHOLOGY

There are many other areas of research and study in the field of industrial/organization psychology. Table B.1 briefly lists some of the areas of specialization.

TABLE B.1 AREAS IN I/O PSYCHOLOGY

Areas in Industry	Areas in Organizations
Job analysis	Social behavior of work teams
Job evaluation and compensation	Job satisfaction
Characteristics critical to effective management	Personality characteristics critical to job performance
Personnel recruiting, selection, and placement	Relationships between management and workers
Occupational training	Leadership characteristics and training
Examination of working conditions	Consumer psychology
Interviewing and testing	Motivational concerns
Performance appraisal and feedback	Conflict management

Pick the best answer.

1. Bernard works in a factory and is responsible for making sure that the office equipment made in the factory is practical and easy to use. He sometimes suggests changes in the design of certain equipment to accomplish this goal. Bernard is most likely what type of psychologist?
a. forensic
b. human factors
c. industrial/organizational
d. management/design

2. One of the early figures in I/O psychology who examined the behavior of eyewitnesses in the courtroom was
a. Wilhelm Wundt.
b. Walter D. Scott.
c. Hugo Munsterberg.
d. Robert Yerkes.

3. The theory that assumes workers want to work and will be more productive if they are committed to the company in some way is
a. Theory X.
b. Theory Y.
c. Theory Z.
d. management by objectives.

4. Fosbender Electronics recently instituted a monthly meeting in which representatives from all areas of the company, from the factory assembly-line workers to upper management personnel, are asked for their input concerning decisions the company is about to make. This style of management is called
a. participant management.
b. management by objectives.
c. quality circles.
d. management by committee.

Applying Psychology to Everyday Life: Techniques Used by Sports Psychologists

B.7 *What are some techniques used in sports psychology?*

Many athletes become frustrated when their performance seems to be less than it could be or when they reach some "roadblock" on their way to achieving new goals. The techniques that follow are designed to help athletes get around the roadblocks and get the most out of their performance. The same techniques are also helpful in the careers of acting, musical performance, professional speaking, teaching, or any career in which there is an element of performance in front of others.

1. *Visualization.* In this technique, athletes try to "see" their performance in their minds as if watching from the sidelines before actually doing it.

2. *Imagery/mental rehearsal.* Similar to visualization, imagery can be used to mentally rehearse the desired performance. Instead of visualizing oneself as if from the sidelines, however, imagery/mental rehearsal involves actually "seeing" and "feeling" the performance in one's mind from one's own viewpoint. This helps prepare the muscles that will be used for action.

3. *Distraction desensitization.* Athletes can be trained to ignore distractions, such as the shouts of spectators.

4. *Thought stopping.* People often have negative thoughts about things that might happen: "I'm going to miss it, I just know it!" is a good example of a negative, self-defeating thought. Sports psychologists train athletes to stop such thoughts in the making, replacing them with more positive thoughts: "I can do this, I've done it before and it was easy."

5. *Confidence training.* Another thing that sports psychologists do is try to build confidence and self-esteem in the athletes who come to them for help. Lack of confidence in one's own abilities is a major roadblock.

Relaxation training is becoming a very important part of any athlete's training. Here, the Wisconsin Badgers college football team participates in a relaxation exercise before the big game. What other career areas might be improved by relaxation training?

6. *Focus training.* Athletes can also be trained to focus attention, often through the use of hypnosis, concentrative meditation, or similar psychological techniques.

7. *Relaxation training.* Athletes can be trained to use special breathing methods, tension and relaxation of muscles, and other tricks for relaxation to reduce anxiety and tension before a performance.

8. *Autogenic training.* Autogenic essentially means "from within the self." In the sense used here, autogenic training involves helping athletes learn about their physiological responses to stress. Once learned, athletes can gain control over these responses, such as learning to slow one's heart rate or lower anxiety.

9. *Fostering realistic goals and expectations.* Sports psychologists try to teach athletes that although setting goals is important, setting unrealistic goals can lead to burnout, frustration, and feelings of failure. Sports psychologists try to help athletes modify their expectations and goals to be more realistic.

10. *Fostering team unity.* Sports psychologists may also work with entire teams of athletes, helping them to become a unit that works as one single "organism" while still providing support for each individual athlete.

A

CHAPTER SUMMARY

What Is Applied Psychology?

B.1 *What is the definition of applied psychology?*

- Applied psychology refers to using psychological principles and research to solve problems in the real world.

Psychology as a Career

B.2 *What are the different types of psychological professionals?*

- The different types of psychological professionals are psychiatrists, psychoanalysts, psychiatric social workers, and psychologists.

- Psychologists hold either a Ph.D. or Psy.D. degree.

B.3 *What kinds of careers are available to someone with a bachelor's degree in psychology?*

- Education, statistical consulting, administration and other business careers, as well as health services are examples of careers that a person with a bachelor's degree in psychology might enter.

B.4 *What are the areas of specialization in psychology?*

- Areas of specialization include clinical and counseling psychology, developmental, experimental, social, personality, physiological, and comparative psychology.

Psychology and Health, Education, Sports, Law, and the Environment

B.5 *How does psychology interact with the fields of health, education, sports, law, and the environment?*

- Health psychology is an area in which the goal is to discover relationships between human behavior, including stress factors, and physical health with the intention of preventing and treating ill health.

- Educational psychologists study the processes of human learning to develop new techniques and methods, whereas school psychologists apply those methods in the school, administer assessments, recommend placement, and provide counseling and diagnosis of educational problems.

- Sports psychologists help athletes prepare themselves mentally for participation in sports.

- Psychologists may act as expert witnesses for legal matters, help in jury selection, provide clinical services to defendants or prisoners, or produce personality profiles of various types of criminals in the field of forensic psychology.

- Environmental psychology looks at the relationship between human behavior and the physical environment in which that behavior takes place.

Psychology and Work

B.6 *What are industrial/organizational psychology and human factors psychology?*

- Industrial/organizational psychology is concerned with how people function in and are affected by their work environments.

- Human factors is a type of I/O psychology in which the focus is on the way humans and machines interact with each other, designing or helping to design the machines used by people in various science and industrial settings.

- Scientific management (Theory X) assumed that work was primarily motivated by money and that there was only one best way to perform any task.

- Theory Y assumes that work should be meaningful for employees, who should have a commitment to the company's goals.

- Other management strategies include participant management, management by objectives, and quality circles.

Applying Psychology to Everyday LifE: Techniques Used by Sports Psychologists

B.7 *What are some techniques used in sports psychology?*

- Sports psychologists use many techniques to help athletes better their performances, including visualization, imagery, thought stopping, confidence training, relaxation training, and fostering team unity.

TEST YOURSELF

Pick the best answer.

1. Carrie would like to work as a psychological professional, but she is not interested in scientific research or in becoming a medical doctor. She would like to be able to call herself a psychologist and provide therapy for her clients. What type of degree would be best for Carrie to pursue?
   a. a master's degree in psychology
   b. a Ph.D.
   c. a Psy.D.
   d. a master's degree in social work

2. The professional most likely to use Freudian concepts in therapy is a
   a. psychiatrist.
   b. psychoanalyst.
   c. psychologist.
   d. psychiatric social worker

3. What type of professional would help people with adjustments to stress, work problems, or marital difficulties?
   a. clinical psychologist
   b. personality psychologist
   c. developmental psychologist
   d. counseling psychologist

4. Dr. Trentenelli is studying the changes that occur in people's memories as they age from youth to late adulthood. Dr. Trentenelli's area of specialization is most likely in _____ psychology.
   a. social
   b. personality
   c. comparative
   d. developmental

5. _____ psychologists do research and conduct experiments with people and animals in the areas of learning, memory, thought processes, perception, and language
   a. Experimental
   b. Comparative
   c. Developmental
   d. Social

6. The view that panic attacks occur because of a malfunction in a small area of the brain normally responsible for alerting the person to real danger is most compatible with which area of specialization in psychology?
   a. developmental
   b. health
   c. physiological
   d. human factors

7. What type of psychologist would be most likely to put together a personality profile of a criminal for the FBI?
   a. industrial/organizational
   b. clinical
   c. forensic
   d. environmental

8. City planners who want the new public library to be accessible to all and logically organized into different areas, each with a different function, might consult what type of psychologist?
   a. developmental
   b. physiological
   c. social
   d. environmental

9. Which type of psychologist is most concerned with increasing productivity of workers by increasing morale and manipulating work shifts?
   a. industrial/organizational
   b. clinical
   c. forensic
   d. environmental

10. The assumption that money is the only true motivator for work is a major feature of
    a. Theory X.
    b. Theory Y.
    c. Theory Z.
    d. quality circles.

11. McGregor's Theory Y was heavily influenced by which of the following theorists?
    a. Darwin
    b. Watson
    c. Maslow
    d. Rogers

12. At Courtland Electronics, the employees responsible for manufacturing a certain product meet on a regular basis to brainstorm solutions to problems in production. This is most like which of the following?
    a. participant management
    b. quality circles
    c. management by objectives
    d. management by committee

13. Suzanne is about to compete on the balance beam and begins to have second thoughts about her ability. She realizes that such negative thoughts will not help and tells herself that this is something she has done perfectly in practice and that she can do it perfectly now. Suzanne's ability to replace her negative thinking with more helpful, positive thinking is a form of
    a. visualization.
    b. thought stopping.
    c. distraction desensitization.
    d. autogenic training.

14. The psychologist tells Michaela that she needs to "be the ball," or try to see herself actually hitting the ball over the net. The psychologist is using
    a. distraction desensitization.
    b. thought stopping.
    c. imagery/mental rehearsal.
    d. focus training.

Answers: 1-c, 2-b, 3-d, 4-d, 5-a, 6-c, 7-c, 8-d, 9-a, 10-a, 11-c, 12-b, 13-b, 14-c.

For more sample quizzes and other review activities that will help you get a better grade, be sure to check out your accompanying study guide. To access tests and your own personalized study plan that will help you focus on the areas you need to master before your next class test, be sure to go to the on-line Psychology web site available with the access code packaged with your book.

Glossary

absolute threshold: the smallest amount of energy needed for a person to consciously detect a stimulus 50 percent of the time it is present. 85

accommodation: as a monocular clue, the brain's use of information about the changing thickness of the lens of the eye in response to looking at objects that are close or far away. 114

acculturative stress: stress resulting from the need to change and adapt a person's ways to the majority culture. 429

acquired (secondary) drives: those drives that are learned through experience or conditioning, such as the need for money or social approval. 337

acrophobia: fear of heights. 531

action potential: the release of the neural impulse consisting of a reversal of the electrical charge within the axon. 47

action therapy: therapy in which the main goal is to change disordered or inappropriate behavior directly. 562

activation-information-mode model (AIM): revised version of the activation-synthesis explanation of dreams in which information that is accessed during waking hours can have an influence on the synthesis of dreams. 141

activation-synthesis hypothesis: explanation that states that dreams are created by the higher centers of the cortex to explain the activation by the brain stem of cortical cells during REM sleep periods. 141

activity theory: theory of adjustment to aging that assumes older people are happier if they remain active in some way, such as volunteering or developing a hobby. 283

adaptive theory: theory of sleep proposing that animals and humans evolved sleep patterns to avoid predators by sleeping when predators are most active. 129

adolescence: the period of life from about age 13 to the early twenties, during which a young person is no longer physically a child but is not yet an independent, self-supporting adult. 274

adrenal glands: endocrine glands located on top of each kidney that secrete over 30 different hormones to deal with stress, regulate salt intake, and provide a secondary source of sex hormones affecting the sexual changes that occur during adolescence. 74

aerial perspective: the haziness that surrounds objects that are farther away from the viewer, causing the distance to be perceived as greater. 112

affect: in psychology, an emotional reaction. 541

afterimages: images that occur when a visual sensation persists for a brief time even after the original stimulus is removed. 92

aggression: actions meant to harm or destroy. 415

aggression: behavior intended to hurt or destroy another person. 505

agonists: chemical substances that mimic or enhance the effects of a neurotransmitter on the receptor sites of the next cell, increasing or decreasing the activity of that cell. 50

agoraphobia: fear of being in a place or situation from which escape is difficult or impossible. 531

agreeableness: the emotional style of a person that may range from easygoing, friendly, and likeable to grumpy, crabby, and unpleasant. 461

AIDS or acquired immune deficiency syndrome: sexually transmitted viral disorder that causes deterioration of the immune system and eventually results in death due to complicating infections that the body can no longer fight. 396

alcohol: the chemical resulting from fermentation or distillation of various kinds of vegetable matter. 151

algorithms: very specific, step-by-step procedures for solving certain types of problems. 298

all-or-none: referring to the fact that a neuron either fires completely or does not fire at all. 48

all-or-nothing thinking: the tendency to believe that one's performance must be perfect or the result will be a total failure. 534

alpha waves: brain waves that indicate a state of relaxation or light sleep. 131

altered state of consciousness: state in which there is a shift in the quality or pattern of mental activity as compared to waking consciousness. 126

altruism: prosocial behavior that is done with no expectation of reward and may involve the risk of harm to oneself. 509

amphetamines: stimulants that are synthesized (made) in laboratories rather than being found in nature. 147

amygdala: brain structure located near the hippocampus, responsible for fear responses and memory of fear. 66

anal expulsive personality: a person fixated in the anal stage who is messy, destructive, and hostile. 449

anal retentive personality: a person fixated in the anal stage who is neat, fussy, stingy, and stubborn. 449

anal stage: second stage occurring from about 1 to 3 years of age, in which the anus is the erogenous zone and toilet training is the source of conflict. 449

analytical intelligence: the ability to break problems down into component parts, or analysis, for problem solving. 318

androgens: male sex hormones. 374

androgyny: characteristic of possessing the most positive personality characteristics of males and females regardless of actual sex. 379

andropause: gradual changes in the sexual hormones and reproductive system of males. 280

anorexia nervosa: a condition in which a person reduces eating to the point that a weight loss of 15 percent below the ideal body weight or more occurs. 350

antagonists: chemical substances that block or reduce a cell's response to the action of other chemicals or neurotransmitters. 50

anterograde amnesia: loss of memory from the point of injury or trauma forward, or the inability to form new long-term memories. 220

antianxiety drugs: drugs used to treat and calm anxiety reactions, typically minor tranquilizers. 586

antidepressant drugs: drugs used to treat depression and anxiety. 586

antipsychotic drugs: drugs used to treat psychotic symptoms such as delusions, hallucinations, and other bizarre behavior. 584

antisocial personality disorder: disorder in which a person has no morals or conscience and often behaves in an impulsive manner without regard for the consequences of that behavior. 549

anxiety disorders: disorders in which the main symptom is excessive or unrealistic anxiety and fearfulness. 530

applied behavior analysis (ABA): modern term for a form of behavior modification that uses shaping techniques to mold a desired behavior or response. 190

applied psychology: the use of psychological concepts in solving real-world problems. B-2

approach–approach conflict: conflict occurring when a person must choose between two desirable goals. 417

approach–avoidance conflict: conflict occurring when a person must choose or not choose a goal that has both positive and negative aspects. 418

arbitrary inference: distortion of thinking in which a person draws a conclusion that is not based on any evidence. 574

archetypes: Jung's collective, universal human memories. 452

arousal theory: theory of motivation in which people are said to have an optimal (best or ideal) level of tension that they seek to maintain by increasing or decreasing stimulation. 341

artificial intelligence (AI): the creation of a machine that can think like a human. 300

association areas: areas within each lobe of the cortex responsible for the coordination and interpretation of information, as well as higher mental processing. 69

attachment: the emotional bond between an infant and the primary caregiver. 270

attitude: a tendency to respond positively or negatively toward a certain person, object, idea, or situation. 488

attribution: the process of explaining one's own behavior and the behavior of others. 496

attribution theory: the theory of how people make attributions. 496

auditory canal: short tunnel that runs from the pinna to the eardrum. 96

auditory learners: people who learn best by hearing and saying things out loud. I-2

auditory nerve: bundle of axons from the hair cells in the inner ear. 97

authenticity: the genuine, open, and honest response of the therapist to the client. 567

autobiographical memory: the memory for events and facts related to one's personal life story. 239

automatic encoding: tendency of certain kinds of information to enter long-term memory with little or no effortful encoding. 229

autonomic nervous system (ANS): division of the PNS consisting of nerves that control all of the involuntary muscles, organs, and glands. 56

autonomy versus shame and doubt: second stage of personality development in which the toddler strives for physical independence. 273

aversion therapy: form of behavioral therapy in which an undesirable behavior is paired with an aversive stimulus to reduce the frequency of the behavior. 570

avoidance–avoidance conflict: conflict occurring when a person must choose between two undesirable goals. 418

axon: tube like structure that carries the neural message to other cells. 45

axon terminals: branches at the end of the axon. 49

barbiturates: depressant drugs that have a sedative effect. 150

basal metabolic rate (BMR): the rate at which the body burns energy when the organism is resting. 347

basic anxiety: anxiety created when a child is born into the bigger and more powerful world of older children and adults. 453

basic level type: an example of a type of concept around which other similar concepts are organized, such as "dog," "cat," or "pear." 296

behavior modification or applied behavior analysis: the use of learning techniques to modify or change undesirable behavior and increase desirable behavior. 570

behavior modification: the use of operant conditioning techniques to bring about desired changes in behavior. 190

behavior therapies: action therapies based on the principles of classical and operant conditioning and aimed at changing disordered behavior without concern for the original causes of such behavior. 569

behavioral genetics: field of study devoted to discovering the genetic bases for personality characteristics. 462

behaviorism: the science of behavior that focuses on observable behavior only. 10

bell curve: alternate name for the normal curve, which is said to be shaped like a bell. A-3

benevolent sexism: acceptance of positive stereotypes of males and females that leads to unequal treatment. 379

benzodiazepines: drugs that lower anxiety and reduce stress. 151

bilateral cingulotomy: psychosurgical technique in which an electrode wire is inserted into the cingulated gyrus area of the brain with the guidance of a magnetic resonance imaging machine for the purpose of destroying that area of brain tissue with an electric current. 589

bilateral ECT: electroconvulsive therapy in which the electrodes are placed on both sides of the head. 588

bimodal: condition in which a distribution has two modes. A-6

bimodal distribution: frequency distribution in which there are two high points rather than one. a-4

binocular cues: cues for perceiving depth based on both eyes. 112

binocular disparity: the difference in images between the two eyes, which is greater for objects that are close and smaller for distant objects. 114

biofeedback: the use of feedback about biological conditions to bring involuntary responses such as blood pressure and relaxation under voluntary control. 191

biological model: model of explaining behavior as caused by biological changes in the chemical, structural, or genetic systems of the body. 524

biological preparedness: referring to the tendency of animals to learn certain associations, such as taste and nausea, with only one or few pairings due to the survival value of the learning. 174

biomedical therapies: therapies that directly affect the biological functioning of the body and brain. 584

biomedical therapy: therapy for mental disorders in which a person with a problem is treated with biological or medical methods to relieve symptoms. 562

biopsychological perspective: perspective that attributes human and animal behavior to biological events occurring in the body, such as genetic influences, hormones, and the activity of the nervous system. 14

bipolar disorder: severe mood swings between major depressive episodes and manic episodes. 543

bisexual: person attracted to both men and women. 392

blind spot: area in the retina where the axons of the three layers of retinal cells exit the eye to form the optic nerve, insensitive to light. 90

borderline personality disorder: maladaptive personality pattern in which the person is moody, unstable, lacks a clear sense of identity, and often clings to others. 550

bottom-up processing: the analysis of the smaller features to build up to a complete perception. 116

brightness constancy: the tendency to perceive the apparent brightness of an object as the same even when the light conditions change. 108

Broca's aphasia: condition resulting from damage to broca's area, causing the affected person to be unable to speak fluently, to mispronounce words, and to speak haltingly. 69

bulimia: a condition in which a person develops a cycle of "binging" or overeating enormous amounts of food at one sitting, and "purging" or deliberately vomiting after eating. 351

burnout: negative changes in thoughts, emotions, and behavior as a result of prolonged stress or frustration. 428

bystander effect: referring to the effect that the presence of other people has on the decision to help or not help, with help becoming less likely as the number of bystanders increases. 509

caffeine: a mild stimulant found in coffee, tea, and several other plant-based substances. 149

cannon-Bard theory of emotion: theory in which the physiological reaction and the emotion are assumed to occur at the same time. 357

case study: study of one individual in great detail. 22

catastrophe: an unpredictable, large-scale event that creates a tremendous need to adapt and adjust as well as overwhelming feelings of threat. 409

catatonic: type of schizophrenia in which the person experiences periods of statue-like immobility mixed with occasional bursts of energetic, frantic movement and talking. 546

central nervous system (CNS): part of the nervous system consisting of the brain and spinal cord. 53

central-route processing: type of information processing that involves attending to the content of the message itself. 492

centration: in Piaget's theory, the tendency of a young child to focus only on one feature of an object while ignoring other relevant features. 266

cerebellum: part of the lower brain located behind the pons that controls and coordinates involuntary, rapid, fine motor movement. 64

cerebral hemispheres: the two sections of the cortex on the left and right sides of the brain. 67

cerebrum: the upper part of the brain consisting of the two hemispheres and the structures that connect them. 70

character: value judgments of a person's moral and ethical behavior. 444

chromosome: tightly wound strand of genetic material or DNA. 252

circadian rhythm: a cycle of bodily rhythm that occurs over a 24-hour period. 127

classical conditioning: learning to make a reflex response to a stimulus other than the original, natural stimulus that normally produces the reflex. 167

claustrophobia: fear of being in a small, enclosed space. 531

clinical psychology: area of psychology in which the psychologists diagnose and treat people with psychological disorders that may range from mild to severe. B-5

closure: the tendency to complete figures that are incomplete. 109

cocaine: a natural drug derived from the leaves of the coca plant. 147

cochlea: snail-shaped structure of the inner ear that is filled with fluid. 96

cognitive arousal theory: theory of emotion in which both the physical arousal and the labeling of that arousal based on cues from the environment must occur before the emotion is experienced. 358

cognitive development: the development of thinking, problem solving, and memory. 264

cognitive dissonance: sense of discomfort or distress that occurs when a person's behavior does not correspond to that person's attitudes. 493

cognitive perspective: modern perspective that focuses on memory, intelligence, perception, problem solving, and learning. 15

cognitive perspective: modern theory in which classical conditioning is seen to occur because the conditioned stimulus provides information or an expectancy about the coming of the unconditioned stimulus. 175

cognitive psychologists: psychologists who study the way people think, remember, and mentally organize information. 525

cognitive therapy: therapy in which the focus is on helping clients recognize distortions in their thinking and replace distorted, unrealistic beliefs with more realistic, helpful thoughts. 573

cognitive-behavioral therapy (CBT): action therapy in which the goal is to help clients overcome problems by learning to think more rationally and logically. 574

cognitive-mediational theory: theory of emotion in which a stimulus must be interpreted (appraised) by a person in order to result in a physical response and an emotional reaction. 360

cognitive universalism: theory that concepts are universal and influence the development of language. 325

collective unconscious: Jung's name for the memories shared by all members of the human species. 452

College Undergraduate Stress Scale (CUSS): assessment that measures the amount of stress in a college student's life over a one-year period resulting from major life events. 411

companionate love: type of love consisting of intimacy and commitment. 505

comparative psychology: area of psychology in which the psychologists study animals and their behavior for the purpose of comparing and contrasting it to human behavior. B-7

compensation (substitution): defense mechanism in which a person makes up for inferiorities in one area by becoming superior in another area. 433

compliance: changing one's behavior as a result of other people directing or asking for the change. 483

computed tomography (CT): brain-imaging method using computer-controlled X-rays of the brain. 62

concentrative meditation: form of meditation in which a person focuses the mind on some repetitive or unchanging stimulus so that the mind can be cleared of disturbing thoughts and the body can experience relaxation. 432

conception: the moment at which a female becomes pregnant. 255

concepts: ideas that represent a class or category of objects, events, or activities. 295

concrete operations stage: third stage of cognitive development in which the school-age child becomes capable of logical thought processes but is not yet capable of abstract thinking. 266

conditional positive regard: positive regard that is given only when the person is doing what the providers of positive regard wish. 458

conditioned emotional response (CER): emotional response that has become classically conditioned to occur to learned stimuli, such as a fear of dogs or the emotional reaction that occurs when seeing an attractive person. 172

conditioned response (CR): learned reflex response to a conditioned stimulus. 168

conditioned stimulus (CS): stimulus that becomes able to produce a learned reflex response by being paired with the original unconditioned stimulus. 168

conditioned taste aversion: development of a nausea or aversive response to a particular taste because that taste was followed by a nausea reaction, occurring after only one association. 173

cones: visual sensory receptors found at the back of the retina, responsible for color vision and sharpness of vision. 89

confirmation bias: the tendency to search for evidence that fits one's beliefs while ignoring any evidence that does not fit those beliefs. 303

conflict: psychological experience of being pulled toward or drawn to two or more desires or goals, only one of which may be attained. 417

conformity: changing one's own behavior to match that of other people. 481

conscience: part of the superego that produces pride or guilt, depending on how well behavior matches or does not match the ego ideal. 447

conscientiousness: the care a person gives to organization and thoughtfulness of others; dependability. 461

conscious mind: level of the mind that is aware of immediate surroundings and perceptions. 446

consciousness: a person's awareness of everything that is going on around him or her at any given moment. 126

conservation: in Piaget's theory, the ability to understand that simply changing the appearance of an object does not change the object's nature. 266

consolidation: the changes that take place in the structure and functioning of neurons when an engram is formed. 237

constructive processing: referring to the retrieval of memories in which those memories are altered, revised, or influenced by newer information. 231

consumer psychology: branch of psychology that studies the habits of consumers in the marketplace. 482

contiguity: the tendency to perceive two things that happen close together in time as being related. 109

contingency contract: a formal, written agreement between the therapist and client (or teacher and student) in which goals for behavioral change, reinforcements, and penalties are clearly stated. 572

continuity: the tendency to perceive things as simply as possible with a continuous pattern rather than with a complex, broken-up pattern. 109

continuous reinforcement: the reinforcement of each and every correct response. 182

control group: subjects in an experiment who are not subjected to the independent variable and who may receive a placebo treatment. 27

conventional morality: second level of Kohlberg's stages of moral development in which the child's behavior is governed by conforming to the society's norms of behavior. 277

convergence: the rotation of the two eyes in their sockets to focus on a single object, resulting in greater convergence for closer objects and lesser convergence if objects are distant. 114

convergent thinking: type of thinking in which a problem is seen as having only one answer, and all lines of thinking will eventually lead to that single answer, using previous knowledge and logic. 304

conversion disorder: somatoform disorder in which the person experiences a specific symptom in the somatic nervous system's functioning, such as paralysis, numbness, or blindness, for which there is no physical cause. 535

coping strategies: actions that people can take to master, tolerate, reduce, or minimize the effects of stressors. 430

corpus callosum: thick band of neurons that connects the right and left cerebral hemispheres. 67

correlation: a measure of the relationship between two variables. 24

correlation coefficient: a number that represents the strength and direction of a relationship existing between two variables. A-11

cortex: outermost covering of the brain consisting of densely packed neurons, responsible for higher thought processes and interpretation of sensory input. 66

counseling psychology: area of psychology in which the psychologists help people with problems of adjustment. B-6

counterconditioning: replacing an old conditioned response with a new one by changing the unconditioned stimulus. 570

creative intelligence: the ability to deal with new and different concepts and to come up with new ways of solving problems. 318

creativity: the process of solving problems by combining ideas or behavior in new ways. 304

critical periods: times during which certain environmental influences can have an impact on the development of the infant. 257

critical thinking: making reasoned judgments about claims. 33

cross-sectional design: research design in which several different age groups of participants are studied at one particular point in time. 250

cross-sequential design: research design in which participants are first studied by means of a cross-sectional design but also followed and assessed for a period of no more than six years. 250

cult: any group of people with a particular religious or philosophical set of beliefs and identity. 512

cultural relativity: the need to consider the unique characteristics of the culture in which behavior takes place. 526

culture-bound syndromes: disorders found only in particular cultures. 526

curve of forgetting: a graph showing a distinct pattern in which forgetting is very fast within the first hour after learning a list and then tapers off gradually. 234

cybertherapy: psychotherapy that is offered on the Internet. Also called online, Internet, or Web therapy or counseling. 583

cyclothymia: disorder that consists of mood swings from moderate depression to hypomania and lasts two years or more. 542

dark adaptation: the recovery of the eye's sensitivity to visual stimuli in darkness after exposure to bright lights. 91

decay: loss of memory due to the passage of time, during which the memory trace is not used. 235

declarative memory: type of long-term memory containing information that is conscious and known. 221

deep lesioning: insertion of a thin, insulated wire into the brain through which an electrical current is sent that destroys the brain cells at the tip of the wire. 60

delta waves: long, slow waves that indicate the deepest stage of sleep. 132

delusional disorder: a psychotic disorder in which the primary symptom is one or more delusions. 545

delusions: false beliefs held by a person who refuses to accept evidence of their falseness. 545

dendrites: branchlike structures that receive messages from other neurons. 45

denial: psychological defense mechanism in which the person refuses to acknowledge or recognize a threatening situation. 433

dependent variable: variable in an experiment that represents the measurable response or behavior of the subjects in the experiment. 27

depersonalization disorder: dissociative disorder in which a person feels detached and disconnected from themselves, their bodies, and their surroundings. 539

depressants: drugs that decrease the functioning of the nervous system. 146

depth perception: the ability to perceive the world in three dimensions. 111

descriptive statistics: a way of organizing numbers and summarizing them so that patterns can be determined. A-1

developmental psychology: area of psychology in which the psychologists study the changes in the way people think, relate to others, and feel as they age. B-6

developmentally delayed: condition in which a person's behavioral and cognitive skills exist at an earlier developmental stage than the skills of others who are the same chronological age. A more acceptable term for mental retardation. 312

deviation IQ scores: a type of intelligence measure that assumes that IQ is normally distributed around a mean of 100 with a standard deviation of about 15. 309

diffusion of responsibility: occurring when a person fails to take responsibility for actions or for inaction because of the presence of other people who are seen to share the responsibility. 509

direct observation: assessment in which the professional observes the client engaged in ordinary, day-to-day behavior in either a clinical or natural setting. 469

directive: therapy in which the therapist actively gives interpretations of a client's statements and may suggest certain behavior or actions. 565

discrimination: treating people differently because of prejudice toward the social group to which they belong. 489

discriminative stimulus: any stimulus, such as a stop sign or a doorknob, that provides the organism with a cue for making a certain response in order to obtain reinforcement. 181

disorganized: type of schizophrenia in which behavior is bizarre and childish and thinking, speech, and motor actions are very disordered. 546

displaced aggression: taking out one's frustrations on some less threatening or more available target, a form of displacement. 415

displacement: psychological defense mechanism in which emotional reactions and behavioral responses are shifted to targets that are more available or less threatening than the original target. 415

display rules: learned ways of controlling displays of emotion in social settings. 355

dispositional cause: cause of behavior attributed to internal factors such as personality or character. 496

dissociative amnesia: loss of memory for personal information, either partial or complete. 537

dissociative disorders: disorders in which there is a break in conscious awareness, memory, the sense of identity, or some combination. 536

dissociative fugue: traveling away from familiar surroundings with amnesia for the trip and possible amnesia for personal information. 537

dissociative identity disorder: disorder occurring when a person seems to have two or more distinct personalities within one body. 538

distress: the effect of unpleasant and undesirable stressors. 407

disuse: another name for decay, assuming that memories that are not used will eventually decay and disappear. 235

divergent thinking: type of thinking in which a person starts from one point and comes up with many different ideas or possibilities based on that point. 304

dizygotic twins: often called fraternal twins, occurring when two eggs each get fertilized by two different sperm, resulting in two zygotes in the uterus at the same time. 255

DNA (deoxyribonucleic acid): special molecule that contains the genetic material of the organism. 252

dominant: referring to a gene that actively controls the expression of a trait. 253

door-in-the-face technique: asking for a large commitment and being refused, and then asking for a smaller commitment. 483

double approach–avoidance conflict: conflict in which the person must decide between two goals, with each goal possessing both positive and negative aspects. 419

double-blind study: study in which neither the experimenter nor the subjects knows if the subjects are in the experimental or control group. 29

drive: a psychological tension and physical arousal arising when there is a need that motivates the organism to act in order to fulfill the need and reduce the tension. 337

drive-reduction theory: approach to motivation that assumes behavior arises from physiological needs that cause internal drives to push the organism to satisfy the need and reduce tension and arousal. 337

dysthymia: a moderate depression that lasts for two years or more and is typically a reaction to some external stressor. 541

echoic memory: the brief memory of something a person has just heard. 215

eclectic therapies: therapy style that results from combining elements of several different therapy techniques. 580

educational psychology: area of psychology in which the psychologists are concerned with the study of human learning and development of new learning techniques. B-7

ego: part of the personality that develops out of a need to deal with reality, mostly conscious, rational, and logical. 447

egocentrism: the inability to see the world through anyone else's eyes. 265

ego ideal: part of the superego that contains the standards for moral behavior. 447

eidetic imagery: the ability to access a visual memory for 30 seconds or more. 214

elaboration likelihood model: model of persuasion stating that people will either elaborate on the persuasive message or fail to elaborate on it, and that the future actions of those who do elaborate are more predictable than those who do not. 492

elaborative rehearsal: a method of transferring information from STM into LTM by making that information meaningful in some way. 220

electroconvulsive therapy (ECT): form of biomedical therapy to treat severe depression in which electrodes are placed on either one or both sides of a person's head and running an electric current through the electrodes that is strong enough to cause a seizure or convulsion. 587

electroencephalograph (EEG): machine designed to record the brain wave patterns produced by electrical activity of the surface of the brain. 60

embryo: name for the developing organism from two weeks to eight weeks after fertilization. 257

embryonic period: the period from two to eight weeks after fertilization, during which the major organs and structures of the organism develop. 257

emotion: the "feeling" aspect of consciousness, characterized by a certain physical arousal, a certain behavior that reveals the emotion to the outside world, and an inner awareness of feelings. 354

emotion-focused coping: coping strategies that change the impact of a stressor by changing the emotional reaction to the stressor. 431

emotional intelligence: the awareness of and ability to manage one's own emotions as well as the ability to be self-motivated, able to feel what others feel, and socially skilled. 319

empathy: the ability of the therapist to understand the feelings of the client. 567

encoding: the set of mental operations that people perform on sensory information to convert that information into a form that is usable in the brain's storage systems. 210

encoding failure: failure to process information into memory. 235

encoding specificity: the tendency for memory of information to be improved if related information (such as surroundings or physiological state) available when the memory is first formed is also available when the memory is being retrieved. 225

endocrine glands: glands that secrete chemicals called hormones directly into the bloodstream. 72

environmental psychology: area of psychology in which the focus is on how people interact with and are affected by their physical environments. B-9

episodic memory: type of declarative memory containing personal information not readily available to others, such as daily activities and events. 222

equal status contact: contact between groups in which the groups have equal status, with neither group having power over the other. 502

escape or withdrawal: leaving the presence of a stressor, either literally or by a psychological withdrawal into fantasy, drug abuse, or apathy. 416

estrogens: female sex hormones. 374

eustress: the effect of positive events, or the optimal amount of stress that people need to promote health and well-being. 407

evolutionary perspective: perspective that focuses on the biological bases of universal mental characteristics that all humans share. 15

excitatory neurotransmitter: neurotransmitter that causes the receiving cell to fire. 50

expectancy-value theories: incentive theories that assume the actions of humans cannot be predicted or fully understood without understanding the beliefs, values, and the importance that a person attaches to those beliefs and values at any given moment in time. 342

experiment: a deliberate manipulation of a variable to see if corresponding changes in behavior result, allowing the determination of cause-and-effect relationships. 26

experimental group: subjects in an experiment who are subjected to the independent variable. 29

experimental psychology: area of psychology in which the psychologists primarily do research and experiments in the areas of learning, memory, thinking, perception, motivation, and language. B-6

experimenter effect: tendency of the experimenter's expectations for a study to unintentionally influence the results of the study. 29

explicit memory: memory that is consciously known, such as declarative memory. 222

extinction: the disappearance or weakening of a learned response following the removal or absence of the unconditioned stimulus (in classical conditioning) or the removal of a reinforcer (in operant conditioning). 170

extinction: the removal of a reinforcer to reduce the frequency of a behavior. 573

extraversion: dimension of personality referring to one's need to be with other people. 461

extraverts: people who are outgoing and sociable. 461

extrinsic motivation: type of motivation in which a person performs an action because it leads to an outcome that is separate from or external to the person. 336

eye-movement desensitization reprocessing (EMDR): controversial form of therapy for post-traumatic stress disorder and similar anxiety problems in which the client is directed to move the eyes rapidly back and forth while thinking of a disturbing memory. 579

facial feedback hypothesis: theory of emotion that assumes that facial expressions provide feedback to the brain concerning the emotion being expressed, which in turn causes and intensifies the emotion. 360

false positive: error of recognition in which people think that they recognize some stimulus that is not actually in memory. 228

family counseling (family therapy): a form of group therapy in which family members meet together with a counselor or therapist to resolve problems that affect the entire family. 577

fertilization: the union of the ovum and sperm. 255

fetal period: the time from about eight weeks after conception until the birth of the child. 259

fetus: name for the developing organism from eight weeks after fertilization to the birth of the baby. 259

figure–ground: the tendency to perceive objects, or figures, as existing on a background. 109

five-factor model (Big Five): model of personality traits that describes five basic trait dimensions. 461

fixation: disorder in which the person does not fully resolve the conflict in a particular psychosexual stage, resulting in personality traits and behavior associated with that earlier stage. 448

fixed interval schedule of reinforcement: schedule of reinforcement in which the interval of time that must pass before reinforcement becomes possible is always the same. 184

fixed ratio schedule of reinforcement: schedule of reinforcement in which the number of responses required for reinforcement is always the same. 183

flashbulb memories: type of automatic encoding that occurs because an unexpected event has strong emotional associations for the person remembering it. 229

flat affect: a lack of emotional responsiveness. 545

flooding: technique for treating phobias and other stress disorders in which the person is rapidly and intensely exposed to the fear provoking situation or object and prevented from making the usual avoidance or escape response. 571

foot-in-the-door technique: asking for a small commitment and, after gaining compliance, asking for a bigger commitment. 483

forensic psychology: area of psychology concerned with people in the legal system, including profiling of criminals, jury selection, and expert witnessing. B-9

formal concepts: concepts that are defined by specific rules or features. 296

formal operations: Piaget's last stage of cognitive development in which the adolescent becomes capable of abstract thinking. 266

free association: Freudian technique in which a patient was encouraged to talk about anything that came to mind without fear of negative evaluations. 565

free-floating anxiety: anxiety that is unrelated to any realistic, known source. 530

frequency count: assessment in which the frequency of a particular behavior is counted. 469

frequency distribution: a table or graph that shows how often different numbers or scores appear in a particular set of scores. A-2

frequency theory: theory of pitch that states that pitch is related to the speed of vibrations in the basilar membrane. 98

frontal lobes: areas of the cortex located in the front and top of the brain, responsible for higher mental processes and decision making as well as the production of fluent speech. 68

frustration: the psychological experience produced by the blocking of a desired goal or fulfillment of a perceived need. 414

fully functioning person: a person who is in touch with and trusting of the deepest, innermost urges and feelings. 458

functional fixedness: a block to problem solving that comes from thinking about objects in terms of only their typical functions. 303

functionalism: early perspective in psychology associated with William James, in which the focus of study is how the mind allows people to adapt, live, work, and play. 8

fundamental attribution error (actor-observer bias): the tendency to overestimate the influence of internal factors in determining behavior while underestimating situational factors. 496

g factor: the ability to reason and solve problems, or general intelligence. 317

gender: the psychological aspects of being male or female. 274, 374

gender identity: the individual's sense of being male or female. 274, 374

gender roles: the culture's expectations for masculine or feminine behavior, including attitudes, actions, and personality traits associated with being male or female in that culture. 374

gender schema theory: theory of gender identity acquisition in which a child develops a mental pattern, or schema, for being male or female and then organizes observed and learned behavior around that schema. 378

gender stereotype: a concept held about a person or group of people that is based on being male or female. 378

gender typing: the process of acquiring gender role characteristics. 374

gene: section of DNA having the same arrangement of chemical elements. 252

general adaptation syndrome (GAS): the three stages of the body's physiological reaction to stress, including alarm, resistance, and exhaustion. 420

generalized anxiety disorder: disorder in which a person has feelings of dread and impending doom along with physical symptoms of stress, which lasts six months or more. 533

generativity: providing guidance to one's children or the next generation, or contributing to the well-being of the next generation through career or volunteer work. 282

genetics: the science of inherited traits. 252

germinal period: first two weeks after fertilization, during which the zygote moves down to the uterus and begins to implant in the lining. 256

Gestalt psychology: early perspective in psychology focusing on perception and sensation, particularly the perception of patterns and whole figures. 9

Gestalt therapy: form of directive insight therapy in which the therapist helps clients to accept all parts of their feelings and subjective experiences, using leading questions and planned experiences such as role-playing. 567

gifted: the 2 percent of the population falling on the upper end of the normal curve and typically possessing an IQ of 130 or above. 314

glial cells: grey fatty cells that provide support for the neurons to grow on and around, deliver nutrients to neurons, produce myelin to coat axons, and clean up waste products and dead neurons. 46

glucagons: hormones that are secreted by the pancreas to control the levels of fats, proteins, and carbohydrates in the body by increasing the level of glucose in the bloodstream. 346

gonads: the sex glands that secrete hormones that regulate sexual development and behavior as well as reproduction. 74

grammar: the system of rules governing the structure and use of a language. 323

groupthink: kind of thinking that occurs when people place more importance on maintaining group cohesiveness than on assessing the facts of the problem with which the group is concerned. 482

gustation: the sensation of taste. 101

habits: in behaviorism, sets of well-learned responses that have become automatic. 455

habituation: tendency of the brain to stop attending to constant, unchanging information. 86

hallucinations: false sensory perceptions, such as hearing voices that do not really exist. 545

hallucinogens: drugs that cause false sensory messages, altering the perception of reality. 154

halo effect: tendency of an interviewer to allow positive characteristics of a client to influence the assessments of the client's behavior and statements. 467

hardy personality: a person who seems to thrive on stress but lacks the anger and hostility of the Type A personality. 425

hassles: the daily annoyances of everyday life. 411

health psychology: area of psychology in which the psychologists focus on the relationship of human behavior patterns and stress reaction to physical health. B-7

hermaphroditism: the condition of possessing both male and female sexual organs. 382

heroin: narcotic drug derived from opium that is extremely addictive. 153

hertz (Hz): cycles or waves per second, a measurement of frequency. 96

heterosexual: person attracted to the opposite sex. 389

heuristic: an educated guess based on prior experiences that helps narrow down the possible solutions for a problem. Also known as "rule of thumb." 299

higher-order conditioning: occurs when a strong conditioned stimulus is paired with a neutral stimulus, causing the neutral stimulus to become a second conditioned stimulus. 171

hindsight bias: the tendency to falsely believe, through revision of older memories to include newer information, that one could have correctly predicted the outcome of an event. 231

hippocampus: curved structure located within each temporal lobe, responsible for the formation of long-term memories and the storage of memory for location of objects. 65

histogram: a bar graph showing a frequency distribution. A-2

homeostasis: the tendency of the body to maintain a steady state. 338

homosexual: person attracted to the same sex. 389

hormones: chemicals released into the bloodstream by endocrine glands. 72

human development: the scientific study of the changes that occur in people as they age from conception until death. 250

human factors psychology: area of industrial/organizational psychology concerned with the study of the way humans and machines interact with each other. B-10

humanistic perspective: the "third force" in psychology that focuses on those aspects of personality that make people uniquely human, such as subjective feelings and freedom of choice. 457

hypnosis: state of consciousness in which the person is especially susceptible to suggestion. 142

hypochondriasis: somatoform disorder in which the person is terrified of being sick and worries constantly, going to doctors repeatedly, and becoming preoccupied with every sensation of the body. 535

hypothalamus: small structure in the brain located below the thalamus and directly above the pituitary gland, responsible for motivational behavior such as sleep, hunger, thirst, and sex. 65

hypothesis: tentative explanation of a phenomenon based on observations. 19

iconic memory: visual sensory memory, lasting only a fraction of a second. 213

id: part of the personality present at birth and completely unconscious. 446

ideal self: one's perception of whom one should be or would like to be. 457

identification: defense mechanism in which a person tries to become like someone else to deal with anxiety. 433, 450

identity versus role confusion: fifth stage of personality development in which the adolescent must find a consistent sense of self. 278

imaginary audience: type of thought common to adolescents in which young people believe that other people are just as concerned about the adolescent's thoughts and characteristics as they themselves are. 276

immune system: the system of cells, organs, and chemicals of the body that responds to attacks from diseases, infections, and injuries. 421

implicit memory: memory that is not easily brought into conscious awareness, such as procedural memory. 221

implicit personality theory: sets of assumptions about how different types of people, personality traits, and actions are related to each other. 495

impression formation: the forming of the first knowledge that a person has concerning another person. 494

incentive approaches: theories of motivation in which behavior is explained as a response to the external stimulus and its rewarding properties. 342

incentives: things that attract or lure people into action. 342

independent variable: variable in an experiment that is manipulated by the experimenter. 26

individualized educational program (IEP): a special education plan drawn up by teachers for children with special needs such as giftedness or mental retardation. B-1

industrial/organizational (I/O) psychology: area of psychology concerned with the relationships between people and their work environment. B-10

industry versus inferiority: fourth stage of personality development in which the adolescent strives for a sense of competence and self-esteem. 273

infantile amnesia: the inability to retrieve memories from much before age 3. 239

inferential statistics: statistical analysis of two or more sets of numerical data to reduce the possibility of error in measurement and to determine if the differences between the data sets are greater than chance variation would predict. A-1

information-processing model: model of memory that assumes the processing of information for memory storage is similar to the way a computer processes memory in a series of three stages. 211

in-groups: social groups with whom a person identifies; "us." 499

inhibitory neurotransmitter: neurotransmitter that causes the receiving cell to stop firing. 50

initiative versus guilt: third stage of personality development in which the preschool-aged child strives for emotional and psychological independence and attempts to satisfy curiosity about the world. 273

insight: the sudden perception of relationships among various parts of a problem, allowing the solution to the problem to come quickly. 195

insight therapies: therapies in which the main goal is helping people to gain insight with respect to their behavior, thoughts, and feelings. 562

insomnia: the inability to get to sleep, stay asleep, or get a good quality of sleep. 137

instinct approach: approach to motivation that assumes people are governed by instincts similar to those of animals. 337

instinctive drift: tendency for an animal's behavior to revert to genetically controlled patterns. 189

instincts: the biologically determined and innate patterns of behavior that exist in both people and animals. 336

insulin: a hormone secreted by the pancreas to control the levels of fats, proteins, and carbohydrates in the body by reducing the level of glucose in the bloodstream. 346

integrity: sense of wholeness that comes from having lived a full life and the ability to let go of regrets; the final completion of the ego. 282

intelligence: the ability to learn from one's experiences, acquire knowledge, and use resources effectively in adapting to new situations or solving problems. 306

intelligence quotient (IQ): a number representing a measure of intelligence, resulting from the division of one's mental age by one's chronological age and then multiplying that quotient by 100. 306

interneuron: a neuron found in the center of the spinal cord that receives information from the sensory neurons and sends commands to the muscles through the motor neurons. Interneurons also make up the bulk of the neurons in the brain. 54

interpersonal attraction: liking or having the desire for a relationship with another person. 503

interposition (overlap): the assumption that an object that appears to be blocking part of another object is in front of the second object and closer to the viewer. 112

intersex: alternate term for hermaphroditism. 383

intersexed, intersexual: a person who possesses ambiguous sexual organs, making it difficult to determine actual sex from a visual inspection at birth. 382

interview: method of personality assessment in which the professional asks questions of the client and allows the client to answer, either in a structured or unstructured fashion. 466

intimacy: an emotional and psychological closeness that is based on the ability to trust, share, and care, while still maintaining a sense of self. 281

intrinsic motivation: type of motivation in which a person performs an action because the act itself is rewarding or satisfying in some internal manner. 345

introversion: dimension of personality in which people tend to withdraw from excessive stimulation. 460

introverts: people who prefer solitude and dislike being the center of attention. 461

irreversibility: in Piaget's theory, the inability of the young child to mentally reverse an action. 266

James-Lange theory of emotion: theory in which a physiological reaction leads to the labeling of an emotion. 357

"jigsaw classroom": educational technique in which each individual is given only part of the information needed to solve a problem, causing the separate individuals to be forced to work together to find the solution. 502

just noticeable difference (jnd or the differential threshold): the smallest difference between two stimuli that is detectable 50 percent of the time. 84

kinesthetic learners: people who prefer to learn by doing and being active. I-2

kinesthetic sense: sense of the location of body parts in relation to the ground and each other. 104

language: a system for combining symbols (such as words) so that an unlimited number of meaningful statements can be made for the purpose of communicating with others. 323

latency: fourth stage occurring during the school years, in which the sexual feelings of the child are repressed while the child develops in other ways. 451

latent content: the symbolic or hidden meaning of dreams. 564

latent learning: learning that remains hidden until its application becomes useful. 194

Law of Effect: law stating that if a response is followed by a pleasurable consequence, it will tend to be repeated, and if followed by an unpleasant consequence, it will tend not to be repeated. 176

learned helplessness: the tendency to fail to act to escape from a situation because of a history of repeated failures in the past. 195

learning style the particular way in which a person takes in information. I-2

learning/performance distinction: referring to the observation that learning can take place without actual performance of the learned behavior. 196

leptin: a hormone that, when released into the bloodstream, signals the hypothalamus that the body has had enough food and reduces the appetite while increasing the feeling of being full. 349

levels-of-processing model: model of memory that assumes information that is more "deeply processed," or processed according to its meaning rather than just the sound or physical characteristics of the word or words, will be remembered more efficiently and for a longer period of time. 212

libido: the instinctual energy that may come into conflict with the demands of a society's standards for behavior. 446

light adaptation: the recovery of the eye's sensitivity to visual stimuli in light after exposure to darkness. 91

limbic system: a group of several brain structures located under the cortex and involved in learning, emotion, memory, and motivation. 65

linear perspective: the tendency for parallel lines to appear to converge on each other. 112

linguistic relativity hypothesis: the theory that thought processes and concepts are controlled by language. 324

longitudinal design: research design in which one participant or group of participants is studied over a long period of time. 250

long-term memory (LTM): the system of memory into which all the information is placed to be kept more or less permanently. 218

lowball technique: getting a commitment from a person and then raising the cost of that commitment. 484

LSD (lysergic acid diethylamide): powerful synthetic hallucinogen. 154

Müller-Lyer illusion: illusion of line length that is distorted by inward-turning or outward-turning corners on the ends of the lines, causing lines of equal length to appear to be different. 56, 114

magnetic resonance imaging (MRI): brain imaging method using radio waves and magnetic fields of the body to produce detailed images of the brain. 62

magnification: the tendency to interpret situations as far more dangerous, harmful, or important than they actually are. 534

magnification and minimization: distortions of thinking in which a person blows a negative event out of proportion to its importance (magnification) while ignoring relevant positive events (minimization). 574

maintenance rehearsal: practice of saying some information to be remembered over and over in one's head in order to maintain it in short-term memory. 217

major depression: severe depression that comes on suddenly and seems to have no external cause. 542

maladaptive: anything that does not allow a person to function within or adapt to the stresses and everyday demands of life. 524

mammary glands: glands within the breast tissue that produce milk when a woman gives birth to an infant. 373

manic: having the quality of excessive excitement, energy, and elation or irritability. 543

manifest content: the actual content of one's dream. 564

marijuana (pot or weed): mild hallucinogen derived from the leaves and flowers of a particular type of hemp plant. 155

MDMA (Ecstasy or X): designer drug that can have both stimulant and hallucinatory effects. 155

mean: the arithmetic average of a distribution of numbers. A-4

means–end analysis: heuristic in which the difference between the starting situation and the goal is determined and then steps are taken to reduce that difference. 299

measures of central tendency: numbers that best represent the most typical score of a frequency distribution. A-4

measures of variability: measurement of the degree of differences within a distribution or how the scores are spread out. A-7

median: the middle score in an ordered distribution of scores, or the mean of the two middle numbers; the 50th percentile. A-5

meditation: mental series of exercises meant to refocus attention and achieve a trancelike state of consciousness. 432

medulla: the first large swelling at the top of the spinal cord, forming the lowest part of the brain, which is responsible for life-sustaining functions such as breathing, swallowing, and heart rate. 63

memory: an active system that receives information from the senses, organizes and alters it as it stores it away, and then retrieves the information from storage. 210

memory trace: physical change in the brain that occurs when a memory is formed. 235

menopause: the cessation of ovulation and menstrual cycles and the end of a woman's reproductive capability. 279

menstrual cycle: monthly shedding of the blood and tissue that line the uterus in preparation for pregnancy when conception does not occur. 373

mental images: mental representations that stand for objects or events and have a picture-like quality. 294

mental set: the tendency for people to persist in using problem-solving patterns that have worked for them in the past. 303

mescaline: natural hallucinogen derived from the peyote cactus buttons. 155

microsleeps: brief sidesteps into sleep lasting only a few seconds. 128

minimization: the tendency to give little or no importance to one's successes or positive events and traits. 534

misinformation effect: the tendency of misleading information presented after an event to alter the memories of the event itself. 231

mnemonic: a strategy or trick for aiding memory. I-11

mode: the most frequent score in a distribution of scores. A-6

modeling: learning through the observation and imitation of others. 572

monocular cues (pictorial depth cues): cues for perceiving depth based on one eye only. 112

monozygotic twins: identical twins formed when one zygote splits into two separate masses of cells, each of which develops into a separate embryo. 255

mood disorders: disorders in which mood is severely disturbed. 541

morphemes: the smallest units of meaning within a language. 323

morphine: narcotic drug derived from opium, used to treat severe pain. 153

motion parallax: the perception of motion of objects in which close objects appear to move more quickly than objects that are farther away. 113

motivation: the process by which activities are started, directed, and continued so that physical or psychological needs or wants are met. 336

motor cortex: section of the frontal lobe located at the back, responsible for sending motor commands to the muscles of the somatic nervous system. 68

motor neuron: a neuron that carries messages from the central nervous system to the muscles of the body. Also called efferent neuron. 54

motor pathway: nerves coming from the CNS to the voluntary muscles, consisting of motor neurons. 56

multiple approach–avoidance conflict: conflict in which the person must decide between more than two goals, with each goal possessing both positive and negative aspects. 419

myelin: fatty substances produced by certain glial cells that coat the axons of neurons to insulate, protect, and speed up the neural impulse. 46

narcolepsy: sleep disorder in which a person falls immediately into REM sleep during the day without warning. 138

narcotics: a class of opium-related drugs that suppress the sensation of pain by binding to and stimulating the nervous system's natural receptor sites for endorphins. 146

natural concepts: concepts people form as a result of their experiences in the real world. 296

natural killer cell: immune system cell responsible for suppressing viruses and destroying tumor cells. 423

nature: the influence of our inherited characteristics on our personality, physical growth, intellectual growth, and social interactions. 251

need: a requirement of some material (such as food or water) that is essential for survival of the organism. 337

need for achievement (nAch): a need that involves a strong desire to succeed in attaining goals, not only realistic ones but also challenging ones. 339

need for affiliation (nAff): the need for friendly social interactions and relationships with others. 340

need for power (nPow): the need to have control or influence over others. 340

negative reinforcement: the reinforcement of a response by the removal, escape from, or avoidance of an unpleasant stimulus. 179

negative symptoms: symptoms of schizophrenia that are less than normal behavior or an absence of normal behavior; poor attention, flat affect, and poor speech production. 547

negatively skewed: a distribution of scores in which scores are concentrated in the high end of the distribution. A-4

neo-Freudians: followers of Freud who developed their own competing theories of psychoanalysis. 451

nerves: bundles of axons coated in myelin that travel together through the body. 46

nervous system: an extensive network of specialized cells that carries information to and from all parts of the body. 44

neurofeedback: form of biofeedback using brain-scanning devices to provide feedback about brain activity in an effort to modify behavior. 192

neuron: the basic cell that makes up the nervous system and that receives and sends messages within that system. 45

neuroscience: a branch of the life sciences that deals with the structure and function of neurons, nerves, and nervous tissue, especially focusing on their relationship to behavior and learning. 45

neurotic personalities: maladaptive ways of dealing with relationships in Horney's theory. 453

neuroticism: degree of emotional instability or stability. 461

neurotransmitter: chemical found in the synaptic vesicles that, when released, has an effect on the next cell. 50

neutral stimulus (NS): stimulus that has no effect on the desired response. 168

nicotine: the active ingredient in tobacco. 148

nightmares: bad dreams occurring during REM sleep. 135

night terrors: relatively rare disorder in which the person experiences extreme fear and screams or runs around during deep sleep without waking fully. 133

nondirective: therapy style in which the therapist remains relatively neutral and does not interpret or take direct actions with regard to the client, instead remaining a calm, nonjudgmental listener while the client talks. 566

norm of reciprocity: assumption that if someone does something for a person, that person should do something for the other in return. 484

normal curve: a special frequency polygon in which the scores are symmetrically distributed around the mean, and the mean, median, and mode are all located on the same point on the curve with scores decreasing as the curve extends from the mean. A-3

NREM (non-REM) sleep: any of the stages of sleep that do not include REM. 131

nurture: the influence of the environment on personality, physical growth, intellectual growth, and social interactions. 251

obedience: changing one's behavior at the command of an authority figure. 485

object permanence: the knowledge that an object exists even when it is not in sight. 265

objective introspection: the process of examining and measuring one's own thoughts and mental activities. 7

observational learning: learning new behavior by watching a model perform that behavior. 196

observer bias: tendency of observers to see what they expect to see. 21

observer effect: tendency of people or animals to behave differently from normal when they know they are being observed. 21

obsessive-compulsive disorder: disorder in which intruding, recurring thoughts or obsessions create anxiety that is relieved by performing a repetitive, ritualistic behavior (compulsion). 532

occipital lobe: section of the brain located at the rear and bottom of each cerebral hemisphere containing the visual centers of the brain. 67

Oedipus complex: situation occurring in the phallic stage in which a child develops a sexual attraction to the opposite-sex parent and jealousy of the same-sex parent. 450

olfaction (olfactory sense): the sensation of smell. 103

olfactory bulbs: areas of the brain located just above the sinus cavity and just below the frontal lobes that receive information from the olfactory receptor cells. 65

olfactory bulbs: two projections just under the front of the brain that receive information from the receptors in the nose located just below. 104

openness: one of the five factors; willingness to try new things and be open to new experiences. 461

operant: any behavior that is voluntary. 177

operant conditioning: the learning of voluntary behavior through the effects of pleasant and unpleasant consequences to responses. 175

operational definition: definition of a variable of interest that allows it to be directly measured. 26

opium: substance derived from the opium poppy from which all narcotic drugs are derived. 152

opponent-process theory: theory of color vision that proposes four primary colors with cones arranged in pairs: red and green, blue and yellow. 92

optimists: people who expect positive outcomes. 425

oral stage: first stage occurring in the first year of life in which the mouth is the erogenous zone and weaning is the primary conflict. 449

organic or stress-induced dysfunction: sexual problem caused by physical disorder or psychological stress. 393

orgasm: a series of rhythmic contractions of the muscles of the vaginal walls or the penis, also the third and shortest phase of sexual response. 384

out-groups: social groups with whom a person does not identify; "they." 498

ovaries: the female gonads. 372

ovaries: the female sexual glands. 74

overgeneralization: distortion of thinking in which a person draws sweeping conclusions based on only one incident or event and applies those conclusions to events that are unrelated to the original. 534

overgeneralization: the tendency to interpret a single negative event as a never-ending pattern of defeat and failure. 574

ovum: the female sex cell, or egg. 255

pancreas: endocrine gland that controls the levels of sugar in the blood. 73

panic attack: sudden onset of intense panic in which multiple physical symptoms of stress occur, often with feelings that one is dying. 532

panic disorder: disorder in which panic attacks occur frequently enough to cause the person difficulty in adjusting to daily life. 532

panic disorder with agoraphobia: fear of leaving one's familiar surroundings because one might have a panic attack in public. 533

parallel distributed processing (PDP) model: a model of memory in which memory processes are proposed to take place at the same time over a large network of neural connections. 212

parameter: a number representing some measure of central tendency or variability within a population. A-1

paranoid: type of schizophrenia in which the person suffers from delusions of persecution, grandeur, and jealousy, together with hallucinations. 546

paraphilia: a sexual disorder in which the person's preferred method of sexual arousal and fulfillment is through sexual behavior that is unusual or socially unacceptable. 395

parapsychology: the study of ESP, ghosts, and other subjects that do not normally fall into the realm of ordinary psychology. 117

parasympathetic division: part of the ANS that restores the body to normal functioning after arousal and is responsible for the day-to-day functioning of the organs and glands. 57

parietal lobes: sections of the brain located at the top and back of each cerebral hemisphere containing the centers for touch, taste, and temperature sensations. 67

partial reinforcement effect: the tendency for a response that is reinforced after some, but not all, correct responses to be very resistant to extinction. 182

participant modeling: technique in which a model demonstrates the desired behavior in a step-by-step, gradual process while the client is encouraged to imitate the model. 572

participant observation: a naturalistic observation in which the observer becomes a participant in the group being observed. 21

PCP: synthesized drug now used as an animal tranquilizer that can cause stimulant, depressant, narcotic, or hallucinogenic effects. 154

peak experiences: according to Maslow, times in a person's life during which self-actualization is temporarily achieved. 344

pedophile: a person who has recurring sexual thoughts, fantasies, or engages in sexual actions toward prepubescent (nonsexually mature) children. 395

pedophilia: deriving sexual arousal and pleasure from touching or having sexual relations with prepubescent (nonsexually mature) children or fantasizing about such contact. 395

perception: the method by which the sensations experienced at any given moment are interpreted and organized in some meaningful fashion. 108

perceptual set (perceptual expectancy): the tendency to perceive things a certain way because previous experiences or expectations influence those perceptions. 116

peripheral nervous system (PNS): all nerves and neurons that are not contained in the brain and spinal cord but that run through the body itself. 56

peripheral-route processing: type of information processing that involves attending to factors not involved in the message, such as the appearance of the source of the message, the length of the message, and other noncontent factors. 492

personal fable: type of thought common to adolescents in which young people believe themselves to be unique and protected from harm. 276

personal unconscious: Jung's name for the unconscious mind as described by Freud. 452

personality: the unique and relatively stable ways in which people think, feel, and behave. 444

personality disorders: disorders in which a person adopts a persistent, rigid, and maladaptive pattern of behavior that interferes with normal social interactions. 549

personality inventory: paper and pencil or computerized test that consists of statements that require a specific, standardized response from the person taking the test. 469

personality psychology: area of psychology in which the psychologists study the differences in personality among people. B-6

personalization: distortion of thinking in which a person takes responsibility or blame for events that are unconnected to the person. 574

person-centered therapy: a nondirective insight therapy based on the work of Carl Rogers in which the client does all the talking and the therapist listens. 567

persuasion: the process by which one person tries to change the belief, opinion, position, or course of action of another person through argument, pleading, or explanation. 491

pessimists: people who expect negative outcomes. 425

phallic stage: third stage occurring from about 3 to 6 years of age, in which the child discovers sexual feelings. 450

phobia: an irrational, persistent fear of an object, situation, or social activity. 530

phonemes: the basic units of sound in language. 323

phototherapy: the use of lights to treat seasonal affective disorder or other disorders. 552

physiological psychology: area of psychology in which the psychologists study the biological bases of behavior. B-6

pineal gland: endocrine gland located near the base of the cerebrum that secretes melatonin. 73

pitch: psychological experience of sound that corresponds to the frequency of the sound waves; higher frequencies are perceived as higher pitches. 98

pituitary gland: gland located in the brain that secretes human growth hormone and influences all other hormone-secreting glands (also known as the master gland). 73

place theory: theory of pitch that states that different pitches are experienced by the stimulation of hair cells in different locations on the organ of Corti. 98

placebo effect: the phenomenon in which the expectations of the participants in a study can influence their behavior. 28

pleasure principle: principle by which the id functions; the immediate satisfaction of needs without regard for the consequences. 447

polygon: line graph showing a frequency distribution. A-2

pons: the larger swelling above the medulla that connects the top of the brain to the bottom and that plays a part in sleep, dreaming, left–right body coordination, and arousal. 63

population: the entire group of people or animals in which the researcher is interested. 23

positive psychology movement: a viewpoint that recommends shifting the focus of psychology away from the negative aspects to a more positive focus on strengths, well-being, and the pursuit of happiness. 363

positive regard: warmth, affection, love, and respect that come from significant others in one's life. 458

positive reinforcement: the reinforcement of a response by the addition or experiencing of a pleasurable stimulus. 179

positive symptoms: symptoms of schizophrenia that are excesses of behavior or occur in addition to normal behavior; hallucinations, delusions, and distorted thinking. 547

positively skewed: a distribution of scores in which scores are concentrated in the low end of the distribution. A-4

positron emission tomography (PET): brain-imaging method in which a radioactive sugar is injected into the subject and a computer compiles a color-coded image of the activity of the brain with lighter colors indicating more activity. 62

post-traumatic stress disorder (PTSD): a disorder resulting from exposure to a major stressor, with symptoms of anxiety, nightmares, poor sleep, reliving the event, and concentration problems, lasting for more than one month. 409

postconventional morality: third level of Kohlberg's stages of moral development in which the person's behavior is governed by moral principles that have been decided on by the individual and which may be in disagreement with accepted social norms. 277

postpartum depression: depression occurring within a year after giving birth in about 10 percent of women and that includes intense worry about the baby, thoughts of suicide, and fears of harming the baby. 520

postpartum psychosis: a rare and severe form of depression that occurs in women just after giving birth and includes delusional thinking and hallucinations. 520

practical intelligence: the ability to use information to get along in life and become successful. 319

pragmatics: aspects of language involving the practical ways of communicating with others, or the social "niceties" of language. 324

preconscious mind: level of the mind in which information is available but not currently conscious. 444

preconventional morality: first level of Kohlberg's stages of moral development in which the child's behavior is governed by the consequences of the behavior. 277

prefrontal lobotomy: psychosurgery in which the connections of the prefrontal lobes of the brain to the rear portions are severed. 588

prejudice: negative attitude held by a person about the members of a particular social group. 498

preoperational stage: Piaget's second stage of cognitive development in which the preschool child learns to use language as a means of exploring the world. 265

pressure: the psychological experience produced by urgent demands or expectations for a person's behavior that come from an outside source. 414

primacy effect: tendency to remember information at the beginning of a body of information better than the information that follows. 226

primary appraisal: the first step in assessing a stress, which involves estimating the severity of a stressor and classifying it as either a threat or a challenge. 407

primary drives: those drives that involve needs of the body such as hunger and thirst. 337

primary reinforcer: any reinforcer that is naturally reinforcing by meeting a basic biological need, such as hunger, thirst, or touch. 178

primary sex characteristics: sexual organs present at birth and directly involved in human reproduction. 372

proactive interference: memory retrieval problem that occurs when older information prevents or interferes with the retrieval of newer information. 236

problem solving: process of cognition that occurs when a goal must be reached by thinking and behaving in certain ways. 298

problem focused coping: coping strategies that try to eliminate the source of a stress or reduce its impact through direct actions. 430

procedural (nondeclarative) memory: type of long-term memory including memory for skills, procedures, habits, and conditioned responses. These memories are not conscious but are implied to exist because they affect conscious behavior. 220

projection: defense mechanism involving placing, or "projecting," one's own unacceptable thoughts onto others, as if the thoughts actually belonged to those others and not to oneself. 433

projection: psychological defense mechanism in which unacceptable or threatening impulses or feelings are seen as originating with someone else, usually the target of the impulses or feelings. 468

projective tests: personality assessments that present ambiguous visual stimuli to the client and ask the client to respond with whatever comes to mind. 468

prosocial behavior: socially desirable behavior that benefits others. 509

prostate gland: gland that secretes most of the fluid holding the male sex cells or sperm. 372

prototype: an example of a concept that closely matches the defining characteristics of a concept. 297

proximity: physical or geographical nearness. 109

proximity: the tendency to perceive objects that are close to each other as part of the same grouping. 503

pseudopsychologies: systems of explaining human behavior that are not based on or consistent with scientific evidence. 34

psilocybin: natural hallucinogen found in certain mushrooms. 155

psychiatric social worker: a social worker with some training in therapy methods who focuses on the environmental conditions that can have an impact on mental disorders, such as poverty, overcrowding, stress, and drug abuse. 17, B-3

psychiatrist: a medical doctor who has specialized in the diagnosis and treatment of psychological disorders. 16, B-3

psychoactive drugs: drugs that alter thinking, perception, and memory. 145

psychoanalysis: an insight therapy based on the theory of Freud, emphasizing the revealing of unconscious conflicts. 10

psychoanalysis: Freud's term for both the theory of personality and the therapy based on it. 451

psychoanalysis: the theory and therapy based on the work of Sigmund Freud. 564

psychoanalyst: either a psychiatrist or a psychologist who has special training in the theories of Sigmund Freud and his method of psychoanalysis. 16, B-3

psychodynamic perspective: modern version of psychoanalysis that is more focused on the development of a sense of self and the discovery of other motivations behind a person's behavior than sexual motivations. 13

psychodynamic therapy: a newer and more general term for therapies based on psychoanalysis, with an emphasis on transference, shorter treatment times, and a more direct therapeutic approach. 565

psychogenic drugs: drugs including hallucinogens and marijuana that produce hallucinations or increased feelings of relaxation and intoxication. 146

psychological defense mechanisms: unconscious distortions of a person's perception of reality that reduce stress and anxiety. 432

psychological dependence: the feeling that a drug is needed to continue a feeling of emotional or psychological well-being. 146

psychological disorders: any pattern of behavior that causes people significant distress, causes them to harm others, or harms their ability to function in daily life. 524

psychologist: a professional with an academic degree and specialized training in one or more areas of psychology. 17, B-3

psychology: the scientific study of behavior and mental processes. 4

psychoneuroimmunology: the study of the effects of psychological factors such as stress, emotions, thoughts, and behavior on the immune system. 421

psychopathology: the study of abnormal behavior. 522

psychopharmacology: the use of drugs to control or relieve the symptoms of psychological disorders. 584

psychophysiological disorder: modern term for psychosomatic disorder. 535

psychosexual stages: five stages of personality development proposed by Freud and tied to the sexual development of the child. 449

psychosomatic disorder: disorder in which psychological stress causes a real physical disorder or illness. 535

psychosurgery: surgery performed on brain tissue to relieve or control severe psychological disorders. 588

psychotherapy: therapy for mental disorders in which a person with a problem talks with a psychological professional. 562

psychotic: the break away from an ability to perceive what is real and what is fantasy. 545

puberty: the physical changes that occur in the body as sexual development reaches its peak. 274

punishment: any event or object that, when following a response, makes that response more likely to happen again. 186

punishment by application: the punishment of a response by the addition or experiencing of an unpleasant stimulus. 186

punishment by removal: the punishment of a response by the removal of a pleasurable stimulus. 187

random assignment: process of assigning subjects to the experimental or control groups randomly, so that each subject has an equal chance of being in either group. 27

range: the difference between the highest and lowest score in a distribution. A-7

rapid eye movement (REM): stage of sleep in which the eyes move rapidly under the eyelids and the person is typically experiencing a dream. 131

rating scale: assessment in which a numerical value is assigned to specific behavior that is listed in the scale. 469

rational-emotive behavior therapy (REBT): cognitive-behavioral therapy in which clients are directly challenged in their irrational beliefs and helped to restructure their thinking into more rational belief statements. 575

rationalization: psychological defense mechanism in which a person invents acceptable excuses for unacceptable behavior. 433

reaction formation: psychological defense mechanism in which a person forms an opposite emotional or behavioral reaction to the way he or she really feels to keep those true feelings hidden from self and others. 433

real self: one's perception of actual characteristics, traits, and abilities. 457

realistic conflict theory: theory stating that prejudice and discrimination will be increased between groups that are in conflict. 499

reality principle: principle by which the ego functions; the satisfaction of the demands of the id only when negative consequences will not result. 447

recall: type of memory retrieval in which the information to be retrieved must be "pulled" from memory with very few external cues. 226

recency effect: tendency to remember information at the end of a body of information better than the information ahead of it. 227

receptive meditation: form of meditation in which a person attempts to become aware of everything in immediate conscious experience, or an expansion of consciousness. 434

receptor sites: holes in the surface of the dendrites or certain cells of the muscles and glands, which are shaped to fit only certain neurotransmitters. 50

recessive: referring to a gene that only influences the expression of a trait when paired with an identical gene. 254

reciprocal determinism: Bandura's explanation of how the factors of environment, personal characteristics, and behavior can interact to determine future behavior. 456

reciprocity of liking: tendency of people to like other people who like them in return. 504

recognition: the ability to match a piece of information or a stimulus to a stored image or fact. 226

reflection: therapy technique in which the therapist restates what the client says rather than interpreting those statements. 567

reflex arc: the connection of the sensory neurons to the interneurons to the motor neurons, resulting in a reflex action. 54

refractory period: time period in males just after orgasm in which the male cannot become aroused or achieve erection. 384

regression: psychological defense mechanism in which a person falls back on childlike patterns of responding in reaction to stressful situations. 433

reinforcement: the strengthening of a response that occurs when that response is followed by a pleasurable consequence. 572

reinforcement: the strengthening of a response by following it with a pleasurable consequence or the removal of an unpleasant stimulus. 177

reinforcer: any event or object that, when following a response, increases the likelihood of that response occurring again. 170

relative size: perception that occurs when objects that a person expects to be of a certain size appear to be small and are, therefore, assumed to be much farther away. 112

reliability: the tendency of a test to produce the same scores again and again each time it is given to the same people. 308

REM behavior disorder: a rare disorder in which the mechanism that blocks the movement of the voluntary muscles fails, allowing the person to thrash around and even get up and act out nightmares. 135

REM rebound: increased amounts of REM sleep after being deprived of REM sleep on earlier nights. 135

replicate: in research, repeating a study or experiment to see if the same results will be obtained in an effort to demonstrate reliability of results. 20

representative sample: randomly selected sample of subjects from a larger population of subjects. 22

repression: psychological defense mechanism in which the person refuses to consciously remember a threatening or unacceptable event, instead pushing those events into the unconscious mind. 433

residual: type of schizophrenia in which there are no delusions and hallucinations, but the person still experiences negative thoughts, poor language skills, and odd behavior. 547

resistance: occurring when a patient becomes reluctant to talk about a certain topic, either changing the subject or becoming silent. 565

resolution: the final phase of the sexual response in which the body is returned to a normal state. 384

resting potential: the state of the neuron when not firing a neural impulse. 47

restorative theory: theory of sleep proposing that sleep is necessary to the physical health of the body and serves to replenish chemicals and repair cellular damage. 130

reticular formation (RF): an area of neurons running through the middle of the medulla and the pons and slightly beyond that is responsible for selective attention. 64

retrieval: getting information that is in storage into a form that can be used. 211

retrieval cue: a stimulus for remembering. 224

retroactive interference: memory retrieval problem that occurs when newer information prevents or interferes with the retrieval of older information. 236

retrograde amnesia: loss of memory from the point of some injury or trauma backwards, or loss of memory for the past. 238

reuptake: process by which neurotransmitters are taken back into the synaptic vesicles. 52

reversible figures: visual illusions in which the figure and ground can be reversed. 109

rods: visual sensory receptors found at the back of the retina, responsible for noncolor sensitivity to low levels of light. 89

romantic love: type of love consisting of intimacy and passion. 505

Rorschach inkblot test: projective test that uses 10 inkblots as the ambiguous stimuli. 468

S factor: the ability to excel in certain areas, or specific intelligence. 317

sample: group of subjects selected from a larger population of subjects, usually selected randomly. A-1

scaffolding: process in which a more skilled learner gives help to a less skilled learner, reducing the amount of help as the less skilled learner becomes more capable. 267

scheme (plural schemas): a mental concept formed through experiences with objects and events. 264

schizophrenia: severe disorder in which the person suffers from disordered thinking, bizarre behavior, hallucinations, and is unable to distinguish between fantasy and reality. 544

school psychology: area of psychology in which the psychologists work directly in the schools, doing assessments, educational placement, and diagnosing educational problems. B-8

scientific management: older theory of management, also known as Theory X, in which it is assumed that workers do not want to work and only do so because they are getting paid, and also that there is only one correct way to perform any task. B-11

scientific method: system of gathering data so that bias and error in measurement are reduced. 18

scrotum: external sack that holds the testes. 372

Seasonal Affective Disorder (SAD): a mood disorder caused by the body's reaction to low levels of sunlight in the winter months. 552

secondary appraisal: the second step in assessing a threat, which involves estimating the resources available to the person for coping with the stressor. 408

secondary reinforcer: any reinforcer that becomes reinforcing after being paired with a primary reinforcer, such as praise, tokens, or gold stars. 178

secondary sex characteristics: sexual organs and traits that develop at puberty and are indirectly involved in human reproduction. 372

selective attention: the ability to focus on only one stimulus from among all sensory input. 215

selective thinking: distortion of thinking in which a person focuses on only one aspect of a situation while ignoring all other relevant aspects. 574

self: archetype that works with the ego to manage other archetypes and balance the personality. 457

self-actualization: according to Maslow, the point that is seldom reached at which people have sufficiently satisfied the lower needs and achieved their full human potential. 343

self-actualizing tendency: the striving to fulfill one's innate capacities and capabilities. 457

self-concept: the image of oneself that develops from interactions with important, significant people in one's life. 457

self-determination theory (SDT): theory of human motivation in which the social context of an action has an effect on the type of motivation existing for the action. 345

self-efficacy: individual's perception of how effective a behavior will be in any particular circumstance. 456

self-fulfilling prophecy: the tendency of one's expectations to affect one's behavior in such a way as to make the expectation more likely to be occur. 501

self-help groups (support groups): a group composed of people who have similar problems and who meet together without a therapist or counselor for the purpose of discussion, problem solving, and social and emotional support. 578

semantic memory: type of declarative memory containing general knowledge, such as knowledge of language and information learned in formal education. 221

semantic network model: model of memory organization that assumes information is stored in the brain in a connected fashion, with concepts that are related stored physically closer to each other than concepts that are not highly related. 223

semantics: the rules for determining the meaning of words and sentences. 323

seminal fluid: fluid released from the penis at orgasm that contains the sperm. 384

sensation: the activation of receptors in the various sense organs. 84

sensation seeker: someone who needs more arousal than the average person. 341

sensorimotor stage: Piaget's first stage of cognitive development in which the infant uses its senses and motor abilities to interact with objects in the environment. 264

sensory adaptation: tendency of sensory receptor cells to become less responsive to a stimulus that is unchanging. 86

sensory conflict theory: an explanation of motion sickness in which the information from the eyes conflicts with the information from the vestibular senses, resulting in dizziness, nausea, and other physical discomforts. 107

sensory memory: the very first stage of memory, the point at which information enters the nervous system through the sensory systems. 213

sensory neuron: a neuron that carries information from the senses to the central nervous system. Also called afferent neuron. 54

sensory pathway: nerves coming from the sensory organs to the CNS consisting of sensory neurons. 56

serial position effect: tendency of information at the beginning and end of a body of information to be remembered more accurately than information in the middle of the body of information. 226

sexism: prejudice about males and/or females leading to unequal treatment. 379

sexual deviance: behavior that is unacceptable according to societal norms and expectations. 389

sexual dysfunction: a problem in sexual functioning. 392

sexual orientation: a person's sexual attraction preference for members of a particular sex. 389

shape constancy: the tendency to interpret the shape of an object as being constant, even when its shape changes on the retina. 108

shaping: the reinforcement of simple steps in behavior that lead to a desired, more complex behavior. 181

short-term memory (STM) (working memory): the memory system in which information is held for brief periods of time while being used. 215

significant difference: a difference between groups of numerical data that is considered large enough to be due to factors other than chance variation. A-10

similarity: the tendency to perceive things that look similar to each other as being part of the same group. 109

single-blind study: study in which the subjects do not know if they are in the experimental or the control group. 29

situational cause: cause of behavior attributed to external factors, such as delays, the action of others, or some other aspect of the situation. 496

situational context: the social or environmental setting of a person's behavior. 523

size constancy: the tendency to interpret an object as always being the same actual size, regardless of its distance. 108

skewed distribution: frequency distribution in which most of the scores fall to one side or the other of the distribution. A-4

skin senses: the sensations of touch, pressure, temperature, and pain. 104

sleep apnea: disorder in which the person stops breathing for nearly half a minute or more. 137

sleep deprivation: any significant loss of sleep, resulting in problems in concentration and irritability. 128

sleepwalking (somnambulism): occurring during deep sleep, an episode of moving around or walking around in one's sleep. 133

social categorization: the assignment of a person one has just met to a category based on characteristics the new person has in common with other people with whom one has had experience in the past. 495

social cognition: the mental processes that people use to make sense of the social world around them. 494

social cognitive: referring to the use of cognitive processes in relation to understanding the social world. 500

social cognitive learning theorists: theorists who emphasize the importance of both the influences of other people's behavior and of a person's own expectancies on learning. 456

social cognitive view: learning theory that includes cognitive processes such as anticipating, judging, memory, and imitation of models. 456

social comparison: the comparison of oneself to others in ways that raise one's self-esteem. 500

social facilitation: the tendency for the presence of other people to have a positive impact on the performance of an easy task. 487

social identity: the part of the self-concept including one's view of self as a member of a particular social category. 500

social identity theory: theory in which the formation of a person's identity within a particular social group is explained by social categorization, social identity, and social comparison. 500

social influence: the process through which the real or implied presence of others can directly or indirectly influence the thoughts, feelings, and behavior of an individual. 480

social learners: people who prefer to learn with other people or in groups. I-2

social loafing: the tendency for people to put less effort into a simple task when working with others on that task. 488

social phobia: fear of interacting with others or being in social situations that might lead to a negative evaluation. 531

social psychology: area of psychology in which the psychologists focus on how human behavior is affected by the presence of other people. B-6

social psychology: the scientific study of how a person's thoughts, feelings, and behavior are influenced by the real, imagined, or implied presence of others. 480, B-6

Social Readjustment Rating Scale (SRRS): assessment that measures the amount of stress in a person's life over a one-year period resulting from major life events. 410

social role: the pattern of behavior that is expected of a person who is in a particular social position. 507

social support system: the network of family, friends, neighbors, coworkers, and others who can offer support, comfort, or aid to a person in need. 429

social-cognitive theory of hypnosis: theory that assumes that people who are hypnotized are not in an altered state but are merely playing the role expected of them in the situation. 145

sociocultural perspective: perspective that focuses on the relationship between social behavior and culture. 15

soma: the cell body of the neuron responsible for maintaining the life of the cell. 45

somatic nervous system: division of the PNS consisting of nerves that carry information from the senses to the CNS and from the CNS to the voluntary muscles of the body. 56

somatization disorder: somatoform disorder in which the person dramatically complains of a specific symptom such as nausea, difficulty swallowing, or pain for which there is no real physical cause. 535

somatoform disorders: disorders that take the form of bodily illnesses and symptoms but for which there are no real physical disorders. 535

somatosensory cortex: area of neurons running down the front of the parietal lobes responsible for processing information from the skin and internal body receptors for touch, temperature, body position, and possibly taste. 67

somesthetic senses: the body senses consisting of the skin senses, the kinesthetic sense, and the vestibular senses. 104

source traits: the more basic traits that underlie the surface traits, forming the core of personality. 460

spatial neglect: condition produced by damage to the association areas of the right hemisphere resulting in an inability to recognize objects or body parts in the left visual field. 69

specific phobia: fear of objects or specific situations or events. 531

spinal cord: a long bundle of neurons that carries messages to and from the body to the brain that is responsible for very fast, lifesaving reflexes. 53

spontaneous recovery: the reappearance of a learned response after extinction has occurred. 171

sports psychology: area of psychology in which the psychologists help athletes and others to prepare themselves mentally for participation in sports activities. B-8

standard deviation: the square root of the average squared deviations from the mean of scores in a distribution; a measure of variability. A-7

statistic: a measure of central tendency or variability computed from a sample. A-1

statistically significant: referring to differences in data sets that are larger than chance variation would predict. A-10

statistics: branch of mathematics concerned with the collection and interpretation of numerical data. A-1

stem cells: special cells found in all the tissues of the body that are capable of manufacturing other cell types when those cells need to be replaced due to damage or wear and tear. 55

stereotype: a concept held about a person or group of people that is based on superficial, irrelevant characteristics. 378

stereotype: a set of characteristics that people believe is shared by all members of a particular social category. 495

stereotype vulnerability: the effect that people's awareness of the stereotypes associated with their social group has on their behavior. 501

stimulants: drugs that increase the functioning of the nervous system. 147

stimulatory hallucinogenics: drugs that produce a mixture of psychomotor stimulant and hallucinogenic effects. 155

stimulus discrimination: the tendency to stop making a generalized response to a stimulus that is similar to the original conditioned stimulus because the similar stimulus is never paired with the unconditioned stimulus. 170

stimulus generalization: the tendency to respond to a stimulus that is only similar to the original conditioned stimulus with the conditioned response. 170

stimulus motive: a motive that appears to be unlearned but causes an increase in stimulation, such as curiosity. 340

stimulus substitution: original theory in which Pavlov stated that classical conditioning occurred because the conditioned stimulus became a substitute for the unconditioned stimulus by being paired closely together. 174

storage: holding onto information for some period of time. 211

stress: the term used to describe the physical, emotional, cognitive, and behavioral responses to events that are appraised as threatening or challenging. 406

stressors: events that cause a stress reaction. 406

stress-vulnerability model: explanation of disorder that assumes a biological sensitivity, or vulnerability, to a certain disorder will develop under the right conditions of environmental or emotional stress. 549

structuralism: early perspective in psychology associated with Wilhelm Wundt and Edward Titchener, in which the focus of study is the structure or basic elements of the mind. 7

subjective: referring to concepts and impressions that are only valid within a particular person's perception and may be influenced by biases, prejudice, and personal experiences. 468

subjective discomfort: emotional distress or emotional pain. 524

sublimation: channeling socially unacceptable impulses and urges into socially acceptable behavior. 433

subordinate concept: the most specific category of a concept, such as one's pet dog or a pear in one's hand. 296

successive approximations: small steps in behavior, one after the other, that lead to a particular goal behavior. 181

superego: part of the personality that acts as a moral center. 447

superordinate concept: the most general form of a type concept, such as "animal" or "fruit." 296

surface traits: aspects of personality that can easily be seen by other people in the outward actions of a person. 460

sympathetic division (fight-or-flight system): part of the ANs that is responsible for reacting to stressful events and bodily arousal. 57

synapse (synaptic gap): microscopic fluid-filled space between the synaptic knob of one cell and the dendrites or surface of the next cell. 50

synaptic knob: rounded areas on the end of the axon terminals. 49

synaptic vesicles: saclike structures found inside the synaptic knob containing chemicals. 49

synesthesia: disorder in which the signals from the various sensory organs are processed in the wrong cortical areas, resulting in the sense information being interpreted as more than one sensation. 82

syntax: the system of rules for combining words and phrases to form grammatically correct sentences. 323

systematic desensitization: behavior technique used to treat phobias, in which a client is asked to make a list of ordered fears and taught to relax while concentrating on those fears. 570

tactile learners: people who need to touch objects in order to learn about them. I-2

temperament: the behavioral characteristics that are fairly well established at birth, such as easy, difficult, and slow to warm up. 270

temperament: the enduring characteristics with which each person is born. 444

temporal lobes: areas of the cortex located just behind the temples containing the neurons responsible for the sense of hearing and meaningful speech. 67

teratogen: any factor that can cause a birth defect. 258

testes (testicles): the male sex glands. 372

testes: the male gonads. 74

texture gradient: the tendency for textured surfaces to appear to become smaller and finer as distance from the viewer increases. 113

thalamus: part of the limbic system located in the center of the brain; this structure relays sensory information from the lower part of the brain to the proper areas of the cortex and processes some sensory information before sending it to its proper area. 65

that's-not-all technique: a sales technique in which the persuader makes an offer and then adds something extra to make the offer look better before the target person can make a decision. 484

Thematic Apperception Test (TAT): projective test that uses 20 pictures of people in ambiguous situations as the visual stimuli. 468

therapeutic alliance: the relationship between therapist and client that develops as a warm, caring, accepting relationship characterized by empathy, mutual respect, and understanding. 582

therapy: treatment methods aimed at making people feel better and function more effectively. 562

theta waves: brain waves indicating the early stages of sleep. 131

thinking (cognition): mental activity that goes on in the brain when a person is organizing and attempting to understand information and communicating information to others. 294

thyroid gland: endocrine gland found in the neck that regulates metabolism. 73

time-out: an extinction process in which a person is removed from the situation that provides reinforcement for undesirable behavior, usually by being placed in a quiet corner or room away from possible attention and reinforcement opportunities. 573

token economy: the use of objects called tokens to reinforce behavior in which the tokens can be accumulated and exchanged for desired items or privileges. 572

token economy: type of behavior modification in which desired behavior is rewarded with tokens. 190

top-down processing: the use of preexisting knowledge to organize individual features into a unified whole. 116

trait: a consistent, enduring way of thinking, feeling, or behaving. 459

trait–situation interaction: the assumption that the particular circumstances of any given situation will influence the way in which a trait is expressed. 462

trait theories: theories that endeavor to describe the characteristics that make up human personality in an effort to predict future behavior. 459

transference: In psychoanalysis, the tendency for a patient or client to project positive or negative feelings for important people from the past onto the therapist. 565

transvestism: deriving sexual arousal and pleasure from dressing in the clothing of the opposite sex. 395

trial and error (mechanical solution): problem-solving method in which one possible solution after another is tried until a successful one is found. 298

triarchic theory of intelligence: Sternberg's theory that there are three kinds of intelligences: analytical, creative, and practical. 318

trichromatic theory: theory of color vision that proposes three types of cones: red, blue, and green. 91

trust versus mistrust: first stage of personality development in which the infant's basic sense of trust or mistrust develops as a result of consistent or inconsistent care. 273

t-test: type of inferential statistical analysis typically used when two means are compared to see if they are significantly different. A-10

Type A personality: person who is ambitious, time conscious, extremely hardworking, and tends to have high levels of hostility and anger as well as being easily annoyed. 423

Type B personality: person who is relaxed and laid-back, less driven and competitive than Type A, and slow to anger. 423

Type C personality: pleasant but repressed person, who tends to internalize his or her anger and anxiety and who finds expressing emotions difficult. 424

unconditional positive regard: positive regard that is given without conditions or strings attached. 458

unconditional positive regard: referring to the warmth, respect, and accepting atmosphere created by the therapist for the client in client-centered therapy. 567

unconditioned response (UCR): an involuntary response to a naturally occurring or unconditioned stimulus. 168

unconditioned stimulus (UCS): a naturally occurring stimulus that leads to an involuntary response. 167

unconscious mind: level of the mind in which thoughts, feelings, memories, and other information are kept that are not easily or voluntarily brought into consciousness. 446

undifferentiated: type of schizophrenia in which the person shows no particular pattern, shifting from one pattern to another, and cannot be neatly classified as disorganized, paranoid, or catatonic. 546

unilateral ECT: electro-convulsive therapy in which the electrodes are placed on only one side of the head and the forehead. 588

uterus: the womb in which the baby grows during pregnancy. 372

vagina: the tube that leads from the outside of a female's body to the opening of the womb. 372

validity: the degree to which a test actually measures what it's supposed to measure. 308

variable interval schedule of reinforcement: schedule of reinforcement in which the interval of time that must pass before reinforcement becomes possible is different for each trial or event. 185

variable ratio schedule of reinforcement: schedule of reinforcement in which the number of responses required for reinforcement is different for each trial or event. 184

vestibular senses: the sensations of movement, balance, and body position. 104

vicarious conditioning: classical conditioning of a reflex response or emotion by watching the reaction of another person. 173

visual accommodation: the change in the thickness of the lens as the eye focuses on objects that are far away or close. 89

visual learners: people who learn best by seeing, reading, and looking at images. I-2

volley principle: theory of pitch that states that frequencies above 100 Hz cause the hair cells (auditory neurons) to fire in a volley pattern, or taking turns in firing. 98

waking consciousness: state in which thoughts, feelings, and sensations are clear, organized, and the person feels alert. 126

weight set point: the particular level of weight that the body tries to maintain. 347

Wernicke's aphasia: condition resulting from damage to Wernicke's area, causing the affected person to be unable to understand or produce meaningful language. 69

withdrawal: physical symptoms that can include nausea, pain, tremors, crankiness, and high blood pressure, resulting from a lack of an addictive drug in the body systems. 146

Yerkes-Dodson Law: law stating performance is related to arousal; moderate levels of arousal lead to better performance than do levels of arousal that are too low or too high. This effect varies with the difficulty of the task: easy tasks require a high-moderate level while more difficult tasks require a low-moderate level. 341

zone of proximal development (ZPD): Vygotsky's concept of the difference between what a child can do alone and what that child can do with the help of a teacher. 267

z score: a statistical measure which indicates how far away from the mean a particular score is in terms of the number of standard deviations which exist between the mean and that score. A-8

zygote: cell resulting from the uniting of the ovum and sperm. 255

References

AAA Foundation for Traffic Safety. (1997). *Aggressive driving: Three studies*. Washington, DC.

Abadinsky, H. (1989). *Drug abuse: An introduction*. Chicago: Nelson-Hall Series in Law, Crime, and Justice.

Abe, K., Amatomi, M., & Oda, N. (1984). Sleepwalking and recurrent sleep talking in children of childhood sleepwalkers. *American Journal of Psychiatry, 141*, 800–801.

Abel, G. G., & Osborn, C. A. (1992). The paraphilias: The extent and nature of sexually deviant and criminal behavior. In J. M. W. Bradford (Ed.), *Psychiatric Clinics of North America, 15*(3) (pp. 675–687). Philadelphia: W. B. Saunders Company.

Abela, J. R. Z., & D'Allesandro, D. U. (2002). Beck's cognitive theory of depression: The diathesis-stress and causal mediation components. *British Journal of Clinical Psychology, 41*, 111–128.

Abraham, S., Llewellyn-Jones, D. (2001). *Eating disorders, the facts*. 5th ed. London: Oxford University Press.

Abraham, W. C., & Williams, J. M. (2003). Properties and mechanisms of LTP maintenance. *The Neuroscientist, 9*(6), 463–474.

Abramson, L. Y., Garber, J., & Seligman, M. E. P. (1980). Learned helplessness in humans: An attributional analysis. In J. Garber, & M. E. P. Seligman (Eds.) *Human Helplessness* (pp. 3–34). New York: Academic Press.

Abramson, L. Y., Seligman, M. E. P., & Teasdale, J. D. (1978). Learned helplessness in humans: Critique and reformulation. *Journal of Abnormal Psychology, 87*, 49–74.

Acar, N., Chardigny, J. M., Darbois, M., Pasquis, B., & Sebedio, J. L. (2003). Modification of the dopaminergic neurotransmitters in striatum, frontal cortex and hippocampus of rats fed for 21 months with trans isomers of alpha-linolenic acid. *Neuroscience Research, 45*(4), 375–382.

Adam, K. (1980). Sleep as a restorative process and a theory to explain why. *Progressive Brain Research, 53*, 289–305.

Adams, D. B. (1968). The activity of single cells in the midbrain and hypothalamus of the cat during affective defense behavior. *Archives Italiennes de Biologie, 106*, 243–269.

Adams, R. J. (1987). An evaluation of colour preferences in early infancy. *Infant Behaviour and Development, 10*, 143–150.

Adler, A. (1954). *Understanding human nature*. New York: Greenburg Publisher.

Adolph, K. E. (1995). Psychophysical assessment of toddlers' ability to cope with slopes. *Journal of Experimental Psychology: Human Perception and Performance, 21*, 734–750.

Adolph, K. E., Eppler, M. A., & Gibson, E. J. (1993). Crawling versus walking infants' perception of affordances for locomotion over sloping surfaces. *Child Development, 64*, 1158–1174.

Adolphs, R., & Tranel, D. (2003). Amygdala damage impairs emotion recognition from scenes only when they contain facial expressions. *Neuropsychologia, 41*, 1281–1289.

Aghajanian, G. K., & Marek, G. J. (1999). Serotonin and hallucinogens. *Neuropsychopharmacology, 21*, 16S–23S.

Agnati, L. F., Bjelke, B., & Fuxe, K. (1992). Volume transmission in the brain. *American Scientist, 80*, 362–373.

Agresti, A., & Finlay, B. (1997). *Statistical methods for the social sciences*, 3rd ed. Upper Saddle River, NJ: Prentice Hall.

Aguiar, A., & Baillargeon, R. (2003). Perseverative responding in a violation-of-expectation task in 6.5-month-old infants. *Cognition, 88*(3), 277–316.

Ahern, G. L., & Schwartz, G. E. (1985). Differential lateralization for positive and negative emotion in the human brain: EEG spectral analysis. *Neuropsychologia, 23*(6), 745–755.

Ahlskog, J. E. (2003). Slowing Parkinson's disease progression: Recent dopamine agonist trials. *Neurology, 60*(3), 381–389.

Ahn, W. (1998). Why are different features central for natural kinds and artifacts? The role of causal status in determining feature centrality. *Cognition, 69*, 135–178.

Ahokas, A., Aito, M., & Rimon, R. (2000). Positive treatment effect of estradiol in postpartum psychosis: a pilot study. *Journal of Clinical Psychiatry, 61*(3), 166–169.

Aiello, J. R., & Douthitt, E. A. (2001). Social facilitation from Triplett to electronic performance monitoring. *Group Dynamics: Theory, Research, and Practice, 5*(3), 163–180.

Ainsworth, M. D. S. (1985). Attachments across the life span. *Bulletin of the New York Academy of Medicine, 61*, 792–812.

Ainsworth, M. D. S., Blehar, M. C., Waters, E., & Wall, S. (1978). *Patterns of attachment: A study of the strange situation*. Hillsdale, NJ: Erlbaum.

Aitchison, J. (1992). Good birds, better birds, & amazing birds: The development of prototypes. In P. J. Arnaud & H. Béjoint (Eds.), *Vocabulary and applied linguistics* (pp. 71–84). London: Macmillan.

Ajzen, I. (2001). Nature and operation of attitudes. *Annual Review of Psychology, 52*, 27–58.

Ajzen, I., & Fishbein, M. (2000). Attitudes and the attitude–behavior relation: Reasoned and automatic processes. In W. Stroebe & M. Hewstone (Eds.), *European review of social psychology* (pp. 1–33). New York: John Wiley & Sons.

Akil, M., Kolachana, B. S., et al. (2003). Catechol-o-methyltransferase genotype and dopamine regulation in the human brain. *Journal of Neuroscience, 23*(6), 2008–2013.

Albarracin, D., & Wyer, R. S. (2000). The cognitive impact of past behavior: Influences on beliefs, attitudes, and future behavioral decisions. *Journal of Personality and Social Psychology, 79*, 1–17.

Albert, D. J., & Richmond, S. E. (1977). Reactivity and aggression in the rat: Induction by alpha–adrenergic blocking agents injected ventral to anterior septum but not into lateral septum. *Journal of Comparative and Physiological Psychology, 91*, 886–896 [DBA] *Physiology and Behavior, 20*, 755–761.

Alderfer, C. P. (1972). *Existence, relatedness and growth: Human needs in organisational settings*. New York: Free Press.

Aldridge-Morris, R. (1989). *Multiple personality: An exercise in deception*. Hillsdale, NJ: Erlbaum.

Alexander, G., DeLong, M. R., & Strick, P. L. (1986). Parallel organization of functionally segregated circuits linking basal ganglia and cortex. *Annual Review of Neuroscience, 9*, 357–381.

Aligne, C. A., Auinger, P., Byrd, R. S., & Weitzman, M. (2000). Risk factors for pediatric asthma contributions of poverty, race, and urban residence. *American Journal of Respiratory Critical Care Medicine, 162*(3), 873–877.

Alkon, D. (1989). Memory storage and neural systems. *Scientific American, 261*(1), 42–50.

Allen, F. (1994). *Secret formula*. New York: HarperCollins.

Allen, G., & Parisi, P. (1990). Trends in monozygotic and dizygotic twinning rates by maternal age and parity. Further analysis of Italian data, 1949–1985, and rediscussion of US data, 1964–1985. *Acta Genetic Medicine & Gemellology, 39*, 317–328.

Allen, I. V. (1991). Pathology of multiple sclerosis. In W. B. Matthews (Ed.). *McAlpine's multiple sclerosis*. Edinburgh: Churchill Livingstone, 341–378.

Allen, J. J., & Iacono, W. G. (1997). A comparison of methods for the analysis of event-related potentials in deception detection. *Psychophysiology, 34*, 234–240.

Allen, L. S., & Gorski, R. A. (1991). Sexual dimorphism of the anterior commissure and massa intermedia of the human brain. *Journal of Comparative Neurology, 312*, 97–104.

Allen, L. S., Hines, M., Shryne, J. E., & Gorski, R. A. (1989). Two sexually dimorphic cell groups in the human brain. *Journal of Neuroscience, 9*(9), 496–506.

Alloy, L. B., & Clements, C. M. (1998). Hopelessness theory of depression: Tests of the symptom component. *Cognitive Therapy and Research, 22,* 303–335.

Allport, G. W., & Odbert, H. S. (1936). Trait names: A psycho-lexical study. *Psychological Monographs, 47*(211).

Alperstein, L. (2001). For two: Some basic perspectives and skills for couples therapy. Paper presented at the XXXIII Annual Conference of the American Association of Sex Educators, Counselors, and Therapists. San Francisco, May 2–6.

Amabile, T. M. (1982). The social psychology of creativity: A consensual assessment technique. *Journal of Personality and Social Psychology, 43,* 997–1013.

Amabile, T. M., DeJong, W., & Lepper, M. R. (1976). Effects of externally imposed deadlines on subsequent intrinsic motivation. *Journal of Personality and Social Psychology, 34,* 92–98.

Amabile, T., Hadley, C. N., & Kramer, S. J. (2002). Creativity under the gun. *Harvard Business Review, 80*(8), 52–60.

American Academy of Pediatrics. (1995). Health supervision for children with Turner syndrome. *Pediatrics, 96*(6), 1166–1173.

American Association of University Women. (1992). *How schools shortchange girls.* Washington, DC: American Association of University Women.

American Association of University Women. (1998). *Separated by sex: A critical look at single-sex education for girls.* Washington, DC: American Association of University Women.

American Association on Mental Retardation. (2002). Mental retardation: Definition, classification, and systems of supports (10th ed.). Washington, DC: American Association on Mental Retardation.

American Foundation for Suicide Prevention. **www.afsp.org**.

American Psychiatric Association (2000b). Practice guidelines for the treatment of patients with major depressive disorder (revision). *American Journal of Psychiatry, 157*(4, Supplement): 1–45.

American Psychiatric Association Committee on Electroconvulsive Therapy. (2001). *The practice of electroconvulsive therapy: Recommendations for treatment, training, and privileging,* 2nd ed. Washington, DC: American Psychiatric Association.

American Psychiatric Association. (2000). *DSM-IV-TR: Diagnostic and statistical manual of mental disorders* (4th ed., Text Revision). Washington, DC: APA.

American Psychiatric Association. (2000). *DSM-IV-TR: Diagnostic and statistical manual of mental disorders* (4th ed., Text Revision). Washington, DC. [Appendix I: Outline for Cultural Formulation and Glossary of Culture-Bound Syndromes].

American Psychological Association. (1992). Ethical principles of psychologists and code of conduct. *American Psychologist, 47*(12), 1597–1611.

American Social Health Association. (2004). STD statistics. Retrieved from the Internet on November 18, 2004, at **www.ashastd.org/stdfaqs/statistics.html**.

Anand, B. K., & Brobeck, J. R. (1951.) Hypothalamic control of food intake in rats and cats. *Yale Journal of Biological Medicine, 24,* 123–146.

Anastasi, A., & Urbina, S. (1997). *Psychological testing* (7th ed.). Upper Saddle River, NJ: Prentice-Hall.

Anch, M., Browman, C. P., Mitler, M. M., & Walsh, J. (1988). *Sleep: A scientific perspective.* Englewood, NJ: Prentice Hall.

Anderson, C. A. (1987). Temperature and aggression: Effects on quarterly, yearly, and city rates of violent and nonviolent crime. *Journal of Personality and Social Psychology, 52*(6), 1161–1173.

Anderson, C. A. (2003). Video games and aggressive behavior. In D. Ravitch & J. P. Viteritti (Eds.), *Kid stuff: Marketing sex and violence to America's children* (p. 157). Baltimore and London: The Johns Hopkins University Press.

Anderson, C. A., & Bushman, B. J. (2001). Effects of violent video games on aggressive behavior, aggressive cognition, aggressive affect, physiological arousal, and prosocial behavior: A meta–analytic review of the scientific literature. *Psych Science, 12*(5), 353–359.

Anderson, C. A., & Dill, K. E. (2000). Video games and aggressive thoughts, feelings, and behavior in the laboratory and in life. *Journal of Personality and Social Psychology, 78*(4), 772–790.

Anderson, C. A., Berkowitz, L., Donnerstein, E., Huesmann, R. L., Johnson, J., Linz, D., Malamuth, N., & Wartella, E. (2003). The influence of media violence on youth. *Psychological Science in the Public Interest, 4,* 81–110.

Anderson, D. (1964 June 10). 4 Kew Gardens residents testify to seeing woman slain on street. *The New York Times* p. 50.

Anderson, M. C., & Neely, J. H. (1995). Interference and inhibition in memory retrieval. In E. L. Bjork & R. A. Bjork (Eds.), *Handbook of perception and cognition, Volume 10, Memory.* San Diego, CA: Academic Press.

Andrews, J. D. W. (1989). Integrating visions of reality: Interpersonal diagnosis and the existential vision. *American Psychologist, 44,* 803–817.

Anschuetz, B. L. (1999). The high cost of caring: Coping with workplace stress. *The Journal, the Newsletter of the Ontario Association of Children's Aid Societies, 43*(3).

Antuono, P. G., Jones, J. L., Wang, Y., & Li, S. (2001). Decreased glutamate + glutamine in Alzheimer's disease detected in vivo with (1)H-MRS at 0.5 T. *Neurology, 56*(6), 737–742.

Aral, S. O., & Holmes, K. K. (1999). Social and behavioral determinants of the epidemiology of STDs: Industrialized and developing countries. In K. K. Holmes, P. A. Mardh, P. F. Sparling, S. M. Lemon, W. E. Stamm, & P. Piot, (Eds.), *In sexually transmitted diseases* (pp. 39–76). New York: McGraw-Hill.

Archer, J. (1991). The influence of testosterone on human aggression. *British Journal of Psychology, 82,* 1–28.

Argamon, S., Koppel, M., Fine, J., & Shimoni, A. (2003 August). Gender, genre, and writing style in formal written texts., *Text, 23*(3).

Argyle, M. (1986). Rules for social relationships in four cultures. *Australian Journal of Psychology, 38,* 309–318.

Armstrong, R. (1997). When drugs are used for rape. *Journal of Emergency Nursing, 23*(4), 378–381.

Arnett, P. A., Smith, S. S., & Newman, J. P. (1997). Approach and avoidance motivation in psychopathic criminal offenders during passive avoidance. *Journal of Personality and Social Psychology, 72*(6), 1413–1428.

Aron, A., Aron, E. N., & Coups, E. (2005). *Statistics for the behavioral and social sciences: A brief course,* 3rd ed. Upper Saddle River, NJ: Prentice Hall.

Aronson, E. (1997). Back to the future. Retrospective review of Leon Festinger's—A theory of cognitive dissonance. *American Journal of Psychology, 110,* 127–137.

Aronson, E., Blaney, N., Stephan, C., Sikes, J., & Snapp, M. (1978). *The jigsaw classroom.* Beverly Hills, CA: Sage.

Arrigo, J. M., & Pezdek, K. (1998). Textbook models of multiple personality: Source, bias, and social consequences. In S. Lynn (Ed.), *Truth in memory* (pp. 372–393). New York: Guilford Press.

Asarnow, R. F., Granholm, E., & Sherman, T. (1991). Span of apprehension in schizophrenia. In H. A. Nasrallah (Ed.), *Handbook of Schizophrenia, Vol. 5,* S. R. Steinhauer, J. H. Gruzelie, & J. Zubin, (Eds.), *Neuropsychology, psychophysiology and information processing.* (pp. 335–370). Amsterdam: Elsevier.

Asch, S. E. (1951). Effects of group pressure upon the modification and distortion of judgement. In H. Guetzkow (Ed.), *Groups, leadership and men.* Pittsburgh, PA: Carnegie Press.

Asch, S. E. (1956). Studies of independence and conformity: A minority of one against a unanimous majority. *Psychological Monographs, 70* (Whole No. 416).

Aserinsky, E., & Kleitman, N. (1953). Regularly occurring periods of eye motility, and concomitant phenomena, during sleep. *Science, 118,* 273–274.

Ash, M. G. (1998). *Gestalt psychology in German culture, 1890–1967: Holism and the quest for objectivity.* Cambridge: Cambridge University Press.

Asimov, I. (1968). *I, robot.* London: Grafton Books.

Atkinson, D. R. (1983). Ethnic similarity in counseling psychology: A review of research. *Counseling Psychologist, 11,* 79–92.

Atkinson, R. C., & Shiffrin, R. M. (1968). Human memory: A proposed system and its control processes. In K. W. Spence & J. T. Spence (Eds.), *The psychology of learning and motivation* (vol. 2, pp. 89–105). New York: Academic Press.

Augenbraun, M. H. (2002). Treatment of syphilis 2001: Nonpregnant adults. *Clinical Infections and Disorders, 35*(Suppl 2), S187–90.

Aylward, E. H., Richards, T. L., Berninger, V. W., Nagy, W. E., Field, K. M., Grimme, A. C., Richards, A. L., Thomson, J. B., & Cramer, S. C. (2003). Instructional treatment associated with changes in brain activation in children with dyslexia. *Neurology, 61,* 212–219.

Backer, B., Hannon, R., & Russell, N. (1994). *Death and dying: Understanding and care,* 2nd ed. Albany, NY: Delmar Pub.

Baddeley, A. (1988). Cognitive psychology and human memory. *Trends in Neurosciences, 11,* 176–181.

Baddeley, A. D. (1986). *Working memory.* London/New York: Oxford University Press.

Baddeley, A. D. (1996). Exploring the central executive. *Quarterly Journal of Experimental Psychology, 49A,* 5–28.

Baddeley, A. D. (2003). Working Memory: Looking back and looking visual forward. *Nature Reviews Neuroscience, 4*(10), 829–839.

Baddeley, A. D., & Hitch, G. (1974). Working memory. In G. A. Bower (Ed.), *The psychology of learning and motivation, 8,* (pp. 47–89). New York: Academic Press.

Baehr, E. K., Revelle, W., & Eastman, C. I. (2000). Individual difference in the phase amplitude of the human circadian temperature rhythm: With an emphasis on morningness-eveningness. *Journal of Sleep Research, 9,* 117–127.

Baer, D. M., Wolf, M. M., & Risley, T. R. (1968). Some current dimensions of applied behavior analysis. *Journal of Applied Behavior Analysis, 1,* 91–97.

Baglio, C., Benavidiz, D., Compton, L., Matson, J., & Paclawskyj, T. (1996). Behavioral treatment of autistic persons: A review of research from 1980 to present. *Research in Developmental Disabilities, 17,* 433–465.

Bahrick, H. (1984). Fifty years of second language attrition: Implications for programmatic research. *Modern Language Journal, 68,* 105–118.

Bahrick, H. P., Hall, L. K. & Berger, S. A. (1996, September). Accuracy and distortion in memory for high school grades. *Psychological Science, 7,* 265–271.

Bailey, J., Dunne, M. P., & Martin, N. G. (2000). Genetic and environmental influences on sexual orientation and its correlates in an Australian twin sample. *Journal of Personality and Social Psychology Volume, 78*(3), 524–536.

Bailey, J. M., & Pillard, R. C. (1991). A genetic study of male sexual orientation. *Archives of General Psychiatry, 48,* 1089–1096.

Bailey, J. M., & Zucker, K. J. (1995). Childhood sex-typed behavior and sexual orientation: A conceptual analysis and quantitative review. *Developmental Psychology, 31,* 43–55.

Bailey, J. M., Pillard, R. C., Neale, M. C., & Agyei, Y. (1993). Heritable factors influence sexual orientation in women. *Archives of General Psychiatry, 50,* 217–223.

Baillergeon, R. (1986). Representing the existence and location of hidden objects: Object permanence in 6- and 8-month-old infants. *Cognition, 23,* 21–24.

Ball, K., Berch, D. B., Helmers, K. F., Jobe, J. B., Leveck, M. D., Marsiske, M., Morris, J. N., Rebok, G. W., Smith, D. M., Tennstedt, S. L., Unverzagt, F. W., & Willis, S. L. (2002). Advanced Cognitive Training for Independent and Vital Elderly Study Group. Effects of cognitive training interventions with older adults: A randomized controlled trial. *Journal of the American Medical Association, 288,* 2271–2281.

Baltes, P. B., Reese, H. W., & Nesselroade, J. R. (1988). *Introduction to research methods, life-span developmental psychology.* Hillsdale, NJ: Lawrence Erlbaum Associates, Inc.

Bandura, A. (1965). Influence of models' reinforcement contingencies on the acquisition of imitative responses. *Journal of Social Psychology, 1,* 589–595.

Bandura, A. (1980). The social learning theory of aggression. In R. A. Falk & S. S. Kim (Eds.), *The war system: An interdisciplinary approach* (p. 146). Boulder, CO: Westview Press.

Bandura, A. (1986). *Social foundations of thought and action.* Englewood Cliffs, NJ: Prentice-Hall.

Bandura, A. (1986). *Social foundations of thought and action: A social cognitive theory.* Englewood Cliffs, NJ: Prentice Hall.

Bandura, A. (1989). Human agency in social cognitive theory. *American Psychologist, 44,* 1175–1184.

Bandura, A. (1998). Exploration of fortuitous determinants of life paths. *Psychological Inquiry, 9,* 95–99.

Bandura, A. Jeffrey, R. W., & Wright, C. L. (1974). Efficacy of participant modeling as a function of response induction aids. *Journal of Abnormal Psychology, 83,* 56–64.

Bandura, A., & Rosenthal, T. L. (1966). Vicarious classical conditioning as a functioning of arousal level. *Journal of Personality and Social Psychology, 3,* 54–62.

Bandura, A., Blanchard, E. B., & Ritter, B. (1969). Relative efficacy of desensitization and modeling approaches for inducing behavioral, affective, and attitudinal changes. *Journal of Personality and Social Psychology, 13,* 173–199.

Bandura, A., Ross, D., & Ross, S. A. (1961). Transmission of aggression through imitation of aggressive models. *Journal of Abnormal and Social Psychology, 63,* 575–582.

Barabasz, A., & Barabasz, M. (2000). Treating AD/HD with hypnosis and neurotherapy. *Child Study Journal, 30*(1), 25–42.

Barak, A. (1999). Psychological applications on the Internet: A discipline on the threshold of a new millennium. *Applied and Preventive Psychology, 8,* 231–246.

Bard, P. (1934). On emotional expression after decortication with some remark on certain theoretical views. *Psychological Review, 41,* 309–329, 424–449.

Bargh, J. A., Chen, M., & Burrows, C. (1996). Automaticity of social behavior: Direct effects of trait construct and stereotype activation on action. *Journal of Personality & Social Psychology, 71*(2), 230–244.

Barker, E. (1983). The ones who got away: People who attend Unification Church workshops and do not become Moonies. In E. Barker (Ed.), *Of gods and men: New religious movements in the West.* Macon, GA: Mercer University Press.

Barkley, R. A. (1998). *Attention deficit hyperactivity disorder: A handbook for diagnosis and treatment.* New York: Guilford Press.

Barkley, R. A., Fischer, M., Fletcher, K., & Smallish, L. (2001). *Young adult outcome of hyperactive children as a function of severity of childhood conduct problems, I: Psychiatric status and mental health treatment.* Submitted for publication.

Barnes, A. M., & Carey, J. C. (2002). Common problems of babies with trisomy 18 or 13. Rochester, NY, *Support Organization for Trisomy 18, 13, and Related Disorders,* January 11.

Barnes, V., Schneider, R., Alexander, C., & Staggers, F. (1997). Stress, stress reduction, and hypertension in African Americans: An updated review. *Journal of the National Medical Association, 89*(7), 464–476.

Barnyard, P., & Grayson, A. (1996). *Introducing psychological research.* London: MacMillan Press.

Baron, J. N., & Reiss, P. C. (1985). Same time, next year. Aggregate analyses of the mass media and violent behavior. *American Sociological Review, 50,* 347–363.

Barondes, S. H. (1998). *Mood genes: Hunting for origins of mania and depression.* New York: W. H. Freeman.

Barone, J. J., & Roberts, H. R. (1996). Caffeine consumption. *Food Chemistry and Toxicology, 34,* 119–129.

Barsalou, L. W. (1992). *Cognitive psychology: An overview for cognitive scientists.* Hillsdale, NJ: Lawrence Erlbaum Associates.

Barsch, J. (1996). *Barsch learning style inventory* (rev. ed.). Novato, CA: Academic Therapy Publications.

Barsh, G. S., Farooqi, I. S., & O'Rahilly, S. (2000). Genetics of body-weight regulation. *Nature, 404,* 644–651.

Bartels, A., & Zeki, S. (2000). The neural basis of romantic love. *NeuroReport, 11,* 3829–3834.

Barth, J. M., & Boles, D. B. (1999). Positive relations between emotion recognition skills and right hemisphere processing. Paper presented to the *11th Annual Convention of the American Psychological Society,* Denver.

Bartholomew, K. (1990). Avoidance of intimacy: An attachment perspective. *Journal of Social and Personal Relationships, 7,* 147–178.

Bartlett, F. C. (1932). *Remembering: A study in experimental ad social psychology.* Cambridge: Cambridge University Press.

Bartlett, N. R. (1965). Dark and light adaptation. Chapter 8. In C. H. Graham, (Ed.), *Vision and visual perception.* New York: John Wiley and Sons, Inc.

Barton, M. E., & Komatsu, L. K. (1989). Defining features of natural kinds and artifacts. *Journal of Psycholinguistic Research, 18,* 433–447.

Bartoshuk, L. M. (1993). The biological basis for food perception and acceptance. *Food Quality and Preference, 4*(1/2), 21–32.

Barzega, G., Maina, G., Venturello, S., & Bogetto, F. (2001). Gender-related distribution of personality disorders in a sample of patients with panic disorder. *European Psychiatry, 4*(3), 173–179.

Basadur, M., Pringle, P., & Kirkland, D. (2002). Crossing cultures: Training effects on the divergent thinking attitudes of Spanish-speaking South American managers. *Creativity Research Journal, 14*(3, 4), 395–408.

Bates, J. E. (1989). Applications of temperament concepts. In G. A. Kohnstamm, J. E. Bates, & M. K Rothbart (Eds.), *Temperament in childhood* (pp. 323–355). New York: Wiley.

Battaglia, M., Bernardeschi, L., Franchini, L., Bellodi, L., & Smeraldi, E. (1995). A family study of schizotypal disorder. *Schizophrenia Bulletin, 21*(1), 33–45.

Battan, J. (1999). The "rights" of husbands and the "duties" of wives: Power and desire in the American bedroom, 1850–1910. *Journal of Family History, 24*(2), 165–186.

Baumrind, D. (1964). Some thoughts on ethics of research: After reading Milgram's "Behavioral Study of Obedience." *American Psychologist, 19*, 421–423.

Baumrind, D. (1997). Necessary distinctions. *Psychological Inquiry, 8*, 176–182.

Beardsley, T. (1995), January. For whom the bell curve really tolls. *Scientific American*, 14–17.

Beck, A. T. (1976). *Cognitive therapy and the emotional disorders*. New York: International Universities Press.

Beck, A. T. (1979). *Cognitive therapy and the emotional disorders*. New York: Penguin Books.

Beck, A. T. (1984). Cognitive approaches to stress. In C. Lehrer & R. L. Woolfolk (Eds.), *Clinical guide to stress management*. New York: Guilford Press.

Beckman, M. & Pierrehumbert, J. (1986). Intonational structure in English and Japanese. *Phonology Year Book III*, 15–70.

Beehr, T. A., Jex, S. M., Stacy, B. A., & Murray, M. A. (2000). Work stressors and coworker support as predictors of individual strain and job performance. *Journal of Organizational Behavior, 21*(4), 391–405.

Beer, J. M., & Horn, J. M. (2000). The influence of rearing order on personality development within two adoption cohorts. *Journal of Personality, 68*, 789–819.

Bellizzi, J. A., & Crowley, A. E. (1983). The effects of color in store design. *Journal of Retailing, 59*, 21–45.

Bem, D. J., & Honorton, C. (1994). Does psi exist? *Psychological Bulletin, 115*(1), 4–18.

Bem, S. L. (1975). Sex role adaptability: The consequence of psychological androgyny. *Journal of Personality and Social Psychology, 31*, 634–643.

Bem, S. L. (1981). Gender schema theory: A cognitive account of sex typing. *Psychological Review, 88*, 354–364.

Bem, S. L. (1981). The BSRI and gender schema theory: A reply to Spence and Helmreich. *Psychological Review, 88*, 369–371.

Bem, S. L. (1987). Gender schema theory and the romantic tradition. In P. Shaver & C. Hendrick (Eds.), *Review of personality and social psychology* (Volume 7). Newbury Park, CA: Sage.

Bem, S. L. (1993), Is there a place in psychology for a feminist analysis of the social context? *Feminism & Psychology, 3*, 247–251.

Bemporad, J. R. (1997). Cultural and historical aspects of eating disorders. *Theor Med 18*(4), 401–420.

Benasich, A. A., & Tallal, P. (1996). Auditory temporal processing thresholds, habituation, and recognition memory over the 1st year. *Infant Behavior & Development, 19*(3), 339–357.

Benis, A. M. (1990). A theory of personality traits leads to a genetic model for borderline types and schizophrenia. *Speculations in Science and Technology, 13*(3), 167–175.

Benis, A. M. (2004). *Toward self & sanity: On the genetic origins of the human character*. New York: Psychological Dimensions Publishers.

Benjafield, J. J. G. (1996). *A history of psychology*. Boston: Allyn and Bacon.

Benjamin, S. L. (1996). An interpersonal theory of personality disorders. In J. F. Clarkin & M. F. Lenzenweger (Eds.), *Major theories of personality disorder*. New York: Guilford Press.

Benowitz, N. L. (1996). Pharmacology of nicotine: Addiction and therapeutics. *Annual Review of Pharmacology and Toxicology, 36*, 597–613.

Ben-Shakhar, G., Bar-Hillel, M., Bliu, Y., Ben-Abba, E., & Flug, A. (1986). Can graphology predict occupational success? Two empirical studies and some methodological ruminations. *Journal of Applied Psychology, 71*, 645–653.

Benson, H. (1975). *The relaxation response*. New York: Morrow.

Benson, H., Beary, J. F., & Carol, M. P. (1974). The relaxation response. *Psychiatry, 37*, 37–46.

Benson, H., Beary, J., & Carol, M. (1974a). The relaxation response. *Psychiatry, 37*, 37–46.

Benson, H., Rosner, B. A., Marzetta, B. R., & Klemchuk, H. M. (1974b). Decreased blood pressure in pharmacologically treated hypertensive patients who regularly elicited the relaxation response. *Lancet, 1*(7852), 289–291.

Benton, D., & Parker, P. Y. (1998). Breakfast, blood glucose, and cognition. *American Journal of Clinical Nutrition, 67*(S):772S–778S.

Berenbaum, S. A., & Snyder, E. (1995). Early hormonal influences on childhood sex-typed activity and playmate preferences: Implications for the development of sexual orientation. *Developmental Psychology, 31*, 31–42.

Berent, S. (1977). Functional asymmetry of the human brain in the recognition of faces. *Neuropsychologia, 15*. 829–831.

Berg, F. (1999). Health risks associated with weight loss and obesity treatment programs. *Journal of Social Issues, 55*(2), 277–297.

Berk, L. S., Felten, D. L., Tan, S. A., Bittman, B. B., & Westengard, J. (2001, March). Modulation of neuroimmune parameters during the eustress of humor-associated mirthful laughter. *Alternative Therapy Health Medicines, 7*(2), 62–72, 74–76.

Berkowitz, L. (1993). *Aggression: Its causes, consequences and control*. New York: McGraw-Hill.

Bermond, B., Nieuwenhuyse, B., Fasotti, L., & Schuerman, J. (1991). Spinal cord lesions, peripheral feedback, and intensities of emotional feelings. *Cognition and Emotion, 5*, 201–220.

Berndt, T. (1992). Friendship and friends' influence in adolescence. *Current Directions in Psychological Science, 1*(5), 156–159.

Berry, J. W., & Kim, U. (1998). Acculturation and mental health. In P. R. Dasen, J. W. Berry, & N. Sartorius (Eds.), *Health and cross-cultural psychology: Toward applications* (pp. 207–236). Newbury Park, CA: Sage Publications.

Berry, J. W., & Sam, D. L. (1997). Acculturation and adaptation. In J. W. Berry, M. H. Segall, & C. Kagitcibasi (Eds.), *Handbook of cross-cultural psychology, Vol. 3: Social behaviour and applications* (2nd ed., pp. 291–326). Boston: Allyn & Bacon.

Berscheid, E., & Reis, H. T. (1998). Attraction and close relationships. In D. T. Gilbert & S. T. Fiske et al. (Eds.), *The handbook of social psychology, Vol 2* (4th ed. pp. 193–281), New York: McGraw-Hill.

Bértolo, H., Paiva, T., Pessoa, L., Mestre, T., Marques, R., & Santos, R. (2003). Visual dream content, graphical representation and EEG alpha activity in congenitally blind subjects. *Cognitive Brain Research, 15*, 277–284.

Best, D. L., & Williams, J. E. (2001). Gender and culture. In D. Matsumoto (Ed.), *The handbook of culture and psychology* (pp. 195–212). New York: Oxford University Press.

Betancourt, J. R., & Jacobs, E. A. (2000). Language barriers to informed consent and confidentiality: The impact on women's health. *Journal of American Medical Women's Association, 55*, 294–295.

Beyer, B. K. (1995). *Critical thinking*. Bloomington, IN: Phi Delta Kappa Educational Foundation.

Bigler, E. D., Johnson, S. C., Anderson, C. V., Blatter, D. D., Gale, S. D., Russo, A. A., Ryser, D. K., Macnamara, S. E., Bailey, B. R., & Hopkins, R. O. (1996). Traumatic brain injury and memory: The role of hippocampal atrophy. *Neuropsychology, 10*, 333–342.

Binet, A., & Simon, T. (1916). *The development of intelligence in children*. Baltimore: Williams & Wilkins.

Bishop, K. M., & Wahlsten, D. (1997). Sex differences in the human corpus callosum: Myth or reality? *Neurosience and Biobehavioral Review, 21*, 581–601.

Bjork, R. A. & Bjork, E. L. (1992). A new theory of disuse and an old theory of stimulus fluctuation. In A. Healy, S. Kosslyn, & R. Shiffrin (Eds.), *From learning processes to cognitive processes: Essays in honor of William K. Estes* (vol. 2, pp. 35–67). Hillsdale, NJ: Erlbaum.

Bjork, R. A., & Whitten, W. B. (1974). Recency-sensitive retrieval processes in long-term free recall. *Cognitive Psychology, 6*, 173–189.

Black, D. W., & Andreasen, N. C. (1999). Schizophrenia, schizophreniform disorder, and delusional (paranoid) disorders. In R. E. Hales et al., (Eds.), *Textbook of psychiatry* (3rd ed., pp. 425–477). Washington, D.C.: American Psychiatric Press.

Blair, R. J. R., Sellars, C., Strickland, I., Clark, F., Williams, A. O., Smith, M., & Jones, L. (1995). Emotion attributions in the psychopath. *Personality and Individual Differences, 19* (4), 431–437.

Blakeslee, S. (2002, September 12). Actor regains some movement, doctor says. *New York Times*.

Blanchard, M., & Main, M. (1979). Avoidance of the attachment figure and social-emotional adjustment in day-care infants. *Developmental Psychology, 15*, 445–446.

Blass, T. (1991). Understanding behavior in the Milgram obedience experiment: The role of personality, situations, and their interactions. *Journal of Personality and Social Psychology, 60*, 398–413.

Blass, T. (1999). The Milgram paradigm after 35 years: Some things we now know about obedience to authority. *Journal of Applied Social Psychology, 25*, 955–978.

Blatt, S. D., Meguid, V., & Church, C. C. (2000). Prenatal cocaine: What's known about outcomes? *Contemporary Ob/Gyn, 9*, 67–83.

Blazer, D. G., Kessler, R. C., McGonagle, K. A., & Swartz, M. S. (1994). The prevalence and distribution of major depression in a national community sample: The National Comorbidity Survey. *American Journal of Psychiatry, 151*, 979–986.

Bledsoe, C. H., & Cohen, B. (1993). *Social dynamics of adolescent fertility in Sub-Saharan Africa*. Washington DC: National Academy Press.

Blehar, M. C., & Oren, D. A. (1997). Gender differences in depression. *Medscape General Medicine, 1*(2). Retrieved from the Internet on June 27, 2004, at **www.medscape.com/viewarticle/408844**.

Bleuler, E. (1911, reissued 1950). *Dementia praecox or the group of schizophrenias*. New York: International Universities Press.

Bloom, L. (1974). Talking, understanding and thinking. In R. Schiefelbusch, & L. L. Lloyd (Eds.), *Language perspectives: Acquisition, retardation and intervention*. New York: Macmillan.

Bloom, L., Lightbown, P., & Hood, L. (1975). Structure and variation in child language. *Monographs of the Society for Research in Child Development, 40*, (Serial No. 160).

Bloom, P. (1996). Intention, history, and artifact concepts. *Cognition, 60*, 1–29.

Bloom, P. (2000). *How children learn the meaning of words*. Cambridge, MA: MIT Press.

Blumer, D. (2002). The illness of Vincent van Gogh. *American Journal of Psychiatry, 159*(4), 519–526.

Bock, R. (1993). *Understanding Klinefelter Syndrome: A guide for XXY males and their families*. National Institutes of Health, Office of Research Reporting. Publication No. 93-3202 (August).

Bodrova, E., & Leong, D. J. (1996). *Tools of the mind: The Vygotskian approach to early childhood education*. Englewood Cliffs, NJ: Prentice Hall.

Bogle, K. D. (2000). Effect of perspective, type of student, and gender on the attribution of cheating. *Proceedings of the Oklahoma Academy of Science, 80*, 91–97.

Bond, R. A. & Smith, P. B. (1996). Culture and conformity: A meta–analysis of studies using Asch's (1952, 1956) line judgment task. *Psychological Bulletin, 119*, 111–137.

Bondarenko, L. A. (2004). Role of methionine in nocturnal melatonin peak in the pineal gland. *Bulletin of Experimental Biological Medicine, 137*(5), 431–432.

Bonnelykke, B. (1990). Maternal age and parity as predictors of human twinning. *Acta Genetic Medicine & Gemellology, 39*, 329–334.

Bonnet, M., & Arand, D. (1995). We are chronically sleep deprived. *Sleep, 18*(10), 908–911.

Boor, M. (1982). The multiple personality epidemic: Additional cases and inferences regarding diagnosis, etiology, dynamics, and treatment. *Journal of Nervous and Mental Disease, 170*, 302–304.

Booth-Butterfield, S. (1996). Message characteristics. *Steve's primer of practical persuasion and influence*. Document retrieved from the Internet on August 2, 2004 from **www.as.wvu.edu/~sbb/comm221/chapters/message.htm**.

Borgeat, F., & Goulet, J. (1983, June). Psychophysiological changes following auditory subliminal suggestions for activation and deactivation. *Perceptual & Motor Skills, 56*(3), 759–766.

Borges, M. A., Stepnowsky, M. A., & Holt, L. H. (1977). Recall and recognition of words and pictures by adults and children. *Bulletin of the Psychonomic Society, 9*, 113–114.

Bornstein, M. H. (1985). Habituation of attention as a measure of visual information processing in human infants: summary, systematization, and synthesis. In G. Gottleib & N. A. Krasnegor (Eds.), *Measurement of audition and vision in the first year of postnatal life: A methodological overview* (pp. 253–300). Norwood: Ablex.

Bornstein, M. H., & Benasich, A. A. (1986). Infant habituation: Assessments of individual differences and short-term reliability at 5 months. *Child Development, 57*, 87–99.

Boswell, S. (2002). Former Miss America receives cochlear implant. *The ASHA Leader Online*. AGS Publishing. Retrieved from the Internet March 2003 at **www.asha.org/about/publications/leader-online/archives/2002/q4/021109a.htm**.

Bosworth, H. B., & Schaie, K. W. (1997). The relationship of social environment, social networks, and health outcomes in the Seattle Longitudinal Study: Two analytical approaches. *Journals of Gerontology Series B: Psychological Sciences and Social Sciences, 52*(5), 197–205.

Botwin, M. D., & Buss, D. M. (1989). The structure of act data: Is the five-factor model of personality recaptured? *Journal of Personality and Social Psychology, 56*, 988–1001.

Bouchard, C. (1997). Genetic determinants of regional fat distribution. *Human Reproduction, 12*(Suppl 1), 1–5.

Bouchard, C., Tremblay, A., Nadeau, A., Dussault, J., Despres, J. P., Theriault, G., Lupien, P. J., Serresse, O., Boulay, M. R., & Fournier, G. (1990). Long-term exercise training with constant energy intake. 1: Effect on body composition and selected metabolic variables. *International Journal on Obesity, 14*(1), 57–73.

Bouchard, T. (1994). Genes, environment, and personality. *Science, 264*, 1700–1701.

Bouchard, T. J., Jr. (1997). Whenever the twain shall meet. *The Science, 37*, 5, 52–57.

Bouchard, T. J., & Segal, N. L. (1985). Environment and IQ. In B. B. Wolman (Ed.), *Handbook of intelligence: Theories, measurements, and applications* (pp. 391–464). New York: John Wiley.

Bouchard, T. J., Lykken, D. T., McGue, M., Segal, N. L., & Tellegen, A. (1990). Sources of human psychological differences: The Minnesota study of twins reared apart. *Science, 250*(4978), 223.

Bowden, C. L., Calabrese, J. R., McElroy, S. L., Gyulai, L., Wassef, A., Petty, F., Pope, H. G. Jr., Chou, J. C., Keck, P. E. Jr., Rhodes, L. J., Swann, A. C., Hirschfeld, R. M., & Wozniak, P. J. (2000). For the Divalproex Maintenance Study Group. A randomized, placebo-controlled 12-month trial of divalproex and lithium in treatment of outpatients with bipolar I disorder. *Archives of General Psychiatry, 57*(5), 481–489.

Bowers, K. S., & Woody, E. Z. (1996). Hypnotic amnesia and the paradox of intentional forgetting. *Journal of Abnormal Psychology, 105*, 381–390.

Bowman, E. S. (1996). Delayed memories of child abuse: Part II: An overview of research findings relevant to understanding their reliability and suggestibility. *Dissociation: Progress in the Dissociative Disorders, 9*, 232–243.

Boyd, C. H., & Peeler, C. M. (May, 2004). *Highlighting vs note taking: A comparison of students' performance on tests*. Poster presented at 16th Annual Convention of the American Psychological Society, Chicago.

Boyd, L. A., & Winstein, C. J. (2004). Cerebellar stroke impairs temporal but not spatial accuracy during implicit motor learning. *Neurorehabilitation and Neural Repair, 18*(3), 134–143.

Boyson-Bardies, B., deHalle, P., Sagart, L., & Durand, C. (1989). A cross-linguistic investigation of vowel formats in babbling. *Journal of Child Language, 16*, 1–17.

Bracey, G. (1997). A few facts about poverty. *Phi Delta Kappan, 79*, 163–164.

Bradshaw, W. (1997). Evaluating cognitive-behavioral treatment of schizophrenia: Four single-case studies. *Research in Social Work Practice, 7*, 419–445.

Bradshaw, W. (1998). Cognitive-behavioral treatment of schizophrenia: A case study. *Journal of Cognitive Psychotherapy: An International Journal, 12*(1), 13–25.

Braio, A., Dunn, R., Beasley, T. M., Quinn, P., & Buchanan, K. (1997). Incremental implementation of learning style strategies among urban low achievers. *Journal of Educational Research, 91*, 15–25.

Brauen, C. M., & Bonta, J. L. (1979). Cross-cultural validity, reliability, and stimulus characteristics of the Luscher Color Test. *Journal of Personality Assessment, 43*, 459–460.

Braun, B. G. (Ed.) (1986). *Treatment of multiple personality disorder*. Washington, DC: American Psychiatric Press.

Braun, S. (1996). *Buzz: The science and lore of alcohol and caffeine*. New York: Oxford University Press, 107–192.

Brawman-Mintzer, O., & Lydiard, R. B. (1997). Biological basis of generalized anxiety disorder. *Journal of Clinical Psychiatry, 58*(3), 16–25.

Brazelton, T. B. (1992). *Touchpoints: Your child's emotional and behavioral development*. Reading, MA: Addison-Wesley Publishing Co.

Brecher, M., Wang, B. W., Wong, H., & Morgan, J. P. (1988). Phencyclidine and violence: Clinical and legal issues. *Journal of Clinical Psychopharmacology, 8*, 397–401.

Breger, L. (2000). *Freud: Darkness in the midst of vision*. New York: John Wiley & Sons.

Breggin, P. R. (2003/2004). Suicidality, violence and mania caused by selective serotonin reuptake inhibitors (SSRIs): A review and analysis. *International Journal of Risk & Safety in Medicine, 16*, 31–49.

Breggin, P. R., & Breggin, G.R. (1994). *Talking back to Prozac*. New York: St. Martin's Press.

Breier A., Albus M., Pickar D., Zahn, T. P., Wolkowitz, O.M., & Paul, S. M. (1987). Controllable and uncontrollable stress in humans: Alterations in mood, neuroendocrine and psychophysiological function. *American Journal of Psychiatry, 144*, 1419–1425.

Breland, K., & Breland, M. (1961). The misbehavior of organisms. *American Psychologist. 16*, 681–684.

Brennan, J. F. (2002). *History and systems of psychology*, 6th ed. Upper Saddle River, NJ: Prentice Hall.

Brennan, P. A., Raine, A., Schulsinger, F., Kirkegaard-Sorensen, L., Knop, J., Hutchings, B., Rosenberg, R., & Mednick, S. A. (1997). Psychophysiological protective factors for male subjects at high risk for criminal behavior. *American Journal of Psychiatry, 154*, 853–855.

Breslau, N., Chilcoat, H. D., Kessler, R. C., Peterson, E. L., & Lucia, V. C. (1999). Vulnerability to assaultive violence: Further specification of the sex difference in posttraumatic stress disorder. *Psychological Medicine, 29*, 813–821.

Breslau, N., Davis, G. C., Andreski, P., & Peterson, E. L. (1997). Sex differences in posttraumatic stress disorder. *Archives of General Psychiatry, 54*(11), 1044–1048.

Breuer, J. & Freud, S. (1895). *Studies on hysteria (cathartic method). Special Edition, 2*, 1–309.

Brewer, M. B. (2001). Ingroup identification and intergroup conflict: When does ingroup love become outgroup hate? In R. D. Ashmore, L. Jussim, & D. Wilder (Eds.), *Social identity, intergroup conflict, and conflict reduction*. New York: Oxford University Press.

Brick, J. (2003). The characteristics of alcohol: Chemistry, use and abuse. In J. Brick (Ed.), *Handbook of the medical consequences of alcohol and drug abuse* (pp. 1–11). New York: Haworth Medical Press.

Briggs, K. C., & Myers, I. B. (1998). *The Myers-Briggs Type Indicator-Form M*. Palo Alto, CA: Consulting Psychologists Press.

Brigham, A. (1844). Asylums exclusively for the incurably insane. Classic article in *The American Journal of Psychiatry, 151*, 50–70.

Broadbent, D. (1958). *Perception and communication*. Elmsford, NY: Pergamon.

Brockington, I. F., Winokur, G., & Dean, C. (1982). Puerperal psychosis. In I. F. Brockington, & R. Kumar, (Eds.), *Motherhood and mental illness* (pp. 37–69). London: Academic Press.

Brondolo, E., Rieppi, R., Erickson, S. A., Bagiella, E., Shapiro, P. A., McKinley, P., & Sloan, R. P. (2003). Hostility, interpersonal interactions, and ambulatory blood pressure. *Psychosomatic Medicine, 65*, 1003–1011.

Brooks, J. G., & Brooks, M. G. (1993). *In search of understanding: The case for constructivist classrooms*. Alexandria, VA: The Association for Supervision and Curriculum Development.

Brotman, E. (2001). *How to Toilet Train Your Cat: The Education of Mango*. Sherman Oaks, CA: Bird Brain Press.

Brown, C., Taylor, J., Green, A., Lee, B. E., Thomas, S. B., & Ford, A. (2003). *Managing depression in African Americans: Consumer and provider perspectives*. (Final Report to Funders). Pittsburgh: Mental Health Association of Allegheny County.

Brown, G. L., & Linnoila, M. I. (1990). CSF serotonin metabolite (5–HIAA) studies in depression, impulsivity, and violence. *Journal of Clinical Psychiatry, 51*(4)(suppl), 31–43.

Brown, J. (1958). Some tests of the decay theory of immediate memory. *Quarterly Journal of Experimental Psychology, 10*, 12–21.

Brown, P. K., & Wald, G. (1964). Visual pigments in single rods and cones of the human retina. *Science, 144*, 45.

Brown, R. (1973). *A first language: The early stages*. Cambridge, MA: Harvard University Press.

Brown, R. W. A. (1973). *First language: The early stages*. London: George Allen and Unwin.

Brown, R., & McNeill, D. (1966). The "tip of the tongue" phenomenon. *Journal of Verbal Learning & Verbal Behavior, 5*(4), 325–337.

Brown, Y. A., Barlow, D. H., & Liebowitz, M. R. (1994). The empirical basis of generalized anxiety disorder. *American Journal of Psychiatry, 151*, 1272–1280.

Brubaker, D. A., & Leddy, J. J. (2003). Behavioral contracting in the treatment of eating disorders. *The Physician and Sportsmedicine, 31*(9).

Brunner, E. J., Hemingway, H., Walker, B., Page, M., Clarke, P., Juneja, M., Shipley, M. J., Kumari, M., Andrew, R., Seckl, J. R., Papadopoulos, A., Checkley, S., Rumley, A., Lowe, G. D., Stansfeld, S. A., & Marmot, M. G. (2002). Adrenocortical, autonomic and inflammatory causes of the metabolic syndrome: Nested case-control study. *Circulation, 106*, 2659–2665.

Brunner, L., Nick, H. P., Cumin, F., Chiesi, M., Baum, H. P., Whitebread, S., Stricker-Krongrad, A., & Levens, N. (1997). Leptin is a physiologically important regulator of food intake. *International Journal of Obesity Related Metabolic Disorders, 21*, 1152–1160.

Bryan, E. B., & Hallett, F. (2001). *Guidelines for professionals. Twins and triplets: The first five years and beyond*. London: Multiple Births Foundation.

Bryan, J., & Freed, F. (1982). Corporal punishment: Normative data and sociological and psychological correlates in a community college population. *Journal of Youth and Adolescence, 11*(2), 77–87.

Bryant, R. A., & McConkey, K. M. (1989). Hypnotic blindness: A behavioral and experimental analysis. *Journal of Abnormal Psychology, 98*, 71–77.

Brzustowicz, L. M., Simone, J., Mohseni, P., Hayter, J. E., Hodgkinson, K. A., Chow, E. W., & Bassett, A. S. (2004). Linkage disequilibrium mapping of schizophrenia susceptibility to the CAPON region of chromosome 1q22. *American Journal of Human Genetics, 74*(5), 1057–1063.

Bucher, B. D., & Lovaas, O. I. (1967). Use of aversive stimulation in behavior modification. In M. R. Jones (Ed.), *Miami Symposium on the Prediction of Behavior 1967: Aversive Stimulation*, 77–145.

Buck, R. (1980). Nonverbal behavior and the theory of emotion: The facial feedback hypothesis. *Journal of Personality and Social Psychology, 38*, 811–824.

Budney, A. J., Hughes, J. R., Moore, B. A., & Novy, P. L. (2001). Marijuana abstinence effects in marijuana smokers maintained in their environment. *Archives of General Psychiatry, 58*, 917–924.

Buller, D. B., Burgoon, M., Hall, J., Levine, N., Taylor, A., Beach, B., Melcher, C., Buller, M. K., Bowen, S., Hunsaker, F., & Bergen, A. (2000). Using language intensity to increase the success of a family intervention to protect children from ultraviolet radiation: Predictions from language expectancy theory. *Preventive Medicine, 30*, 103–114.

Bunge, M. (1984). What is pseudoscience? *The Skeptical Inquirer, 9*(1), 36–46.

Bunge, M. B., & Pearse, D. D. (2003). Transplantation strategies to promote repair of the injured spinal cord. *Journal of Rehabilitative Research & Development, 40*(4), 55–62.

Burger, J. J. M. (1997). The psychoanalytic approach: Neo-Freudian theory, application, and assessment. *Personality*, (4th ed.). Pacific Grove, CA: Brooks/Cole.

Burger, J. M. & Petty, R. E. (1981). The low-ball compliance technique: Task or person commitment? *Journal of Personality and Social Psychology, 40*, 492–500.

Burger, J. M. (1986). Increasing compliance by improving the deal: The that's not all technique. *Journal of Personality and Social Psychology, 51*, 277–283.

Burgio, K. L. (1998). Behavioral vs. drug treatment for urge urinary incontinence in older women: A randomized controlled trail. *Journal of the American Medical Association, 280*, 1995–2000.

Burke, D. M., MacKay, D. G., Worthley, J. S., & Wade, E. (1991). On the tip of the tongue: What causes word finding failures in young and older adults. *Journal of Memory and Language, 30*, 542–579.

Burks, N., & Martin, B. (1985). Everyday problems and life change events: Ongoing versus acute sources of stress. *Journal of Human Stress, 11*, 27–35.

Bushman, B. J. (1997). Effects of alcohol on human aggression: Validity of proposed explanations. In M. Galanter (Ed.), *Recent developments in alcoholism. Vol. 13* (pp. 227–243). New York: Plenum Press.

Bushman, B. J., & Huesmann, L. R. (2000). Effects of televised violence on aggression. In D. G. Singer & J. L. Singer (Eds.), *Handbook of children and the media* (pp. 223–254). Thousand Oaks, CA: Sage Publications.

Buss, D. M., Larsen, R. J., Westen, D., & Semmelroth, J. (1992). Sex differences in jealousy: Evolution, physiology, and psychology. *Psychological Science, 3*, 251–255.

Bussa, B., & Kaufman, C. (2000). What can self-help do? *The Journal of the California Alliance of the Mentally Ill, 2*(2).

Butcher, J. N., & Rouse, S. V. (1996). Personality: Individual differences and clinical assessment. *Annual Review of Psychology, 47*, 87–111.

Butcher, J. N., Graham, J. R., Ben-Poarth, Y. S., Tellegen, A., Dahlstrom, W. G., & Kaemmer, B. (2001). *Minnesota Multiphasic Personality Inventory-2. Manual for administration, scoring, and interpretation* (rev. ed.). Minneapolis, MN: University of Minnesota Press

Butcher, J. N., Rouse, S. V., & Perry, J. N. (2000). Empirical description of psychopathology in therapy clients: Correlates of MMPI-2 scales. In J. N. Butcher (Ed.), *Basic sources on the MMPI-2*, (pp. 487–500). Minneapolis, MN: University of Minnesota Press.

Butler, A. B. (2000). Chordate evolution and the origin of craniates: An old brain in a new head. *The Anatomical Record, 261*, 111–125.

Butler, K. (1993). Too good to be true? *Networker, 6*, 19–31.

Byne, W. (1995). Science and belief: Psychobiological research on sexual orientation. *Journal of Homosexuality, 28*, 303–344.

Cabeza, R., Anderson, N. D., Locantore, J. K. & McIntosh, A. R. (2002). Aging gracefully: Compensatory brain activity in high-performing older adults. *NeuroImage, 17*(3), 1394–1402.

Cain, D., & Seeman, J. (Eds.). (2001). *Humanistic psychotherapies: Handbook of research and practice*. Washington, DC: APA Publications.

Califia, P. (1997). *Sex changes: The politics of transgenderism*. San Francisco: Cleis Press.

Calvert, D. R. (1992). *Descriptive phonetics*. New York, Stuttgart: Thieme.

Camara, W. J., Nathan, J. S., & Puente, A. E. (2000). Psychological test usage: Implications in professional psychology. *Professional Psychology: Research and Practice, 31*(2), 141–154.

Cameron, J. A., Alvarez, J. M., Ruble, D. N., & Fuligni, A. J. (2001). Children's lay theories about ingroups and outgroups: Reconceptualizing research on prejudice. *Personality and Social Psychology Review, 5*, 118–128.

Cameron, J. R., Hansen, R., & Rosen, D. (1989). Preventing behavioral problems in infancy through temperament assessment and parental support programs. In W. B. Carey & S. C. McDevitt (Eds.), *Clinical and educational applications of temperament research* (pp. 155–165). Amsterdam: Swets & Zeitlinger.

Cameron, J., Banko, K. M., & Pierce, W. D. (2001). Pervasive negative effects of rewards on intrinsic motivation: The myth continues, *The Behavior Analyst, 24*, 1–44.

Cami, J., Farre, M., Mas, M., Roset, P. N., Poudevida, S., Mas, A., San, L., & de la Torre, R. (2000). Human pharmacology of 3,4-methylenedioxymethamphetamine ("ecstasy"). Psychomotor performance and subjective effects. *Journal of Clinical Psychopharmacology, 20*, 455–466.

Campbell, J. C., & Wolf, A. D. (2003). Risk factors for femicide in abusive relationships: Results from a multisite case control study. *American Journal of Public Health, 93*(7).

Campos, J. J., Langer, A., & Krowitz, A. (1970). Cardiac responses on the visual cliff. *Science, 170*, 196–197.

Cannon, W. B. (1927). The James-Lange theory of emotion: A critical examination and an alternative theory. *American Journal of Psychology, 39*, 10–124.

Cannon, W. B., & Washburn, A. L. (1912). An explanation of hunger. *American Journal of Physiology, 29*, 444–454.

Capek, J., & Capek, K. (1923). "*R.U.R.*" (*Rossum's Universal Robots*). London: Oxford University Press.

Carducci, B. (1998). *The psychology of personality*. Pacific Grove, CA: Brooks/Cole Publishing Co.

Carlson, G. A., Jensen, P. S., & Nottelmann, E. D. (Eds.) (1998). Special issue: Current issues in childhood bipolarity. *Journal of Affective Disorders, 51*.

Carpenter, P. A., Just, M. A., & Shell, P. (1990). What one intelligence test measures: A theoretical account of the processing in the Raven Progressive Matrices test. *Psychological Review, 97*(3), 404–431.

Carr, E. G., & Lovaas, O. I. (1983). Contingent electric shock as a treatment for severe behavior problems. In S. Axelrod & J. Apsche (Eds.), *The effects of punishment on human behavior* (pp. 221–245). New York: Academic Press.

Carroll, R. T. (2000). Eye movement desensitization and reprocessing (EMDR). The Skeptic's Dictionary. Retrieved from the Internet on July 14, 2004 at **www.skepdic.com/pseudosc.html**.

Carroll, R. T. (2002). ESP: Extrasensory perception. *Skeptic's Dictionary*. Retrieved from the Internet March 2003 at **http://skepdic.com/esp.html**.

Carruthers, M. (2001). A multifactorial approach to understanding andropause. *Journal of Sexual and Reproductive Medicine, 1*, 69–74.

Carson, R. C. (1969). *Interaction concepts of personality*. Chicago: Aldine.

Carter, C., Bishop, J., Kravits, S. L., & D'Agostino (ed. consultant). (2002). *Keys to college studying: Becoming a lifelong learner*. Upper Saddle River, NJ: Prentice-Hall.

Carver, C. S., & Antoni, M. H. (2004). Finding benefit in breast cancer during the year after diagnosis predicts better adjustment 5 to 8 years after diagnosis. *Health Psychology, 26*, 595–598.

Carver, L. J., & Bauer, P. J. (2001). The dawning of a past: The emergence of long-term explicit memory in infancy. *Journal of Experimental Psychology: General, 130*, 726–745.

Cassiday, K. L., & Lyons, J. A. (1992). Recall of traumatic memories following cerebral vascular accident. *Journal of Traumatic Stress, 5*, 627–631.

Cassidy, A., Bingham, S., & Setchell, K. D. R. (1994). Biological effects of a diet of soy protein rich in isoflavones on the menstrual cycle of premenopausal women. *American Journal of Clinical Nutrition, 60*, 333–340.

Castellanos, F., Giedd, J. N., Marsh, W. L., Hamburger, S. D., Vaituzis, A. C., Dickstein, D. P., Sarfatti, S. F., Vauss, Y. C., Snell, J. W., Lange, N., Kaysen, D., Krain, A. L., Ritchie, G. F., Rajapakse, J. C., & Rapoport, J. L. (1996). Quantitative brain magnetic resonance imaging in attention-deficit hyperactivity disorder. *Archives of General Psychiatry, 53*, 607–616.

Castillo, R. J. (1997). Eating disorders. In R. J. Castillo (Ed.), *Culture and mental illness: A client-centered approach* (p. 152). Pacific Grove, CA: Brooks/Cole Publishing Co.

Cattell, R. B. (1950). *Personality: A systematic, theoretical, and factual study*. New York: McGraw-Hill.

Cattell, R. B. (1990). Advances in Cattellian personality theory. In L. A. Pervin (Ed.), *Handbook of personality: Theory and research* (pp. 101–110). New York: Guilford.

Cattell, R. B. (1994). *Sixteen Personality Factor Questionnaire* (5th ed.). Champaign, Illinois: Institute for Personality and Ability Testing, Inc.

Cattell, R. B. (1995). Personality structure and the new fifth edition of the 16PF. *Educational & Psychological Measurement, 55*(6), 926–937.

Cattell, R. B. (Ed.). (1966). *Handbook of multivariate experimental psychology*. Chicago: Rand McNally.

Cattell, R. B., & Kline, P. (1977). *The scientific analysis of personality and motivation*. New York: Academic Press.

Cautela, J. R., & Kearney, A. J. (Eds.). (1994). *The covert conditioning casebook*. Pacific Grove, CA: Brooks/Cole.

Cautela, J. R., & Wisocki, P. A. (1971). Covert sensitization for the treatment of sexual deviations. *Psychological Record, 21*, 37–48.

Cave, K. R., & Kim, M. (1999). Top-down and bottom-up attentional control: On the nature of interference from a salient distractor. *Perception & Psychophysics, 61*, 1009–1023.

Centers for Disease Control and Prevention (CDC). (1992). *Smoking and health in the Americas: The Surgeon General's report*. National Center for Chronic Disease Prevention and Health Promotion.

Centers for Disease Control and Prevention (CDC). (1994). *Addressing emerging infectious disease threats: A prevention strategy for the United States*. Atlanta, GA: U.S. Department of Health and Human Services, Public Health Service.

Centers for Disease Control and Prevention (CDC). (1999). Achievements in public health, 1900–1999: Impact of vaccines universally recommended for children, United States 1990–1998. *Morbidity and Mortality Weekly Report, 48*, 243–248. Atlanta, GA: U.S. Department of Health and Human Services, Public Health Service.

Centers for Disease Control and Prevention (CDC). (2000). *What would happen if we stopped vaccinations?* Atlanta, GA: U.S. Department of Health and Human Services, Public Health Service. Retrieved from the Internet on August 23, 2004 at **www.cdc.gov/nip/publications/fs/gen/WhatIfStop.htm**.

Centers for Disease Control and Prevention (CDC). (2002). Annual smoking-attributable mortality, years of potential life lost, and economic costs—United States, 1995–1999. *Morbidity and Mortality Weekly Report, 51*, 300–303.

Centers for Disease Control and Prevention (CDC). (2004). *Parents' guide to childhood immunization*. Atlanta, GA: U.S. Department of Health and Human Services, Public Health Service.

Centerwall, B. S. (1989). Exposure to television as a risk factor for violence. *American Journal of Epidemiology, 129*, 643–652.

Cermak, L., & Craik, F. (1979). *Levels of processing in human memory*. Hillsdale, NJ: Erlbaum.

Cha, J. H., & Nam, K. D. (1985). A test of Kelley's cube theory of attribution: A cross-cultural replication of McArthur's study. *Korean Social Science Journal, 12*, 151–180.

Chang, P. P., Ford, D. E., Meoni, L. A., Wang, N., & Klag, M. J. (2002). Anger in young men and subsequent premature cardiovascular disease: The precursors study. *Archives of Internal Medicine, 162*, 901–906.

Chapelon-Clavel, F., Paoletti, C., & Benhamou, S. (1997). Smoking cessation rates 4 years after treatment by nicotine gum and acupuncture. *Preventive Medicine 26*, 25–28.

Charlesworth, W. R., & Kreutzer, M. A. (1973). Facial expression of infants and children. In P. Ekman (Ed.), *Darwin and facial expression: A century of research in review*. New York: Academic.

Chen, R., & Ende, N. (2000). The potential for the use of mononuclear cells from human umbilical cord blood in the treatment of amyotrophic lateral sclerosis in SOD1 mice. *Journal of Medicine, 31*, 21–31.

Cheng, H., Cao, Y., & Olson, L. (1996). Spinal cord repair in adult paraplegic rats: Partial restoration of hind limb function. *Science, 273*, 510–513.

Cherry, E. C. (1953). Some experiments on the recognition of speech, with one and with two ears. *Journal of the Acoustical Society of America, 25*(5), 975–979.

Chess, S., & Thomas, A. (1986). *Temperament in clinical practice*. New York: Guilford.

Chesterton, L. S., Barlas, P., Foster, N. E., Baxter, G. D., & Wright, C. C. (2003). Gender differences in pressure pain threshold in healthy humans. *Pain., 101*, 259–266.

Chiu, C., Hong, Y., & Dweck, C. S. (1997). Lay dispositionism and implicit theories of personality. *Journal of Personality and Social Psychology, 73*, 19–30.

Choi, I., & Nisbett, R. E. (1998). Situational salience and cultural differences in the correspondence bias and in the actor–observer bias. *Personality and Social Psychology Bulletin, 24*, 949–960.

Choi, I., Nisbett, R. E., & Norenzayan, A. (1999). Causal attribution across cultures: Variation and universality. *Psychological Bulletin, 125*, 47–63.

Chomsky, N. (1957). *Syntactic structures*. The Hague: Mouton.

Chomsky, N. (1964). *Current issues in linguistic theory*. The Hague: Mouton.

Chomsky, N. (1981). Principles and parameters in syntactic theory. In N. Hornstein & D. Lightfoot (Eds.), *Explanation in linguistics: The logical problem of language acquisition*. London: Longman.

Chomsky, N. (1986). *Knowledge of language: Its nature, origin and use*. New York: Praeger.

Chou, S. Y., Grossman, M., & Saffer, H. (2004). An economic analysis of adult obesity: Results from the behavioral risk factor surveillance system. *Journal of Health Economics, 23*, 565–587.

Christensen, A., Jacobson, N. S., & Babcock, J. C. (1995). Integrative behavioral couple therapy. In N. S. Jacobson & A. S. Gurman (Eds.), *Clinical handbook of couple therapy* (pp. 31–64). New York: Norton.

Christopher Reeve Paralysis Foundation. (2002). *Christopher Reeve Recovery Q & A*. Retrieved from the Internet on September 10, 2002 at **www.christopherreeve.org/news/NewsPrint.cfm?ID=328&c=30**.

Chu, J. A., Frey, L. M., Ganzel, B. L., & Matthews, J. A. (1999). Memories of childhood abuse: Dissociation, amnesia, and corroboration. *American Journal of Psychiatry, 156*, 749–755.

Chwalisz, K., Diener, E., & Gallagher, D. (1988). Autonomic arousal feedback and emotional experience: Evidence from the spinal cord injured. *Journal of Personality and Social Psychology, 54*, 820–828.

Cialdini, R. B., Trost, M. R., & Newsom, J. T. (1995). Preference for consistency: The development of a valid measure and the discovery of surprising behavioral implications. *Journal of Personality and Social Psychology, 69*, 318–328.

Cialdini, R., Vincent, J., Lewis, S., Catalan, J., Wheeler, D., & Darby, B. (1975). Reciprocal concessions procedure for inducing compliance: The door–in–the–face technique. *Journal of Personality and Social Psychology, 31*, 206–215.

Cialdini, R., Wosinska, W., Barrett, D., Butner, J., & Gornik–Durose, M. (1999). Compliance with a request in two cultures: The differential influence of social proof and commitment/consistency on collectivists and individualists. *Personality and Social Psychology Bulletin, 25*, 1242–1253.

Ciardiello, A. (1998). Did you ask a good question today? Alternative cognitive and metacognitive strategies. *Journal of Adolescent & Adult Literacy, 42*, 210–219.

Cincirpini, P. M., Lapitsky, L., Seay, S., Wallfisch, A., & Kitchens, K. V. V. H. (1995). The effects of smoking schedules on cessation outcome: Can we improve on common methods of gradual and abrupt nicotine withdrawal? *Journal of Consulting and Clinical Psychology, 63*(3), 388–399.

Cioffi, F. (1998). *Freud and the question of pseudoscience* (pp. 210–239). Chicago: Open Court.

Clark, D. A., Beck, A. T., & Brown, G. (1989). Cognitive mediation in general psychiatric outpatients: A test of the content-specificity hypothesis. *Journal of Personality and Social Psychology, 56*, 958–964.

Clarke, A., Harvey, M. L., & Kane, D. J. (1999). Attitudes and behavior: Are produce consumers influenced by eco-labels? Paper presented at a National Conference on Eco-labels, "Making Change in the Marketplace," October 22–23, 1998, at the Governor Hotel in Portland, Oregon. Sponsored by the Food Alliance. Retrieved from the Internet on August 1, 2004 at **www.ssi.nrcs.usda.gov/SSIEnvPsy/nrcs/ecopaper.pdf**.

Clarke, J. (1994). Pieces of the puzzle: The jigsaw method. In S. Sharan (Ed.), *Handbook of cooperative learning methods* (pp. 34–50). Westport, CT: Greenwood Press.

Coates, J. (1986). *Women, men, and language*. New York: Longman.

Coccaro, E. F., & Kavoussi, R. J. (1996). Neurotransmitter correlates of impulsive aggression. In D. M. Stoff & R. B. Cairns (Eds.), *Aggression and violence* (pp. 67–86). Mahwah, NJ: Lawrence Erlbaum.

Coffield, F., Moseley, D., Hall, E., & Ecclestone, K. (2004). Should we be using learning styles? What research has to say about practice. *Learning and Skills Research Centre*. **www.WSRD.ac.uk**.

Cohen, L. J. (1997). Rational drug use in the treatment of depression. *Pharmacotherapy, 17*, 45–61.

Cohen, L., Berzoff, J., & Elin, M. (1995). *Dissociative identity disorder: Theoretical and treatment controversies*. New York: Human Sciences Library.

Cohen, N. J., Eichenbaum, R., Decedo, J. C., & Corkin, S. (1985). Preserved learning capacity in amnesia: Evidence for multiple memory systems. In L. S. Squire & N. Butters (Eds.), *Neuropsychology of memory*. New York: The Gilford Press.

Cohen, S., & Herbert, T. B. (1996). Health psychology: Psychological factors and physical disease from the perspective of human psychoneuroimmunology. *Annual Review of Psychology, 47*, 113–142.

Colapinto, J. (2000). *As nature made him: The boy who was raised as a girl*. New York: HarperCollins.

Colcombe, S. J., Erickson, K. I., Raz, N., Webb, A. G., Cohen, N. J., McAuley, E., & Kramer, A. F. (2003). Aerobic fitness reduces brain tissue loss in aging humans. *Journal of Gerontology Series A: Biological Sciences and Medical Sciences, 58*, 176–180.

Colligan, J. (1983). Musical creativity and social rules in four cultures. *Creative Child and Adult Quarterly, 8*, 39–44.

Collins, A. M., & Loftus, E. F. (1975). A spreading activation theory of semantic processing. *Psychological Review, 82*, 407–428.

Collins, A. M., & Quillian, M. R. (1969). Retrieval time from semantic memory. *Journal of Verbal Learning and Verbal Behaviour, 8,* 240–247.

Collins, C. J., Hanges, P. J., & Locke, E. A. (2004). The relationship of achievement motivation to entrepreneurial behavior: A meta-analysis. *Human Performance, 17*(1), 95–117.

Collins, D. (1996). How and why participatory management improves a company's social performance: Four gainsharing case studies. *Business and Society 35*(2), 176–210.

Committee on Animal Research and Ethics. (2004). *Research with animals in psychology.* APAOnline. Retrieved from the Internet on October 12, 2004, at **www.apa.org/science/animal2.html.**

Concar, D. (1997). Blow your mind (does Ecstasy cause lasting damage to the human brain?). *New Scientist, 156,* 7.

Conrad, R., & Hull, A. J. (1964). Information, acoustic confusion, and memory span. *British Journal of Psychology, 55,* 429–432.

Consumer Reports. (1995, November). Mental health: Does psychotherapy help? 734–739.

Conway, M. (1995). *Flashbulb memories.* Hove, UK: Lawrence Erlbaum Associates, Publishers.

Conway, M. A., Cohen, G., & Stanhope, N. (1992). Very long-term memory for knowledge acquired at school and university. *Applied Cognitive Psychology, 6,* 467–482.

Cook, R. L., St. George, K., Lassak, M., Tran, N., Anhalt, J. P., & Rinaldo, C. R. (1999). Screening for Chlamydia trachomatis infection in college women with a polymerase chain reaction assay. *Clinical Infectious Diseases, 28,* 1002-1007.

Cooper, L. A., Gonzales, J. J., Gallo, J. J., Rost, K. M., Meredith, L. S., Rubenstein, L. V., Wang, N. Y., & Ford, D. E. (2003). The acceptability of treatment for depression among African-American, Hispanic, and white primary care patients. *Medical Care, 41*(4), 479–489.

Cormier, J. F., & Thelen, M. H. (1998). Professional skepticism of multiple personality disorder. *Professional Psychology: Research and Practice, 29,* 163–167,

Cosgrove, G. R., & Rauch, S. L. (1995). Psychsurgery. *Neurosurgery Clinics of North America, 6,* 167–176.

Costa P. T., Jr., & McCrae. R. R. (1989). Personality continuity and the changes of adult life. In M. Storandt & G. R. VandenBos (Eds.), *The adult years: Continuity and change* (pp. 45–77). Washington, DC: American Psychological Association,.

Costa, P. T., Jr., & McCrae, R. R. (2000). The Revised NEO Personality Inventory (NEO PI-R). In J. Cheek, & E. M. Donahue (Eds.), *Handbook of personality inventories.* New York: Plenum.

Courage, M. L., & Howe, M. L. (2002). From infant to child: The dynamics of cognitive change in the second year of life. *Psychological Bulletin, 128,* 250–277.

Cowan, N. (1988). Evolving conceptions of memory storage, selective attention, and their mutual constraints within the human information processing system. *Psychological Bulletin, 104,* 163–191.

Coye, R. W., & Belohlav, J. A. (1995). An exploratory analysis of employee participation. *Group and Organization Management 20*(1), 4–17.

Crago, M. B., Shisslak, C. M., & Estes, L. S. (1996). Eating disturbances among American minority groups: A review. *International Journal of Eating Disorders, 19,* 239–248.

Craik, F. I. M. (1970). The fate of primary memory items in free recall. *Journal of Verbal Learning and Verbal Behavior, 9,* 143–148.

Craik, F. I. M. (1994). Memory changes in normal aging. *Current Directions in Psychological Science, 3*(5), 155–158.

Craik, F. I. M., & Lockhart, R. S. (1972). Levels of processing. A framework for memory research. *Journal of Verbal Learning and Verbal Behaviour, 11,* 671–684.

Craik, F. I. M., & Tulving, E. (1975). Depth of processing and the retention of words in episodic memory. *Journal of Experimental Psychology: General, 104,* 268–294.

Cramer, P. (2000). Defense mechanisms in psychology today: Further processes for adaptation. *American Psychologist, 55,* 637–646.

Crawford, M., & Unger, R. (2004). *Women and gender: A feminist psychology* (4th ed.). Boston: McGraw-Hill.

Crowley, A. E., & Hoyer, W. D. (1994). "An integrative framework for understanding two–sided persuasion," *Journal of Consumer Research, 20,* 561–574.

Csernansky, J. G., Mahmoud, R., & Brenner, R. (2002). A comparison of reperidone and hloperidol for the prevention of relapse in patients with schizophrenia. *New England Journal of Medicine, 346,* 16–22.

Csikszentmihalyi, M. (1996). *Creativity: Flow and the psychology of discovery and Invention.* New York: Harper Perennial.

Csikszentmihalyi, M. (1997). *Finding flow: The psychology of engagement with everyday life.* New York: Basic Books.

Cua, A. B., Wilhelm, K. P., & Maibach, H. I. (1990). Elastic properties of human skin: Relation to age, sex and anatomical region. *Archives of Dermatology Research, 282,* 283–288.

Culbertson, F. (2003). *The phobia list.* Retrieved from the Internet on June 22, 2004 at **www.phobialist.com.**

Cummings, J. L., & Coffey C. E. (1994). Neurobiological basis of behavior. In C. E., Coffey, & J. L., Cummings, (Eds.), *Textbook of geriatric neuropsychiatry* (pp. 72–96). Washington, DC: American Psychiatric Press.

Cummings, S. R., & Melton, L. J. III. (2002). Epidemiology and outcomes of osteoporotic fractures. *Lancet, 359*(9319), 1761–1767.

Cup of Heaven. (2000). F.Y.I.: For your information: Caffeine. Document retrieved from the Internet on October 19, 2004 at **www.cupofheaven.com/fyi.htm.**

Curtis, R. C., & Miller, K. (1986). Believing another likes or dislikes you: Behaviors making the beliefs come true. *Journal of Personality and Social Psychology, 51,* 284–290.

Curtis, R. H. (1993). *Great lives: Medicine.* New York: Scribner's.

Cytowic, R. E. (1989). Synesthesia and mapping of subjective sensory dimensions. *Neurology, 39,* 849–850.

Czeisler, C. A. (1995). The effect of light on the human circadian pacemaker. In D. J. Chadwick & K. Ackrill (Eds.), *Circadian clocks and their adjustment* (pp. 254–302). West Sussex, England: John Wiley & Sons.

Czeisler, C. A., Weitzman, E. D., Moore-Ede, M. C., Zimmerman, J. C., & Knauer, R. S. (1980). Human sleep: Its duration and organization depend on its circadian phase. *Science, 210,* 1264–1267.

Dalenberg, C. J. (1996). Accuracy, timing and circumstances of disclosure in therapy of recovered and continuous memories of abuse. *The Journal of Psychiatry and Law, 24*(2), 229–275.

Dallman, M., Pecoraro, N., Akana, S., la Fleur, S. E., Gomez, F., Houshyar, H., Bell, M. E., Bhatnagar, S., Laugero, K. D., & Manalo, S. (2003). Chronic stress and obesity: A new view of "comfort food." *Proceedings of the National Academy of Sciences, 100*(20), 11696–11701.

Daly, M., Wilson, M., & Weghorst, S. J. (1982). Male sexual jealousy. *Ethology and Sociobiology, 3,* 11–27.

Damasio, H., Grabowski, T., Frank, R., Galaburda, A. M., & Damasion, A. R. (1994). The return of Phineas Gage: Clues about the brain from the skull of a famous patient. *Science, 264,* 1102–1105.

Darley, J. M., & Latané, B. (1968). Bystander intervention in emergencies: Diffusion of responsibility. *Journal of Personality and Social Psychology, 8,* 377–383.

Darvill, T., Lonky, E., Reihman, J., Stewart, P. & Pagano, J. (2000). Prenatal exposure to PCBs and infant performance on the Fagan test of infant intelligence. *Neurotoxicology, 21*(6), 1029–1038.

Darwin, C. (1859). *The origin of species by means of natural selection.* London: John Murray.

Darwin, C. (1898). *The expression of the emotions in man and animals.* New York: D. Appleton & Co.

Daum, I., & Schugens, M. M. (1996). On the cerebellum and classical conditioning. *Current Directions in Psychological Science, 5,* 58–61.

Davidson, R. J., Ekman, P., Saron, C. D., Senulis, J. A., & Friesen, W. V. (1990). Approach-withdrawal and cerebral asymmetry: Emotional expression and brain physiology I. *Journal of Personality and Social Psychology, 58*(2), 330–341.

Davidson, R. J., Putman, K. M. & Larson, C. L. (2000). Dysfunction in the neural circuitry of emotion regulation-A possible prelude to violence. *Science, 289,* 591–594.

Davies, I. R. L., Laws, G., Corbett, G. G., & Jerrett, D. J. (1998a). Crosscultural differences in colour vision: Acquired "colour blindness" in Africa. *Personality and Individual Differences, 25,* 1153–1162.

Davies, I. R. L., Sowden, P., Jerrett, D. T., Jerrett, T., & Corbett, G. G. (1998b). A cross-cultural study of English and Setswana speakers on a colour triads task: A test of the Sapir-Whorf hypothesis. *British Journal of Psychology, 89,* 1–15.

Davis, C. J., Harding, J. W., & Wright, J. W. (2003). REM sleep deprivation-induced deficits in the latency-to-peak induction and maintenance of long-term potentiation within the CA1 region of hippocampus. *Brain Research, 973*, 293–297.

Davis, K. L., Kahn, R. S., Ko, G., & Davidson, M. (1991). Dopamine in schizophrenia: A review and reconceptualization. *American Journal of Psychiatry, 148*, 1474–1486.

Davis, M., & Whalen, P. J. (2001). The amygdala: Vigilance and emotion. *Molecular Psychiatry 6*, 13–34.

Dawood, K., Pillard, R. C., Horvath, C., Revelle, W., & Bailey, J. M. (2000). Familial aspects of male homosexuality. *Archives of Sexual Behavior, 29*(2).

Day, R. H., & McKenzie, B. E. (1981). Infant perception of the invariant size of approaching and receding objects. *Developmental Psychology, 17*, 670–677.

Dean, G., & Kelly, I. W. (2000). Does astrology work? Astrology and skepticism 1975–2000. In P. Kurtz (Ed), *Skepticism: A 25 Year Retrospective*, (pp. 191–207) Amherst NY: Prometheus Books.

Dean, G., Kelly, I. W., Sakolfske, D. H., & Furnham, A. (1992). Graphology and human judgment. In B. L. Beyerstein & D. F. Beyerstein, (Eds.). *The write stuff: Evaluations of graphology—the study of handwriting analysis*, (pp. 342–396) Amherst NY: Prometheus Books.

DeAngelis, T. (2002). Promising treatments for anorexia and bulimia: Research boosts support for tough-to-treat eating disorders. *APA Monitor on Psychology, 33*(3), 38–43.

DeCasper, A. J., & Fifer, W. P. (1980). Of human bonding: Newborns prefer their mothers' voices. *Science, 208*, 1174–1176.

DeCasper, A. J., & Spence, M. J. (1986). Prenatal maternal speech influence on newborns' perception of sounds. *Infant Behaviour and Development, 9*, 133–150.

deCharms, R. (1968). *Personal causation*. New York: Academic Press.

Deci, E. L., & Ryan, R. M. (1985). *Intrinsic motivation and self–determination in human behavior*. New York: Plenum.

Deci, E. L., Eghrari, H., Patrick, B. C., & Leone, D. R. (1994). Facilitating internalization: The self-determination theory perspective. *Journal of Personality, 62*, 119–142.

Deci, E. L., Koestner, R., & Ryan, R. M. (1999). A meta-analytic review of experiments examining the effects of extrinsic rewards on intrinsic motivation. *Psychological Bulletin, 125*, 627–668.

DeCoster, J., & Claypool, H. M. (2004). A meta-analysis of priming effects on impression formation supporting a general model of informational biases. *Personality and Social Psychology Review, 8*(1), 2–27.

DeGrandpre, R. J. (2000). A science of meaning: Can behaviorism bring meaning to psychological science? *American Psychologist, 55*, 721–739.

Dehaene, S., Naccache, L., Cohen, L., Le Bihan, D., Mangin, J. F., Poline, J. B., & Riviere, D. (2001). Cerebral mechanisms of word masking and unconscious repetition priming. *Nature Neuroscience, 4*, 752–758.

Deinzer, R., Kleineidam, C. H., Winkler, R., Idel, H., & Bachg, D. (2000). Prolonged reduction of salivary immunoglobulin A (slgA) after a major academic exam. *International Journal of Psychophysiology, 37*, 219–232.

Delagrange, P., & Guardiola-Lemaitre, B. (1997). Melatonin, its receptors, and relationships with biological rhythm disorders. *Clinical Neuropharmacology, 20*, 482–510.

Delfiner, R. (2001, November 16). "Kitty Left at Death's Door." *The New York Post.*

DeLongis, A., Lazarus, R. S. & Folkman, S. (1988). The impact of daily stress on health and mood: Psychological and social resources as mediators. *Journal of Personality and Social Psychology, 54*(3), 486–495.

Dement, W. (1997). Sleepless at Stanford: What all undergraduates should know about how their sleeping lives affect their waking lives. Article retrieved from the Internet on October 19, 2004 at **www.stanford.edu/~dement/sleepless.html.**

Dement, W. C. (1960). The effect of dream deprivation. *Science, 131*, 1705–1707.

Dement, W. C., Henry, P., Cohen, H., & Ferguson, J. (1969). Studies on the effect of REM deprivation in humans and animals. In K. H. Pribram (Ed.), *Mood, states, and mind*. Baltimore: Penguin.

Demers, R. A. (1988). Linguistics and animal communication. In Newmeyer (Ed.), *Language form and language function*. 314–335.

Deming, E. (2000). *Out of the Crisis*. Cambridge, MA: The MIT Press.

Denno, D. W. (2002). Crime and consciousness: Science and involuntary acts. *Minnesota Law Review, 87*, 269–399.

Deregowski, J. B. (1969). Perception of the two-pronged trident by two- and three-dimensional perceivers. *Journal of Experimental Psychology, 82*, 9–13.

DeRubeis, R. J., Gelfand, L. A., Tang, T. Z., & Simons, A. D. (1999). Medications versus cognitive behavior therapy for severely depressed outpatients: Mega-analysis of four randomized comparisons. *American Journal of Psychiatry, 156*(7), 1007–1013.

DeStefano, A., & Hurtado, P. (1995, July 25). Dredging the past; Kitty Genovese convict takes stand. *Newsday.*

De Valois R. L., & Jacobs G. H. (1968). Primate color vision, *Science, 162*, 533–540.

DeVry University. (2004). *DeVry University Online Learning Styles Assessment*. Retrieved from the Internet on September 8, 2004, at **www.devry.edu/online/ online_styles.html.**

Diamond, L. M. (2003). What does sexual orientation orient? A biobehavioral model distinguishing romantic love and sexual desire. *Psychological Review, 110*, 173–192.

Diamond, M. (1995). Biological aspects of sexual orientation and identity. In L. Diamant & R. McAnulty (Eds.), *The psychology of sexual orientation, behavior and identity: A handbook* (pp. 45–80). Westport, CT: Greenwood Press.

Diamond, M. C. (1991). Hormonal effects on the development of cerebral lateralization. *Psychoneuroendocrinology, 16*, 121–129.

Diamond, M., & Sigmundson, H. K. (1997). Sex reassignment at birth. Long-term review and clinical implications. *Archives of Pediatric Adolescent Medicine, 151*(3), 298–304.

Dickens, W. T., & Flynn, J. R. (2001 April). Heritability estimates vs. large environmental effects: The IQ paradox resolved. *Psychological Review, 108*(2), 346–369.

Dickerson, F., Ringel, N., Parente, F., & Boronow, J. (1994). Seclusion and restraint, assaultiveness, and patient performance in a token economy. *Hospital and Community Psychiatry, 45*, 168–170.

Digman, J. M. (1990). Personality structure: Emergence of the five-factor model. *Annual Review of Psychology, 41*, 417–440.

Dillard, J. (1990). Self-inference and the foot–in–the–door technique: Quantity of behavior and attitudinal mediation. *Human Communication Research, 16*, 422–447.

Dillard, J. (1991). The current status of research on sequential–request compliance techniques. *Personality and Social Psychology Bulletin, 17*, 282–288.

Dimberg, U., Thunberg, M., & Elmehed, K. (2000). Unconscious facial reactions to emotional facial expressions. *Psychological Science, 11*, 86–89.

Dinges, D. F. (1995). An overview of sleepiness and accidents. *Journal of Sleep Research, 4*(2), 4–14.

Dion, K., Berscheid, E., & Walster, E. (1972). What is beautiful is good. *Journal of Personality & Social Psychology, 24*, 285–290.

Dodge, K. A., Bates, J. E., & Pettit, G. S. (1990). Mechanisms in the cycle of violence. *Science, 250*, 1678–1683.

Dollard, J., & Miller, N. (1950). *Personality and psychotherapy: An analysis in terms of learning, thinking and culture*. New York: McGraw-Hill.

Dollard, J., & Miller, N. F. (1950). *Personality and psychotherapy*. New York: McGraw-Hill.

Dollard, J., Doob, L. W., Milller, N. E., Mowrer, O. H., & Sears, R. R. (1939). *Frustration and aggression*. New Haven: Yale University Press.

Domhoff, G. W. (1996). *Finding meaning in dreams: A quantitative approach*. New York: Plenum Publishing Co.

Domhoff, G. W. (2000). The problems with activation-synthesis theory. Retrieved from the Internet on February 10, 2005 at **www.dreamresearch.net/Library/ domhoff_2000e.html.**

Dominy, N. J., & Lucas, P. W. (2001). Ecological importance of trichromatic vision to primates. *Nature, 410*, 363–366.

Domjan, M., Cusato, B., & Villarreal, R. (2000), Pavlovian feed-forward mechanisms in the control of social behavior. *Behavioral and Brain Sciences, 23*, 235–282.

Dorahy, M. J. (2001). Dissociative identity disorder and memory dysfunction: The current state of experimental research and its future directions. *Clinical Psychology Review, 21*(5), 771–795.

Dougherty, D. D., Baer, L., Cosgrove, G. R., Cassem, E. H., Price, B. H., Nierenberg, A. A., Jenike, M. A., & Rauch, S. L. (2002). Prospective long-term follow-up of 44 patients who received cingulotomy for treatment-refractory obsessive-compulsive disorder. *The American Journal of Psychiatry, 159*(2), 269–275.

Dove, A. (1971). The "Chitling" Test. In Lewis R. Aiken, Jr. *Psychological and educational testings*. Boston: Allyn and Bacon.

Dreger, A. D. (1998). "Ambiguous sex"—or ambivalent medicine? Ethical issues in the treatment of intersexuality. *Hastings Center Report, 28*(3), 24–35.

Dreger, A. D. (1999). *Intersex in the age of ethics*. Hagerstown, MD: University Publishing Groups Inc.

Drenth, P. J., Thierry, H., Willems, P. J., & de Wolff, C. J. (1984) *Handbook of work and organizational psychology*. Chichester: John Wiley and Sons, Inc.

Druckman, D., & Bjork, R. A. (Eds.). (1994). *Learning, remembering, believing: Enhancing human performance*. (Study conducted by the National Research Council). Washington, DC: National Academy Press.

Dryer, D. C., & Horowitz, L. M. (1997). When do opposites attract? Interpersonal complementarity versus similarity. *Journal of Personality and Social Psychology, 72*, 592–603.

Drysdale, M. T. B., Ross, J. L., & Schulz, R. A. (2001). Cognitive learning styles and academic performance in 19 first-year university courses: Successful students versus students at risk. *Journal of Education for Students Placed at Risk, 6*(3), 271–289.

Duben, A., & Behar, C. (1991). *Istanbul households: Marriage, family and fertility 1880–1940*. Cambridge: Cambridge University Press.

Duker, P. C., & Seys, D. M. (1995). *Long-term use of electrical aversion treatment with self-injurious behavior* Paper presented at BILD Conference.

Duncan, R. M. (1995). Piaget and Vygotsky revisited: Dialogue or assimilation? *Developmental Review, 15*, 458–472.

Duncker, K. (1945). On problem solving. *Psychological Monographs, 58* (5, Whole No. 270).

Dunn, R., Beaudry, J. S., & Klavas, A. (1989). Survey of research on learning styles. *Educational Leadership, 46*(6), 50–57.

Dunn, R., Della Valle, J., Dunn, K., Geisert, G., Sinatra, R., & Zenhausern, R. (1986). The effects of matching and mismatching students' mobility preferences on recognition and memory tasks. *Journal of Educational Research, 79*, 267–272.

Dunn, R., Denig, S., & Lovelace, M. K. (2001, February 1). Multiple intelligences and learning styles: Two sides of the same coin or different strokes for different folks? *Teacher Librarian, 28*, 9–15.

Dunn, R., Griggs, S. A., Olson, J., Gorman, B., & Beasley, M. (1995). A meta-analytic validation of the Dunn and Dunn model of learning-style preferences. *Journal of Educational Research, 88*, 353–361.

Durrant, M. (Ed.). (1993). *Aristotle's De anima in focus*. London: Routledge.

Durso, F., Rea, C., & Dayton, T. (1994). Graph-theoretic confirmation of restructuring during insight. *Psychological Science, 5*, 94–98.

Durston, S. (2003). A review of the biological bases of ADHD: What have we learned from imaging studies? *Mental Retardation and Developmental Disabilities Research Reviews, 9*, 184–195.

Dweck, C. (1986). Motivational processes affecting learning. *American Psychologist, 41*(10), 1040–1048.

Dweck, C. S. (1999). *Self-theories: Their role in motivation, personality and development*. Philadelphia: Psychology Press.

Dweck, C. S., & Leggett, E. L. (1988). A social-cognitive approach to motivation and personality. *Psychological Review, 95*, 256–273.

Dweck, C. S., Chiu, C., & Hong, Y. (1995). Implicit theories and their role in judgments and reactions: A world from two perspectives. *Psychological Inquiry, 6*, 267–285.

Dweck, C., & Elliott, E. (1983). Achievement motivation. In P. Mussen (Ed.), *Handbook of child psychology. Vol. 4. Socialization, personality, and social development* (pp. 643–691). New York: Wiley.

Dykens, E. M., Hodapp, R. M., & Leckman, J. F. (1994). *Behavior and development in Fragile X syndrome*. Thousand Oaks, CA: Sage Publications.

Eagly, A. H. (1987). *Sex difference in social behavior: A social-role interpretation*. Hillsdale, NJ: Lawrence Erlbaum.

Eagly, A. H., & Chaiken, S. (1993). *The psychology of attitudes*. Fort Worth, TX: Harcourt Brace.

Eagly, A. H., & Chaiken, S. (1998). Attitude structure and function. In D. T. Gilbert, S. T. Fiske, & G. Lindzey (Eds.), *The handbook of social psychology* (4th ed. pp. 269–322). New York: McGraw-Hill.

Eagly, A. H., Ashmore, R. D., Makhijani, M. G., & Longo, L. C. (1991). What is beautiful is good, but…: A meta-analytic review of the physical attractiveness stereotype. *Psychological Bulletin, 110*, 109–128.

Eagly, A. H., Wood, W., & Diekman, A. B. (2000). Social role theory of sex differences and similarities: A current appraisal. In T. Eckes & H. M. Trautner (Eds.), *The developmental social psychology of gender* (pp. 123–174). Mahwah, NJ: Lawrence Erlbaum..

Eagly, A., & Chaiken, S. (1975). An attribution analysis of the effect of communicator characteristics on opinion change: The case of communicator attractiveness. *Journal of Personality and Social Psychology, 37*, 136–144.

Eaker, E. D., & Castelli, W. P. (1988). Type A behavior and mortality from coronary disease in the Framingham Study. *New England Journal of Medicine, 319*, 1480–1481.

Eaton, W. W., Kessler, R. C., Wittchen, H. U., & Magee, W. J. (1994). Panic and panic disorder in the United States. *American Journal of Psychiatry 151*(3), 413–420.

Ebbinghaus, H. (1913). *Memory: A contribution to experimental psychology*. New York: Teachers College Press. (Translated from the 1885 German original.)

Eddy, J., Fitzhugh, E., & Wang, M. (2000). Smoking acquisition: Peer influence and self-selection. *Psychological Reports, 86*, 1241–1246.

Edelmann, R. J., & Iwawaki, S. (1987). Self-reported expression of embarrassment in five European cultures. *Psychologia: An International Journal of Psychology, 30*, 205–216.

Egner, T., Strawson, E., & Gruzelier, J. H. (2002). EEG signature and phenomenology of alpha/theta neurofeedback training versus mock feedback. *Appl Psychophysiol Biofeedback, 27*(4), 261–70.

Eich, E., & Metcalfe, J. (1989). Mood dependent memory for internal vs. external events. *Journal of Experimental Psychology: Learning, Memory and Cognition, 15*, 443–455.

Eiser, J. R., & van der Pligt, J. (1984). Attitudinal and social factors in adolescent smoking: In search of peer group influence. *Journal of Applied Social Psychology, 14*, 348–363.

Ekman, P. (1973). Darwin and cross-cultural studies of facial expression. In P. Ekman (Ed.), *Darwin and facial expression: A century of research in review*. New York: Academic Press.

Ekman, P. (1980). Asymmetry in facial expression. *Science, 209*, 833–834.

Ekman, P., & Friesen, W. (1969). The repertoire of nonverbal behavior: Categories, origins, usage, and coding. *Semiotica, 1*, 49–98.

Ekman, P., & Friesen, W. (1971). Constants across cultures in the face and emotion. *Journal of Personality and Social Psychology, 17*(2), 124–129.

Ekman, P., & Friesen, W. V. (1978). *The facial action coding system*. Palo Alto, CA: Consulting Psychologists Press.

Ekman, P., Sorensen, E. R., & Friesen, W. V. (1969). Pan-cultural elements in facial displays of emotion. *Science, 164*, 86–88.

Elkind, D. (1985). Egocentrism redux. *Developmental Review, 5*, 218–226.

Elliott, E., & Dweck, C. (1988). Goals: An approach to motivation and achievement. *Journal of Personality and Social Psychology, 54*, 5–12.

Ellis, A. (1997). *The practice of rational emotive behavior therapy*. New York: Springer Publishing Company.

Ellis, A. (1998). *The Albert Ellis reader: A guide to well-being using rational emotive behavior therapy*. Secaucus, NJ: Carol Publishing Group.

Ellis, B. J., McFadyen-Ketchum, S. A., Dodge, K. A., Pettit, G. S., & Bates, J. E. (1999). Quality of early family relationships and individual differences in the timing of pubertal maturation in girls: A longitudinal test on an evolutionary model. *Journal of Personality and Social Psychology, 77*, 387–401.

Ellis, H. D. (1983). The role of the right hemisphere in face perception. In A. W. Young (Ed.), *Functions of the right cerebral hemisphere.* London: Academic Press.

Ellis, L., Ames, M. A., Peckham, W., & Burke, D. (1988). Sexual orientation of human offspring may be altered by severe maternal stress during pregnancy. *The Journal of Sex Research, 25,* 152–157.

Ellis, L. K., Gay, P. E., & Paige, E. (2001). Daily pleasures and hassles across the lifespan. Poster presented at the annual meeting of the American Psychological Association, San Francisco, CA.

Emmert, D. H., & Kirchner, J. T. (2000). Sexually transmitted diseases in women: Gonorrhea and syphilis. *Postgraduate Medicine, 107*(2), 181–197.

Endler, N. S. (1988). The origins of electroconvulsive therapy (ECT). *Convulsive Therapy, 4,* 5–23.

Engle, R. W., & Kane, M. J. (2004). Executive attention, working memory capacity, and a two-factor theory of cognitive control. *The Psychology of Learning and Motivation, 44,* 145–199.

Enns, J. T., & Coren, S. (1995). The box alignment illusion: An orientation illusion induced by pictorial depth. *Perception & Psychophysics, 57,* 1163–1174.

Epping-Jordan, M., Waltkins, S. S., Koob, G. F., & Markou, A. (1998). Dramatic decreases in brain reward function during nicotine withdrawal. *Nature (Lond), 393,* 76–79.

Epstein, J. (1990). Either/or—neither/both: Sexual ambiguity and the ideology of gender. *Genders, 7,* 99–142.

Erdley, C. A., & Dweck, C. S. (1993). Children's implicit personality theories as predictors of their social judgments. *Child Development, 64,* 863–878.

Erikson, E. (1980). Elements of a psychoanalytic theory of psychosocial development. In S. Greenspan, & G. Pollock, (Eds.), *The Course of Life, Vol. 1* (pp. 11–61). Washington, DC: U.S. Dept. of Health and Human Services.

Erikson, E. H. (1950). *Childhood and society.* New York: Norton.

Erikson, E. H. (1959). Growth and crises of the healthy personality. *Psychological Issues, 1,* 50–100.

Erikson, E. H. (1982). *The life cycle completed.* New York: Norton.

Erikson, E. H., & Erikson, J. M. (1997). *The life cycle completed.* New York: Norton.

Eriksson, P., Jakobsson, E., & Fredriksson, A. (2001). Brominated flame retardants: A novel class of developmental neurotoxicants in our environment? *Environmental Health Perspectives, 109*(9), 903–908.

Eskenazi, B., Bradman, A., & Castorina, R. (1999). Exposures of children to organophosphate pesticides and their potential adverse health effects. *Environmental Health Perspectives, 107*(Suppl. 3), 409–419.

Evans, D., Hodgkinson, B., O'Donnell, A., Nicholson, J., & Walsh, K. (2000). The effectiveness of individual therapy and group therapy in the treatment of schizophrenia. In *Best Practice, 5*(3), 1–54. Published by the Joanna Briggs Institute for Evidence Based Nursing and Midwifery.

Evans, I. M. & Meyer, L. H. (1985). *An educative approach to behavior problems: A practical decision model for interventions with severely handicapped learners.* Baltimore: Paul H. Brookes.

Evans, W. H., Evans, S. S., & Schmid, R. E. (1989). *Behavior and instructional management: An ecological approach.* Boston: Allyn and Bacon.

Everson, S. (1995). Psychology. In J. Barnes (Ed.), *The Cambridge companion to Aristotle* (pp. 168–194). Cambridge, England: Cambridge University Press.

Exner, J. E. (1980). But it's only an inkblot. *Journal of Personality Assessment, 44,* 562–577.

Eysenck, H. (1994). *Test your IQ.* Toronto: Penguin Books.

Eysenck, H. J. (1957). The effects of psychotherapy: An evaluation. *Journal of Consulting Psychology, 16,* 319–324.

Eysenck, H. J. (1994). Synergistic interaction between psychosocial and physical factors in the causation of lung cancer. In C. Lewis, C. O'Sullivan, & J. Barraclough (Eds.), *The psychoimmunology of human cancer* (pp. 163–178). London: Oxford University Press.

Eysenck, H. J., & Eysenck, S. B. G. (1993). *Eysenck Personality Questionnaire [Revised].* London: Hodder & Stoughton Educational.

Fagot, B. I., & Hagan, R. (1991). Observations of parent reactions to sex-stereotyped behaviours: Age and sex effects. *Child Development, 62,* 617–628.

Fahey, V. (1993). How sleep deprived are you? *Health, 7*(5), 3–4.

Fanselow, M. S., & Gale, G. D. (2003). The amygdala, fear, and memory. *Annals of the New York Academy of Sciences, 985,* 125–134.

Fantz, R. L. (1961). The origin of form perception. *Scientific American, 204,* 66–72.

Fantz, R. L. (1964). Visual experience in infants: Decreased attention to familiar patterns relative to novel ones. *Science, 146,* 668–670.

Faraone, S. V., Biederman, J., & Friedman, D. (2000). Validity of DSM-IV subtypes of attention-deficit/hyperactivity disorder: A family study perspective. *Journal of the American Academy of Child and Adolescent Psychiatry, 39,* 300–307.

Faraone, S. V., Biederman, J., Lehman, B. K., Keenan, K., Norman, D., Seidman, L. J., Kolodny, R., Kraus, I., Perrin, J., & Chen, W. J. (1993). Evidence for independent familial transmission of attention deficit hyperactivity disorder and learning disabilities: Result from a family genetic study. *American Journal of Psychiatry, 150,* 891–895.

Faraone, S. V., Tsuang, M. T., & Tsuang, D. W. (1999). *Genetics of mental disorders: A guide for students, clinicians, and researchers.* New York: Guilford Press.

Farmer, A. E. (1996). The genetics of depressive disorders. *International Review of Psychiatry, 8*(4).

Farthing, W. (1992). *The psychology of consciousness.* Upper Saddle River, NJ: Prentice-Hall.

Faucett, J., Gordon, N., & Levine, J. (1994). Differences in postoperative pain severity among four ethnic groups. *Journal of Pain Symptom Management, 9,* 383–389.

Fawzy, F. I., Fawzy, N. W., Hyun, C. S., Elashoff, R., Guthrie, D., Fahey, J. L., & Morton, D. L. (1993). Malignant melanoma effects of an early structured psychiatric intervention, coping, and affective state on recurrence and survival 6 years later. *Archives of General Psychiatry, 50*(9), 681–689.

FDA MedWatch Safety Alert. (October 15, 2004). Public health advisory: Suicidality in children and adolescents being treated with antidepressant medications. Retrieved from the Internet on December 15, 2004 at **www.fda.gov/medwatch/SAFETY/2004/safety04.htm#ssri**.

Fechner, G. T. (1860). *Elemente der Psykophysik.* Leipzig: Breitkopf und Härtel.

Fedoroff, I. C., & McFarlane, T. (1998). Cultural aspects of eating disorders. In S. S. Kazarian & D. R. Evans (Eds.). *Cultural clinicalm psychology: Theory, research and practice* (pp. 152–176). New York: Oxford University Press.

Feingold, A. (1992). Good-looking people are not what we think. *Psychological Bulletin, 111,* 304–341.

Felder, R. (1993). Reaching the second tier: Learning and teaching styles in college science education. *Journal of College Science Teaching, 23*(5), 286–290.

Felder, R. (1996). Matters of style. *ASEE Prism, 6*(4), 18–23.

Feldman, D. H. (2003). Cognitive development in childhood. In R. M. Lerner, M. A. Easterbrooks, et al. (Eds.), *Handbook of psychology: Developmental psychology, Vol. 6* (pp. 195–201). New York: Wiley.

Ferguson, N. B., & Keesey, R. E. (1975). Effect of a quinine-adulterated diet upon body weight maintenance in male rats with ventromedial hypothalamic lesions. *Journal of Comparative Physiological Psychology, 89*(5): 478–488.

Fernandez, E., & Sheffield, J. (1996). Relative contributions of life events versus daily hassles to the frequency and intensity of headaches. *Headache, 36*(10), 595–602.

Feroah, T. R., Sleeper, T., Brozoski, D., Forder, J., Rice, T. B., & Forster, H. V. (2004). *Circadian slow wave sleep and movement behavior are under genetic control in inbred strains of rat.* Paper presented at the American Physiological Society Annual Conference, April 17–21, 2004, at the Washington, DC, Convention Center.

Ferron, F., Considine, R. V., Peino, R., Lado, I. G., Dieguez, C., & Casanueva, F. F. (1997). Serum leptin concentrations in patients with anorexia nervosa, bulimia nervosa and non-specific eating disorders correlate with the body mass index but are independent of the respective disease. *Clinical Endocrinology (Oxford), 46,* 289–293.

Festinger, L. (1954). A theory of social comparison processes. *Human Relations, 7,* 117–140.

Festinger, L. (1957). *A theory of cognitive dissonance.* Stanford, CA: Stanford University Press.

Festinger, L., & Carlsmith, J. (1959). $1/$20 Experiment: Cognitive consequences of forced compliance. *Journal of Abnormal and Social Psychology, 58.*

Fiatarone, M. (1996). Physical activity and functional independence in aging. *Research Quarterly for Exercise & Sport, 67,* 70–75.

Fiatarone, M. A., O'Neill, E. F., Doyle, N., Clements, K. M., Roberts, S. B., Kehayias, J. J., Lipsitz, L. A., & Evans, W. J. (1993). The Boston FICSIT study: The effects of resistance training and nutritional supplementation on physical frailty in the oldest old. *Journal of American Geriatrics, 41*, 333–337.

Fieve, R. R. (1997). *Moodswing: Dr. Fieve on depression*, 2nd rev. ed. New York: Bantam Books.

Fincham, F. D., Harold, G. T., & Gano–Phillips, S. (2000). The longitudinal association between attributions and marital satisfaction: Direction of effects and role of efficacy expectations. *Journal of Family Psychology, 14*, 267–285.

Fink, M. (1984). Meduna and the origins of convulsive therapy. *American Journal of Psychiatry, 141*, 1034–1041.

Finke, R. (1995). Creative realism. In S. Smith, T. Ward, & R. Finke (Eds.), *The creative cognition approach* (pp. 301–326). Cambridge: Cambridge University Press.

Finkel, D., & McGue, M. (1997). Sex differences and nonadditivity in heritability of the Multidimensional Personality Questionnaire scales. *Journal of Personality and Social Psychology, 72*, 929–938.

Fischer, A. (1993). Sex differences in emotionality: Fact or Stereotype? *Feminism & Psychology, 3*, 303–318.

Fischer, S., Hallschmidt, M., Elsner, A. L., & Born, J. (2002). Sleep forms memory for finger skills. *Procedures of the National Academy of Science: USA, 99*, 11987–11991.

Fischl, B., Liu, A., & Dale, A. M. (2001). Automated manifold surgery: Constructing geometrically accurate and topologically correct models of the human cerebral cortex. *IEEE Transactions on Medical Imaging, 20*, 70–80.

Fiske, S. T. (1998). Stereotyping, prejudice, and discrimination. In D. T. Gilbert & S. T. Fiske (Eds.), *The handbook of social psychology* (4th ed., Vol. 2, pp. 357–411). New York: McGraw–Hill.

Fitzgerald, J. (2004). 'Superman' star Christopher Reeve, an advocate for spinal cord research, dies at age 52. *Associated Press*, Monday, October 11.

Fivush, R., & Nelson, K. (2004). Culture and language in the emergence of autobiographical memory. *Psychological Science, 15*(9), 573.

Fivush, R., Haden, C., & Reese, E. (1996). Remembering, recounting, and reminiscing: The development of autobiographical memory in social context. In D. C. Rubin (Ed.), *Remembering our past. Studies in autobiographical memory* (pp. 341–359). New York: Cambridge University Press.

Flaherty, J. A., & Adams, S. A. (1998). Therapist–patient race and sex matching: Predictors of treatment duration. *Psychiatric Times, 15*(1).

Flaskerud, J. H. (1991). Effects of an Asian client therapist language, ethnicity and gender match on utilization and outcome of therapy. *Community Mental Health Journal, 27*, 31–42.

Flavell, J. H. (1999). Cognitive development: Children's knowledge about the mind. *Annual Review of Psychology, 50*, 21–45.

Fleming, M. F., & Barry, K. L. (1992). Clinical overview of alcohol and drug disorders. In M. F. Fleming & K. L. Barry (Eds.), *Addictive disorders*. St. Louis: Mosby Year Book.

Fleming, N. D., & Mills, C. (1992). *VARK a guide to learning styles*. Retrieved September 7, 2004, from **www.vark-learn.com/English/index.asp.**

Flemons, W. W. (2002). Obstructive sleep apnea. *New England Journal of Medicine, 347*, 498–504.

Foa, E. B., & Franklin, M. E. (2000). Psychotherapies for obsessive-compulsive disorder: A review. In M. Maj, N. Sartorius, A. Okasha, & J. Zohar, (Eds.), *Obsessive-compulsive disorder* (pp. 93–115). New York: John Wiley & Sons.

Foa, E. B., Keane, T. M., Friedman, M. J. (Eds.) (2000). *Effective treatments for PTSD*. New York: Guilford.

Folkman, S. (1997). Positive psychological states and coping with severe stress. *Social Science & Medicine, 45*, 1207–1221.

Folkman, S., & Chesney, M. A. (1995). Coping with HIV infection. In M. Stein and A. Baum (Eds.), *Perspectives in behavioral medicine* (pp. 115–133). Hillsdale, NJ: Lawrence Erlbaum.

Folkman, S., & Lazarus, R. S. (1980). An analysis of coping in a middle-aged community sample. *Journal of Health and Social Behavior, 21*(3), 219–239.

Ford, N., & Chen, S. Y. (2001). Matching/mismatching revisited: An empirical study of learning and teaching styles. *British Journal of Educational Technology, 32*(1), 5–22.

Foulkes, D. (1982). *Children's dreams*. New York: Wiley.

Foulkes, D., & Schmidt, M. (1983). Temporal sequence and unit comparison composition in dream reports from different stages of sleep. *Sleep, 6*, 265–280.

Frank, D. A., Augustyn, M., Knight, W. G., Pell, T., & Zuckerman, B. (2001). Growth, development, and behavior in early childhood following prenatal cocaine exposure. *Journal of the American Medical Association, 285*(12): 1613–1625.

Franke, R. H., & Kaul, J. D. (1978). The Hawthorne experiments: First statistical interpretation. *American Sociological Review 43*, 623–643.

Frankel, B. R., & Piercy, F. P. (1990). The relationship among selected supervisor, therapist, and client behaviors. *Journal of Marital and Family Therapy, 16*, 407–421.

Fredrickson, B. L., Maynard, K. E., Helms, M. J., Haney, T. L., Siegler, I. C., & Barefoot, J. C. (1999). Hostility predicts magnitude and duration of blood pressure response to anger. *Journal of Behavioral Medicine, 23*(3), 229–243.

Freedman, J., & Fraser, S. (1966). Compliance without pressure: The foot-in-the-door technique. *Journal of Personality and Social Psychology, 4*, 195–202.

Freeman, A., Simon, K. M., Beutler, L. E., & Arkowitz, H. (Eds.) (1989). *Comprehensive handbook of cognitive therapy*. New York: Plenum Press.

Freeman, J. (2001). *Gifted children grown up*. London: David Fulton Publishers Ltd.

Freeman, W., & Watts, J. W. (1937). Prefrontal lobotomy in the treatment of mental disorders. *Southern Medical Journal, 30*, 23–31.

Freese, J., Powell, B., & Steelman, L. C. (1999). Rebel without a cause or effect: Birth order and social attitudes. *American Sociological Review, 64*, 207–231.

Frensch, P. A., & Runger, D. (2003). Implicit learning. *Current Directions in Psychological Science, 12*, 13–18.

Freud, A. (1946). *The ego and the mechanisms of defense. American Edition.*, New York: I.U.P.

Freud, S. (1900). *The interpretation of dreams. S.E., 4–5.* (cf. Joyce Crick, Trans., 1999). London: Oxford University Press.

Freud, S. (1900). *The interpretation of dreams.* Translated by A. A. Brill, 1913. New York: Macmillan.

Freud, S. (1901). *The psychopathology of everyday life, S.E., 6, 1–290.*

Freud, S. (1904). *Freud's psycho-analytic procedure, S.E., 7, 249–254.*

Freud, S. (1904). *Psychopathology of everyday life.* New York: Macmillan; London: Fisher Unwin.

Freud, S. (1915). *Repression, S.E., 14*, 146–158.

Freud, S. (1915). *Repression, The Standard Edition of the Complete Psychological Works of Sigmund Freud, Vol. 14.* Edited by James Strachey. London: The Hogart Press and the Institute of Psychoanalysis, 1974.

Freud, S. (1923). *The ego and the id, S.E., 19*, 12–66.

Freud, S. (1930). *Civilization and its discontents.* New York: Jonathon Cape and Co.

Freud, S. (1931.) Female sexuality. *Pelican Freud Library, 7*, 367.

Freud, S. (1933). *New introductory lectures on psycho-analysis*, London: Hogarth.

Freud, S. (1940). Splitting of the ego in the process of defence. *International Journal of Psychoanalysis, 22*, 65 [1938], S.E., 23:275–278.

Freud, S., & Gay, P. (1977). *Inhibitions, symptoms and anxiety. Standard edition of the complete works of Sigmund Freud.* New York: W. W. Norton.

Freud, S., Strachey, J., & Riviere, J. (1990). *The ego and the id (The Standard Edition of the Complete Psychological Works of Sigmund Freud).* New York: W. W. Norton and Company.

Friedman, J. M. (2000). Obesity in the new millennium. *Nature, 404*, 632–634.

Friedman, J. M. (2003). A war on obesity, not the obese. *Science, 299*(5608), 856–858.

Friedman, J. M., & Halaas, J. L. (1998). Leptin and the regulation of body weight in mammals. *Nature, 395*, 763.

Friedman, M., & Kasanin, J. D. (1943). Hypertension in only one of identical twins. *Archives of Internal Medicine, 72*, 767–774.

Friedman, M., & Rosenman, R. H. (1959). Association of specific behavior pattern with blood and cardiovascular findings. *Journal of the American Medical Association, 169*, 1286–1296.

Frontera, W. R., Hughes, V. A., Lutz, K. J., & Evans, W. J. (1991). A cross-sectional study of muscle strength and mass in 45- to 78-year-old men and women. *Journal of Applied Physiology, 71*, 644–650.

Fujii, Y., Suzuki, K., Sato, T., Murakami, Y., & Takahashi, T. (1998). Multiple personality disorder in Japan. *Psychiatry and Clinical Neurosciences, 52*(3), 299.

Fulcher, J. S. (1942). "Voluntary" facial expression in blind and seeing children. *Archives of Psychology, 38*, 1–49.

Fumeron, F., Betoulle, D., Aubert, R., Herbeth, B., Siest, G., & Rigaud, D. (2001). Association of a functional 5–HT transporter gene polymorphism with anorexia nervosa and food intake. *Molecular Psychiatry, 6,* 9–10.

Furumoto, L. (1979). Mary Whiton Calkins (1863–1930): Fourteenth president of the American Psychological Association. *Journal of the History of Behavioral Sciences, 15,* 346–356.

Gado, M. (2004). A cry in the night: The Kitty Genovese murder. *Court TV's Crime Library: Criminal Minds and Methods.* Article retrieved from the Internet on August 2, 2004 at **www.crimelibrary.com/serial_killers/predators/kitty_genovese/ 1.html?sect=2.**

Galanter, M. (1983). Unification Church ("Moonie") dropouts: Psychological readjustment after leaving a charismatic religious group. *American Journal of Psychaiatry, 140*(8), 984–989.

Galanti, G. A. (1997). *Caring for patients from different cultures* (2nd ed.). Philadelphia: University of Pennsylvania Press.

Galea, S., Resnick, H., Kilpatrick, D., Bucuvalas, M., Gold, J., & Vlahov, D. (2002, March 28). Psychological sequelae of the September 11 terrorist attacks in New York City. *New England Journal of Medicine, 346*(13), 982–987.

Gamwell, L., & Tomes, N. (1995). *Madness in America: Cultural and medical perspectives of mental illness before 1914.* Ithaca, NY: Cornell University Press.

Ganchrow, J. R., Steiner, J. E., & Munif, D. (1983). Neonatal facial expressions in response to different qualities and intensities of gustatory stimuli. *Infant Behavior Development, 6,* 473–478.

Ganellen, R. J. (1996). *Integrating the Rorschach and the MMPI-2 in personality assessment.* Mahwah, NJ: Erlbaum.

Garb, H. N., Florio, C. M., & Grove, W. M. (1998). The validity of the Rorschach and the Minnesota Multiphasic Personality Inventory: Results from meta-analyses. *Psychological Science, 9,* 402–404.

Garcia, J., & Koelling, R. A. (1966). Relation of cue to consequence in avoidance learning. *Psychonomic Science, 4,* 123.

Garcia, J., Brett, L. P., & Rusiniak, K. W. (1989). Limits of Darwinian conditioning. In S. B. Klein & R. R. Mowrer (Eds.), *Contemporary learning theories: Instrumental conditioning theory and the impact of biological constraints on learning* (pp. 237–275). Hillsdale, NJ: Erlbaum.

Garcia, J., Hawkins, W. G., & Rusiniak, K. W. (1974). Behavioral regulation of the milieu interne in man and rat. *Science, 185,* 823–831.

Gardner, H. (1993a). *Creating minds: An anatomy of creativity seen through the lives of Freud, Einstein, Picasso, Stravinsky, Eliot, Graham, and Ghandi.* New York: Basic Books.

Gardner, H. (1993b). *Multiple intelligences: The theory in practice.* New York: Basic Books.

Gardner, H. (1998). Are there additional intelligences? The case for naturalist, spiritual, and existential intelligences. In J. Kane (Ed.), *Education, information, and transformation* (pp. 111–131). Upper Saddle River, NJ: Merrill-Prentice Hall.

Gardner, H. (1999a). *Intelligence reframed: Multiple intelligences for the 21st century.* New York: Basic Books.

Gardner, H. (1999b, February). Who owns intelligence? *Atlantic Monthly,* 67–76.

Gardner, H., Kornhaber, M. L., & Wake, W. K. (1996). *Intelligence: Multiple perspectives.* Orlando, FL: Harcourt Brace & Co.

Gardner, J., & Oswald, A. J. (2004). How is mortality affected by money, marriage, and stress? *Journal of Health Economics, 23*(6), 1181–1207.

Gardner, R. J. M., & Sutherland, G. R. (1996). Chromosome abnormalities and genetic counseling. *Oxford Monographics on Medical Genetics No. 29.* New York: Oxford University Press.

Garland, E. J., & Smith, D. H. (1991). Simultaneous prepubertal onset of panic disorder, night terrors, and somnambulism. *Journal of American Academic Child and Adolescent Psychiatry, 30*(4), 553–555.

Garner, D. M., & Garfinkel, P. E. (1980). Socio-cultural factors in the development of anorexia nervosa. *Psychological Medicine, 10,* 647–656.

Gathercole, S. E., & Hitch, G. J. (1993). Developmental changes in short-term memory: A revised working memory perspective. In A. F. Collins, S. E. Gathercole, M. A. Conway, & P. E. Morris (Eds.), *Theories of memory* (pp. 189–209). Hove: Erlbaum.

Gauld, A. (1992). *A history of hypnotism.* New York: Cambridge University Press.

Geary, D. C. (2000). Evolution and proximate expression of human paternal investment. *Psychological Bulletin, 126,* 55–77.

Gebhard, P. H., & Johnson, A. B. (1979/1998). *The Kinsey data: Marginal tabulations of 1938–1963 interviews conducted by the Institute for Sex Research.* Philadelphia: W. B. Saunders.

Geddes, D. P. (Ed.), (1954). *An analysis of the Kinsey reports.* New York: New American Library.

Geddes, J. R., Carney, S. M., Davies, C., Furukawa, T. A., Kupfer, D. J., Frank, E., & Goodwin, G. M. (2003). Relapse prevention with antidepressant drug treatment in depressive disorders: A systematic review. *Lancet, 361*(9358), 653–661.

Geddes, J., & Butler, R. (2002). Depressive disorders. *Clinical Evidence, 7,* 867–882.

Geen, R. G., & Thomas, S. L. (1986). The immediate effects of media violence on behavior. *Journal of Social Issues, 42,* 7–27.

Gelder, M. (1976). Flooding. In T. Thompson & W. Dockens (Eds.), *Applications of behavior modification.* New York: Academic Press.

Geliebter, A. (1988). Gastric distension and gastric capacity in relation to food intake in humans. *Physiological Behavior, 44,* 665–668.

Geller, B., Williams, M., Zimerman, B., Frazier, J., Beringer, L., & Warner, K. L. (1998). Prepubertal and early adolescent bipolarity differentiate from ADHD by manic symptoms, grandiose delusions, ultra-rapid or ultradian cycling. *Journal of Affective Disorders, 51*(2), 81–91.

Gelman, S. A. (1988). The development of induction within natural kind and artifact categories. *Cognitive Psychology, 20,* 65–95.

Gelman, S. A., & Markman, E. M. (1986). Categories and induction in young children. *Cognition, 23,* 183–209.

Gershoff, E. (2000). The short- and long-term effects of corporal punishment on children: A meta-analytical review. In D. Elliman & M. A. Lynch. *The physical punishment of children, 83,* 196–198.

Gershoff, E. T. (2002). Parental corporal punishment and associated child behaviors and experiences: A meta-analytic and theoretical review. *Psychological Bulletin, 128,* 539–579.

Gibbons, J. L., Stiles, D. A., & Shkodriani, G. M. (1991). Adolescents' attitudes toward family and gender roles: An international comparison. *Sex Roles, 25,* 625–643.

Gibson, E. J., & Walk, R. D. (1960). The "visual cliff." *Scientific American, 202,* 67–71.

Gibson, J. J. (1966). *The senses considered as perceptual systems.* Boston: Houghton Mifflin.

Gibson, J. J. (1977). The theory of affordances. In R. E. Shaw & J. Bransford (Eds.), *Perceiving, acting, and knowing.* Hillsdale, NJ: Lawrence Erlbaum Associates.

Gibson, J. J. (1979). *The ecological approach to visual perception.* Boston: Houghton Mifflin.

Giedd, J. N., Blumenthal, J., Jeffries, N. O., Castellanos, F. X., Liui, H., Zijdenbos, A., Paus, T., Evans, A. C., & Rapoport, J. L. (1999). Brain development during childhood and adolescence: A longitudinal MRI study. *Nature Neuroscience, 2*(10), 861–863.

Gil-Verona, J. A., Pastor, J. F., De Paz, F. J., Barbosa M., Macias, J. A., Picornell, I., Rami-Gonzalez L., Canizares, S., & Boget, T. (2001). Neuropsychological study of the sleep–learning relationship. *Neurobiology of Sleep-Wakefulness Cycle, 1* (2), 82–86.

Gilberg, C., & Coleman, M. (2000). *The biology of the autistic syndromes.* (3rd ed.). London: Mac Keith Press.

Gilbert, P. B., Peterson, M. L., Follmann, D., Hudgens, M. G., Francis, D. P., Gurwith, M., Heyward, W. L., Jobes, D. V., Popovic, V., Self, S. G., Sinangil, F., Burke, D., & Berman, P. W. (2005). Correlation between immunologic responses to a recombinant glycoprotein 120 vaccine and incidence of HIV-1 infection in a phase 3 HIV-1 preventive vaccine trial. *Journal of Infectious Diseases, 191,* 666–677.

Gilbert, S. J. (1981). Another look at the Milgram obedience studies: The role of the graduated series of shocks. *Personality and Social Psychology Bulletin, 7*(4), 690–695.

Gill, S. T. (1991). Carrying the war into the never-never land of psi. *Skeptical Inquirer, 15*(1), 269–273.

Gillespie, M. A., Kim, B. H., Manheim, L. J., Yoo, T., Oswald, F. L., & Schmitt, N. (2002). The development and validation of biographical data and situational judgment tests in the prediction of college student success. Presented in A. M.

Ryan (Chair), *Beyond g: Expanding thinking on predictors of college success.* Symposium conducted at the 14th Annual Convention of the American Psychological Society, New Orleans, LA.

Gillham, B., Tanner, G., Cheyne, B., Freeman, I., Rooney, M., & Lambie, A. (1998). Unemployment rates, single parent density, and indices of child poverty: Their relationship to different categories of child abuse and neglect. *Child Abuse and Neglect, 22*(2), 79–90.

Gilligan, C. (1982). *In a different voice: Psychological theory and women's development.* Cambridge, MA: Harvard University Press.

Gillund, G., & Shiffrin, R. M. (1984). A retrieval model for both recognition and recall. *Psychological Review, 91*, 1–67.

Gilmour, J., & Skuse, D. (1999). A case-comparison study of the characteristics of children with a short stature syndrome induced by stress (hyperphagic short stature) and a consecutive series of unaffected "stressed" children. *Journal of Child Psychology and Psychiatry and Allied Disciplines, 40*(6), 969–978.

Ginzburg, K., Solomon, Z., Koifman, B., Keren, G., Roth, A., Kriwisky, M., Kutz, I., David, D., & Bleich, A. (2003). Trajectories of post-traumatic stress disorder following myocardial infarction: A prospective study. *Journal of Clinical Psychiatry, 64*(10), 1217–1223.

Gittelman-Klein, R. (1978). Validity in projective tests for psychodiagnosis in children. In R. L. Spitzer & D. F. Klein (Eds.), *Critical issues in psychiatric diagnosis* (pp. 141–166). New York: Raven Press.

Gleaves, D. H. (1996). The socio-cognitive model of dissociative identity disorder: A reexamination of the evidence. *Psychological Bulletin, 20*, 42–59.

Glick, P., & Fiske, S. (2001). An ambivalent alliance: Hostile and benevolent sexism as complementary justifications for gender inequality. *American Psychologist, 56*, 109–118.

Glynn, S. M. (1990). Token economy approaches for psychiatric patients: Progress and pitfalls over 25 years. *Behavior Modification, 14*, 383–407.

Godden, D. R., & Baddeley, A. D. (1975). Context dependent memory in two natural environments: On land and underwater. *British Journal of Psychology, 66*, 325–331.

Goel, V., & Grafman, J. (1995). Are the frontal lobes implicated in "planning" functions? Interpreting data from the Tower of Hanoi. *Neuropsychologia, 33*(5), 623–642.

Goin, M. K. (2005). Practical psychotherapy: A current perspective on the psychotherapies. *Psychiatric Services, 56*(3), 255–257.

Goldman-Rakic, P. S. (1998) The prefrontal landscape: Implications of functional architecture for understanding human mentation and the central executive. In A. C. Roberts, T. W. Robbins, & L. Weiskrantz, (Eds.), *The prefrontal cortex: Executive and cognitive functions* (pp. 87–102). Oxford: Oxford University Press.

Goldsmith, H. H., & Campos, J. (1982). Toward a theory of infant temperament. In R. Emde & R. Harmon (Eds.), *The development of attachment and affiliative systems: Psychobiological aspects* (pp. 161–193). New York: Plenum Press.

Goldstein, S. (1997). *Managing attention and learning disorders in late adolescence and adulthood. A guide for practitioners.* New York: John Wiley.

Goleman, D. (1982). Staying up: The rebellion against sleep's gentle tyranny. *Psychology Today, 3,* 24–35.

Goleman, D. (1995). *Emotional intelligence: Why it can matter more than IQ.* New York: Bantam Books.

Gonsalves, B., Reber, P. J., Gitelman, D. R., Parrish, T. B., Mesulam, M. M., & Paller, K. A. (2004). Neural evidence that vivid imagining can lead to false remembering. *Psychological Science, 15,* 655–660.

Gonzales, P. M., Blanton, H., & Williams, K. J. (2002). The effects of stereotype threat and double–minority status on the test performance of Latino women. *Personality and Social Psychology Bulletin, 28*(5), 659–670.

Gonzalez, J. S., Penedo, F. J., Antoni, M. H., Duran, R. E., Fernandez, M. I., McPherson-Baker, S., Ironson, G., Klimas, N. G., Fletcher, M. A., & Schneiderman, N. (2004). Social support, positive states of mind, and HIV treatment adherence in men and women living with HIV/AIDS. *Health Psychology, 23*(4), 413–418.

Goodglass, H., Kaplan, E., & Barresi, B., (2001). *The Assessment of Aphasia and Related Disorders*, 3rd ed., Baltimore: Lippincott, Williams and Wilkins.

Goodman, E. S. (1980). Margaret Floy Washburn (1871–1939) first woman Ph.D. in psychology. *Psychology of Women Quarterly, 5,* 69–80.

Gordon, T., (1989). *Discipline that works.* New York: Plume Books.

Gosselin, R. E., Smith, R. P., Hodge, H. C., & Braddock, J. E. (1984). *Clinical toxicology of commercial products.* (5th ed.). Sydney: Williams & Wilkins.

Gotlib, I. H., Sivers, H., Canli, T., Kasch, K. L., & Gabrieli, J. D. E. (2001). Neural activation in depression in response to emotional stimuli. In I. H. Gotlib (Chair), *New directions in the neurobiology of affective disorders.* Symposium presented at the Annual Meeting of the Society for Research in Psychopathology, Madison, WI.

Gottesman, I. I., & Shields, J. (1976). A critical review of recent adoption, twin and family studies of schizophrenia: Behavioural genetics perspectives. *Schizophrenia Bulletin, 2,* 360–401.

Gottesman, I. I., & Shields, J. (1982). *Schizophrenia, the epigenetic puzzle.* New York: Cambridge University Press.

Gottman, J. M., & Krokoff, L. J. (1989). Marital interaction and satisfaction: A longitudinal view. *Journal of Consulting and Clinical Psychology, 57,* 47–52.

Gough, H. G. (1995). *California Psychological Inventory* (3rd ed.). Palo Alto, CA: Consulting Psychologist-Press.

Gould, J. L., & Gould, C. G. (1994). *The animal mind.* New York: Scientific American Library.

Gould, S. J. (1981). *The mismeasure of man.* New York: Norton.

Gould, S. J. (1996). *The mismeasure of man.* New York: W. W. Norton.

Gouldner, A. W. (1960). The norm of reciprocity: A preliminary statement. *American Sociological Review, 25,* 161–178.

Graber, J. A., Brooks-Gunn, J., & Warren, M. P. (1995). The antecedents of menarcheal age: Heredity, family environment, and stressful life events. *Child Development, 66,* 346–359.

Grandjean, P., Weihe, P., White, R. F., Debes, F., Araki, S., Yokoyama, K., Murata, K., Sorensen, N., Dahl, R., & Jorgensen, P. J. (1997). Cognitive deficit in 7-year-old children with prenatal exposure to methylmercury. *Neurotoxicology and Teratology, 19*(6), 417–428.

Greenberg, R., & Perlman, C. (1993). An integrated approach to dream theory: Contributions from sleep research and clinical practice. In A. Moffitt, M. Kramer & R. Hoffmann (Eds.), *The functions of dreaming* (pp. 363–380). Albany, NY: State University of New York Press.

Greenwald, A. G., Draine, S. C., & Abrams, R. L. (1996). Three cognitive markers of unconscious semantic activation. *Science, 273,* 1699–1702.

Gregory, R. L. (1990). *Eye and brain, the psychology of seeing.* Princeton, NJ: Princeton University Press.

Gresham, L. G., & Shimp, T. A. (1985). Attitude toward the advertisement and brand attitudes: A classical conditioning prospective. *Journal of Advertising, 14*(1), 10–17, 49.

Gribbons, B., & Herman, J. (1997). True and quasi-experimental designs. *Practical Assessment, Research & Evaluation, 5*(14).

Grocer, S., & Kohout, J. (1997). The 1995 APA Survey of 1992 Psychology Baccalaureate Recipients. American Psychological Association.

Groden, G., Stevenson, S., & Groden, J. (1996). *Understanding challenging behavior: A step-by-step behavior analysis guide.* Providence, RI: Groden Center Publications.

Gross, C. G. (1999). A hole in the head. *The Neuroscientist, 5,* 263–269.

Grumbach, M. M., & Kaplan, S. L. (1990). The neuroendocrinology of human puberty: An ontogenetic perspective. In M. M. Grumbach, P. C. Sizonenko, & M. L. Aubert (Eds.), *Control of the Onset of Puberty* (pp. 1–6). Baltimore: Williams & Wilkins.

Grumbach, M. M., & Styne, D. M. (1998). Puberty: Ontogeny, neuroendocrinology, physiology, and disorders. In J. D. Wilson, D. W. Foster, H. M. Kronenberg, & P. R. Larsen (Eds.), *Williams Textbook of Endocrinology*, 9th ed. (pp. 1509–1625). Philadelphia: W. B. Saunders Co.

Grünbaum, A. (1984). *The foundations of psychoanalysis: A philosophical critique.* Berkeley, CA: University of California Press.

Guerin, D. A., Park, Y., & Yang, S. (1995). Development of an instrument to study the meaning of color in interior environments. *Journal of Interior Design, 20*(2), 31–41.

Guilford, J. P. (1967). *The nature of human intelligence.* New York: McGraw-Hill.

Gupta, M. (1994). Sexuality in the Indian sub-continent. *Sex and Marital Therapy, 9,* 57–69.

Gustavson, C. R., Kelly, D. J., Seeney, M., & Garcia, J. (1976). Prey lithium aversions I: Coyotes and wolves. *Behavioral Biology, 17,* 61–72.

Guthrie, R. V. (2004). *Even the rat was white: A historical view of psychology.* Boston: Allyn and Bacon.

Haase, J., Halama, P., & Horr, R. (1996). Effectiveness of brief infusions with Ginkgo biloba Special Extract EGb 761 in dementia of the vascular and Alzheimer type. *Gerontology and Geriatrics, 29*(4), 302–309.

Haber, R. N. (1979). Twenty years of haunting eidetic imagery: Where's the ghost? *The Behavioral and Brain Sciences, 2,* 583–619.

Hajek, P., & Belcher, M. (1991). Dream of absent-minded transgression: An empirical study of a cognitive withdrawal symptom. *Journal of Abnormal Psychology, 100,* 487–491.

Hajek, P., & Stead, L. F. (2000). *Aversive smoking for smoking cessation.* Oxford, UK: The Cochrane Library.

Hall, C. (1966). Studies of dreams collected in the laboratory and at home. *Institute of Dream Research Monograph Series* (No. 1). Santa Cruz, CA: Privately printed.

Hamann, S., Herman, R. A., Nolan, C. L., & Wallen, K. (2004). Men and women differ in amygdale response to visual sexual stimuli. *Nature Neuroscience, 7*(4), 411–419.

Hamer, D. H., Hu, S., Magnuson, V. L., Hu, N., & Pattatucci, A. M. L. (1993). A linkage between DNA markers on the X chromosome and male sexual orientation. *Science, 261,* 321–327.

Hamilton, D. L., & Gifford, R. K. (1976). Illusory correlation in interpersonal perception: A cognitive basis of stereotypic judgments. *Journal of Experimental Social Psychology, 12,* 392–407.

Hamilton, J. A. (1982). The identity of postpartum psychosis. In I. F. Brockington, & R. Kumar, (Eds.), *Motherhood and mental illness* (pp. 1–17). London: Academic Press.

Hammond, D. C. (2001a). Neurofeedback treatment of depression with the Roshi. *Journal of Neurotherapy, 4*(2), 45–56.

Hammond, D. C. (2001b). Treatment of chronic fatigue with neurofeedback and self-hypnosis. *NeuroRehabilitation, 16,* 295–300.

Hammond, D. C. (2003). QEEG-guided neurofeedback in the treatment of obsessive compulsive disorder. *Journal of Neurotherapy, 7*(2), 25–52.

Hampton, J. A. (1998). Similarity-based categorization and fuzziness of natural categories. *Cognition, 65,* 137–165.

Handel, S. (1989). *Listening: An introduction to the perception of auditory events.* Cambridge, MA: MIT Press.

Hansen, C. P. (1988). Personality characteristics of the accident involved employee. *Journal of Business and Psychology, 2*(4), 346–365.

Harlow, H. F. (1958). The nature of love. *American Psychologist, 13,* 573–685.

Harlow, H. F. (1959). Love in infant monkeys. *Scientific American, 200,* 68, 70, 72–73.

Harman, G. (1999). Moral philosophy meets social psychology: Virtue ethics and the fundamental attribution error. *Proceedings of the Aristotelian Society, 1998–99, vol. 99,* 315–331.

Harrison, P. J. (1999). The neuropathology of schizophrenia: A critical review of the data and their interpretation. *Brain, 122,* 593–624.

Hart, P. (1998). Preventing groupthink revisited: Evaluating and reforming groups in government. *Organizational Behavior & Human Decision Processes, 73*(2–3), 306–326.

Hartfield, E. (1987). Passionate and companionate love. In R. J. Sternberg & M. L. Barnes (Eds.), *The psychology of love* (pp. 191–217). New Haven, CT: Yale University Press.

Hartfield, E., & Rapson, R. L. (1992). Similarity and attraction in intimate relationships. *Communication Monographs, 59,* 209–212.

Hassold, T., & Patterson, D. (Eds.). (1998). *Down syndrome: A promising future, together.* New York: Wiley.

Hauck, S. J., & Bartke, A. (2001). Free radical defenses in the liver and kidney of human growth hormone transgenic mice. *Journal of Gerontology and Biological Science, 56,* 153–162.

Havighurst R. J., Neugarten B. L., & Tobin S. N. S. (1968). Disengagement and patterns of aging. In B. L. Neugarten (Ed.), *Middle age and aging: A reader in social psychology* (pp. 161–172). Chicago: University of Chicago Press.

Hawks, S. R., Madanat, H. N., Merrill, R. M., Goudy, M. B., & Miyagawa, T. (2003). A cross-cultural analysis of "motivation for eating" as a potential factor in the emergence of global obesity: Japan and the United States. *Health Promotion International, 18*(2), 153–162.

Hay, P., & Bacaltchuk, J. (2002). Bulimia nervosa. *Clinical Evidence,* (8), 914–926.

Hayflick, L. (1977). The cellular basis for biological aging. In C. E. Finch & L. Hayflick (Eds.), *Handbook of biology of aging* (p. 159). New York: Van Nostrand Reinhold Co.

Hazan, C., & Shaver, P. (1987). Romantic love conceptualized as an attachment process. *Journal of Personality and Social Psychology, 52,* 511–524.

Heavey, C. L., Layne, C., & Christensen, A. (1993). Gender and conflict structure in marital interaction: A replication and extension. *Journal of Consulting and Clinical Psychology, 61,* 16–27.

Hebb, D. O. (1955). Drives and the C.N.S. (Conceptual Nervous System). *Psychological Review, 62,* 243–254.

Hechtman, L., Weiss, G., & Perlman, T. (1984). Hyperactives as young adults: Past and current substance abuse and antisocial behavior. *American Journal of Orthopsychiatry, 54,* 415–425.

Heesacker, M., Petty, R. E., & Cacioppo, J. T. (1983). Field dependence and attitude change: Source credibility can alter persuasion by affecting message–relevant thinking. *Journal of Personality, 51,* 653–666.

Heider, F. (1958). *The psychology of interpersonal relations.* New York: John Wiley & Sons.

Heil, G., Maslow, A., & Stephens, D. (1998). *Maslow on management.* New York: John Wiley and Sons, Inc.

Heilman, K., Watson, R., & Valenstein, E. (1993). "Neglect and Related Disorders," In *Clinical Neuropsychology,* K. Heilman and E. Valenstein (Eds.). New York: Oxford University Press.

Heinicke, C. M., Goorsky, M., Moscov, S., Dudley, K., Gordon, J., Schneider, C., & Guthrie, D. (2000). Relationship-based intervention with at-risk mothers: Factors affecting variations in outcome. *Infant Mental Health Journal, 21,* 133–155.

Heinrich, B. (2000). Testing insight in ravens. In C. Heyes & L. Huber (Eds.), *The evolution of cognition.* Cambridge, MA: MIT Press.

Helms, J. E. (1992). Why is there no study of cultural equivalence in standardized cognitive ability testing? *American Psychologist, 47*(9), 1083–1101.

Henning, H. (1916). Die qualitätenreihe des geschmacks. *Zsch. f. Psychol., 74,* 203–219.

Henningfield. J. E. (1995). Nicotine medications for smoking cessation. *New England Journal of Medicine, 333*(18), 1196–1203.

Henningfield. J. E. Clayton, R., & Pollin, W. (1990). Involvement of tobacco in alcoholism and illicit drug use. *British Journal of Addition, 85,* 279–292.

Hensleigh, P. A., Andrews, W. W., Brown, Z., Greenspoon, J., Yasukawa, L., & Prober, C. G. (1997). Genital herpes during pregnancy: Inability to distinguish primary and recurrent infections clinically. *Obstetrics and Gynecology, 89,* 891–895.

Herberman, R. B., & Ortaldo, J. R. (1981). Natural killer cells: Their role in defenses against disease. *Science, 214,* 24–30.

Herman, L. M., Pack, A. A., & Morrell-Samuels, P. (1993). Representational and conceptual skills of dolphins. In H. L., Roitblatt, L. M. Herman, & P. E. Nachtigall (Eds.), *Language and communcation: comparative perspectives.* Hillsdale, NJ: Erlbaum.

Hernandez, D., & Fisher, E. M. (1996). Down syndrome genetics: Unravelling a multifactorial disorder. *Human Molecular Genetics, 5,* 1411–1416.

Herrnstein, R. J., & Murray, C. (1994). *The bell curve.* New York: The Free Press.

Herrnstein, R. J., & Murray, C. (1994). *The bell curve: The reshaping of american life by differences in intelligence.* New York: Free Press.

Hersh, S. M. (2004, May 10). Annals of national security: Torture at Abu Ghraib. *The New Yorker.*

Hershberger, S. L., Plomin, R., & Pedersen, N. L. (1995, October). Traits and meta-traits: Their reliability, stability, and shared genetic influence. *Journal of Personality and Social Psychology, 69*(4), 673–685.

Hetherington, A. W., & Ranson, S. W. (1940). Hypothalamic legions and adiposity in rats. *Anatomical Records, 78*, 149–172.

Hewstone, M., Rubin, M., & Willis, H. (2002). Intergroup bias. *Annual Review of Psychology, 53*, 575–604.

Heyes, C. M. (1998). Theory of mind in nonhuman primates. *Behavior and Brain Science, 21*, 101–148.

Hicklin, J., & Widiger, T. A. (2000). Convergent validity of alternative MMPI-2 personality disorder scales. *Journal of Personality Assessment, 75*(3), 502–518.

Hilgard, E. R. (1991). A neodissociation interpretation of hypnosis. In Lynn & Rhue (Eds.), *Theories of hypnosis* (pp. 83–104). New York: Guilford Press.

Hilgard, E. R., & Hilgard, J. R. (1994). *Hypnosis in the relief of pain* (rev. ed.). New York: Brunner/Mazel.

Hill, D. (1990). Causes of smoking in children. In B. Durston & K. Jamrozik, *Smoking and health 1990—the global war. Proceedings of the Seventh World Conference on Smoking and Health,* 1–5 April. Perth: Health Department of Western Australia, 205–209.

Hill, J. A. (1998). Miscarriage risk factors and causes: What we know now. *OBG Management, 10*, 58–68.

Hill, P. C., & Butter E. M. (1995). The role of religion in promoting physical health. *Journal of Psychology and Christianity, 14*(2), 141–155.

Hilton, J. L., & von Hipple, W. (1996). Stereotypes. *Annual Review of Psychology, 47*, 237–271.

Hinton, G. E., McClelland, J. L., & Rumelhart, D. E. (1986). Distributed representations. In D. E. Rumelhart, J. L. McClelland, & the PDP Research Group (Eds.), *Parallel distributed processing: Explorations in the microstructure of cognition, volume 1: Foundations* (pp. 77–109). Cambridge, MA: MIT Press.

Hintze, J. M. (2002). Interventions for fears and anxiety problems. In M. R. Shinn, H. R. Walker, & G. Stoner (Eds.), *Interventions for academic and behavior problems II: Preventive and remedial approaches* (pp. 939–954). Bethesda, MD: National Association of School Psychologists.

Hirshfield, C. (1983). Quality circles in the classroom: An experiment in the pedagogical uses of Japanese management methods. Paper presented at the Annual Conference of the Eastern Community College Social Science Association, Williamsburg, Virginia, March 23–26.

Hobson, J. (1988). *The dreaming brain*. New York: Basic Books.

Hobson, J., Pace-Schott, E., & Stickgold, R. (2000). Dreaming and the brain: Towards a cognitive neuroscience of conscious states. *Behavioral and Brain Sciences, 23*(6), 793–1121.

Hobson, J. A., & McCarley, R. (1977). The brain as a dream state generator: An activation-synthesis hypothesis of the dream process. *American Journal of Psychiatry, 134,* 1335–1348.

Hochman, J. (1994). Buried memories challenge the law. *National Law Journal, 1*, 17–18.

Hodges, J. R. (1994). Retrograde amnesia. In A. Baddeley, B. A. Wilson, & F. Watts (Eds.), *Handbook of memory disorders* (pp. 81–107). New York: Wiley.

Hodgson, B. (2001). *In the arms of Morpheus: The tragic history of laudanum, morphine, and patent medicines*. New York: Firefly Books.

Hodson, D. S., & Skeen, P. (1994). Sexuality and aging: The hammerlock of myths. *The Journal of Applied Gerontology, 13*, 219–235.

Hoebel, B. G., & Teitelbaum, P. (1966). Weight regulation in normal and hypothalamic hyperphagic rats. *Journal of Comparative Physiological Psychology, 61,* 189–193.

Hoffmann, A. (1998). *Paradigms of artificial intelligence: A Methodological and computational analysis*. London: Springer-Verlag.

Hoffrage, U., Hertwig, R., & Gigerenzer, G. (2000). Hindsight bias: A by product of knowledge updating? *Journal of Experimental Psychology: Learning, Memory, and Cognition, 26*, 566–581.

Hofstede, G. H. (1980). *Culture's consequences, international differences in work-related values*. Beverly Hills, CA: Sage Publications.

Hofstede, G. J., Pedersen, P. B., & Hofstede, G. H. (2002). *Exploring culture: Exercises, stories, and synthetic cultures*. Yarmouth, ME: Intercultural Press.

Hogg M. A. & Hains S. C. (1998). Friendship and group identification: a new look at the role of cohesiveness in groupthink. *European Journal of Social Psychology, 28*(1), 323–341.

Holahan, C. K. & Sears, R. R. (1996). *The gifted group at later maturity*. Stanford, CA: Stanford University Press.

Holcomb, W. R. (1986). Stress inoculation therapy with anxiety and stress disorders of acute psychiatric patients. *Journal of Clinical Psychology, 42*, 864–872.

Holden, C., & Vogel, G. (2002). Plasticity: Time for a reappraisal? *Science, 296*, 2126–2129.

Hollon, S., These, M., & Markowitz, J. (2002). Treatment and prevention of depression. *Psychological Science in the Public Interest, 3*, 39–77.

Hollon, S. D., & Beck, A. T. (1994). Cognitive and cognitive-behavioral therapies. In A. E., Bergin, & and S. L. Garfield, (Eds.), *Handbook of psychotherapy and behavior change* (4th ed., p. 428). Chichester, UK: John Wiley & Sons.

Holmes, C. B., Wurtz, P. J., Waln, R. F., Dungan, D. S., & Joseph, C. A. (1984). Relationship between the Luscher Color Test and the MMPI. *Journal of Clinical Psychology, 40*, 126–128.

Holmes, T. H., & Masuda, M. (1973). Psychosomatic syndrome: When mothers-in-law or other disasters visit, a person can develop a bad, bad cold. *Psychology Today, 5*(11), 71–72, 106.

Holmes, T. H., & Rahe, R. H. (1967). The Social Readjustment Rating Scale. *Journal of Psychosomatic Research II*, 213–218.

Holroyd, J. (1996). Hypnosis treatment of clinical pain: Understanding why hypnosis is useful. *International Journal of Clinical and Experimental Hypnosis, 44*, 33–51.

Holt-Lunstad, J., Uchino, B. N., Smith, T. W., Cerny, C. B., & Nealey-Moore, J. B. (2003). Social relationships and ambulatory blood pressure: Structural and qualitative predictors of cardiovascular function during everyday social interactions. *Health Psychology, 22*, 388–397.

Hood, D. C. (1998). Lower-level visual processing and models of light adaptation. *Annu. Rev. Psychology, 49*, 503–535.

Hopfinger, J. B., Buonocore, M. H., & Mangun, G. R. (2000). The neural mechanisms of top-down attentional control. *Nature Neuroscience, 3*, 284–291.

Horne, J. A., & Staff, C. H. (1983). Exercise and sleep: Body heating effects. *Sleep, 6*, 36–46.

Horney, K. (1939). *New ways in Psychoanalysis*. New York: W. W. Norton.

Horney, K. (1967/1973). *Feminine psychology*. New York: W. W. Norton.

Horowitz, D. L. (1985). *Ethnic groups in conflict*. Berkeley, CA: University of California Press.

Hortaçsu, N. (1999). The first year of family and couple initiated marriages of a Turkish sample: A longitudinal investigation. *International Journal of Psychology, 34*(1), 29–41.

Hothersall, D. (1995). *History of psychology*. New York: McGraw-Hill, Inc.

Howard, K. I., Moras, K., Brill, P. L., Martinovich, Z., & Lutz, W. (1996). Evaluation of psychotherapy: Efficacy, effectiveness, and patient progress. *American Psychologist, 51*, 1059–1064.

Howe, M. L., & O'Sullivan, J. T. (1990). The development of strategic memory: Coordinating knowledge, metamemory, and resources. In D. F. Bjorklund (Ed.), *Children's strategies: Contemporary views of cognitive development* (pp. 129–155). Hillsdale, NJ: Erlbaum.

Hu, P., & Meng, Z. (1996). *An examination of infant–mother attachment in China*. Poster presented at the meeting of the International Society for the Study of Behavioral Development, Quebec City, Quebec, Canada.

Hu, S., Pattatucci, A. M. L., Patterson, C., Li, L., Fulker, D. W., Cherny, S. S., Kruglyak, L., & Hamer, D. H. (1994). Linkage between sexual orientation and chromosome Xq28 in males but not in females. *Nature Genetics, 11*, 248–256.

Hubble, M. A., Duncan, B. L., & Miller, S. D. (1999). Directing attention to what works. In M. A. Hubble, B. L. Duncan, & S. D. Miller (Eds.), *The heart and soul of change: What works in therapy* (pp. 407–447). Washington, DC: American Psychological Association.

Huesmann, L. R., & Miller, L. S. (1994). Long-term effects of repeated exposure to media violence in childhood. In L. R. Huesmann (Ed.), *Aggressive behavior: Current perspectives* (pp. 153–183). New York: Plenum Press.

Huesmann, L. R., Moise, J. F., & Podolski, C. L. (1997). The effects of media violence on the development of antisocial behavior. In D. M. Stoff, J. Breiling, & J. D. Maser (Eds.), *Handbook of antisocial behavior* (pp. 181–193). New York: John Wiley.

Huesmann, L. R., Moise-Titus, J., Podolski, C. L., & Eron, L. D. (2003). Longitudinal relations between children's exposure to TV violence and their aggressive and violent behavior in young adulthood: 1977–1992. *Developmental Psychology, 39*(2), 201–221.

Hugenberg, K., & Bodenhausen, G. V. (2003). Facing prejudice: Implicit prejudice and the perception of facial threat. *Psychological Science, 14*, 640–643.

Hughes, J. (1993). Behavior therapy. In T. R. Kratochwill & R. J. Morris (Eds.), *Handbook of psychotherapy with children and adolescents* (pp. 185–220). Boston: Allyn and Bacon.

Hull, C. L. (1943). *Principles of behavior*. New York: Appleton-Century.

Hummer, R. A., Rogers, R. G., Nam, C. B., & Ellison, C. G. (1999). Religious involvement and U.S. adult mortality. *Demography, 36*(2), 273–285.

Hunt, E. (2001). Multiple views of multiple intelligence. [Review of Intelligence reframed: Multiple intelligence in the 21st century.] *Contemporary Psychology, 46*, 5–7.

Hunt, M. (1993). *The Story of Psychology*. New York: Doubleday.

Hurley, D. (1989). The search for cocaine's methadone. *Psychology Today, 23*(7/8), 54.

Hurst, S., & Milkewicz, N. (2000). Eye movement desensitization and reprocessing: A controversial treatment technique. Retrieved from the Internet on July 14 2004 at **www.netpsych.com/health/emd.htm**.

Hurvich, L. M. (1969). Hering and the scientific establishment. *American Psychologist, 24*, 497–514.

Hurwitz, T. A. (1989). Approach to the patient with psychogenic neurological disturbance. In W. N. Kelley (Ed.), *Textbook of internal medicine. Volume 2* (pp. 2518–2521). Philadelphia: J. B. Lippincott.

Hutcheson, J., & Snyder, H. M. (2004). Ambiguous genitalia and intersexuality. *eMedicine Journal, 5*(5). Retrieved from the Internet on November 17, 2004 at **http://author.emedicine.com/PED/topic1492.htm**.

Hyde, J. S., & Kling, K. C. (2001). Women, motivation, and achievement. *Psychology of Women Quarterly, 25*, 264–378.

Hyde, J. S., & Plant, E. A. (1995). Magnitude of psychological gender differences. *American Psychologist, 50*, 159–161.

Hyman, I. E., Gilstrap, L. L., Decker, K., & Wilkinson, C. (1998). Manipulating remember and know judgements of autobiographical memories. *Applied Cognitive Psychology, 12*, 371–386

Hyman, I. E., Jr. (1993). Imagery, reconstructive memory, and discovery. In B. Roskos-Ewoldsen, M. J. Intons-Peterson, & R. E. Anderson (Eds.), *Imagery, creativity, and discovery: A cognitive perspective* (pp. 99–121). The Netherlands: Elsevier Science Publishers.

Hyman, I. E., Jr., & Loftus, E. F. (1998). Errors in autobiographical memories. *Clinical Psychology Review, 18*, 933–947.

Hyman, I. E., Jr., & Loftus, E. F. (2002). False childhood memories and eyewitness memory errors. In M. L. Eisen, J. A. Quas, & G. S. Goodman (Eds.) *Memory and suggestibility in the forensic interview* (pp. 63–84). Mahwah, NJ: Erlbaum.

Imaizumi, Y. (1998). A comparative study of twinning and triplet rates in 17 countries, 1972–1996. *Acta Genetic Medicine & Gemellology, 47*, 101–114.

Ioannidis, J. P. A. (1998, January 28). Effect of the statistical significance of results on the time to completion and publication of randomized efficacy trials. *Journal of the American Medical Association, 279*, 281–286.

Irwin, A. R., & Gross, A. M. (1995). Cognitive tempo, violent video games, and aggressive behavior in young boys. *Journal of Family Violence, 10*(3), 337–350.

Irwin, M., Mascovich A., Gillin, J. C., Willoughby, R., Pike, J., Smith, T. L. (1994). Partial sleep deprivation reduces natural killer cell activity in humans. *Psychosomatic Medicine, 56*, 493–498.

Irwin, M., McClintick, J., Costlow, C., Fortner, M., White, J. & Gillin, J. C. (1996). Partial night sleep deprivation reduces natural killer and cellular immune responses in humans. *The Federation of American Societies for Experimental Biology Journal, 10*, 643–653.

Isabel, J. (2003). *Genetics: An introduction for dog breeders*. Loveland, CO: Alpine Publications.

Iwamoto, E. T., & Martin, W. (1988). A critique of drug self-administration as a method for predicting abuse potential of drugs. *National Institute on Drug Abuse Research Monograph, 1046*, 81457–81465.

Izard, C. (1988). Emotion-cognition relationships and human development. In C. Izard, J. Kagan, and R. Zajonc (Eds.). *Emotions, cognition, and behavior* (Chapter 1). New York: Cambridge University Press.

Jackson, R. (2001). *Plato: A Beginner's Guide*. London: Hoder & Stroughton.

Jackson, T., Iezzi, T., Gunderson, J., Fritch, A., & Nagasaka, T. (2002). Gender differences in pain perception: The mediating role of self-efficacy beliefs. *Sex Roles, 47*, 561–568.

Jacobson, S. G., Cideciyan A. V., Regunath, G. et al. (1995). Night blindness in Sorsby's fundus dystrophy reversed by vitamin A. *Nat Genet., 11*, 27–32.

Jaeger, J. J., Lockwood, A. H., Van Valin, R. D., Kemmerer, D. L., Murphy, B. W., & Wack, D. S. (1998). Sex differences in brain regions activated by grammatical and reading tasks. *Neuroreport, 9*, 2803–2807.

James, W. (1884). What is an emotion? *Mind, 9*, 188–205.

James, W. (1890). *Principles of psychology*. New York: Henry Holt .

James, W. (1890, 2002). *The principles of psychology (Vols. 1 and 2)*. Cambridge, MA: Harvard University Press.

James, W. (1894). The physical basis of emotion. *Psychological Review, 1*, 516–529.

Jang, K. L., Livesley, W. J., & Vernon, P. A. (1996). Heritability of the Big Five personality dimensions and their facets: A twin study. *Journal of Personality, 64*, 577–591.

Jang, K. L., McCrae, R. R., Angleitner, A., Riemann, R., & Livesley, W. J. (1998). Heritability of facet-level traits in a cross-cultural twin sample: Support for a hierarchical model of personality. *Journal of Personality and Social Psychology, 74*, 1556–1565.

Janicki, M. P., Heller, T., Seltzer, G., & Hogg, J. (1995). *Practice guidelines for the clinical assessment and care management of Alzheimer and other dementias among adults with mental retardation*. Washington, DC: American Association on Mental Retardation.

Janis, I. (1972). *Victims of groupthink*. Boston: Houghton-Mifflin.

Janis, I. (1982). *Groupthink* (2nd ed.) Boston: Houghton-Mifflin.

Janos, P. M. (1987). A fifty-year follow-up of Terman's youngest college students and IQ-matched agemates. *Gifted Child Quarterly, 31*, 55–58.

Janowitz, H. D. (1967). Role of gastrointestinal tract in the regulation of food intake. In C. F. Code (Ed.), *Handbook of physiology: Alimentary canal 1*. Washington, DC: American Physiological Society.

Janus, S. S., & Janus, C. L. (1993). *The Janus report on sexual behavior*. New York: John Wiley & Sons, Inc.

Jarusiewicz, B. (2002). Efficacy of neurofeedback for children in the autistic spectrum: A pilot study. *Journal of Neurotherapy, 6*(4), 39–49.

Jay, S. M., & Elliot, C. H. (1990). A stress inoculation program for parents whose children are undergoing medical procedures. *Journal of Consulting and Clinical Psychology, 58*, 799–804.

Jensen, A. R. (1969). How much can we boost IQ and scholastic achievement? *Harvard Educational Review, 39*, 1–123.

Jester, C. (2000). Introduction to the DVC Learning Style Survey for College. Adapted for the Web by Suzanne Miller, Instructor, Math and Multimedia © Copyright 2000. Retrieved from the Internet on September 7, 2004 at **www.metamath.com/lsweb/dvclearn.htm**.

Jimerson, D. C., Wolfe, B. E., Metzger, E. D., Finkelstein, D. M., Cooper, T. B., & Levine, J. M. (1997). Decreased serotonin function in bulimia nervosa. *Archives of General Psychiatry, 54*, 529–534.

Joanna Briggs Institute. (2001). Smoking cessation interventions and strategies. In *Best Practice, 5*(3), 1329–1874. Published by the Joanna Briggs Institute for Evidence Based Nursing and Midwifery.

John, O. P., Angleitner, A., & Ostendorf, F. (1988). The lexical approach to personality: A historical review of trait taxonomic research. *European Journal of Personality, 2*, 171–203.

Johnson, D., Johnson, R., & Smith, K. (1991). *Active learning: Cooperation in the college classroom*. Edna, MN: Interaction Book Company.

Johnson, G. (1995, June 6). Chimp talk debate: Is it really language? *The New York Times*.

Johnson, J., Cohen, P., Pine, D. S., Klein, D. F., Kasen, S., & Brook, J. S. (2000). Association between cigarette smoking and anxiety disorders during adolescence and early adulthood. *Journal of the American Medical Association, 284*(18), 2348–2351.

Jones, E. E., & Harris, V. A. (1967). The attribution of attitudes. *Journal of Experimental Social Psychology, 3,* 1–24.

Jones, E. J., Krupnick, J. L., & Kerig, P. K. (1987). Some gender effects in a brief psychotherapy. *Psychotherapy, 24,* 336–352.

Jones, G. W. (1997). Modernization and divorce: Contrasting trends in Islamic Southeast Asia and the West. *Population and Development Review, 23*(1), 95–113.

Jones, H. M., & Pilowsky, L. S. (2002). Dopamine and antipsychotic drug action revisited. *British Journal of Psychiatry, 181,* 271–275.

Jones, M. C. (1924). A laboratory study of fear: The case of Peter. *Pedagogical Seminary, 31,* 308–315.

Joscfso, D. (2002, March 23). Psychologists allowed to prescribe drugs for mental illness. *British Medical Journal 324,* 698.

Juffer, F., & Rosenboom, L. G. (1997). Infant–mother attachment of internationally adopted children in the Netherlands. *International Journal of Behavioral Development, 20*(1), 93–107.

Jung, C. (1933). *Modern man in search of a soul.* New York: Harcourt Brace.

Köhler, W. (1925). *Mentality of apes* (E. Winter, Trans.). London: Routledge & Kegan Paul.

Kabat-Zinn, J., Lipworth, L., & Burney, R. (1985). The clinical use of mindfulness meditation for the self-regulation of chronic pain. *Journal of Behavioral Medicine, 8,* 163–190.

Kabat-Zinn, J., Lipworth, L., Burney, R., & Sellers, W. (1986). Four year follow-up of a meditation-based program for the self regulation of chronic pain: Treatment outcomes and compliance. *Clinical Journal of Pain, 2,* 159–173.

Kahan, M., & Sutton, N. (1998). Overview: Methadone treatment for the opioid-dependent patient. In B. Brands & J. Brands (Eds.), *Methadone maintenance: A physician's guide to treatment* (pp. 1–15). Toronto, ON: Addiction Research Foundation.

Kaiser, P. K. (1984). Physiological response to color: Critical review. *Color Research and Application, 9,* 29–36.

Kales, A., Soldatos, C., Bixler, E., Ladda, R. L., Charney, D. S., Weber, G., & Schweitzer, P. K. (1980). Hereditary factors in sleepwalking and night terrors. *British Journal of Psychiatry, 137,* 111–118.

Kamin, L. J. (1995, February). Behind the curve. *Scientific American,* 99–103.

Kamphaus, R. W. (1993). *Clinical assessment of children's intelligence.* Boston: Allyn & Bacon.

Kandel, E. R., & Schwartz, J. H. (1982). Molecular biology of learning: Modulation of transmitter release. *Science, 218,* 433–443.

Kanigel, R. (1997). *The one best way: Frederick Winslow Taylor and the enigma of efficiency.* New York: Penguin.

Kanne, S. M., Balota, D. A., Storandt, M., McKeel, D. W. Jr., & Morris, J. C. (1998). Relating anatomy to function in Alzheimer's disease: Neuropsychological profiles predict regional neuropathology 5 years later. *Neurology, 50*(4), 979–985.

Karau, S. J., & Williams, K. D. (1993). Social loafing: A meta-analytic review and theoretical integration. *Journal of Personality and Social Psychology, 65,* 681–706.

Karau, S. J., & Williams, K. D. (1997). The effects of group cohesiveness on social loafing and social compensation. *Group Dynamics: Theory, Research and Practice, 1,* 156–168.

Karayiorgou, M., Altemus, M., Galke, B., Goldman, D., Murphy, D., Ott, J., & Gogos, J. (1997). Genotype determining low catechol-O-methyltransferase activity as a risk factor for obsessive-compulsive disorder. *Proceeds of the National Academy of Science, 94,* 4572–4575.

Karney, B. R., & Bradbury, T. N. (2000). Attributions in marriage: State or trait? A growth curve analysis. *Journal of Personality and Social Psychology, 78,* 295–309.

Kastenbaum, R., & Costa, Jr., P. T. (1977). Psychological perspective on death. *Annual Review of Psychology, 28,* 225–249.

Katada, E. K., Sato, K., Sawaki, A., Dohi, Y., Ueda, R., & Ojika, K. (2003). Long-term effects of donepezil on P300 auditory event-related potentials in patients with Alzheimer's disease. *Journal of Geriatric Psychiatry and Neurology, 16*(1), 39–43.

Kaufman, J., & Zigler, E. (1993). The intergenerational transmission of abuse is overstated. In R. J. Gelles & D. R. Loseke (Eds.), *Current controversies on family violence.* Newbury Park, CA: Sage Publications.

Kaufmann, G. R., Bloch, M., Zaunders, J. J., Smith, D., & Cooper, D. A. (2000). Long-term immunological response in HIV-1 infected subjects receiving potent antiretroviral therapy. *AIDS, 14,* 959–969.

Kaveny, M. C. (2001). The case of conjoined twins: Embodiment, individuality, and dependence. *Theological Studies, 62.*

Kazdin, A. E. (1980). Acceptability of time out from reinforcement procedures for disruptive behavior. *Behavior Therapy, 11*(3), 329–344.

Keane, T. M., Fairbank, J. A., Caddell, J. M., & Zimering, R. T. (1989). Implosive (flooding) therapy reduced symptoms of PTSD in Vietnam combat veterans. *Behavior Therapy, 20,* 245–260.

Kearney, C. A., & Silverman, W. K. (1998). A critical review of pharmacotherapy for youth with anxiety disorders: Things are not as they seem. *Journal of Anxiety Disorders, 12,* 83–102.

Keillor, J., Barrett, A., Crucian, G., Kortenkamp, S., & Heilman, K. (2002). Emotional experience and perception in the absence of facial feedback. *Journal of the International Neuropsychological Society, 8*(1), 130–135.

Keirsey, D. (1998). *Please understand me II: Temperament, character, intelligence.* Del Mar, CA: Prometheus Nemesis Book Co., Inc.

Keller, M. B., McCullough, J. P., Klein, D. N., Arnow, B., Dunner, D., Gelenberg, A., Markowitz, J. C., Nemeroff, C. B., Russell, J. M., Thase, M. E., Trivedi, M. H., & Zajecka, J. (2000). A comparison of nefazodone, the cognitive behavioral-analysis system of psychotherapy, and their combination for the treatment of chronic depression. *New England Journal of Medicine, 342*(20), 1462–1470.

Keller, M. B., Ryan, N. D., Strober, M., Klein, R. G., Kutcher, S. P., Birmaher, B., Hagino, O. R., Koplewicz, H., Carlson, G. A., Clarke, G. N., Emslie, G. J., Feinberg, D., Geller, B., Kusumakar, V., Papatheodorou, G., Sack, W. H., Sweeney, M., Wagner, K. D., Weller, E. B., Winters, N. C., Oakes, R., & McCafferty, J. P. (2001). Efficacy of paroxetine in the treatment of adolescent major depression. A randomized, controlled trial. *Journal of the Academy of Child and Adolescent Psychiatry, 40*(7), 762–772.

Kellner, R. (1986). *Somatization and hypochondriasis.* New York: Praeger-Greenwood.

Kelly, I. (1980). The scientific case against astrology. *Mercury, 10.*13.

Kendall, P. (1983). Stressful medical procedures: Cognitive-behavioral strategies for stress management and prevention. In D. Meichenbaum & M. Jaremko (Eds.), *Stress reduction and prevention.* New York: Plenum Press.

Kendler, K. S. (1985). Diagnostic approaches to schizotypal personality disorders: A historical perspective. *Schizophrenia Bulletin, 11,* 538–553.

Kendler, K. S., & Prescott, C. A. (1999). A population-based twin study of lifetime major depression in men and women. *Archives of General Psychiatry, 56*(1), 39–44.

Kendler, K. S., & Walsh, D. (1995). Schizotypal personality disorder in parents and the risk for schizophrenia in siblings. *Schizophrenia Bulletin, 21*(2), 47–52.

Kennedy, D. O., Scholey, A. B., & Wesnes, K. A. (2000). The dose-dependent cognitive effects of acute administration of Ginkgo biloba to healthy young volunteers. *Psychopharmacology (Berl), 151*(4), 416–423.

Kennedy, D. O., Scholey, A. B., & Wesnes, K. A. (2001). Differential, dose-dependent changes in cognitive performance following actue administration of a Ginkgo Biloba/Panax ginseng combination to healthy young volunteers. *Nutrition and Neuroscience, 4*(5), 399–412.

Kenny, A. (1968). "Mind and Body," in *Descartes: A study of his philosophy* (p. 279). New York: Random House.

Kenny, A. (1994). Descartes to Kant. In A. Kenny, (Ed.), *The Oxford History of Western Philosophy* (pp. 107–192). Oxford, England: Oxford University Press.

Keromoian, R., & Leiderman, P. H. (1986). Infant attachment to mother and child caretaker in an East African community. *International Journal of Behavioral Development, 9,* 455–469.

Kessler, S. (1998). *Lessons from the intersexed.* Piscataway, NJ: Rutgers University Press.

Kety, S. S., Wender, P. H., Jacobsen, B., Ingraham, L. J., Jansson, L., Faber, B., & Kinney, D. K. (1994). Mental illness in the biological and adoptive relatives of schizophrenic adoptees. *Archives of General Psychiatry, 51,* 442–455.

Kiecolt-Glaser, J. K., Fisher, L. D., Ogrocki, P., Stout, J. C., Speicher, C. E., & Glaser, R. (1987). Marital quality, marital disruption, and immune function. *Psychosomatic Medicine, 49*, 13–34.

Kiecolt-Glaser, J. K., Glaser, R., Gravenstein, S., Malarkey, W. B., & Sheridan, J. (1996). Chronic stress alters the immune response to influenza virus vaccine in older adults. *Processes of the National Academy of Science, 93*(7), 3043–3047.

Kiecolt-Glaser, J. K., Marucha, P. T., Malarkey, W. B., & Marcado, A. M. (1995). Slowing of wound healing by psychological stress. *Lancet, 346*, 1194–1196.

Kiecolt-Glaser, J. K., McGuire, L., Robles, T., & Glaser, R. (2002). Psychoneuroimmunology: Psychological influences on immune function and health. *Journal of Consulting and Clinical Psychology, 70*, 537–547.

Kihlstrom, J. F. (1985). Hypnosis. *Annual Review of Psychology, 36*, 385–418.

Kihlstrom, J. F. (1987). The cognitive unconscious. *Science, 237*, 1445–1452.

Kihlstrom, J. F. (1999). Conscious and unconscious cognition. In R. J. Sternberg (Ed.), *The nature of cognition* (pp. 173–203). Cambridge, MA: MIT Press.

Kihlstrom, J. F. (2001). Hypnosis and the psychological unconscious. In Howard S. Friedman (Ed.), *Assessment and therapy: Specialty articles from the Encyclopedia of Mental Health.* Adelman (Ed.), San Diego, CA: Academic Press.

Kihlstrom, J. F. (2002). Memory, autobiography, history. *Proteus: A Journal of Ideas, 19*(2), 1–6.

Kihlstrom, J. F., Couture, L. J., Schacter, D. L., & Cork, R. L. (1998). Anesthesia, effects on cognitive functions. In G. Adelman (Ed.), *The Encyclopedia of Neuroscience,* (2nd ed.), Amsterdam: Elsevier Science Publishers.

Kihlstrom, J., Mulvaney, S., Tobias, B., & Tobis, I. (2000). The emotional unconscious. In E. Eich, J. Kihlstrom, G. Bower, J. Forgas, & P. Niedenthal (Eds.), *Cognition and emotion* (pp. 30–86). New York: Oxford University Press.

Kim, H., & Markus, H. R. (1999). Deviance or uniqueness, harmony or conformity? A cultural analysis. *Journal of Personality and Social Psychology, 77*, 785–800.

Kimura, D. (1999). *Sex and cognition.* Cambridge, MA: MIT Press.

Kimura, D. (2002, May 13). Sex differences in the brain. *Scientific American.*

King, S. (1979). *The dead zone.* New York: Viking Peguin.

Kinsey, A. C., Pomeroy, W. B., & Martin, C. E. (1948). *Sexual behavior in the human male.* Philadelphia: W. B. Saunders.

Kinsey, A. C., Pomeroy, W. B., Martin, C. E., & Gebhard, P. H. (1953). *Sexual behavior in the human female.* New York: W. B. Saunders.

Kirby, J. S., Chu, J. A., & Dill, D. L. (1993). Correlates of dissociative symptomatology in patients with physical and sexual abuse histories. *Comprehensive Psychiatry 34*, 250–263.

Kirchner, J. T., & Emmert, D. H. (2000). Sexually transmitted diseases in women. Chlamydia trachomatis and herpes simplex infections. *Postgraduate Medicine, 107*, 55–65.

Kirmayer, L. J. (1991). The place of culture in psychiatric nosology: Taijinkyofusho and the DSM-III-R. *Journal of Nervous and Mental Disease, 179*, 19–28.

Kirsch, I. (2000). The response set theory of hypnosis. *American Journal of Clinical Hypnosis, 42*, 3/42, 4, 274–292.

Kirsch, I., & Lynn, S. J. (1995). The altered state of hypnosis: Changes in the theoretical landscape. *American Psychologist, 50*, 846–858.

Kitayama, S., & Markus, H. R. (1994). Introduction to cultural psychology and emotion research. In S. Kitayama & H. R. Markus (Eds.), *Emotion and culture: Empirical studies of mutual influence* (pp. 1–22). Washington, DC: American Psychological Association.

Klaver, C. C., Wolfs, R. C., Vingerling, J. R., Hofman, A., & de Jong, P. T. (1998). Age-specific prevalence and causes of blindness and visual impairment in an older population: The Rotterdam Study. *Arch Ophthalmol, 116*, 653–658.

Klein, D., Schwartz, J., Rose, S., & Leader, J. (2000). Five-year course and outcome of dysthymic disorder: A prospective, naturalistic follow-up study. *American Journal of Psychiatry, 157*(6), 931–939.

Klein, S. B., & Mowrer, R. R. (1989). *Contemporary learning theories: Pavlovian conditioning and the status of traditional learning theory.* Hillsdale, N.J.: Lawrence Erlbaum Associates.

Kleinot, M. C., & Rogers, R. W. (1982). Identifying effective components of alcohol misuse prevention programs. *Journal of Studies on Alcohol, 43*, 802–811.

Kligman, A. M., & Balin, A. K. (1989). Aging of human skin. In A. K. Balin & A. M. Kligman (Eds.), *Aging and the skin* (pp. 1–42). New York: Raven Press.

Klorman, R., Hilpert, P.L., Michael, R., LaGana, C., & Sveen, O. B. (1980). Effects of coping and mastery modeling on experienced and inexperienced pedodontic patients' disruptiveness. *Behavior Therapy, 11*, 156–168.

Kluft, R. P. (1984). Introduction to multiple personality disorder. *Psychiatric Annals, 14*, 19–24.

Kluft, R. P. (1988). The phenomenology and treatment of extremely complex multiple personality disorder. *Dissociation, I*, 47–58.

Klüver, H., & Bucy, P. C. (1939). Preliminary analysis of functions of the temporal lobes in monkeys. *Archives of Neurological Psychiatry, 42*, 979–1000.

Knauth, P. (1993). The design of shift systems. *Ergonomics, 36*(1–3), 15–28.

Knight, A. (1996). *The life of the law: The people and cases that have shaped our society, from King Alfred to Rodney King.* New York: Crown Publishing Group.

Knight, J. A. (1998). Free radicals: Their history and current status in aging and disease. *Annals of Clinical and Laboratory Science, 28*, 331–346.

Knight, W. (2003). Man vs. machine chess match ends in stalemate. *NewScientist.com News Service, February.* Retrieved from the Internet on November 4, 2004 at **www.newscientist.com/news/news.jsp?id=ns99993370**.

Kobasa, S. (1979). Stressful life events, personality, and health: An inquiry into hardiness. *Journal of Personality and Social Psychology, 37*(1), 1–11.

Koenig, H. G., Hays, J. C., Larson, D. B., George, L. K., Cohen, H. J., McCullough, M. E., Meador, K. G., & Blazer, D. G. (1999). Does religious attendance prolong survival? A six-year follow-up study of 3,968 older adults. *Journal of Gerontology, 54A*, M370–M377.

Koenig, H. G., McCullough, M. E., & Larson, D. B. (2001). *Handbook of religion and health.* Oxford, UK: Oxford University Press.

Koh, J. K. (1996). A guide to common Singapore spiders. *BP Guide to Nature* series. Singapore: Singapore Science Center.

Kohlberg, L. (1969). Stage and sequence: the cognitive-developmental approach to socialization. In D. A. Goslin (Ed.), *Handbook of socialization: Theory in research* (pp. 347–480). Boston: Houghton-Mifflin.

Kohlberg, L. (1973). Continuities in childhood and adult moral development revisited. In P. Baltes & K. W. Schaie (Eds.), *Life-span development psychology: Personality and socialization.* San Diego, CA: Academic Press.

Kohler, W. (1992). *Gestalt psychology: An introduction to new concepts in modern psychology (reissue).* New York: Liveright.

Kolodny, R. C. (2001, August). In memory of William H. Masters. *Journal of Sex Research.*

Konowal, N. M., Van Dongen, H. P. A., Powell, J. W., Mallis, M. M., & Dinges, D. F. (1999). Determinants of microsleeps during experimental sleep deprivation. *Sleep, 22* (1 Suppl.), 328.

Korn, S. (1984). Continuities and discontinuities in difficult/easy temperament: Infancy to young adulthood. *Merrill Palmer Quarterly, 30*, 189–199.

Kosslyn, S. M. (1983). Mental imagery. In Z. Rubin (Ed.), *The psychology of being human.* New York: Harper and Row.

Kosslyn, S. M., Ball, T. M., & Reiser, B. J. (1978). Visual images preserve metric spatial information: Evidence from studies of image scanning. *Journal of Experimental Psychology: Human Perception and Performance, 4*, 47–60.

Kosslyn, S. M., Ganis, G., & Thompson, W. L., (2001). Neural foundations of imagery. *Nature Reviews Neuroscience 2*, 635–642.

Kosslyn, S.M., Alpert, N. M., Thompson, W. L., Maljkovic, V., Weise, S. B., Chabris, C. F., Hamilton, S. E. and Buonano, F. S., (1993). Visual mental imagery activates topographically organized visual cortex: PET investigations. *Journal of Cognitive Neuroscience 5*, 263–287.

Kosslyn, S. M., Pascual-Leone, A., Felician, O., Camposano, S., Keenan, J. P., Thompson, W. L., Ganis, G., Sukel, K. E., & Alpert, N. M. (1999). The role of area 17 in visual imagery: Convergent evidence from PET and rTMS. *Science 284*, 167–170.

Kosslyn, S. M., Thompson, W. L., Wraga, M. J., & Alpert, N. M. (2001). Imagining rotation by endogenous and exogenous forces: Distinct neural mechanisms for different strategies. *Neuroreport, 12*, 2519–2525.

Kotkin, M., Daviet, C., & Gurin, J. (1996). The *Consumer Reports* mental health survey. *American Psychologist, 51*(10), 1080–1082.

Kouri, E. M., Pope, H. G., & Lukas, S. E. (1999). Changes in aggressive behavior during withdrawal from long-term marijuana use. *Psychopharmacology, 143*, 302–308.

Kourtis, A. P., Bulterys, M., Nesheim, S. R., & Lee, F. K. (2001). Understanding the timing of HIV transmission from mother to infant. *Journal of the American Medical Association, 285*(6), 709–712.

Kratofil, P. H., Baberg, H. T., & Dimsdale, J. E. (1996). Self mutilation and severe self-injurious behavior associated with amphetamine psychosis. *General Hospital Psychiatry, 18,* 117–120.

Kreipe, R. E. (1992). Normal somatic adolescent growth and development. In E. McAnarney, R. E., Kreipe, D. Orr, & G. Comerci (Eds.), *Textbook of adolescent medicine.* (pp. 44–68). Philadelphia: W.B. Saunders & Co.

Kryger, M., Lavie, P., & Rosen, R. (1999). Recognition and diagnosis of insomnia. *Sleep, 22,* S421–S426.

Kubler-Ross, E. (1997). *The wheel of life: A memoir of living and dying.* New York: Touchstone.

Kuhn, H. W., & Nasar, S. (Eds.) (2001). *The essential John Nash.* Princeton, NJ: Princeton University Press.

Kulik, J. A., & Mahler, H. I. M. (1989). Social support and recovery from surgery. *Health Psychology, 8,* 221–238.

Kulik, J. A., & Mahler, H. I. M. (1993). Emotional support as a moderator of adjustment and compliance after coronary bypass surgery: A longitudinal study. *Journal of Behavioral Medicine, 16,* 45–63.

Kumar, R. (1994). Postnatal mental illness: A transcultural perspective. *Social Psychiatry and Psychiatric Epidemiology, 29*(6), 250–264.

Kumar, S., & Oakley-Browne, M. (2002). Panic disorder. *Clinical Evidence, 7,* 906–912.

Kunkel, P., & Mead, K. P. (1991). How to Toilet Train Your Cat: 21 Days to a Litter-Free Home. New York: Workman Publishing Company.

Kupfer, D. J., & Reynolds, C. F. III. (1997). Management of insomnia. *New England Journal of Medicine, 336*(5), 341–346.

LaBar, K. S., LeDoux, J. E., Spencer, D. D., & Phelps, E. A. (1995). Impaired fear conditioning following unilateral temporal lobectomy to humans. *Journal of Neuroscience, 15,* 6846–6855.

LaBar, K. S., LeDoux, J. E., Spencer, D. D., & Phelps, E. A. (1995). Impaired fear conditioning following unilateral temporal lobectomy to humans. *Journal of Neuroscience, 15,* 6846–6855.

LaBerge, D. (1980). Unitization and automaticity in perception. In J. H. Flowers (Ed.), *Nebraska symposium on motivation* (pp. 53–71). Lincoln, NB: University of Nebraska Press.

Lacayo, A. (1995). Neurologic and psychiatric complications of cocaine abuse. *Neuropsychiatry, Neuropsychology, and Behavioral Neurology, 8*(1), 53–60.

LaFromboise, T., Coleman, H. L. K., & Gerton J. (1993). Psychological impact of biculturalism: Evidence and theory. *Psychological Bulletin, 114,* 395–412.

Laguna, F., Adrados, M., Alvar, J., Soriano, V., Valencia, M. E., Moreno, V., Polo, R., Verdejo, J., Jimenez, M. I., Martinez, P., Martinez, M. L., & Gonzalez-Lahoz, J. M. (1997). Visceral leishmaniasis in patients infected with the human immunodeficiency virus. *European Journal of Clinical Microbiology and Infectious Diseases, 16,* 898–903.

Lal, S. (2002). Giving children security: Mamie Phipps Clark and the radicalization of child psychology. *American Psychologist, 57*(1), 20–28.

Lalancette, M-F, & Standing, L. G. (1990). Asch fails again. *Social Behavior and Personality, 18*(1), 7–12.

Lambert, M. J., & Ogles, B. M. (2003). The efficacy and effectiveness of psychotherapy. In M. J. Lambert (Ed.), *Handbook of psychotherapy and behavior change* (5th ed.). New York: Wiley.

Lance, C. E., & LaPointe, J. A. (1994). Tests of three causal models of halo rater error., *Academic Press, Inc., 57,* 83–96.

Lance, C. J., LaPointe, & S. Fisicaro. (1994). Tests of three causal models of halo rater error. *Organizational Behavior and Human Decision Performance, 57,* 83–96.

Lane, R. D., Kivley, L. S., DuBois, M. A. Shamasundara, P., & Schwartz, G. E. (1995). Levels of emotional awareness and the degree of right hemisphere dominance in the perception of facial emotion. *Neuropsychologia, 33,* 525–538.

Lange, C. (1885/1967). The emotions. Reprinted in Lange and James (Eds.), *The emotions.* New York: Harper Publishing Co.

Langer, E. J., & Rodin, J. (1976). The effects of enhanced personal responsibility for the aged: A field experiment in an institutional setting. *Journal of Personality and Social Psychology, 34,* 191–198.

Langford, C. (2002). *Sexually transmitted diseases: Frequently asked questions.* National Women's Health Information Center, U.S. Department of Health and Human Services.

Langone, M. C. (1996). Clinical update on cults. *Psychiatric Times, 13*(7).

Lanphear, B. P., Dietrich, K., Auinger, P., & and Cox, C. (2000). Cognitive deficits associated with blood lead concentrations <10 micrograms/dL in U.S. children and adolescents. *Public Health Reports, 115*(6), 521–529.

Lapsley, D. K., Milstead, M., Quintana, S. M., Flannery, D., & Buss, R. R. (1986). Adolescent egocentrism and formal operations: Tests of a theoretical assumption. *Developmental Psychology, 22,* 800–807.

Larzelere, R. (1986). Moderate spanking: Model or deterrent of children's aggression in the family? *Journal of Family Violence, 1*(1), 27–36.

Lashley, K. S. (1938). The thalamus and emotion. *The Psychological Review, 45,* 21–61.

Lasnik, H. (1990). Metrics and morphophonemics in early English verse. *University of Connecticut Working Papers in Linguistics, Vol. 3,* 29–40.

Latane, B., & Darley, J. M. (1969). Bystander "apathy." *American Scientist, 57*(2), 244–268.

Latane, B., Williams, K., & Harkins, S. (1979). Many hands make light the work: The causes and consequences of social loafing. *Journal of Personality & Social Psychology, 37*(6), 822–832.

Lauer, J., Black, D. W., & Keen, P. (1993). Multiple personality disorder and borderline personality disorder: Distinct entities or variations on a common theme? *Annals of Clinical Psychiatry, 5,* 129–134.

Laumann, E. O., Paik, A., & Rosen, R. C. (1999). Sexual dysfunction in the United States: Prevalence and predictors. *Journal of the American Medical Association, 281*(6), 537–544.

Launer, L., Masaki, K., Petrovitch, H., Foley, D., & Havlik, R. (1995). The association between midlife blood pressure levels and late-life cognitive function. *Journal of the American Medical Association, 272*(23), 1846–1851.

Lavergne, G. M. (1997). *A sniper in the tower: The true story of the Texas Tower massacre.* New York: Bantam.

Laws, G., Davies, I., & Andrews, C. (1995). Linguistic structure and nonlinguistic cognition: English and Russian blues compared. *Language and Cognitive Processes, 10,* 59–94.

Lay, C., & Nguyen, T. T. I. (1998). The role of acculturation-related and acculturation non-specific daily hassles: Vietnamese-Canadian students and psychological distress. *Canadian Journal of Behavioural Science, 30*(3), 172–181.

Lazarus, A. A. (1963). The results of behavior therapy in 126 cases of severe neurosis. *Behaviour Research and Therapy, 1,* 69–79.

Lazarus, R. S. (1991). *Emotion and adaptation.* New York: Oxford University Press.

Lazarus, R. S. (1993). From psychological stress to the emotions: A history of changing outlooks. *Annual Review of Psychology, 44.*

Lazarus, R. S. (1999). *Stress and emotion: A new synthesis.* New York: Springer.

Lazarus, R. S., & Folkman, S. (1984). *Stress, appraisal and coping.* New York: Springer.

Leary, M. R., & Forsyth, D. R. (1987). Attributions of responsibility for collective endeavors. *Review of Personality and Social Psychology, 8,* 167–188.

Leask, J., Haber, R. N., & Haber, R. B. (1969). Eidetic imagery in children: II. Longitudinal and experimental results. *Psychonomic Monograph Supplements, 3,* 25–48.

Leavitt, H. J., & Pondy, L. R. (1964). *Readings in managerial psychology.* Chicago: University of Chicago Press.

Le Bars, P. L., Kieser, M., & Itil, K. Z. (2000). A 26-week analysis of a double-blind, placebo-controlled trial of ginkgo biloba extract EGb 761 in dementia. *Dementia and Geriatric Cognitive Disorders, 11*(4), 230–237.

Le Bars, P. L., Velasco, F. M., Ferguson, J. M., Dessain, E. C., Kieser, M., & Hoerr, R. (2002). Influence of the severity of cognitive impairment on the effect of the Ginkgo biloba extract EGb 761 in Alzheimer's disease. *Neuropsychobiology, 45*(1), 19–26.

Leccese, A. P., Pennings, E. J. M. & De Wolff, F. A. (2000). Combined use of alcohol and psychotropic drugs. A review of the literature. *Academisch Ziekenhuis Leiden (AZL),* Leiden.

LeDoux, J. (1994). Emotion, memory and the brain. *Scientific American, 270,* 32–39.

Lee, F., Hallahan, M., & Herzog, T. (1996). Explaining real life events: How culture and domain shape attributions. *Personality and Social Psychology Bulletin, 22,* 732–741.

Lee, M., & Shlain, B. (1986). *Acid dreams: The complete social history of LSD: The CIA, the sixties, and beyond.* Grove Press.

Lee, P. A. (1995). Physiology of puberty. In K. L. Becker (Ed.), *Principles and Practice of endocrinology and metabolism* (pp. 822–830). Philadelphia: J.B. Lippincott Company.

Lee, S. (1995). Self-starvation in context: Towards a culturally sensitive understanding of anorexia nervosa. *Social Science Medicine, 41,* 25–36.

Lehr, U., & Thomae, H. (Hrsg.) (1987). Patterns of psychological aging. *Results from the Bonne Aging Longitudinal Study (BOLSA).* Stuttgart: Enke.

Leibel, R. L., Rosenbaum, M., & Hirsch, J. (1995). Changes in energy expenditure resulting from altered body weight. *The New England Journal of Medicine, 332,* 621–628.

Leonard, L. (1997). *Children with specific language impairment.* Cambridge: MIT Press, pp. 89–117.

Leong, F. T. L., Hartung, P. J., Goh, D., & Gaylor, M. (2001). Appraising birth order in career assessment: Linkages to Holland's and Super's models. *Journal of Career Assessment, 9,* 25–39.

LePoncin, M. (1990). *Brain fitness.* New York: Ballantine Books.

Leroy, C., & Symes, B. (2001). Teachers' perspectives on the family backgrounds of children at risk. *McGill Journal of Education, 36*(1), 45–60.

Lesch, K. P., Bengel, D., Heils, A., Sabol, S. Z., Greenberg, B. D., Petri, S., Benjamin, J., Muller, C. R., Hamer, D. H., & Murphy, D. L. (1996). Association of anxiety-related traits with a polymorphism in the serotonin transporter gene regulatory region. *Science, 274*(5292), 1527–1531.

Leslie, M. (2000, July/August). The vexing legacy of Louis Terman. *Stanford Magazine.*

LeVay, S. (1991). A difference in hypothalamic structure between heterosexual and homosexual men. *Science, 253,* 1034–1037.

LeVay, S., & Hamer, D. (1994). Evidence for a biological influence in male homosexuality, *Scientific American, 270,* 44–49.

Levenson, R. W. (1992). Autonomic nervous system differences among emotions. *Psychological Sciences, 3,* 23–27.

Levenson, R. W., Ekman, P., Heider, K., & Friesen, W. V. (1992). Emotion and autonomic nervous system activity in the Minangkabau of West Sumatra. *Journal of Personality and Social Psychology, 62,* 972–988.

Levy, B. R., Slade, M. D., Kunkel, S. R., & Kasl, S. V. (2002). Longevity increased by positive self-perceptions of aging. *Journal of Personality and Social Psychology, 83,* 261–269.

Levy, S. R., Stroessner, S. J., & Dweck, C. S. (1998). Stereotype formation and endorsement: The role of implicit theories. *Journal of Personality and Social Psychology, 74,* 1421–1436.

Lewin, K. (1935). *A dynamic theory of personality.* New York: McGraw-Hill.

Lewin, K. (1936). *Principles of topological psychology.* New York: McGraw-Hill.

Lewis, D. K. (1996, June). A cross-cultural model for psychotherapy: Working with the African-American client. *Perspectives on Multiculturalism and Cultural Diversity,* VI (2).

Liberman, A., & Chaiken, S. (1992). Defensive processing of personally relevant health messages. *Personality and Social Psychology Bulletin, 18*(6), 669–679.

Like, R., Steiner, P., & Rubel, A. (1996). Recommended core curriculum guidelines on culturally sensitive and competent care. *Family Medicine, 27,* 291–297.

Lilienfeld, S. O. (1999). Projective measures of personality and psychopathology: How well do they work? *Skeptical Inquirer, 23*(5), 32–39.

Lin, P. J., & Schwanenflugel, P. J. (1995). Cultural familiarity and language factors in the structure of category knowledge. *Journal of Cross-Cultural Psychology, 26,* 153–168.

Lin, P. J., Schwanenflugel, P. J., & Wisenbaker, J. M. (1990). Category typicality, cultural familiarity, and the development of category knowledge. *Developmental Psychology, 26,* 805–813.

Lindemann, B. (1996) Taste reception. *Physiological. Review, 76,* 719–766.

Linden, M., Habib, T., & Radojevic, V. (1996). A controlled study of the effects of EEG biofeedback on cognition and behavior of children with attention deficit disorder and learning disabilities. *Biofeedback and Self Regulation, 21*(1), 35–49.

Lipsitt, L. P., Kaye, H., & Bosack, T. N. (1966). Enhancement of neonatal sucking through reinforcement. *Journal of Experimental Child Psychology, 4,* 163–168.

Lisanby, S. H., Maddox, J. H., Prudic, J., Devanand, D. P., & Sackeim, H. A. (2000). The effects of electroconvulsive therapy on memory of autobiographical and public events. *Archives of General Psychiatry, 57,* 581–590.

Livesley, J. W., (Ed.). (1995). *The DSM-IV Personality disorders.* New York: Guilford Press.

Lock, M. (1994). Menopause in cultural context. *Experimental Gerontology, 29*(3–4), 307–317.

Loehlin, J. C. (1992). *Genes and environment in personality development.* Newbury Park, CA: Sage.

Loehlin, J. C., McCrae, R. R., Costa, P. T., Jr., & John, O. P. (1998). Heritabilities of common and measure-specific components of the Big Five personality factors. *Journal of Research in Personality, 32,* 431–453.

Loehlin, J. C., Willerman, L., & Horn, J. M. (1985). Personality resemblances in adoptive families when the children are late-adolescent or adult. *Journal of Personality and Social Psychology, 48,* 376–392.

Loftus, E. (1975). Leading questions and the eyewitness report. *Cognitive Psychology, 7,* 560–572.

Loftus, E. (1987, June 29). Trials of an expert witness. *Newsweek.*

Loftus, E. F., & Pickrell, J. E. (1995). The formation of false memories. *Psychiatric Annals, 25,* 720–725.

Loftus, E. F., Miller, D. G., & Burns H. J. (1978). Semantic integration of verbal information into a visual memory. *Journal of Experimental Psychology: Human Learning, 4,* 19–31.

Logue, M. W., Vieland, V. J., Goedken, R. J., & Crowe, R. R. (2003). Bayesian analysis of a previously published genome screen for panic disorder reveals new and compelling evidence for linkage to chromosome 7. *American Journal of Medical Genetics, 121B,* 95–99.

Lohr, J. M., Kleinknecht, R. A., Tolin, D. F., & Barrett, R. H. (1995). The empirical status of the clinical application of eye movement desensitization and reprocessing. *Journal of Behavior Therapy and Experimental Psychiatry, 26,* 285–302.

Lohr, J. M., Tolin, D. F., & Lilienfield, S. O. (1998). Efficacy of eye movement desensitization and reprocessing: Implications for behavior therapy. *Behavior Therapy, 29,* 123–156.

Lopes da Silva, F. H. (2003). Visual dreams in the congenitally blind? *Trends in Cognitive Sciences, 7,* 328–330.

Lord, T. R. (2001). 101 reasons for using cooperative learning in biology teaching. *The American Biology Teacher, 63*(1), 30–38.

Lovaas, O. I. (1964). Cue properties of words: The control of operant responding by rate and content of verbal operants. *Child Development, 35,* 245–256.

Lovaas, O. I. (1987). Behavioral treatment and normal educational and intellectual functioning in young autistic children. *Journal of Consulting and Clinical Psychology, 55,* 3–9.

Lovaas, O. I. Berberich, J. P., Perloff, B. F., & Schaffer, B. (1966). Acquisition of imitative speech by schizophrenic children. *Science, 151,* 705–707.

Lu, S., & Ende, N. (1997). Potential for clinical use of viable pluripotent progenitor cells in blood bank stored human umbilical cord blood. *Life Sciences, 61,* 1113–1123.

Lubinski, D. (2000). Scientific and social significance of assessing individual differences: "Sinking shafts at a few critical points." *Annual Review of Psychology, 51,* 405–444.

Luborsky, L., Singer, B., & Luborsky, L. (1975). Comparative studies of psychotherapies: Is it true that "everyone has won and all must have prizes"? *Archives of General Psychiatry, 32,* 995–1008.

Luchins, A. S. (1957). Primacy-recency in impression formation. In C. Hovland (Ed.), *The order of presentation in persuasion* (pp. 33–40, 55–61). New Haven, CT: Yale University Press.

Lucy, J. A., & Shweder, R. A. (1979). Whorf and his critics: Linguistic and nonlinguistic influences on color memory. *American Anthropologist, 81,* 581–615.

Luria, A. R. (1968). *The mind of a mnemonist.* (pp. 24, 25). New York: Basic Books.

Lurito, J. T., Dzemidzic, M., Mathews, V. P., Lowe, M. J., Kareken, D. A., Phillips, M. D., & Wang, Y. (2000). Comparison of hemispheric lateralization using four language tasks. *Neuroimage, 11,* S358.

Lüscher, M. (1969). *The Lüscher Color Test.* New York: Random House.

Lutkenhaus, P., Grossmann, K. E., & Grossman, K. (1985). Infant–mother attachment at twelve months and style of interaction with a stranger at the age of three years. *Child Development, 56,* 1538–1542.

Lykken, D. T. (1995). *The antisocial personalities.* Hillsdale, NJ: Laurence Erlbaum.

Lykken, D. T. & Tellegen, A. (1996). Happiness is a stochastic phenomenon. *Psychological Science, 7,* 186–189.

Lynch, E. B., Coley, J. D., & Medin, D. L. (2000). Tall is typical: Central tendency, ideal dimensions, and graded category structure among tree experts and novices. *Memory & Cognition, 28*(1), 41–50.

Lytton, H., & Romney, D. M. (1991). Parents' sex-differentiated socialization of boys and girls: A meta-analysis. *Psychological Bulletin, 109*, 267–296.

Lyubomirsky, S. (2001). Why are some people happier than others?: The role of cognitive and motivational processes in well-being. *American Psychologist, 56*, 239–249.

Lyvers, M. (2003). The neurochemistry of psychedelic experiences. *Science & Consciousness Review, 1*, 1–5.

Lyznicki, J. M., Doege, T. C., Davis, R. M., & Williams, M. A. (1998). Sleepiness, driving, and motor-vehicle crashes. Council on Scientific Affairs, American Medical Association. *Journal of the American Medical Association, 279*(23), 1908–1913.

Maccoby, E. E. (1998). *The two sexes: Growing up apart: Coming together.* Cambridge, MA: Belknap Press of Harvard University Press.

MacDonald, A. P. (1970). Internal-external locus of control and the practice of birth control. *Psychological Reports, 27*, 206.

MacDonald, D., Kabani, N., Avis, D., & Evens, A. C. (2000). Automated 3D extraction of inner and outer surfaces of cerebral cortex from MRI. *NeuroImage, 12*, 340–356.

Mack, J. E. (1994). *Abduction.* New York: Scribner.

MacKenzie, S. B., Lutz, R. J., & Belch, G. E. (1986, May). The role of attitude toward the ad as a mediator of advertising effectiveness: A test of competing explanations. *Journal of Marketing Research, 23*, 130–143.

Macquet, P., & Franck, G. (1996). Functional neuroanatomy of human rapid eye movement sleep and dreaming. *Nature, 383*, 163–166.

Macrae, C. N., & Bodenhausen, G. V. (2000). Social cognition: Thinking categorically about others. *Annual Review of Psychology, 51*, 93–120.

Maddi, S., & Kobasa, S. C. (1984). *The hardy executive: Health under stress.* Homewood, IL: Dow Jones-Irwin.

Madsen, K. M., Hviid, A., Vestergaard, M., Schendel, D., Wohlfahrt, J., Thorsen, P., Olsen, J., & Melbye, M. (2002). A population-based study of measles, mumps, rubella vaccine and autism. *New England Journal of Medicine, 347,* 1477–1482.

Magarinos, M., Zafar, U., Nissenson, K., & Blanco, C. (2002). Epidemiology and treatment of hypochondriasis. *CNS Drugs, 16*(1), 9–22.

Maguire, E. A., Burgess, N., Donnett, J. G., O'Keefe, J., & Frith, C. D. (1998). Knowing where things are: Parahippocampal involvement in encoding object locations in virtual large-scale space. *Journal of Cognitive Neuroscience, 10*(1), 61–76

Mahe, V., & Dumaine, A. (2001). Oestrogen withdrawal associated psychoses. *Acta Psychiatrica Scandinavica, 104*(5), 323–331.

Mahowald, M. W., & Schenck, C. H. (1996). NREM sleep parasomnias. *Neurologic Clinics, 14*, 675–696.

Mai, J. K., Triepel, J., & Metz, J. (1987). Neurotensin in the human brain. *Neuroscience, 22*, 499–524.

Maier, S. F., & Watkins, L. R. (1998). Cytokines for psychologists: Implications of bidirectional immune-to-brain communication for understanding behavior, mood, and cognition. *Psychological Review, 105*, 83–107.

Main, M., & Cassidy, J. (1988). Categories of response to reunion with the parent at age 6: Predictable from infant attachment classifications and stable over a 1-month period. *Developmental Psychology, 24*, 415–426.

Main, M., & Hesse, E. (1990). Parents' unresolved traumatic experiences are related to infant disorganized attachment status; Is frightened and/or frightening parental behaviour the linking mechanism? In M. T. Greenberg, D. Cicchetti, & E. M. Cummings (Eds.), *Attachment in the preschool years: Theory, research and intervention* (pp. 161–182). Chicago: University of Chicago Press.

Main, M., & Solomon, J. (1990). Procedures for identifying infants as disorganized/disoriented during the Ainsworth Strange Situation. In M. T. Greenberg, D. Cicchetti, & E. M. Cummings (Eds.), *Attachment in the preschool years: Theory, research and intervention* (pp. 121–160). Chicago: University of Chicago Press.

Makeig, S., Delorme, A., Westerfield, M., Jung, T., Townsend, J., Courchesne, E., & Sejnowski, T. J. (2004). Electronic brain dynamics following manually responded visual targets. *Public Library of Science: Biology, 2*(6), e176.

Mandler, G. (1967). Organization and memory. In K. W. Spence & J. T. Spence (Eds.), *The psychology of learning and motivation, Vol. 1* (pp. 327–372). New York: Academic Press.

Mandler, J. M. (2000). Perceptual and conceptual processes. *Journal of Cognition and Development, 1*, 3–36.

Mandler, J. M. (2003). Conceptual categorization. In D. H. Rakison & L. M. Oakes (Eds.), *Early category and concept development: Making sense of the blooming, buzzing confusion* (pp. 103–131). Oxford, England: Oxford University Press.

Mann, J. (1972). Vicarious desensitization of test anxiety through observation of videotaped treatment. *Journal of Counseling Psychology, 19*, 1–7.

Mann, R. A. (1972). The behavior-therapeutic use of contingency contracting to control an adult behavior problem: Weight control. *Journal of Applied Behavior Analysis, 5*, 99–109.

Manson, J., Greenland, P., LaCroix, A. Z., Stefanick, M. L., Mouton, C. P., Oberman, A., Perri, M. G., Sheps, D. S., Pettinger, M. B., & Siscovick, D. S. (2002). Walking compared with vigorous exercise for the prevention of cardiovascular events in women. *The New England Journal of Medicine, 347*(10), 716–725.

March, J., Silva, S., Petrycki, S., Curry, J., Wells, K., Fairbank, J., Burns, B., Domino, M., McNulty, S., Vitiello, B., & Severe, J. [Treatment for Adolescents with Depression Study (TADS) Team]. (2004). Fluoxetine, cognitive-behavioral therapy, and their combination for adolescents with depression: Treatment for Adolescents with Depression Study (TADS) randomized controlled trial. *Journal of the American Medical Association, 292*(7), 807–820.

Maren, S., & Fanselow, M. S. (1996). The amygdala and fear conditioning: Has the nut been cracked? *Neuron, 16*, 237–240.

Margolin, S., & Kubic, L. S. (1944). An apparatus for the use of breath sounds as a hypnogogic stimulus. *American Journal of Psychiatry, 100*, 610.

Marik, P. E. (2000). Leptin, obesity, and obstructive sleep apnea. *Chest, 118*, 569–571.

Markovitz, J. H., Lewis, C. E., Sanders, P. W., Tucker, D., & Warnock, D. G. (1997). Relationship of diastolic blood pressure with cyclic GMP excretion among young adults (the CARDIA study): Influence of a family history of hypertension. *Journal of Hypertension, 15*(9), 955–962.

Markwell, J. (2004). The human side of science education: Using McGregor's Theory Y as a framework for improving student motivation. *Biochemistry and Molecular Biology Education 32*(5), 323–325.

Marlatt, G. A., & Perry, M. A. (1975). Modeling methods. In F. H. Kanter & A. P. Coldstein (Eds.), *Helping people change.* Elmsford, NY: Pergamon Press.

Mars, A. E., Mauk, J. E., & Dowrick, P. (1998). Symptoms of pervasive developmental disorders as observed in prediagnostic home videos of infants and toddlers. *Journal of Pediatrics, 132*, 500–504.

Martin, C. L. (2000). Cognitive theories of gender development. In T. Eckes & H. M. Trautner (Eds.), *The developmental social psychology of gender* (pp. 91–121). Mahwah, NJ: Lawrence Erlbaum.

Martin, J. A., & Buckwalter, J. J. (2001). Telomere erosion and senescence in human articular cartilage chondrocytes. *Journal of Gerontology and Biological Science, 56*(4), 172–179.

Martin, L. (2004). Can sleepwalking be a murder defense? Document retrieved from the Internet on October 19, 2004 at: **www.mtsinai.org/pulmonary/Sleep/sleep-murder.htm.**

Maruta, T., Colligan, R. C., Malinchoc, M., & Offord, K. P. (2002, August). Optimism-pessimism assessed in the 1960s and self-reported health status 30 years later. *Mayo Clinic Proceedings. 77*, 748–753.

Maslow, A. (1971). *The farther reaches of human nature.* New York: The Viking Press.

Maslow, A. (1987). *Motivation and personality*, 3rd ed. New York: Harper & Row.

Maslow, A. H. (1943). A theory of human motivation. *Psychological Review 50*, 370–396.

Maslow, A. H. (1968). *Toward a psychology of being.* Princeton, NJ: Van Nostrand Reinhold.

Maslow, A., & Lowery, R. (Ed.). (1998). *Toward a psychology of being*, 3rd ed. New York: Wiley & Sons.

Massaro, D. W., & Cowan, N. (1993). Information processing models: Microscopes of the mind. *Annual Review of Psychology, 44*, 383–426.

Masters, J. C., Burish, T. G., Holton, S. D., & Rimm, D. C. (1987). *Behavior therapy: Techniques and empirical finding.* San Diego: Harcourt Brace Jovanovich, Inc.

Masters, W. H., & Johnson, V. E. (1970). *Human sexual inadequacy* (pp. 316–351). Boston: Little, Brown.

Masters, W., & Johnson, V. (1966). *Human sexual response.* Boston: Little, Brown.

Masters, W., Johnson, V., & Kolodny, R. (1995). *Human sexuality* (5th ed.). New York: Harpers-Collins.

Masuda, T., & Kitayama, S. (2004). Perceiver-induced constraint and attitude attribution in Japan and the US: A case for the cultural dependence of the correspondence bias. *Journal of Experimental Social Psychology, 40*, 409–416.

Matsumoto, D. (1994). *People: Psychology from a cultural perspective* (pp. 144–147). Pacific Grove, CA: Brooks-Cole.

Matthews, K. A., Gump, B. B., Harris, K. F., Haney, T. L., & Barefoot, J. C. (2004). Hostile behaviors predict cardiovascular mortality among men enrolled in the Multiple Risk Factor Intervention Trial. *Circulation, 109*, 66–70.

Maurer, D., & Young, R. (1983). Newborns' following of natural and distorted arrangements of facial features. *Infant Behaviour and Development, 6*, 127–131.

Mavromatis, A. (1987). *Hypnagogia: The unique state of consciousness between wakefulness and sleep.* London: Routledge & Kegan Paul.

Mavromatis, A., & Richardson, J. T. E. (1984). Hypnagogic imagery. *International Review of Mental Imagery, 1*, 159–189.

Mayer, J. D. (September 1999). Emotional intelligence: Popular or scientific psychology? *APA Monitor Online, 30*(8) [*Shared Perspectives* column]. Washington, DC; American Psychological Association. Retrieved from the Internet on June 12, 2004 at **www.apa.org/monitor/sep99/sp.html**.

Mayer, J. D., & Geher, G. (1996). Emotional intelligence and the identification of emotion. *Intelligence, 22*, 89–113.

Mayer, J. D., Salovey, P., & Caruso, D. R. (2000). Models of emotional intelligence. In R. J. Sternberg (Ed.), *Handbook of human intelligence* (2nd ed., pp. 396–420). New York: Cambridge.

Maziade, M., Bissonnette, L., Rouillard, E., Martinez, M., Turgeon, M., Charron, L., Pouliot, V., Boutin, P., Cliché, D., Dion, C., Fournier, J. P., Garneau, Y., Lavallee, J. C., Montgrain, N., Nicole, L., Pires, A., Ponton, A. M., Potvin, A., Wallot, H., Roy, M. A., & Merette, C. (1997). 6p24–22 region and major psychoses in the Eastern Quebec population. Le Groupe IREP. *American Journal of Medical Genetics, 74*, 311–318.

Mazzoni, G. A. L., Loftus, E. F., & Kirsch, I. (2001). Changing beliefs about implausible autobiographical events: A little plausibility goes a long way. *Journal of Experimental Psychology: Applied, 7*(1), 51–59.

McAloon, M., & Lester, D. (1979). The Luscher Color Test as a measure of anxiety in juvenile delinquents. *Psychological Reports, 45*, 228.

McCann, S. J. H., & Stewin, L. L. (1988). Worry, anxiety, and preferred length of sleep. *Journal of Genetic Psychology, 149*, 413–418.

McCarthy, J. (1959). Programs with common sense. In *Mechanisation of thought processes, proceedings of the Symposium of the National Physics Laboratory* (pp. 77–84). London: Her Majesty's Stationery Office.

McCauley, C. (1998). Group dynamics in Janis's theory of groupthink: Backward and forward. *Organizational Behavior & Human Decision Processes, 73*(2–3), 142–162.

McClelland, D. C. (1961). *The achieving society.* Princeton, NJ: Van Nostrand.

McClelland, D. C. (1987). *Human motivation.* Cambridge, MA: Cambridge University Press.

McClelland, J. L., & Rumelhart, D. E. (1988). Explorations in parallel distributed processing. Cambridge, MA: MIT Press.

McCrae, R. R., & Costa, P. T. (1990). *Personality in Adulthood.* New York: Guilford Press.

McCrae, R. R., & Costa, P. T., Jr. (1996). Toward a new generation of personality theories: Theoretical contexts for the five-factor model. In J. S. Wiggins (Ed.), *The five-factor model of personality: Theoretical perspectives* (pp. 51–87). New York: Guilford.

McCrae, R. R., Costa, P. T., Jr., Ostendorf, F., Angleitner, A., Hrebickova, M., Avia, M. D., Sanz, J., Sanchez-Bernardos, M. L., Kusdil, M. E., Woodfield, R., Saunders, P. R, & Smith, P. B. et al. (2000). Nature over nurture: Temperament, personality, and life span development. *Journal of Personality and Social Psychology, 78*, 173–186.

McDermott, J. F. (2001). Emily Dickinson revisited: a study of periodicity in her work. *American Journal of Psychiatry, 158*(5), 686–690.

McDonald, J., Becker, D., Sadowsky, C., Jane, J., Conturo, T., & Schultz, L. (2002). Late recovery following spinal cord injury. *Journal of Neurosurgery: Spine, 97*, 252–265.

McDougall, W. (1908). *An introduction to social psychology.* London: Methuen & Co.

McEwen, B. S. (2000). The neurobiology of stress: From serendipity to clinical relevance. *Brain Research, 886*, 172–189.

McGinn, L. K. (2000). Cognitive behavioral therapy of depression: Theory, treatment, and empirical status. *American Journal of Psychotherapy, 54*, 254–260.

McGinnis, J. M., & Foege, W. H. (1993). Actual causes of death in the United States. *Journal of the American Medical Association, 270*(18), 2207–2212.

McGrath, E., Keita, G. P., Strickland, B. R., & Russo, N. F. (1992). *Women and depression: Risk factors and treatment issues.* Washington, DC: American Psychological Association.

McGregor, D. (1960). *The human side of enterprise.* New York: McGraw-Hill.

McGuire, F. (1994). Army alpha and beta tests of intelligence. In R. J. Sternberg (Ed.), *Encyclopedia of intelligence* (Vol. 1, pp. 125–129). New York: Macmillan.

McGwin, G. (1999). Characteristics of traffic crashes among young, middle-aged, and older drivers. *Accident Analysis and Prevention, 31*(3), 181–198.

McHugh, P. R. (1993). Multiple personality disorder. *Harvard Mental Health Newsletter, 10*(3), 4–6.

McKenzie, B. E., Tootell, H. E., & Day, R. H. (1980). Development of visual size constancy during the 1st year of human infancy. *Developmental Psychology, 16*, 163–174.

McLaughlin, S. K. & Margolskee, R. F. (1994). Vertebrate taste transduction. *American Scientist, 82*, 538–545.

McMillan, H. L., Boyle, M. H., Wong, M. Y., Duku, E. K., Fleming, J. E., & Walsh, C. A. (1999). Slapping and spanking in childhood and its association with lifetime prevalence of psychiatric disorders in a general population sample. *Canadian Medical Association Journal, 161*, 805–809.

McMonagle, T., & Sultana, A. (2002). Token economy for schizophrenia (Cochrane Review). In *The Cochrane Library, Issue 2.* Oxford: Update Software.

McPherson, M., Smith-Lovin, L., & Cook, J. M. (2001). Birds of a feather: Homophily in social networks. *Annual Review of Sociology, 27*, 415–444.

Meador, B. D., & Rogers, C. R. (1984). Person-centered therapy. In R. J. Corsini (Ed.), *Current psychotherapies* (3rd ed., pp. 142–195). Itasca, IL: Peacock Publishers.

Meadow, P. W., & Clevans, E. G. (1978). A new approach to psychoanalytic teaching. *Modern Psychoanalysis, 3*(1), 29–43.

Medical Economics Staff. (1994). *PDR family guide to women's health & prescription drugs.* Montvale, NJ: Medical Economics Company.

Medicine, B. (2002). Directions in gender research in American Indian societies: Two spirits and other categories. In W. J. Lonner, D. L. Dinnel, S. A. Hayes, & D. N. Sattler (Eds.), *Online Readings in Psychology and Culture* (Unit 3, Chapter 2), (**www.wwu.edu/~culture**), Center for Cross-Cultural Research, Western Washington University, Bellingham, WA.

Mehrabian, A. (2000). Beyond IQ: Broad-based measurement of individual success potential or "emotional intelligence." *Genetic, Social, and General Psychology Monographs, 126*, 133–239.

Meichenbaum, D. (1996). Stress inoculation training for coping with stressors. *The Clinical Psychologist, 49*, 4–7.

Melzack, R., & Wall, P. D. (1965). Pain mechanisms: A new theory. *Science, 150*, 971–979.

Melzack, R., & Wall, P. D. (1996). *The challenge of pain.* London: Penguin Books.

Menon, T., Morris, M., Chiu, C. Y., & Hong, Y. I. (1999). Culture and the construal of agency: Attribution to individual versus group dispositions. *Journal of Personality and Social Psychology, 76*, 701–727.

Merikle, M. P. (2000). Subliminal perception. In A. E. Kazdin (Ed.), *Encyclopedia of Psychology* (Vol. 7, pp. 497–499). New York: Oxford University Press.

Merriam-Webster. (2003). *Merriam-Webster's collegiate dictionary*, 11th ed. Merriam-Webster, Publisher.

Merritt, J. M., Stickgold, R., Pace-Schott, E., Williams, J., & Hobson, J. A. (1994). Emotion profiles in the dreams of men and women. *Consciousness and Cognition, 3*, 46–60.

Merskey, H. (1992). The manufacture of personalities: The production of multiple personality disorder. *British Journal of Psychiatry, 160*, 327–340.

Mervis, C. B., & Rosch, E. (1981). Categorization of natural objects. *Annual Review of Psychology, 32*, 89–115.

Messina, C. R., Lane, D. S., Glanz, K., West, D. S., Taylor, V., Frishman, W., & Powell, L. (2004). Relationship of social support and social burden to repeated breast cancer screening in the Women's Health Initiative. *Health Psychology 23*(6), 582, 592–594.

Meyrick, J. (2001). Forget the blood and gore: An alternative message strategy to help adolescents avoid cigarette smoking. *Health Education, 101*(3), 99–107.

Mezzich, J. E., Kleinman, A., Fabrega, H., & Parron, D. L. (1996). *Culture and psychiatric diagnosis.* Washington DC: American Psychiatric Association.

Michaels, J. W., Blommel, J. M., Brocato, R. M., Linkous, R. A., & Rowe, J. S. (1982). Social facilitation and inhibition in a natural setting. *Replications in Social Psychology, 2,* 21–24.

Miles, D. R., & Carey, G. (1997). Genetic and environmental architecture of human aggression. *Journal of Personality and Social Psychology, 72,* 207–217.

Milgram, S. (1964a). Behavioral study of obedience. *Journal of Abnormal and Social Psychology, 67,* 371–378.

Milgram, S. (1964b). Issues in the study of obedience: A reply to Baumrind. *American Psychologist, 19,* 848–852.

Milgram, S. (1974). *Obedience to authority: An experimental view.* New York: Harper and Row.

Miller, G. A. (1956). The magical number seven, plus or minus two: Some limits on our capacity for processing information. *Psychological Review, 63,* 81–97.

Miller, H. G., Cain, V. S., Rogers, S. M., Gribble, J. N., & Turner, C. F. (1999). Correlates of sexually transmitted bacterial infections among U.S. women in 1995. *Family Planning Perspectives, 311,* 4–9, 23.

Miller, J. G. (1984). Culture and the development of everyday social explanation. *Journal of Personality and Social Psychology, 46,* 961–978.

Miller, K. E., & Graves, J. C. (2000). Update on the prevention and treatment of sexually transmitted diseases. *American Family Physician, 61,* 379–386.

Miller, K., & Doman, J. M. R. (1996, April). Together forever. *Life Magazine,* 46–56.

Miller, L. H., & Smith, A. D. (1993). *The stress solution.* New York: Pocket Books.

Miller, M., & Kantrowitz, B. (1999, January 25). Unmasking Sybil: A re-examination of the most famous psychiatric patient in history. *Newsweek*.

Miller, M. & Rahe, R. H. (1997). Life changes scaling for the 1990s. *Journal of Psychosomatic Research, 43*(3), 279–292.

Miller, M. E., & Bowers, K. S. (1993). Hypnotic analgesia: Dissociated experience or dissociated control? *Journal of Abnormal Psychology, 102,* 29–38.

Miller, M. N., & Pumariega, A. (1999). Culture and eating disorders. *Psychiatric Times, 16*(2): 1–4.

Miller, N. E., Sears, R. R., Mowrer, O. H., Doob, L. W., & Dollard, J. (1941). The frustration-aggression hypothesis. *Psychological Review, 48,* 337–342.

Miller, P. M. (1976). *Behavioral treatment of alcoholism.* Elmsford, NY: Pergamon Press.

Milligan, B. (1998). *An interview with Chris Burke on living with Down's syndrome.* Retrieved from the Internet on July 10, 2004 at **www.arcark.org/drbethinterview.html**.

Milner, B., Corkin, S., & Teuber, H. L. (1968). Further analysis of the hippocampal syndrome: 14-year follow-up study of H. M. *Neuropsychologia, 6,* 215–234.

Milner, J. (1992, January). Risk for physical child abuse: Adult factors. *Violence Update.*

Milton, J., & Wiseman, R. (2001). Does psi exist? Reply to Storm and Ertel (2001). *Psychological Bulletin, 127,* 434–438.

Miner, M. H., & Dwyer, S. M. (1997). The psychosocial development of sex offenders: Differences between exhibitionists, child molesters, and incest offenders. *International Journal of Offender Therapy and Comparative Criminology, 41,* 36–44.

Mintz, L. B., & Betz, N. E. (1988). Prevalence and correlates of eating disordered behaviors among undergraduate women. *Journal of Counseling Psychology, 35,* 463–471.

Mischel, W. (1966). A social learning view of sex differences in behaviour. In E. E. Maccoby (Ed.), *The development of sex differences* (pp. 56–81). Stanford, CT: Stanford University Press.

Mischel, W., & Shoda, Y. (1995). A cognitive-affective system theory of personality: Reconceptualizing situations, dispositions, dynamics, and invariances in personality structure. *Psychological Review, 102,* 246–268.

Mishell, D. R. (2001). Menopause. In M.A. Stenchever et al. (Eds.), *Comprehensive Gynecology,* 4th ed. (pp. 1217–1258). St. Louis: Mosby.

Mitchell, J. E. (1985). *Anorexia nervosa & bulimia, diagnosis and treatment.* Minneapolis, MN: University of Minnesota Press.

Mitchell, S. A., & Black, M. J. (1996). *Freud and beyond: A history of modern psychoanalytic thought.* New York: HarperCollins Publishers, Reprint Edition.

Miyatake, A., Morimoto Y., Oishi, T., Hanasaki, N., Sugita, Y., Iijima, S., Teshima. Y., Hishikawa, Y., & Yamamura, Y. (1980). Circadian rhythm of serum testosterone and its relation to sleep: Comparison with the variation in serum luteinizing hormone, prolactin, and cortisol in normal men. *Journal of Clinical Endocrinology and Metabolism, 51*(6), 1365–1371.

Mokdad, A, H., Bowman, B. A., Ford, E. S., Dietz, W. H., Vinicor, F., Bales, V. S., & Marks, J. S. (2001). Prevalence of obesity, diabetes, and obesity related health risk factors. *Journal of the American Medical Association, 289,* 76–79.

Moldofsky, H. (1995). Sleep and the immune system. *International Journal of Immunopharmacology, 17*(8), 649–654.

Möller, A., & Hell, D. (2002). Eugen Bleuler and forensic psychiatry. *International Journal of Law and Psychiatry, 25,* 351–360.

Monastra, V. J., Monastra, D. M., & George, S. (2002). The effects of stimulant therapy, EEG biofeedback, and parenting style on the primary symptoms of attention-deficit/hyperactivity disorder. *Applied Psychophysiology & Biofeedback, 27*(4), 231–249.

Money, J. (1994). *Sex errors of the body and related syndromes.* Baltimore: Paul H. Brookes Publishing Co.

Money, J., & Mathews, D. (1982). Prenatal exposure to virilizing progestins: An adult follow-up study of 12 women. *Archives of Sexual Behavior, 11*(1), 73–83.

Money, J., & Norman, B. F. (1987). Gender identity and gender transposition: Longitudinal outcome study of 24 male hermaphrodites assigned as boys. *Journal of Sex and Marriage Therapy, 13,* 75–79.

Montgomery, R. W., & Ayllon, T. (1994). Eye movement desensitization across subjects: Subjective and physiological measures of treatment efficacy. *Journal of Behavior Therapy and Experimental Psychiatry, 25,* 217–230.

Moody, R., & Perry, P. (1993). *Reunions: Visionary encounters with departed loved ones.* London: Little, Brown and Company.

Moore, T. E. (1988). The case against subliminal manipulation. *Psychology and Marketing, 5,* 297–316.

Moore-Ede, M. C., Sulzman, F. M., & Fuller, C. A. (1982). *The clocks that time us.* Cambridge, MA: Harvard University Press.

Moorhead, G., Neck, C. P. & West, M. S. (1998). The tendency toward defective decision making within self-managing teams: The relevance of groupthink for the 21st century. *Organizational Behavior & Human Decision Processes, 73*(2–3), 327–351.

Mora, G. (1985). History of psychiatry. In H. I. Kaplan & B. J. Sadock (Eds.), *Comprehensive textbook of psychiatry* (pp. 2034–2054). Baltimore: Williams & Wilkins.

Moreland, R. L., & Zajonc, R. B. (1982). Exposure effects in person perceptions: Familiarity, similarity, and attraction. *Journal of Experimental Social Psychology, 18*(5), 395–415.

Morey, L., Warner, M. B., & Boggs, C. D. (2002). Gender bias in the personality disorders criteria: An investigation of five bias indicators. *Journal of Psychopathology & Behavioral Assessment, 24*(1), 55–65.

Morgan, C. D., & Murray, H. A. (1935). A method for investigating fantasies: The Thematic Apperception Test. *Archives of Neurology and Psychiatry, 34,* 298–306.

Morris, J. S., Friston, K. J., Buche, L. C., Frith, C. D., Young, A. W., Calder, A. J., & Dolan, R. J. (1998). A neuromodulatory role for the human amygdala in processing emotional facial expressions. *Brain, 121,* 47–57.

Morris, M. W., & Peng, K. (1994). Culture and cause: American and Chinese attributions social and physical events. *Journal of Personality and Social Psychology, 67,* 949–971.

Morris, M., Nisbett, R. E., & Peng, K. (1995). Causal understanding across domains and cultures. In D. Sperber, D. Premack, & A. J. Premack (Eds.), *Causal cognition: A multidisciplinary debate.* Oxford: Oxford University Press.

Morrison, J. (1995). *The clinician's guide to diagnosis.* New York: Guilford Press.

Moruzzi, G., & Magoun, H. W. (1949). Brainstem reticular formation and activation of the EEG. *Electroencephalographs in Clinical Neurophysiology, 1,* 455–473.

Mowat, F. (1988). *Woman in the mists: The story of Dian Fossey and the mountain gorillas of Africa.* New York: Warner Books.

Mueller, H. H., Donaldson, C. C. S., Nelson, D. V., & Layman, M. (2001). Treatment of fibromyalgia incorporating EEG-driven stimulation: A clinical outcomes study. *Journal of Clinical Psychology, 57*(7), 933–952.

Muller-Oerlinghausen, B., Berghofer, A., & Bauer, M. (2002). Bipolar disorder. *Lancet, 359,* 241–247.

Mullington, J., & Broughton, R. (1993). Scheduled naps in the management of daytime sleepiness in narcolepsy. *Sleep, 16,* 444–456.

Munroe, R. (1980). Male transvestism and the couvade: A psychocultural analysis. *Ethos, 8,* 49–59.

Munsterberg, H. (1907). *On the witness stand.* New York: Doubleday, Page & Company.

Munsterberg, H. (1913). *Psychology and industrial efficiency.* Boston and New York: Houghton Mifflin Company.

Murdock, B. B., Jr. (1962). The serial position effect in free recall. *Journal of Experimental Psychology, 64,* 482–488.

Muris, P., Harald, M., Irit, H., & Sijsenaar, M. (1998). Treating phobic children: Effects of EMDR versus exposure. *Journal of Consulting and Clinical Psychology, 66,* 193–198.

Murphy, C. C., Boyle, C., Schendel, D., Decouflé, P., & Yeargin-Allsopp, M. (1998). Epidemiology of mental retardation in children. *Mental Retardation and Developmental Disabilities Research Reviews, 4,* 6–13.

Murphy, K. R., & LeVert, S. (1995). *Out of the fog: Treatment options and coping strategies for adult attention deficit disorder.* New York: Hyperion.

Murphy, L. R. (1995). Managing job stress: An employee assistance/human resource management partnership. *Personnel Review, 24*(1), 41–50.

Murphy, M., & Donavan, S. (1997). *The physical and psychological effects of meditation: A review of contemporary research with a comprehensive bibliography.* Petaluma, CA: Institute of Noetic Sciences.

Murray, C. J. L., & Lopez, A. D., (Eds.). (1996). *Summary: The global burden of disease: A comprehensive assessment of mortality and disability from diseases, injuries, and risk factors in 1990 and projected to 2020.* Cambridge, MA: Published by the Harvard School of Public Health on behalf of the World Health Organization and the World Bank, Harvard University Press.

Murray, F. (1996). *Ginkgo biloba: Therapeutic and antioxidant properties of the "tree of health" (Keats Good Herb Guide).* Keats Publishing.

Murray, S. L., Holmes, J. G., MacDonald, G., & Ellsworth, P. C. (1998). Through the looking glass darkly? When self-doubts turn into relationship insecurities. *Journal of Personality and Social Psychology, 75,* 1459–1480.

Muter, P. (1978). Recognition failure of recallable words in semantic memory. *Memory & Cognition, 6*(1), 9–12.

Myers, D. (1993). *The pursuit of happiness: Who is happy, and why?* Avon.

Nadeau, K. G. (1995). *A comprehensive guide to attention deficit disorder in adults: Research, diagnosis, and treatment.* New York: Brunner/Mazel.

Nadeau, K. G., Quinn, P., & Littman, E. (2001). *AD/HD Self-Rating Scale for Girls.* Springfield, MD: Advantage Books.

Naitoh, P., Kelly, T. L., & Englund, C. E. (1989). *Health effects of sleep deprivation.* Naval Health Research Centre, Report No. 89–46.

Nasar, S. (1998). *A beautiful mind: A biography of John Forbes Nash, Jr., winner of the Nobel Prize in economics 1994.* New York: Simon & Schuster.

Nash, A. (2004). Christopher Reeve: A hero onscreen and off. *The Reader's Digest,* October, 23–25.

National Commission on Sleep Disorders. (1997). Lack of sleep America's top health problem, doctors say. CNN Interactive: Health Story Page. Retrieved from the Internet on October 19, 2004 at **www.cnn.com/HEALTH/9703/17/nfm/sleep.deprivation/index.html.**

National Institute of Allergy and Infectious Diseases. (2001). Human papillomavirus and genital warts. Retrieved from the Internet on November 18, 2004 at **www.niaid.nih.gov/factsheets/stdhpv.htm.**

National Institute of Child Health and Human Development. (1997). *National Institute of Health fact sheet: Sudden Infant Death Syndrome.* Bethesda, MD. Available on the Internet at **www.nichd.nih.gov/sids/sids_fact.htm.**

National Institute of Child Health and Human Development. (2004). *Targeting Sudden Infant Death Syndrome (SIDs): A strategic plan.* Bethesda, MD. Available on the Internet at: **www.nichd.nih.gov/strategicplan/cells/SIDS_Syndrome.pdf.**

National Institute of Mental Health (NIMH). (2001). The numbers count: Mental disorders in America. *NIH Publication No. 01-4584.* Bethesda, MD.

National Institute of Mental Health (NIMH). (2001). The numbers count: Mental disorders in America. Retrieved from the Internet on June 22, 2004 at **www.nimh.nih.gov/publicat/numbers.cfm.**

National Institute on Drug Abuse (NIDA). (2002). Research report series—Prescription drugs: Abuse and addiction. National Institutes of Health (NIH). Retrieved from the Internet on July 19 at **www.drugabuse.gov/ResearchReports/Prescription/prescription5.html.**

National Institutes of Health. (1998). *Understanding vaccines.* NIH Publication #98–4219.

National Institutes of Health. (2000). *NIH publishes final guidelines for stem cell research,* Retrieved from the Internet on August 23, 2004, at: **www.nih.gov/news/pr/aug2000/od-23.htm.**

Neale, M. C., Rushton, J. P., & Fulker, D. W. (1986). The heritability of items from the Eysenck Personality Questionnaire. *Personality and Individual Differences, 7,* 771–779.

Neary, N. M., Goldstone, A. P., & Bloom, S. R. (2004). Appetite regulations: From the gut to the hypothalamus. *Clinical Endocrinology, 60*(2): 153–160.

Neimark, J. (1996). The diva of disclosure, memory researcher Elizabeth Loftus. *Psychology Today, 29*(1), 48–80.

Neimeyer, R. A., & Mitchell, K. A. (1998). Similarity and attraction: A longitudinal study. *Journal of Social and Personality Relationships, 5,* 131–148.

Neisser, U. (1982). Snapshots or benchmarks? In U. Neisser (Ed.), *Memory observed: Remembering in natural contexts* (pp. 43–48). San Francisco: W. H. Freeman.

Neisser, U., & Harsch, N. (1992). Phantom flashbulbs: False recollections of hearing the news about *Challenger.* In E. Winograd & U. Neisser (Eds.), *Affect and accuracy in recall: Studies of "flashbulb memories."* New York: Cambridge University Press.

Neisser, U., Boodoo, G., Bouchard, T. J., Boykin, A. W., Brody, N., Ceci, S. J., Halpern, D. F., Loehlin, J. C., Perloff, R., Sternberg, R. J., & Urbina, S. (1996). Intelligence: Knowns and unknowns. *American Psychologist, 51,* 77–101.

Nelson, K. (1978). Semantic development and the development of semantic memory. In K. E. Nelson (Ed.), *Children's language, Vol 1.* New York: Gardner Press.

Nelson, K. (1993). The psychological and social origins of autobiographical memory. *Psychological Science, 4,* 7–14.

Nelson, K. (1993). The psychological and social origins of autobiographical memory. *Psychological Science, 4,* 1–8.

Neto, F. (1995). Conformity and independence revisited. *Social Behavior and Personality, 23*(3), 217–222.

Neumarker, K. (1997). Mortality and sudden death in anorexia nervosa. *International Journal of Eating Disorders, 21,* 205–212.

Neumeister, A., Bain, E., Nugent, A. C., Carson, R. E., Bonne, O., Luckenbaugh, D. A., Eckelman, W., Herscovitch, P., Charney, D. S., & Drevets, W. C. (2004). Reduced serotonin Type 1_a receptor binding in panic disorder. *The Journal of Neuroscience, 24*(3), 589–591.

Neville, H. J., & Bavelier, D. (2000). Specificity and plasticity in neurocognitive development in humans. In M.S. Gazzaniga, (Ed.) *The New Cognitive Neurosciences* (2nd ed. pp. 83–99). Cambridge, MA: The MIT Press.

Nicholson, N., Cole, S., & Rocklin, T. (1985). Conformity in the Asch situation: A comparison between contemporary British and US students. *British Journal of Social Psychology, 24,* 59–63.

Nickerson, R. S., & Adams, J. J. (1979). Long-term memory for a common object. *Cognitive Psychology, 11,* 287–307.

Nieto, F., Young, T. B., Lind, B. K., Shahar, E., Samet, J. M., Redline, S., D'Agostino, R. B., Newman, A. B., Lebowitz, M. D., & Pickering, T. G. (2000). Association of sleep-disordered breathing, sleep apnea, and hypertension in a large, community-based study. *Journal of the American Medical Association, 283*(14), 1829–1836.

Nigg, J. T., & Goldsmith, H. H. (1994). Genetics of personality disorders: Perspectives from personality and psychopathology research. *Psychological Bulletin, 115,* 346–380.

Nijenhuis, E. R. (2000). Somatoform dissociation: Major symptoms of dissociative disorders. *Journal of Trauma and Dissociation, 1*(4), 7–29.

NIMH Genetics Workgroup. (1998). *Genetics and mental disorders.* NIH Publication No. 98-4268. Rockville, MD: National Institute of Mental Health.

Nisbett, R. E. (1972). Hunger, obesity, and the ventromedial hypothalamus. *Psychological Review, 79,* 433–453.

Nolen-Hoeksema, S. (1990). *Sex differences in depression.* Palo Alto, CA: Stanford University Press.

Norenzayan, A., Choi, I., & Nisbett, R. E. (1999). Eastern and Western perceptions of causality for social behavior: Lay theories about personalities and situations. In D. A. Prentice & D. T. Miller (Eds.), *Cultural divides* (pp. 239–272). New York: Russell Sage Foundation.

Norrbrink Budh, C., Lund, I., Hultling, C., Levi, R., Werhagen, L., Ertzgaard, P., & Lundeberg, T. (2003). Gender-related differences in pain in spinal cord injured individuals. *Spinal Cord, 41*, 122–128.

Norris, S. L., Lee, C. T., Burshteyn, D., & Cea-Aravena, J. (2001). The effects of performance enhancement training on hypertension, human attention, stress, and brain wave patterns: A case study. *Journal of Neurotherapy, 4*(3), 29–44.

NSF/NIH/USED/NEH/USDA/NASA. (2000). Survey of Earned Doctorates. Arlington, VA: National Science Foundation.

Nyberg, L., & Tulving, E. (1996). Classifying human long-term memory: Evidence from converging dissociations. *European Journal of Cognitive Psychology, 8*(2), 163–183.

Ocholla-Ayayo, A. B. C., Wekesa, J. M., & Ottieno, J. A. M. (1993). *Adolescent pregnancy and its implications among ethnic groups in Kenya.* International Population Conference, Montreal, Canada: International Union for the Scientific Study of Population.

Ochsner, K., & Kosslyn, S. M. (1994). Mental imagery. In V. S. Ramaschandran (Ed.), *Encyclopedia of human behavior.* New York: Academic Press.

O'Connor, L. E. (1994). Empirical studies of shame and guilt: Development of a new measure, the Interpersonal Guilt Questionnaire. *Process Notes, 1*(1), 12–15.

O'Connor, L. E., Berry, J. W, Weiss, J., Bush, M., & Sampson, H. (1997). The Interpersonal Guilt Questionnaire: Development of a new measure. *Journal of Clinical Psychology, 53*(1), 74–89.

O'Connor, R. D. (1972). Relative efficacy of modeling, shaping, and the combined procedures for modification of social withdrawal. *Journal of Abnormal Psychology, 79*, 327–334.

O'Dell, S. (1974). Training parents in behavior modification: A review. *Psychological Bulletin, 81*, 418–433.

Offit, P. A., & Bell, L. M. (1998). *What every parent should know about vaccines.* New York: Macmillan.

Ofshe, R., & Watters, E. (1994). *Making monsters: False memories, psychotherapy and sexual hysteria.* New York: Scribners.

O'Leary, K. D., & Drabman, R. (1971). Token economy programs in the classroom: A review. *Psychological Bulletin, 75*, 379–398.

Olin, B. R., (Ed.). (1993). Central nervous system drugs, sedatives and hypnotics, barbiturates. In *Facts and comparisons drug information* (pp. 1398–1413). St. Louis, MO: Facts and Comparisons.

Oliver, J. E. (1993). Intergenerational transmission of child abuse: Rates, research, and clinical interpretations. *American Journal of Psychiatry, 150*, 1315–1324.

Ollendick, T. H., & King, N. J. (1998). Empirically supported treatments for children with phobic and anxiety disorders: Current status. *Journal of Clinical Child Psychology, 27*(2), 156–167.

Olsen, P. (1975). *Emotional flooding.* Baltimore, MD: Penguin Books.

Olson, H. C., & Burgess, D. M. (1997). Early intervention for children prenatally exposed to alcohol and other drugs. In M. J. Guralnick (Ed.), *The effectiveness of early intervention.* Baltimore: Brookes.

Oman, C. M. (1990). Motion sickness: A synthesis and evaluation of the sensory conflict theory. *Canadian Journal of Physiological Pharmacology, 68*, 294–303.

Onken, L. S., Blaine, J. D. & Battjes, R. J. (1997). Behavioral therapy research: A conceptualization of a process. In S. W. Henggeler & A.B. Santos (Eds.), *Innovative approaches for difficult-to-treat populations* (pp. 477–485). Washington, DC: American Psychiatric Press.

Oswald, I. (1959). Sudden bodily jerks on falling asleep. *Brain, 82*, 92–103.

Oswalt, R., Anderson, M., Hagstrom, K., & Berkowitz, B. (1993). Evaluation of the one-session eye-movement desensitization reprocessing procedure for eliminating traumatic memories. *Psychological Reports, 73*, 99–104.

Overeem, S., Mignot, E., Gert van Dijk, J., & Lammers, G. J. (2001). Narcolepsy: Clinical features, new pathophysiological insights, and future perspectives. *Journal of Clinical Neurophysiology, 18*(2), 78–105.

Overmier, J. B., & Seligman, M. E. P. (1967). Effects of inescapable shock on subsequent escape and avoidance behavior. *Journal of Comparative Physiology and Psychology, 63*, 23–33.

Owen, M. T., Easterbrooks, M. A., Chase-Lansdale, L., & Goldberg, W. A. (1984). The relation between maternal employment status and the stability of attachments to mother and to father. *Child Development, 55*, 1894–1901.

Padayatty, S. J., & Levine, M. (2001). New insights into the physiology and pharmacology of vitamin C [editorial]. *Canadian Medical Association Journal, 164*(3), 353–355.

Padian, N. S., Shiboski, S. C., & Jewell, N. P. (1991). Female-to-male transmission of human immunodeficiency virus. *Journal of the American Medical Association, 266*(12), 1664–1667.

Pagi, P., & Abramovich, H. (1984). Death: A cross-cultural perspective. *Annual Review of Anthropology, 13*, 385–417.

Paivio, A. (1971). *Imagery and verbal processes.* New York: Holt, Rinehart & Winston.

Paivio, A. (1986). *Mental representations: A dual coding approach.* New York: Oxford University Press.

Palefsky, J., Holly, E. A., Ralston, M. L., Da Costa, M., Bonner, H., Jay, N., Berry, J. M., & Darragh, T. M. (2001). Effect of highly active antiretroviral therapy on the natural history of anal squamous intraepithelial lesions and anal human papillomavirus infection. *Journal of Acquired Immune Deficiency Syndrome, 28*, 422–428.

Palmer, S. E. (1992). Common region: A new principle of perceptual grouping. *Cognitive Psychology, 24*(3), 436–447.

Pan, A. S. (2000). Body image, eating attitudes, and eating behaviors among Chinese, Chinese-American and non-Hispanic White women. *Dissertation Abstracts International, Section B: The Sciences and Engineering, 61*(1-B), 544.

Papousek, I., & Schulter, G. (2002). Covariations of EEG asymmetries and emotional states indicate that activity at frontopolar locations is particularly affected by state factors. *Psychophysiology 39*, 350–360.

Pargament, K. I. (1997). *The psychology of religion and coping: Theory, research, and practice.* New York: Guilford.

Paris, J. (2004). Gender differences in personality traits and disorders. *Current Psychiatry Reports, 6*, 71–74.

Park J., Turnbull A. P., & Turnbull H. R. (2002). Impacts of poverty on quality of life in families of children with disabilities. *Exceptional Children, 68*, 151–170.

Parkinson, W. L., & Weingarten, H. P. (1990). Dissociative analysis of ventromedial hypothalamic obesity syndrome. *American Journal of Physiology: Regulatory, Integrative, and Comparative Physiology, 259*, R829–R835.

Parobek, V. M. (1997). Distinguishing conversion disorder from neurologic impairment. *Journal of Neuroscience Nursing, 29*(2), 128.

Parsons, H. M. (1992). Hawthorne: An early OBM experiment. *Journal of Organizational Behavior Management 12*(1), 27–43.

Partonen, T., & Lonnqvist, J. (1998). Seasonal affective disorder. *Lancet, 352*(9137), 1369–1374.

Passantino, G. (1992). The Feds meet self-styled "God's Anointed Avenger." *World Magazine.* Retrieved from the Internet on June 28, 2004 at **http://answers.org/cultsandreligions/koresh.html.**

Pattie, F. A. (1994). *Mesmer and animal magnetism: A chapter in the history of medicine.* Place: Edmonston Publishing, Inc.

Paul, G. L., & Shannon, D. T. (1966). Treatment of anxiety through systematic desensitization in therapy groups. *Journal of Abnormal Psychology, 71*, 124–135.

Paunonen, S. V., Keinonen, M., Trzbinski, J., Forsterling, F., Grishenko-Roze, N., Kouznetsova, L., & Chan, D. W. et al. (1996). The structure of personality in six cultures. *Journal of Cross Cultural Psychology, 27*, 339–353.

Pavlov, I. (1926). *Conditioned reflexes.* London: Oxford University Press.

Peng, K., Ames, D. R., & Knowles, E. D. (2000). Culture and human inference: Perspectives from three traditions. In D. Matsumoto (Ed.), (2001). *The handbook of culture and psychology* (pp. 245–264). New York: Oxford University Press.

Penn, D. L. (1998). Assessment and treatment of social dysfunction in schizophrenia. *Clinicians Research Digest, Supplemental Bulletin, 18*, 1–2.

Peplau, L. A., & Taylor, S. E. (1997). *Sociocultural perspectives in social psychology: Current readings.* Upper Saddle River, NJ: Prentice-Hall.

Pepperberg, I. M. (1998). Talking with Alex: Logic and speech in parrots. *Scientific American Presents: Exploring Intelligence, 9*(4), 60–65.

Pereira, M. A., Kartashov, A. I., Van Horn, L., Slattery, M., Jacobs, D. R. Jr., & Ludwig, D. S. (2003). Eating breakfast may reduce risk of obesity, diabetes, heart disease. Paper presented March 6 at the American Heart Association's 2003 Annual Conference on Cardiovascular Disease Epidemiology and Prevention in Miami.

Perls, F. (1951). *Gestalt therapy.* New York: Julian Press.

Perls, F. (1969). *Gestalt therapy verbatim*. Moab, UT: Real People Press.

Perlstein, W. M., Carter, C. S., Noll, D. C., & Cohen, J. D. (2001). Relation of prefrontal cortex dysfunction to working memory and symptoms in schizophrenia. *American Journal of Psychiatry, 156*, 1105–1113.

Perrin, S., & Spencer, C. (1980). The Asch effect—a child of its time. *Bulletin of the British Psychological Society, 33*, 405–406.

Persaud, R. (2001). *Staying sane: How to make your mind work for you*. New York: Bantam.

Peters, W. A. (1971). *A class divided*. Garden City, NY: Doubleday.

Peterson, D. R. (1976). Need for the doctor of psychology degree in professional psychology. *American Psychologist 31*, 792–798.

Peterson, D. R. (1982). Origins and development of the doctor of psychology concept. In G. R. Caddy, D. C. Rimm, N. Watson, & J. H. Johnson (Eds.), *Educating professional psychologists* (pp. 19–38). New Brunswick, NJ: Transaction Books.

Peterson, L. R., & Peterson, M. J. (1959). Short-term retention of individual items. *Journal of Experimental Psychology, 58*, 193–198.

Petrak, J., & Keane, F. (1998). Cultural beliefs and the treatment of sexual dysfunction: An overview. *Sexual Dysfunction, 1*, 13–17.

Petrakis, I. L, Gonzalez, G., Rosenheck, R., & Krystal, J. H. (2002). Comorbidity of alcoholism and psychiatric disorders. *Alcohol Research and Health, 26*(2), 81–89.

Petri, H. (1996). *Motivation: Theory, research and application*, 4th ed., Belmont, CA: Wadsworth.

Petrova, P. K., Cialdini, R. B., & Sills S., J. (2003). Compliance, consistency, and culture: Personal consistency and compliance across cultures. *Journal of Experimental Social Psychology* [Submitted]. Retrieved from the Internet on August 6, 2004 at **www.public.asu.edu/~liulang/Compliance.pdf**.

Pettigrew, T. F., & Tropp, L. R. (2000). Does intergroup contact reduce prejudice? Recent meta-analytic findings. In S. Oskamp (Ed.), *Reducing prejudice and discrimination: Social psychological perspectives* (pp. 93–114). Mahwah, NJ: Erlbaum.

Petty, R. E. (1995). Attitude change. In A. Tesser (Ed.), *Advances in social psychology* (pp. 194–255). New York: McGraw-Hil.

Petty, R. E., Wheeler, S. C., & Tormala, Z. L. (2003). Persuasion and attitude change. In T. Millon & M. J. Lerner (Eds.), *Handbook of psychology: Volume 5: Personality and social psychology* (pp. 353–382). Hoboken, NJ: John Wiley & Sons.

Petty, R., & Cacioppo, J. (1986). *Communication and persuasion: Central and peripheral routes to attitude change*. New York: Springer-Verlag.

Petty, R., & Cacioppo, J. (1996). *Attitudes and persuasion: Classic and contemporary approaches*, reprint. Boulder, CO: Westview Press.

Pezdek, K., & Hodge, D. (1999). Planting false childhood memories in children: The role of event plausibility. *Child Development, 70*, 887–895.

Pezdek, K., Finger, K., & Hodge, D. (1997). Planting false childhood memories: The role of event plausibility. *Psychological Science, 8*, 437–441

Pfeiffer, W. M. (1982). Culture-bound syndromes. In I. Al-Issa (Ed.), *Culture and psychopathology* (pp. 201–218). Baltimore: University Park Press.

Phan, T., & Silove, D. (1999). An overview of indigenous descriptions of mental phenomena and the range of traditional healing practices amongst the Vietnamese. *Transcultural Psychiatry, 36*, 79–94.

Phillips, K. A. (2001). Somatoform and factitious disorders. *Review of Psychiatry, 20*(3), 27–65.

Piaget, J. (1926). *The language and thought of the child*. New York: Harcourt Brace.

Piaget, J. (1952). *The origins of intelligence in children*. New York: W. W. Norton.

Piaget, J. (1954) *The construction of reality in the child*. New York: Basic Books.

Piaget, J. (1962). *Play, dreams and imitation in childhood*. New York: W. W. Norton.

Piaget, J. (1983) Piaget's theory. In W. Kessen (Ed.), *Handbook of child psychology, Volume 1* (pp. 103–128). New York: Wiley.

Pierce, S. H., & Lange, G. (2000). Relationships among metamemory, motivation, and memory performance in young school age children. *The British Journal of Developmental Psychology, 18*, 121–135.

Pilkington, J. (1998). "Don't try and make out that I'm nice": The different strategies women and men use when gossiping. In J. Coates (Ed.), *Language and gender: A reader*. Oxford: Blackwell.

Pimentel, E. E. (2000). Just how do I love thee? Marital relations in urban China. *Journal of Marriage and Family, 62*(1), 32.

Pinker, S. (1995). Language acquisition. In Gleitman et al., (Eds.), *An invitation to cognitive science*, 2nd ed. Cambridge: MIT Press.

Pinker, S., & Bloom, P. (1990). Natural language and natural selection. *Behavioral and Brain Sciences, 13*(4), 707–784.

Pinsof, W. M., & Wynne, L. C. (1995). The efficacy of marital and family therapy: An empirical overview, conclusions, and recommendations. *Journal of Marital and Family Therapy, 21*, 585–613.

Pittam, J., Gallois, C., Iwawaki, S., & Kroonenberg, P. (1995). Australian and Japanese concepts of expressive behavior. *Journal of Cross-Cultural Psychology, 26*(5), 451–473.

Pizarro, D. A., & Salovey, P. (2002). On being and becoming a good person: The role of emotional intelligence in moral development and behavior. In J. Aronson (Ed.), *Improving academic achievement: Impact of psychological factors on education* (pp. 247–266). San Diego: Academic Press.

Plomin, R. (1994). The nature of nurture: The environment beyond the family. In R. Plomin, (Ed.), *Genetics and experience: The interplay between nature and nurture* (pp. 82–107). Thousand Oaks, CA: Sage.

Plomin, R. N. L., Pederson, G. E., McClearn, J. R., Nesselroade, C. S., & Bergman, H. F. (1988). EAS temperaments during the last half year of the life span: Twins reared apart and twins raised together. *Psychology of Aging, 4*, 43–50.

Plomin, R., & DeFries, J. C. (1998, May). Genetics of cognitive abilities and disabilities. *Scientific American*, 62–69.

Plug, C., & Ross, H. E. (1994). The natural moon illusion: A multi-factor angular account. *Perception, 23*, 321–333.

Plum, F., & Posner, J. B. (1985). *The diagnosis of stupor and coma*. Philadelphia: F. A. Davis.

Pollitt, E., & Matthews, R. (1998). Breakfast and cognition: An integrative summary. *American Journal of Clinical Nutrition, 67*(S), 804S–813S.

Pormerleau, C. S., & Pormerleau, O. F. (1994). Euphoriant effects of nicotine. *Tobacco Control, 3*, 374.

Postman, L. (1975). Tests of the generality of the principle of encoding specificity. *Memory & Cognition, 3*, 663–672.

Powers, M. H. (1984). A computer assisted problem solving method for beginning chemistry students. *The Journal of Computers in Mathematics and Science Teaching, 4*(1), 13–19.

Pratkanis, A. R. (1992). The cargo-cult science of subliminal persuasion. *Skeptical Inquirer, 16*, 260–272.

Pratkanis, A.R., & Greenwald A. G., (1988). Recent perspectives on unconscious processing: Still no marketing applications. *Psychology and Marketing, 5*, 337–353.

Pratt, J. A. (1991). Psychotropic drug tolerance and dependence: Common underlying mechanisms? In E. Pratt (Ed.), *The biological bases of drug tolerance and dependence*. London: Academic Press, Harcourt Brace Jovanovich.

Priester, J. M., & Petty, R. E. (1995). Source attributions and persuasion: Perceived honesty as a determinant of message scrutiny. *Personality and Social Psychology Bulletin, 21*, 637–654.

Prigerson, H. G., Bierhals, A. J., Kasi, S. V., Reynolds, C. F., Shear, M. K., Day, N., Beery, L. C., Newsome, J. T., & Jacobs, S. (1997). Traumatic grief as a risk factor for mental and physical morbidity. *American Journal of Psychiatry, 154I*, 616–623.

Prochaska, J. O., & Norcross, J. C. (2003). *Systems of psychotherapy* (5th ed.). Belmont, CA: Wadsworth.

Pullum, G. K. (1991). *The great Eskimo vocabulary hoax: And other irreverent essays on the study of language*. Chicago: The University of Chicago Press.

Pumariega, A. J., & Gustavson, C. R. (1994). Eating attitudes in African-American women: The essence. *Eating Disorders: Journal of Treatment and Prevention, 2*, 5–16.

Purcell, S. (1985). Relation between religious orthodoxy and marital sexual functioning. Paper presented at a meeting of the American Psychological Association, Los Angeles, August 25.

Putnam, J. A. (2001). EEG biofeedback on a female stroke patient with depression: A case study. *Journal of Neurotherapy, 5*(3), 27–38.

Putnam, S. P., & Stifter, C. A. (2002). Development of approach and inhibition in the first year: Parallel findings for motor behavior, temperament ratings and directional cardiac response. *Developmental Science, 5*, 441–451.

Quintero, J. E., Kuhlman, S. J., & McMahon, D. G. (2003). The biological clock nucleus: A multiphasic oscillator network regulated by light. *Journal of Neuroscience, 23*, 8070–8076.

Raaijmakers, J. G. W., & Shiffrin, R. M. (1992). Models for recall and recognition. *Annual Review of Psychology, 43*, 205–234.

Rachman, S. (1990). The determinants and treatments of simple phobias. *Advances in Behavioral Research and Therapy, 12*(1), 1–30.

Rachman, S. J., & Hodgson, R. J. (1980). *Obsessions and compulsions.* Englewood Cliffs, NJ: Prentice Hall.

Radford, B. (2004). New technique used in treating A.D.D. Article retrieved from the Internet on August 28, 2004 at **www.kansascity.com/mld/kansascity**.

Raikkonen, K., Matthews, K. A., & Salomon, K. (2003). Hostility predicts metabolic syndrome risk factors in children and adolescents. *Health Psychology, 22,* 279–286.

Ramón y Cajal, S. (1995.) *Histology of the nervous system of man and vertebrates.* New York: Oxford University Press. English translation by N. Swanson and L. M. Swanson.

Ramachandran, V. S., & Blakeslee, S. (1998). *Phantoms in the brain.* New York: Quill William Morrow.

Randi, J. (1980). *Flim-flam!* New York: Lippincott/Crowell.

Randi, J. (1982). *Flim-flam! Psychics, ESP, unicorns and other delusions.* Buffalo, NY: Prometheus.

Ranke, M. B., & Saenger, P. (2001, July 28). Turner's syndrome. *Lancet, 358*(9278), 309–314.

Rao, S. C., Rainer, G., & Miller, E. K. (1997) Integration of what and where in the primate prefrontal cortex. *Science, 276,* 821–824.

Raynor, H. A., & Epstein, L. H. (2001). Dietary variety, energy regulation and obesity. *Psychological Bulletin, 127*(3), 325–341.

Reder, L. M., Anderson, J. R., & Bjork, R. A. (1974). A semantic interpretation of encoding specificity. *Journal of Experimental Psychology, 102,* 648–656.

Regier, D. A., Narrow, W. E., Rae, D. S., Manderscheid, R. W., Locke, B. Z., & Goodwin, F. K. (1993). The de facto mental and addictive disorders service system. Epidemiologic Catchment Area prospective 1-year prevalence rates of disorders and services. *Archives of General Psychiatry, 50*(2), 85–94.

Reinders, A., Quak, J., Nijenhuis, E. R., Korf, J., Paans, A. M., Willemsen, A. T., & den Boer, J. A. (2001). Identity state-dependent processing of neutral and traumatic scripts in Dissociative Identity Disorder as assessed by PET. Oral Presentation: 7th Annual Meeting of the Organisation for Human Brain Mapping, June 10–14, Brighton, UK. *NeuroImage 13* (supplement), S1093.

Reiner, W. G. (1999). Assignment of sex in neonates with ambiguous genitalia. *Current Opinions in Pediatrics, 11*(4), 363–365.

Reiner, W. G. (2000). The genesis of gender identity in the male: Prenatal androgen effects on gender identity and gender role. Talk given at New York University Child Study Center, Grand Rounds Summary.

Reinsel, R., Antrobus, J., & Wollman, M. (1992). Bizarreness in dreams and waking fantasy. In J. Antrobus & M. Bertini (Eds.), *The neuropsychology of sleep and dreaming* (pp. 157–184). Hillsdale, NJ: Erlbaum.

Reinsel, R., Wollman, M., & Antrobus, J. (1986). Effects of environmental context and cortical activation on thought. *Journal of Mind and Behavior, 7,* 259–275.

Reiseberg, B., Doody, R., Stoffler, A., Schmitt, F., Ferris, S., & Mobius, H. J. (2003). Memantine in moderate to severe Alzheimer's disease. *New England Journal of Medicine, 348*(14), 1333–1341.

Reisenzein, R. (1983). The Schachter theory of emotion: Two decades later. *Psychological Bulletin, 94,* 239–264.

Reisenzein, R. (1994). Pleasure-arousal theory and the intensity of emotions. *Journal of Personality and Social Psychology, 7*(6), 1313–1329.

Reiter, R., & Milburn, A. (1994). Exploring effective treatment for chronic pelvic pain. *Comtemporary Ob/Gyn, 3,* 84–103.

Renchler, R. (1993). Poverty and learning. *ERIC Digests,* ERIC Clearinghouse on Educational Management, Eugene, OR. Retrieved from the Internet on June 1, 2004 at **www.ed.gov/databases/ERIC_Digests/ed357433.html**.

Renfrey, G., & Spates, R. C. (1994). Eye movement desensitization: A partial dismantling study. *Journal of Behavior Therapy and Experimental Psychiatry, 25,* 231–239.

Renner, M. J., & Mackin, R. S. (1998). A life stress instrument for classroom use. *Teaching of Psychology, 25,* 47.

Rescorla, R. (1988). Pavlovian conditioning—It's not what you think. *American Psychologist, 43,* 151–160.

Rescorla, R. A. (1968). Probability of shock in the presence and absence of CS in fear conditioning. *Journal of Comparative and Physiological Psychology, 66,* 1–5.

Rescorla, R. A., & Lolordo, V. M. (1965). Inhibition of avoidance behavior. *Journal of Comparative and Physiological Psychology, 59,* 406–412.

Reynolds, J. (2002). *Succeeding in college: Study skills and strategies.* Upper Saddle River, NJ: Prentice-Hall.

Reynolds, J. K., & Pezdek, K. (1992). Face recognition memory: The effects of exposure duration and encoding instructions. *Applied Cognitive Psychology, 6,* 279–292.

Rezvani, A. H., & Levin, E. D. (2001). Cognitive effects of nicotine. *Biological Psychiatry, 49,* 258–267.

Rhine, J. B. (1935). *Extrasensory perception.* Boston: Bruce Humphries.

Richards, C. F., & Lowe, R. A. (2003). Researching racial and ethnic disparities in emergency medicine. *Academic Emergency Medicine, 10*(11), 1169–1175.

Rideout, T. M. (2005). Eating disorders: Anorexia and bulimia. Holistic-online.com: Eating Disorders Infocenter. Retrieved from the Internet on March 30, 2005 at **www.holistic-online.com/Remedies/EatingD/EatD_anorxia-bulemia.htm**.

Ridley, M. (1999). *Genome: The autobiography of a species in 23 chapters.* London: Fourth Estate Ltd.

Rieber, R. W., & Robinson, D. K. (2001). *Wilhelm Wundt in history: The making of a scientific psychology.* New York: Kluwer Academic Publishers.

Rieger, E., Touyz, S. W., Swain, T., & Beumont, P. J. (2001). Cross-cultural research on anorexia nervosa: Assumptions regarding the role of body weight. *International Journal of Eating Disorders, 29*(2), 205–215.

Ritenbaugh, C., Shisslak, C., Prince, R. (1992). Eating disorders: A cross-cultural review in regard to DSM-IV. In J. E. Mezzich, A. Kleinman, & H. Farega et al., (Eds.), *Cultural Proposals for DSM-IV.* Submitted to the DSM-IV Task Force by the NIMH Group on Culture and Diagnosis. Pittsburgh: University of Pittsburgh.

Ritts, V. (1999). Infusing culture into psychopathology: A supplement for psychology instructors. Retrieved from the Internet on June 19, 2004 at **www.stlcc.cc.mo.us/mc/users/vritts/psypath.htm**.

Robins, L. N. (1996). *Deviant children grown up.* Baltimore: Williams & Wilkins.

Robinson, F. P. (1970). *Effective study* (4th ed.). New York: Harper & Row.

Robinson, J. W., & Preston, J. D. (1976). Equal status contact and modification of racial prejudice: A reexamination of the contact hypothesis. *Social Forces, 54,* 911–924.

Robinson, P. (1993). *Freud and his critics.* Berkeley, CA: University of California Press.

Rodgers, J. E. (1992). *Psychosurgery: Damaging the brain to save the mind.* New York: HarperCollins.

Rodin, J. (1981). Current status of the internal-external hypothesis for obesity. *American Psychologist, 36,* 361–372.

Rodin, J. (1985). Insulin levels, hunger, and food intake: An example of feedback loops in body weight regulation. *Health Psychology, 4,* 1–24.

Rodin, J., & Langer, E. J. (1977). Long-term effects of a control-relevant intervention among the institutionalized aged. *Journal of Personality and Social Psychology, 35,* 275–282.

Roediger, H. L. (1990). Implicit memory: Retention without remembering. *American Psychologist, 45,* 1043–1056.

Roediger, H. L. III (2000). Why retrieval is the key process to understanding human memory. In E. Tulving (Ed.), *Memory, consciousness and the brain: The Tallinn Conference* (pp. 52–75). Philadelphia: Psychology Press.

Roediger, H. L., III, & Crowder, R. G. (1976). A serial position effect in recall of United States presidents. *Bulletin of the Psychonomic Society, 8,* 275–278.

Roediger, H. L. III, & Guynn, M. J. (1996). Retrieval processes. In E. L. Bjork & R. A. Bjork (Eds.), *Memory* (pp. 197–236). New York: Academic Press.

Roethlisberger, F. J., & Dickson, W. J. (1939). *Management and the worker: An account of a research program conducted by the Western Electric Company, Hawthorne Works, Chicago.* Cambridge, MA: Harvard University Press.

Roffman, R. A., Stephens, R. S., Simpson, E. E., & Whitaker, D. L. (1988). Treatment of marijuana dependence: Preliminary results. *Journal of Psychoactive Drugs, 20*(1), 129–137.

Rogers, C. (1961). *On becoming a person: A therapist's view of psychotherapy.* Boston: Houghton/Mifflin.

Rogers, C. F. (1961). *On becoming a person.* Boston: Houghton Mifflin.

Rogers, R. W., & Mewborn, C. R. (1976). Fear appeals and attitude change: Effects of a threat's noxiousness, probability of occurrence, and the efficacy of the coping responses. *Journal of Personality and Social Psychology, 34,* 54–61.

Rogoff, B. (1994). Developing understanding of the idea of communities of learners. *Mind, Culture, and Activity, 1*(4), 209–229.

Rohde, A., & Marneros, A. (1993). Postpartum psychoses: Onset and long-term course. *Psychopathology, 26,* 203–209.

Roos, P. E., & Cohen, L. H. (1987). Sex roles and social support as moderators of life stress adjustment. *Journal of Personality and Social Psychology, 3,* 576–585.

Roper, G., Rachman, S., & Marks, I. (1975). Passive and participant modeling in exposure treatment of obsessive-compulsive neurotics. *Behaviour Research and Therapy, 13,* 271–279.

Rorschach, H. (1921). *Psychodiagnostik.* Bern: Bircher.

Rosch, E. (1973). On the internal structure of perceptual and semantic categories. In T. E. Moore (Ed.), *Cognitive development and the acquisition of language,* New York: Academic Press.

Rosch, E. (1977). Human categorization. In N. Warren (Ed.), *Advances in cross-cultural psychology, 1.* London: Academic Press.

Rosch, E., & Mervis, C. (1975). Family resemblances: Studies in the internal structures of categories. *Cognitive Psychology, 7,* 573–605.

Rosch, E., Mervis, C. B., Gray, W. D., Johnson, D. M., & Boyes-Braem, P. (1976). Basic objects in natural categories. *Cognitive Psychology, 8,* 382–439.

Rosch-Heider, E. (1972). Universals in color naming and memory. *Journal of Experimental Psychology, 93,* 10–20.

Rosch-Heider, E., & Olivier, D. C. (1972). The structure of the color space in naming and memory for two languages. *Cognitive Psychology, 3,* 337–354.

Rose, S., Kamin, L. J., & Lewontin, R. C. (1984). *Not in our genes: Biology, ideology and human nature.* Harmondsworth, UK: Penguin.

Roselli, C. E., Larkin, K., Resko, J. A., Stellflug, J. N., & Stormshak, F. (2004). The volume of a sexually dimorphic nucleus in the ovine medial preoptic area/anterior hypothalamus varies with sexual partner preference. *Endocrinology, 145*(2), 478–483.

Rosenman, R. H., Brand, R. I., Jenkins, C. D., Friedman, M., Straus, R., & Wurm, M. (1975). Coronary heart disease in the Western Collaborative Group Study, final follow-up experience of $8\frac{1}{2}$ years. *Journal of the American Medical Association, 233,* 812–817.

Rosenthal, A. M. (1964). *Thirty-eight witnesses: The Kitty Genovese case.* New York: McGraw-Hill.

Rosenthal, R., & Jacobson, L. (1968). *Pygmalion in the classroom.* New York; Holt, Rinehart and Winston.

Rosenthal, T. L. (1976). Modeling therapies. In M. Hersen, R. M. Eisler, & P. M. Miller (Eds.), *Progress in behavior modification. Vol. 2.* New York: Academic Press.

Rosenzweig, M. R., Leiman, A. L., & Breedlove, A. M. (1996). *Biological psychology.* Sunderland, MA: Sinaur Associates Inc.

Rossiter, T. R., & La Vaque, T. J. (1995). A comparison of EEG biofeedback and psychostimulants in treating attention deficit hyperactivity disorders. *Journal of Neurotherapy,* 48–59.

Rothenberg, A. (2001). Bipolar illness, creativity, and treatment. *Psychiatric Quarterly, 72*(2), 131–147.

Rotter, J. B. (1954). *Social learning and clinical psychology.* New York: Prentice Hall.

Rotter, J. B. (1966). Generalized expectancies for internal versus external control of reinforcements. *Psychological Monographs, 80,* Whole No. 609.

Rotton, J., & Frey, J. (1985). Air pollution, weather, and violent crime: Concomitant time-series analysis of archival data. *Journal of Personality and Social Psychology, 49,* 1207–1220.

Rotton, J., Frey, J., Barry, T., Milligan, M., & Fitzpatrick, M. (1979). The air pollution experience and physical aggression. *Journal of Applied Social Psychology, 9,* 397–412.

Rouse, B. A. (1998). *Substance and mental health statistics source book.* Rockville, MD: Department of Health and Human Services, Substance Abuse and Mental Health Services Administration (SAMHSA).

Rovet, J. (1993). The psychoeducational characteristics of children with Turner's syndrome. *Journal of Learning Disabilities, 26,* 333–341.

Rowan, J. (2001). *Ordinary ecstasy.* Hove, UK: Brunner-Routledge.

Rowe, D. C., Almeida, D. A., & Jacobson, K. C. (1999). School context and genetic influences on aggression in adolescence. *Psychological Science, 10,* 277–280.

Roysircai-Sodowsky, G. R., & Maestas, M. V. (2000). Acculturation, ethnic identity, and acculturative stress: Evidence and measurement. In R. H. Dana (Ed.), *Handbook of cross-cultural and multicultural assessment* (pp. 131–172). Mahwah, NJ: Lawrence Erlbaum.

Ruble, D., Alvarez, J., Bachman, M., Cameron, J., Fuligni, A., Garcia Coll, C., & Rhee, E. (2004). The development of a sense of "we": The emergence and implications of children's collective identity. In M. Bennett & F. Sani (Eds.), *The development of the social self.* New York: Psychology Press.

Rudd, P., & Osterberg, L. G. (2002). Hypertension: Context, pathophysiology, and management. In E. J. Topol (Ed.), *Textbook of cardiovascular medicine* (pp. 91–122). Philadelphia: Lippincott Williams and Wilkins.

Rumelhart, D. E., Hinton, G. E., & McClelland, J. L. (1986). A general framework for parallel distributed processing. In D. E. Rumelhart, J. L. McClelland, & the PDP Research Group (Eds.), *Parallel distributed processing: Explorations in the microstructure of cognition. Vol. 1: Foundations.* Cambridge, MA: MIT Press.

Rundus, D. (1971). An analysis of rehearsal processes in free recall. *Journal of Experimental Psychology, 89,* 63–77.

Ruscio, A. M., Borkovec, T. D., & Ruscio, J. (2001). A taxometric investigation of the latent structure of worry. *Journal of Abnormal Psychology, 110,* 413–422.

Russell, D. E. (1986). *The secret trauma: Incest in the lives of girls and women..* New York: Basic Books.

Rutherford, A. (2000). Mary Cover Jones (1896–1987). *The Feminist Psychologist, 27*(3), 25.

Rutherford, E. (1886). A new theory of hearing. *Journal of Anatomy and Physiology, 21,* 166–168.

Ryan, R. M., & Deci, E. L. (2000). Intrinsic and extrinsic motivations: Classic definitions and new directions. *Contemporary Educational Psychology, 25,* 54–67.

Rynn, M., Scherrer, J., & True, W. R. (2000, November). Generalized anxiety disorder. *Best Practice of Medicine.*

Sackeim, H. A., Prudic, J., Devanand, D. P., Nobler, M. S., Lisanby, S. H., Peyser, S., Fitzsimons, L., Moody, B. J., & Clark, J. (2000). A prospective, randomized, double-blind comparison of bilateral and right unilateral electroconvulsive therapy at different stimulus intensities. *Archives of General Psychiatry, 57,* 425–434.

Sacks, O. (1990). *The Man who mistook his wife for a hat and other clinical tales.* New York: HarperPerennial.

Sacks, O. (1995). *An anthropologist on Mars.* London: Picador.

Sadker, M., & Sadker, D. (1994). *Failing at fairness: How America's schools cheat girls.* New York: Scribner.

Salend, S. J. (1987). Contingency management systems. *Academic Therapy, 22,* 245–253.

Salovey, P., & Mayer, J. D. (1990). Emotional intelligence. *Imagination, Cognition, and Personality, 9,* 185–211.

Salovey, P., Rothman, A. J., Detweiler, J. B., & Steward, W. (2000). Emotional states and physical health. *American Psychologist, 55,* 110–121.

Salthouse, T. A. (1984). The skill of typing. *Scientific American, 250*(2), 128–135.

Sands, L. P., & Meredith, W. (1992). Intellectual functioning in late midlife. *Journal of Gerontological and Psychological Science, 47,* 81–84.

Sapir, E. S. (1921). *Language: An introduction to the study of speech.* New York: Harcourt, Brace.

Sapolsky, R. M. (2004). *Why zebras don't get ulcers* (3rd ed., pp. 1, 144–145). New York: Owl Books.

Sarbin, T. R., & Coe, W. C. (1972). *Hypnosis: A social psychological analysis of influence communication.* New York: Holt, Rinehart, & Winston.

Sartori, G., & Umilta, C. (2000). How to avoid the fallacies of cognitive subtraction in brain imaging. *Brain and Language, 74,* 191–212.

Satcher, D. (1999). *The surgeon general's call to action to prevent suicide.* Washington, DC: Office of the Surgeon General of the United States.

Satcher, D. (2001). *The surgeon general's national strategy to prevent suicide.* Washington, DC: Office of the Surgeon General of the United States.

Satterly, D. (1987). Piaget and education. In R. L. Gregory (Ed.), *The Oxford companion to the mind.* Oxford: Oxford University Press.

Sattler, J. M. (1977). The effects of therapist–client racial similarity. In A. S. Gurman, A. M. Razin. (Eds.), *Effective psychotherapy: A handbook of research* (pp. 252–290). Elmsford, NY: Pergamon.

Saunders, B., & Goddard, C. R. (1998). Why do we condone the "physical punishment" of children? *Children Australia, 23,* 23–28.

Savage-Rumbaugh, S., & Lewin, R. (1994). *Kanzi.* New York: Wiley.

Savage-Rumbaugh, S., Shanker, S., & Taylor, T. J. (1998). *Apes, language and the human mind.* Oxford: Oxford University Press.

Schachter, S., & Singer, J. E. (1962) Cognitive, social and physiological determinants of emotional states. *Psychological Review, 69,* 379–399.

Schaefer, H. H., & Martin, P. L. (1975). *Behavioral therapy* (2nd ed.). New York: McGraw-Hill.

Schafer, M., & Crichlow S. (1996). Antecedents of groupthink: A quantitative study. *Journal of Conflict Resolution, 40,* 415–435.

Schillemans, L., De Grande, L., & Remmen, R. (1989). Using quality circles to evaluate the efficacy of primary health care. In R. F. Conner & M. Hendricks (Eds.), *International innovations in evaluation methodology. New directions in program evaluation 42* (pp. 19–27). San Francisco: Jossey-Bass.

Schmitt, D. P. (2002). Personality, attachment and sexuality related to dating relationship outcomes: Contrasting three perspectives on personal attribute interaction. *British Journal of Social Psychology, 41*(4), 589–610.

Schmitz, C., Wagner, J., & Menke, F. (2001). The interconnection of childhood poverty and homelessness: Negative impact/points of access. *Families in Society, 82*(1), 69–77.

Schneider, K. J., Bugental, J. F. T., & Fraser, J. F. (Eds.). (2001). *Handbook of Humanistic Psychology.* Thousand Oaks, CA: Sage.

Schneider, R. H., Staggers, F., Alexander, C. N., Sheppard, W., Rainforth, M., Kondwani, K., Smith, S., & King, C. G. (1995). A randomized controlled trial of stress reduction for hypertension in older African Americans. *Hypertension, 26*(5), 820–827.

Schneider, W., Dumais, S., & Shriffrin, R. (1984). *Automatic and control processing and attention.* London: Academic Press.

Schneidman, E. (1983). *Death of man.* New York: Jason Aronson, Inc.

Schneidman, E. (1994). *Death: Current perspectives.* New York: McGraw-Hill.

Schols L., Haan J., Riess O., Amoiridis G., Przuntek H. (1998). Sleep disturbance in spinocerebellar ataxias: Is the SCA3 mutation a cause of restless legs syndrome? *Neurology, 51,* 1603–1607

Schreiber, F. R. (1973, reissued 1995). *Sybil.* New York: Warner.

Schroeder, S. R. (2000). Mental retardation and developmental disabilities influenced by environmental neurotoxic insults. *Environmental Health Perspectives 108* (Suppl. 3), 395–399.

Schroth, M. L., & McCormack, W. A. (2000). Sensation seeking and need for achievement among study-abroad students. *The Journal of Social Psychology, 140,* 533–535.

Schultz, D. P., & Schultz, S. E. (2004). *A history of modern psychology* (pp. 239–242). Belmont, CA: Wadsworth.

Schwanenflugel, P., & Rey, M. (1986). Interlingual semantic facilitation: Evidence from common representational system in the bilingual lexicon. *Journal of Memory and Language, 25,* 605–618.

Schwartz, B., Ward, A. H., Monterosso, J., Lyubomirsky, S., White, K., & Lehman, D. (2002). Maximizing versus satisficyng: Happiness is a matter of choice. *Journal of Personality and Social Psychology, 83,* 1178–1197.

Schwartz, S. K. (2000). Working your degree. *CNNMoney.* Retrieved from the Internet on January 17, 2005 at **http://money.cnn.com/2000/12/08/career/q_degreepsychology.**

Schweickert, R. (1993). A multinomial processing tree model for degradation and redintegration in immediate recall. *Memory and Cognition, 21,* 168–175.

Schwitzgebel, E. (1999). Representation and desire: A philosophical error with consequences for theory-of-mind research. *Philosophical Psychology, 12,* 157–180.

Scott, S. K., Young, A. W., Calder, A. J., Hellawell, D. J., Aggleton, J. P., & Johnson, M. (1997). Impaired auditory recognition of fear and anger following bilateral amygdala lesions. *Nature, 385*(6613), 254–257.

Scott, W. D. (1908). *The psychology of advertising: A simple exposition of the principles of psychology in their relation to successful advertising.* Boston: Small, Maynard and Company.

Scull, A. T., MacKenzie, C., & Hervey, N. (1996). *Masters of bedlam.* Princeton, NJ: Princeton University Press.

Searight, H. R., Burke, J. M., & Rottnek, F. (2000). Adult ADHD: Evaluation and treatment in family medicine. *American Family Physician, 62*(9), 2077–2086, 2091–2092.

Segall, M. H., Campbell, D. T., & Herskovits, M. J. (1966). *The influence of culture on perception.* Indianapolis: Bobbs-Merrill Co.

Segerstrom, S. C., Taylor, S. E., Kemeny, M. E., & Fahey, J. L. (1998). Optimism is associated with mood, coping, and immune change in response to stress. *Journal of Personality and Social Psychology, 74*(6), 1646–1655.

Seligman, L. (1998). *Selecting effective treatments: A comprehensive guide to treating mental disorders.* San Francisco, CA: Jossey-Bass.

Seligman, M. (1975). *Helplessness: Depression, development and death.* New York: W. H. Freeman.

Seligman, M. (1989). *Helplessness.* New York: W. H. Freeman.

Seligman, M. E. P. (1970). On the generality of the laws of learning. *Psychological Review, 77,* 406–418.

Seligman, M. E. P. (1975). *Helplessness—On depression, development, and death.* San Francisco: Freeman.

Seligman, M. E. P. (1995). The effectiveness of psychotherapy: The *Consumer Reports* study. *American Psychologist, 50,* 965–975.

Seligman, M. E. P. (1998). *Learned optimism: How to change your mind and your life* (2nd ed.). New York: Pocket Books.

Seligman, M.E.P. (2002). *Authentic happiness.* New York: Free Press.

Seligman, M. E. P., & Maier, S. F. (1967). Failure to escape traumatic shock. *Journal of Experimental Psychology, 74,* 1–9.

Sellin, D. J., & Birch, J. W. (1981). *Psycho-educational development of gifted and talented learners.* Rockville, MD: Aspen Systems Corporation.

Selye, H. (1956). *The stress of life.* New York: McGraw-Hill.

Selye, H. (1976). *The stress of life* (rev. ed.). New York: McGraw-Hill.

Selye, H. A. (1936). Syndrome produced by diverse nocuous agents. *Nature, 138,* 32.

Shackelford, T. K., Buss, D. M., & Bennett, K. (2002). Forgiveness or breakup: Sex differences in responses to a partner's infidelity. *Cognition and Emotion, 16*(2), 299–307.

Shadish, R., Cook, T. D., & Campbell, D. T. (2002). *Experimental and quasi-experimental designs for generalized causal inferences.* New York: Houghton Mifflin Company.

Shafto, P., & Coley, J. D. (2003). Development of categorization and reasoning in the natural world. Novices to experts, naive similarity to ecological knowledge. *Journal of Experimental Psychology: Learning, Memory & Cognition, 29,* 641–649.

Shafton, A. (1995). *Dream reader: Contemporary approaches to the understanding of dreams (S U N Y series in dream studies)* (pp. 40–46). New York: State University of New York Press.

Shah, P. M. (1991). Prevention of mental handicaps in children in primary health care. *Bulletin of the World Health Organization, 69,* 779–789.

Shapiro, A. K., & Shapiro, E. (1997). *The powerful placebo.* Baltimore: Johns Hopkins University Press.

Shapiro, F. (1989). Eye movement desensitization: A new treatment for post-traumatic stress disorder. *Journal of Behavior Therapy and Experimental Psychiatry, 20,* 211–217.

Shapiro, F. (1995). *Eye movement desensitization and reprocessing: Basic principles, protocols, and procedure.* New York: Guilford.

Shapiro, K. L., Jacobs, W. J., & LoLordo, V. M. (1980). Stimulus relevance in Pavlovian conditioning in pigeons. *Animal Learning and Behavior, 8,* 586–594.

Shaywitz, S. E. (1996). Dyslexia. *Scientific American, 275*(5), 98–104.

Shean, R. E., de Klerk, N. H., Armstrong, B. K., & Walker, N. R. (1994). Seven-year follow-up of a smoking-prevention program for children. *Australian Journal of Public Health, 18,* 205–208.

Sheeber, L. B., & Johnson, J. H. (1992). Child temperament, maternal adjustment, and changes in family life style. *American Journal of Orthopsychiatry, 62*(2), 178–185.

Shekelle, P. G., Hardy, M. L., Morton, S. C., Maglione, M., Mojica, W. A., Suttorp, M. J., Rhodes, S. L., Jungvig, L., & Gagné, J. (2003). Efficacy and safety of ephedra and ephedrine for weight loss and athletic performance: A meta-analysis. *Journal of the American Medical Association, 289*(12), 1537–1545.

Shelley, M. (1818/1969). *Frankenstein* (12th ed.). Oxford: Oxford University Press.

Shepard, R. N., & Metzler, J. (1971). Mental rotation of three-dimensional objects. *Science, 171,* 701–703.

Shepard, T. H. (2001). *Catalog of teratogenic agents,* 10th ed. Baltimore, MD: Johns Hopkins University Press.

Sherif, M. (1936). *The psychology of social norms.* New York: Harper & Row.

Sherif, M., Harvey, O. J., White, B. J., Hood, W. R., & Sherif, C. W. (1961). *Intergroup conflict and cooperation: The Robber's Cave experiment.* Norman, OK: University of Oklahoma Book Exchange.

Sherry, P. (1991). Person environment fit and accident prediction. *Journal of Business and Psychology, 5,* 411–416.

Sherry, P., Gaa, A., Thurlow-Harrison, S., Graber, K., Clemmons, J., & Bobulinski, M. (2003). Traffic accidents, job stress, and supervisor support in the trucking industry. Paper presented at the International Institute for Intermodal Transportation at the University of Denver, CO.

Shore, L. A. (1990). Skepticism in light of scientific literacy. *Skeptical Inquirer, 15*(1), 3–4.

Shorey, G. (2001). Bystander non-intervention and the Somalia incident. *Canadian Military Journal,* 19–27.

Shorter E. (1997). *A history of psychiatry: From the era of the asylum to the age of Prozac.* New York: John Wiley & Sons.

Showalter, E. (1997). *Hysteries: Hysterical epidemics and modern culture.* New York: Columbia University Press.

Shuglin, A. (1986). The background chemistry of MDMA. *Journal of Psychoactive Drugs, 18*(4), 291–304.

Shurkin, J. N. (1992). *Terman's kids; The groundbreaking study of how the gifted grow up.* Boston: Little, Brown & Company Limited.

Siegel, S. (1969). Effects of CS habituation on eyelid conditioning. *Journal of Comparative and Physiological Psychology, 68*(2), 245–248.

Siegler, I. C., Costa, P. T., Brummett, B. H., Helms, M. J., Barefoot, J. C., Williams, R. B., Dahlstrom, G., Kaplan, B. H., Vitaliano, P. P., Nichaman, M. Z., Day, S., & Rimer, B. K. (2003). Patterns of change in hostility from college to midlife in the UNC alumni heart study predict high-risk status. *Psychosomatic Medicine, 65,* 738–745.

Siegler, R. S. (1989). Mechanisms of cognitive development. *Annual Review of Psychology, 40,* 353–379.

Siegler, R. S. (1996). *Emerging minds: The process of change in children's thinking.* New York: Oxford University Press.

Silva, C. E., & Kirsch, I. (1992). Interpretive sets, expectancy, fantasy proneness, and dissociation as predictors of hypnotic response. *Journal of Personality & Social Psychology, 63,* 847–856.

Silver, F. W. (1996). Management of conversion disorder. *American Journal of Physical Medicine and Rehabilitation, 75,* 134–140.

Silver, L. (2000). Attention deficit/hyperactivity in adult lives. *Child & Adolescent Psychiatric Clinics of North America, 9,* 511–523.

Silver, S. M., Brooks, A., & Obenchain, J. (1995). Eye movement desensitization and reprocessing treatment of Vietnam war veterans with PTSD: Comparative effects with biofeedback and relaxation training. *Journal of Traumatic Stress, 8*(2), 337–342.

Simeon, D., Guralnik, O., Hazlett, E. A., Spiegel-Cohen, J., Hollander, E., & Buchsbaum, M. S. (2000). Feeling unreal: A PET study of depersonalization disorder. *American Journal of Psychiatry, 157,* 1782–1788.

Singer, M. T., & Lalich, J. (1995). *Cults in our midst.* San Francisco: Jossey-Bass.

Singh-Manoux, A., Richards, M., & Marmot, M. (2003). Leisure activities and cognitive function in middle age: Evidence from the Whitehall II study. *Journal of Epidemiology and Community Health, 57,* 907–913.

Siqueland, E. R., & Lipsitt, L. P. (1966). Conditioned head-turning in human newborns. *Journal of Experimental Child Psychology, 3,* 356–376.

Skinner, B. F. (1938). *The behavior of organisms: An experimental analysis.* Upper Saddle River, NJ: Prentice-Hall.

Skinner, B. F. (1938). *The behavior of organisms: An experimental analysis.* New York: Appleton-Century-Crofts.

Skinner, B. F. (1953). *Science and human behavior.* New York: MacMillan.

Skinner, B. F. (1954). The science of learning and the art of teaching. *Harvard Educational Review, 24*(2), 86–97.

Skinner, B. F. (1956). A case history in scientific method. *American Psychologist, 11,* 221–233.

Skinner, B. F. (1961). *Cumulative record: Definitive edition.* New York: Appelton-Century-Crofts.

Skinner, B. F. (1971). *Beyond freedom and dignity.* New York: Alfred A. Knopf, Inc.

Skinner, B. F. (1974). *About behaviorism.* New York: Alfred A. Knopf.

Skinner, B. F. (1989). The origins of cognitive thought. *American Psychologist, 44,* 13–18.

Skolnick, A. (1986). Early attachment and personal relationships across the life course. In P. B. Baltes, D. L. Featherman, & R. M. Lerner (Eds.), *Life-span development and behavior* (Vol. 7). Hillsdale, NJ: Erlbaum.

Skrandies, W., Reik, P., & Kunze, C. (1999). Topography of evoked brain activity during mental arithmetic and language tasks: Sex differences. *Neuropsychologia, 37,* 421–430.

Slater, A. (2000). Visual perception in the young infant: Early organisation and rapid learning. In D. Muir and A. Slater (Eds.), *Infant development: The essential readings.* Oxford: Blackwells.

Slater, A., Mattock, A., & Brown, E. (1990). Size constancy at birth: Newborn infants' responses to retinal and real size. *Journal of Experimental Child Psychology, 49,* 314–322.

Slater, A., Murison, V., & Rose, D. (1984). Habituation in the newborn. *Infant Behavior Development, 7,* 183–200.

Slipp, S. (1993). *The Freudian mystique: Freud, women and feminism.* New York: New York University Press.

Sloan, D. M., & Mizes, J. S. (1999). Foundations of behavior therapy in the contemporary healthcare context. *Clinical Psychology Review, 19,* 255–274.

Sloop, E. W. (1975). Parents as behavior modifiers. In W. D. Gentry (Ed.), *Applied behavior modification.* St. Louis: Mosby.

Smith, D. (2001). Shock and disbelief. *Atlantic Monthly, 2,* 79–90.

Smith, J. D. & Mitchell, A. (2001). "Me? I'm not a drooler. I'm the assistant": Is it time to abandon mental retardation as a classification. *Mental Retardation, 39*(2), 144–146.

Smith, J. W. (1988). Long term outcome of clients treated in a commercial stop smoking program. *Journal of Substance Abuse Treatment, 5*(1), 33–36.

Snyder, M., Tanke, E. D., & Berscheid, E. (1977). Social perception and interpersonal behavior: On the self-fulfilling nature of social stereotypes. *Journal of Personality and Social Psychology, 35,* 656–666.

Snyder, S. H. (1986). *Drugs and the Brain.* New York: Scientific American Books.

Sodowsky, G. R., Lai, E. W., & Plake, B. S. (1991). Moderating effects of socio-cultural variables on acculturation attitudes of Hispanics and Asian Americans. *Journal and Counseling and Development, 70,* 194–204.

Solomon P. R., Adams F., Silver A., Zimmer J. & DeVeaux, R. (2002). Ginkgo for memory enhancement: A randomized controlled trial. *Journal of the American Medical Association, 288*(7), 835–840.

Soomro, G. M. (2001). Obsessive-compulsive disorder. *Clinical Evidence, 6,* 754–762.

Southeast Asia and the West. *Population and Development Review, 23*(1), 95–113.

Sowell, E. R., Thompson, P. M., Holmes, C. J., Jernigan, T. L., & Toga, A. W. (1999). In vivo evidence for post-adolescent brain maturation in frontal and striatal regions. *Nature Neuroscience, 2*(10), 859–861.

Spangler, W. D. (1992). Validity of questionnaire and TAT measures of need for achievement: Two meta-analyses. *Psychological Bulletin, 112,* 140–154.

Spangler, W. J., Cosgrove, G. R., Ballantine, H. T., Jr., Cassem, E. H., Rauch, S. L., Nierenberg, A., & Price, B. H. (1996). Magnetic resonance image-guided stereotactic cingulotomy for intractable psychiatric disease. *Neurosurgery, 38,* 1071–1076.

Spanos, N. P. (1994). Multiple identity enactments and multiple personality disorder: A socio-cognitive perspective. *Psychological Bulletin, 116,* 143–165.

Spanos, N. P. (1996). *Multiple identities and false memories: A socio-cognitive perspective.* Washington, DC: American Psychological Association.

Spanos, N. P., Weekes, J. R., & Bertrand, L. D. (1985). Multiple personality: A social psychological perspective. *Journal of Abnormal Psychology, 94,* 362–376.

Sparing, R., Mottaghy, F., Ganis, G., Thompson, W. L., Toepper, R., Kosslyn, S. M., & Pascual-Leone, A. (2002). Visual cortex excitability increases during visual mental imagery—A TMS study in healthy human subjects. *Brain Research, 938,* 92–97.

Spearman, C. (1904). "General intelligence" objectively determined and measured. *American Journal of Psychology, 15,* 201–293.

Speca, M., Carlson, L. E, Goodey, E., & Angen, E. (2000). A randomized wait-list controlled clinical trial: The effects of a mindfulness meditation-based stress reduction program on mood and symptoms of stress in cancer outpatients. *Psychosomatic Medicine, 6,* 2613–2622.

Spencer, J. (2004, June 1). States extend prescription-writing powers to growing range of non-physicians. *The Wall Street Journal,* p. 1.

Sperling, G. (1960). The information available in brief visual presentations. *Psychological Monographs, 74*(11), 1–29.

Speroff, L., Glass, R. H., & Kase, N. G. (1999). Recurrent early pregnancy loss. In *Clinical Gynecologic Endocrinology and Infertility*, (pp. 1042–1055). Philadelphia: Lippincott Williams and Wilkins.

Sperry, R. W. (1968). Mental unity following surgical disconnection of the cerebral hemispheres. *The Harvey Lectures.* Series 62, 293–323. New York: Academic Press.

Spiegel, D., Bloom, J. R., & Gottheil, E. (1989). Effects of psychosocial treatment on survival of patients with metastatic breast cancer. *Lancet, 2*, 888–891.

Spiegel, H., & Borch-Jacobsen, M. (1997). Sybil—The making of a disease. *New York Review of Books, 44*(7).

Springer, S. P., & Deutsch, G. (1998). *Left brain, right brain: Perspectives from cognitive neuroscience*, 5th ed. New York: Freeman.

Squire, L., & Kandel, E. (1999). *Memory: From mind to molecule*. New York: Scientific American Library.

Squire, L. R., & Slater, P. C. (1978). Anterograde and retrograde memory impairment in chronic amnesia. *Neuropsychologia, 16*, 313–322.

Squire, L. R., Knowlton, B., & Musen, G. (1993). The structure and organization of memory. *Annual Review of Psychology, 44*, 453–495.

Squire, L. R., Slater, P. C., & Chace, P. M. (1975). Retrograde amnesia: Temporal gradient in very long-term memory following electroconvulsive therapy. *Science, 187*, 77–79.

Stanberry, L. R., Cunningham, A. L., Mindel, A., Scott, L. L., Spruance, S. L., Aoki, F. Y., & Lacey, C. J. (2000). Prospects for control of herpes simplex virus disease through immunization. *Clinical Infectious Diseases, 30*, 549–566.

Standing, L., Conezio, J., & Haber, R. N. (1970). Perception and memory for pictures: Single-trial learning of 2500 visual stimuli. *Psychonomic Science, 19*, 73–74.

Steele, C. M. (1992). Race and the schooling of black Americans. *The Atlantic Monthly, 269*(4), 68–78.

Steele, C. M. (1997). A threat in the air: How stereotypes shape intellectual identity and performance. *American Psychologist, 52*, 613–629.

Steele, C. M. (1999, August). Thin ice: "Stereotype threat" and Black college students. *The Atlantic Monthly, 284*, 44–54.

Steele, C. M., & Aronson J. (1995). Stereotype threat and the intellectual test performance of African Americans. *Journal of Personality and Social Psychology, 69*, 797–811.

Steele, J., James, J. B., & Barnett, R. C. (2002). Learning in a man's world: Examining the perceptions of undergraduate women in male-dominated academic areas. *Psychology of Women Quarterly, 26*, 46–50.

Steen, C. (1996). Synesthesia. *Health Report with Robin Hughes*. ABC Radio National Transcripts.

Stein, H. T. (2001). Adlerian overview of birth order characteristics. Alfred Adler Institute of San Francisco. Retrieved from the Internet on June 16, 2004 at **http://ourworld.compuserve.com/homepages/hstein/birthord.htm**.

Stein, S. (1984). *Girls and boys: The limits of non-sexist rearing* (pp. 12–14). London: Chatto and Windus.

Stein-Behrens, B., Mattson, M. P., Chang, I., Yeh, M., & Sapolsky, R. (1994). Stress exacerbates neuron loss and cytoskeletal pathology in the hippocampus. *Journal of Neuroscience, 14*, 5373–5380.

Steinberg, L., & Silverberg, S. B. (1987). Influences on marital satisfaction during the middle stages of the family life cycle. *Journal of Marriage and the Family, 49*, 751–760.

Stephenson, M. T., & Witte, K. (1998). Fear, threat, and perceptions of efficacy in frightening skin cancer messages. *Public Health Reviews, 26*, 147–174.

Steriade, M., & McCarley, R.W. (1990). *Brainstem control of wakefulness and sleep*. New York: Plenum.

Sterman, M. B. (2000). Basic concepts and clinical findings in the treatment of seizure disorders with EEG operant conditioning. *Clinical Electroencephalography, 31*(1), 45–55.

Sterman, M. B., & Lantz, D. (2001). Changes in lateralized memory performance in subjects with epilepsy following neurofeedback training. *Journal of Neurotherapy, 5*, 63–72.

Stern, W. (1912). The psychological methods of testing intelligence. (translated by G. M. Whipple). *Educational Psychology Monographs*, no. 13.

Sternberg, R. J. (1986). A triangular theory of love. *Psychological Review, 93*, 119–135.

Sternberg, R. J. (1988). *The triarchic mind: A new theory of human intelligence*. New York: Viking-Penguin.

Sternberg, R. J. (1988). Triangulating love. In R. Sternberg & M. Barnes (Eds.), *The psychology of love* (pp. 119–138). New Haven: Yale University Press.

Sternberg, R. J. (1996). *Successful intelligence: How practical and creative intelligence determine success in life*. New York: Simon & Schuster.

Sternberg, R. J. (1997). Construct validation of a triangular love scale. *European Journal of Social Psychology, 27*, 313–335.

Sternberg, R. J. (1997). The triarchic theory of intelligence. In P. Flannagan, J. L. Genshaft, & P. L. Harrison (Eds.), *Contemporary intellectual assessment: Theories, tests, and issues* (pp. 92–104). New York: Guilford Press.

Sternberg, R. J., & Grigorenko, E. L. (2000). *Teaching for successful intelligence: To increase student learning and achievement*. Arlington Heights, IL: Merrill-Prentice Hall.

Sternberg, R. J., & Kaufman, J. C. (1998). Human abilities. *Annual Review of Psychology, 49*, 479–502.

Sternberger, R. R. et al. (1995). Social phobia: An analysis of possible developmental factors. *Journal of Abnormal Psychology, 194*, 526–531.

Stickgold, R., Hobson, J. A., Fosse, R., & Fosse, M. (2001). Sleep, learning, and dreams: Off-line memory reprocessing. *Science, 294*(11), 1052–1057.

Stiff, J. B., & Mongeau, P. A. (2002). *Persuasive communication* (2nd ed.). New York: Guilford Publications.

Stiles, W. B., Agnew-Davies, R., Hardy, G. E., Barkham, M., & Shapiro, D. A. (1998). Relations of the alliance with psychotherapy outcome: Findings in the second Sheffield Psychotherapy Project. *Journal of Consulting and Clinical Psychology, 66*, 791–802.

Stitzer, M. L., & De Wit, H. (1998). Abuse liability of nicotine. In N. L. Benowitz (Ed.), *Nicotine safety and toxicity* (pp. 119–131). New York: Oxford University Press.

Stockhorst, U., Gritzmann, E., Klopp, K., Schottenfeld-Naor, Y., Hübinger, A., Berresheim, H., Steingrüber, H. & Gries, F. A. (1999). Classical conditioning of insulin effects in healthy humans. *Psychosomatic Medicine, 61*, 424–435.

Stoler, M. H. (2000). Human papillomaviruses and cervical neoplasia: A model for carcinogenesis. *International Journal of Gynecology and Pathology, 19*, 16–28.

Storch, A. (2004). Conversion of adult bone marrow cells in to stem cells for transplantation. Paper presented at the American Academy of Neurology 56th Annual Meeting in San Francisco, CA, April 24–May 1, 2004.

Stowell, J. R., Kiecolt-Glaser, J. K., & Glaser, R. (2001). Perceived stress and cellular immunity: When coping counts. *Journal of Behavioral Medicine, 24*(4), 323–339.

Strassman, R. J. (1984). Adverse reactions to psychedelic drugs: A review of the literature. *Journal of Nervous Mental Disease, 172*, 577–595.

Stratton, K., Gable, A., & McCormick, M. C. (Eds.) (2001a). *Immunization safety review: Thimerosal-containing vaccines and neurodevelopmental disorders*. Washington, DC: The National Academies Press.

Stratton, K., Wilson, C. B., & McCormick, M. C. (Eds.). (2001b). *Immunization safety review: Measles-mumps-rubella vaccine and autism*. Washington, DC: The National Academies Press.

Straus, M. A. (2000). Corporal punishment of children and adult depression and suicidal ideation. *Beating the devil out of them: Corporal punishment in American families and its effects on children*, New York: Lexington Books, 60–77.

Straus, M. A., & Stewart, J. H. (1999). Corporal punishment by American parents: National data on prevalence, chronicity, severity, and duration, in relation to child, and family characteristics. *Clinical Child and Family Psychology Review, 2*, 55–70.

Straus, M. A., & Yodanis, C. L. (1994). Physical abuse. In M. A. Straus (Ed.), *Beating the devil out of them: Corporal punishment in American families* (pp. 81–98). San Francisco: New Lexington Press.

Strawbridge, W. J., Cohen, R. D., Shema, S. J., & Kaplan, G. A. (1997). Frequent attendance at religious services and mortality over 28 years. *American Journal of Public Health, 87*, 957–961.

Strober, M., Freeman, R., Lampert, C., Diamond, J., & Kaye, W. (2000). Controlled family study of anorexia nervosa and bulimia nervosa: Evidence of shared liability and transmission of partial syndromes. *American Journal of Psychiatry, 157*, 393–401.

Stromeyer, C. F. III, & Psotka, J. (1971). The detailed texture of eidetic images. *Nature, 237*, 109–112.

Stubbs, R. J., van Wyk, M. C. W., Johnstone, A. M., & Harbron, C. G. (1996). Breakfasts high in protein, fat or carbohydrate: Effect on within-day appetite and energy balance. *European Journal of Clinical Nutrition, 50*, 409–417.

Stuss, D. T., Binns, M. A., Murphy, K. J., & Alexander, M. P. (2002). Dissociations within the anterior attentional system: Effects of task complexity and irrelevant information on reaction-time speed and accuracy. *Neuropsychology, 16*(4).

Sue, D. W., & Sue, D. (2003). *Counseling the culturally different: Theory and practice* (4th ed.). New York: John Wiley & Sons.

Sue, S. (1977). Community mental health services to minority groups: Some optimism, some pessimism. *American Psychologist, 32*, 616–624.

Sue, S. (1992). Ethnicity and mental health: Research and policy issues. *Journal of Social Issues, 48*(2), 187–205.

Sue, S., Fujino, D. C., Hu, L., Takeuchi, D. T., & Zane, N. W. S. (1991). Community mental health services for ethnic minority groups: A test of the cultural responsiveness hypothesis. *Journal of Consulting and Clinical Psychology, 59*, 533–540.

Sue, S., Zane, N., & Young, K. (1994). Research on psychotherapy in culturally diverse populations. In A. Bergin, & S. Garfield (Eds.), *Handbook of Psychotherapy and Behavior Change* (pp. 783–817). New York: Wiley.

Sulloway, F. J. (1996). *Born to rebel: Birth order, family dynamics, and creative lives.* New York: Pantheon.

Suryani, L., & Jensen, S. (1993). *Trance and possession in Bali: A window on western multiple personality, possession disorder, and suicide.* New York: Oxford University Press.

Sutcliffe, N., Clarke, A. E., Levinton, C., Frost, C., Gordon, C., & Isenberg, D. A. (1999). Associates of health status in patients with systemic lupus erythematosus. *Journal of Rheumatology, 26*, 2352–2356.

Sutherland, P. (1992). *Cognitive development today: Piaget and his critics.* London: Paul Chapman.

Swann, J. (1998). Talk control: An illustration from the classroom of problems in analyzing male dominance of conversation. In J. Coates (Ed.), *Language and gender: A reader.* Oxford: Blackwell.

Swanson, H. (1994). Index of suspicion. Case 3. Diagnosis: Failure to thrive due to psychosocial dwarfism. *Pediatric Review, 15*(1), 39, 41.

Swanson, J. W., Swartz, M. S., & Elbogen, E. B. (2004). Effectiveness of atypical antipsychotic medications in reducing violent behavior among persons with schizophrenia in community-based treatment. *Schizophrenia Bulletin, 30*(1), 3–20.

Swartz, M. (1990). Somatization Disorder. In L. N. Robins, (Ed.), *Psychiatric disorder in America* (pp. 220–257). New York: Free Press.

Swartz, M., Blazer, D., George, L., & Winfield, I. (1990). Estimating the prevalence of borderline personality disorder in the community. *Journal of Personality Disorders, 4*(3), 257–272.

Swayze V. W. II, (1995). Frontal leukotomy and related psychosurgical procedures in the era before antipsychotics (1935–1954): A historical overview. *American Journal of Psychiatry, 152*(4), 505–515.

Taglialatela, J. P., Savage-Rumbaugh, E. S., & Baker, L. A. (2003). Vocal production by a language-competent bonobo (Pan Paniscus). *International Journal of Comparative Psychology, 24*, 1–17.

Tajfel, H., & Turner, J. C. (1986). The social identity theory of intergroup behaviour. In S. Worchel & W. G. Austin (Eds.), *The psychology of intergroup relations* (Vol. 2). New York: Nelson Hall.

Takeuchi, T., Ogilvie, R. D., Murphy, T. I., & Ferrelli, A. V. (2003). EEG activities during elicited sleep onset. REM and NREM periods reflect difference mechanisms of dream generation. *Clinical Neurophysiology, 114*(2), 210–220.

Talbott, G. D. & Crosby, L. R. (2001). Recovery contracts: Seven key elements. In R. H. Coombs (Ed.), *Addiction recovery tools* (pp. 127–144). Thousand Oaks, CA: Sage Publications, Inc.

Tamminga, C. A. (2002). Partial dopamine agonists in the treatment of psychosis. *Journal of Neural Transmission, 109*, 411–420.

Tart, C. (1986). *Waking up: Overcoming the obstacles to human potential.* Boston: New Science Library.

Tart, C. T. (1970). Marijuana intoxication: Common experiences. *Nature, 226*, 701.

Taylor, B., Miller, E., Farrington, C. P., Petropoulos, M. C., Favot-Mayaud, I., Li, J., & Waight, P. A. (1999). Autism and measles, mumps, and rubella vaccine: No epidemiological evidence for a causal association. *Lancet, 353*, 2026–2029.

Taylor, D. M., & Moghaddam, F. M. (1994). *Theories of intergroup relations: International social psychological perspectives* (2nd ed.). Westport, CT: Praeger.

Taylor, F. W. (1985). (Originally 1911). *Principles of scientific management* (pp. 5–29). New York: Harper Bros.

Taylor, M. J., Carney, S., Geddes, J., & Goodwin, G. (2004). Folate for depressive disorders (Cochrane Review). In *The Cochrane Library*, Issue 2, 2004. Chichester, UK: John Wiley & Sons, Ltd.

Teigen, K. (1994). Yerkes–Dodson: A law for all seasons. *Theory & Psychology, 4*, 525–547.

Temoshok, L., & Dreher, H. (1997). *The Type C connection: The behavioral links to cancer and your health.* New York: Random House.

Terman, J. S. (2001). Circadian time of morning light administration and therapeutic response in winter depression. *Archives of General Psychiatry, 58*, 69–75.

Terman, L. M. (1916). *The measurement of intelligence.* Boston: Houghton Mifflin.

Terman, L. M. (1925). *Mental and physical traits of a thousand gifted children (I).* Stanford, CA: Stanford University Press.

Terman, L. M., & Oden, M. H. (1947). *The gifted child grows up: 25 years' follow-up of a superior group: Genetic studies of genius (V. 4).* Stanford, CA: Stanford University Press.

Terman, L. M., & Oden, M. H. (1959). *The gifted group at mid-life, thirty-five years follow-up of the superior child: Genetic studies of genius (V. 3).* Stanford, CA: Stanford University Press.

Terr, L. C. (1981). Psychic trauma in children: Observations following the Chowchilla bus kidnapping. *American Journal of Psychiatry, 138*, 14–19.

Terr, L. C. (1983). Chowchilla revisited: The effects of trauma four years after a school bus kidnapping. *American Journal of Psychiatry, 140*, 1543–1550. **http://www.theness.com/index.htm**

Terry, A. V. Jr., Hill, W. D., Parikh, V., Waller, J. L., Evans, D. R., & Mahadik, S. P. (2003). Differential effects of haloperidol, risperidone, and clozapine exposure on cholinergic markers and spatial learning performance in rats. *Neuropsychopharmacology, 28*(2), 300–309.

Terry, A. V. Jr., Hill, W. D., Parikh, V., Evans, D. R., Waller, J. L., & Mahadik, S. P. (2002). Differential effects of chronic haloperidol and olanzapine exposure on brain cholinergic markers and spatial learning in rats. *Psychopharmacology, 164*(4), 360–368.

Thase, M. E. (1999). When are psychotherapy and pharmacotherapy combinations the treatment of choice for major depressive disorders? *Psychiatric Quarterly, 70*(4), 333–346.

Thase, M. E., & Sachs, G. S. (2000). Bipolar depression: Pharmacotherapy and related therapeutic strategies. *Biological Psychiatry, 48*(6), 558–572.

The Arc (1982). *The prevalence of mental retardation.* Hartford, CT: The Arc.

Thiedke, C. C. (2001). Sleep disorders and sleep problems in childhood. *American Family Physician, 63*, 277–284.

Thigpen, C. H., & Cleckley, H. M. (1992, revised). *The three faces of Eve.* London: Secker & Warburg.

Thomas, A., & Chess, S. (1977). *Temperament and development.* New York: Brunner/Mazel.

Thomas, M., Thorne, D., Sing, H., Redmond, D., Balkin, T., Wesensten, N., Russo, M., Welsh, A., Rowland, L., Johnson, D., Aladdin, R., Cephus, R., Hall, S., & Belenky, G. (1998). The relationship between driving accidents and microsleep during cumulative partial sleep deprivation. *Journal of Sleep Research, 7*(2), 275.

Thomas, N. J. T. (2001). Mental Imagery. In E. N. Zalta, (Ed.), *The stanford encyclopedia of philosophy* (Winter 2001 Edition).

Thoresen, C. E., & Harris, H. S. (2002). Spirituality and health: What's the evidence and what's needed? *Annals of Behavioral Medicine, 24*, 3–13.

Thorndike, E. L. (1911). *Animal Intelligence: Experimental studies.* New York: MacMillan.

Thorndike, E. L. (1920). A constant error on psychological rating. *Journal of Applied Psychology, vol. IV*, 25–29.

Thornton, A., & Hui-Sheng, L. (1994). Continuity and change. In A. Thornton & L. Hui-Sheng (Eds.). *Social change and the family in Taiwan.* Chicago: University of Chicago Press.

Thurstone, L. L. (1938). *Primary mental abilities.* Chicago: University of Chicago Press.

Thyer, B. A. (1991). Diagnosis and treatment of child and adolescent anxiety disorders. *Behavior Modification, 15*(3), 310–325.

Tjio, J. H., & Levan, A. (1956). The chromosome number of man. *American Journal of Obstetrics and Gynecology, 130*, 723–724.

Tobach, E. (2001). Development of sex and gender. In Worell (Ed.), *Encyclopedia of women and gender* (pp. 315–332). San Diego, CA: Academic Press.

Toga, A. W., & Thompson, P. M. (2003). Mapping brain asymmetry. *Natural Neuroscience, 4*, 37–48.

Tohen, M., Vieta, E., Calabrese, J., Ketter, T. A., Sachs, G., Bowden, C., Mitchell, P. B., Centorrino, F., Risser, R., Baker, R. W., Evans, A. R., Beymer, K., Dube, S., Tollefson, G. D., & Breier, A. (2003). Efficacy of olanzapine and olanzapine-fluoxetine combination in the treatment of bipolar I depression. *Archives of General Psychiatry, 60*(11), 1079–1088.

Tolman, E. C. (1932). *Purposive behavior in animals and man*. New York: Century.

Tolman, E. C., & Honzik, C. H. (1930). Introduction and removal of reward and maze learning in rats. *University of California Publications in Psychology, 4*, 257–275.

Torgersen, S. (2000). Genetics of patients with borderline personality disorder. *Psychiatric Clinics of North America, (23)*, 1–9.

Torrance, E. P. (1993). The Beyonders in a thirty-year longitudinal study of creative achievement. *Roeper Review, 15*(3), 131–135.

Torrey, E. F. (1986). *Witchdoctors and psychiatrists. The common roots of psychotherapy and its future*. New York: Harper & Raw.

Torrey, E. F. (1987). Prevalence studies in schizophrenia. *British Journal of Psychiatry, 150*, 598–608.

Trappey, C. (1996). A meta-analysis of consumer choice and subliminal advertising. *Psychology and Marketing, 13*, 517–530.

Tremblay, A., Doucet, E., & Imbeault, P. (1999). Physical activity and weight maintenance. *International Journal of Obesity, 23*(3), S50–S54.

Tresniowski, A. (1999, July 12). Troubled sleep. *People Weekly*, 56–59.

Triandis, H. (1971). *Attitude and attitude change*. New York: Wilcy.

Trocmé, N., MacLaurin, B., Fallon, B., Daciuk, J., Billingsley, D., Tourigny, M., Mayer, M., Wright, J., Barter, K., Furford, G., Hornick, J., Sullivan, R., & McKenzie, B. (2001). Canadian incidence study of reported child abuse and neglect: Final report, pp. 30–31. Ottawa, ON: Minister of Public Works and Government Services Canada.

Troisi, A., & McGuire, M. (2002). Darwinian psychiatry and the concept of mental disorder. *Human Ethology & Evolutionary Psychology, 23*(4), 31–38.

Trudeau, D. L. (2000). The treatment of addictive disorders by brain wave biofeedback: A review and suggestions for future research. *Clinical Electroencephalography, 31*(1), 13–22.

Trujillo, K. A., & Chinn, A. B. (1996). Antidepressants. *Drugs and the Brain*: California State University. Retrieved from the Internet on July 20, 2004 at **www.csusm.edu/DandB/AD.html#history.**

Trut, L. M. (1999). Early canid domestication: The Farm-Fox Experiment. *Science, 283*.

Tsai, J. L., Simeonova, D. I., & Watanabe, J. T. (2004). Somatic and social: Chinese Americans talk about emotion. *Personality and Social Psychology Bulletin, 30*(9), 1226–1238.

Tugade, M. M., & Fredrickson, B. L. (2004). Resilient individuals use positive emotions to bounce back from negative emotional experiences. *Journal of Personality and Social Psychology, 86*(2), 320–333.

Tukuitonga, C. F., & Bindman, A. B. (2002). Ethnic and gender differences in the use of coronary artery revascularisation procedures in New Zealand. *New Zealand Medical Journal, 115*, 179–182.

Tulving, E., & Thomson, D. M. (1973). Encoding specificity and retrieval processes in episodic memory. *Psychological Review, 80*, 352–373.

Turner, W. J. (1995). Homosexuality, Type 1: An Xq28 phenomenon. *Archives of Sexual Behavior, 24*(2), 109–134.

Tusel, D. J., Piotrowski, N. A., Sees, K., Reilly, P. M., Banys, P., Meek, P., & Hall, S. M. (1994). Contingency contracting for illicit drug use with opioid addicts in methadone treatment. In L. S., Harris, (Ed.), *Problems of drug dependence. Proceedings of the 56th Annual Scientific Meeting. National Institute on Drug Abuse research monograph 153* (pp. 155–160). Washington, DC: U.S. Goverment Printing Office.

Tversky, A., & Kahneman, D. (1974). Judgment under uncertainty: Heuristics and biases. *Science, 185*, 1124–1130.

Tversky, A., & Shafir, E. (1992). The disjunction effect in choice under uncertainty. *Psychological Science, 3*(5), 305–309.

U.S. Department of Education. (2000). *A guide to the individualized education program*. Washington, DC: Educational Publications.

UNAIDS. (2003). AIDS epidemic update. Publication of the Joint United Nations Programme on HIV/AIDS.

Unger, R. (1979). Toward a redefinition of sex and gender. *American Psychologist, 34*, 1085–1094.

Uretsky, S. D. (2002). Antianxiety drugs. *Gale Encyclopedia of Medicine*. The Gale Group. Retrieved from the Internet on July 19, at **www.healthatoz.com/healthatoz/Atoz/ency/antianxiety_drugs.html#.**

Vail, A. (1976). Factors influencing lower class, black patients' remaining in treatment. *Clinical Psychology, 29*, 12–14.

Vaillant, G. E. (2002). Adaptive mental mechanisms: Their role in a positive psychology. *American Psychologist, 55*, 89–98.

Van de Castle, R. (1994). *Our dreaming mind*. New York: Ballantine Books.

van der Merwe, A., & Garuccio, A. (Eds.). (1994). *Waves and particles in light and matter*. New York: Plenum Press.

Van Dongen, H. P. A., Maislin, G., Mullington, J. M., & Dinges, D. F. (2003). The cumulative cost of additional wakefulness: Dose-response effects on neurobehavioral functions and sleep physiology from chronic sleep restriction and total sleep deprivation. *Sleep, 26*, 117–126.

van Dongen, M. C., van Rossum, E., Kessels, A. G., Sielhorst, H. J., & Knipschild, P. G. (2000). The efficacy of ginkgo for elderly people with dementia and age-associated memory impairment: New results of a randomized clinical trial. *Journal of the American Geriatric Society, 48*, 1183–1194.

Van Til, R. (1997). *Lost daughters: Recovered memory therapy and the people it hurts*. Grand Rapids, MI: Eerdmand.

Vartanian, L. R. (2000). Revisiting the imaginary audience and personal fable constructs of adolescent egocentricism: A conceptual review. *Adolescence, 35*(140), 639–661.

Vaughan, K., Armstrong, M. S., Gold, R., O'Connor N., Jenneke, W., & Tarrier, N. (1994). A trial of eye movement desensitization compared to image habituation training and applied muscle relaxation in post-traumatic stress disorder. *Journal of Behavior—Therapy and Experimental Psychology, 25*, 283–291.

Vaughan, S. (2000). *Half empty, half full: The psychological roots of optimism*. New York: Harcourt.

Veasey, S. C. (2003). Serotonin agonists and antagonists in obstructive sleep apnea: Therapeutic potential. *American Journal of Respiratory Medicine, 2*(1), 21–29.

Vernon, S. W., & Roberts, R. E. (1982). Use of RDC in a tri-ethnic community survey. *Archives of General Psychiatry, 39*, 47.

Villani, S. (2001). Impact of media on children and adolescents: A 10-year review of the research. *Journal of the American Academy on Child and Adolescent Psychiatry, 40*(4), 392–401.

Vink, T., Hinney, A., Van Elburg, A. A., Van Goozen, S. H., Sandkuijl, L. A., Sinke, R. J., Herpertz-Dahlman, B. M., Henebrand, J., Remschmidt, H., Van Engeland, H., & Adan, R. A. (2001). Association between an agouti-related protein gene polymorphism and anorexia nervosa. *Molecular Psychiatry, 6*(3), 325–328.

Virkkunen, M., & Linnoila, M. (1996). Serotonin and glucose metabolism in impulsively violent alcoholic offenders. In D. M., Stoff, & R. B., Cairns, (Eds.), *Aggression and violence* (pp. 87–100). Mahwah, NJ: Lawrence Erlbaum.

Visser, P. S., & Krosnick, J. A. (1998). Development of attitude strength over the life cycle: Surge and decline. *Journal of Personality and Social Psychology, 75*(6), 1389–1410.

Vogel, G. W. (1975). A review of REM sleep deprivation. *Archives of General Psychiatry, 32*, 749–761.

Vogel, G. W. (1993). Selective deprivation, REM sleep. In M. A. Carskadon (Ed.), *The encyclopedia of sleep and dreaming*. New York: Macmillan Publishing Company.

Vokey, J. R., & Read J. D., (1985). Subliminal messages: Between the devil and the media. *American Psychologist, 40*, 1231–1239.

von Helmholtz, H. (1852). On the theory of compound colours. *Philosophical Magazine, 4*, 519–535.

von Helmholtz, H. L. F. (1863). *Die Lehre von den Tonempfindungen als physiologische Grundlage fur die Theorie der Musik* published in translation (1954). *On the sensations of tone as a physiological basis for the theory of music*. New York: Dover.

Voyer, D., & Rodgers, M. (2002). Reliability of laterality effects in a dichotic listening task with nonverbal material. *Brain & Cognition, 48*, 602–606.

Voyer, D., Voyer, S., & Bryden, M. (1995). Magnitude of sex differences in spatial abilities: A meta-analysis and consideration of critical variables. *Psychological Bulletin, 117*(2), 250–270.

Vygotsky, L. S. (1934/1962). *Thought and language.* Cambridge, MA: MIT Press.

Vygotsky, L. S. (1978). *Mind in society: The development of higher psychological processes.* Cambridge, MA: Harvard University Press.

Vygotsky, L. S. (1987). Thought and word. In R. W. Riebe, & A. S. Carton (Eds.), *The collected works of L. S. Vygotsky, Vol. 1: Problems of general psychology* (pp. 243–288). New York: Plenum.

Wahlberg, D. (2001, October 11). We're more depressed, patriotic, poll finds. *Grand Rapids Press,* p. 535.

Wahlsten, D. (1997). The malleability of intelligence is not constrained by heritability. In B. Devlin, S. E. Fienberg, & K. Roeder, *Intelligence, genes, and success: Scientists respond to the bell curve* (pp. 71–87). New York: Springer.

Walker, J. (2004). The death of David Reimer: A tale of sex, science, and abuse. *Reason Online* at **http://reason.com/links/links052404.shtml**.

Walker, L. J. (1991). Sex differences in moral reasoning. In W. M. Kurtines & J. L. Gewirtz (Eds.), *Handbook of moral behavior and development: Vol. 2. Research* (pp. 333–364). Hillsdale, NJ: Lawrence Erlbaum.

Wampold, B. E. (1997). Methodological problems in identifying efficacious psychotherapies. *Psychotherapy Research, 7,* 21–43.

Ward, A. S., Li, D. H., Luedtke, R. R., & Emmett-Oglesby, M. W. (1996). Variations in cocaine self-administration by inbred rat strains under a progressive-ratio schedule. *Psychopharmacology, 127*(3), 204–212.

Ward, C., & Rana-Deuba, A. (1999). Acculturation and adaptation revisited. *Journal of Cross-Cultural Psychology, 30,* 422–442.

Ward, I. L. (1992). Sexual behavior: The product of parinatal hormonal and prepubertal social factors. In A. A. Gerall, H. Moltz, & I. L. Ward. (Eds.), *Handbook of behavioral neurobiology, vol. 11, Sexual differentiation.* New York: Plenum Press.

Ward, J., Mattic, K. R. P., & Hall, W. (1999). *Methadone maintenance treatment and other opioid replacement therapies.* Sydney: Harwood Academic Publishers.

Ward, M. M., Lotstein, D. S., Bush, T. M., Lambert, R. E., van Vollenhoven, R., & Neuwelt, C. M. (1999). Psychosocial correlates of morbidity in women with systemic lupus erythematosus. *Journal of Rheumatology, 26,* 2153–2158.

Wartner, U. G., Grossmann, K., Fremmer-Bombik, E., & Suess, G. (1994). Attachment patterns at age six in south Germany: Predictability from infancy and implications for preschool behavior. *Child Development, 65,* 1014–1027.

Washburn, M. F., (1908). *The animal mind: A text-book of comparative psychology.* New York: Macmillan.

Washington University in St. Louis, School of Medicine (2002, September). Questions and answers about Christopher Reeve's recovery of movement and the Washington University spinal cord injury program.

Wasserman, E. A., & Miller, R. R. (1997). What's elementary about associative learning? *Annual Review of Psychology, 48,* 573–607.

Watkins, C. E., Campbell, V. L., Nieberding, R., & Hallmark, R. (1995). Contemporary practice of psychological assessment by clinical psychologists. *Professional Psychology: Research and Practice, 26,* 54–60.

Watkins, C. E., Jr., & Savickas, M. L. (1990). Psychodynamic career counseling. In W. B. Walsh & S. H. Osipow (Eds.), *Career counseling: Contemporary topics in vocational psychology* (pp. 79–116). Hillsdale, NJ: Lawrence Erlbaum.

Watson, D. L., Hagihara, D. K., & Tenney, A. L. (1999). Skill-building exercises and generalizing psychological concepts to daily life. *Teaching of Psychology, 26,* 193–195.

Watson, J. B. (1913). Psychology as the behaviorist views it. *Psychological Review, 20,* 158–177.

Watson, J. B. (1924). *Behaviorism.* New York: W. W. Norton and Company.

Watson, J. B., & Rayner, R. (1920). Conditioned emotional responses. *Journal of Experimental Psychology, 3,* 1–14.

Watt, H. M. G. (2000). Measuring attitudinal change in mathematics and English over the 1st year of junior high school: A multi-dimensional analysis. *Journal of Experimental Education, 68,* 331–361.

Webb, C. T., & Levinson, D. F. (1993). Schizotypal and paranoid personality disorder in the relatives of patients with schizophrenia and affective disorders: A review. *Schizophrenic Research, 11*(1), 81–92.

Webb, W. B. (1992). *Sleep: The gentle tyrant* (2nd ed.). Bolton, MA: Ander.

Wechsler, D. (1975). *The collected papers of David Wechsler.* New York: Academic Press.

Wechsler, D. (1981). *Weschler Adult Intelligence Scale—Revised.* San Antonio, TX: The Psychological Corporation.

Wechsler, D. (1990). *Wechsler Preschool and Primary Scale of Intelligence—Revised.* Sidcup, Kent: The Psychological Corporation.

Wechsler, D. (1991). *Wechsler Intelligence Scale for Children-Third Edition.* New York: Psychological Corporation.

Wedding, D. (2004). Cross-cultural counseling and psychotherapy. In R. J. Corsini & D. Wedding (Eds.), *Current Psychotherapies* (7th ed. p. 485). Itasca, IL: Peacock.

Wegner, D. M., Wenzlaff, R. M., & Kozak, M. (2004). Dream rebound: The return of suppressed thoughts in dreams. *Psychological Science, 15*(4): 232–236.

Weinberger, D. R. (1987). Implications of normal brain development for the pathogenesis of schizophrenia. *Archives of General Psychiatry, 44,* 660–668.

Weiner, B. (1985). An attributional theory of achievement motivation. *Psychological Review, 92,* 548–573.

Weiner, I. B. (1997). Current status of the Rorschach Inkblot Method. *Journal of Personality Assessment, 68,* 5–19.

Weiner, R. D. (2000). Retrograde amnesia with electroconvulsive therapy: Characteristics and implications. *Archives of General Psychiatry, 57,* 591–592.

Weis, S., Klaver, P., Reul, J., Elger, C. E., & Fernandez, G. (2004). Temporal and cerebellar brain regions that support both declarative memory formation and retrieval. *Cerebral Cortex, 14,* 256–267.

Weisman, A. (1972). *On dying and denying.* New York: Behavioral Publications.

Weiss, J. M. (1972). Psychological factors in stress and disease. *Scientific American, 26,* 104–113.

Weisse, C. S. (1992). Depression and immunocompetence: A review of the literature. *Psychological Bulletin, 111,* 475–489.

Weissman, M. M., & Klerman, G. L. (1977). Sex differences and the epidemiology of depression. *Archives of General Psychiatry, 34,* 98–111.

Weissman, M. M., Bland, R. C., Canino, G. J., Faravelli, C., Greenwald, S., Hwu, H. G., Joyce, P. R., Karam, E. G., Lee, C. K., Lellouch, J., Lepine, J. P., Newman, S. C., Oakley-Browne, M. A., Rubio-Stipec, M., Wells, J. E., Wickramaratne, P. J., Wittchen, H. U., & Yeh, E. K. (1997). The cross-national epidemiology of panic disorder. *Archives of General Psychiatry, 54,* 305–309.

Weissman, M. M., Bland, R., Joyce, P. R., Newman, S., Wells, J. E., & Wittchen, H. U. (1993). Sex differences in rates of depression: Cross-national perspectives. *Journal of Affective Disorders, 29,* 77–84.

Weizenbaum, J. (1976). *Computer Power and Human Reason.* San Francisco: W. H. Freeman and Company.

Wen-Shing, T., & Strelzer, J. (Eds.). (1997). *Culture and psychopathology: A guide to clinical assessment.* Bristol, PA: Brunner/Mazel.

Wender, P. H., Wolf, L. E., & Wasserstein, J. (2001). Adults with ADHD. An overview. *Annals of the New York Academy of Sciences, 931,* 1–16.

Wenneberg, S. R., Schneider, R. H., Walton, K. G., Maclean, C. R., Levitsky, D. K., Mandarino, J. V., Waziri, R., & Wallace, R. K. (1997). Anger expression correlates with platelet aggregation. *Behavioral Medicine, 22*(4), 174–177.

Werker, J. F., & Lalonde, C. E. (1988). Cross-language speech perceptions: Initial capabilities and developmental change. *Developmental Psychology, 24,* 672–683.

Wertheimer, M. (1982). *Productive thinking.* Chicago: University of Chicago Press.

Westen, D. (in press). Cognitive neuroscience and psychotherapy: Implications for psychotherapy's second century. In G. Gabbard, J. Beck, & J. Holmes (Eds.), *Oxford textbook of psychotherapy.* Oxford: Oxford University Press.

Wetherell, J. L. (2002). Behavior therapy for anxious older adults. *Behavior Therapist, 25,* 16–17.

White, G. L. (1980). Physical attractiveness and courtship progress. *Journal of Personality and Social Psychology, 39,* 660–668.

White, S. (2000). *The transgender debate (the crisis surrounding gender identity).* Reading: Garnet Publishing Ltd.

Whittington, C. J., Kendall, T., Fonagy, P., Cottrell, D., Cotgrove, A., & Boddington, E. (2004). Selective serotonin reuptake inhibitors in childhood depression: Systematic review of published versus unpublished data. *Lancet, 363*(9418), 1341–1345.

WHO International Consortium in Psychiatric Epidemiology. (2000). Cross-national comparisons of the prevalences and correlates of mental disorders. *Bulletin of the World Health Organization, 78*(4), 413–426.

Whorf, B. L. (1956). *Language, thought and reality.* New York: Wiley.

Wicker, A. W. (1971). An examination of the "other variables" explanation of attitude–behavior inconsistency. *Journal of Personality and Social Psychology, 19,* 18–30.

Widiger, T. A., & Weissman, M. M. (1991). Epidemiology of borderline personality disorder. *Hospital and Community Psychiatry, 42,* 1015–1021.

Williams, M. E. (1995). *The American Geriatrics Society's complete guide to aging and mental health.* New York: Random House, Inc.

Williams, R. B. (1999). A 69-year-old man with anger and angina. *Journal of the American Medical Association, 282,* 763–770.

Williams, R. B., Haney, T. L., Lee, K. L., Kong, Y. H., Blumenthal, J. A., & Whalen, R. E. (1980). Type A behavior, hostility, and coronary atherosclerosis. *Psychosomatic Medicine, 42*(6), 539–549.

Williams, T. P. (1981). *The relative role of alcohol as a contributing factor in the over-representation of young drivers in highway crashes.* Albany, NY: New York State Division of Alcoholism and Alcohol Abuse, Bureau of Alcohol and Highway Safety.

Williamson, A. M., & Feyer, A. M. (2000). Moderate sleep deprivation produces impairments in cognitive and motor performance equivalent to legally prescribed levels of alcohol intoxication. *Journal of Occupational and Environmental Medicine, 57*(10), 649–655.

Wilson, S., Becker, L., & Tinker, R. (1995). Eye movement desensitization and reprocessing (EMDR) treatment for psychologically traumatized individuals. *Journal of Consulting and Clinical Psychology, 63,* 928–937.

Wilson. R. S., Mendes de Leon, C. F., Barnes, L. L., Schneider, J. A., Bienias, J. L., Evans, D. A., & Bennet, D. A. (2002). Participation in cognitively stimulating activities and risk of incident Alzheimer disease. *Journal of the American Medical Association, 287,* 742–748.

Winningham, R. G., Hyman, I. E., Jr., & Dinnel, D. L. (2000). Flashbulb memories? The effects of when the initial memory report was obtained. *Memory, 8,* 209–216.

Wisner, K., & Stowe, Z. (1997). Psychobiology of postpartum mood disorders. *Seminar on Reproductive Endocrinology, 15,* 77–89.

Witelson, S. F. (1991). Neural sexual mosaicism. Sexual differentiation of the human temporo-parietal region for functional asymmetry. *Psychoneuroendocrinology, 16,* 131–153.

Wolberg, L. R. (1977). *The technique of psychotherapy.* New York: Grune & Stratton.

Wolpe, J. (1958). *Psychotherapy by reciprocal inhibition.* Stanford: Stanford University Press.

Wolpe, J. (1991). *The practice of behavior therapy.* Boston: Allyn & Bacon.

Wood, J. M., Nezworski, M. T., & Stejskal, W. J. (1996). The comprehensive system for the Rorschach: A critical examination. *Psychological Science, 7*(1), 3–10, 14–17.

WordIQ.com. (2002). Cults. Article retrieved from the Internet on August 13, 2004 at **www.wordiq.com/definition/Cult.**

Wu, C., Tashkin, D., Djahed, B., & Rose, J. E. (1988). Pulmonary hazards of smoking marijuana as compared with tobacco. *New England Journal of Medicine, 318,* 347–351.

Wynne, C. (1999). Do animals think? The case against the animal mind. *Psychology Today, 32*(6), 50–53.

Yalom, I. (1995). *The theory and practice of group psychotherapy* (4th ed.). New York: Basic Books.

Yamaguchi, S., Isejima, H., Matsuo, T., Okura, R., Yagita, K., Kobayashi, M., & Okamura, H. (2003). Synchronization of cellular clocks in the suprachiasmatic nucleus. *Science, 302,* 1408–1412.

Yerkes, R. M. (Ed.) (1921). Psychological examining in the United States Army. *Memoirs of the National Academy of Sciences, 15,* 1–890.

Yerkes, R. M., & Dodson, J. D. (1908). The relation of strength of stimulus to rapidity of habit formation. *Journal of Comparative Neurology and Psychology, 18,* 459–482.

Ying, Y. W. (1990). Explanatory models of major depression and implications for help-seeking among immigrant Chinese-American women. *Culture, Medicine, and Psychiatry, 14,* 393–408.

Young, T. (1802). On the theory of light and colors. *Philosophical Transactions of the Royal Society, 91,* 12–49.

Yule, G. (1996). *Pragmatics.* Oxford: Oxford University Press.

Zajonc, R. B. (1965). Social facilitation. *Science, 149,* 269–274.

Zajonc, R. B. (1968). Attitudinal Effects of Mere Exposure. *Journal of Personality and Social Psychology Monographs, 9*(2), 1–27.

Zajonc, R. B. (1980). Feeling and thinking: Preferences need no inferences. *American Psychologist, 35,* 151–175.

Zajonc, R. B. (1984). On the primacy of affect. *American Psychologist, 39,* 117–123.

Zajonc, R. B. (1998). Emotions. In D. T. Gilbert & S. T. Fiske (Eds.), *Handbook of social psychology* (4th ed., Vol. 1, pp. 591–632). New York: McGraw-Hill.

Zajonc, R. B., Heingartner, A., & Herman, E. M. (1970). Social enhancement and impairment of performance in the cockroach. *Journal of Social Psychology, 13*(2), 83–92.

Zamrini, E., McGwin, G., & Roseman, J. M. (2004). Association between statin use and Alzheimer's disease. *Neuroepidemiology, 23,* 94–98.

Zanarini, M. C. (2000). Childhood experiences associated with the development of borderline personality disorder. *Psychiatric Clinics of North America, 23*(1), 89–101.

Zeki, S. (2001). Localization and globalization in conscious vision. *Annual Review of Neuroscience, 24,* 57–86.

Zentall, T. R. (2000). Animal intelligence. In R. J. Sternberg (Ed.), *Handbook of intelligence.* Cambridge: Cambridge University Press.

Zhou, J. N., Hofman, M. A., Gooren, L. J. G., & Swaab, D. F. (1995). A sex difference in the human brain and its relation to transsexuality. *Nature, 378,* 68–70.

Zilles, K. (1990). Cortex. In G. Paxinos (Ed.), *The human nervous system* (pp. 757–802). San Diego: Academic.

Zillmann, D., Baron, R., & Tamborini, R. (1981). Social costs of smoking: Effects of tobacco smoke on hostile behavior. *Psychology Journal of Applied Social, 11,* 548–561.

Zimbardo, P. (1971). The pathology of imprisonment. *Society, 9*(4–8), 4.

Zimbardo, P. G., & Hartley, C. F. (1985). Cults go to high school: A theoretical and empirical analysis of the initial stage in the recruitment process. *Cultic Studies Journal, 2,* 91–148.

Zimbardo, P. G. (1970). The human choice: Individuation, reason, and order versus deindividuation, impulse, and chaos. In N. J. Arnold & D. Levine (Eds.), *Nebraska Symposium on Motivation, 1969.* Lincoln: University of Nebraska Press.

Zimbardo, P., Maslach, C., & Haney, C. (2000). Reflections on the Stanford Prison Experiment: Genesis, transformations, consequences. In T. Blass (Ed.), *Obedience to authority: Current perspectives on the Milgram paradigm.* London: Lawrence Erlbaum.

Zisapel, N. (2001). Circadian rhythm sleep disorders: pathophysiology and potential approaches to management. *CNS Drugs, 15*(4), 311–328.

Zorilla, E. P., Luborsky, L., McKay, J. R., Rosenthal, R., Houldin, A., Tax, A., McCorkle, R., Seligman, D. A., & Schmidt, K. (2001). The relationship of depression and stressors to immunological assays: A meta-analytic review. *Brain, Behavior, and Immunity, 15,* 199–226.

Zuckerman, M. (1979). *Sensation seeking: Beyond the optimal level of arousal.* Hillsdale, NJ: Lawrence Erlbaum.

Zuckerman, M. (1994). *Behavioral expression and biosocial bases of sensation seeking.* New York: Cambridge University Press.

Zuckerman, M. (2002). Zuckerman-Kuhlman Personality Questionnaire (ZKPQ): An alternative five-factorial model. In B. De Raad & M. Perugini (Eds.), *Big five assessment* (pp. 377–396). Seattle: Hogrefe & Huber Publishers.

Zuo, L., & Cramond, B. (2001). An examination of Terman's gifted children from the theory of identity. *Gifted Child Quarterly, 45*(4), 251–259.

Zvolensky, M. J., Schmidt, M. B., & Stewart, S. H. (2003). Panic disorder and smoking. *Clinical Psychology: Science and Practice, 10,* 29–51.

Credits

PHOTO CREDITS

INTRODUCTION

Page I-2 Geri Engberg Photography. Page I-3 David Joel; David Joel/Getty Images, Inc. Page I-4 Joe Sohm/Chromosohm; The Stock Connection. Page I-5 Tom Stewart; Corbis/Bettmann. Page I-7 (Top) David Butow; Corbis/SABA Press Photos, Inc. (Bottom) Bill Varie; Corbis/Bettmann. Page I-9 (Top) Andy Sacks/Stone/Getty Images. (Bottom) © Dex Images/CORBIS. Page I-10 Corbis Royalty Free. Page I-11 Paul Barton; Corbis/Bettmann. Page I-12 Andersen Ross/Photodisc/Getty Images.

Chapter 1

Page 3 1-A Ryan McVay/Photodisc/Getty Images. 1-B Stockbyte. 1-C GK Hart/Vikki Hart/Photodisc/Getty Images. 1-D Marc Romanelli/Photodisc/ Getty Images Page 7 (Middle) Nancy R. Cohen; Getty Images, Inc.- Photodisc. (Bottom) Corbis/Bettmann. Page 8 Archives of the History of American Psychology - The University of Akron. Page 10 Getty Images Inc. - Hulton Archive Photos. Page 11 Corbis/Bettmann. Page 12 G. Paul Bishop. Page 13 Nina Leen; Getty Images/Time Life Pictures. Page 14 (Top) Michael Rougier; Getty Images/Time Life Pictures. (Bottom) Courtesy, Dr. Arthur W. Toga, Laboratory of Neuro Imaging. Page 15 Stockbyte. Page 17 Michael Grecco; Stock Boston. Page 19 Bob Daemmrich; The Image Works. Page 21 (Top) Michael K. Nichols; Michael K. Nichols/National Geographic Image Collection. (Bottom) Jonathan Nourok; PhotoEdit. Page 22 (Top) Hanna Damasio, M.D.; From H. Damasio, T. Grabowski, R. Frank, A.M. Galaburda, A.R. Damasio, The Return of Phineas Gage: Clues about the brain from the skull of a famous patient. Science 264:1102-1105, 1994. Department of Neurology and Image Analysis Facility, University of Iowa. (Bottom) The Warren Anatomical Museum, Francis A. Countway Library of Medicine, Harvard Medical School. Page 23 © The New Yorker Collection 1989 George Price from cartoonbank.com. All Rights Reserved. Page 24 © The New Yorker Collection 1994 Leo Cullum from cartoonbank.com. All Rights Reserved. Page 26 Bill Aron; PhotoEdit. Page 27 © The New Yorker Collection 2005 Peter Mueller from cartoonbank.com. All Rights Reserved. Page 28 Mendil; Photo Researchers, Inc. Page 30 Ellen Senisi. Page 32 © The New Yorker Collection 1999 Tom Chalkley from cartoonbank.com. All Rights Reserved. Page 33 Hulton Archive/Getty Images.

Chapter 2

Page 43 2-A Gary Rhijnsburger; Masterfile Corporation. 2-B © Dorling Kindersley. 2-C Amos Morgan/Photodisc/Getty Images. 02-D Amos Morgan/Photodisc/Getty Images. Page 45 (Right) Juergen Berger/Max-Planck Institute; Photo Researchers, Inc.; Illustration ©Dorling Kindersley. Page 49 (Right) E.R. Lewis, T.E. Everhart, Y.Y. Zeevi; Visuals Unlimited; Illustration ©Dorling Kindersley. Page 51 (Top) C. Allan Morgan; Peter Arnold, Inc. (Bottom) Image Source; Creatas/Dynamic Graphics. Page 55 Andrew Paul Leonard; Photo Researchers, Inc. Page 57 Peter Hvizdak; The Image Works. Page 58 (Top) Kai Pfaffenbach; Corbis/Reuters America LLC. (Bottom) Joel Gordon Photography; Page 61 (Top Left) SPL, Photo Researchers, Inc. (Top Right) Alfred Pasieka; Photo Researchers, Inc. (Bottom Left) CORBIS - NY. (Bottom Right) Tim Beddow; Photo Researchers, Inc. Page 64 David Longstreath; AP Wide World Photos. Page 66 Michael Newman; PhotoEdit. Page 68 (Top) Howard Grey; Getty Images Inc. - Stone Allstock. (Bottom) Chapman, Gary S. and Vivian; Getty Images Inc. - Image Bank. Page 70 Linnea Lenkus; Getty Images Inc. - Stone Allstock. Page 75 David R. Frazier.

Chapter 3

Page 83 3-A Dave King © Dorling Kindersley. Page 84 Steve Taylor; Getty Images Inc. - Stone Allstock. Page 86 (Top) Lester Lefkowitz; Getty Images, Inc. - Taxi. (Bottom) Joel Gordon Photography. Page 89 Photo Researchers, Inc.; Illustration ©Dorling Kindersley. Page 91 Bryan Allen; Corbis/Bettmann. Page 92 Fritz Goro; Getty Images/Time Life Pictures. Page 93 (Left) © Copyright Lowell Handler. (Right) © Copyright Lowell Handler. Page 94 (Left) Ishihara, "Test for Color Deficiency". Courtesy Kanehara & Co., Ltd. Offered Exclusively in The USA by Graham-Field, Inc., Bay Shore, New York (Right) Hart-Davis/Science Photo Library; Photo Researchers, Inc. Page 96 © The New Yorker Collection 1998 Charles Barsotti from cartoonbank.com. All Rights Reserved. Page 99 Corbis/Bettmann; Illustration ©Dorling Kindersley. Page 100 Ron Edmonds; AP Wide World Photos. Page 102 Omikron/Photo Researcher, Inc.; Illustration ©Dorling Kindersley. Page 104 Robin Sachs; PhotoEdit. Page 105 AP Wide World Photos. Page 107 Lionel Cironneau; AP Wide World Photos. Page 109 © The New Yorker Collection 2000 John O'Brien from cartoonbank.com. All Rights Reserved. Page 111 Mark Richards/PHOTOEDIT. Page 113 (Top Left) Faint, Grant V.; Getty Images Inc. - Image Bank. (Top Right) Shaen Adey © Dorling Kindersley. (Bottom Left) Robin Smith; Photolibrary.com. (Bottom Right) Tom Mareschal; Creative Eye/MIRA.com. Page 115 Larry Landolfi; Photo Researchers, Inc.

Chapter 4

Page 125 4-A Getty Images - Digital Vision. 4-B Photodisc/Getty Images. 4-C Getty Images, Inc.-Photodisc. 4-D Richard Cash; PhotoEdit. 4-E Photodisc 4-F Deximage/Shigeru Bando/Getty Images, Inc. Page 127 Stockbyte. Page 128 (Top) Michael Newman; PhotoEdit. (Bottom Left) SW Productions; Getty Images, Inc.- Photodisc. Page 129 (Top) David Tejada; Getty Images Inc. - Stone Allstock. (Bottom Left) Michael Dick; Animals Animals/Earth Scenes. (Bottom Right) Stephen Frink; Corbis/Bettmann. Page 131 James Holmes; Photo Researchers, Inc.; Illustration ©Dorling Kindersley. Page 133 (Top) Chuck Nacke; Woodfin Camp & Associates. (Bottom) © The New Yorker Collection J. Dator from cartoonbank.com. All Rights Reserved. Page 134 William C. Dement, MD, Ph.D. Page 136 Pool/Getty Images, Inc. Page 137 (Top) Bill Bachmann; Photo Researchers, Inc. (Bottom) Custom Medical Stock Photo, Inc. Page 138 www.CartoonStock.com. Page 139 © The New Yorker Collection 1973 Dana Fradon from cartoonbank.com. All Rights Reserved. Page 140 Omni-Photo Communications, Inc. Page 144 Joel Gordon Photography. Page 146 Ken Graham; Bruce Coleman Inc. Page 147 The Granger Collection. Page 148 Michael Newman; PhotoEdit. Page 149 (Top Left) Spencer Grant/Grantpix; Photo Researchers, Inc. (Top Right) Billy E. Barnes; PhotoEdit. (Bottom) Stewart Tilger; Corbis/Bettmann. Page 150 © The New Yorker Collection 1989 George Price from cartoonbank.com. All Rights Reserved. Page 151 Drew Crawford; The Image Works. Page 155 Burke/Triolo/Brand X; Creatas/Dynamic Graphics. Page 156 Lee Powers; Photo Researchers, Inc. Page 158 Doug Menuez; Getty Images, Inc., PhotoDisc.

Chapter 5

Page 165 5-A Photodisc/Getty Images. 5-B Photodisc/Getty Images. 5-C Photodisc/Getty Images. 5-D Photodisc/Getty Images. Page 166 © Reprinted with special permission of King Features Syndicate. Page 167 © CORBIS Page 168 Shelley Rotner; Omni-Photo Communications, Inc. Page 169 Dagmar Ehling; Photo Researchers, Inc. Page 173 Professor Ben Harris, University of New Hampshire. Page 174 Frank Greenaway © Dorling Kindersley, Courtesy of the Natural History Museum, London. Page 177 (Top) © The New Yorker Collection 2005

Inc. - Brand X Pictures. 12-E James Darell/Photodisc/Getty Images. Page 445 Courtesy of A.W. Freud et al./Collection of the Library of Congress. Page 449 (Top) Pearson Education/PH College. (Bottom) Margaret Miller; Photo Researchers, Inc. Page 450 Michale Newman/PhotoEdit. (Bottom) © The New Yorker Collection 1978 Everett Opie from cartoonbank.com. All Rights Reserved. Page 452 Getty Images Inc. - Hulton Archive Photos. Page 453 (Top Left) Getty Images Inc. - Hulton Archive Photos. (Top Middle) Corbis/Bettmann. (Top Right) Courtesy of the Library of Congress. Page 457 © The New Yorker Collection 1990 Peter Steiner from cartoonbank.com. All Rights Reserved. Page 460 Lee Lorenz; © The New Yorker Collection 1994 Lee Lorenz from cartoonbank.com. All Rights Reserved. Page 464 Bob Sacha Photography. Page 465 (Top) Stephen Crowley/The New York Times. (Bottom) Gamma Press USA, Inc. Page 466 © The New Yorker Collection 1997 Robert Weber from cartoonbank.com. All Rights Reserved. (Top) Laura Dwight; PhotoEdit. Page 468 (Bottom) Don Martinetti.

Chapter 13

Page 479 13-A Getty Images/Digital Vision. 13-B Hans Neleman/Stone/Getty Images. Page 481 © The New Yorker Collection 2003 Alex Gregory from cartoonbank.com. All Rights Reserved. Page 482 Bruce Weaver; AP Wide World Photos. Page 484 Romanelli, Marc; Getty Images Inc. - Image Bank. Page 487 Javier Pierini; © Bettmann/CORBIS All Rights Reserved. Page 490 AP Wide World Photos. Page 491 Reprinted by the permission of the American Cancer Society, Inc. Page 492 Ron Chapple/Taxi; Getty Images, Inc. - Taxi. Page 495 © Reuters New Media Inc./CORBIS. Page 496 Lon C. Diehl; PhotoEdit. Page 498 Corbis/Bettmann. Page 499 © The New Yorker Collection 2002 Charles Barsotti from cartoonbank.com. All Rights Reserved. Page 500 Allan Tannnbaum; Gamma Press USA, Inc. Page 501 J. Nettis; IPNstock.com. Page 503 Zigy Kaluzny; Getty Images Inc. - Stone Allstock. Page 505 Sheila McKinnon; Creative Eye/MIRA.com. Page 507 (Top) Philip G. Zimbardo, Inc. (Bottom) Washington Post/Agence France Presse/Getty Images. Page 512 Corbis/Bettmann.

Chapter 14

Page 521 14-A Kevin Mackintosh; Getty Images. Page 523 (Top) Francisco Goya, "El Hechizo", 1787-88, Fundacion Lazaro Galdiano. (Bottom) © The New Yorker Collection 1986 George Price from cartoonbank.com. All Rights Reserved. Page 524 Robert Ginn; PhotoEdit. Page 525 Brian Lowe; ZUMA Press, Inc./Keystone Press Agency. Page 530 Jeff Greenberg; Omni-Photo Communications, Inc. Page 531 Michael Caulfield; AP Wide World Photos. Page 532 © The New Yorker Collection 2003 Michael Shaw from cartoonbank.com. All Rights Reserved. Page 533 David Young-Wolff; PhotoEdit. Page 535 © The New Yorker Collection 2000 Robert Mankoff from cartoonbank.com. All Rights Reserved. Page 537 New York Daily News. Page 538 David Longstreath; AP Wide World Photos. Page 540 AP Wide World Photos. Page 541 © The New Yorker Collection 1992 Mike Twohy from cartoonbank.com. All Rights Reserved. Page 543 (Top) Kevin Lamarque; Corbis/Reuters America LLC. (Bottom) Jonathan Exley; Getty Images, Inc - Liaison. Page 545 Eli Reed; Everett Collection. Page 546 Getty Images, Inc. Page 548 Spencer Grant; PhotoEdit. Page 549 Nick Downes. Page 552 Michael Newman; PhotoEdit.

Chapter 15

Page 561 15-A Burke/Triolo Productions; Getty Images, Inc - Brand X Pictures. 15-B Daly & Newton/Image Bank/Getty Images. Page 563 Charles Ciccione; Photo Researchers, Inc. Page 564 David Young-Wolff; PhotoEdit. Page 565 © The New Yorker Collection 1991 Lee Lorenz from cartoonbank.com. All Rights Reserved. Page 567 Getty Images Inc. - Stone Allstock. Page 568 D. Young-Wolff; PhotoEdit. Page 570 (Top) Sidney Harris. (Bottom) Lester Sloan; Woodfin Camp & Associates. Page 573 Bob Daemmrich; The Image Works. Page 576 George Dodson; Pearson Education/PH College. Page 577 (Top) © Dan Piraro. Reprinted with special permisison of King Features Syndicate. (Bottom) David Young-Wolff; PhotoEdit. Page 578 Mary Kate Denny; PhotoEdit. Page 583 Reprinted with special permission of King Features Syndicate. Page 587 James Wilson/Woodfin Camp & Associates. Page 589 © Bettmann/CORBIS All Rights Reserved. Page 590 Cleo Freelance; Index Stock Imagery, Inc.

Appendix B

Page B-3 Michal Heron Photography. Page B-4 Peace Corps. Page B-5 David Young-Wolff; PhotoEdit. Page B-6 Richard Nowitz; Phototake NYC. Page B-7 Will & Deni McIntyre/Science Source; Photo Researchers, Inc. Page B-8 Laura Dwight; PhotoEdit. Page B-9 AP Wide World Photos. Page B-10 Brian Smith. Page B-11 (Top) Property of AT&T Archives, reprinted with permission of AT&T. (Bottom) © 2007 The New Yorker Collection, David Sipress from cartoonbank.com. All Rights Reserved. Page B-12 ©2001 Charles Barsotti from cartoonbank.com. All Rights Reserved. Page B-13 Dan McCoy; Rainbow.

TEXT CREDITS

Chapter 3

Page 82 Extract from "Synesthesia" on the Health Report by Robin Hughes first broadcast on ABC Radio National Monday 8 July 1996, reprinted by permission of the Australian Broadcasting Corporation and ABC Online. © 1996 ABC. All rights reserved. The full text is available at: http://www.abc.net.au/rn/talks/8.30/helthrpt/hstories/hr080796.htm.

Chapter 4

Page 131 Figure 4.1 Reprinted with permission from Roffwarg, et al., *Science* 152:604 (1996). Page 143 Table 4.2 From HYPNOTIC SUSCEPTIBILITY by E. Hilgard, published by Harcourt Brace & World. Copyright 1965. Reprinted with permission from the estate of Ernest R. Hilgard. Page 150 Table 4.4 Reprinted from publication FOOD & CHEMICAL TOXICOLOGY, Vol. 34, Barone et al., CAFFEINE CONSUMPTION, pages 119-129. Copyright 1996, with permission from Elsevier. Page 153 Table 4.5 Adapted from *How to Control Your Drinking* by William Miller and Ricardo Munoz. Reprinted by permission of University of Wisconsin-Eau Claire.

Chapter 5

Pages 198-201 Reprinted by permission of Karawynn Long.

Chapter 6

Page 225 Fig. 6-7 D.R. Godden and A.D. Baddeley: "Context-dependent memory in two natural environments", the British Journal of Psychology, Vol. 66, Part 3 (August 1975), pp. 325-331. Reproduced with permission from the British Journal of Psychology, © The British Psychological Society. Page 235 Fig. 6-10 Reprinted from *Cognitive Psychology*, Vol 11, 1979, pp. 297–307, Nickerson, et al. "Long-Term Memory for a Common Object" with permission from Elsevier.

Chapter 7

Page 273 Table 7.4 Shepard, T. H. Catalog of Teratogenic Agents, 10th Edition. Copyright © 2001. Reprinted with permission of Johns Hopkins University Press.

Chapter 8

Page 295 Fig 8-1 From DISCOVERING PSYCHOLOGY, 3/E by Don H. Hockenbury and Sandra E. Hockenbury. © 1998, 2001, 2004 by Worth Publishers. Used with permission. Page 307 Table 8.3 From Gail H. Roid, STANFORD-BINET INTELLIGENCE SCALES, Fifth Edition (SB5). Copyright 2004. The Riverside Publishing Company. All rights reserved. Page 308 Table 8.4 Wechsler Adult Intelligence Scale, Third Edition. Copyright © 1997 by Harcourt Assessment, Inc. Reproduced with permission. All rights reserved. Page 311 Table 8.5 From Lewis R. Aiken *Psychological and Educational Testing* published by Allyn and Bacon, Boston, MA. Copyright © 1971 by Pearson Education. Reprinted by permission of the publisher. Page 313 Table 8.6 Reprinted with permission from the *Diagnostic and Statistical Manual of Mental Disorders, Fourth Edition, Text Revision*, (Copyright © 2000). American Psychiatric Association.

Chapter 9

Page 341 Table 9.2 Adapted from Zuckerman-Kuhlman Personality Questionnaire (ZKQPP: An Alternative Five-Factorial Model" in b. De Raad and M. Perugini, eds. *Big Five Assessment* (Cambridge: Hogrefe & Huber, 2002).

Chapter 10

Page 385 Figures 10.4 and 10.5 Reprinted by permission of the Estate of William Masters. Page 387 Table 10-1 Reprinted by permission of The Kinsey Institute for Research in Sex, Gender and Reproduction, Inc. Page 388 Table 10-2 Reprinted by

Name Index

Subject Index